戴志騫文集

下　冊

韦庆媛　邓景康　主编

国家圖書館出版社
National Library of China Publishing House

目 录

中文著作

图书馆学术讲稿

序言 ·· (5)
第一章　图书馆组织法 ·· (7)
第二章　图书馆管理法 ·· (10)
　　第一节　图书选择法 ··· (12)
　　第二节　图书出纳法 ··· (13)
　　第三节　杂志书籍登录式 ·· (15)
　　第四节　管理、出纳、选择、装订等之参考书 ··························· (18)
第三章　图书馆之建筑 ·· (19)
第四章　论美国图书馆 ·· (23)
第五章　图书馆分类法 ·· (27)
　　第一节　勃郎氏分类法(Brown Classification) ························ (30)
　　第二节　美国国会图书馆之分类法 ··· (31)
　　第三节　克脱氏展开分类法(Cutter's Expansive Classification) ·· (31)
　　第四节　杜威氏十分分类法(Dewey's Decimal Classification) ···· (33)
　　第五节　清华学校图书馆分类法 ·· (36)
　　第六节　日本帝国图书馆分类法 ·· (43)
　　第七节　图书馆分类法之评断 ··· (47)
第六章　图书馆编目法 ·· (48)
和汉图书目录编纂概则 ··· (57)
西书著者、书名目录编纂略则 ··· (59)

英文著作

Professional Education for Librarianship

Preface ·· (69)
Introduction ··· (71)
Part I　The Development of Modern Libraries and Librarianship ········ (80)
Part II　Training and Education for Librarianship ··························· (109)
Part III　A Proposed Scheme of Professional Education for Librarianship ··· (164)

Appendix I　Suggested Curriculum for the Proposed Library School at the State University of Iowa …………………………………………………………（193）
Appendix II　A Budget for the Proposed Library School at the University of Iowa ………（200）
译文：图书馆学专业教育………………………………………………冯立昇、司宏伟审（223）
　　前言 ………………………………………………………………………… 王媛译（227）
　　序言 ………………………………………………………………………… 王媛译（229）
　　第一部分　现代图书馆与图书馆事业的发展………王媛、杨玲、郭兰芳、张秋译（237）
　　第二部分　图书馆学专业教育与培训 …………………………………韦庆媛译（261）
　　第三部分　图书馆学专业教育的提案 ……………………………………胡冉译（313）
　　附录 I ……………………………………………………………………… 胡冉译（337）
　　附录 II ……………………………………………………………………… 胡冉译（343）

Bibliography on China：1900—1918（关于中国的书目：1900—1918）

Preface ……………………………………………………………………………（348）
Abbreviations ……………………………………………………………………（349）
Bibliographical Aids ……………………………………………………………（352）
General Works …………………………………………………………………（354）
Philosophy and Religion ………………………………………………………（356）
Missions …………………………………………………………………………（361）
Economic & Political Organizations …………………………………………（363）
Education ………………………………………………………………………（368）
Social Life & Customs …………………………………………………………（370）
Science and Useful Arts ………………………………………………………（375）
Fine Arts …………………………………………………………………………（378）
Language and Literature ………………………………………………………（382）
Travels & Description …………………………………………………………（384）
Manchuria ………………………………………………………………………（391）
Mongolia …………………………………………………………………………（392）
Tibet ……………………………………………………………………………（394）
Turkestan ………………………………………………………………………（397）
Biography ………………………………………………………………………（399）
History …………………………………………………………………………（402）
International Relations …………………………………………………………（406）
Boxer Uprising 1900 ……………………………………………………………（411）
Revolution 1911 …………………………………………………………………（413）
Author Index ……………………………………………………………………（416）

后　　记…………………………………………………………………………韦庆媛（425）

中文著作

图书馆学术讲稿

序 言

图书馆事业之发达,实为普及平民、社会、专门教育之母。中国图书馆事业,尚在胚胎时代,不得不竭力提倡,以促平民、社会、专门教育之进步。北高前校长陈筱庄先生有鉴于此,乃于去夏组织北高暑假图书馆讲习会,委骞充该会讲席。骞以一人担任图书馆各科讲演,精力有所不逮,乃函商武昌文华大学图书馆主任沈祖荣先生襄赞一切。会其时直皖交哄,交通中断,沈君未即来都。幸得邓芝园、王仲达、李守常、李翼庭、程伯庐诸先生之赞助,始获如期开讲。两星期后,沈君既来,遂竣骞未尽之业,讲习会于以告一结束。莅会听讲者男女约计八十余人,其中亦有来自厦门、奉天、湖北等处者。骞每日讲演数小时,而关于图书馆学术之中文书籍,又无善本可以参考。不得已选择西文图书馆学术之纲领,临时译成中文,作为讲演之资料。所编讲义,但用纲要式,以求简明。脱稿时间极形匆促;潦草之处,知所不免。尚希宏达之士,随时指教,以匡不逮焉。

编者识

第一章　图书馆组织法

图书馆与人生有密切之关系，其重要理由厥有数端：
（一）扶助学校教育之不足；并可为国民终身学校。
（二）增进专门职业智识。
（三）修养精神。
图书馆能辅助以上人生之三要素，设立图书馆之必要，实基于此。
美国图书馆管理名家台拿John C. Dona（泥滑克公立图书馆主任）曾论图书馆有益于社会之事共有六端：
（一）社会上大多数人，竟日奔走事务；少暇翻阅小说记事等书籍，可娱悦精神。
（二）图书馆收藏文学、艺术、理化各种图书，攻学者可就其学业所近得自修之机会。
（三）图书馆搜集古今政治经济之争议、专门大家之思想学术，能陶冶国民政治智识。
（四）图书馆可养成国民品学兼备之美风。（Culture）
（五）图书馆可抵抗败坏风化、耗时之游戏；养成青年好学之习惯。
（六）图书馆常可辅助学校教职之学理。
参见 Dona：Library Primer
图书馆设立之必要既如上述，则其组织及管理法亦必须详加研究。
各种图书馆之组织及管理稍有不同，惟组织大纲约有三条：
（一）须得适当主任：促进图书馆之发达，如抚育儿童，然孩童不得良好之保姆，易生疾病，易染不良之习惯。图书馆创办之初，能得优美之领袖，则其进步速而费不糜，公众且获其利益焉。
（二）须选择图书：近来书籍出版，日增月盛；图书馆经济有限，势不能齐备各种书籍，故选择必须慎重。而所选之书又须投大多数阅览者之所好，其能增进公众之常识者宜多购置，切不可购置管理员本身嗜好之书籍而置公众之嗜好于不顾。图书馆愈小，选择愈求精当，所以利公众而节费用也。
（三）图书馆之建筑及馆内之布置：建筑须庄严，各室之配置务求适合于管理各方面，以达到少数管（馆）员能顾及出纳书籍与阅览者之全部为范围。馆内家具宜舒服而坚固；整齐清洁，尤须特别注意焉。

图书馆

图书馆不可入政治或党派范围。
各国官立图书馆主任及馆员，均受文官事务法之保障。
公立及私立图书馆须设图书馆董事会。
（甲）董事：人数宜少；最适宜之数五人或七人。惟大都市之图书馆董事人数，以事情多寡为比例。
（乙）资格及任期：资格须具有威望而并重视教育者。任期以二年半或三年为限；改选时一半连任,以资熟手。

（丙）职务:1. 经费;2. 审查用度;3. 图书馆经营;4. 图书馆规程;5. 主任馆员之选定。

图书馆之经费

（一）创办费

（甲）标准 1. 人口之多寡;2. 经常费之多寡。

建筑费表

岁入额	公债偿还金	建筑费	设备费	建物容积
10,000 元	2,500 元	36,000 元	4,000 元	72 立方英尺

创办费各种费用之分配表

（二）经常费

（甲）薪俸

（乙）图书

（丙）需用

英国图书馆经常费预算表

岁入额（磅）	公债偿还金（磅）	建筑费（磅）	设备费（磅）	建物容积（立方英尺）	地基（平方英尺）	藏书数	阅览人数
1,000	250	3,600	400	72,000	4,412	34,000	200
2,000	500	7,200	800	144,000	8,824	68,000	400 分馆合计
3,000	750	10,800	1,200	216,000	13,236	102,000	600 同
4,000	1,000	14,400	1,600	288,000	19,200	136,000	800 同
5,000	1,250	18,000	2,000	360,000	24,000	170,000	1,000 同
10,000	2,500	36,000	4,000	720,000	48,000	340,000	2,000 同

创办费总额(元)	建筑费(元)	设备费(元)	图书费(元)	事务费(元)
500	300	100	50	50
1,000	600	200	100	100
5,000	3,000	1,000	500	500
10,000	6,000	2,000	1,000	1,000
50,000	35,000	7,000	5,000	3,000
100,000	70,000	10,000	8,000	12,000
150,000	100,000	25,000	10,000	15,000
200,000	140,000	30,000	1,000①	18,000

---

① 【编者注】此数字有误,但原文如此,已无从查考。

岁入总额（磅）	偿还借款及利息（磅）	维持费总额（磅）	薪俸（磅）	图书费（磅）	需用费（磅）
3,000	750	2,250	1,007	790	459
2,500	620	1,880	877	640	358
2,000	500	1,500	757	480	263
1,500	375	1,125	604	330	191
1,000	250	750	456	180	114
500		500	254	105	141
100		100	40	22	38
平均百分率		100	49.1	31.3	19.6

创办费:创办费当如何定其多寡?

(甲)以人口为标准。

(乙)勃郎氏(Brown)云:人口不能定为标准,不如以图书馆之岁入额为标准,如:第一表,以岁入额之多寡,而算定其相当之建筑费。

创办费中分:1. 建筑费;2. 设备费;3. 图书费。此三者应如何分配,方为适当?今分配如第二表。此表约略算定各费之分配问题。如用公地者,应加入土地购入费。

经常费或维持费:经常费或维持费分:1. 薪俸;2. 图书;3. 需用。此三者可分配如第三表及第四表。第三表为勃郎氏(Brown)之图书馆岁出预算表。(英国设立图书馆时,其建筑费及设备费均以借款充之,故每年有从岁入中偿还借金及利息之支出。)

第四表

国名	薪俸	图书	需用
1. 英国	百分之四十九	百分之三十一	百分之二十
2. 美国	百分之五十二	百分之二十五	百分之二十三
3. 日本	百分之四十三	百分之二十七	百分之三十
4. 中国无锡	百分之四十九	百分之二十八	百分之二十三
5. 中国清华	百分之四十	百分之五十	百分之十

备注:

1. 英国图书馆协会报告。
2. 美国图书馆协会报告。
3. 日比谷、大阪、京都三图书馆。
4. 无锡县立图书馆汇刊(薪俸项内,包括膳食费)
5. 清华九年度图书馆预算。

以上各表,不可作为一定之标准。各费之分配,均有图书馆规模之大小、种类之相异而定其分配。

图书馆之创办之方法:

(一)公开小学校附属之图书室。

（二）用校友会、青年会或小学校之一室，设简易图书馆。

（三）教育会及个人捐款，设参考图书馆、普通图书馆等。

（四）创设良好图书馆，须要国家及省、县、市、乡村等公共团体之实力赞助。

（五）嘉仪盛典之纪念，宣扬英雄豪杰之功业，忠勇义烈之声名，皆可为建设图书馆之机会。

（六）请富豪捐助，冠其名为图书馆之名。

卡纳奇氏（Carnegie）捐助图书馆之条件：

（一）受捐之都市，需捐助图书馆基地。

（二）市民亦须负担卡氏助金一成之金额，作经常费。

关于图书馆组织及管理法之书籍杂志：

1. Brown, J. D. Manual of Library Economy, London.

2. Brown, J. D. Guide to Librarianship, London.

3. Dona, J. C. Library Primer, Chicago.

4. Hetcher, W. I. Public Libraries in America, Boston.

5. Morel, E. Bibliotheques Vols, Paris.

6. Plummer, M. W. Hints to Small Libraries. N. Y.

7. A. L. A. Bulletin, Chicago.

8. Library Journal, N. Y.

9. Public Libraries, Chicago.

10. Bostwick, A. E. Library Essays, Wilson, N. Y.

11. Hardy, E. A., Public Library, Toronto.

12. The Libraries, London.

关于图书馆教育之书籍杂志：

1. Library Journal
2. Public Libraries　} 见前。
3. The Libraries

4. Adams H. B. Public Libraries and Popular Education, Albany.

5. Ayres & Mckinzie. The Public Libraries and The Public School, Cleveland.

6. Powell S. H. Children's Library, a dynamic factor in Education N. Y.

第二章　图书馆管理法

近世图书馆于社会上须具一种自进之活动，故图书馆之管理及馆员服务之热心，实为重大之关键。

（甲）大图书馆管理事务之组织：

(1)管理部—图书馆馆长 ⎰ 参考主任 ⎰ 文学参考主任
　　　　　　　　　　　　　　　　　　　　工程学参考主任
　　　　　　　　　　　　　　　　　　　　其他可视图书馆之大小,以定其多寡
　　　　　　　　　　　　　编目主任
　　　　　　　　　　　　　选书主任
　　　　　　　　　　　　　采办主任(有时兼收入主任)
　　　　　　　　　　　　　收入主任
　　　　　　　　　　　　　出纳主任
　　　　　　　　　　　　　藏书主任
　　　　　　　　　　　　　装订主任
　　　　　　　　　　　　　分馆馆长(有时总馆长兼任)
　　　　　　　　　　　　　书记主任
　　　　　　　　　　　　　庶务主任

管理部之大小,照图书馆之大小而定。馆内一切行政之方针,皆由管理部议决施行。

(2)顾问部 ⎰ 参考科馆员
　　　　　　儿童图书科馆员
　　　　　　出纳科馆员
　　　　　　阅览室馆员
　　　　　　其他

阅览人有违背图书馆规则者,馆员均得施行相当之惩罚。如有故意毁坏公产者,可送警局惩戒。

(乙)图书馆员会议:

(1)图书馆各科讨论会。

(2)图书馆馆内之布告:(一)日刊,(二)周刊,此种布告适用于大图书馆,专为周知图书馆员对于图书馆各种新闻或一切办法而设。

(丙)图书馆馆员之待遇:

(1)时间:(一)晚上,(二)放假,(三)修养假,(四)病假。

(2)薪津:(一)每月公积法,(二)养老金,(三)加薪法。

每日办事时间,约七小时;惟管理员值晚班或放假日班,其薪水稍优,以资鼓励。

划到积记时间片

○○○纽约图书馆										
1920　　　八月	上午		下午		晚上		总记	迟到	迟出	备注
	到	出	到	出	到	出				
1										
2										
3										
4										

续表

○○○纽约图书馆										
1920＼八月	上午		下午		晚上		总记	迟到	迟出	备注
	到	出	到	出	到	出				
5										
6										
7										
8										
9										

第一节　图书选择法

图书馆于图书之选择甚为紧要,然此事极不易为,而选择之标准,亦不易定。概括言之:如美国图书馆协会对于选择图书之训语,曾有"最多之图书费,应购最多之书籍,以供最多数阅览者。"此训语可谓包括选择图书之要诀。选择图书应加注意之各点如下:

(一)应供给图书馆所在地社会之希望及需要。

(二)小说流动之统计及每书流动之次数,均不可作为选择图书之标准。

(三)关于图书馆所在地之图书应在搜罗之列:

1. 图书地图及其他相类之图书。

2. 本地人士之著述及其传记肖像等。

3. 本地发行之新闻及杂志。(大城不在此列)

4. 本地官厅之出版物。

(四)关于人民道德、学问、生活上有扶助能力之图书。

(五)选择书籍之参考书:

1. 中外古书目录。

2. 各图书馆之印刷目录。

3. 各种新刊图书之评论目录。

4. 图书馆协会选定之新刊图书目录。

(六)购置重本书籍问题之商榷:

购置重本书籍,须按各馆之特性而定,不能拘执于一定条例。兹就习惯上定之下列各条以为购置:

1. 学校图书馆如设有分科阅览室,一书须供数科参考者。

2. 新出版之著名书籍,同时须阅览者甚多。如 B. Russell 之 *Theory and Practice of Bolshevism* 及 H. G. Wells 之 *Outline of History* 等书。

3. 著名小说同时要求借阅者太多时。

4. 某类书籍具有参考及流动两种性质者。

（七）购置已得选择之图书手续有下列数端：

1. 应制有图书馆费预算表。
2. 应预备得选各图书之书片或书单。
3. 选择书店。
4. 留意再版及预约等事项。
5. 图书馆应得之折扣。

购置图书之书牌

著作者 Author	
书名 Title	
地名及发行所 Place, Publisher	经理 Agent
价格 Cost	
签名 Signature	
摘要 Remarks	
	○

尚未购置
非重本
……………………
购置年月日
……………………
收入年月日
……………………
馆长签名处
……………………

已译成中文之图书馆管理法书籍如下：

（一）图书馆小识，通俗教育研究会编辑。
（二）图书馆指南，顾实，上海医学书局。
（三）图书馆管理法，商务印书馆。
（四）图书馆学指南，杨昭悊，法政学报社。

第二节 图书出纳法

（一）馆内阅览：1.最好不收阅览费；2.普通参考书、杂志、词典等书，须任人检阅；3.阅览证须简便；4.一书一证，便于作每日之统计。

馆内借览证之格式

	纽约省立图书馆	
书号	著作者	书名
坐号……姓名……		

(二)馆外阅览：
(1)请求借览证之正面格式

Registration Card

第　号		年　月　日
今蒙　贵馆认某某为有借览图书之资格者,请即交付借览证,贵馆一切规则,借书人理应遵守。		
姓名(签名盖印)		
住址		
职业		
保证人(签名盖印)		
保证人住址		

背面格式

姓名
号数
住址

(2)借览证

Borrower's Card

号数					
姓名					
住址					
书号	借	还	书号	借	还

此系存馆内之借览证,如许借览者能将此证带出馆外,须备有效期限于号数之后。

(3)馆外阅览书片

Book Card

332.4-L69					
梁启超著					
币制论					
借	人号	还	借	人号	还

人号即借览证之号数。

每书的后书面或前书面,贴附一纸袋,插置馆外阅览书片。如允许借书者,将借览证带出馆外,于借书时,出纳员可将书内馆外览书片抽出,而将借书证置于此袋内,盖印借出日期于纸袋左右边,或右边之空白纸上,纸袋有数种格式,今将最普通之纸袋式绘列于下:

(4)书牌纸袋

阅览室及出纳台之馆员,时与阅览人及借书人接触;其举动态度,务使来馆者得愉快之心理。以下五条阅览室及出纳台之馆员,往往于无意中忽略之,此实须注意者也。

(1)不可常答人以"否"之一字。
(2)闭馆时慎勿作匆忙状,露不耐烦之态度。
(3)交付图书于借书人不可作性急状。
(4)须不惮烦,不畏劳,而介绍馆中之图书于阅览者。
(5)应学商人之待遇顾客,务使其满足。

第三节 杂志书籍登录式

杂志及日刊登录式
(1)杂志登录片

正面

号数								杂志名					
年	卷	一月	二月	三月	四月	五月	六月	七月	八月	九月	十月	十一月	十二月
出版地								出版者					
价格								每年之卷数					
出版次数								(已装订者)					

背面

○			定价＿＿＿
定购或续定之年月日	终止	来源	实价

(2) 日刊登录片

正面

	日刊名														份数											终止					
	1	2	3	4	5	6	7	8	9	10	11	12	13	14	15	16	17	18	19	20	21	22	23	24	25	26	27	28	29	30	31
一月																															
二月																															
三月																															
四月																															
五月																															
六月																															
七月																															
八月																															
九月																															
十月																															
十一月																															
十二月																															

背面

定购处			价格	
年　月　日				
付款期				

年　月　日

□A+2

（一）西文图书登录簿式

登录号数 Number	著作者 AUTHOR	书名 TITLE	出版地及出版者 PLACE& PUBLISHER	出版年 Year	页数 Pages	大小 Size	装订 Binding	来源 Source	价格 Cost	类名 Class	书号 Book	卷 Vol	备注 REMARKS
1226	Beecher Hu.	Speeches on The Rebellion	N. Y. Sowell	1887	368	□	Paper	Putnam	80 34	g37.71	B39		Cd. 3reg. g188
27	Mahoffy, J. P.	Social Life		1875	15十140	□		Stechert	1 50	g3.38	mg4		
28													
29													
30													
1231													
32													

(二) 中日文图书登录模式

年 月 日	登录号数	类名	号数	册数	著作者	书名	出版地及出版者	出版年	页数	大小	装订	价格	摘要
	四一	二七〇	五	一	中学教育社	读书法	东京中学教育社	明治三一		小	洋	三〇	
	四二	三〇〇	一〇	一	三岛毅	福泽全集	东京	明治一二		中	日	二五	
	四三												
	四四												
	四五												
	四六												

第四节　管理、出纳、选择、装订等之参考书

一、学校图书馆管理法之书籍：

1. Dana. J. C. School Department (Modern American Library Economy) Elm Tree Press, woodstock Vermont.

2. Ward G. O. High School Library. A. L. A. Chicago.

3. Hall, M. E. Report of the committee on high school libraries N. E. A. Proceedings 1912.

4. Hall. M. E. Vocational guidance through the Library A. L. A. Chicago.

5. Wilson, Martha, Comp. Books for high Schools A. L. A. Chicago.

6. Gibson, M. L. Course of study for normal school students on the use of a library. Wilson, N. Y.

7. Ward, G. O. Practical use of books and Libraries. Boston Book Co. Boston.

8. Wyer, J. I. College and University Library A. L. A. Chicago.

9. Ward G. O. Suggestive outlines of methods for Teaching the use of the Library. Faxon, Boston.

二、关于出纳、选择图书等之书籍：

1. Dana. J. C. Modern American Library Economy, Booklists and other publications. Elm Tree Press, woodstock Vermont.

2. Carr, S. C. Vonde, Modern American Library Economy the Lending Department. Elm Tree

Press, woodstock Vermont.

3. Carr, S. C. Vonde, Administration of Lending Department (Modern Amer. Lib. Economy) Elm Tree Press woodstock Vermont.

4. Dana J. C. and Ball, S. B. Business Branch (Modern Amer. Lib. Economy) Elm Tree Press, woodstock Vermont.

5. Dana, J. C. Advertising (Modern Amer. Lib. Economy) Elm Tree Press, woodstock Vermont.

6. Carr, S. C. Vonde. Charging System (Modern Lib. Economy) Elm Tree Press woodstock Vermont.

7. Brown, J. D. Small Library Routledge, London.

8. Roebuck & Thorne. Primer of Library Practice for Junior Assistants Putnam, N. Y.

9. Oregon Library Commission. Books for high School Library Salem. Oregon.

三、关于图书馆装订之书籍：

1. Adam, Pane, Practical Bookbinding Van Nostrand, N. Y.

2. Bailey. A. L. Library Bookbinding. Wilson, N. Y.

3. Brown, M. W. Mending & Repair of Books A. L. A. Chicago.

4. Chivers Cedric. Relative Value of leathers & other binding materials chivers N. Y.

5. Cockerell, D. Bookbinding and care of Books appleton N. Y.

6. Coutts and Stephen: Manual of Library Bookbinding. Libraco London.

7. Dana, J. C. Bookbinding for libraries. Library Bureau, Chicago.

8. Philip, A. J. Business of bookbinding from the Viewpoint of the binder, the publisher, the librarian and the general reader.

第三章　图书馆之建筑

图书馆之建筑，与图书馆之作用，有密切关系；故其建筑，须具以下诸点：
（一）坚固；（二）美观；（三）便利；（四）避火险；（五）易扩张。
在建筑之先，于各点务必研究：
（一）当先筹内部诸室之配合，然后及于外观。
（二）不能以建筑上之理由，而疏忽内部配合之便利。
（三）光线务使充足，而书库之窗，当对于书架，而设其左右之空间。
（四）阅览室及事务室必须宽敞。
（五）阅览室当留意者，即以少数馆员能监视一切。
（六）书库应与出纳书籍台接近。
（七）锅炉、暖气管、气窗、电灯之装置，务求充分。

今略举数图以资参考：

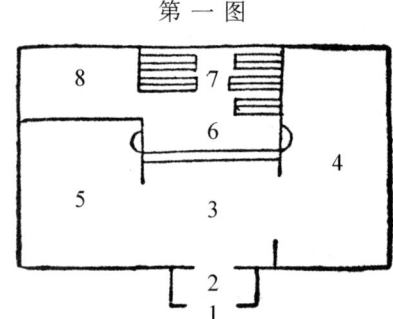

第 一 图

1. 入口
2. 门房
3. 馆外贷出室
4. 阅览室
5. 参考室或杂志室
6. 出纳书籍台
7. 书库
8. 事务室

可容图书 2000 册

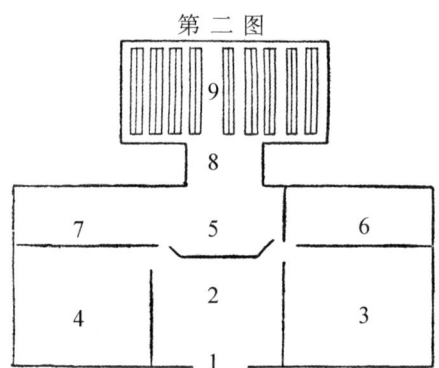

第 二 图

1. 入口
2. 馆外贷出室
3. 普通阅览室
4. 儿童阅览室(分割为目录室或新闻室均可)
5. 出纳书籍台
6. 特别阅览室或妇女阅览室
7. 事务室
8. 走廊
9. 书库

可容图书 60,000 册

第三图
Zadoc Long Free Library
Gold $ 2,800

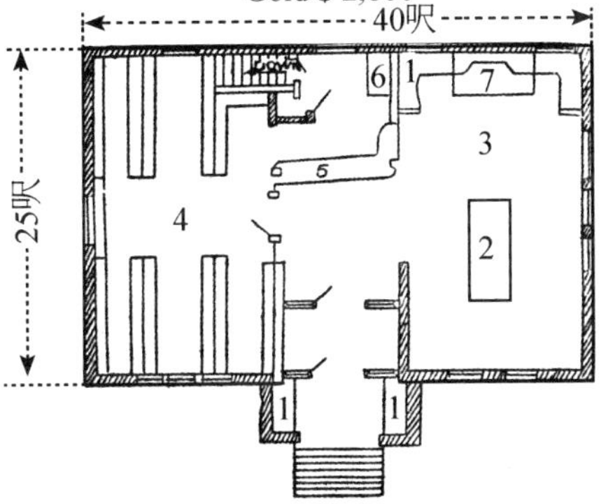

1. Seat 座位
2. Table 桌子
3. Reading Room 阅览室
4. Stack Room 书库
5. Delivery 出纳书籍台
6. Desk 书桌
7. Fire Place 火炉处

可容图书 8000 册

建筑工程师 T. C. Stone

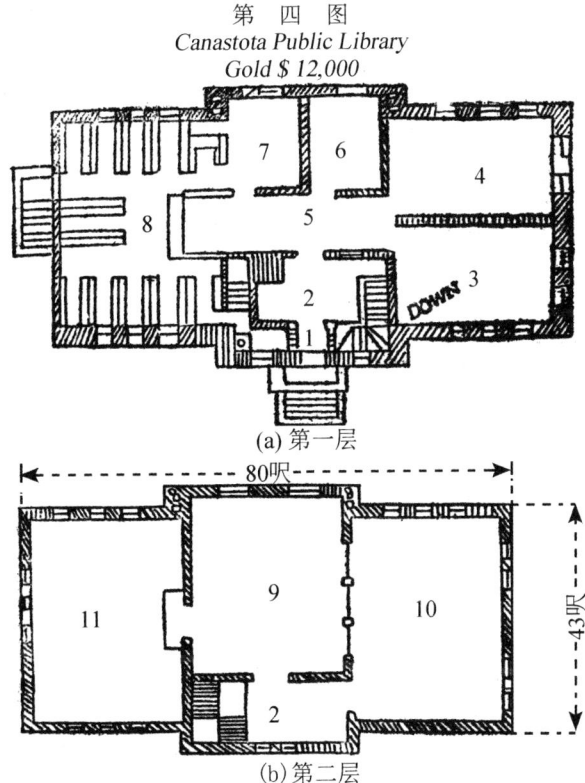

第 四 图
Canastota Public Library
Gold $ 12,000

(a) 第一层

(b) 第二层

1. Vestibule　　　　　　　　（入口）

2. Hall　　　　　　　　　　（门厅）

3. Reading Room　　　　　　（阅览室）

4. Children's Room　　　　　（儿童阅览室）

5. Lobby　　　　　　　　　（休息室）

6. Reference Room　　　　　（参考室）

7. Librarians Room　　　　　（馆长室）

8. Stock Room　　　　　　　（书库）

9. Lecture Room　　　　　　（讲演室）

10. Museum　　　　　　　　（陈列室）

11. Upper part of Stack Room　（上层书库）

可容图书 15,000 册

建筑工程师：A. Russell

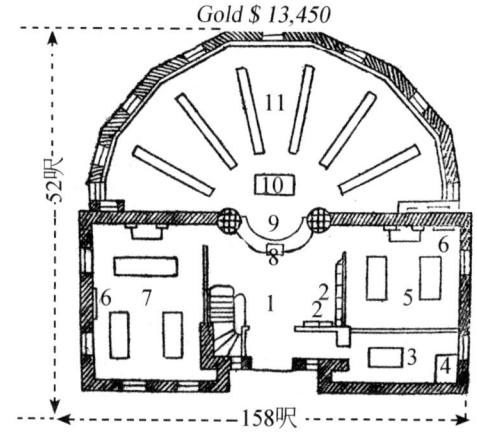

第 五 图
Lindsay Public Library
Gold $ 13,450

1. Rotunda　　　　　　　　（休息室）

2. Paper　　　　　　　　　（报纸）

3. Librarian　　　　　　　　（馆长室）

4. Desk　　　　　　　　　（桌）

5. Children's Room　　　　　（儿童阅览室）

6. Periodicals　　　　　　　（杂志）

7. Reading Room　　　　　　（阅览室）

8. Card Index　　　　　　　（目录片）

9. Delivery Desk　　　　　　（出纳书籍台）

10. Table　　　　　　　　　（桌）

11. Stack Room　　　　　　（书库）

可容图书 12,500 册

建筑工程师：G. M. Miller

图书馆建筑参考书：

1. Burgoyne, F. J. Library Construction London.
2. Eastman, W. R. Library Building Plans Albany.
3. Eastman, W. R. Library Buildings A. L. A. Chicago.
4. Marvin, C. Small Library Buildings A. L. A. Chicago.
5. Fletcher, W. L. Public Libraries in America Boston.
6. Snead & Co. Library Planning, Book stack & shelving. New Jersey.
7. Buildings, J. S. On Ventilation and Heating New York
8. Clark, J. W. Care of Books Camb England.
9. Chandler, A. G. The Country Library versus the Dener and the Architect, Boston.

第四章　论美国图书馆

西人游历中国城镇，普通所见者，城隍庙也，省有省城隍，县有县城隍，市乡有市乡之城隍。吾人游美国城乡，普通所见者，有四特色：即教堂、邮政局、学校及图书馆也。以前三者，为各文明国国民必要之物，而图书馆亦林立其中，不得不有疑问焉。盖国民教育已操之于学校，而图书馆之设立，如星罗，如棋布，用意何在？而有益于国民教育之关系亦何在？作者请暂不论图书馆与学校及国民教育之密切关系，先言美国图书馆发达史之梗概，以饷留心图书馆诸君。

一六七九年，有英国牧师勃兰氏（Dr. Thomas Bray）始创图书馆于新大陆之教堂内，如曼尔兰一省（Maryland），创教堂图书馆三十所，共有书籍二千五百四十五册，为教士参考而设，惟亦允每教堂区域内之人民，自由借阅。此可谓美国图书馆史之开辟时代。至一八零三年，始有学校区域图书馆之设。如纽约省在一八三五年，立专律以维持各学校区域之图书馆，教士学生有专所观览典籍。然而当时普通人民仍未免有向隅之叹，故法兰恩格林（Benjamin Franklin）集股创合股图书馆（Subscription Library）于费立特城（Philadelphia），不但认股诸人有借览该馆图籍之权利，而近处人民亦能同受该馆之利益焉。各埠商人，悯商铺学徒无从研究学问，而商人图书馆（Mereantile Library）于一八二〇年亦创于纽约、波士顿、圣路易三城矣。至于大学校图书馆之鼻祖，首推哈佛，此馆之设立，始于 Rev. John Harvard 在一六三八年，迄今为全国大学校图书馆之冠。至美国公共图书馆者，向以税饷维持，亦可谓人民之图书馆。英国国会议员（William Ewart）通过一议案，此公共图书馆之根本也。一六九七年，美国有（Sir Francis Nichilson）者发起，由曼尔兰省市政厅上禀于英皇惠廉第三，请抽军火税之一分，为设公共图书馆之用。不意此禀竟遭无结果之打消。至一八三三年纽哈姆省（New Hampshire）首创公共省图书馆①。二十六年后，纽极才省（New Jersey）亦创公共省图书馆。至十九世纪之初，人民稍稍知公共图书馆有益于社会，南加落立那省（South Carolina）设省图

---

① 【编者注】：原文为177年。现在一般认为美国的第一个公共图书馆是1833年在新罕布什尔州（New Hampshire）的一个小镇成立的，原文应为印刷错误。资料来源：陈同丽.追求卓越：美国公共图书馆的绩效评估.山东图书馆学刊, 2010(6)

书馆于一八一四年,纽约省(New York)于一八一八年,始设省图书馆,二年后,本薛佛尼Pennsylvania省图书馆成立。今首都华盛顿之国立图书馆,始创于一八〇〇年,虽已二次被焚,然迄今藏书之富,不但为全国之冠,而已为全世界之冠矣。

美国图书馆受个人捐资而成立者,始于波士顿之迭格拿氏(George Ticknor)一八五一年之义举。迭氏愿建一图书馆,与公共图书馆不同,愿多数之人民,能同时读一种有益之书籍。盖当时美国图书馆,亦如现今中国之藏书楼,专为保藏书籍,非为人民自修而设也。以图书馆为普通人民自修之所,为普通人民教育之关键,始于一八七六年。介绍此图书馆之新理想于人民之脑海中者,皆美国图书管理员会之力也。

美国图书管理员会,首由Professor Charles Jewett在纽约城于一八五三年发起,到会者共八十人,在闭会时,Jewett虽云愿该会作永久图书管理员会之母,然无教育界中人相助,而受一顿挫。直至二十三年后,该会始正式成立。会纲由全会会员一〇三人选定,并出图书管理月刊一种,作该会之出版物,以后每年有年会一次,以互相研究图书管理法,而以普及教育为目的。故现今美国图书馆之发达,而人民得无限之利益者,均此会之力也。该会对于图书管理法,详细研究,不厌烦屑,对于如何设立图书馆,如何购办书籍杂志,如何分类编目,均详细印成最简明之小本,分发于各处之有意设立图书馆者,并请驻会书记一人,筹划通信事。除此全国图书管理员会外,现各省有各省图书管理员会。骞初应美国图书管理员会之请,今夏特赴该会年会于纽约之散落托加泉(Saratoga Springs),默察该会会员之精神,皆悉心擘画图书管理法,会员互相切实砥砺。后又应纽约全省图书管理员会之招,而再赴波兰雪湖(Lake Placid)之会。该会会员之团结精神,互相砌磨,研究图书管理之法,实令人崇拜。该会之种种出版物,关于该省之图书管理法,亦详细研究,且助各图书馆改正管理上之缺点。

全国图书管理员会,始创于美国,后一年英国亦创立斯会,发起于英国国立图书馆长John Winter Jones。近年来,欧洲诸邦,如法、德、意均有全国图书管理员会之建设矣。美国图书管理法之完备适当,亦全仗诸发明家,如Cutter,Dewey,Winsor,Bowker等之力居多。至南北美战争时,方有美国妇女崛起,而为图书馆管理员矣。如将三十年前美国图书馆之数目,书籍之多寡,与现在之图书馆及书籍之数目比较,有天地之别。现不但省有省图书馆,市乡有市乡图书馆,而大城如纽约、芝加哥、波士顿等,一城之中有数十之图书馆,并有无数幼孩图书馆、盲人图书馆、医院图书馆、旅行图书馆、银行图书馆、工艺图书馆、大学校图书馆、高等学校图书馆、中学校、小学校图书馆及种种专门职业图书馆。自去年美国加入欧战以来,全国图书管理员会,即全力提倡军营图书馆、战场图书馆。美陆军总长Baker云,此次战争之胜负,非枪械之精,战术之娴,能决最后之胜利,其真能决最后之胜利者,在兵士能用书与否耳。骞为美国图书管理员之精神所动,故今夏毕业后,竭力思得军营图书馆之阅历,现已蒙政府许可,将赴军营图书馆为实地之练习矣;希日后还国有所贡献于我国之健儿也。

美国图书馆林立,得力于富翁慨捐者甚多。如纽勃兰氏(Walter Newberry)之三百万元之图书馆,建于芝加哥;飞斯刻氏(Fiske's)以一百五十万元之图书馆,赠于康奈尔大学;波兰忒氏(Enoch Pratt's)一百五十万元之图书馆,设于排尔跌城(Baltimore);卡纳奇氏(Carnegie's)二百五十万元之图书馆,建于Pittsburg;天尔登氏(Tilden's)之一千万元,赠于纽约图书馆。诸富翁中捐资建筑图书馆之最豪者,惟推卡纳奇氏,几乎各城各乡,均有卡纳奇氏之图书馆。去年军营图书馆,需一百七十万元之款,卡氏立助其半。若将美国富翁,曾捐助图书馆之芳名汇刻,必成一巨册。然而图书馆如此之多,藏书如此之富,则需有人理其事,是则图书管理学学校之设尚矣。在一八八七年,纽约省大学列图书管理科,为大学院之一专门科。在此三十一年内,全国设立专门图书管理学学校十四处。欧洲诸邦,均逐年遣有阅历、有心得之图书管理员,到美国专门图书管理学学校留学矣。故各国之图书馆管理,均取法于美国。由此可见美国图书馆,实甲于天下,而否则欧洲各国多典章文物之旧邦,岂肯俯首推重。今请细察下方纽约全省图书馆及二十五年来流通书籍之比较表,则可知美国图书馆尚有日增月盛之势焉。

纽约全省图书馆及流通书籍二十五年之比较表 1893—1917

年份 Year	图书馆数目 No of Libraries	书籍册数 Volumes in Libraries	流通书籍之总数 Total circulation	每日流通书籍数目 Circulation per day	每千个人中使用流通书籍之人数 Circulation per 1,000 population
1893	238	849995	2293861	6285	352
1894	293	1049869	2766973	7581	425
1895	309	1127199	3146405	8620	483
1896	351	1313299	3933623	10777	604
1897	375	1446874	4904793	13438	753
1898	408	1755036	6439999	17644	989
1899	431	1979319	7395527	20262	1135
1900	460	2187125	8452445	23157	1163
1901	529	2425260	9232697	25350	1290
1902	550	2598472	10063703	27571	1385
1903	555	2804628	10897126	29855	1500
1904	573	3108365	11347802	31089	1561
1905	*377	*2953177	*11685889	33115	1663
1906	678	3645662	13835639	37906	1715
1907	661	3782609	14968722	41010	1855
1908	686	4050563	16479457	45146	2043
1909	689	4227665	18749849	51364	2324
1910	710	4341103	19254729	52753	2387
1911	661	4635716	20122745	50131	2208
1912	*464	*4421901	*20309176	55641	2228
1913	*477	*4707472	*21530294	58987	2362
1914	*493	*5074650	*22918026	62762	2515
1915	*536	*5330826	*26003009	71241	2853
1916	*544	*5570271	*28223898	77326	2913
1917	*551	*5775115	*27259840	73693	2814

* 高等学校图书馆不包括在内

图书馆与教育,有极密切不能分开之关系。教育者,智力生长之义也;如不生长,即至灭绝。学校即教育之初步也,教少年人民以温故知新之识。然学校不能教育国民之终身,人人有出学校之一日,若社会中无图书馆,则多数学子出学校后,即于智力上不能生长。如要国民有终身智力生长之机,除图书馆外,别无较良美之法,故图书馆,可称国民之终身学校也。美国人民因知此义,故不惜数亿兆之金钱,造就全国国民终身之大学校,今者途人问答皆曰,"该村之图书馆在何处?"而不问"该村有无图书馆?"于此语,则知美国人民之教育与图书馆如手足,有不能分离之势矣。美国图书管理家Dewey云:学校者,锥也,图书馆者,大理石也,二者缺一,虽能工刻者,亦不能产美丽之石像。夫图书馆既为国民之终身学校,则该学校之教授法,不得不悉心研究。因该校学生程度之不齐,年龄之不一,各种职业,莫不代表,自专门有心得之大学教员,至目不识字之工人小贩;自耄耋之士,至四五龄之婴孩,故当此特制学校之教员者,须有适当之教授法,而应以上种种学生之要求,否则虽有国民终身学校之设,而于事实上,则等于无有。故设立图书馆之至要者,不在屋宇之宏丽庄严,亦不在藏书有汗牛充栋之富,首要者,在图书之管理法。管理适当,虽少数之有用书籍,皆能应多数人民之参考。管理不完备,虽有极多之书籍,而不能应少数人民之参考。仆在中国时,参观数处之公立图书馆,及通俗图书馆,管理法曾注重于保藏主义,而轻忽书籍流动主义。善本希珍之书籍保藏之,亦图书管理员之天职,然切不可不注意书籍流动主义焉。馆长应想种种法则,诱劝地方多数之人民,日常到馆;并于离馆时,多借流动书籍回家,为茶余饭后之消遣品,则该馆虽每年书籍因用而损坏之数不少,然而该馆馆长之天职尽矣!造福于社会,岂可胜数哉?

现我国最缺少亦最要者,莫如管理良美之图书馆。吾全国有无数之藏书楼,而可谓无一处有良美图书馆。中国历年来,派留学生之数,可称甲于天下;而留学生之在各国者,于学问上,均有极深之心得。然观近来三十年之留学史,虽为总长、局长者,比比皆是,然真能于科学上、文学上、工艺上,而有所发明,而能造福于国民,并能造福于世界者,其数少若晨星。鄙见非谓我中国学生之智力迟钝,实缺乏良美图书馆,为回国后参考之用,是一大原因也。留学诸君回国后,因无适当之图书馆,并于幼时未养成好读之习惯,故一遇此境,智力生长,骤遭停顿。而数年在异邦所得之学问,亦日退而无进境矣,故极愿我诸同学于设立良美之图书馆,希慷慨出全力相助,为发育国民智力日进之基础。

如欲设立有实用之图书馆,希留意以下诸事:

(一)切不可设在偏僻交通不便之处。

(二)虽不必有极华丽之屋宇,然终要整齐、清洁、干燥、空气流通、光线充足之所。

(三)若限于款项,所购书籍,不必出重价购善本希珍之书籍,应先购有实用而多参考资料之书籍。

(四)所购之书籍,应详细分类编目,以便检查,以省阅者宝贵之时光,以免书籍陈列架上,终无与阅览者。

(五)开门借书时刻,应日夜、星期、假日皆不闭馆,为利便人民起见;惟此项于人民极有益,而于图书馆款项上,稍有妨碍,因须加增馆员人数,并值星期及假日馆员之薪金应稍优,以示鼓励。然于人民有益,此层终须力行。

(六)馆长之对于书籍,切不可有守财奴对于金钱之观念。应想各种方法,使人民多用书籍杂志,而少窨藏书籍;须具商铺掌柜之资格,望每日夜皆有主顾,愈多愈善。切不可具局长之威严,有"图书馆为重地,闲人莫入"之牌示。

以上六项，实普通图书馆管理法之要素，希有意捐资设立公共图书馆者，三注意焉。美国图书馆管理员会格言之一云："出少数之金钱，购多数有用之书籍，与大多数人民享受。"此格言每图书馆管理员应当作金科玉律。骞参观美国各种大小图书馆百余处，而反顾我国图书馆之状况，不禁受无穷之感触，拉杂书此，希我国人于图书馆问题，有所激动，则于中国之教育前途，有厚望焉。

第五章　图书馆分类法

一、定义：

分类之法（Classification）自古以来，立论颇多，而良善者绝少。今先将其定义说明如下：

甲、英哲学家迈尔（Mill）云：凡物之属于一类者，必须有自然之顺序。今假定某种事物属于某类，而某类又按某种之排列。盖欲吾人易于辨别或记忆某种事物排列之法则耳。

乙、赫胥黎（Huxley）云：各种事物之分类，即用实在的或意像的整理法，将同类之事物放置一处，而将异类的事物另置他处，以明其性质之不同。排列之目的，在使易于鉴别，及记忆某种事物之特质耳。

丙、图书馆管理家克脱（Cutter）云：分类时集各种之书籍择其性之所同者，置于一处，是谓分类。

二、分类时其大纲有二：

甲、自然的或论理的（natural or logical），即检其性质类似者置于一处。

乙、人为的（artificial），即将形式类似者排列于一处。

图书馆书籍若用严格论理的分类，势有所不能。图书馆书籍分类法，应多少采用人为的分类法。此法对于书籍的排列、出纳手续及种种整理方法，应较论理的分类简便而适当一也。

按书与书论理的关系：同是一书，其排列之次序，亦因各图书馆性质而异。今举一例以证明之：譬如，研究莎士比亚之哈母来式①的神经症，普通图书馆置该书于莎士比亚所著书一类，而医学图书馆将该书排列于神经症一类二也。

一种书籍往往包含数种的学说，若用严格论理的分类，实有所不便。因一书在架上只能占一号数，而此一号数决不能包含数种的学说。故多少须应用人为的分类法，以济其穷，三也。

三、古时分类法：

甲、中国如诗、书、易、礼之分类法。

乙、希腊亚力士多德分人类智识为三大类。

1. 理想哲学：

$$\text{Theoretical Philosophy} \begin{cases} \text{Physics} & 物理 \\ \text{Mathematics} & 数学 \\ \text{Metaphysics} & 形而上学 \end{cases}$$

---

① 【编者注】今译哈姆雷特。

2. 实用哲学：

Practical Philosophy $\begin{cases} \text{Ethics} & 伦理 \\ \text{Economics} & 经济 \\ \text{Politics} & 政治 \end{cases}$

3. 外感哲学：

Productive Philosophy $\begin{cases} \text{Rhetoric} & 辞 \\ \text{Poetics} & 诗 \\ \text{Arts} & 美术 \end{cases}$

四、1603 至 1623，英国哲学家倍根①氏的分类法如下：

1. History 史记(memory) 记忆

（a）Natural History 博物学史，astronomy 天文，Physicgraphy 地志，Physic 物理，Biology 生物

（b）Civil History 民事史，ecclesiastical 宗教，literary 文学，memorials 奏记议，annals 通鉴，Biographies 传记

2. Poesy(Imagination) 虚想

（a）Narrative 叙事的

（b）Dramatic 戏曲的

（c）Prabolical(Mythology) 譬喻的

3. Science 科学(Reason) 理性

（a）Philosophy 哲学，Theology 神导学，Natural philosophy 自然哲学

（b）Human Philosophy 人类哲学，Physiology 生理，Speech 言语

（c）Civil Philosophy 民事哲学，Law 法律，government 政治，Society 社会

再孔德(Comte)、斯宾塞(Spencer)等各有学术分类法

图书馆分类法

美国创始有统系并有记号之图书分类法自哈理司(Harris W. T. 1870)始。哈理司分类法又名（倒置培根分类法）(Inverted Baconian)

A. Science(科学)

1. Philosophy(哲学) 2. Religion(宗教)

3. Jurisprudence(法理) 4. Politics(政治)

5. Natural Science(自然科学) 6. Useful Arts(应用技术)

7. Mathematics(数学)

B. Art(艺术)

12. Fine arts(美术) 13. Poetry(诗) 14. Pure Fiction(小说)

C. History(史记) 16. Geography Travel(地理及游记)

D. Appendix(附录)

哈理司同时，有法人薄洛纳(G. C. Brunet)亦发明一种有记号之图书分类法，名薄洛纳法，普通名之曰法国法(French Scheme)

---

① 【编者注】今译培根。

Class I:Theology（神学）（将各种神学为十小分类）
Class II:Jurisprudence（法理）
 1. General Treatises on Law（普通法理）
 2. Natural Law（自然法）
 3. International Law（国际法）
 4. Political Law（政治法）
 5. Civil Law（民事法）
 6. Criminal Law（刑事法）
 7. Canon and Ecclesiastical Law（教会法）
Class III:Sciences Arts（科学及艺术）
 1. Dictionaries and Encyclopaedia（词典及百科全书）
 2. Philosophical Sciences（哲理学）
 3. Physical and Chemical Sciences（物理及化学）
 4. Natural Sciences（博物学）
 5. Medical Sciences（医学）
 6. Mathematical Sciences（数学）
 7. Mnemonics（记忆学）
 8. Fine Arts（美术学）
 9. Technical Arts（技术学）
 10. Gymnastics（体育学）
Class Ⅳ:Polite literature（优美文学）
Class Ⅴ:History（史记）

欲知近时图书馆分类法,须先知各种图书记号之特长及书库中图书之排列法。图书排列法之沿革,约可分为五时期:

（一）照登录号数之先后排列:一书之排列,按书籍购入之先后为次序,并不顾及书籍之性质及形式为何如。

（二）照图书之大小排列,完全不顾及书籍性质为何若,仅就表面形式而排列。

（三）照字母记号之先后排列,或数目记号之先后排列。

（四）照图书与书库及书库内部函架之固定排列（Fixed Location）,如126430即知该书在第一层楼第二号房间第六架上第四排之第三十号。此种数号,仅表明该书在书架上之固定位置,与分类号数毫不相涉。

（五）照书籍分类号数排列,书籍分类法,即采用论理的及人为的分类法混合而成。

普通所用之图书记号法如下:

（1）字母法;（2）数目法;（3）代名字法,如天干地支或千字文等;（4）字母及数目集合法。此四种记号法,欲判其优劣,须先察其能否具有下述之五特点:

（1）易读;（2）易写;（3）易记;（4）易识;（5）易增减。

第一节　勃郎氏分类法（Brown Classification）

Class A. Religion and Philosophy（宗教及哲学）
  1. Bible（圣经）   2. Church（教堂）
  3. Theology（神学）   4. Philosophy（哲学）

Class B. History, Travel and Topography（历史游记及地形）
    National History and Topography（国史及地形学）
  1. Europe（欧洲）   2. Aisa（亚洲）
  3. Africa（非洲）   4. America（美洲）
  5. Australasia（澳洲）   6. Polar Regions（南北两极）

Class C. Biography（传记）
    Dictionaries and General Collections（辞典及丛书）

Class D. Social Science（社会学）
  1. Society（社会）   2. Government and Politics（行政及政治）
  3. Law（法律）   4. Political Economy（法制）
  5. Education（教育）   6. Commerce（商学）

Class E. Science（科学）
  1. Biology（生物学）   2. Zoology（动物学）
  3. Botany（植物学）   4. Geology（地质学）
  5. Chemistry（化学）   6. Physiography（地文学）
  7. Astronomy（天文学）   8. Physics（物理学）
  9. Mathematics（数学）

Class F. Fine and Recreative Arts（美术及娱乐）
  1. Architecture（建筑学）   2. Painting（油画学）
  3. Sculpture & Carving（雕刻术） 4. Decoration（装饰学）
  5. Engraving（雕版术）   6. Music（音乐）
  7. Amusements（娱乐）   8. Sports（游戏）

Class G. Useful Arts（应用技术）
  1. Engineering（工学）   2. Building and Mechanical（建筑法及机械学）
  3. Manufactures（制造学）   4. Agriculture & Gardening（农学园艺学）
  5. Sea & Navigation（航海术） 6. Health and Medicine（卫生及医学）
  7. Household Arts（家政学）

Class H. Language and Literature（语言学及文学）
  1. Philology（语言学）   2. Literary History（文学史）
  3. Bibliography（书目提要） 4. Libraries（图书馆学）

Class I. Poetry and the Drama（诗及戏曲）
  1. Poetry（诗）   2. Drama（戏曲）

Class J. Fiction（小说）

1. Collections(集合)　　2. Miscellanies(杂记)
3. Collected Words(集合著作)　　4. Periodicals not in other classes(杂志之不在他类者)

第二节　美国国会图书馆之分类法

A. General Works(总记)

B. Philosophy Religion(哲学及宗教)

C. History Auxiliary Sciences[史——扶(辅)助科学]

D. History & Topography(except American)[各国史及地形(除美国)]

E-F American(美国史及地形)

G. Geography Anthropology(地理及人类学)

H. Social Science(社会学)

M. Music(音乐)

N. Fine Arts(美术)
　　NA Architecture(建筑学)
　　NB Sculpture & Related arts(雕刻术)
　　NC Graphic arts in general Drawing & design(绘图)
　　ND Painting(油画)
　　NE Engraving(雕版术)
　　NF Photography(in art)(摄影术)See TR.
　　NK Art applied to industry Decoration & Ornament(应用美术,装饰学)

P. Language & Literature(语言学及文学)

PN-PV Literary History Literature(文学史,文学)

Q. Science(科学)

R. Medicine(医学)

S. Agriculture, Plant & Animal Industry(农学,植物学及动物学)

T. Technology(工艺学)

U. Military Science(陆军学)

V. Naval Science(海军学)

Z. Bibliography & Library Science(目录学及图书馆学)

第三节　克脱氏展开分类法(Cutter's Expansive Classification)

A. General Works(总计)
　　Ap General Periodicals(普通杂志)
　　Ar Reference Works(参考书)
　　As General Society(学会)

B. Philosophy(哲学)

  Bh Logic(论理学)

  Bi Psychology(心理学)

  Bm Ethics(伦理学)

  Br Religions(宗教)

  Cc Christianity(基督教)

E. Biography(传记)

F. History, Antiquities(古代历史)

G. Geography, Travels, Maps, Manners & Customs(地理,游记,地图,民情及风俗)

H. Social Science(社会学)

  Hb Statistics(统计学)

  Hc Economics(经济学)

  Hk Commerce(商学)

  Ht Finance(财政学)

I. Social problems(社会问题)

  Ik Education(教育)

J. Government(政治)

K. Law(法律)

L. Natural Science(自然科学)

  Lb Mathematics(数学)

  Lh Physics(物理学)

  Lo Chemistry(化学)

  Lr Astronomy(天文学)

M. Natural history(博物史)

  Mg Geology(地质学)

  My Biology(生物学)

N. Botany(植物学)

O. Zoology(动物学)

Pw Anthropology, Ethnology(人类学,人种学)

Q. Medicine(医学)

R. Arts(General Works, Exhibitions, Patents, Metric arts)[技术(总记,展览,专卖,尺度法)]

  Rd Mining & Metallurgy(矿学及冶金术)

  Rg Agriculture(农学)

  Rt Chemic & Electric arts(化学及电学技术)

  Ry Domestic arts(家政)

S. Engineering & Building(工程及建筑)

T. Manufactures & Handicrafts(制造及手艺)

U. Military & Naval arts(陆军及海军学)

V. Athletic & Recreative arts(竞技及娱乐)

  Vv Music(音乐)

W. Graphic & plastic arts（书画及黏土术）
　　We Landscape Gardening（园艺学）
　　Wf Architecture（建筑）
　　Wg Sculpture（雕刻术）
　　Wp Painting & drawing（彩色画及图画）
　　Wq Engraving（雕版术）
　　Wr Photography（摄影术）
　　Ws Decorative arts（including costume）［装饰术（包括服装）］
X. Language（语学）
Y. Literature（文学）
　　Yf Fiction（小说）
Z Book Arts
　　Zp Libraries（图书馆学）
　　Zt Bibliography（目录学）
　　Zy Literary History（文学史）

第四节　杜威氏十分分类法（Dewey's Decimal Classification）

000 General Works（总记）
　　010 Bibliography（目录学）
　　020 Library Economy（图书馆经济学）
　　030 General cyclopaedias（普通百科全书）
　　040 General Collections（丛书）
　　050 General periodical（periodicals on special subjects are classed with that subject）（专门杂志分列于专门各部）
　　060 General Societies（学会）
　　070 Newspapers（新闻纸）
　　080 Special Libraries polygraph（i. e. Collected works）（特别文库，摘录）
　　090 Book rarities（古书抄本）
100 Philosophy（哲学）
　　110 Metaphysics（形而上学）
　　120 Special metaphysical topics（形而上学之特别著作）
　　130 Mind & body（心理及身体）
　　140 Philosophical Systems（哲学系统）
　　150 Mental Faculties（心理学）
　　160 Logic（论理学）
　　170 Ethics（伦理学）
　　180 Ancient Philosophers（古代哲学）
　　190 Modern Philosophers（近世哲学）

200 Religion(宗教)

    210 Natural theology(自然神学)

    220 Bible(圣经)

    230 Doctrinal theology Dogmatics(信条神学教义)

    240 Devotion & practical(信仰及实用)

    250 Homiletic, pastoral, parochial(宣教师)

    260 Church, Institution & Work(教堂事业及功绩)

    270 Religions History(宗教史)

    280 Christian churches & sects(基督教会及宗派)

    290 Non-christian religious(杂教)

300 Sociology(社会学)

    310 Statistics(统计)(Statistics of a special subject are classed with that subject)特别事件之统计分列于各部

    320 Political science(政治学)

    330 Political economy(法制学)

    340 Law(法律)

    350 Administration(行政)

    360 Association & Institutions(社会及制度)

    370 Education(教育)

    380 Commerce(商学)

    390 Customs, Costumes, Folk lore(风俗,服装,及民俗学)

400 Philology(语学)

    410 Comparative(比较语学)

    420 English(英语)

    430 German(德语)

    440 French(法语)

    450 Italian(意语)

    460 Spanish(西班牙语)

    470 Latin(拉丁语)

    480 Greek(希腊语)

    490 Minor language(其他各国语)

500 Natural science(自然科学)

    510 Mathematics(数学)

    520 Astronomy(天文学)

    530 Physics(物理学)

    540 Chemistry(化学)

    550 Geology(地质学)

    560 Paleontology(古代生物学)

    570 Biology(生物学)

580 Botany(植物学)

590 Zoology(动物学)

600 Useful Arts(应用技术)

610 Medicine(医学)

620 Engineering(工学)

630 Agriculture(农学)

640 Domestic economy(家政)

650 Communication,commerce(交通学,商务)

660 Chemical technology(化学工艺)

670 Manufactures(制造学)

680 Mechanical trades(机械学)

690 Building(建筑法)

700 Fine arts(美术)

710 Landscape gardening(园艺学)

720 Architecture(建筑学)

730 Sculpture(雕刻)

740 Drawing Design,Decoration(图书装饰)

750 Painting(油画)

760 Engraving(雕版术)

770 Photography(摄影术)

780 Music(音乐)

790 Amusements(娱乐)

800 Literature,including Fiction(文学,包括小说)

810 American(美国文学)

820 English(英国文学)

830 German(德国文学)

840 French(法国文学)

850 Italian(意国文学)

860 Spanish(西班牙文学)

870 Latin(拉丁文学)

880 Greek(希腊文学)

890 Minor Languages(其他各国文学)

900 History(历史)

910 Geography & Travel(地理及游记)

920 Biography(传记)

930 Ancient History(古代史)

940 Modern History-Europe(近代史—欧)

950 Modern History-Asia(近代史—亚)

960 Modern History-Africa(近代史—非)

970 Modern History-N. America(近代史—北美)
980 Modern History-S. America(近代史—南美)
990 Modern History Oceanica & Polar Regions(近代史—大洋及地极)

克脱氏格式分类法：
1. Theory(理论)
2. Bibliography(目录)
3. Biography(传记)
4. History(史记)
5. Dictionaries(字典)
6. Handbooks(手册)
7. Periodical(杂志)
8. Societies[会(社)]
9. Collected works(集)

杜威氏格式分类法
01 or. 1 Theory(理论)
02 or. 2 Outlines(概略)
03 or. 3 Dictionaries(字典)
04 or. 4 Essays(论文)
05 or. 5 Periodicals(杂志)
06 or. 6 Societies[会(社)]
07 or. 7 Study & Teaching(教课,学业诸书)
08 or. 8 Polygraph(丛书)
09 or. 9 History(史)

第五节　清华学校图书馆分类法

书目分类,包涵哲学学理,实为一种专门之学。虽古往今来研究斯学者不乏其人;而新书之出版无穷,分类之准绳亦因之递变。我国目录之兴,始于《汉书·艺文志》;四部之别,肇于唐秘府藏书;而集大成于清四库提要。丛书汇刻,昉于宋左禹锡之《百川学海》。迨清张南皮《书目答问》出,遂于四部外别标丛书为专部。于是经、史、子、集、丛书五部目,遂为吾国旧籍分类之准绳。西国书目分类之学,起于英之培根(Bacon),其后研究者项背相望,如斯宾塞(Spencer)、哈理司(Harais)、勃郎(Brown)、克脱(Cutter)、杜威(Dewey)、美国国立图书馆,各有分类法,而其中尤以杜氏之十分法为最便利适用。其在泰西之价值,以视吾国之四库提要,犹驾而上之。然尤不能无訾议。盖天下事理有较善而无至善,殆进化之公理也。吾人向者以为博览群书,即可极编目之能事。然按之事实,未必尽然。见仁见智,本自不同。每一书出,各种学理互相牵连,往往有一书归入此类,归入彼类,各有理者。分析愈微,此种困难愈觉层见叠出。推乎西书分类亦何独不然? 故分类之在今日,正值研究时代,未可据一家之言以为断也。图书馆之编目,固当根据分类之举,然与研究分类者不同。盖彼主学理,而此重应用;于应用上倘无窒碍,则不复深求。本馆分类但使一般阅书者,易于检寻而关于管理图书者之便利,亦并及焉。兹分述如下:

(一)编目应代阅书者设想,使所有书籍如何定分类之号数,如何定顺置之次序;如何定皮藏之方法;俾阅书者一检即得也。我国旧时编目,只有分类,并无分类号数。故欲使阅书者检寻容易,当使该书在所置之架上,或所藏之箱内,有一定之位置而后可。然或箱架皆满,而又有同类之书添入,势必至无地可容,而另设箱架;久则同一类之书分置数处。一图书馆中之书如此藏置,不独表面失整齐划一之美观,且欲阅一类之书,势必分赴各处捡取,仍感不便。本馆编目,参照欧美最近编目方法:首编分类号数;次定各类各属之目,分隶于号数之后,成一有系统之组织;然后将各书纳入。于是每书各有其属于何类何属之号数。藏书者按号数属类之次序,顺置架上,则凡同类同属之书,永置一处。即每类有新添书籍亦易插入。因照此法编制书在架上,尽可伸缩移动。只须其号数之次序不变,即无纷乱之虞;且有任意扩张之余地,以备后来之子目,源源添入。盖一种编目不仅为当代载籍之用,必阅数十载后亦能入我范围,乃为难能而可贵耳。

(二)编目应为掌书籍出纳者设想:研究如何而使借书手续简便;如何而使逾限及已借出之书籍系何人何日借去,一查便得。盖一图书馆之设,必每日有数十百人借阅,亦能应付裕如。故编目之外,应编一种借书片及藏书片之袋置于书内。该书借出时,即将借书片登记借书人姓名、日期后留下(其详另载)。如此既省手续,又便检查,且一借书片可用数十次之多,亦断无靡费之虞。

(三)编目应参用世界各国通例,不能墨守一国之故习也。我国向用经、史、子、集、丛书为分类部目,历年以来,编目者悉尊用之。然自万国沟通,世界图籍流入中国者,科目繁复,卷帙纷杂,断非五部所能概括;即强令新籍纳入旧籍之中,旧时之籍有限,而新出之书无穷。势必此一部之书,逐渐增加;彼一部之书,相形见少。且古代之书,以科学眼光观之,往往时而经济,时而军事,时而哲学,时而物理,不能与科学书合而为一;强相牵附,只增纷扰耳。今欧美图书编目分类,条分缕析,纲举目张,其界限厘然划然,用之于西籍及科学各书固当;若以吾国性质笼统含混之旧籍入之,殊觉枘凿难容。故本馆编目将新旧各书分开,旧书仍照原有经、史、子、集、丛书分为五部;新书则参用杜威十分法分为十部。合新旧书共为十五部,以概括吾国一切书籍。庶使后出之书,亦得次第加入。惟是本馆编目事出草创;贻讥之处,知所不免。所望海内宏达,进而教之,使吾国书目,日臻完善,则岂惟为本馆之私幸哉。

暂定清华图书馆分类简目

(附注)本馆中文书籍分类,暂定旧籍新籍两种:旧籍分为经、史、子、集、丛书五门,新书仿杜威十类分类法分为十门而稍加变通。新书细目可参看杜氏分类法原本,兹从略。

旧籍分类纲目

经部

经000 群经类

  经000 群经合刻本

  经010 群经总义

经100 易类

经 200 书类
经 300 诗类
经 400 礼类
　　经 410 周礼
　　经 420 仪礼
　　经 430 礼记
经 500 春秋类
　　经 510 左传
　　经 520 公羊
　　经 530 谷梁
经 600 四书类
　　经 610 学庸
　　经 620 论语
　　经 630 孟子
经 700 孝经类
经 800 尔雅类
经 900 小学类
　　经 910 说文
　　经 920 字书
　　经 930 训诂
　　经 940 韵书
史部
史 000 总史类
　　史 000 正史合刻本
　　史 010 正史分刻本
　　史 020 编年
　　史 030 纪事本末
　　史 040 古史
　　史 050 别史
　　史 060 载记
　　史 070 杂史
　　史 080 传记
史 100 诏令奏议类
　　史 110 诏令
　　史 120 奏议
史 200 时令类
史 300 地理类
　　史 300 总志(附图)
　　史 310 都会郡县志(附图)

史 320 河渠

　　史 330 山川

　　史 340 边防

　　史 350 外纪

　　史 360 游记

　　史 370 舆地丛记

史 400 政书类

　　史 410 历代通制

　　史 420 各代旧制

　　史 430 仪制

　　史 440 法令

　　史 450 军政

　　史 460 邦讨

　　史 470 外交

　　史 480 考工

　　史 490 掌故杂记

史 500 职官类

　　史 510 官制

　　史 520 官箴

史 600 谱录类

　　史 610 书目

　　史 620 家乘年谱

　　史 630 姓名年齿

　　史 640 盛事题名

史 700 金石类

　　史 710 目录

　　史 720 文字

　　史 750 图象

　　史 760 义例

史 800 史钞类

史 900 史评类

　　史 910 论史法

　　史 920 论史事

子部

子 000 诸子类

　　子 000 诸子合刻本

　　子 010 诸子分刻本

　　子 020 杂家

　　子 030 类书

子 100 儒家类

子 200 兵家类

子 300 法家类

子 400 农家类

子 500 医家类

子 600 天文算法类

子 700 艺术类

子 800 释道阴阳类

    子 810 释家

    子 820 道家

    子 830 术家

子 900 小说类

集部

集 000 总集类

    集 010 诗文

    集 020 文

    集 030 骈文

    集 040 经世文

    集 050 书牍

    集 060 课艺

    集 070 诗赋

    集 080 词曲

    集 090 科举文

集 100 楚词类

集 200 先唐别集类

集 300 唐别集类

集 400 宋别集类

集 500 金元别集类

集 600 明别集类

集 700 清代集类

集 800 现代别集类

集 900 诗文评类

丛书部

(附注一)丛书所收,四部兼赅。故本馆于每书编有总目片外,其中细目另备分析目片,附入四部内,以便检查。

(附注二)丛书总目片分类号数,仿西书传记编法,概以丛字冠于著者朝代及其姓氏笔画数之上。

新籍分类简目

000 总记部
  010 目录学类
  020 图书馆组织法类
  030 百科全书类
  040 丛书选集类
  050 普通杂志类
  060 普通学会及学术陈列所类
  070 报章类
  080 特别文库类（系他人存储另藏一处者）
  090 善本类
100 哲学类
  110 理学类
  120 理学各论类
  130 心理学类
  140 伦理学类
  150 论理学类
  160 哲学派别类
  170 古代哲学家类
  180 近世哲学家类
  190 宗教类
200 教育部
  210 国家教育类
  220 教育学类
  230 管理法类
  240 教授法类
  250 学校体育卫生类
  260 学校出版类
  270 幼稚园及家庭教育类
  280 特殊教育类
  290 社会教育类
300 政法部
  310 统计类
  320 政治类
  330 经济类
  340 法制类
  350 行政法规类
  360 社会学类
  370 会社院馆类（指慈善事业者）

380 实业政务类
　　390 习俗礼制类
400 兵事部
　　410 军政类
　　420 兵法类
　　430 训练类
　　440 工程类
　　450 器械类
　　460 陆军类
　　470 海军类
　　480 航空战术类
　　490 军事余项类
500 科学部
　　510 数学类
　　520 天文类
　　530 物理类
　　540 化学类
　　550 地质学类
　　560 化石学类
　　570 生物学类
　　580 植物学类
　　590 动物学类
600 实业艺术部
　　610 医学类
　　620 工程汽机学类
　　630 农业类
　　640 家政类
　　650 交通及商业类
　　660 化学工艺类
　　670 制造类
　　680 手艺类
　　690 土木工程类
700 美术部
　　710 风景庭园术类
　　720 建筑学类
　　730 石工雕刻术类
　　740 装饰术类
　　750 绘画类
　　760 雕版术类

770 摄影术类

　　780 音乐类

　　790 游艺类

800 文学语学部

　　810 文典及修辞学类

　　820 文学读本类

　　830 诗歌类

　　840 戏曲类

　　850 演说类

　　860 文牍类

　　870 新文学类

　　880 小说类

　　890 杂著类

　　(附注)此部书籍关于各国地理号数悉照杜威氏所定者加入各类分类号数之后

900 历史地理部

　　910 地理游记类

　　920 世界名人传记类

　　930 外国古代史类

　　940 欧洲近世史类

　　950 亚洲近世史类

　　960 非洲近世史类

　　970 北美近世史类

　　980 南美近世史类

　　990 澳洲及地极近世史类

　　(附注)关于史舆部书籍各国地理记号悉用杜威氏原定号数

第六节　日本帝国图书馆分类法

第一门　神书及宗教
　　一、总记
　　二、神书
　　三、佛教
　　四、基督教
　　五、杂教
第二门　哲学及教育
　甲　哲学
　　一、总记
　　二、论理
　　三、心理

四、伦理

　乙　教育

　　一、总记

　　二、普通教育

　　三、高等教育

　　四、特种教育

　　五、学校外教育

第三门　文学及语学

　甲　文学

　　一、总记

　　二、日本文学(总记、和歌、和文、戏曲、俳歌、滑稽文学)

　　三、欧美文学

　　四、小说

　　五、演说及论说

　　六、书目

　乙　语学

　　一、总记

　　二、国语

　　三、外国语

　　四、速记法

第四门　历史,传记,地理,纪行

　甲　历史

　　一、总记及万国史

　　二、日本史

　　三、外国史

　乙　传记

　　一、总记

　　二、日本人传记(附系谱)

　　三、外国人传记

　丙　地理

　　一、总记及万国地志

　　二、日本地志

　　三、外国地志

　丁　纪行

　　一、内国纪行

　　二、外国纪行

第五门　国家,法律,经济,财政,社会及统计学

　甲　国家学

　　一、总记

二、政治学

　　三、国家学及宪法

　　四、行政学及行政法

乙　法律学

　　一、总记

　　二、刑法

　　三、民法

　　四、商法

　　五、证据法

　　六、诉讼法

　　七、国际法

　　八、现今法令及议会纪事

丙　经济及财政学

　　一、总记

　　二、经济学

　　三、财政学

丁　社会学（附风俗）

戊　统计学

第六门　数学,理学,医学

甲　数学

　　一、总记

　　二、算术

　　三、代数

　　四、几何

　　五、三角法,微分,积分

乙　理学

　　一、总记

　　二、物理学

　　三、化学

　　四、天文

　　五、地文,气象学

　　六、博物学

　　　　（1）总记

　　　　（2）生理学,植物学,人类学,动物学

　　　　（3）地质学

　　　　（4）矿物学

丙　医学

　　一、总记

　　二、生理及解剖

三、药物及调剂

四、内科学

五、外科学

六、皮肤病学

七、眼科学

八、齿科学

九、产科妇科学

十、小儿科学

十一、法医学

十二、卫生学

十三、兽医学

第七门　工学,兵事,美术,诸艺及产业

甲　工学

一、总记

二、土木工学

三、机械科学

四、电气工学

五、建筑学

六、采矿学

七、造船学

八、航海

乙　兵事

一、总记

二、陆军

三、海军

丙　美术及诸艺

一、美术

(1)总记

(2)书画

(3)雕刻

(4)金漆绘及漆器

二、音乐(附乐舞)

三、写真及印刷

四、武艺及体操

五、游技及娱乐(茶道,围棋,能乐,演剧,相扑等)

丁　产业

一、总记

二、农业(附茶叶)

三、园艺(附果树栽培)

四、山林

五、牧畜及养禽

六、水产及渔业

七、蚕桑及制丝

八、商业(附度量衡,交通,簿记)

九、工艺(机械工艺,化学工艺,附手艺)

十、家政

第八门　类书,业书,随笔,杂书,杂志,新闻纸

一、类书

二、丛书

三、随笔

四、杂书

五、杂志

六、新闻纸

第七节　图书馆分类法之评断

(一)勃郎氏分类法:(1)科学及书用科学之工艺品等类,尚未分析清楚;(2)记号法缺乏增减之能力;(3)未有别种分类法之长处。

(二)美国国会图书馆分类法:(1)只能适用于最大之图书馆;(2)记号法兼用字母及数目故易混杂;(3)缺乏论理的分类式;(4)尚未完全编就。

优美之点如下:

(1)极易增减;(2)适用于最大之图书馆;(3)注重地理(Geographical)分类法。

(三)克脱氏分类法:

优劣诸点各如下列:

(1)清楚;(2)与现世学术及论理的分类甚相似;(3)记号法简单易记忆;(4)含有弹力性;(5)注重地理分类法;(6)排列图书时之手续不易;(7)各种轻重不一;(8)无索引目录;(9)非熟于分类者,不能使用。

(四)杜威氏分类法之优点如下:

(1)简单;(2)有柔韧性;(3)记号易记易识,有前述之五特点;(4)小册、信札、簿记,均适用此种分类法;(5)数目记号已通行于全世界;(6)有详细索引目录;(7)门类轻重划一;(8)便于参用。

曾有攻讦杜威氏分类法者曰:(1)机械式;(2)无科学上之统系;如语学与文学相离极远,哲学制一类夹入于实验心理及心理学之中间,卞士克(Biscol)及尔力吉特生(Richardson)等(二人皆分类学名家)曰:杜威未曾云其分类法为理想中完全之分类法;然此法之奥妙,正在不以分类者之主观而分类,故其法有实用之功效,现时各图书馆采用此法者,占总数百分之七十五,岂偶然哉?

理想之分类法,务必包括以下五点:

1. Logical(论理的)

2. Geographical(地理的)

3. Chronological(依年代的)

4. Alphabetical(字母的)

5. Linguistic(方言的)

论分类法有价值之书籍如下:

1. Brown, J, D, Library Classification and Catalogicing; pub. by Grafton London.

2. Richardson, E. C. Classification, pub. by Scribners N. Y.

3. Sayers, W, C, B, Canons of Classification pub. by Grafton London.

4. Bostwick, A. E. American Public Library, pub. by Appleton, N. Y. (Chap. 12)

5. Bacon, Corinne, Classification pub. by American Library Association Chicago.

6. Dewey, Melvil, Decimal Classification and Relatives Index, Forest Press, Lake Placid, N. Y.

7. Cutter, C. A. Expansive Classification Boston.

第六章　图书馆编目法

图书是一种宝库,而目录者,宝库之键也。图书馆虽有多数可读之书,而不讲编目之方,利用之法,于阅者终无利益。其编目方法愈善,则阅者愈得便益。然编成目录极难,而手续亦繁。今先将目录必具之特点叙述之:

(一)目录须可阻止购置复本。

(二)目录须为图书馆各种册籍之主要,并须能划一各种记载之方法。

(三)目录须使阅览者在最短时间内,得悉该馆有此种书籍或论著与否。

(四)目录须能省管理者之强记。

(五)目录须使出纳科之手续,迅速便利。

目录之种类,可分三种:

(一)书片目录;

(二)书簿目录;

(三)印刷目录。

无论书片或书簿目录,均应包括以下四种之目录:

(一)著者目录　著作者置于片上之第一行。

(二)书名目录　书名置于片上之第一行。

(三)件名目录　用红色书于片之最高部,余按著者目录片式。

(四)分类目录　按类名排列于目录片抽屉内,如杜威分类哲学书籍,皆置于宗教书籍之前。

今将此数种书片目录各列一式如下。

(1)西文书著者目录片

973.3	著者之姓名	子爵
T81	美国革命史	新版
	出版地,出版者,出版年,(最初出版年——最后出版年)	
	三册,地图,廿一生基米突	

(2)西文书书名目录片

973.3	美国革命史	出版年
T81	三册	
	著者之姓名	

(3)西文书件名目录

973.3	合众国史,革命史,1775年至1783年
T81	著者之姓名　　　　　　　　　　　　　　　子爵
	美国革命史　　　　　　　　　　　　　　新版…
	出版地,出版者,出版年(最初出版年——最后出版年)
	三册　地图　廿一生基米突

(1)主要目录片之背面记录式①

第一册 登录号数	第二册	编目者之姓名
		合众国史一八一二年之战争
		海权
		编辑者之姓名
		第二合著之姓名
		丛书名
		书名
		已查得之著者姓名(书内无此姓名)

(2)件名目录片之参照式

飞禽学
可查得于此目录中在
鸟属

(3)同上

古传,	参考
神话	
寓言	
神仙谭	

---

① 【编者注】原稿序号即如此排列。

(4) 编译者目录片

842	编译者之姓名,名	翻译及编辑
M12	原著者之姓,名	
	书名…………1876—77 年 三册	

(5) 合著者之目录片

915	姓,名,及 姓,名
A43	书名
	出版地 出版者 出版年(最初出版年)二三四页　　插画

(6) 合著者之件名目录片

915	亚洲　游记	
A43	姓,名,及　姓,名	
	书　名…………	
	出版地,出版者,出版年(最初出版年)二三四页	插画
	肖像一九五生基米突	

(7) 合著之第二著者目录片

915	第二著者之姓,名及第一著者之姓,名
A43	书名…………………………出版年

(8) 合著之书名目录片

915	书名…………………………出版年
A43	姓,名及姓,名(名可缩写)

(9) 参照著者称号目录片

姓名	第一次男爵 Auebury
看	(地名)
爵号地名,名,姓	第一次男爵

(10) 参照著者最习知之姓名之目录片

女子未婚时姓,名	参看
已婚后姓,名	(未婚时姓)

(11) 同上

已婚后姓,名	参看
女子未婚时姓,名	

(12) 参照著者译名目录片

Göthe　　（著者之姓）	看
Goethe	
凡德语之 A,ö,ü 即 oe,æ,ue,之省略	

(13) 丛书编辑者目录片

姓,名	编辑
美国平民政治	
属于此类丛书之书籍于此目录中可于标目	
美国平民政治者觅得	

(14) 丛书目录片

	万国科学丛书	
613.7	卷六六　著者之姓,名	书名………………
L17	……………………	出版年
581	卷六三,著者之姓,名	书名………………
H52	……………………	
5237	卷三四　著者之姓,名	书名　出版年
Y69		

(15) 丛书中一种之著者目录片

975.5	著者之姓,名		
C77	书名…	出版地,	出版者
	出版年(最初出版年)五二三页,地图　一八生基米突		
	（美国平民政治）		

(16) 丛书与编辑者目录片

	美国平民政治；	（名）	（姓）	
975.5		H. E.	Scudder,	编辑
C77	书名；（名）	（姓）		
		J. E.	Cooke 著	出版年
G74.7	书名；（名）	（姓）		
		E. H.	Roberts 著	出版年
G77.4	书名；（名）	（姓）		
C77		T. M.	Cooley 著	出版年

(17)匿名著者目录片

817	（著者之真姓,名.）
C625	书名　　Mark Twain 著（著者之变称）
	出版地，　出版者（最初出版年——最后出版年）
	二册合订一册　　图　　二〇·五生基米突

(18)匿名著者书名目录片

817	书名	（最初出版年——最后出版年）
C625t	（著者之真姓名）	

(19)匿名著者参考目录片

姓,名,	（变名）	参看
（真）姓,名		

(20)主要分析目录片

821	著者姓(名)	
A736	书名及各篇著者之姓	出版地　出版者，
	出版年　　二八一页	廿一·五生基米突

(21)著者分析目录片

821	第二篇　著者之姓,名		
	书名	（在第一篇著者姓名）	书名
	及各篇著者之姓　　出版年　　九九页至二三〇页		

(22)主要分析目录片

821	第一篇著者姓,名
C693r	…书名,及第二篇书名,著者名姓
	出版地　　出版者　　出版年（最初出版年）
	五八页两篇　　十九生基米突

(23)书名分析目录片

821	…书名	出版年
C693r	第一篇著者姓,名(用缩写)	

(24)著者分析目录片

821	第二篇著者姓,名	
C693r	第二篇书名	（在第一篇著者）
	姓,名　…第一篇书名	出版年（三三页至五八页）

(25)书名分析目录片

821 C693r	第二篇书名 第二篇著者姓,名 (在第一篇著者姓,名)　　　　…第一篇书名 出版年　(三三页至五八页)

(26)主要分析目录片

948.1 K24	著者姓,名 书名　　　　出版地　出版者,　出版年 四〇七页　　地图,　　一七,五生基米突 包括挪威野花一章,著者姓名姓在三七四页至三九四页

(27)著者分析目录片

948.1 K24	挪威野花著者姓,名 　挪威野花一章之名　　　　(在著者姓,名　书名 出版年　　　三七四页至三九四页)

(28)件名分析目录片

948.1	植物学·野花类·挪威 挪威野花著者姓,名 　挪威野花一章之名　　　(在著者姓,名　　书名 出版年三七四页至三九四页)

(29)一书有两事项之件名分析目录片

917.3 C77	迦拿大·游记 著者姓,名 　第二册　书名 　　在著者之论美洲一书内　　　出版年　　第二册 　(三九七页至五一四页)

(30)同上

914.2 B79	园名,苏格兰·叙述 著者姓,名(未婚时姓) 书名 (在著者之述七园——皇宫书内　出版年(一一九页至二三四页)

(31—35)著者与件名分析目录片,此书有两著者各著一篇,其页数亦不连接。

(31)主要目录片(31—32)页数相连接之书名分析目录片

T27a	著者姓,名		
	书名(另一篇)传记名		出版地
	出版者	一八八八年	二九〇页	一九·五生基米突

(32)分析目录片

T27a	传记名
	著者姓,名
	(在著者之书名 一八八八年(一三九页至一九五页)

(33)主要目录片

916	书名	第二篇书名	著者名姓
W52	出版地 出版者 一八三三年 一二四页至一七七页		
	一七·五×一〇生基米突		

(34)著者分析目录片(题名纸各别)

916	第二篇著者姓,名		
W52	第二篇书名…	出版地	出版者
	一八三三年 一七七页 一七·五×一〇生基米突		
	(在第一篇书名 一八三三年〔第二篇〕)		

(35)件名分析目录片

216	贩奴业		
W52	第二篇著者之姓,名		
	第二三篇书名… 出版地 出版者		
	一八三三年 一七七页 一七·五×一〇生基米突		
	(在第一篇书名一八三三年〔第二篇〕)		

杂志编目法

(1)主要目录片(卷帖子完全者)

905	英国历史杂志	一八八六年——
E58	出版地	出版者
	本馆有	
	第一卷至第十卷	一八八六至一八九五年
	第十一卷至二十卷	一八九六至一九〇五年
	第二十一卷至第二十七卷	一九〇六至一九一二年

续下片

中文著作

	2			
905	英国历史杂志,索引目录…第一至第二十卷,			
E58	一八八六至一九〇五年　　　　出版地			
	零册一　　出版者　　一九〇六年　　至九页　　二五・五生基米突			
		○		续下片

	3
905	每年出版四次
E58	第一至第五卷　　　　克雷登编
	第六卷　　　　　　　克雷登加笛拿及蒲尔编
	第七至十六卷　　　　加笛拿及蒲尔编
	第十七卷至――　　　　蒲尔编
	○

(2)件名目录片

905	历史　　　　　　杂志
E58	英国历史杂志
	关于本馆所有此杂志之卷数,希参观
	英国历史杂志

(3—5)编辑者目录片

905	克雷登,名　　　　编辑
E58	英国历史杂志　　一八八六至一八九一年
一至六卷	第一至六卷

905	加笛拿,名　　　　编辑
E58	英国历史杂志　　一八九一至一九〇一年
六至十六卷	第六至第十六卷

905	满尔,名　　　　编辑
E58	英国历史杂志　　一八九一――一九〇一年
六卷至卷――	

（6）主要目录片（卷帖不完全者）

051	世界杂志　　一九〇〇年十一月——出版地	
W92	出版者　　插画	
	本馆有	
	第一至第九卷　　　　一九〇〇年十一月至一九〇五年四月	
	第十二至第十八卷　　一九〇六年五月至一九〇九年十月	
	○	续下片

	2	
051	每月出版一次	
W92	第一至第十八卷　　　　互奇编	

（7）编辑者目录片

051	互奇，名　　　　　　　　　编辑
W92	世界杂志　　　　　第一至第九，第十二至第十八卷
	（一九〇一年）至一九〇九年

关于编目应用之书籍：

1. Crawfard, E Cataloguing. Lib. Bureau. Chicago

2. Cutter, C. A. Rules for a Dictionary Catalog Government Printing Office Washington.

3. Cutter, C. A. Explanation of the Cutter-sanborn Auther marks. Lib. Bureau Chicago

4. Cutter, C. A. Alfabetic-order Table, Lib Bureau Chicago

5. Drwey, M. Library School Rules. Lib. Bureau Chicago

6. A. L. A. Catalog Rules. A. L. A. Chicago

7. N. Y. State Library School Cataloguing Rules, Albary.

8. Bishop, W. W. Practical Handbook of modern Library Cataloguing, N. Y.

9. Foote F. R. Cataloguing for small College Libraries. A. L. A. Bulletin, A. L. A. Chicago.

10. Hitchler, T. Cataloguing for small Libraries A. L. A. Publishing Board, Chicago

和汉图书目录编纂概则

（节录图书馆小识111页至117页）

第一、书名

（一）书名以记诸卷首为主，不可删改变更。

（二）卷首无书名，则就标签封面或半封面所题，择书其最适当者。

（三）标签封面或半封面所记书名，与卷首书名不同，或同为一书而有异名者，宜加补注并备参照。

（四）缺书名者可另选适当之名称，其不备者则补正之。

（五）合订书及有独立书名之附录，应将书名一一分出。

（六）分期刊行之书名，可除其顺序之号数，而仅标其书名。

第二、著者

（一）记录著者以书其本名为原则；如著者用别号或其他名时，应加补注，以备参照。但关于文学艺术著者以其最通行之名号代其本名时，亦宜附列本名，并备参照。

（二）著者本名有一部分不令知者，可于不知之处用其别名。

（三）丛书可取编者之名，所收之书则用著者之名。

（四）府、县、市、町、村、协会及其他团体所著者，则取用团体之名，如有特记著者之名者，宜加补注，并备参照。

（五）翻译书、较订书、注释书等，于原著者、翻译者、较订者、注释者均应分列记名。但注释书不载本文者，原著书人名可以省略。

（六）二人合著者，则记二人；三人以上合著者，则取最先一人名记之。应于必要，亦得将各著者之名，一一记出。

（七）著者如系外国人，则记录著者之名外，并宜揭其国籍。

第三、出版及书写之条件

书名及著者之后，宜记下列诸项；但在括弧内者，编纂时随意取舍。

（一）刊本写本之区别。

（二）出版地。

（三）出版年月。

（四）版式及书写之种类。

（五）出版次数。

（六）卷数及册数。

（七）图书之尺寸。

（八）装订之种类。

（九）出版人。

（十）地图及肖像或不在本文中之图画。

第四、目次备考及杂件

(一)目次但记书名,并揭载书中难解之处。

(二)便于搜索图书之参照,及明了其性质之备考,必一体附入。

(三)略语符号及书式,宜从别定之式规定。

第五、排列

(一)书名及其他之排列,都按五十音顺序。

(二)书名及著者之名有二种以上读法者,宜择其最适当者而排列之,并附列其他读法,以备参照。

(三)书名有冠称者,可别除之;但按本称排列,如冠称取舍不定者,应于必要可附以参照。

(四)同一之书有刊本、写本二种者,则先列刊本。

(五)同一之书共为刊本者,则先列其刊行在前之本。

附录

概则第二之注:

(七)可记入英、美、法、唐、宋、清、高丽、朝鲜等。

概则第三之注:

(二)记入发行所之地点。

(四)写真版影写等。

(八)和装、洋装、轴帖等。

(九)无出版署名人者,可记入博文馆、三省堂等发行所名。

概则第四之三项:

(其一)略语:

(甲)著:一著述、著作、撰述、撰著、讲述、口授等。

(乙)编:一编辑、编纂、辑录、纂辑、编次等。

(丙)译:一翻译、译述等。

(丁)注:一标注、旁注、增注、冠注等。

(戊)补:一增补。

(己)写:一写本。

(庚)刊:一刊本。

(其二)符号:

(甲)[ ]补足文字用者。

(乙)( )补注用者。

(丙)？示疑义者。

(丁),示绝句者。

(其三)书式:

书之形式,原无一定。

西书著者、书名目录编纂略则

（节录图书馆小识 134 页至 144 页）

编定此略则，系以美国图书馆协会共同事业委员所编者为蓝本，稍加取舍，而折衷者也。此中于东馆（东京帝国大学附属图书馆）不采用事项，用◎以为区别。文中所称东馆，即指东京帝国大学附属图书馆而言。

（一）记入书籍，应用下列之语：

一、著者姓字：苟著者之名不存，则以 anon（anonym，即"无名"之义）一语代之。

二、著者之名之首字：（Initials）须以其最后者，置诸最初之部位。

三、无著者真名时，则从其化名。

四、丛书编辑者之名。同时所采各著述，一一分出记入。

五、对于出版物，有责任之国都市、团体等之名。

六、分期刊行及不知著者名之书籍，可除其号数，记其最初之语，而移其号数于后部适当之处。所谓最初之语，当除其冠词计之，示格言（Motto）或分统（Series）等语，冠于书名之前者，亦须除去，而以其次为真正书名之第一语。

七、随本文之注释及一切翻译，可记入原著标目（Heading）之下。其不随本文之注释，应于注释者名下，题"就于某书之注释"。即随本文者，亦应将注释者名，记原书标目之下。

八、圣书（Bible）或其一部，（含有 Apocrypha 者）不论系何国语，可记入 Bible 语下。

九、"犹太经传"及"回回经典"（并其一部）可记入 Talmud Koran 之下。其他宗教之圣典，可计入该圣典于世人尽知者名称之下。

惟本书编辑者、翻译者等之名，可附列本书参照。Reference

十、书籍具有二人以上之著者，可记入最初一人名字之下；其他一一附列，以备参照。

十一、民事诉讼报告，可记入原告者姓名之下；刑事诉讼报告，则记入被告者姓名之下。关于船舶之法律事件，可记于该船舶名之下。

十二、贵族可记于其称号（Title）之下。惟其姓名，世多知者，则不在此限。

十三、宗教之上贵显，除法王及国君外，其他均记于其姓名之下。

十四、国君，除（希腊、罗马之国君）凡有土之君长、东方之著者及法王等，仅其最初之名，见知于世者，则记于最初之名之下。

十五、结婚之妇人，及其他更变姓名之人，皆记于其最知于世之姓名之下。（大都列最终之姓名，而以他姓名与之参照。）

十六、变名（Pseudonym）。得用以代其姓名；但以该著者变名当世知者较多为限，仍应附列本名，以备参照。

十七、团体可记于最初名称（除冠词）之下。其他名称见知于世者，亦宜附列，以备参照。（大概标出团体本部所在地之名称，再记团体之名称于其后；惟此以地名为团体名称之一部者为限。）

十八、参照(Reference)。若一著作有二个以上姓名见知于世者,不采为标目(Heading)之名称,应与采为标目者,施以参照。

十九、凡小说、戏曲、诗歌等,往往据书名而检索,故宜就其书名与著者,施以参照。

二十、从其他所著之书名。

二一、无著者姓名,则从书籍题名中之用语。

二二、传记书类,则从主人公之名。

二三、分期刊行物中,有称编辑者之名者,则从其编辑者之名。

二四、从重要之翻译者(如诗歌之翻译者),及注释者之名。

二五、从宗教上贵显之称号,但限于本书用此称号者。

二六、其他为便于检索计,均宜施以参照。

(二)标目:

一、以书名为标目时,著者姓名,必须明列,且宜从著者之国语。惟腊丁语①最为通行,可径用腊丁语。其用他国语者,则加括弧以为别。(又法王及国君,均可用一定之英语。)

二、英法语姓名中,以前置语(法语除及)始者,则并前置语记入,英法以外(外)国语,则记入前置语以后之语。

三、英语之复合姓名,宜记其中最后一部分;他国语则记最初一部分。

四、就国名著者,明彼此之区别,宜与以相当之注意。

五、表示著者阶级或职业之前置语,宜加记标目之中。

(三)书名:Title

一、书名所用标题纸(Title page),以精密确实为佳,不可加入订正、翻译、变更等事。但格言、著者学位、称号等重复事项,及一切不要紧者,可省略之。

视精密之必要,于可省事项宜用三点…为识。古书或罕见本等之书名,宜精密记列;假令其缀字与近代形式有异者,可一切照原形记之。

二、为明了书名之故,补入之附加,宜用括弧,示与文本有别。

三、大字(Capital letter)用法,宜据规定。

(四)出版事项(Imprint):

书名之后,应列事项,可按下列之顺序,但有[ ]者可随意。

一、出版次数(Edition)。

二、出版地。

三、出版者姓名。

以上三件与书名同,均用国语记列。

四、出版年,用亚剌伯②数字。

五、版权许可之年:如知实际出版年,与表题纸之出版年有异者,则以 C(Copyright 之略)置诸版权许可年之前;以 P(Actual publication 之略)置诸实际出版年之前。

六、册数。(如只一册,则按其页数)

七、地图,肖像,及不含于文中之插画。

---

① 【编者注】今译拉丁语。

② 【编者注】今译阿拉伯。

八、大小:表示大小有二法:(甲)按纸之折数,示其大略。如120,80,40,等;(乙)"用生基米突"精细表示,就图幅而言,必用"生基米突"纵横表示,其法式如下:125x87Cm。

九、属于该书籍系统(Series)之名称,于前记诸项既终后,记入括弧之内。

十、古书之出版地与印刷地有异者,宜于出版地后,记其印刷地。

十一、页数:书中各部最后页,可用"十"之符号连续之;无页数之部分,则计算其页数,记入括弧( )内。(若有三数以上之页数,则合之而示其通计亦可。)

十二、书籍出版事项,宜据本书籍,或由他资料而得知之事实、通例,据表题纸采用者(即出版之次数、出版地、出版者姓名及丛书名),书名宜从其国语。若有订正及附加语,可记入括弧内(地图、肖像等语,及册与页之略语,均可用英语记列)。

(五)目次:(Content)及备考(Notes):

备考(用英语记载)及目次,宜记其与书籍有关者,均可用小形之字。

(六)杂伴:

一、单线:(Single dash)示前行标目之省略,其下单线则示省略第二标目者。

二、连续数字之单线示起讫之意,数字以后之单线,示继续之意。

三、一语或一记列之后加?符号者,乃表示推定及存疑之义。

四、括弧示书名或出版事项之添加,或形式上之有变更。(此所谓括弧者[ ]是也。)

五、数字宜用亚刺伯文,惟国君、侯、伯及法王名之后所用数字(即第某世之意),常用小形之罗马数字。

六、目录编纂上所用略语宜别据定。

(七)排列(arrangement)

一、仅有姓者宜置诸兼有名者之前。

二、仅有名之首字者宜置诸同一首字而不全名者之前(但同一人物不在此限,此等处详悉之方宜有一定)。

三、前置语(Prefix) N. M., Mc., S., St., Messrs., Mr., Mrs 即 Mac, Sanctus, Saint, Messieurs, Mistress 之省略宜悉照排列。

四、一人之著述宜按下例顺序排列之

    甲、全集

    乙、一部分之地

    丙、个个(人)之著述宜除冠词用书名之初语顺序排列。

五、"字母"当按英语之顺序。

六、人名可排列于同样地名之前,地名可排列于同样书名初语之前。

原载:《教育丛刊》1923年第3卷第6集

英文著作

PROFESSIONAL EDUCATION FOR LIBRARIANSHIP

PROFESSIONAL EDUCATION FOR LIBRARIANSHIP

BY
TSE-CHIEN TAI, B. L. S., Ph. D.
Librarian, Tsing Hua University, Peking, China; Chairman of the Executive
Board of the Chinese Library Association; Author of
Recent Literature on China, etc.

With an Introduction
BY
JOHN BOYNTON KAISER, M. L. S.
Director of Libraries, University of Iowa

NEW YORK
THE H. W. WILSON COMPANY
1925

Published November, 1925
Printed in the United States of America

CONTENTS[①]

PREFACE	69
INTRODUCTION	71
PART I. THE DEVELOPMENT OF MODERN LIBRARIES AND LIBRARIANSHIP	
CHAPTER I. The Democratic Ideal in Education	81
II. The Spirit of Research in Higher Education	86
III. Increase of Printed Material	95
IV. Library Philanthropy	101
V. The Library Associations	105
PART II. TRAINING AND EDUCATION FOR LIBRARIANSHIP	
CHAPTER VI. The Librarians in Ancient Times	110
VII. The Medieval and Early Modern Librarians	120
VIII. The Professional Education of the Modern Librarian	130
IX. Changing Conceptions of Librarianship and Its Educational Requirements	142
X. American Library Schools	152
PART III. A PROPOSED SCHEME OF PROFESSIONAL EDUCATION FOR LIBRARIANSHIP	
CHAPTER XI. The Library School as a School of a University	165
XII. A Proposed Library School for the State University of Iowa	175
XIII. Requirements for Admission, Degrees and Curriculum for a Library School	183
APPENDIX I. Suggested Curricula for Both Graduate and Under-graduate Work in the Library School	193
APPENDIX II. A Budget for the Proposed Library School at the University of Iowa	200
INDEX	203

---

① 【编者注】该书原版为前言在前,按照现行出版习惯,将目录调整到前面。此外,为方便查阅,目录页码为本书中页码。

PREFACE

This study deals primarily with professional education for librarianship in the United States. Since the publication of Dr. Charles C. Williamson's report on *Training for Library Service* to the Carnegie Corporation authorized in 1919 and published in 1923, the American library world has had much discussion of the problem of training professional librarians. But none of the criticism and comment on this report nor the general widespread discussion which has followed has been based on a proper realization of the existing inter-relations between the development of libraries, the dominant factors in the determination of the character of library service, past and present training, and education for librarianship including the development of professional library schools.

The method employed in this work is, first, to present a theoretical analysis of the social, educational and intellectual factors which have been and still are dominant in the development of libraries and the determination of the character of their service and are, consequently, the dominant factors in the determination of the character of professional education for librarianship.

For practically every other recognized profession there is available the recorded history of its scientific and cultural development and of the training and education of its masters from the past to the present. But in the field of education for librarianship such is not the case. Without knowing the qualifications of the librarians during the various stages in the evolution of the office from ancient times to the present and without knowing definitely the reasons for establishing professional library schools and their origin and development in different countries, there is small wonder at having no proper instrument for detecting the factors at present changing the conceptions of librarianship and its educational requirements. The systematic study of the past casts light on the development of librarianship today and the careful analysis of the present may illumine the path to the future.

This historical method is applied in studying systematically the training and education for librarianship and the origin and development of professional library schools on the continent, in England, and in America. Especially have the merits and defects of the professional library schools of the last named country been critically analyzed. This constitutes the second part of this study.

From the theoretical analysis of the social, educational and intellectual factors in the development of librarianship, advanced in the first part of this study, and the historical study of the origin and development of librarianship and professional library training agencies in the second, a definite program for the future is formulated. The program receives concrete illustration in the specific proposal for a Library School at the State University of Iowa. This, including the curriculum and budget found in Appendixes 1 and 2 constitute the third part of this study. If in reading the chapters which follow it is felt that proportionally too much space has been devoted in a treatise on professional education for librarianship to a description of the various types of libraries that have developed from ancient times to the present, it must be kept in mind that this is necessary in order to show the character of service for which librarians during these periods had to be educated.

Throughout this study almost all the quotations of various authorities whether agreed with or not are directly quoted with two distinct purposes: (1) to avoid the unintentional accident of misinterpretation and (2) to give due credit to those who have before dealt with the particular points involved.

The writer wishes to apologize to the woman-librarian. Whenever there is occasion to use the pronoun, the masculine "he" is generally used. But it does not mean that he neglects the valuable feminine contributions to the profession. He may be permitted to assert that wherever the word "librarian" is used, it is meant to include both men and women.

The writer wishes gratefully to acknowledge his indebtedness to those whose writings or opinions he has quoted. The number of persons contributing in this respect is so large that it is not possible to mention them individually. However, special acknowledgements of his indebtedness are due to the following: to Professor John Boynton Kaiser, Director of the University Libraries, and Dean Paul Clifford Packer and Professor Forest C. Ensign of the College of Education, for their suggestion that this study be undertaken. The writer is further indebted to Professor John Boynton Kaiser for his valuable suggestions in procedure, helpful criticisms in development and untiring labor in the revision of the entire work. Without his deep interest and constant aid, this task would have been impossible.

The writer wishes to mention that the broad scientific attitude and scholarly atmosphere prevailing in the Graduate College of the State University of Iowa, exemplified by its leader, Dean Carl Emil Seashore and his colleagues, Professors G. T. W. Patrick, Carl F. Taeusch, Giles M. Ruch and other members of the College, have been a constant inspiration. He has been conscious of the fact that something was expected of him, and he has put forth his best efforts in striving toward this ideal.

Thanks are extended for the courtesy of the Board of Education for Librarianship of the American Library Association. It gave the writer the opportunity of attending its two conferences from which he got much inspiration and information from leaders of the profession in this country. To the members of the staff of the University Libraries, special thanks are due for their prompt service.

To Mrs. John F. Loeck who kindly read portions of the manuscript and to Mr. Jackson E. Towne, Superintendent of Departmental Libraries of the University of Iowa, who patiently read the entire manuscript and made many valuable corrections especially in the use of English idioms, grateful acknowledgement is returned. Finally much indebtedness is acknowledged to the writer's wife, Julie Rummelhoff Tai, without whose constant devotion, enthusiasm, and systematic effort in checking over the translations from German books and periodicals and painstaking labor in reading the final typewritten copy, this work would not have been possible in its present condition.

May 11, 1925   TSE-CHIEN TAI
Iowa City, Iowa

INTRODUCTION

Dr. Tai in his preface virtually supplies an introduction to his subject. If more were needed one could not do better than read the recently published *Annual Report*, the first, of the Board of Education for Librarianship of the American Library Association wherein the board expresses its convictions that "the repeated assertions concerning the scarcity of well-qualified librarians are in no way exaggerated." Indeed, this volume seems in itself almost a direct answer to what the board says so convincingly on the effect of the shortage of librarians and the means necessary for increasing the supply of those properly qualified for this work in all its manifold ramifications. That Dr. Tai differs somewhat from this board of experts in his conclusions and ably defends his position, and that others may with sincerity and reason differ with both argue well rather than ill for a subject in a stage of transition such as this and of such potential significance in the economic, cultural and educational life of the nation.

Readers of this volume will naturally have a special interest in the biography and personality of a foreigner who comes to us from the Orient and gives us not only the most substantial but what bids fair to remain for some time our most thorough and most stimulating history and commentary on a phase of professional education in which America admittedly already leads the world.

Tse-Chien Tai was born in Chuchiakoh, Kiangsu, China, February 27, 1888. His early education was at the hands of private tutors from 1894 through 1903 and as a student at St. John's Preparatory College, Shanghai, from 1904 to 1907, when he graduated from this institution receiving the Prince Pu Medal for excellent scholarship and the St. John's Alumni Medal for the best oration. This early education, as was usual in China at the time, included a study of the Chinese classics and history and it was then Mr. Tai's aim to enter the Imperial Competitive Examination under the regime of the Tsing Dynasty. Following this Mr. Tai taught history and grammar in the Jui-An High School, Wenchow, 1907 to 1909, when he entered St. John's University at Shanghai and became its assistant librarian. From this institution he received his Bachelor's degree in 1912 achieving again the medal for oratory, and here he pursued graduate studies for another year, becoming at the same time librarian of the University. The graduate work taken by Tai included special study in the realms of philosophy, sociology and education. At the end of 1913 his health was such that he was obliged to give up, for the time being, the thought of continuing graduate studies.

It was in 1908 when Theodore Roosevelt was President, and Elihu Root Secretary of State, that the United States government decided to return to China part of the Boxer indemnity funds, an "international act which was at the same time graceful and just," to quote Chinese comment on the matter. The Chinese government, recognizing the friendly spirit of America in this, decided to use the funds thus made available for the purpose of sending students to study in American colleges and universities. "The Chinese Educational Mission, as the resulting organization was called, stands then, as a witness to the friendliness of the great occidental republic for her oriental sister-republic. At the very beginning it was realized that, owing to the lack of college material in China, a school to prepare the students to be sent abroad would be necessary and in this way Tsing Hua College came into existence."① To Tsing Hua College Mr. Tai was called as librarian in 1914.

Mr. Tai's first trip to America was in 1917, as secretary of the Chinese Educational Mission to this country. Later that same year he entered the New York State Library School at Albany and completed, in less than twelve months and in spite of language difficulties, a professional training course, two years in length, and received the degree Bachelor of Library Science. Few of our own people have done as much. When asked whether he could speak English on coming to this country the first time, Mr. Tai naively remarked (with as near a twinkle as the oriental comes) "Oh, yes! But nobody could understand me." In the fall of 1919 Mr. Tai resumed his post as chief librarian at Tsing Hua, which he continues to hold. He is also a member of the Faculty Council and the Administrative Council of that institution. The library occupies a beautiful building of its own in the attractive grounds of the college some seven miles from the Northwestern Gate of Peking.

To write with authority on education for librarianship one should not only have been through the best education that has been provided in that field but one should have had experience both in various kinds of library work and in other educational fields as well. Mr. Tai meets these requirements. In 1920 he was the director of the Library Science School, Summer Course, at the National Teachers' University, Peking, and the following year organized the commercial library of the Chinese General Chamber of Commerce at Shanghai. From 1919 to 1922 he was adviser to the Nankai University Library at Tientsin and for the past five years has served in a similar capacity to the General Tsai-Soong-Po Memorial Library in Peking. Mr. Tai is one of a committee of seven appointed by the President of China as the Organization Committee for a Chinese National Library to be established in Peking, other members of the committee all being present or former cabinet ministers of the Chinese Republic. While in America recently he received word of his election to the position of chairman of the Executive Board of the newly formed Chinese Library Association, a board made up largely of statesmen, university presidents and other educational leaders. In 1923 the Order of Knighthood of Dannebroge was conferred on Mr. Tai by His Majesty, the King of Denmark, for special services rendered the Danish government.

Mr. Tai's standing in his profession at home is further evidenced by his election, twice, to the presidency of the Peking Library Association and his presidency from 1922 to date of the Library Science Section of the Chinese National Association for the Advancement of Education. For six years he has been a member also of the American Library Association and has kept fully in touch with library affairs in this country. Other interests are revealed in his membership in the Science Society of China for some seven years, the College Men's Club of Peking, the Advisory Committee of the National Defense League of China, the Peking Literary Club and the American College Club

---

① *Tsing Hua* 1911-1921: *A Review*, published on the Tenth Anniversary of the Founding of Tsing Hua College. Peking. May 1, 1921. 5op.

in Peking. Mr. Tai is a member of the Presbyterian Church.

This personal history is not given to show that the author of this volume has a right to speak with authority on the subject he discusses; that is quite evident from his volume itself. It is given primarily as biography but secondarily to show that were the geographical and institutional names changed to names of places and institutions in America the author's experience and record would be seen to parallel at nearly all points the experience and record of many of the leaders in the library field in America itself. In other words, we need not discount what is said because it is said to us by one from another clime. Indeed that has its advantages for us. The commentaries of De Tocqueville and Bryce have remained at par.

With the subject of this sketch already a quarter of the way around the globe from where these lines are written in Norway on his return to China via England, the Continent, Russia and Siberia—perhaps an even more intimate touch may be forgiven in this foreword. A friend and classmate of mine, Professor Carroll B. Malone, went to China early in 1911 as a member of the original faculty of Tsing Hua College when it was first opened in that year, while T. C. Tai was still at St. John's. A request soon came back from Professor Malone for information and books that would guide the new faculty in having the library of the new institution organized along American lines. Some advice and some technical publications were secured, largely through the generosity of the individual authors of several of our leading texts on various phases of library work. Some years later, in 1917 it was, a note in the library press revealed the presence of Tsing Hua's librarian at the New York State Library School, a matter naturally of special interest to me and I soon was in touch with him. Later came our entrance into the war and the development of the Library War Service of the American Library Association. When I reached Camp Upton as camp librarian in January of 1919, it was my pleasant surprise to find there T. C. Tai who had joined the library staff in October of the previous year. Acquaintance soon ripened into friendship and it is only the truth to record that Mr. Tai's industry and ability and his fine spirit of service at all times won for him the genuine admiration of all associated in the work of the camp library. Many a delightful midnight chat around the fire on Confucianism, the evolution of the written language of the Chinese and other oriental subjects, is now recalled with the keenest delight. Mr. Tai also assisted in the Library War Service exhibit of the American Library Association at the Asbury Park Conference, June 1919, and returned to China later that year via the Pacific. A year's furlough was granted him by Tsing Hua College beginning in August, 1924 and he and his wife (formerly Julie Rummelhoff, B. L. S., New York State Library School 1919) came to America for a year of professional experience and study, Mr. Tai being in charge during the trip of Tsing Hua's contingent of new students to America, to the number of some one hundred and thirty. The Tais' plans were a little uncertain. Mr. Tai hoped perhaps to lecture on oriental literature at some university; Mrs. Tai was engaged to work in the Cataloging Department of the New York Public Library. It proved possible to change this arrangement eventually; and, primarily at the suggestion of President Jessup of the University of Iowa, Mr. Tai came to the university and continued his graduate work. The studies pursued were educational statistics, mental measurements, school administration, university administration, modern philosophy and library education.

7   The dissertation prepared is the volume in hand which the university was prepared to publish at once, but, as matters developed, it was decided to publish through trade channels.

For a time it was thought that it might be well to revise the manuscript a little for general distribution as it concludes with a specific proposal for the establishment of a library school at the University of Iowa, but the more the question was considered the more definite became the conviction that no change was necessary. The general principles stated are widely applicable; the specific proposal is but a concrete illustration of how they may be applied in detail in any one of scores of institutions or adapted by existing library schools in a revision of their own curricula if the principles are approved. For the individual library, the prospective library school student, and for many others, the illustration has special value due to its very detailed and specifically concrete character.

In the pages that follow, as was indicated earlier, Dr. Tai differs from the Board of Librarianship of the American Library Association in regard to its proposed reorganization of the program of professional education for librarianship. Whereas the board proposes a fourfold system involving Junior and Senior Undergraduate Library Schools with Graduate and an Advanced Graduate School, Dr. Tai recommends a school in a university, organized as are most other schools, with an undergraduate and a graduate department. He would begin the study of library work in the junior year and continue it through the senior year, granting the B. A. and B. S. degree and would provide additional graduate work leading to the M. A. and Ph. D. It should be stated, however, in fairness to all concerned, that Dr. Tai's comments relate to the *Provisional Minimum Standards for Library*

8   *Schools* as outlined by the Board of Education for discussion and criticism in April, 1925 and not in the final form of the board's proposals in its first *Annual Report* which appear in print June 20. Dr. Tai's work was completed early in May. The changes between the board's *Provisional Standards*, however, and those subsequently advocated are so slight that we may safely assume that Dr. Tai's comments would not be materially altered now. It should be said further that the points of agreement between the board and Dr. Tai's proposals are as interesting and significant as are the points of difference.

It will be seen that Dr. Tai attaches considerable importance to Professor Robert J. Leonard's insistence on a proper differentiation in professional education between the highest-level professional group and the middle-level occupational group and intimates that failure to make such a differentiation has been as great a mistake in education for librarianship as Professor Leonard claims it has been in other fields, such as law, dentistry, engineering, agriculture, business administration and education. It is an interesting speculation whether Professor Leonard's later discussion of professional education in junior colleges,② which appeared after this work was completed, contains suggestions which can be applied with profit to education for some of the "lower levels" of librarianship.

Whether one accepts or not this theory of levels and its application to education for librarianship, it has been clear for some time that librarians, those in the business of educating librarians,

---

② *Teachers College Record*. 26:724-33. May, 1925.

and those who use libraries have not differentiated sufficiently between the different types of work that must go on within a library and the necessary and corresponding differences in training which different types of work predicate.

  It is probably obvious to all that library work may be divided at least into two types, professional and subprofessional. It is almost equally obvious that a fourfold division into mechanical, clerical, technical and professional can logically be adopted and fairly consistently applied, although there will be overlapping in some positions. *The Brief and Specifications for Library Service in the Federal Government* submitted to the Personnel Classification Board by a committee of government librarians for the District of Columbia Library Association in 1923 proposed the following detailed classification of library personnel and outlined the duties and responsibilities, qualifications and salaries for each class specified (except the first two):

I. Custodial Service
II. Clerical Service
III. Sub-professional Library Service

Minor Library Assistant	Grade 1
Under Library Assistant	Grade 2
Junior Library Assistant	Grade 3
Library Assistant	Grade 4
Main Library Assistant	Grade 5

IV. Professional and Scientific Library Service
  1. Library Administration

Junior Administrative Librarian	Grade 1
Assistant Administrative Librarian	Grade 2
Associate Administrative Librarian	Grade 3
Administrative Librarian	Grade 4
Senior Administrative Librarian	Grade 5
Senior Administrative Consulting Librarian	Grade 5
Chief Administrative Librarian	Grade 6
Librarian, Public Library, District of Columbia; Assistant Librarian of Congress	
Special Administrative Librarian	Grade 7

  2. Reference, Research and Bibliography

Junior Reference Librarian	Grade 1
Assistant Reference Librarian	Grade 2
Associate Reference Librarian	Grade 3
Associate Bibliographical Librarian	Grade 3
Reference Librarian	Grade 4

  3. Technical

Junior Librarian	Grade 1

Junior Cataloging Librarian	Grade 1
Assistant Cataloging Librarian	Grade 2
Associate Cataloging Librarian	Grade 3

4. Special Work

Junior Children's Librarian	Grade 1

In the Class Specifications for Positions in the Departmental Service issued by the Personnel Classification Board of 1924 this grouping of positions in libraries was altered but little and a few changes were made in terminology. The "sub-professional" group became the "library assistant" group with seven instead of five grades and the "professional and scientific" group became the "librarian group" with six grades instead of the sub-divisions noted above.

If all this seems carrying the classification of positions in a library a little far let it be stated at once this is but a beginning with more to follow, much of which is already well under way. Indeed personnel experts tell us that if we will accept their definition of a "class," there are at least two hundred and fifty true classes of library positions in public, university, college, normal school and high school libraries. There is much in all this for the consideration of those who are formulating both policies and details in the field of preparation for librarianship.

As a matter of fact this question of education for librarianship is at least a four-fold problem. There is involved, first, the question of an understanding of the place and purpose of libraries in our system of social organization and an understanding of the specific function of each of the numerous types of libraries that has developed to meet recognized needs. Next comes the necessity for knowing exactly what work is required of each member of a library staff in order that the institution may function properly in every respect; selecting those persons who are best fitted to perform these several tasks follows; and, lastly, is the building of a curriculum of instruction that will best fit prospective librarians for their respective tasks. In other words, there is the philosophy of the work and the "job analysis," the education of prospective candidates, and the fitting of the candidate himself to the "job" he can perform best.

The editor of the *Bulletin* of the National Education Association stated last year that we could easily absorb seven thousand new recruits each year into our libraries. The chapter on "Library Education" in the Cleveland Foundation's *Survey of Higher Education in Cleveland* published within a few months states that there are only forty-four hundred graduates of American library schools now actually engaged in library work in all the nine or ten thousand libraries of the United States and Canada, and not a few from abroad are included in this number who have gone back into library work in their own countries.

Libraries have an increasingly important function to perform in helping to achieve, in the broadest sense, all the social aims of education. Dr. William S. Learned has recently characterized librarians as "the new clergy of the mind", the "community's intelligence service," and a few years ago, Dr. Osier, the beloved physician and bibliographer, suggested for them the title (or, was it the degree?) *doctor perplexorum*. These titles suggest in a measure the relation of the librarian both to the community and to the individual. In a letter two years ago, while China was in the midst of troublous times (from which she has not yet emerged) the author of this book wrote: "My friends and I all believe that the only salvation for China's future is the problem of educating the mass. " Is that not democracy's problem everywhere? In it there is a challenge for the library and a challenge which the agencies for training librarians must prepare to meet.

There is comfort for the writer in the saying of Emerson that "Consistency is the hobgoblin of little minds!" He has frankly stated that Dr. Tai provided his own introduction and then he proceeded at length to provide another. His excuse is that he was invited so to do by the author in a way that could not be refused. He admits having said some things that the modesty of the author would not have permitted to appear in a foreword to this book. But distance has put the author at the mercy of his introducer; and, indeed, there is much more that might be said.

One final word: In commending this volume wholeheartedly to the largest possible audience, the writer of this introduction realizes somewhat the feeling of the condemned criminal when he assists the hangman to adjust the noose about his own neck. Three authorities — the Association of American Universities, the Board of Education of the American Library Association, and his friend, Dr. Tai—now agree that the only two professional degrees that the writer holds must be abandoned. But we recall McCarthy, McCarthy of *The Wisconsin Idea*, who cheerfully drafted a bill for an irate legislator to abolish the splendid Legislative Reference Bureau which he, McCarthy, had founded and managed so successfully for so many years. After all, the play's the thing. Cheerfully, *Morituri te salutamus*.

JOHN BOYNTON KAISER

SOME PUBLICATIONS BY DR. TAI[①]

In Chinese

"Influence of Modern Education." *St. John's Echo.* Nov., 1912.

"Library and Popular Education." *Democracy and Education.* Nov., 1919.

"Library Profession." *St. John's Echo.* (Alumni Number) Feb., 1920.

"Chinese Wood-Block Printed Books and Provincial Libraries." *New Education.* (Proceedings Number) Feb., 1922.

"Outlines of Library Science." National Teachers' University Press. Peking. 1922. 120p.

"Library Science and Normal Schools." *New Education.* (Proceedings Number) Feb., 1923.

"Comments on Library Science." *New Education.* Mar., 1924.

"Principles of Classification of Books." *Peking Library Association Bulletin.* Feb., 1925.

In English

"Recent Literature on China with Annotations." *Chinese Students' Monthly.* Vol. 13. No. 1—Vol. 14. No. 8. Nov., 1918-June, 1919. (about) 80p. A monthly contribution of six to ten pages.

"Library Movement in China" *Bulletin of the National Association for the Advancement of Education.* Vol. 2. No. 3. Peking. 1923. 20p. (Also reprinted by the Commercial Press. Shanghai. 1924. 22p.)

Written for the Chinese delegates to the International Education Conference at Los Angeles, 1923.

"A Brief Sketch of Chinese Libraries." *Library Journal.* 44:423-9. July, 1919.

"Present Library Conditions in China." *Public Libraries.* 24:37-40. Feb., 1919.

"Library Excitements." *Philadelphia Record.* May, 1919.

(Prize Story of War Service)

"Library Service in China." *American Library Association, Annual Reports*, 1920-21. p. 58-63. 1921.

"An Advanced School of Librarianship—Aim of Curriculum." *Public Libraries.* 30:59-61. Feb., 1925.

---

① Many of the publications containing Dr. Tai's writings are not available in this country, hence the incomplete bibliographical details.

In French

"Les Bibliothèques Chinois." *La Politique de Pekin.* Jan. ,1920.
Publications Edited
Library Science. Commercial Press. 2vols. Shanghai.
1924. (In Chinese)
Supplements to Dewey's Decimal Classification for Chinese Books. Tsing Hua College. Peking. 1924. 33p. (In English and Chinese)

PART I
THE DEVELOPMENT OF MODERN LIBRARIES AND LIBRARIANSHIP

CHAPTER   I.   The Democratic Ideal in Education
CHAPTER   II.   The Spirit of Research in Higher Education
CHAPTER   III.   Increase of Printed Material
CHAPTER   IV.   Library Philanthropy
CHAPTER   V.   The Library Associations

CHAPTER I
THE DEMOCRATIC IDEAL IN EDUCATION

Throughout history many different forces have been at work moulding the character of the modern library. The democratic ideal of education is to give every citizen the opportunity of schooling. It is his or her birthright to be brought into contact with the rudiments of learning—reading, writing, and arithmetic. The democratic tendency in education since Rousseau's *Emile* has been gradually developed in this country. In the second half of the nineteenth century the establishment of free public schools by the government of all the states was already a matter of fact. That impressive situation was well described by the French Commission to the Centennial Exposition of 1876.

The great zeal for the education of the youth which grows as the population increases, penetrates into the public mind more and more, and manifests itself in more and more decided ways. What may have seemed at first a transient glow of enthusiasm, a generous impulse, has in time assumed all the force of a logical conviction, or rather of a positive certainty. It is no longer a movement of a few philanthropists or of a few religious societies, but it is an essential part of the public administration for which the states, the cities and townships appropriate every year more money than any other country in the world has hitherto devoted to the education of the people. Far from limiting this generosity as much as possible to primary instruction, it goes so far as to declare free for all not only primary but even secondary schools. ①

The period between 1835 and 1861 in American history was a great epoch of territorial expansion toward the west, of industrial development in the east, and of educational awakening, especially in the New England states. It was a period of growth in democratic ideas and of belief in human betterment. The statesmen, the religious thinkers, the social reformers, and others all believed that the extension of the franchise, growth of industrial prosperity, and social betterment of the masses from poverty and crime must call for a new system of democratic education. If all citizens were entitled to the right to vote, they must be qualified to vote intelligently. Education for the masses was conceived as the means of realizing the ideals. As early as 1852 the state of Massachusetts introduced the law of compulsory attendance. Many public schools were established and all children were required to attend school to receive regular training in reading and thinking.

This great period of educational awakening and establishing public schools for the masses resulted, among other things, in the formation of modern libraries. Educators knew that the period of formal schooling was limited. The method of teaching in schools was only to teach pupils how to read, to spell, and to write, but seldom taught the pupils how to educate themselves. The educators also saw clearly that it would be unfortunate if young people after quitting the schools and becoming

---

① F. V. N. Painter. *History of Education.* Appleton. New York. 1903. p. 321-2.

bread-winners were to have no agency to furnish them good and desirable reading. Charles Francis Adams, Jr., in an address delivered before the teachers of Quincy, Massachusetts, in 1877, expressed a pessimistic view of the smattering education accorded the youth of that day.

The child was made to learn some queer definition in words, or some disagreeable puzzle in figures, as if it were in itself an acquisition of value… The result was that the scholars acquire with immense difficulty something which they forgot with equal ease; and when they left our grammar schools, they had what people are pleased to call the rudiments of education, and yet not one in twenty of them could sit down and write an ordinary letter, in a legible hand, with ideas clearly expressed, in words correctly spelled; and the proportion of those who left school with either the ability or desire to further educate themselves was scarcely greater… A man or woman whom a whole childhood spent in the common schools has made able to stumble through a newspaper, or labor through a few trashy books, is scarcely better off than one who cannot read at all. Indeed, I doubt if he or she is as well off, for it has long been observed that a very small degree of book knowledge almost universally takes a depraved shape, the animal will come out. The man who can barely spell out his newspaper confines his labor in nine cases out of ten to these highly seasoned portions of it which relate to acts of violence and especially to murders. A little learning is proverbially a dangerous thing; and the less the learning the greater the danger. ②

Many great educators at that time felt the need of better methods of teaching in the public schools and also of some educational agency which would continue what the school had begun. They desired to have something which could exert a continuous educational influence over the young as well as the old; which could supply a stimulus for the development of individuality among the citizens; and which could gratify those who had a strong love for reading. This something was bound to be the public library. Since the first half of the nineteenth century, modern public libraries have been gradually founded side by side with the public schools. The public schools not only taught pupils how to read, to spell, and to write, but also began to give them the tools with which to educate themselves in the form of books available in the more modern type of public libraries. From that time, schools and libraries joined together to do their educational work. The library became a natural complement of the school. Between teachers and librarians of vision there has been from the beginning close cooperation.

Samuel S. Green performed a hitherto untried experiment in Worcester, Massachusetts, in 1887, when he placed four little libraries, made up of books most likely to be useful in school work, in the rooms of the sixth, seventh, eighth, and ninth grades. The results of the use of these books were as follows during the two hundred days of the school year 1886-1887: ③

Grade 9   Home use 856   Reference use 2522

---

② C. F. Adams, Jr. The Public Library and the Public Schools. *Library Journal.* 1:437-8. August, 1877.

③ S. S. Green. The Public Library and the Schools in Worcester. *Library Journal.* 12: 119-21. March, 1887, and *Library Journal.* 12:400-2. September-October, 1887.

Grade 8   Home use 595   Reference use 1565

Grade 7   Home use 650   Reference use 1032

Grade 6   Home use 595   Reference use 908

This encouragement to the use of modern public library facilities by school teachers and scholars produced satisfactory results. Many superintendents of schools and school principals have felt and still feel that the modern public library is not only useful but indispensable to the system of public schools. The democratic ideal in education would not have fully developed if there had been instituted only the public schools without their natural and necessary complement, modern public libraries. Without the library the work in schools would become the rigid method of memorizing text-books, and the desire for knowledge awakened in classrooms would have to go unsatisfied. Melvil Dewey emphasized this very point in his address before the convocation of the University of the State of New York in 1888.

Our schools, at best, will only furnish the tools(how rudimentary these tools for most people); but in the ideal libraries, towards which we are looking today, will be found the materials with which these tools may be worked up into good citizenship and higher living. The schools give the chisel; the libraries the marble; there can be no statues without both. ④

Thus, the movement of education for the masses resulted in the founding of public schools, which, in turn, was one of the influential factors in bringing about the development of public libraries. The children who are educated in the public schools must continue their training after they leave the classroom or the endeavors of their teachers will not have been of much use. But besides the young, there are adults in every community to be educated. Therefore, it is the duty of the state to establish and maintain by taxation not only schools for the young but public libraries both for the young and the mature. A democratic state cannot compromise with the idea that the sphere of the common people is merely to work and not to read and to think. In order to live up to the democratic ideal of education the state took up the task of providing public libraries for the people who saw clearly the merit and importance of their service. These people, then, willingly allowed themselves to be taxed for the purpose of sustaining these libraries.

The recognition of public libraries as an essential part of the system of public education was first advocated in 1826 by DeWitt Clinton, Governor of the state of New York. In 1838 General John A. Dix, Secretary of state for New York, was "charged with the execution of the law giving to the school districts \$55,000 a year to buy books for their libraries, and requiring them to raise by taxation an equal amount for the same purpose."⑤

---

④ Melvil Dewey. Libraries as Related to the Educational Work of the State. *Library Notes*. 3:340. June, 1888.

⑤ Moses Coit Tyler. Historical Evolution of the Free Public Library in America and Its True Function in the Community. *Library Journal*. 9:40-7. March, 1884; reprinted in A. E. Bostwick. *Library and Society*. Wilson. New York. 1920. p. 17-32.

Thus, New York has the honor of being the first state to recognize the full significance of public libraries in the realization of the democratic ideal of education for the masses. Soon the school district libraries were also advocated in the state of Massachusetts by the eminent educator, Horace Mann. He had been personally benefited by the service of a little library at Franklin. The significance of this is shown by Mr. A. E. Winship in his story of Mann in *Great American Educators*: "As this library furnished the only books that Horace Mann had in his boyhood and youth, without it he would probably have developed no taste for scholarship, and the world would not have known this most brilliant American educator. Mr. Mann was so much indebted to this library, that in speaking of it in later years, he said he would like to scatter libraries broadcast over the land as a farmer sows his wheat."⑥ Through Mann's enthusiasm and influence the school district library law was passed in Massachusetts in 1837.

Michigan adopted and incorporated similar provisions into its school law in 1837. Then the tide swept over the seventeen other states in the following chronological order: Connecticut in 1839; Rhode Island and Iowa in 1840; Indiana in 1841; Maine in 1844; Ohio in 1847; Wisconsin in 1848; Missouri in 1853; California and Oregon in 1854; Illinois in 1855; Kansas and Virginia in 1870; New Jersey in 1871; Kentucky and Minnesota in 1873; and Colorado in 1876.

Although this first movement to establish public libraries with the school district as a unit was a failure through sheer lack of proper administration, yet it had a threefold effect in connection with the development of modern public libraries in America. First, it was the forerunner of the movement for town or city libraries. Had it not been for this pioneer legislation in the establishment of school district libraries, it is improbable that the first city library for which a special state law was enacted would have been born in the city of Boston as early as the year 1848. The present modern libraries of American cities and counties are all the prosperous descendants of that humble ancestor.

The second great effect was to stimulate the love of books and the diffusion of knowledge among the masses of the people. To make people understand that the free public libraries were the popular universities of the young and the old, of the poor and the rich, of the well-educated and the uneducated.

The full recognition of the free public libraries as a part of the system of public education, and, therefore, entitled to be supported by public taxation, was the third great main effect of the movement. From the above discussions we realize that the public schools will not yield their fullest return unless they are supplemented by free public libraries. Besides being a complement to the public schools, the free public library is a people's university, whose wonderful development since 1835 has depended upon and illustrated the democratic ideal of education.

SELECTED BIBLIOGRAPHY

Adams, C. F. Public library and the public schools. Library Journal. 1:437-41. Aug., 1877.
Bostwick, A. E. Co-operation with schools. (*In* his The American public library. Appleton. New York. 1923. p. 13-

---

⑥ A. E. Winship. *Great American Educators*. Werner School Book Co. New York. 1900. p. 17-18.

英文著作

14).

Bostwick, A. E. The library and the school. (*In* his The American public library. Appleton. New York. 1923. p. 100-13).

Chamberlain, Mellon. Public library and public school. Library Journal. 5:299-302. Nov. -Dec. ,1880.

Dana, John Cotton. Relations of libraries and schools. (*In* his Libraries. Wilson. New York. 1916. p. 92-4).

Dewey, Melvil. Libraries as related to the educational work of the state. Library Notes. 3:333-40. June,1888.

Foster, W. E. Relation of the libraries to the school system. Library Journal. 5:99-104. April,1880.

Foster, W. E. The school and the library:their mutual relation. Library Journal. 4:319-25. Sept. -Oct. ,1879.

Gilbert, Charles B. The public library and the public school. Library Journal. 29:169-73. April,1904.

Green, Samuel Swett. Libraries and schools:the results of a new experiment in Worcester, Mass. Library Journal. 12:400-2. Sept. -Oct. ,1887.

Green, Samuel Swett. The public library and the schools in Worcester. Library Journal. 12:119-21. Mar. ,1887.

Green, Samuel Swett. The relation of the public library to the public schools. Library Journal. 5:235-45. Sept. -Oct. , 1880.

Green, S. S. , and others. Work between libraries and schools—a symposium. Library Journal. 22:181-7. April,1897.

Hoag, J. P. Co-operation of public library and public school. Public Libraries. 9:225-7. May,1904. Howes, H. A. Legislation for public libraries. Library Journal. 4:262-7. June-July,1879.

Howes, H. A. Library legislation. (Chronological list of state library laws). Library Journal. 5:79-80. Mar. ,1880.

Ogle, John J. The public library and the public elementary school. Library. 8:93-5. 1896.

Painter, F. V. N. History of education. Appleton. New York. 1903. p. 321-2.

Poole, W. F. State legislation in the matter of libraries. Library Journal. 2:7-12. Sept. ,1877.

Ranck, Samuel H. How to make the library of greater service to the student of school age. Library Journal. 34:52-4. Feb. ,1909.

Rathbone, Josephine A. Co-operation between libraries and schools:an historical sketch. Library Journal. 26:187-91. April,1901.

Stephens, T. E. Rise and growth of public libraries in America. Library Association of the United Kingdom. Transactions and Proceedings. 1883. p. 17-30.

Tyler, Moses Coit. Historical evolution of the free public library in America and its true function in the community. Library Journal. 9:40-7. Mar. ,1884. Reprinted in Bostwick, A. E: Library and society. Wilson. New York. 1920. p. 17-32.

United States. Bureau of Education. Free town libraries. (*In* United States Bureau of education. Special report, 1876. p. 445-56).

United States. Bureau of Education. General statistics of all public libraries in the United States. (*In* United States Bureau of education. Special report, 1876. chap. 39).

Winship, A. E. Great American educators. Werner School Book Co. New York. 1900. p. 17-18.

CHAPTER II
THE SPIRIT OF RESEARCH IN HIGHER EDUCATION

The conception of college studies a century ago was quite different from that of the present time. In former days students regarded their teachers as a sort of walking encyclopedia. They took down all the sayings of their professors and studied their text-books word by word without looking further into other authorities. The subjects were limited mainly to Latin, Greek, mathematics, and philosophy. Theology, law, and medicine were the only so-called special subjects for post-graduate students.

The early university libraries under a limited curriculum of classical courses and cultural studi3es did not have need of enormous collections of books. The rigid method of text-book teaching required very little use of a college library. A library in a university was a museum of rare books, or was regarded as "an elegant concomitant of higher instruction."① The librarian was generally a professor with regular work in class instruction. The office was a sinecure. Opening the library three or four hours per week to loan a few books of interest was a courteous act to the professors. The library was virtually a place of storing and hiding books. Under such an atmosphere the students had no pleasure in or desire to use the college libraries and furthermore they were neither welcome nor wanted by the librarians. The eminent librarian of Harvard University, Justin Winsor, well illustrated the vogue of the university libraries at that time in his address before the American Social Science Association at Saratoga, September 10, 1879.

Time was when the student in college came up to the library once or twice a week on sufference, under the impression that it would never do to have too much of a good thing. "Boys!" cried the warder of one of the first of our college libraries, within the memory of the present generation, "Boys! What are you doing here—this is no place for you!" The poor craving creatures slunk away to Euclid and Horace in the seclusion of their bedrooms. ②

The enlargement of the field of knowledge in the last century has had a profound effect on the methods of academic teaching. The students, in view of the very rapid increase of new subjects for study, realized that they could not pursue all. The administrators and professors recognized the situation and hence pushed forward a set of new methods of instruction with all effort. They accelerated the wide adoption of the elective system, they introduced the topical study by syllabi and emphasized collateral readings. All these methods encourage and direct the students not to confine them-

---

① C. E. Lowrey. University Library, Its Larger Recognition in Higher Education. *Library Journal.* 19:264. August, 1894.

② Justin Winsor. Coliege and Other Higher Libraries. *Library Journal.* 4:401. November, 1879.

selves to their textbooks alone. The students select the subject they like. The professors aim more to suggest than to direct their pupils to the various authorities on the subject. This results in a much freer expression of opinions and judgments in the classroom, for the topic taught is no longer restricted to recitations from a single textbook.

Besides these innovations in instruction the German form of seminary method conducted in the university libraries was also introduced. In the last century many American scholars experienced and later reflected the academic influence of Göttingen, Berlin, Leipzig, Halle, and other German universities. Their influence in the founding of seminar-collections in American university libraries ushered in the epoch of departmental libraries in universities in this country.

These new methods of instruction were based on the deep conception of freedom of thought and breadth of view which are the essentials in the spirit of research. No view will be broad and no thought impartial without studying the works of various authorities. Such changes in instruction have necessitated an unavoidable change in the administration of a university library and concurrently contributed an important factor in the development of modern university and special research libraries. As President Thwing remarked, "The causes of the growth of the library of the college are comprehended in a single movement. It is the movement toward research. The college has come to stand for scholarship. Scholarship is at once the cause and the result of the book. The continuity of learning is embodied in the library. The library gathers up the wealth of the past. It represents all that man has struggled for or achieved. The library is, therefore, the treasure-house of the linguist, the philologist, the philosopher, the historian. Even the scientist finds in the library the records of experiments, be they successful or of failures."③

This theory regarding the growing significance of modern libraries is well sustained by the established facts concerning the greater use and rapid growth of college libraries during the last fifty years. Limited was the use and slow the growth of the American college library before 1875. There are striking contrasts between a college library of today and that of about the middle of the nineteenth century if we compare the hours open, the size of collections, and annual expenditures for the purchase of books. Harvard College Library was founded as early as 1638, but after more than two hundred years, through the efforts of many faithful and enthusiastic librarians, it only contained about forty-one thousand volumes. Professor John Langton Sibley effectively remarked in his address to the American librarians in 1879, "It was open for consultation from 9 o'clock to 1, and from 2 until 4, on the first four secular days of the week, and on Fridays in the forenoon. There was one hour when the sophomores on Tuesdays and the freshmen on Wednesdays took out books, and one on Mondays and on Thursdays for seniors and juniors. There were no shelves in the galleries, and Gore Hall was considered large enough to accommodate all the additions that would be made during the century. The total income from the permanent fund for purchasing, repairing and binding

---

③ Charles F. Thwing. *A History of Higher Education in America*. Appleton. New York. 1906. p. 413.

books was exactly $250 a year."④ The modern college librarian would take such a condition as a joke. Nevertheless, it actually existed in one of the most renowned American colleges only eighty-four years ago. Harvard College Library was at that time the leading institution in the length of hours kept open. It also advocated liberal principles for use of the books by students. As to the other college libraries their collections were less accessible than those of Harvard. Some amusing facts on the opening hours of the college libraries in 1850 are given us by Librarian Koch of Northwestern University. He says, "In 1850 the libraries at Amherst and Trinity, for example, were open once a week from 1 to 3 P. M. , at Princeton one hour twice a week, at the University of Missouri one hour every two weeks. At the University of Alabama there was a rule that 'the books shall ordinarily be received at the door, without admitting the applicant in the library room.' Harvard with its 28 hours of opening per week was as usual in the vanguard of progress, but contrast even these liberal hours with present-day schedules of 89 hours and even more per week and you will see that there has been considerable progress along this line."⑤

We learn at the conclusion of the above illustration the length of opening hours of the present college and university library. Every college and university librarian can testify that the library is well patronized by teachers and students during every hour that it is open. Longer hours of opening went into effect when the required reading of source-materials for study and research was introduced. Not only the increase in the length of opening hours of the university library, but also the increase in the use as well as the rapid enlargement of the collections and the establishment of new libraries have been regarded as results of the new methods of instruction. In order to give a clear and definite idea of the rapid growth of the college and university libraries from 1876-1920, a comparative table of their collections and the average annual increase of the sixty principal college libraries is here submitted. The data compared are taken from the statistical tables of the Special Report of 1876 on libraries published by the United States Bureau of Education, and also from statistical table No. 24 on colleges and universities of the United States Bureau of Education, Bulletin No. 29, 1923.

A TABLE OF SIXTY COLLEGE AND UNIVERSITY LIBRARIES SHOWING
THEIR AVERAGE GROWTH FROM THE DATE OF ORIGIN
TO 1876 AND FROM 1876 TO 1920.

---

④ John Langton Sibley. An Address before the American Library Association. *Library Journal.* 4:307. August, 1879.

⑤ T. W. Koch. *On University Libraries.* Paris. 1924. p. 23.

State	Name	Date of Origin	Number of Volumes in 1876	Number of Bound Volumes in 1920	Average Annual Increase from Date of Origin to 1876	Average Annual Increase from 1876–1920
CALIFORNIA						
	Univ. of California	1869	13,600	479,000	1,944	10,886
CONNECTICUT						
	Trinity College	1824	15,000	85,000	288	1,589
	Wesleyan Univ.	1833	26,000	120,000	605	2,136
	Yale College Univ.	1700	95,200	1,250,000	541	26,245
DISTRICT OF COLUMBIA						
	Georgetown College(Univ.)	1791	28,000	140,000	329	2,545
CEORGIA						
	Univ. of Georgia	1831	21,600	66,500	480	1,020
ILLINOIS						
	Chicago Univ.	1857	18,000	599,492	947	13,215
	Northwestern Univ.	1856	33,000	193,662	1,650	3,651
INDIANA						
	Wabash College	1833	10,482	56,000	244	1,033
	Indiana Univ.	1828	5,300	134,370	110	2,933
	Univ. of Notre Dame	1843	10,000	103,000	303	2,113
LOWA						
	Iowa State Univ. ⑥	1860	8,823	162,000	551	3,481

---

⑥ According to the history of the General Library of the State University of Iowa, the first collection of books for a general library began in the fall of 1855. *See* University of Iowa, *The University Libraries. Facilities and Service.* 1924. p. 29.

续表

State	Name	Date of Origin	Number of Volumes in 1876	Number of Bound Volumes in 1920	Average Annual Increase from Date of Origin to 1876	Average Annual Increase from 1876–1920
MAINE						
	Bowdoin College	1802	22,760	125,000	307	2,323
	Bates College	1859	6,800	47,000	400	913
	Colby Univ.	1813	11,100	56,000	176	1,020
MARYLAND						
	Mt. St. Mary's College	1808	7,000	20,000	103	295
MASSACHUSETTS						
	Amherst College	1821	30,406	125,000	553	2,150
	Harvard College Univ.	1638	212,050	2,028,100	891	41,274
	Mass. Institute of Tech	1866	2,500	140,737	250	3,142
	Tufts College	1854	16,000	80,000	727	1,454
	Williams College	1793	17,500	96,320	211	1,791
MICHIGAN						
	Univ. of Michigan	1841	27,500	432,394	785	9,202
MINNESOTA						
	Univ. of Minnesota	1869	10,000	300,000	1,428	6,591
MISSISSIPPI						
	Univ. of Mississippi	1848	6,192	31,000	221	564
MISSOURI						
	Univ. of Missouri	1840	11,000	223,670	305	4,883
	St. Louis Univ.	1829	17,000	75,000	362	1,318
	Washington Univ.	1853	4,500	176,013	196	3,898
NEW HAMPSHIRE						
	Dartmouth College	1770	25,500	150,000	240	2,829

英文著作

续表

State	Name	Date of Origin	Number of Volumes in 1876	Number of Bound Volumes in 1920	Average Annual Increase from Date of Origin to 1876	Average Annual Increase from 1876–1920
NEW JERSEY						
	Rutgers College	1770	6,814	106,000	64	2,254
	College of New Jersey(Princeton Univ.)	1775	29,500	444,268	244	9,426
NEW YORK						
	Hamilton College	1812	22,000	87,000	344	1,477
	Cornell Univ.	1868	39,000	630,637	4,874	13,446
	College of the City of N. Y.	1850	20,000	71,000	769	1,159
	Columbia College(Univ.)	1757	31.390	737,448	264	16,274
	Vassar College	1865	9,881	116,300	898	2,419
	Univ. of Rochester	1850	12,000	83,003	461	1,614
	Union College	1795	19,800	58,450	244	878
	Syracuse Univ.	1871	10,000	109,500	2,000	2,261
	United States Military Acad.	1812	25,000	103,620	390	1,787
NORTH CAROLINA						
	Univ. of North Carolina	1795	8,394	93,914	103	1,944
OHIO						
	Univ. of Cincinnati	1875	500	125,000	500	2,830
	Oberlin College	1834	7,000	204,501	167	4,488
	Ohio Wesleyan Univ.	1856	10,400	90,000	520	1,809
	Marietta College	1835	15,130	83,000	369	1,543
PENNSVLVANIA						
	Dickinson College	1783	7,765	34,000	83	596
	Lafayette College	1832	16,400	49,098	373	743
	Pennsylvania College	1832	7,200	35,000	164	632
	Haverford College	1833	7,000	81,000	163	1,682
	Franklin and Marshall Col.	1853	3,500	48,000	152	1,011
	Univ. of Pennsylvania	1755	23,250	503,572	192	10,916
RHODE ISLAND						
	Brown Univ.	1768	45,000	270,000	417	5,114

34

续表

State	Name	Date of Origin	Number of Volumes in 1876	Number of Bound Volumes in 1920	Average Annual Increase from Date of Origin to 1876	Average Annual Increase from 1876–1920
SOUTH CAROLINA						
	College of Charleston	1825	8,000	21,902	157	316
	Univ. of South Carolina	1805	27,000	65,000	380	864
VERMONT						
	Univ. of Vermont	1800	13,521	105,000	178	2,079
	Middlebury College	1800	12,000	50,000	158	864
VIRGINIA						
	Univ. of Virginia	1825	40,000	120,300	784	1,825
	Washington and Lee Univ.	1796	11,000	50,000	137	863
	College of William and Mary	1700	5,000	21,000	28	363
WISCONSIN						
	Beloit Colege	1848	8,300	65,000	296	1,289
	Univ. of Wisconsin	1849	6,670	276,000	247	6,121

The sixty cases in the above table indicate a more rapid average increase of every library from 1876-1920 than that from the dates of their origins to the year 1876. From 1876 to 1920 Columbia College library has had an average annual increase, the equivalent of 61 times its increase between 1757 and 1876 and from 1876 to 1920 Yale has had about 48 times its increase between 1700 and 1876. Before 1876 the average annual increase of Columbia was 264 books and that of Yale 541 books. Some may say that the average annual increase of any library before 1876 cannot be taken as a reliable record, due to several serious factors, namely, fire, war, absence of records, and irregularity of annual purchase. For example Harvard College Library, nominally dating back from 1678, does not really take its origin until after the fire of 1764. It is true that we cannot take too seriously the figures of annual increase before 1876, but nevertheless, the above table shows very definitely the rapid growth of the college library from 1876 to the present day. It is not alone in the old universities that the rapid growth of the library has taken place, but the more recent universities and colleges have awakened to the same important truth. For instance several college libraries were not founded until 1876 or later and their growth was also very rapid. The libraries of Johns Hopkins University and the University of Oregon both began in 1876 and within the period of the last forty-four years, i. e. 1876-1920, they have acquired two hundred and twenty-five thousand and ninety-four thousand bound volumes, respectively. In the year 1883 the library of the University of Texas was established and in about thirty-seven years it has grown to a collection of 194,459 volumes. This rapid development of college libraries has just begun. The momentum of acceleration of growth is and will be increased, as the spirit of research in the universities intensifies the method of instruction in every branch of scientific and professional subjects. The slogan now-a-days is "use and more use" of the college and university libraries. The present methods of college teaching increase the use of the university libraries. They have become mental laboratories for every phase of human knowledge.

The important role to be played by university libraries in the sphere of the university teaching functions was well described by President Harper of the University of Chicago in his address read at the dedication of the Library of Colorado College, March 14, 1894. He began his paper by painting the college libraries of the third quarter of the nineteenth century:

A quarter of a century ago the library in most of our institutions, even the oldest, was scarcely large enough, if one were to count volumes, or valuable enough, if one were to estimate values, to deserve the name of library. So far as it had location, it was the place to which the professor was accustomed to make his way occasionally, the student almost never... Today the chief building of a college, the building in which is taken greatest pride, is the library. With the stack for storage purposes, the reading room for reference books, the offices of delivery, the rooms for seminar purposes, it is the center of the institutional activity. The director of the library is not infrequently one of the most learned men of the faculty; in many instances certainly, the most influential. Lectures are sometimes given by him on bibliography, or classes organized for instruction in the use of books. The staff of assistants is often larger than the entire faculty in the same institution thirty years ago. Volumes are added to the number of 3,000; 5,000; 10,000; or 20,000 in a single year; the periodical literature of each department is on file; the building is open day and night... That factor of our college and university work, the library, fifty years ago was almost unknown, today already the center of the institution's intellectual activity, half a century hence — with its sister, the laboratory, almost equally unknown fifty years back—will, by absorbing all else, have become the institution itself. ⑦

This is a very enthusiastic statement. As the spirit of research advances in universities, the university library will be the heart of intellectual activities and it will constantly supply life and strength to the faculty and to the students.

SELECTED BIBLIOGRAPHY

Adams, John. College library (*In* Mellen Chamberlain's John Adams and addresses. Houghton. Boston. 1899. p. 392-425).

---

⑦ William Rainey Harper. *Trend in Higher Education.* University of Chicago Press. Chicago. 1905. p. 120-2.

Bicknell, Percy F. University and college libraries and their relation to the library movement of today. Public Libraries. 2: 301-4. June, 1897.

Canfield, James H. The library of the American university. Public Libraries. 9: 385-8. Oct., 1904.

Carlton, W. N. Chattin. College libraries in the midnineteenth century. Library Journal. 32: 479-86. Nov., 1907.

College Libraries. (*In* United States Bureau of education. Special report, 1876. p. 60-126).

Compton, Charles H. Library in relation to the university. Library Journal. 35: 494-503. Nov., 1910.

Fletcher, W. I. Yearly report on college libraries. Library Journal. 10: 267-9. Sept. -Oct., 1885.

Guild, Reuben A. The college library. Library Journal. 10: 216-21. Sept. -Oct., 1885.

Hadley, Arthur T. The library in the university. Public Libraries. 14: 115-17. April, 1909.

Harper, William Rainey. The trend in higher education. Chicago University Press. Chicago. 1905. Chap. 5.

Johnston, W. Dawson. Librarian as an educator. Library Journal. 35: 437-41. Oct., 1910.

Koch, Theodore Wesley. On university libraries. Paris. 1924.

Lowrey, C. E. University library, its larger recognition in higher education. Library Journal. 19: 264-8. Aug., 1894.

Poole, W. F. The university library and the university curriculum. Library Journal. 18: 470-3. Nov., 1893.

Richardson, E. C. The place of the library in a university. American Library Association Bulletin. 10: 1-13. Jan., 1916.

Robinson, Otis H. College library administration. (*In* United States Bureau of education. Special report, 1876. p. 505-25).

Robinson, Otis H. The relation of libraries to college work. Library Journal. 6: 97-104. April, 1881.

Robinson, Otis H. Rochester university library—administration and use. (*In* United States Bureau of education. Circulars of information No. 1, 1880. p. 15-27).

Scudder, Horace E. College libraries a hundred years ago. (*In* United States Bureau of education. Special report, 1876. p. 21-31).

Sibley, John Langton. An address before the American library association. Library Journal. 4: 305-8. Aug., 1879.

Thwing, C. F. University libraries. (*In* his A short history of higher education in America. Appleton. New York. 1906. p. 408-17).

United States. Bureau of Education. Bulletin No. 29, 1923. Biennial survey of education, 1918-1920. Washington, D. C. 1923.

University of Iowa. The university libraries, facilities and service. Iowa City. 1924.

Wharey, James B. Modern teaching and the library. Library Journal. 32: 153-6. April, 1907.

Winsor, Justin. College library. (*In* United States Bureau of education. Circulars of information, No. 1. 1880. p. 7-14).

Winsor, Justin. College and other higher libraries. Library Journal. 4: 339-402. Nov., 1879.

Woodruff, Edwin H. University libraries and seminary methods of instruction. Library Journal. 11: 219-24. July, 1886.

CHAPTER III
INCREASE OF PRINTED MATERIAL

The last quarter of the nineteenth century marked the beginning of an age of publication, scientific, philosophic, social, ephemeral and what not. In science it was the time of crystallization of the experimental methods of the last two hundred and fifty years. It was the fruit produced from a great period of scientific revolution. In philosophy and natural science, empiricism and the theory of evolution had filled the mind of intellectuals and laymen alike with skeptical curiosity. In the social sciences the results of industrial revolution started afresh the new conception of the organization of society. Modern inventions and wonderful discoveries in applied chemistry have revolutionized the ordinary conditions and views of life. The everyday working man has been bewildered by the miracles around him. He has been restless to learn about the miracles of scientific invention and to inform himself of the new interpretations of life. This desire of the working man has called forth a flood of publications. The great age of printing is characterized by a headlong rush into the wide production of reading material. Scientists publish the results of their investigations, philosophers their new interpretations of life and knowledge, psychologists their advanced theories of mental tests, jingoists their war talk, and business men their clever advertisements. Not only have books, monographs and pamphlets on various subjects been published, but periodicals and newspapers have increased daily in numbers and in variety.

If one compares the newspapers of 1875 with those of today, he will be greatly surprised to find the extraordinary voluminousness of the modern dailies. They publish news, national, local, and international, irrespective of its significance or scandalous nature. Stock exchange news, financial markets, interesting stories, scientific discussions, and talks on arts occupy many pages of the metropolitan dailies. Advertisements and crossword puzzles give no less pleasure to the readers. Papers of yesterday had only two to four pages, but papers of today take more than twenty. The items are so numerous that they necessitate an index.

People read not only dailies, but weeklies and monthlies. According to Mr. John Cotton Dana's estimates ten years ago of the publication of dailies, weeklies, and monthlies in the United States of America in a single year, the figures were as follows:[①]

    Weeklies ············ 1,208,190,000
    Dailies ··············· 2,865,466,000 copies
    Monthlies ············ 263,452,000
    Total ················ 4,337,108,000 copies

Before going on to speak of the profound effect of this age of publication on the development

---

① J. C. Dana. *Libraries*. Wilson. New York. 1916. p. 43-9

of modern libraries, two important factors should not be overlooked. First the cost of paper today is cheaper than fifty years ago and second the improvement of printing machinery has made possible the great success of multitudinous publications. Mr. Dana, librarian of the Newark Public Library, succinctly pointed out these facts in an address delivered before the Pennsylvania Library Association as follows: "In 1870 a poor quality of printing paper cost 16 cents a pound. Paper of better quality is sold today for 2 cents a pound… Up to 1880 type was made and set very much as it had been from its first invention several hundred years before. Now the punches, one of the most expensive of the things required in typesetting, are cut almost automatically from one model for type of any size of a given style. The Wicks typecasting machine is reported as about to reduce the cost of type one half… The Lanston monotype casts and sets and justifies lines—does all that a hand compositor can do—automatically and with astonishing rapidity, under the guidance of a strip of paper properly perforated by a machine almost as easy to operate as a typewriter. The linotype machine casts solid bars of type with almost any desired changes of face. All large papers and most books are stereotyped before printing. A machine now makes the stereotype plates in a fraction of a minute from a matrix formed in a few seconds… Presses are now obtainable which will deliver in one hour one hundred thousand newspapers complete and folded and printed in twelve colors."②

With the improvements of manufacturing paper and of printing machinery, the production of printed material is much easier and also much cheaper. Consequently the demand for things to read has been easily filled. At the same time the schools and the colleges turn out more graduates whose tendency to read has been stimulated and because of this the public and university libraries have more readers of a serious type. The view of every man and woman is wider and the habit of reading and wishing to know more about things are constantly increased. These tendencies have been anticipated by the commercialized publications. Excellent writers, now-a-days somewhat more than their forefathers, who were more likely to write prompted by their genuine convictions, may be hired to compose propaganda. To produce a work to satisfy the popular fancy may yield a much bigger financial return than a work of plain truth. Many publishers will publish any book, provided that it will have a chance of commanding a sale. Thus the book-market is flooded not only with scientific publications but also with commercialized literature of every conceivable sort.

And what has resulted from this enormous output of publications, of ephemeral or even more or less permanent value? One of the direct results has been the rapid development of modern libraries of every type and particularly state libraries and special libraries. In general the increase of printed material has created the need for special libraries. The more books a library has the more complicated is the administration. The librarian must be able to handle books with less labor and expense. No matter how big the income of a library is, it cannot keep pace with the production of books. Then book-selection and sharper differentiation in the nature and scope of different libraries are more emphasized than ever before.

Libraries hitherto bought standard works of well-known authors irrespective of their subjects.

---

② Ibid. p. 77-8.

But such a purchasing policy in this age of quantity production will not satisfy the interests of the patrons of a library. The patrons will not get what they want to read. To avoid their disappointment the library has adopted two policies of development. First, it defines its scope and nature and only purchases those books within its sphere. Second, it recognizes that it is more economical and efficient to have a division of the field of purchase between different libraries of the same region. For instance, the John Crerar Library of Chicago aims to buy only scientific and technical books, and leaves the purchase of books in the humanities to the Newberry Library, while the Chicago Public Library through its branches looks after the buying of fiction and of books of general culture and recreation.

As has been already mentioned, the increase of printed material has influenced the growth of two particular orders of libraries, namely state and special libraries. The state libraries go back rather far in the history of American libraries. Originally these were reference collections of law books and public documents, housed in state capitols for the use of state legislators and officials. In general, all the collections of the state libraries outgrew their limitations and they were and are immensely influenced by the tremendous increase of things to read. The state libraries could not expect to stand against the tide and in time some of them became general reference libraries, and some, special reference libraries on legislative problems or on history. The scope of the state library has been widened and its contents enriched by the increase of printed material. Mr. G. S. Godard illuminates this point in his article *Development of the State Library*, as follows:

> The area of human knowledge is unlimited and getting more so. Books! Books! Books! See how they grow. A dozen or more new ones every hour, 24 hours a day, 365 days in a year. Good books and bad books. Standard books and books to stand, and some one, somewhere, desiring to see, not necessarily read, each one sometime. Think of it! From eternity to eternity is a long time, and each decade must learn and unlearn so much, but apparently print it all. It is no longer possible within any sort of reason for any one library—town, county, state or national—to think of enveloping everything printed. The expense of purchasing, collecting, cataloging and housing is prohibitive. Therefore, is it not desirable—as has in some instances been done—that each state library select its departments or fields of work which may thus be made approximately complete, leaving the other departments of knowledge which are thus either neglected or deficient to be covered by other libraries which may in turn be deficient or neglected in some lines covered in this. ③

In the same manner as the growth of the state library, the Library of Congress has been greatly effected by the increase of printed material at the close of the last century. Any one who is familiar with the history of the Library of Congress knows that its rapid development occurred only recently. Besides its acquisition from deposits under the copyright law and from gifts and exchanges, the annual appropriation for the purchase of books amounts, approximately, to $100,000. In 1852, immediately after the second fire of the Congressional Library, Congress generously voted $75,000 for the immediate purchase of books. That amount was then an enormous sum to spend for books, but it

---

③ G. S. Godard. Development of the State Library. *Library Journal*. 30:38-9. September, 1905; reprinted in *Library and Its Organization*, ed. by G. G. Drury. Wilson. New York. 1924. p. 281-6.

is small in comparison to the present annual appropriation, already cited. From 1800, the date of birth of the Library of Congress, to the year 1860, partly because of two destructive fires, it had grown to but seventy-five thousand volumes. ④ Sixteen years later it had grown to about three hundred and sixty thousand volumes including pamphlets. In 1897 the library was removed to its new building and at that time it had a collection of seven hundred and fifty thousand volumes. During the last twenty-five years the collection of books and pamphlets has grown to about three millions. It is a wonderful development which indirectly reflects the tremendous increase of the printed material of the present age. Some may suppose that the growth is not primarily due to the increase of books to read and that it may be due to a considerable extent to the buying of much material printed before the improvement of the printing press, such as the Peter Force Library, purchased in 1867. The Library of Congress does buy old European and Oriental books, but the large annual appropriation for useful books and pamphlets in conjunction with current copyrighted books has certainly been the chief force in moulding and influencing its scope and development. Dr. Putnam, the present librarian, remarks on this very fact in an address delivered at the Portland conference of the American Library Association in 1905:

And its appropriation for the purchase is now $98,000 a year. Freed from any expenditure for current copyrighted books and a considerable mass of other material, this may go far. It might do much even in the purchase of the rare and curious books suited to a museum library. It is not, however, being applied to these. It is being applied to the acquisition of the material not precious from its form or rarity merely, but useful from its contents. ⑤

Therefore, the increase of printed material does effect the development of the modern libraries and it has moulded the state libraries into general and special reference libraries, and the Library of Congress into a monstrous reference and research library for the whole country.

Special libraries are of two types which might be termed the static and the dynamic. The static type, such as the Union Theological Seminary Library of New York, the Philadelphia Law Association Library, and the Boston Medical Library, was established for the convenience and learning of the members of a certain profession. But most of these libraries were not very rich in collections even as late as 1876. If we refer to Professor Theodore Gill's article on scientific libraries in the United States, made as a special report to the Bureau of Education for the year 1876 we learn that at that time only the libraries of a few learned societies contained the chief sources of scientific information. The societies which could afford the requisite facilities were extremely few. In fact there were considerably less than a dozen of these libraries. ⑥ The medical library of the Surgeon-General's Office, the applied science library of the Patent Office, the Astronomical Library of the

---

④ A. R. Spofford. *Library of Congress or National Library*. (*In* United States Bureau of Education, Special Report, 1876. p. 256).

⑤ Herbert Putnam. The Library of Congress as a National Library. *Library Journal*. 30:29. September, 1905.

⑥ Theodore Gill. *Scientific Libraries in the United States*. (*In* United States Bureau of Education, Special Report, 1876. p. 183-4).

United States Naval Observatory, the Boston Society Library of natural history, and a few other scientific libraries in New York, Philadelphia, and Boston, were the leaders.

Within the period of the last fifty years the tremendous advances made in pure and applied science have resulted in the production of numberless scientific and technical publications. That in turn has immensely enlarged the collections of the early scientific and technical libraries, and promoted the establishment of many new ones. The library data on pages 391 and 392 of the Encyclopaedia Americana, 1924 edition, show that at present the United States has seventy-six principal libraries representing thirty-four special subjects of human knowledge. For example, the Prudential Life Insurance Company of Newark, N. J. has an insurance library of one hundred thousand volumes. The sociological library of the Russell Sage Foundation has 15,695 volumes. The art library of the Metropolitan Museum of New York City has twenty-nine thousand volumes. The agricultural library of the United States Department of Agriculture has 131,693 volumes. The scientific library of the Smithsonian Institution has 521,616 volumes. This is the wonderful progress of the special libraries of the static type.

The dynamic type of special library has been developing especially since 1909 in commercial corporations and industrial plants. Its purpose is to supply managers, submanagers, engineers, accountants, foremen and others in important positions with scientific information pertaining to their work and to the work of the industry or organization as a whole. These libraries are not like the static type of special libraries for investigation and research. They are primarily time-saving machines for information for the creative and managerial minds of a big concern. The old proverb "knowledge is power" is taken deeply to heart by the ever insistent business man, but he finds that he has no time to get "power" from the great flood of modern business, scientific, and technical literature. As the industrial and commercial organizations were growing and expanding rapidly, new problems concerning management, science, and technique were daily rising. They demanded of the managers, experts, foremen, salesmen and other heads of departments fresh ideas, new devices, greater efficiency, and broader views. Advice and suggestions from the treasury of publications were sought. Thus trade journals and professional publications grew by leaps and bounds. Great organizations found that the printed trade material was so helpful in increasing their knowledge that they needed a tool to supply them with the maximum information within the minimum time. Thus came the establishment of commercial and industrial libraries.

Both in scope and function these differ from the special libraries of the static type. The special libraries of the dynamic type deal chiefly with the latest data on current problems, while the special libraries of the static type include primarily well-authenticated though not necessarily current material on special subjects. They are for scholars and investigators. The one collects books and periodicals to be preserved and the other discards printed material which is no longer of use. Utilitarianism of an extreme form is the guiding principle of the commercial and industrial libraries. Let us borrow a paragraph regarding the nature, method, and use of the special libraries of the dynamic type.

The special library (Mr. John A. Lapp means the special library of the dynamic type) is an organization serving a specific institution which seeks to gather all of the experiences available with regard to that institution's problems, to classify it in such a way as to make it quickly available, to digest and prepare the same in usable form, to study the actual problems which confront the institution and to attempt to bring the information gathered to the right man at the right place, so that it may function in the work of the institution which it serves. ⑦

SELECTED BIBLIOGRAPHY

Babock, Laura E. Reference library in a manufacturing plant. Special Libraries. 2:13-15. Feb. ,1911.

Billings, J. S. Medical libraries in the United States. (*In* United States Bureau of education. Special report,1876. p. 171-82).

Bishop, W. W. How the Library of Congress serves the people. Public Libraries. 19:331-4. Oct. ,1914.

Dana, John Cotton. Libraries. Wilson. New York. 1916. p. 43-9,77-8.

Dudgeon, M. S. The scope and purposes of special libraries. Special Libraries. 3:129-32. June,1912.

Dudgeon, M. S. The Wisconsin legislative library. Yale Review. 16:288-95. Nov. ,1907.

Encyclopaedia Americana. Special libraries. (*In* Encyclopaedia Americana. 1924 ed. Vol. 17, p. 363-5).

Gill, Theodore. Scientific libraries in the United States. (*In* United States Bureau of education. Special report,1876. p. 183-217).

Godard, George Seymour. Development of the state library. Library Journal. 30:37-40. Sept. 1905; reprinted in Library and its organization, ed. by G. G. Drury. Wilson. New York. 1924. p. 281-6.

Griswold, Stephen B. Law libraries. (*In* United States Bureau of education. Special report,1876. p. 161-70).

Lapp, J. A. Growth of a big idea. Special libraries. 9:157-9. Sept. -Oct. ,1918.

Lee, George Winthrop. Library of Stone and Webster, Boston. Special Libraries. 1:44-7. June,1910.

Marion, G. E. The special library field. Special Libraries. .9:59-64. March,1918.

Putnam, Herbert. The Library of Congress as a national library. Library Journal. 30:27-34. Sept. ,1905.

Spofford, Ainsworth Rand. Library of Congress or national library. (*In* United States Bureau of education. Special report,1876. p. 253-61).

Theological Libraries in the United States. (*In* United States Bureau of education. Special report,1876. p. 127-60).

Whitten, Robert Harvey. Library of the New York Public service commission. Special Libraries. 1: 18-20. March,1910.

Williamson, C. C. The importance of special libraries to the public library. Special Libraries. 1:115-16. Jan. ,1913.

---

⑦ John A. Lapp. Growth of a Big Idea. *Special Libraries.* 9:157. September-October,1918.

CHAPTER IV
LIBRARY PHILANTHROPY

The last three chapters have dealt with certain important forces of outstanding significance in the development of modern libraries. The functions and contents of these libraries have been so moulded that each type has had a special service to render to society. This is a very important point in connection with the duties, work, training, and education of a librarian, and will be fully treated in the second part of this thesis. In addition to the democratic ideal in education, the spirit of research, and the increase of printed material, there are two immediate factors which have accelerated the development of modern libraries. They are library philanthropy and library organizations.

In the history of library donations in America, two early events heralded the beginning of this magnificent epoch. In the year 1700 Reverend John Sharp bequeathed his books to the city of New York and the second event was the establishment of subscription and society libraries for the benefit of the common people. These events directed the attention of wealthy men to a productive field for philanthropy. ①

Benjamin Franklin in Philadelphia was the first to organize a subscription library and later the movement spread to the other parts of the early colonies. Men like James Logan, John McKenzie, Abraham Redwood, and others, started to bequeath either books or money to found public libraries for the intellectual benefit of the people. The movement of library philanthropy reached its maturity in the generous donations of John Jacob Astor and James Lenox to the New York City Library; the munificent gifts of Joshua Bates of London to the Boston Public Library; the princely bequests of Walter L. Newberry to found the well-known Newberry Library for the citizens of Chicago; the $1,000,000 left by James Rush to the Ridgeway Branch of the Philadelphia Public Library for the erection of a magnificent building; several gifts of James Lick to the libraries of San Francisco; and the generous donation of Enoch Pratt to the people of Baltimore for maintaining and developing a library and branches. A list of the names of all the great library philanthropists would be too long to include here.

Andrew Carnegie has been, of course, the greatest of all donors of libraries. According to Dr. William S. Learned, the total number of library buildings in the United States, Canada, Hawaii and Porto Rico given by Mr. Carnegie and his corporation amounts to eighteen hundred and four. The total amount of money for those buildings reaches the sum of $43,665,513.47. ②

---

① H. E. Scudder. *Public Libraries a Hundred Years Ago*. (*In* United States Bureau of Education. Special Report, 1876. p. 14).

② Wm. S. Learned. *The American Public Library and the Diffusion of Knowledge*. Harcourt. New York. 1924. table 1.

We have seen that many rich men have been awakening to the worthiness of the library field to receive their philanthropy. Those who have accumulated millions in the keen competition of modern industry and commerce who are willing to spend their fortunes for the benefit of their fellowmen have shown themselves possessed of a penetrating and farsighted view of social problems. To them enlightenment and education for the mass is a royal way to peace and prosperity. Many modern millionaires realize that they are not especially created by providence to own their millions for their private comfort and luxury, but that their wealth is a sacred trust for them wisely to administer for the welfare of the human race. Mr. Carnegie expressed the most philanthropic sentiments concerning the disposal of what he regarded as the surplus wealth of multi-millionaires in an inspiring article entitled, "Wealth," which appeared in the June number of the *North American Review* in 1889.

Mr. Carnegie would not give his money to libraries if they were to be but decorations to the community. The librarians of Carnegie libraries are not afraid of the accusation of belonging to a class of professionals who trumpet the importance of their own calling. For in the first place the Carnegie library has not developed only in those localities where enormous gifts have made it easy. It has come into being in regions where the need for a library was strongly felt by the community. The golden rule of Mr. Carnegie's philanthropy has been to help those who can help themselves. As Dr. Bostwick remarks of the library donations, "Most of the larger library gifts, too, have been of such a nature that they require public cooperation, so that, in the long run, the private benefaction that is the nucleus of the library snowball is almost as nothing within the accreted mass of public contributions that clings around it."③

Library philanthropy has not created the need of free libraries for the public, but in helping to meet the need it has accelerated a movement which was already well under way. The need for a certain institution is first felt and then comes the institution. Any institution artificially installed by a whimsical person cannot flourish normally and permanently and it will wither away as a hot-house plant as soon as it is exposed under natural conditions. The determination to spread popular education through free public schools has taken firm hold on the public mind and one of the continuing natural results of that determination has been more and more readers of books. The need of free public libraries is only a necessary incident of the movement. The more the need is fulfilled, the more readers and users of the free public libraries will be produced and the more available will be the popular books. These factors are interdependent quantities.

We have seen that it has become the desire and conviction on the part of many rich men to help their fellows. In Mr. Carnegie's article "The Best Field for Philanthropy," he presented seven of the best uses of the surplus wealth of a millionaire. He placed donations to free public libraries at the top of his scheme. He said, "the result of my own study of the question, what is the best gift which can be given to a community is that a free library occupies the first place, provided the com-

---

③ A. E. Bostwick. *Library Philanthropy.* (*In* his *The American Public Library.* Appleton. New York. 1923. p. 215).

munity will accept and maintain it as a public institution, as much a part of the city property as its public schools, and, indeed, an adjunct to these. It is, no doubt, possible that my own personal experience may have led me to value a free library beyond all other forms of beneficence... No millionaire will go far wrong in his search for one of the best forms for the use of his surplus who chooses to establish a free library in any community that is willing to maintain and develop it."④Mr. Carnegie's donations not only accelerated the growth of the public libraries of America, but also the growth of the public libraries of British municipalities, where Mr. Carnegie and other British men of wealth, notably Passmore Edwards donated large amounts to help their less fortunate fellowmen secure access to books thru free public libraries. ⑤

Another result produced by the library donations of millionaires was to impart a great stimulus to librarians, some of whom were not, previous to that time, fully awakened to the value and great possibilities of their calling. The original concept of a library was a reservoir of knowledge, a mere storehouse of books. No words can better or more fully indicate the meaning of "library," in the former sense than the Chinese terminology. Formerly a library in Chinese was "Ch'on Ssu Lou." It literally mean *to store* (Ch'on) *books* (Ssu) in the *upper story of a house* (Lou). Why in the upper story of a house? This meant two important factors in storing books, namely, keeping off dampness and making access difficult. The above term for library was always used after Lao-Tse's time from about the sixth century B. C. Lao-Tse was the first librarian of the archives of the Chow Dynasty. The term was recently discarded and the Chinese have adopted in its place a modern name, Tu Ssu Ku'an, which means as follows: Tu(maps) Sssu(books) Ku'an(house).

Thus we see a great change in the concept of the functions of a library in its community. It is no longer a mere reservoir for storing books, but a fountain, a vital force and a progressive element in the solution of the problem of education. It is a "continuing university" of the people, free to all and supported by all. Hence the librarians are not only custodians of books, but active agents supplementing the work of teachers and professors in the function of teaching the people. Library donations hastened the realization of modern librarians of their responsibilities and helped to prepare them the better for discharging their duties as public servants.

SELECTED BIBLIOGRAPHY

Baker, Ernest A. The Public library. Grafton. London. 1924. Chap. 1.
Bostwick, A. E. , ed. Library and society. Wilson. New York. 1920. p. 49-54, 75-99, 149-67.
Bostwick, A. E. Library philanthropy. (*In* his The American public library. Appleton. New York. 1923. Chap. 15).
Carnegie, Andrew. Autobiography. Houghton. Boston. 1920. Chap. 4.
Carnegie, Andrew. The best field for philanthropy. North American Review. 149:682-98. Dec. ,1889.
Carnegie, Andrew. Wealth. North American Review. 148:653-64. June, 1889.

---

④ Andrew Carnegie. The Best Field for Philanthropy. *North American Review.* 149:688-90. December, 1889.
⑤ Ernest A. Baker. *The Public Library.* Grafton. London. 1924. P-24-5.

Koch, T. W. Carnegie libraries. Library Journal. 30:78-81. Sept., 1905.

Learned, William S. The American public library and the diffusion of knowledge. Harcourt. New York. 1924. Chap. 4.

Lydenberg, H. M. History of the New York public library. New York Public Library. New York. 1923.

Patronymic Libraries. (*In* United States Bureau of education. Special report, 1876. p. 456-9).

Scudder, H. E. Public libraries a hundred years ago. (*In* United States Bureau of education. Special report, 1876. p. 1-37).

CHAPTER V
THE LIBRARY ASSOCIATIONS

American librarians were the first to have a national library association. On October 6, 1876, the American Library Association now commonly known as the A. L. A., was organized in Philadelphia, with one hundred and three members. In 1879 it was chartered in the state of Massachusetts. ① As early as 1853 Charles C. Jewett, of the Smithsonian Institution, and eighty others interested in bibliography and libraries, had convened in New York to discuss various ways of forming a permanent organization of librarians. This plan did not materialize until twenty-three years later. The organization of national library associations, started in the United States, was enthusiastically sponsored by the librarians of Great Britain who besides holding an international librarians' conference in London in 1877 formed the Library Association of the United Kingdom in that same year. John Winter Jones, librarian of the British Museum, and president of the International Librarians' Conference, gave due credit to American librarians in his inaugural address, "We live in an age of congresses and conferences—which means that we live in an age when the advantages of the interchange of thoughts, ideas, and experiences are fully appreciated, and the benefits to be derived from unity of action in the affairs of life are recognized. The idea of holding a conference of librarians originated in America—in that country of energy and activity which has set the world so many good examples, and of which a conference of librarians is not the least valuable, looking to the practical results which may be anticipated from it."②

The spirit of The International Librarian's Conference at London was taken home by many librarians of different countries, and soon the growing interest in the modern library movement was manifested in the founding of many national library associations. For instance the National Library Association of Australia was founded in 1896; the Verein Deutscher Bibliothekare in Germany was founded in 1900; and the Kansai Bunko Kyokai of Japan was established in 1901. Later Italy, France, Denmark, Norway, Sweden, and other countries followed and established national library associations. Today almost all civilized nations have some sort of a national association with local subsidiary organizations.

American librarians were not only the first to found a national library association, but were also the first to found library clubs, state library associations, special library associations, the American Library Institute, and the Library Workers' Association. Library clubs are in general organized

---

① American Library Association: Charter. (*In* its *Bulletin.* 18:396. September, 1924).

② J. W. Jones. Inaugural Address at the Conference of Librarians held in London, October, 1877. First International Library Conference in London. *Transactions and Proceedings*, 1877. p, 1; or *Library Journal.* 2:99. November-December, 1877.

by the librarians of a single city, as the New York or the Chicago Library Club. State library associations have been founded by librarians serving within the boundaries of a single state. Librarians of special libraries have organized a Special Libraries' Association.

A glance at the organization of the American Library Institute will suggest to us a mental picture of the House of Elders of Japan or the House of Peers of England. Its members consist of all ex-presidents, members of the Executive Board, and members of the Council of the American Library Association, and elected Fellows. Their chief duty is to deliberate on difficult questions in connection with library administration and economy. In reality the Institute is a body like the learned societies and scientific academies. The majority of the members of the American Library Association have, however, considered the members of the Institute as powerful elders. This subjective view is probably due to the fact that most of the American Library Institute members are either directors of libraries or head-librarians. They have the actual power of giving positions to their fellow-librarians. This represents, to some extent, a difference between the American Library Institute and most scientific academies. So far the Institute has not affiliated with the American Library Association but has existed as an independent organization.

In 1920 the Library Workers' Association was formed at Atlantic City. Its main purpose is to act as an employment agency for library assistants without library school training, and to look after their welfare intellectually and materially. ③ The formation of this association appears to outside observers, perhaps, as a weak link in the strong chain of American library organizations. Its organization implies that the American Library Association has not been sufficiently active in looking after the employment, and welfare of the "library workers". The Library Workers' Association is nearly the opposite of the American Library Institute. Roughly speaking the members of the former are the plebeians and those of the latter are the aristocrats of the library profession. However, if one analyzes further the duty and service of any library organization he finds it totally different from that of any capitalistic or labor organization. The essential difference is perhaps summed up in the slogan of the American Library Association i. e. "The best reading for the largest number at the least cost."

The American Library Association bases itself on two principles, service to society and mutual aid among the members. The wonderful progress of the library movement since 1876 has been due largely to those librarians of the American Library Association who have been vitally concerned about these two principles. They give their best service to the poor as well as to the rich. Social inequality and racial prejudice are beyond the conception of a true librarian. In effective library management, emphasis on efficiency is stressed, but the human touch is never lacking. No capable librarian will treat his staff members as mere machines. There is always a sympathetic relation. As Dr. Dana of the Newark Public Library remarked in one of his addresses, "In union is strength; but the worth of strength is in its use. An association tends to the academic and to hold its members to a standard, often a narrow one… The conclusion is, encourage your colleagues, confer with them, work with them, and as opportunity permits join with them in organized effort to attain certain defi-

---

③ Constitution of the Library Workers' Association. *Library Journal.* 45:839-40. October, 1920.

nite results. So doing you get wisdom for yourself and growth in esteem and efficiency for your profession."④

Since the formation of the American Library Association the members have always taken a noteworthy interest in problems of self-advancement. They have always been mentally alert. They take much interest in the meetings of library clubs and local library associations, in staff training classes in the large libraries, in attendance at summer schools, and many, after a number of years' experience in a library, are still anxious to study a year or two in a library school. Every librarian feels that his or her service will be better if he or she keeps on advancing in the profession. And so the motive of the American Library Association to promote larger library interests through the means of better service has been well realized. Better service can be rendered only through the incessant self-improvement of the librarians in professional knowledge. Dr. Learned in his book, *The American Public Library and the Diffusion of Knowledge*, declares that there is probably no group of responsible men and women which can more safely be trusted as the custodian of its own professional standards and qualifications. ⑤ The present writer feels that this is not too sweeping a statement. Dr. Learned is not himself a librarian but a professional educator of high rank.

A brief review of what the American Library Association has accomplished in the field of technical aids and of interpretive material for readers, should satisfy any hostile critic as to its unquestionably helpful influence in the development of modern libraries. First, the American Library Association emphasized uniformity in methods in order to enable librarians to do better work at less expense. Then library supplies, such as shelf-lists, accession books, book-covers, book-supports, binders, call slips, and other useful appliances were introduced. This was followed by publications dealing with book selection, indexes, building plans, classification, cataloging, book-buying, organization, administration, library legislation and other technical matters. They enable librarians to administer their libraries more efficiently and more scientifically. Any new theory, method, or appliance is always fully discussed in the official publication of the association. This has benefited not only American librarians but the librarians of other countries.

The official mouth-piece of the American Library Association from 1876 to 1907 was the *Library Journal*. From 1907 the association has published its own *Bulletin*. Besides the journals called *Public Libraries* and *Special Libraries*, some of the state libraries and large public libraries have issued their own *Bulletins*, as for instance *New York State Library Bulletin*, the *New York Public Library Bulletin*, and the *Carnegie Library of Pittsburgh Monthly Bulletin*.

As to interpretive material for readers, roughly there are two classes. One is for quick information on how ideas are to be found in print at libraries. There are numerous forms used to give this information such as posters, placards, leaflets, book-lists and hand-books from which readers can

---

④ J. C. Dana. What State and Local Library Associations Can Do for Library Interests. *Library Journal*. 30: 20-1. September, 1905; or, *in* his *Libraries*. Wilson. New York. 1916. p. 132-3.

⑤ *American Library Association*. Publications of the American Library Association. (*In Bulletin*. 18:419-26. September, 1924).

easily learn what, where, and how to find in print needed facts. The other class of material is for the systematic study of students and scholarly readers. Extensive indexes, impartial book-notes, and bibliographies for research are prepared. ⑥

The influence of the American Library Association in the growth of modern libraries and librarianship is incalculable. Its service in organizing printed knowledge for popular use is very extensive. Its attitude toward the library activities of other countries is genuinely sympathetic and internationally cooperative. Such is the brilliant record of the American Library Association. Every American librarian should be proud of its great success. During this age of economic unrest and class struggle, may the American Library Association set a lofty example in rendering a bigger service to human society through the united effort of its members to provide trustworthy information to all who seek after truth. With this as its aim there should be no cleavage between head-librarians and library workers. They are brothers and sisters of one family. Their common mission is to spread the Gospel of Knowledge which is the key to the Hall of World Democracy.

SELECTED BIBLIOGRAPHY

American Library Association. An editorial. Library Journal. 3:43-4. April, 1878.

American Library Association. Charter, constitution and by-laws of the American library association. (*In* its Bulletin. 18:396, 398-403. Sept., 1924).

American Library Association. Publications of the American library association. (*In* its Bulletin. 18:419-26. Sept., 1924).

American Library Institute. Public Libraries. 11:108. Mar., 1906.

Bostwick, A. E. Organizations of librarians. (*In* his The American public library. Appleton. New York. 1923. Chap. 27).

Brett, Wm. H. Address of the president of the American library association. Library Journal. 22:1-5. Oct., 1897.

Dana, J. C. What state and local library associations can do for library interests. Library Journal. 30:17-21. Sept., 1905; or, *in* his Libraries, Wilson. New York. 1916. p. 123-33.

Dewey, Melvil. American library association. Library Journal. 1:245-7, Mar., 1877.

Dewey, Melvil. Origin of American library association motto. Public libraries. 11:55. Feb., 1906.

First Convention of Librarians. 1853. Proceedings of the librarians' convention held in New York City, Sept., 15-17, 1853. Reprinted for William H. Murray. 1915.

Friedel, J. H. Library association. (*In* his Training for librarianship. Lippincott. Philadelphia. 1921. Chap. 18).

Hadley, C. History and aims of the American library association. Educational Bi-Monthly. 4:293-5. April, 1910.

Iles, George. A headquarters for our association. Library Journal. 28:24-8. July, 1903.

Jones, John Winter. Inaugural address at the conference of librarians held in London, Oct., 1877. Library Journal. 2:99-119. Nov.-Dec., 1877.

Learned, William S. The American public library and the diffusion of knowledge. Harcourt. New York. 1924. p. 57-63.

Library Workers Association. Constitution. Library Journal. 45:839-40. Oct., 1920.

Work and needs of the American Library Association. Library Journal. 30:858-60. Sept., 1905.

---

⑥ W. S. Learned. *The American Public Library and the Diffusion of Knowledge.* Harcourt. New York. 1924. p. 63.

PART II
TRAINING AND EDUCATION FOR LIBRARIANSHIP

CHAPTER   VI.   The Librarians in Ancient Times
CHAPTER   VII.   The Medieval and Early Modern Librarians
CHAPTER   VIII. The Professional Education of the Modern Librarian
CHAPTER   IX.   Changing Conceptions of Librarianship and Its Educational Requirements
CHAPTER   X.   American Library Schools

CHAPTER VI
THE LIBRARIANS IN ANCIENT TIMES

The primitive library takes its origin from the desire for the preservation of some record either of the worship of supernatural beings or of political events. Because of the lack of proper tools for recording and of the elementary state of the written language, the records were not so abundant that it was necessary to have a special keeper. Therefore, before the beginning of large collections of books for the use of scholars, the librarian discharged numerous offices and the keeping of records was only one of his functions.

Before taking up the discussion of the education and the function of a librarian among the ancients, two terms, "library" and "librarian" as understood by the ancients, should be defined. [1] At one time a misunderstanding about the interpretation of these two terms existed between Professor Max Müller and Dr. E. C. Richardson, after the publication of the latter's interesting book on *Old Egyptian Librarians*. [2] To counteract the tendency to confuse modern librarians with the keepers of libraries of about four thousand years ago, Dr. Richardson's definitions in reply to Professor Max Müller's criticisms are fully quoted:

Turning to the facts as to library usage, one may first set right the implication that a library is not a library when it is an archive. At a later period in Egypt, as the Papyri show, a man could send a book (biblion) to a keeper of books (bibliophylax) and have it put in a library (bibliotheke), and this library not be a library, according to Professor Müller, because it was a depository of official records! Yet the word used is the word that was used, and has been used constantly ever since, and is now used in all languages except English for library. The Egyptians themselves thus called a library a library, even if it was an archive, and this is the practice with the best modern experts in book-history (Birt. Buchrolle, p. 247), "when the library was an archive of account books and official documents." Library is the generic word for all collections of written documents, their place and their keeper. And why, indeed, does Professor Max Müller object to attributing to "librarians" the keeping of copies of the divine oracles? Is the keeper of a special library of Bibles not a librarian? When the people of Sparta made their kings custodians of the responses from the various shrines, sent for by the State through their special oracle bringers and deposited in the public collections, and the laws for which, one by one or in quantity, they had likewise sent and received the approval of the oracle, also the Athenian oracles captured by Cleomenes, were not these kings "librarians?" If these "keepers" of books were not librarians, what were they? They, of course, were not "librarians," because "liber" and the Latin tongue had not been invented when these began to be used, but they were keepers of books, just as the

---

[1] William Max Müller. Richardson's Some Old Egyptian Librarians. *Library Journal*. 37:217. April, 1912.

[2] E. C. Richardson. Definitions of the Library. (*In his Beginnings of Libraries*. Princeton University Press. 1914. Chapter 3).

keeper of printed books or the keeper of manuscripts in the British Museum today. ③

As to the accounts of ancient libraries, the material is quite scanty and of their librarians, almost all traces have disappeared. Only fragmentary passages of references dug out here and there must suffice from which we may infer the education and function of the librarians of the past. Human beings are always interested in their ancestors and genealogy is a fascinating study to many scholars. Modern librarians are no exception. A study of the librarians of the past may satisfy the pride of modern librarians that their professional ancestors came from no mean origin and that the professional services of these accomplished much benefit to humanity and civilization. That notion may stimulate modern librarians to place their useful deeds against the accomplishments of their ancestors.

There are two prominent facts about the earliest of librarians. They were as a class above the average in knowledge. They were intellectual leaders. It is invariably true in the ancient histories of Babylonia, Egypt, India, China, Greece, and Rome, that the earliest librarians were either priests, or kings, or archivists, or teachers. They had many duties and the keeping of official records was only one of their functions. The multiplication of library-duties and the specialized work of the present day librarians evolved from this simple origin of keeping official documents. The process of training and the function of the librarians of the past leading on up to the librarians of the present suggests Spencer's law of evolution, *i. e.* "from their initial state of simplicity to their ultimate state of complexity," or Spencer's more exact and philosophical definition, "evolution is an integration of matter and concomitant dissipation of motion; during which the matter passes from an indefinite incoherent homogeneity to a definite, coherent heterogeneity." Beginnings, though simple, are the roots of the present complex organization. To approach the past is a method of understanding the present and to study the present is a means of predicting the future.

Before getting into contact with the lives of the librarians of the past and learning something from their experiences in managing libraries, a brief explanation regarding the divisions of the periods of time and the continuity of function at the different ages may be necessary. The evolution of the training of librarians can be conveniently divided into three periods, ancient, medieval and early modern, and modern. The ancient period begins with history and ends with the fall of the Western Empire in 476 A. D. The medieval and early modern period starts with the invasions of the northern barbarians and closes at the end of the eighteenth century. The modern period begins with the wonderful development of modern libraries and the recognition of the professional status of the librarian in the nineteenth century. As to the function of the librarians from the past to the present, it is a continuous development from the simplest state to the most complex, though the development was arrested for some time at the beginning of the medieval age.

According to old and reliable records of Chinese history there were libraries for storing official

---

③ E. C. Richardson. The Facts about Old Egyptian Librarians—a Reply. *Library Journal.* 37:317-18. June, 1912.

documents as early as 2650 B. C. ④ The writer has seen several pieces of bone full of old Chinese hieroglyphics excavated from a place in the province of Honan. The authorities on Chinese antiquities consider that the "bone-book" is the oldest written record of the Chinese archives. Several prominent scholars, Chinese, Japanese, and western sinologists, have been and are studying these earliest hieroglyphics. As to the earliest Chinese librarians, no instance has yet been found before 600 B. C.

The first Chinese librarian who appeared in the history of China was Laotse, founder of Taoism and author of the *Tao-Te-King* (Book of the Way and Virtue). He was regarded by his contemporaries as a great scholar who had profound knowledge about the literatures of the ancients. Laotse was appointed keeper of the royal archives of the Chou dynasty about 553 B. C. Confucius once consulted him for material for his works. In this period there was not only a royal library but each feudal prince had a place for keeping his books. Confucius' great work, *Spring and Autumn Annals* was compiled from the official records of one hundred and twenty archives of the feudal princes.

According to the records of history, a royal custodian was usually appointed by a ruler to look after the archives of former reigns and to keep the records of the important events of the ruler's own reign. About the sixth century B. C. the staff of the royal custodian was increased until it included five separate offices under the supervision and direction of the chief royal custodian, whose official title was T'ai Shih (Head Archivist). He recorded the ruler's actions (in the manner of a modern court circular) besides his duty of supervising the library. The Hsiao Shih's (assistant archivist) function was to take care of the records of the important events of the country and the Wai Shih (reference librarian in the present sense) was to keep archives and geographical records. The Nai Shih was the head archivist's secretary. The Yu Shih watched and recorded the actions of various officials in the library. The Hsiao Yin Jen were the assistants.

From Chinese history and other records there are sufficient references about the development of Chinese libraries from Laotse's time in 600 B. C. to the present. As to the functions and education of the keepers of books, these can be traced from the books of reliable, as remarked by the eminent sinologist, Dr. Berthold Laufer. "The marked historical sense of the Chinese is one of their most striking characteristics. Hardly any other nation can boast of such a long and well-authenticated record of a continuous uninterrupted historical tradition extending over a millennium and a half down to 1644… excluding the present one, there are in existence the official records of twenty-four previous dynasties, known as the 'Twenty-Four Histories', comprising altogether 3,264 extensive chapters, with pedantic accuracy, all events are there registered, not only year by year, but also month by month, and even frequently day by day."⑤ After 1910 the custodians of the libraries have gradually begun to enlarge their duties into the realm of modern library economy. The tendency

---

④ T. C. Tai. A Brief Sketch of Chinese Libraries. *Library Journal.* 44:423-9-July,1919.

⑤ Berthold Laufer. *East Asiatic Collection.* Newberry Library. Publication No. 4. 1913-P. 15.

in library administration now inclines toward the American system. ⑥

The Near East has been a rich field for the studies of archaeologists. The researches which followed the discoveries of P. E. Potta and H. Layard in 1850 at Kouyunjik, on the Tigris, have revealed the fact that the ancient Babylonians and Assyrians had libraries. The clay tablets with cuneiform characters are the contents of the palace-library of Assur-bani-pal, King of Nineveh. These tablets have been arranged according to the following subjects, namely: History, Law, Science, Magic, Dogma, and Legends. ⑦ From such orderly arrangement we can infer that there must have been a keeper. He was probably a priest, because priests were the learned men par excellence of the ancients. Three points can be definitely inferred: (1) There was a special functionary to look after the tablets. (2) The keeper was learned enough to be able to arrange them in their proper sequence. (3) In ancient times the learned persons were generally priests and the keeping of the official documents was one of the priestly duties. Such a big library as Assur-bani-pal's might demand the entire time of a priest. When we read the history of the early libraries of Babylonia, Assyria and ancient Egypt we learn that the priests were concurrently the librarians. They had "the power to communicate with gods." That power of communication might mean merely the power of reading the records of the ancients.

The ancient librarians of the priestly type were gradually supplanted by learned teachers. The substitution took place in the normal process of evolution. As the intellect of the ancients advanced, more people were able to read the records of the dead. This was a heavy blow to the power of the priestly librarian. It was only natural for the great kings such as the Ptolemies of Alexandria, Antiochus the Great of Pergamum, and Augustus of the Roman Empire, to look for outstanding scholars and learned teachers of the age to be the librarians of their splendid libraries. The qualifications of a librarian then were that he must possess more than the mere knowledge to read all kinds of books, modern and ancient. His power to communicate with the records of the dead has ceased to be a charm, because abundant scholars by that time could do the same, and, therefore, in knowledge he had to know more than his contemporaries; in thought he was expected to be a creator; and in literary works he was required to be a master.

The functions of the librarians of that period were mainly three: (1) preservation and arrangement of books (rolls), as the librarians of Babylonia and Assyria did in their temple-libraries; (2) compilations of bibliographies and catalogs of the libraries; and (3) encouragement of scholars to use libraries and to permit readers to take out books. In the libraries of Alexandria and Rome there was systematic organization and the chief librarian had supervision and direction of his staff-members as one of his duties. Two distinctive functions which have been outstanding considerations in building up the professional education of a librarian took their origin in this golden age of ancient civilization. First, the compilation of bibliographies and the making of library catalogs were originally

---

⑥ T. C. Tai. *Library Movement in China*. Chinese National Association for the Advancement of Education. Vol. 2. Bulletin 3. Peking. 1923.

⑦ John Willis Clark. *Care of Books*. Cambridge University Press. 1902. p. 3-4.

experiments of the Alexandrian librarians. In the course of making a library catalog, according to the arrangement of rolls on shelves, the idea of book-classification probably crept into the minds of the ancient librarians. Bibliographies, cataloging, and classification are still the main technical subjects taught in library schools. The second distinctive function was the encouragement of scholars to use the books in, and to draw out the books from, the library. This was certainly a new departure from the established custom of the earliest libraries. These two new lines of development complicated and increased the amount of work for the librarian, and necessitated the introduction of some organization among the staff-members of a library.

According to Silvestrede Sacy's *Abdu-I-Lattif's Compendium of the History of Egypt*, there were four famous Alexandrian libraries, (1) the Library of the Brucheion, collected and founded by the early Ptolemies; (2) the Library of the Serapeum; (3) the Library of the Temple of Augustus; and (4) the Library of the School of Alexandria. Among the librarians of the Library of the Brucheion, five famous learned men are known. They were Zenodotus, Callimachus, Eratosthenes, Apollonius, and Aristonymus, or Aristophanes of Byzantium.⑧ The story runs that Zenodatus the Ephesian, about 280 B. C. was the first librarian. He rejected the unauthorized additions to Homer and produced the earliest scientific edition of the Greek poet. His successors were all scholars and grammarians of equal or greater eminence. They not only preserved their collections with care, but they also took an inventory and revised their library catalogs once in every five years.⑨ Two lists of the Alexandrian collections on tragedies and comedies were prepared by these famous librarians, and Callimachus compiled a catalog of all the principal books in Alexandria under one hundred and twenty classes. A fragment of that catalog, the philosophical works, from a papyrus found near Alexandria, is among the Greek manuscripts in the Library of Leningrad (formerly the Imperial Library of St. Petersburg.)⑩

The names of the librarians Callimachus and Aris-tonymus have occasioned much dispute. According to the references in the *Dictionary of Greek and Roman Biography*, the *Encyclopedia Britannica*, Edward's *Memoirs of Libraries*, and Clark's *Care of Books*, Callimachus was well established as the chief librarian of the Library of Alexandria under the reign of Ptolemy Philadelphus. Gardthausen's recent book, *Handbuch der Wissenschaftlichen Bibliothekskunde*, however, denies Callimachus the honor of being the chief librarian of the Alexandrian library. Gardthausen bases his evidence on the finding of a papyrus Oxyrynch. 10 p. 99 no. 124 of the second century including an old list of the names of the Alexandrian librarians which gives us the name of one of Callimachus's students but does not mention Callimachus himself.

Regarding Aristonymus, Edwards with his sources from the text of Suidas' and Meineke's *Apud Bonamy ut supra*, concludes that Aristonymus, the grammarian, succeeded Apollonius as the chief

---

⑧ Edward Edwards. *Memoirs of Libraries.* Trübner. London. 1859. Vol. 1. p. 22.

⑨ Victor Gardthausen. *Handbuch der Wissenschaftlichen Bibliothekskunde.* Quelle. Leipzig. 1920. Vol. 2, Book 8. Chap. 1.

⑩ J. W. Clark. *Care of Books.* 1902. p. 21.

librarian of the Brucheion. But the information in Savage's *Story of Libraries and Book Collecting*, and other references, point to Aristophanes of Byzantium as the successor of Apollonius and the fifth of the eminent Alexandrian librarians.

An interesting story about the appointment of Aristophanes of Byzantium to the position of chief librarian is worth repeating from Dr. Edwards's version of Vitruvius.

It was the practice of the Ptolemies to invite literary men to come to Alexandria on certain festive occasions to recite their compositions before seven appointed judges; those who were deemed to have surpassed their rivals being honored and rewarded for their works. On one such occasion, the king had selected six judges but could not so readily satisfy himself as to the seventh. In his strait, he applied to the officers of the Library for their aid, and was told that one Aristophanes had long been a most diligent reader there—so diligent, indeed, that he seemed to be steadily working his way through the collection. He, it was thought, might worthily acquit himself of this duty. Aristophanes, accordingly, took his place amongst the judges. The recitations proceeded. Some were loudly applauded. Others were listened to in cold silence. When the time came for distribution of the prizes, six of the judges were speedily of one mind, but the seventh—our plodding student, Aristophanes—was of quite another. The best poet, said he, has had little applause or none. The king grew impatient and the people grew angry. Aristophanes, however, persisted in his opinion. These he said, are not poets, but plagiarists. One man only recited what he had himself composed. Summoned to bring proof of his allegations, he named the books in the library from which the thefts had been committed. The upshot of the matter was, of course, the disgrace of the plagiarists, and the elevation of Aristophanes to the superintendence of the library. ⑪

The eminent Alexandrian librarians were not without rivals in neighboring countries. A royal library was founded by the kings of Pergamum, and Antiochus the Great appointed Euphorion of Chalcis, the poet and grammarian, to be the librarian. Euphorion's literary fame was as high as that of Callimachus of the Alexandrian library. His works were highly esteemed by the Romans. Under his administration, the royal library of Pergamum became a worthy rival of the libraries of the Ptolemies.

The duties of the library officials under the Roman Empire assumed a more definite form than those of the Alexandrian librarians. The Roman emperors were anxious to have eminent scholars as their librarians. The collections of the libraries at that time were bigger and the scholars more numerous. Some authorities have claimed that there were twenty-eight, possibly twenty-nine, public libraries in ancient Rome. Regardless of the various opinions concerning the number of Roman public libraries, we know that new developments took shape in library management. It was the first time in the history of libraries that the general public was allowed to use the books and to take the books out of the library. From this innovation in the field of library management sprang the work of reference and circulation. The duties of librarians became more complex and the organization of the library staff-members and the division of labor in library work had their beginnings.

According to Professor Boyd's *Public Libraries and Literary Culture in Ancient Rome*, the evi-

---

⑪ Edward Edwards. *Memoirs of Libraries*. Vol. I. p. 23-4.

dence for the management of the ancient Roman libraries is taken chiefly from inscriptions and secondly from Roman literature. A rough diagram of the personnel organization of the libraries of ancient Rome is here given from Dr. Boyd's descriptions of the duties of library officials of various grades. ⑫

PERSONNEL ORGENIZATION OF THE ROMAN LIBRARIES

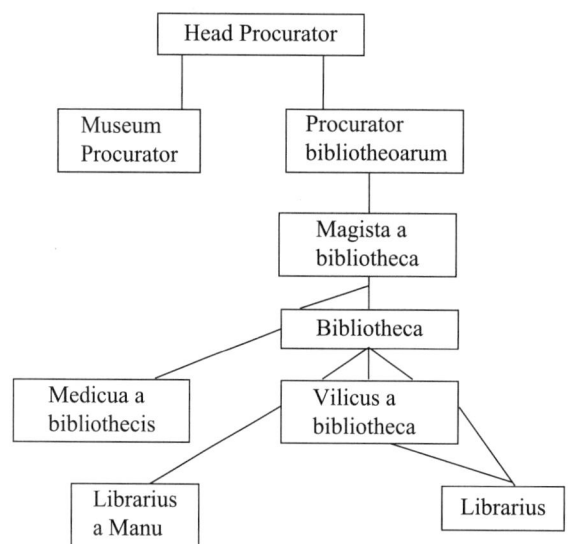

The head procurator might correspond to the position of a cabinet-minister. He might have several vice-ministers and one of them might have the duty of looking after the development of the public libraries. According to Mommsen and Hirschfeld, the "Procurator bibliothecarum" was subordinate to the head procurator and his duty was to look after the imperial finances available for library purposes. One of the Greek inscriptions (CIG, 5900) gives a reference to the effect that the position of procurator bibliothecarum (chief director of libraries) was once occupied by the eminent scholar, L. Julius Vestinus. He concurrently held positions as curator of museum, high priest of Alexandria, imperial secretary to Emperor Hadrian, and philologist. Gardthausen concludes in his *Handbuch der Wissenschaftlichen Bibliothekskunde*, Vol. 2, Chapter 1, p. 69-70, that these procurators were never called librarians, but actually were directors of Greek and Latin libraries. They had somehow the same functions as the curators of the German universities in dealing with the administration of external and economic affairs. These directors at the same time held positions as imperial secretaries for Greek correspondence and also study-councilors to the emperor. To be such a curator was a high honor. He had a salary of 60,000 sesterces (about \$3,000 United States currency). It is quite evident that the procurator bibliothecarum in the organization of Roman libraries is the highest administrative officer, and a great scholar with marked executive abilities.

Since the procurator bibliothecarum had many duties, the libraries must have had an official

---

⑫ C. E. Boyd. *Public Libraries and Literary Culture in Ancient Rome.* University of Chicago Press. 1915. Chap. 4. p. 41-51.

who took charge of the central administration. This official was probably the magista a bibliotheca. Under him there were a number of librarians, bibliothecas, and each of them took charge of a special library. The bibliothecas' names were usually recorded with the names of special libraries, as in one of the inscriptions (CIL, VI, 4433) "a bibliotheca Graeca Porticus Octaviae." The bibliotheca must have been a man of literary training and professional efficiency. His culture and knowledge must have had to command the respect of scholars. In an epigram of Martial, one Sextus is spoken of as officially connected with the Palatine Library, "O Sextus, thou eloquent devotee of Palatine Minerva, who possesses intelligence approaching that of a god..."⑬

Asinius Pollio, Pompeius Macer, and C. Julius Hyginus were the prominent librarians in the reign of the Emperor Augustus. Augustus appointed Asinius Pollio to take over the uncompleted task of Varro of founding libraries in Rome. Pollio was a prominent literary man, a noted orator, a learned historian, and a Roman general. Pompeius Macer was delegated to put the Palatine Library in order; and C. Julius Hyginus, a freedman of Augustus, and an intimate friend of Ovid and of C. Licinius, the historian, was in turn appointed to the librarianship of the Palatine. Caius Melissus, the librarian of the Porticus Octaviae, was a great grammarian and author of *loci*. All the ancient Roman librarians were worthy successors of the famous Varro, selected by Julius Caesar to be the first organizer and director of the Roman libraries.

Vilicus a bibliotheca was some sort of a departmental head of a library in the modern sense. He had a special duty. Medicus a bibliothecis might be the librarian of a collection of medical books and concurrently a special physician to the library employees. One of the inscriptions tells us that Hymenaeus, medicus a bibliothecis, had the duty of looking after the health of all the library employees of the emperor and that he was efficient in his work.

Near the end of the nineteenth century many men-librarians, especially in England and Europe, regarded the presence of women in library work as savoring of novelty and inappropriate.⑭ But they forgot that women took up library work almost as early as men. Both men and women did library work under the Roman emperors. According to one of the inscriptions (CIL, VI, 6314) a woman is regarded as quite capable to fill the office of "librarius a manu," which means a secretary on the library staff or a copyist.

The work of "librarius," which had several meanings, copyist, or transcriber, or bookseller (who had books copied), was divided under various heads, as servus librarius, doctus librarius, benignus librarius and other kinds of librarius. These heads performed various minor tasks, clerical and literary. They might correspond to the assistants of a modern library. All evidence that survives indicates that literary training, knowledge of both Greek and Latin books, high intellectuality and library efficiency were the important qualifications of the several upper grades of Roman library administrators. Assistants, secretaries, copyists, scribes and clerks were locally trained in library tech-

---

⑬ C. E. Boyd. *Public Libraries and Literary Culture in Ancient Rome.* p. 48.

⑭ H. R. Tedder. *Librarianship as a Profession.* Library Association of the United Kingdom. Transactions and Proceedings. 1882. p. 171.

nique. Most of the secretaries, copyists, scribes and clerks were well-educated and intelligent slaves. They were especially qualified for their numerous duties. This fact is well brought out in Cicero's three letters to his friend Atticus about the rearrangement of his library. ⑮

First letter: "I wish you would send me any two fellows out of your library, for Tyrannio to make use of as pasters and assistants in other matters. Remind them to bring some vellum with them to make those titles (indices) … "

Second letter: "Your men have made my library gay with their carpentry-work and their titles. I wish you would commend them." When the arrangement of his library was completed, Cicero wrote the third letter. "Now that Tyrannio has arranged my books, a new spirit has been infused into my house. In this matter the help of your men Dionysius and Menophilus has been invaluable. Nothing could look neater than these shelves of yours (illa tua pegmata), since they smartened up my books with their titles."

Callimachus's system of classification might have been improved by later Roman librarians and the technique of cataloging bettered for public use. "Further, it's evident, from the passages which I have quoted," says Mr. J. W. Clark, "that catalogs must have been in use. But, besides this inference, such a document is distinctly mentioned by Quintilian and the younger Pliny. The former remarks that anybody could increase his list of Greek authors by transferring a library catalog (index) to his pages; and the latter, speaking of his uncle's works, says that he could supply the want of a catalog (index) and record the very order in which they had been written." ⑯

The Roman conquests brought the Romans into direct contact with other civilizations, notably the Hellenic and the Egyptian. Julius Caesar, Augustus, and other emperors encouraged civic ideals and the attainment of a high intellectual standard. All those incentives made for the development of ancient Roman libraries. The use of the libraries increased in proportion as the literary and cultural tendencies of the citizens developed. The practice of lending books from libraries was introduced. There are many references to this. One occurs in the writings of Aulus Gellius. On a very hot summer day Gellius and some of his friends were assembled in a rich man's villa and began to drink melted snow. They discussed whether such cold water was healthful. One member of the party was a philosopher and he asserted that Aristotle and many physicians had strongly condemned the use of cold water. In order to convince his companions of the truth of his argument, he ran to the public library in the temple of Hercules to take out a copy of Aristotle's book dealing with the subject and read to them the statement. ⑰

This instance clearly shows that ancient public libraries in Rome allowed readers to take books out of the library.

The splendid Roman public libraries fell into decline at the repeated invasions of the northern

---

⑮ J. W. Clark. *Care of Books*. 1902. p. 35.

⑯ Ibid. p. 2o-I.

⑰ Aulus Gellius. *Noctes Atticae*. XIX. 5, 4. (original quotation in Boyd's *Public Libraries and Literary Culture in Ancient Rome*. p. 30).

barbarians. Literary activity at Rome as well as at Constantinople rapidly collapsed. Books were either burnt or destroyed and librarians were not wanted. This marks the end of the library development among the ancients and practically ended the labors of their librarians.

SELECTED BIBLIOGRAPHY

Boyd, Clarence Eugene. Public libraries and literary culture in ancient Rome. Univ. of Chicago Press. 1915.

Brittanica. 11th ed. Ancient, medieval and modern libraries. Vol. 16. p. 545-77.

Clark, John Willis. Care of books. Cambridge Univ. Press. 1902. Chap. 1.

Edwards, Edward. Memoirs of libraries. Trübner. London. 1859. Vol. 1. Chap. 1-5.

Gardthausen, Victor. Handbuch der wissenschaftlichen bibliothekskunde. Quelle. Leipzig. 1920. Vol. 2. Book 8. Chap. 1.

Laufer, Berthold. East Asiatic collection. Publication No. 4. Newberry Library. Chicago. 1913.

Lipsius, Justus. History of libraries; trans. from the 2nd ed. John Moretus. (The Plantin Press Antwerp. 1607) by Dana, J. C. and Kent, H. W. McClurg. Chicago. 1907.

Müller, William Max. Richardson's some old Egyptian libraries. Library Journal. 37:217. April, 1912.

Richardson, E. C. Beginnings of libraries. Milford. London. 1914.

Richardson, E. C. Facts about old Egyptian librarians. Library Journal. 37:316-19. June, 1912.

Richardson, E. C. Old Egyptian librarians. Scribner. New York. 1911.

Savage, Ernest A. Story of libraries and book collecting. Routledge. London. Chap. 1-2.

Smith, William, ed. Dictionary of Greek and Roman biography and mythology. Walton. London. 1869. 3 vol.

Spofford, Ainsworth Rand. A book for all readers. Putnam. New York. 1900. Chap. 15.

Tai, T. C. A brief sketch of Chinese libraries. Library Journal. 44:423-9. July, 1919.

Tai, T. C. Library movement in China. Chinese National Association for the Advancement of Education. Vol. 2. Bulletin 3. Peking. 1923.

Tedder, Henry R. Evolution of the public library. Second International Library Conference. Transactions. London. 1897. p. 13-18.

Tedder, Henry R. Librarianship as a profession. Library Association of the United Kingdom. Transactions and Proceedings, 1882. p. 171.

CHAPTER VII
THE MEDIEVAL AND EARLY MODERN LIBRARIANS

The library movement during the Middle Ages had a weak and narrow beginning and a powerful and broad ending. The medieval age can be divided into two parts. The first period covers the growth of the monastic libraries when the members of the library profession all wore the garb of monks. Biblical literature, theological dogma, and biographies of saints and martyrs were the principal collections of the monastic library of the first period. The second period covers the great strides made by libraries in institutions of learning after the invention of printing had multiplied the number of books, and when a revival of true learning and science made the libraries the indispensable tools of scholars. Learned monks and great savants were again summoned to the tasks of librarianship.

In the development of the training of librarians, the Order of Saint Benedict, the Cistercians, the Augustinians, and the other orders, contributed several valuable factors as to the methods of arranging books, repairing, binding, loaning, and cataloging. The care and preservation of books in libraries was much emphasized. Annual reports and stock-taking were a few of the important duties of a monk-librarian who at the same time was the leader of the choir, superintendent of the transcription of manuscripts, and occasionally the master of ceremonies. The monk-librarian was an all-round person in a monastery. Only in large and wealthy monasteries was there a special monk to take charge of the library. Usually the old manuscripts in the monastery were kept in the treasury room and the new books in the scriptorium. Therefore, there was no use for a special monk-librarian.

Some of the regulations governing the use and the loaning of books in modern collegiate libraries have their origin in the rules of the monastic libraries. In the early monastery no stranger could borrow a book. The privilege of taking out a book for a week was only granted to the brothers of the monastery. In the evening the "Second", *i. e.* the second in command, took charge of the books, counted them, and locked them in a cupboard in the thickness of the wall.[①] As a result of the encouragement of reading in the various Orders and the diligent and extensive labors in scriptoria, the production of books was much increased. Some of the large monasteries began to keep their books in a separate room and to publish regulations governing circulation to monks and to strangers. Regarding the loan of books to strangers, there was much variety in the regulations of the different orders. In general the system of loan on pledge was adopted.

Saint Benedict was the first to issue a set of rules regarding the reading and the loaning of books. These rules were further modified by the Cluniacs. The Carthusians maintained the principle

---

① J. W. Clark. *Care of Books*. Cambridge University Press. 1902. 54-5.

of loaning two books to each brother of the House. The Cistercians, the Augustinians, and the other orders all allowed the circulation of books. In a way the monasteries were the collegiate libraries to the monks and the public libraries to any others who were anxious to read. The following passages from J. W. Clark's translations in his *Care of Books* will illustrate the viewpoints on library economy held by the monk-librarians.

"Between Easter and the Calends of October let them apply themselves to reading from the fourth hour till near the sixth hour. From the Calends of October to the beginning of Lent let them apply themselves to reading until the second hour... During Lent, let them apply themselves to reading from morning until the end of the third hour... and, in these days of Lent, let them receive a book apiece from the library, and read it straight through."② This was the famous rule of Saint Benedict. "Then shall he read aloud a note of the books which a year before had been given out to brethren for their reading. When a brother's name is called, he rises, and returns the book that has been given to him; and if it should happen that he has not read it through, he is to ask forgiveness for his want of diligence. A carpet on which these books are to be laid out is to be put down in the Chapter-House; and the titles of those which are distributed to brethren afresh are to be noted, for which purpose a tablet is to be made of somewhat larger size than usual."③

About 1070 Archbishop Lanfranc gave decrees to the English Benedictines. The section relating to books and the duty of the librarian is as follows, "On the Monday after the first Sunday in Lent... before the brethren go into Chapter, the librarian (custos librorum) ought to have all the books brought together into the Chapter-House and laid out on a carpet, except those which had been given out for reading during the past year; these the brethren ought to bring with them as they come into Chapter, each carrying his book in his hand. Of this they ought to have had notice given to them by the aforesaid librarian on the preceding day in Chapter... Next let the librarian read a document (breve) setting forth the names of the brethren who have had books during the past year; and let each brother, when he hears his own name pronounced, return the book which had been entrusted to him for reading; and let him who is conscious of not having read the book through which he had received, fall down on his face, confess his fault and pray for forgiveness. Then let the aforesaid librarian hand to each brother another book for reading; and when the books have been distributed in order, let the aforesaid librarian in the same Chapter put on record the names of the books and of those who receive them."④

The fourteenth chapter of the customs of the Augustinian Order, "of the safe keeping of the books, and of the office of librarian," represents the general trend of the administration of monastery libraries in Great Britain as well as in Europe. Many phases of present day library training can be traced to the practices of the monastic and collegiate libraries of the Middle Ages. Dr. C. C. Williamson's report on "Training for Library Service," deplores the present condition of the library schools in that they do not differentiate clearly between professional and clerical training. This lack

---

② Ibid. p. 56.
③ Ibid. p. 57.
④ Ibid. p. 57-8.

of differentiation has been due, Dr. Williamson thinks, to the mixture in library administration of the two types of services (professional and clerical). Many duties of a twentieth century librarian are simply the inherited traditions of the past. For example, modern library schools give a course in binding. It is not expected that professionally trained librarians are to be binders after graduation. The course is given in part merely because of the age old tradition that every librarian should know how to mend and to bind books just as the monk-librarian of the Middle Ages did. The following excerpt illustrates the scope of the functions and training of a monk-librarian.

  The librarian, who is called also precentor, is to take charge of the books of the church; all which he ought to keep and to know under their separate titles; and he should frequently examine them carefully to prevent any damage or injury from insects or decay. He ought also, at the beginning of Lent, in each year, to show them to the convent in Chapter, when the souls of those who have given them to the church, or of the brethren who have written them, and laboured over them, ought to be absolved, and a service in convent be held over them. He ought also to hand to the brethren the books which they see occasion to use, and to enter on his roll the titles of the books, and the names of those who receive them. These, when required, are bound to give surety for the volumes they receive; nor may they lend them to others, whether known or unknown, without first obtaining permission from the librarian. Nor ought the librarian himself to lend books unless lie receive a pledge of equal value; and then he ought to enter on his roll the name of the borrower, the title of the book lent, and the pledge taken. The larger and more valuable books he ought not to lend to anyone, known or unknown, without permission of the Prelate…

  Books which are to be kept at hand for daily use, whether for singing or reading, ought to be in some common place, to which all the brethren can have easy access for inspection, and selection of anything which seems to them suitable. The books, therefore, ought not to be carried away into the chambers, or into corners outside the Cloister or the Church. The librarian ought frequently to dust the books carefully, to repair them, and to point them, lest brethren should find any error or hindrance in the daily service of the church, whether in singing or in reading. No other brother ought to erase or change anything in the books unless he have obtained the consent of the librarian…

  The press in which the books are kept ought to be lined inside with wood that the damp of the walls may not moisten or stain the books. This press should be divided vertically as well as horizontally by sundry shelves on which the books may be ranged so as to be separated from one another; for fear they be packed so close as to injure each other or delay those who want them.

  Further, as the books ought to be mended, pointed, and taken care of by the librarian, so ought they to be properly bound by him. ⑤

  From the above passages we see that the monasteries encouraged monks to study and that generally there was some sort of a library in spite of the difficulty of acquiring books. Special care against the theft and the soiling of books was usually taken by the medieval librarians. The preservation of books was regarded, perhaps, as the most important problem of medieval library administration. The scarcity of books and the laborious task of copying made the monk-librarians realize their responsibility in looking after their collections. There were rules regarding the handling of books in reading. "When the religious are engaged in reading in cloister or in church," says an Order of the General Benedictine Chapter, "they shall if possible hold the books in their left hands, wrapped in the sleeve of their tunics, and resting on their knees; their right hands shall be uncov-

---

⑤ Ibid. p. 61.

ered with which to hold and turn the leaves of the aforesaid book." Thomas à Kempis advised the youthful student how to use a book in his Doctrinale Juvenum. He said, "take thou a book into thine hands as Simeon the Just took the Child Jesus into his arms to carry Him and kiss Him. And when thou hast finished reading, close the book and give thanks for every word out of the mouth of God; because in the Lord's field thou hast found a hidden treasure."⑥ What would a present day student who unscrupulously cuts the pages of an encyclopedia or mercilessly drags a heavy book about by one of the covers say about these injunctions? To curb vandalism in libraries is as difficult today as it was several centuries ago. It is still an unsolved problem in library administration. An imprecation like that on a book plate of a book belonging to the house of Saint Mary of Robert's Bridge, "This book belongs to Saint Mary of Robert's Bridge: Whosoever steals it, or sells it, or takes it away from this house in any way, or injures it, let him be anathema-maranatha," will certainly not serve as a restraining influence today. Small likelihood a youth of the present generation on getting hold of such a book would keep it and write on the title page as the Bishop of Exeter flippantly did, "*I*, John, Bishop of Exeter, do not know where the said house is: I did not steal this book, but got it lawfully."⑦ Of course the word "lawfully" may have been used with ironic intent, and would surely be so used by the modern library vandal.

Indications of careful methods and of minute accuracy are to be found in some of the monastic catalogs, though others were mere inventories with no classification. In general the monastic libraries emphasized the compilation of catalogs. There are monastic manuscript catalogs in the Library of Munich, in Jesus College, Cambridge, and in other libraries. The classifications are general and hardly have any subdivisions. The letters of the alphabet are used to signify classes. The books are arranged in the manner of fixed location. The divisions of the catalogs of the Library of the Monastery of Rievaux and the main classes of the catalog of the Library of the Monastery of Tychefeld are respectively reprinted in Edwards' *Memoirs of Libraries* and Clark's *Care of Books*. In plan they were defective and in classification unscientific; but we must remember that they mark only the beginnings. The development in the technique of cataloging and in the science of bibliography, during a period generally characterized by a low ebb of the intellectual life of the masses, compares very favorably with any other intellectual undertakings at that time.

Modern university librarians favor the installation of carrells in the stacks for graduate students. This is only a revival of a phase of the administration of monastery-libraries in the Middle Ages. The carrell system in monastery-libraries was quite prevalent. The privilege of occupying carrells belonged only to the older monks who were engaged either in copying, in illuminating, or in reading, as was the case at Durham. According to Clark, the carrells in the south cloister at Gloucester were built between 1370 and 1412. Each carrell was four feet wide, nineteen inches deep and six feet nine inches high, and was lighted by a small window of two lights.

As to the organization of some large cloister-libraries, there were two officers, a precentor and

---

⑥ Ibid. p. 67.
⑦ T. W. Koch. *On University Libraries*. 1924. p. 3-4.

a succentor. The former had a seat in front of the press, which doubtless stood against the wall, and his carrell was generally located at no great distance. The latter had his seat and his carrell near the press.⑧ They, or at least one of them, was always at hand to give service to brethren who wished to seek some information about the books. The precentor was the librarian and the succentor was the sub-librarian. They were always ready to answer questions somewhat in the manner of modern reference librarians.

In summing up, the monastery-librarian was a learned monk of high rank in his order. In earlier monasteries when the books were not numerous, he was an all-round monk with many duties. Later his chief functions were to look after the cloister-libraries, to mend books, to circulate books, to compile catalogs, and to serve as a reference librarian. His status was not changed but his functions increased during the growth of cathedral libraries in the fifteenth century.

Early collegiate libraries, for instance some of the earlier colleges at Oxford and Cambridge, developed in the manner of the cloister libraries. Scholars borrowed books under pledges. The annual audit and distribution of books was carried out somewhat as directed in Lanfranc's statutes for English Benedictines. An examination of the statutes of Oriel College or of Merton College, Oxford, or of Peterhouse, Cambridge, leads us to the definite conclusion that the library regulations were directly derived from monastic practice. Modern library management, especially modern university library management, has inherited many of the customs of the monastic libraries.

For about a millennium the task of managing libraries and of looking after books was in the hands of monks. By the fifteenth century, the monasteries, cathedrals, and universities throughout Europe were vieing with each other in collecting books, building libraries, compiling catalogs, and framing liberal regulations to make libraries useful not only to monks but to the public. The development was arrested in the sixteenth century by the Huguenot movement in France and the suppression of the monasteries in England. Many monasteries were pulled down and their contents destroyed. Manuscripts were either burned or scattered. How terrible the loss was has been bitterly recorded by many writers. One writer who was especially aware of the worth of the monastery-libraries wrote emphatically to King Edward VI, in 1549, protesting "that in turning over of the superstitious monasteries so little respect was had to their libraries, for the safeguard of these noble and precious monuments... Avarice was the other dispatcher which hath made an end both of our libraries and books... A great number of them which purchased those superstitious mansions, reserved of those library books, some... to scour their candlesticks, and some to rub their boots; some they sold to the grocers and soap-sellers, and some they sent over sea to the bookbinders, not in small number but at times whole ships full, to the wondering of the foreign nations... I judge this to be true, and utter it with heaviness—that neither the Britons under the Romans and Saxons, nor yet the English people under the Danes and Normans, had ever such damage of their learned monuments as we have seen in our time. Our posterity may well curse this wicked fact of our age, this unreasonable spoil of

---

⑧ J. W. Clark. Care of Books. Cambridge University Press. 1902. p. 92.

England's most noble antiquities."⑨... This devastation of monastic libraries and manuscripts, coupled with the protests and lamentations of many learned persons, prepared the ground for a new and forceful development of the library movement.

In the seventeenth and eighteenth centuries books were rapidly multiplied by the use of movable type. Freedom of thought budded forth as the first fruit of the Renaissance and the Reformation. Authorship in literature and science was much more prolific than under the ecclesiastical yoke of monasticism. On one hand the dispersion of the medieval monastery libraries was a loss to human knowledge, and on the other hand the conception of making libraries free to all and not merely sacred store-houses open only to a few privileged scholars and monks would probably not have developed so fully had monk-librarians continued to exercise the sole power as library administrators and educators. Would the administrators of cloister-libraries have been liberal enough to collect and to catalog the irreligious and radical books of the early modern era within their sacred walls, if the type of dogmatic monk who believed that to ward off the evils of the Hebrews it would be best to commit all the Jewish books except the Bible to the flames, had continued to control the fountain of knowledge? Modern librarians are indebted to the monks in many ways both in library economy and in bibliography, but the spirit of impartiality toward the contents of books and the idea of democracy in the free library movement are the new wine. Had it happened to be put into the old bottles of the monastery libraries, there would today have been no battle-cry to promote the advanced education for librarianship.

After the suppression of many monasteries the management of libraries began to pass into the hands of secular scholars and clergymen. In the seventeenth century there were many scholars who at the same time were eminent librarians. Men like Gabriel Naudé, John Durie, James Kirkwood, Antonio Magliabecchi, and others, have contributed much to the foundation of modern library science. They were book lovers and they wished to collect books, to enlarge libraries, and to systematize library service. The eighteenth century's librarians were no less prominent than their predecessors. Jean Des Houssayes, David Hume, Gotthold Ephraim Lessing, and many other learned persons were once the keepers of the treasures of knowledge. Some contributed to the library profession by the eminence of their literary standing and some gave their suggestions for the advancement of the science of bibliography. As a class they were chiefly learned professors and prominent writers, but nevertheless a few of them had visions of administering libraries in accordance with the new order of society.

One of the great librarians of the seventeenth century was Gabriel Naudé, who was born at Paris in February, 1600. He studied philosophy and rhetoric under Padet and Belurget. The last named teacher was a free thinker in matters of religion and belief. Naudé was a prolific writer and his knowledge was very encyclopedic. At the age of twenty, his literary reputation attracted Henri de Mesmes, President of the Parliament, who appointed young Gabriel to take charge of his library. In 1630 Naudé became the librarian of Cardinal de Bagni. This office took him to Italy, and when

---

⑨ Edward Edwards. *Memoirs of Libraries*. Trübner. London. 1859. Vol. 1, p. 360-1.

Bagni died, Naudé became librarian to Cardinal Barberini. In 1642 Cardinal Richelieu recalled him to Paris. After Richelieu's death he became librarian to Mazarin. During Mazarin's exile from Paris he was engaged by Queen Christina of Sweden to be the librarian of her famous library. In spite of his wide interest in various controversial subjects, he was by nature a born librarian. He loved to collect books and was an expert in bargaining. When he started a book hunting expedition, he took a foot rule in his hand. As soon as he entered a book shop, he would ask a bookseller to name a price for several piles of books. The latter would suggest some amount all too hastily and Naudé would then begin to bully and to storm and would generally carry the books he wanted at a very low figure. He often struck bargains and the bookseller, only after stopping to think over the matter, would realize that he had been duped and left lamenting over the deal and wishing that he had sold those papers to the butterman or the grocer. When Naudé found nothing more to buy in Paris, he went to Belgium and there bought the best books on the market. Italy having been ransacked, Germany and England were next attacked. Wherever he visited, the booksellers' shops seemed to be devastated by a whirlwind. Gabriel Naudé was the librarian who made the Mazarin Library "the eighth wonder of the world." ⑩ in the seventeenth century.

We realize Naudé's grasp of the problem of library science when we survey his brilliant achievements. When he was only twenty-six and still librarian to President de Mesmes, he wrote a book, *Advis pour Dresser une Bibliotheque*, in honor of his patron. It was first published in 1627, a second edition came out in 1644, and other editions in the same year and in 1668. In 1661 John Evelyn translated it into English and in 1703 it was translated into Latin. This book consists of nine chapters, the first five giving reasons for forming a library, the sort of books of which it should be composed, and by what means to obtain them. The sixth chapter deals with library architecture; the seventh introduces a scheme of classification divided into twelve main classes, with several sub-divisions. ⑪ The eighth chapter treats of bookbinding, and the ninth deals with the principal aims of a library.

According to George Smith, Naudé's *Advis pour Dresser une Bibliotheque* was the first "practical" treatise on libraries and Naudé was the first librarian to sketch out in full a plan for the arrangement of a library. "The basis he (Naudé) adopted," says George Smith, "was not much dissimilar to some of the most successful schemes of the present day. Accessions he proposed to keep separately for six months, at the end of which time, they were to be placed on the shelves in their respective classes, opportunity then being seized of dusting the rest of the books, which in many cases would require to be moved to make room for the newcomers; he thus avoids, in a practical manner, the constant re-arrangement necessitated by immediately shelving new books in their respective

---

⑩ Naudé, G. Plea to Parliament for the Preservation of the Mazarin Library, 1652. (Reprinted in Dana and Kent, eds. *Literature of Libraries in the Seventeenth and Eighteenth Centuries*. 1907. Vol. 6. p. 72).

⑪ J. D. Brown. *Library Classification and Cataloguing*. Grafton. London. 1916. p. 29-30.

classes."⑫

Not only did Naudé conceive the idea of throwing open the library to the public, but he actually persuaded Cardinal Mazarin to open his rich library on every Thursday, from eight until eleven and from two until five. Anybody was admitted and could freely consult the valuable collections. Naudé not only advocated the policy of free library service, but also urged the appointment of capable librarians to draw up catalogs of both authors and subjects as well as to minister in every way to the needs of all earnest students. No one has payed a more respectful tribute to Naudé, the forerunner of the modern library profession, than Albert de la Fizelière in his *Rymaille sur les plus Célebres Bibliolieres de Paris*: "As long as there are in France men devoted to literature and to a discriminating love of books, Gabriel Naudé will remain the type of the model librarian. It is true that there were bibliophiles and bibliographers before his day, but the science of books had not been coordinated. He was the first to set a proper standard for it, and, thanks to his encyclopedic knowledge, he was able to make it take its place beside the science and letters of the seventeenth century on their lofty eminence."⑬

During the eighteenth century royal libraries, libraries of learned institutions and private libraries developed extensively in various countries. It was often a matter of pride to the owners to obtain learned men, great thinkers and well-known bibliographers to be their librarians. The position offered more honor than remuneration. The use of libraries was generally granted to scholars by royal collectors, who took this means of giving scholars their encouragement and of expressing their love for literature and science. The value of those libraries would have been increased, had the well-known authors and thinkers been engaged to take charge. Learned men like Hume, Lessing, and others were as important assets to their libraries as many valuable manuscripts would have been. Famous scholars sometimes took a library appointment with two reasons: to receive charity under the name of a salary for library service; and to have free use of the books of the library while carrying on their work.

David Hume was elected to succeed Ruddiman in 1752 as the librarian of the Library of the Advocates in Edinburgh. According to Hume, it was a petty office of about forty guineas a year. Though the salary was insignificant, he accepted the offer, because it gave him the command of a large library. His assistant, Walter Goodall, who was "seldom sober," spent a part of his time in writings designed to white-wash Queen Mary, and Hume's primary interest lay in composing a history of England. Ernest A. Savage has remarked, "We may well wonder how the library was administered under them." (Hume and Goodall.)⑭ It was the same in the case of Lessing's acceptance of the offer to be the librarian of the Wolfenbüttel Library in 1770. His chief purpose was to make

---

⑫ George Smith. Gabriel Naudé, a Librarian of the Seventeenth Century. *Library Association Record*. 1:425-6. July, 1899.

⑬ R. S. Granniss. Gabriel Naudé, Biographical Sketch. (In Dana and Kent, eds. *Literature of Libraries in the Seventeenth and Eighteenth Centuries*. McClurg. Chicago. 1906. Vol. 6. p. 37-8).

⑭ E. A. Savage. *Story of Libraries and Book Collecting*. Routledge. London, p. 169.

personal use of the rich manuscript-collection of the library, though he wished also to give the contents of these manuscripts to the world by their publication. ⑮

In spite of the laissez-faire attitude of not a few of the most famous scholar-librarians, the standards for being a librarian have been raised by such types of learned as well as public spirited men as those among whom we must include Jean-Baptiste Cotton Des Houssayes, elected librarian of the Society of the Sorbonne about 1776. In his discourse on the "Duties and Qualifications of a Librarian," Des Houssayes sets up classical professional standards. As to qualifications, "A librarian truly worthy of the name should, if I may be permitted the expression, have explored in advance every region of the empire of letters, to enable him afterwards to serve as a faithful guide to all who may desire to survey it. And though it is by no means my intention to give the preference above all other sciences to the science of bibliography, which is nothing more than an exact and critical acquaintance with the productions of the intellect, it will nevertheless be permitted me to consider this science as the forerunner of all the others… Thus the superintendent of a library, whatever be its character, should be no stranger to any department of learning; sacred and profane literature, the fine arts, the exact sciences, all should be familiar to him." As to the administration of a library, Des Houssayes emphasized that, "it should be administered by a librarian distinguished for soundness of judgment no less than for the readiness and accuracy of his memory… He will therefore not admit indiscriminately every book into his collection, but will select such only as are of genuine merit and of well approved utility; and his acquisitions, guided by the principles of an enlightened economy, will be rendered still more valuable by the substantial merits of an able classification." ⑯

The qualifications prescribed by the learned librarians of the eighteenth century fortunately set up a fine scholarly standard for their successors. Following this, the highly useful service rendered by the librarians of the first three-quarters of the nineteenth century introduced training for library work to the hall of professional studies.

SELECTED BIBLIOGRAPHY

Axon, William F. A. Antonio Magliabecchi. Library Association Record. 5;59-76. Feb., 1903.
Brown, James Duff. Library classification and cataloging. Grafton. London. 1916. Chap. 3.
Clark, John Willis. Care of books. Cambridge Univ. Press. Cambridge. 1902.
Clark, J. W. Mediaeval and Renaissance libraries. Macmillan. Cambridge. 1894.
Clarke, A. Lessing as a librarian. Library, n. s. 2;376-83. 1901.
Dana, J. C. and Kent, H. W., eds. Literature of libraries in the seventeenth and eighteenth centuries. McClurg. Chicago. 1906. 6vols.
Des Houssayes, Jean-Baptiste Cotton. Duties and qualifications of a librarian. (In Dana and Kent, eds. Literature of

---

⑮ V. Gardthausen. *Handbuch der Wissenschaftlichen Bibliothekskunde.* Quelle. Leipzig. 1920. Vol. 2. p. 82.

⑯ Des Houssayes. Discourse on the Duties and Qualifications of a Librarian. (In Dana and Kent, eds. *Literature of Libraries in the Seventeenth and Eighteenth Centuries.* McClurg. Chicago. 1906. Vol. 1, p. 37-8, 43-4).

英文著作

libraries in the seventeenth and eighteenth centuries. McClurg. Chicago. 1906. Vol. 1).

Edwards, Edward. Libraries and founders of libraries. Trübner. London. 1864.

Edwards, Edward. Memoirs of libraries. Trübner. London. 1859. 2vols. Book II. Chap. 6-9; Book III. Chap. 1-2, 7.

Gardthausen, Victor. Handbuch der wissenschaftlichen bibliothekskunde. Quelle. Leipzig. 1920. Vol. 2, Book 8. p. 82-4.

Garnett, Richard. Essays in librarianship and bibliography. Allen. London. 1899. p. 166-8, 174-90.

Gibson, Strickland. Some Oxford libraries. Oxford Univ. Press. 1914.

Kirkwood, James. Two tracts on the founding and maintaining of parochial libraries in Scotland. (In Dana and Kent, eds. Literature of libraries in seventeenth and eighteenth centuries. McClurg. Chicago. 1906. Vol. 3).

Koch, T. W. On university libraries. Paris. 1924.

Maitland, S. R. The dark ages. Hodges. London. 1890. p. 477-91.

Naudé, Gabriel. The library of Cardinal Mazarin. (In Dana and Kent, eds. Literature of libraries in seventeenth and eighteenth centuries. McClurg. Chicago. 1906. Vol. 6).

Savage, Ernest A. Old English libraries. Methuen. London. 1912. Chap. 3, 5, 11.

Savage, Ernest A. Story of libraries and book collecting. Routledge. London.

Smith, George. Gabriel Naudé: a librarian of the seventeenth century. Library Association Record. 1: 423-31, 483-93. July, Aug., 1899.

Tedder, Henry R. Evolution of the public library. Second International Library Conference in London. Transactions. 13-18. 1897.

CHAPTER VIII
THE PROFESSIONAL EDUCATION OF THE MODERN LIBRARIAN

During the first half of the nineteenth century libraries were increasingly used, many books were bought, and buildings were multiplied. The "book worm" type of librarian could not handle the situation efficiently. Up to this time the typical librarian was supposed to have read everything and was looked upon as a living catalog. Soon after the middle of the century, however, the administrative aspects of librarianship began to be more fully recognized, and the literature of various subjects became so voluminous that a librarian, even though possessed of a Magliabecchi's zeal and brain, could not be expected to have read all of the books on any single subject. The compilation and use of bibliographies rather than prodigious learning, and the introduction of mnemonic methods in library technique naturally developed as characteristics of librarianship in evolution.

The people at that time began to feel that they had the right to ask the state to supply free schools and public libraries. Hence legislation for this was introduced and libraries were thrown open to young and old and to the uneducated as well as the learned. Under such circumstances the demand for a new type of librarian who possessed not only scholarly attainments but also organizing power and business capacity was necessary. Men like Sir Anthony Panizzi of England and Professor Charles C. Jewett of America are splendid examples of both the scholarly and the newer professional type of librarian during the great transitional period of which we speak. The pendulum of librarianship has since swung to the side of practicability and library economy. By the middle of the nineteenth century also many prominent advocates of modern librarianship urged the importance of proper training in library administration. They wrote treatises on library science and popular articles to convince the public of the necessity of having trained librarians. They started to form associations, to publish journals, to advocate the establishment of training agencies, and were themselves careful to render efficient and modern library service. The public reluctantly began to give the librarian the formal status of a person engaged in a profession. For all this modern librarians are deeply indebted to the untiring efforts of their immediate forerunners.

In regard to the training and qualifications of a modern librarian, F. A. Ebert, the learned Dresden librarian, commonly referred to as Germany's greatest librarian, in his *Bildung des Bibliothekars*, 2nd edition, Leipzig, 1820, set up an ideal standard for a librarian involving encyclopedic knowledge, zeal and interest in every phase of human knowledge, and an extreme love of orderliness. He should devote his entire time to library work and above all he must be prepared to find the only reward in the work itself. Ebert lived up to what he preached, but this was too high and impractical a standard for the average individual to achieve.

As Mr. Tedder, librarian of the Athenaeum Club, London, remarked, "Such universality as he

(Ebert) asked for might be desirable, but it was very rarely to be obtained in one individual."①

Instead of attempting Ebert's almost utopian ideal, librarians of Mr. Tedder's type planned to work out a system which could train an average person of general culture to become a professional librarian. As early as 1829, Martin Schrettinger had published in Munich his *Versuch eines Vollstandigen Lehrbuchs der Bibliothek-Wissenschaft*, in which was emphasized the value of training in a special librarians' training school. "No man," said Schrettinger, "with a literary education, however highly educated he is, even if he is a great scholar, is fitted to be a librarian without a special study, preparation and practice… There should be a kind of librarians' training school connected with a national library; from that the other libraries could be supplied with its able graduates. Thus the methods of administration could be carried on in a uniform way."② Mr. Frank K. Walter, librarian of the University of Minnesota, is right in saying that Schrettinger was probably first to suggest a special school for training librarians.③ Schrettinger did not outline any definite program as to how a special library school could be established in a national library, nor suggest any schedule of courses to be offered. He simply expressed the idea.

No extensive plea for library training was made in Germany until the publication of Dr. Anton Klette's *Die Selbständigkeit des Bibliothekarischen Berufes*, Leipzig, 1871. Then the practice of recognizing librarianship as an independent profession had its beginning in Germany. Librarians and university professors became keenly interested in the new-born profession and in their discussions stressed methods of training. Thus the way was somewhat prepared for F. Rullman, librarian of the University of Freiburg, to outline in 1874 a university course of three years in library science.④

Mr. F. Rullman suggested a meeting of German librarians to discuss two things, namely, (1) the formation of an organization of German libraries, (2) the establishment of a library school for professional training. The decisions of the meeting were to be carried out by the states. This meeting was never held due to objections raised by some of the librarians. Dr. Steffenhagen, librarian of the University of Kiel, criticized the project as entirely too theoretical. In the first place the decisions of the librarians at the meeting could have no authoritative effect on the state governments since the meeting would be financially dependent upon the states. In the second place, the courses outlined were too theoretical and put too much emphasis on the bibliographical side rather than the practical problems of library administration. Rullman and Steffenhagen carried on a bitter fight in various papers for a long time. After 1876, Rullman, with the assistance of Julius Petzholdt, referred his fellow-librarians to the success of the conference of the American Librarians at Philadelphia in the formation of the American Library Association. However the formation of the American Library As-

---

① Henry R. Tedder. Librarianship as a Profession. Library Association of the United Kingdom. *Translation*. 5:163-4. 1882.

② Martin Schrettinger. *Versuch eines Vollstandigen Lehrbuchs der Bibliothek-Wissenschaft*. Munich. 1829. Vol. 2. p. 187-8.

③ Frank K. Walter, Library Training. *Encyclopaedia Americana*. Vol. 17-p. 393-4.

④ F. Rullman. *Outlines of Library Science*. (United States Bureau of Education. Special Report, p. XXIII-XVI. 1876).

sociation proved but a slight incentive to the German librarians. ⑤ In short, the time was not yet ripe for the majority of the German librarians to regard librarianship seriously as an independent profession requiring a thorough school training and an organization for professional cooperation and improvement.

The question of training librarians was finally settled for Prussia by a proclamation issued by the Department of Public Instruction on December 15, 1893. ⑥ The first meeting of German librarians was called under the leadership of Karl Dziatzko in 1897 as a section of the Association of Philologists and Educators in Dresden. ⑦ Fifty-one librarians gathered together to discuss various problems. Three years later the Verein Deutscher Bibliothekare was formally organized.

According to James Ross in his essay "Technical Training in Librarianship in England and Abroad" (*Library Association Record.* 12:114. February, 1910) "As early as 1861 the Library of the Bonn University was used as a training school for intending librarians by Friedrich Ritschl. Subsequently in 1886 a professorship of Library Science (Bibliotheks-Hilfswissenschaften) was created at Göttingen, and consequently instruction in that science must have been offered." In a letter from Professor R. Fick, Director of the Göttingen University Library to Director John Boynton Kaiser of the University Libraries of the State University of Iowa, Dr. Karl Dziatzko is designated as the first one to systematize courses of library training at Göttingen University. Professor Fick quotes a paragraph from P. Schwenke's article about Dziatzko's work in *Zentralblatt für Bibliothekswesen* (20: 135. March, 1903). This is translated as follows: "He (Dziatzko) organized a course of four semesters of two to three hours' lectures which gradually developed and also included courses on library management (or, as he called it later, history and development of the modern library science), books and writing to solve the problem of the best professional education and of the book-trade (before and after the Reformation). Besides there were also lectures on manuscripts of Latin authors and authors' and publishers' rights in the history of bookselling. There was also regular practice work in bibliography as Mr. Dziatzko lectured on certain subjects or gave practical bibliographical problems to the students to solve. During the last years his subjects were chiefly description of the Göttingen incunabula and the ascertaining of the printing types and printing practice during the fifteenth century. Dziatzko's work as a teacher and as director of the Examination Commission founded in 1896, which for the first time with us prescribed the extent and nature of the long desired professional library training, will always be a landmark in the history of the Prussian and German library development." Professor Fick adds that among Dziatzko's papers, manuscripts on which he had based his lectures on library science were also found. "As far as I have seen, these manuscripts correspond with the subjects of his lectures as given in the university bulletins... There are

---

⑤ Arnin Graesel. *Handbuch der Bibliothekslehre.* Weber. Leipzig. 1902. p. 486-7.

⑥ Prussian Act Defining the Qualifications of a Librarian, 1893. *Zentralblatt für Bibliothekswesen.* 11:77-9. January-February, 1894; or, *Library Journal.* 19:170. May, 1894.

⑦ German Librarians' Conference at Dresden. 1897. *Zentralblatt für Bibliothekswesen.* 14:321. June-July, 1897.

some insufficient references in Georg Schneider's *Handbuch der Bibliographie*, 1923, page 25 and page 195. In connection with these references it should be noticed that already before Dziatzko there were then at Göttingen assistant professors acting as librarians who created interest in bibliography and lectured on the literary history of their subjects…"

Dr. Ernest A. Baker, Director of the University of London School of Librarianship in his new book, *The Public Library*, has a concise chapter on training in librarianship, in which he traces the history of professional library training. He says, "certain general colleges, also, hold courses in bibliography, paleography and kindred subjects, useful not only to the librarian but also to the research student. Germany, Italy and Sweden preceded us in the establishment of library schools, the first-named in 1861."[8] The references in Graesel's *Bibliothekslehre*, or in Gardthausen's *Handbuch der Wissenschaftlichen Bibliothekskunde*, or in Dr. Fick's letter to Director Kaiser about professional library training in Germany, or in Dziatzko's *Present State of Libraries and Librarianship in Germany* (*Library Chronicle*. 4:57-63. 1887) or in Mr. Ambrose's *Dr. Dziatzko on German Libraries* (*Library Journal*. 21:53-9. February, 1896), speak only of innovations in the catalog, rearrangement of books on the shelves, and of other purely administrative improvements put into effect at Bonn from 1854 to 1865 by the eminent scholar and chief librarian, Friedrich Ritschl. For the introduction of professional library training in Germany most of the references give the honor to Karl Dziatzko as the first professor of library science at Göttingen University. The year 1886 has been generally considered as the date of the establishment of the first chair of library science in a German university.

When Dziatzko was a student at the University of Bonn, Friedrich Ritschl, professor of philology and university librarian, made it a rule for the students of the philological seminar to assist in the library, and so Dziatzko probably made his first acquaintance with library methods in the circulation department of the library at Bonn. Professor Ritschl entirely reorganized the library and did much for its development. Dr. Richard Pietschmann, Director of the University Library of Göttingen, remarked in his memorial sketch of Dziatzko, "Many of the best librarians of Germany received their training from Ritschl, of whom I mention only Aug. Wilmanns, general director in Berlin, Jos. Ständer, director of the university library at Bonn, and Wilhelm Brambach, until recently librarian at the Court Library in Karlsruhe."[9] From this we might assume that Professor Ritschl gave his student-assistants in the library and other students some instruction in library methods and bibliography, just as some of the present American universities and colleges give courses in how to use books in the library and in bibliography. It cannot be said that such American universities and colleges have library schools for the purpose of training persons intending to be librarians. Professor Ritschl may have given considerable extra-curriculum instruction in library management to his library assistants, who, though working in the university library, might not have had any intention of making library work their vocation, as in the case of Dziatzko. Upon his graduation

---

[8] Ernest A. Baker. *The Public Library*. Grafton. London. 1924. p. 220,

[9] Richard Pietschmann. Karl Dziatzko: A Memorial Sketch; translated by Miss Selina Nachmann. *Library Journal*. 29:c87-8. December, 1904.

in 1863, Dziatzko chose the career of teacher. Had the University of Bonn had a library school as early as 1861, Dziatzko's natural inclination toward the library profession, and his long connection with the university library under Professor Ritschl, would surely have inclined him to graduate as a librarian rather than a teacher. If Friedrich Ritschl had founded a library school in the University of Bonn, Rullman's outline of a university course of three years in library science would not have created so great a sensation among his contemporaries in 1874. It was not unusual for professors of German universities to give courses in bibliography and in the history of books and libraries, but these courses were not regarded as constituting in any sense professional library training comparable to that offered by a professional library school.

Since the Prussian Act of 1893 defining the qualifications of a librarian, and the appointment of a Library Examination Commission in 1896, the entire German system of examining librarians and certification has been revised several times. In 1917 two decrees about examinations were issued. They were (1) for "middle officials" at scientific libraries, (2) for "workers" in public libraries. The decrees prescribed certain courses for the assistants in scientific libraries. These courses had to be taken by the assistants before they might enter the libraries to do practice work. Due to the Great War, the entire matter was neglected. In 1918 the question of examination and training of library assistants was taken up again and it was decided to find a happy medium between theoretical training and practical work. The aim was that practice work should be done at the libraries and studies of library science in universities be simultaneously carried on. A new act was accordingly published in 1919. After the end of the war the development in the library field was very rapid, so that courses for library science were started with the winter semester of 1919-1920 in several of the universities.

In order to give some general idea of the library courses in Germany, the following extract from the *Leipzig University Bulletin* may serve as an example. "(1) Courses for higher library training (in connection with the University Library). The candidates will, during the two semesters' lectures, problems and practice work, get the necessary theoretical knowledge for passing the diploma examination. But this is only the preliminary training for a special examination. (2) Special studies for future librarians. The candidates taking these special studies must first have two years' practice work at a large library. The theoretical studies may be covered in one year and then the second year only is devoted to practical library work."[⑩]

Lecture Courses for Winter Semester 1919-1920

1. History of Libraries, Director Dr. Boysen.
2. Manuscript I, Professor Dr. Rörig.
3. Encyclopedias and Bibliography, Professor Dr. Minde-Pouet.
4. History of the German Booktrade, Dr. Goldfriedrich.

---

⑩ Library Science in Saxony and Library Courses in Leipzig University. (*In Zentralblatt für Bibliothekswesen.* 36:230-1. September-October 1919).

5. History of Printing, Professor Dr. Schramm.

6. Greek Palaeography, Professor Dr. Gardthausen.

7. Chronology of the Middle Ages and Modern Time, Professor Dr. Seeliger.

8. Palaeographical Problems, Professor Dr. Rörig.

9. Problems of Diplomatics, Professor Dr. Rörig.

The last four courses, i. e. Nos. 6-9, are also intended for general students.

The qualifications for candidates to enter professional library service in Prussia are (1) final examination from a humanistic gymnasium, (2) testimony of successful studies in one of the four colleges in a German university, (3) a doctor's or a licentiate degree, (4) certificate of good health, (5) two years' practice work in one of the large Prussian libraries, (6) a successful examination by a state commission. In Saxony the German Printers' Association has recently started in Leipzig a library school for lower functionaries, since the government has started library courses at the university for higher functionaries. This plan has been adopted by other German states.

In Austria examination for library positions was already required in 1862. Lectures in bibliography, history of books and other subjects were undertaken by the Institute of Historical Enquiry as early as 1874. The contents of the examination were modified and rearranged in November 1895. Italy has had tentative regulations governing public libraries and examinations for library officials since 1876. These were drawn up by Signor Ruggero Bonghi, Minister of Public Instruction. The examination in bibliography and librarianship was not actually given by the government until 1885.[11] An international library school on American lines was projected at Florence in 1905. The Scandinavian countries recognized the profession of librarianship in the latter part of the nineteenth century. Some of the descendants of the Vikings have crossed the Atlantic to be trained in American library schools. Sweden started its first summer school of librarianship in 1908 at Stockholm.

In France the examination for librarianship has been given by the Minister of Public Instruction since 1879. There are two types of examination, one for the higher and the other for the lower functionaries. The qualifications for the higher functionaries require candidates to produce (1) their birth-certificates with diplomas, (2) a statement of the work they have done, their library experience of two years and their knowledge of languages. The examination is partly written and partly oral. Both the oral and written examinations for the lower functionaries or sub-librarians include:

I Printed Books

    1. Cataloging of twelve books including incunabula and books in foreign languages.

    2. Arrangement of twelve order slips.

    3. Classification in the National Library and questions about bibliography, history of printing, binding, exhibits, etc.

II Manuscripts

    1. Description of four or five manuscripts.

    2. Questions about palaeography and bibliography of manuscripts.

---

[11] Examination open to all citizens. *Library Chronicle.* 2:76. 1885.

3. History of libraries and the chief collections of the National Library since the seventeenth century.

In 1894 the Sorbonne commenced to give lectures in bibliography and a few courses in library economy. But there was no independent library school either in Paris or in any province until June, 1923. The American Library School in Paris was founded by the American Committee for Devastated France. The plan for a regular full-time library school for French librarians was matured in the fall of 1924. It has been conducted by the American Library Association. [12] However, we must remember that although France has no modern library school, yet she has one of the finest schools in the world to teach scholars and bibliophiles how to study and interpret her rich stores of documents. One who reads Delisle's *Souvenirs de Jeunesse* cannot help but realize that the "Ecole des Chartes" of Paris has produced many brilliant archivists. It has rendered civilization a great service, as Sir William Osier remarked in his address at the opening of the Aberystwyth Summer School of Library Service in July 1917. "When, as we may hope, library schools are organized, opportunities will be offered to students on the same wide and liberal lines as the 'Ecole des Chartes' of Paris, whose students have been well named the modern Benedictines." [13]

The Library Association of the United Kingdom has always enthusiastically promoted the training of librarianship and rigorously defined the proper qualifications of librarians in England. The first examination of library assistants in accordance with a syllabus drawn up by the Library Association was held in July 1885, and three candidates presented themselves for the occasion. Many librarians at that time felt that an organization to train candidates for examination under the auspices of the Library Association was quite necessary. Mr. J. J. Ogle, Librarian of the Bootle Public Library, read a paper on "A Summer School of Library Science" at the fifteenth annual meeting of the Library Association. In response to his appeal the first Summer School of Library Science in England was inaugurated in 1893. By the inspiration of Mr. H. D. Roberts, Librarian of St. Saviour Public Library, the Library Association changed the name of the Summer School Committee to the Education Committee, and the regular training of library assistants began in February, 1898. The courses were modified to a certain extent when the Library Association decided in 1902 to cooperate with the London School of Economics. Since that time the London School has been for nearly a decade the place for English would-be librarians to receive their training in bibliography, classification, cataloging, library law and library economy. The library assistants in the provinces were without opportunity for training, and so the Library Association commenced correspondence classes in 1904, and urged certain leading provincial colleges and universities to give lectures on library economy and bibliography for the convenience of the library assistants in their neighboring districts. This proposal of the Library Association has been put into effect by the Manchester School of Technology, the John Rylands Library, Manchester, Leeds University and Armstrong College, Newcastle.

---

[12] Library School in Paris. *Public Libraries.* 28:440-1. October, 1923; 29:435-7. October, 1924.

[13] William Osier. Library School in the College. *Library Association Record.* 19:306. August-September, 1917.

The lectures and methods of training in the English summer schools, correspondence classes, and universities and colleges have been nearly the same. The syllabus published by the Library Association has always been closely followed and students have been prepared with the one aim to pass the examinations conducted by the Library Association every year. Certificates have been granted in separate subjects and each subject has formed a section of an examination. There have been six sections, namely: literary history, bibliography, classification, cataloging, library organization and library routine. When one has passed all these six sections and shown some knowledge of Latin and of a foreign language with a satisfactorily written thesis on an appropriate subject, he has been entitled to a full diploma. This system has had the advantage of standardizing the training of library assistants, but it has not been sufficiently broad in scope to cover the entire field of library subjects. The shortcomings of the system were taken into account in the establishment of the School of Librarianship in the University of London in 1919. The plan of this school offers a thorough training in library science. The school is the result of close cooperation between the Carnegie United Kingdom Trust and the Library Association.

"The school is a department of University College... its curriculum fits into the scheme of the Faculty of Arts." Dr. Baker adds, "the nominal course of training occupies two years, and students must devote their whole time to lectures, private study, and practice work; but for the benefit of assistants who cannot throw up their occupation, and also of booksellers, publishers' assistants ... part time attendance is allowed, by which the training is spread over a period varying from three to five years. But it must be continuous. This and the thoroughness of a college training, coupled with the initial requirement of a general education of matriculation standard, make the advent of the school a great stride forward. In time the training may develop into a postgraduate course."⑭ The present curriculum is as follows: (1) English Composition, (2) Latin or Greek or Sanskrit or Classical Arabic, (3) A Modern Language other than English, (4) Bibliography, (5) Library Organization(including Public Library Law), (6) Library Routine, (7) Cataloging and Indexing, (8) Literary History and Book Selection, (9) Classification, (10) Palaeography and Archives, (11) Special Lectures in Library Topics by special authorities. The instruction in the purely technical subjects is both theoretical and practical. The students are required to do practice work under expert supervision. One year's salaried work in a library is necessary before receiving the diploma.

The beginning of systematic library training in America is chiefly due to Dr. Melvil Dewey, who had the vision to foresee the development in the United States of a library movement unparalleled in history. To him it was especially clear that the growth of education, journalism, and industry and the general progress of American achievements would inevitably result in libraries in America far different from those of the old world. The "jailer of books" of yesterday could not very well understand the significance of the modern public library which Mr. Dewey has called in Carlyle's phraseology "the peoples' university." Dr. Dewey has spent much of his energy in advocating a type of librarian trained to utilize libraries as channels for the diffusion of knowledge among all the people.

---

⑭　E. A. Baker. *The Public Library*. Grafton. London. 1924. p. 213-14.

As early as 1879 Dr. Dewey wrote, "We need a training school for preparation for the special work. The village school-mistress is provided with normal schools by the hundred, where the best methods of teaching are taught. Physicians, lawyers, preachers, yes even our cooks have special schools for special training. But the librarian, whose profession has been so much exalted, must learn his trade by his own experiments and experience."⑮

Dr. Dewey's advocacy of a regular library school was enthusiastically received by many eminent American librarians. Dr. William F. Poole, C. A. Cutter, Samuel S. Green, R. C. Davis and many others joined him to push the project. The plan for a library school was accepted in 1884 by Columbia College after a full meeting of its trustees. The school of Library Economy was finally opened on January 5, 1887, at Columbia College, New York City. When Dr. Dewey was appointed librarian of the New York State Library in 1889 the school was transferred to Albany. It was renamed the New York State Library School and it became a part of the University of the State of New York. This was an important step in library history, because librarianship was thus to a certain extent officially acknowledged as a profession of equal standing with those of teaching, law, medicine, etc. It was natural that other schools should be established, once the New York State Library School had proved itself of value to the library profession and to libraries. Since 1902 the rules of the regents of the university have required graduation from a registered college for admission to the New York State Library School.

The Pratt Institute School of Library Science, Brooklyn, New York, opened in 1890. It was followed by the Drexel Institute, Philadelphia, in 1892, which was discontinued in 1914 and re-established in 1922. According to a recent announcement, admission to Drexel will require graduation from college or university and this rule will be in force from the fall term of 1925. In 1893 a library training class was started in the Armour Institute of Technology, Chicago, which was transferred to the University of Illinois, Urbana, in September, 1897, becoming then a full-fledged Library School. Since 1911 only college graduates have been admitted. The other "accredited" library schools in America today are as follows:

1897. Syracuse University Library School, Syracuse, New York.
1900. Carnegie Library School, Pittsburgh, Pa.
1902. Simmons College, School of Library Science, Boston, Mass.
1904. Western Reserve University Library School, Cleveland, Ohio.
1905. Library School of the Carnegie Library of Atlanta, Ga.
1906. University of Wisconsin Library School, Madison, Wis.
1911. Library School of the New York Public Library, New York City, N. Y.
1911. University of Washington Library School, Seattle, Wash.
1914. Library School of the Los Angeles Public Library, Los Angeles, Cal.
1917. St. Louis Library School, St. Louis, Mo.

In 1915 the Association of American Library Schools was formed. "This Association consists

---

⑮ Melvil Dewey. Apprenticeship of Librarians. *Library Journal.* 4:147. May, 1879.

only of schools deemed by the Association itself to be of the first grade," says Dr. Bostwick, adding, "It has from time to time admitted other schools until in 1922 it included thirteen. Its requirements have never been formulated and published, but it is generally acknowledged to have acted wisely in the admission of schools."⑯ The Association affiliated with the American Library Association in December, 1922.

The library schools named above give courses of either one or two school years. All of them are connected with large libraries providing facilities for study and practice. In the main the subjects taught in these schools are the same. They include library administration, buildings and equipment, loan work, binding, cataloging, classification, reference work, bibliography, book selection, history of libraries and books, and many other technical and social subjects related to library work. The training emphasizes the theoretical as well as the practical side.

Other library schools are the University of Texas, School of Library Science, Austin, Texas⑰; University of California, Course in Library Science, Berkeley, Cal.; Riverside Library Service School, Riverside, Cal.; University of Buffalo Library Science Course, Buffalo, N. Y.; Washington Training School for Business Librarians, Washington, D. C.; and University of Minnesota Library Course for Hospital Library Service, Minneapolis, Minn.

Besides these regular training schools, many universities, colleges, libraries and library commissions give elementary courses of three or more weeks' duration in the summer months and the courses are intended for librarians of small public or school libraries and library assistants of subprofessional grade. Let us place this last type of instruction in the second category of training for librarianship.

The classes generally conducted by the large libraries for their assistants will then occupy the third category of training for librarianship in America. The courses given are elementary and the instruction is usually local in emphasis.

In the fourth category we will place the library institutes or library conferences which are conducted by library commissions or local library associations. These conferences are helpful forces in promoting a professional spirit and in encouraging library training. Sometimes a library organizer is employed by a state to give library instruction to librarians of small libraries.

In a fifth category are correspondence and extension courses in library work. They have so far made very little progress. But at present many normal schools, colleges and universities give a course in how to use the library intelligently, how to select the best books, and how to compile a bibliography. The primary purpose of such a course is to familiarize students with the contents of libraries and not to train them as librarians or library assistants.

In 1916 the American Library Association Council appointed a committee on Standardization of Libraries and Certification of Librarians. After three years, the outlines of a national certification

---

⑯ A. E. Bostwick. Training for Librarianship. (*In* his *American Public Library*. Appleton. New York. 1923. p. 347-8.)

⑰ Discontinued late in 1925. (Ed. note)

system were presented to the Association at the Asbury Park Conference of 1919. The outlines were informally approved and referred to the Council. After another lapse of two years, a report of the committee on National Certification and Training, with a suggested plan of certification, was again submitted to the Association. By 1923 two states, Wisconsin and New York, had passed laws requiring some form of certificate for persons employed in public libraries. Four states, California, Iowa, Minnesota, and South Dakota had adopted some scheme of voluntary certification under the charge of either state library association or library commission. A national certification system is still under discussion. Some American librarians believe that it would provide a very effective means for furthering professional progress and efficient library service, and others fear that a certification system will stifle librarians of the "original genius" type now in the library field. Whether the national certification system of librarianship will be useful or not depends upon certain objective measurements scientifically valid and reliable. So far the arguments for and against are chiefly emotional and subjective in nature.

The American Library Association, anxious to have the whole question scientifically considered, is studying it in all its aspects through a number of important boards, commissions and committees. One committee is conducting a comprehensive survey of all library activities in America. Another is cooperating with the Bureau of Personnel Administration of the Institute for Government Research in conducting a series of personnel surveys involving elaborate job analyses to be followed by suggested psychological tests of fitness for the various jobs analyzed. There is also a Board of Education for Librarianship studying the whole question of professional education which has visited all existing library schools and has held several public hearings attended by prominent educators, including various specialists in the field of professional education. But of the association's part in helping to solve the problem of the best professional education for librarianship more will be said later.

SELECTED BIBLIOGRAPHY

Ambrose, Lodilla. Dr. Dziatzko on German libraries. Library Journal. 21:53-9. Feb., 1896.

American Library Association. Report of the Committee on apprentice and training classes. Bulletin. 11:284-6. July, 1917.

American Library Association. Report of the Committee on summer school. Bulletin. 11:279-84. July, 1917.

Baker, Ernest A. The public library. Grafton. London. 1924. Chap. 6.

Balzani, Ugo. On the regulations of Italian public libraries. Library Journal. 4:83-187. June, 1879.

Bostwick, Arthur E. American public library. Appleton. New York. 1923. Chap. 26.

Camper, Etta L. State certification of librarians. Public Libraries. 27:95-8. Feb., 1922.

Certification of librarians. Library Journal. 46:891-2. Nov. 1, 1921.

Dana, John Cotton. Certification and civil service control. Library Journal. 46:881-3. Nov. 1, 1921.

Delisle, Leopold. Souvenirs de Jeunesse. Library. n. s. 9:201-11, 245-56. April-July, 1908.

Dewey, Melvil. Apprenticeship of librarians. Library Journal. 4:147-8. May, 1879.

Dziatzko, Karl. Present state of libraries and librarianship in Germany. Library Chronicle. 4:57-63. 1887.

英文著作

Evans, H. R. Library instruction in universities, colleges and normal schools. (United States Bureau of education. Bulletin 606. Washington, D. C. 1914).

Friedel, J. H. Training for librarianship. Lippincott. Philadelphia. 1921. Chap. 17.

Gardthausen, Victor. Handbuch der wissenschaftlichen bibliothekskunde. Quelle. Leipzig. 1920. Book 8. p. 77-82.

German librarians' conference at Dresden, 1897. Zentralblatt fur Bibliothekswesen. 14:321. June-July, 1897.

Glenn, Frank M. Technical training in librarianship in England and abroad. Library Association Record. 12:118-29. Mar., 1910.

Graesel, Arnin. Handbuch der bibliothekslehre. Weber. Leipzig. 1902. p. 457-92.

Hottinger's library school for women in Berlin. Library Journal. 27:84-5. Feb., 1902.

Library instruction. Library Notes. 2:286-306. Mar., 1888.

Library school in Paris. Public Libraries. 28:440-1, Oct., 1923; 29:435-7. Oct., 1924.

Library schools and training classes and special training for librarians, a symposium by American librarians. Library Journal (Conf. No.). 23:59-84. Aug., 1898.

Library science in Saxony and library courses in Leipzig University. Zentralblatt für Bibliothekswesen. 36:230-1. Sept.-Oct., 1919.

London. University College. Library school. Library Association Record. 21:121-8. May, 1919.

Minnesota, University of. A course of training for hospital librarians. School and Society. 19:304. Mar. 15, 1924.

Morel, Eugene. Bibliothèques. Mercure de France. Paris. 1908. 2vols. Vol. 1. Chap. 9; Vol. 2. Chap. 11, 12.

Neumann, Felix. Karl Dziatzko, 1842-1903; an obituary and bibliography. Library Journal. 28:105-10. Mar., 1903.

Ogle, J. J. A summer school of library science. Library. 4:319-23. 1892.

Osler, William. Library school in the college. Library Association Record. 19:287-308. Aug.-Sept., 1917.

Paris. Librarianship examination. Library Chronicle. 1:26. 1884.

Pietschmann, Richard. Karl Dziatzko; a memorial sketch; trans. by Miss Selina Nachmann. Library Journal. 29:87-8. Dec., 1904.

Piper, A. Cecil. Technical training in librarianship in England and abroad. Library Association Record. 14:332-51. July, 1912.

Plummer, Mary W. Training for librarianship. American Library Association. Chicago. 1923.

Prussian act defining the qualifications of a librarian, 1893. Zentralblatt für Bibliothekswesen. 11:77-9. Jan.-Feb., 1894; Library Journal. 19:170. May, 1894.

Roberts, Henry D. Education of the librarian; elementary stage. Library Association Record. 8:556-72. Nov., 1906.

Roberts, Henry D. Some remarks on the education of the library assistant; a plea. Library. 9:103-12. 1897.

Ross, James. Technical training in librarianship in England and abroad. Library Association Record. 12:99-117. Feb., 1910.

Rullman, F. Outlines of library science. (United States Bureau of education. Special Report. p. xxiii-xxvi. 1876).

Sanborn, Henry N. Standardization of library service. Library Journal. 44:351-8. June, 1919.

School of Library Economy. Library Journal. 8:285-94. Sept.-Oct., 1883.

School of Library Economy. Library Notes. 1:85-9. Oct., 1886.

Schrettinger, Martin. Versuch eines vollstandigen lehrbuchs der bibliothek-wissenschaft. Munich. 1829. 2vols. Vol. 2. p. 187-96.

Schwenke, P. Karl Dziatzko. Zentralblatt für Bibliothekswesen. 20:133-7. Mar., 1903.

Tedder, Henry. Librarianship as a profession. Library Association of the United Kingdom. Transactions. 5:163-72. 1882.

Walter, Frank K. Library training. (In Encyclopedia Americana. Vol. 17. p. 393-4).

CHAPTER IX
CHANGING CONCEPTIONS OF LIBRARIANSHIP AND ITS EDUCATIONAL REQUIREMENTS

As we survey the librarian's qualifications and preparation for his calling from ancient times to the present, as was done in the last three chapters, it appears that the one fundamental qualification for librarianship, common to all ages and peoples, is education. The librarian must be an educated man. Different personalities have given different interpretations to the office. Varying techniques have developed. Yet, the foundation has been and is ever the same.

The question then naturally arises whether the changing conceptions of librarianship will necessitate for the future any other foundation than this.

The answer must be, "Yes." Even this first essential must be changed; the very foundation broadened. The librarian of the future must not simply be educated, but in a very definite sense he must be liberally educated. And, what it is to be liberally educated has been well stated by President Charles F. Thwing in these words: "The primary purpose of the ideal college is to give a liberal education, or if one prefer the active voice, to give an education which liberalizes the human mind and character... The liberally educated man, we sometimes say, is the scholar. But we all know men who are scholars who do not embody an education of a liberal type... The liberally educated man, it is sometimes said, is the thinker. The man who can reason, judge, assess a truth at its proper value, relate truth to truth, or infer a new truth, is the thinker. But there are men whose minds are as accurate in their movements, as Babbage's famous machine, who would never be judged guilty of having a liberal education. One knows such men—orderly, precise, correct, their mental operations are more regular than the movements of the heavenly bodies—but they are not liberally educated.

"The man of a liberal education is a scholar, or at least is scholarly; he is a thinker, or at least is thoughtful, but he is also more than either the thinker or the scholar, in fact, more than both. This man, liberally educated, has entered the arena of learning, yet he is not cumbered by, nor made heavy with the treasures which he bears forth. He is still intellectually alert... Every faculty acts, every function is complete. Reason *plus* sympathy *plus* appreciation equals fullness of life. Fullness of life equals the man himself liberally educated."① A liberal education then, in President Thwing's meaning best describes the *primary* qualification of the future librarian.

President Thwing has aimed to present an ideal standard of a liberally educated man, but we must realize that to set one's standard high—higher even than one is able to reach—is the surest way to attain real excellence in any profession. It is very true that human beings seldom reach per-

---

① Charles F. Thwing. *The American College.* Platt and Peck. New York. 1914. p. 3-8.

fection, nevertheless, it is the business of the liberally educated man to aim at it. The higher the ideal, the nearer one is likely to come to success in the profession one has voluntarily chosen. A high aim is necessary in the future not only to librarians but to all professional men.

Any adequate program of professional education for librarianship in America must be fully cognizant of the fact that here there has developed both from the standpoint of administration and of library service an American type; and, furthermore, this program must recognize definitely the several significant factors which have produced this distinctly American type of library organization and library service. In successive chapters the principal factors which have influenced the development of American libraries have been shown to be the democratic ideal of education, the spirit of research, the growth of print, library philanthropy and library associations.

These and doubtless other influences are still at work. The American type of library is still evolving. The process is one of at least semi-conscious evolution.

Today a certain method of training for librarianship may admirably serve the needs of American library administration but tomorrow it will need modification. American methods of training for librarianship are also a resultant of the spirit and influence of these same factors which have acted upon and affected the development and organization of American libraries. If some defects in the modern methods and system of library training have been felt it will be worth-while to examine into the matter. It is quite possible that these defects may be traced to a failure to recognize the factors that have influenced library development here in America and to adjust professional instruction accordingly.

Some seem to think that the present-day librarian is too mechanical and not as scholarly or learned as his predecessor. The library school graduate is felt to be too practical and machine-minded. Perhaps the training in library schools does lay too much emphasis on technique. Mr. J. H. Friedel describes the situation thus: "It is the watch-spring all wound up, not the brain that knows when or how to wind. The emphasis is thus continually on memory, since to the technician memory is more essential than the ability to cope with new situations. Yet it is the latter faculty which we should try to develop. The end of all library science, as of all education, should be development of character not of mere skill… Or they may be subjects involving skill of performance. Of these three, those involving skill of performance undoubtedly cover a major part of the subjects taught in the library schools, since library work is largely an occupation involving skill of performance. The special danger of such subjects is that they tend to become performed mechanically, thereby restricting independent thought. The accomplishment tends to become an end in itself. Cataloging may be cited as an example. How frequently do we hear the fact bemoaned that trained catalogers center their attention so much on commas and periods and use so little grey matter."②

It is true that many library processes are mechanical, others highly technical, and that at one time the emphasis in training agencies was such that "practical" and often, no doubt, "mechanical" librarians were the result. But these qualifications were once, at a certain stage in the development

---

② J. H. Friedel. Training for Librarianship. *Library Journal*. 44:570-1. September, 1919.

of libraries and librarianship, very useful. Existing conditions almost necessitated the production of such mechanical librarians, at least of librarians capable of taking an intelligent interest in seeing that the necessary mechanical processes were well done. And, while this is not the place to digress at length upon the subject, it should be pointed out that one must not confuse in his mind those library processes which are admittedly mechanical with those like cataloging and classification which are always technical, as opposed to mechanical, and which may be and often are highly professional and scholarly pursuits.

But to return to the question of preparation for librarianship, note that it is the American librarians themselves who have become conscious of the inadequacy of their training agencies who are taking the lead in the movement for improvement. They are demanding a new standard for professional training. There are evidences too that this desire for a change in the system of training has been prompted, in part at least, by a further recognition of the requirements of the still evolving American type of library administration and service and the factors that have produced it.

After the middle of the nineteenth century, the democratic ideal of education aimed primarily to lift the level of education for the masses of the people, and the American public library attempting to play its part became both an adjunct to the public schools and in truth an independent "people's university." The public demanded only quick and in the main superficial service from the librarians of public libraries. Consequently mechanical aids and administrative methods conducive to machine-like staff-management were urgently sought by students of library schools and the higher principles of library science and humanistic studies in general were neglected. The popular demand for librarians of a technical type was great and naturally the training agencies centered their efforts on skill in technique rather than on the development of the broadest possible grasp of the problems of the profession.

The movement of library philanthropy increased the need for trained librarians in ever increasing numbers. The demand for librarians to operate the host of newly founded libraries had to be supplied as quickly as possible from library schools, training classes, and apprentice courses. The donors' idea was that the library was the place to diffuse knowledge among the masses of the people, and the community which received the gift frequently regarded the library as merely a social center with books for recreation. A librarian who could keep the place clean and who could arrange books in order was hired to supply library service. The donors, the people, and the librarians, all proceeded to carry out too mechanically an idea of popular education which constituted one of the essentials of American democracy.

With the twentieth century there dawned a new spirit in library service. Librarians have now begun to realize that the exactness of the catalog, the neatness of the loan-system, and the careful arrangement of scheduled hours for staff-members are not ultimate aims, but merely means to the economical utilization of books. The right books cannot be brought to the right people by librarians who are interested only in mechanical systems. A type of librarian who knows how to perform library service of quality, whose eyes are open to social needs, and whose administration does not lack human sympathy is needed. Present-day librarians are conscious of their short-comings and some requirements for the future have been outlined by Mr. Carl B. Roden, librarian of the Chicago Public Library, in one of his thoughtful addresses read at the twenty-seventh annual meeting of the Illinois Library Association, Peoria, on September 26, 1923. "Thanks to their labors we are the legatees of a well-nigh perfect body of doctrine and practice, which we have but to follow to achieve a satisfactory measure of mechanical efficiency. The principles of classification, so far as they concern most of us, were established when Melvil Dewey evolved the Decimal System. The rules for cataloging have long since been so far stabilized that little remains even for catalogers to talk about, and the craft is in danger of being embedded like the well-known fly in a rigid translucence that promotes both permanence and finality. So in other departments, our work, save for occasional innovation born of personal ingenuity, has been standardized to a degree that should leave little room for further fruitful discussions... The outward and visible form of our calling is clear and sharply defined." He continues by emphasizing the spiritual value which he feels should characterize the future librarianship. "Books are spiritual goods; they are imponderables. To attempt to apply quantitative standards to their distribution or to the measurement of their power is as futile as the Dean (Dean Inge of Saint Paul's Cathedral, London) declares these methods to be in the realm of Philosophy... It is the mission of the librarian, not merely to supply even the best books to the greatest number, not yet 'at the least cost,' but to bring together the right book and the right reader—at any cost! That, in my opinion, will be the next step in library administration, if there is to be one. Thus, in the end, and thus alone, will be manifested that inward and spiritual grace which is the soul of librarianship."③

Hitherto library donors have fixed their attention upon building more and larger libraries. Only recently have they shifted their gaze to a new aspect of the library movement. It has been pointed out by many librarians and recognized by many donors that the essential factor in enabling a library to perform better service and to function on a greater scale is a sufficiently large and competently trained personnel. The repeated grants by the Carnegie Corporation for library service as distinguished from buildings and books herald the new aspect of the library movement. Dr. William S. Learned's expectation of the future librarianship and the library schools is as follows, "The provision of a sufficient number of thoroughly educated and technically trained library workers under conditions suitable for a permanent career is the salient feature in a properly reorganized library service, and should receive immediate attention... If a rapid and wholesome development is to take place in the process of adjusting libraries to their users, the most vigorous and drastic changes should be made at this point. Expert duties in libraries must be distinguished from routine duties of a purely clerical sort, and the personnel developed accordingly; full-time teachers and adequate equipment must be provided; and professional curricula for the higher, responsible positions must

---

③ Carl B. Roden. On a Certain Reticence or Inarticulateness among Librarians. *Public Libraries.* 28:492. November, 1923.

doubtless be associated with comparable professional curricula in the universities."④

Before the spirit of research was fully felt in American universities, the professional qualifications and specialized education of their librarians were neglected. Any person was employed who had a little library training in classification and cataloging. His chief work was to keep records and his status among the faculty was frequently only that of a book-clerk. In America the methods of library training were not much influenced by the earlier college and university libraries. Only recently have American universities begun to vie in the achievements of their research with European universities, and only recently have the American university libraries been brought face to face with problems, the solutions of which require the tact, energy, and initiative of a highly trained librarian. For instance such problems as the efficient organization of departmental libraries, the centralization of administration, the building up of special collections, the teaching function of the library, conferences with the deans of various schools, the estimating of yearly budgets, and the problem of the best service to all library users require the most careful thought of a liberally educated as well as a technically trained librarian. Today the importance of a library in the life and work of a university is beginning to be generally recognized. From an introductory statement in the 1924 Report of the Commission on the Future Policy of the University Libraries of the University of Chicago we learn that "The library is the heart of the University. The rectifying of these conditions is essential to the life of the University."⑤ On November 30, 1912, Dean Kendric C. Babcock of the University of Illinois presented a paper, "Bibliographical Instruction in College," at the Conference of Eastern College Librarians, at Columbia University. He thought that instruction in bibliographical method should be given by the librarian and the members of the library staff. He said, "This plea for required accredited instruction in bibliography is not based wholly upon theory. It certainly would not be satisfied by chance instruction through the insistence of departmental heads or enthusiastic instructors in different departments. Several institutions have already tried the scheme and find that it works well. They have reasoned rightly that the work should be under the direction of the librarian and carried on by his trained assistants, and that when so done it is entitled to recognition."⑥ Dr. E. C. Richardson of Princeton believes that the question of the position of the library in the university will in the end be determined by this matter of the methods by which it fulfills its teaching function.⑦

The ranking of the university librarian as a dean and of the trained members of the staff as professors and instructors will be adopted by American universities when the university libraries become the dominating forces as well as the indispensable tools of research work. This admission of

---

④ William S. Learned. *The American Public Library and the Diffusion of Knowledge.* Harcourt. New York. 1924. p. 78-9.

⑤ University of Chicago. *Commission on the Future Policy of the University Libraries.* Tentative Report. 1924. p. vii.

⑥ Kendric C. Babcock. Biographical Instruction in College. *Library Journal.* 38:135. March, 1913.

⑦ E. C. Richardson. The Place of the Library in a University. *American Library Association Bulletin*, 10:12. January, 1916.

librarians into the sacred circle of the instructional faculties will be a test of the education and professional training of the graduates of library schools.

Occasionally unfavorable criticisms of trained librarians come from the field to special libraries. It is intimated that the library school graduates are specialists in methods of checking, of classifying, and of cataloging books, but not in knowledge of current research material on industrial conditions, for instance. The growth of print has influenced all types of libraries and the flood of commercial and industrial literature has necessitated many special and business libraries. It is expected of the library school graduate that he be well versed not only in library methods but also in the concrete knowledge of a few highly specialized subjects. Sometimes a young library school graduate who either lacks broad educational background or has not the aptitude to master the literature of a specific field disappoints the employers of special librarians.

In 1919 Mr. J. H. Friedel, then editor of *Special Libraries*, vividly wrote: "But this should not blind us to the need of teaching the student to be self-dependent, to think for himself and to be able to solve new problems when these are encountered. A problem frequently met in the newly organized special library is that of preparing a special classification that will best meet the needs of the particular library. The capable, experienced special librarian is invariably of the opinion that a special classification is essential to the best functioning of the library. The writer's experience has been that few library school graduates know how to prepare such classifications and this observation is confirmed by inquiry from other special librarians. Where standard methods, such as the Dewey, are adopted, the library school graduate appears at a loss to make necessary expansions. Scientific classification is cast to the winds and a method of patchwork is resorted to, followed by consequent patching of patches. Instances might be enumerated galore, but the necessity of politeness prevents specific mention of cases encountered… The courses given are in many cases capable of improvement… Our courses, however, should not be designed for appearance only. Catch-fly methods may be efficient for flies; they cannot honestly deserve the name of education, much less the dignity of classification as scholarship or science."⑧

If one wished to answer Friedel's criticisms of the trained librarian's inability to function well as a special librarian he might point out that particularly in the early days of the special library movement it was the noticeably mediocre librarian, dissatisfied with his or her lot, and more interested in salary than in service, who rushed in and filled the ranks of the so-called "special librarians." That there were notable exceptions does not disprove the fact. Moreover, many of these special librarians had no professional training at all but were opportunists alert for a change whose small learning did much to discredit those who came later to the field well prepared.

The failure on the part of some of the library school graduates to meet the requirements of certain special libraries does not necessarily mean that the standard of any of the library schools is low. The number of library school students entering the field of special libraries is constantly in-

---

⑧ J. H. Friedel. Training for Librarianship. *Library Journal*. 44:570-1, September, 1919.

creasing, and in a large proportion of the cases the students succeed in their work.⑨ Again, the sudden increase of special libraries and of special divisions in large public libraries has disturbed the equilibrium of the preparation for the work and strained the resources of the library training agencies, which are primarily schools to train assistants for general public rather than for special libraries. When the schools want to prepare their students for special library work, their finances are insufficient to cover the cost of new courses, equipment, and the salaries of extra teachers. Professional libraries, those of medical, legal, theological, sociological, educational, industrial, financial, technological, and scientific institutions are calling for trained librarians. The existing schools cannot give the specific training for such work, and can supply only graduates with a general library training.

Again, suppose that some of the library schools should try to specialize in preparing for work in special libraries, whether there will be enough students to take special library training is a grave conjecture. In general students ask themselves two questions before choosing special library work. Will the salary be enough to justify an extra year or years in special library training, and how can one be sure of employment in the kind of special library for which one has trained? As to the salary, the employers of special librarians frequently do not wish to put too much money into what they regard as a new experiment, and to most business men a librarian is only a sort of clerk and bookkeeper. Though there is a demand, it is not a certain one for the exact position for which the student may have specialized. The fault is not that of the existing library training agencies nor the library school graduates. The entire situation is in a stage of transition. Special libraries are the sign of a further development of American libraries, and the ultimate demands of special libraries will exert great influence on the training and qualifications of the future librarian.

One of the most influential factors in moulding the course of professional training for librarianship in America has been the American Library Association which was and is the guiding spirit of the profession. The plan of the first American library school was presented by Dr. Melvil Dewey to the American Library Association in 1883. This plan was approved by the association in spite of strong opposition on the part of several of its leading members. The actual operation of the first library school at Columbia College, New York City, in 1887, was followed as we have already seen by the establishment of other library schools, training classes, apprentice classes and summer schools. The policies and the curricula of the library schools have always been influenced by those members of the American Library Association who have actually been engaged in library work. Their opinions have to a large extent been respected by the library schools.

In the earlier years of library schools, technical subjects were greatly emphasized because libraries at that time laid much emphasis on cataloging, classification, and subject-headings. One needs only to turn to the reports and discussions of the conferences of the American Library Association to learn how absorbed in such matters the profession was.

---

⑨ Frank K. Walter. The Future Training of the Business Librarian. *Special Libraries*. 10:4. January-February, 1919.

In 1890 the first standing committee on training for librarianship was established by the association. In 1903 Miss Mary W. Plummer, on behalf of the committee, gave an exhaustive report. It summarizes reports from nine library schools, ten summer schools, thirty-three apprentice classes, fifteen college courses in bibliography, twelve normal school courses in library economy and four correspondence courses. In view of the rapid growth of the library training agencies and in order to protect the professional standard of librarianship, the American Library Association established a Professional Training Section in 1909.

In the summer of 1919, at the tenth annual meeting of the Professional Training Section, several papers all of which stressed the importance of specialized library training were read. There was a paper on "Advanced Library Training for Research Workers" by Mr. Andrew Keogh, librarian of Yale University; Miss Sarah Bogle, then principal of the Carnegie Library School, Pittsburgh, Pa., presented a paper entitled "Training for High School Librarianship;" "Training for the Librarian of a Business Library or a Business Branch" was the subject of a paper by Mr. Frank K. Walter, then vice-director of the New York State Library School, Albany, N. Y.; and Miss Mary E. Robbins gave a paper on "Training Teacher-Librarians in Normal Schools."

Regarding the subject of certification, Dr. C. C. Williamson, now with the Rockefeller Foundation, strongly urged the American Library Association at the Asbury Park Conference in 1919 to form an American Library Association Board with a permanent staff and a competent expert as its executive. This board should have three main functions, he said. "(1) The formulation of a standard scheme of grading library positions which would necessarily resemble the best schemes of service now in use, but which would be so extended as to cover all kinds of professional library work, and possibly include also at least the higher grades of the clerical service, (2) Its second task would be, first to decide, with the advice and council of the whole profession, what should be the minimum standard of qualification in the way of training and experience for each grade; and then to issue certificates of the appropriate grade to all applicants who qualify, (3) The third task would relate to the training agencies. Having decided that library school training of a certain character constitutes the desirable minimum for one or more of the higher grades of library service, the board could proceed, as the Association of Library Schools does now, to examine and approve such schools as meet a reasonable standard. Graduates of these schools who have a minimum period of successful experience could be given a Training Board certificate of high grade without further question. Similarly, successful completion of an accredited training class course, combined with a minimum period of experience in a library approved for practice work, might almost automatically entitle one to a Training Board certificate of an appropriate grade."[10] A Committee on National Certification and Library Training was appointed by the association in 1920 to consider this problem carefully. Due to the uncertainty of post-war conditions and the duplication of duties and the powers of interlocking committees of the association, the Committee on National Certification and

---

[10] C. C. Williamson. Some Present-Day Aspects of Library Training. (In *American Library Association. Papers and Proceedings.* 41:122. July, 1919).

Library Training recommended that a Library Training Board which should have powers wide enough to cover library training, library service, and library certification should be appointed. In May, 1923, the president, on the authority of the Executive Board of the Association, appointed the Temporary Library Training Board. In the summer of 1924 the board presented a thorough report with findings and recommendations including a recommendation for the formation of a permanent Board of Education for Librarianship. It was formed in July, 1924, and Mr. Adam Strohm, librarian of the Detroit Public Library, was appointed chairman. Since its establishment the board has held four regular meetings, the first in July at Saratoga Springs immediately after its appointment; the second the following September in Chicago; the third, December 30 and 31, 1924, in Chicago; and the fourth, April 15 and 16, 1925, in Chicago. It has made a thorough investigation of the problems of library training in relation to other important library questions. The writer was invited by the board to take part in the program on the advisability of founding an advanced school of librarianship at the open meetings of December 31, 1924, and of April 16, 1925. As a student of the problem of library training and an active worker in and organizer of libraries for the last fifteen years, he is confident that the American Library Association will formulate before long a satisfactory program of training for professional librarianship suited to various types of libraries and for various grades of library service. The rapid changes of American life and of American views in education after the close of the Great War have necessitated corresponding changes in library service and thus indirectly in the field of library training. "To exist is to change, to change is to mature, to mature is to go on creating oneself endlessly"[⑪] according to Bergson's philosophy of creative evolution. Does the same principle apply to the problem of library training and its final solution?

In summing up, the future American librarian will have a fine structure of professional training on the solid foundation of a liberal education. His administration will be cultured and scholarly. In work we know that he will be faithful; in scholarship he will be an earnest student, and in service he will be an inspiring as well as a helpful guide. The various types of libraries mentioned in the pages of this chapter are at present pressing library schools for graduates with some of these ideal qualifications. Can the existing library schools meet the challenge?

SELECTED BIBLIOGRAPHY

American Library Association. Board of education for librarianship. (*In* its Papers and Proceedings. 46:197-9, 257-88. 1924).

American Library Association. Committee on library training. Reports. (*In* its Papers and Proceedings. 12:91-5. 1890;14:31-4. 1892;16:116-20. 1894;25:83-101. 1903).

American Library Association. Committee on national certification and library training. Reports. (*In* its Papers and Proceedings. 42:311-13. 1920;45:194-7. 1923;46:239-41. 1924. ;*In* its Annual Reports. 78-89. 1921).

American Library Association. Professional training section. Reports. (*In* its Papers and Proceedings. 31:427-36,

---

⑪ Henri Bergson. *Creative Evolution*, translated by Arthur Mitchell. Holt. New York. 1911. p. 7.

442. 1909;32:776-86. 1910;36:228-45. 1914;41:395-7. 1919;42:334-5. 1920;43:183-4. 1921;45:246-9. 1923).

American Library Association. Report of the temporary library training board. (*In* its Papers and Proceedings. 46: 257-88. 1924).

Babcock, Kendric C. Bibliographical instruction in college. Library Journal. 38:133-6. Mar. ,1913.

Bogle, Sarah C. N. Training for high school librarianship. American Library Association. *In* Papers and Proceedings. 41:277-8. 1919.

Buell, D. C. Sources of information for business men. Special Libraries. 7:142-4. Oct. ,1916.

Donnelly, June Richardson. The library school and the library. Library Journal. 35:109-11. Mar. ,1910.

Dudgeon, M. S. The scope and purposes of special libraries. Special Libraries. 3:129-33. June, 1912.

Evans, Henry R. Library instruction in universities, colleges and normal schools. United States Bureau of education. Bulletin. No. 606. Government Printing Office. Washington. 1914.

Fairchild, Salome Cutler. Function of the library. Public Libraries. 6:527-32. Nov. ,1901.

Friedel, J. H. Training for librarianship. Library Journal. 44:569-74. Sept. ,1919.

Hasse, Adelaide R. The great release. Special Libraries. 10:2-3. Jan.-Feb. ,1919.

Henry, W. E. Librarianship as a profession. Library Journal. 42:350-5. Sept. ,1917.

Herbert, Clara A. Librarianship—a profession. Library Journal. 48:605-9. July, 1923.

Hitchler, Theresa. Library school training versus practical experience. Library Journal. 42:931-8. Dec. ,1917.

Keogh, Andrew. Advanced library training for research workers. Library Journal. 44:581-2. Sept. ,1919; American Library Association. Papers and Proceedings. 41:165-7. 1919.

Learned, William S. The American public library and the diffusion of knowledge. Harcourt. New York. 1924. p. 75-80.

New York State Library School. Librarianship as a profession. Albany. 1911.

Plummer, Mary W. Forecast of the next twenty-five years for library schools. Library Journal. 35:251-3. June, 1910.

Richardson, E. C. The place of the library in a university. American Library Association Bulletin. 10: 1-13. Jan. ,1916.

Robbins, Mary E. Training teacher-librarians in normal schools. American Library Association. Papers and Proceedings. 41:279-81, 1919.

Roden, Carl B. On a certain reticence or inarticulateness among librarians. Public Libraries. 28: 489-94. Nov. ,1923.

Shearer, Augustus H. What constitutes adequate library training? Library Journal. 47:1073-4. Dec. 15, 1922.

Thompson, C. Seymour. Librarianship—a profession or a business? Library Journal. 47:1063-6. Dec. 15, 1922.

Thwing, Charles Franklin. The American college. Platt and Peck. New York. 1914. p. 1-23.

Tyler, Alice S. Education for librarianship; as it is and as it might be. Public Libraries. 29:389-90. Oct. ,1924.

University of Chicago. Commission on the future policy of the university libraries. Tentative Report. 1924.

Walter, Frank K. The future training of the business librarian. Special Libraries. 10:3-4. Jan.-Feb. ,1919.

Walter, Frank K. Training for the librarians of a business library or a business branch. Library Journal. 44:578-80. Sept. ,1919; American Library Association. Papers and Proceedings. 41:273-6, 1919.

Williamson, Charles C. Some present-day aspects of library training. Library Journal. 44:563-8, Sept. ,1919; American Library Association. Papers and Proceedings. 41:120-6, 1919.

CHAPTER X
AMERICAN LIBRARY SCHOOLS

The first professional school of library economy was founded in the United States. Though Göttingen University, Germany, established a professional chair of library science in 1886, about six months earlier than the date of the formal opening of the library school at Columbia College, New York City, the American school is generally considered the first professional school of library science. The number of the subjects taught at Göttingen was by no means so extensive as those offered at the American school. The latter was a full-fledged professional school; the former was not even a department of a university. The founder of the first American library school, Dr. Melvil Dewey, has written about the matter in the following characteristic fashion. Simplified spelling has long been a passionate hobby of Dr. Dewey's. "We have always supposed that the Columbia Library School was the 1st in the world. If anything had been done anywhere in that line it was in so small a way that it cud not count. Just as we say about starting the card catalog, or the loose leaf system. It is inevitable that sumbody sumwhere had tied sheets together and had set cards on ej, but those don't count any more than the experiments with the string and mustard boxes cud be counted as the invention of the telephone. The Albany school I think is universally recognized as the 1st real library school in the world."①

In this age of speedy transportation and easy communication many foreign students come every year to the United States to take up various studies in American universities and schools and conversely many American students betake themselves to European countries. But in the field of library economy and technique, it is rather significant that though foreign students have very often come to American library schools to study, it has not yet proved worth-while for any American student to go to any library school of any other country.

The following figures regarding the number of foreign students of different countries who have graduated from the New York State Library School, Albany, since 1887, are taken from a letter of Miss Edna M. Sanderson, vice-director of the school:②

Australia	1
Canada	8
China	4
Denmark	4

---

① Melvil Dewey. The First Library School, a letter to J. B. Kaiser, November 19, 1924.

② Edna M. Sanderson. The Number of Foreign Students Graduated from the New York State Library School, a letter to T. C. Tai, April 14, 1925.

  Germany ··· 1
  Holland ·· 1
  Nova Scotia ··· 3
  Norway ··· 38
  Philippine Islands ······································· 1
  Sweden ·· 1
             ———
  Total ··· 67

  The other American library schools have had the same international atmosphere as a result of their foreign students. In the Report of the Pratt Institute School of Library Science for 1923-1924, Miss Josephine A. Rathbone, vice-director, comments, "The class, in the first place, was unusually large, containing, as it did, twenty-seven members, two more than our normal quota. It is a commonplace of the school that every person over the limit makes more trouble in adjustments and re-adjustments than any five people below it, but 1924 proved the exception to that rule, for the additional members, two scholarship holders from Europe, added so much to the interest and pleasure of us all that they more than repaid the extra efforts of the faculty and staff. In addition to the two continental students, were two from Great Britain, so the class had a distinctly international flavour..." ③ The Library School of the New York Public Library, the Library School of the University of Illinois, the Carnegie Library School of Pittsburgh and a few others have all been attended by foreign students.

  The priority of the founding of the American library schools and the large percentage of students from the old world who attend them received due emphasis from Edwin H. Anderson, director of the New York Public Library, in his address delivered before the Pennsylvania Library Club, at Atlantic City, May 2, 1924. "It strikes me as curious that in a survey of the library school situation in this country Dr. Williamson should not even mention the fact that the first library schools in the world were established here, and that we are still the recognized leaders in this field. Universities have had exemplars in Europe for a thousand years, but America was the first to wake up to the need for library schools; and that significant fact is entirely ignored. 'We were the first that ever burst into that silent sea'—and the fact that the first school here was established only thirty-seven years ago, and for a number of years occupied the field almost alone, explains many of the short-comings to which he calls attention. Nor is there any mention of the significant fact that library science or technique is one of the few things for which Europe has come to school to us. Americans have always gone to Europe to study art; and practically all our art and architecture have come to us from across the sea. American students have flocked to the great universities of Europe; but who ever heard of an American librarian going to Europe to study library methods or technique? Almost from the beginning the library schools in this country have had a considerable por-

---

③ The Pratt Institute. *School of Library Science. Report.* 1924 p. 17.

tion of foreign students, and as one of the results, library schools have been established in several European countries, one even in Moscow, and another in China. A summer school was conducted in Paris last summer; and the American Committee for Devastated France has provided the funds to maintain a full-fledged library school in France for the next two years, after which time it is hoped that the French may continue it on their own account."④ Although the American library schools have led the world as to the methods and the technique of library training, yet in an allied field such as archives, and in the more scholarly sort of bibliographical study such as that dealing with incunabula, other countries have had much to contribute to library science as a whole.

The publication of Dr. C. C. Williamson's Report on *Training for Library Service* by the Carnegie Corporation of New York, has shaken the equanimity of librarians and centered their attention on the American library schools and other training agencies. Mr. Frank K. Walter prefaces his review of the report with a complimentary reference to the stimulating value of the special reports of the Carnegie Corporation. "Dr. Flexner's report on medical education in the United States practically revolutionized the medical curricula of the whole country. Redlich's report on legal education did not stampede the law schools but it did lead to the modification of the courses in many of them. Dr. Pritchett's comments on the cost and value of education, in his last published annual report caused many rejoinders, pro and con. In this respect Dr. Williamson's report will certainly run true to form. There is nothing sedative about it."⑤

Opinion among American librarians on the quality of the professional training offered by American library schools is much divided. Some believe that the present educational agencies for librarianship are capable of training the type of librarians needed for the future and some think that if the American library schools do not effect a radical change in their faculties, curricula, entrance requirements and what not, they will hardly be able to maintain their position of leadership in the realm of library training.

Current opinion including criticisms of the existing order and theories of what ought to be can be conveniently summarized under six main divisions.

I. Academic affiliation.

Library schools lack general recognition and professional prestige because their entrance requirements are not on a par with those of other professional schools; because their curricula include courses of too conglomerate a nature; and because their teaching staff has neither the size, nor the usual academic qualifications of instructors and professors nor the quality of productive scholarship. In general the appearance, the nature of the work, and the entire make-up of library schools suggest those of vocational schools rather than those of professional schools of university grade. Hence some librarians prefer an academic atmosphere and to raise the standards of library schools to those of the professional schools of universities. This sentiment was well voiced by Edith M.

---

④ Edwin H. Anderson. Training for Library Service. *Library Journal*. 49:463. May 15, 1924.
⑤ Frank K. Walter. A Dynamic Report. *Library Journal*. 48:709. September 1, 1923.

Coulter in her paper presented at the college and reference section of the American Library Association Conference at Detroit, June, 1922: "Furthermore, library schools should be connected with institutions of higher learning. There is at present an encouraging tendency in this direction. The newer schools of librarianship are connected with state universities, and it would seem a great advance if the present schools now under the administration of public libraries would affiliate with colleges and universities. In my opinion to have all professional training connected with recognized universities, together with the granting of uniform professional degrees would do more than anything else to make the library profession comparable to engineering, law, or medicine... University librarians and instructors in our library schools should be holders of such an advanced degree. It is certain that if our library schools connected with universities are to hold their place with other technical and professional schools, the instructors must hold a degree higher than that granted to graduates of the school."⑥

Let us remember that we have seen that the American library schools were organized at a time when it was chiefly essential to master the details of library technique and methods rather than the broader theories and principles of library science. The primary aim of the schools was to impart to the students the practical training necessary to meet the demands of the service in public libraries. At present it is still true that the majority of the library school graduates enter public library work. To attach all the existing agencies for training for librarianship to academic institutions at the expense of the practical training these agencies have heretofore been able to give their students for service in public libraries would be to lose touch with the reality of the situation as a whole. The public would suffer in consequence. Dr. Edwin H. Anderson says, "The dictum that library schools should be connected with universities and not with public libraries is, I think, entirely too sweeping. That depends upon local circumstances and conditions. If, for instance, the public library is a live institution, striving day in and day out to better its services to the public, while the college or university is slow in solving its own library problems, or is indifferent to library progress in general, certainly that public library is a better place for the school than the college or university."⑦

II. Entrance requirements.

Great variation exists in the entrance requirements of the present library schools. Roughly tabulated these requirements are as follows:⑧

1. High school diploma and entrance examinations or degree from an approved college. In the list below, any variation from this requirement follows the name of the school in parentheses.

    a. Library School of the Carnegie Library of Atlanta.

---

⑥ Edith M. Coulter. The University Librarian: His Preparation, Position and Relation to the Academic Department of the University. (*In American Library Association. Papers and Proceedings.* 44:272-3. July, 1922.)

⑦ Edwin H. Anderson. Training for Library Service. *Library Journal.* 49:464. May 15, 1924.

⑧ American Library Association. Temporary Library Training Board. Report. *American Library Schools*, Appendix H. (*In* its *Papers and Proceedings.* 46:277-88. August, 1924.)

b. Drexel Institute, School of Library Science (beginning in the fall of 1925, will only admit applicants with degree from an approved college).

c. Chautauqua School for Librarians (no entrance examinations, but requires library position or that student be under definite library appointment).

d. Library School of the New York Public Library.

e. Carnegie Library School of Pittsburgh (also admits applicants having senior standing in an affiliated college).

f. Pratt Institute of Library Science.

g. St. Louis Library School.

h. Syracuse University Library School (entrance examination may be waived, if applicant intends to be candidate for certificate, only on evidence of satisfactory ability).

i. Library School of Western Reserve University (also admits applicants without examination who have had three years in College for Women of Western Reserve University if applicant is candidate for degree of that college).

j. Library School of the University of Wisconsin (admits applicants who have had three years in the College of Letters and Science of the University of Wisconsin).

2. Junior standing or two years in an approved college. Any variation of this requirement follows the name of the school in parentheses.

a. University of Buffalo, Course in Library Science.

b. Simmons College School of Library Science (applicant for the one year program should have a degree from an approved college or three years in an approved college).

c. Riverside Library Service School (admits applicants with two years college work and entrance examination).

d. University of Texas, Department of Library Science⑨ (admits applicants with a degree from an approved college).

3. Senior standing or degree from an approved college. Any variation of this requirement follows the name of the school in parentheses.

a. Library School of the Los Angeles Public Library (admits applicants with satisfactory equivalents to entrance examination and library experience).

b. University of Washington Library School.

4. Degree from an approved college.

a. University of California, Department of Library Science.

b. University of Illinois Library School.

c. New York State Library School.

The entrance requirements for the above nineteen library schools can thus be roughly grouped under four main classes. No one can say that the library schools are not elastic enough in their entrance requirements to admit the exceptional person who may prove a real genius as a librarian but

⑨ This school discontinued the fall of 1925.

who lacks certain formal phases of preliminary academic training.

Dr. C. C. Williamson in his report to the Carnegie Corporation regards the entrance requirements of the schools as too elastic and he feels that "Much can be said in favor of simplifying entrance requirements of specifying a full college course for all students in professional library schools and at least a high school course for admission to training classes. If desired, the school can call for the applicant's college record and accept only those whose work is of high grade. If classes must be further limited, other tests can be applied to applicants."[⑩]

The present writer feels that in the matter of entrance requirements the library schools had better specify a certain definite and uniform standard similar to that of other professional schools. The exceptional person or genius without the hall mark of a college degree might still be admitted upon sufficient evidence of his or her creditable experience and scholarship. Such a well-known educational institution as Yale University sometimes admits an exceptional person to the graduate school on probation. "It is part of Yale's general plan to admit to its graduate and professional courses all students who are adequately equipped. Each case is considered on its merits, and if the applicant is admitted, he is not enrolled at the beginning as a candidate for a higher degree, but as a so-called 'special student.' If his work should prove equal in quantity and quality to the regular students, he can take the final examinations and get his degree."[⑪] Mr. Andrew Keogh, librarian of Yale University, brought out this fact in his paper, "Advanced Library Training for Research Workers," read before the Professional Training Section of the American Library Association at Asbury Park, June 25, 1919.

The present entrance requirements of some of the library schools are rather anomalous. They stipulate that a high school graduate must pass an entrance examination but they admit a college graduate from an approved college without examination to the same course. This procedure is a frank admission that a four-years' college course is easily the equivalent of their entrance examination as a means of selecting qualified students for the school. It is not an assumption on the part of the library school that their entrance examination is the equivalent of a four-years' college course. On the other hand, this procedure places college graduates on a par with high school graduates who have been successful in passing certain examinations and produces as a result an illogical grouping of students for professional training purposes.

The present writer doubts that examination questions can be made comprehensive enough to measure satisfactorily the unmistakable qualities of an exceptional person adaptable to library training. The result of admission by examination also is a mixture of students with widely varying cultural background. Such a grouping of students is not particularly stimulating mentally to the more intellectual type of college graduates. Furthermore it is difficult for an instructor to devise a course suited and interesting to such widely varying elements of a class. Surely it is much better for the

---

⑩ C. C. Williamson. *Training for Library Service.* New York. 1923. P-32.

⑪ Andrew Keogh. Advanced Library Training for Research Workers. *In American Library Association. Papers and Proceedings.* 41:166-7. July, 1919; or. *Library Journal.* 44:582. September, 1919.

schools to admit only either high school graduates or college graduates. The director or the principal of a library school might still have authority to admit the very exceptional person when he appears. The policy of the Yale graduate school should not be disregarded entirely. As for psychological tests as a means of limiting the number of candidates for library schools, it may be said there is much value in the psychological testing of many vocational abilities, but the problem of constructing tests applicable to the library profession has not yet been solved by psychologists or others though investigations with that in view are in progress. If classes must be further limited, surely those who have had satisfactory practical experience in a library plus a college education are entitled to prior consideration for admission.

III. Curriculum.

The curricula of library schools have been hastily built as the different types of library work have happened to develop. They are not planned out as they ought to be. If subjected to careful critical analysis the average library school curriculum reveals glaring defects. The grouping of several closely related subjects under one course-heading is not followed and there is an unnecessary number of odds and ends. For instance returning books to their proper places on the shelves, shelf-reading, accessioning, alphabeting and book-numbering are all listed as separate subjects for professional library training, but in reality such subjects constitute but relatively insignificant phases of library routine. Strictly speaking such subjects should be taught only in the training class or undergraduate library schools. It is necessary for every trained librarian to have mastered such subjects, but they are not subjects appropriate in the curriculum of a graduate, professional library school. They should be classified as pre-requisites for professional library studies in a graduate school. Any professional school has two principal purposes in planning a curriculum. One is that it should conform to the highest professional standards of the profession and the other is that it should stimulate the professional initiative of the student. The library school curriculum at present too often over-emphasizes the unprofessional aspects of library work and neglects the promotion of professional initiative in the student.

Improvements have been concretely suggested by Dr. Williamson: "While it manifestly would not be desirable to bring about strict uniformity in the content of the various courses in the curriculum, there seems to be need for a certain degree of standardization of both the major and minor courses given in the first year of professional library school study. Nomenclature should be standardized and standard courses worked out and officially adopted by the proper professional body. The term 'book selection' means far different things in different schools, and terms used in presenting the subject do not have at all the same meaning everywhere. The situation is similar in other parts of the curriculum. It is impossible to tell what instruction a student has had in book selection from the mere fact he had a course in that subject in an accredited library school. The fundamental courses in library schools, as in schools of law and engineering, should all have the same scope."[12]

---

[12] C. C. Williamson. *Training for Library Service.* New York. 1923. P. 23.

IV. Instructional staff.

The chapter on the Teaching Staff in Dr. Williamson's *Training for Library Service* is one of the most fault-finding portions of the entire report. In summing up, Dr. Williamson points out that:

Analysis of the training and experience of instructors in library schools indicates that many of them are not fitted to give instruction of high professional character to college graduates. The statistics show that:

a. Only 52 percent of the members of instructional staffs of the library schools in 1921 were college graduates;

b. 42 percent were teaching in the same library school in which they received their own training;

c. 93 percent of the instructors had no training in the science of teaching;

d. 80 percent had no experience in teaching before joining the library school staff;

e. 32 percent without adequate experience in practical library work. ⑬

The oldest library school in America has only been in existence thirty-eight years. If we compare American professional schools of law, medicine, and theology, with those of the library schools, the comparison does reveal some tendency to mere apprenticeship training in the latter. As stated before, the training in the library schools has been chiefly aimed to meet the need of the public libraries. So long as the instructors were proficient in some phase of library technique they were considered capable teachers regardless of their educational background. In the days when technique and method only were emphasized, the college degree and teaching experience were not so essential for library school instructors.

On the other hand is it fair to measure the teachers of library schools with the same criteria by which we measure those of the other professional schools? Do the colleges as yet insist sufficiently on *ability to teach* or training in the art of teaching for their faculties and do the other professional schools, even the older ones like law, medicine, and theology? In realizing that instructors in library schools should be experts at teaching as well as experts in their respective fields the library profession is a step ahead, it would seem, of some of its older professional colleagues. Dr. Williamson's criticism of the teachers of the present library schools was based on his ideal conception of a future professional library school.

If we take into consideration the unfavorable environment of the instructors of library schools in comparison with that of the instructors of colleges and universities, their achievement and success are worthy of praise. First, the salaries of library school instructors are very meagre. Secondly, they have practically no opportunity of meeting great scholars and authorities on certain subjects as the instructors of colleges and universities have. Their daily contact is either with library school students or with general readers of public libraries. Unconsciously their views become narrow and they fall into a mental rut. Thirdly, they have no long vacations or leaves of absence for self-study

---

⑬ Ibid. p. 138.

and improvement. Under such circumstances library schools are naturally often up against a real problem to secure competent instructors.

Besides increase of salary and the introduction of septennial furloughs for research and study, the present library schools should tentatively engage qualified and promising persons from the library field and then give them an opportunity to prepare themselves in graduate schools of education. Such a policy would serve to build up a strong teaching staff. In nearly every university the young and prominent instructors always have the chance of completing their special and advanced studies in graduate schools, and at the same time they are allowed to teach the lower classes of under-graduates. Library schools which are not connected with universities ought to give their most capable instructors some similar opportunity for further education. The library school directors and the American Library Association should unite in the effort to secure an endowment fund for the use of training library school instructors. Otherwise there is no possibility of obtaining ideal library school instructors with library school training plus college education and training in the science and art of teaching.

V. Professional education and technical training.

One of the most common criticisms of the methods of training in library schools is that there is no differentiation between professional education and technical training. Library schools have not done much to make their students grasp the broader principles and methods of library science but have been content to drill them in the routine processes of hand-work in minute detail, and to force them to memorize arbitrary rules and forms of library technique. The over-emphasis on mere technical skill discourages the coming of many fine types of college men and women to library schools. On the other hand many practical librarians hold the view that the technical training taught them in library school is the very thing which enables them successfully to direct their assistants. Library work includes a large amount of routine. It is necessary and desirable for every library school graduate to have mastered mere technical skill.

Library work necessarily involves both professional education and clerical routine. It is not easy nor always necessary to have a very definite distinction between them. Too much emphasis on the principles and methods of library science leads to speculative theories of professional education. It is also true that too much stress laid on technical skill and clerical efficiency reduces professional library training to the level of a trade school. Overemphasis of one and negligence of the other and vice-versa will surely result in injury to the library profession. William E. Henry, Director of the Library and the Library School of the University of Washington, Seattle, comments as follows on Dr. C. C. Williamson's Report. "His distinction of the types of training—professional and clerical— is one that the library schools cannot longer afford to disregard. We cannot make a profession out of high school graduates by nine or ten months training—not education—in clerical details. Such meagre educational equipment does not prepare for educational leadership. We might as well admit it first as last. The strongest man and woman will not compete in such a race. The cheaper drives out the better values, and salaries remain low in perfect justice."[14] The existing library schools may have committed the mistake of overstressing mere technical skill.

VI. Standardization of library training agencies.

A study of the history of library training for the past thirty-eight years reveals development of training agencies in various localities. Their work and growth have been in accordance with their environments. In consequence great variations exist in their standards of entrance requirements, curricula, facilities and aims. Variations in the terminology of library training likewise exist which have been no less a puzzle to librarians than to laymen. Dr. Williamson remarks, "The term 'book selection' means far different things in different schools, and terms used in presenting the subject do not have at all the same meaning everywhere… The fundamental courses in library schools, as in schools of law and engineering, should all have the same scope."[15] In view of such widely varying conditions, the Temporary Library Training Board recommended twelve measures to be carried out by the new Board of Education for Librarianship with the consent of the library training agencies. It was specifically recommended that the Board of Education for Librarianship:

1. Study library service and its changing needs and promote the further development of education for librarianship;

2. Investigate the extent to which existing agencies meet the needs of the profession;

3. Formulate for the approval of the Council standards for library schools, for summer library courses, for courses on school library work in normal schools and teachers' colleges for training and apprentice classes, for correspondence and extension courses, and for such other educational agencies as may arise;

4. Classify these agencies in accordance with the standards thus adopted;

5. Publish annually a list of the accredited agencies;

6. Plan for the correlation of the work offered by the agencies; so that a unified system of education for librarianship may be developed;

7. Establish throughout the different agencies a uniform system of credits consistent with collegiate practice;

8. Assign to the technical terms used in library education meanings which will promote accurate and uniform application;

9. Establish close relations with other bodies having similar purposes;

10. Serve in an advisory capacity in regard to grants of funds for library education;

11. Serve in any other matters which would fall logically within the functions of the Board;

12. Report annually to the American Library Association Council on the progress of education

---

[14] William E. Henry. The Williamson Report, Comment from the Library Schools. *Library Journal*, 48:910. November 1, 1923.

[15] C. C. Williamson. *Training for Library Service*. New York. 1923. p-23.

for librarianship.⁽¹⁶⁾

While the existing library training agencies are at present too little standardized, the Board of Education for Librarianship must guard itself against swinging the pendulum of standardization to the other extreme. Over-standardization inevitably destroys initiative and reduces to rule of thumb methods. The introduction of certain minimum standards for the existing training agencies, the adoption of a uniform nomenclature, and the enforcement of all the standards agreed upon, are the important problems for the Board of Education, for Librarianship to solve.

In reviewing the current criticisms and theories concerning library training agencies, many of the short-comings appear to be due to lack of system rather than bad management. The schools attempt to train their students to give all sorts of service in all sorts of libraries. It is too ambitious a policy in this age of specialization. As a result an overcrowded curriculum is unavoidable and thoroughness in certain subjects has to be sacrificed. In the near future the demand for specialization in library service will grow, and at the same time the general and mechanical work in libraries will proportionately increase. It is bad economy for any library administration to have highly trained assistants in library science doing most of the routine work, therefore, the different grades of library work will sooner or later have to be definitely recognized. This is the right time for the existing library training agencies to formulate and to agree upon their classification. Each school should then adhere to its scope and do its best to promote the full development of the library profession.

The provisional scheme for accrediting the agencies which offer education for librarianship has been outlined by the American Library Association Temporary Library Training Board as follows:⁽¹⁷⁾

1. Library Courses, Correspondence and Extension;
2. Courses in Normal Schools and Teachers' Colleges for School Librarians;
3. Library Apprentice Classes;
4. Library Training Classes;
5. Summer Library Courses;
6. Junior Under-graduate Library School;
7. Senior Under-graduate Library School;
8. Graduate Library School.

As to the length of curriculum; entrance requirements; credits; certificate; qualifications and number of the instructional staff; and library facilities, quarters and equipment, there seems to have been a general agreement among the librarians and the authorities of the library training agencies listed above from 1 to 5. The schools classed under 6 to 8 are still in the stage of discussion and formulation by the Board of Education for Librarianship, especially a new type of advanced gradu-

---

⑯ American Library Association. Report of the Temporary Library Training Board. (*In* its *Papers and Proceedings.* 46:259. August, 1924).

⑰ American Library Association. Report of the Temporary Library Training Board. (*In* its *Papers and Proceedings.* 46:261-75. August, 1924).

ate library school in connection with some university which so far is hardly beyond the embryonic stage. Whether an under-graduate library school, or a graduate library school, or both, should be connected with a university will be fully discussed in the next chapter.

SELECTED BIBLIOGRAPHY

American Library Association—Temporary Library Training Board. Report of American library schools, Appendix H. (*In* its Papers and Proceedings. 46:277-88. Aug., 1924).

American Library Association. Meetings of the professional training section at the 46th Annual conference of the American library association. July, 1924.

American Library Association. Report of the Committee on training class standards. July, 1924.

American Library Association. Report of the Temporary library training board. (*In* its Papers and Proceedings. 46: 257-60. Aug., 1924).

Anderson, Edwin H. Training for library service. Library Journal. 49:462-6. May 15, 1924.

Baldwin, Emma V. Training of professional librarians. Library Journal. 44:574-6. Sept., 1919.

Bostwick, Arthur E. The Carnegie Corporation report on library training. Public Libraries. 28:496-7. Nov., 1923.

Bostwick, Arthur E. Standardization. Library Journal. 48:799-802. Oct. 1, 1923.

Coulter, Edith M. The university librarian: his preparation, position and relation to the academic department of the university. (*In* American Library Association. Papers and Proceedings. 44:271-5. July, 1922).

Curtis, Florence R. Present status of the entrance requirements of the library schools. (*In* Papers of the Professional Training Section of the American Library Association. July, 1924. p. 14-18).

District of Columbia Library Association. Specifications for library service in the Federal government. Washington, D. C. 1923.

Donnelly, June R. A unified system of education for librarianship. (*In* Papers of the Professional Training Section of the American Library Association. July, 1924. p. 29-32).

Keogh, Andrew. Advanced library training for research workers. (*In* American Library Association. Papers and Proceedings. 41:165-7. July, 1919; Library Journal. 44:581-2. Sept., 1919).

Morgan, Joy Elmer. Professional librarians for the nation. Public Libraries. 29:464-5. Nov., 1924.

Pendry, Eliza R. Scientific methods of vocational guidance applied to the problem of recruiting for the library profession. Public Libraries. 28:349-54. July, 1923.

Pratt Institute. School of Library Science. Report. 1924. p. 17-21.

Reece, Ernest J. Some possible developments in library education. American Library Association. Chicago. 1924.

Walter, Frank K. A dynamic report. Library Journal. 48:709-11. Sept. 1, 1923.

Williamson, Charles C. Some present day aspects of library training. Library Journal. 44:563-8. Sept., 1919.

Williamson, Charles C. Training for library service. New York. 1923.

Williamson Report. Comment from librarians. Library Journal. 48:999-1006. Dec. 1, 1923.

Williamson Report. Comment from the library schools. Library Journal. 48:883-910. Nov. 1, 1923,

Wyer, James I. A unified system of education for librarianship. (*In* Papers of the Professional Training Section of the American Library Association. July, 1924. p. 27-8).

PART III
A PROPOSED SCHEME OF PROFESSIONAL EDUCATION FOR LIBRARIANSHIP

CHAPTER XI. The Library School as a School of a University
CHAPTER XII. A Proposed Library School for the State University of Iowa
CHAPTER XIII. Requirements for Admission, Degrees and Curriculum for a Library School

CHAPTER XI
THE LIBRARY SCHOOL AS A SCHOOL OF A UNIVERSITY

The organization of another type of library school is a live question among American librarians. The close affiliation of any new library school with some university will be advisable for the library profession, in the opinion of the writer, but there are those who do not share this opinion.

The existing schools in connection with public libraries have performed and are performing vital work in training librarians. They have the equipment, facilities, and quarters in most cases the equal of other standard library schools. The curricula as they stand at present require much demonstration work in all types of library routine. The well-organized public libraries offer excellently equipped laboratories for library school students. In general the public library in America is better organized and more adequately supported than the university library. Considering such conditions, an affiliation with a university may seem unnecessary.

Some librarians who favor the affiliation of library schools with universities reason that the money appropriated for public library service should not be diverted to support a professional library school. To these men and women the training of professional librarians appears a task for educational institutions. The equipment and facilities of the public libraries for library school students need not be wasted if the library schools be located in universities not too far distant. It could be managed similarly to the way in which the medical school students of a university use nearby hospital facilities. The primary duty of a municipal public library is to provide library service to the city tax-payers and not to maintain a professional school for librarianship.

It has been the tendency of professional education to center in universities. For example, medical schools before conducted as adjuncts to medical practice or hospital service have now been organized as integral parts of universities. Education for the law has long been primarily under university control. The majority of law schools offer a full-time professional training of three years based on a preliminary education of two years of college work, in some instances requiring a college degree for admission.

The same university affiliations exist in regard to engineering education and pharmaceutical training. Table No. 23 of the *Biennial Survey of Education* 1918-1920, published by the United States Bureau of Education, lists some one hundred and twenty-four schools of engineering of which eighty-eight are professional engineering schools in universities, and twenty-nine are attached to colleges, either state or private; and only the remaining seven are separate technical schools. The same Table No. 23 includes forty-seven schools of pharmacy. Thirty-eight are departments or schools in universities, six are with state and private colleges, and only three are separate and independent schools. ①

The same tendency in the direction of affiliation with universities prevails in the preparation for all the other professions. No one can fail to note that education, dentistry, journalism, architecture, and business administration have also become members of the university family. The Temporary Library Training Board has listed nineteen library schools. Ten of them connect with universities and colleges, two with institutes, one with an agency for educational extension, and six with public libraries. ② Ten out of nineteen library schools are either a department or a school in a university or a college, but unfortunately most of the library schools are not operated on the same basis as the other professional schools of engineering, law, medicine, agriculture, etc. Therefore, in general, librarians as well as laymen have a hazy impression that library schools are connected with public libraries and that some are independent schools, not connected with universities. Such a wrong impression is frequently augmented by the small size of the library school, the paucity of productive scholarship from the instructional staff, and the inferior rank of the instructional staff in the faculty hierarchy. The personality of the library school or the department of library science is often markedly unimpressive to the general faculty and students, when it should rank with the other professional schools in the same institution. Local institutional comment on existing library schools connected with universities may not directly reveal this fact but it is made apparent when university administrative councils are asked officially to allow graduate school credit for professional library school courses.

The tendency of professional education to center under university control is, without doubt, correct. Professor Robert J. Leonard has exhaustively treated this subject in his *Trends in Professional Education*, an address delivered at the opening Convocation of Columbia University, September 24, 1924. As to the reasons for university affiliation, he says:

Professional schools of yesterday and to-day have little in common. In the main, professional schools of yesterday were isolated from all other educational institutions, under proprietary or commercial control, and, perforce, colored or dominated by monetary considerations. In the main, professional schools of to-day are either a part of, or associated with, our great universities, and removed thereby from commercial influence...

What has the development of professional schools within universities meant to the professional schools themselves?

It has heightened the ideals of professional training and service. It has given impetus to research, without which professional schools soon degenerate into technical schools. It has led to the adoption of curricula of appropriate length, resting upon a sound general education in which the deferred as well as the immediate values are recognized. It has made possible the attraction of scholarly men as instructors. It has attracted students of high intelligence with extensive preparation, who are willing to invest in themselves sufficient time and money for adequate training.

---

① United States Bureau of Education. *Biennial Survey of Education of* 1918-1920. Bulletin No. 29. Washington, D. C. 1923. p. 309-82.

② American Library Association. Report of the Temporary Library Training Board. Appendix H. (*In its Papers and Proceedings.* 46:277-88. August, 1924).

And so, the university has provided the environment necessary for professional schools to achieve the well-rounded development of which the leaders in each of the professions have dreamed.

To the universities, the professional schools have made worthy contributions. They have added to the vitality and strength which characterize modern institutions. They have contributed to the assemblage of students thousands of mature men and women of driving purpose and varying interests. Complacency and provincialism have been prevented and broad tolerance and mutual respect developed among student groups. Vital contacts with the current problems of the day have been made possible and productive research has been fostered. The public belief in higher education has been strengthened greatly…

Each decade brings a fuller participation of universities in professional education. The trend is unmistakably toward incorporating within the systems of higher education facilities for education for all professions necessary for the public good. By responding to this trend, our universities are adding new chapters to their usefulness. They have placed culture and professionalism in a co-operative rather than a competitive relation. ③

Under the present era of high specialization, library service will also grow more and more highly specialized. In discussing the modern library movement in one of the previous chapters, the tendency for special libraries and special departments of public libraries to develop has been seen to be very strong. In the practice of other professions, specialization in actual work is promptly followed by a similar specialization in the schools for professional education. For instance specialization in medical work has forced medical schools to provide specialized courses. No intelligent patient with appendicitis is willing to have his appendix removed by a general physician. The service of a skilled surgeon is sought. It will be the same sooner or later in library service. Therefore, adequate provision for specialized library training should be provided.

Specialized training under any high standard of professional education involves two pre-requisites, broad cultural education and general professional training. Although two of the existing library schools admit only college graduates and give a two-year general course, yet it is quite evident that under their present organization they are financially or otherwise unable to handle the problem of training librarians primarily for special libraries.

Let us take the comparatively simple problem of training qualified high school librarians. According to the qualifications outlined in the Report of the Committee on Library Organization and Equipment of the National Education Association and of the North Central Association of Colleges and Secondary Schools:

The standard requirements for future appointments of librarians in high schools should be a college or university degree with major studies in literature, history, sociology, education, or other subjects appropriate to any special demands, as, for example, those of the technical high school, upon the library. In addition the librarian should have at least one year of post graduate library training in an approved library school and one year's successful library experience in work with young people in a library of standing. ④

---

③ Robert J. Leonard. Trends in Professional Education. *Teachers College Record*. 26: 177-9. November, 1924.

④ C. C. Certain. *Standard Library Organization and Equipment for Secondary Schools of Different Sites*. American Library Association. Chicago. 1920. p. 16.

This standard appears high in the light of the fact that at the present time most of the library schools only require that their students be graduates of high schools who can pass entrance examinations, yet it falls below Dr. C. C. Williamson's specifications.

Dr. Williamson emphatically says:

In states that have the best educational standards the high school librarian must have the qualifications of a high school teacher—which means a college degree with special training in education and some graduate study—in addition to a certain amount of professional library training. A college education and one year's study in a library school do not give adequate preparation for high school librarianship. A second year of special preparation is coming to be essential, the course to consist of three elements: (1) special study of high school library problems, supplementing and adapting the general course; (2) special study and training in educational subjects: history of education, educational psychology, and the high school curriculum; (3) extensive field practice, consisting of quite long periods devoted to actual service in well-organized high school libraries under the close supervision and direction of able and experienced high school librarians. At the end of this second year's work the student would be much better equipped to organize and administer a high school library than he can be at the end of the second year's work in one of the two-year schools at the present time. ⑤

The second year as suggested by Dr. Williamson for the training of high school librarians cannot be had by any student in the existing library schools, for under the present organization these schools have no arrangement which will allow students to major in library training and minor in any study offered by a standard university. Library training in America has reached a place where the entire system requires a re-adjustment. Supposing that a big banking library or a big education library wishes to have an assistant, well versed in library science as well as in some knowledge of banking or of education. To which library school can that special library write for such an assistant?

A person graduated from a *special* school of a university might go to a graduate library school for one or two years' study and then be well equipped to fill a position in a special library. It is a possible case, but a very rare one. For, in the first place, any successful graduate of a professional school of a university is not likely to change his profession. In the second place the further investment in one or two years' additional library training will probably not give him a better financial return after his later graduation from the library school. In the third place if he is not capable of being successful in his special line of work, the present graduate library schools will discourage him from taking up librarianship. Taking all these difficulties into consideration, very few desirable persons who graduate from a professional school of a university will enter a library school, even if there is a great demand for specialized librarians. Furthermore the salary of a librarian of a special library has no particular attraction to many young ambitious persons who already have some professional knowledge of another special calling.

In the main, a person who has already inclined to a certain profession and who has been well grounded in a professional school of a university by years of training will not make a good special librarian. He is apt to be a *specialist* rather than a *special librarian.* At the Special Library Associa-

---

⑤ C. C. Williamson. *Training for Library Service.* New York. 1923. p. 94.

tion Conference at Ottawa, Canada, June 27, 1912, Mr. A. G. S. Josephson led a discussion as to whether the proper method of making a special librarian is to take a person already a trained librarian and give him the knowledge of a special subject, or to take a specialist on a subject and give him library training, saying at that time:

 It has been said that the librarian of a special library must be a specialist first of all, and only secondarily a librarian. To this I cannot agree... A librarian must first of all be a librarian. Some persons seem to think that all there is to a librarian is technique, knowledge of the rules and practices that have grown up among libraries and are taught in library schools. This is the very smallest part of a librarian's equipment. No librarian was yet made in the library school alone.

 Take an engineer, or a minister, or a professor of history, let him take a special course in library "science", and he will never become anything but an engineer, or a minister, or a professor, any more than a course in a business college would make him an expert accountant unless he possesses the inborn feeling for books, the real scent of the bibliographer. ⑥

 It seems wisest to the writer neither to take an already trained librarian and give him one or two years' study in a professional school of a special subject, nor to take a specialist on a subject and give him one or two years' library training. As the best solution of the problem and the most satisfactory from both the economic and educational points of view it is proposed to train special librarians in a professional university library school offering both graduate and under-graduate professional courses with an opportunity for further collateral study of other special subjects. The accepted applicants of such a school should show adequate pre-requisites in library subjects, general cultural subjects, and a few special subjects, in their four years' under-graduate studies. The curriculum of the graduate year should consist of approximately ten hours of library subjects and five hours of special subjects per week. Under the present organization of the library schools, without closer university affiliation, such an arrangement is impossible.

 Some may argue that the schools without university affiliation at all would be able to train special librarians by engaging part-time professors of special subjects. It is a feasible scheme, provided that the library schools are ready to incur the almost prohibitive expense and to establish an educational policy not commonly recognized.

 Any one who reads Dr. C. C. Williamson's report on "Training for Library Service" and the multitudinous comments on it by library school directors and librarians will notice the consensus of opinion that the library schools are in a condition of extreme poverty. The salaries of vice-principals and full-time instructors are so low that teaching positions in a library school have no appeal to ambitious librarians. Consequently the library profession has a constant shortage of able instructors. Therefore, the argument for existing library schools to engage part-time specialists to teach certain special subjects is financially an impracticable one.

 To have special professors teaching in library schools is logically unsound from an educational viewpoint. Any professional school which attempts to branch out into the unrelated subjects of other

---

⑥ A. G. S. Josephson. What Is a Special Library? *Special Libraries*. 3:146. September, 1912.

professional studies is trying to build a miniature university within its curriculum. Therefore, a plan of giving instruction in special subjects by cooperating with educational institutions in the same locality will be much more feasible, though it is inferior to the scheme of close university affiliation.

When a re-adjustment of library schools comes into operation, we will have to take the complex occupational situation and the opportunity for advanced research work into careful consideration. Professor R. J. Leonard said:

Professions, formerly complete units, have been divided, redivided, and divided again. Each new fractional part of the unit profession has become as extensive and exacting as the profession from whence it originated. As illustrated by the field of dentistry, the development of levels has accompanied this process of division. Dentistry was a unit profession only thirty years ago. Now it embraces at least fifteen different callings representing at least two distinct levels. In the highest level, there is the dentist, the orthodentist⑦, the research dentist, and the dental surgeon. The other level, which may be characterized as the middle level, includes the dental nurse, the dental mechanic, and the dental hygienist.

The same process of subdivision, and the development of levels, has occurred in medicine, law, engineering, business administration, and education; in fact, in all the professions…

We dwell upon these developments because professional schools frequently do not recognize the differentiation between the middle and the higher levels. The failure to recognize this differentiation is one of the gravest problems in professional education. An illustration may be helpful. There is almost universal dissatisfaction with the colleges of agriculture, engineering, and commerce, particularly as found in our state-supported universities. Farmers condemn colleges of agriculture as being too theoretical, and agriculturalists condemn them as too practical. Some engineers condemn colleges of engineering as being too theoretical, others as being too practical. The same criticisms are made of colleges of commerce and business administration. Both types of criticisms should be heeded. ⑧

It is equally true in the library profession. Some librarians who condemn the advanced studies of library schools as being useless and theoretical are thinking of the "middle-level occupational groups," chiefly characterized by the need of technical efficiency. Those who criticize the library school graduates as being too mechanical are thinking of the "highest-level professional groups," chiefly characterized by the need of cultural, bibliographical and research studies.

The existing library schools are open to these criticisms, because they have attempted to train both levels, *i. e.* the "middle-level occupational group" and the "highest-level professional group." In so doing they have struck the average between these two groups and have been unable to fulfill the requirements of either level.

Whenever the re-adjustment of the organization of the present library schools takes place, a clear differentiation between the requirements for these two levels should be made. The graduate library schools in universities should confine their efforts entirely to professional studies of library science and certain specialized subjects, or to advanced research work. To train the librarians of the "middle-level occupational group" is a task for the under-graduate library schools.

That the proper standard of the library profession be advanced, there must be graduate library

---

⑦ 【译者注】疑为 orthodontist,正牙医生,牙齿矫正医师。
⑧ R. J. Leonard. Trends in Professional Education. *Teachers College Record.* 26: 180. November, 1924.

schools in universities to train for leadership in administration as well as research workers and library school professors. Any profession that lacks the opportunity and facility of training the highest type of practitioners and research workers is bound to sink to the level of a vocation. Comparatively speaking, in research work and professional training, a standard university has a more inspiring atmosphere, better facilities, and richer opportunities to rub shoulders with various scholars than an isolated professional school. The training for leadership in a profession requires something more than the mere "dishing out" of intensive instruction in the professional technicalities. It requires that the students be given a vision of great usefulness and an appreciation of those humanistic principles which deepen human sympathies. The university professional school is able to impart the broader ideals essential for really advanced professional training much more satisfactorily than the isolated professional school.

This general plea for a university professional school of library training with graduate studies is not new. Mr. W. P. Cutter, librarian of Arthur D. Little Chemistry Library, Boston, Massachusetts, urged a graduate school for librarians about twenty years ago. He said about a year ago: "I wish to repeat the suggestion which I made in a little leaflet published twenty years ago. I was then giving rather desultory instruction in library work in evening classes at the Library of Congress, with the cordial consent of the Librarian of Congress, and under the nominal auspices of the Columbian (now the George Washington) University. The leaflet in question was prepared at the suggestion of President Whitman of that institution, to summarize the advantages of Washington as a place where advanced library instruction should be carried on."⑨

In 1910 Miss Mary W. Plummer thought of formulating a university professional school in library training. Her article, *Forecast of the Next Twenty-five Years for Library Schools*, seems to have been written today and not fifteen years ago. She believed that the level of the library profession would have been perceptibly raised, if it had held certain attractions for mature and cultivated persons who at that time turned to what then seemed to them more scholarly pursuits. She placed her finger on the weak spot of the library schools at that time and suggested a thorough re-adjustment on a larger scale than anything the librarians had tried.

There are two things that will probably serve as factors to determine the line of development of library schools in this country... One is, the American tendency toward organization and system, and the other the less distinctively American tendency to supply a state demand.

Both tendencies are affecting the school-problem to-day, as the demand for specialization grows in extent and intensity. The more intense the need and demand, the greater the pressure on the schools to supply it and the greater their effort to do so; while the greater the variety of demand, the greater the necessity of systematization. So that, the demand being what it is, the two tendencies work together to meet it.

Law is law and medicine is medicine, but librarianship is called upon to cover the entire field of knowledge. The medical society wants its librarians versed to some extent in medicine; and trained to apply the general principles of librarianship to the medical library; the bar asks for legal knowledge and the same application of

---

⑨ W. P. Cutter. Graduate School for Librarians. *Special Libraries*. 15: 81. April, 1924.

principles to the law library. State and city governments are forming their libraries and calling for the application of librarianship to civics and economics. Large manufacturing concerns, laboratories, daily papers, are realizing the necessity of the special library for their needs and demanding trained administrators who shall be also specialists, potential if not actual... ⑩

Her solution for this dilemma was as follows:

  Let the general courses continue for the younger people, for the general work, always having in view the discovery of talents and aptitudes for specializing, and let there be two or three schools in the country, connected with universities and an integral part of them, in which the study of technique and administration may be connected with an outline course in medicine, law, theology, science, pure and applied, civics, child study or whatever other specialty calls for training. A university frequently carries on a course followed by one or two students only, so that a paucity of applicants in any one division of the work would not mean discouragement or bankruptcy.

The discussion in the preceding pages of this chapter tries to bring out the need for professional library schools in connection with universities. In order to re-adjust the existing library schools to the tendencies and needs of the time, closer affiliations of independent library schools with universities have been suggested. Those which have some nominal connections with universities should improve their relations.

This suggestion of affiliation involves practical difficulties. Whether any university wishes to shoulder the responsibility of adopting an existing library school, or conversely whether any existing library school is willing to be a member of a university, is a practical problem. In this respect the Board of Education for Librarianship and the Association of American Library Schools can cooperatively exert great influence on the universities as well as on the library schools, provided that the two boards are in agreement as to the principles on which the university professional schools are now organized.

Perhaps some of the existing library schools prefer to be connected with public libraries or with any other agency except a college or university. They can be so connected, provided that they conform to the minimum requirements outlined by the Board of Education for Librarianship of the American Library Association. Nothing can ruin the standing of a profession so much as to have every school of that profession have its own standards, entrance requirements, and nomenclature. Certain minimum standards outlined and enforced by a professional association and willingly followed by all the professional schools form one of the best guarantees against the development of spurious schools and one of the surest ways of upholding the standard of professional education. For instance the standardization of medical education at the hands of the American Medical Association has been very successful in improving the general standard of the medical profession.

The Board of Education for Librarianship of the American Library Association has formulated provisional minimum standards for four grades of library schools, namely, Junior Under-graduate Library School, Senior Under-graduate Library School, Professional Library School, and Graduate

---

  ⑩ Mary W. Plummer. Forecast of the Next Twenty-five Years for Library Schools. *Library Journal.* 35: 251-2. June, 1910.

School of Librarianship. This division of the library schools into four classes is somewhat unnatural in scope and confusing in terminology.

Since these provisional minimum standards for library schools have not yet been adopted and are still in the discussion stage, it may not be too late to suggest an alternative scheme. The plan is to change the arbitrary divisions of library schools from four grades into two, namely, Under-graduate Library Schools and Graduate Library Schools. Both the schools are to be regarded as two distinctive functions of a single unit, under the common name of a library school within the jurisdiction of a university. The status should be like any of the other professional schools of education, business administration, engineering, dentistry, pharmacy, et cetera.

SELECTED BIBLIOGRAPHY

American Library Association. Report of the temporary library training board on American library schools. Appendix H. (*In* its Papers and Proceedings. 46:277-88. Aug., 1924).

American Library Association. Report of the temporary library training board on provisional grouping for agencies which offer education for librarianship. Appendix B. (*In* its Papers and Proceedings. 46:261-73. Aug., 1924).

Capon, S. P. Tendencies in professional education. Bulletin of the American Association of University Professors. 10:35-9. Oct., 1924.

Carleton, W. N. C. Universities and librarians. Public Libraries. 20:451-6. Dec., 1915.

Certain, C. C. Standard library organization and equipment for secondary schools of different sizes. American Library Association. Chicago. 1920.

Compton, Charles H. Comparison of qualifications, training, demand and remuneration of the library profession with social work. (*In* American Library Association. Professional Training Section of the Forty-sixth Annual Conference, July, 3-4, 1924. p. 19-27); reprinted under the title "Comparison of library profession with social work." Public Libraries. 30:115-21. Mar., 1925.

Craig, Florence M. Education of librarians: —a fantasy. Library Journal. 44:577. Sept., 1919.

Cutter, W. P. Graduate School for librarians. Special Libraries. 15:81-2. April, 1924.

Dudgeon, Matthew S. The scope and purposes of special libraries. Special Libraries. 3:129-33. June, 1912.

Dudgeon, Matthew S. What has an employer the right to expect from library school graduates? (*In* American Association. Professional Training Section of the Forty-Sixth Annual Conference, July, 3-4, 1924. p. 5-7).

Hedrick, Ellen A. Education of a librarian. Special Libraries. 15:79-81. April, 1924.

Josephson, A. G. S. What is a special library? Special Libraries. 3:145-7. Sept., 1912.

Kaiser, John Boynton. The special library and the library school. Library Journal. 37:175-9. April, 1912.

Leonard, Robert Josselyn[⑪]. Trends in professional education. Teachers College Record. 26:177-83. Nov., 1924.

Plummer, Mary W. Forecast of the next twenty-five years for library schools. Library Journal. 35:251-3. June, 1910.

Training for the professions and allied occupations. Bureau of Vocational Information. New York. 1924.

Tufts, James H. Education and training for social work. Russell Sage Foundation. New York. 1923.

United States Bureau of Education. Biennial survey of education. 1918-1920. Bulletin No. 29. Government Printing Office. Washington, D. C. 1923. p. 309-83.

---

⑪ 【译者注】疑为 Joselyn。

Walter, Frank K. A course of training for hospital librarians. Library Journal. 49:381. April 15, 1924.

198 Wilbur, Ray Lyman. Maintaining standards without excessive standardization. School and Society. 20:607-12. Nov. 15, 1924.

Williamson, Charles C. Training for library service. New York. 1923. p. 86-102.

CHAPTER XII
A PROPOSED LIBRARY SCHOOL FOR THE STATE UNIVERSITY OF IOWA

The distribution of professional library schools in America is more uneven than that of other professional schools. The eighteen library schools offering not less than one full academic year of library training are roughly scattered in five regions: (1) The Pacfic① coast has four library schools. (2) The southern states two; Texas and Georgia have one library school each. (3) The states around the Great Lakes, Wisconsin, Illinois, and Ohio have three library schools. (4) The northeastern states, Pennsylvania, New York, and Massachusetts, take the lead, having eight library schools. (5) The Mississippi Valley and the great west extending to the Rocky Mountains have only one library school, which is connected with the St. Louis Public Library, Missouri.

In order to divide the task of training professional librarians more evenly, the states between the Mississippi River and the Rocky Mountains should have more library schools of a high standard. In training for professional librarianship this great region is certainly behind the states along the Pacific coast or those along the northern coast of the Atlantic. Furthermore, local needs and conditions are important considerations in library service. For example, many administrative problems of a medium sized library in the mid-west are different from those of a library of the same size in the east. Occupations and the environment, which characterize the life of the community are most significant factors in conducting a public library.

The University of Minnesota has seen the need of special librarians for special libraries and has recently established a library school to train librarians for hospital library service. Visits to the principal libraries in Minnesota, Iowa, Missouri, Illinois, and Wisconsin, and the information obtained from several of the prominent librarians of these states, have led to the conclusion that the states in the Mississippi valley have need not only of special librarians but also a larger number of "unspecialized" but well-trained librarians. The 1924 reports of the library schools all expressed regret that their facilities, equipment, and quarters did not permit them to take more applicants.

The writer was once asked to give an address at the Des Moines Library Club. After the talk he had the opportunity of meeting many Iowa librarians. During the course of conversation on library conditions of the state, and during the visit to the headquarters of the travelling libraries conducted by the Iowa Library Commission, he was informed that the demand for trained librarians in all types of library work exceeds the supply.

This fact has been further substantiated during recent years by the increasing number of applicants seeking admission to the summer courses in library training under the auspices of the State

---

① 【译者注】疑为 Pacific。

University of Iowa. Every summer many universities in America conduct summer schools in library training and all of them are well attended by active and prospective library workers as well as by college students. The new *Bulletin of the State University of Iowa* on "Summer Courses in Library Training" tells us of the great demand for trained librarians in this part of the country:

To-day the demand for trained librarians is constantly greater than the supply. Especially opportune is the time for training. The librarian of the old school was a fine scholarly type, more or less—often less—willing to share his treasures with a few like-minded souls. The modern librarian finds himself charged with the responsibilities of an executive, an administrator, and an educator as well as those of a scholar. Trained minds are needed to apply the suggestions being made by those studying the question of the significance of the public library in the new program of adult education. By a wiser choice of material, by dignified publicity, by improved methods of distribution the librarian of to-day endeavors to bring his world of print to the very doors of the public. He is a propagandist for learning and culture. ②

The spring semester of 1925, the University of Iowa offered a new one-hour, one-credit course in "Instruction in the Use of Books and Library Methods" known as Library 2. Immediately after the tentative announcement of this course from the office of the Registrar, twenty-five students registered in spite of the already crowded schedule of courses offered to under-graduate students of the Liberal Arts College. The registrants were assigned to two sections and were given ample facilities to solve practical problems in this elementary library course. This and the popularity of similar courses elsewhere are illustrations of the fact that college students are beginning to be interested in the comparatively new subject of library science.

Quite evidently the trend is such that the professional library school will be the next addition to the university family in America. Formerly the conception of a university education was limited to the seven liberal arts and it was thought below the dignity of any university to train students in the practical callings of every-day life. This barrier between the academic and the practical has been broken down. Today educators are realizing that cultural education and professional training in no way conflict with each other, but are two phases of preparation for the same thing—life.

This new movement of harmonizing the academic and the practical in university education has been carried out in America chiefly by the state universities. It is only in recent years that nearly all universities in this country, including such historical institutions of cultural learning as Harvard and Yale, have extended their curricula to include such subjects as pharmacy, dentistry, business administration, and engineering. In this age of combining professional instruction with cultural studies in universities, no profession fits into the trend of the new movement better than the library profession.

Within this generation the university that is fully conscious of its obligations and of the best educational thought of the time will gladly takes the responsibility of training future librarians. Dr. W. N. C. Carlton, the librarian of Williams College feels that professional library education should

---

② University of Iowa. *Summer Courses in Library Training.* Iowa City. April 23, 1925. (*Bulletin.* n. s. No. 317).

most certainly be taught by a university library school. He has expressed the matter thus: "The isolated library school and the library apprentice class, necessary as they have been and still are to meet pressing immediate needs, should eventually become things of the past. Universities should be just as much the cradles and nurseries of librarians as they are of teachers, clergymen, physicians, and lawyers. If the university prepares and equips men and women for positions as principals of city high schools and for the headship of the physics, chemistry, history, mathematics, ancient or modern language departments of such schools, it ought also to prepare the librarian and the chief assistants of the municipal library. We are rapidly passing out of the pioneer period, the self-taught stage of American librarianship. In the future we shall turn increasingly to the universities for the men and women best qualified to meet the ever widening and always exacting demands made upon our libraries."[3]

No educational institution in the state of Iowa can discharge the responsibility of training professional librarians more adequately than the State University. Besides the reasons discussed in the preceding paragraphs of this chapter, this institution already has the practical facilities, specialized equipment, and in part the personnel for carrying on the work of a professional library school. Its nine colleges, four schools, research station, and extension division, providing training in every major profession and offering the opportunity for research work in all fields makes it able to give the fullest range of training for both general and special librarians. The general library and its many departments already possess a workable collection of general and special reference books, national and subject bibliographies, and books on library science in all its aspects. If the present professional staff of the library were supplemented by an instructional staff with at least one professor, one assistant professor, and three full-time instructors, and should have the cooperation of the faculties of the other colleges and schools, a full-fledged professional library school with fifty students could be started without difficulty.

Let us assume that a library school is going to be started in this University in September, 1926. The time from September 1925 to the summer of 1926 can be profitably utilized in re-organizing facilities so as to provide a proper seminar room for students, teachers' offices, and classrooms. A concentrated effort should be made to secure the most competent teachers available anywhere in the country.

The organization, the administration, the qualifications of the instructional staff, the requirements for admission, the courses of studies, and the degrees of the coming library school will be outlined. Certain important financial points involved will be discussed. The various topics will be treated in the form of a general discussion rather than by precise statements, such as are usually seen in the catalogs of colleges and universities. Whenever the writer's opinion is at variance with some of his professional colleagues, reasons for the difference are given.

It has already been argued that any new library school should be connected with an approved degree-conferring institution, preferably with a university which is a member of the Association of

---

[3] W. N. C. Carlton. Universities and Librarians. *Public Libraries*. 20:452-543. December, 1915.

American Universities. As regards the detailed organization of a degree-conferring institution or a university, the Board of Education for Librarianship of the American Library Association to which the profession is now looking for advice in these matters will probably feel that it should not specify, because every individual institution has its own characteristics. It is naturally advisable to let a library school be administered in accordance with the general policy of that institution.

A library school can be organized in the State University of Iowa with three purposes: (1) to train students to be administrators of small libraries and assistants of medium size and large libraries; (2) to train students to be special librarians and bibliographers, such as high school librarians, hospital librarians, medical librarians, etc.; (3) to train instructors for library schools. The courses designed for the first and the second purpose will be given respectively to students with standing in the third and the fourth year of the College of Liberal Arts and in the Graduate College. For the third purpose the curriculum should include work in both the undergraduate and the graduate department with parallel courses in the College of Education. This suggested division of the studies of the library school into undergraduate and graduate is more common and simpler than the scheme of four grades outlined by the Board of Education for Librarianship of the American Library Association. The objections to the scheme of four grades will be discussed elsewhere in connection with the requirements for admission, in the last chapter.

The chief executive officer of the university library school should be the director of the university library. Some librarians may object to this practice on account of the numerous duties and responsibilities already attached to the office of a university librarian. In case he has also the duties and responsibilities of the head of a library school, it is felt by some that he may not be able to discharge both his duties with thoroughness.

The weakness in this apparently reasonable argument lies in vagueness as to the meaning of the word, "thoroughness." Does the thoroughness in question mean that the chief executive officer should be thorough in handling every detail of his library, or simply mean that he should be thorough in the main aspects of administration? Every experienced administrator will agree with the meaning of thoroughness as to important functions. The chief duty of the administrator of a department is similar to that of a chief engineer responsible at all times for the proper functioning of the machinery as a result of the expert and intimate contact with its detailed parts by a corps of cooperating expert workmen. The more detailed duties of the director of a university library can well be delegated to an assistant director or an executive secretary, and the more detailed work of a library school can also be taken care of by a secretary. If the staffs of both the university library and the library school are well organized, the director can discharge all the important functions of both library and school with thoroughness.

Friction and failure in administration frequently result when two or three heads with equal powers and divided responsibilities are filling two or three closely related positions in the same institution. Can any university hope to find a head of a library school and a director of the university library always sure to agree upon theories, policies, and practices in these two necessarily closely cooperating undertakings? An unpleasant result is almost certain to be the outcome of a dual administration of two intimately related units in a university. In fact the university library is the laboratory of a university library school and the actual operation of the former is a demonstration lesson in library administration to the students of the latter. Therefore, the director of a university library concurrently holding the office of the head of a university library school will eliminate all possible friction of administration between these two separate yet closely related units of a university.

Some administrative difficulties as to proper relationships between the teaching staff of a university library school and the professional staff of a university library will undoubtedly be experienced. The main difficulty involved is the problem of salary. At present the instructional staff of a university is paid according to a scale which in general is not applied to the professional staff of a university library. Other difficulties are the length of working hours and the privilege of vacations and furloughs.

In most universities departmental heads in the library are treated on the same basis as other members of the administrative staff. Dr. Walter Lichtenstein, formerly librarian of Northwestern University, has remarked on the unequal treatment of professionally trained library assistants in comparison with trained assistants on the teaching staff of universities. "In general, it is not an exaggeration to say that very few library assistants in a university library occupy in reality, whatever it may be on paper, a position at all comparable to that of even the lowest rank of university teachers. In every way they are made to feel the difference. They are tide down to fixed hours, they have shorter vacations, often they do not receive complimentary tickets to university functions as do the university teachers, etc. In short the library assistants are regarded in the same light as are the stenographers, bookkeepers, etc., employed by the university, tho④ the academic training required of the former is far in excess of that required of the usual office employee. The reason for this is not hard to discover. The university teacher is, or wishes to be regarded, as a specialist and as an expert in some field of human knowledge, and he does not regard highly those who have merely a general knowledge and training to offer. Specialization in mechanical and administrative work will not be accepted as a substitute. This may not be right, but we are not concerned with the question of right or wrong, but with the actual state of affairs, whether right or wrong. The result then is that those who have the necessary qualifications as specialists will seek for those positions which will place them on a pedestal in their communities and where they will have long vacations, easy hours, title and rank, and compared to the salaries in libraries, a good salary."⑤

In case both the library school and the university library are under the administration of one director, it is impossible for him to run his administration successfully on two bases of salaries and other privileges, one for the teaching staff of the library school and the other for the professional staff of the library. The former will be treated as on a par with the instructional staff of the university and the latter will be classed with the general administrative staff in spite of their professional training and experience.

---

④ 【译者注】疑为 though。

⑤ Walter Lichtenstein. Question of a Graduate Library School. *Library Journal*. 43:234. April, 1918.

Some suggest that the teaching in the university library school can be solely carried on by the university library staff. To this suggestion, though it is worthy of consideration, there are several objections. Generally the professional staff of a university library is not large enough to teach the various subjects in the curriculum of a library school including both under-graduate and graduate studies. Some of the professional assistants of a university library may know their work well, but will not necessarily have the ability to teach.

Instruction given by professional assistants of a university library will have the value of theoretical teaching combined with practical experience. But after balancing up the defects and advantages, the writer feels that it is better for a university library school to have a separate instructional staff whose qualifications, experiences, and abilities for scholarly work are on a par with the instructional staff of other professional schools. The professional assistants of the university library can be asked to give lectures on special topics and to supervise the students' practice work, but should not act as regular instructors and professors of the library school.

As regards the salary problem and the question of privileges for the professional assistants of a university library and the teachers of a university library school, an equitable solution may be worked out from the present anomalous situation by introducing a new salary schedule. It should be in such a form that it is applicable to both teachers of the library school and professional assistants of the university library. What types of service the trained librarians can render should not be considered as the primary factor in framing a salary schedule. For example it is a poor and unjust policy to pay an instructor in the university library school more than the reference librarian of the university library. The salary schedule for trained librarians should be framed in accordance with the amount of exact qualifications in the way of liberal and professional training received, the length of successful experience in library service, and a certain amount of recognition accorded to meritorious work. In case a highly specialized librarian with very broad educational background and experience is needed as a reference librarian of a university departmental library, his salary should not be that of an ordinary departmental librarian, but that of a professor of a special subject. In short the exact qualifications of an individual should determine his rank and the amount of salary he is to receive, and it is not the type of position that should determine how much a person should be given. Of course, it is understood that the qualifications needed for every important position should be definitely defined. For instance, if the position of a university reference librarian requires higher qualifications in training, experience and meritorious work than those of an assistant professor of a university library school, the salary for the former should be larger than that of the latter. This method may be able to eliminate the existing difficulties of the salary problem between the instructional staff of a university library school and the professional staff of a university library.

The number of working hours and the length of vacations sometimes constitute another source of friction between the instructional staff of a library school and the professional staff of a university library though in certain instances the inequalities are more apparent than real. There is a big difference between the forty to forty-four hours weekly schedule of the professional library staff in comparison with the twelve to fifteen hours' class-work per week of a library school instructor.

One month's annual vacation for the former and three months' annual vacation for the latter add another issue to the debate over the unequal treatment of the trained professional assistants of a library in comparison with library school teachers.

On the other hand a full-time instructor sometimes has to spend more than forty hours per week in preparation for his teaching. Generally one hour's class-room lecture with preparation is considered at least the equivalent of two hours. Therefore, fifteen hours' class-room work per week will amount to about thirty hours. If we include time spent in individual conferences with students and in revising students' work, an instructor will probably devote more than forty hours per week to his teaching. But to a certain extent it is true that a teacher is freer in arranging his hours. A zealous teacher may devote much time and energy to conferring with his students and have great interest in watching their progress in a subject. He is not only a teacher in a professional subject but an example and adviser to the students in their conduct, thought and life. Therefore, a teacher's time cannot be quantitatively measured.

Regarding the annual vacation, it is a matter of insignificant difference. Some universities only pay their instructional staff ten months' salary for nine months' instructional service. The administrative staff of professional grade receives twelve months' salary for eleven months' work. Under such practice there is no injustice between the instructional staff of a university library school and the professional staff of a university library. In case the instructional staff of a university library school receives twelve months' salary for nine months' work, the professional staff of a university library should be remunerated accordingly.

In the matter of leaves of absence and other privileges there should be the same treatment for the instructional staff of a library school and the professional staff of a library. Although the question of salary, the number of office hours, vacation, and leave of absence are insignificant topics in view of the important mission and service of each professionally trained librarian in an educational institution, yet these small things are often very provoking. Therefore, an administrator on the one hand should attempt to eliminate as completely as possible such causes of irritation in his organization, and on the other hand should try to develop the *esprit de corps* of the professional staff of his library and of the instructional staff of his library school so that inevitable differences will cause a minimum of irritation.

The qualifications of the instructional staff of the library school at the State University of Iowa should at least be on a par with those of the other professional schools of the institution, if a library school is to be established here. The emphasis should be laid upon academic and professional training, practical experience, and ability to teach and to do research work. To be specific, the minimum qualifications of an instructor of a library school should be that he is a graduate of a standard university; a graduate from an approved graduate library school offering two years' professional library training; that he has had three years' successful experience in at least a medium sized library; and has done some creative work, either literary or bibliographical. The success of a library school depends upon the quality of the instructional staff. The responsibility of a teacher in a professional library school is great, for he must teach not only the mastery of professional technique but also the true meaning of library service so that the library school graduate can take his proper place in that group of professional workers which Dr. Learned has ingeniously characterized as "the new clergy of the mind," the "community's intelligence service."

SELECTED BIBLIOGRAPHY

Carlton, W. N. C. University and librarians. Public Libraries. 20:451-6. Dec. ,1915.

Lichtenstein, Walter. The question of a graduate library school. Library Journal. 43:233-5. April,1918.

Reece, Ernest J. Some possible development in library education. American Library Association. Chicago. 1924.

Tufts, James H. Education and training for social work.

Russell Sage Foundation. New York. 1923.

University of Minnesota. Hospital library service. School and Society. 19:304. Mar. 15,1924.

University of the State of Iowa. Summer courses in library training. (Bulletin n. s. No. 317). Iowa City. April 23,1925.

Van Hoesen, Henry B. More thoughts on training for librarianship. Library Journal. 49:360-1. April 15,1925.

Williamson Report. Comment from the library schools. Library Journal. 48:899-910. Nov. 1,1923.

CHAPTER XIII
REQUIREMENTS FOR ADMISSION, DEGREES AND CURRICULUM FOR A LIBRARY SCHOOL

A number of prominent librarians present at the meeting of the Board of Education for Librarianship in Chicago on April 16, 1925, favored a scheme proposing four grades of library schools. The requirements for admission to the first grade, "junior under-graduate library school,"① would be (1) a year's acceptable freshman studies in an approved college or university, (2) at least two months of satisfactory general experience in an approved library, or its equivalent, and (3) an aptitude and personal qualification for library work. The second grade of school, "senior under-graduate library school," would require items (2) and (3) of the "junior under-graduate library school," but item (1) concerning college education, would be raised to three years of acceptable work in an approved college or university instead of one year of freshman studies.

Both the junior and the senior under-graduate library schools would have the same one-year curriculum in library science. After the satisfactory completion of the professional studies of the year, the graduates of the "Junior Under-graduate Library School" would be given a certificate and the graduates of the "Senior Undergraduate Library School" a degree of A. B. and B. S. They would probably not lack employment by libraries and we assume that their remuneration would be in accordance with their academic standing, whether certificate-holders or diploma-holders.

This division of the under-graduate library school into the grades of junior and senior involves, perhaps, slightly ambiguous nomenclature. The ordinary academic use of "junior" is in reference to a student in the third year's college work, and the word is much less frequently applied to a college offering only two years' collegiate work (junior college). The "junior under-graduate library school" requires only one year of freshman work and another year of professional studies in library science. This much-discussed standard for a new professional senior under-graduate library school, then, does not much improve the standard of the existing one-year library schools. The only difference from the existing one-year "accredited" library schools is that it will not admit the mere high school graduate. According to the current reports of the existing "accredited" schools, high school graduates who are able to pass the entrance examinations successfully constitute only a small percentage among entering students.

The weakness of the new scheme lies in having no differentiation in *professional education* between the students of the junior and the senior under-graduate library schools. If the libraries recog-

---

① American Library Association. Provisional Minimum Standards for Library Schools. (Mimeographed by the Board of Education for Librarianship). This provisional document is not to be printed, and was distributed only for discussion by the members who were present at the meeting of April 16, 1925.

nize the distinction and pay the salary of a diploma-holder and of a certificate-holder on a different basis, will the two years of college education make so great a difference in the quality of professional work that any administrator will be justified in distinguishing quite materially in matters of salary and rank between the two grades of graduates? If the graduates of the "senior under-graduate library school" do not show decided superiority in professional work, a fair administrator will hesitate to make any distinction in salary and rank between the graduates of the junior and the senior school. This will eventually lead more students having one year of college work to enter the "junior school" and will discourage ambitious students of senior standing from entering the "senior school. " It will not be felt that two extra years of college education will yield a bigger financial return in the practice of the library profession. Furthermore we must remember that most of the professional schools in universities recruit students of junior that is, third-year standing. And it would place the "senior school" in a disadvantageous position in recruiting students if the "junior school" were to offer exactly the same curriculum of professional studies.

A scheme for an under-graduate library school of two years at the State University of Iowa was proposed in the last chapter. The requirements for admission are as follows: (1) two years of the standard course in liberal arts of an approved college or university, evidenced by a transcript of the college record, (2) two months of satisfactory experience in a medium-sized library, or its equivalent, (3) a reading knowledge of two foreign languages, (4) ability to use a typewriter.

In exceptional cases, applicants over twenty-five years of age who are high school graduates and have been successful library assistants in medium-sized libraries for five or more years, but who are unable to meet the full requirements of the first two years' college work, may be admitted by special permission of the faculty of the Library School and of the College of Liberal Arts upon presenting sufficient evidence of exceptional ability to justify such action. Applicants so admitted should have a probational period of one academic year. If the work and ability of such applicants at the end of the probational period prove to be above the average, they might then be permitted to carry on the work of the senior year. Applicants for admission under these conditions should be discouraged, as the requirement of two years of college education is based on the belief that this is for the best interests of the students as well as for the standards of the library profession. Therefore, all prospective applicants for the Library School are urged to equip themselves with the two years of preliminary education.

The degree of Bachelor of Arts or Bachelor of Science in Library Science is conferred upon the satisfactory completion of one hundred and twenty semester hours, exclusive of credits gained for military and physical training and for freshman lectures. In addition to the requirements of the freshman and sophomore years, the candidate must fulfill the specific requirements of thirty-four semester hours of the Library School Course. (See suggested curricula in Appendix I.) The twenty-eight semester hours for the junior and senior years may be elected, by arrangement, from courses of the College of Liberal Arts or of any of the other colleges and schools in this University, subject to the approval of the students' adviser in the Library School.

The Graduate School for librarianship, should require for admission (1) graduation with an A.

B. or B. S. degree in library science from an approved library school, (2) at least one year of first-class library experience. In exceptional cases candidates without the degree from an approved library school may be admitted for an advanced degree. This exception is provided in order not to close the doors of professional library education to the "original genius" type. Any exceptional candidate without the preliminary degree admitted to the Graduate Library School must amply substantiate his admittance by the excellence of his work.

If any experienced and prominent librarian with or without the first degree of an approved library school, does not desire to work for a degree, he may be admitted to elect any advanced courses for which he is prepared, and will be classified as a special student and not as a candidate for a degree.

In all the above cases, the head and the instructional staff of the Library School are held responsible for the arrangement and approval of the study-schedules of all the candidates admitted to the Graduate Library School. The head must study the qualifications of every individual student, observe the progress of his work in major and minor studies, and confer with him from time to time about his specialization and research.

Every candidate for the degree of M. A. or M. S. in library science shall satisfactorily complete twenty semester hours in professional library courses as his major and ten semester hours of other special and professional courses as his minor. For instance, one who desires to be a high school librarian can register his ten semester hours in the College of Education as his minor, in addition to his major studies in library science. A thesis or a bibliography showing independent scholarship, creative thought, and intensive study of a special topic in the realm of library science, shall be submitted. After passing successfully both written and oral final examinations and after the acceptance of the thesis by the graduate faculty, the degree of M. A. or M. S. in library science will be granted to the candidate.

The degree of Doctor of Philosophy will be open to the graduate students of the Library School. A student shall choose a program of study, subject to faculty approval, along the line of his special interest. He shall have a thorough knowledge of a special subject and also a marked capacity for research. The degree of Doctor of Philosophy shall be conferred upon a graduate student of the Library School in accordance with all the requirements and regulations of the Graduate College of this University governing the granting of this degree.

In studying the "Provisional Minimum Standards for Junior Under-graduate Library School, Senior Undergraduate Library School, Professional Library School and Graduate School of Librarianship" outlined by the Board of Education for Librarianship of the American Library Association, we have seen that divisions of the first two grades of library schools are somewhat ambiguously named and that the standards suggested are open to question. It may not be out of place to continue with a few remarks about the name and the standards suggested for the "professional library school" in connection with our present discussion of requirements and degrees for a graduate library school.

The requirements for admission to the "professional library school"② require (1) graduation from an approved college or university, (2) at least two months of satisfactory general experience in an approved library or its equivalent, and (3) aptitude and personal qualifications for library work, and demonstrated ability to pursue profitably the curriculum. Items (2) and (3) are the same as the requirements for admission to the junior and the senior under-graduate library schools. After the satisfactory completion of the professional study of the first year a certificate will be given to the candidate, and at the end of the second year a degree of Master of Arts or Master of Science will be granted.

The name "professional library school" is ambiguous. The word "professional" is a generic name and its range should include under-graduate as well as graduate library school. It is not for this particular grade of library training to monopolize the name "professional," otherwise the junior and the senior under-graduate library schools might be appropriately designated as sub-professional library schools, and the graduate school for librarianship might be spoken of as a super-professional library school.

If the "professional library school" is graduate in character, the curriculum of the first year should not be practically the same as that of the under-graduate library schools, but such work could better be a pre-requisite. Only candidates who are graduates from the standard library schools with A. B. or B. S. degrees in library science who have this pre-requisite should be admitted to carry on another year's study in advanced library courses and some specialized courses in other professional schools of a standard university. After the satisfactory completion of a year's specialized studies and the acceptance of a thesis or of a bibliography by the faculty, the degree of M. A. or M. S. in library science might be granted to the candidates.

The "provisional minimum standard" for the "professional library school" which demands one more year for the degree of M. A. or M. S. than the other graduate schools of American universities will prove most disadvantageous in recruiting graduate students. The curriculum of the first year has no more advanced quality and character than that of the under-graduate library schools. Prospective candidates for the degree of M. A. or M. S. will have the impression that the school is trying to raise its standard to that of a professional graduate school merely by incorporating an extra year's work.

The second item in the requirements for admission to the "professional library school" lays too little stress on practical experience. A year of general experience in a medium-sized or a large library should be required of every candidate who desires to enroll in a professional graduate library school for an advanced degree.

The entire scheme lacks any ascending features in the courses offered in the junior and the senior undergraduate library schools and the first year of the professional library school. The same professional curriculum of one year will be studied in three different schools supposed to provide

---

② American Library Association. Provisional Minimum Standards for Library Schools, (mimeographed by the Board of Education for Librarianship). This provisional document is not to be printed and was distributed only for discussion by the members who were present at the meeting of April 16, 1925.

three different grades of professional knowledge.

One of the main criticisms against the existing library schools of one year is that they put college graduates, college students, and high school graduates in the same classroom to pursue the same library studies. Now, the provisional scheme outlined by the Board of Education for Librarianship puts students of sophomore standing in the "junior under-graduate library school," students of senior standing in the "senior under-graduate library school," and college graduates in the "professional library school," but although these students with different educational background are separated, in three different schools, yet they study the same professional library course, for which they will receive different credentials namely, "junior under-graduate library school" certificate, "senior under-graduate library school" diploma of A. B. or B. S. in Library Science, and "professional library school" first year certificate.

The library profession needs to have a coordinated system of ascending character in professional education. The standards of the outstanding professional schools of law, medicine, engineering, teaching, and others are fixed according to the major factor of quality and scope of the professional studies given in the schools and the minor or auxiliary factor of general and cultural education involved in the system. Therefore, in formulating the standards of the two types of professional library schools, the successful principles followed by the other professional schools are worthy to be taken into careful consideration.

The writer has the belief that the Board of Education for Librarianship of the American Library Association is going to have a thorough revision of the provisional scheme outlined in the discussion by the librarians and educational experts at the meeting of April 16, 1925 at Chicago. Such experienced and scholarly educators as Dean Russell of Columbia University and such experts in curriculum construction as Professor W. W. Charters of the University of Chicago[3] are now asked to serve on the Board of Education for Librarianship as expert-advisers. So a workable scheme for library education in America may be anticipated. May the final scheme of the Board of Education for Librarianship form a solid foundation for professional library education for the future!

The curriculum of a library school—in fact any professional school—should be constructed with three fundamental aims, specialized knowledge, technical skill and. high ideals. Dean James Earl Russell of Columbia University emphasized the fundamental requisites of a curriculum for a professional school in his address delivered at the inauguration of Dr. Lotus D. Coffman as president of the University of Minnesota: "In its curriculum it should strive to organize and systematize the knowledge available in its particular field so that its students may get the essential facts needed at the beginning of their career; in its teaching it should give inspiration to creative effort and altruistic service; and at some stage of its training provision must be made for gaining technical skill. The pedagogical problems of all professional schools grow out of these three fundamental requisites. These factors, however, are all variable quantities. A professional school may be acceptable in general and yet be weak in one or more of these essentials. The ideals that guide the faculty may be

---

[3] Formerly of the University of Pittsburgh.

rightly conceived, and yet fail to function in the lives of students and graduates. The knowledge gained in course may be defective because of lack of scholarship on the part of instructors, want of intelligence in students, or through bad teaching. Technical skill may be purchased at too great a cost, or neglected to the point of leaving graduates helpless on entering their vocational employment. Right proportion in the adjustment of these essentials is the crux of administration in every type of professional school."④

The specialized knowledge of the library profession should be so organized and systematized that, within the minimum period of time, the maximum amount of the essential knowledge of the profession can be mastered. This means two definite things in the making of a curriculum, namely, (1) that it be not crowded with non-essential courses in professional subjects; (2) that emphasis be put upon the completion of pre-requisite courses for any advanced work. For example, a student in a graduate library school wishing to specialize in bibliographical cataloging should have a thorough knowledge of general cataloging as a pre-requisite.

As to technical skill we all know that every profession demands a certain amount of either manual or clerical work. For instance, in medicine, a skilled surgeon knows how to place a bandage when the interne or the nurse is not around. When and how much the teaching of technical skill should be introduced in the curriculum of a professional school is the keynote of the question.

The length of time spent on it, the nature of it, and the method of teaching technical skill vary in various professional schools. For instance, schools of law, medicine, and engineering give their students competent instruction in professional subjects and some instruction in technical skill, but leave them to acquire thorough technical skill in an office, a hospital or a machine-shop under the guidance and instruction of a skilled master. In other professions such as teaching, agriculture and social work, the graduates of the schools must make good the first day on the job. The writer feels that the library profession is similar to that of teaching, agriculture, and social work. Every library employing a library school graduate expects him or her to possess technical skill as well as specialized knowledge. Instruction imparting a certain amount of technical skill should surely be provided in the curriculum of a professional library school.

To build the curriculum of a professional school and include only the minimum essentials of specialized knowledge and technical skill without consideration of any of the interpretative subjects necessary for the cultivation of high ideals, is surely undesirable. Certain cultural subjects which will broaden the vision and stimulate ideals in human relationships should be included in the curriculum of a professional library school.

The importance of having cultural subjects in the curriculum of professional schools has been strongly emphasized by Professor V. T. Thayer of Ohio State University and Professor R. J. Leonard of Columbia. In his article "Training Teachers for the Profession of Teaching," Professor Thayer remarks: "Democracy is not opposed to specialization except as the latter is specialization and noth-

---

④ James Earl Russell. *University and Professional Training*, reprinted in his *Trend in American Education*. American Book Co. New York. 1922. p. 224-5.

ing else. Democratic education involves knowing and doing one thing well, but with a full appreciation of its intimate implications in a larger context. So a democratic system of teacher training involves that type of procedure which leads the teacher to specialize in her tasks but to bring into this specialization an enriched background. Thus will her daily duties continually take on new meaning and significance and her intellectual horizon constantly expand."⑤

Professor R. J. Leonard gives a special name to the group of cultural subjects in the curriculum of a professional school. He calls them "marginal responsibilities" in his article "Trends in Professional Education." He says: "To be appropriate for the professions, occupational analyses must include what may be characterized as *marginal responsibilities*. By way of contrast with *technical responsibilities* they are of a higher order, more remote and less concrete. But it is obvious that they have meaning and reality, and they are present in every profession. In the medical profession, they may be illustrated by the physician's responsibility to combat quackery and public exploitation by those improperly prepared, to promote social hygiene, sex education, and community health and recreation, and to use his matchless opportunities to foster home and family integrity. In business administration, we may mention business ethics, problems growing out of the increasing jurisdiction of state and nation in private enterprise, and questions arising from complex and involved international relations. In addition to these marginal responsibilities in all the professions there are the common problems of civic leadership which society has a right to expect from all graduates of professional schools."⑥

Those librarians, who are interested in the movement to reorganize professional library schools according to the principles which have successfully governed the development of some of the other professional schools, are naturally anxious to be certain as to the most essential specialized courses in library science, the irreducible minimum of technical skill, and the indispensable "marginal responsibilities" for cultural subjects, to be included in the ideal professional library school. About a decade ago, library school instructors and experienced librarians would probably have talked through a whole day's meeting and eloquently presented subject after subject. Everyone would have felt that this proposed subject was the most important and the most useful study for the student. Those who would have argued most convincingly would have been successful in having their proposed subjects adopted by the meeting. There was danger of this becoming the general practice in building up curricula of professional schools in former days. In 1925 however, experienced librarians and library school instructors can present their experiences and views to be considered as factors to determine "the functional point of view" of a curriculum, as Professor W. W. Charters acutely emphasized it in his talk, "Formulating Curricula Standards for Library Schools," at the April meeting of the Board of Education for Librarianship already mentioned.

The essential element in determining "the functional point of view" of the professional subjects

---

⑤ V. T. Thayer. Training Teachers for the Profession of Teaching. *School and Society*. 20: 676-7. November 29, 1924.

⑥ R. J. Leonard. Trends in Professional Education. *Teachers College Record*. 26: 182-3. November, 1924.

of library schools is to collect and to study facts and ideals. Then the functions of the subjects can be determined and the studies which will tend to realize the functions can be formulated. These methods of "job specifications" can even be carried into neighboring fields of cultural subjects. Professor Charters illuminates this point thus: "In the absence of definite methods for prescribing the extra-vocational material the tendency is to fall back upon those traditional subjects which appeal to any particular faculty. The difficulty is very well illustrated by the inquiry from a professional faculty as follows: ' We have arranged for all our professional curriculum except nine hours, which we have left for cultural subjects, and we should like to know what these should be. ' In this case consensus of opinion was used. But it is generally much better to analyze extra-vocational activities, and make eventual selection on the ground not of how many or how few hours a subject will require, but rather of how much it will be in the students' extra-vocational life."[7]

In spite of knowing the superior advantages in formulating curricula for library schools strictly in accordance with the scientifically objective method of occupational analysis, the writer feels compelled to follow the older traditional method and to formulate two curricula for a professional library school, including under-graduate and graduate studies, in the State University of Iowa. It is hoped that these curricula, which are the representative expression of only one man's training, experience, and study of the problems of training for professional librarianship, may be some slight assistance to the specialists who are going to collect the occupational facts and ideals of library service and to interpret them in terms of the functional theory of scientific curriculum construction for a professional library school.

SELECTED BIBLIOGRAPHY

Charters, W. W. Curriculum construction. Macmillan. New York. 1923.

Henry, W. E. A system of library schools. Library Journal. 49:347-9. April 15, 1925.

Kaiser, John Boynton. The special library and the library schools. Library Journal. 37:175-9. April, 1912.

Kaiser, John Boynton. Library school training for law library employees. Law Library Journal. 5: 52-3. July-Oct., 1912.

Leonard, Robert Josselyn[8]. Trends in professional education. Teachers College Record. 26:177-83. Nov., 1924.

Library Association of the United Kingdom. Syllabus of information on facilities for training in librarianship and the professional examination. Library Association. London. 1924.

Reese, Ernest J. Some possible developments in library education. American Library Association. Chicago. 1924.

Russell, James Earl. University and professional training, (reprinted *in* his Trend in American education. American Book Co. New York. 1922. p. 223-37).

Tai, T. C. An advanced school of librarianship—aim of curriculum. Public Libraries. 30:59-61. Feb., 1925.

Thayer, V. T. Training teachers for the profession of teaching. School and Society. 20:671-7. Nov. 29, 1924.

Tufts, James H. Education and training for social work. Russell Sage Foundation. New York. 1923.

---

⑦ W. W. Charters. *Curriculum Construction.* Macmillan. New York.

⑧ 【译者注】疑为 Joselyn。

英文著作

University of the State of Iowa. Catalogue including announcements, 1922-1925. Iowa City. 1922-1925.

University of Minnesota. Hospital library service. School and Society. 19:304. Mar. 15, 1924.

Williams, Reginald G. Courses of study in library science. Hopkins. Bolton. 1924.

Williamson, C. C. Library school curriculum. (*In* his Training for Library Service. New York. 1923. p. 12-15).

Windsor, Phineas L. Summer school credits in library schools. (*In* American library association. Meetings of the professional training section at the Forty-sixth annual conference of American library association. 1924. p. 10-14).

APPENDIX

APPENDIX I.　　SUGGESTED CURRICULA FOR BOTH GRADUATE AND UNDER-GRADUATE WORK IN THE LIBRARY SCHOOL

APPENDIX II.　　A PROPOSED BUDGET

APPENDIX I

SUGGESTED CURRICULUM FOR THE PROPOSED LIBRARY SCHOOL AT THE STATE UNIVERSITY OF IOWA

SUGGESTED CURRICULUM: A—FOR UNDER-GRADUATES

1. Each junior student must earn 32 semester hours credits in the junior year. Of these 18 semester hours must be in the Library School and 14 semester hours may be earned in any of the under-graduate courses of any of the colleges of the University for which the student is qualified.
2. Each senior student must earn 30 to 32 semester hours credits in the senior year. Credits of 16 to 18 semester hours must be gained in the Library School and credits of 14 semester hours may be earned in any of the under-graduate courses of any of the colleges of the University for which the student is qualified.
3. The courses other than library school courses elected from other colleges of the University should be subject to the approval of the faculty advisers of the Library School.

JUNIOR YEAR

	Credit Hours
I Library Courses	*1st Semester*
Lib. 1 Classification	2
Lib. 3 Cataloging	3
Lib. 5 Reference	2
Lib. 7 Library Technique	2
II Non-Professional Courses	
1 Modern Language	2
2 Electives from Other Colleges	5
	16
I Library Courses	*2d Semester*
Lib. 10 Bibliography	2
Lib. (4) Cataloging	2
Lib. (6) Reference	2
Lib. 12 Field Work	1
Lib. 14 American Library Movement... 2 hrs.	

Lib. 16 Selection of Books⋯⋯⋯⋯⋯2 hrs.
Lib. 18 Library Administration⋯⋯⋯⋯⋯2 hrs.
  (2 semester hours must be elected from this group)   2
 II Non-Professional Courses   *Credit Hours*
  1 Modern Language   2
  2 Electives From Other Colleges   5
                           ―
                           16

SENIOR YEAR

Credit Hours

 I Library Courses   *1st Semester*
Lib. 31 Bibliography   3
Lib. 33 Field Work   1
Lib. 35 *Classification⋯⋯⋯⋯⋯2 hrs.
Lib. 37 *Reference⋯⋯⋯⋯⋯⋯⋯2 hrs.
Lib. 39 *Selection of Books⋯⋯⋯3 hrs.
Lib. 41 *Work with Children⋯⋯⋯2 hrs.
Lib. 43 *Cataloging ⋯⋯⋯⋯⋯⋯⋯2 hrs.
  (4-5 semester hours must be elected from this group)   4-5
 II Non-Professional Courses
  3 Electives From Other Colleges   7
                           ―
                          15-16

 I Library Courses   *2d Semester*
Lib. 46 History of Libraries   2
Lib. 48 Printing and Binding   2
Lib. 18 Library Administration⋯⋯⋯⋯2 hrs.
Lib. (38) Reference⋯⋯⋯⋯⋯⋯⋯⋯⋯2 hrs.
Lib. (44) Cataloging⋯⋯⋯⋯⋯⋯⋯⋯⋯2 hrs.
Lib. (42) Work with Children⋯⋯⋯⋯⋯2 hrs.
Lib. 50 Library Extension⋯⋯⋯⋯⋯⋯1 hrs.
  (4-5 semester hours must be elected from this group)   4-5
 II Non-Professional Courses
  3 Electives From Other Colleges   7
                           ―
                          15-16

---

① * Courses marked with an asterisk are electives

SUGGESTED CURRICULUM: B—FOR GRADUATES

1. Candidates for the advanced degree of M. A. or M. S. in Library Science should fulfill all the requirements of the Graduate College and present

   credits of 30 semester hours. Credits of 20 semester hours must be earned in the graduate department of the Library School and credits of 10 semester hours may be earned in any graduate department of the University.

2. Candidates for the degree of Doctor of Philosophy are required to take at least 60 semester hours after receiving the advanced degree of M. A. or M. S. in Library Science. Credits to the amount of 40 semester hours should be gained in the graduate department of the Library School and credits to the amount of 20 semester hours may be gained in any graduate department of the University. Approximately one-third to one-half of the 40 semester hours in the Library School may be devoted to work on a dissertation, or a complete or select bibliography of a particular subject or author. The bibliography should involve work comparable to that involved in preparing a dissertation for the degree of Doctor of Philosophy. As to the other requirements and conditions for the degree of Doctor of Philosophy, see the detailed regulations of the Graduate College.

3. The minors elected from other departments of the University should be subject to the approval of the faculty advisers of the Library School.

OUTLINES OF COURSES FOR GRADUATES

   I Library Courses

Lib. 201(202) Advanced Library Administration,

  Individual Instruction   2-20 hrs.

  e. Large Public Libraries and County Libraries

  f. High School Libraries

  g. College and University Libraries

  h. Business Libraries

  i. Special Libraries (a) Medical, (b) Hospital, (c) Law, (d) Engineering, (e) Scientific, (f) Educational

Lib. 203(204) Special Subject Bibliography Individual Instruction   2 hrs.

Lib. 205(206) Prints and Book Illustration   2 hrs.

Lib. 207(208) History of Scholarship   3 hrs.

Lib. 209(210) Paleography and Diplomatics   3 hrs.

Lib. 211(212) Advanced Cataloging   2 hrs.

Lib. 213(214) Library School Teaching   3 hrs.

Lib. 215(216) Bibliographical Problems   2 hrs.

DESCRIPTION OF COURSES

Lib. 1 *Classification.* Junior. 1st semester 2 hrs.

A study of the principles of book classification. Particular attention is given to the Dewey Decimal System and its various modifications. Practice in assigning book numbers and practice work in classifying lists of books required throughout the semester.

Lib. 35 *Classification.* Senior. 1st semester 2 hrs.

A hasty review of the principles underlying Decimal Classification will be given at the beginning of the course. Comparative study of different systems of book classification and their schemes of notation will be discussed. Special emphasis laid on the system of the Library of Congress, The Brussels Institute, on Cutter's Expansive Classification and on Brown's Subject Classification. During the course the necessary differences between a classification for books in libraries and a theoretical classification of all knowledge will be discussed.

Lib. 3 (4) *Cataloging.* Junior. 1st semester 3 hrs.

Junior. 2nd semester 2 hrs.

Lectures, problems and practice work confined to the making of a catalog. Assigning subject headings and the use of cross references studied as problems of cataloging. Using and ordering Library of Congress printed catalog cards and shelf-listing are included. Each student is required to make a sample dictionary catalog of 200 books.

Lib. 43 (44) *Cataloging.* Senior. 1st and 2nd semester 2 hrs.

Lectures, problems and practice work giving consideration to the classed catalog; followed by the cataloging of Federal and municipal documents, pamphlets and sheet music. Students who elect this course must have as a pre-requisite Cataloging Lib. 3(4)

Lib. 5 (6) *Reference.* Junior. 1st and 2nd semester 2 hrs.

A study of general and special encyclopedias, dictionaries, annuals, year-books, atlases and indexes to periodicals. Familiarity in using general and special reference books and a knowledge of their relative importance are emphasized. Exercises in the use of reference books follow each lecture.

Lib. 37 (38) *Reference.* Senior. 1st and 2nd semester 2 hrs.

This course is to prepare students especially for the problems of the reference departments of college, university and large public libraries. It includes a study of publications of learned societies, dissertations, indexes to foreign periodicals and government publications. Administration of a reference department and the compilation of reference lists and bibliographies are discussed in detail.

Lib. 7 *Library Technique.* Junior. 1st semester 2 hrs.

Principal topics: Alphabeting, loan systems, inventory, checking of periodicals, care of pamphlets and clippings, order and accession work and library labor-saving devices.

Lib. 12 (33) *Field Work.* Junior. 2nd semester 1 hr.

Senior. 1st semester 1 hr.

Carefully graded and closely supervised field work will be assigned to the junior and senior students in every department of the University libraries and the City Public Library. Three hours' field work per week throughout a semester is equivalent to one semester hour's credit.

Lib. 10 *Bibliography.* Junior. 2nd. semester 2 hrs.

Lectures and problems on American, English, French, Italian, German, and Scandinavian national and trade bibliography. Students are required to compile a selected list of bibliographies for a medium sized public library.

Lib. 31 *Bibliography.* Senior. 1st semester 3 hrs.

Lectures and problems on subject bibliographies of the scholarly, monumental type. Scope, limitations, and utility of subject bibliography are fully discussed.

Lib. 14 *American Library Movement.* Junior. 2nd semester 2 hrs.

A study of the development, organization, personnel, characteristics and tendencies of library work in the United States. Includes a bird's-eye-view of different types of libraries, library associations, library commissions and library training agencies.

Lib. 16 *Selection of Books.* Junior. 2nd semester 2 hrs.

Aims to cultivate students' power of judging books as to their value and adaptability to various types of libraries and readers. Comparison of translations of the classics and foreign fiction, series and editions. The writing of book-notes and book reviews required. Careful examination and rapid reading of books on a wide range of subjects emphasized.

Lib. 39 *Selection of Books.* Senior. 1st semester 3 hrs.

Similar to selection of books Lib. 16. An analytical survey of modern and contemporary drama, poetry, fiction, essays, science, technology and philosophy, from the viewpoint of selecting books for libraries. Checking *Publishers' Weekly*, *Publishers' Circular*, *Booklist*, *Book Review Digest* and second-hand and bargain catalog of book-dealers required as demonstration work in the problems of selecting books for different types of libraries.

Lib. 18 *Library Administration.* Junior and Senior. 2d semester 2 hrs.

Lectures, problems and required reading. Principal topics; library buildings, library budget, accounts and book-keeping, personnel problems, publicity, library and community, library supplies, statistics, annual reports, boards of trustees and other administrative problems.

Lib. 41 (42) *Work with Children.* Senior. 1st and 2nd semester 2 hrs.

A course in three parts. Part I. Lectures and readings on the organization and administration of children's rooms. Special attention given to the collateral school reading of the children. Part II. Determine the principles of book selection for children by a comparative study of different types of children's books and juvenile literature. Part III. Principles of the art of story-telling. Students are supplied with opportunities to practice story-telling to children.

Lib. 46 *History of Libraries.* Senior. 2nd semester 2 hrs.

Lectures and required reading. This extensive course includes ancient, medieval and modern libraries with special attention to their collectors and keepers, and to their management and buildings.

Lib. 48 *Printing and Binding.* Senior. 2nd semester 2 hrs.

This course has two parts. Part I. Printing, including technical terms, hand and machine composition, specifications, paper, design, illustration and proofreading. Aims to make students understand intelligently the processes of printing. Lectures, problems, and required reading, are supplemented by inspections of printing plants. Part II. Binding, including technical processes, binding materials, rebinding, mending, binding records, appearance and cost. Lectures and required readings are supplemented by visits to a bindery.

Lib. 50 *Library Extension.* Senior. 2nd semester 1 hr.

Study of methods and problems of branch libraries, deposit stations, rural libraries, travelling libraries, rural delivery by book automobile, and smaller agencies. Lectures, discussions and required reading.

Lib. 201 (202) *Advanced Library Administration. Individual Instruction.* Graduates. 1st and 2nd semester 2-20 hrs.

This course is designed to give prospective library administrators as much training as their time and ability permit. Any student may study intensively any type of library administration by individual instruction in the following types:

1. Large Public Libraries and County Libraries.
2. High School Libraries.
3. College and University Libraries.
4. Business Libraries including industrial libraries.
5. Special Libraries including.
   (a) Medical libraries.
   (b) Hospital libraries.
   (c) Law libraries.
   (d) Engineering libraries.
   (e) Scientific libraries.
   (f) Educational libraries.

Lib. 203 (204) *Special Subject Bibliography. Individual Instruction.* Graduates. 1st and 2nd semester 2 hrs.

This course is planned to train the student through familiarity with the important sources of information on any subject or subjects which are closely connected with the type of advanced library administration in which he specializes. Every individual case will be specially arranged by the head of the library school with the deans and heads of other departments. It may be taken preferably in connection with a subject given by a professional college or a school of the University.

Lib. 205 (206) *Prints and Book-Illustration.* Graduates, 1st and 2nd semester 2 hrs.

This course has three distinctive parts. Part I. Lectures and discussions on the early history and development of writing materials such as papyrus and vellum, and paper making. Part II. A study of block books, movable type and the evolution of the printed book from manuscript forms. Lectures and required reading on the spread of printing in Germany, Italy, France, Holland, Spain and England with emphasis on the great printers of different periods. Part III. An extensive study covering early woodcuts, engravings, etchings, mezzotint, line engraving and lithography for book illustration. The lives of the leading illustrators are also included.

Lib. 207(208) *History of Scholarship.* Graduates. 1st and 2nd semester 3 hrs.

This extensive course is designed to train students through familiarity with the history of scholarship of six different groups: Latin, Greek, Biblical, Teutonic, Celtic and Romance Scholarship. Lectures and required readings.

Lib. 209(210) *Paleography and Diplomatics.* Graduates. 1st and 2nd semester 3 hrs.

This course is designed to meet the needs of those who wish to study problems in the origin and classification of writing, manuscripts, technical chronology, numismatics, sigillography and medieval linguistics.

Lib. 211(212) *Advanced Cataloging.* Graduates. 1st and 2nd semester 2 hrs.

Comparative study of cataloging rules and methods. Administrative problems of a large catalog department. Cataloging incunabula, collections of coins, pottery, bronze, pictures, jewelry and other miscellaneous objects and curios, is the main practice work. No regular library school student is permitted to elect this course, unless he has as pre-requisites Cataloging Lib. 3(4) and Lib. 43(44).

Lib. 213(214) *Library School Teaching.* Graduates. 1st and 2nd semester 3 hrs.

This course aims to train students to be library school instructors. Emphasis is laid upon (1) methods and preparation of subject-matter, (2) selection and organization of the content to be taught, (3) testing or measuring results, (4) principles of teaching chiefly applied to library schools. Any library school graduate student who aims to be a library school teacher is required to take his minor in the College of Education.

Lib. 215(216) *Bibliographic Problems.* Graduates. 1st and 2nd semester 2 hrs.

A complete or select bibliography of a particular subject or author. The result should be comparable to a master's thesis. The mere fulfilment of two credit hours throughout the year spent in its preparation is not the primary basis for acceptance. It is required of any candidate for an advanced degree of M. A. or M. S. in Library Science who does not elect to prepare a thesis as an alternative. The subject chosen should be subject to the approval of the head of the Library School.

The non-professional and professional courses of other colleges, schools and departments of the University, see the Catalog of the University of Iowa.

APPENDIX II

A BUDGET FOR THE PROPOSED LIBRARY SCHOOL AT THE UNIVERSITY OF IOWA

The proposed budget consists of two divisions. Division A, with its four main sub-divisions, is an annual budget. Division B is a budget estimate for initial outlay.

The proposal for salaries for the administrative and instructional staff suggests the minimum and maximum in each case but no suggestion is made for an automatic or regular yearly increase.

In Division B the proposal for initial capital outlay assumes that the Library School will have all new equipment except the present collection of books on library science. Were the furniture already available, the amount for initial capital outlay would be correspondingly reduced. The number of chairs, desks, and other equipment is based on an estimate of fifty students and about six full-time and seven part-time members of the instructional and administrative staff.

A Proposed Budget for the Suggested Library School at the State University of Iowa

A: PROPOSED ANNUAL BUDGET

I. Personnel Service—Salaries

1	Administration Director	$2,000-$3,000①
1	Executive Secretary	1,800-2,500
1	Stenographer and Clerk	1,020-1,500
	Other Assistance	600-1,200
	Sub-total	$5,420-$8,200

2. Instruction

1	Associate Professor	$3,000-$4,000	
1	Assistant Professor	2,400-3,600	
2	Instructors ($2,000-$2,800)x2	4,000-5,600	
4	Part-time Instructors	($900-$1,100)x4	3,600-4,400
	Lecturers	1,000-1,000	
2	Part-time Revisers ($960-$1,200)x2	1,920-2,400	

---

① The Director of the University Library concurrently acts as the Director of the Library School and gets an additional minimum salary of $2,000 a year from the Library School budget.

Sub-total	$15,920- $21,000

II. Service Other Than Personnel

1	Transportation (for lecturers, trips for investigation, attending conferences, etc.)	$2,000
2	Telegraph	100
3	Telephone	100
4	Postage	200
5	Printing	200
6	Binding theses, reports, etc	200
7	Other expenses	500
	Sub-total	$3,300

III. Equipment

1. Books	$1,500
2. Periodicals, including binding	150
3. Other expenses	500
Sub-total	$2,150

IV. Supplies

1. Office stationery	$800
2. Other expenses	200
Sub-total	$1,000

B: BUDGET ESTIMATES FOR INITIAL CAPITAL OUTLAY

70	Office desks	$2,800
70	Desk chairs	900
24	Chairs	170
70	3-section bookshelves (3 ft. x 3.5 ft.)	800
10	6-section bookshelves (3 ft. x 7 ft.)	200
20	Typewriters	2,100
1	Adding machine with stand	420
10	Steel vertical filing cabinets	780
10	dozen pasteboard pamphlet boxes	30
	Additional books and periodicals of bibliography and library science	2,000
	Other equipment	1,000
	Total	$11,200

SUMMARY

A: Proposed Annual Budget

    I. Personnel Service—Salaries

        1. Administration—Sub-total $5,420- $8,200

        2. Instruction—Sub-total   15,920-21,000

    II. Services other than Personnel   3,300-3,300

    III. Equipment—Sub-total   2,150-2,150

    IV. Supplies—Sub-total   1,000-1,000

    Total $27,790- $35,650

B: Budget Estimates for Initial Capital

    OUTLAY   11,200-11,200

    Grand Total $38,990- $46,850

INDEX

Absence, Leave of, 211

Academic affiliation of library schools, 159-61

"Accredited" library schools, 216

Adams, C. F. 18-19, 24

Adams, John, 37

Administration, Library, Courses in, 242-3

Administration of a library, 106-7

Administration of library schools in universities, 204; difficulties, 206

Administrative librarians, grades, 9

Admission requirements, to graduate school of librarianship, 218-19; professional library school, 220-1; University of Iowa, proposed library school, 217

Advanced education for librarianship, 101

"*Advis pour dresser une biblioiheque*," by G. Naudé, 103

Advocates in Edinburgh, Library of, 105

Affiliation of university and library schools, 181; difficulties, 194

Albany Library School. *See* New York State Library School

Alexandria, Library of the School of, 78

Alexandrian libraries, 78; catalog, 79

Ambrose, Lodilla, 117, 131

America, Library training in, 125-30

American Committee for Devastated France, 122, 158

American Library Association, 4, 114, 130; accomplishments, 63; conducts American Library School in Paris, 122; guiding spirit of the profession, 147; influence, 64; members, 62, 147; organized and chartered, 59; principles, 62; publications, 64; Professional Training Section, 148

American Library Association Board (proposed), 148

American Library Association Council, 129

American Library Institute, 60-1

American library movement, Course in, 241

American Library School in Paris, 122

American type of library, 137

Amherst College Library, statistics, 32

Anderson, E. H., 157-8, 161, 176

Apollonius, 78

Appropriation for books, 21, 46-7

① 【编者注】索引页码为原书页码,即本书的边码。

Archives, 72; Chinese, 74
Aristonymus, 78, 79 Aristophanes of Byzantium, 78, 80
Armour Institute of Technology, library training class, 127
Armstrong College, 123
Assistants, grades, 9; training, 119, 128
Association of American Library Schools, 127-8, 194
Association of American Universities, 204
Association of Library Schools, 149.
Association of Philologists and Educators in Dresden, 115
Assur-bani-pal, 76
Assyrian libraries, 76
Astor, J. J., 54
Atlanta Library School, entrance requirements, 162
Augustinians, 91, 92, 94
Augustus, Emperor, 83
Augustus, Library of the Temple of, 78
Austria, Library training in, 120
Authorship, 100
Axon, W. F. A., 108

Babcock, K. C., 143, 152
Babcock, L. E., 51
Babylonian libraries, 76
Bagni, Cardinal, de, 102
Baker, E. A., 57, 58, 116-17, 125, 131
Baldwin, E. V., 176
Baltimore Public Library, 54
Balzani, Ugo, 131
Barberini, Francesco, Cardinal, 102
Bargaining for books, 102
Bates, Joshua, 54
Bates College Library, statistics, 32
Beloit College Library, statistics, 34
Benedict, Saint, Order of, 91; library rules, 92-3
Bequests. *See* Donations
Bergson, Henri, 150
Bibliographic problems, Course in, 246
Bibliographical librarians, grades, 9
Bibliographical method, Instruction in, 143

Bibliography, 78, 98, 101, 116; courses in, 241; individual instruction in special subjects, 244

Bicknell, P. F., 37

Billings, J. S., 51

Binding, Course in, 243

Bishop, W. W., 51

Board of Education for Librarianship, 7-8, 130, 150, 172-3, 194, 204, 220; report, 1, 8; standards (provisional) for library schools, 195; scheme proposing four grades for library schools, 215-19

Bogle, Sarah, 148, 152

"Bone-book," 74

Bonghi, Ruggero, 121

Bonn, University of, 117; training school for librarians, 115

Book-illustration, Course in, 244

Book selection, 44; courses in, 241-2

"Book worm" type of librarian, 111

Books, Arrangement of, 97; care of, 91, 96

Boston Medical Library, 47

Boston Public Library, 23, 54

Bostwick, A. E., 24, 55, 58, 66, 127-8, 131, 176

Bowdoin College Library, statistics, 32

Boxer indemnity funds, 2

Boyd, C. E., 81, 83, 88 Bramback, Wilhelm, 118

Brett, W. H., 66

Brown, J. D., 103, 108

Brown University Library, statistics, 34

Brucheion, Library of the, 78

Budget for the proposed Library School at the University of Iowa, (appendix II), 247-9

Buell, D. C., 152

Buffalo, University of, 163

Buildings, Library, 54

Bureau of Personnel Administration, 130

Business libraries, 48-9

California, University of, Department of Library Science, entrance requirements, 163; Library, statistics, 32

Callimachus, 78, 79, 85

Camper, E. L., 131

Canfield, J. H., 37

Capen, S. P., 196

Carlton, W. N. C., 37, 196, 202-3, 213

Carnegie, Andrew, 54-5, 56, 58
Carnegie Corporation, 142, 158
Carnegie Library School of Pittsburgh, foreign students, 157; entrance requirements, 162
Carrells, 98
Carthusians, 92
Cataloging, 98, 138; courses in, 239, 245
Catalogs, 78, 86, 104; monastic, 97
Cathedral libraries, 99
Centenial Exposition of 1876, 17
Certain, C. C., 186, 196
Certification and Library Training, National Committee on, 129, 149
Certification of librarians, requirements in England, 124; laws, 129
Challenge for libraries and library training agencies, 12
Chamberlain, Mellon, 24
Changing conceptions of librarianship, (chapter), 135-51; bibliography 152-4
Charleston, College of, Library, statistics, 34
Charters, W. W., 228, 230
Chautauqua School for Librarians, entrance requirements, 162
Chicago Public Library, 45
Chicago University, Committee on the Future Policy of the University Libraries, 143
Chicago University Library, statistics, 32
Children, Work with, Course in, 242
China, library school, 158
Chinese archives, 74
Chinese Educational Mission, 2-3
Chinese General Chamber of Commerce, 4
Chinese librarians, 74, 75-6
Chinese libraries, 57, 74
Chinese Library Association, 4
Chinese National Association for the Advancement of Education, Library Science Section, 4
Chinese National Library, Organization Committee, 4
Christina, Queen of Sweden, 102
Cincinnati, University of, Library, statistics, 33
Circulation, 92
Cistercians, 91, 92
City libraries, 23
Clark, J. W., 85-6, 88, 92, 93-4, 95-6, 98, 108
Clarke, A., 108
Classification, 78, 85, 97; courses in, 238-9; for special libraries, 145

Classification of library positions,9-10

Clergymen as librarians,101

Clerical service,9

Clerical training,94

Cleveland Foundation,11

Clinton,De Witt,21

Cloister libraries,98-9

Cluniacs,92

Colby University Library,statistics,32

College Librarians,Eastern,Conference of,143

College libraries,29;growth,99;growth(statistics),31-5;origin of rules,92

College of the City of New York,Library,statistics,33

Colleges,Library courses in,118,129,201

Columbia College,School of Library Economy,126, 147.155

Columbia University Library,statistics,33

Compton,C. H. ,37,196

Compulsory school attendance,18 Conferences for library instruction,129

Confucius,74-5

Cornell University Library,statistics,33

Correspondence courses,123,129

Coulter,E. M. ,160,176

Courses of study for librarians,Germany,119-20

Courses of study in library schools,115,128;graduate,237-46;undergraduate,235-7

Craig,F. M. ,196

Criticism of library schools,159,222

Curriculum,Library school,124-5,166-8,228;suggested for proposed library school at University of Iowa,(appendix I)235-46

Curtis,F. R. ,176

Custodial service,9

Custodians,Royal Chinese,75

Cultural subjects,226

Cutter,C. A. ,126

Cutter,W. P. ,192,196

Dana,J. C. ,24,42-3,51,62,66,108,131

Dartmouth College Library,statistics,33

Davis,R. C. ,126

Degrees,Advanced,requirements,219-20,237

Degrees of B. A. and B. S. in Library Science,requirements,218

Delisle, Leopold, 122, 131
Democracy in the free library movement, 101
Democratic education, Need of, 18
Democratic ideal of education, (chapter), 17-23; bibliography, 24-6
Departmental libraries, 29
Des Houssayes, J. -B. C. , 101, 106-7, 108
Devastation of monastic libraries, 100
Development of libraries, 44, 53, 99
Dewey, Melvil, 20, 21, 24, 66, 125-6, 131, 141, 147, 155
Dickinson College Library, statistics, 34
Diplomatics, Course in, 245
Director of university library as head of library school, 205-6; salary, 247
District of Columbia Library Association, 9
Division of studies in library schools, 205
Doctor of philosophy, degree, 220 *Doctor perplexorum*, 11
Documents, Chinese, 74
Donations, 53, 56, 57
Donnelly, J. R. , 152, 177
Drexel Institute, School of Library Science, 126; entrance requirements, 162
Dudgeon, M. S. , 51, 153, 197
Duties of librarian, 93
Dynamic type of special library, 48-50
Durie, John, 101
Dziatzko, Karl, 115, 117, 118, 131

Ebert, F. A. , 112
Ecole des Chartes, 122
Education for Librarianship, Board of, *See* Board of Education for Librarianship
Education for librarianship a fourfold problem, 10
Education of the masses, 18, 21, 54-5; in China, 11-12
Educational awakening in America, 18
Educational requirements for librarianship, (chapter), 135-51; bibliography, 152-4
Edwards, Edward, 78-80, 88, 97, 100, 108 Edwards, Passamore, 56
Egyptian libraries, 72, 77
Emerson, R. W. , 12
Employment agency for library assistants, 61
England, Library training in, 122-5
Entrance requirements in library schools, 161-6
Eratosthenes, 78

Euphorion of Chalcis, 81

Evans, H. R., 131, 153

Evelyn, John, 103

Examination Commission, 116, 118

Examinations for librarianship, 165; Austria, 120; England, 122-3; France, 121-2; Germany, 119-20; Italy, 120-1.

Experience, Stress on, 222

Extension courses, 129

Extension, Library, Course in, 243

Fairchild, S. C., 153

Fick, R., 115-16, 117

Field work, 240

Fizelière, Albert de la, 104

Fletcher, W. I., 37

Foreign students in library schools in America, 156

Foster, W. E., 24

France, Library training in, 121-2

Franklin, Benjamin, 53

Franklin and Marshall College Library, statistics, 34

Free library service, 104

Free public libraries, 55, 111

Freiburg, University of, 114

French Commission, 17

Friedel, J. H., 67, 132, 137-8, 144-5, 153.

Functions of library, 11, 57

Functions of subjects in library school, 228

Future librarian, Expectation of, 142

Gardthausen, Victor, 79, 82, 88, 106, 108, 117, 132

Garnett, Richard, 108

Gellius, Aulus, 86

Georgetown University Library, statistics, 32

Georgia, University of, Library, statistics, 32

German Librarians' Conference at Dresden, 115

German libraries, Proposed organization of, 114

German Printers' Association, 120

German universities, Influence of, 29

Germany, Library training in, 113-20

Gibson, Strickland, 108

Gifts. *See* Donations

Gilbert, C. B. , 24

Gill, Theodore, 47-8, 51

Glenn, F. M. , 132

Godard, G. S. , 45-6, 51

Goodall, Walter, 105

Göttingen University, Library training at, 115-17, 155

Grades in library service, 9-10

Grades of library schools, 215

Graesel, Arnin, 114, 117, 132

Graduate library school, curriculum, 237-8; entrance requirements, 218-19; scope, 191

Granniss, R. S. , 104-5

Great Britain Library Association. *See* Library Association of the United Kingdom

Green, S. S. , 20, 24-5, 126

Griswold, S. B. , 51

Growth of libraries, college and university, 31-5, 99; public, 56; monastic, 91; state and special, 45

Guild, R. A. , 37

Hadley, A. T. , 37

Hadley, C. , 67

Hamilton College Library, statistics, 33 Harper, W. R. , 36, 37

Harvard College Library, 30

Harvard University Library, statistics, 32

Hasse, A. R. , 153

Haverford College Library, statistics, 34

Hedrick, E. A. , 197

Henry, W. E. , 153, 171-2, 230

Herbert, C. A. , 153

High school librarians, qualifications, . 185-7

History of libraries, Course in, 242

Hitchler, Theresa, 153

Hoag, J. P. , 25

Homer, 78

Hospital library service, Library school for, 200

Hottinger's Library School for Women, Berlin, 132

Hours, college library, 30-1; library school instructors, 210

Howes, H. A. , 25

Hua, Tsing, 6

Huguenot movement, 99

Hume, David, 101, 105
Hyginus, C. J., 83

Ideals, High, Cultivation of, 225
Iles, George, 67
Illinois, University of, Library School, 127; entrance requirements, 163; foreign students, 157
Illustration of books, Course in, 244
Improvement, Movement for, 139
Indiana University Library, statistics, 32
Individual instruction, 243-4
Inge, W. R., 141
Institute for Government Research, 130
Institutions of learning, Libraries of, 91
International Librarians Conference, London, 59
International library school, projected, 121
Interpretive material, 64
Iowa, State University of, Library, statistics, 32
Iowa, State University of, Library School (proposed), (chapter), 199-213; bibliography 214; budget, 247-9; purpose, 204-5; qualifications of instructors, 211-12; suggested curriculum, (appendix I) 235-46; summary of proposal, 7
Italy, Library training in, 120-1

Jessup, W. A., 6
Jesus College, 97
Jewett, C. C., 59, 111
Job analysis, 11, 130
John Crerar Library, 44
John Rylands Library, 123
Johns Hopkins University Library, 35
Johnston, W. D., 37
Jones, J. W., 59-60, 67
Josephson, A. G. S., 188, 197
Junior under-graduate library school, 215-16

Kaiser, J. B., (introduction), 1-12; 115, 117, 197, 230
Kansai Bunko Kyokai, 60
Kempis, Thomas à, 96
Keogh, Andrew, 148, 153, 165, 177
Kirkwood, James, 101, 109

Klette, Anton, 113
Koch, T. W. , 30-1, 37, 58. 97, 109

Lafayette College Library, statistics, 34
Lanfranc, Archbishop of Canterbury, 93, 99
Laotse, first Chinese librarian, 57, 74
Lapp, J. A. , 50, 51
Laufer, Berthold, 76, 88
Law, Massachusetts school district library, 22; compulsory school attendance, Massachusetts, 18; regarding certification of librarians, 129
Leadership in administration, Training for, 191-2
Learned, W. S. , 11, 54, 58, 63, 67, 142, 153
Learned institutions, Libraries of, 105
Lecture courses, Germany, 120
Lee, G. W. , 51
Leeds University, 123
Leipzig University, Library courses in, 119-20
Lending books, 86, 92
Leningrad, Library of, 79
Lenox, James, 54
Leonard, R. J. , 8, 183-5, 190-1, 197, 226-7, 230
Lessing, G. E. , 101, 106
Levels applied to librarianship, 8
Liberal education, 135-6
Librarians, Demand for, 1, 11, 111-12; early definition, 71-2; modern standards, 112; monks as librarians, 91; priestly type supplanted by learned teachers, 77; qualifications, 106; relation to the community and to the individual, 11; service, 56, 62, 77
Librarians, Ancient, (chapter) 71-87; bibliography, 88-9; duties, 77; qualifications, 77
Librarians, High school, qualifications, 185-7
Librarians, Medieval and early modern, (chapter), 91-107; bibliography, 108-9
Librarianship, Changing conceptions of, (chapter), 135-51; bibliography, 152-4
Libraries, Early definition of, 71-2; first treatise on, 103; relation to social education, 11
Library, American type of, 137
Library administration, Chinese, 76
Library assistants in university, rank, 207
Library Association of the United Kingdom, 59, 122
Library associations, (chapter), 59-65; bibliography, 66-7
Library clubs, 60
Library conferences, 129

Library economy, 93, 101
Library institutes, 129
Library management, 81
Library movement, 91, 100, 125-6
Library of Congress, 46-7
Library Organization and Equipment, Committee on, 185-6
Library School in Paris. *See* American Library School in Paris
Library school(proposed), University of Iowa, (chapter), 199-212; bibliography, 213; budget, 247-9; entrance requirements, 217-19; suggested curriculum, 235-46
Library schools, academic affiliation, 159-61; American, (chapter), 155-78; criticism, 94, 159, 191, 222; curriculum, 166-8, 223-7; distribution, 199; entrance requirements, 161-6; expectation of, 142; finances of, 189. 247-9; first, 147-8, 155; foreign, 113-25; foreign students in American library schools, 156; graduates, 11, 144-6; professional education, 170-2; grades of, 215; quality of professional training offered, 159; re-adjustment, 190-1; staff, 168-70; standardization, 172-5; technical training, 170-2; weak spot in, 193-4
Library Schools, Association of, 149
Library schools and universities. *See* Universities and library schools
Library science, 114; professorship created at Göttingen, 115
Library technique, Course in, 240
Library training, (chapter), 111-30; bibliography, 131-4; in foreign countries, 113-25; in United States, 125-30; standardization, 172-4
Library Training Board. *See* Temporary Library Training Board
Library War Service, American Library Association, 5-6
Library work, Division of, 9
Library Workers' Association, 60-2, 67
Lichenstein, Walter, 207-8, 213
Lick, James, 54
Lipsius, Justus, 88
Logan, James, 53
London, University of, 124
London School of Economics, 123
Los Angeles Public Library, Library School, entrance requirements, 163
Lowrey, C. E., 27, 37 Lydenberg, H. M., 58

M. A. degree in library science, requirements, 219, 237
M. S. degree in library science, requirements, 219, 237
Macer, Pompeius, 83
McKenzie, John, 53
Magliabecchi, Antonio, 101

Maitland, S. R. , 109
Malone, C. B. , 5
Management of libraries, 62, 101
Manchester School of Technology, 123
Mann, Horace, 22
Manuscript catalogs, 97
Marginal responsibilities, 226
Marietta College Library, statistics, 33
Marion, G. E. , 52
Massachusetts Institute of Technology Library, statistics, 32
Massachusetts school law, 1852, 18
Masses, Education of. *See* Education of the masses
Mazarin, 102; library, 103-4
Mechanical librarian, 137-8
Medieval librarians, (chapter), 91-107; bibliography, 108-9
Merton College, 99
Mesmes, Henri de, 102
Methods of teaching in American universities, 28; influence on the use of the library, 35
Methods of training for librarianship, American, 137; English, 123
Michigan, University of, Library, statistics, 33
Middle Ages, Library movement in, 91
Middlebury College Library, statistics, 34
Minnesota, University of, Library, statistics, 33
Mississippi, University of, Library, statistics, 33
Mississippi valley, Need of trained librarians in, 200
Missouri, University of, Library, statistics, 33
Mitchell, Arthur, 150
Monastic libraries, 91-4
Monastic librarians, 91, 95, 98-9, 101; English Benedictines, 93
Morel, Eugene, 132
Morgan, J. E. , 177
Moscow, Library School, 158
Mt. St. Mary's College Library, statistics, 32
Müller, W. M. , 71, 88
Munich, Library of, 97

Nankai University Library, 4
National Certification and Library Training, Committee on, 129, 149
National certification system, 130

National Educational Association, 11, 185-6
National Library Association of Australia, 60
National library associations, 60
National Teachers' University, Peking, Library Science School, 3
Naudé, Gabriel, 101, 102-5, 109
Neumann, Felix, 133
New York City Library, 54
New York Public Library, Library School, entrance requirements, 162; foreign students, 157
New York State Library School, 3, entrance requirements, 163; established, 126, 147, 155; foreign graduates, 156
Newberry, W. L., 54
Newberry Library, 44, 54
Newspapers, 42
Normal schools, Library courses in, 129
North Carolina, University of, Library, statistics, 33
North Central Association of Colleges and Secondary Schools, 186
Northwestern University Library, statistics, 32
Notre Dame, University of, Library, statistics, 32

Oberlin College Library, statistics, 33
Ogle, J. J., 25, 123, 133
Ohio Wesleyan University Library, statistics, 33
Open libraries, 104, 111
Order of Saint Benedict, 91
Organization of librarians, 59
Oriel College, 99
Osier, Dr., 11
Osier, Sir William, 122, 133

Painter, F. V. N., 17, 25
Paleography, 116; course in, 245
Panizzi, Sir Anthony, 111
Paper, 42
Paris, American Library School in. *See* American Library School in Paris
Paris summer school, 158
Peking Library Association, 4
Pendry, E. R., 177
Pennsylvania College Library, statistics, 34
Pennsylvania, University of, Library, statistics, 34

"People's university," 125

Pergamum library, 80-1

Personnel, Library, organization, 81-5; surveys, 130

Personnel Classification Board, proposed classification of library personnel, 9-10

Peter Force Library, 47

Peterhouse, Cambridge, 99

Petzholdt, Julius, 114

Philadelphia Law Assoc. Library, 47

Philadelphia Public Library, 54

Philanthropy, (chapter), 53-7; bibliography, 58; increased need for trained librarians, 139-40

Pietschmann, Richard, 117, 133

Piper, A. C., 133

Pledge, system of loan, 92

Pliny, the Younger, 86

Plummer, M. W., 133, 148, 153, 192-4, 197

Pollio, Asinius, 83

Poole, W. F., 25, 38, 126

Positions in library, Classification of, 9

Practice work, 119

Pratt, Enoch, 54

Pratt Institute, School of Library Science, 126; entrance requirements, 162; foreign students, 156-7; report, 157

Precentor, 98

Preliminary education of library school applicants, 218

Preparation for librarianship, 139

Preservation of books, 91, 96

Priests as librarians, 76-7

Primitive library, 71

Princeton University Library, statistics, 33

Printed material, (chapter), 41-50; bibliography, 51-2

Printing, Course in, 243; effect of its invention on libraries, 91

Printing machinery, 42-3

Prints, Course in, 244

Private libraries, 105

Problems in university libraries, 143

Professional education and university control, 183-5

Professional education for librarianship, (chapter), 111-30; bibliography, 131-4; contrasted with technical education, 74, 170-2; history, 116-17

Professional library schools, Need of, 194; entrance requirements, 220-1; two curricula for, 228

Professional library service,9

Professional staff of university library, proper relationship to teaching staff of university library school,206

Professional Training Section, American Library Association,148

Professor,special,189

Professors as librarians,116

Provisional minimum standards for library schools,215-19,criticism of,7-8,220-3

Prussia. *See* Germany

Prussian Act of 1893 defining the qualifications of a librarian,114-15,118

Psychological tests, Admission to library schools by,166;for library positions,130

Public library, Need of,19;library schools in,181

Public schools,compulsory attendance,18;establishment,17

Publications,commercialized,43-4;increase of,41

Purchasing policy,44

Putnam,Herbert,47,52

Qualifications of instructional staff,University of Iowa Library School(proposed),211-12

Qualifications of librarians,120-2;professional,142;should determine rank,209-10

Quality of professional training offered by American library schools,159

Quintilian,86 Ranck,S. H. ,25

Ranking of university librarian,144

Rathbone,J. A. ,25,156

Reading material,Wide production of,41

Redwood,Abraham,53

Reece,E. J. ,177,213,230

Reference,Courses in,240

Reference librarians,grades,9

Reference libraries,45

Reformation,influence on libraries,100

Renaissance,influence on libraries,100

Requirements for admission to graduate school of librarianship,218-19

Requirements for B. A. or B. S. degree in library science,218

Requirements for future librarian,140-1

Research,(chapter),27-36;bibliography,37-9

Richardson,E. C. ,38,71-2,88,143-4,153

Richelieu,A. J. du P. ,Cardinal,102

Rievaux,Monastery,Library of,97

Ritschl,Friedrich,115,117-18

Riverside Library Service School, entrance requirements, 163
Robbins, M. E., 148, 154
Roberts, H. D., 123, 133
Robinson, O. H., 38
Rochester, University of, Library, statistics, 33
Roden, C. B. 140-1, 154
Roman conquests, influence on libraries, 86
Roman libraries, 81; decline, 87; development, 86; personnel organization, 82-4
Ross, James, 115, 133
Royal libraries, 105
Rullman, F., 113-14, 118, 133
Rush, James, 54
Russell, J. E., 223-4, 230
Rutgers College Library, statistics, 33

Sacy, Silvestrede, 78
St. Johns University, Shanghai, 2
St. Louis Library School, 199; entrance requirements, 162
St. Louis University Library, statistics, 33
Salaries, 83, 105, 209; of teachers in library schools, 169-70, 247-8; of special librarians, 146, 187-8
Sanborn, H. N., 134
Sanderson, E. M., 156
Savage, E. A., 88, 105-6, 109
Saxony, Library School, 120
Scandinavian countries, Librarianship in, 121
Scheme proposing four grades of library schools, 215-17
Schneider, Georg, 116
Scholars as librarians, 101
Scholarship, History of, Course in, 245
School district libraries, 21-2
School librarians, High, qualifications, 185-7
School of Librarianship, University of London, 124
Schools and libraries, Cooperation of, 19-23
Schrettinger, Martin, 113, 134
Schwenke, P., 115, 134
Scientific libraries, 48-9, 119
Scientific library service, 9
Scudder, H. E., 38, 53, 58

Seminary method, German, 28

Senior under-graduate library school, 215-16

Serapeum, Library of the, 78

Sharp, John, 53

Shearer, A. H., 154

Sibley, J. L., 30, 38

Simmons College, School of Library Science, entrance requirements, 163

Smith, George, 103-4, 109

Smith, William, 88

Sorbonne, Society of, 106, 122

South Carolina, University of, Library, statistics, 34

Special libraries, 44, 47-50, 144, 145; courses in, 244; increase in, 146

Special library associations, 60

Special students, 219

Specialization and library service, 185, 224

Spiritual value should characterize future librarians, 141

Spofford, A. R., 46, 52, 89

Staff, Chinese library, 75; library school, 168

Standard of a liberally educated man, 136

Standards for librarianship, 106, 107

Standardization of libraries, 129; of library training, 124; of library training agencies, 172-4

Ständer, Joseph, 117

State and public libraries, 21

State library associations, 60

State libraries, 44, 45

Static type of special library, 47

Steffenhagen, Dr., 114

Stephens, T. E., 25

Stock taking, 91

Strohm, Adam, 150

Student assistants, 117, 118

Study schedules, 219

Sub-professional library service, 9

Subscription libraries, 53

Succentor, 98

Summer schools of library science, China, 3; England, 123; France, 158; University of Iowa, 200-1

Suppression of monasteries, 99

Syracuse University Library, statistics, 33

Syracuse University Library School, entrance requirements, 162

Sweden, Library training in, 121

Tablets, 76

Tai, Julie (Rummelhoff), 6

Tai, Tse-Chien, 11-12, 74, 76, 89; biography, 1-12; books by, 13-14

Taxation, 21, 23

Teaching staff of university library school, relation to professional staff of university library, 206; qualifications, 212

Teaching, Library school, Course in, 245-6

Technical skill, 225

Technical training, 170-2

Technical subjects emphasized in early library schools, 147

Technical type of librarian, demand for, 139

Technique, Emphasis on, 137-8

Tedder, H. R., 84, 89, 109, 112-13, 134

Temporary Library Training Board, 161-3, 172, 173, 174-5, 183; appointed, 150

Texas, University of, Department of Library Science, entrance requirements, 163; University library, 35

Thayer, V. T., 226, 230

Theft, Precaution against, 96

Thomas à Kempis. *See* Kempis

Thompson, C. S., 154

Thwing, C. F., 29, 30, 135-6, 154

Town libraries, 23

Trained librarians, Need of, 1, 11, 111-12

Training Board certificate, 149

Training for librarianship, history, 116

Training school for librarians, first proposed, 113

Trinity College Library, statistics, 32

Tsai-Soong-Po Memorial Library, 4

Tsing Hua College, 3, 5, 6

Tufts, J. H., 197, 213, 231

Tufts College Library, statistics, 32

Tychefeld Monastery, Library of, 97

Tyler, A. S., 154

Tyler, M. C., 21, 25

Type, Movable, 100

Under-graduate library school, curriculum, 235-7

Union College Library, statistics, 33
Union Theological Seminary Library, 47
United States, Library training in, 125-30
United States Military Academy Library, statistics, 33
Universities, Library courses in, 129
Universities and library schools, (chapter), 181-95, 201-3; bibliography, 196-8
University affiliation, 182-3
University librarians, Ranking of, 144
University libraries, 29, 36; early, 27; growth, 31-5; management, 99; problems, 142-3
University library assistants, privileges, 209
University library school, separate instructional staff, 208

Vacations, 210-11
Vandalism, 97
Van Hoesen, H. B., 213
Varro, M. T., 83-4
Vassar College Library, statistics, 33
Verein Deutscher Bibliolhekare, 60, 115
Vermont, University of, Library, statistics, 34
Vestinus, Julius, 82
Virginia, University of, Library, statistics, 34

Wabash College Library, statistics, 32
Walter, F. K., 113, 134, 146, 148, 154, 158-9, 177, 197
Washington, University of, Library, statistics, 33; Library School, 163
Washington and Lee University Library, statistics, 34
Wealth, 55, 56
Wesleyan University Library, statistics, 32
Western Reserve University, library school, entrance requirements, 162
Wharey, J. B., 39
Whitten, R. H., 52
Wilbur, R. L., 198
William and Mary, College of, Library, statistics, 34
Williams College Library, statistics, 32
Williamson, C. C., 52, 148-9, 154, 157; report on Training for Library Service, 94, 158, 164, 167-9, 171-2, 177, 186-7, 189
Wilmanns, Augustus, 117
Windsor, P. L., 231
Winship, A. E., 22, 26

Winsor, Justin, 28, 38

Wisconsin, University of, Library, statistics, 34; Library School, entrance requirements, 162

Wisconsin Legislative Reference Bureau, 12

Wolfenbüttel Library, 106

Women in library work, 84

Woodruff, E. H., 39

Work with children, Course in, 242

Wyer, J. I,, 178

Yale University, admission to graduate school, 164

Yale University Library, 34-5, statistics, 32

Zenodotus, 78

图书馆学专业教育

戴志骞著

译文		冯立昇、司宏伟审
前言		王　媛译
序言		王　媛译
第一部分	1—2 章	王　媛译
	第 3 章	杨　玲译
	第 4 章	郭兰芳译
	第 5 章	张　秋译
第二部分	6—10 章	韦庆媛译
第三部分	11—13 章	胡　冉译
附录 I		胡　冉译
附录 II		胡　冉译

图书馆学专业教育

戴志骞著

图书馆学学士　哲学博士
中国 北京 清华学校图书馆主任,中华图书馆协会执行部部长,《最新关于中国的文献》的作者

约翰·博因顿·凯撒序
图书馆学硕士
爱荷华大学图书馆馆长

纽约 威尔逊出版公司
1925

1925 年 11 月在美国出版发行

目 录

前言 ………………………………………………………………………… (227)
序言 ………………………………………………………………………… (229)

第一部分　现代图书馆与图书馆事业的发展

第一章　教育中的民主思想 ………………………………………………… (238)
第二章　高等教育的研究精神 ……………………………………………… (243)
第三章　纸质印刷材料的增长 ……………………………………………… (250)
第四章　图书馆慈善事业 …………………………………………………… (255)
第五章　图书馆协会 ………………………………………………………… (258)

第二部分　图书馆学专业教育与培训

第六章　古代的图书馆员 …………………………………………………… (262)
第七章　中世纪和近代早期的图书馆员 …………………………………… (273)
第八章　现代图书馆员的专业教育 ………………………………………… (283)
第九章　图书馆学观念的转变和教育要求 ………………………………… (295)
第十章　美国的图书馆学校 ………………………………………………… (303)

第三部分　图书馆学专业教育的提案

第十一章　作为大学学院的图书馆学校 …………………………………… (314)
第十二章　爱荷华州立大学拟建的图书馆学院 …………………………… (322)
第十三章　图书馆学院的入学申请、学位和课程 ………………………… (329)

附录Ⅰ　为爱荷华州立大学图书馆学院研究生和本科生推荐的课程……… (337)
附录Ⅱ　爱荷华州立大学图书馆学院预算建议 …………………………… (343)

索引（略）

前　言

本研究主要涉及美国的图书馆学专业教育。查尔斯·C. 威廉姆森博士（Dr. Charles C. Williamson）[①]1919年受卡内基基金会委托对美国图书馆学校进行质量调查，并于1923年出版了调查报告《图书馆服务培训》（*Training for Library Service*），自从那时开始，美国图书馆界已就培养专业图书馆员这一问题进行了许多讨论。但无论是针对这个报告的批评和评论，还是随之开展的广泛讨论，都没有建立在对图书馆发展、决定图书馆服务品质的主要因素、过去和现在的培训以及包括图书馆专业学校发展在内的图书馆学教育等几方面之间关系的正确认识上。

本文的第一部分所采用的研究方法是理论分析法，对社会因素、教育因素和智力因素进行了理论分析，这些因素过去一直、现在依然主导着图书馆的发展，决定了图书馆服务的品质，并因此成为决定图书馆学专业教育特征的主要因素。

几乎所有其他公认的职业都有一份关于该职业的科学和文化发展以及其专业人员培训和教育的有文字可考的历史。但在图书馆学的专业教育领域却不是这样。既不了解从古至今进化的不同阶段中图书馆员的资格要求，又不清楚建立图书馆专业学校的原因，以及他们在不同国家的起源与发展，这也就难怪当下没有适当的方法来检测那些改变图书馆学内含的因素及其教育需求。系统研究图书馆学的历史对其今天的发展有意义，而仔细分析当下现状则对其未来有启发。

本文还采用的是历史研究法，系统研究了欧洲、英、美等国家图书馆员的培训与教育以及图书馆专业学校起源与发展，尤其是对那些图书馆专业学校的优缺点进行批判性分析。这构成了本文的第二部分。

在第一部分中对图书馆事业发展的社会因素、教育因素和智力因素进行理论分析，以及第二部分对图书馆事业、专业图书馆培训机构的起源与发展进行历史研究之后，本研究的第三部分将为今后图书馆学专业教育的发展制订一个明确的计划。这个计划包括为爱荷华州立大学图书馆学院所设计的具体方案——课程设计和附录1、附录2中预算方案，这构成了本文的第三部分。如果您在阅读接下来的章节中，感到作者在文中撰写图书馆员的专业教育方面、描述从古至今出现的各种类型的图书馆花费了太多笔墨，请一定牢记，这是在强调为了彰显各个时代图书馆员服务的品质而对图书馆员进行教育是非常必要的。

无论是否被授权使用，本文中几乎引文都是直接引用，这有两个目的：(1) 避免意外的曲解；(2) 给那些之前论述的观点以适当的证据。

笔者希望向女性图书馆员致歉。每当需要使用代词时，笔者通常使用的是"他"。但是这并不意味着笔者忽视了女性在行业中的价值和贡献。笔者可以保证，只要使用了"图书馆

---

① 【译者注】查尔斯·C. 威廉姆森博士（Dr. Charles C. Williamson），是纽约公共图书馆读者咨询服务部经济和社会处主任，曾获哥伦比亚大学政治经济学博士学位。威廉姆森因1919年在ALA年会上提交的一篇严厉批评图书馆员教育的论文而闻名。

员"这个词时,既包括了男性图书馆员,也包括了女性图书馆员。

笔者要感谢本文中所引用的那些著作或观点的帮助。给予帮助和支持的人数如此之多,以至于在这里无法一一列出。不过,笔者还是希望向下述人士表达由衷的感谢:爱荷华州立大学图书馆馆长约翰·博因顿·凯撒教授(John Boynton Kaiser)①,和教育学院的保罗·克利福德·帕克主任(Paul Clifford Packer)以及弗雷斯特·C.·恩赛因教授(Forest C. Ensign),感谢他们在本研究进行中所给予的建议。笔者要进一步感谢约翰·博因顿·凯撒教授所给予的宝贵的建议和有益的批评,以及不辞辛劳地对整部作品的修订,没有他的浓厚兴趣和不断援助,这项工作不可能顺利完成。

笔者亦希望感谢爱荷华州立大学研究生院无拘无束的科学态度和学术氛围,以其领导者卡尔·埃米尔·西肖尔(Carl Emil Seashore)②主任为代表,他及其同事 G.T.W. 帕特里克(G. T. W. Patrick)教授、卡尔·F. 托伊施(Carl F. Taeusch)教授、吉尔斯·M. 鲁赫(Giles M. Ruch)教授和学院中的其他成员不断地鼓舞着笔者。笔者感受到他们的期望,于是尽最大的努力去争取实现这个理想。

笔者还要感谢美国图书馆协会图书馆员教育委员会的支持,给予笔者两次参加其专业会议的机会,使笔者得以从行业领导者那里获得良多灵感和很多信息。笔者同样向大学图书馆的馆员表达感谢,感谢他们及时的服务。

约翰·F. 勒克夫人(Mrs. John F. Loeck)耐心阅读了本文的部分手稿,爱荷华州立大学图书馆的部门主管杰克逊·E. 汤先生(Mr. Jackson E. Towne)耐心阅读了全部手稿,他们帮助修正了文中许多英文语法使用,一并致谢。最后,我要将最诚挚的谢意致以我的妻子戴罗瑜丽(Julie Rummelhoff Tai),她帮助我从德文书刊中核对翻译,不辞艰辛地阅读最后的打印稿,没有她持续不断的热情和一以贯之的努力,就不会有这部著作现在的样子。

戴志骞
1925 年 5 月 11 日
于爱荷华州爱荷华城

---

① 【译者注】约翰·博因顿·凯撒教授(John Boynton Kaiser),生于 1887 年,卒于 1973 年,1910 年毕业于纽约州立大学图书馆学院,曾在多个公共图书馆工作过,在多所学校教授图书馆管理,并担任过不同的图书馆协会组织的管理者。著有《法律、立法及内政参考资料》(Law, Legislative And Municipal Reference Libraries)和《南美洲共和国的国家书目》(The National Bibliographies of the South American Republics)他亦是一名集邮爱好者。

② 【译者注】卡尔·埃米尔·西肖尔(Carl Emil Seashore),美国心理学家、音乐心理学家,1866 年出生于瑞典,1949 年去世于美国爱荷华州。他在音乐测量方面做出了突出贡献,主要对音乐能力测量的研究。他创立了音乐心理学实验室,发明心理测试仪器,编制了多种测试量表,研制了音乐测量法,在音乐人才的成长测量方面建立了科学研究体系,被称之为"实验音乐心理学之父"。1905 年,西肖尔获得爱荷华大学全职教授职位,任职心理学系主任。1908 年,他任职爱荷华州立大学研究生院的主任,这个职务一直保持到他退休(1937 年)。

序　　言

　　戴志骞博士在前言中实际上已经介绍了他所研究的题目。如果还需要更多的介绍,我们不如先阅读最近由美国图书馆协会图书馆员教育委员会所出版的《年度报告》(Annual Report)中所表达的更有说服力的说法,"合格图书馆员是匮乏的,这一主张是毫不夸张的。"事实上,本书几乎直接回答了图书馆员教育委员会所确信的图书馆员短缺的影响以及增加合格图书馆员供应的必要手段。

　　戴博士在本书中的结论稍微与图书馆员教育委员会的专家们的观点不同,他巧妙地表明了自己的观点,其他人可以真诚理智地不赞同他们二者的观点,而不是对这个在国家经济、文化和教育生活中具有潜在意义的社会转型期的专题研究内容横加指责。

　　本书的读者自然会对这位外国作者的背景怀有天然的兴趣,他来自东方,带给我们的著作不仅是最有份量的,并且有望在一段时间保留在我们跌宕起伏的历史中,说明美国的图书馆学专业教育无可否认地领先于世界。

　　戴志骞博士1888年2月27日出生于中国江苏省青浦县珠溪镇(今朱家角镇)。1894年至1903年,他开始在私塾接受早期教育,并于1904至1907年就读于上海圣约翰大学预科,毕业时他获得了奖励给最优秀学生的"溥伦贝子奖章"(the Prince Pu Medal)①,并因出众的演说而获颁"圣约翰大学校友奖章"(the St. John's Alumni Medal)。彼时的中国,这样的早期教育主要是对中国传统经典典籍与史册的学习,而戴先生的目标也是能通过清政府的科举考试。1907年到1909年,戴先生到浙江温州瑞安高级中学(Rui-An High School)教授历史和英语文法,之后他又回到上海圣约翰大学,并成为该校图书馆的副馆长。1912年,他在圣约翰大学获得了学士学位,再次因演讲出色而获得奖章,随后他又在圣约翰大学进行了几年研究生阶段的研习,同时也担任图书馆馆长。戴先生在研究生阶段的学习主要包括哲学、社会学和教育学等领域的专门研究。到1913年年底,他的健康状况迫使他不得不暂时放弃继续攻读研究生的想法。

　　1908年,西奥多·罗斯福(Theodore Roosevelt)②担任总统,伊莱休·鲁特(Elihu Root)③担任国务卿期间,美国政府将部分庚子赔款退回给中国,中国方面对此举的评价是"优雅公正的国际行为"。中国政府认识到美国的友好精神,决定利用这笔经费派遣学生到美国的学

---

① 【译者注】溥伦,字彝庵,又字叙斋,姓爱新觉罗氏。镶红旗满洲人。清道光帝长子隐智亲王之长孙,封为贝勒衔贝子。光绪三十一年(1904)赴美国考察海军及渔业等,归后主张实行君主立宪制。民国初年,代表清皇室及八旗王公上劝进表,拥护袁世凯称帝。1915年12月以后出任参政院院长、参政。《圣约翰大学自编校史稿》一文中提及,"伦贝子给与成绩最优之学仁银牌一百方。周玉帅则捐助五百元学校议决。以其利息。制奖章,赠与高级中之善作文论说者"。

② 【译者注】西奥多·罗斯福,1901—1909年担任美国总统。任总统期间,推行公平交易(Square Deal)计划进行社会改革,外交关系上奉行"软嘴加大棒政策"。

③ 【译者注】伊莱休·鲁特,美国律师、政治家。1899—1904年任陆军部长,1905—1909年任国务卿,海牙法庭成员之一,1912年获诺贝尔和平奖。

院和大学学习。"随即出现了被称为留学监督公署(The Chinese Educational Mission)的机构,它见证了西方的伟大共和国对她东方的姐妹共和国的友情。起初,因为意识到中国大学资源的匮乏,成立一个留美预备学校是必要的,清华学堂应运而生"①。1914 年,戴先生在清华担任图书馆主任。

1917 年,戴先生以留学监督公署秘书的身份首次访美,并于当年晚些时候进入位于奥尔巴尼(Albany)的纽约州立大学图书馆学院学习,尽管存在语言上的障碍,戴先生还是用不到一年的时间就完成了两年制的专业培训课程,并获得了图书馆学学士学位。这一点我们本国人都很少能做到。当被问到他第一次来美国就能说英语,戴先生带着东方特有的诙谐,天真地说,(目光炯炯有神。每当东方人前来,你都能看见那种目光),"哦,是的! 就是没有人能听懂我说的"。1919 年秋天,戴先生回到清华,继续担任图书馆主任一职。他同时也是清华学校教授会成员和评议会委员。在距离北京西北城门七英里外的优美校园中,图书馆有了独立馆舍,馆舍建筑恢宏美丽。

写这样一本权威的关于图书馆学专业教育的著作,作者不仅要接受过这一领域最好的教育,而且还应该有图书馆工作各领域和其他教育领域的相关经验。戴先生完全符合这些要求。1920 年,他担任设在北京高等师范学校(the National Teachers' University, Peking)的暑期图书馆学讲习会负责人,次年又参与创办了中华总商会在上海的商业图书馆。从 1919 年到 1922 年,他担任天津南开大学图书馆的顾问,并有五年时间在纪念蔡锷将军的松坡图书馆担任馆务委员会委员。戴先生是由中华民国总统任命的国家图书馆筹建委员会的七名委员之一,该委员会的其余成员均是现任或前任的内阁部长。最近,虽然身在美国,他依然被选为新成立的中华图书馆协会执行部部长,中华图书馆协会董事部绝大多数成员都是政治家、大学校长或其他教育领导者。1923 年,丹麦国王授予戴志骞先生丹尼勃罗格骑士勋位(Knighthood of Dannebroge),以表彰他为丹麦政府提供的特殊服务。

戴先生再被选为北平图书馆协会的会长,1922 年以来一直担任中华教育改进社图书馆教育组的主席,这些都进一步证明了他在中国图书馆专业领域的地位。六年前他成为美国图书馆协会的成员,与美国图书馆界保持了密切联系。戴先生的其他社会身份还包括已达 7 年之久的中国科学社(the Science Society of China)会员、北京高校男子俱乐部(the College Men's Club of Peking)成员、中国国防联盟咨询委员会(the Advisory Committee of the National Defense League of China)成员、北京文学俱乐部(the Peking Literary Club)成员和北京美国大学俱乐部(the American College Club in Peking)成员。他还是长老会(the Presbyterian Church)成员。

罗列戴先生的这些个人经历并不是为了证明他是谈论图书馆学专业教育的权威人士,摆在我们面前的这本著作其实早已是最好的证明。在以上的主要传记内容中,把一些地名或机构名换成美国的地名或机构名,我们会发现戴先生的经历和履历与同时期美国许多图书馆界的领袖在几乎所有点上都是平行的。换句话说,我们不必仅仅因为作者是外国的而低估本书的内容价值。事实上,对我们来说,这本书是很有益的。托克维尔和布莱斯持有同样高水准的评价。

---

① 【原注】*Tsing Hua* 1911—1921: *A Review*, *published on the Tenth Anniversary of the Founding of Tsing Hua College*. Peking. May 1, 1921. 5op.

经由英格兰、欧洲大陆、俄罗斯和西伯利亚,从挪威回到中国的路几乎横跨了四分之一个地球,戴志骞先生在挪威开始本书的写作,并构思了整体的大纲草图——请原谅我在此体现一下我们之间更为密切的联系。1911 年,清华学堂刚刚开办,我的同学兼朋友卡罗尔·麻伦教授(Carroll B. Malone)就作为清华学堂最初的教员于 1911 年年初抵达中国,此时戴志骞先生还在圣约翰大学。很快麻伦教授寄信回美国,要求获取一些信息与书籍,以指导新教职员工按照美国方法办好这所新办学校的图书馆。他获得了一些建议与技术性出版物,多数是来自美国图书馆界各个时期重要作者个人的慷慨捐赠。几年以后,当 1917 年我得知纽约州立大学图书馆学院来了一位来自清华学校的图书馆员时,自然引起了我特别的兴趣,我很快与他取得了联系。随后,美国参加了一战,美国图书馆协会的图书馆战时服务得到了发展。1919 年 1 月,我抵达纽约爱布顿(Upton)军营担任营地图书馆员,我很惊喜地发现戴先生已于前一年的 10 月就加入营地图书馆员的队伍中了。我们认识不久就成了好朋友,营地图书馆的工作不仅真实记录了戴先生的勤勉和能力,贯穿始终的良好的服务精神也为他在所有同事中赢得了美誉。许多个午夜,我们围着篝火愉快地聊天,谈论中国的儒家思想、汉字演化以及其他东方话题,这些回忆现在想来依然令人心生欢喜。1919 年 6 月,戴先生还帮助筹备了美国图书馆学会在阿斯伯里帕克市(Asbury Park)年会上的图书馆战时服务展览,年底他经由太平洋回了中国。1924 年 8 月,戴先生的一年休假被清华学校批准,他携妻子戴罗瑜丽(Julie Rummelhoff,1919 年毕业于纽约州立大学图书馆学院)来到美国进行一年的学习、工作和研究,戴先生在旅行中负责管理 130 人的清华赴美留学生团。起初,夫妇俩的计划并未确定。戴先生希望有可能的话在大学中讲讲东方文学,戴夫人则到纽约市立公共图书馆的编目部工作。后来他们的计划很快就完全改变了,主要因为他们采纳了爱荷华大学杰瑟普(Jessup)校长的建议,戴先生来到爱荷华大学继续他的研究生学习。研究生课程包括教育统计、心理测量、学校管理、大学管理、现代哲学和图书馆教育等。戴先生的博士论文,也就是本书,本计划由大学立即出版,后来随着事情的发展,最终决定通过商业渠道出版。

本书出版发行前,戴先生考虑过修改某些章节,因为这本书最后部分是一个在爱荷华大学成立图书馆学院的特别建议方案,不过,思考越多,戴先生就越坚信不必修改。一般的原则是普遍适用的,但特别的建议则是告诉大家如果方案被批准了,在一个现有院校中增设学院或修订现有的图书馆学教育课程该如何操作的详细具体说明。对图书馆、未来的图书馆学学生和其他人而言,这本书中详细具体的内容也会有特殊的价值。

正如前面所提到的,在如何设计图书馆员的专业教育体系上,戴志骞博士的观点有别于美国图书馆协会图书馆员委员会,后者认为一个完整的图书馆员教育体系包含初级本科图书馆学院、包含研究生的高级本科图书馆学院和高级研究生院,而戴博士则建议在一所综合性大学中设立图书馆学院,建制与其他学院一样,培养本科生和研究生,学生可以在低年级时学习图书馆工作,也可以通过高年级的学习获得文学士和理学士学位,学院同时也培养研究生,将来授以硕士学位和博士学位。然而,应该公平地说,戴博士的观点主要是对 1925 年 4 月图书馆员教育委员会所公布的用以讨论的《图书馆学校最低暂行标准》(Provisional Minimum Standards for Library Schools)而言的,并非 1925 年 6 月 20 日发表在《年度报告》(Annual Report)中的最终版本。戴博士的写作在当年 5 月就已经完成了。不过,《最低暂行标准》和最后推出的正式版本之间的差别是很细微的,我们有把握认为戴博士的观点不会有太大的改变。我还应当进一步指出,委员会与戴博士的一致观点是那么的有趣和显著,一如他们之间的不同观点。

可以看出,戴博士相当重视罗伯特·J.莱纳德(Robert J. Leonard)教授的观点,在高级专业群体和中级职业群体中有所区分,莱纳德教授认为如果不像法律、牙科、工程、农业、商业管理和教育等领域一样做这样的区分将会造成图书馆学教育的失误。这里有一个有趣的猜测,不论莱纳德教授后来是否讨论专科院校中的专业教育①,这项工作完成之后,总会给一些建议以应用在培养"低水平"图书馆员的教育上。

不管是否接受图书馆员专业教育的分层理论及其应用,有一点是明确的,以前在训练图书馆员的过程中,人们并没有充分区分同一个图书馆中不同类型的工作,也没有区分不同工作属性之间的差异。

对所有人而言,这一点是显而易见的,那就是图书馆工作至少可以被分成两种类型:专业工作和半专业工作。另一点也是明确的,图书馆工作可以分为机械、文书、技术和专业四个部分,从逻辑上来讲也是可以接受的,而且也是可以贯彻执行的,虽然工作内容会有些重叠。

1923年,由哥伦比亚特区图书馆协会的政府图书馆员委员会提交给职业分类委员会的《联邦政府图书馆服务简明规范》中对图书馆职业进行了如下详细的划分,并且列出每一种(尤其是在前两种中)分类中图书馆员的职责、义务、资格和薪金。

Ⅰ. 托管服务(Custodial Service)
Ⅱ. 文书服务(Clerical Service)
Ⅲ. 半专业的图书馆服务(Sub-professional Library Service)

低级图书馆助理(Minor Library Assistant)	1级
下级图书馆助理(Under Library Assistant)	2级
初级图书馆助理(Junior Library Assistant)	3级
图书馆助理(Library Assistant)	4级
主要图书馆助理(Main Library Assistant)	5级

Ⅳ. 专业科学的图书馆服务(Professional and Scientific Library Service)
1. 图书馆管理(Library Administration)

初级行政图书馆员(Junior Administrative Librarian)	1级
助理行政图书馆员(Assistant Administrative Librarian)	2级
副行政图书馆员(Associate Administrative Librarian)	3级
行政图书馆员(Administrative Librarian)	4级
高级行政图书馆员(Senior Administrative Librarian)	5级
高级行政顾问图书馆员(Senior Administrative Consulting Librarian)	5级
首席行政图书馆员(Chief Administrative Librarian)	6级
哥伦比亚特区公共图书馆馆长;国会图书馆副馆长,(Librarian, Public Library, District of Columbia; Assistant Librarian of Congress	
特别行政图书馆长 Special Administrative Librarian)	7级

---

① 【原注】*Teachers College Record*. 26:724—33. May,1925.

2. 咨询、研究与参考书目服务（Reference, Research and Bibliography）
  初级咨询馆员（Junior Reference Librarian）   1级
  助理咨询馆员（Assistant Reference Librarian）   2级
  副参考咨询馆员（Associate Reference Librarian）   3级
  副参考书目馆员（Associate Bibliographical Librarian）   3级
  参考咨询馆员（Reference Librarian）   4级
3. 技术（Technical）
  初级图书馆员（Junior Librarian）   1级
  初级编目馆员（Junior Cataloging Librarian）   1级
  助理编目馆员（Assistant Cataloging Librarian）   2级
  副编目馆员（Associate Cataloging Librarian）   3级
4. 特别工作（Special Work）
  初级儿童图书馆员（Junior Children's Librarian）   1级

  1924年由职业分类委员会发布的《服务部门岗位分类规范》（*In the Class Specifications for Positions in the Departmental Service*）中，图书馆这个分组的岗位术语发生了一点改变。"半专业"组变成了"图书馆助理"组，细分成7个级别，而不是原来的5个，"专业科学"组变成了"图书馆员"组，由上述所列的细分改为分为6级。

  一次性说清楚图书馆的所有岗位分类似乎有些难度，但这个分类提供了一个可遵依循的开始，其中大部分都已顺利进行了。事实上，人事专家告诉我们，如果我们接受了这个"分类"的定义，那么未来在公共图书馆、大中小学图书馆中至少有250个图书馆岗位的分类。这些大部分已经在那些筹备图书馆事业的人所考虑的政策和细节中了。

  事实上，图书馆员专业教育至少包含以下问题。首先，理解图书馆在我们的社会组织中的地位和目的，理解现已运行的众多类型图书馆满足公众需求的独特作用；接下来需要面对的问题是，必须确切了解为了使图书馆在各方面都运转正常，每个图书馆员所必须做的工作，并且找到最适合做这些工作的人；最后，建立能帮助准图书馆员们完成各自任务的教育体系。换言之，即是图书馆工作理念、"工作内容分析"、准图书馆员的教育以及找到胜任工作的准图书馆员合适人选。

  去年，《全国教育协会公报》（*the Bulletin of the National Education Association*）编辑说，我们每年很容易吸引到700名新人到图书馆就业。最近几个月克利夫兰基金会①刚刚发布的《克利夫兰高等教育情况调查》（*Survey of Higher Education in Cleveland*）中"图书馆教育"一章中认为，仅有4400名美国图书馆学校的毕业生会真正到美国、加拿大的近万所图书馆中从事图书馆工作，这其中不包含部分来自国外毕业后会回国从事图书馆工作的学生。

  从广义而言，图书馆在帮助实现教育的所有社会目标方面发挥越来越重要的作用。最

---

  ① 【译者注】克利夫兰基金会（Cleveland Foundation）是世界上第一家社区基金会组织，成立于1914年，由克利夫兰信托公司总裁弗雷德里克·戈夫（Fredrick Harris Goff）发起成立。

近，威廉·S. 勒恩德博士（Dr. William S. Learned）①认为图书馆员是"大脑的牧师"，提供"社区的智力服务"，几年前，身为医生和目录学家的奥斯耶博士（Dr. Osier）建议将图书馆员的头衔（或学位）定位为"解惑大夫"（doctor perplexorum）。这个头衔可以测度图书馆员与社区及与个人之间的关系。两年前，中国尚处在最艰难的时刻，本书的作者就在一封信中写到，"我和我的朋友都相信中国未来的唯一出路就是使大众接受教育"。那不就是无处不在的民主问题吗？这对图书馆是一个挑战，对培训图书馆员的机构而言也是一个必须面对的挑战。

对笔者而言，看到爱默生的名言"愚蠢的一致性是头脑狭隘人士的心魔！"颇感到欣慰。其实，戴志骞博士已写了一个简介，笔者又续上一个更详细的介绍文字，实在是因为对作者的邀请盛情难却。笔者也承认的确补充了一些作者因谦虚而不肯在前言中透露的内容，事实上，可能比他能说的内容还要多。

最后要说的是，在竭诚向读者推荐这本著作时，笔者意识到几分罪恶感，仿佛在帮刽子手调整自己颈上的绞索。三个权威——美国大学协会、美国图书馆协会教育委员会和戴博士——都同意笔者仅有的两个专业学位可以扔掉了。但是，我们想起了写有《威斯康辛思想》（The Wisconsin Idea）②的麦卡锡（McCarthy），他兴致勃勃地为愤怒的议员起草了一份废除他创立并成功运行多年的立法咨询办公室的法案。归根到底，这件事本身就是一场戏。但我们依然心甘情愿地说，吾等将亡，为汝致敬（Morituri te salutamus）。

约翰·博伊顿·凯撒（John Boynton Kaiser）

---

① 【译者注】威廉·S. 勒恩德博士（Dr. William S. Learned），生于1876年，卒于1950年，曾为卡耐基基金会工作，著有《美国公共图书馆与知识的扩散》《欧美教育的质量》《班主任——德国校长的社会化与职业化进程研究》等著作。

② 【译者注】威斯康辛思想是20世纪初发端于美国威斯康辛大学的大学办学思想。其认为大学应为本州农业、教育、社会和经济的综合发展提供服务。威斯康辛大学校长提出"州的边界也就是大学校园的边界"，实行开放性入学制度，为本地区公民提供继续教育。1912年，威斯康辛州公共图书馆管理员查尔斯·麦卡锡在其题为《威斯康辛思想》的著作中，首次使用"威斯康辛思想"一词。

戴志骞博士部分出版作品目录①

中文
新中国之道德. 约翰声,1912 年第 5 期②
图书馆与通俗教育. 民主与教育,1919 年 11 月③
图书馆学. 约翰声,1920 年第 4 期④
中国木版书与省级图书馆. 新教育,1922 年第 2 期⑤
图书馆学术讲稿. 北京高等师范学校出版,1922:120⑥
图书馆与学校. 教育丛刊,1923 年 2 月⑦
图书馆学评论. 新教育,1924 年第 5 期⑧
图书分类法几条原则的商榷. 北京图书馆协会会刊,1924 年 8 月⑨

英文
最新关于中国的文献. 中国学生月刊,第 13 卷第 1 期—第 14 卷第 8 期,1918 年 11 月—1919 年 6 月,约 80 页,每期 6—10 页⑩。
中国的图书馆运动. 北京:中华教育改进社会刊,第 2 卷第 3 号,1923,20p(1924 年上海商务印书馆再版),为中国代表团参加 1923 年洛杉矶世界教育大会而作。

---

① 【原注】Many of the publications containing Dr. Tai's writings are not available in this country, hence the incomplete bibliographical details.
② 【编者注】原文为"Influence of Modern Education."(现代教育的影响)*St. John's Echo.* Nov.,1912.,查《约翰声》1912 年第 11 期上没有找到该文,疑为记述有误。
③ 【编者注】原文为"Library and Popular Education."*Democracy and Education.* Nov.,1919.,没有找到该期刊和该文。
④ 【编者注】原文为"Library Profession."*St. John's Echo.* (Alumni Number)Feb.,1920. 查《约翰声》1920 年第 2 期上没有找到该文,疑为记述有误。
⑤ 【编者注】原文为"Chinese Wood-Block Printed Books and Provincial Libraries."*New Education.* (Proceedings Number)Feb.,1922.,查《新教育》1922 年第 2 期上没有找到该文。
⑥ 【编者注】原文为"Outlines of Library Science."National Teachers' University Press. Peking. 1922. 120p.,应为戴志骞 1920 年在北京高师图书馆学讲习会上所编译的讲稿,印刷稿没有找到。后该书刊登在该校出版的《教育丛刊》第 3 卷第 6 期上(1923 年 1 月出版),出版时为 67p。
⑦ 【编者注】原文为"Library Science and Normal Schools."*New Education.* (Proceedings Number)Feb.,1923. 该文刊登在《教育丛刊》第 3 卷第 6 期上(1923 年 1 月出版)。
⑧ 【编者注】原文为"Comments on Library Science."*New Education.* Mar.,1924. 查该刊没有找到该文。
⑨ 【编者注】原文为"Principles of Classification of Books."*Peking Library Association Bulletin.* Feb.,1925. 时间记述有误。
⑩ 【编者注】原文为"Recent Literature on China with Annotations."*Chinese Students' Monthly.* Vol. 13. No. 1—Vol. 14. No. 8. Nov.,1918-June,1919. (about)80p. A monthly contribution of six to ten pages.,查该篇原稿题名为"Recent Literature on China"。

中国图书馆概述.图书馆学刊,1919,44(6):423—429
中国图书馆的现状.公共图书馆(月刊),1919,24(2):37—40
令人振奋的图书馆.费城记录,1919年5月(战地服务获奖故事)①
中国的图书馆运动.美国图书馆协会年度报告,1920-21,1921:58—63②
高等图书馆学校——课程宗旨.公共图书馆,1925,30(2):59—61

法文
中国的图书馆.北京政闻周报,1920年1月③

出版物
图书馆学.商务印书馆,2册,上海,1924(中文)④
杜威书目十类法补编.北京清华学校,1924:33(中、英文)⑤

---

① 【编者注】原文为"Library Excitements." Philadelphia Record. May,1919. (Prize Story of War Service),该文没有找到。

② 【编者注】原文为"Library Service in China." *American Library Association*, *Annual Reports*, 1920-21. p.58—63.1921.,查该篇论文原稿,题名为"Library Movement in China"。

③ 【编者注】原文为"Les Bibliothèques Chinois." *La Politique de Pekin*. Jan.,1920.,查该刊没有找到该文。

④ 【编者注】原文为 Library Science. Commercial Press. 2vols. Shanghai. 1924. (In Chinese),1923年上海上午印书馆出版杨昭悊的《图书馆》,戴志骞为其撰写序言。

⑤ 【编者注】原文为 Supplements to Dewey's Decimal Classification for Chinese Books. Tsing Hua College. Peking. 1924. 33p. (In English and Chinese),该书目在戴志骞的领导下,由清华图书馆馆员查修编辑,戴志骞撰写了序言。

第一部分　现代图书馆与图书馆事业的发展

第一章　教育中的民主思想

第二章　高等教育的研究精神

第三章　纸质印刷材料的增长

第四章　图书馆慈善事业

第五章　图书馆协会

第一章 教育中的民主思想

纵观历史，许多不同的力量在塑造现代图书馆的特征中发挥着作用。教育的民主思想是给予每一个公民受教育的机会。初步学习阅读、写作与算术是每个人与生俱来的权利。自从卢梭的《爱弥儿》①出版，教育的民主化趋势在美国逐步发展起来了。十九世纪下半叶，各州政府广为设立免费公立学校已是不争的事实。1876年费城独立百年纪念博览会②详细描述了这一令人印象深刻的情况。

伴随着人口的增加，对青少年教育的巨大热情越来越渗透进公众心中，并越来越明显地体现在各个方面。起初像是一瞬间的热情光芒或慷慨的冲动，后来都及时呈现出所有合理信念的魄力，或相当积极的正面肯定。教育不再是少数慈善家或宗教社团的活动，而成为公共行政管理的重要组成部分，州、市、镇每年都要拨比世界上任何国家都多的经费投入到教育中。这种"慷慨"并非只限于小学教育，甚至连中学教育都是对公众免费的。③

1835年到1861年这段时期是美国历史的大发展时代，领土不断向西扩张，而东部的工业迅猛发展，教育得以觉醒，尤其是在新英格兰地区。这段时期也是民主思想和人类福祉信念得以发展的时期。政治家、宗教思想家、社会改革家和其他所有人都相信公民权的扩展、工业繁荣发展、社会大众脱离贫穷与犯罪都需要一种新的民主教育体系。如果所有公民都被赋予投票权，那他们必须都能胜任投票。对公众进行教育被认为是实现这一理想的手段。早在1852年，马萨诸塞州就推行了《义务教育法》，州内建立了许多公立学校，所有的儿童被要求上学，接受阅读和思考的训练。

这个教育觉醒和广为设立公立学校的大时代同时促成了另外一件事——现代图书馆的形成。教育者认识到正规学校教育的时间毕竟是有限的，学校教育的教学方法只是教会学生如何阅读、拼写、写作，但很少教学生如何自我教育。教育工作者也清晰地认识到如果年轻人在离开学校、挣钱养家之后，没有机构为他们提供令人满意的读物将是不幸的。在1877年为马萨诸塞州昆西的老师们所做的一次演讲中，小查尔斯·弗朗西斯·亚当斯④表达了对那时年轻人所受的一知半解的教育的悲观看法。

---

① 【译者注】《爱弥儿》，是十八世纪法国启蒙思想家、教育家卢梭的长篇教育哲理小说，对近代教育产生了深远的影响。全名为《爱弥儿，或论教育》，全书共分为5卷。其中1—4卷依次分别论述儿童身心发展的4个时期的特点、教育内容和方法。

② 【译者注】费城独立百年纪念博览会（Centennial Exposition）:1876年在宾夕法尼亚州费城为庆祝美国独立100周年而举办的一次规模庞大的世界博览会。300万名来访者到博览会参观杰出的科学成就和发明。博览会标志着美国已从国内战争时期政治、工业和财政各方面的困境中恢复过来。

③ 【原注】F. V. N. Painter. *History of Education*. Appleton. New York. 1903. p. 321-2.

④ 【译者注】小查尔斯·弗朗西斯·亚当斯（Charles Francis Adams, Jr.）:铁路专家，学者。1856年毕业于哈佛大学。曾参与马萨诸塞州教育改革。著有《铁路的起源与问题》《马萨诸塞的历史与历史学家》《1775—1865年美国军事、外交研究》及自传等。

孩子们被要求学习一些奇怪的单字定义或一些令人不快的数字测验,仿佛这是很有价值的收获……结果是勤奋聪颖的学生获得大量艰涩的知识,但之后他们又很快会忘掉;当他们离开文法学校(grammar schools),他们已成为人们欣然称呼的"教育的雏形",然而他们中二十个没有一个能坐下来使用正确的单词拼写写一封普通的信,准确清晰地表达一个想法;离开学校的人中拥有这种能力或渴望进一步自我教育的比例就更低了……一个全部童年在普通学校度过、能够阅读报纸或书的人并不比一个完全不能阅读的人更好到哪儿去。事实上,我怀疑,因为早就感到书本知识在普遍意义上起不了多少作用,所以即使他或她如此这般地"文明开化"了,也不能避免其依然可能成为"野蛮人"。几乎不能读出报纸的人干的活儿十有八九都只限于暴力尤其是谋杀等这些娴熟"下三烂"手段的行为。众所周知,一知半解是危险的,学的越少越危险。①

当时许多伟大的教育家觉得在公立学校之外需要有更多的教育方法,需要建立一些教育机构以承继学校所拉开的教育帷幕。他们希望有一些机构能发挥持续教育的影响力,不分长幼,可以提供公民个性发展所需,并能满足大家对阅读的热爱。这个机构就注定是公共图书馆。自从十九世纪上半叶,现代公共图书馆已逐步与公立学校一起建立起来了。公立学校不仅教学生如何阅读、如何拼写、如何写作,也开始教他们利用公共图书馆里的书籍进行自我教育。从那时起,学校和图书馆就肩并肩发挥着教育的功用。图书馆成为学校的天然补充。在教师与图书馆员的视野中,二者之间从一开始就有密切地合作。

1887年,塞缪尔·S.格林在马萨诸塞州伍斯特市(Worcester,Massachusetts)进行了一场以前从未尝试过的实验,他在六年级、七年级、八年级、九年级的教室里各布置了一个小图书馆,放了一些对学生们的作业很有帮助的图书。在1886—1887学年中的200多天,这些图书的使用结果如下:②

　　九年级　用作家庭读物856　　用作学习参考2522
　　八年级　用作家庭读物595　　用作学习参考1565
　　七年级　用作家庭读物650　　用作学习参考1032
　　六年级　用作家庭读物595　　用作学习参考908

由学校老师和学者所推动的对现代公共图书馆设施的使用产生了令人满意的效果。许多学校的校长已经意识到现代公共图书馆不仅是有用的,而且是公立学校系统不可或缺的组成部分。如果仅仅设立了公立学校,而没有设立其天然且必要的补充——现代公共图书馆,那教育的民主思想就将得不到充分的发展。没有图书馆,学校中的工作将变成死记硬背教科书上的知识点,而教室中被唤醒的对知识的渴求却得不到满足。1888年,杜威(Melvil Dewey)③在纽约州立大学集会上的演讲也强调了这一观点。

我们的学校充其量只是提供一些工具(这些工具对大多数人而言极其初等),但今天看

---

① 【原注】C. F. Adams, Jr. The Public Library and the Public Schools. *Library Journal*. I:437-8. August, 1877.

② 【原注】S. S. Green. The Public Library and the Schools in Worcester. *Library Journal*. 12:119-21. March, 1887, and *Library Journal*. 12:400-2. September-October, 1887.

③ 【译者注】杜威(Melvil Dewey):美国图书馆学家。《杜威十进分类法》创编人。曾先后任哥伦比亚大学图书馆、纽约州立图书馆馆长,创办《图书馆杂志》并任主编。

来,在理想的图书馆中,我们会发现一些有助于养成良好公民意识和实现更好生活的材料。学校提供凿子,图书馆提供大理石,要想雕出雕像,二者缺一不可。①

因此,面向公众的教育活动导致了公立学校的建立,同时也是公立图书馆发展的重要影响因素之一。在公立学校中受教育的孩子们在离开学校或教师自身发挥不了太大作用时,依然要继续他们的学习训练。除了年轻人之外,每个社区中还有成年人需要受教育。因此,政府的责任不仅包括建立和维护由税收支持的、面向年轻人的学校,还应该包括面向所有年龄群的公共图书馆。民主的政府不能囿于这样的想法,认为普通公众的领域就仅仅是工作,而不包括阅读和思考。为了达成教育的民主思想,政府承担起为那些清楚地认识到公共图书馆服务价值和重要性的公众提供相应服务的责任。然后,这些人就会心甘情愿地为维持图书馆而纳税。

认可公共图书馆作为公共教育体系的基本组成部分,这一理念首倡于 1826 年,由时任纽约州州长的德威特·克林顿(DeWitt linton)②提出。1838 年,纽约州州务卿约翰·亚当斯·迪克斯将军,"负责执行这一法律,每年给予学区 55,000 美金,用于其图书馆购置图书,并要求学区为同样目的而筹集等额的税收"③。

因此,纽约有幸成为第一个充分认识到公共图书馆在实现公众教育的民主思想中的意义的州。不久,马萨诸塞州的图书馆也在著名教育家霍瑞斯·曼(Horace Mann)④倡导下建立起来。霍瑞斯曾亲身受益于富兰克林的小图书馆。温希普先生(A. E. Winship)撰写的《伟大的美国教育家》(*Great American Educators*)一书中记录了这个故事,"这个图书馆提供的书是霍瑞斯·曼在青少年时期唯一能接触到的书,没有这些书他可能就不会获得奖学金,世界也可能就错过了一位才华横溢的美国教育家。曼先生如此地感激这个图书馆,以至于多年后谈及这个图书馆时,他依然非常愿意像农民播撒麦种一样向人们广为传颂图书馆的益处"⑤。凭借曼先生的热情和影响力,马萨诸塞州于 1837 年通过了《学区图书馆法》(*School District Library Law*)。

1837 年,密歇根州也在其学校法案中吸收和接纳了类似的条款。随即浪潮席卷了其他 17 个州:1839 年,康涅狄格州;1840 年,罗德岛和爱荷华州;1841 年,印第安纳州;1844 年,缅因州;1847 年,俄亥俄州;1848 年,威斯康辛州;1853 年,密苏里州;1854 年,加利福尼亚州和俄勒冈州;1855 年,伊利诺伊州;1870 年,堪萨斯州和弗吉尼亚州;1871 年,新泽西州;1873

---

① 【原注】Melvil Dewey. Libraries as Related to the Educational Work of the State. *Library Notes*. 3:340. June,1888.

② 【译者注】德威特·克林顿(DeWitt Clinton),美国政治家,任纽约州州长(1817—1823,1825—1828)期间,修建了"克林顿渠",将哈得逊河与北美五大湖相连接。他还积极支持免费普及教育、艺术和科学。著作有《引论》(1814)、《纽约州西部怀古》(1817)等。

③ 【原注】Moses Coit Tyler. Historical Evolution of the Free Public Library in America and Its True Function in the Community. *Library Journal*. 9:40-7. March,1884; reprinted in A. E. Bostwick. *Library and Society*. Wilson. New York. 1920. p. 17-32.

④ 【译者注】霍瑞斯·曼(Horace Mann),美国教育家。1796 年 5 月 4 日生于马萨诸塞州富兰克林。1827 年起先后任马萨诸塞州众议院议员、州参议院议员。1848—1853 年,任国会议员。他积极宣传教育的重要性,主张国民教育必须是普及的免费的和世俗的。

⑤ 【原注】A. E. Winship. *Great American Educators*. Werner School Book Co. New York. 1900. p. 17-18.

年,肯塔基州和明尼苏达州;1876年,科罗拉多州。

虽然将公共图书馆与学区作为一个整体来建设的第一次运动因为完全缺少适当的管理而失败了,但它仍然对美国现代公共图书馆的发展产生了三重效果。首先,这是城镇或城市图书馆运动的先驱;如果没有建立学校图书馆的先驱法案,第一个城市图书馆就不能得以在特定的州立法颁布后出现在1848年的波士顿市。美国现在市、县里的现代公共图书馆都是早期祖先的后裔发展起来的。

第二个大的作用是激发了公众对书的热爱以及促进了对知识的传播扩散,使人们了解到公共图书馆向不分年龄、不分贫富、不分受教育水平的广大公众免费开放,是受欢迎的大学。

充分地认识到公共图书馆是公共教育体系的一部分,从而有权要求享有公共财政的支持,这是运动第三个重要影响。通过以上的讨论,我们认识到,除非得到公共图书馆的有力补充,否则公立学校不会得到最充分的回馈。除了是公立学校的补充之外,公共图书馆还是人民的大学,自1835年以来,公共图书馆的蓬勃发展依赖且阐明了教育中的民主思想。

SELECTED BIBLIOGRAPHY

Adams, C. F. Public library and the public schools. Library Journal. 1:437-41. Aug., 1877.

Bostwick, A. E. Co-operation with schools. (In his The American public library. Appleton. New York. 1923. p. 13-14).

Bostwick, A. E. The library and the school. (In his The American public library. Appleton. New York. 1923. p. 100-13).

Chamberlain, Mellon. Public library and public school. Library Journal. 5:299-302. Nov. -Dec., 1880.

Dana, John Cotton. Relations of libraries and schools. (In his Libraries. Wilson. New York. 1916. p. 92-4).

Dewey, Melvil. Libraries as related to the educational work of the state. Library Notes. 3:333-40. June, 1888.

Foster, W. E. Relation of the libraries to the school system. Library Journal. 5:99-104. April, 1880.

Foster, W. E. The school and the library: their mutual relation. Library Journal. 4:319-25. Sept. -Oct., 1879.

Gilbert, Charles B. The public library and the public school. Library Journal. 29:169-73. April, 1904.

Green, Samuel Swett. Libraries and schools: the results of a new experiment in Worcester, Mass. Library Journal. 12: 400-2. Sept. -Oct., 1887.

Green, Samuel Swett. The public library and the schools in Worcester. Library Journal. 12:119-21. Mar., 1887.

Green, Samuel Swett. The relation of the public library to the public schools. Library Journal. 5:235-45. Sept. -Oct., 1880.

Green, S. S., and others. Work between libraries and schools—a symposium. Library Journal. 22: 181-7. April, 1897.

Hoag, J. P. Co-operation of public library and public school. Public Libraries. 9:225-7. May, 1904. Howes, H. A. Legislation for public libraries. Library Journal. 4:262-7. June-July, 1879.

Howes, H. A. Library legislation. (Chronological list of state library laws). Library Journal. 5:79-80. Mar., 1880.

Ogle, John J. The public library and the public elementary school. Library. 8:93-5. 1896.

Painter, F. V. N. History of education. Appleton. New York. 1903. p. 321-2.

Poole, W. F. State legislation in the matter of libraries. Library Journal. 2:7-12. Sept., 1877.

Ranck, Samuel H. How to make the library of greater service to the student of school age. Library Journal. 34:52-4.

Feb. ,1909.

Rathbone, Josephine A. Co-operation between libraries and schools: an historical sketch. Library Journal. 26: 187-91. April, 1901.

Stephens, T. E. Rise and growth of public libraries in America. Library Association of the United Kingdom. Transactions and Proceedings. 1883. p. 17-30.

Tyler, Moses Coit. Historical evolution of the free public library in America and its true function in the community. Library Journal. 9: 40-7. Mar. , 1884. Reprinted in Bostwick, A. E: Library and society. Wilson. New York. 1920. p. 17-32.

United States. Bureau of Education. Free town libraries. (In United States Bureau of education. Special report, 1876. p. 445-56).

United States. Bureau of Education. General statistics of all public libraries in the United States. (In United States Bureau of education. Special report, 1876. chap. 39).

Winship, A. E. Great American educators. Werner School Book Co. New York. 1900. p. 17-18.

第二章　高等教育的研究精神

　　一百年前的大学学习概念与今日相比已十分不同。过去学生认为他们的老师是活百科全书。他们记录教授所说的一字一句,逐字学习教科书,并不查阅其他权威读物。所学学科也主要被限制在拉丁语、希腊语、数学和哲学。神学、法律和医学是只针对研究生的特殊学科。

　　基于有限经典课程和文化研究的早期大学图书馆并不需要大量的藏书。僵硬地教科书教学方法很少使用大学图书馆。大学里的图书馆是珍本书的博物馆,或者被认为是"高等教育的优雅伴侣"①。图书馆员通常也是进行常规课堂教学的教授。办公室只是挂名差事,工作只是每周图书馆开放三到四个小时、出借一些感兴趣的图书。图书馆实际上就是储存和收藏图书的地方。在这样的气氛下,学生并不喜欢或渴望使用大学图书馆,从而他们也并不欢迎或需要大学图书馆员。1879 年 9 月 10 日,哈佛大学图书馆的杰出馆长贾斯汀·温泽(Justin Winsor)②在萨拉托加(Saratoga)为美国社会科学协会所做的演讲中描绘了那时大学图书馆的情况。

　　那时,大学生每周勉强能来图书馆一次或两次,在这种印象下绝不会有什么好的效果。"同学们!"在我们这代人的记忆中,我们大学图书馆第一批馆员会喊道,"同学们!你们在干什么呢!这不是适合你呆的地方!"可怜的充满求知欲的学生们只好溜走,躲进寝室里阅读欧几里得和贺拉斯。③

　　知识领域在上世纪的扩大已对学术教学的方法产生了深远的影响。在新学科快速增长的情况下,学生们认识到无法追求所有的知识。大学的管理者和教授也认识到这种情形,并因此竭尽全力推行一套新的教学方法。他们促进了一套选课制度的广泛采用,根据教学大纲推出了专题研究,并强调课外读物。所有这些方法鼓励、指导学生并不仅仅局限于教科书。学生们选择自己喜欢的学科。教授在学科上更多地是向学生推荐各种权威。这样的结果就是课堂上有更自由地观点表达和判断,教学不再仅仅局限于单一的教科书上的知识。

　　除了这些创新的教学方法之外,德国大学图书馆的运行方法也被引进。上个世纪,许多美国学者亲身体验了德国的大学教育,随后深受哥廷根大学、柏林大学、莱比锡大学、哈雷大学和其他德国大学的学术影响。这些影响对建立美国大学图书馆馆藏起了作用,而且在美国创建专业图书馆方面引领风气之先。

　　这些研究的新方法基于思想自由和广阔见识的深层观念,这些都是研究精神的实质。

---

　　① 【原注】C. E. Lowrey. University Library, Its Larger Recognition in Higher Education. *Library Journal*. 19: 264. August, 1894.

　　② 【译者注】贾斯汀·温泽(Justin Winsor),1831—1897,美国图书馆学家。曾任波士顿公共图书馆负责人及哈佛大学图书馆馆长。1876 年创办美国图书馆协会,为第一任会长。是美国早期图书馆界重要领导人之一。编辑过《美国历史述评》(8 卷)。

　　③ 【原注】Justin Winsor. College and Other Higher Libraries. *Library Journal*. 4:401. November, 1879.

观点不是泛泛而谈的,公正的思想也不是泛泛而谈的,要基于对各种权威著作的研读。这些教学方面的演化,为大学图书馆的管理带来了不可避免的改变,同时,也是现代大学图书馆和研究型图书馆发展的重要因素。正如特温校长(President Thwing)①所说的,"大学图书馆增长的原因被理解成单一的活动。事实上,它是面向研究的活动。大学意味着学术,学术研究既是书籍的成因也是书籍的结果。学习的连续性体现在图书馆中。图书馆收藏了过去所有的知识财富。它代表了人们所有为之奋斗或已得到的知识,因此图书馆是语言学家、哲学家和历史学家的宝库,甚至科学家也可以在图书馆中找到过去实验或成功或失败的记录"②。

过去 50 年间,基于大学图书馆的广泛使用和快速增长的既定事实,关于现代图书馆增长重要性的理论经久不衰。1875 年以前,美国大学图书馆的使用量有限,发展缓慢。如果比较开放时间、藏书规模、年度购书经费,我们会发现今日的美国大学图书馆与十九世纪中期时的已有明显不同。哈佛大学图书馆建成于 1638 年,但直到 200 多年后,经过图书馆员的经年努力,仅有 41 000 册馆藏。1879 年,约翰·兰顿·西布利(John Langton Sibley)③教授在给美国图书馆员的演讲中有力地谈到,"经过磋商,图书馆周一到周四上午 9 点到中午 1 点、下午 2 点到 4 点开放,周五只上午开放。大二学生周二、大一学生周三可以带出书籍 1 小时,周一和周四则是大三和大四的学生。走廊里没有书架,戈尔馆被认为大到可以容纳一个世纪的所有增加的馆藏。从永久基金支出的用以购买、修补、装订图书的所有经费每年正好是 250 美元"④。现代大学图书馆员会把这种情况视为一个笑话,但是,84 年前这的确存在于这所美国最负盛名的大学中。那时,哈佛大学图书馆的开放时长处于领先的地位,对于学生使用书籍也采用自由主义的原则。至于其他大学图书馆,他们的馆藏量要远远少于哈佛大学图书馆。关于 1850 年大学图书馆的开放时间的一些有趣事实,西北大学图书馆科赫(Koch)馆长曾说道,"举例来说,1850 年,阿默斯特学院和三一学院的图书馆每周开放一次,下午一点到三点;普林斯顿大学每周开放两次,每次 1 小时;密苏里大学每两周开放一小时。阿拉巴马大学有一个规定,'图书通常只能在门口借还,借书人不允许进入图书馆'。哈佛大学图书馆每周开放 28 小时在当时已是相当地进步了,相比而言,今日长达 89 小时或更长的时间,图书馆的开放时间已取得了长足的进步"⑤。

我们从上述说明中已经了解了当下大学图书馆开放时间的结论。每一所大学图书馆的馆员都能作证,图书馆开放时每小时都会有教师或学生光顾。当新引进一批学习和研究所必须的阅读材料时,图书馆又会施行更长的开放时间。不仅仅是开放时间的延长,伴随着馆藏的增长,图书馆的使用量也在增加,新图书馆的建立被认为是教学新方法的结果。为了清

---

① 【译者注】特温(Charles F. Thwing),1853—1937,生于缅因州纽沙伦镇的一个牧师家庭,从哈佛大学和安多福神学院毕业后,在教会服务多年,后长期担任西储大学(Western Reserve University)校长。他也是一位追求社会进步的活动家,著有《大学校长》《美国高等教育史》《大学管理》《远东教育》等。

② 【原注】Charles F. Thwing. *A History of Higher Education in America*. Appleton. New York. 1906. p. 413.

③ 【译者注】约翰·兰顿·西布利,原文为 John Langton Sibley,亦写作 John Langdon Sibley,1804—1885,1856 到 1877 年担任哈佛大学图书馆馆长。

④ 【原注】John Langton Sibley. An Address before the American Library Association. *Library Journal*. 4:307. August,1879.

⑤ 【原注】T. W. Koch. *On University Libraries*. Paris. 1924. p. 23.

晰地说明1876—1920年间大学图书馆的快速增长,下面将列出60所主要大学图书馆的馆藏量和平均年度增长量的对比表。用于对比的数据来自美国教育部出版的1876年关于图书馆的特别报告统计表,以及美国教育部1923年29号公报(Bulletin No.29,1923)中的关于高等院校的24号统计表(statistical table No.24 on colleges and universities of the United States Bureau of Education)。

60所大学图书馆平均增长量表(创始日至1876年,1876年至1920年)

州名	校名	创始日	1876年馆藏量	1920年的馆藏量	创始日至1876年的平均增长量	1876年至1920年的平均增长量
加利福尼亚州						
	加州大学	1869	13,600	479,000	1,944	10,886
康涅狄格州						
	三一学院	1824	15,000	85,000	288	1,589
	卫斯理大学	1833	26,000	120,000	605	2,136
	耶鲁大学	1700	95,200	1,250,000	541	26,245
哥伦比亚特区						
	乔治城大学	1791	28,000	140,000	329	2,545
佐治亚州						
	佐治亚大学	1831	21,600	66,500	480	1,020
伊利诺伊州						
	芝加哥大学	1857	18,000	599,492	947	13,215
	西北大学	1856	33,000	193,662	1,650	3,651
印第安纳州						
	华佰士学院	1833	10,482	56,000	244	1,033
	印第安纳大学	1828	5,300	134,370	110	2,933
	圣母玛利亚大学	1843	10,000	103,000	303	2,113
爱荷华州						
	爱荷华州立大学①	1860	8,823	162,000	551	3,481
缅因州						
	鲍登学院	1802	22,760	125,000	307	2,323
	贝茨学院	1859	6,800	47,000	400	913
	科尔比大学	1813	11,100	56,000	176	1,020

---

① 【原注】According to the history of the General Library of the State University of Iowa, the first collection of books for a general library began in the fall of 1855. See University of Iowa, *The University Libraries. Facilities and Service*. 1924. p.29.

续表

州名	校名	创始日	1876年馆藏量	1920年的馆藏量	创始日至1876年的平均增长量	1876年至1920年的平均增长量
马里兰州						
	圣玛丽山学院	1808	7,000	20,000	103	295
马萨诸塞州						
	阿默斯特学院	1821	30,406	125,000	553	2,150
	哈佛大学	1638	212,050	2,028,100	891	41,274
	麻省理工学院	1866	2,500	140,737	250	3,142
	塔夫茨学院	1854	16,000	80,000	727	1,454
	威廉姆斯学院	1793	17,500	96,320	211	1,791
密歇根州						
	密歇根大学	1841	27,500	432,394	785	9,202
明尼苏达州						
	明尼苏达大学	1869	10,000	300,000	1,428	6,591
密西西比州						
	密西西比大学	1848	6,192	31,000	221	564
密苏里州						
	密苏里大学	1840	11,000	223,670	305	4,883
	圣路易斯大学	1829	17,000	75,000	362	1,318
	华盛顿大学	1853	4,500	176,013	196	3,898
新罕布什尔州						
	达特茅斯学院	1770	25,500	150,000	240	2,829
新泽西州						
	罗格斯学院	1770	6,814	106,000	64	2,254
	新泽西学院(普林斯顿大学)	1775	29,500	444,268	244	9,426
纽约州						
	汉密尔顿学院	1812	22,000	87,000	344	1,477
	康奈尔大学	1868	39,000	630,637	4,874	13,446
	纽约城市学院	1850	20,000	71,000	769	1,159
	哥伦比亚大学	1757	31.390	737,448	264	16,274
	瓦瑟学院	1865	9,881	116,300	898	2,419
	罗切斯特大学	1850	12,000	83,003	461	1,614
	联合学院	1795	19,800	58,450	244	878
	雪城大学	1871	10,000	109,500	2,000	2,261
	西点军校	1812	25,000	103,620	390	1,787

续表

州名	校名	创始日	1876年馆藏量	1920年的馆藏量	创始日至1876年的平均增长量	1876年至1920年的平均增长量
北卡罗来纳州						
	北卡罗来纳大学	1795	8,394	93,914	103	1,944
俄亥俄州						
	辛辛那提大学	1875	500	125,000	500	2,830
	欧柏林学院	1834	7,000	204,501	167	4,488
	俄亥俄卫斯理大学	1856	10,400	90,000	520	1,809
	玛瑞埃塔学院	1835	15,130	83,000	369	1,543
宾夕法尼亚州						
	迪金森学院	1783	7,765	34,000	83	596
	拉法耶特学院	1832	16,400	49,098	373	743
	宾夕法尼亚学院	1832	7,200	35,000	164	632
	哈弗福德学院	1833	7,000	81,000	163	1,682
	富兰克林与马歇尔学院	1853	3,500	48,000	152	1,011
	宾夕法尼亚大学	1755	23,250	503,572	192	10,916
罗德岛州						
	布朗大学	1768	45,000	270,000	417	5,114
南卡罗来纳州						
	查尔斯顿学院	1825	8,000	21,902	157	316
	南卡罗来纳大学	1805	27,000	65,000	380	864
佛蒙特州						
	佛蒙特大学	1800	13,521	105,000	178	2,079
	明德学院	1800	12,000	50,000	158	864
弗吉尼亚州						
	弗吉尼亚大学	1825	40,000	120,300	784	1,825
	华盛顿和李大学	1796	11,000	50,000	137	863
	威廉玛丽学院	1700	5,000	21,000	28	363
威斯康辛州						
	贝洛伊特学院	1848	8,300	65,000	296	1,289
	威斯康辛大学	1849	6,670	276,000	247	6,121

以上表中60所高校图书馆的例子表明每一所图书馆在1876至1920年间馆藏平均增长速度比其创始日至1876年间要更快。1876至1920年间，哥伦比亚大学图书馆的年均增

长率是 1757 至 1876 年间的 61 倍,而在此期间耶鲁大学图书馆的年均增长率是 1700 至 1876 年间的 48 倍。1876 年以前,哥伦比亚大学年均增长 264 册图书,耶鲁年均增长 541 册图书。有人可能会说,因为一些严重的因素,比如火灾、战争、档案缺失和每年订购的不规律性,1876 年以前的图书馆年均增长率并不能被视为可靠的记录。比如,哈佛大学图书馆名义上创始于 1678 年,事实上直到 1764 年大火之后才是其真正的起源。的确,对于 1876 年之前图书馆每年增加的馆藏量我们无法采取更为精确的数字,但尽管如此,上表所列数字已非常明确地显示了 1876 至 1920 年间高校图书馆馆藏量的快速增长。不单单是那些老牌大学里的图书馆已经快速发展了,更多地后起大学已经有了同样的觉醒。例如,有一些学院图书馆 1876 年或之后都还没有建立,他们的发展也很迅速。约翰·霍普金斯大学图书馆和俄勒冈大学图书馆均开始于 1876 年,在过去 44 年间(1876—1920),他们各自拥有了 225,000 册、94,000 册馆藏。1883 年,德克萨斯大学成立,经过大约 37 年的发展,已拥有馆藏 194,459 册。大学图书馆的快速发展期已经开始了,并且随着大学里研究精神加剧了科学与专业学科各个分支教学方法的改进,这种发展仍将保持加速增长的势头。现今,我们的口号是"使用,更多地使用大学图书馆"。当下大学的教学方法提高了图书馆的使用量,图书馆已经成为人类知识每个阶段的精神实验室。

芝加哥大学校长哈珀在 1894 年 3 月 14 日给科罗拉多学院图书馆的献辞中很好地描述了大学图书馆在大学教育功能中的重要角色,文章一开始他描绘了十九世纪中后叶的大学图书馆:

如果计算馆藏数量或评估馆藏的价值以配上图书馆之名,25 年前,我们大部分机构的图书馆都不是足够大的,即使是最古老的图书馆也不例外。只要有场所,图书馆就是教授们习惯偶尔前去的场所,学生几乎从不去……今天大学里的主要建筑,校园中最值得骄傲的建筑就是图书馆。拥有储存书库、参考书阅览室、传递办公室、讨论室,图书馆就是大学活动的中心。极少情况下,图书馆馆长不是员工中最博学的人之一,在许多情况下,还是最有影响力的人之一。有时,他要给学生做有关书目的报告,或组织图书使用辅导的课程。30 年前,图书馆助理的数量要比整个机构的所有教员数量都多。馆藏单年就可增加 3000 册、5000 册、10000 册或 20000 册,各学科的期刊文献也归档了,整个图书馆建筑日夜开放……50 年前,我们对大学工作的要素——图书馆几乎一无所知,半个世纪后的今天它已经成为大学智力活动的中心,图书馆与其姐妹——50 年前也同样未知的实验室一道,正变成为大学本身。①

这是一个非常热情的声明。随着大学研究精神的发展,大学图书馆将成为智力活动的心脏,源源不断地向教师和学生提供生命和力量。

SELECTED BIBLIOGRAPHY

Adams, John. College library (*In* Mellen Chamberlain's John Adams and addresses. Houghton. Boston. 1899. p.392-425).

---

① 【原注】William Rainey Harper. *Trend in Higher Education.* University of Chicago Press. Chicago. 1905. 120-2.

英文著作

Bicknell, Percy F. University and college libraries and their relation to the library movement of today. Public Libraries. 2:301-4. June, 1897.

Canfield, James H. The library of the American university. Public Libraries. 9:385-8. Oct., 1904.

Carlton, W. N. Chattin. College libraries in the midnineteenth century. Library Journal. 32:479-86. Nov., 1907.

College Libraries. (*In* United States Bureau of education. Special report, 1876. p. 60-126).

Compton, Charles H. Library in relation to the university. Library Journal. 35:494-503. Nov., 1910.

Fletcher, W. I. Yearly report on college libraries. Library Journal. 10:267-9. Sept.-Oct., 1885.

Guild, Reuben A. The college library. Library Journal. 10:216-21. Sept.-Oct., 1885.

Hadley, Arthur T. The library in the university. Public Libraries. 14:115-17. April, 1909.

Harper, William Rainey. The trend in higher education. Chicago University Press. Chicago. 1905. Chap. 5.

Johnston, W. Dawson. Librarian as an educator. Library Journal. 35:437-41. Oct., 1910.

Koch, Theodore Wesley. On university libraries. Paris. 1924.

Lowrey, C. E. University library, its larger recognition in higher education. Library Journal. 19:264-8. Aug., 1894.

Poole, W. F. The university library and the university curriculum. Library Journal. 18:470-3. Nov., 1893.

Richardson, E. C. The place of the library in a university. American Library Association Bulletin. 10:1-13. Jan., 1916.

Robinson, Otis H. College library administration. (*In* United States Bureau of education. Special report, 1876. p. 505-25).

Robinson, Otis H. The relation of libraries to college work. Library Journal. 6:97-104. April, 1881.

Robinson, Otis H. Rochester university library—administration and use. (*In* United States Bureau of education. Circulars of information No. 1, 1880. p. 15-27).

Scudder, Horace E. College libraries a hundred years ago. (*In* United States Bureau of education. Special report, 1876. p. 21-31).

Sibley, John Langton. An address before the American library association. Library Journal. 4:305-8. Aug., 1879.

Thwing, C. F. University libraries. (*In* his A short history of higher education in America. Appleton. New York. 1906. p. 408-17).

United States. Bureau of Education. Bulletin No. 29, 1923. Biennial survey of education, 1918-1920. Washington, D. C. 1923.

University of Iowa. The university libraries, facilities and service. Iowa City. 1924.

Wharey, James B. Modern teaching and the library. Library Journal. 32:153-6. April, 1907.

Winsor, Justin. College library. (*In* United States Bureau of education. Circulars of information, No. 1. 1880. p. 7-14).

Winsor, Justin. College and other higher libraries. Library Journal. 4:339-402. Nov., 1879.

Woodruff, Edwin H. University libraries and seminary methods of instruction. Library Journal. 11:219-24. July, 1886.

第三章　纸质印刷材料的增长

十九世纪最后的 25 年标志着出版时代的开始,这是一个包括科学的、哲学的、社会学的以及刚冒头还什么也不是的学科的出版时代。在科学领域,这是实证研究方法具体化的最后 250 年,这是从科技革命伟大时期产生的硕果。在哲学和自然科学领域,经验主义和进化论使得知识分子和普通人的心中都充满了持怀疑态度的好奇。在社会科学领域,工业革命的成果使得人们对社会团体重新产生了新的认知。现代发明和应用化学领域的美妙发现彻底改变了人们的普通生活条件和人生观。日常工作的人们已经被他们周围发生的奇迹搞得手足无措,他们开始马不停蹄地学习这些科技发明的奇迹,并不断地重新向自己诠释生活的真谛。这些人们的需求唤起了一大批出版物的发行。印刷大时代以迅猛之势涌现的阅读材料的大生产为特点。科学家们出版他们的研究成果;哲学家们出版他们对生活和知识的新阐释;心理学家们出版他们关于智力测验的先进理论;沙文主义者们出版他们的战争言论;企业家发布他们构思巧妙的商品广告。这期间不仅有各学科的书籍、专著和宣传册的出版,期刊和报纸的数量和品种也日渐增多。

如果将 1875 年的报纸与现今的报纸相比较,人们会因当今报纸极其冗长的版面而大吃一惊。今天的报纸只顾着出版新闻了,不论是当地新闻、国家新闻还是国际新闻也好,却都没有考虑这些新闻是否是重要的,或者是否是针砭时弊的。股票交易所信息、金融市场、逸闻趣事、科学辩论和艺术讲座占据着当今都市日报的很多版面。报纸上的广告和填字游戏也带给读者很多乐趣。过去,报纸只有 2 到 4 页,而今天的报纸通常超过 20 页,以至于需要版面索引的引导。

人们阅读的不仅有日报,还有周刊和月刊。根据约翰·科顿·丹纳先生的估计,10 年前的美国在 1 年中出版的日报、周刊和月刊的数量如下①:

  日报　　··················　2.865.466.000 本
  周刊　　··················　1.208.190.000 本
  月刊　　··················　　263,452,000 本
  共计　　··················　4,337,108,000 本

在叙述出版时代对现代图书馆业发展的深刻影响前,有两个重要的因素不容忽视。首先,今天的纸张价格比 50 年前还要便宜;其次,印刷机械设备的改进使得海量出版成为现实。纽瓦克市公共图书馆馆员丹纳先生在一次于宾夕法尼亚州图书馆协会的演讲中曾简明扼要地指出:"1870 年,一张质量不良的印刷纸张成本为 16 美分一磅,而如今,一张质量上乘的印刷纸张仅为 2 美分一磅……截止到 1880 年,铅字距离它最初的发明已经经过了几百年的历史,铅字技术也因而已经十分成熟和固定。现在的打孔机,作为排版所需中最贵的因素之一,几乎也可以自动地根据模子进行切割,用于任何大小、任何给定样式的铅字。据报

---

① 【原注】J. C. Dana. *Libraries.* Wilson. New York. 1916. p. 43-9

道,维克斯(Wicks)铸造机大约减少了铅字制作的一半费用……兰斯顿(Lanston)发明的莫诺铸排机——可以完成一个排字工人手工所能完成的所有任务——可以自动地以惊人的速度来铸造、安置铅字和修正文字排版,而它只需要一条恰当穿孔的纸带,并且操作起来几乎与操作一个打字机一样简单容易。莱诺整行铸排机(Linotype)可以铸造几乎任何我们所需要的表面的固体铅字。所有大型论文和大部分书籍都被浇铸成铅版以用于打印。现在的机器根据几秒之内建立的矩阵再制作成铅板,只需要几分之一分钟……现在我们已经可以获得能在一小时内完成十万份报纸的十二色印刷、折叠的印刷机。"①

随着造纸术和印刷术的进步,纸质材料的生产不仅更加容易,而且成本更低,人们的阅读需求也因此得以满足。与此同时,学校和大学里涌现出更多喜爱阅读的学生,公共图书馆和大学图书馆也因此拥有更多类型的读者。人们的视野变得更加宽广,阅读习惯逐渐养成,求知欲不断增强。这些趋势已经在商业性出版物的预料之中了。优秀的作家,相对于那些凭借真诚信仰而写作的老一辈作家来讲,更倾向于编写宣传册,而不是出版专著。因为能够迎合大众兴趣的出版物比朴素的描述真理的作品能够获得更多的经济回报。任何书籍,只要有市场,出版商便愿意出版。因此,图书市场上不仅有学术著作,还有很多五花八门的商业化的文学出版物。

这些具有短期价值甚至长期价值的出版物的大量出版,带来了什么影响呢?其中一项最直接的影响就是现代各类型图书馆的快速发展,尤其是州立图书馆和专业图书馆。总体来讲,纸质出版物的增加使得专业图书馆显得非常必要。图书馆的藏书量越大,书籍管理工作就越复杂,图书馆员需要能够以较少的人力和有限的经费管理这些书籍。无论一家图书馆的收入有多高,它都无法跟得上出版物增长的速度。因此,书籍选择和明确区分不同类型图书馆的性质和馆藏范围比以往任何时候都显得重要。

到目前为止,图书馆购买标准著作的时候关注的都是那些知名作家的作品,而不是考虑作品的学科分类。在海量出版物的时代,图书馆采用这样的采购政策并不能满足一个图书馆所有读者的需求。因为这样读者得不到他们想读的书。为了避免使读者失望,图书馆开始采用两种采购政策。首先,图书馆先对自己的馆藏范围和性质进行明确界定,然后只购买与此相关的书籍。其次,他们认识到,与同地区的不同图书馆进行学科分工来采购图书更加经济和高效。例如,芝加哥的约翰克里勒图书馆只购买科学技术类书籍,人文领域的书籍由纽贝里图书馆购买,而芝加哥公共图书馆的各个分馆分别采购小说类、大众文化类和娱乐类书籍。

正如前文所说,出版物的增多促进了两类图书馆在资源采购方面的发展,这两类图书馆分别是州立图书馆和专业图书馆。在美国图书馆历史上,州立图书馆在这方面发展更快。最开始时,只有法律类图书和公文等参考性书籍才被保管在州议会大厦,供立法者和官员使用。通常而言,所有这些参考性书籍就足以超过州立图书馆的馆藏容量,而在参考性书籍之外,有着数目更加庞大的出版物,这样的情形影响着这些州立图书馆的决策。州立图书馆并不期望能够抵制馆藏增长潮流,因此,一些州立图书馆顺应时代潮流,及时地转变成了综合性的参考型图书馆,也有一些州立图书馆转变成法律或历史学科的专业图书馆。随着印刷版材料的增多,州立图书馆的馆藏范围逐渐扩大、馆藏内容逐渐丰富。G.S.戈达德先生在他

---

① 【原注】J. C. Dana. *Libraries*. Wilson. New York. 1916. p. 43-9

的文章《州立图书馆的发展》中这样描述这个观点：

> 人类的知识是无限的，并且它还在继续增长。书籍！书籍！书籍！越来越多。每小时都有一打或者更多的新书问世，而每天有 24 小时，每年有 365 天。这些书籍或许有价值、或许没有，或许是标准书籍、或许不是，或许有读者愿意阅读、或许根本没有。想象一下！从一个永恒到另一个永恒，人们在每一个十年都需要学多少知识，而无论是否学习，这些知识都将被印刷成纸质材料永久保存。任何图书馆，无论是乡镇图书馆、城市图书馆、州立图书馆还是国家图书馆，都不可能馆藏所有的出版物。购买、整理、编目和仓储全部出版物的费用往往让图书馆望而却步。因此，几乎每家州立图书馆都只选择自己的学科范畴的出版物，而非所有学科，以争取尽量完整覆盖其学科的所有书籍，而其他学科的出版物则由别的州立图书馆进行购买和馆藏。①

和州立图书馆的发展相同，国会图书馆在十九世纪末也受到了纸质出版物增长的巨大影响。熟悉国会图书馆历史的人都知道，它是近年来才开始迅速发展的。除了从版权法保护下的存缴本制度获取书籍、获得捐赠以及交换等方式获取书籍外，国会图书馆每年得到的用于采购书籍的政府拨款约为 10 万美元。1852 年，在国会图书馆第 2 次失火后，国会慷慨地为高达 7.5 万美元的图书购置拨款投票。尽管这笔钱在现在对图书馆而言微不足道，但当时却是一笔很大的数额。从 1800 年国会图书馆建馆，到 1860 年，国会图书馆的藏书量虽然有所增长，但也由于这两次毁灭性的大火的部分原因，其馆藏量也仅为 7.5 万册②。16 年后，其藏书量包括宣传册在内就已经增长至 36 万册。在 1897 年，国会图书馆移至新址，当时的馆藏量为 75 万册。而在过去 20 年，包括图书和宣传册在内的馆藏量更是增至 300 万册。这一惊人的增长也从侧面反映出当今印刷材料的激增。或许有人认为馆藏量的增长并非因为出版行业的快速发展，而可能是因为在出版行业快速发展前的图书购置行为，例如皮特福斯图书馆在 1867 年购买了大量的书籍。国会图书馆确实购买了欧洲和亚洲的古老图书，但是用于购买当代有价值的正版书籍和宣传册的大额财政年度拨款才是真正影响国会图书馆定位、促进国会图书馆发展的主要因素。现任国会图书馆馆员普特南博士，在美国图书馆协会于 1905 年在波兰举办的一次会议上讲到：

> 现在的政府拨款为 9.8 万美元/年。这一经费用于购买当代正版书籍及其他出版物已绰绰有余，甚至有盈余部可以购买那些适合博物馆图书馆的珍稀书籍。但这些经费并没有用于购买那些在外形上珍稀或者罕见的书籍，而是用于购买在内容上真正有价值的书籍。③

因此，出版物的增多确实影响了现代图书馆的发展，并使州立图书馆逐渐转变为综合性参考型图书馆和专业参考型图书馆，而将国会图书馆转变为全国性的参考型和研究型图书馆。

---

① 【原注】G. S. Godard. Development of the State Library. *Library Journal*. 30:38-9. September, 1905; reprinted in *Library and Its Organization*, ed. by G. G. Drury. Wilson. New York. 1924. p. 281-6.

② 【原注】A. R. Spofford. *Library of Congress or National Library*. (*In* United States Bureau of Education, Special Report, 1876. p. 256).

③ 【原注】Herbert Putnam. The Library of Congress as a National Library. *Library Journal*. 30:29. September, 1905.

专业图书馆分为静态和动态两类。静态的专业图书馆,诸如纽约协和神学院图书馆、费城法律协会图书馆和波士顿医学图书馆,都是为方便专业协会会员的学习而建立。这类图书馆的馆藏大多并不丰富,即便到1876年的时候亦是如此。根据西奥多·吉尔教授关于美国科学类图书馆的文章(这篇文章在1876年曾作为专题报告呈交给美国联邦教育署),我们可以得知那些为数不多的知名团体的图书馆是当时科学信息的主要来源。而能够支付图书馆所需设备经费的这类学术团体是相当有限的,因此实际上这类图书馆少之又少,不足十余家①。这类图书馆的主要代表是美国国家卫生总监下属的医学图书馆、专利局的应用科学图书馆、美国海军天文台的天文图书馆、波士顿协会自然历史图书馆,以及少数几家位于纽约、费城和波士顿的科学图书馆。

过去50年间自然科学和应用科学领域的巨大进步促进了科技出版物的生产,而科技出版物的生产极大促进了早期的科学技术图书馆的馆藏发展,并且促进了一些新的图书馆的建立。1924年版的《美国百科全书》其中第391—392页中揭示了美国当时有76家最主要的图书馆,这些图书馆的馆藏能够代表当前人类知识的34门学科。例如,纽瓦克市的保诚保险公司(the Prudential Life Insurance Company)N. J. 拥有一家具有10万册藏书量的保险图书馆。罗素塞奇基金会的社会学图书馆拥有15,695册藏书。纽约大都会博物馆的艺术图书馆拥有2.9万册藏书。美国农业部的农业图书馆拥有131,693册藏书。史密森学会的科学图书馆拥有521,616册藏书。这是静态专业图书馆的巨大进步。

动态的专业图书馆于1909年后在商业公司和工厂中得以发展。这类图书馆的目标是为经理、副经理、工程师、会计、工长等工作在重要岗位上的人员提供与工作有关的科技知识,以及为行业工作或者行业组织整体提供支持。与为科学研究服务的静态专业图书馆不同,动态专业图书馆主要为创新人才和管理人员服务,他们是节省时间的信息机器。商人们深知"知识就是力量",但他们却发现自己没有时间去从浩瀚的商业与科技文献中获取"力量"。然而随着工业机构和商业机构的不断增多和扩张,涉及的管理问题、科学问题、技术问题层出不穷。这使得经理、专家、工长、销售员以及其他单位的领导者需要获取新思维、购置新设备以不断提高工作效率并在行业发展上拥有更广阔的视野。他们需要从出版物这样的宝库中寻求解决方案。因此商业杂志和专业出版物激增。一些大型组织机构发现纸质贸易类出版物在增长知识方面对他们非常有益,现在他们需要的是一种在短时间内获得大量的知识的方式,于是商业图书馆和工业图书馆诞生了。

无论从馆藏范围上还是功能上,动态专业图书馆都有别于静态专业图书馆。动态专业图书馆关注的是关于当前问题的最新资料,而静态专业图书馆的收藏大多是关于专门学科的权威思想成果,这些资料不一定就是现在所需资源,他们主要供学者和研究人员使用。一个是专门收藏用于保存的图书和期刊;另一个则是丢弃那些不再使用的印刷资源。商业图书馆和工业图书馆的收藏原则具有很强的功利性。让我们引用一段话来说明动态专业图书馆的特性、方式以及使用:

专业图书馆(约翰·A·拉普先生特指动态专业图书馆)旨在为特定的机构服务,收藏能够解决机构里具体问题的经验性资料。可以这样区分出动态专业图书馆,即它提供的这

---

① 【原注】Theodore Gill. *Scientific Libraries in the United States.* (*In* United States Bureau of Education, Special Report, 1876. p. 183-4).

些资料供快速取阅,机构和组织借此来应对运作过程中的实际问题的挑战。专业图书馆试图为适合他的人和地方提供知识和信息,因此在其所服务的机构中扮演着重要的角色。①

SELECTED BIBLIOGRAPHY

Babock, Laura E. Reference library in a manufacturing plant. Special Libraries. 2:13-15. Feb. ,1911.

Billings, J. S. Medical libraries in the United States. (*In* United States Bureau of education. Special report,1876. p. 171-82).

Bishop, W. W. How the Library of Congress serves the people. Public Libraries. 19:331-4. Oct. ,1914.

Dana, John Cotton. Libraries. Wilson. New York. 1916. p. 43-9,77-8.

Dudgeon, M. S. The scope and purposes of special libraries. Special Libraries. 3:129-32. June,1912.

Dudgeon, M. S. The Wisconsin legislative library. Yale Review. 16:288-95. Nov. ,1907.

Encyclopaedia Americana. Special libraries. (*In* Encyclopaedia Americana. 1924 ed. Vol. 17, p. 363-5).

Gill, Theodore. Scientific libraries in the United States. (*In* United States Bureau of education. Special report,1876. p. 183-217).

Godard, George Seymour. Development of the state library. Library Journal. 30:37-40. Sept. 1905; reprinted in Library and its organization, ed. by G. G. Drury. Wilson. New York. 1924. p. 281-6.

Griswold, Stephen B. Law libraries. (*In* United States Bureau of education. Special report,1876. p. 161-70).

Lapp, J. A. Growth of a big idea. Special libraries. 9:157-9. Sept. -Oct. ,1918.

Lee, George Winthrop. Library of Stone and Webster, Boston. Special Libraries. 1:44-7. June,1910.

Marion, G. E. The special library field. Special Libraries. . 9:59-64. March,1918.

Putnam, Herbert. The Library of Congress as a national library. Library Journal. 30:27-34. Sept. ,1905.

Spofford, Ainsworth Rand. Library of Congress or national library. (*In* United States Bureau of education. Special report,1876. p. 253-61).

Theological Libraries in the United States. (*In* United States Bureau of education. Special report,1876. p. 127-60).

Whitten, Robert Harvey. Library of the New York Public service commission. Special Libraries. 1: 18-20. March,1910.

Williamson, C. C. The importance of special libraries to the public library. Special Libraries. 1:115-16. Jan. ,1913.

---

① 【原注】John A. Lapp. Growth of a Big Idea. *Special Libraries.* 9:157. September-October,1918.

第四章　图书馆慈善事业

前三章探讨了在现代图书馆发展过程中，具有突出意义的重要因素。图书馆的功能和馆藏各异，决定了其为社会提供的服务各具特色。这点非常重要，与图书馆员的职务、工作、培训及教育紧密相连，我们将在本文的第二部分详细介绍。除了教育之民主思想、研究精神及印刷资料的增加，还有两个直接因素加速了现代图书馆的发展，分别是图书馆慈善事业和图书馆组织。

在美国的图书馆捐赠史上，两起早期事件预示了这个恢弘时代的到来。1700年，教士约翰·夏普捐书给纽约市，第二件事是面向民众开放的会员图书馆及社会图书馆的建立。这两件事将富人的目光吸引到了富有成效的慈善领域[1]。

费城的本杰明·富兰克林是组建会员图书馆的第一人，此后这项运动扩展到了早期殖民地的其他地方。像詹姆士·洛根、约翰·麦肯齐、亚伯拉罕·雷德伍德等一批人，捐出书籍或钱财，建立公共图书馆，以提高民众素养。约翰·雅各布·阿斯特及詹姆士·雷诺克斯为纽约市图书馆的慷慨捐赠，使图书馆慈善运动步入成熟阶段。伦敦的约书亚·贝茨为波士顿公共图书馆做出了丰厚捐赠；沃尔特·卢米斯·纽贝里为芝加哥市民建造了闻名的纽贝里图书馆；詹姆士·拉什为费城公共图书馆里韦奇分馆留下1,000,000美金，用于建造一座宏伟的馆舍；詹姆士·利克为旧金山的图书馆进行过多次捐赠；伊诺克·普拉特为巴尔的摩民众慷慨捐资，用于维持和发展一家图书馆及其分馆。伟大的图书馆慈善家不胜枚举。

当然，安德鲁·卡耐基是所有图书馆捐赠者中最伟大的一位。根据威廉·勒尼德博士统计，在美国、加拿大、夏威夷及波多黎各，卡耐基先生和他的基金会累计捐建1804座馆舍，花费总额共计43,665,513.47美元[2]。

我们可以看到，富人们已经意识到，图书馆领域可以更好地实现慈善事业的价值。那些在现代工商业激烈的竞争中积累了数百万资产，同时又愿意让同胞受益于自己财富的有钱人，表现出了对社会问题的洞察力和前瞻性。在他们看来，教化民众是实现和平与繁荣的首要途径。很多现代富人已经认识到，造物主创造他们，并非只让其支配财富，独享舒适与奢华，这些财富是造物主赋予他们的神圣信任，让其管理，谋求人类福祉。在发人深省的文章《财富》一文中，卡耐基先生对于被其视为富翁们剩余财富的支配，表达出了最仁慈的情感，该文刊登在1889年《北美评论》的六月刊上。

如果仅仅是社区的装饰，卡耐基先生就不会把钱捐给图书馆。对于吹嘘自身行业重要性的指责，卡耐基图书馆馆员并不害怕。因为，首先卡耐基图书馆并不只在那些因受捐赠而有能力修建图书馆的地方发展，在那些无力修建而又迫切需要图书馆的地区，卡耐基图书馆

---

[1]　【原注】H. E. Scudder. *Public Libraries a Hundred Years Ago.* (*In* United States Bureau of Education. Special Report, 1876. p.14).

[2]　【原注】Wm. S. Learned. *The American Public Library and the Diffusion of Knowledge.* Harcourt. New York. 1924. table 1.

同样存在。在慈善事业上,卡耐基先生的黄金准则是,帮助那些可以自助的人群。就像博斯特威克博士关于图书馆捐赠的评论,"大部分数目可观的捐赠需要有公众配合,因此,长远来说,私人捐赠作为图书馆捐赠这个大雪球的核心,在逐渐被日益增加的公众捐款所覆盖,显得微不足道"①。

图书馆慈善没有促使公共免费图书馆的诞生,但是为了满足这一需求,它加速了一场正在开展的运动。有需求,公共机构方可被建立。任何公共机构,因异想天开之人的主观臆断而建立,都不能正常发展,更谈不上长盛不衰,其终究会像温室里的花草一样,一旦进入自然环境就会衰败、凋零。通过公共免费学校来推广公民教育已深入人心,由此带来的结果是读书之人逐渐增多。对公共免费图书馆的需求只是这场运动所带来的一个必然结果。随着需求不断被满足,公共免费图书馆的读者和用户将日益增多,大众书籍也将更方便借阅。这些因素彼此间相互依赖。

可以看出,帮助自己的同胞已经成为许多富人的愿望和信念。卡耐基在《慈善事业的最佳领域》一文中,提到了对富人剩余财富的七种最佳利用方式,并将为公共免费图书馆捐赠置于榜首。他讲道:"我本人对该问题的研究结果是,如果社区可以把图书馆当作公共机构,像学校一样,作为城市财产的一部分来接受并且维护,虽然实际上,图书馆是学校的辅助机构,那么给社区的最好礼物是为其建立免费图书馆。无疑,我的个人经验可能会导致我认为,公共免费图书馆是最好的慈善方式。任何富人,在愿意维护和发展图书馆的社区,建立一座公共免费图书馆,都是对其剩余财富的最佳利用方式。"②卡耐基的捐赠不仅加速了美国公共图书馆事业的发展,而且也加速了英国城市公共图书馆的发展,卡耐基先生和一些英国富人,尤其是爱德华兹,捐赠巨资,帮助穷人进入免费公共图书馆借阅书籍③。

富人为图书馆捐赠所带来的另一个结果,是唤醒了图书馆员,他们中的一部分人此前并没有充分认识到图书馆行业的价值和潜力。图书馆的原始概念是知识库,是保存书籍的地方。早期,在所有表示"图书馆"的词汇中,没有哪种语言可以与汉语所用术语相媲美。最早,汉语里图书馆被称作"藏书楼"。字面意思是藏书于楼上。为什么是在楼上?这涉及藏书过程中的两个重要因素,一是防潮,二是难入。这个词在老子之后一直被使用,约公元前六世纪,老子是周朝档案室首位管理员。这个词新近才被舍弃,取而代之的是一个现代称谓,图书馆,意思是:Tu(图)Ssu(书)Ku'an(馆)。

因此,我们可以看到,概念当中所体现出的图书馆功能发生了很大变化。它不再只是书库,而已然是源泉,充满了生命力,是解决教育问题的先进因素。它还是民众的"继续教育大学",对所有人免费开放,也得到所有人的支持。因此,图书馆员不只保管图书,同时也在教师教育民众的过程中承担着积极的补充作用。捐赠在加快现代图书馆员职能实现的同时,也帮助他们更好地去履行公仆的义务。

---

① 【原注】A. E. Bostwick. *Library Philanthropy*. (*In his The American Public Library*. Appleton. New York. 1923. p. 215).

② 【原注】Andrew Carnegie. The Best Field for Philanthropy. *North American Review*. 149:688-90. December, 1889.

③ 【原注】Ernest A. Baker. *The Public Library*. Grafton. London. 1924. P-24-5.

SELECTED BIBLIOGRAPHY

Baker, Ernest A. The Public library. Grafton. London. 1924. Chap. 1.

Bostwick, A. E., ed. Library and society. Wilson. New York. 1920. p. 49-54, 75-99, 149-67.

Bostwick, A. E. Library philanthropy. (*In* his The American public library. Appleton. New York. 1923. Chap. 15).

Carnegie, Andrew. Autobiography. Houghton. Boston. 1920. Chap. 4.

Carnegie, Andrew. The best field for philanthropy. North American Review. 149:682-98. Dec., 1889.

Carnegie, Andrew. Wealth. North American Review. 148:653-64. June, 1889.

Koch, T. W. Carnegie libraries. Library Journal. 30:78-81. Sept., 1905.

Learned, William S. The American public library and the diffusion of knowledge. Harcourt. New York. 1924. Chap. 4.

Lydenberg, H. M. History of the New York public library. New York Public Library. New York. 1923.

Patronymic Libraries. (*In* United States Bureau of education. Special report, 1876. p. 456-9).

Scudder, H. E. Public libraries a hundred years ago. (*In* United States Bureau of education. Special report, 1876. p. 1-37).

第五章　图书馆协会

　　美国图书馆员建立了世界上第一个国家级图书馆协会。1876年10月6日,美国图书馆协会在费城成立,拥有103位会员。随后,协会于1879年在马萨诸塞州注册①。早在1853年,史密森学会的查尔斯·朱伊特以及其他8位对文献学和图书馆感兴趣的人士曾聚集在纽约讨论设立永久性图书馆协会的多种方式。这些计划直至23年后才得以实现。国家图书馆协会始于美国,而国际图书馆员大会由热心的英国图书馆员发起,1877年国际图书馆员大会在伦敦召开,同年,英国成立了图书馆协会。国际图书馆员大会主席、英国博物馆馆长约翰·温特·琼斯在他的就职演说中这样赞许了美国图书馆员:"我们生活在一个充满各种代表大会和其他各种会议的时代——这意味着,我们生活在一个鼓励思想碰撞和经验交流的时代,同时这个时代也认可社会事务的统一行动。召开图书馆员大会的想法起源于美国——美国在活力和行动上已经为世界树立了典范——而在图书馆员大会方面也具有参考价值和实际效果"②。

　　伦敦国际图书馆员大会精神被众多与会图书馆员们带回到不同国家,随之而来的是众多国家对现代图书馆运动的兴趣高涨以及众多国家图书馆协会的创立。例如,澳大利亚国家图书馆协会成立于1896年,德意志国家图书馆协会成立于1900年,日本国家图书馆协会成立于1901年。此后,意大利、法国、丹麦、挪威和瑞典等国也纷纷效仿,创立了自己的国家图书馆协会。如今,几乎所有的文明国家都以某种方式创建了国家图书馆协会。

　　美国的图书馆员们不仅在世界上首次创建了图书馆协会,也首次创建图书馆俱乐部、州立图书馆协会、专业图书馆协会、美国图书馆学会和图书馆工会。图书馆俱乐部(如纽约图书馆俱乐部和芝加哥图书馆俱乐部)一般由一个城市的图书馆员主办。州立图书馆协会由同一个州内的图书馆员组成。而专业图书馆的馆员则组成了专业图书馆协会。

　　美国图书馆学会给人的印象宛如日本的元老院或英国的上议院。美国图书馆学会成员包括全部前总统、行政长官、美国图书馆协会的理事会成员以及当选院士的学者。他们的主要职责是审议图书馆管理和经济方面的难题。在现实中,学会类似于学术团体或科研院校。大部分美国图书馆协会的成员都将学会会员视为地位较高的长老。这种主观看法可能源自一个事实,即大部分的美国图书馆学会的会员都是图书馆的管理人员,他们拥有提拔同事的实际权力。这在一定程度上也决定了美国图书馆学会与大多数学术团体的不同。迄今为止,该学会并不隶属于美国图书馆协会,而是一直以一个独立组织的身份存在。

　　图书馆工会于1920年成立于大西洋城。其主要目的是作为招聘无专业训练的图书

---

①　【原注】American Library Association:Charter. (*In its Bulletin.* 18:396. September,1924).

②　【原注】J. W. Jones. Inaugural Address at the Conference of Librarians held in London, October, 1877. First International Library Conference in London. *Transactions and Proceedings*, 1877. p,1; or *Library Journal*. 2: 99. November-December, 1877.

助理的机构,并维护他们的精神福利和物质福利①。或许对外人而言,该协会看似是强大的美国图书馆链条中的薄弱环节。它的成立暗示着美国图书馆协会在雇佣工作和"图书馆工人"的福利保证方面存在不足。美国图书馆工会几乎恰好是美国图书馆学会的另一个极端,前者的成员都是普通民众,而后者的成员则是图书馆专家。然而,如果进一步分析任何图书馆的职责和服务,你会发现这与其他资本主义的或劳工的组织完全不同,最本质的区别或许正如美国图书馆协会的口号所言:"以最低的成本为最广大的读者提供最好的阅读体验。"

美国图书馆协会立足于两个原则:服务社会和成员互助。始于1876年的蓬勃发展的图书馆运动在很大程度上是由遵循这些原则的美国图书馆协会会员推动的。美国图书馆协会将最好的服务不分贫富地提供给读者。对于一位真正的图书馆员而言是没有社会不公和种族歧视的。在有效的图书馆管理中,效率往往被着重强调,但人情味也永远不会缺乏。没有一位有能力的图书馆员会将同事视为单纯的机器,他们之间总会有一种和谐互助的关系。正如纽华克公共图书馆的丹纳博士在他的演说中所言:"在团体中具有优势,但优势的真正价值在于发挥优势本身。一个趋向于学术并以统一标准维持成员的组织往往是很狭隘的……因此,鼓励和认可你的同事,与他们合作,并以此为契机共同努力从而达到特定的目的。这样一来,你自己会收获智慧,并获得尊重,且能提高专业技能。"②

由于美国图书馆协会的成员一直很关注自我发展问题,因此他们也往往思维敏捷。他们对图书馆俱乐部和当地图书馆协会的会议有着很大兴趣,并积极参与到大型图书馆的员工培训和暑期学校中,并且其中的大部分人在拥有数年的图书馆工作经验后,还能够到图书馆学校进行1—2年的学习。每一个馆员都认为他的服务将会更好,并认为自己在专业技能上有着持续进步。这样一来,美国图书馆协会通过更好的服务促进图书馆利益的目标得以实现。更好的服务只能通过图书馆员持续的自我完善来实现。勒尼德博士在他的著作《美国公共图书馆与知识传播》一书中称,行业协会作为各自行业标准和资质的监管人,可能再没有这样一批有责任心的人能够比他们更值得放心的信任了③。我们并不认为这是一个以偏概全的观点。勒尼德博士自己本身不是图书馆员,而是一位高级职业教育家。

美国图书馆协会为读者提供的技术援助和资料,应该使任何不友善的评论家都无话可说,而这些评论家对现代图书馆事业的发展无疑是有积极影响的。首先,美国图书馆协会强调相同的方法,旨在确保图书馆员以更低的成本做到更好地工作。其次是图书馆用品,包括书架、书籍、书籍封面、书籍附件、粘合剂、电话单以及其他有用的设备。再次是出版物,这些出版物的内容包括选书、索引、预算、归类、编目、图书采购、组织、管理、图书馆立法以及其他技术问题。他们使图书馆员能够更加有效和科学地管理自己的图书馆。任何新的理论、方法和设备都会在协会的官方出版物中进行描述和讨论。这不仅使美国的图书馆员受益,也使其他国家的图书馆员受益。

从1976年至1907年,表达美国图书馆协会的官方"声音"是《图书馆学刊》。从1907年

---

① 【原注】Constitution of the Library Workers' Association. *Library Journal.* 45:839-40. October,1920.

② 【原注】J. C. Dana. What State and Local Library Associations Can Do for Library Interests. *Library Journal.* 30:20-1. September,1905;or, in his *Libraries.* Wilson. New York. 1916. p. 132-3.

③ 【原注】*American Library Association.* Publications of the American Library Association. (*In Bulletin.* 18:419-26. September,1924).

起,美国图书馆协会出版了自己的通报:《公共图书馆》和《专业图书馆》。此外,州立图书馆和大型图书馆也出版了自己的通报,例如《纽约州立图书馆通报》《纽约公共图书馆通报》和《匹兹堡卡内基图书馆月报》。

至于为读者提供的解释材料,大致分为两类。一类是如何在图书馆内快速找到所需指示的快速指南。这类快速指南具有多种形式,例如海报、标语、传单、书籍列表和指导读者应于何处以何种方法查找信息的指导手册。另一类是为学生和学者的系统研究提供的材料,诸如索引、笔记和参考目录①。

美国图书馆协会对现代图书馆和图书馆事业的影响是无法估量的。它在整合纸质知识方面的服务非常广泛,对其他国家的图书馆活动的态度也是真诚且具有合作性的。这正是美国图书馆协会的辉煌成就,并使得每一位美国图书馆员都引以为豪。在这个经济动荡和充满阶级斗争的时代,美国图书馆协会或许缔造了这样的典范:通过其成员的共同努力,为人类社会中所有追寻真理的人提供可靠的知识保障。正是因为这样的目标,图书馆馆长和图书馆工作者之间并无分歧,他们是同一个家庭中的兄弟姐妹。他们的共同使命是传播知识,而这正是世界民主的关键所在。

SELECTED BIBLIOGRAPHY

American Library Association. An editorial. Library Journal. 3:43-4. April,1878.

American Library Association. Charter, constitution and by-laws of the American library association. (*In* its Bulletin. 18:396,398-403. Sept. ,1924).

American Library Association. Publications of the American library association. (*In* its Bulletin. 18:419-26. Sept. ,1924).

American Library Institute. Public Libraries. 11:108. Mar. ,1906.

Bostwick, A. E. Organizations of librarians. (*In* his The American public library. Appleton. New York. 1923. Chap. 27).

Brett, Wm. H. Address of the president of the American library association. Library Journal. 22:1-5. Oct. ,1897.

Dana, J. C. What state and local library associations can do for library interests. Library Journal. 30:17-21. Sept. , 1905; or, *in* his Libraries, Wilson. New York. 1916. p. 123-33.

Dewey, Melvil. American library association. Library Journal. 1:245-7, Mar. ,1877.

Dewey, Melvil. Origin of American library association motto. Public libraries. 11:55. Feb. ,1906.

First Convention of Librarians. 1853. Proceedings of the librarians' convention held in New York City, Sept. ,15-17, 1853. Reprinted for William H. Murray. 1915.

Friedel, J. H. Library association. (*In* his Training for librarianship. Lippincott. Philadelphia. 1921. Chap. 18).

Hadley, C. History and aims of the American library association. Educational Bi-Monthly. 4:293-5. April,1910.

Iles, George. A headquarters for our association. Library Journal. 28:24-8. July,1903.

Jones, John Winter. Inaugural address at the conference of librarians held in London, Oct. ,1877. Library Journal. 2: 99-119. Nov. -Dec. ,1877.

Learned, William S. The American public library and the diffusion of knowledge. Harcourt. New York. 1924. p. 57-63.

Library Workers Association. Constitution. Library Journal. 45:839-40. Oct. ,1920.

Work and needs of the American Library Association. Library Journal. 30:858-60. Sept. ,1905.

---

① 【原注】W. S. Learned. *The American Public Library and the Diffusion of Knowledge.* Harcourt. New York. 1924. p. 63.

第二部分 图书馆学专业教育与培训

第六章　古代的图书馆员

第七章　中世纪和近代早期的图书馆员

第八章　现代图书馆员的专业教育

第九章　图书馆学观念的转变和教育要求

第十章　美国的图书馆学校

第六章 古代的图书馆员

最早的图书馆起源于保存一些拜神或争权谋政事件的文献,由于缺乏合适的记录工具,以及书面语言还处于原始状态,留下的文献并不多,不需要有专门的保管员。因此,在学者开始大量使用文献资料之前,图书管理员还承担着很多公务,保存文献只是他的职责之一。

在开始讨论古代图书馆员的教育和职责之前,需要定义古代人理解的两个词,"图书馆"和"图书馆员"①。在理查德森博士出版《古埃及图书馆员》之后②,曾经在马克斯·穆勒(Max Müller)教授和理查德森(E. C. Richardson)博士之间,出现了对这两个词不同的解释。为了避免将现代图书馆员和四千年前的图书保管员相混淆,本文对理查德森博士回应马克斯·穆勒(Max Müller)教授的批评引述如下:

回到图书馆使用的事实,首先,也许有人会说,当它存放档案时,它不是图书馆。在古埃及晚期,正如纸草纸(Papyri)所示,一个人送书(biblion)给书的管理者(bibliophylax),将它放在图书馆(bibliotheke)。按照穆勒教授的说法,这个图书馆不是图书馆,因为这是一个官方记录的存放处!然而,图书馆(bibliotheke),是从开始到现在一直使用的词,是现在除了英语之外所有语言都使用的词,埃及人自己也这样叫"library"为"图书馆",尽管它是档案馆。当代杰出学者在书史中也有应用,德国古典语言学家西奥多·波特写到,"当时的图书馆是存放账册和官方文件的档案馆,"③图书馆是所有书写文件藏品、地点和保管者的总称。马克斯·穆勒教授确实反对把保管神谕抄本的人归为图书馆员?圣经的保管者不是图书馆员?那些由国家派出的专门神谕传送者从不同神庙带回神谕,保存在公共储藏所中;他们还把法律条文,一件一件地,或者大批地送往神庙,并收回神谕的批件;以及克莱奥梅尼(Cleomenes)捕获的雅典人的神谕;当斯巴达人让他们的国王成为神谕的监管者时,这些国王不是"图书馆员"?如果这些图书"保管者"不是图书馆员,那他们是什么?当然,他们不是"图书馆员",因为当这些词开始使用时,"书籍"(liber)和拉丁语还没有创造出来,而他们就是书籍的保管者,正如印刷书籍的保管者或今天大英博物馆的手稿保管者一样。④

关于古代图书馆的记述,材料非常少,而关于他们的图书馆员,几乎毫无线索。但是,仅靠挖掘出来的参考文献零星碎片,足以推断出过去图书馆员的教育和职责。人们总是对自己的祖先感兴趣,对于很多学者来说,宗谱学是一个很有吸引力的研究课题,现代图书馆员也不例外。对过去图书馆员的研究,使现代图书馆员感到自豪,因为他们的祖先出身不凡,

---

① 【原注】William Max Müller. Richardson's Some Old Egyptian Librarians. *Library Journal*. 37:217. April,1912.

② 【原注】E. C. Richardson. Definitions of the Library. (*In his Beginnings of Libraries*. Princeton University Press. 1914. Chapter 3).

③ 【译者注】Birt,原名 Theodor Birt(西奥多·波特),德国古典语言学家,其著作 Buchrolle,原名为 Die Buchrolle in Der Kunst(《卷轴的艺术》),引文出自该书 P247。

④ 【原注】E. C. Richardson. The Facts about Old Egyptian Librarians—a Reply. *Library Journal*. 37:317-18. June,1912.

为人类的文明和进步提供了有益的专业服务,这个观念能够激励现代图书馆员切实行动起来,追随他们的祖先,取得更大的成就。

关于最早的图书馆员,有两个明显的事实:他们是在平均知识水平之上,他们是智慧的领袖。在巴比伦、埃及、印度、中国、希腊和罗马的古代历史中,最早的图书馆员一直是牧师,或者是国王、档案保管员、教师,他们有很多职责,保存官方记录只是职责之一。现今图书馆功能的多样性和图书馆员的专业化工作,都是从最初简单的保存官方文件发展而来的。过去图书馆员的培训过程和作用,一直延续至现代的图书馆员,这表明了斯宾塞(Spencer)[①]的演变法则,也就是"从简单的初始状态到复杂的终了状态",或斯宾塞更加精确的哲学定义,"进化是物质及伴随运动耗散的结合,在这个过程中,物体经历了从不确定的、不相干的同质状态到确定的、相干的异质状态的过程"。起源看似简单,却是现代复杂组织结构的本源。回顾过去是理解现实的方法,而研究现在是预测未来的一种方法。

在了解过去图书馆员的生活,以及学习他们管理图书馆的经验之前,有必要简单解释一下关于时间阶段的划分和各个时代职责的衔接。图书馆员培训的演变可以简单地分为三个时期:古代、中世纪和近代早期、现代。古代是从有历史开始到公元476年西罗马帝国灭亡,中世纪和近代早期是从北方蛮族的入侵开始到十八世纪末结束,现代开始于十九世纪新式图书馆的大发展和图书馆员专业地位的确立。从过去到现在,图书馆员的职责从最简单到最复杂不断发展,纵然这种发展在中世纪初期一度停滞。

根据中国历史古老的、可靠的记录,早在公元前2650年,就有收藏官方文件的图书馆[②],笔者已经看到一些从(中国)河南省出土的写满中国古代象形文字的甲骨。中国文物权威人士认为,这些"骨书"(bone-book)是最早书写的中国档案记录。中国、日本和西方汉学家等一些著名学者,一直在研究这些最早的象形文字。但关于最早的中国图书管理员的记录,还没有发现早于公元前600年。

中国历史上最早的图书馆员是老子,道教的创始人,作品有《道德经》(Book of the Way and Virtue),他具有渊博的古文献知识,被同时代人看作是一位伟大的学者。约公元前553年,老子被任命为周朝的皇家档案保管员,孔子曾为著书问礼老子。那时,不仅有皇家图书馆,而且每个封建贵族都有自己保存书籍的地方。孔子的伟大作品《春秋》,就是根据120个诸侯国的官方档案汇编而成的。

根据历史记载,皇帝通常任命皇家主管看管先朝政事档案和保存当朝重要事件的文献。大约在公元前六世纪,皇家主管下辖的工作人员增多,分成了五个职能部门。主管史官被称为太史(档案主管),负责监督和指导工作,除了要监管图书馆外,还要记录当朝皇帝的活动(类似现代的宫廷通报);小史(助理档案管理员)的职责是管理记录国家重要事件的文献;外史(类似现在的参考馆员)负责管理档案和地理文献;内史是档案主管的秘书;右史观察和记录官员们的活动;小尹仁是助手。

在中国历史和其他文献中,大量资料记录了公元前600年老子时代直至现代中国图书馆发展的历史。有关图书保管员的职责和教育,都可以追溯到可靠的记载,正如著名汉学家

---

① 【译者注】赫伯特·斯宾塞(Herbert Spencer,1820—1903),英国哲学家,以"社会达尔文主义之父"著称。

② 【原注】T. C. Tai. A Brief Sketch of Chinese Libraries. *Library Journal*. 44:423-9-July,1919.

贝特霍尔德·劳费尔(Berthold Laufer)①的评论:"中国人强烈的历史意识是他们最显著的特点之一,几乎没有任何一个国家能够如此自豪的留下了从未间断的历史文献,拥有漫长和可信的记录,绵延1500年,一直持续到公元1644年……除了现存政权之外,存有二十四个前朝的官方记录,称之为《二十四史》,共由3264卷组成,所有的事件都被精确地记录下来,不是一年接一年,而是一个月接一个月,甚至频繁到一天接一天。"②公元1910年以后,图书馆的管理者开始逐渐扩大他们的职责,从而进入现代图书馆管理时期,现在图书馆管理趋势倾向于学习美国的管理方法③。

在近东,考古学家们已经在广阔的领域开展研究。随着1850年保罗·埃弥尔·博塔(P. E. Potta)④和奥斯丁·亨利·莱亚德(Austen Henry Layard)⑤在底格里斯河(Tigris)库云吉克(kouyunjik)的考古发现,研究显示,古巴比伦人(Babylonians)和亚述人(Assyrian)已经有了图书馆。刻有楔形文字的泥板包含尼尼微(Nineveh)⑥国王阿述尔巴尼帕尔(Assur-ba-ni-pal)宫廷图书馆的目录⑦,这些泥板已经按照下列主题进行排列:历史、法律、科学、巫术、教义和传说⑧,从这样有序的摆放可以推断,在那里一定有一个保管者,他很可能是一个牧师,因为牧师是古代最优秀的学者。由此可以推断出三点:(1)有一个特殊的人照看这些泥板。(2)保管者有足够的知识,能够按照合适的顺序进行排列。(3)在古代,有学问的人通常是牧师,保存官方文献是牧师的职责之一。像亚述巴尼帕尔这样一个大图书馆,可能需要一个全职的牧师。当我们阅读巴比伦、亚述和古埃及的早期图书馆历史时,我们知道牧师同时也是图书馆员,他们有"与上帝交流的能力",这个能力可能不过是指阅读古代文献的能力。

在不知不觉的演化过程中,僧侣型的古代图书馆员逐渐被博学的教师所取代。伴随着古代人智力的进步,更多人能够阅读先人的记录,这对于僧侣图书馆员的权力是一个沉重的

---

① 【译者注】贝特霍尔德·劳费尔(Berthold Laufer,1874—1934),美籍德国学者,生于德国科隆,肄业于柏林大学,1897年在莱比锡大学获博士学位。通晓波斯文、梵文、巴利文、马来语、汉语、藏语、蒙古语、满语和日语。1898年移居美国,代表作《中国伊朗编》等。

② 【原注】Berthold Laufer. *East Asiatic Collection.* Newberry Library. Publication No. 4. 1913-P. 15.

③ 【原注】T. C. Tai. *Library Movement in China.* Chinese National Association for the Advancement of Education. Vol. 2. Bulletin 3. Peking. 1923.

④ 【译者注】保罗·埃弥尔·博塔(P. E. Potta),法国驻摩苏尔领事,第一个主持法国在近东的考古挖掘活动,1842年12月,博塔开始主持库云吉克的考古发掘,确定是古代的尼尼微城。

⑤ 【译者注】奥斯丁·亨利·莱亚德(Austen Henry Layard,1817—1894),英国考古学家,近东考古学的创建者,被称为"英国西亚考古学之父"。

⑥ 【译者注】尼尼微(Nineveh),西亚古城,新亚述帝国都城。位于底格里斯河上游东岸今伊拉克摩苏尔附近。意为"上帝面前最伟大的城市"。

⑦ 【译者注】亚述巴尼帕尔(Assur-bani-pal)(公元前668—约631年在位)是亚西利亚(Assyria,即巴比伦帝国的后身)末代大皇帝。十九世纪,考古学家在伊拉克发现了亚述巴尼帕尔王的尼尼微泥版图书馆,3900年前的楔形文字泥版,记述了距今4600年前的苏美尔史诗《吉尔伽美什》,叙述了乌鲁克王吉尔伽美什与勇士恩奇都的爱情故事。

⑧ 【原注】John Willis Clark. *Care of Books.* Cambridge University Press. 1902. p. 3-4.

打击。伟大的国王,比如亚历山大(Alexandria)的托勒密(Ptolemies)①、大帕加马(Pergamum)的阿塔罗斯(Antiochus)②、塞琉西王国的安提奥克斯(Antiochus)③、罗马皇帝奥古斯都④,自然去寻找那个时代杰出的学者和博学的教师,去管理他们无以伦比的图书馆。那时,成为图书馆员的资格是他必须掌握超过普通人应有的知识,能够阅读包括现代和古代所有的图书,阅读先人记录的能力不再具有优势,因为大量的学者都能做到这一点,因此,在知识方面,他必须知道的比同时代的人更多,在思想方面,他应该是一个创造者,在文学写作方面,要求他是一个大师。

那时,图书馆员的职责主要有三项:

(1)保存和整理图书(卷轴),就像巴比伦和亚述的图书馆员在他们神庙图书馆的工作一样;(2)汇编书目和图书馆目录;(3)鼓励学者使用图书馆,允许读者借走图书。

亚历山大和罗马图书馆有系统化的组织机构,馆长的职责之一是监管和指导图书馆工作人员。建立图书馆员专业教育时必须考虑的两个特殊职责,溯源于这个古代文明发展的黄金时代。首先,亚历山大图书馆员最早尝试汇编书目和创立图书馆目录,在创立图书馆目录的过程中,按照书卷在书架上的排列顺序为图书进行分类的思想,可能渐渐在古代图书馆员头脑中产生,书目、编目和分类一直是图书馆学校教学的主要技术科目。其次,鼓励学者在图书馆内使用图书,或从图书馆借走图书,这无疑是创建图书馆服务的新起点。这两条新的发展线索增加了图书馆员的工作量,使图书馆员的工作更加复杂,从而有必要对图书馆员的工作进行分类。

根据西尔维斯特·德·萨西(Silvestre de Sacy)⑤在《阿波杜·拉提夫的埃及史纲》中所述,有四个著名的亚历山大图书馆:(1)布鲁却姆图书馆(Library of the Brucheion),由早期托勒密王朝建立。(2)塞拉皮雍图书馆(Library of the Serapeum)。(3)奥古斯都神庙图书馆

---

① 【译者注】亚历山大城(Alexandria)由希腊北部马其顿王国菲利普二世之子亚历山大建立。亚历山大20岁即位,33岁病死,在这13年中,他远征小亚细亚、叙利亚.埃及、美索不达米亚、印度西部等地,建立了庞大的亚历山大帝国。首都亚历山大城是希腊——东方文化的中心,最有名的是亚历山大博物馆,其中有一所古代最大的图书馆——亚历山大图书馆,其藏书量据不同说法在10万至70万册之间。

② 【译者注】原文为Antiochus the Great of Pergamum,意为"大帕加马的安提奥克斯",此处似乎有误。据杨威理《西方图书馆史》(商务印书馆,1988)记载,帕加马和安提奥克斯非属同一个国家。帕加马位于小亚细亚(今土耳其)西北部,地近爱琴海岸,公元前三世纪至二世纪一度很繁荣。在首都帕加马城建有图书馆,藏书20万卷,可与亚历山大图书馆媲美,他们还创制了羊皮纸,代替了埃及的纸草纸。

③ 【译者注】安提奥克斯(Antiochus),在亚历山大帝国分裂后建立了塞琉西王国,领有西起小亚细亚,叙利亚,东达伊朗高原东部的广大地区,首都安提奥克位于土耳其南部,奥龙特斯河畔。安提奥克斯三世时,在首都安提奥克建造了剧院、美术馆和图书馆

④ 【译者注】奥古斯都(Augustus),建立了两所图书馆。第一所图书馆于公元前33年建造,是献给奥古斯都的姐姐屋大维亚的,故命名为屋大维亚门廊。门廊的第一层是人走廊,图书馆在第二层。这所图书馆开办了一百多年,直到公元80年梯特皇帝时被大火烧毁。第二所图书馆于公元前28年设置在帕拉丁丘上的阿波罗神庙内,分为希腊文图书部和拉丁文图书部。

⑤ 【译者注】西尔维斯特·德·萨西(Silvestre de Sacy,1758—1838),法国东方学家,是欧洲第一位学院化的研究伊斯兰、阿拉伯文学、德鲁兹教派和萨桑王朝时代波斯的现代东方学家;1831年在《皇家文库稿本著作提要与摘录》第4卷中,对曾经保存在中国开封府犹太教堂中的一部五经稿本做了提要,其中包括《旧约》《雅歌》和各种经文的叙利亚文本。

(Temple of Augustus)。(4)亚历山大学校图书馆(Library of the School of Alexandria)。在布鲁却姆图书馆的馆长中,有5位博学学者最为著名,他们是:泽诺多托斯(Zenodotus)、卡利马科斯(Callimachus)、厄拉多塞斯(Eratosthenes)、阿波罗尼斯(Apollonius)、阿利司托尼莫斯(Aristonymus),或拜占庭(Byzantium)的阿里斯托芬(Aristophanes)①。据记载,公元前280年,以弗所(Ephesian)的泽诺多托斯是第一任图书馆馆长,他拒绝擅自对荷马史诗进行添加,编辑了希腊诗人最早的诗歌版本。他的继任者都是学者、文法学家,和他同样甚至比他更加有名。他们不仅小心地保存这些藏品,而且还编制了目录,每五年校订一次②。这些著名图书馆馆长保存了亚历山大人收藏的两张悲剧和喜剧清单,卡利马科斯编辑了亚历山大图书馆120种主要书籍的目录。在亚历山大附近发现的纸莎草纸上有关哲学著作的目录残片以及其他希腊文稿一起保存在列宁格勒图书馆(原圣彼得堡帝国图书馆)③。

卡利马科斯和阿利司托尼莫斯的图书馆馆长身份引起了很多争论。按照《希腊和罗马传记词典》《不列颠百科全书》、爱德华的《图书馆纪要》和克拉克的《照管图书》的说法,卡利马科斯在托勒密·费拉德尔甫斯(Ptolemy Philadelphus)④统治时代是地位稳固的亚历山大图书馆的馆长。然而,在嘎斯奥森(Viktor Emil Gardthausen)最近出版的《图书馆科学手册》中,否认卡利马科斯是亚历山大图书馆的馆长。嘎斯奥森的证据是在俄克喜林库斯(Oxyrynchus)⑤发现的2世纪纸草纸《俄克喜林库斯古卷》第10卷第99页第124条,包括原亚历山大图书馆馆长的名单,其中有一个是卡利马科斯的学生,但是没有提到卡利马科斯本人。

关于阿利司托尼莫斯,爱德华兹根据《苏达辞书》⑥课本和梅耐克的 Apud Bonamy ut supra 得出结论,文法学家阿利司托尼莫斯继阿波罗尼斯之后成为布鲁却姆图书馆的馆长。但是,萨维奇(Ernest Albert Savage)⑦根据《图书馆和藏书的故事》以及其他的一些参考资料,指出拜占庭的阿里斯托芬才是阿波罗尼斯的继任者,是第五位杰出的亚历山大图书馆馆长。

关于任命拜占庭的阿里斯托芬任图书馆馆长,还有一个有趣的故事,爱德华兹复述维特鲁威(Vitruvius)⑧的记载如下:

---

① 【原注】Edward Edwards. *Memoirs of Libraries.* Trübner. London. 1859. Vol. 1. p. 22.

② 【原注】Victor Gardthausen. *Handbuch der Wissenschaftlichen Bibliothekskunde.* Quelle. Leipzig. 1920. Vol. 2, Book 8. Chap. 1.

③ 【原注】J. W. Clark. *Care of Books.* 1902. p. 21.

④ 【译者注】托勒密二世.

⑤ 【译者注】俄克喜林库斯位于开罗西南约160公里,是重要的考古遗址。十九世纪末至二十世纪,在俄克喜林库斯发现大量纸草纸古文书,可以追溯至托勒密和古罗马时期的埃及,出土的古卷被陆续出版,目前已出版70多卷。

⑥ 【译者注】《苏达辞书》是拜占庭学者在公元十至十一世纪编纂的一部百科全书性质的辞书,收录辞条约30,000条。该书保存了大量已散失的古籍的内容,成为后世的重要史料。

⑦ 【译者注】厄内斯特·艾伯特·萨维奇(Ernest Albert Savage, 1877—1966),1922—1942年为爱丁堡公共图书馆负责人,1929—1931年任苏格兰图书馆协会主席。

⑧ 【译者注】马尔库斯·维特鲁威(Marcus Vitruvius)是公元前1世纪罗马工程师,他所作的《建筑十书》是现存欧洲最完备的建筑专著,书中提出了"坚固、适用、美观"的建筑原则,奠定了欧洲建筑科学的基本体系。

托勒密王朝有一个惯例,在某些节日的场合,邀请一些文人到亚历山大,在指定的七位裁判面前朗诵自己的作品,那些被认为超过竞争对手的人,将会获得荣誉和奖励。有一次,国王已经选了6位裁判,但是他不容易找到令人满意的第7位,在这种窘境下,他请图书馆官员帮忙,图书馆官员告诉他,有一个人叫阿里斯托芬,很长时间以来,他是那里最勤奋的读者,真的,非常勤奋,他利用图书馆的藏品稳步地推进自己的工作,他被认为也许值得作为裁判表现一下。于是,阿里斯托芬成为第7位裁判。在朗诵过程中,一些人获得热烈的掌声,一些人则没有多少掌声。评奖的时间到了,对于获奖选手,6位裁判迅速统一了意见,但是,第7位,我们勤奋的学生,阿里斯托芬,选了完全不同的人。他说,最好的诗人,是获得很少掌声或没有掌声的人。国王不耐烦了,人们愤怒了,然而,阿里斯托芬坚持自己的意见。他说,那些不是诗人,而是剽窃者,因为一个人只能朗诵自己的作品。当要求举出证据时,他列出了图书馆里剽窃者们利用的图书目录。当然,事情的结果,是剽窃者的丢脸,而阿里斯托芬被提升为图书馆的馆长。①

亚历山大图书馆的杰出馆长在邻国也有竞争对手。帕加马国王建立了皇家图书馆,安提奥克斯三世格瑞特(Antiochus III the Great)②任命卡尔基斯(Chalcis)③的诗人和文法学家尤福利翁(Euphorion)为图书馆馆长。尤福利翁的文学知名度与亚历山大图书馆的卡利马科斯④一样高,他的作品受到罗马人的高度推崇,在他的领导下,帕加马的皇家图书馆成为托勒密图书馆强有力的竞争对手。

罗马帝国图书馆员的职责比亚历山大图书馆员更加明确,罗马皇帝渴望任用杰出的学者作为图书馆员。那时,罗马图书馆的藏品更丰富,学者更多,一些权威人士声称古罗马有28个,也许有29个公共图书馆。抛开关于罗马公共图书馆数量的各种说法,我们知道,那时图书馆管理形成了新的发展模式,在图书馆历史上第一次允许普通民众使用书籍,并可以借走图书馆的图书。从图书馆管理领域的变革中,分化出了参考和流通工作,图书馆员的职责变得更加复杂,图书馆工作人员组织和部门开始建立。

根据博伊德教授(Boyd)的《古罗马的公共图书馆与文学文化》一书,古罗马图书馆管理工作的证据,主要来源于碑文,其次来源于罗马文学作品。博伊德博士展示了不同等级图书馆职员的职责,描述了古罗马图书馆的人员组织简图⑤:

---

① 【原注】Edward Edwards. *Memoirs of Libraries.* Vol. I. p. 23-4.

② 【译者注】安提奥克斯三世格瑞特(Antiochus III the Great,公元前241—公元前187),塞琉西王国的国王,是塞琉西王国的第6位统治者,公元前222—公元前187在位。

③ 【译者注】卡尔基斯(Chalcis)是希腊东南部的一个港口城市。

④ 【译者注】卡利马科斯(约公元前305年—公元前240年),古希腊著名诗人、学者以及目录学家,亚历山大里亚派诗歌的代表,曾在亚历山大图书馆工作,为亚历山大图书馆编纂了一份详尽的书目《卷录》(Pinakes),共120卷,今有残卷传世。

⑤ 【原注】C. E. Boyd. *Public Libraries and Literary Culture in Ancient Rome.* University of Chicago Press. 1915. Chap. 4. p. 41-51.

罗马图书馆的人员组织

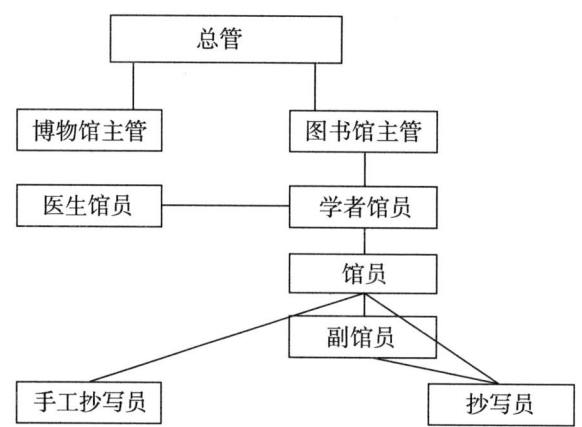

总管可能相当于内阁部长的位置,他可能有几个副总管,其中之一负责公共图书馆的发展。按照蒙森(Mommsen)①和赫斯菲尔德(Hirschfeld)的说法,图书馆主管是总管的下级,他的责任是管理罗马帝国可供图书馆使用的财政经费。一则希腊的碑文②为我们对图书馆主管(procurator bibliothecarum)职位的影响力提供了参考,图书馆的主管(chief director of libraries)曾经由杰出的学者卢修斯·朱利叶斯·维斯提努斯(Lucius Julius Vestinus)③担任,同时,他也是亚历山大博物馆的馆长、亚历山大主教、哈德良皇帝④的秘书、语言学家。按照嘎斯奥森的《图书馆科学手册》第2卷第1章第69—70页的说法,这些主管并不称为图书馆馆长,而实际上是古希腊和古罗马图书馆的监督,在管理外部和经济事务方面,他们的职能就像德国大学学监的职能一样。这些监督同时兼任为皇帝处理信件的秘书和学习顾问。成为这样的监督享有很高的荣誉,他的工资是60,000赛斯特斯⑤(约合3000美元),很明显,罗马图书馆组织里的图书馆主管是最高行政长官、优秀学者,具有很高的行政权力。

因为图书馆主管具有很多职责,图书馆就必须有一个行政官员负责核心行政管理事务,这个官员也许就是学者馆员(馆长)(magista a bibliotheca),他的下面还有一些馆员,每个人

---

① 【译者注】特奥多尔·蒙森(Theodor Mommsen,1817—1903),德国历史学家、文学家、政治家,1902年获诺贝尔文学奖。他研究罗马历史,关于罗马法和债法的研究成果,对德国民法典有重大影响。

② 【译者注】CIG,5900,即 Corpus Inscriptium Graecarum《希腊碑铭集成》第5900条,是德国古典学家柏克(August Bockh,1785—1867)最早发起编纂的,第一卷于1825年出版,1860年普鲁士科学院在柏克《希腊铭文集成》基础上,组织汇编更为全面的《希腊铭文集成》,后改由柏林——布兰登堡科学院主持,作为系列出版物,至今仍在出版。

③ 【译者注】卢修斯·朱利叶斯·维斯提努斯(Lucius Julius Vestinus)于公元59—62年任罗马图书馆主管,他曾担任过家庭教师,后来又主持过亚历山大博物馆。

④ 【译者注】普布利乌斯·埃利乌斯·哈德良(Publius Aelius Hadrianus,公元76—138),罗马帝国安敦尼王朝的第三位皇帝,117—138年在位。在位期间,停止东方战争,与帕提亚国王缔结和约,改革官僚制度和法律,是一位博学多才的皇帝。

⑤ 【译者注】Seserce 古罗马货币单位。

管理一个专业图书馆,馆员的名字通常和专业图书馆的名字记录在一起,就像一则碑文①里写的"希腊屋大维亚图书馆馆员(a bibliotheca Graeca Porticus Octaviae)"。学者馆员必须是一个接受过文学培训和有专业能力的人,他的文化和知识一定要受到学者的推崇。在马提亚尔(Martial)的《隽语》(Epigrams)②里,塞克斯都(Sextus)③被认为是神灵与帕拉丁图书馆(Palatine Library)的联系人,"至高无上的赛克斯都,你真诚的热爱帕拉丁密涅瓦神(Minerva)④,她拥有智慧去传达上帝的旨意……"⑤

阿西尼乌斯·波利奥(Asinius Pollio)⑥、庞贝乌斯·马赛尔(Pompeius Macer)⑦、尤里乌斯·希津努斯(C. Julius Hyginus)⑧是奥古斯都当政时的杰出图书馆馆长。奥古斯都任命阿西尼乌斯·波利奥接替瓦罗(Varro)⑨未完成的在罗马建立(第一座)图书馆的任务,波利奥是一个杰出的文学家、著名的演说家、博学的历史学家、罗马将军;庞贝乌斯·马赛尔被派去管理帕拉丁图书馆(罗马的第二座图书馆);尤里乌斯·希津努斯是奥古斯都的自由民、奥维德(Ovid)⑩和卢库卢斯(C. Licinius)⑪的亲密朋友、历史学家,后被任命为帕拉丁图书馆馆长;屋大维亚图书馆(罗马的第三座图书馆)馆长凯乌斯·梅利苏斯(Caius Melissus)是一个杰出的文法学家和《笑话》(Ioci)⑫的作者;尤利乌斯·凯撒(Julius Caesar)⑬选择著名的瓦罗

---

① 【译者注】CIL,Ⅵ,4433,即 Corpus Inscriptionum Latinarum《拉丁碑铭集成》第五卷第4433条,该书主要收藏古代拉丁碑文,包括公共的和个人的碑文,记载了罗马的历史和生活,直到现在,一直在出版新版本和增补本。

② 【译者注】马提亚尔(Marcus ValeriusMartialis,约公元40—103/104年),罗马帝国诗人,在西班牙接受教育,在罗马图密善王朝时代出版了12卷《隽语》(Epigrams),其中包括1500多首短诗,大部分以挽歌对句写成。这些作品描述了当时罗马社会的复杂景象,多带有讽刺性,通常为短篇,在结尾处带有诙谐的点睛之笔或讽刺点。

③ 【译者注】赛克斯都·恩披里柯(SextusEmpiricus,公元160—210年),古罗马哲学家、医生、怀疑论派代表之一。有三种哲学著作流传下来,其中记载了古代怀疑论者的主张以及他们对各派学说的反驳,是研究古代哲学的重要史料。

④ 【译者注】密涅瓦神(Minerva),古罗马神话中的智慧女神,传说她把纺织、缝纫、制陶、园艺等技艺传给了人类,因此,她最受雅典人的尊敬,栖落在她身上的猫头鹰因此成了智慧的象征。

⑤ 【原注】C. E. Boyd. *Public Libraries and Literary Culture in Ancient Rome.* p. 48.

⑥ 【译者注】盖乌斯·阿西尼乌斯·波利奥(Gaius Asinius Pollio,公元前76—公元4年),写过一部共17册的历史,记述凯撒和庞培之间的内战以及这之前的内战,叙述时间起于公元前60年,后散佚。

⑦ 【译者注】庞贝乌斯·马赛尔(Pompeius Macer),是奥古斯都建立的帕拉丁阿波罗神庙图书馆的第一任馆长,该馆最初的书籍是由马塞尔收集的。

⑧ 【译者注】尤里乌斯·希津努斯(C. Julius Hyginus,约公元前64—公元17年),文法学家,是奥古斯都时代最负盛名的学人之一。

⑨ 【译者注】马库斯·特伦提乌斯·瓦罗(Marcus Terentius Varro,公元前116—公元前27年)是古罗马学者和作家,先后写有70多部著作,以渊博学识受到当时和中世纪学者的尊崇。他唯一流传到现在的完整作品是晚年的《论农业》,是研究古罗马农业生产的重要著述,曾奉凯撒之命在罗马建造第一座图书馆。

⑩ 【译者注】奥维德(Ovid,公元前43—公元18)古罗马诗人,一生创作丰富,早期诗歌主要反映生活、爱情,多为哀歌体情诗。

⑪ 【译者注】卢库卢斯(C. Lucullus,约公元前117—前56),罗马将军和执政官。

⑫ 【译者注】Ioci 是拉丁词汇,大意可以翻译成笑话或幽默,本书译为《笑话》。

⑬ 【译者注】尤利乌斯·凯撒(Julius Caesar),史称凯撒大帝,罗马共和国杰出的军事统帅、政治家。

作为罗马图书馆第一个组织者和领导者，其后所有古罗马图书馆馆长的继任者都是杰出人物。

副馆员在现代管理观念里是图书馆里的部门主管，他有专门的职责；医学馆员可能是管理医学藏书的馆员，同时也是图书馆员的专门医生，一块碑文告诉我们，医学馆员许米乃①有照料所有皇家图书馆员健康的职责，他的工作很有成效。

十九世纪末期，特别是在英格兰和欧洲，很多男性图书馆员认为女性参加图书馆工作是新奇的、不合适的②。但是，他们忘记了，女性做图书馆工作几乎和男性一样早。男性和女性都曾在罗马帝国的图书馆里工作。根据一块碑文记载③，女性被认为很适合做办公室的"librarius a munu"工作，意思是图书馆的秘书或抄写员。

"librarius"的工作有几个意思，抄写员、誊写员、售书员（售卖抄写本），他们作为奴隶抄写员、熟练抄写员、高级抄写员和其他种类的抄写员，被分配在不同的人领导之下，这些领导者要完成各种各样的文书、公文等任务，他们可能和现代图书馆的助理差不多。所有保存下来的证据都表明，文学素养、希腊和拉丁书籍的知识、高智商、管理成效是不同罗马图书馆高级管理者的重要资质，助理、秘书、抄写员、誊写员、书记员都在本地接受图书馆技术培训。很多秘书、抄写员、誊写员和书记员都是受过良好教育、具有聪明才智的奴隶，他们非常胜任自己的各项工作。这个事实在西塞罗（Cicero）④给他的朋友阿提库斯（Atticus）⑤关于重新整理其图书馆的三封信中很好地体现出来⑥。

第一封信："我希望你从你的图书馆里派两位助手来，帮助泰勒诺（Tyrannio）⑦贴标签和做其他事情，请提醒他们带一些牛皮纸来做书卷的标签……"

第二封信："我很满意你（派来）的人做的木工活，又做了书卷的标签，使我的图书馆明亮宜人，我希望你表扬他们。"

当整理图书馆的工作完成时，西塞罗写了第三封信，"现在泰勒诺已经整理好了我的书，我的家充满了新的气象，这与你派来的狄奥尼修斯（Dionysius）和门诺菲卢斯（Menophilus）出色的工作是分不开的，没有什么看上去能比这些书架更整洁了，那些标签使我的书焕然一新"。

卡利马科斯的分类系统可能已经被后来的罗马图书馆员们改进了，编目技术更好了，"很明显，从我引用的材料来看"，J. W. 克拉克先生说，"那个目录一定一直在使用，而且，除

---

① 【译者注】许米乃（Hymenaeus），圣经人物。

② 【原注】H. R. Tedder. *Librarianship as a Profession*. Library Association of the United Kingdom. Transactions and Proceedings. 1882. p. 171.

③ 【原注】《拉丁碑铭集成》第五卷第 6314 条。

④ 【译者注】马库斯·图利乌斯·西塞罗（Marcus Tullius Cicero，公元前 106—前 43），罗马哲学家、政治家、律师、作家、雄辩家，其思想深深影响欧洲的哲学和政治学说。

⑤ 【译者注】阿提库斯（Titus Pomponius Atticus，公元前 109—前 32）罗马贵族、学者、藏书家，西塞罗之友，早年接受良好教育，公元前 65 年从雅典回国后创办了古罗马第一家正规的抄本出版社。

⑥ 【原注】J. W. Clark. Care of Books. 1902. p. 35.

⑦ 【译者注】泰勒诺（Tyrannio），罗马学者、教师，负责管理亚里斯多德的苏兰图书馆，整理西塞罗的安提乌姆图书馆。

了这个推断之外,显然昆体良(Quintilian)①和小普林尼(younger Pliny)②都明确提到了图书目录。前者(昆体良)说,任何人都可以从图书馆的目录(索引)中抄下书名,补充到自己的有关希腊作家的名单中。后者(小普林尼)在谈到他叔叔(老普林尼)的作品时,说他可以按照这些书的写作顺序提供图书目录"③。

罗马的征服带来了罗马与其他文明的直接融合,尤其是希腊和埃及。凯撒大帝、奥古斯都和其他的皇帝都鼓励人们拥有公民意识和高智力的学识,这些动机都有利于古代罗马图书馆的发展。随着市民文学素养和文化旨趣的提高,图书馆的使用也成比例地增加,允许从图书馆借书的实践从此开始了,很多文献资料都提到了这一点。在奥卢斯·格利乌斯(Aulus Gellius)④的作品里记录了一件事。在一个炎热的夏日,格利乌斯和他的朋友们齐聚在一幢富人的别墅里喝融雪饮料,他们讨论这样的冰水是否有益于健康,其中一位是哲学家,他说亚里士多德(Aristotle)⑤和很多医生都强烈反对饮用冰水,为了说服同伴儿相信他的话,他跑到海克力斯神庙(Temple of Hercules)⑥的公共图书馆里,借出亚里士多德论述这个主题的图书,给他们读这段陈述⑦。这个例子清晰地说明了古罗马公共图书馆允许读者把书借出馆外。

北方蛮族的不断入侵,使辉煌的罗马公共图书馆走向没落,罗马以及君士坦丁堡(Constantinople)的文学活动迅速衰落,图书被焚烧,或者被毁掉,不再需要图书馆员。这标志着古代图书馆发展的结束,实际上也是古代图书馆员职业的终结。

SELECTED BIBLIOGRAPHY

Boyd, Clarence Eugene. Public libraries and literary culture inancient Rome. Univ. of Chicago Press. 1915.
Brittanica. 11th ed. Ancient, medieval and modern libraries. Vol. 16. p. 545-77.
Clark, John Willis. Care of books. Cambridge Univ. Press. 1902. Chap. 1.
Edwards, Edward. Memoirs of libraries. Trübner. London. 1859. Vol. 1. Chap. 1-5.
Gardthausen, Victor. Handbuch der wissenschaftlichenbibliothekskunde. Quelle. Leipzig. 1920. Vol. 2. Book 8.

---

① 【译者注】昆体良(Marcus Fabius Quintilianus,约公元35—95年)古罗马时期的著名律师、教育家,是皇室委任的第一位修辞学教授,担任拉丁语修辞术学校的主持(校长)达20年,培养了很多人才,小普林尼就是他的著名学生,著有《雄辩术原理》《演说术原理》等。

② 【译者注】小普林尼(Gaius Plinius Caecilius Secundus,约公元61/62—113),古罗马帝国律师、作家和元老,史称小普林尼,以区别于老普兰尼(公元23/24—公元79,古罗马百科全书式作家,小普林尼的叔叔)。小普林尼的很多信件流传下来,成为研究当时历史的珍贵资料。

③ 【原注】J. W. Clark. *Care of Books*. 1902. p. 20-21.

④ 【译者注】奥卢斯·格利乌斯(Aulus Gellius),是活跃于1世纪的古罗马作家,他留下的《阿提卡之夜》一书,记下了他所见所闻所读,为后世提供了一部关于那时代的重要史料。

⑤ 【译者注】亚里士多德(公元前384—前322年),柏拉图的学生,古希腊伟大的哲学家。他的作品涉及伦理学、形而上学、心理学、经济学、神学、政治学、修辞学、自然科学、教育学等多种学科。

⑥ 【译者注】海克力斯神庙(Temple of Hercules Victor),约建于公元前二世纪晚期,是一座圆形的古罗马神庙建筑,位于意大利罗马的屠牛广场,周围环绕着希腊风格的柱廊。

⑦ 【原注】Aulus Gellius. *Noctes Atticae*. XIX. 5, 4. (original quotation in Boyd's *Public Libraries and Literary Culture in Ancient Rome*. p. 30).

Chap. 1.

Laufer, Berthold. East Asiatic collection. Publication No. 4. Newberry Library. Chicago. 1913.

Lipsius, Justus. History of libraries; trans. from the 2nd ed. John Moretus. (The Plantin Press Antwerp. 1607) by Dana, J. C. and Kent, H. W. McClurg. Chicago. 1907.

Müller, William Max. Richardson's some old Egyptian libraries. Library Journal. 37:217. April, 1912.

Richardson, E. C. Beginnings of libraries. Milford. London. 1914.

Richardson, E. C. Facts about old Egyptian librarians. Library Journal. 37:316-19. June, 1912.

Richardson, E. C. Old Egyptian librarians. Scribner. New York. 1911.

Savage, Ernest A. Story of libraries and book collecting. Routledge. London. Chap. 1-2.

Smith, William, ed. Dictionary of Greek and Roman biography and mythology. Walton. London. 1869. 3vol.

Spofford, Ainsworth Rand. A book for all readers. Putnam. New York. 1900. Chap. 15.

Tai, T. C. A brief sketch of Chinese libraries. Library Journal. 44:423-9. July, 1919.

Tai, T. C. Library movement in China. Chinese National Association for the Advancement of Education. Vol. 2. Bulletin 3. Peking. 1923.

Tedder, Henry R. Evolution of the public library. Second International Library Conference. Transactions. London. 1897. p. 13-18.

Tedder, Henry R. Librarianship as a profession. Library Association of the United Kingdom. Transactions and Proceedings, 1882. p. 171.

第七章 中世纪和近代早期的图书馆员

中世纪的图书馆运动在脆弱的、有限的范围内开始,而在强大的、宽广的范围内结束。中世纪可以分成两个时期,第一个时期包括修道院图书馆的成长,那时图书馆员都是修道士的装束,圣经文献、神学教义、圣徒和殉道者的档案,是第一个时期修道院图书馆的主要藏品。第二个时期包括作为学习机构的图书馆的巨大进步,印刷术的发明使图书的数量大量增加,学术和科学的真正复兴,使图书馆成为学者不可缺少的工具,博学的修道士和杰出的学者被召集起来,重新开展图书馆工作。

在图书馆员培训的发展过程中,圣本笃会(Order of Saint Benedict)①、西多会(Cistercians)②、奥斯定会(Augustinians)③和其他修会,对图书排架、修补、装订、借出和编目等方法做出了贡献。图书馆特别强调保护和保存图书,年度报告和书库盘点是一些修道士图书馆员的重要职责,修道士图书馆员同时还是唱诗班的领班、手稿抄本的管理者,偶尔也是宗教仪式的主持者,他们是修道院里的多面手。仅在大的和富有的修道院里,才有专门的修道士管理图书馆,普通教堂里的古老手稿保存在珍藏室,新书保存在缮写室,因此,不需要设立专门的修道士图书馆员。

现代大学图书馆的一些使用和借书管理条例,都源自于修道院图书馆规则。在早期修道院图书馆里,非教友不能借书,仅准许修道院的教友有借走图书一周的特权。每到晚上,"助手",也就是管理这些图书的副手,负责清点图书,然后把书锁在厚墙中的壁橱里④。由于许多天主教修会鼓励阅读,以及抄写员的勤奋和大量的工作,图书增加很快,一些大的修道院开始把图书保存在不同的房间里,颁布针对修道士和非教友读者的图书流通管理条例。关于非教友读者借书,在不同的条例里有很多不同的规定,通常采用担保的借书方法。

本笃会最早发布了一套关于阅览和借书的规则,这些规则被克吕尼修会(Cluniacs)⑤进

---

① 【译者注】本笃会(Order of Saint Benedict)为天主教隐修会之一,又译为本尼狄克派,由意大利人圣本笃于 529 在意大利创办。本笃会会规共七十三章,规定会士不可婚娶,不可有私财,一切服从长上;会士每日按时进经堂诵经,视游手好闲为罪恶,余暇时从事各种劳动,该会规后来成为天主教修会制度的范本。

② 【译者注】西多会(Cistercians)为天主教隐修会之一,由法国人罗贝尔于 1098 年在法国勃艮第地区第戎附近的西多旷野创办,因此得名。会服为白色,又称白衣修士,该会严格遵守本笃会规则,推行静默、祈祷、垦荒等隐修制度。

③ 【译者注】奥斯定会(Augustinian)是天主教托钵修会之一,又译奥古斯丁派,是遵行圣奥斯定会规生活的男女修会的总称。会规要求抛弃家庭和财产而追随基督,在教会内集体过清贫生活,脱离世俗事务;除日常祈祷外,从事济贫和传教工作等。

④ 【原注】J. W. Clark. *Care of Books*. Cambridge University Press. 1902. 54-5.

⑤ 【译者注】克吕尼修会(Cluniacs Order)是天主教隐修院修会,又称重整本笃会。十世纪初由法国人伯尔诺在克吕尼修院创建。该会主张整顿修院纪律,严守本笃所订会规,得到很多修院的响应。十一到十二世纪改革修院之风遍及西部教会,世称克吕尼改革运动,后该运动的领导者希尔得布兰成为教皇,即格列高利七世。

一步修改。加尔都西会(Carthusians)①保留了借给每位教友2本书的原则,西多会、奥斯定会和其他修会都允许图书的流通。在某种意义上,修道院对于修道士来说就是大学图书馆,对于其他那些渴望读书的人来说就是公共图书馆,下面译自约翰·威利斯·克拉克所著《照管图书》中的一段话,说明了修道士图书馆员管理图书馆的情况:

"从复活节(Easter)到十月的第一天(Calends of October),他们(教友)应当从第4小时开始阅读,直到接近第6小时;从十月的第一天到大斋节(Lent)②,他们应当阅读到第2小时;在大斋节期间,他们应当从早晨开始阅读,直到第3小时结束;在这期间,每人可以从图书馆领到一本书通读"③。这是著名的本笃会规则,"然后,他(图书馆员)应该大声朗读一年前分给教友阅读的图书名单,当叫到教友名字时,他要站起来,交回分给他的图书,如果他还没有读完,他应因为缺乏勤奋而请求原谅。还回的图书放在修道院大厅的地毯上,再把重新分配给教友的书名记下来,列在一张表格上,表格的篇幅比通常要大一些"④。

约在1070年,兰弗朗克大主教(Archbishop Lanfranc)⑤颁布英国本笃会教令,下面是关于图书和图书馆员职责的部分:"在大斋节第一个星期日之后的星期一……在教友进入大厅之前,除了上一年已经送出阅读的图书之外,图书馆员应该把所有的图书都放在大厅的地毯上。当教友进入大厅时,应该每个人的手里都拿着上一年分发的图书,这些应该由图书馆员前一天在大厅里发布通知……接下来,图书馆员宣读去年领书教友的名单,当听到自己名字时,教友还回分给他们阅读的图书,让收到图书而没有读完的人颜面尽失,忏悔他的错误,请求原谅。然后让图书馆员发给每一位教友另外的图书去阅读。当图书井然有序地分配完毕后,图书馆员要把书名和借书人的名字当场记录下来。"⑥

奥斯定会规则第十四章"有关图书的安全保存和图书馆员职责"的规定,是英国以及欧洲修道院图书馆管理的通用模式,现在图书馆培训的很多方面都可以追溯到中世纪修道院和大学图书馆的实践。威廉姆森博士(C.C Williamson)在《图书馆服务培训》⑦的报告中,强烈反对现在图书馆学校没有明显区分培养专业馆员和办事员的情况,威廉姆森博士认为,这种区别的缺乏,归因于图书馆服务两种管理类型(专业馆员和办事员)的混杂。二十世纪图书馆员的很多职责是简单地继承过去的传统,例如,现代图书馆学校设立装订课程,而我们并不希望经过专业培训的图书馆员,在毕业之后成为装订员,设立这个课程仅仅是因为古老的传统认为,每个图书馆员都应该像中世纪修道院图书馆员一样,知道怎样修补和装订图

---

① 【译者注】加尔都西会(Carthusians Order)天主教隐修院修会之一。1084年法国人圣布鲁诺创立于法国加尔都西山中。以本笃会会规做蓝本,但更严格。修士各居一小室,以便独自专务苦身、默想、诵经;终身严守静默,只能在每周六聚谈一次;在每年四十天的封斋期内,仅食面包和清水,有"苦修会"之称。

② 【译者注】大斋节(Lent),大斋节亦称"封斋节",是基督教的斋戒节期。复活节前的40天,是信友准备耶稣复活及更新自己的日子。

③ 【原注】J. W. Clark. *Care of Books*. Cambridge University. 1902. p.56.

④ 【原注】J. W. Clark. *Care of Books*. Cambridge University. 1902. p.57.

⑤ 【译者注】兰弗朗克(Lanfranc,约1005—1089),生于意大利,天主教神父,约1042年进入法国诺曼底卡特莱特修道院,1045年成为修道院院长和修道院学校的校长,1070年至1089年任坎特伯雷大主教。

⑥ 【原注】J. W. Clark. *Care of Books*. Cambridge University. 1902. p.57-8.

⑦ 【译者注】威廉姆森于1923年在卡内基基金会任职,他出版的《图书馆培训报告》,提出大学应该提供图书馆学培训。

书,下面这段摘录说明了修道院图书馆员的职责和工作的范围。

图书馆员,又称为教堂唱诗班的领班,负责管理教堂的图书。他应该保管并熟悉每一本图书,他应该经常仔细检查图书,预防虫蛀和腐烂造成破损或伤害。每年大斋节开始,当修道院为那些给教堂捐献的人,或那些辛辛苦苦地抄写图书而应该得到灵魂宽恕的教友举行宗教仪式时,他还应该在修道院大厅里展示图书。他应该送给教友随手翻看的图书,并记录书名和借书人的名字,同时要求借书人保证细心保管图书,没有获得图书馆员的允许,不得把图书转借给别人,不论是否熟识。图书馆员自己也不应该随意借出图书,除非收到等值的抵押品,并在登记簿上记下借书人的名字、借出的书名和收到的抵押品。对于大部头的、珍贵的图书,没有经过修道院院长的允许,图书馆员不应该借给任何人,不管是否熟识。

无论是吟唱还是阅读,日常使用的图书,应该放在公共的地方,便于教友取阅,选择适合于他们使用的图书。因此,这些书不应该带进内室,或带到回廊及修道院以外的角落。图书馆员应该经常细心地打扫图书、修补图书、标点图书,以免教友在吟唱或阅读等日常使用时,发现错误而带来不便。任何教友都不能抹去或改动书中的字句,除非得到图书馆员的同意……

存放图书的书柜,应该在内层安装木板,不能让墙壁的潮气使图书受潮或变脏。书柜内部应该用横向和竖向的各种架子隔开,以便图书成排摆放,互不干扰,要避免把图书排得太紧而损坏,或延误取阅者的时间。

此外,图书馆员应该修补、标点以及细心保护图书,还应该装订图书。①

从上面一段话中,我们看到,修道院鼓励修道士学习,通常那里有图书馆,尽管获得图书比较困难。中世纪图书馆员非常细心保护图书,防止偷窃和弄脏,或许,图书的保存是中世纪图书馆管理中最重要的问题。图书的缺乏和抄写的辛劳,使修道士图书馆员意识到他们保管藏书的责任。有一些关于读书时持书的规则,"当教士们在教堂或回廊内阅读时",本笃会规则规定,"他们应该尽可能左手拿书,用长袍的衣袖将左手裹起来,把书放在膝盖上;右手应该露在外面翻书"。托马斯·肯比斯(Thomas à Kempis)在他的《青年神父》(*Doctrinale Juvenum*)②中教导青年学生应该怎样使用图书,他说,"把你的书拿在手中,就像圣者西面(Simeon the Just)③把圣婴耶稣抱在臂上,带着他、亲吻他。当你阅读完毕,合上书本,要感谢上帝说的每一个词,因为在主的领地,你已经找到了隐藏的宝藏"④。当现在的学生肆无忌惮地剪下百科全书的书页,或者持着一本厚重图书的封面无情地拖来拽去的时候,关于这些规定能说什么?今天在图书馆里阻止故意破坏图书就像几个世纪以前一样困难,这仍然是图书馆管理中没有解决的问题。像罗伯特桥圣玛丽修道院(the house of Saint Mary of

---

① 【原注】J. W. Clark. *Care of Books*. 1902. p. 61.
② 【译者注】托马斯·肯比斯(Thomas Kempis,1379—1471),德国神学家,著有《青年神父》(Doctrinale Juvenum)。
③ 【译者注】西面是圣经故事中的先知,是期盼救主的人之一。传说圣灵引领他到圣殿去,当玛利亚和约瑟带着耶稣进来的时候,西面接过圣婴耶稣,称颂他是上帝派来的救主。
④ 【原注】J. W. Clark. *Care of Books*. 1902. p. 67.

Robert's Bridge)①那样,在图书的藏书票上有一条咒语,"这本书属于罗伯特桥圣玛丽修道院,无论是谁偷走它,或卖掉它,或者用任何方式从这间房子里拿走它,或损坏它,都会被诅咒"。今天,这当然不起作用,当代年轻人一旦偶尔获得这样的图书,将会占有它,并像埃克塞特主教(Bishop of Exeter)②那样草率地在题名页上写道,"我,约翰,埃克塞特主教,不知道上述房子在哪里:我没有偷这本书,而是合法地获得"③。当然,这里使用的"合法地"一词也许带有讽刺意味,现代图书馆破坏者无疑已经习惯使用这个词了。

在一些修道院目录里,发现了使用精细方法和精确编目的痕迹,尽管其余的仅仅是清单而没有分类。通常修道院图书馆强调汇编目录,在慕尼黑图书馆、剑桥耶稣学院以及其他图书馆都有一些修道士手稿目录,通常进行综合分类,一般没有进行细分。字母表用来表示类别,图书以固定架位的方式排列。里沃兹修道院(Monastery of Rievaulx)④图书馆分目录和蒂奇菲尔德修道院(Monastery of Tychefeld)⑤图书馆主目录分别在爱德华兹的《图书馆纪要》和克拉克的《照管图书》中再版。他们的设计是有缺陷的,分类是不科学的,但是我们必须记住,这标志着分类的开始。在民众精神生活处于较低水平的时代,编目技术和书目科学的发展,和那时任何脑力工作的发展情况相比毫不逊色。

现代大学图书馆员喜欢在书库里为研究生放置分隔式单人桌,而这只是中世纪修道院图书馆管理方式的再现。修道院图书馆的分隔式小书房很盛行,使用小书房的特权只属于那些从事抄写、著述,或阅读的年长修道士,就像杜伦大教堂(Durham)⑥的情况一样。根据克拉克的记载,格洛斯特大教堂(Gloucester)⑦南回廊的分隔式小书房,建于1370—1412年之间,每个小书房4英尺宽,19英寸长、6尺9寸高,通过两个小窗户照明。

一些大教堂图书馆一般有两个工作人员,即领班和副领班。前者在书柜的前面有一个座位,多半儿是紧靠着墙,他的小书房通常也离此不远,后者的座位和小书房在书柜旁边⑧。他们,或至少是他们中的一个人,总是随时为那些希望寻找图书信息的教友提供服务。领班是馆长,副领班是副馆长,他们随时准备回答教友的问题,从某种意义上说,就像现代图书馆的参考馆员一样。

---

① 【译者注】1176年,阿留雷德(Alured de St. Martin)和他的兄弟罗伯特(Robert),在英国东苏塞克斯郡(East Sussex)塞勒赫斯特(Salehurst)附近建立了圣玛丽修道院(the monastery of St. Mary's),不久,罗伯特在罗瑟河谷(Rother)建了一座桥,称为罗伯特桥(Robert's Bridge),该修道院也称"罗伯特桥圣玛丽修道院"。

② 【译者注】埃克塞特大教堂位于英国德文郡的埃克塞特,是埃克塞特的主教堂,建于1400年,是世界上哥特式建筑最好的典范之一。

③ 【原注】T. W. Koch. *On University Libraries*. 1924. p. 3-4.

④ 【译者注】里沃兹修道院(Rievaulx Abbey)位于英格兰约克郡,石雕精美,柱子高耸,拱门优雅,现在只有修道院遗址。

⑤ 【译者注】位于英国汉普郡蒂奇菲尔德镇。

⑥ 【译者注】杜伦大教堂(Durham Cathedral)建于1093年,位于北英格兰杜伦郡,是英国最典型的诺曼底式教堂,建立之初是本笃会修士交流的场所。

⑦ 【译者注】格洛斯特大教堂(Gloucester Cathedral)位于英格兰南部的格洛斯特郡,681年在一个为圣彼得修建的修道院上扩建而成。在克拉克《照管图书》一书中,收藏有格洛斯特大教堂南回廊一排小书房的照片。

⑧ 【原注】J. W. Clark. *Care of Books*. Cambridge University Press. 1902. p. 92.

总之，修道院图书馆员是有文化的高级修道士，在早期修道院，当图书还不是很多时，他是一个多面手，负有很多职责。后来他的主要职责是照管图书、修补图书、流通图书、编制目录、担任参考馆员。他的地位没有改变，但是他的职责在十五世纪大教堂图书馆的增长过程中增多了。

早期大学图书馆，比如牛津大学、剑桥大学较早的一些学院，就是以修道院图书馆的方式发展起来的。学者借书要支付押金，每年进行图书清查和发放，在某种程度上，是按照类似英国本笃会兰弗朗克章程（Lanfranc）执行的。对牛津大学奥里尔学院①、墨顿学院②，剑桥大学彼得学院③图书馆章程的考察，得出一个明确的结论，图书馆规则直接来源于修道院的实践。现代图书馆管理，特别是现代大学图书馆管理，继承了很多修道院图书馆的传统。

近千年以来，管理图书馆和保管图书的任务一直由修道士负责。到了十五世纪，遍布欧洲的修道院、大教堂和大学，在收藏图书、建造图书馆、汇编目录、设计开放的规章制度等方面互相竞争，使图书馆不仅对修道士，而且也对公众更加有用。然而，由于十六世纪法国胡格诺运动（Huguenot movement）④和英国镇压修道院⑤的行动，图书馆的发展停滞了，很多修道院被破坏，书籍被毁掉，手稿或者被烧掉，或者散落，很多作者痛苦地记录下这些可怕的损失。一位深知修道院图书馆价值的作者，断然于1549年给爱德华六世（King Edward VI）⑥写信，抗议到："解散修道院，亵渎图书馆，庄严、珍贵的历史遗迹得不到保护……贪婪是另外导致图书馆和图书终结的祸首……大量接管修道院的人，接管了图书馆的图书，其中的一些……用来擦洗烛台，一些用来擦皮靴；一些卖给杂货店和肥皂商人，一些发送给海外的装订商，这不是小数目，有时甚至所有的船只都装满了，连外国人都感到奇怪……我断定这是事实，并且沉痛地说——不管是罗马人和撒克逊人⑦统治下的不列颠人，还是丹麦人⑧和诺

---

① 【译者注】奥里尔学院（Oriel College, Oxford），又名国王学院（King's College），是牛津大学的一个学院，建于1326年，位于英国牛津市奥里尔广场。

② 【译者注】墨顿学院（Merton College, Oxford）是牛津大学最古老的学院之一，建于1264年，位于英国牛津市墨顿街，以悠久的历史和出色的学术著称。

③ 【译者注】彼得学院（Peterhouse, Cambridge）是剑桥大学最早的学院，建于1284年。

④ 【译者注】十六世纪四十年代，加尔文教在法国传播，称为胡格诺教（新教）。法国南部的大封建贵族信奉新教，企图利用宗教改革运动达到夺取教会地产的目的，他们与北方有分裂倾向的信奉天主教大封建贵族有深刻的利害冲突，最终演变为长期内战。1562—1598年连续八次天主教和新教的激烈对抗，给十六世纪的法国造成了严重破坏。

⑤ 【译者注】英王亨利八世（1491—1547）在英国推行宗教改革，1529年创立英国国教，教会宣布脱离罗马教廷，亨利八世成为英格兰最高宗教领袖，确立了英国王权至尊的地位。1542年英格兰修道院全数解散，其财产收归皇室，取消修道院和隐修院在英国上议院的席位，只保留大主教和主教席位。

⑥ 【译者注】爱德华六世（Edward VI, 1537—1553），亨利八世之子，他坚持其父英国国教政策，是英格兰首位信奉新教的统治者。

⑦ 【译者注】撒克逊人是古代日耳曼人的分支，原居北欧日德兰半岛、丹麦诸岛和德国西北沿海一带，公元五世纪至六世纪，盎格鲁、撒克逊两部都有人群南渡北海移民大不列颠岛，在此后的三四百年间，两部逐渐融合为盎格鲁·撒克逊人。

⑧ 【译者注】公元八世纪，诺曼人在法国北部建立了诺曼底公国，诺曼底公爵威廉说服他的邻国丹麦国王，组成攻打英国的欧洲联盟军，建立了英国诺曼底王朝（1066—1154）。

曼人①统治下的英国人,都从未像我们现在见到的这样,破坏他们的文化遗迹,我们的子孙将诅咒我们这个时代无理破坏英格兰最珍贵古老遗迹的邪恶行为"②。修道院图书馆和手稿的毁坏,伴随着很多有识之士的抗议和悲恸,为图书馆运动新的强劲发展做好了准备。

十七、十八世纪,活字印刷术的使用,使图书迅速增加。自由思想的萌芽成为文艺复兴和宗教改革的第一个成果,文学和科学著作比在教会束缚下更多产。一方面中世纪修道院图书馆的湮灭是人类知识的损失,另一方面如果修道士图书馆员继续拥有图书馆管理者和教育者的专属权利,建立向所有人开放的图书馆,而不只是建立一些仅向几个享有特权的学者和修道士开放的神圣储藏所的理念,或许不会发展得如此充分。如果听任那些相信阻挡希伯来人(Hebrew)③的罪恶最好的办法,是烧掉除了《圣经》之外所有犹太人图书的修道士继续控制知识的源泉,修道院图书馆的管理者还有足够的自由,去收藏、编目那些藏在圣墙里的近代早期无宗教色彩和激进的图书吗?现代图书馆员在图书馆管理和编制书目的很多方面都从修道士那里受惠,然而,公平对待书中所包含的精神和自由图书馆运动中的民主思想,在免费图书馆运动中是一杯新酒④,如果它装进了修道院图书馆的旧皮袋,就不会有今天提升高等图书馆学教育的呐喊。

在很多修道院被镇压之后,图书馆的管理权逐渐转移到世俗学者和牧师手中,十七世纪的很多学者,同时也是杰出的图书馆馆长。加布里埃尔·诺德(Gabriel Naudé)⑤、约翰·杜里(John Durie)⑥、詹姆斯·科克伍德(James Kirkwood)⑦、安东尼奥·马利亚贝基(Antonio Magliabecchi)⑧等都为建立现代图书馆学做出了很多贡献。他们是爱书者,愿意收藏图书,扩大图书馆,建立图书馆服务系统。十八世纪的图书馆员像他们的前辈一样杰出,简·德休

---

① 【译者注】诺曼人(Normans),是八世纪至十一世纪自北欧日德兰半岛和斯堪的纳维亚半岛等原住地,向欧洲大陆各国进行掠夺性和商业性远征的日耳曼人,发动了殖民诺曼底、入侵英格兰、建立西西里和南意大利国家、十字军东征等,是中世纪北欧、地中海和近东的重要部族。

② 【原注】Edward Edwards. *Memoirs of Libraries*. Trübner. London. 1859. Vol. 1, p. 360-1.

③ 【译者注】希伯来人是犹太人的祖先。

④ 【译者注】马太福音中有 new wine in old bottles,译为"新酒装在旧皮袋里"。在耶稣时代,人们使用酒皮袋盛酒,新酒装在旧皮袋里,皮袋会因弹性不足而裂开。耶稣用这一比喻启示,如果将福音限制在摩西的律法下,就会浪费福音信息并毁坏律法。也就是说,如果接纳了基督教,而没有改变人生是毫无意义的。

⑤ 【译者注】加布里埃尔·诺德(Gabriel Naude,1600—1653),法国图书馆学家,历史学家、哲学家。1627 年出版《关于图书馆建设的意见》,最早阐述公共图书馆的理想,强调"将书提供给公众使用""即使对最卑微的能多少获益的人也不要限制"等。

⑥ 【译者注】约翰·杜里(John Durie,又作 John Dury,1596—1680)苏格兰人,加尔文教派牧师,曾致力于基督新教的加尔文教派和路德派的结合。1650 年任圣马丁教区图书馆管理员,著有《图书管理员制度改革》。

⑦ 【译者注】詹姆斯·科克伍德(James Kirkwood,1650—1708/1709),苏格兰长老会牧师,毕业于爱丁堡大学,提倡建立免费教区图书馆。

⑧ 【译者注】安东尼奥·马利亚贝基(Antonio Magliabecchi,1633—1714),意大利图书馆学家、学者、藏书家,1673 年任托斯卡纳大公国图书馆馆长。他的私人图书馆收藏 4 万册图书和 1 万件手稿,他去世后,以他的 3 万多册图书和 3 千多件手稿遗赠,建立了 Magliabechiana 图书馆(马利亚贝基图书馆),1861 年该馆与巴拉蒂那(Palatina)图书馆合并,改称佛罗伦萨国立图书馆,即今佛罗伦萨国家中心图书馆的前身。

赛思(Jean Des Houssayes)①、戴维·休谟(David Hume)②、戈特霍尔德·埃夫莱姆·莱辛(Gotthold Ephraim Lessing)③以及很多知识渊博的学者,都曾经是知识财富的保存者,他们中的一些人通过其显赫的文学声望,为图书馆专业发展做出贡献,一些人推动了书目学的进步。作为一个群体,他们主要是博学的教授和杰出的学者,然而他们中的一些人,具有与新的社会秩序相适应的管理图书馆的广阔视野。

加布里埃尔·诺德是十八世纪杰出的图书馆馆长之一。1600年2月,诺德出生于巴黎,曾跟随派代特(Padet)和布拉格特(Belurget)教授研究哲学和修辞学,他最后一位著名的老师是一位宗教和信仰领域的自由思想者。诺德是一位多产作者,他的学问非常渊博,20岁时,他的文学声望引起亨利·德麦兹姆斯议长(Henri de Mesmes)④的注意,议长任命年轻的加布里埃尔主持他的图书馆。1630年,诺德成为意大利(罗马)红衣主教⑤巴尼(Bagni)图书馆馆长;巴尼去世后,诺德成为红衣主教巴贝里尼(Barberini)图书馆馆长;1642年,红衣主教黎塞留(Richelieu)召他去巴黎;黎塞留去世后,他成为红衣主教马萨林(Mazarin)图书馆馆长;在马萨林从巴黎流亡出走⑥期间,他成为瑞典女王克里斯蒂娜(Christina)著名图书馆的馆长。尽管他对很多有争议的学科都有广泛的兴趣,但他是一位天生的图书馆馆长,他热爱收藏图书,是购书交易的专家。当他开始一次寻书之旅时,手里拿上一把尺,一进入书店,他就拿出好几堆书向店员询价,店员来不及细想,匆忙报出价格,然后诺德开始大折扣讨价,通常都能以很低的价格带走想要买的图书。他经常能做成交易,而店员仅仅是在卖完之后才仔细考虑,意识到上当了,悔恨这档交易,只当是把那些书卖给了卖奶油的人或是杂货商。当诺德发现在巴黎再也没有可买的图书时,他去了比利时,在那儿的市场上买到了最好的图书。意大利被搜遍了,德国和英格兰成为下一个目标,不管他到哪里,书店都像被旋风掠过一样,损失惨重。诺德是让马萨林图书馆成为十七世纪"世界第八大奇迹"的图书馆馆长⑦。

---

① 【译者注】简·德休赛思(Jean-Baptiste Cotton des Houssayes,1727—1783),法国图书馆学家,1776年任索邦大学(今巴黎大学的前身)图书馆馆长。

② 【译者注】戴维·休谟(David Hume,1711—1776),苏格兰哲学家,苏格兰启蒙运动和西方哲学历史中最重要的人物之一,1752年任爱丁堡大学图书馆馆长,图书馆的丰富资源为他研究《大不列颠史》提供了帮助。

③ 【译者注】戈特霍尔德·埃夫莱姆·莱辛(Gotthold Ephraim Lessing,1729—1781),是德国十八世纪启蒙运动的主要代表人物之一,杰出的剧作家、文艺批评家和美学家。1770年任沃芬比特的赫尔措格·奥古斯特大公图书馆(Herzog August Bibliothek)馆长。

④ 【译者注】亨利·德麦兹姆斯(Henri de Mesmes,1575—1650)法国鲁瓦西地区的领主,巴黎市长和治安官。

⑤ 【译者注】红衣主教又称枢机主教,因穿戴红衣红帽,被教外人士称为红衣主教,是天主教会神职人员中仅次于教宗的职位,通常是各大教区大主教上级的都会主教和宗主教,或是梵蒂冈教廷的内阁成员,教宗出缺时,按法律只有他们才有权选举教宗。

⑥ 【译者注】1648年8月26日,巴黎市民武装暴动,要求处死马萨林,要求进行改革、大幅减税、整肃腐败与扩大法院职权,因市民主要使用投石器(Fronde)作为武器,故称投石党之乱。1850年爆发第二次投石党之乱,马萨林宣布引退流亡,1853年暴动平息,马萨林回到巴黎,依赖法王路易十四,建立了巩固的权利体系。

⑦ 【原注】Naudé, G. Plea to Parliament for the Preservation of the Mazarin Library, 1652. (Reprinted in Dana and Kent, eds. *Literature of Libraries in the Seventeenth and Eighteenth Centuries*. 1907. Vol. 6. p. 72).

当回顾诺德耀眼的成就时,我们意识到他抓住了图书馆学的要害问题。当他 26 岁仍在担任德麦兹姆斯图书馆馆长时,为了向德麦兹姆斯表达敬意,写下了《关于创办图书馆的意见书》(Advis pour Dresser une Bibliotheque),第一版于 1627 年出版,1644 年出版第二版,同年以及 1668 年又再版。1661 年约翰·伊夫林(John Evelyn)①将其译为英文,1703 年被译为拉丁文。这本书共分为九章,前五章给出了成立图书馆的理由、应该收藏图书的种类以及获得藏书的方法,第六章论述了图书馆体系结构,第七章介绍了图书分类体系,共分为十二个大类和几个细分子类②,第八章论及装订,第九章论述图书馆的主要目标。

根据乔治·史密斯(George Smith)的研究,诺德《关于创办图书馆的意见书》是第一个"实用的"关于图书馆的专著,诺德是第一个全面描述图书馆完整计划的图书馆馆长。"他(诺德)采用的原则,"乔治·史密斯说,"与现在最成功的设计很相似,他建议新书另行保存六个月,利用这段时间给其余的图书除尘,到时间后,再把这些书按类放在合适的书架上,以便给后续新书腾出空间。这样,在实际操作中,避免了新书立刻按类上架而带来的不断重新排架的麻烦。"③

诺德不仅提出图书馆向公众开放的设想,在实践中,他还说服红衣主教马萨林在每个星期四开放他那丰富的图书馆,开放时间为上午 8:00—11:00,下午 2:00—5:00,任何人都可以去图书馆,免费查阅那些有价值的藏品。诺德不仅提倡实行免费图书馆服务,而且主张任用有才能的图书馆员编制作者和主题目录,在各方面满足所有读者的需求。诺德是现代图书馆专业的先驱,阿尔伯特·德拉费热利赫(Albert de la Fizelière)④在他的《1649 年巴黎著名图书馆介绍》中,给予诺德最高的赞扬:"在法国,如果说有人钟爱文献和书籍,加布里埃尔·诺德就是图书馆馆长的模范典型。实际上,在他之前有藏书家和书目学家,但是图书学并未同步发展,他是第一个为图书学制定正式标准的人,正是由于他百科全书式的知识体系,使图书学在十七世纪令人高山仰止的科学与文学成就之侧,占据了一席之地。"⑤

十八世纪,皇家图书馆、学习机构图书馆和私人图书馆在许多国家广泛发展,通常对于图书馆的所有者来说,聘请有学问的人、伟大的思想家、知名的书目学家做他们的图书馆馆长是非常自豪的,这个职位获得的尊敬胜过酬劳。皇家图书馆通常允许学者使用图书馆的藏品,以此鼓励学者,表达他们对文学和科学的热爱。如果知名学者和思想家致力于管理图书馆,那么图书馆的价值将更加提高。像休谟、莱辛等博学学者,就像很多宝贵的手稿一样,是图书馆的重要资产。著名学者任图书馆馆长有两个理由:一是收到为图书馆服务的薪俸;二是在他从事这项工作时,可以自由使用图书馆里的图书。

---

① 【译者注】约翰·伊夫林(John Evelyn,1620—1706),英国作家,英国皇家学会的创始人之一,曾撰写过有关美术、宗教等著作三十余部。

② 【原注】J. D. Brown. *Library Classification and Cataloguing*. Grafton. London. 1916. p. 29-30.

③ 【原注】George Smith. Gabriel Naudé, a Librarian of the Seventeenth Century. *Library Association Record*. 1:425-6. July, 1899.

④ 【译者注】原文书名为 Rymaille Sur Les Plus CélèbresBibliotières De Paris,根据查证,书名应为 Rymaillesur les plus célèbresbibliotières de Paris en 1649,译为《1649 年巴黎著名图书馆介绍》,作者为奥伯特·德拉费热利赫(Albert de la Fizeliere,1819—1878),法国文学家、文艺评论家、历史学家。

⑤ 【原注】R. S. Granniss. Gabriel Naudé, Biographical Sketch. (In Dana and Kent, eds. *Literature of Libraries in the Seventeenth and Eighteenth Centuries*. McClurg. Chicago. 1906. Vol. 6. p. 37-8).

戴维·休谟作为鲁迪曼(Ruddiman)①的继任者,1752年被选为爱丁堡爱德沃凯特(Advocates)图书馆馆长。根据休谟的描述,那是一个薪资很低的职位,一年大约40几尼②,虽然这点薪金微不足道,他还是接受了这份工作,因为他可以掌管一个大图书馆。他的助理瓦尔特·古德尔(Walter Goodall)③是一个"很少清醒"的人,他的一部分时间用来写作,粉饰玛丽皇后④。休谟把主要兴趣用于撰写英格兰历史,厄内斯特·萨费基(Ernest A. Savage)⑤曾说:"我们很好奇他们是如何管理图书馆的"(休谟和古德尔)⑥。莱辛的情况也一样,他于1770年接受了沃芬布特尔(Wolfenbüttel)图书馆馆长的职位,虽然他也希望通过他们的出版物,让世界了解该馆收藏的手稿内容,但是,他的主要目的是自己方便使用图书馆丰富的馆藏⑦。

尽管不少著名的学者馆长对图书馆管理采取放任的态度,然而,这种学者型的、具有公益精神的人还是提升了图书馆馆长的标准,像他们中的简·德休赛思(Jean-Baptiste Cotton des Houssayes),1776年被选为索邦社区(大学)图书馆馆长。在有关"图书馆馆长的职责与资格"的论述中,德休赛思设定了图书馆馆长的经典职业标准,关于馆长的资格:"请允许我说,一个真正当之无愧的图书馆馆长,应该提前研究每个领域的文献,使他以后能够成为一个忠实的向导,为所有想要查找这些文献的人服务。书目学就是要准确、严谨地熟悉人类智力成果,尽管将文献学置于其他所有科学之上绝不是我的本意,但请允许我把书目学看作是所有其他科学的先锋……因此,不管图书馆的属性如何,图书馆的管理者都应该对任何知识领域不陌生,包括宗教和世俗文学、艺术、精密科学等,所有学科他都应该熟悉。"对于图书馆管理,德休赛思强调:"图书馆应该由这样的馆长来管理,他不仅具有非凡的记忆力,而且具有准确的判断力,因而他不允许不加选择地让每本书都进入他的图书馆,而只是选择那些真正有价值和有用的图书。在开明经营的原则指导下获得的图书,通过准确合理的分类,体现更大的价值。"⑧

---

① 【译者注】托马斯·鲁迪曼(Thomas Ruddiman,1674—1757),苏格兰学者,1930—1752年任爱德沃凯特图书馆馆长。

② 【译者注】几尼(guineas),英国的旧金币,值一镑一先令。

③ 【译者注】瓦尔特·古德尔(Walter Goodall,1796—1766),苏格兰史学家,毕业于阿伯丁大学国王学院,后来成为爱丁堡爱德沃凯特图书馆馆长助理。

④ 【译者注】玛丽·安托瓦内特(Queen Mary,即Marie An-toinette,1755—1793),原奥地利公主,生于维也纳,1770年成为法国王储路易·奥古斯特·德·波旁(即日后的路易十六)的王太子妃,1792年巴黎人民起义被判死刑,1793年10月被处死。

⑤ 【译者注】厄内斯特·萨费基(Ernest A. Savage,1877—1966),1922—1942年任爱丁堡公共图书馆馆长,1929—1931年任苏格兰图书馆协会主席,1936年任图书馆协会(CILIP,即现在的"英国图书馆与情报专家学会")主席,长期从事图书馆员培训和专业教育,他的著述广泛涉猎图书馆和图书馆学。

⑥ 【原注】E. A. Savage. *Story of Libraries and Book Collecting*. Routledge. London, p. 169.

⑦ 【原注】V. Gardthausen. *Handbuch der Wissenschaftlichen Bibliothekskunde*. Quelle. Leipzig. 1920. Vol. 2. p. 82.

⑧ 【原注】Des Houssayes. Discourse on the Duties and Qualifications of a Librarian. (In Dana and Kent, eds. *Literature of Libraries in the Seventeenth and Eighteenth Centuries*. McClurg. Chicago. 1906. Vol. 1, p. 37-8, 43-4).

十九世纪学者馆长描述的馆长资格,为他们的继任者建立了一个良好的学术标准,在此基础上,十九世纪中后期,馆长们提供了非常实用的图书馆服务,并把图书馆学培训引进专业学习的课堂。

SELECTED BIBLIOGRAPHY

Axon, William F. A. Antonio Magliabecchi. Library Association Record. 5;59-76. Feb. ,1903.

Brown, James Duff. Library classification and cataloging. Grafton. London. 1916. Chap. 3.

Clark, John Willis. Care of books. Cambridge Univ. Press. Cambridge. 1902.

Clark, J. W. Mediaeval and Renaissance libraries. Macmillan. Cambridge. 1894.

Clarke, A. Lessing as a librarian. Library, n. s. 2;376-83. 1901.

Dana, J. C. and Kent, H. W. , eds. Literature of libraries in the seventeenth and eighteenth centuries. McClurg. Chicago. 1906. 6vols.

Des Houssayes, Jean-Baptiste Cotton. Duties and qualifications of a librarian. (*In* Dana and Kent, eds. Literature of libraries in the seventeenth and eighteenth centuries. McClurg. Chicago. 1906. Vol. 1).

Edwards, Edward. Libraries and founders of libraries. Trübner. London. 1864.

Edwards, Edward. Memoirs of libraries. Trübner. London. 1859. 2vols. Book II. Chap. 6-9;Book III. Chap. 1-2 ,7.

Gardthausen, Victor. Handbuch der wissenschaftlichen bibliothekskunde. Quelle. Leipzig. 1920. Vol. 2, Book 8. p. 82-4.

Garnett, Richard. Essays in librarianship and bibliography. Allen. London. 1899. p. 166-8 ,174-90.

Gibson, Strickland. Some Oxford libraries. Oxford Univ. Press. 1914.

Kirkwood, James. Two tracts on the founding and maintaining of parochial libraries in Scotland. (*In* Dana and Kent, eds. Literature of libraries in seventeenth and eighteenth centuries. McClurg. Chicago. 1906. Vol. 3).

Koch, T. W. On university libraries. Paris. 1924.

Maitland, S. R. The dark ages. Hodges. London. 1890. p. 477-91.

Naudé, Gabriel. The library of Cardinal Mazarin. (*In* Dana and Kent, eds. Literature of libraries in seventeenth and eighteenth centuries. McClurg. Chicago. 1906. Vol. 6).

Savage, Ernest A. Old English libraries. Methuen. London. 1912. Chap. 3 ,5 ,11.

Savage, Ernest A. Story of libraries and book collecting. Routledge. London.

Smith, George. Gabriel Naudé: a librarian of the seventeenth century. Library Association Record. 1;423-31 ,483-93. July, Aug. ,1899.

Tedder, Henry R. Evolution of the public library. Second International Library Conference in London. Transactions. 13-18. 1897.

第八章 现代图书馆员的专业教育

十九世纪上半叶,图书馆的建设如雨后春笋,使用人数及藏书量也大大增加,"书虫"式的图书馆员再也不能有效地应付这种局面。在此之前,人们一直认为,典型的图书馆员应博览群书,被视为活目录。然而,十九世纪中期以后,人们开始更加充分认识图书馆的管理形态,由于不同学科的文献大量增加,图书馆员即使有马利亚贝基的热情和头脑,也不可能通读任一学科的所有图书。不仅仅是掌握庞大的知识量,而是编制和应用书目,以及引进辅助人们记忆的技术方法,自然而然地成为图书馆变革的特征。

这一时期,人们开始认识到,他们有权要求国家提供免费学校和公共图书馆,因此,有了关于图书馆要向少年和老年、未受过教育和受过教育的人开放的立法意识。在这种情况下,要求新型的图书馆员,不仅要有学术成就,而且要有组织能力和经营能力。像英国的安东尼·帕尼齐爵士(Sir Anthony Panizzi)①和美国的查尔斯 C. 朱厄特(Charles C. Jewett)教授②,都是在我们所谈到的巨大变革时代被推崇的学者型和新型职业图书馆馆长的典型。图书馆学经过曲折的发展,逐渐偏向实用性和经营管理。十九世纪中期,很多现代图书馆学的积极支持者,强调对图书馆经营进行适当培训的重要性,他们撰写图书馆学术论文和通俗读物,使公众明白图书馆员培训的必要性。他们开始组织协会,出版刊物,提倡建立培训机构,他们自己也认真提供高效和现代的图书馆服务,公众开始接受图书馆员从事图书馆职业的正式地位,所有现代图书馆员都深深地受惠于先驱们的不懈努力。

关于现代图书馆员的培训和资格,德国最伟大的图书馆馆长德累斯顿图书馆馆长弗里德里希·阿道夫·艾伯特(F. A. Ebert)③在他的《图书馆员的教育》④一书中,提出了一个理想的标准:包括百科全书式的知识,对人类各方面知识都充满热情和兴趣,特别喜欢有条不紊,应该把全部时间都贡献给图书馆工作,最重要的是,他必须做好准备,认识到他所获得的唯一奖赏就是工作本身。艾伯特以身作则,但是作为平均要求,这个标准未免太高,不切实际。

---

① 【译者注】安东尼·帕尼齐(Anthony Panizzi,1797—1879),英国图书馆学家。1856—1866 年任大不列颠博物院图书馆(现大英图书馆)馆长。他主张实施呈缴本法,争取充裕的经费,使大不列颠博物院图书馆藏书增加 4 倍;他亲自筹划和设计了世界上第一座容量为 130 万册的大型书库和有 450 个座位的阅览大厅;他所著的《91 条著录规则》,成为编目著录的原则;他改革借阅工作,制定借书程序,为不列颠博物馆图书馆向读者免费开放做出了贡献。

② 【译者注】查尔斯 C. 朱厄特(Charles Coffin Jewett,1816—1868),美国图书馆学家。1841 年任布朗大学第一位专职图书馆馆长(过去均由教授兼任),1847—1855 年任史密森宁研究院图书馆馆长。1855 年入波士顿公共图书馆供职,先后担任编目馆员和采访馆员。1858 年任该馆第一位督导。

③ 【译者注】弗里德里希·阿道夫·艾伯特(Friedrich Adolf Ebert,1791—1834),德国图书馆学家。1706 年开始在莱比锡市立图书馆工作,此后学习文献学,1812 年获得博士学位。1813—1814 年分别在莱比锡大学图书馆和德累斯顿皇家图书馆任职。出版了大量图书馆及图书馆学著作,影响最大的是《图书馆员的教育》(1820)。

④ 【原注】弗里德里希·阿道夫·艾伯特.图书馆员的教育(Bildung des Bibliothekars).第二版,莱比锡,1820.

正像伦敦绅士俱乐部图书馆馆长亨利·理查德·泰德(henry Richard Tedder)①所说的那样:"他(艾伯特)提出的这种普适性要求也许是理想的,但是在同一个人身上很难达到。"②

与艾伯特近乎乌托邦式的理想不同,泰德式的图书馆馆长设计了一个解决办法,能够将具有平均文化水平的人培养成为专业图书馆员。早在1829年,马丁·施莱廷格(Martin Schrettinger)③就在慕尼黑出版的《图书馆学综合性试用教科书》中,强调在专业图书馆员培训学校接受培训的价值,"没有人",施莱廷格说,"尽管他在文学方面受过高等教育,即使他是一个伟大的学者,不经过专业学习、准备和实践,就能适合做图书馆员……应该有一种图书馆学校与国家图书馆衔接,从而能够为其他图书馆提供有才能的毕业生,这样,图书馆管理的方法就能以一贯的方式延续下去。"④明尼苏达大学图书馆馆长弗兰克 K.瓦尔特(Frank K. Walter)说得很对,施莱廷格可能是第一个建议建立培训图书馆员专业学校的人⑤,然而,施莱廷格既没有明确列出怎样在国家图书馆建立专业图书馆学校的计划,也没有提供任何课程表,他只是简单地表达了这样的思想。

图书馆培训没有在德国引起更广泛的呼吁,直到1871年安东·克莱特(Anton Klette)博士在莱比锡出版《独立的图书馆员职业》⑥一书。此后,德国开始认识图书馆员是一个独立的职业。新职业的出现,引起图书馆员和大学教授的强烈兴趣,他们讨论研究培训的方法。德国弗赖堡大学图书馆馆长鲁尔曼(F. Rullman)为此做好准备,1874年制定了图书馆学三年大学课程草案⑦。

鲁尔曼先生建议德国图书馆员开会讨论两件事:(1)成立德国图书馆组织,(2)建立图书馆专业培训学校。会议决定该会由国家组织召开,由于一些图书馆员的反对,会议一直没有召开。德国基尔大学图书馆馆长斯特芬哈根(Steffen Hagen)博士批评这个计划太理想化。第一,因为会议依赖国家财政支持,图书馆员会议的决议对政府部门没有权威效应。第二,

---

① 【译者注】亨利·理查德·泰德(henry Richard Tedder,1850—1924)历史学家,伦敦绅士俱乐部图书馆馆长。伦敦绅士俱乐部(The Athenaeum Club,Pall Mall,London)1824年由当时的英国海军部长 J·W·Croker 发起建立,成立之初是为英国的上层人士(如内阁,上院议员等)提供一个私人交流的场所,后来推广至科学、文化、艺术等学术界等人士参加,他们中间已经有52人获得诺贝尔奖,涵盖各个领域。

② 【原注】Henry R. Tedder. Librarianship as a Profession. Library Association of the United Kingdom. *Translation.* 5:163-4. 1882.

③ 【译者注】马丁·施莱廷格(Martin Schrettinger,1772—1851),德国牧师和图书馆管理员。1800年任修道院图书馆管理员,1802年前往慕尼黑皇家图书馆工作。1829年出版《图书馆学综合性试用教科书》(Versuch eines Vollstandigen Lehrbuchs der Bibliothek-Wissenschaft),首次把图书馆作为一门理论学科正式提出来。

④ 【原注】Martin Schrettinger. *Versuch eines Vollstandigen Lehrbuchs der Bibliothek-Wissenschaft.* Munich. 1829. Vol. 2. p. 187-8.

⑤ 【原注】Frank K. Walter, Library Training. *Encyclopaedia Americana.* Vol. 17-p. 393-4.

⑥ 【译者注】安东·克莱特(Anton Klette,1834—1879/1896年),德国图书馆学家,1870—1878年任耶拿大学图书馆馆长,主张图书馆员专业具有独立性,著作有《独立的图书馆员职业》(*Die Selbständigkeit des Bibliothekarischen Berufes*,莱比锡,1871)。

⑦ 【原注】F. Rullman. *Outlines of Library Science.* (United States Bureau of Education. Special Report, p. XXIII-XVI. 1876).

课程草案太理论化,过分强调书目问题,而不是图书馆管理的实际问题。在很长一段时间里,鲁尔曼和斯特芬哈根在很多文章中进行了针锋相对的斗争。1876 年以后,鲁尔曼在尤利乌斯·彼得佐特(Julius Petzholdt)的协助下,向他的支持者介绍了在美国费城召开的美国图书馆员会议上,成功建立了美国图书馆协会。然而,美国图书馆协会的建立,只给德国图书馆员带来微小的影响①。总之,对于大多数德国图书馆员来说,真正把图书馆学看作是一门独立的专业,而要求进行全面的学校培训和建立专业合作组织的时机尚未成熟。

1893 年 12 月 15 日,图书馆员培训的问题终于由普鲁士公共教育部发布公告而得到了解决②。德国第一次图书馆员会议是在卡尔·齐亚茨科(Karl Dziatzko)③的召集下,作为语言学家和教育家协会的分支,于 1897 年在德累斯顿举行④,51 名图书馆员聚集在一起,讨论各种各样的问题,3 年后,德国图书馆协会(Verein Deutscher Bibliothekare)正式建立。

正如詹姆斯·罗斯(James Ross)在《英国和国外的图书馆技术培训》中所说:"早在 1861年,弗里德里希·里奇尔(Friedrich Ritschl)⑤就将波恩大学图书馆作为培训学校,为想要成为图书馆员的人提供培训。随后,1886 年在哥廷根大学设立了图书馆学教授职位(Bibliotheks-Hilfswissenschaften),因此那里一定提供了图书馆学课程。"⑥在哥廷根大学图书馆馆长费克(R. Fick)教授写给爱荷华大学图书馆馆长约翰·博因顿·凯撒(John Boynton Kaiser)的信中说,卡尔·齐亚茨科教授是第一位被委任为在哥廷根大学设计图书馆学系统化培训课程的人,费克教授引用了一段施文克(P. Schwenke)在《图书馆文摘》中描述卡尔·齐亚茨科工作情况的文章,译文如下:"他(齐亚茨科)安排四个学期两到三小时的讲座课程,后来课程又逐渐完善,包括有关图书馆管理(或后来他称之为"现代图书馆学的历史与发展")、图书和写作的课程,解决专业教育和图书交易的问题(改革前后)。此外,还有关于拉丁作者的手稿、图书出版史上作者和出版商版权的讲座。当齐亚茨科先生做专题讲座时,还有关于编制书目的常规实践,让学生解决有关书目编制的实际问题。最后一年,他的主题是重点讲述哥廷根古版书,了解十五世纪的印刷类型和印刷情况。作为教师和成立于 1893 年

---

① 【原注】Arnin Graesel. *Handbuch der Bibliothekslehre.* Weber. Leipzig. 1902. p. 486-7.

② 【原注】Prussian Act Defining the Qualifications of a Librarian, 1893. *Zentralblatt für Bibliothekswesen.* 11:77-9. January-February, 1894; or, *Library Journal.* 19:170. May, 1894.

③ 【译者注】齐亚茨科(Karl Franz Otto Dziatzko, 1842—1903)德国图书馆学家,生于上西里西亚的诺伊施塔特镇,1859 年入布雷斯劳大学(今弗罗茨瓦夫大学)学习,1862 年就读波恩大学,在该校图书馆工作,毕业后任该校教师,1872 年起任布雷斯劳大学图书馆馆长,对该校图书馆的管理进行改革,修订编目条例,称为《齐亚茨科规则》。1886 年任哥廷根大学图书馆馆长和图书馆学教授,1893 年任图书馆员考试委员会主席。1896 年,德国根据著名的《齐亚茨科规则》,制订了各图书馆共同遵守的著录规则,1899 年《普鲁士图书馆字顺目录适用规则》(即《普鲁士规则》)问世。1900 年齐亚茨科参与创立德国图书馆协会,并任英语刊物《图书馆》的特约编辑。

④ 【原注】German Librarians' Conference at Dresden. 1897. *Zentralblatt für Bibliothekswesen.* 14:321. June-July, 1897.

⑤ 【译者注】弗里德里希·威廉·里奇尔(Friedrich Wilhelm Ritschl, 1806—1876),德国文字学家,著名学者。

⑥ 【原注】英国和国外的图书馆学技术培训,图书馆协会记录,1910,12(2):114.

的普鲁士图书馆职位考试委员会的主席①，齐亚茨科第一次为我们指明了期盼已久的图书馆专业培训的范围和性质。齐亚茨科的工作，永远是普鲁士和德国图书馆发展历史上的里程碑。"费克教授补充到，在齐亚茨科的资料中，发现了他的图书馆学讲座手稿："据我所见，这些手稿与他在大学公告上发布的讲座主题完全一致……在乔治·施耐德（Georg Schneider）1923年出版的《参考书目手册》（Handbuch der Bibliographie）第5页和第195页上有一些不完整的介绍。在与此有关的介绍中，还应该注意到，在齐亚茨科之前，哥廷根大学已经有对书目感兴趣的助理教授担任图书馆馆长，并开设本学科文献学史讲座……"②

伦敦大学图书馆学院院长厄内斯特·艾伯特·贝克（Ernest A. Baker）博士在他的新书《公共图书馆》中，有简短的一章讲到图书馆培训，追溯了图书馆专业培训的历史。他说："某些普通高校也开设书目、古文字学以及相似学科的课程，这不仅对图书馆员有用，而且对做研究工作的学生也有用。德国、意大利和瑞典在我们之前建立了图书馆学校，最早的是在1861年。"③

参考格雷塞尔（Graesel）的《图书馆管理学》、嘎斯奥森的《图书馆科学手册》、费克博士给凯撒馆长的信中关于德国图书馆专业培训的问题、齐亚茨科的《德国图书馆和图书馆学教育现状》④、安布罗斯（Ambrose）先生的《齐亚茨科博士论德国图书馆》⑤等著述，其中只提到杰出学者、图书馆馆长弗里德里希·里奇尔于1854—1865年在波恩大学进行了编目创新、重新排架，以及其他纯管理工作的改进，而关于德国图书馆学专业培训的介绍，大多数人把第一个图书馆学教授的荣誉给予哥廷根大学的卡尔·齐亚茨科，通常认为1886年是德国大学设立第一个图书馆学教授职位的时间。

当齐亚茨科还是波恩大学的学生时，波恩大学语言学教授和图书馆馆长弗里德里希·里奇尔制定了一个规定，要求语言学研讨班的学生们去做图书馆助理，因此，齐亚茨科可能最早在波恩大学图书馆的流通部门了解到图书馆的管理方法。里奇尔教授全面改组图书馆，为图书馆的发展做了很多工作。哥廷根大学图书馆馆长理查德·匹兹曼（Richard Pietschmann）⑥在对齐亚茨科的回忆中谈道："很多德国最优秀的图书馆员都在里奇尔那里得到培训，我只提其中的几位，如德国皇家图书馆总干事奥古斯特·威廉姆斯（Aug. Wilmanns）⑦，波恩大学图书馆馆长乔斯·斯旦德（Jos. Ständer），直到最近一直担任卡尔斯鲁厄大学法律图书馆馆长的威廉姆·布兰巴赫（Wilhelm Brambach）。"⑧从以上这些情况来看，我

---

① 【译者注】据《世界图书馆与情报服务百科全书》（美国图书馆协会，1993：260）关于Dziatzko Karl的介绍，1893年齐亚茨科被任命为普鲁士的图书馆职位考试委员会主席。但原记为1896年，疑为此处时间记载有误，译文中更正。

② 【原注】图书馆文摘.1903,20(3):135.

③ 【原注】Ernest A. Baker. *The Public Library*. Grafton. London. 1924. p. 220.

④ 【原注】图书馆编年.1887,4:57—63.

⑤ 【原注】图书馆杂志.1896,21(2):53—59.

⑥ 【译者注】路德维希·威廉·理查德·匹兹曼（1851—1923），哥廷根大学图书馆馆长，东方和埃及古物学者。

⑦ 【译者注】奥古斯特·威廉姆斯（1833—1917），德国古典学者。

⑧ 【原注】Richard Pietschmann. Karl Dziatzko: A Memorial Sketch; translated by Miss Selina Nachmann. *Library Journal*. 29:c87-8. December,1904.

们可以想象,里奇尔教授教给他的图书馆学生助理和其他学生一些图书馆管理方法和对书目的指导,就像现在一些美国高校开设如何使用图书馆的图书和书目的课程一样,这并不是说,这样的美国高校有了旨在培训未来图书馆员的图书馆学院。里奇尔教授可能给他的图书馆助理们很多关于图书馆管理的课外指导,虽然这些助理只是在大学图书馆实习,而没有任何意向要以图书馆工作作为他们的职业,就像齐亚茨科一样。1863 年,齐亚茨科毕业时,选择了教师职业,假如早在1861年波恩大学就有图书馆学校,齐亚茨科自然倾向于图书馆职业,他在里奇尔教授指导下,长时间建立的与大学图书馆的关系,使他一定倾向于毕业时成为一位图书馆员,而不是一位教师。如果弗里德里希·里奇尔已经在波恩大学建立了图书馆学校,那么,1874年鲁尔曼制定的图书馆学三年大学课程草案,就不会在他的同龄人中引起强烈的反响。作为德国大学教授,提供书目、书史、图书馆的课程是很正常的,但是这些课程与专业图书馆学校提供的课程相比,无论如何也不能看成是图书馆专业的培训。

自从1893年任命图书馆职位考试委员会①以及1899年颁布《普鲁士规则》②给出了图书馆员资格的定义,德国图书馆员考试和取得证书制度已经修订过若干次。1917年颁布了两个关于考试的法令,它们是:(1)关于科学图书馆的"助理馆员",(2)关于公共图书馆的"职员"。法令规定了科学图书馆助理馆员考试的某些课程,在助理馆员进入图书馆做实际工作之前,必须完成这些课程。由于第一次世界大战的爆发,所有关于德国图书馆员资格考试的问题都被搁置了。1918年,重新提出了助理馆员培训和考试的问题,并决定在理论培训和实际工作之间找到一个折衷的办法,目标是实际工作在图书馆里完成,图书馆学理论学习在大学里完成,两项工作同时进行,新法令于1919年出版。第一次世界大战结束之后,图书馆的发展非常迅速,于是1919—1920年冬季学期,有几个大学开设了图书馆学课程。

为了对德国图书馆学课程有一个整体印象,下面以《莱比锡大学公告》摘录为例,"(1)高级图书馆培训课程(与大学图书馆联合)。报考者在两学期的教学、解题和实际工作课程中,获得通过毕业考试必需的理论知识,这只是为了参加专业考试的初级培训;(2)为未来图书馆员做准备的专业学习。报考者必需先在大型图书馆做二年实际工作,才能接受专业学习,理论学习可能用一年的时间,第二年全部用于做图书馆实际工作。"③

1919—1920冬季学期教学课程

    1. 图书馆历史   主任鲍森(Boysen)博士

    2. 手稿 I   教授尤瑞(Rörig.)

    3. 百科全书和书目   教授明德·波特(Minde-Pouet)博士

    4. 德国书业史   古德·弗里德瑞兹(Gold-friedrich)博士

    5. 印刷史   教授雪姆(Schramm)博士

    6. 希腊古文书学   教授嘎斯奥森(Gardthausen)博士

    7. 中世纪和现代大事记   教授西利格(Seeliger)

---

① 【译者注】见【译者注】146。

② 【译者注】普鲁士规则(Prussian Act),于1896年开始制定,1899年出版,原文记为1893年颁布,疑为时间记载有误。见【译者注】141。

③ 【原注】Library Science in Saxony and Library Courses in Leipzig University. (*In Zentralblatt für Bibliothekswesen*. 36:230-1. September-October 1919).

8. 古文书学疑难问题　　　　　　教授卢瑞兹(Rorig)
9. 对外交往疑难问题　　　　　　教授卢瑞兹(Rorig)

后四个课程,也就是6—9,也为普通学生开设。

在普鲁士从事图书馆专业服务的资格是:(1)通过中学毕业考试;(2)在德国大学四个学院之一学习合格的证明;(3)博士或硕士学位;(4)健康证书;(5)在普鲁士大型图书馆做两年实际工作;(6)国家图书馆职位委员会考试及格。自从政府在大学里为高级馆员开设图书馆课程以后,萨克森德国印刷者协会最近在莱比锡为初级馆员开设了图书馆学校,这个计划也已经被德国其他的州所采纳。

在奥地利,1862年开始,申请图书馆职位需要考试。早在1874年,历史调查研究所(Institute of Historical Enquiry)就提供书目、书史及其他科目课程,1895年修改和重新调整了考试内容。在意大利,1876年开始,就已经有了公共图书馆管理和图书馆官员考试试行规定,公共教育部部长西诺·鲁杰罗·波飞(Signor Ruggero Bonghi)①制定了草案,但是,直到1885年,政府才提供书目和图书馆学考试②,1905年计划在佛罗伦萨建立美国式的国际图书馆学校。在斯堪的纳维亚国家③,十九世纪后期承认图书馆职业,一些维京人④的后裔穿越大西洋到美国图书馆学校接受培训。在瑞典,1908年在斯德哥尔摩第一次开办图书馆学夏季学校。

在法国,1879年由公共教育部组织图书馆员职位考试,有两类考试,一类是高级馆员考试,另一类是初级馆员考试。申请高级馆员资格,要求报考者出示:(1)出生证、毕业证;(2)已经做过的工作,两年的图书馆工作经历,语言知识的证明。考试一部分是笔试,一部分是口试,初级馆员或助理馆员的口试和笔试包括:

Ⅰ. 印刷本

1. 12本书的编目,包括古版书和外语书。
2. 12本书排架的对错。
3. 国家图书馆的分类,以及书目、印刷史、装订、展览等问题。

Ⅱ. 手稿

1. 4本或5本手稿的描述。
2. 关于古文书和手稿目录的问题。
3. 十七世纪以来的图书馆历史和国家图书馆的主要藏品。

1894年,索邦大学开始提供书目讲座和一些图书馆经营的课程,但直到1923年6月,在巴黎和其他省份都没有独立的图书馆学校。巴黎的美国图书馆学校,是由"美国救援法国减

---

① 【译者注】西诺·鲁杰罗·波飞(Signor RuggeroBonghi,1826—1895),意大利学者、作家和政治家。
② 【原注】Examination open to all citizens. *Library Chronicle*. 2:76.1885.
③ 【译者注】在地理上是指斯堪的纳维亚半岛,包括挪威和瑞典,文化与政治上则包含丹麦。这些国家互相视对方属于斯堪的纳维亚,虽然政治上彼此独立,但共同的称谓显示了其文化和历史有深厚的渊源。
④ 【译者注】维京人(Viking)生活在1000多年前的北欧,即今天的挪威、丹麦和瑞典一带,从公元八到十一世纪,他们一直侵扰欧洲沿海和英国岛屿,其足迹遍及从欧洲大陆至北极的广阔疆域,欧洲这一时期被称为"维京时期"(Viking Age)。

灾委员会"①建立,1924年秋,制订了为法国图书馆员开设正规全日制图书馆学校的计划,由美国图书馆协会组织实施②。然而,我们不能忘记,虽然法国没有现代图书馆学校,但是他有一个世界上最好的学校,教会学者和藏书家怎样研究和利用丰富的档案藏品。阅读德利尔(Delisle)《青春的回忆》③,能够帮助我们认识"巴黎文献学院"④,那里培养出了众多才华横溢的档案管理员,为人类文明做出了贡献,正如1917年7月,威廉·奥斯勒爵士(Sir William Osier)⑤在阿伯里斯特维斯大学⑥图书馆服务夏季学校开幕式上讲到的那样:"我们希望,当图书馆学校建立起来的时候,能为学生们提供像'巴黎文献学院'那样广阔和自由的机会,那所学院的学生被称为现代本笃会修士。"⑦

英国图书馆协会一直积极推进图书馆学培训,严格定义英国图书馆员的资格。按照图书馆协会制定的教学大纲,1885年7月英国举行了第一次助理馆员考试,三个报考者参加了考试。那时,很多图书馆员感到,在图书馆协会支持下成立一个机构,对参加考试者进行培训,是非常必要的。布特尔公共图书馆馆长奥格勒(J. J. Ogle)先生在图书馆协会十五周年年会上宣读了论文《图书馆学夏季学校》,为了回应他的呼吁,1893年英国创立了第一个图书馆学夏季学校。由圣塞维尔(St. Saviour)公共图书馆馆长罗伯特(H. D. Roberts)提议,图书馆协会将夏季学校委员会改为教育委员会,1898年2月开始举办助理馆员定期培训。1902年,图书馆协会决定与伦敦经济学院合作,对课程进行了一些修订。从那时起,伦敦学院在近十年的时间里,为英国有志成为图书馆员的人提供书目、分类、编目、图书馆法、图书馆经营培训。由于各省的助理馆员没有机会接受培训,于是,1904年图书馆协会开始设置函授班,鼓励某些顶尖的省属高等院校提供图书馆管理和书目课程,方便邻近地区的助理馆员学习。图书馆协会的这项计划已经在曼彻斯特技术学院、曼彻斯特约翰·里兰兹图书馆、利兹大学、纽卡斯尔安姆斯壮学院实施。

英国的夏季学校、函授班、高等院校培训的课程和方法大致相同,他们严格遵循图书馆协会编辑出版的教学大纲,学生只有一个目的,就是参加图书馆协会组织的每年一次的考试,并取得合格的成绩。考试分为六个科目,即文献学史、书目、分类、编目、图书馆组织、图书馆日常工作,每个科目考试通过后,单独授予合格证书。当一个人通过六科考试,并掌握适当的拉丁语和外语知识,撰写一篇具有合适主题、符合要求的毕业论文,就有资格获得毕

---

① 【译者注】美国救援法国减灾委员会,是一小群美国妇女自愿帮助法国从第一次世界大战的破坏中恢复的民间救援组织,由慈善家安妮·摩根(Anne Morgan,1873—1952)和她的朋友安妮·穆雷·迪科(Anne Murray Dike,1879—1929)创立。

② 【原注】Library School in Paris. *Public Libraries*. 28:440-1. October,1923;29:435-7. October,1924.

③ 【译者注】德利尔(Léopold Victor Delisle,1826—1910)法国史学家、图书馆学家。1871—1874年任法国国家图书馆写本部主任,1874—1905年任馆长,为该馆的扩建和改进做出贡献,著有《青春的回忆》。

④ 【译者注】巴黎文献学院(Ecole des Chartes)。

⑤ 【译者注】威廉·奥斯勒爵士(Sir William Osler,1849—1919),加拿大医生,约翰·霍普金斯医院的四个创始教授之一,他还是一个藏书家、历史学家、作家。

⑥ 【译者注】阿伯里斯特维斯大学(Aberystwyth, University of Wales)始建于1872年,是威尔士历史上第一所大学。该校提供高质量的教学及优秀的研究工作,在世界上享有很高的声誉。

⑦ 【原注】William Osier. Library School in the College. *Library Association Record*. 19:306. August-September,1917.

业文凭。这个制度有助于馆员培训的标准化,但是还没有足够大的范围去覆盖所有的图书馆学科领域。1919年在伦敦大学建立图书馆学院时,考虑到了这个制度的不足,计划提供全面的图书馆学培训,学院是卡内基英国信托基金和图书馆协会密切合作的成果。

"学院是大学学院的一个系……课程纳入文学院计划,"贝克博士(Baker)说到:"例行培训课程用时两年,学生必须投入所有的时间去上课、自学、实习,为了照顾那些不能放弃现有工作的助理馆员、售书助理、出版助理……允许他们兼职参加学习,培训时间延至3—5年,但培训必须连贯。完全学院式的培训,加上入学标准的基本教育要求,使图书馆学校前景广阔,迟早培训课程能够发展成为研究生课程。"①

现在的课程如下:
(1)英语作文
(2)拉丁语,或希腊语、梵文、经典阿拉伯语
(3)非英语的一门现代语言
(4)书目
(5)图书馆组织(包括公共图书馆法)
(6)图书馆日常工作
(7)编目和索引
(8)文献史和史籍选
(9)分类
(10)古文书学和档案
(11)权威学者开设的图书馆主题专业课程

纯技术科目的教学包括理论与实践,学生要在专业人士的指导下做实际工作,在获得毕业文凭之前,需要在图书馆完成一年带薪工作。

在美国,图书馆系统培训的开端,主要归功于麦维尔·杜威博士(Melvil Dewey),他敏锐地洞察到史上空前的图书馆运动在美国的发展。他清晰地认识到,教育、新闻、工业的增长和各项成就的不断取得,必将带来与过去时代完全不同的美国图书馆的发展。旧时的"图书保管员"已经不能较好地体现现代公共图书馆的意义,杜威先生引述卡莱尔(Carlyle)②的说法,称现代图书馆为"人民的大学"。他花费大量精力,提倡任用受过培训的图书馆员引导使用图书馆,将之作为向广大民众传播知识的渠道。

早在1879年,杜威博士写到:"我们需要一个培训学校,为专业工作做准备。数百所师范学校为乡村提供女教师,在那里,她们学到了最好的教学方法。医生、律师、传教士,甚至还有我们的厨师,都有专门学校进行专门培训。但是,专业要求更高的图书馆员,却必须通过自己的实践和经历去学习管理。"③

杜威博士关于建立正规图书馆学校的倡议,得到很多美国知名图书馆员的热情支持,威廉姆 F. 普尔(William F. Poole)④博士、C. A. 卡特(C. A. Cutter)、塞缪尔 S. 格林(Samuel S.

---

① 【原注】E. A. Baker. *The Public Library*. Grafton. London. 1924. p. 213-14.
② 【译者注】卡莱尔(Carlyle Thomas,1795—1881),英国作家。
③ 【原注】Melvil Dewey. Apprenticeship of Librarians. *Library Journal*. 4:147. May,1879.
④ 【译者注】威廉姆 F. 普尔(William Frederick Poole,1821—1894),美国书目学家、图书馆馆长。

Green)、R. C. 戴维斯（R. C. Davis）等都加入他的行列，共同推动此项计划。1884年，哥伦比亚学院董事会全体会议接受了建立图书馆学校的计划，1887年1月5日，哥伦比亚学院图书馆管理学校在纽约城正式建立。1889年，当杜威博士被任命为纽约州立图书馆馆长时，他把该校迁到奥尔巴尼，改称纽约州立大学图书馆学院，成为纽约州立大学的一部分，这是图书馆发展历史上的重要一步，因为，在某种程度上，正式承认了图书馆学与教育、法律、医学等具有相等的专业地位。纽约州立大学图书馆学院证明了自身对于图书馆专业和图书馆发展的价值，其他学校的建立也就是自然而然的了。1902年开始，纽约州立大学董事会规定，学生从高等学院毕业后，才能进入纽约州立大学图书馆学院学习。

1890年，位于纽约布鲁克林的普瑞特图书馆学院建立，紧随其后的是1892年位于费城的德雷克塞尔学院，该学院1914年一度中断，1922年重新建立。根据最新公告，进入德雷克塞尔就读，需要从高等学校毕业，这个规定将从1925年秋季学期开始执行。1893年，在芝加哥阿默技术学院①开设了图书馆学培训班，1897年9月该培训班转入厄巴纳伊利诺伊大学②，后来发展成为一所成熟的图书馆学院，从1911年开始，规定只有大学毕业生才允许进入该院学习。

美国现在"公认的"图书馆学校如下：

1897. 锡拉丘兹大学③图书馆学院，锡拉丘兹，纽约

1900. 卡内基图书馆学校，匹兹堡，宾夕法尼亚州

1902. 西蒙斯学院，图书馆学学校，波士顿，马萨诸塞州

1904. 西储大学图书馆学院，克里夫兰，俄亥俄州

1905. 亚特兰大卡内基图书馆的图书馆学校，亚特兰大，佐治亚州

1906. 威斯康星大学图书馆学院，麦迪逊，威斯康星州

1911. 纽约公立图书馆的图书馆学校，纽约城，纽约州

1911. 华盛顿大学图书馆学院，西雅图，华盛顿州

1914. 洛杉矶公立图书馆的图书馆学校，洛杉矶，加利福尼亚州

1917. 圣路易斯图书馆学校，圣路易斯，密苏里州

1915年建立了美国图书馆学校协会，"该协会仅由被协会视为第一流的学校组成，"鲍士伟（Bostwick）博士说，他补充到："它不时接纳其他学校，到1922年，包括了13所学校（院）。它从未明确制定和公布要求，但是人们普遍认为，这些学校在准入方面采用了高标准。"④1922年12月，该协会成为美国图书馆协会分会。

上述图书馆学校（院）提供一年或二年的课程，所有学校（院）都与大图书馆联合，提供学习和实践的设施。这些学校所教的主要科目都是一样的，包括图书馆管理、建筑、设备、借书、装订、编目、分类、参考、书目、采选、图书馆史、书史，以及其他与图书馆工作有关的技术

---

① 【译者注】原为Armour Institute of Technology，现为阿默工程学院（Armour College of Engineering），隶属于伊利诺伊理工大学。

② 【译者注】今伊利诺伊大学厄巴纳—香槟分校。

③ 【译者注】又称雪城大学。

④ 【原注】A. E. Bostwick. Training for Librarianship. (*In his American Public Library*. Appleton. New York. 1923. p. 347-8.)

和社会学科，培训强调理论和实践两个方面。

其他的图书馆学校有：

德克萨斯大学图书馆学学院①，奥斯汀，德克萨斯州

加利福尼亚大学图书馆学课程，伯克利，加利福尼亚州

河滨图书馆服务学校，河滨市，加利福尼亚州

布法罗大学②图书馆学课程，布法罗，纽约

华盛顿商业图书馆员培训学校，华盛顿，D.C.

明尼苏达大学医学图书馆服务课程，明尼阿波利斯，明尼苏达州

除了这些正规的培训学校之外，很多大学、学院、图书馆和图书馆委员会在夏季提供三周或数周的初级课程，这些课程主要提供给小的公立图书馆、小的学校图书馆和半专业助理馆员，我们把这种教学类型归入第二种图书馆学培训类型之中。

美国图书馆学培训的第三种类型，主要是由大图书馆组织，为他们的助理馆员开办培训班，提供初级课程，教学通常强调在当地进行。

第四种类型，是由图书馆机构，或由图书馆委员会、当地图书馆协会组织的图书馆会议，这些会议有助于提升图书馆专业精神和鼓励图书馆培训。有时，图书馆的组织者受州政府的委派，为小图书馆的馆员们提供图书馆课程。

第五种类型是图书馆工作的函授和进修课程，到目前为止，这类课程几乎还未开展。但是现在很多师范学校、学院、大学等，都提供如何灵活使用图书馆、如何选择好的图书、如何编制书目等课程，此类课程的主要目的是让学生了解图书馆所包含的内容，而不是培训他们成为图书馆员或助理馆员。

1916年，美国图书馆协会理事会成立"图书馆标准化和图书馆员认证委员会"，三年以后，1919年在美国图书馆协会阿斯伯里帕克（Asbury Park）会议上介绍了国家认证系统草案，草案得到非正式批准，并提交给理事会，沉寂了两年之后，"国家认证和培训委员会"提出了实行认证计划的报告，再次递交给美国图书馆协会。1923年前，威斯康星和纽约两个州通过立法，要求对受雇于公共图书馆的人实行某种形式的认证，加利福尼亚、爱荷华、明尼苏达和南达科他四个州，在州立图书馆协会或图书馆委员会的主持下，实行自愿认证的方案。而国家认证系统仍然在讨论中，一些美国图书馆员相信，认证系统将提供更有效的方法，促进专业发展和高效的图书馆服务，另一些人则害怕认证系统扼杀活跃在图书馆领域的"天才"型馆员。不管图书馆的国家认证系统是否有用，它都应该依赖于某种有效的和可靠的客观科学标准，但到目前为止，双方的争论和对抗主要是情绪化的和主观化的。

美国图书馆协会正在通过各种重要的董事会、委员会，研究该项认证系统的所有情况，希望能够科学地考虑到所有的问题。一个委员会正在对美国所有图书馆的活动进行综合性的调查；另一个委员会正在与"政府研究所"（Institute for Government Research）的人事管理局合作，进行一系列的人员调查，围绕详细的职位分析、心理测试，研究某人是否适合这类岗位；还有一个图书馆学教育委员会，研究所有的专业教育问题，他们已经访问了所有现存的图书馆学校，举办了几场由著名教育家参加的、包括在不同专业领域的教育专家参加的公开

---

① 【原注】Discontinued late in 1925. (Ed. note)

② 【译者注】现为"纽约州立大学布法罗分校"，又称纽约州立大学水牛城分校。

听证会。更多有关图书馆协会帮助解决图书馆学专业教育的问题,将在后面章节讲到。

SELECTED BIBLIOGRAPHY

Ambrose, Lodilla. Dr. Dziatzko on German libraries. Library Journal. 21:53-9. Feb. ,1896.

American Library Association. Report of the Committee on apprentice and training classes. Bulletin. 11:284-6. July, 1917.

American Library Association. Report of the Committee on summer school. Bulletin. 11:279-84. July,1917.

Baker, Ernest A. The public library. Grafton. London. 1924. Chap. 6.

Balzani, Ugo. On the regulations of Italian public libraries. Library Journal. 4:83-187. June,1879.

Bostwick, Arthur E. American public library. Appleton. New York. 1923. Chap. 26.

Camper, Etta L. State certification of librarians. Public Libraries. 27:95-8. Feb. ,1922.

Certification of librarians. Library Journal. 46:891-2. Nov. 1,1921.

Dana, John Cotton. Certification and civil service control. Library Journal. 46:881-3. Nov. 1,1921.

Delisle, Leopold. Souvenirs de Jeunesse. Library. n. s. 9:201-11,245-56. April-July,1908.

Dewey, Melvil. Apprenticeship of librarians. Library Journal. 4:147-8. May,1879.

Dziatzko, Karl. Present state of libraries and librarianship in Germany. Library Chronicle. 4:57-63. 1887.

Evans, H. R. Library instruction in universities, colleges and normal schools. (United States Bureau of education. Bulletin 606. Washington, D. C. 1914).

Friedel, J. H. Training for librarianship. Lippincott. Philadelphia. 1921. Chap. 17.

Gardthausen, Victor. Handbuch der wissenschaftlichenbibliothekskunde. Quelle. Leipzig. 1920. Book 8. p. 77-82.

German librarians' conference at Dresden,1897. Zen-tralblatt fur Bibliothekswesen. 14:321. June-July,1897.

Glenn, Frank M. Technical training in librarianship in England and abroad. Library Association Record. 12:118-29. Mar. ,1910.

Graesel, Arnin. Handbuch der bibliothekslehre. Weber. Leipzig. 1902. p. 457-92.

Hottinger's library school for women in Berlin. Library Journal. 27:84-5. Feb. ,1902.

Library instruction. Library Notes. 2:286-306. Mar. ,1888.

Library school in Paris. Public Libraries. 28:440-1,Oct. ,1923;29:435-7. Oct. ,1924.

Library schools and training classes and special training for librarians, a symposium by American librarians. Library Journal(Conf. No.). 23:59-84. Aug. ,1898.

Library science in Saxony and library courses in Leipzig University. Zentralblatt für Bibliothekswesen. 36:230-1. Sept. -Oct. ,1919.

London. University College. Library school. Library Association Record. 21:121-8. May,1919.

Minnesota, University of. A course of training for hospital librarians. School and Society. 19:304. Mar. 15,1924.

Morel, Eugene. Bibliothèques. Mercure de France. Paris. 1908. 2vols. Vol. 1. Chap. 9;Vol. 2. Chap. 11,12.

Neumann, Felix. Karl Dziatzko,1842-1903:an obituary and bibliography. Library Journal. 28:105-10. Mar. ,1903.

Ogle, J. J. A summer school of library science. Library. 4:319-23. 1892.

Osier, William. Library school in the college. Library Association Record. 19:287-308. Aug. -Sept. ,1917.

Paris. Librarianship examination. Library Chronicle. 1:26. 1884.

Pietschmann, Richard. Karl Dziatzko:a memorial sketch:trans. by Miss Selina Nachmann. Library Journal. 29:87-8. Dec. ,1904.

Piper, A. Cecil. Technical training in librarianship in England and abroad. Library Association Record. 14:332-51.

July, 1912.

Plummer, Mary W. Training for librarianship. American Library Association. Chicago. 1923.

Prussian act defining the qualifications of a librarian, 1893. Zentralblatt für Bibliothekswesen. 11:77-9. Jan.-Feb., 1894; Library Journal. 19:170. May, 1894.

Roberts, Henry D. Education of the librarian: elementary stage. Library Association Record. 8:556-72. Nov., 1906.

Roberts, Henry D. Some remarks on the education of the library assistant: a plea. Library. 9:103-12. 1897.

Ross, James. Technical training in librarianship in England and abroad. Library Association Record. 12:99-117. Feb., 1910.

Rullman, F. Outlines of library science. (United States Bureau of education. Special Report. p. xxiii-xxvi. 1876).

Sanborn, Henry N. Standardization of library service. Library Journal. 44:351-8. June, 1919.

School of Library Economy. Library Journal. 8:285-94. Sept.-Oct., 1883.

School of Library Economy. Library Notes. 1:85-9. Oct., 1886.

Schrettinger, Martin. Versucheinesvollstandigenlehrbuchs der bibliothek-wissenschaft. Munich. 1829. 2vols. Vol. 2. p. 187-96.

Schwenke, P. Karl Dziatzko. Zentralblatt für Bibliothekswesen. 20:133-7. Mar., 1903.

Tedder, Henry. Librarianship as a profession. Library Association of the United Kingdom. Transactions. 5:163-72. 1882.

Walter, Frank K. Library training. (In Encyclopaedia Americana. Vol. 17. p. 393-4).

第九章 图书馆学观念的转变和教育要求

像前三章讲到的那样,当我们研究图书馆员的资格以及他们从古代到现在为职业所做的准备时,所有时代和所有人显示出的共同之点,图书馆学的基本要求是教育。图书馆员一定是一个受过教育的人,不同的人对职务有不同的理解,各种各样的技术不断更新,然而,这个基本要求始终未变。

那么问题自然产生了,随着图书馆学观念的转变,未来是否需要除教育之外的其他基本要求?

回答一定是:"是的",甚至这个最基本的要求也必须改变,变得更加宽广。未来的图书馆员不是简单地受过教育,而是确定无疑的,他必须接受通识教育。什么是通识教育?查尔斯·F·施文(Charles F. Thwing)①校长这样表述:"理想大学的基本目标是提供通识教育,或者,如果喜欢用主动语态表述的话,那就是,理想大学提供的教育应使学生的思想和性格自由和开放。我们有时说,受过通识教育的人是学者,但是我们认识一种人,他们虽然是学者,但并未体现出受过通识教育……人们有时说,受过通识教育的人是思想家,一个人,能够推理、判断、评判真理的价值,将真理与真理联系起来,或推导出一个新的真理,是思想家。然而,有些人,思维像巴贝奇(Babbage)②发明的著名机器一样精确,他们绝不会犯受过通识教育的人的'罪行',这种人:遵守规则、思维缜密、不犯错误,举止呆板,他们的思维活动比天体活动更有规律——他们不是受过通识教育的人。

受过通识教育的人是一个学者,或至少是学者型的人。他是一个思想家,或至少是思考型的人,但是他不只是思想家或学者,事实上,他要超过二者。受过通识教育的人,已经进入了知识的竞技场,在他前进的道路上,既没有阻碍,也没有沉重的负担,他始终思维敏捷……每种才能、每种职责的表现都是完美的,理智+同情+欣赏=完美的生活,完美的生活等于他受过通识教育。"③施文校长所说的通识教育,非常清楚地描述了未来图书馆员的基本资格。

施文校长旨在为受过通识教育的人提出一个理想的标准。我们必须意识到,设置一个高标准,甚至比一个人能够达到的标准还高,是任何一个专业真正达到卓越最可行的方法。事实上,人类很少能够达到完美,尽管如此,追求完美还是接受过通识教育的人的目标,理想越高,一个人在自主选择的专业领域就越可能获得成功,不仅对于图书馆员,而且对于所有专业人士来说,将来设立一个较高的目标都是必要的。

制订任何完备的图书馆学专业教育计划,都必须充分认识到一个事实,美国式图书馆管理和服务的观念已经形成,同时,必须明确知晓产生美国式图书馆管理和服务的几个重要因

---

① 【译者注】查尔斯·F·施文(Charles Franklin Thwing,1853—1937),生于缅因州纽沙伦镇的一个牧师家庭,从哈佛大学和安多佛神学院毕业后,在教会服务多年,后长期担任西部保留地大学校长。
② 【译者注】查尔斯·巴贝奇(Charles Babbage,1791—1871),英国数学家,计算机先驱,发明差分机。
③ 【原注】Charles F. Thwing. *The American College*. Platt and Peck. New York. 1914. p.3-8.

素。在以下的论述中将会看到这些影响美国图书馆发展的重要因素,其表现为教育的民主思想、研究的精神、印刷的增长、图书馆慈善和图书馆协会。

这些因素以及其他影响因素仍然存在,美国式图书馆仍在发展,至少这个过程是在下意识的演变之中。

今天的某些美国图书馆学培训方法,可能较好地满足了美国图书馆管理的需求,但是明天可能将需要修改。美国图书馆学培训的方法,同样是那些已经对美国图书馆的发展产生影响的相同因素作用的结果。如果感到现代图书馆培训的系统和方法有一些瑕疵,那就值得做进一步调查,很可能这些瑕疵可以追溯到那些没有意识到的影响美国图书馆发展的因素,并相应地做出调整。

一些人似乎认为,当今的图书馆员太机械化,不像他的前辈那样是学者和有学问的人,图书馆学校毕业生让人感到太讲究实用和思想僵化。也许图书馆学校的培训过分强调技能,弗里多(J. H. Friedel)先生这样描述这种情况:"那是上足了发条的弹簧表,而不是知道什么时候和怎样上发条的大脑。由于对技术人员而言,记忆比应对新情况的能力更重要,因此一直强调记忆。然而,我们应该尝试开发后一种能力,就像所有的教育一样,图书馆学的目的,应该是个性的发展,而不仅仅是技能……否则将会退化为只提供操作技能的科目,图书馆工作是一项很大程度上与操作技能相关的职业,涉及操作技能的三个部分,无疑是图书馆学校所教科目的主要内容。这些科目的严重危害是,学生往往变成操作机器,从而限制了独立思考。技能最终将走入自身的死胡同,编目就是一个可以引证的例子。我们常常听到令人叹息的事实,受过培训的编目员把很多注意力集中在逗号和句号上,而很少使用脑力。"①

不错,很多图书馆流程是机械性的,其他是技术性的。教育机构一度强调培训"实用型"的馆员,往往"机械型"馆员就是教育的结果。但是这些"实用型"的馆员,曾经在图书馆和图书馆学发展的某个阶段很有用。现实需要培养机械型的图书馆员,至少需要当看到顺畅的机械流程时能够产生思考兴趣的图书馆员。尽管这里不是一个离开本题而详细讨论这个话题的适当位置,但是应该指出,在我们的头脑中,一定不能把那些公认的机械操作性的流程和那些像编目和分类等技术性的、而非机械性的工作混为一谈,后者,如编目和分类,可能或常常是专业性很强和学术性探索的工作。

回到为图书馆学做准备的问题上,我们注意到,美国图书馆员自己已经意识到率先进行改良运动的培训机构存在的不足,要求专业培训要有一个新的标准。他们深刻认识到仍在变革中的美国式图书馆管理、服务以及各种影响因素的需求,表明了至少部分地改革培训系统的愿望。

十九世纪中叶以后,教育的民主思想旨在提高民众的教育水平,美国公共图书馆尝试在其中发挥自己的作用,成为公共学校的辅助系统,以及真正独立的"人民的大学"。公众只要求从公共图书馆的馆员那里得到快速和基本的服务,因此,图书馆学校的学生急切寻找有助于机器般人力管理的方法,而普遍忽略了更高标准的图书馆学和人文知识的学习。大众对技能型图书馆员的需求很大,培训机构自然努力把技术技能放在首位,而不是培养他们尽可能最广泛地了解专业的发展问题。

图书馆慈善运动增加了对受过培训的图书馆员的需求,使之达到前所未有的数量。大

---

① 【原注】J. H. Friedel. Training for Librarianship. *Library Journal.* 44:570-1. September,1919.

量新建图书馆,需要图书馆学校、培训班、入门班等各类培训机构尽快提供图书馆员。图书馆的捐赠人,认为图书馆是在公众中传播知识的地方;受益的公众,通常认为图书馆仅仅是一个有图书的社会消遣中心;而图书馆员,认为只要能保持图书馆清洁和有序整理图书,就可以被聘用去提供图书馆服务。捐赠人、公众、图书馆员都过分机械化地遵循构成美国民主基础之一的普通教育观念。

到了二十世纪,图书馆服务出现了新气象,图书馆员开始意识到,准确的编目、清晰的借书系统、详细安排工作人员值班时间表都不是图书馆的终极目标,而仅仅是意味着图书的管理使用。只对机械操作感兴趣的图书馆员,没有能力将合适的书送给合适的人。图书馆需要的馆员类型是:知道如何高质量地完成图书馆服务,关注社会的需求,实行人性化的管理。现在,图书馆员意识到了自己的不足。关于未来馆员的要求,1923年9月26日在皮奥里亚举行的伊利诺伊州图书馆协会第27周年纪念会上,芝加哥公共图书馆馆长卡尔·罗顿(Carl B. Roden)①先生在演讲中描绘到:"由于他们(前辈)的努力,我们是理论和实践完美体系的受惠者,我们只要遵循他们的规则,就能达到令人满意的效果。对我们大多数人而言,分类的原则是在麦维尔·杜威十进位分类法创立时建立的,编目的规则早就固定了,即使是编目员,也几乎没有可以讨论的空间了,编目技术有被嵌入记忆的危险,就像众所周知的昆虫在一个刚性半透明的物体中,加速了它的永恒和终结。我们其他部门的工作也一样,除了出于个人独创性的偶尔创新之外,已经标准化到了几乎没有进一步讨论的空间,我们行业外在的和表面的形式,是清晰的和明确的。"他继续强调应该塑造未来图书馆学的精神价值,"书是精神产品,他们的价值无法估量,尝试应用量化标准来对他们进行分类或衡量其影响力都是徒劳的,就像伦敦圣保罗大教堂的英奇教长②所说,这些量化方法是无效的……这是图书馆员的任务,不只是'以最小的成本',为尽可能多的人提供好书,而且要将合适的书提供给合适的读者——不记代价。我认为,如果有这样一步,那将是图书馆管理的下一个台阶,这终将证明内在的和精神的魅力是图书馆学的灵魂。"③

今天,图书馆的捐赠人把注意力集中在图书馆建筑越来越多、越来越大。直到最近,他们才把目光转移到图书馆运动的新方向上。很多图书馆员指出,很多图书馆的捐赠人也意识到,能使图书馆实行更好服务和在更大规模上发挥作用的重要因素,是拥有一支足够规模的、有竞争力的、受过培训的图书馆员队伍。卡内基基金会多次为图书馆服务,而不是为建筑或购买图书提供基金,预示图书馆运动的新方向。威廉姆·S. 勒恩德(William S. Learned)期望未来的图书馆学和图书馆学校如下:"大量受过良好教育和技术培训的图书馆工作人员将图书馆工作作为永久职业,是重建图书馆服务的显著特征,应该尽快受到重视……如果希望在图书馆适时调整适应读者需求的过程中,取得快速的、健康的发展,就必须在这一点上进行疾风暴雨式的改革。图书馆专家的职责必须有别于纯文书类的日常工作,而相应

---

① 【译者注】卡尔·罗顿(Carl B. Roden),1918—1950年任芝加哥公共图书馆馆长。

② 【译者注】威廉·拉尔夫·英奇(William Ralph Inge, 1860—1954),英国作家,英国圣公会牧师,剑桥大学教授,伦敦圣保罗大教堂教长。他是这样描述功利主义:"尝试应用量化标准去测量精神产品,相当于称量一个无法称量的东西。"("an attempt to apply quantitative standards of measurement to spiritual goods——an attempt to weigh the imponderable。")

③ 【原注】Carl B. Roden. On a Certain Reticence or Inarticulateness among Librarians. *Public Libraries*. 28: 492. November, 1923.

地进行人才培养;必须提供全时教师和足够的设备;重要职位的高等专业课程,必须与大学的专业课程相媲美。"①

在美国大学形成研究风气之前,图书馆员的专业资格和专业教育一直被忽视,只要受过一点儿图书馆分类和编目的培训,就可以成为图书馆员,他的主要工作是保管资料,在学校教职员中的地位通常仅仅是一个书记员。在美国,图书馆培训方法几乎没有受到早期大学图书馆的影响,仅在最近,美国大学开始与欧洲大学竞争,也仅在最近,美国大学图书馆已经正视出现的问题,这些问题的解决,需要训练有素的图书馆员拥有机智、活力和创造性。受过通识教育和技术培训的图书馆员需要认真思考一些问题,比如图书馆分馆的有效组织、集中化管理、特色馆藏的积累、图书馆的教学功能、各类图书馆学院院长会议、年度预算的评估、为所有读者提供最好的服务等。今天,人们已经普遍认识到图书馆在大学生活和工作中的重要性。1924年芝加哥大学的"大学图书馆未来政策委员会"报告引言中指出:"图书馆是大学的心脏,这些问题的解决是大学中的核心问题。"②1912年11月30日,伊利诺伊大学肯德里克 C. 巴布科克(Kendric C. Babcock)③院长在哥伦比亚大学举行的"东方学院图书馆员会议"上的论文《学院的书目课程》中,认为书目教学方法应该由图书馆员和助理馆员提供,他说:"我们呼吁需要合格的书目课程,这并非完全建立在理论基础上。通过不同系列的主任和热心教师提供的不定期课程,确实不能令人满意。一些机构已经尝试实施培训计划,发现运行良好。他们明确认识到,课程应该在图书馆员的指导下,由受过培训的助理馆员执行,学习完成后,他们有资格获得承认。"④普林斯顿的 E. C. 理查德森博士相信,大学图书馆在大学里的地位问题,最终将通过其实现教学功能来确立。⑤

当大学图书馆成为研究工作中的首要角色和不可缺少的工具时,美国大学将把图书馆馆长归为学院院长,把受过培训的图书馆工作人员归为教授和指导教师,图书馆员进入神圣的教师队伍,将是对图书馆学校毕业生教育和专业培训质量的检验。

偶尔,接受过培训的图书馆员会受到来自专业图书馆领域的负面批评。比如,批评指出图书馆学校毕业生是检索、分类、图书编目等方法的专家,但不了解工业环境下的最新研究进展。印刷品的增长影响所有类型的图书馆,商业洪流和工业文献需要很多专业和商业图书馆,人们对图书馆学校毕业生寄予厚望,希望他们不仅精通图书馆管理方法,而且了解一些高度专业化的学科知识。有时,一个年轻的图书馆学校毕业生,既缺乏宽广的教育背景,又没有掌握专业领域文献的能力,会使专业馆员的聘用者感到失望。

1919年,时任《专业图书馆》编辑的 J. H. 弗里多先生生动地写到:"然而,我们不应该对这些需求视而不见,而是需要教会学生自立自强、独立思考、解决新问题。新建专业图书馆

---

① 【原注】William S. Learned. *The American Public Library and the Diffusion of Knowledge.* Harcourt. New York. 1924. p. 78-9.

② 【原注】University of Chicago. *Commission on the Future Policy of the University Libraries.* Tentative Report. 1924. p. vii.

③ 【译者注】肯德里克·C. 巴布科克(Kendric Charles Babcock,1864—1932),伊利诺伊大学文理学院院长。

④ 【原注】Kendric C. Babcock. Biographical Instruction in College. *Library Journal.* 38:135. March,1913.

⑤ 【原注】E. C. Richardson. The Place of the Library in a University. *American Library Association Bulletin*, 10:12. January,1916.

经常遇到的问题是进行专业分类以满足特色图书馆的需求，有才能、有经验的专业图书馆员，始终认为专业分类对充分发挥图书馆的功能非常重要。笔者的经验是，几乎没有图书馆学校毕业生知道怎样做这样的分类，其他专业图书馆员通过调查也证实了这个结论。比如采用杜威的标准方法，图书馆学校毕业生不知道如何对分类进行必要的扩充，科学分类的概念被抛到九霄云外，通常先采取拼凑的方法，然后再修修补补。这样的例子可能会举出很多，但是出于礼貌的需要，这里不谈具体遇到的案例。学校提供的课程，在很多情况下需要改进，而且，我们的课程，不应该仅仅设计为表面文章。捕蝇的方法也许对捕捉苍蝇很有效，然而，坦率地说，他们不值得被冠以教育的名义，何况去维护作为学术或科学分类的尊严。"①

关于受过培训的图书馆员不能充分发挥专业馆员作用的问题，如果有人愿意回应弗里多的批评，他可能会指出，特别是在专业图书馆运动早期，一个很普通的图书馆员，急冲冲地加入所谓的"专业图书馆员"队伍之中，他或她并不满意这份工作，对薪水的兴趣比服务更浓厚，虽有一些值得注意的例外，但那并不是反驳的理由。而且，毕竟很多专业图书馆员没有经过专业培训，只是机会主义者意识到社会需求的转变，那些人学习得很少，极大地损害了为这一领域做了良好准备的后来者的信誉。

一些图书馆学校毕业生不能满足某些专业图书馆的要求，并不意味着所有图书馆学校的标准都很低，图书馆学校学生进入专业图书馆领域的数目不断增加，在工作中取得成功的学生占很大比例②。而且，专业图书馆和大的公共图书馆专业部门的突然增加，打破了职业准备的供求平衡，造成图书馆培训机构资源紧张，因为这些机构主要是为普通公众提供初级助理培训，而不是为专业图书馆培训人才。当学校想为专业图书馆工作培训学生时，他们的财政支出不够支付新课程、设备、新增教师薪水的费用。那些医学、法律、神学、社会学、教育、工业、商业、技术、科研机构等专业图书馆，都需要受过培训的图书馆员，现存学校不能为这样的专业图书馆提供专业毕业生，而只能提供受过普通图书馆培训的毕业生。

再者，假如一些图书馆学校尝试为专业图书馆工作提供专业化培训，是否就有足够的学生愿意接受专业图书馆培训也是很重要的问题。通常在选择专业图书馆工作之前，学生会自问两个问题：薪水是否足够值得多花一年或几年时间接受专业图书馆培训？怎样确保能够聘用到所受培训类型的专业图书馆工作？至于薪水，专业图书馆员的聘用者，通常不希望把太多的钱投给他们所称的新人试验，而对于很多商业人士来说，图书馆员只是书记员和记账员，即使有需求，也不是与某一学生所学专业对应的专业职位，这个缺陷不在于现存的图书馆培训机构，也不是图书馆学校毕业生，而是整个图书馆界处于一个转折时期。专业图书馆是美国图书馆进一步发展的信号，最终，专业图书馆的需求将对未来图书馆员的资格和培训产生重大影响。

影响美国图书馆学专业培训课程的重要因素之一，是一直引导图书馆专业精神的美国图书馆协会。1883年麦维尔·杜威博士向美国图书馆协会提出建立第一个美国图书馆学校的计划，尽管遇到一些领导成员的强烈反对，协会最终还是支持了这个计划。1887年，在纽

---

① 【原注】J. H. Friedel. Training for Librarianship. *Library Journal*. 44:570-1, September, 1919.

② 【原注】Frank K. Walter. The Future Training of the Business Librarian. *Special Libraries*. 10:4. January-February, 1919.

约城的哥伦比亚学院,正式建立了第一个图书馆学校,此后,就像我们看到的一样,又建立了其他图书馆学校、培训班、入门班、夏季学校。图书馆学校的法规和课程,一直受到实际从事图书馆工作的美国图书馆协会会员的影响,在很大程度上,图书馆学校接受了他们的意见。

在早期图书馆学校里,非常强调技术科目,因为那时的图书馆很强调编目、分类和主题词,人们只需要查阅美国图书馆协会会议的讨论和报告,就能了解当时图书馆专业是怎样聚焦在这样的问题上。

1890年,美国图书馆协会建立了第一个"图书馆学培训常务委员会",1903年,玛丽W. 普卢默(Mary W. Plummer)[①]女士代表委员会提交了一份详尽的报告,概括了来自9个图书馆学校、10个夏季学校、33个入门班、15个大学的书目课程、12个师范学校图书馆管理课程、4个函授课程的报告,鉴于图书馆培训机构的迅速增长,为了保证图书馆学的专业标准,1909年美国图书馆协会建立了"专业培训部"。

1919年夏,在"专业培训部"十周年会议上,宣读的几篇论文都着重强调图书馆培训专业化的重要性,其中有耶鲁大学图书馆馆长安卓·基奥堡(Andrew Keogh)先生的论文《为研究人员提供高级图书馆培训》、时任宾夕法尼亚州匹兹堡卡内基图书馆学校校长莎拉·伯格(Sarah Bogle)女士的论文《高中图书馆学培训》、时任奥尔巴尼纽约州立大学图书馆学院副校长弗兰克K. 瓦尔特(Frank K. Walter)的论文《商业图书馆或商业分馆的图书馆员培训》、玛丽·罗宾斯(Mary E. Robbins)女士的论文《师范学校的图书管理员兼教师的培训》。

关于认证的科目,1919年在阿斯伯里帕克召开的美国图书馆协会会议上,现在洛克菲勒基金会任职的威廉姆森博士强烈主张建立美国图书馆协会董事会,由一位固定职员和一位称职专家作为执行者。他说,这个董事会应该有三个主要功能:"(1)制定图书馆职位等级标准方案,这个方案必须与现行服务最佳方案相类似,但须扩充到覆盖所有图书馆的专业工作,至少还包括高级文书服务。(2)根据所有专业委员会的建议,首先决定什么应该是与每个等级相对应的教育和经验方面的最低资格标准,然后向所有合格的申请人颁发相应的等级证书。(3)应该与培训机构建立联系,首先决定某类图书馆学校培训能够授予一个或多个高级等级的最少数量,然后董事会就像现在图书馆学校协会所做的一样,检查、批准那些达到合理标准的学校。在这些学校一个最短期限内顺利毕业的学生,无需进一步考核就可以获得由培训委员会颁发的高级证书。同样,读完有资质的培训班课程,并在被批准的图书馆有一个最短期限的实际工作经历,就可以自动获得培训董事会认证的适当等级证书。"[②] 1920年图书馆协会任命"图书馆培训和国家认证委员会",认真研究这个问题。由于第一次世界大战后不稳定的环境、成倍的工作以及协会中各委员会权利的交织,"图书馆培训和国家认证委员会"建议,应该任命有足够能力覆盖图书馆培训、图书馆服务、图书馆认证的图书馆培训董事会。1923年5月,图书馆协会执行董事会主席经董事会授权任命"临时图书馆培训董事会",1924年夏,理事会提交了一份详尽的研究成果和报告,包括成立永久性的"图

---

① 【译者注】玛丽·莱特·普卢默(Mary Wright Plummer,1856—1916),曾任普拉特学院免费图书馆的馆长(1890—1894),普拉特图书馆学院院长(1895—1911),纽约公共图书馆图书馆学院第一任院长(1911—1916),纽约州图书馆协会主席(1906),美国图书馆协会的第二任女主席(1915—1916)。

② 【原注】C. C. Williamson. Some Present-Day Aspects of Library Training. (In *American Library Association. Papers and Proceedings*. 41:122. July,1919).

书馆学教育董事会"的建议,1924年7月,该理事会正式建立,底特律公共图书馆馆长亚当·斯特罗姆(Adam Strohm)先生被任命为主席。自从该理事会建立后,已经举行了四次定期会议,第一次会议是在该理事会成立后不久,于7月在萨拉托加泉(Saratoga Springs)举行;第二次会议于9月在芝加哥举行;第三次会议于1924年12月30—31日在芝加哥举行;第四次会议于1925年4月15—16日在芝加哥举行,这些会议详尽调查了涉及其他重要图书馆疑难问题的图书馆培训相关问题。1924年12月31日和1925年4月16日,笔者受理事会邀请,参加了建立图书馆学高等学校可行性计划的公开会议,作为一个研究图书馆学培训问题的学生,一个从事图书馆工作15年的工作者和组织者,我确信,美国图书馆协会不久将制订出令人满意的、适合各种类型图书馆和各种等级图书馆服务的培训计划。第一次世界大战结束后,美国人的生活方式以及教育观念迅速转变,需要图书馆服务和图书馆培训领域同步转变。按照柏格森(Bergson)创世进化的哲学,"存在是为了改变,改变是为了成熟,成熟就是不断地创造自己"①。同样原则适用于图书馆培训问题及其最终解决方案吗?

综上所述,未来的美国图书馆员,将接受建立在通识教育基础上的专业培训,他的管理工作将是有文化的、学术型的。这样,在工作中,他将是诚实守信的;在学术上,他将是诚挚认真的学生;在服务中,他是给人启迪的向导。本章提到的多种类型图书馆,目前迫切需要图书馆学校为毕业生提供理想资格,现有图书馆学校能否迎接这个挑战?

SELECTED BIBLIOGRAPHY

American Library Association. Board of education for librarianship. (In its Papers and Proceedings. 46:197-9,257-88. 1924).

American Library Association. Committee on library training. Reports. (In its Papers and Proceedings. 12:91-5. 1890;14:31-4. 1892;16:116-20. 1894;25:83-101. 1903).

American Library Association. Committee on national certification and library training. Reports. (In its Papers and Proceedings. 42:311-13. 1920;45:194-7. 1923;46:239-41. 1924. ;*In* its Annual Reports. 78-89. 1921).

American Library Association. Professional training section. Reports. (In its Papers and Proceedings. 31:427-36, 442. 1909;32:776-86. 1910;36:228-45. 1914;41:395-7. 1919;42:334-5. 1920;43:183-4. 1921;45:246-9. 1923).

American Library Association. Report of the temporary library training board. (In its Papers and Proceedings. 46:257-88. 1924).

Babcock, Kendric C. Bibliographical instruction in college. Library Journal. 38:133-6. Mar. ,1913.

Bogle, Sarah C. N. Training for high school librarianship. American Library Association. In Papers and Proceedings. 41:277-8. 1919.

Buell, D. C. Sources of information for business men. Special Libraries. 7:142-4. Oct. ,1916.

Donnelly, June Richardson. The library school and the library. Library Journal. 35:109-11. Mar. ,1910.

Dudgeon, M. S. The scope and purposes of special libraries. Special Libraries. 3:129-33. June,1912.

Evans, Henry R. Library instruction in universities, colleges and normal schools. United States Bureau of education.

---

① 【原注】Henri Bergson. *Creative Evolution*, translated by Arthur Mitchell. Holt. New York. 1911. p. 7.
【译者注】亨利·柏格森(Henri Bergson,1859—1941),法国哲学家,文笔优美,思想富于吸引力,曾获诺贝尔文学奖。

Bulletin. No. 606. Government Printing Office. Washington. 1914.

Fairchild, Salome Cutler. Function of the library. Public Libraries. 6:527-32. Nov. ,1901.

Friedel, J. H. Training for librarianship. Library Journal. 44:569-74. Sept. ,1919.

Hasse, Adelaide R. The great release. Special Libraries. 10:2-3. Jan. -Feb. ,1919.

Henry, W. E. Librarianship as a profession. Library Journal. 42:350-5. Sept. ,1917.

Herbert, Clara A. Librarianship—a profession. Library Journal. 48:605-9. July,1923.

Hitchler, Theresa. Library school training versus practical experience. Library Journal. 42:931-8. Dec. ,1917.

Keogh, Andrew. Advanced library training for research workers. Library Journal. 44:581-2. Sept. ,1919; American Library Association. Papers and Proceedings. 41:165-7. 1919.

Learned, William S. The American public library and the diffusion of knowledge. Harcourt. New York. 1924. p. 75-80.

New York State Library School. Librarianship as a profession. Albany. 1911.

Plummer, Mary W. Forecast of the next twenty-five years for library schools. Library Journal. 35:251-3. June,1910.

Richardson, E. C. The place of the library in a university. American Library Association Bulletin. 10: 1-13. Jan. ,1916.

Robbins, Mary E. Training teacher-librarians in normal schools. American Library Association. Papers and Proceedings. 41:279-81. 1919.

Roden, Carl B. On a certain reticence or inarticulateness among librarians. Public Libraries. 28: 489-94. Nov. ,1923.

Shearer, Augustus H. What constitutes adequate library training? Library Journal. 47:1073-4. Dec. 15,1922.

Thompson, C. Seymour. Librarianship—a profession or a business? Library Journal. 47:1063-6. Dec. 15,1922.

Thwing, Charles Franklin. The American college. Platt and Peck. New York. 1914. p. 1-23.

Tyler, Alice S. Education for librarianship: as it is and as it might be. Public Libraries. 29:389-90. Oct. ,1924.

University of Chicago. Commission on the future policy of the university libraries. Tentative Report. 1924.

Walter, Frank K. The future training of the business librarian. Special Libraries. 10:3-4. Jan. -Feb. ,1919.

Walter, Frank K. Training for the librarians of a business library or a business branch. Library Journal. 44:578-80. Sept. ,1919; American Library Association. Papers and Proceedings. 41:273-6. 1919.

Williamson, Charles C. Some present-day aspects of library training. Library Journal. 44:563-8,Sept. ,1919; American Library Association. Papers and Proceedings. 41:120-6. 1919.

第十章　美国的图书馆学校

第一个专业图书馆管理学校在美国建立。尽管1886年德国哥廷根大学设立了图书馆学专业教授职位,约早于纽约城的哥伦比亚学院图书馆学校正式开放6个月,但通常认为美国学校是第一个图书馆学专业学校。哥廷根大学所教的科目并不像美国学校提供的那样宽广,后者是成熟的专业学校,而前者甚至不是大学的一个系。第一个美国图书馆学校的缔造者,麦维尔·杜威博士,用特色文字记录了这一事件(简单拼写是杜威博士长时间的强烈嗜好):"我们始终认为哥伦比亚图书馆学校是世界上第一个图书馆学校,即使国内外其他地方在图书馆教育方面也做了一些事情,那也是因为微不足道而可以忽略不计。就像我们谈到卡片目录或活页卡片的开端,尽管偶然某人在某处把纸片边缘串起来,但是那并不意味着他首先发明了卡片目录或活页卡片,就如同用绳子和深黄色的盒子做实验,不能被看作是发明了电话一样。我认为,人们普遍认可奥尔巴尼的学校,是世界上第一个真正的图书馆学校。"①

在这个传输快捷、通讯便利的时代,每年都有很多外国学生来到美国,进入美国不同的学校学习,反过来也有很多美国学生去欧洲国家。然而在图书馆管理和图书馆技术领域,一个重要的事实是,尽管外国学生经常到美国图书馆学校学习,但还没有先例证明,美国学生值得去任何国家的任何图书馆学校学习。

下面的数字摘自纽约州立大学图书馆学院副院长埃德那 M. 桑德森(Edna M. Sanderson)女士的书信②,记录了自1887年以来,来自不同国家的奥尔巴尼纽约州立大学图书馆学院毕业生的人数:

澳大利亚	1
加拿大	8
中国	4
丹麦	5
英国	4
德国	1
荷兰	1
新苏格兰③	3
挪威	38
菲律宾群岛	1

---

①【原注】Melvil Dewey. The First Library School, a letter to J. B. Kaiser, November 19, 1924.

②【原注】Edna M. Sanderson. The Number of Foreign Students Graduated from the New York State Library School, a letter to T. C. Tai, April 14, 1925.

③【译者注】新斯科舍(Nova Scotia)拉丁语意为"新苏格兰"。加拿大东南部的一省,是早期欧洲移民加拿大的登陆点,也是历史上英法殖民者利益争夺的焦点地之一。

瑞典	1
总计	67

其他的美国图书馆学校,由于有外国学生,也具有相同的国际氛围。在 1923—1924 年普拉特图书馆学院副院长约瑟芬 A. 瑞士朋(Josephine A. Rathbone)女士的报告中提到:"从一开始,班级规模就很大,实际有 27 名学生,比我们预定的班额多 2 人。对超额的学生进行调整和再调整带来的麻烦比计划内招收的 5 个人还多,这种情况在学校里很常见。但是对于超额的学生来说,1924 年是个例外,超额的是来自欧洲的两位奖学金获得者,他们为我们增添了很多乐趣,所带来的回报大大超过教师和员工的付出。除了两个欧洲大陆的学生,还有两个英国学生,这样,班级有明显的国际化氛围……"①纽约公共图书馆学校、伊利诺伊大学图书馆学院、匹兹堡卡内基图书馆学校和其他一些学校都有外国学生。

1924 年 5 月 2 日,纽约公共图书馆馆长埃德温 H. 安德森(Edwin H. Anderson)在大西洋城的宾夕法尼亚图书馆俱乐部的演讲中,突出强调了美国率先成立图书馆学校以及学生较高比例来自欧洲大陆(old world)②的事实:"让我感到好奇的是,威廉姆森博士在关于美国图书馆学校状况的调查中,竟然没有提及这样一个事实,即世界上第一所图书馆学校在这里建立,而我们一直是这个领域公认的领袖。欧洲大学领先世界已经有一千年了,但美国第一个认识到对图书馆学校的需求,这个重要的事实却完全被忽略了,'我们是这里的第一批来客,闯进这一片沉寂的海面'③——这里的第一所学校建立仅 37 年,多年以来一直在本领域独占鳌头,几乎是孤独前行,这个事实解释了他注意到还存在的很多不足。他的调查也没有任何地方提到另一个重要事实,图书馆学或图书馆技术是欧洲学生到美国学校学习的几项主要内容之一。美国人总是去欧洲学习艺术,我们几乎所有的艺术和建筑都来自于大洋彼岸,美国学生成群地赴欧洲著名大学去留学,但是有谁听说美国图书馆员去欧洲学习图书馆管理方法和技术?几乎从一开始,美国的图书馆学校就有很多外国学生,作为影响之一,是在一些欧洲国家已经建立了图书馆学校,莫斯科也有一个,另一个在中国④,去年夏天在巴黎建立了一个夏季学校,'美国救援法国减灾委员会'⑤已经为法国提供了两年的运行基金,此后的经费问题希望法国自己解决,继续办学。"⑥虽然美国图书馆学校已经在图书馆培训的方法和技术上领先世界,然而,在档案等相近学科领域,在古版书等很多学术性书目研究方面,总体而言,其他国家也为图书馆学做出了大量贡献。

由纽约卡内基基金会出版的 C. C. 威廉姆森《图书馆服务培训》的报告,已经搅动了图书馆员队伍的平静,把他们的注意力集中在美国图书馆学校和其他培训机构上。弗兰克 K. 瓦尔特(Frank K. Walter)先生在威廉姆森报告的序言中,肯定了卡内基基金会专业报告的促进作用:

---

① 【原注】The Pratt Institute. *School of Library Science. Report.* 1924 p. 17.
② 【译者注】旧大陆对应的是新大陆,新大陆是指哥伦布发现的美洲,旧大陆指欧洲大陆。
③ 【译者注】选自英国诗人塞缪尔·T·柯勒律治(Samuel Taylor Coleridge)的《古舟子咏》,即《古代水手的诗韵》(The Rime of the Ancient Mariner)。
④ 【译者注】1920 年韦棣华创办武昌文华大学图书科,同年戴志骞创办北京高师图书馆夏季学校。
⑤ 【译者注】见第三章【译者注】37.
⑥ 【原注】Edwin H. Anderson. Training for Library Service. *Library Journal.* 49:463. May 15,1924.

"弗莱克斯纳(Abrahan Flexner)①博士关于美国医学教育的报告,实际上是整个国家医学课程的革命。瑞第力希(Redlich)关于法制教育的报告,没有吓跑法律学校,而是带来很多学校课程的改革。普里切特(Pritchett)博士在他最新出版的年度报告中,谈到教育的成本和价值,引起很多来自正反两方面的争论。从某种意义上说,威廉姆森博士的报告必定会一如既往地带来争论。"②

美国图书馆员对美国图书馆学校提供专业培训质量的认识颇不一致,一些人相信现在的图书馆教育培训机构,有能力培训满足未来需求的各种图书馆员,一些人认为如果美国图书馆学校不在教师、课程、入学要求等方面进行彻底转变,他们就不能保持在图书馆培训领域的领导地位。

目前对现行制度和理论评价的观点,可以总结为6点:

I. 学术合作

图书馆学校缺乏认同感和专业威望,因为他们的入学要求不同于其他专业学校,课程性质太杂,教师既没有规模,也没有像其他专业一样的讲师和教授的学术资历,更没有创新研究的素养。通常情况下,图书馆的工作性质和图书馆学校的构成,让人联想到的是那些职业学校,而不是那些大学级别的专业学校。因此,一些图书馆员更喜欢学术氛围,希望将图书馆学校的水准提高到大学专业学院的标准。1922年6月,伊迪丝 M. 库尔特(Edith M. Coulter)在底特律召开的"美国图书馆协会学院和参考分会"年会上提交的论文中,清楚地表达了这种情绪:"此外,图书馆学校应该与高等院校联合,目前有令人鼓舞的朝着这个方向发展的趋势,新建的图书馆学校已经与州立大学联合。如果现有公共图书馆下辖的图书馆学校与大学联合,这是一个很大的进步。我认为让所有的专业培训与有授权的大学联合,一起授予统一的专业学位,会使图书馆专业教育与其他任何工程、法律、医学教育相媲美……大学图书馆学校的图书馆员和教师,应该拥有这样的高等学位,毫无疑问,如果我们的图书馆学校与大学联合,保持与其他的技术和专业学校同等的地位,教师必须拥有比授予该校毕业生更高的学位。"③

然而,请大家注意,我们已经看到,在美国图书馆学校创立时,首先需要掌握的是详细的图书馆技术和方法,而不是宽泛的图书馆学理论和原则。学校的最初目标是对学生进行必须的实践培训,以满足公共图书馆服务的需求。目前,实际情况仍然是,大部分图书馆学校毕业生进入公共图书馆工作。此前培训机构提供的实践培训,为学生提供了进入公共图书馆工作的机会,如果要求所有现存图书馆培训机构以牺牲实践培训为代价,与学术机构挂钩,总体来看是脱离实际,公众获得的服务将受到影响。埃德温 H. 安德森(Edwin H. Anderson)博士说:"我认为,图书馆学校应该与大学联合而不是与公共图书馆联合的说法太绝对了。这依赖于本地的环境和情况,比如,如果公共图书馆是一个充满活力的机构,他将日复

---

① 【译者注】弗莱克斯纳(Abrahan Flexner)于1910年发表的Flexner报告(简称弗氏报告),奠定了美国现代医学教育的基础。

② 【原注】Frank K. Walter. A Dynamic Report. *Library Journal*. 48:709. September 1, 1923.

③ 【原注】Edith M. Coulter. The University Librarian: His Preparation, Position and Relation to the Academic Department of the University. (*In American Library Association. Papers and Proceedings.* 44:272-3. July, 1922.)

一日地努力改进对公众的服务。而大学则不急于解决图书馆自身存在的问题,或常常对图书馆的进步漠不关心,对于图书馆学校来说,无疑与公共图书馆联合比大学更好。"①

Ⅱ. 入学要求

现存图书馆学校入学要求存在很大差异。大致可以列出以下要求②：

1. 高中毕业文凭加上入学考试,或国家承认的大学授予的学位。在下列学校名单中,校名后面的括号里注明了该校与本要求不同的地方。

a. 亚特兰大卡内基图书馆的图书馆学校

b. 德雷克赛尔学院图书馆学学校(从1925年秋季学期开始,必须获得国家承认的大学授予的学位才能申请)

c. 肖托夸图书馆员学校(没有入学考试,但是要求有图书馆职位或明确签约图书馆职位的学生)

d. 纽约公共图书馆学校

e. 匹兹堡卡内基图书馆学校(也招收相关学院四年级学生)

f. 普拉特学院图书馆学校

g. 圣路易斯图书馆学校

h. 锡拉丘兹大学图书馆学院(可以免除入学考试,如果申请人想要学位证书,只需要证明具有符合要求的能力)

i. 西储大学图书馆学院(如果申请人有三年西储大学女子学院学习经历,攻读该学院学位,不用考试)

j. 威斯康星大学图书馆学院(要求申请人有3年威斯康星大学文理学院的学习经历)

2. 在国家承认的大学就读三年或两年,括号里是该类学校的不同要求。

a. 布法罗大学图书馆学课程

b. 西蒙斯学院图书馆学学校(一年期学习计划的申请人,应该具有国家承认的大学学位或在国家承认的大学三年的学习经历)

c. 河滨图书馆服务学校(申请人有两年大学工作经历,并参加入学考试)

d. 德克萨斯大学图书馆学系③(申请人具有国家承认大学的学位)

3. 大学四年级或获得国家承认的大学学位,括号里是该类学校的不同要求。

a. 洛杉矶公共图书馆的图书馆学校(申请人参加符合要求的同等入学考试,并具有图书馆工作经历)

b. 华盛顿大学图书馆学院

4. 具有国家承认的大学学位

a. 加利福尼亚大学图书馆学系

b. 伊利诺伊大学图书馆学院

---

① 【原注】Edwin H. Anderson. Training for Library Service. *Library Journal*. 49:464. May 15,1924.

② 【原注】American Library Association. Temporary Library Training Board. Report. *American Library Schools*, Appendix H. (*In its Papers and Proceedings*. 46:277-88. August,1924.)

③ 【原注】This school discontinued the fall of 1925.

c. 纽约州立大学图书馆学院

以上19所图书馆学校的入学要求,大体上可以分为四种主要类型。图书馆学校在入学要求上有足够的弹性,对于杰出的人来说,只要能证明他是天才的图书馆员,而只是缺乏某些阶段正式的专业培训,可以允许进入图书馆学校学习。

C.C.威廉姆森博士在他给卡内基基金会的报告中认为,图书馆学校的入学要求过于烦琐,他感到:"可以说出很多理由支持简化入学要求,只要完成大学课程就可以进入专业图书馆学校,至少完成高中课程就可以进入图书馆培训班。如果有需要,学校可以查阅申请者的大学学习成绩,只招收那些成绩优秀的人。如果需要进一步限制招生规模,可以应用其他方法进行测试。"①

笔者认为,在图书馆入学要求问题上,图书馆专业学校最好制定类似于其他专业学校的明确和统一的标准。那些杰出人才或有特殊才能的人,即使没有大学学位,但只要可以提供足够的证据,证明其具有可信的经验和学术水平,仍然可以被录取。像耶鲁大学这样著名的教育机构,也允许杰出人才去研究生院试读。"招收所有具有充分知识储备、有非凡才能的学生进研究生院以及进行专业课程学习,是耶鲁大学正规教育计划的一部分。根据每个个体的特点单独考虑,如果申请人被录取,开始时他并不是一个高级学位的候选人,而是作为所谓的'特别生'录取的。如果证明他的学习在数量上和质量上都与正式学生相同,他就可以参加毕业考试,并获得学位。"②耶鲁大学图书馆馆长安德鲁·基奥(Andrew Keogh)先生于1919年6月25日在阿斯伯里帕克举行的"美国图书馆协会专业培训分会"上,宣读他的论文《研究人员高级图书馆培训》时,提到了这个做法。

目前,一些图书馆学校的入学要求很不正常,他们规定高中毕业生必须通过入学考试才能学习图书馆课程,而国家承认的大学毕业生不经过考试,就可以学习相同的课程。这个做法相当于坦率地承认,作为学校选拔合格学生的一种手段,四年的大学课程与他们的入学考试等效,而对于图书馆学校而言,不能想当然把入学考试与四年大学课程等效。另一方面,这个做法把大学毕业生放在与通过入学考试的高中毕业生相等的地位,结果是为了进行专业培训而把学生不合逻辑地组合在一起。

对于通过综合性考试,令人满意地测试出杰出图书馆人才质量的做法,笔者持怀疑态度。通过考试录取的结果同样是不同文化背景学生的混合,这样的组合尤其不能促进高智商大学毕业生的智力发展。而且,教师很难设计出合适的、能够使这样一个多元化的班级感兴趣的课程。的确,学校或者只允许高中毕业生,或者只允许大学毕业生入学可能更好。当遇到优秀人才时,图书馆学校的主任或校长仍然有权允许他们入学,我们不应该完全漠视耶鲁大学研究生院的做法。至于心理测试,很多职业能力的心理测试可谓是很有价值的,然而作为一种限制报考图书馆学校人数的手段,设计适合图书馆专业测试的问题,心理学家或其他人还没有解决,调查还在进行之中。如果人数需要进一步限制,那些具有图书馆实践经验加上受过大学教育的人,当然有资格被优先考虑录取。

---

① 【原注】C. C. Williamson. *Training for Library Service*. New York. 1923. P-32.
② 【原注】Andrew Keogh. Advanced Library Training for Research Workers. *In American Library Association. Papers and Proceedings*. 41:166-7. July,1919;or. *Library Journal*. 44:582. September,1919.

Ⅲ. 课程

为了适应不断发展的不同类型的图书馆工作,图书馆学校的课程体系已经匆忙建立起来了,但并没有很好地规划。如果进行仔细地批判性分析,则图书馆学校课程显示出明显的缺陷。同一课程下几个相近主题的组合是不关联的,有大量不必要的琐碎事务,比如,还回的书放到正确的架上、开架阅读、登录、字母表、书号等都列为图书馆专业培训的单独科目。然而,在现实工作中,这些科目只是图书馆日常工作中相对琐碎的工作,严格来说,这些科目的教学只需要在培训课程或本科图书馆学校中完成。的确,每一位受过培训的图书馆员都必须掌握这些科目,但这并不适合专门图书馆学校的研究生课程,而应该作为进入研究生院进行图书馆专业学习的先决条件。任何专业学校在设计课程时都有两个主要要求:一个是应该遵照本专业的最高标准,另一个是应该鼓励学生的专业创造性。目前的图书馆学校课程,通常过分强调图书馆工作的非专业方面,而忽视学生专业创造性的提升。

威廉姆森博士提出的具体改进建议是:"尽管对于各种各样的课程在内容上实行严格统一是不合适的,但似乎需要对专业图书馆学校第一学年的主修课和辅修课实行一定程度的标准化。相应的专业团体应该规范专业术语,设计标准化的课程供官方采用。术语'采选'在不同的学校代表不同的意义,一门科目使用的术语,在其他科目不一定具有相同的意义,其他课程也有类似的情况。所以,即使学生在正式的图书馆学校上过'采选'课程,我们也不可能确定他到底在'采选'课程中学到了什么。就像法律和工科学校一样,图书馆学校的基础课程,都应该有相同的涵盖范围。"①

Ⅳ. 教学人员

威廉姆森的《图书馆服务培训》中的有关教育工作者一章,是全部报告中责难最多的部分之一,在总结中,威廉姆森博士指出:

分析图书馆学校教师的教育背景和经验表明,他们中的许多人不适合为大学毕业的高级专业人才提供教学,统计显示:

a. 1921年,只有52%的图书馆学校教学人员是大学毕业生。

b. 42%的教师是在同一所图书馆学校接受的图书馆教育,而后成为该校教师。

c. 93%的教师没有经过教育科学的学习。

d. 80%的人在成为图书馆学校教师之前没有教学经历。

e. 32%的教师没有足够的图书馆实际工作经验。②

美国最老的图书馆学校存在也只有38年,如果我们把图书馆学校与那些美国的法律、医学、神学等专业学校相比较,就能显示出图书馆学校只是学徒式的培训。如前所述,图书馆学校培训的主要目的是满足公共图书馆的需要,只要教师精通某些方面的图书馆技术,不管他们的教育背景如何,就被认为是能胜任工作的教师。在只强调技术和方法的时代,对于图书馆教师来说,大学学位和教学经验都不是很重要的因素。

另一方面,我们用衡量其他专业学校的标准,去衡量图书馆学校的教师是公平的吗?目

---

① 【原注】C. C. Williamson. *Training for Library Service.* New York. 1923. P-32.
② 【原注】C. C. Williamson. *Training for Library Service.* New York. 1923. P-138.

前大学还强调教师的教学能力吗？还强调为教师提供教学艺术培训吗？其他专业学校，甚至像更老的法律、医学和神学学校，也一样强调吗？我们认识到，图书馆学校的教师应该是教学专家，也是超越前辈同行的专业领域专家，威廉姆森博士对现在图书馆学校教师的批评，是建立在未来图书馆专业教育理念基础上的。

如果我们考虑到图书馆学校教师与其他高等学校教师相比的不利环境，那么，他们的成就和成功就是值得赞扬的。首先，图书馆学校教师的薪水很微薄，其次，实际上他们没有机会像其他高等学校教师那样，与某些学科的著名学者和权威人士接触。他们每天接触的要么是图书馆学校的学生，要么是公共图书馆的普通读者，不知不觉，他们的眼界变得狭窄，陷入思想禁锢。再次，他们没有长假或休假进行自学和提高。在这种情况下，图书馆学校自然经常面临一个实际问题，即如何能够留住有能力的教师。

除了增加薪水和采用七年一次的休假制度以便进一步研究和学习之外，现在的图书馆学校，应该尝试从图书馆领域聘用合格的、有潜力的人，给他们机会，去教育专业的研究生院进修提高，这样的政策将有助于建立一支强大的教师队伍。差不多每一所大学年轻的和杰出的教师都有机会到研究生院完成专业学习和高级学习，同时允许他们去教低年级本科生。那些没有与大学联合的图书馆学校，也应该提供给最有才华的教师相似的深造机会。图书馆学校校长和美国图书馆协会应该一起努力，保证捐赠基金用来培训图书馆学校的教师。否则，就不可能得到受过图书馆学校教育的，再加上大学教育，以及经过教育科学和教学艺术培训的、理想的图书馆学校教师。

V. 专业教育和技术培训

不区分专业教育和技术培训，是最受批评的图书馆学校培训方法之一，有人认为图书馆学校没有尽力让学生掌握较宽的图书馆学普遍原理和方法，只是满足于培训他们在日常工序中的细枝末节，强迫他们记忆那些主观制定的规则和技术形式，只是过分强调专门技能，阻碍了很多优秀大学生进入图书馆学校。而另一方面，很多从事实际工作的图书馆员则认为，图书馆学校教给她们的技术方法，是他们成功指导助理馆员的重要法宝，图书馆工作包括大量的日常工作，对于每个图书馆学校毕业生来说，掌握专门技能都是必需的。

图书馆工作需要包括专业技能和办事员的日常工作，我们不容易、也没有必要总是明确区分这两种工作，太强调图书馆学的原理和方法，可能导致专业教育的纯理论化。当然，如果太过分强调专门技术和办事效率，势必将专业图书馆教育降格为中等专业学校的水平。过分强调一个，而忽视另一个，或者反过来，都会伤害图书馆专业。西雅图华盛顿大学图书馆学校校长和该校图书馆馆长威廉姆 E. 亨利（William E. Henry）对威廉姆森博士的报告发表如下评论："他关于教育类型的区分——专业人员和办事人员——是图书馆学校再也不能漠视的问题之一，我们不能通过 9 个月或 10 个月的培训——不是教育——而只是培训办事细节，就把高中毕业生培养成为专业人员。这样贫乏的教育素养，不可能造就专业教育的领袖，我们得承认这一点。男、女精英学生不会参加这样的竞争比赛，廉价的投入失去了好的教育效果，作为公平的回报就是图书馆员的低薪。"[①]现存图书馆学校犯了过分强调纯技术

---

① 【原注】William E. Henry. The Williamson Report, Comment from the Library Schools. *Library Journal*, 48:910. November 1, 1923.

训练的错误。

Ⅵ. 图书馆培训机构的标准化

对过去 38 年图书馆培训历史的研究表明,培训机构在不同地区发展起来,他们的经营和成长与各自所处的环境相一致,因此他们的入学要求、课程、设备、目标等标准存在很大差异。图书馆培训中同样存在"术语"的差异,图书馆员和外行人一样,对这些差异感到困惑。正像威廉姆森博士所说的那样:"术语'采选'在不同的学校代表不同的意义,一门科目使用的术语,在其他科目不一定具有相同的意义……就像法律和工科学校一样,图书馆学校的基础课程,都应该有相同的涵盖范围。"①鉴于这样多变的环境,"临时图书馆培训董事会"推荐 12 个测量标准,征得图书馆培训机构的同意,由新的"图书馆学教育董事会"负责执行。"图书馆学教育董事会"建议执行的标准如下:

1. 研究图书馆服务的变化和需求,促进图书馆学教育的进步;
2. 调查现存图书馆培训机构是否能满足现在的需要;
3. 制定图书馆学校、夏季图书馆课程、师范学校图书馆工作课程、师范学院培训和入门课程、函授课程、进修课程以及未来可能出现的像这样的教育机构的标准,提请委员会批准执行;
4. 按照标准对培训机构进行分类;
5. 每年印刷出版被批准的培训机构名单;
6. 设法使各培训机构互相联络,以期形成图书馆学教育的统一制度体系;
7. 依照大学学分办法,建立各培训机构统一的学分制度;
8. 明确图书馆教育中使用专门术语的含义和范围,促进准确和统一的使用;
9. 与其他学术机关互相联络;
10. 提供关于图书馆培训机构经费使用的顾问咨询服务;
11. 提供关于其他图书馆教育事宜的服务;
12. 每年向美国图书馆协会委员会提交图书馆学教育进展的报告。②

虽然现存图书馆培训机构标准化程度较低,但是"图书馆学教育董事会"必须把握方向,不要让摇摆不定的标准化走向另一个极端,过度标准化不可避免地会破坏创造性和降为经验法则③。在现有培训机构中引入最低标准,采用统一术语,强化大家认同的所有标准,是"图书馆学教育董事会"需要解决的重要问题。

回顾现有对图书馆培训机构的批评和理论研究,很多不足是由于体系的缺失,而不是由于管理不善造成的。学校试图为学生提供所有类型图书馆的所有类别服务的培训,在这个专业化时代,这是太过雄心勃勃的策略。结果,不可避免地造成课程过多,不得不牺牲某些科目的严谨性和完整性。在不远的将来,专业化图书馆服务的需求将不断增长,同时,图书

---

① 【原注】C. C. Williamson. *Training for Library Service.* New York. 1923. p-23.
② 【原注】American Library Association. Report of the Temporary Library Training Board. (*In its Papers and Proceedings.* 46:259. August,1924).
③ 【译者注】拇指规则(RULE OF THUMB),中文又译为"大拇指规则",也叫"经验法则",是一种可用于多种情况的、简单的、经验性的、探索性的,但不是很准确的原则。

馆常规工作和机械性工作也将相应地增加。对于普通图书馆管理工作来说,让受过高等图书馆学教育的馆员去做大量的日常工作,并不是一个好的经营策略,因此,最终会确定图书馆工作的不同等级。现在正是现有图书馆培训机构制定规则、确定归类的大好时机,每个学校都应该坚持自己的目标,竭尽全力,促进图书馆专业的全面发展。

"美国图书馆协会临时图书馆培训董事会"已经为图书馆学教育培训机构的分类制订了临时计划草案,略述如下:①

1. 图书馆函授和进修课程;
2. 师范学校和师范学院对学校图书馆员开设的课程;
3. 图书馆入门课程;
4. 图书馆培训课程;
5. 夏季图书馆学校课程;
6. 图书馆学校低年级大学生;
7. 图书馆学校高年级大学生;
8. 图书馆学研究生院。

关于课程的课时、入学要求、学分、证书、资格和教师的数量,以及图书馆设施、宿舍和设备,已经在上面1—5中的图书馆员和图书馆培训机构之间达成共识;列入6—8中的图书馆学校,"图书馆学教育董事会"仍然在讨论之中,特别是新型的与一些大学联合的高级图书馆研究生院,到目前为止,仍然处在萌芽阶段。是否大学图书馆学校,或图书馆研究生院,或两者都应该与大学联合的问题,将在下一章进行充分讨论。

SELECTED BIBLIOGRAPHY

American Library Association—Temporary Library Training Board. Report of American library schools, Appendix H. (*In* its Papers and Proceedings. 46:277-88. Aug.,1924).

American Library Association. Meetings of the professional training section at the 46th Annual conference of the American library association. July,1924.

American Library Association. Report of the Committee on training class standards. July,1924.

American Library Association. Report of the Temporary library training board. (*In* its Papers and Proceedings. 46:257-60. Aug.,1924).

Anderson, Edwin H. Training for library service. Library Journal. 49:462-6. May 15,1924.

Baldwin, Emma V. Training of professional librarians. Library Journal. 44:574-6. Sept.,1919.

Bostwick, Arthur E. The Carnegie Corporation report on library training. Public Libraries. 28:496-7. Nov.,1923.

Bostwick, Arthur E. Standardization. Library Journal. 48:799-802. Oct. 1,1923.

Coulter, Edith M. The university librarian: his preparation, position and relation to the academic department of the university. (*In* American Library Association. Papers and Proceedings. 44:271-5. July,1922).

Curtis, Florence R. Present status of the entrance requirements of the library schools. (*In* Papers of the Professional Training Section of the American Library Association. July,1924. p.14-18).

---

① 【原注】American Library Association. Report of the Temporary Library Training Board. (*In* its *Papers and Proceedings*. 46:261-75. August,1924).

District of Columbia Library Association. Specifications for library service in the Federal government. Washington, D. C. 1923.

Donnelly, June R. A unified system of education for librarianship. (*In* Papers of the Professional Training Section of the American Library Association. July, 1924. p. 29-32).

Keogh, Andrew. Advanced library training for research workers. (*In* American Library Association. Papers and Proceedings. 41:165-7. July, 1919; Library Journal. 44:581-2. Sept., 1919).

Morgan, Joy Elmer. Professional librarians for the nation. Public Libraries. 29:464-5. Nov., 1924.

Pendry, Eliza R. Scientific methods of vocational guidance applied to the problem of recruiting for the library profession. Public Libraries. 28:349-54. July, 1923.

Pratt Institute. School of Library Science. Report. 1924. p. 17-21.

Reece, Ernest J. Some possible developments in library education. American Library Association. Chicago. 1924.

Walter, Frank K. A dynamic report. Library Journal. 48:709-11. Sept. 1, 1923.

Williamson, Charles C. Some present day aspects of library training. Library Journal. 44:563-8. Sept., 1919.

Williamson, Charles C. Training for library service. New York. 1923.

Williamson Report. Comment from librarians. Library Journal. 48:999-1006. Dec. 1, 1923.

Williamson Report. Comment from the library schools. Library Journal. 48:883-910. Nov. 1, 1923,

Wyer, James I. A unified system of education for librarianship. (*In* Papers of the Professional Training Section of the American Library Association. July, 1924. p. 27-8).

第三部分 图书馆学专业教育的提案

第十一章 作为大学学院的图书馆学校

第十二章 爱荷华州立大学拟建的图书馆学院

第十三章 图书馆学院的入学申请、学位和课程

第十一章　作为大学学院的图书馆学校

　　组织另外一种类型的图书馆学校是美国图书馆热点问题。在笔者看来,新成立的图书馆学校与某个大学保持密切的隶属联系,这对图书馆专业的发展是明智的选择,但是有人并不这么认为。

　　现有的与公共图书馆保持联系的图书馆学校正在并且已经在培养图书馆员方面发挥着至关重要的作用。这些学校基本上具备与其他优秀的图书馆学校一样的设备、工具和校舍。目前这些学校设置的课程需要演示各类型图书馆的日常工作。运行良好的公共图书馆为图书馆学校的学生提供了很好的配备齐全的"实验室"。总的来说,美国的公共图书馆比大学图书馆管理得好,并会得到更多的支持。考虑到这种情况,成为大学的从属机构看起来也许就没有必要了。

　　支持"将图书馆学校纳入大学"观点的图书馆员解释说,拨给公共图书馆服务使用的款项是不应该转而作为专业图书馆学校运行费用的。持这种观点的人认为,培养专业的图书馆员是教育机构的任务。如果公共图书馆附近的大学里设有图书馆学校,那么公共图书馆为图书馆学校学生准备的设备和工具也不至于浪费。这种模式的管理方式类似于大学医学院的学生利用附近医院的设施。市政公共图书馆的基本任务就是为城市的纳税人提供图书馆服务,而不是为图书馆行业维持一所专业学校。

　　专业的教育集中在大学已经是一个趋势了。比如,医学学校原来是医疗实践①或者医院服务的从属部分,现在都成了大学不可或缺的组成部分。法律教育早已主要由大学来实行。多数法学院在学院二年基础教育②的基础上,提供三年的全日制职业训练,但有的法学院要求首先要获得大学的学位。

　　同样被大学接纳的还有工程教育和制药培训。美国教育署③发布的《1918—1920 美国教育调查》④第 23 个表中,列出了大约 124 个工程学校,其中有 88 个是大学工程专业学院,29 个从属于州立或私立大学,只有 7 个是独立的技术学校。另外,表 23 里还列出了 47 所药学学校。其中 38 所是大学的学院或者系,6 所从属于州立或者私立大学,只有 3 所是单独的学校⑤。

　　在所有其他专业的筹备中都同样出现了依附于大学的趋势。任何人都会注意到教育学、牙医学、新闻学、建筑学和工商管理专业也都成为大学这个大家庭中的一员。临时图书

---

　　① 【译者注】原文是 medical practice。

　　② 【译者注】原文是 preliminary education。

　　③ 【译者注】原文是 the United States Bureau of Education。根据有关资料显示,当时美国教育署隶属于美国内务部(Department of the Interior)。

　　④ 【译者注】原文是 the Biennial Survey of Education 1918—1920。

　　⑤ 【原注】United States Bureau of Education. *Biennial Survey of Education of* 1918-1920. Bulletin No. 29. Washington, D. C. 1923. p. 309-82.

馆培训委员会①列出了19所图书馆学校,其中10所学校与大学或者学院有联系,2所与研究机构有联系,1所与教育进修机构有联系,6所与公共图书馆联系②。19所中的10所是大学或者学院的一个学院或者系,但不幸的是,图书馆专业院系的运行基础与工程、法律、医学、农业等其他专业院系并不一样。一般来说,图书馆员和对图书馆不了解的人,同样都有一个模糊认识,那就是图书馆学校或者与公共图书馆有联系或者独立存在,但与大学无关。特别是一些小规模的图书馆学校教师的学术成果少,在全校教师中的排名靠后,又常常成为这种错误想法的有力证据。同一学校里与其他专业院系相比,图书馆学院系没什么特色,不能给师生们留下深刻印象。地方机构有关与大学有联系的图书馆学校的评论,可能不会直接揭示这一事实,但当大学管理委员会正式为图书馆学专业课程分配研究生院学分的时候,就显而易见了。

专业教育集中于大学的趋势,毋庸置疑,是对的。罗伯特 J·伦纳德教授在1924年9月24日哥伦比亚大学开学典礼上,发表题为《专业教育的趋势》的演讲,对这个方面的问题进行了充分的阐述。关于设置大学从属机构的原因,他是这么说的:

现在的专业学校和过去的已经大不相同了。大体来说,过去,专业学院是在所有人和商业利益的控制之下,独立于其他教育机构的,必然会带有金钱的色彩或者为金钱所控制。大体上讲,现在的专业学校本身就是我们优秀的大学的一部分,或者与之联合,而从商业的影响中解脱出来……

在大学里的专业学院的发展对专业学院自身来说意味着什么?

首先是使专业培训和服务的理想得到加强,并给了开展研究的推动力,如果没有这些,专业学院将会很快退化成一所技术学校。专业学院率先在课程设置方面采用了合适的长度,依靠于良好的通识教育,人们已经认识到专业学院的潜在的和当前的价值。专业学院不仅在吸引学者作为教师方面成为可能,还吸引了有充分准备的高智商学生,而这些学生愿意为获得足够的培训而投入大量的时间和金钱。

这样大学就为专业学院提供了全面发展所必须的环境,而这种环境是每个专业的佼佼者所一直梦想拥有的。

对大学而言,专业学院也做出了有价值的贡献。他们带来了现代教育机构所应该具有的活力和力量。他们聚集了成千上万的有明确目标的和多种兴趣的青年人。在学生团体中,自满和地方狭隘主义受到摈弃,而宽容和彼此之间的尊重得到了发展。与当前的社会问题保持必不可少的联系已经成为可能,富有成效的研究得以培养。公众对高等教育的信任度大大加强……

每个十年都会使大学更充分地参与到专业教育中。无论是对于教育,对于专业需要,对于公众利益,专业教育纳入高等教育系统的趋势都是显而易见的。我们的大学顺应这个趋势,为自己的社会价值谱写了新的篇章。他们把文化和专业化结合起来,而不是放在一种竞

---

① 【译者注】原文是 the Temporary Library Training Board。
② 【原注】American Library Association. Report of the Temporary Library Training Board. Appendix H. (*In its Papers and Proceedings.* 46;277-88. August,1924).

争的关系中。①

在现在高度专业化的时代,图书馆服务也会变得越来越高度专业化。在前面讨论现代图书馆运动的章节中指出,专业图书馆和公共图书馆的专门业务部门的发展趋势是很强劲的。在其他行业的实践中,实际工作中的专业化会很快引起学校相关教育的专业化。比如医疗工作的专业化迫使医学学校提供专业化课程。任何一个明智的阑尾炎患者都不会心甘情愿地找一个普通外科医生切除阑尾。大家一般都会去寻求技术精湛的外科医生(来给自己做手术)。这种情况迟早会出现在图书馆服务中。因而,应该为专业图书馆培训提供充分的准备。

所有高水准的专业教育中的专业训练都包括两个首要条件:广泛的文化教育和普通专业教育。虽然两所现有图书馆学校只接收大学毕业生,并提供两年的通识课程,但是很明显,在现有的情况下,由于财务或者其他方面的原因,这两所学校是无力解决为专业图书馆培训图书馆员的问题的。

让我们以培养合格中学图书馆员这个相对简单的问题为例。根据国家教育协会图书馆组织和设备委员会和大学、中等学校北方中心协会的②报告中列出的任职条件:

未来中等学校图书馆员任职的规范要求应该是拥有大学或学院的学位,主修是文学、历史、社会学、教育或者适合针对图书馆的任何专门需求——比如,那些技术高中对图书馆的需求——的其他学科。除此之外,图书馆员还要在国家承认的图书馆学校进行至少一年的研究生阶段的图书馆培训,以及在固定的图书馆,与青年人一起工作一年的成功经历。③

比照实际情况,这个标准看起来有点高,目前的大部分图书馆学校只要求他们的学生是能通过入学考试的高中毕业生,然而相比C.C.威廉姆森博士的标准,这个要求不高。

C.C.威廉姆森博士强调说:

那些有最好的教育水平的州,中等学校图书馆馆员必须有中等学校教师的资格条件——这就意味着具有大学的学位,受过教育方面专门训练,有的还有研究生阶段的学习经历——除此之外还要有一定量的专业图书馆培训。大学教育和一年的图书馆学校学习并不能给中等学校图书馆管理业务提供足够的准备。第二年的特别训练变得很重要,课程包括三个要素:(1)专门学习中等学校图书馆问题,并结合常规课程内容进行补充和修改;(2)教育方面科目的专门研究和培训:教育的历史、教育心理学和中等学校的课程;(3)拓展领域的实践,包括在有能力和经验丰富的中等学校图书馆馆员的近距离指导和管理下,相当长的一段时期的投入组织良好的中等学校图书馆的实际服务中。在第二学年学业结束的时候,相比在目前任何一个两年制学校学习结束的学生,应该具备了更出色的组织和管理中等学校

---

① 【原注】Robert J. Leonard. Trends in Professional Education. *Teachers College Record*. 26:177-9. November,1924.

② 【译者注】原文是 the Committee on Library Organization and Equipment of the National Education Association and of the North Central Association of Colleges and Secondary Schools。

③ 【原注】C. C. Certain. *Standard Library Organization and Equipment for Secondary Schools of Different Sites.* American Library Association. Chicago. 1920. p. 16.

图书馆的能力。①

目前现有图书馆学校的学生不可能有威廉姆森博士推荐的关于中等学校图书馆员第二年的培训经历，因为学校里没有这样的安排，目前的学校只允许学生主修图书馆训练，辅修大学里提供的其他课程。美国的图书馆培训已经到了整个体系都要需要重新调整的地步。假如一个规模较大的银行图书馆或者教育图书馆希望招聘一个助理馆员，深谙图书馆学，以及银行业务或者教育方面的一些知识，这个专业图书馆能给哪个图书馆学校写信去要这样的助理？

一个人从大学的某个专业②学院毕业，有可能会到图书馆研究生学院学习一年或两年，就足以胜任专业图书馆的职位。可能会有这种情况发生，但是特别少见。因为首先，任何一个大学专业学院顺利毕业的毕业生是不太可能改变他的专业。第二，一年或两年额外的图书馆培养要有更多的投入，而从图书馆学院毕业后可能也不会给他更好的资金回报。第三，如果不能够在他的专业做得成功，目前的图书馆研究生院也会阻止他从事图书馆行业的工作。即使有大量的专业图书馆馆员的需求，考虑所有这些困难，只有非常少的其他专业学院令人满意的学生毕业之后进入图书馆学院学习。此外，专业图书馆馆员的工资，对于许多已经具备了其他专业知识的雄心勃勃的年轻人来说，没有特别的吸引力。

大体上，一个人喜欢某个专业，并且在专业学院受到了几年训练，有了很好的专业基础，那么他不会成为一个优秀的专业图书馆员。他适合成为一位专家③，而不是专业图书馆员④。1912年6月27日在加拿大渥太华专业图书馆协会的会议上，A. G. S. 约瑟夫森先生发起了一个关于哪个是培养专业图书馆员的更好方法的讨论，即是选择一个训练有素的图书馆员，给他专业学科的知识，还是选择某个学科的专家，对他进行图书馆方面的培训。当时他说：

有人说专业图书馆员必须首先是位专家，其次才是图书馆馆员。我对这个不敢苟同……一个图书馆员必须首先是位图书馆馆员。有些人似乎认为，对图书馆员而言，掌握形成于图书馆，并在图书馆学校里教授的技术、规则和做法就足够了。其实这只是一个图书管理员的必备素质中最微不足道的一部分。图书馆员绝不仅仅是在图书馆学校中培养出来的。

比如一个工程师，部长或者历史学教授，让他学习图书馆"科学"的专门课程，他绝不会成为别的什么，他还是一名工程师，或者部长，或者教授，就好比上商学院的一门课也不会成为熟练的会计一样，除非他拥有目录学家的真正潜质——对书籍天生的感觉。⑤

在笔者看来最明智的既不是采取安排训练有素的图书管理员，在专业学院学习一两年专业课程，也不是针对某个学科的专家进行一两年图书馆方面的培训。从经济的和教育的观点来看，最令人满意的，解决问题的最好办法就是在正规大学图书馆学院培养专业图书馆

---

① 【原注】C. C. Williamson. *Training for Library Service.* New York. 1923. p.94.
② 【译者注】原文是斜体 *special*。
③ 【译者注】原文是斜体 *specialist*。
④ 【译者注】原文是斜体 *special librarian*。
⑤ 【原注】A. G. S. Josephson. What Is a Special Library? *Special Libraries.* 3:146. September, 1912.

员,学院为本科生和研究生开设专业课程,而且还能附带着学习其他学科的课程。图书馆学院接收的申请人在其本科四年中,要有足够的图书馆学各个科目的先修课程、一般的文化学科以及一些其他专业的课程。研究生这一年的课程应包括大约每星期 10 小时图书馆学科的课程和 5 个小时某个专业的课程。根据目前图书馆学校的组织状况,没有关系密切的高校,这样的课程安排是不可能实现的。

有些人可能会争辩说,实在没有隶属关系的大学,学校可以雇佣专业学科的兼职教授来培养专门的图书馆员。这是一个可行的方案,但前提是图书馆学校已经准备好承担过于昂贵的费用和创建一个并不会被普遍认可的教育政策。

任何一个人如果读了 C.C. 威廉姆森博士的《图书馆服务培训》的报告,以及图书馆学校负责人、图书馆馆长针对报告的大量评论,会注意到,评论一致认为,图书馆学校的条件太恶劣了。副校长及全职教师的薪水是如此之低,对有抱负的图书馆员没有什么吸引力。因此图书馆专业也长期缺少有能力的教师。因此,这也证明了现在一些图书馆学校吸引兼职专家教授某些专业课程的说法是不可行的。

从教育学的观点上看,安排某个专业的教授任教于图书馆学校是不合逻辑的。任何试图拓展与自己专业无关的专业学习科目的专业学校,都是试图在自己的课程体系里建立一个微型大学。因此,通过与在同一地区的教育机构合作,开展某个专业课程的教学计划将会更加可行,虽然这不如与大学建立密切关系的计划好。

当重新调整的图书馆学校投入运行的时候,我们将不得不慎重考虑到复杂的职业状况和开展深入研究工作的时机。R.J. 伦纳德教授说:

职业,最早是没有细分的整体,后来被划分,再划分,又一次划分。每个新分出来的小部分,就像最早起源的那个职业一样,已经成为全面而严格的行业。就以牙科科学为例来说明,牙科发展各个阶段一直伴随着分工的过程。牙科三十年前是一个单一的职业。现在它在至少包含十五种不同的职业,至少代表了两种不同的水平。最高水平包括牙医,正牙学家,从事研究的牙医和牙科矫形医生。其他的水平,也可以被认为是中等水平,包括牙科护士,牙科技工和牙科保健员。

医学、法律、工程、工商管理以及教育行业都已经发生了同样细分的过程和不同等级的发展过程,事实上,在所有的行业(都已出现这种情况)……

现在专业学院常常不能识别中等水平和更高水平之间的差异,无法意识到这种分化是职业教育最严重的问题之一,我们要仔细研究这些发展变化。举一个例子会更能说明问题。现在几乎普遍存在对农业、工程学和商业的院校的不满,特别是在我们州政府支持的大学。农场主谴责农学院过于理论化,农学家则谴责农学院太注重实际了。有些工程师谴责工学院过于理论化,另一些则认为太注重实际了。商业和工商管理学院也受同样的批评。这两种类型的批评都应该得到重视。①

在图书馆行业中也是这样。那些谴责图书馆学院的深入研究是无用的、空论的图书馆员,被认为是"中级水平的职业群体",其主要特点是有技术的实力。那些批评图书馆学校毕

---

① 【原注】R. J. Leonard. Trends in Professional Education. *Teachers College Record*. 26:180. November, 1924.

业生太过于机械的人们,被认为是图书馆行业中"最高水平的职业群体",其主要特点是有文化素养的,编文纂目和研究探索的高级需要。

现有的图书馆学校很容易受到这些批评,因为他们试图培养两种水平的学生,也就是说,"中等水平的职业群体"和"最高水平的职业群体"。这样做,虽然他们达到了两个职业群体的平均水平,但是却无法满足两种"职业群体"的需求。

不论目前图书馆学校的组织机构何时重新调整,都应该明确两种"职业群体"的需求之间明显的区别。大学图书馆研究生院应该将他们的全部努力放到图书馆学和某些专门科目的研究上,或者更高级的研究工作上。培养"中等水平的职业群体"的图书馆员,则是本科图书馆学院的任务。

图书馆专业的适用的标准提高了,在大学里一定要有图书馆研究生院来培养行政管理、研究人员和图书馆学院教授方面的领军人物。任何专业,如果缺乏培养最高类型的从业人员和科研工作者的机遇和能力,势必下降到一般职业的水平。比较而言,在研究工作和专业培训方面,一个标准的大学相比孤立的职业学校,有更多鼓舞人心的氛围,更好的设备,更多的机会,有与各方面的学者打交道的机会。培养某个行业中的具有领导力的人才,需要的不仅仅是在专业技能方面给予大量、集中地培养。它要求给予学生非常有用的愿景和对于加深人类同情心的人道主义原则的领会。大学专业学院能够给予学生更广阔的理想,这对于真正的进一步的专业训练来说是最基本的,在这方面,相比独立的专业学校,大学做得更令人满意。

呼吁大学图书馆学专业学院对毕业生进行图书馆专业的培训教育,这种请求并不是刚被提出来。马萨诸塞州波士顿亚瑟 D. 李特尔化学图书馆①的图书馆员 W. P. 卡特先生,二十年前就大力主张为图书馆员设立研究生院。一年前他说道:"我想重新提一下二十年前我出版的一个小册子里的建议。当时在哥伦比亚大学(现在的乔治华盛顿大学)的名义赞助下,在国会图书馆馆长的热情支持下,我在美国国会图书馆的夜校讲授有关图书馆工作的课程,授课内容没有按照常规内容,有点散乱。刚才提到的那个小册子就是在哥伦比亚大学惠特曼校长的提议下准备的,主要是总结了在华盛顿推行高级图书馆教学的几个有利条件。"②

1910 年,玛丽 W. 普卢默构想了一个图书馆培训的大学专业学院。她的文章《预测未来二十五年的图书馆学校》③,就像是现在刚写的,而不是 15 年前写的。她提到,她相信如果图书馆行业一定程度上能吸引那些成熟而又有修养却转向了其他他们认为更具有学术性的工作的人,就能切实提高自身水平。当时她触及到了图书馆学校的薄弱点,并且建议图书馆员要进行相比他们已经做的还要更大规模的全面调整。

在我们国家,决定图书馆学校的发展道路有两个因素……一个是美国国家对组织和系统的倾向,另外一个区别不大,是美国国家满足一个州需求的倾向。

当专门化的需求在广度和深度上增长时,这两种倾向同时影响了当今学校问题的解决。要求和需求越迫切,学校的压力就越大,就要付出更大的努力去满足需求;当需求多样化的

---

① 【译者注】原文是 Arthur D. Little Chemistry Library。
② 【原注】W. P. Cutter. Graduate School for Librarians. *Special Libraries*. 15:81. April,1924.
③ 【译者注】原文是 *Forecast of the Next Twenty-five Years for Library Schools*。

越大,系统化的需求就越大。所以,需求就是这样存在,两种倾向应联合起来满足需求。

法律就是法律,医学就是医学,但是"图书馆管理业务"这个称呼却涵盖了整个知识领域。医学界想让图书馆员具备一定的医学知识,并且能运用图书馆管理一般规律管理医学图书馆;当咨询台有读者咨询法律知识,法律图书馆员也要能够应对自如。州政府和市政府建设图书馆,需要按照市民和经济的要求进行图书馆管理。大型制造业相关的,实验室,日报,都认识到专业图书馆的必要性,并需要专家级或具有这种潜质的训练有素的管理者……①

她对这个困境的解决办法是:

为年青人、为一般的工作提供通识课程,常常希望发现他们从事这项工作的才能和潜质,在全国设立两到三所学校,与大学建设联系,成为大学的院系,教授技术和管理,也许涉及以下方面的概论性课程:医学、法律、神学、纯科学或者应用科学、市政、儿童教育等任何需要学习的专门课程。在大学里,开设只有一两个学生选修的课程是常事儿,所以就算开设的课程缺少申请人,也不是一个让人感到沮丧、彻底失败的事情。

在这一章里前面的内容主要是提出专业图书馆学校与大学建立联系的必要性。为了把现有的图书馆学校改造成符合时代需求和发展趋势,建议进一步拉近独立图书馆学校和大学的关系。那些与大学只有象征性关系的图书馆学校,要加强这种合作关系。

成为大学从属机构的建议存在着实际操作的困难。不管是大学要去承担起接纳现有图书馆学校的责任,还是反过来图书馆学校愿意成为大学的成员,都是一个实践的问题。如果图书馆学教育董事会②和美国图书馆学校协会③如果能在大学专业学院的基本组织原则上持有一致意见,那么他们可以在在这方面联合起来,对大学和图书馆学校发挥重要的影响。

也许有些图书馆学校倾向于和公共图书馆或者大专院校之外的其他机构建立联系。假如这些图书馆学校符合美国图书馆协会图书馆学教育董事会列出来的最低要求,他们可以这样建立联系。如果跟某个专业有关的学校都有自己的标准、入学要求和命名方式,没有什么比这个更能影响这个专业的长久存在了。某些最低标准被专业协会列出来并强制实施,所有专业学校都情愿遵守,是抵制弄虚作假的学校发展的最保险的方法之一,也是维护专业教育标准的最有把握方式之一。例如美国医学协会④实现了医学教育的标准化,这非常成功地提高了医学专业的一般标准。

美国图书馆协会图书馆学教育董事会已经为四个等级的图书馆学校规划了临时性的最低标准,即两年制本科图书馆学校⑤,四年制本科图书馆学校,图书馆职业学校,图书馆管理研究生学校。这种把图书馆学校划分成四个类别,在规模上差别有点大,另外,在专业术语上也容易引起混乱。

---

① 【原注】Mary W. Plummer. Forecast of the Next Twenty-five Years for Library Schools. *Library Journal*. 35:251-2. June,1910.
② 【译者注】原文是 the Board of Education for Librarianship,译文下同。
③ 【译者注】原文是 the Association of American Library Schools,译文下同。
④ 【译者注】原文是 the American Medical Association,译文下同。
⑤ 【译者注】根据第十三章的内容,将此处译成两年制本科图书馆学校。

因为这些为图书馆学校制定的临时性的最低标准,还没有被完全采纳,并且仍然处于讨论阶段,如果另外再提出方案可能不会太晚。现在是随意把图书馆学校分成了四个等级,可以将其合并成两个,即本科图书馆学校和研究生图书馆学校。这两类学校都被认为是一个单位的两个不同的分支,在一所大学的管辖范围内,有共同的名字"图书馆学院"。这个学院的地位应该与教育、工商管理、工程、牙医、药学等其他任何的专业学院一样。

SELECTED BIBLIOGRAPHY

American Library Association. Report of the temporary library training board on American library schools. Appendix H. (*In* its Papers and Proceedings. 46:277-88. Aug.,1924).

American Library Association. Report of the temporary library training board on provisional grouping for agencies which offer education for librarianship. Appendix B. (*In* its Papers and Proceedings. 46:261-73. Aug.,1924).

Capen, S. P. Tendencies in professional education. Bulletin of the American Association of University Professors. 10:35-9. Oct.,1924.

Carleton, W. N. C. Universities and librarians. Public Libraries. 20:451-6. Dec.,1915.

Certain, C. C. Standard library organization and equipment for secondary schools of different sizes. American Library Association. Chicago. 1920.

Compton, Charles H. Comparison of qualifications, training, demand and remuneration of the library profession with social work. (*In* American Library Association. Professional Training Section of the Forty-sixth Annual Conference, July, 3-4, 1924. p. 19-27); reprinted under the title "Comparison of library profession with social work." Public Libraries. 30:115-21. Mar.,1925.

Craig, Florence M. Education of librarians:—a fantasy. Library Journal. 44:577. Sept.,1919.

Cutter, W. P. Graduate school for librarians. Special Libraries. 15:81-2. April,1924,

Dudgeon, Matthew S. The scope and purposes of special libraries. Special Libraries. 3:129-33. June,1912.

Dudgeon, Matthew S. What has an employer the right to expect from library school graduates? (*In* American Association. Professional Training Section of the Forty-Sixth Annual Conference, July,3-4,1924. p. 5-7).

Hedrick, Ellen A. Education of a librarian. Special Libraries. 15:79-81. April,1924.

Josephson, A. G. S. What is a special library? Special Libraries. 3:145-7. Sept.,1912.

Kaiser, John Boynton. The special library and the library school. Library Journal. 37:175-9. April,1912.

Leonard, Robert Josselyn. Trends in professional education. Teachers College Record. 26:177-83. Nov.,1924.

Plummer, Mary W. Forecast of the next twenty-five years for library schools. Library Journal. 35:251-3. June,1910.

Training for the professions and allied occupations. Bureau of Vocational Information. New York. 1924.

Tufts, James H. Education and training for social work. Russell Sage Foundation. New York. 1923.

United States Bureau of Education. Biennial survey of education. 1918-1920. Bulletin No. 29. Government Printing Office. Washington, D. C. 1923. p. 309-83.

Walter, Frank K. A course of training for hospital librarians. Library Journal. 49:381. April 15,1924.

Wilbur, Ray Lyman. Maintaining standards without excessive standardization. School and Society. 20:607-12. Nov. 15,1924.

Williamson, Charles C. Training for library service. New York. 1923. p. 86-102.

第十二章　爱荷华州立大学拟建的图书馆学院

美国图书馆专业学校相比其他的专业学校而言，分布是不均衡的。提供不少于一个学年的图书馆专业教学的图书馆学校有十八所，大致分布在五个地区：(1)太平洋沿岸有四个；(2)南方各州有两所，得克萨斯州和佐治亚州各有一所；(3)大湖区①周围的三个州，威斯康星州、伊利诺伊州和俄亥俄州，有三所图书馆学校；(4)北方各州，宾夕法尼亚州、纽约州、马萨诸塞州，图书馆学校的数量居于首位，有八所；(5)密西西比河流域②向西一直到落基山脉③的地区，只有一个图书馆学校，这个学校与密苏里州的圣路易斯公共图书馆④联合。

为了更均匀地分担培养专业图书馆员的任务，密西西比河和落基山脉之间的几个州应设立更多的高标准的图书馆学校。在专业图书馆员培训方面，这一大片地区确实落在了位于太平洋海岸区⑤和北大西洋海岸⑥各州后面。而且，当地的需求和环境也是图书馆服务应该考虑的重要因素。比如，美国中西部地区中等规模的图书馆与东部地区同等规模的图书馆的管理问题是不一样的。职业和环境，是描述人的社会生活的重要指标，也是公共图书馆管理中的最重要的影响因素。

明尼苏达大学⑦已经意识到专业图书馆对专业图书馆员的需求，最近设立了一个图书馆学校，为医学图书馆培训图书馆员。笔者参观了明尼苏达州、爱荷华州、密苏里州、伊利诺伊州和威斯康星州的重要图书馆，从这些州的几个著名的图书馆馆长那里得到的信息，可以得出这样的结论，密西西比河流域的几个州，不仅需要专业图书馆员，而且需要很多训练有素的"非专业化的"图书馆员。图书馆学校1924年的报告中都非常遗憾地表示，他们的设备、工具和职位不允许他们录用更多的申请人。

笔者曾经在得梅因图书馆俱乐部⑧发表演讲。演讲之后，得以拜会几位爱荷华州图书馆馆长。从中了解到爱荷华州图书馆的现有状况，并参观了爱荷华州图书馆委员会的流动图书馆总部，了解到训练有素的图书馆员在各类型的图书馆工作中，都是供不应求的。

最近几年，爱荷华州立大学主办的图书馆培训暑期课程，收到的入学申请的数量逐年增加，也进一步证实上述事实。每个夏天，一些美国大学就会安排图书馆培训的暑期学校，所有这些培训受到积极活跃、有发展潜力的图书馆工作人员的欢迎，也受到大学生的欢迎。最新一期的《爱荷华州立大学通报》关于"图书馆培训的暑期课程"报道，告诉我们这个州对训练有素的图书馆员有很大的需求。

---

① 【译者注】原文是 the Great Lakes。
② 【译者注】原文是 the Mississippi Valley。
③ 【译者注】原文是 Rocky Mountain。
④ 【译者注】原文是 St. Louis Public Library。
⑤ 【译者注】原文是 the Pacific Coast。
⑥ 【译者注】原文是 the northern coast of the Atlantic。
⑦ 【译者注】原文是 the University of Minnesota。
⑧ 【译者注】原文是 the Des Moines Library Club。

现在对训练有素的图书馆员经常是供不应求的。很明显是到了该培训的时候了。过去学校的图书馆员是纯粹学者类型,或多或少,经常是很少愿意和有类似想法的人分享他的精神财富。现代图书馆员发现他们被赋予了行政人员、管理者、教育者、学者职责。那些研究公共图书馆在成人教育新方案之意义的学者,提出一些建议,这些建议需要训练有素的馆员去实施。通过明智的选择材料,高质量的宣传,改进分发的方法,今天的图书馆员尝试着把他的印刷品的世界带到公众的家门口。他是知识和文化的宣传员。①

1925年春季学期,爱荷华大学新开设了一门一小时的、一学分的课程"利用图书和图书馆的方法指导",代号是"library 2"。在注册办公室尝试性的发布这个课程不久,就有二十五个学生注册,虽然他们已经选了很多文理学院为本科生开设的课程。在这个图书馆学基础课程中,选课的学生被分成两部分,并且被提供了足够设备学习解决实际问题。这个课程与在其他地方受欢迎的同类课程说明一个事实,即大学生们都开始对图书馆学这个相对比较新的学科产生了兴趣。

很明显的趋势是专业图书馆学校将成为美国大学这个大家庭的新成员。以前大学教育的概念局限于"七艺"②,培训学生做日常生活相关的实用职业被认为是一件有失大学尊严的事情。现在这个学术和实践之间的屏障已经被打破了。今天的教育者意识到文化教育和职业训练之间绝不是冲突的,只不过都是在为同样的事情——人生做准备。

这次大学教育中融合学术和实践的新运动主要是由美国州立大学推动起来的。只是在最近几年来,几乎全国所有的大学,包括诸如历史悠久的文化学习机构哈佛或者耶鲁,已经将他们的课程延伸到制药、牙医、工商管理和工程等科目上。在这个时代在大学里将职业教育和文化学习结合起来,没有什么其他专业比图书馆专业更符合这次新运动发展的趋势了。

在这一时代里,能充分意识自己的责任,并具有当代最好的教育思想的大学,将会很乐意承担起培养未来图书馆员的责任。W. N. C. 卡尔顿博士③,威廉姆斯学院图书馆馆长,认为专业图书馆教育确实应该由大学图书馆学院来承担。他说:"孤立的图书馆学校和图书馆学徒式的课堂教学,在过去和现在都满足了当时迫切的需要,都是必须存在的,但最终将成为过去。大学应该成为培养图书馆员的摇篮和苗圃,正如大学是教师、神职人员、医师和律师的摇篮一样。如果大学使得青年男女具备了城市中等学校校长的职位需要的能力,具备了物理、化学、历史、数学、古代或现代语言等院系的领导者需要的能力,那么大学也应该培养市立图书馆馆长和馆长助理。我们快速完成了美国图书馆事业初始阶段和自我教育阶段。在未来,我们将越来越多地转向大学教育,通过培养有很好资质的学生,满足图书馆更广阔却常常是精益求精的需求。"④

---

① 【原注】University of Iowa. *Summer Courses in Library Training*. Iowa City. April 23, 1925. (*Bulletin*. n. s. No. 317).

② 【译者注】原文是 seven liberal arts,译为七艺,包括三艺和四艺,前者指语法学、修辞学和逻辑学,后者包括算术、几何、音乐和天文学,两者和在一块即所谓的"七门自由艺术",简称"七艺"。这是在中世纪的教会学校中必修的课程。

③ 【译者注】Carlton, W. N. C. (William Newnham Chattin), 1873—1943. 出生于英国, 1882年来到美国, 1909—1920 任 Newberry Library 第三任馆长,后来曾在包括威廉姆斯学院在内的多个图书馆任职。

④ 【原注】W. N. C. Carlton. Universities and Librarians. *Public Libraries*. 20; 452-543. December, 1915.

在爱荷华州除了爱荷华州立大学之外,没有其他教育机构更能充分履行培养专业图书馆的职责了。除了在这一章前面段落中讨论的几个原因,爱荷华州立大学已经有了实用的设施,专业的设备,以及一些专业图书馆学院运行的人力资源储备。爱荷华州立大学有九个学院、四个系,一个研究机构和推广部①,提供各个主要专业的培养以及进行研究的机会,这些使得它能够为综合和专业图书馆员提供全方位的培训。综合图书馆以及各个部门已经有了可利用的普通或者专业参考图书,国家书目和主题书目,还有涉及图书馆科学方方面面的图书。如果目前图书馆员的专业馆员,再增补一些教学人员,至少包括一位教授,一个助理教授,三个全职的教师,再加上其他院系可以合作的教师,创建一个有五十个学生的齐全完备的图书馆专业学院应该是没有问题的。

我们假设爱荷华州立大学在1926年9月成立图书馆学院。可以很好地利用从1925年9月到1926年夏天的时间,重新组织各种设施,准备学生研讨间,教师办公室和教室。还要尽最大努力从全国范围内招聘到最称职的教师。

即将成立的图书馆学院教学人员的组织、管理、资格条件,入学申请条件、课程设置、授予的学位都要进行规划。重要的财政安排也要进行讨论。各方面的问题将进行一般讨论的形式,而不是通过诸如通常看到的学校院系目录等严密声明的形式。每当笔者的观点跟同行有分歧的时候,都会给出之所以不同的原因。

任何一个新的图书馆学校应该跟一个国家承认的能够授予学位的机构联合,最好是一所美国大学联合会②成员的大学,这种说法是有道理的。至于学位授予机构或者大学的组织细节,同行们希望得到这方面的建议,而美国图书馆协会图书馆学教育董事会③可能认为不需要太详细,因为每个独立的机构有其自身的特点。图书馆学校与管理单位的总体政策相一致,这无疑是非常明智的。

在爱荷华州立大学建立一个图书馆学院有三个目的:(1)培养学生成为小型图书馆的管理者和中等以上规模图书馆的管理者助手;(2)培养学生成为专业图书馆员和编目人员,比如中学图书馆员、医院图书馆员、医学图书馆员等;(3)培养图书馆学校的教学人员。为第一个和第二个目的设计的课程,将分别给文理学院三、四年级和研究生院的学生开设。为第三个目的设计的课程,应该在本科生和研究生中都开设,同时要并行开设教育学校的课程。这种将图书馆学院的教学分成本科生和研究生阶段的做法,相比美国图书馆协会图书馆学教育董事会四年制的设计,更有普遍性和易操作性。反对这种四年制做法的意见将结合入学条件,在最后一章中一起讨论。

大学图书馆学院的首席执行官应该是学校图书馆的馆长。一些图书馆馆长可能反对这种做法,因为大学图书馆馆长办公室已经承担很多责任和职责了。假如他还要承担领导图书馆学院的责任和义务,有些人认为他可能不能完全履行图书馆馆长和图书馆学院院长两种职责。

这个表面上合情合理的争论的弱点在于"完全"④这个词的意思模糊不清。难道这个所

---

① 【译者注】原文是 extension division。
② 【译者注】原文是 the Association of American University。
③ 【译者注】原文是 the Board of Education for Librarianship of the American Library Association。
④ 【译者注】原文是 thoroughness。

谓的"完全"的含义就是作为首席执行官就要从头到尾的掌控他的图书馆每一个细节,或者仅仅意味着他应该对管理的方方面面都要考虑周全?每个有经验的管理者都会同意"完全"是指重要的功能。一个部门管理者的主要责任就好比是总工程师的责任,总工程师负责一台机器各种功能一直都能正常运行,因为他能通过一群相互协作有经验的工人,专业而及时的掌握机器各个部分的运行情况。大学图书馆主管越是能将具体工作委托给主管助理或者执行秘书,图书馆学院就能有越多的具体工作交给秘书来负责。如果大学图书馆和图书馆学院的员工都能被很好的组织起来,领导者就能"完全地"执行图书馆和图书馆学院的所有重要职能了。

在同一机构里,当两三个领导有同等的权力,不同的职责,管理两三个密切相关的职位,那么常常会发生管理上的摩擦和失误。难道大学能够找到一个图书馆学院院长和一个图书馆馆长,在这两个必须密切合作的事业上,理论、政策、实践等方面都能观点一致吗?在大学里对于两个密切相关的单位实行双重管理,往往会导致令人感到不愉快的结果。实际上,大学图书馆是大学图书馆学院的实验室,大学图书馆的良好运行,对图书馆学院的学生而言就是图书馆管理的示范课。因此,大学图书馆馆长同时掌管大学图书馆学院主任办公室,将会消除一个大学里两个相对独立然而又密切联系的单位管理上所有可能的冲突。

毋庸置疑,在妥善处理大学图书馆学院教师和大学图书馆专业馆员之间的关系方面,会存在一些管理的困难。主要的困难是薪水问题。目前大学的教学人员的工资支付标准,总的来说并没有应用于大学图书馆的专业馆员。另外一个困难是工作时间的长度和休假的福利。

在大部分大学,图书馆的各部门主任的待遇标准跟学校其他管理行政人员是一样的。沃尔特·利希滕斯坦博士①,前西北大学图书馆馆长,曾经批评过大学里训练有素的教学助理和训练有素的专业图书馆助理之间这种不公平的待遇。"大体上,毫不夸张地说,在现实中,几乎没有大学图书馆助理能够排在大学教师前面,即使排名最靠后的教师前面,也许只有在理论上是可以。在各方面图书馆员都能感受到不一样。他们被束缚于②固定的工作时间,他们只有相对比较短的假期,他们常常得不到送给大学的免费招待券,而教师往往能享受到,等等。总之,图书馆助理被认为和受聘于大学的速记员、记账人等是一样的,但是前者所需要的学术训练是远远超过了一般的办公室职员③。这里面的原因是不难发现的。大学教师是,或者希望被当作是人类知识某些领域的专家能手,但他不会很重视那些仅仅能提供普通的知识和培训的人。机械、管理工作上的专门化是不能被替代的。这种说法可能不对,但我们不关注问题本身是正确还是错误,而是关心事件真实的情况,是对还是错。现状就是那些具有专家水平的人将会寻找那些能够让他们在自己的交际圈子里受尊敬、崇拜的职位,在这个职位上,可以享受很长的假期,宽松的工作时间,头衔及排名,以及与图书馆的薪水比

---

① 【译者注】Dr. Walter Lichtenstein(1880—1964)沃尔特·利希滕斯坦出生在德国,1908—1918年任西北大学图书馆馆长。之后在芝加哥第一国家银行任职(the First National Bank of Chicago),最终任银行副总裁。利希滕斯坦任馆长期间,曾在1911年到欧洲,1913年到南美洲,为西北大学图书馆及学校其他机构采购图书资料。

② 【译者注】原文是 are tide down to,译者认为应该为 are tied down to。

③ 【译者注】原文是 tho the academic training required of the former is far in excess of that required of the usual office employee,tho 有误,猜测是 the。

起来,一份很不错的工资待遇"①。

假如图书馆学院和大学图书馆在一个领导的管理之下,对这位领导来说,基于两套工资福利标准进行管理,一套是给图书馆学院的教学人员,一套是给图书馆的专业馆员,这样的管理是不可能成功的。前者是按照大学教学人员的标准对待,后者尽管具有专业的教育和工作经历,将被归为一般管理人员。

有人建议,大学图书馆学院的教学可以只让大学图书馆馆员来承担。这个建议虽然可以称得上是深思熟虑,但有几个反对的理由。一般来说,大学图书馆的专业馆员人数不够多,不足以承担图书馆学院的本科生和研究生的各个科目的课程。有些大学图书馆的专业助理馆员可能对自己的工作非常了解,但是不一定具备教学能力。

优点是大学图书馆专业助理的教学具有将理论教学与实践经验相结合的特点。在权衡了缺点和长处之后,笔者觉得大学图书馆学院配备独立的教学人员会更好,这些人开展学术工作的资格、经验、能力与其他专业院系的教学人员具有同样的标准。大学图书馆的专业助理会就专门的主题做演讲、管理学生的实习工作,但是不应该担当图书馆学院的正规的教师和教授。

关于处理大学图书馆助理和大学图书馆学院教师的薪水问题和特权问题,建立新的工资明细表不失为解决目前不合理状况的一个好办法。这对于图书馆学院的教师和图书馆专业馆员都是适用的。"训练有素的图书馆员能提供哪种服务"不应该被当作一个构架工资明细的基本因素。例如,给大学图书馆学院教学人员支付的工资要多于大学图书馆的参考馆员,这就是不好和不公平的政策。自由教育②

和专业培训获得的真实的资格条件,成功的从事图书馆服务的时间,值得称赞的工作获得荣誉的数量,这些才是决定图书馆员工资表的因素。假如在大学系图书馆的参考馆员,有很高专业化水平,很广阔的教育背景和丰富的经验,那他的工资就不能与普通的系图书馆馆员一样,而应该和专业学科的教授一样。总之,一个人确切的资格,应该决定他的排名,和得到的工资数额,并不是一个人所在的岗位决定他能得到多少工资。当然,要明确的规定每个重要岗位必需的资格条件是可以理解的。例如,大学参考馆员相对大学图书馆学院的助理教授而言,在培训、经验、资历和有建树的工作方面需要更高的任职要求,那么前者的工资应该比后者更多一些。这个方法也许可以消除大学图书馆学院教学人员和大学图书馆专业馆员工资问题上存在的困难。

工作时间和假期的长度有时候构成了大学图书馆学院教学人员和大学图书馆专业馆员之间冲突的另一个来源,虽然在某些情况下,不平等是表面的现象,而非实际情况。专业图书馆员每周40—44个小时的工作安排,和图书馆学院教师每周12—15个课时相比,区别是很大的。

---

① 【原注】Walter Lichtenstein. Question of a Graduate Library School. *Library Journal*. 43:234. April,1918.
② 【译者注】liberal training,自由教育,不同的时代,自由教育有不同的含义。十八、十九世纪以来,自然科学兴起,并逐渐与人文学科并驾齐驱,使自由教育的概念又有所发展。1868年,英国生物学家、教育家赫胥黎在其著作《论自由教育》中,把自由教育解释为文、理兼备的普通教育,中国通常把这一时代的"自由教育"意译为"通才教育"或"文雅教育",以别于学习各种专门知识的专业教育(摘自百度百科)。

前者每年一个月的假期和后者每年 3 个月的假期,是图书馆训练有素的专业助理相比图书馆学院教师不公平待遇的另一个有争论的话题。

另一方面,全职的教师有时候每周不得不花费超过 40 个小时的时间来准备他的教学。一般来说,一个小时的课堂教学,至少要用 2 个小时来准备。因此,每周 15 个小时的课时意味着就是大概 30 个小时。如果我们把花在与学生单独讨论和修改学生作业的时间都算上,那么一个教师投入到教学上的时间每周要超过 40 个小时。但是某种程度上讲,教师在安排自己的时间上更自由一些,确实是不争的事实。一个充满热情的教师可能投入很多的时间和精力去跟学生交流,看着学生们在自己的专业上有进步是件让他很感兴趣的事儿。他不仅是专业学科的教师,而且在学生的举止行为、思想和生活方面是一个榜样和导师。因此,教师的时间是不能以数量来测量的。

至于每年的假期,这只是微不足道的差异。一些大学只为他们的教师 9 个月的教学服务支付 10 个月的工资。专业级别的管理人员工作 11 个月能收到 12 个月的工资。在这种实际情况下,大学图书馆学院的教学人员和大学图书馆的专业馆员之间没有什么不公平的。假如大学图书馆学院的教师因为 9 个月的工作收到了 12 个月的工资,一个大学图书馆的专业馆员应该相应的得到同样的酬劳。

图书馆学院的教师和图书馆的专业馆员应该在休假和其他特权得到统一的对待。虽然鉴于一个教育机构里每个受过专业训练馆员的所担负的重要使命和所提供的服务,工资的问题,办公时间数量和休假的问题都是微不足道的话题,然而这些小事情却常常是很让人恼火的。因此,管理者一方面应该尝试去尽可能彻底地消除他的机构里的这些令人恼火的事情的起因,另一方面,还应该尽力去发展所在图书馆的专业馆员和所属图书馆学院教师的团队精神①,这样不可避免的差异将只会产生最少的刺激。

如果爱荷华州立大学要建立图书馆学院,那么图书馆学院教师的资格至少应该是和其他的专业院系一样的标准。重点应该放在学术和专业训练、实践经验、教学和从事研究工作的能力上。具体一点说,图书馆学院的教师最低的资格条件是正规大学的毕业生;国家承认的提供两年专业图书馆教育的图书馆学校的研究生;有三年中等规模以上的图书馆成功工作的经验;做过一些文学或者著录书目方面的创新工作。图书馆学院的成功依赖于教师的品质。在一个专业图书馆学院教师的责任是重大的,因为他不仅要教授掌握专业技能,还要教授图书馆服务的真正含义,使得图书馆学院的毕业生能在专业人员的群体中找到自己的正确位置,勒尼德博士②已经巧妙地将这个特征描述为"心灵的新牧师""社区的情报服务"。

SELECTED BIBLIOGRAPHY

Carlton, W. N. C. University and librarians. Public Libraries. 20:451-6. Dec., 1915.

Lichtenstein, Walter. The question of a graduate library school. Library Journal. 43:233-5. April, 1918.

Reece, Ernest J. Some possible development in library education. American Library Association. Chicago. 1924.

Tufts, James H. Education and training for social work.

---

① 【译者注】原文是 *esprit de corps*,斜体字,法语,团结精神,集体精神;集体荣誉感(或自豪感)。

② 【译者注】原文是 Dr. Learned。

Russell Sage Foundation. New York. 1923.

University of Minnesota. Hospital library service. School and Society. 19:304. Mar. 15,1924.

University of the State of Iowa. Summer courses in library training. (Bulletin n. s. No. 317). Iowa City. April 23,1925.

Van Hoesen, Henry B. More thoughts on training for librarianship. Library Journal. 49:360-1. April 15,1925.

Williamson Report. Comment from the library schools. Library Journal. 48:899-910. Nov. 1,1923.

第十三章　图书馆学院的入学申请、学位和课程

1925年4月16日,很多杰出的图书馆馆长出席了芝加哥图书馆学教育董事会的会议,赞成了四个等级①的图书馆学院的提议。第一个等级,"图书馆学院两年制本科生"②-③,入学的条件是(1)在国家承认的大学或学院接受了第一年的教育,(2)在国家承认的图书馆至少两个月比较让人满意的工作经验,或者是相当的条件,(3)对图书馆工作的态度和个人资质。图书馆学院第二个等级,"图书馆学院四年制本科",入学条件包括"图书馆学院两年制本科生"的第(2)条和第(3)条,但是第(1)条中关于大学教育部分,第一年的新生学习被替换成在国家承认的大学或学院三年令人满意的工作经历。

图书馆学院两年制和四年制本科生将同样有一年的图书馆学的课程。圆满完成这一年的课程后,"图书馆学院两年制本科生"的毕业生将颁发结业证书,"图书馆学院四年制本科生"的毕业生获得了文学学士和理学学士学位④。他们将可能不会缺乏在图书馆的就业机会,我们认为无论是持有结业证书或者学位证书,他们的薪酬将与他们的学术水平相一致。

将本科生图书馆学院分成两年制和四年制两个等级,也许命名稍微有点模棱两可。通常学术上使用"三年级"⑤是就一个学生在大学第三年学习而言,而这个词不经常应用到只提供两年大学学习的学院(两年制学院)。"图书馆学院两年制本科生"只需要一年的新生学习,另一年学习图书馆学的专业知识。至于那个被大量讨论的新的"图书馆学校四年制本科生"专业标准,并没有对现行的一年制的图书馆学校的标准有多大的改进。与"官方认可的"⑥现存的一年制图书馆学校唯一的区别是不接受高中毕业生。而根据现有官方认可的图书馆学校的最近报告,能成功通过入学考试的高中毕业生在所有录取学生中占很少的比例。

新方案的缺点在于,在图书馆学院本科生两年制和四年制学生的专业教育⑦上没有什么区别。如果图书馆承认这个区别,并按不同标准给持有结业证书和毕业证书者发工资,难道两年的学院教育会使专业工作的质量上产生如此大的不同,以至于任何管理者都有合适的

---

① 【译者注】原文是 four grades,是指图书馆学校的四个等级,即两年制本科图书馆学校,四年制本科图书馆学校,图书馆专业学校,图书馆管理研究生学校。

② 【译者注】原文是"junior under-graduate library school",参照后面段落的这句话"The ordinary academic use of 'junior' is in reference to a student in the third year's college work, and the word is much less frequently applied to a college offering only two years' collegiate work"。因此,"junior college",翻译成两年制。

③ 【原注】American Library Association. Provisional Minimum Standards for Library Schools. (Mimeographed by the Board of Education for Librarianship). This provisional document is not to be printed, and was distributed only for discussion by the members who were present at the meeting of April 16, 1925.

④ 【译者注】原文是 a degree of A. B. and B. S. ,下文同。

⑤ 【译者注】原文是 junior。

⑥ 【译者注】原文是"accredited" library schools。

⑦ 【译者注】原文用斜体, *professional education*。

理由在两个级别毕业生的工资和职级上有相当大区别？如果"图书馆学校四年制本科"的毕业生在专业工作上没有表现明显的优势，那么，一个公平的管理者就不愿意对于两年制和四年制学校的毕业生在薪水和排名上区别对待。这最终导致更多的学生上了一年大学之后进入"两年制学校"，并将持续阻止优秀的有抱负的高年级学生进入"四年制学校"。在图书馆行业现实情况是，两年额外的大学教育并不能让人觉得能产生更大的经济回报。而且，我们一定要记住，多数大学里的专业学院招收三年级的学生。如果"两年制学校"确实能提供同样专业学习的课程，那么"四年制学校"在招收学生方面将处于一个很不利的位置。

在最后一章，将提出爱荷华州立大学建立二年制的本科生图书馆学院的计划。入学条件主要包括：(1)在国家承认的大学或学院两年正规的人文科学课程学习，出示院系学习成绩报告单；(2)在中等规模的图书馆，两个月的令人满意的工作经历，或者相当的条件；(3)两种外语的阅读能力；(4)能熟练运用打字机。

有一些例外的情况，比如，二十五岁以上的申请者，是高中毕业生，已经在中等规模的图书馆成功担任五年或五年以上的图书馆助理，但是他不符合必备条件里的第一个条件——两年的大学学习，如果可以提供证明自己具有这样杰出能力的充分证据，图书馆学院和人文社科学院的老师也许可以特别批准录取。获得准许的申请人，应该有一个学年的试用期。如果在试用期结束的时候，申请人的学习和能力都在平均水平之上，他们应该被允许继续完成最后一年的学业。而不能满足条件的申请人将被劝阻，因为两年制的大学教育是建立在这样的信念的基础之上的，这个信念就是这种做法既符合学生的最大利益，也符合图书馆专业的标准规范。因而，呼吁所有未来要申请图书馆学院的学生，都要求他们自己完成二年的基础教育①。

要获得图书馆学文学学士学位和理学学士学位，除了从大学新生课程和军训、体育训练得到的学分，要很好地完成120个学时。除了一二年级的一般要求，申请人还必须完成图书馆学院课程34学时的特殊要求(请见附录Ⅰ的推荐课程)。三四年级还有28学分的选修课，可以从人文科学学院②或者大学其他院系的课程里选修，但要获得图书馆学院导师的批准。

图书馆研究生院，入学条件是(1)被认证图书馆学院的毕业生，获得图书馆学专业的文学学士或者理学学士学位；(2)至少一年的一流图书馆工作经历。特殊情况下，如果申请人没有被认证的图书馆学校学位，那么就要求有更高的学位。提供这个例外的机会，就是为了向"具有独创性天才人物"敞开图书馆专业教育的大门。任何破例录用的申请人，如果没有被图书馆学院研究生院承认的最基本的学位，必须用他的出色的学业来证明他具有被录取的资格。

如果任何有经验的、杰出的图书馆馆员具有或者不具有国家承认的图书馆学校的第一学位，不是为了学位而去学习，他可能会来选修一些他感兴趣的高级课程，也会被当作一个特殊的学生，而不只是一个学位申请人来对待。

在上面所有的情况中，图书馆学院的领导和老师要承担起安排、批准图书馆学研究院所有录取的申请人学习计划的任务。院长必须了解每个学生的资历，观察他在主修和辅修课

---

① 【译者注】原文是 preliminary education。
② 【译者注】原文是 the degree of M. A. or M. S.。

程的进展,时常就他的专业和研究进行商谈。

每个图书馆学文学硕士和理学硕士学位的申请人[56]都要完成20个学分的专业图书馆的主修课程,10个学分辅修其他专门或者专业的课程。比如,如果一个学生将来想成为中等学校图书馆员,除了他的图书馆学的主修课程,还可以在教育学院注册10个学分的课程作为辅修。申请硕士学位还要提交一份学位论文或参考书目,要能够体现出作者独立的学术水平,创造性思维以及对图书馆学领域的某个专题深入研究。在成功通过最后笔试和口试,研究生导师验收通过学位论文后,申请人即可获得图书馆学文学硕士或者理学硕士。

图书馆学院的研究生可以攻读哲学博士的学位。学生可以选择研究项目,得到老师的批准认可,并且符合个人的特殊兴趣。他应该具备某个专题的全面的知识,还要有突出的研究能力。并根据这个大学研究生院管理授予学位的所有要求和规则,授予图书馆学院研究生哲学博士的学位。

美国图书馆协会图书馆学教育董事会概述了的"图书馆两年制本科,图书馆学院四年制本科,专业图书馆学校,图书馆管理研究生院暂行最低标准",在研究这个标准的时候,我们发现前两个等级的图书馆学校划分有些模糊,并且这个推荐的标准还是值得商榷的。结合我们现在讨论的图书馆研究生院的入学资格和学位,继续就"专业图书馆学校"的命名和标准进行评论并不是不合时宜的。

"专业图书馆学校"①入学的条件是(1)国家承认的学院或大学的毕业生;(2)在国家承认的图书馆或者相当机构,至少两个月的令人满意的工作经历;(3)从事图书馆工作个人资格和态度,展现出来的很好学习的能力。第(2)条和第(3)条与图书馆学院两年制和四年制本科的入学条件是一样的。在圆满完成第一学年的专业学习后,会发给申请人一个结业证书,第二学年末就会授予文学硕士和理学硕士学位。

"专业图书馆学校"的命名是模棱两可的。"职业"这个词是一个总的名称,它的范围应该包括图书馆学院本科生和研究生,并不是图书馆研究生院②这个特定的图书馆培训等级独享"职业"这个名称,要不然,从某种观点来说,图书馆学院两年制和四年制本科相当于图书馆准专业学校,图书馆学研究生院可以称之为高级图书馆专业学校。

如果"专业图书馆学校"的特点是有学位的,那么第一年的课程将不应该和本科图书馆学校几乎一样,不过这些课程可以作为先修课。只有选修完这些先修课,从正规图书馆学校获得文学学士或者理学学士学位的申请人,才能被允许继续一年的图书馆高级课程和大学其他专业学院的相关专业课程的学习。一年的专业学习圆满完成后,学位论文或者书目被教师批准通过后,学生就可以获得文学硕士和理学硕士学位了。

"暂行最低标准"中规定"专业图书馆学校"授予文学硕士或者理学硕士,比美国大学其他的研究生院,要多花费一年多的时间,这在招收研究生方面是个非常不利的因素。第一年的课程相比本科生阶段没有更加深入,也没有特色。未来的文学硕士和理学硕士的申请人

---

① 【原注】American Library Association. Provisional Minimum Standards for Library Schools, (mimeographed by the Board of Education for Librarianship). This provisional document is not to be printed and was distributed only for discussion by the members who were present at the meeting of April 16, 1925.

② 【译者注】原文是 this particular grade of library training,根据上下文的意思,判断特指研究生阶段的图书馆学校。

会有一个印象就是,学校只是试图通过增加额外一年的学习将自己升级到专业研究生院的水平。

"专业图书馆学校"入学条件的第二项,对实际工作经验上强调的太少。所有的希望到图书馆专业研究生院获得更高学位的申请人都应该有中等或者大型的图书馆一年的工作经历。

图书馆学院二年制、四年制本科和专业图书馆学校的一年级的整个的课程计划缺少逐渐提高的特点。同样的一年的专业课程,将要在三个不同的学校里学习,而这三个学校本应该提供三种不同级别的专业知识。

反对现在一年制的图书馆学校批评的主要观点之一是把研究生、大学生、高中毕业生放在一个教室里,学习同样的图书馆学课程。现在,图书馆学教育董事会制定的临时方案,用把二年级学生归到"图书馆学院两年制本科",四年级的学生归到"图书馆学院四年制本科",大学毕业生归到"专业图书馆学校",虽然他们学习同样的图书馆专业的课程,但是这些有不同教育背景的人被分在了三个不同的学校,所以他们得到了三种不同的资格证书,即,"图书馆学院两年制本科"的结业证书,"图书馆学院四年制本科"图书馆科学的文学学士或者理学学士的学位证书,"专业图书馆学校"第一年结业证书。

在专业教育方面,图书馆专业需要一个协同体系,来不断提高专业教育的自身特色。法律、医学、工程、教育等优秀的专业学院都有固定的标准,主要决定因素是学院提供的专业学习的质量和范围,以及次要或辅助因素教学体系所能提供的通识教育和文化教育。因而,在制定两种类型的专业图书馆学校的标准时,其他专业学院的成功原则也值得认真考虑。

笔者相信在芝加哥1925年4月16日会议上,以图书馆长和教育专家讨论提出的临时提案为基础,美国图书馆协会图书馆学教育董事会一定会制定出一个暂行方案完整版本。这些有经验的学者型教育者有如哥伦比亚大学的罗素院长①,还有课程构建专家芝加哥大学②的查特斯教授③,现在都是图书馆学教育董事会的专家顾问。在美国的图书馆教育方面能有这样一个具有可行性的方案是很让人期待的。图书馆学教育董事会的最终方案将为未来的图书馆专业教育奠定一个坚实的基础!

图书馆学院的课程——实际上,任何专业学院——应该围绕着三个基本的目标构成,那就是专业的知识,技术技能,崇高的理想。在明尼苏达州大学校长的就职典礼上,哥伦比亚

---

① 【译者注】James Earl Russell,詹姆斯·厄尔·罗素(1864—1945)在二十世纪早期的教育家和大学教务长,1897年至1927年发展师范学院成为全国领先的小学和中学教师,管理人员和监事的高级培训。

② 【原注】Formerly of the University of Pittsburgh.

③ 【译者注】Professor W. W. Charters of the University of Chicago, Werrett Wallace Charters 1875年10月24日出生于加拿大一个苏格兰移民家庭。查特斯1901年从多伦多大学毕业后赴美进入芝加哥大学学习,受教于杜威门下并获博士学位。查特斯一生深受杜威实用主义哲学和进步教育的影响,他首倡"教育工程"的概念对教育技术领域影响深远,这使他成为教育技术领域为数不多的思想先驱之一。在其1928年加入美国俄亥俄州立大学之前,查斯特先后在六机构担任教员或系主任,其中包括匹兹堡大学、芝加哥大学。

大学的詹姆斯·厄尔·罗素院长①在他的演讲中强调,专业学院课程体系的最基本的条件是:"在全部课程中,应该把某一个特定领域的知识系统化地组织起来,使得学生毕业进入工作岗位的时候,就可以获得掌握专业领域的基本要素。在教学活动中,应该给予学生进行创造性的努力和无私服务的灵感;并且在培养过程的某个阶段上必须为培养学生的技术技能有所准备。所有专业学院的教学问题,都产生于这三个基本的要素。这些因素,当然,都是可变的量。一个专业学院总体来说也许是令人满意的,然而在一个或者更多的基本条件上会差一些。也许指导教师的理想被恰当地设想出来,然而却不能在在校学生和毕业生的实际生活中发挥什么作用。由于教师的学术水平有限、学生智力水平不够或者教学水平不高等原因,从课堂上获得的知识也许是有缺陷的。技术技能的获得也许投入过大,或被忽视了,以至于毕业生就业之后处于无助的境地。把这三个要素按照合适的比例进行配置,是管理各种类型的专业学院的关键问题"②。

图书馆学科的专业知识应该被系统地组织起来,让学生在最短的时间里,掌握最大量的基本专业知识。这意味着在课程设置的时候,有两个明确的事情,也就是,(1)在专业学科中,不要设置非基本的课程,(2)重点放在完成所有的高级课程的先修课程上。比如,如果一个图书馆研究生院的学生希望专攻书目编目,那么他就应该把学习全面的普通编目知识作为先修课。

关于技术技能,我们都知道,每个专业需要一定量的手工或者事务性的工作。举个例子,医学上,如果实习医生或者护士不在场,一个熟练的外科医生知道怎样去用绷带。在一个专业学院的课程中,什么时间,要介绍多少技术技能,是问题的关键。

在不同的专业学院,教授技术技能花费的时间、教学特点、教学方法都是不一样的。举个例子,法学院、医学院、工程学院会在专业科目方面给予学生们充分的指导,也会在技术技能方面给予一些指导,但是会让他们到律师事务所、医院、加工车间,在熟练的技师的指导和教授下,获得全面的技能。在另外一些专业,比如教育、农业和社会科学学院的毕业生在上班的第一天就要表现得很好。笔者觉得图书馆专业情况与教育、农业和社会科学学院类似。每个聘用了图书馆专业毕业生的图书馆,都希望他或者她既拥有技术技能又有专业知识。图书馆专业学院确实应该在课程中教授一定量的技术技能。

建立专业学院的课程体系,仅仅包括很少的基本专业知识和专业技能,不考虑任何的培养"崇高理想"所必须的解释性课程,确实是不符合需求的。某些文化方面的学科能够在人

---

① 【译者注】詹姆斯·罗素 1895 年获莱比锡大学博士学位,师从著名的心理学家冯特(Wilhelm Wundt)。在留学期间,开始对英、法、德等国的中等教育展开研究。德国的留学经历使他更加坚信教育在国家当中的作用,同时也坚定了他的一个看法,即必须通过专业教育的手段来培养未来的教师。1897 年,詹姆斯·罗素加盟纽约市的师范学院。这时的师范学院还不是哥伦比亚大学的正式组成部分,两者的合作关系面临着中断的威胁。为解决师范学院与哥伦比亚大学之间的矛盾,詹姆斯·罗素建议将师范学院并入哥伦比亚大学,成为和法学院、医学院一样的专业学院。该方案获得了双方的接受,刚刚进入师范学院 3 个月的罗素被委任为哥伦比亚大学师范学院的首任院长。在罗素看来,师范学院在培养专业教师的过程中,最为重要的是以下四部分的内容:①一般的文化(博雅教育);②各学科专业的知识;③教育类的专业知识(理论、心理学、教育史);④技能(教学法的理论与实践)。

② 【原注】James Earl Russell. *University and Professional Training*, reprinted in his *Trend in American Education*. American Book Co. New York. 1922. p.224-5.

际关系方面拓宽想象力和激发理想,也应该包含在图书馆专业学院的课程中。

俄亥俄州立大学的 V.T. 塞耶教授①和哥伦比亚大学的 R.J. 伦纳德教授强调了在专业学院的课程中设置文化课的重要性。伦纳德教授在他的文章《为教育行业培养教师》中提到,"民主和专制不是对立的,除非专制是完完全全的专制"。民主教育不仅指了解和做好一件事,在更大范围的背景下,全面的领会事物之间固有的密切关系。所以,一个培养教师的民主系统,是这样一个教学过程,它能引导教师学会把她的教学任务专门化,并且在更广阔的背景上使之专门化。这样使她每天工作具有新的意义,她的精神视野也会不断的扩大。②

R.J. 伦纳德教授给了专业学院的文化课程一个专门的名字。在他的文章《专业教育的趋势》中,他称之为"边际责任"。他说:"为了更适合一个行业,职业分析必然涉及'边际责任'③的特征是什么。与'技术的责任'④比起来,'边际责任'具有更高的有序性,更加模糊,少集中的特点,但是很显然具有人生意义和现实意义,并且在每个行业里都存在。在医学领域,'边际责任'表现为,医生的责任是与医学骗术及庸医对公众的压榨作斗争,促进社会卫生学,性教育和社区健康、娱乐,并利用其无与伦比的条件,以促进家庭和谐与团圆。在工商管理领域,我们可能会提到商业道德,问题产生于州政府和国家对于私人企业的管制越来越多,也产生于有关的复杂的国际关系。除了这些所有的行业都有的'边际责任',还有一个共同的问题就是公民领导力,整个社会有权利(在这方面)对专业学院的毕业生们有所期待。"⑤

那些对于按照一定原则——这个原则成功地指导了一些其他专业学院的发展——重组图书馆专业学院的运行感兴趣的图书馆员们,自然急切地想要明确在理想的图书馆学院里,图书馆科学最基本的专业课程,最低限度的技术技能和必不可少的"边际责任"文化类课程。大约十年之前,图书馆学院的教师和有经验的馆员,可能会开一个整天的会议,一门课程接着一门课程的进行辩论。每个人都会认为自己提出的那门课程对于学生来说是最重要最有用的。那些最有说服力的参会者提出的课程将被会议采纳。在以前,这种构建专业学院课程方式,如果变成一般做法是很危险的。然而,1925 年有经验的图书馆馆员和图书馆学院教师提出他们的经验和观点,就被认为是课程"功能"⑥的决定因素,正如 W.W. 查特斯教授在前面提到的图书馆学教育董事会四月会议上的讲话中强调的那样,"系统地阐述了图书馆学院的课程标准"。

决定图书馆学院专业课程的"功能"的基本因素是收集、研究事实和理念。课程的作用确定了以后,那么就可以规划实现这些功能的学习研究了。这种"操作规范"⑦的方法甚至能运用到相关的文化课程领域。查斯特教授这样描述这个情况:"如果缺少确定的方法来规

---

① 【译者注】V.T. 塞耶(1886—1979)美国著名教育家,曾任教于俄亥俄州立大学等多所学校。
② 【原注】V.T. Thayer. Training Teachers for the Profession of Teaching. *School and Society*. 20:676-7. November 29,1924.
③ 【译者注】原文是斜体,*marginal responsibilities*。
④ 【译者注】原文是斜体,*technical responsibilities*。
⑤ 【原注】R.J. Leonard. Trends in Professional Education. *Teachers College Record*. 26:182-3. November, 1924.
⑥ 【译者注】原文是"the functional point of view"。
⑦ 【译者注】原文是 job specifications。

定职业教育之外的教学内容,那就回归能吸引某个专业教师的传统课程上。来自一个专业教师的调查很好地说明了其中的困难:'我们已经安排好专业课程了,并且为文化类科目预留了九个学时,我们要知道这九个小时将怎么安排。'在这种情况下,一般会采用大多数人的意见。不过这样的做法可能会更好一些,那就是分析学生职业教育之外的活动,不是根据一个科目需要课时数的多少,而是根据这门课程将在学生的业余生活中有多大价值,做出最终的抉择[①]。

尽管知道为图书馆学院制定课程最好严格按照科学客观的职业分析方法,但是笔者还是感到被迫追随老旧的传统方法,制定了爱荷华州立大学专业图书馆学院的本科生和研究生两个课程体系。这些课程只是个人的教育素养和工作经验的代表性体现,是针对图书馆专业教育问题的研究,希望(这个成果)对于试图收集图书馆服务的职业的事实和理想,对于根据功能理论构建图书馆专业学院科学课程进而诠释这些职业的事实和理想的专家,有所帮助。

SELECTED BIBLIOGRAPHY

Charters, W. W. Curriculum construction. Macmillan. New York. 1923.

Henry, W. E. A system of library schools. Library Journal. 49:347-9. April 15, 1925.

Kaiser, John Boynton. The special library and the library schools. Library Journal. 37:175-9. April, 1912. ct., 1912.

Leonard, Robert Josselyn. Trends

Kaiser, John Boynton. Library school training for law library employees. Law Library Journal. 5:52-3. July-O in professional education. Teachers College Record. 26:177-83. Nov., 1924.

Library Association of the United Kingdom. Syllabus of information on facilities for training in librarianship and the professional examination. Library Association. London. 1924.

Reese, Ernest J. Some possible developments in library education. American Library Association. Chicago. 1924.

Russell, James Earl. University and professional training, (reprinted in his Trend in American education. American Book Co. New York. 1922. p. 223-37).

Tai, T. C. An advanced school of librarianship—aim of curriculum. Public Libraries. 30:59-61. Feb., 1925.
戴志骞. 高等图书馆学校——课程宗旨. 公共图书馆. 1925 年 2 月第 30 期,第 59－61 页.

Thayer, V. T. Training teachers for the profession of teaching. School and Society. 20:671-7. Nov. 29, 1924.

Tufts, James H. Education and training for social work. Russell Sage Foundation. New York. 1923.

University of the State of Iowa. Catalogue including announcements, 1922-1925. Iowa City. 1922-1925.

University of Minnesota. Hospital library service. School and Society. 19:304. Mar. 15, 1924.

Williams, Reginald G. Courses of study in library science. Hopkins. Bolton. 1924.

Williamson, C. C. Library school curriculum. (In his Training for Library Service. New York. 1923. p. 12-15).

Windsor, Phineas L. Summer school credits in library schools. (In American library association. Meetings of the professional training section at the Forty-sixth annual conference of American library association. 1924. p. 10-14).

---

① American Library Association. Provisional Minimum Standards for Library Schools. (Mimeographed by the Board of Education for Librarianship). This provisional document is not to be printed, and was distributed only for discussion by the members who were present at the meeting of April 16, 1925.

附录 I　为爱荷华州立大学图书馆学院研究生和本科生推荐的课程[*]

附录 II　爱荷华州立大学图书馆学院预算建议[**]

---

[*] 原文为 Suggested Curricula for Both Graduate and Undergraduate Work in the Library School, 现题目为编者所加。

[**] 原文为 A Proposed Budget, 现题目为编者所加。

附录Ⅰ 为爱荷华州立大学图书馆学院研究生和本科生推荐的课程

推荐课程:A——本科生

1. 每个三年级的学生要在第三学年完成32个学分,其中要完成18个学分的图书馆学院课程,另外14个学分,在符合课程选修条件的前提下,可以通过完成大学其他各院系开设的本科生课程来获得。

2. 每个四年级的学生要在第四年完成30—32个学分,其中要完成16—18个学分的图书馆学院课程,另外14个学分,在符合课程选修条件的前提下,可以通过完成大学其他各院系开设的本科生课程来获得。

3. 选修图书馆学院之外的院系的课程,要得到图书馆学院指导老师的认可。

三年级	
第一学期(总计16学分)	
Ⅰ 图书馆课程	学分
Lib.1 分类	2
Lib.3 编目	3
Lib.5 参考	2
Lib.7 图书馆技术	2
Ⅱ 非专业课程	
现代语言	2
选修2门其他院系的课程	5
第二学期(总计16学分)	
Ⅰ 图书馆课程	学分
Lib.10 文献目录	2
Lib.(4) 分类	2
Lib.(6) 参考	2
Lib.12 实习工作	1
Lib.14 *美国图书馆运动(2学分) Lib.16 *挑选图书(2学分) Lib.18 *图书馆管理(2学分) (必须从加*的课程里选修一门)	2
Ⅱ 非专业课程	
现代语言	2
选修2门其他院系的课程	5

注:带*的课程是选修课。

四年级	
第一学期(总计15—16学分)	
Ⅰ 图书馆课程	学分
Lib.31 文献目录	3
Lib.33 实习工作	1
Lib.35 * 分类(2学分) Lib.37 * 参考(2学分) Lib.39 * 挑选图书(3学分) Lib.41 * 儿童图书馆工作(2学分) Lib.43 * 编目(2学分) (必须从加 * 的课程里完成4—5个学分)	4—5
Ⅱ 非专业课程	
选修3门其他院系的课程	7
第二学期(总计15—16学分)	
Ⅰ 图书馆课程	
Lib.46 图书馆历史	2
Lib.48 印刷和装订	2
Lib.18 * 图书馆管理(2学分) Lib.(38) * 参考(2学分) Lib.(44) * 编目(2学分) Lib.(42) * 儿童图书馆工作(2学分) Lib.50 图书馆推广(1学分) (必须从加 * 的课程里完成4—5学分)	4–5
Ⅱ 非专业课程	
选修3门其他院系的课程	7

注:带 * 的课程是选修课。

推荐的课程:B——研究生

1.图书馆学文学硕士或者理学硕士学位的申请人,要符合研究生院的所有条件,完成30个学分,其中要在图书馆学院研究生部①完成20个学分,另外10个学分时可以在大学各研究生部完成。

2.哲学博士学位的申请人,要在获得图书馆学文学硕士或者理学硕士之后,完成至少60个学时。其中40个学时要在图书馆学院研究生部完成,另外20个学分可以在大学其他研究生部获得。在图书馆学院的40个学分时中,大约三分之一到二分之一要投入到博士论文的写作中,或者有关某一专题(作者)的著作的全部或部分书目编辑工作中。书目工作应该与准备哲学博士学位论文的工作量相当。关于哲学博士学位的其他条件和要求,可参考研

---

① 【译者注】原文是 graduate department of the Library School,翻译成图书馆学院研究生部。

究生部的详细规定。

3.选修大学其他院系的辅修课程,要获得图书馆学院指导教师的同意。

研究生课程大纲

Ⅰ 图书馆课程	学分
Lib.201(202)高级图书馆管理 个案指导: 1.大型公共图书馆和国家图书馆 2.中学图书馆 3.大学图书馆 4.商业图书馆 5.专业图书馆(a)医学,(b)医院,(c)法律,(d)工程,(e)科学,(f)教育	2—20
Lib.203(204)专业主题书目个案指导	2
Lib.205(206)印刷和图书插图	2
Lib.207(208)学术发展史	3
Lib.209(210)古文书学①	3
Lib.211(212)高级编目	2
Lib.213(214)图书馆学院教学	3
Lib.215(216)有关书目的问题	2

课程说明

Lib.1 分类	三年级第一学期.2学分
	学习图书分类的基本原理。重点学习《杜威十进分类法》,及其若干次修改。分配书号和给图书进行分类的实践会贯穿整个学期的学习
Lib.35 分类	四年级第一学期.2学分
	在课程开始的部分会快速地介绍十进制分类的基本原理。比较研究不同图书分类系统,探讨这些不同分类系统的符号体系。重点学习美国国会图书馆、布鲁塞尔研究所、克特展开式分类法②、布朗主题分类法③的分类体系。在课程中,将讨论图书馆的图书分类法和知识的分类理论之间必然的差异

---

① 【译者注】原文为"Paleography and Diplomatics",均指古文书学,译者著。

② 【译者注】Cutter's Expansive Classification 克特对于美国图书馆学事业的发展有很大贡献。他在1869—1893年担任波斯顿图书馆馆长。1898年克特出版《波斯顿图书馆分类法》第一版,后又修订并改名为后世著名的《展开式分类法》终其一生,克特展开式分类法仍未完成,但为日后《美国国会图书馆分类法》奠定了基础,影响深远。

③ 【译者注】詹姆斯·达夫·布朗(1982—1914)著名的英国图书馆员。1898年布朗为补救一般图书馆排架效率低下的缺点,发明可调整分类法,1906年又发展为主题分类法。

续表

Lib.3(4)编目	三年级第一学期.3学分 三年级第二学期.2学分
	主要围绕着词典编目进行讲授、质疑和实践工作。分配主题词表和交叉引用的运用研究是学习编目的疑难问题。对美国国会图书馆印刷编目卡片进行利用和排序,并且按照卡片进行排架。每个学生都要求尝试进行200本样本词典的编目工作
Lib.43(44)编目	四年级第一学期和第二学期2学分
	课程主要围绕分类编目进行讲授、解决问题和实践工作;还要学习联邦、地方政府的文件、小册子、乐谱的编目。选修这门课程的学生要先修编目课程Lib.3(4)
Lib.5(6)参考	三年级第一学期和第二学期.2学分
	关于综合和专业百科全书、词典、年度报告、年鉴、地图册和期刊索引的研究。学会熟练运用综合和专业的参考书,并且重点学习这些参考书互相关联的知识。每次课后都有使用参考书的练习
Lib.37(38)参考	四年级第一学期和第二学期.2学分
	这门课程主要是帮助解决学生应对大学图书馆和大型公共图书馆参考部门会遇到的一些问题。这包括学术团体的出版物、学位论文、外文期刊和政府出版物的索引方面的研究。详细讨论参考部门的管理和参考书目书单编辑的有关工作
Lib.7 图书馆技术	三年级第一学期.2学分
	主要主题:符号系统、馆际互借系统、盘点、期刊清点,管理小册子和剪报,订购和接收工作,节省图书馆人力的装备
Lib.12(33)实习工作	三年级第二学期.1学分 四年级第一学期.1学分
	三年级和四年级的学生将被分配到大学图书馆和城市公共图书馆的每一个部门,在严密指导下,分门别类开展工作。一个学期每周三个小时的实践工作可以获得一个学分时
Lib.10 文献目录	三年级第二学期.2学分
	针对美国、英国、法国、意大利、德国、斯堪的纳维亚的国家、传统目录进行讲授和质疑。要求学生为中等规模公共图书馆编辑一个精选的书单目录
Lib.31 文献目录	四年级第一学期.3学分
	针对学术性、纪念类的主题目录进行讲授和质疑。主要讲解主题书目的规模、局限和利用
Lib.14 美国图书馆运动	三年级第二学期.2学分
	研究美国图书馆事业的发展、组织、人员、特点、发展趋势。还要概括介绍不同类型的图书馆、图书馆协会、图书馆委员会和图书馆培训机构

续表

Lib.16 挑选图书	三年级第二学期.2 学分
	目标是培养学生甄别图书的能力,使学生能够根据图书的价值和对不同类型图书馆和读者的适应性选择图书。经典外国小说译本、丛书和版本的比较。撰写所需要的图书笔记和图书评论。强调仔细检查、快速阅读各个重要学科的图书
Lib.39 挑选图书	四年级第一学期.3 学分
	与课程 Lib.16 类似。从图书馆选书的角度,对现当代戏剧、诗歌、小说、散文、科学、技术、哲学进行分析调查。挑选《出版商周刊》①《出版社通告》②《书单》③《书评文摘》④和书商的便宜、二手的书单,作为(解决)各类图书馆选书问题的示范工作
Lib.18 图书馆管理	三年级和四年级第二学期.2 学分
	讲课、质疑和阅读必读书。主要的话题:图书馆建筑、图书馆预算、账目和薄记,人事问题,宣传工作,图书馆和社区,图书馆用品,统计,年度报告,董事会和其他的管理问题
Lib.41(42) 儿童图书馆工作	四年级第一学期和第二学期.2 学分
	课程分三个部分。第一部分:关于组织和管理儿童阅览室的讲演和阅读,特别关注附属学校的儿童阅读。第二部分:通过比较研究不同类型的儿童图书和儿童文学,确定为儿童选书的基本原则。第三部分:讲故事的艺术原则,为学生提供给孩子讲故事的机会
Lib.46 图书馆的历史	四年级第二学期.2 学分
	讲义和指定读物。这个内容全面的课程包括古代、中世纪和现代的图书馆,重点关注不同时代的收藏家、保管人,以及图书馆管理和建筑
Lib.48 印刷和装订	四年级第二学期.2 学分
	这门课程包括两个部分。第一部分:印刷,包括技术术语、人员和机器构成、规格规范、纸张、设计、插图和校对。目标是让学生很好的领悟印刷的过程。讲授,质疑和阅读必读书,还包括参加印刷厂。第二部分:装订,包括技术过程、装订材料、重新装订、修补、装订记录、外观和成本。讲授和阅读必读书,以及参观装订厂
Lib.50 图书馆推广	四学年第二学期.1 学分
	研究有关分馆、图书寄存处、乡村图书馆、流动图书馆、乡村送书车⑤,以及一些更小的机构。讲授、讨论和阅读必读书

---

① 【译者注】原文是 *Publishers'Weekly*。
② 【译者注】原文是 *Publishers'Circular*。
③ 【译者注】原文是 *Booklist*。
④ 【译者注】原文是 *Book Review Digest*。
⑤ 【译者注】原文是 rural delivery by book automobile。

续表

Lib.201(202) 高级图书馆管理	个别指导.研究生.第一个学期和第二个学期.2—20个学分
	这门课程在学生时间和能力允许的范围内,尽可能多为"这些未来的图书馆管理者"提供培训。该课程将给予学生个别的指导,使之能集中研究学习以下各类型的图书馆管理: 1. 大型公共图书馆和国家图书馆① 2. 中学图书馆 3. 大专院校图书馆 4. 商业图书馆包括工厂的图书馆 5. 专业图书馆包括如下: (a)医学图书馆 (b)医院图书馆 (c)法律图书馆 (d)工程图书馆 (e)科学图书馆 (f)教育图书馆
Lib.203(204) 专门主题书目	个别指导.研究生.第一学期和第二学期 2 学分
	这门课程要训练学生全面熟悉某个学科或者某些学科重要的信息来源,这与学生专门研究的高级图书馆管理的类型密切相关。每个单独案例都由图书馆学院和其他系的领导专门安排。如果能与大学专业学院开设的课程联系起来将会有更好的效果
Lib.205(206) 印刷和图书插图	研究生.第一学期和第二学期.2 学分
	这门课程有三个有特色的部分。第一部分,关于莎草纸和羊皮纸等书写材料的早期历史和发展以及造纸方面的讲座和讨论。第二部分研究木板纸、活字以及从手稿格式到印刷书的发展演变。有关的讲座和指定读物主要包括有关印刷术在德国、意大利、法国、荷兰、西班牙和英国的传播,重点是每个时期重要的印刷工人。第三部分,针对图书插图用到的各种技法,比如早期的木刻画、雕版印刷品、蚀刻版画、金属版印刷法、线雕金属板、石板印刷术等全面研究,还包括重要的插图画家生平的了解研究
Lib.207(208) 学术史	研究生.第一学期和第二学期.3 学分
	这个课程内容丰富,主要训练学生透彻熟悉六个不同语系的学术史:拉丁文,希腊语,圣经相关的,日耳曼语,凯尔特语,罗曼语。讲义和必读书目

---

① 【译者注】原文是 County Library。

Lib. 209(210) 古文书学	研究生.第一学期第二学期.3 学分
	这门课程是主要是为了满足那些希望研究以下问题的学生:文字的起源和分类、手稿、年表、货币学、印记学、中世纪语言学
Lib. 211(212) 高级编目	研究生.第一学期第二学期 2 学分
	编目规则和方法的比较研究。大的编目部门的管理问题。主要的实践工作包括:古版本的编目,硬币、陶器、青铜器、绘画、珠宝和其他不同种类的物品和古玩的收藏。正式的图书馆学院学生,先修了编目课程 Lib. 3(4) 和 Lib. 43(44),才可以选修这门课
Lib. 213(214) 图书馆学校教学	研究生.第一学期和第二学期.3 个学分
	这门课程主要是培养学生成为图书馆学院的教师。课程重点是(1)教学方法和教学主题的准备;(2)教学内容的选择与组织;(3)结果的测试或测试;(4)适用于图书馆学院的主要教学原则。任何以成为图书馆学院教师为目标的图书馆学院研究生要求在教育学院选修辅修课程
Lib. 215(216) 目录学问题	研究生.第一学期和第二学期.2 学分
	完成某个主题或者作者的全部或部分书目著录。成果相当于硕士的学位论文。选修的学生花费一年的时间准备,并不是主要为了完成仅有的两个学分。申请图书馆科学文学硕士和理学硕士这些更高级学位的申请者,如果没有准备学位论文,就要选修这门课。选修该课程要得到图书馆学院领导的认可
学校其他院系开设的专业和非专业课程的情况,参见爱荷华州立大学课程目录	

附录Ⅱ 爱荷华州立大学[①]图书馆学院预算建议

提出的预算包括两个部分。A 部分是年度预算,包括四个小部分;B 部分原始投资的预算估计。

提出了每种类型的管理人员和教师薪水的最大最小值,但是没有提出不同等级每年自动或者规律性的年度增长额度。

B 部分原始资金投资的提议,是假设图书馆学院除了目前关于图书馆学的藏书之外,要全部配备新的设备。如果有可以利用的家具,那么原始投资的资金数量要相应地减少。估计图书馆学院的规模有五十个学生、大约六个全职和七个兼职的管理人员和教师,桌椅等家具设备的数量要以此为依据。

---

① 【译者注】原文是 THE UNIVERSITY OF IOWA,根据上下文的翻译成爱荷华州立大学。

为设立爱荷华州立大学图书馆学院制定的预算

A:年预算的提议

Ⅰ.人事服务——薪水	
1.管理者	
院长	$2,000— $3,000①
行政助理	1,800—2,500
速记员和办事员	1,020—1,500
其他助理	600—1,200
小计	$5,420— $8,200
2.教师	
副教授	$3,000— $4,000
助理教授	2,400—3,600
教师($2,000— $2,800)*2	4,000—5,600
兼职教师($900— $1,100)*4	3,600—4,400
讲师	1,000—1,000
兼职校订人($960— $1,200)*2	1,920—2,400
小计	$15,920— $21,000
Ⅱ.人事之外的服务	
1.交通(给授课者,调查、参加会议费用,等等)	$2,000
2.电报	100
3.电话	100
4.邮费	200
5.打印	200
6.装订论文、报告,等	200
7.其他花费	500
小计	$3,300
Ⅲ.设备	
1.图书	$1,500
2.期刊,包括装订	150
3.其他花费	500
小计	$2,150
Ⅳ.办公费用	
1.办公用品	$800
2.其他花费	200
小计	$1,000

---

① 大学图书馆馆长同时是图书馆学院主任,每年从图书馆学院的预算中至少获得额外的$2,000薪水。

B:原始投资预算估计

70个办公桌	$2,800
70个办公桌配套的椅子	900
24把椅子	170
70个三层书架(3英尺*3.5英尺)	800
10个六层书架(3英尺*7英尺)	200
20个打字机	2,100
1台立式加法机	420
10个钢档案立柜	780
10打装小册子的硬纸板盒	30
新增的①目录学和图书馆科学的图书和期刊	2,000
其他设备	1,000
合计	$11,200

摘要

A:每年预算	
Ⅰ.人事服务——薪水	
1.管理——小计	$5,420— $8,200
2.教师——小计	15,920—21,000
Ⅱ.人事之外的服务	3,300—3,300
Ⅲ.设备——小计	2,150—2,150
Ⅳ办公费用——小计	1,000—1,000
合计	$27,790— $35,650
B:原始投资预算估计	11,200—11,200
总计	$38,990— $46,850

---

① 【译者注】原文是 Additional,因为前面的预算内容提到,现存有一些图书馆科学方面的馆藏图书,这里可以理解为除了现有馆藏图书之外新增图书。

Bibliography on China:1900—1918
关于中国的书目:1900—1918

T. C. Tai
戴志骞

北京清华学校图书馆
TSING HUA COLLEGE LIBRARY
PEKING, CHINA.
Dec. 9. 1920

The Librarian

Mr. Paul. H. Baagoe,
Young Men Christian Association,
Antung Manchuria.

Dear My Baagoe:

 Under a separate cover I am sending you a typewritten copy of my bibliography on China. It might have many typographical mistakes, due to the rush business here, I have not read the proofs. I hope it will give you some help in selecting books on China for your State Library.

Yours sincerely,
T. C. Tai
Librarian

PREFACE

Since the unfortunate Boxer uprising in 1900, the Russo-Japanese war of 1904, and the Chinese revolution of 1911, the English speaking people have been more interested in the affairs of the "Middle Kingdom". Naturally the printed matter increased with this interest and attention. Thus the book-market is flooded with books and articles on China. Some who happen to read pessimistic books biased by personal grievance against, China are led to think that country should be wiped off the map. Others who read the works of successful adventurers and sympathetic missionaries are led to think that China is the utopia of the East. However there are books impartial in view and accurate in statements. This list has been compiled with a view of aiding the reader in choosing and comparing the best and most accurate accounts of all activities in China.

Books published since 1900 are much more interesting to the present reader, so that date (1900) has been selected as the starting point. However, revised editions of books published before 1900 have been included. In order to keep the list within usable limits only books in English and certain selected documentary publications having close connections with important subjects are included. Magazine literature has been entirely omitted because of its accessibility through the various indexes and guides to that material.

The titles selected are arranged in classed order. This seeming more practical since the reader is generally interested rather in a subject and its related topics than in the works of any particular author. The classification is primarily arranged according to Decimal Classification with minor variations. The table of contents shows the system in outline and an author index has also been added.

Entries are annotated with descriptive and critical notes, these so far as possible having been taken from critical reviews of the book in question, whether condensed or quoted exactly. Other views are also noted. As a further aid to the reader these books considered excellent by authorities are marked with an asterisk. Most of the books in this bibliography have been examined by the compiler.

T. C. Tai

ABBREVIATIONS

Volume and page numbers are separated by a colon; e. g. 4:333 means vol. 4 and page 333. The abbreviations, which are not self-explanatory and the abbreviations of the periodicals from which the reviews are noted, are as follows:

Acad-Academy
Am Econ R-American Economic Review
Am Hist R-American Historical Review
A L A Bkl-American Library Association Booklist
Am Pol Sci R-American Political Science Review
Ann Am Acad-Annals of the American Academy of Political and Social Science
Ath-Athenaeum

Bib W-Biblical World
Bio-Biography
Bk R D-Book Review Digest
Bookm-Bookman
Bost Trans-Boston Transcript(evening)
Box Up-Boxer Uprising
Cath W-Catholic World
Ch S M-Chinese Students' Monthly
C L S-Christian Literature Society
Cont R-Contemporary Review
Crit-Critic

Econ & Pol Organ-Economic and Political Organizations
Econ J-Economic Journal
Educ-Education
Educ R-Educational Review
Eng Hist R-English Historical Review

Fine A-Fine Arts

Gen Works-General works

Hib J-Hibbert Journal

Hist-History

Ind-Independent
Int J Ethics-International Journal of Ethics
Int Rel-International relations
Int Stu-International studio

J Geol-Journal of Geology
J Pol Econ-Journal of Political Economy

Lang & Lit-Language and Literature
Lit D-Literary Digest
Lond T-London Times

Man-Manchuria
Mil R-Millard's Review
Miss-Missions
Mon Mongolia

Na-Nation
Nat-Nature
N Y T-New York Times Book Review
No Am-North American Review
No C. B. R. A. Soc J-North China Branch Royal Asiatic Society Journal

Outk-Outlook

Ped Sem-Pedagogical Seminary
Phi & Rel-Philosophy and Religion
Pol Sci Q-Political Science Quarterly

R of Rs-American Review of Reviews
Rev-Revolution

Sat R-Saturday Review
Sc n. s. -Science(new series)
Sc & U. A-Science and Useful Arts
Soc L & C-Social life and customs
Spec-Spectator

Sur-Survey

The Time(London)Lit Sup-The times Literary Supplement
Tra & Des-Travels and Description
Turk-Turkestan

Yale R,n. s. -Yale Review(new series)

BIBLIOGRAPHICAL AIDS

Principal bibliographical aids consulted.

A L A catalog 1904.
A L A catalog supplement 1904-11.
A L A Booklist 1911-date.
Bashford, J. W. China, 1916. Bibliographies at the end of each chapter.
Birmingham(England), City Free Libraries. -Books pamphlets, etc. on China, 1901.
Book Review Digest, 1901-date.
Boston Public Library, card catalog.
British Museum Library, Subject Index 1901-10.
Brooklyn Public Library, Books in the B. P. L. On the Far East, 1904.
Carnegie Library of Pittsburgh, Classed catalog, 1895-date.
Clements, P. H. Boxer rebellion, 1915, p. 223-33.
Columbia University Library, Card catalog.
Coolidge, M. R. Chinese immigration, 1909, p. 505-17.
Cordier, Henry. Bibliotheca sinica, 1904-08.
Cowan, R. E. Bibliography of the Chinese question in the United States, 1909.
English catalog of books, 1900-16.
Giles, H. A. Civilization of China, 1911, p. 251-53.
Gowon, H. H. Outline history of China, 1913, pt. 1, p. 194-98.
Griffin, A. P. C. Select list of references on Chinese immigration, 1904.
Kelly and Walsh catalog, 1909-date.
Latourette, K. S. Development of China, 1917, p. 261-67.
New York(City) Pub. Lib. Card Catalog.
New York(State) Library. Card Catalog.
New York(State) Traveling Library, List of books on China.
North China Branch Royal Asiatic Society Catalog, 1909.
Tsing Hua College Library, Peking, List of books on China.
United States Catalog, 1912.
United States Catalog Supplements, 1915-17.
U. S. Library of Congress, Select list relating to the Far East, 1904.
U. S. Library of Congress, select list(typewritten lists) relating to the Far East, 1905-date.
Wang, C. Y. Bibliography of the mineral wealth and geology of China, 1912.
White, M. G. Reading List on China.

英文著作

CONTENTS[①]

Preface	348
Abbreviation	349
Bibliographical Aids	352
Bibliography	
General Works	354
Philosophy and Religion	356
Missions	361
Economic & Political Organization	363
Education	368
Social Life & Customs	370
Science and Useful Arts	375
Fine Arts	378
Language and Literature	382
Travels & Description	384
Manchuria	391
Mongolia	392
Tibet	394
Turkestan	397
Biography	399
History	402
International Relations	406
Boxer Uprising 1900	411
Revolution 1911	413
Author Index	416

---

① 为方便阅读，目录中页码为本书中页码。

GENERAL WORKS

Ball, James Dyer. Things Chinese: or, Notes Connected with China. 4th ed., rev. and enl., New York, C. Scribner's sons, 1904. 2p. 1, vii-xii, 816p. 22.5cm.

  This revised and enlarged edition is still arranged like an encyclopedia. Very useful for general readers or intending tourists to know something about things Chinese.

  Reviewed in Crit 23:287m Nov. 4, 1893. Na 57:475, Dec:21, 1893.

Bashford, James Whitford. China: An Interpretation. New York, Abingdon Press 1916, 620p. front., ports. 22.5cm.

  Contains bibliographies at the end of each chapter.

  No other book will help the peoples of the western nations to understand China better than this remarkable work of Bishop Bashford. For one who wishes to have an intelligent grasp of China's history, her present condition and her future possibility, this is the best book published in a single volume. Fourteen appendices consist of most valuable tables and original document.

  Reviewed in Bost. Trans p4 June 7, 1916; Dial 61:317, Oct. 19, 1916; Ind 87:461 Sept 25 1916; R of Rs 54:120 July 1916.

Couling, Samuel. The Encyclopaedia Sinica. Shanghai, Keely and Walsh, Limited, 1917. viii, 633p. 27.5cm.

  This general work contains about 3000 references which fill 600 well printed pages. It is the first attempt made to cover in book of reference all Chinese matters useful to the students of things Chinese. As Sir Fraser says, "It fact the whole treatment of a vast and exceedingly complex subject seems as catholic as it is satisfactory as far as can be judged..."

  Reviewed in No C B R A Soc Jour, vol. 49.

Crow, Carl. The travelers' handbook for China. With 8 maps and plans and 32 illustrations...Shanghai, Hwa-Mel book concern, 1913. Rev. ed. 1915 4p. -243-1p. front., illus. Plated. plans, 17.5cm.

  Very comprehensive guidebook and contains good map and useful informations.

Dingle, Edwin John. ed. The New Atlas and Commercial gazetteer of China. Shanghai, North China Daily News & Herald, 1917. 374p. (various paging). illus. diagr. maps, 55.5cm.

  A work devoted to its geography and resources and economic and commercial development. Containing 25 bi-lingual maps with complete indexes in Chinese and English and many colored groups; compiled and translated from the latest and most authoritative surveys and records by the staff of the Far Eastern Geographical Establishment.

Millard's review calls it "the biggest and best book on the resources of China...especially a book for the thousands of business men in America and Europe who are looking toward China as a possible field for enterprise and investment."

Far Eastern Geographical Establishment, Shanghai...The new map of China. Shanghai, The Far eastern geographical establishment, 1916. sheet. 168 x 186 cm. fold to 40 x 30 cm.

——Index to the New map of China. Shanghai. The Far eastern geographical establishment 1916. 3p. 1. ,72p. 27.5 cm.

The lettering are in Chinese and English. Accompanied by a very good index with a geographical survey of China by W. Sheldon Ridge.

* Imperial Japanese government railways. An official guide to eastern Asia; trans-continental connections between Europe and Asia by Imperial Japanese government railways. Tokyo, Japan, 1913. v. illus. ,plates, (part col.) maps, plans, 16cm.

In order to facilitate the western travellers in the eastern Asia, the Imperial Japanese government railways issued this set of new guides in English. The four volumes are devoted to: Manchuria and Chosen (Korea); Southwestern Japan; Northeastern Japan, and China. Maps and illustrations are many and they are all very useful and helpful.

Reviewed in Ind 85:460, Mar 37,1916; Lit D 53:622. Sep 9,1916.

* Richard, L. L Richard's Comprehensive Geography of the Chinese Empire and Dependencies. Shanghai, T'usewei Press, 1908. 2p. 1. , xviii, 713p. incl. tables diagrs. maps (fold in pockets)24cm.

"This work is rightly named 'comprehensive', for it contains a great deal of information which cannot be strictly classed as geographical, all of which, however, is of considerable value to the student". H. A. Giles.

Stanford, Edward. Atlas of the Chinese Empire. London, Morgan & Scott, ltd. 1908 Second edition, 1917. Xii,16p. 22 (i.e. 23) map. 34.5cm.

It contains maps of each separate province and dependency and an index to 8000 geographical names. Protestant mission stations are marked with a cross and cities, railroads and telegraph stations are indicated by distinguishing marks. A very clear and accurate atlas.

PHILOSOPHY AND RELIGION

Benoy, Kumar Sarkar, Chinese Religion Though Hindu Eyes: With an Introduction by Wu Ting-Fang. Shanghai, Commercial press, 1916. 331p. 23.5cm. Bibliography pref. p. 29-32. Works relating to India and Hindu culture, appendix p. 1-4. English and Bengali works by the same author, pref. p. 1-4.

    The first two chapters of this work were read before the "International Institute in connection with the studies in comparative religion. A very good study on the oriental philosophy and religion.

Broomhall, Marshall. Islam in China: A Neglected Problem. London, Morgan & Scott, ltd; etc. 1910. xx, 332p. front., plates, maps, facsim, 25.5cm.

    Through Islam has never been prominent in China, yet the north western part has many followers. Mr. Broomhall as a Christian missionary could not neglect the Mohammedan influence in certain parts of the country. Very interesting book on Islam and missions in China.

Chuang Thsze. Musings of a Chinese Mystic…With Introduction by Lionel Giles…London, J. Murray, 1906. 112p. 17cm. (Half-title: The wisdom of the East series. ed. By L. Cranmer-Byng, Dr. S. A. Kapadia).

    Chuang Thsze was a mystic philosopher, moralist and social reformer, who flourished in the third and fourth centuries before Christ. This work is a translation of this leading Taoist philosopher's.

* Clennell, Walter James. The Historical Development of Religion in China. Lond, T. F. Unwin ltd. 1917. 260p. 19.5 cm.

    "The relation between religion and history in China, and the attitude of the Chinese towards religious beliefs and practices, are set before the readers, together with accounts of Confucianism, Taoism, Buddhism in China, and Lamaism, the modern transformation of China, and other matters of interest". Ath.

    Reviewed in Ath p. 94 Feb 1917; Survey 39:446 Jan 19 1918; Na 105:125 Aug 2 1917.

Confucius. The Ethics of Confucius. With a foreword by Wu Ting Fang. New York, G. P. Putnam's Sons, 1915. xxi, 323p, front(ports.)20cm.

    Mr. Dawson has arranged the sayings of Confucius and his disciples according to the scheme laid down as that of Confucius himself in 'The Great Learning'. They are bound together by a running commentary that shows the relationships of one to the other and tells from what book each is taken.

Reviewed in Mis R 39:477 June 1916;Na 102:261 Mar 2 1916.

* Giles, Herbert Allen. Confucianism and Its Rivals. New York, Scribner's Sons, 1915. ix, 271p. illus. 22cm. (The Hibbert lectures. 2d ser.)

This volume consists of Hebert lectures for 1914, delivered in London by the professor of Chinese at Cambridge. In these lectures Dr. Giles deals with Confucianism in connection with Taoism, Buddhism, Mazsaism, Judaism, Mohammedanism and various forms of Christianity.

Reviewed in Ath 2:109 Aug 15 1915; Hib J 14:217 Oct 1915; Spec 115:118 July 24 1915.

Giles, Herbert Allen. Religions of ancient China. London, A. Constable & Co. ltd., 1905. 691p. 17.5cm.

Very brief and clear outlines of the different faiths and religions in ancient China. To the general readers it serves as an introductory chapter to the various religions in the "Celestial kingdom".

Groot, Jan Jacob Maria De. Religion in China. (cont.) New York, G. P. Putnam's Sons, 1912. XV, 327P. 20.5cm.

Contents: The Tao or order of the universe; The Tao of man; Perfection, Holiness, or divinity; Ascetism; Worship of the universe; Social and political universism; Fung-Shai.

"A book of great importance, being the work of a scholar who has spent half a life time on his subject." Na Mar 1913.

Reviewed in Na 96:313 Mar 27 1913; Outk 102:695 Nov 23 1913; Sat R 115:524 Apr 26 1913.

Groot, Jan Jac B Maria de. Religion of the Chinese. N. Y. Macmillan 1910, 230p. 19.5cm. (Half-title: The Hatford-Lanson lectures on the religion of the world).

Contents: Introduction; Universalistic animism; Polydemonism; The struggle against spectators; Ancestral worship; Confucianism; Taoism; Buddhist;.

Reviews the primitive elements on which all Chinese religions except Buddhism are based.

Reviewed in A L A Bkl 7:60 Oct 1910; Bib W 35:216 Mar 1910; Educ R 39:535 May 1910; Na 91:190 Sep 1 1910.

Heuen-Tsang. Si-yu-ki. London, Trubner & Co., 1884. 2v. fold. map. 22cm (Half-title: Trubner's oriental series) Rev. ed. 1906

It contains 12 books, description, geography, manner and religion of the people of India by the early Chinese pilgrims. Very interesting to know how the early Chinese pilgrims have gone to India thru the interior part of western China. A helpful work to study the development of Buddhism in China. References and notes at the foot of each page are very valuable for further studies.

Hoei-li. Heuen Tsang(Hiuen-Tsiang)

Life of Hiuen Tsiang by the Shaman Hwui Li with an introduction containing an account of the works of I-Tsing by Samuel Beal...New Ed with a preface by L. Cranmer-Byng. London, Kegan Paul, 1911. 218p. 22cm. (Trubner's oriental series).

A very good biography of Heuen-Tsant told by his disciples, Hoei-Li. Heuen-Tsang's services to Buddhist literature in China is very difficult to overestimate. When he returned to China with no less than 657 volumes of the sacred books, 74 of which he translated into Chinese. Incidentally this work also shows the Augustan age of Tai-Tsung of Tang Dynasty 629 A. D.

A very valuable piece of work for the students to reconstruct the world and ways of the Buddhist India of the centuries that have passed. This translation is undoubtedly a treasure to the western scholars of Oriental religions.

* Johnston, Reginald Fleming. Buddhist China. New York, E. P. Dutton & Co., 1913. xvi, 403-1p. front., plates, map. 23cm.

The author has intimately associated with Buddhist monks and Confucian scholars for 15 years in China. This work covers very fully and scientifically all phases of the surviving religions of China. It has interesting myths as well as histories. This will interest the general reader as well as the student of comparative religion.

Reviewed in Bid W 44:64 July 1914; Dial 56:305 Apr 1 1914m Spec 112:831 May 16 1914.

Laotzu. Sayings of Laotzu; translated from the Chinese with an introduction by Lionel Gilles. N. Y. Dutton, 1908. 54p. 17cm. (Wisdom of the East series)

Sayings of Laotzu, "The Taote King" is traditionally attributed to Laotzu, the old philosopher. Lately it has attracted considerable attention among the students of philosophy. This translation in English, the small in size, is full of food for reflection.

Reviewed in Ath 125:13 Jan 7 1905.

* Parker, Edward Harper. China and Religion, London, J. Murray, 1905. xxvii, 317-1p, 12 pl. (incl. front., port.)22.5cm.

"We cannot conclude without congratulating him upon the research he has displayed and upon the readable style which makes and abstruse subject easily grasped by the general reader."

Reviewed in Am His R 11:727 Apr 1906; Lond 4:455 Dec 22 1905; Spec 97:270 Aug

25 1906.

Parker, Edward Harper. Studies in Chinese Religion. New York, E. P. Dutton & Co., 1910. xi, 3-3081. front., plates, ports, 23cm.

  This work consists of intensive religions topics which have been excluded from his "China and religion" published in 1905. It is a complete summary about the controversy over Taoism and its founder. The translation of Tao-teh is very well done.

  Reviewed in Ind 70:310 Feb 9 1911; Na 92:344 Apr 6 1911; Sat R 111:193 Feb 11 1911.

Rose, John. The Original Religion of China. Edinburgh, Oliphant, Anderson & Ferrier 1909 327p. front., 2 fold. diagr. 20cm.

  "A fascinating book, the chief interest of which lies in its quotations (from the sacred book of China) Dr. Rose is familiar with the ancient literature of China and he quotes his authorities at every step." Spec. 1910.

* Soothill, William Edward. The Three Religions of China. London, Hodder and Stoughton 1913. xii, 324p. front. 20.5cm.

  One of the best summaries on religions of China.

* Wang, Yang-ming. The Philosophy of Wang Yang-ming, tr. from the Chinese by Frederick Goodrich Henke. London, The Open court publishing Co., 1916. xvii, 512p. pl. front. 23.5cm.

  Wang Yang-ming was a Chinese philosopher and statesman of the late 15th and early 16th centuries. As Dr. Henke says, "Wang Yang-ming was an idealist of the monistic type". The translator adds a very valuable volume of philosophy to the western library.

  Reviewed in J Ethics 27:241 Jan 1917; Lit D 53:418 Aug 19, 1916; R of Rs 54:460 Oct 16, 1916.

Wieger, Leon. Dr. L Wieger's Moral Tenets and Customs in China. Texts in Chinese, translated and annotated by L Davrout. Ho-Kien-fu, Catholic Mission Press, 1913. 604p. front., illus, pl. 26.5cm.

  The moral treatises in this volume are selected from Chinese literature. One generation ago the ceremonies described herein are regarded as essentials of an educated man, but now the readers must bear in mind that those moral precepts are no more followed by many a modern educated and Christian families. The pages are printed in double columns in Chinese (Romanized character) and in English. While on the opposite page appears the same thing in Chinese characters.

  Reviewed in Spec 111:143 July 26 1913.

Yang Chu. Yang chu's Garden of Pleasure, tr. from the Chinese by Prof. Anton Forke, with an introduction by high Granmer-Byng. London, J. Murray, 1912. 64p. 17cm. (Half-title: The wisdom of the East series…)

  This little volume is another valuable addition to the Wisdom of the East series. Yang Chu's philosophy of "Oriental Hedonism" is always condemned by Confucian scholars. This translation will give this egoistic eastern philosopher of four centuries B. C. a chance to be discussed by the western scholars.

MISSIONS

Bashford, James Whitford. China and Methodism. Cincinnati, Jennings and Graham. 1906 118p. 16cm.

"A brief outline which will enable American Methodists to understand the problem which confronts them and to make preparations for a suitable participation in the Centennial celebration of the founding of protestant missions in China!" Bk R D 1907.

Small as the size is, it has fresh and stirring information. Reviewed in Mis. R 31:799 Oct 1907.

Bitton, Nelson. The Regeneration of New China. London, United council for missionary education. 1914 xxii, 282p. front., plates, ports. 19cm. " A select list of book" P. 269-277.

A book giving the account of the first revolution of 1911 and treating its underlined causes largely attributed to the Christian influence.

Reviewed in Mis R 38:80 Jan 1915.

* Broomhall, Marshall. The Chinese Empire: A general & missionary survey. London, Morgan & Scott, etc., pref. 1907 xxiv, 472p. front., plates, ports., fold. map. 22cm.

"The preparation of the various articles was entrusted to those who, by long residence in the field, were specially qualified to write as experts upon their own particular provinces." Editor's preface. A very good missionary survey with useful tables and workable indexes.

* Cecil, Lord William Rupert Ernest Gascoyne. Changing China. New York, D. Appleton & Co., 1912. vii, 1342p. incl, map. plates. 20.5cm.

This volume deals chiefly in three main topics. The first relates the early missions and the various religions of China; the second with the missions proper; and the third treats of questions of education. A very readable book on China and full of information.

Reviewed in N Y T 15:287 May 21, 1910; Spec 104:883 May 28 1910.

* China Mission Year Book. Shanghai, C. L. S. v. fold. maps, fold. tab. 19cm. Published annually.

A full compendium of things Chinese up to date and the information are very accurate.

Lin Shao-Yang. A Chinese Appeal to Christendom Concerning Christian Missions. New York and London, G. P. Putnam's Sons, 1911. iv p., 1 l., 321p. 22cm.

"He does not criticise Christian missions in general, but a particular kind of Christian mission. This kind is not the medical mission, nor is it the educational mission...what he does criticise, as might be expected is that very narrow type which we call the orthodox or evangelical mission. "Outk 1911.

Reviewed in Na 93:574 Dec 14 1911; Outk 99:46 Sep 2 1911; R of Rs 44:724 Dec 1911.

Osgood, Elliott I. Breaking Down Chinese Walls, from a Doctor's Viewpoint. New York, F. H. Revell Company 1908. 9 p., 1 l., 11-217p. front., plates, ports. 20cm.

On missionary work in China and the introduction is by Archibald McLean.

A very clear exposition of Chinese conditions and of the value of medical missionary work in Christianizing China. The author emphasizes greatly that the dispensaries, hospitals and schools are great factors in spreading the Christian civilization and above all that the home-life of the missionary is a very effective agency in regeneration.

Reviewed in Ann Am Acad 31:717 May 1908; Ind 64:1451 June 25 1908; Outk 89:312 June 6 1908.

* Scott, Charles Ernest. China From Within. New York. Fleming H Revell Company 1917. 327p. front. (port) Plates. 21cm. (Students' lectures on missions, Princeton theological seminary, 1914-1815).

This book consists of lectures delivered at Princeton theological seminary in the winter of 1914-15. It touches very little about politics, revolutions, etc. but points out the real regenerative forces those are at work in the development of China. Very interesting to general readers as well as to missionaries.

Reviewed in Bost Trans p. 6, Nov. 17 1917; Ind 93:200 Feb 2 1918; Outk 117:476 Nov 21 1917.

Smith, Arthur Henderson. The Uplift of China. New York, Missionary education movement of the United States and Canada, 1912. xvi, 2, 282p. incl. illus., fold. tab. front., plates, ports., fold. map. 20cm.

A general summary of pointing out the defects of the strength and weakness of the religions and problems of missionary work. It is a text-book for mission study but also a handy volume for the general readers. References for advances study at the end of chapters.

Speicher, Jacob. The Conquest of the Cross in China. N. Y. Revell, 1907. 369p. pl. port. chart. 21.5cm.

The author's lectures are a first hand view of the conditions to be met by missionaries in southern China. Full of sane advice concerning to what kind of missionary that China needs and what kind of training the missionary needs.

Reviewed in Ind 63:942 Oct 17 1907; N. Y. T. 12:665 Oct 19 1907.

ECONOMIC & POLITICAL ORGANIZATIONS

* American Academy of Political and Social Science. Philadelphia. China, social and economic conditions. Philadelphia, American academy of political and social science, 1912. v. 229p. 25cm.

　　This volume contains 16 articles on social and economic conditions of China. All the contributors are either men of experience or profound scholars. A very handy volume for the students of oriental affairs. Its usefulness is further increased by a good index.

Chau Ju Kua. Chau Ju Kua; his work on the Chinese and Arab trade in the 12th and 13th centuries, entitled Chu-fan-chi, translated from the Chinese and annotated by Friedrich Hirth and W. W. Rockhill. St Petersburg, Imperial acad. of science, 1911. 288p. 1 fold. map. 27cm.

　　Notes with bibliographical references with each chapter.

　　This Chinese treatise dealing with medieval trade falls into two parts. The first treats with various countries with which the Chinese traded and the second numerates the products which were brought to China from foreign lands. This volume is a store house of very valuable informations regarding to Chinese medieval trade and its reference use is greatly enhanced by a very full index.

　　Reviewed in Na 98:82 Jan 22 1914.

* Chen Han-Chang. The Economic Principles of Confucius and His School. New York, 1911. 2v. 25cm.

　　Dr. Chen is a prominent confucianist with the wide acquaintance of the best economic literature of the western countries. Confucianism is a great economic as well as a great moral and religious system. "The reader will find in this book a great deal more than the dry bones of political economy. T. L. Bullock".

　　Reviewed in Am Hist R 17:645 Apr 1912; Eng Hist R27:531 July 1912; Na 95:173 Aug 22 1912; Spec 109:456 Sep 28 1912.

Chen, Shao-Kwan. The System of Taxation in China in the Tsing Dynasty, 1644-1911. N. Y. Columbia University, 1914. 118p. 24.5cm.

　　"This survey of the political and financial organization of China seems especially designed for the reader who wishes a brief description of salient facts which hitherto have been available only for oriental readers. It is to be regretted that author was prevented by the catholic condition of the financial accounts on many of the provinces of China from obtaining sufficient statistical material to establish more detailed conclusions". J. Pol. Econ 23:102

Han 1915.

  Reviewed in Am Econ R 5:119 Mar 1915;ANN Am Acad 61:291 Sep 1915;Eng Hist R 30:189 Jan 1915.

China, Inspectorate General of Customs. ——Decennial reports on the trade, navigation, industries, etc., of the ports open to foreign commerce in China and Corea, and on the condition and development of the treaty port provinces. 1892-1901. Shanghai, 1904. 2v. fold. plates, maps. plans, (partly fold.) tables, diagrs., profile. 28cm.

  Authoritative and accurate statistics of the exports and imports of the Chinese trade industries. Very valuable for the business men and students of commerce.

* The China Year Book. 1912—— London, G. Routledge & Sons, Ltd. 1912-v. 19.5cm.

  "The table of contents show 30 main heads, ranging from geography to trade-marks, each of these heads minutely subdivided for easy reference, and each subdivision treated seemingly with painstaking accuracy and in surprising detail. The book should lie upon the desk of every newspaper man who writes either as editor or as report about the Far East, and on the shelves of all students of the orient or of contemporary international affairs."

  Reviewed in Dial 61:539 Dec 14 1916;N Y T 22:6 Jan.7,1917.

Chu, Chin. The Tariff Problem in China. N. Y., Columbia University, 1916. 4p. 1, 5-192p. 24.5cm.

  "Being deprived of tariff protection, having been subjected to unfavorable and unjust commercial regulations, many industries in China are deranged to such an extent that the general condition is deplorable. With a view to showing the Chinese government and people how far they themselves have been responsible for such unreasonable arrangements in the past, to what extent they may expect their removal at present and what should be China's economic policy in the near future." Preface. Besides five useful appendices the treatment is very well arranged, but with no index and bibliography.

  Reviewed in AM Econ R 6:828 Dec 1916;Ann Am Acad 68:321 Nov 1916.

* Coolidge, Mrs. Mary Elizabeth Burroughs (Roberts) Smith. Chinese Immigration. New York, H. Holt & Co.,1909. x,531p. incl. tables,19cm.

  Outlines the complete history of Chinese immigration to the Pacific coast. Good appendices and bibliographies.

  Reviewed in Ann Am Acad 34:617 Nov 1909;Na 89:574 Dec 0 1909;R of Rs 40:511 Oct,1909.

Gibson, Rowland R. Forces Mining and Undermining China. New York, The Century Co. 1914 xii, 301,1p. front. (port)23cm.

"Lacking in that orderly analysis and mastery of material which wins the confidence of the reader in the judgment of the writer…The book contains valuable information. But it looks maturity of judgment and dignity of expression". O. D. Wannamaker.

Reviewed in Dial 58:20 Han 1 1915;N Y T 19:377 Sep 13 1914;R of Rs 50:381 Sep 1914.

Hsu, Mongton, Chih. Railway Problems in China. New York, Columbia University. 1915. 184p. fold. map. 25cm.

"An especial advantage of this monograph over other books on the subject is the author's acquaintance with Chinese sources and correspondingly his ability to present sympathetically the Chinese view of the controversial points of which the subject in so large part consists". A. P. Winston.

Reviewed in Am Econ R 6:121 Mar 1916;J Pol Econ 24:206 Feb 1906;Na 101:441 Oct. 7 1915.

* Jernigan, Thomas R. China in Law and Commerce. N. Y., The Macmillan Company, 1905. vii, 408p. 21cm.

The volume supplies the knowledge of the political and commercial life of the people and also treats the resources, the state, provincial district, town and family organizations, business customs, weights, measures, etc. very fully. Statements are carefully sifted and tested.

Reviewed in Ath 2:398 Sep 23 1905;Na 81:84 July 27 1905;Spec 95:sup 795 Nov 18 1905.

Jernigan, Thomas R. China's Business Methods and Policy. Shanghai, Kelly & Walsh, Limited. 1904. 4p. 1., 439. 1p. 21.5cm

The author outlines a clear and accurate treatment of the administrative system, land tenure, sources of revenue, law courts, finances, social regulations, commercial trend, educational and consular systems and foreign relations. A very useful reference book on economic and political organizations.

Reviewed in Spec. 94:121 Jan 28 1905.

* Kent, Percy Horace Braund. Railway Enterprise in China. London E. Arnold 1907. ix p., 1 1; 304p. maps. 23cm.

This interesting work traces the development and history of the Chinese railway thru the various stages up to the present era of concessions and foreign control.

Reviewed in Na 87:82 July 23 1907;N. Y. T. 13:2 Jan 4 1907;Spec 100:105 Jan 18 1908.

Morse, Hosea, Ballou. The Gilds of China…London, Longmans, Green and Co. 1909. ix 92p. 1pl.

(incl. front.)23cm.

"The historical and comparative material which includes an account of the famous gild merchant of cohong of Canton, has been effectively presented, the author's previous experience well fitting him for the task. " J. Pol Econ

Reviewed in J Pol Econ 18:152 Feb 1910; Pol Sci Q 25:182 Mar 1910.

* Morse, Hosea Ballou. The Trade and Administration of China. New York, Longmans, Green & Co. 1913. xii 466p. incl tables. plates, fold. map. facsim, diagr. 22.5cm.

The first two chapters written by Dr. Pott, President of St John's University, present a condensed, but readable sketch of Chinese history from the earliest time to the beginning of foreign relations. The rest 11 chapters by Mr. Morse deal systemically and exhaustively the conditions of the trade, finance and system of the government.

Reviewed in Ath 2:365 Sep 26 1908; N Y T 13:294 May 23 1908.

Sargent, Arthur John. Anglo-Chinese Commerce and Diplomacy. Oxford, The Clarendon Press, 1907. xi 1 332p. incl. front. , diagrs. 23cm.

One of the best summaries regarding the religions of Great Britain and China, solely viewed in their bearings on the interests of commerce. Statements are reliable and style is lucid.

Reviewed in Ann Am Acad. 31:720 May 1908. J Pol Econ 16:634 Nov 1908.

Tsu, Yu Yue. i. e. Andrew Yu Yue. The Spirit of Chinese Philanthropy: A Study in Mutual Aid. New York, 1912. 2p. 1. , 7-123p. 25cm.

This monograph consists of six chapters: Chinese philanthropy, in thought and practice; Population and social well-being; Charity: Mutual benefit; Civic betterment; Rise of national self-consciousness and solidarity. The arrangement is systematic and the outlines of the history and practice of the Chinese charitable organizations are well drawn.

Reviewed in Am Econ R 3:435 June 1913.

Wagel Srinivas R. Chinese Currency and Banking. Shanghai, North China daily news and herald ltd; , 1915. 6p. 1. , 457p. 25cm.

"A sequel to my finance in China". Pref. Notes and reviews, see author's "Finance in China".

* Wagel, Srinivas R. Finance in China. Shanghai, North China daily news and herald Ltd. , 1914. 4p. 1. , 503p. tables(1 fold). 25cm.

These two bulky volumes "Finance in China" and "Chinese currency and banking" are an attempt to make a comprehensive survey of the very chaotic economic conditions of China as they exist today. The treatment is uneven and unexhaustive, but judging from the sheer magnitude of the task, Mr. Wagel ought to be congratulated to attain such a fair degree of success.

Reviewed in Econ J 25:417 Sept 1915.

Wei, Wen Pin. The Currency Problem in China. New York, Columbia University, 1914. 156p, illus, 25cm.

The sphere of this work supplies the reader to know the history and different phases of the currency problem in China. By no means this treatise is to solve the very complicated conditions of the Chinese monetary system and it does outline the difficulties.

Reviewed in Am Econ R 5:362 June 1915.

Yen, Hawkling Lugine. A survey of Constitutional Development in China. New York, 1911. 136p. 11.25.5cm.

"It should have special value to those students of political science and sociology who are anxious to know something about the evolution of Chinese political institutions and the principal basis of the Chinese political system. But for a person who desires to get a glimpse of the contemporary political situation in that Far Eastern country, this monograph cannot be much relied, upon, for it almost entirely deals with Chinese political philosophy". Chinese Young.

Reviewed in Ann Am Acad. 39:218 Jan 1912; Eng Hist R 27:204 Jan 1912; Na 75:172 Aug 22 1912.

EDUCATION

* Burton, Margaret Ernestine. The Education of Women in China. New York, Fleming H. Revell Co. 1911 232p. front. , plates, ports. 21.5cm.

 Miss Burton's book is a suggestive study of the home and school life of Chinese women and girls with the attitude of men towards their woman education. The system of women education has been greatly improved and developed since the publication of that book.

 Reviewed in Bib W 39: 144 Feb 1912; Dial 52: 89 Feb 1 1912; Na 93: 574 Dec 14 1911.

Eddy, Sherwood. The Student of Asia. N. Y. 1916. 223p. port. pl. 18.5cm. (Student volunteer movement for foreign missions)

 An unpretentious but very inclusive review of the progress of education in Asia. It deals with student life in India, Japan and China.

 Reviewed in Bib W 47: 343 May 1916; Bost Trans p. 9 Mar 25 1916; Ind 85; 459 Mar 27 1916.

* Educational Directory of China. Shanghai, Educational directory of China publishing Co., 1912-21cm.

 A first hand and reliable reference book for all interested in western education in China. It mainly consists of three parts, the first on general information, the second a directory of professors, lecturers, teachers, librarians and others connected with western education and the third is a list of universities, colleges and schools where English and other foreign languages are taught.

Eryer, John. Admission of Chinese Students to American Colleges. Washington, Gov't print. off., 1909. xiii, 221p. 23cm. (U. S. Bureau of education. Bulletin 1909: No. 2, whole No. 399)

 This bulletin contains the entrance requirements of a number of typical institutions and the special facilities offered to Chinese students by certain of the higher educational establishments in the different states. Dr. Fryer is the professor of oriental languages and literature in the University of California.

King, Harry Edwin. The Educational System of China as Recently Reconstructed. Washington, Gov't print. off. 1911. 105p. 23cm. (U. S. Bureau of education. Bulletin 1911, no. 15. Whole number 462).

 This monograph consists of two parts. The first part is to trace the development of new education in China in three periods and the second part to describe the ruling agencies of the new educational system and the grades of educational institutions.

Reviewed in Educ R 43:427 Apr 1912;Ped. Sem. 19:129 Mar 1912.

* Kuo,Ping Wen. The Chinese System of Public Education. New York City,Teachers college,Columbia University,1915. xii,209p. 23.5cm.

Dr. Kuo outlines the history of Chinese educational system from 2357 B. C. to 1911 A. D. besides the interesting topics of the reorganization under the Republic and present day problems.

Reviewed in Ped Sem 22:304 June 1915.

SOCIAL LIFE & CUSTOMS

Ball, James Dyer. The Chinese at Home, or the Man of Tong and His Land. N. Y. , Fleming H. Revell Co. , 1912. lp. 1. , vii-xii, 370p. 23pl. (incl. front.)21.5cm.

　　To know something Chinese is better to read author's "Things Chinese". This is a volume of Chinese social life and customs only. Mr. Ball's lack of acquaintance with the life of northern China, where the people do things differently, is decidedly a drawback in this entertaining book.

　　Reviewed in Ann Am Acad. 42:353 July 1912; Ind. 72:468 Feb 29 1912; Na 95:331 Oct 10 1912; Sepc 107:1078 Dec 16 1911.

* Bard, Emile. Chinese Life in Town and Country. New York, G. P. Putnam's Sons, 1905. 2p. 1. , iii-xii p. , 1 l. , 285p. front. , 15pl. 19cm.

　　The chief value of this book is free from bias. The chapters, though brief, are full of interesting informations.

　　Reviewed in Critic 47:206 Sep 1906; Dial 39:245 Oct 16 1905; Na 81:227 Sept 14 1905.

Blake, Henry Arthur. China. N. Y. Macmillan 1909. 138p. illus. col. pl. 26cm. (Menpes crown series)

　　"A work whose art value is of the first importance. This accompanying text sketches the physical features, the manners and customs of the various people in China, their status in the educational affairs and their prospects for future commercial activity." Bk R D 1999.

　　Reviewed in Ath 2:490 Oct 23 1909; Dial 47:445 Dec. 1 1909; Na 89:569 Dec 9 1909.

Boggs, Lucinda Pearl. Chinese Womanhood. Cincinnati, Jennings and graham, 1913 129p. 18.5cm.

　　"This work is the reflection of author's thought and observation on the mother, the wife, the illustrious women of China, education of women, western civilization and Chinese women."

　　Reviewed in Ped Sem 21:158 Mar 1918.

Broomhall, Marshall. Present Conditions in China. N. Y. , F. H. Revell Co. , 1908. vii, 1 58p. incl. facsim, diagrs. , plates, maps. 22cm.

　　This little book consists of quotations from Chinese newspaper, maps, tables, and text and they all bear witness to the fact that there is a great movement in China. The age of rapid change is golden opportunity for missionaries to christianize the Chinese people.

Reviewed in Ind 66:342 Feb 11 1909; N Y T 13:673 May 23 1908; Spec 100:835 May 23 1908.

Carus, Paul. Chinese Life and Customs. Chicago, The Open Court publishing Co. 1907. vi p., 2 l., 114p. front., illus. 24cm.

 Very interesting book about the Chinese life and customs. The costumes shown in the illustrations now no longer exist in the new republic of the Far East. Illustrations are produced from common Chinese pen drawing.

Chitty, Joseph R. Things Seen in China. Lond. Seeley, 1909. 252p. pl. 15.5cm.

 "There is little excuse for the appearance of the present work, since the information which it contains appears to be eminently commonplace". Ath 1909.

 Reviewed in Ath 1:40 Jan 9 1909; Ind 66:325 Feb 11 1909; N Y T 14:20 Jan 9 1909.

* Cooper, Mrs. Elizabeth. My Lady of the Chinese Courtyard. New York, Frederick A. Stokes Co 1914 xvi p., 1 l., 262p. front., plates. 21.5cm.

 A collection of letters purporting to be those of a Chinese lady, Kwei-Li, to her husband, describing life during his absence. A very entertaining book which contrast between the old China and the new.

 Reviewed in Bookm 39:327 May 1914; Bost Trans p. 22 Apr 15 1914; Na 98:575 May 14 1914.

* Derling, princess, (Mrs. T. C. White). Two Years in the Forbidden City…First lady in waiting to the Empress Dowager. N. Y. Moffat, 1911. 383p. front. pl. ports. 21.5cm.

 It gives the very pompous air of an oriental place. The depiction of the crafty, vain and wise Empress Dowager is exceptionally entertaining. In few places the authenticity of the accounts is rather doubtful.

 Reviewed in Dial 52:89 Feb 1 1912; Ind 71:1403 Dec 21 1911; Na 94:639 June 27, 1912. Spec 108:553 Apr 6 1912.

Dickinson, Goldsworthy Lowes. Letters from a Chinese Official. N. Y. McClure, Phillips & Co. 1903. xiv. 75p. 18cm.

 The purpose of these letters brings out a contrast between eastern and western ideals. They are imaginary letters written by Mr. Dickinson.

 Reviewed in Crit 84:192 Feb 1904.

Dore, Henri. Researches into Chinese Superstitions: translated from the French with notes, historical and explanatory, by M. Kennelly, Shanghai, T'Usewei printing press, 1914-v. 1, 2, 3, -continued, illus. col. pl.

Illustrations of charms and other superstitions signs are fully reproduced from the Chinese sources. A very valuable book for investigating and discussing the Chinese religions and the popular superstitions.

Giles, Herbert Allen. China and the Chinese. N. Y. The Columbia University Press, The Macmillan Co, agents, 1902. ix 229p 18.5cm.

Lectures delivered in Mar 1902 at Columbia University to inaugurate the foundation of a professorship of Chinese. Author is an English scholar will versed in Chinese. A well written book with accuracy.

* Giles, Herbert Allen. The Civilization of China. Lond. Williams and Norgate 1911. 256p. 17cm.

"The author has successfully accomplished an account of history, manners and customs, art, literature and religion into a small book but still keeping it readable". A. L. A. Bkl Apr 1912. An admirable work on China for small libraries with limited means.

Reviewed in Cath W 95:251 May 1912; Ind 72:488 Feb 29 1912; N Y T 17:80 Feb 18 1912; R of Rs 46:120 July 1912.

* Goodrich, Joseph King. The Coming China. Chic. A. C. McClurg & Co. 1911. xx p., 1 1., 298p. front., plates. 19.5cm.

This volume if the reflections and observations of the author's 45 years acquaintances with China and the Chinese. The information though brief, they are thorough and reliable.

Reviewed In Na 93:575 Dec 14 1911; N Y T 16:709 Nov 12 1911; R of Rs 44:723 Dec 1911.

Headland, Isaac Taylor. Court Life in China. New York, F. H. Revell Co. 1909 2p. 1., 372p. col. front. plates. port. 21.5cm.

A very delightful book about the court procedure and conditions at the time of the Empress Dowager, but the descriptions are too much colored.

Reviewed in Dial 47:455 Dec 1 1909; Ind 67:1044 Nov 4 1909; R of Rs 40:758 Dec 1909.

Headland, Isaac Taylor. Home Life in China. N. T. Macmillan Co. 1914. xii, 319 p. col. front., plates. 19.5cm.

The author's knowledge about the home life in China is exceptional, but sometimes unreliable. Delightful book for the general readers.

Reviewed in Sat R 119, sup 6 June 19 1915; Spec 114:395 Feb 27 1915.

Johnston, Reginald Fleming. Lion and Dragon in Northern China. N. Y. E. P. Dutton and Co. 1910. xiv, 461, 1p, front., plates(photos), map. 22.5cm.

The chief value of this book is to study the social organism of a typical community of northern China. Anyone who wishes to know the customs, the observances and institutions which are not yet influenced by the western civilization will be immensely profited by this sympathetic work.

Reviewed in Dial 50:130 Feb 16 1911; N 92:65 Jan 19 1911 E of R's 43:123 Jan 1911.

* Liang, Y K. Village and Town Life in China. N. Y. The Macmillan Co. 1915 xi. 155p 22cm.

"This work is a valuable addition to the growing literature on Chinese institutions written by natives of China educated in occidental scientific method and writing for Europeans and Americans". A. P. Winston. Is reference value is somewhat decreased on account of having no index.

Reviewed in Am Econ R 5:840 Dec 1915; Ath 2:57 July 24 1915.

* Macgowan, John, Missionary. Men and Manners of Modern China. Lond. , T. F. Unwin, 1912 351,1 p. front. plates. 23cm.

The author has a long residence of fifty years in China and his knowledge of Chinese life is quite thorough. His description regarding to the present upheaval is very clear and vigorous. Style is unusually animated.

Reviewed in Ann Am Acad. 47:301 May 1913; Ath 2:334 Sept 28 1912; Dial 43:48 Jan 16 1913.

Macgowan, John, Missionary. Sidelights on Chinese Life. Lond. K. Paul Trench, Trubner & Co. , Ltd. 1907. viii,367,1 p. 12 col. pl. 34pl on 281. ,25.5cm.

This volume is a series of essays which are attempted to depict the various phases of Chinese life from the cradle to the grave. Interesting description with ready anecdotes makes the book very attractive for general readers.

Reviewed in Ath 1:785 June 27 1908; Dial 45:410 Dec 1 1908; Spec 100:151 Jan 25, 1908.

Martin, William Alexander Parsons. The Lore of Cathay. N. Y. Fleming H. Revell Co. 1912 4p. 1. , 480p. front. (ports)plates. 21.5cm.

A comprehensive history of the Chinese intellectual life, as arts and sciences, literature, religion, philosophy and education. A very good summary of the Chinese civilization.

Reviewed in Crit 39:573 Dec 1901; Dec 31:316 Nov 1 1901; Na 73:422 Nov 28 1901.

Merwin Samuel. Drugging a nation. N. Y. F. H. Revell Co. 1908 2p. 1. ,3-212p. front. (port) 8 pl. 20cm.

"An unusually frank statement of facts, made after a searching investigation into both the literature of the subject and actual conditions in China, may be found in the book of Mr. Merwin."Na June 1909. The author holds England directly responsible for the introduction of opium into China.

  Reviewed in Ind 66:325 Feb 11 1909; Na 88:633 June 24 1909.

Miller, George Amos. China Inside Out. N. Y. Cincinnati. The Abingdon Press 1917 18p incl. front. , illus. 21cm.

  In order to know intimately the daily lives of the Chinese people, the author traveled far and near on foot and sometimes by boat. This book gives you how the Chinese amuse themselves, what the Chinese say, what the Chinese ideals of religion are, the occupation of the Chinese and their toil and also with few chapters on Christian missions.

  Reviewed in Bost Trans p6 Apr 4 1917; Dial 62:315 Apr 5 1917; Ind 90:439 June 2 1917.

* Ross, Edward Alsworth. The Changing Chinese. N. Y. The Century Co. ,1911. xii,356p. incl illus. , plates. front. 21.5cm.

  "So interesting is the treatment throughout, so vivid the descriptions, so incisive the arguments, so clear the conclusions, that the volume will appeal to an unusually wide public and must be considered a notable contribution to the literature on that remarkable land". P. J. Treat.

  Reviewed in Dial 51:388 Nov 16 1911; Ind 71:1206 Nov 30 1911; Na 93:574 Dec 14 1911.

SCIENCE AND USEFUL ARTS

* Chan, Shiu Wong. The Chinese Cook Book...N. Y. Frederick A. Stokes company 1917 xiii p. ,1 1. ,201 p. illus. ,plates. 19.5cm.

"More than one hundred tested recipes of palatable Chinese dishes, explicit enough for every housewife and practicable for the restauranteur. Aside from the novelty of the dishes, the recipes are to be recommended for the success they achieve in furnishing a desirable mixed diet. One feature that recommends itself to housewives who are practicing Hoover restraint and economy is the substitution of peanut oil for butter". Rk R D 1917.

Reviewed in Ind 92:343 Nov 17 1917;Ch S M 13:290 Mar 1918.

Jefferys, William Hamilton and James L. Maxwell. . The Diseases of China, Including Formosa and Korea, Philadelphia, P. Blakiston's Sons & Co. ,1910. xvi,716 p. incl. illus. ,xi maps. v col pl. 24.5cm.

The two authors as medical missionaries in China have had much experience in the diseases which prevail in that country. It is a very valuable book not only to physicians and surgeons in Chinese hospitals, but to the medical world as well. The book is profusely illustrated.

* King, Franklin Hiram. Farmers of Forty Centuries; or Permanent Agriculture in China, Korea and Japan. Madison, Wis. ,Mrs. F. H. King,1011. ix,441 p. front. (port.)illus. 19.5cm.

"The soul of the book lies in its appreciative maintenance through many centuries of perhaps the highest average productivity ever attained by great peoples and its chief lesson lies in the realization of this by simple domestic means. They style of the book is excellent and the two hundred and forty odd half tones effectively illustrate the text."Sc n s Jan 1912.

Reviewed in Ann Am Acad. 49:270 Mar 1912;J Pol Econ 20:534 May 1912. Nat 89:500 July 19 1912;Sc n s 35:72 Jan 12 1912.

Lanning George. Wild Life in China; or Chats on Chinese Birds and Beasts. Shanghai, National Review office,1911. 255p. 22.5cm.

Very interesting volume on Chinese birds and beasts. The author travels wildly in the interior parts of China. The material first appeared in the form of series in the"National review" which ended its existence in 1915. Delightful book for travellers and hunters.

Laufer, Berthold. Chinese Clay Figures; or, Chinese Defensive Armour. Chicago,1914. 245p. illus. (Field museum of natural history. Publication 177. Anthropological series v,13, no. 2)

Pt. 1, prolegomena of the history of defensive armour.

"The Mrs. T. B Blackstone expedition".

"The somewhat ponderous title of the work before us rather obscures the subject of this monograph, which is upon the origin and history of defensive armour, a theme of considerable cultural importance and here treated systematically for the first time...A word of high praise must also be given to the illustrations, which are well chosen and significant; and the photographic plates, 64 in number are beautifully reproduced". L. A. Waddell.

Reviewed in Nat 96:229 Oct 28 1915.

Meyer, Frank Nicholas. Agricultural Explorations in the Fruit and Nut Orchards of China. Washington, Gov't print. Off. , 1911. 62p. illus. , vi. pl. 23cm(U. S. Dept. of agriculture. Bureau of plant industry. Bulletin no. 204).

"The Chinese as a race are great lovers of fruits and to satisfy their taste they grow these wherever there is a chance to do so. They understand the arts far less successful in their attempts to originate new varieties". Intro. This bulletin is remarkable both in its treatment and photographic illustrations, besides a workable index.

Shaw, Norman. Chinese Forest Trees and Limber Supply. Lond. Unwin 1914 351p. front. pl. fold. map. 22cm.

Bibliography: p. 333-39.

"The volume as uncritical compilation from various books, journals and official reports, which are indicated in a bibliographical list". Nat 1915. Altho not scientific in its treatment yet it contains some valuable information regarding to the forest conditions of different provinces of China.

Reviewed in Nature 95:556 July 22 1915.

Sowerby, Arthur de Carle. Fur and Feather in North China. Tientsin, Tientsin Press, 1914. 190p. illus. ports. pl. 24.5cm.

A volume of natural history of the vertebrates, especially the game animals in the northern China, is clearly described with sporting experiences. Besides 43 good photographic reproductions there are numerous drawings drawn by the author.

* Wallace, Harold Frank. The Big Game of Central and Western China: Being an Account of a Journey from Shanghai to London Overland across the Gobi Desert. London, J. Murray, 1913. xviii, 318p. front. , illus. , plates, maps. 23.5cm.

The work of a naturalist as well as a hunter. The author began his journey from civilized Shanghai to the semi-barbarous tribes near Omsk. His description of strange people, strange beasts and strange scenes are simply wonderful. It is one of the best and most recent books of hunting on Central Asia.

Reviewed in Ath 1:465 Apr 26 1913. Bost Trans p. 18-Aug 20 1913; Na 97:415 Oct 30

1913.

* Willis, Bailey. Research in China, in three volumes and atlas...by Bailey, Willis, Eliot Blackwelder and R. H. Sargent. Washington, D. C. Carnegie institution of Washington, 1907-1913. 3v. illus. pl. (incl maps. partly double, partly fold.) tabs. 29.5cm x 33.5cm.

 On verso of t. p.: Carnegie institution of Washington. Publication No. 54.

 Cover-title of atlas: research in China, 1903-04. Geographical and geological maps. Bailey, Willis, geologist in Charge...1906.

 Contents:

 v. 1. pt. 1 Descriptive topography and geology, by B. Willis, E. Blackwelder and R. H. Sargent.

 pt. 2 Petrography and zoology, by E. Blackwelder. Syllabary of Chinese sounds by Friedrich Hirth.

 v. 2. Systematic geology by B. Willis.

 v. 3. The Cambrian faunas of China, by C. D. Walcott. A report on Ordovician fossils collected in eastern Asia in 1903-04, by Stuart Weller. A report on upper Paleozoic fossils collected in China in 1903-04, by G. H. Girty.

 A remarkable storehouse, well classified and arranged for the research students of geology and mineralogy of China.

 Reviewed in J Geol 16:389 May 1907; Nat 76:345 Aug 8 1907.

* Wilson, Ernest Henry. A Naturalist in Western China, with Vasculum, Camera, and Gun; Being Account of Eleven Years' Travel, Exploration and Observation in the More Remote Parts of the Flowery Kingdom. Lond. Methuen & Co. Ltd. 1913 2v. fronts. (v. 1, port.) plates, map 23cm.

 This two volume work is remarkable in every way. It contains, botanist, ethnologist, sportsman, general traveller, merchant and any person who interests in things Chinese. The half-tone plates are sharp and attractive and it should be recommended to every library, small and large.

 Reviewed in Ath 2: sup 437 Oct 18 1913; Bost Trans p 22 Dec 31 1913; Dial 56:137 Feb 16 1914.

FINE ARTS

Binyon, Laurence. i. e. Robert Laurence. The Flight of the Dragon: An Essay On the Theory and Practice of Art in China and Japan, Based On Original Sources. Lond. J. Murray, 1911. 112p. 17cm. (Half-title: The Wisdom of the East Series, ed. by L. Cranmer-Byng, Dr. S. A. Kapadia).

The aim of this essay is to bring the westerners to understand the fundamental ideals and philosophy of the art of China and Japan. It is rather useful and adaptable to study clubs and students of art.

Reviewed in A L A Bkl 8:198 Jan 1912; Ath 2:428 Oct 7 1911.

Binyon, Laurence. Painting in the Far East. Lond. E. Arnold, 1908. xvi, 295 2 p. front., xxxpl. 25cm. Rev. ed. 1913.

"His book is a notable one, comprehensive in its outlook, clear in its statements and irrefragable in its philosophy". F. W. Gookin. Besides the accounts about the painting in the Far East, a great deal of space is devoted to the Chinese art. This is a revised edition of 1908.

Reviewed in Dial 46:257 Apr 16 1909; Int Stu 37:83 Mar 1909; Spec 102:541 Apr 3 1909.

*Bushell, Stephen Wootton. Chinese Art. 2d ed. rev. Lond. Printed for H. M. Stationery off. by Eyre and Spottiswoode, Ltd. 1909. 2 v. fronts., illus., plates. 21.5cm.

A very comprehensive book on the various subjects of Chinese art. Useful both for art students and collectors.

*Chu Yen. Description of Chinese Pottery and Porcelain: Being a Translation of the T'ao Shuo. Oxford, The Clarendon Press, 1910. xxxi, 222p, 22cm.

"First special work written upon the subject of Chinese ceramics, and... still generally considered by native connoisseurs as the chief authority on the subject". Translator's introduction. A very good translation for the western art world.

Fenollosa, Ernest Francisco. Epochs of Chinese and Japanese Art: An Outline History of East Asiatic Design. Lond. W. Heinemann, 1912. 2v. col. fronts., 187 pl. 26cm.

A systematic history of the art of Eastern Asia. Very interesting not only to scholars and art collectors but to the general readers on oriental topics and observing travellers.

Reviewed in Ath2:484 Oct 26 1912; Int Stu 48, Sup 20 Nov 1912.

Giles, Herbert Allen. An Introduction to the History of Chinese Pictorial Art. Shanghai, Kelly & Walsh, Ltd. 1905. xp. ,1 l. ,178p. ,1 l. illus. ,plates. 25cm.

  A handbook on the lives and works of over three hundred painters of all ages. They are chiefly translated from the writings of Chinese art-critics, with 16 reproductions of famous Chinese pictures.

* Gorer, Edgar. Chinese Porcelain and Hard Stones…Lond. B. Quaritch, 1911. 2v. 254pl. 32. 5cm.

  Illustrated by 254 Plates in oriental colors of the gems of Chinese ceramic and glyptic art. The work traces Chinese ceramic history thru the period covered by the reigns of K'ang His, Yung Cheng and ch'ien Lung, extending from 1662 to 1795.

  Reviewed in Na 94:220 Feb 29 1912; Sat R 113:20 Jan 6 1912. Spec 108:65 Jan 13 1912.

Gulland, W G. Chinese Porcelain…With Notes by T. J. Larkin 2d ed. London, Chapman & Hall, Ltd. ,1902. 2v. illus. plates. 23cm.

  "Treatise on Chinese art based upon the previous authorities who have written in England and France, and founded as it should be, upon a well set forth statement of the national characteristics alike as the religion, history, beliefs, literature, and their influence upon the popular mind. "Magazine of art, 1899. Vol. 1 is a more elementary treatise for collector-beginner and vol. 2 is useful to connoisseurs.

  Reviewed in Crit 34:278 Mar 1899; Na 76:276 Apr 2 1903.

Hirth, Friedrich. Scraps from a Collector's Note Book. Leiden, Formerly E. J. Brill; N. Y. G. E. Stechert & Co. 1915. 2p. l. ,135 1 p. front. ,plates. 25cm.

  This volume is chiefly devoted to some painters of the Manchu dynasty, 1644-1905 with 21 reproductions of famous pictures. The appendices give biographical notes on some ancient painters and art historians. It forms a supplement to Dr. Giles' "History of Chinese pictorial art".

* Hobson, Robert Lockhart. Chinese Pottery and Porcelain…Lond. Cassel & Co. Ltd. 1915. 2v. col. front. ,illus. pl. 24 5cm.

  Mr. Hobson's knowledge of Chinese ceramic wares is so profound that any book on this subject by him always has some value. The information given is so full and so concisely put that the collector will find it of great value is studying the particular period or style. To the general student of art the description is very entertaining and the plates are of excellent quality.

  Reviewed in Ath 1:432 May 8 1915; Int Stu 55:298 June 1915.

* Hsiang Yuan-p'ien, 16th cent. Chinese Porcelain … Oxford Clarendon Press, 1908. 45. 81p. 80pl. 31cm.

"A work of great importance to the task of reconstructing the story of Chinese ceramics. It is a reproduction of the famous album prepared by Hsiang Yuan-p'ien in 1575 in which are described and illustrated 83 pieces of porcelain", Bk R D. 1909.

Reviewed in Ath 2:615 Nov 14 1908;Spec 102:381 Mar 6 1909.

Laufer, Berthold. Chinese Pottery of the Han Dynasty. Leiden, E. J. Brill, Ltd. 1909. xvi. 339p illus. plates. 26. cm.

This book summarizes the results of three years' investigation conducted in China under an endowment provided by Mr. Schiff. By this first-hand monograph Dr. Laufer brings this neglected subject of Chinese pottery to the attention of museum curators and connoisseurs.

Reviewed in Na 91:229 Sept 29 1910.

* Laufer, Berthold…Jade; a Study in Chinese Archaeology and Religion. Chicago, 1912. 2p. 1., xiv, 370p. illus., LXVIII pl. (6 col). 24. 5cm.

"A remarkable complete and discerning monograph, which will appeal alike to connoisseurs, artist, ethnologists and students of comparative religion and folklore". Haddon. This volume is the first of a series of volumes which will be the result of an expedition to China and Tibet carried on by the gift of Mrs. T. B. Blackstone.

Reviewed in Ind. 73:210 July 25 1912;Na 96:42 Jan 9 1913;Nat 91:226 Mat 1 1913.

Lockhart, Sir James Haldane Stewart…The Stewart Lockhart Collection of Chinese Copper Coins,. Shanghai, Kelly & Walsh, Ltd. 1915. 2p. 1., xv. 174, 36p. illus. 31. 5cm.

Mr. Lockhart has a beautiful collection of the old Chinese copper coins. The engravings and photo-lithographs of 2967 ancient coins obverse and reverse are well illustrated. The description of each coin is carefully arranged and numbered for easy reference.

* Strehlneek, E. A. Tr. Chinese Pictorial Art. Shanghai, Commercial Press, 1915.

Due to inability of getting this book here, no close bibliographical collation given.

The descriptions and notes on the history of Chinese drawing, writing, etc. are very entertaining. The translations from the standard Chinese authors are well down. Bound in light blue Chinese silk and colored collotyped reproductions are excellent.

Tokyo. Imperial University. Decorations of the Imperial Palace of Peking. Tokyo, Ogawa, 1906. No pagination, 80 plates, mostly in original colors, 48 x 38cm. Limited edition of 1000 copies.

This is a companion volume to the "Imperial city of Peking". It, besides furnishing an accurate idea of the whole palace buildings to the students of architecture, interests the general reader also in building decorations. The English translation has been done by Tomoyoshi Torniogi, Bungakushi, lecturer of the college, and O. Tatsuru.

Tokyo. Imperial University. Imperial City of Peking; Compiled by the Imperial Museum of Tokyo and Collotyped from the Negatives Taken by K. Ogawa; With Explanatory Notes in Japanese, English and Chinese. Tokyo, Ogawa, 1906. 2v. 170 collotype prints. 48 x 38cm.

  The 170 pictures of these two volumes form such a comprehensive set that the important views and edifices of the place grounds and the capitol are represented therein. The Japanese notes have been written by Professor Ito and translated into English by Tomoyoshi Torniogi, Bungakushi, lecturer of the college of engineering and into Chinese by Atsutsune Aoyagi, lecturer of the Waseda University. A very good work on Chinese architecture.

Treadwell, Winfred Reed. Chinese Art Motives Interpreted N. Y. G. P. Putnam's sons, 1915. xiiip., 1 l., 110p. 23 pl on 11 l. (incl. front). 21.5cm.

  "A rather slight and casual compilation of the chief subjects which appear on Chinese porcelains and textiles. It will meet the needs of those who want bare elements...There are 23 well chosen illustrations." Na 1916.

  Reviewed in Ath p. 282 June 1916; Bost Trans p. 24 Feb 23 1916; Na 102: 655 June 15 1916.

LANGUAGE AND LITERATURE

Brown, C. Campbell. China in Legend and Story. N. Y. F. H. Revell Co. , 1907. 253p. 12pl. 20cm.
　　"The influence of Christianity of character has seldom been more impressively exemplified than in the tales which compose the latter half of the volume. "Spec.
　　Reviewed in Ind 64:451 June 25 1908; Spec 100:540 Apr 4 1908.

Budd, Charles, tr. Chinese Poems, tr. by C. Budd. Lond. F. Frowde, 1912. 174p. 19.5cm.
　　This translated anthology from the Chinese poems contains a wide variety of subjects, but chiefly are the lyricals. Considering the great technical difficulty, the translations are excellent in spite of loosing some of the original naivete and limpid simplicity.
　　Reviewed in Ath 140:161 Aug 17 1912.

* Crammer-Byng, Launcelot Alfred...A Feast of Lanterns. Lond. , J. Murray, 1916. 95, 1p. 17cm.
　　"In 'the Wisdom of the east series'...There is now published a treasure for students of poetry. 'A feast of lanterns', translations from the work of 20 Chinese poets. The introduction explains the tenets of Chinese poetic art, their reverence and love for flowers, symbolism in poetry, and the lore of the dragon, one of the four spiritually endowed creatures of China. There are also interesting comments of the epochs of Chinese poetry and on the great storehouse of verse that remains untranslated into western tongues. "R of Rs 1917.
　　Reviewed in Ind 91:78 July 14 1917; Kit D. TRN 54:1862 June 16 1917; R of Rs 56: 105 July 1917.

Giles, Herbert Allen. A Chinese-English Dictionary. 2d ed. rev. & enl. Shanghai, Kelly & Walsh, Ltd. 3v. 33 x 26.5cm.
　　A standard Chinese-English dictionary.

* Giles, Herbert Allen. A History of Chinese Literature. N. Y. D. Appleton & co. 1901. viii, 488p. 19.5cm.
　　First attempt of the kind that has been made to produce a history of Chinese literature. Altho name follows name, yet such unavoidable difficulties are considerably reduced by the author's clear and brisk expositions.
　　Reviewed in Acad 60:99 Feb 2 1901; Ath 117:139 Feb 2 1901.

* Headland, Isaac Taylor. Chinese Mother Goose Rhymes. N. Y. Fleming H. Revell Co. 1900. 157, 3p. incl. front. , illus. 23.5cm.

Collections of rhymes taken from Chinese children's poems and translated into English by Professor Headland. Insects, birds, animals, and children are the popular subjects. They are very well translated.

Reviewed in Na 71:392 Nov. 15 1900.

Hearn, Lafcadio. Some Chinese Ghosts ... Boston, Little, Brown and Co. 1906. viii, 5, 14-203 p. 19.5 cm.

This book consists of six tales: The soul of the great bell; the story of Ming-Y; The legend of Tchi-niu; The return of Yen Ychin-kny; The tradition of the tea plant and the tale of the porcelain god. They all, possess poetical beauty and natural touch of human passions.

Reviewed in N. Y. T. 11:801 Dec 1 1906; Outk 85:503 Nov 9 1906.

Pitman, Norman Hinsdale. Chinese Fairy Stories. N. Y. Crowell 1910 183 p. col. front., col. Pl. 20.5 cm.

"Where these Chinese fairy stories differ from those of other countries is in their admirably instructive local color and in a certain happy matter-of-fact style which might tempt a child to forget that they are mere dream stuff". N. Y. T 1910.

Reviewed in Ind 69:706 Sept 29 1910; N Y T 15:618 Nov 5 1910.

* Waddell Helen. Lyrics from the Chinese. 2d impress on. Lond. Constable & Co. Ltd. 1914. Xiv, 41 1 p. 20.5 cm.

"Miss Waddell's 'Lyrics from the Chinese' are interesting historically and not less interesting as poetry. How much is Chinese and how much the translator's we do not know, but the poetic value of these little poems is very high". Spec. 1914.

Reviewed in Ath 2:749 Dec 27 1913; Bookm 39:202 Apr 1915; Sepc 112:sup677 Apr 25 1914.

Wieger, Leon. Chinese Characters: Their Origin, Etymology, History, Classification and Signification: A Thorough Study from Chinese Documents. Tr into English by L. Davrout......Ho-Kien-fu, Catholic Mission Press, 1915. 2v. pl., 25.5 cm.

Very painstaking work and translation is excellent.

Williams, Samuel Wells. A Syllabic Dictionary of the Chinese Language: Arranged According to the Wu-Fang Yuan Yin, Tung Chou, Near Peking, No. China Union College, 1909. lxxxiv, 1056 p. 23 cm.

This is one of the standard dictionaries of the Chinese language for the westerners. Dr. Williams is as authority of etymology and rhymes of Chinese. The first edition was published by American Presbyterian Mission Press, Shanghai, in 1874.

Reviewed in Chinese Recorded 5:226, 1874; North China Herrld Oct 15 1874.

TRAVELS & DESCRIPTION

Bell, Archie. The Spell of China. Boston, The Page Co. , 1917. xiv, 404p. col. front. , plates, ports. , fold. map. 20. 5cm.

 A typical volume of a hasty traveller. Inaccuracies and errors are rather the fuel than exceptions, as the author claims that Hangchow was the first city to receive Christian missions. The value of such book is as Dr. Smith says that they have stalked in boldly with hat on and umbrella spread and have taken a front seat. Nevertheless the chapters on Yangtze cities and Peking are well worth reading.

 Reviewed in Mis R 41:559 July 1918; Ch S M 13:235 Feb 1918.

Borel, Henri. The New China; A Traveller's Impressions. Lond. T. F. Unwim, 1912. 282p. , 1 1. front. , plates, ports. 23cm.

 A volume of descriptions of Peking the legation quarter, the forbidden city, the streets of Peking, the yellow temple, the lama temple, the temple of Confucius, the Summer palace and the funeral of the empress Dowager. The style is vivid and the illustrations from photographs are good.

 Reviewed in Ath 1:359 Mar 30 1912; Ind 73:729 Sept 26 1912.

Conger, Sarah(Pike) "Mrs. E. H. Conger". Old China and Young America. Chicago, E. G. Browne & Co. , 1913. 160p. front. , plates, ports. 18. 5cm.

 A group of stories and sketches about the tings, Chinese for the American children. The tales are simply and entertainingly told and the author's knowledge about China is pretty fair.

 Reviewed in Na 97:148 Aug 14 1913; R of Rs 77:635 May 1913.

* Daly, Emily Lucy(French) "Mrs de Burgh Daly". An Irishwoman in China. Lon. , T. W. Laurie, led. 1915, xi, 294, 1p. col front. , plates. 22. 5cm.

 The author spent about twenty years in China and this book covered the period of the Chinese-Japanese war, and the Boxer uprising, the Russo-Japanese war, and the downfall of the Manchu dynasty. It is entertainingly written with many interesting anecdotes. The illustrations are from photographs and drawings by Chinese artists.

 Reviewed in Ath p. 39 Jan 1916; Bost Trand p9 Oct 28 1916; Dial 61:476 Nov 30 1916.

Denby, Charles. China and Her People: Being the Observations, Reminiscences and Conclusions of an American Diplomat. Bost. , Page, 1906. 2v. fronts. pl. ports. fold. map. 19cm.

 Reminiscences of author's stay in China and his personal impressions of the land and the accounts of court life at Peking and social life and customs of the Chinese form the first volume. Chinese politics and industrial and commercial problems form the second. These two handy size volumes are very readable and interesting.

Reviewed in Ann Am Acad 27:416 Mar 1906;Dial 38445 Dec 16 1905;R of Rs 33:113 Jan 1906.

* Dingle, Edwin J. Across China on Foot. N. Y. , Holly & Co. , 1911. xvi, 445. 1p. front. (port) plates, fold, map. 22cm.

Mr. Dingle was anxious to have a journey across China on foot and altogether he traveled 3100 miles from Shanghai both by river and walking overland. His keen observation gives us a very interesting account about the revolutionary tendencies among the people in the far interior. The antifootbinding campaign in western China is also vividly described. The book is full of clear tones reproduce form author's photographs.

Reviewed in In 71:1038 Nov 9 1911;R of Rs 44:723 Dec 1911.

Farrer, Reginald John. On the Eaves of the World. London. Arnold, 1917. 2v. fronts. pl. fold. map. 23cm.

The author spent two years 1914 and 1915 at the Kansu-Tibet border for searching plant life adaptable to the British climate. This two volume work deals traveling on one hand and plant life on the other.

Mr. Farrer has succeeded in his aim to satisfy the general reader as well as the botanist.
Reviewed in Sat R 124:528 Dec 28 1917;Spec 119:717 Dec 15 1917.

Gamewell, Mrs. Mary Ninde (Porter). Gateway to China: Pictures of Shanghai. N. Y. Revell 1916 252p. illus. pl. ports. 21.5cm.

This is a very entertaining and descriptive book on Shanghai, "Paris of the East." The author reviews the history of that city from the time that Great British opened it as a port by treaty in 1842 to the present. Everything ancient and modern of that popular sea-port is vividly described.

Reviewed in Sat R 124:528 Dec 29 1917;Spec 119:717 Dec 15 1917.

* Gaunt, Mary Eliza Bakewell. Woman in China. Philadelphia, Lippincott, 1914. 390p. pl. (incl. front) 22.5cm.

"One of the most entertaining and pleasing of books on the subject. Artistic by temperament, Mrs. Gaunt has filled her pages with sketches from life, vivid and delightful. Wannamaker. The description dwells chiefly on the northern part of China."

Reviewed in Dail 58:20 Jan 1 1915;Lit D 50:156 Jan 23 1915;Sat R 119:67 Jan 16 1915.

Geil, William Edgar. Eighteen Capitals of China. Philadelphia & London, J. B. Lippincott Co. 1911 xx, 429p R front, illus. , plates, ports. , maps. 22.5cm.

  Besides the descriptions of the provincial capitals of China, the author weaves into his narration with curious legends, poems and anecdotes. A Chinese proverb is on the top of every other page.

  Reviewed in Ind 71:921 Oct 26 1911; Lit D 43:1105 Dec 9 1911; R of Rs 44:723 Dec 1911.

Geil, William Edgar. The Great Wall of China. N. Y. Sturgis & Walton Co. , 1909. xvi, 383p. front. , illus. , plates, ports. , maps. 23.5cm.

  The author was a rare quality to make a general description book interesting but sometimes sacrifices accuracy too much. This is a new edition of a book that came out in 1909.

  Reviewed in A. L. A Bkl 8:186 Dec 1911; N Y T 16:704 Nov 5 1911.

Jack, Robert Logan. The Back Blocks of China. Lond. , E. Arnold. 1904. xxii, 269p. xvi. pl. fold. maps. 23cm.

  Interesting journey and entertaining tales of adventures among the western and southwestern provinces of China and other frontier territories.

  Reviewed in Ath 123:693 May 28 1904: Spec 92:341 Feb 21 1904.

Johnston, Lena E. China, by L. E. Johnson…illus. in colour by Norman H. Hardy, Lond. , A. &C. Black, 1910. vii, 87, 1p. incl. map. col. front. , col. plates. 20cm.

  A book for young people, interesting and sympathetic but inaccurate. No one expects to have definite and accurate statements of a strange country from "People".

  Reviewed in L A Bkl 6:359 May 1910; Spec 103: sup 820 Nov 20 1909.

Johnston, Reginald Fleming. From Peking to Mandalay. Lond. J. Marry, 1908. 2p. 1. , ix-xii, 460p. front. illus. , plates, map. 23cm.

  A valuable book of travel in the interior and frontier of China. There is a great deal of matter that will interest travellers, adventurers, ethnologists, geologists and religionists.

  Reviewed in Ath 1:721 June 13 1908; N Y T 13:513 Sept 19 1908; Spec 101:257 Aug 22 1908.

Kemp, Miss E. G. The Face of China. London. Chatto & Windus, 1909. xv, 275, 1p. , 1 1. 63pl. fold. map. 24.5cm.

  Thru the whole book Miss Kemp comparers here and there with the trying conditions attending travel in China in 1893 and the comfortable ones apparent today and also shows the advancement along the commercial, political, social and educational lines has been made. A well written book of adventure, but its whole atmosphere is too optimistic.

Reviewed in Ath 2:491 Oct 23 1909; Dial 47:455 Dec 1 1909; Spec 103:650 Oct 23 1909.

* Kendall, Elizabeth Kimball. A Wayfarer in China. Boston, Houghton Mifflin Co., 1913. xivp., 1 1., 388p., 11. front., plates, maps. 21.5cm.

  Professor Kendall made up her mind to see certain parts of China which have not been contaminated by the Western material civilization, so she traveled alone from Tonkin into Yunnan and Szechuan, two western provinces. Narratives in this book chiefly concern her experience in these lands and impressions of the people she met. She also traveled to the Siberian railroad thru Mongolia by the native wagon. Very lucid style and many original illustrations make the volume more attractive.

  Reviewed in Ath 1:248 Mar 1 1913; Bost Trans p6 May 21 1913; Dial 54:383 May 1 1913; Na 97:103 July 31 1913.

Lesdain, Count de. From Pekin to Sikkim Through the Ordos, the Gobi Desert and Tibet. N.Y., E.P. Duton & Co., 1908. xii, 301p. 32pl. fold. map. 23cm.

  "A remarkable wedding journey made by Count de Lesdain and his nineteen year old bride, from Peking across northern China, the Ordosland, the Gobi desert, then south over the highland of Tibet into India. It was undertaken to gratify a wish to cross country hitherto unknown and to increase the geographical knowledge of the day". Bk R E 1908.

  Reviewed in Ath 2:178 Aug 15 1908; Ind 64:1451 June 25 1908; Na 86:577 June 25 1908.

Liddell, T. Hodgson. China, Its Marvel and Mystery. Lond., G. Allen & sons, 1909. xiii, 202, 1p. 40. col. pl. facsim. 20.5cm.

  "The main interest of the text in connection with his paintings (which in their original form must constitute a most charming collection) centers in the last two chapters, where he describes his stay in the Summer Palace and certain interesting events in Peking." K. K. Kawakami

  Reviewed in Ath 1:39 Jan 8 1910; Na 90:510 May 19 1910; Spec 10.5:523 Oct 1 1910.

Little, Alicia Helen Neva (Bewicke) "Mrs Archibald Little." Round About My Peking Garden. London, T. Fisher Unwin; Phil. J. B. Lippincott Co., 1905. 5-284, Col, front., 85pl. 22.5cm.

  This volume might be called as a collection of sketches of North china. But her description is quite picturesque and her style is vivid. It is profusely illustrated from original photographs.

  Reviewed in Ath 1:14 Jan 6 1906; Crit 48:478 May 190 6; Na 82:145 Feb 14 1906.

Little, Archibald, John. The Far East. Oxford, Clarendon Press 1905. 334p. illus. pl. maps. 23.5cm. (The Regions of the World)

"The book is no mere compilation, but written out of a full experience. Most of the chapters are occupied with China, historically and geographically……There are also interesting chapters on Mongolia and Turkestan and very good and full account of Tibet and the various approaches to that land". Spec 1905.

Reviewed in Ath 2:361 Sep 16 1905; Dial 39:276 Nov 1 1905; Nat 72:636 Oct 26 905, Spec 95:528 Oct 7 1905.

* Little, Archibald John. Gleanings from Fifty Years in China……revised by Mrs. Archibald Little. Lond., S. Low, marston & Co., Ltd., 1910. xvip., 1 l., 335, 1p. front., plates, ports 23.5cm.

"We have only one fault to find with the volume, It does not inform us as much as we would like concerning the anti-footbinding movement." Outk May 1911. Mr. Little is one of the forerunners who liberates the Chinese women from the agony of Footbinding.

Reviewed in Dial 50:477 June 16 1911; Na 93:574 Dec 14 1911; Outk 98:128 May 20 1911; Spec 107:sup520 Oct 7 1911.

Little, Archibald, John. Mount Omi and Beyond, Lond., W. Heinemann, 1901. xivp., 1 l., 272p. front. port. plates. fold. map. 23cm.

It is an admirable account of Mount Omi and the Tibetan border. Those places regarded by the Chinese always as the very beautiful spots of the empire and the shrines of Buddha's disciples. This is one of the best descriptive books on those regions.

Morse, Edward Sylvester. Glimpses of China and Chinese Homes. Bost., Little, 1902. 216p. front. illus. 21cm.

It might be called a volume of Chinese architecture. The author describes the interior of the Chinese houses, the streets of Chinese villages, theaters, temples, soldiers drillroom and other institutions in detail. Most of the material first appeared in American archived under the title, "Journal sketches in China."

Reviewed in Crit 43:288 Sep 1903; Dial 33:468 Dec 16 1902; Na 76:18 Jan 1 1903.

Moule, Arthur Evans. Half a Century in China. N. Y. Hodder and Stoughton 1911, xii, 343p. fold. front., plates, fold. map. 22.5cm.

The author begins the story with Taiping rebellion 1961-64 and then outlines the daily life and customs of the Chinese people.

Reviewed in Ann Am Acad 44:177 Nov 1912; Sat R 112:496 Oct 14 1911; Spec 107 sup 521 Oct 7 1911.

Ollone, Henri Marie Gustave. Vicomte D'ollone, In Forbidden China. Boston, Small Maynard & Company 1912. 318p. ,1 1. front plates, ports. , fold. map. 23.5cm.

"A narrative of Ollone mission 1906-09 undertaken for the purpose of solving the problem of the origin and affiliation of the powerful non Chinese peoples in the highlands of southern and western China, and also on the western and northern borders. The outcome of the mission is recorded in 11 volumes, published by the order of the French parliament. This volume contains only a record of the journey, its joys and hardships, adventures and hairbreadth escapes. Good illustrations accompany text with index. " Bk R D 1912. The style is vivid but its research value is lessened by the extreme condensation.

Reviewed in Ath 2:136 Aug 29 1912; Ind 73:726 Sept 26 1913; Na 94:190 Aug 29 1912.

* Richard, Timothy. Forty-Five Years in China: Reminiscences; N. Y. , Frederick A. Stokes Company, 1916. 384p. front. , plates. ports. , facsim. 22.5cm.

A wonderful book relates both material and spiritual development of China during the past half century. Not only it gives you the trouble history of that country as large as the whole of Europe but also brings to the light about the menace of Japanese policy in the Far East.

Reviewed in Bost Trans p3 Nov 22 1916; The Times London lit Sup p478 Oct 1916.

Roe, A. S. China As I Saw It, A Woman's Letters from the Celestial Empire. London, Hutchinson & Co. ,1910. vii 2 330,2p. front. , plates. 21.5cm.

An interesting book of a traveler's first impression on China. Those impressions always pale on closer acquaintance of the social conditions. He places traveled by the aut or are usually called the northern part of China. It can only be taken as a book of vivid but colored descriptions.

Reviewed in Ann A, Acad 36:460 Sep 1910; Spec 104:680 Apr 23 1910.

Ronaldshay, Lawerence John Lumley Dundas. earl of. The Wandering Student in the Far East. In two vols. Edinburgh and London, W, Blackwood and sons, 1908. 2v. front. , plates, ports, map. 21cm.

These two volumes are written with a definite purpose of finding the clues to the future development in China and Japan. The main points emphasized are mercantile, industrial and the British interests in the Far East.

Reviewed in Ath 2:677 Nov 28 1908; Sat R 106:793 Dec 26 1908; Spec 101:944 Dec 5 1908.

Scidmore, Eliza Ruhamah. China, the Long-lived Empire. N. Y. Century 1911. 466p. incl front. illus. pl. ports. 21cm.

This volume is a collection of descriptions of metropolitan cities, the Empress Dowager,

Tsze Hsi, Great wall, Tsungli Women and other interesting topics. The style is readable and delightful.

Reviewed in Acad 59:68 July 28 190; Dial 29:71 Aug 1 1900.

Thomson, John Stuart. The Chinese, Indianapolis, The Bobbs-Merrill Company 1909 5p. 1. ,441p. front. , plates, ports, maps. 22cm.

Some of the chapters dealing with antiquity, daily life, religions and superstitions are very picturesque and delightful. A book enlivened with incidents and anecdotes.

Reviewed in A L A Bkl 6:86 Nov 1909; Dial 47:456 Dec 1 1909; R of Rs 40:512 Oct 1909.

Yule Sir Henry. Cathay and the way thither. London. Printed for the Hakluyt Society, 1913-16. 4v fronts. (v. 1-2; v. 1 port.)illus. , pl. , maps(part fold.)23cm.

"I have not to praise a work which has been for a long time the vade-mecum of all those engaged in the study of the Far East in Ancient and Middle ages. All agree in considering it as the indispensable guide of all those interested in the historical geography not only in China, not only Central Asia, but also of Asia at large. "H. Cordier.

Reviewed in Ath 146:478 Dec 25 1915.

MANCHURIA

* Christie Dugald. Thirty Years in Moukden…Ed. By his wife. ,London. Constable and Co. Ltd. , 1913. xiv p. ,11. ,303p. front. ,plates. ,ports. ,fold,map. ,fold. plam. 22. 5cm.

"Dr. Christie's many adventures have given him material for thirty chapters of interesting sketches of men,places and things in and around Moukden that are either new to the American readers or presented from a new viewpoint."F. L. W.

Reviewed in Ath 2:225 Aug 29 1914; Dial 58:20 Jan 1 1915; Sat R 117:711 May 1914.

Hosie,Sir Alexander…Manchuria. Boston and Tokyo. J. R. Millet company ᶜ1910. x,320p. incl col front. plates. 25cm.

A very detailed account is devoted to describe the physical features of the country,the agricultural and mineral products and the people with their special industries. A very entertaining description also given to the author's journeys from New Chwang to Kirin and thru Siberia in 1900. A discussion death with the conditions of the Russo-Japanese War. Treatment is impartial besides 30 excellent photogravures.

Reviewed in Na 79:36 July 14 1904.

Kemp,Miss E. G. The Face of Manchuria,Korea & Russian,Turkestan…Lond. Chatto & Windus, 1910. xv,274,1p,xxiv pl. (part col,,incl. front)fold. map. 24cm.

This guide book describes a four months journey along the trans-Siberian lines and connecting lines into Korea. The author was in the"Hermit Kingdom",before the annexation by Japan. Those chapters on Manchuria are also very interesting. The whole attitude of the book is somewhat marred by English prejudice.

Reviewed in Ind 70:524 Mar 9 1911; Lit D 42:636 Apr 1 1911; Spec 106:63 Jan 14 1911.

Tisdale,Alice. Pioneering Where the World is Old. N. Y. H. Holt & Co. 1917. xvi,227p. front. plates. 20cm.

The accounts of the primitive living and the wretched condition of the people in Manchuria are interesting and humorous. Traveling in a mule cart and Northern China. The authoress features Northern China and gives vivid pictures of a strange race without sacrificing much accuracy. The author accompanied her husband,a business man in his travels in Manchuria,and she is possessed with a love of adventure.

Reviewed in Ind 93:372 Mar 2 1918;Na 106:20 Jan 3 1918;R of Rs 57:219 Feb 1918.

MONGOLIA

Carruthers, Alexander Douglas Mitchell. Unknown Mongolia…Lond. Huchinson & Co., 1913. 2v. front., illus., plates(part fold) maps(part fold) 24.5cm. Paged continously. Bibliography: v. 2, p. 635-639.

A record of exploration and journey thru Mongolia to Kumul, ending with a survey of Karlik Tagh and Barkul mountains. Those two volumes are of great interest and value to geographer, traveler, ethnologist, hunters and the student of Chinese-Russian questions.

Reviewed in Ath 1:188 Feb 7 1914; Dial 57:142 Sep 1 1914; Spec 112:21 Jan 3 1914.

Curtin, Jeremiah. The Mongols. Boston, Little, Brown and Co. 1908 1907 xxvi, 426p. front. (port.) map. 23.5cm.

"Notwithstanding the imperfections of this work…It puts before the public the outlines, at least, of an epic of such wonderful interest and which is so little known to us, that we must be thankful that it has seen the light." W. W. Rockhill.

Reviewed in Am Hist R 13:562 Apr 1908; Dial 44:178 Mar 16 1908; Ind 65:789 Oct 1 1908.

Curtin, Jeremiah. The Mongols in Russia. Boston, Little Brown and Co. 1908. xx, 481p. front., fold. map. 23.5cm.

A companion volume to Mr. Curtin's "The Mongols, a history". It is a detailed history of the Mongols in Russia from the Mongol invasion down to the break up of the Golden Horde at Sarai in 1505.

Reviewed in Lit D 37:850 Dec 5 1908; N Y T 13:669 Nov 14 1908.

* Hedley, John. Tramps in dark Mongolia. N. Y. C. Scribner's sons; 1910. xii, 371, 1p. front., plates. ports., fold, map. 23cm.

"Mr. Hedley is evidently a born traveler, and he was well chosen in his mission authorities to carry a knowledge of the Gospel into the remote districts of eastern Mongolia. In the volume before us he describes his experience in three division, two being narratives of his adventures as a colporteur and the third and most important relating to his work as a pioneer in an untrodden territory." Ath May 1910.

Reviewed in Ath 1:677 May 28 1910; N Y T 15:583 Oct 22 1910.

Perry-Ayscough, Henry George Charles. With the Russians in Mongolia. by H. G. C. Perry-ayscough and R. B. Otter-Barry; with a preface by sir Claude macDonald. Lond. Lane 1913 344p. pl., map. 22.5cm.

Records of the personal experiences of two British travellers who visited Mongolia at different periods. One before the Chinese revolution and the other after China had become a republic. The special value of this book is the clear analysis of the present political situation in Mongolia.

Reviewed in Ath 1:335 Mar 7 1914; Dial 57:142 Sep 1,1914; Spec 112:351 Feb 28 1914.

TIBET

Candler, Edmund. The Unveiling of Lhasa. London, E. Arnold, 1905. xvi, 304p. Col. front., plates, fold. map. 23.5cm.

    More journalistic in style and less authoritative than London's Opening of Tibet; but the author's clear-cut sketches describing the every-day life the Tibetans are very valuable.

    Reviewed in Ath 1:147 Feb 4, 1905; Bookm 21:305 May 1905; Na 80:273 Apr 6 1905; Spec 94:178 Feb 4 1905.

* Fergusson, W. N. Adventure, Sport and Travel on the Tibetan Steppes. With illustrations from photographs by author and the late Lieut. Brooke. Lond. Constable and Co. Ltd. 1911. xvi, 343, 1p. front., illus., plates, ports., fold maps. 25cm.

    This book gives a great deal of material valuable to any traveller who attempts to see the western China and eastern Tibet. The atmosphere of the book is full of interest and animation.

    Reviewed in Ath 1:476 Apr 29 1911; Na 93:245 Sep 14 1911; Spec 106:739 May 13 1911.

Hedin, Sven Anders. Central Asia and Tibet towards the Holy City of Lassa. London, Hurst and Blackett, Ltd. N. Y. C. Scribner's sons, 1903. 2v. fronts. illus., plates. fold, maps. 24.5cm.

    A record of journeys in 1899-1901 in Central Asia and Tibet. The style is clear and simple. The atmosphere of the book is full of human interests.

    Reviewed in Dial 36:194 Mar 16 1904; Na 78:112 Feb 11 1904; Spec 92:156 Jan 30 1904.

* Hedin, Sven Anders. Trans-Himalaya. Lond., Macmillan & Co. Ltd. 1909-13. 3v. front., plates. ports., maps. 23cm.

    Volume 1 and 2 of Mr. Hedin's Trans-Himalaya were published in 1909. The third volume in uniform size with proceeding ones was published in 1913. This set is a monumental work for the scientific explorer, geographer and ethnologist as well as the adventurer and commonplace traveler. Illustration and maps are good.

    Reviewed in Ath 1:675 June 21 1913; Dial 55:118 Aug 16 1913; Sat R 116:145 Aug 2 1913; Spec 111:353 Sep 6 1913.

* Holdich, Sir Thomas Hungerford. Tibet, the Mysterious. N. Y. F. A. Stokes Co. 1906. xiip., 1l., 356p. front., plates., ports., maps. 22.5cm.

    "The immediate interest in the Tibetan situation is sufficiently acute to demand a handbook which will serve both as an introduction and a summary of the various expeditions and travels, and of the geographical and political features of that well-night impregnable land ... Colonial Holdich has made an exhaustive investigation of all the literature relating to that country and has summarized his studies in an accurate and systematic manner." Dial Jan 1907.

 Reviewed in Ath 1:55 Jan 12 1907;Dial 42:44 Jan 16 1907;Na 84:15 July 4 1907;R of Rs 35:384 Mar 1907.

Landon,Perceval. The Opening of Tibet. N. Y. Doubleday Page & Co,1905. xv,484p. col. front. , 48pl. 26.5cm.

 The special correspondent of the London Times has told the story of the English expedition to Tibet 1903-04 with enthusiasms and the descriptions of customs, religion and scenery is fascinating. His style is singularly attractive. The book is profusely illustrated with reproductions of photographs, sketches and maps. Published in England in 2 volumes under the title "Lhasa".

 Reviewed in Ath 1:231 Feb 25 1905; Bookm 21:305 May 1905; Na 80:273 Apr 6 1908.

Landor,Arnold Henry savage. An Explorer's Adventures in Tibet. N. Y. And Lond. Harper & brothers,1910. vii,1p.,L 1.,275,1p. front. (ports.)plates. 21cm.

 It is an abridgment of the author's "Forbidden Land". The sensational atmosphere of author's reckless but plucky and endurable attempt to reach. Lhasa is interesting for the reader who loves a tale of thrilling adventure.

 Reviewed in Ind 89:707 Sep 28 1910;Na 90:652 June 30 1910.

Rawling,Captain cecil Godfrey. The Great Plateau;being an account of explorations in central Tibet,1903 and of the Gartok expedition 1904-1905. N. Y. Longmans,1905. 324p. pl. maps. 23.5cm.

 "An excellent record of two remarkable expedition, one in company with his friend captain Hargreaves to central Tibet in 1903…The other thru eastern Tibet after the British Indian force had occupied Lhasa. The first journey was undertaken at a time when Tibet was rigidly closed to foreigners; the second was rendered possible by the success of the Young husband mission." Sat R Jan 1906.

 Reviewed in Ath 1:18 Jan 1906;Dial 40:35 Apr 1 1906;Sat R 101:23 Jan 6 1906;Spec 46:503 Mar 31 1906.

Rijnhart,Mrs. Susie Carson. With the Tibetans in Tent and Temple. Edinburgh,Oliphant,Anderson & Ferrier,1901 6P. 1.,9 406p. front.,plates,ports.,fold. map. 20.5cm.

 An interesting narrative of four years' residence of a medical missionary in the interior of the "Forbidden land". The description of the journey is very entertaining.

Reviewed in Na 73:116 Aug 8 1901; Spec 89:299 Aug 30 1902.

* Waddell Laurence Austine. Lhasa and Its Mysteries, with a Record of the Expedition of 1903-04. London. Murray 1905. xxii, 530p. 11. col. front illus., plates, ports., maps, plans, facsim. 24cm.

The author subordinates the report of the expedition of 1903-1904 to its scientific results and to an authoritative study of the Tibetans and their religion. Contains about 200 illustrations and maps.

Reviewed in Ath 1:123 Apr 8 1905; Na 80:484 June 15 1905; Spec 95:320 Sep 2 1905.

TURKESTAN

Church, Percy William Palmer. Chinese Turkestan, with Caravan and Rifle. Lond. Rivingtons, 1901. xi,1 207p. front,plates,fold map. 23cm.

"Accounts of an interesting journey in 1898 and of hunting the great stag of the Tien Sgan from the attractive story and history of this unknown region. The descriptions of life and history of the people and the trade of China and Russia are also very vivid and entertaining."

Reviewed in Ath 119:176 Feb 8 1902; Na 73:435 Dec 6 1901; Spec 87:882 Sup Dec 7 1901.

* Curtis, William Eleroy. Turkestan: "the heart of Aisa.". N. Y. Hodder & Stoughton, Geo. H. Doran Co. 1911 5p. 1. ,3-334p. front. plates, ports. fold. map. 21.5cm.

"Much of the book is, of course, devoted to ancient Turkestan, to Tamerlane and his times; but its real value lies in the account of present conditions along the line of Mr. Curtis's travels. The excellent illustrations are from photographs by Mr. John T. McCutcheon." Dial Aug 1911.

Reviewed in Dial 51:108 Aug 16 1911; Na 93:345 Oct 12 1911; R of Rs 44:255 Aug 1911.

Stein, Mark Aurel. Ancient Khotan: Detailed Report of Archaeological Explorations in Chinese Turkestan, carried out and described under the orders of H. M. Indian government. Oxford Clarendon Press, 1907. 2v. illus., 153pl. (part. col,; incl. plans. facsims.) fold. map in pocket. 32cm.

From the Russian explorer. (Pjewtsow Prehevalski) and the Swedish traveler Sven Hedin, the scientific world begins to pay attention to the very rich field of archaeological research in that very little known dependency of China. De Stein's present work is very valuable in the archaeological point of view and by this work many collections of the forged central Asiatic antiquities in London, Paris, St Petersburg have been exposed. The maps illustrations, photographs and plates in those two volumes are also beyond praise. The tutor contributes a great value to the knowledge of the scientific world.

Reviewed in Na 86:332 Apr 9 1908; Spec 132:134 Aug 1 1908.

* Stein, Mark Aurel. Ruin of Desert Cathay. Lond. , Macmillan & Co. , Ltd 1912. 2v. col. fronts. , plates, ports. , maps. 24.5cm.

Dr. Stein's archaeological and geographical explorations in Central Asia, the Kun Lun range, the plateau of Tibet and other inaccessible regions between 1906 and 1908 contribute a great value to the scientific researches and a fascinating and informative work for traveler. The illustrations in those two volumes are excellent.

Reviewed in Am Hist R 18:113 Oct 1912; Ath 1:159 Feb 10 1912.

BIOGRAPHY

Allan, C Wilfrid. The Makers of Cathay. Shanghai, Presbyterian Mission Press, 1909. 1p. 1. , iip. , 1 1. , 242. v. p. 2pl. 22cm.

　　A volunteer of collective biographies of distinguished Chinese philosophers, moral reformers, poets, generals, emperors. Etc. For the past 40 centuries. An interesting book for general readers.

Beach, Harlan Page. Princely Men in the Heavenly Kingdom. Boston and Chicago, United society of Christian endeavor. 1903. 244p. incl. front. plates. ports. , fold. map. 19cm.

　　The author formerly a missionary in China, a member of the American Oriental society and educational secretary of the student volunteer movement for foreign missions. This is a very good collective biographies for any one who wishes to know the Protestant pioneers and the martyrs of 1900 in China.

Burton, Margaret Ernestine. Notable Women of Modern China. N, Y. , Chic. , Fleming H. Revell Co. , 1912. 271p. front. plates, ports. 21cm.

　　"The author's previous work on the general topic of women's education in China gains widespread interest. This volume of biographies should be welcomed even more, for it has that living appeal which the study of personality alone gives. "Bost Tran Dec 1912.

　　Reviewed in Bost Trans p18 Dec 24 1912; Dial 54:102 Feb 1 1913; N Y T 17:700 Dec 1 1912.

Virgil C. Hart. Missionary Statesman, Founder of the American and Canadian Missions in Central and West China. N. Y. Doran 1917. 334p. port. pl. 19. 5cm.

　　Foreword by F. C. Stephenson who says, "Two great missions in China of which Dr. V. C. Hart was the founder, testify to the comprehensive insight he had of China's needs, his recognition of her potential powers, and his appreciation of the forces which would free her from her age long stagnation and life her into new life and influence. "

　　Reviewed in Bib W 50:375 Dec 1917; R of Rs 55:667 June 1917.

Thompson, Ralph Wardlaw. Griffith John: The Story of Fifty Years in China. N. Y. A. C. Armstrong and son, 1906. xvi, 544p. front. , plates, ports. 22. 5cm.

　　"This book is one of the best ever written for its frank portrayal of the ups and downs of a great missionary's aggressive work and his countless hope for China. "Ind Oct 1907.

　　Reviewed in Ind 63:942 Oct 17 1909; Outk 85:524 Mar 2 1907.

* Bland, John Otway Percy. Li Hung-Chang. Lond. Constable & Co. Ltd. , 1917. vi p. , ll. , 327p. (front. port). 23cm. (Makers of the nineteenth century.) "Bibliographic note. " p. 313-314.

"This present volume by Mr. Bland may, however, be regard as authoritative. The author has had ample opportunities to know China in general and Li Hung-Chang in particular. He has written an admirable biography, one which should be in every public library and in the hands of all students of China and of international affairs. " Mis R Feb 1918.

Reviewed in Ch S M 13345 Apr 1908.

Little, Alicia Helen Neva(Bwicks). "Mrs. Archibald Little. "Li Hung-Chang; His Life and Times. Lond. , Paris, N. Y. And Melbourne. Cassell & Co. Ltd. , 1903. 1p. l. , viii, 356p. 5 port(incl. front.)fold. map. 22cm.

In this biography of the distinguished Chinese statesman Mrs. Little practically gives us a history of China from 1851, outbreak of the Taiping rebellion to 1901, the European occupation of Peking. She has an intimate knowledge of Chinese life and character and it is a very entertaining biography.

Reviewed in Ath 122:650 Nov 14 1903; Cont R 85:149 Jan 1904; Spec 92:161 Jan 30 1904.

William Francis Mannix. Memoirs of Li Hung Chang. ed. By Wm Francis Mannis, with an introduction by Hon John W. Foster, Huston and New York, Houghton Mifflin Co. 1913. xxvii, 298p. , ll. front. (port. group)22. 5cm.

"It was a fascinating volume which we read and reread with keen interest; but also, it was declared to be a literary fraud. A man who could manufacture such a book must have remarkable gifts even the veracity is not one of them. " Mis R 41:160 Feb 1918.

Brown, Colin Campbell. A Chinese St. Francis, or, the Life of Brother Mao. Lond. New York, Hodder and Stoughton 1911 xv, 264p, front. , plates, ports. 20cm.

This biography of the little Chinese shoemaker is related with force and sympathy. Mr. Brown has taken great pains to gather the facts of Mao's career and ministry from his(Mao's) friends and relatives. The life is interesting drawn in detail and it is an inspiring book for missionaries.

Reviewed in Mis R 36:209 Mar 1913.

Cantlie, James; Jones, C Sheridan. Sun Yat Sen and the Awakening of China. N. Y. , Chicago etc. Fleming H. Revell Co 1912 252p. front. illus. maps, facsims, plates, ports, map. 20. 5cm.

The first seven chapters are full of interesting facts about Dr. Sun's life and his revolutionary works, and the rest of the book dealing with Chinese current topics has nothing specially striking.

Reviewed in Ind 73:793 Oct 3 1912;Lit D 45:728 Oct 26 1912;Spec 108:1051 June 24 1912.

* Bland,John Otway Percy. China Under the Empress Dowager: Being the History of the Life and Times of Tzu Hsi, Compiled From state Papers of the Comptroller of Her Household, by J. O. P. Bland and E. Backhouse. New and Rev, Cheaper ed. Illus. Boston and N. Y., Houghton Mifflin Co.,1914. xxvi,322p. front. plates,ports,map. 22.5cm.

"Some of the document have never before been published and the whole book in its sound learning, lack of bias and wealth of information, is a revelation of the empress' personality and of Chinese diplomacy." A. L. A. Bkl Jan 1911.

Reviewed in Ath 1:9 Jan 7 1911;Dial 49:518 Dec 6 1910;Na 92:214 Mar 2 1911.

Carl,Katharine Augusta. With the Empress Dowager. N. Y. The Century Co., 1905. xxv,306p. front.,plates,ports. 21.5cm.

Chatty records of impressions and experiences at the Chinese court during 11 months' resident as the Empress' portrait painter. Delightful book for general readers.

Reviewed in Crit 47:573 Dec 1905;Dial 39:379 Dec 1 1905;Ind 59:1378 Dec 14 1905.

Sergeant,Philip Walsingham. The Great Empress Dowager of China. London. Hutchinson & Co., 1910. xii,344p. front.,plates,ports. 22.5cm.

"The portrait which the author gives us of the Empress dowager is exceptionally just and fair considering the circumstances. Mr. Sergeant's book has the neither intimate charm nor historic value of a few books which have already publishes Miss Carl's, or Mrs. Conger's 'Letters from China', for examples. And it may be added that the empress dowager of the two American ladies Books is a much truer portrait of Her Majesty than Mr. Sergeant's. With all, Mr. Sergeant' book is valuable as a fair story of China in the days of her transition." R of Rs Dec 1911.

Reviewed in Na 94:638 June 27 1912;R of Rs 44:724 Dec 1911.

* Yung Wing. My Life in China and America. N. Y., H. Holt and Company, 1909. 2p. 1,iii-vi, 286p. front. (port.)24.5cm.

Dr. Yung was the first Chinese student in the United States and the first to introduce the American educational methods to China. This autobiography is modestly and singularly told and the style is written in Excellent in English. Dr. Yung's step now followed by hundreds of young Chinese students who are all anxious to come to this free land for quenching their thirst for knowledge and for acquiring the truth spirit of democracy.

Reviewed in Ann Am Acad 35:734 May 1910;Dial 48:154 Mar 1 1910;Na 90:508 May 19 1910;Yale R 19:192 Aug 1910.

HISTORY

* E. Backhouse and J. O. P. Bland. Annals & Memoirs of the Court of Peking (From the 16th to the 20th Century). Boston and N. Y., Houghton Mifflin Company, 1914.

x, 531, 1p. front., plates, ports. 25.5cm.

"The present volume includes four centuries of Chinese history written for the most part by contemporaries. Annals and memoirs have been carefully scrutinized, and these that have historical significance have been embodied in this work in chronological order. The reader thus gets his information from original documents, and he is kept in Chinese Atmosphere through his reading." Bost. Trans.

Reviewed in Am Hist R 19:906 July 1914; Am Pol Sci R 8:510 Aug 1914; Ath 2: sup 197 Oct 11 1913; Dial 56:425 May 16 1914.

Chang Chih-tung. China's Only Hope: An Appeal by Her Greatest Viceroy, With the Sanction of the Present Emperor, Kwang Su; N. Y., Chic., F. J. Revell Co., 1900. 2p, 1., 151p. front. (port.) 19.5cm.

Viceroy Chang is a scholar of first magnitude in the late Manchu regime. After the Chine-Japanese war he strongly advocates reform and free intercourse with the western nations. In short he is a grand scholar and broadminded statesman.

Reviewed in Na 71:390 Nov 15 1900; Spec 86:949 Sup June 1901.

Colquhoun, Archibald Ross. China in Transformation. N. Y. and London, Harper and Brothers, 1912. v, 1p., 1 l., 302, 1 P. maps. 21cm.

"A revision and enlargement of the edition that made its appearance in 1897. The author styles it a new 'China in transformation' so thoroughly has the old matter been worked over and so judiciously has new matter been added to make the whole embody the progress of the past 14 years." Bk R D 1912.

Reviewed in Ind 73:727 Sep 26 1912; Na 95:216 Sep 5 1912; Outk 101:132 May 18 1912.

* Conger, Sarah (Pike) "Mrs. E. H. Conger". Letters from China, With Particular Reference to the Empress Dowager and the Women of China. Chicago, A. C. McClurg & Co., 1909.

"Fully as valuable as Mrs. Fraser's 'Letters from Japan' are Mrs. Conger's 'Letters from China'. Her richly illustrated and well indexed book is vivid and fascinating and as a whole is likely to hold its own as a permanent contribution to our knowledge, not only of China, but of the less known half of it, the Chinese woman." Na 1909. It covers the period 1898-1908. With particular references to the Empress Dowager and the women of China.

  Reviewed in Bookm 30:59 Sep 1909; Dial 46:254 Apr 16 1909; Na 88:633 June 24 1909.

* Giles, Herbert Allen. China and the Manchus. Cambridge, Eng. The University Press; New York, G. P. Putnam's Sons, 1912. vii, 148p. front. , pl. , map. 17cm.

  "Mr. Giles has succeeded in sketching the career of the Manchu conguerors with a picturesqueness and clearness which gives to the study a certain fascination, notwithstanding the brevity of the statement."Winston. A systematic and well written history of the Ching dynasty.

  Reviewed in Am Hist R 18:432 Jan 1913; Ann Am Acad 47:301 May 1913; Ath 2:443 Oct 19 1912; Educ R 46:94 June 1913.

Gowen, Herbert Henry. An Outline History of China. Bost. , Sher, man, French & Company, 1917. lp. l. , iv p. , 3 l. , 402p. front. , plates, ports. 21cm.

  Mr. Gowen's purpose is to supply the students of oriental history through knowledge of the four millenniums prior to the Manchu occupation. The dates in the text do not exactly agree with those in the dynastic tables. Burdened with too much detail and too many proper names for the student unfamiliar with Chinese history.

  Reviewed in Dial 54:387 May 1 1913; Educ R 46:310 Oct 1913; Na 96:366 Apr 10 1913.

Griffis, William Elliot. China's Story in Myth, Legend, Art and Annals. Boston and New York, Houghtom, Mifflin Co. , 1911. xii, p. , 1 l. , 302p. , 1 l. front, plates, ports. 19cm.

  A very condensed and elementary sketch of the Chinese history. Suitable for young people who want to know something about Chinese history.

  Reviewed in A L A Bkl 7:378 May 1911; Dial 50:481 June 16 1911; Na 9:575 Dec 14 1911.

Hart sir Robert, lst vart. "These from the land of Sinim"; Essays on the Chinese Question. London, Chapman & Hall Ltd. 1901. 4p. l. , 254p. 22.5cm.

  Series of essay on different phases of the Chinese questions, the Peking legations, China and her foreign trade, China and reconstruction, the Boxers 1900, etc. The author was the inspector-general of the Imperial maritime customs. The picture mainly represent the standpoint of Peking.

  Reviewed in Ath117:523 Apr 27 1901.

Hirth, Friedrich. The Ancient History of China to the End of the Chou Dynasty. N. Y. The Columbia University Press, 1908. xx, 383p. map. 20.5cm.

Dr. Hirth begins with a chapter on the mythological and legendary period and comes down to the 3rd century B. C. It is an excellent text of ancient history of China for students and a useful book of reference for general readers.

Reviewed in Am Hist R 13:675 Apr 1908;Na 87:138 Aug 13 1908;R of Rs 37:509 Apr 1908.

* Latourette, Kenneth Scott. The Development of China. Boston and N. Y. Houghton Mifflin Co., 1917. xi,lp.,1 l.,273,1 p. l l. front(double map)21cm.

"The characteristic feature of this book is successful condensation...The book is well written, well printed and should prove very valuable for the purpose for which it is intended. It bring together with brief compass a variety of essential information which will greatly facilitate the work of classes in oriental history and contemporary politics."S. K. Horback.

Reviewed in Am Hist R 22:857 July 1917;Dial 62:524 June 14 1917;Na 104:681 June 8 1917;Sur 38:360 July 21 1917.

Li Ung Bing. Outlines of Chinese History. Shanghai The Commercial Press,Limited 1914. 4p. l.,iii l 644,xxx p. front.,illus.,maps. 22. 5cm.

This is in English and is edited by a foreigner. Systematically arranged and very valuable for reference use. Illustrations and maps are also very good.

Martin,william alexander parsons. The Awakening of China. N. Y. Doubleday,Pahe & Co.,1907. xvi,328p. front. plates,ports. 26. 5cm.

It is a very valuable and comprehensive column of Chinese affairs. Judging from the author's clear discussions Dr. Martin was certainly the leading authority on things Chinese. But the reference use of this volume is cheapened by a hopeless index.

Reviewed in Ath 2:439 Oct 12 1907;N Y T 12:440 July 1 Re 1907;Spec 99:743 Nov 16 1907.

Parker,Edward Harper. Ancient China Simplified. London,Chapman & Hall,Ltd.,1908. xxxi, 332p. front.,port. Maps. facsim. 23cm.

This book has clear conceptions of China's civilization government, social customs, law, literature and religious conditions as far back as 872 B. C. Its arrangement is very helpful to the English speaking public. The chapters are brief and the Chinese names are gradually introduced.

Reviewed in Ath 1:39 Jan 9 1909;Eng Hist R 24:107 Jan 1909;Na 88:252 Mar 11 1909;Outk 90:967 Dec 1908.

* Parker,Edward Harper. China,Her History,Diplomacy,and Commerce from the Earliest Times to the Present Day. Lond.,J. Murray,1901. xx,332p. front. 19maps. 21cm.

Professor Parker of the Victoria University of Manchester has added three chapters to his remar kable volume 'China', first published in 1901. The last chapter contains valuable information regarding the rise of the republic besides many clear maps which are of great help to the inquiry readers of the Eastern affairs.

Reviewed in Ath p474 Sep 1917; The Times(Lond.)lit Sup 1483 Oct 11 1917.

Pott, Francis Lister Hawks. A Sketch of Chinese History. Shanghai, Kelly & Walsk, Ltd., 1903. x p., 1 l., 206p. fold maps. 21cm. Rev. Ed. 1915.

This is probably one of the best and most comprehensive Chinese history. The author has a very clear back-ground of the historical knowledge of China. The political events of the late Manchu dynasty are fully discussed. But too many Chinese names for the foreigners unfamiliar with Chinese history.

Reviewed in Bk R D 1905.

Simpson, Bertram Lenox. Manchu and Muscovite. London, N. Y., Macmillan and Co., Ltd 1904. xx 552p. front., plates. maps, 23cm.

This was a timely book published just at the moment of the outbreak of the Russo-Japanese war. The author is the authority on the questions of the Far East. The author books is interesting to those who wish to understand the true position of Russia in Manchuria at the moment of the out-break of the Russo-Japanese war. It is a popular survey which strongly condemns Russian policy.

Reviewed in Cont R 86:299 Aug 1904; Crit 45:478 N 1904; Na 79:140 Apr 18 1904; Spec 93:225 Aug 13 1904.

INTERNATIONAL RELATIONS

Blakeslee, George Hubbard. Ed. China and the Far East. N. Y. T. Y. Crowell and Co. 1910. 2p. 1., iii-xxii, 455p. 21.5cm. (Clark University lectures).

 Twenty-two lectures delivered by different men of experience and authority as addresses during the second decennial celebration of the founding of Clark University. They mainly deal with the conditions in China, Japan and Korea and with the relations of these countries to various nations. The use of the book is lessened by lack of an index.

 Reviewed in Ann Am Acad 36:230 July 1910; Educ R 40:426 Nov 1910; Na 90:510 May 19 1910.

Eames, James Bromley. The English in China. Lond. Sir I. Pitman and Sons, Ltd. 1909. xi, 622p. 7 pl. maps. 22Cm,

 A history of commercial intercourse between England and China from 1600-1843. The author ends by appealing the Englishmen to make amends for many acts of injustice towards China by supporting her to suppress the opium trade.

 Reviewed in Ath 134:264 Sept 4 1909.

Herslet, Sir Edward. Hertslet's China Treaties. Lond., Printed for H. M. Stationery off., by Harrison and Sons., 1908 2v. fold. maps, plam. 24.5cm.

 These two volume work of China treaties recently revised under the supervision of the Foreign office library by G. E. P. Hertslet and E. Parkes. The first volume contains the treaties and the Acts of Parliament and Orders in Council which affect the position of British subjects in China.

 Reviewed in Ath 132:69 July 18 1908.

Holcombe, Chester. China's Past & Future...Britain's Son & Folly, by B. Broomhall. Lond., Morgan & Scott, 1904. xxii, 198p. front., plates. parts., maps. 20cm.

 The author's view in regard to opium dealing of the British government is quite frank and the description of the Chinese misery and other social and international topics are quite interesting. The style is attractive and animated.

 Reviewed in Na 72:98 Jan 31 1901.

* Hornbeck Stanley Kuhl. Contemporary Politics in the Far East. N. Y. Appleton and Co., 1916. xii, B 466p. map. 22.5cm.

 "Professor S. K. Hornbeck has given us a really valuable study in the field of Far Eastern politics. He has rarely permitted his feeling to affect his judgment. For the period it covers his book will win a place as a sound and useful work of reference. "P. J. Treat.

Reviewed in Am Hist R 22:654 Apr 1917;Ch S M 13:173 Jan 1918;Na 104:681 June 7 1917 Yale R n. s. 6:661 Apr 1917.

Jones,Jefferson. The Fall of Tsingtau, With a Study of Japan's Ambitions in China. Boston & N. Y. , Houghton Mifflin Co. ,1915. xvii,1 214 ,2 p. front. (port). plates. 21cm.

"The Japan's part in the seizure of the German protectorate of Kiaochow was essentially a blind move in the making over of the Gelestial kingdom into a dependency of Japan, cannot be doubted by any one who follows closely the moves of the Tokyo government from the opening of the European war until China, after much harassing acceded to the demands of Japan in May. "writes the author in his preface. This is a first hand record of events at the fall of Tsingtau. Unusually clear and logical exposition of the point of views.

Reviewed in Dial 60:82 Jan 20 1916;R of Rs 52:754 Dec 1915.

* Koo,Vi Kyuin wellington. The Status of Aliens in China. N. Y. 1912. 2p. 1. ,7-361p. 25cm.

"This is a study of the relations between foreigners in China and the Chinese government…The first division of the book comprises the history of the entrance of foreigners into China, their privileges and protection, and of their subjugation to the Chinese criminal jurisdiction while in the second part are mentioned the origin of the extraterritorial jurisdiction in China, its extent, its limitation, the privileges of foreign merchants in the interior, and of the Christian missionaries. " Ind Sep 26. 1912.

Reviewed in Am Ool Sci R 7:298 May 1913;Ath 1:545 May 17 1913;Eng Hist R 28: 61 July 1913;Na 96:288 Mar 20 1913.

Millard,Thomas Franklin Fairfaz. American and the Far Eastern Question. N. Y. , Moffat, Yard and Co. ,1909. xxii,576p. front. , plates, fold. maps. 23. 5cm.

Roughly this work may be divided into five sections: Japan's foreign relation and internal condition;Japan in Korea;Japan in Manchuria;China of today and American in the Philippine. Those appealing pages should be ready by all who are interested in the Far eastern politics. The 13 appendices greatly increase the usefulness of the book.

Reviewed in Ann Am Acad 34:296 July 1909;Ath 2:261 Nov. 20 1909;Dial 46:324 May 16 1909.

* Millard,Thomas Franklin Fairfax. Our Eastern Question: America's Contact with the Orient and the Trend of Relations with China and Japan. N. Y. , century 1916. 543p. front, port. Plates. maps. 21.5cm.

The author was the editors of China Press, Shanghai, for five years. The aim of this book is"to extract the more pertinent and significant matters from the tremendous and complex movement of political economical and sociological forces in the Orient, with intent expose their direction and controlling elements and tendencies and with special attention to America." Intro. The appendices which contain texts of all the treaties, notes, agreements, issued in connection with the events narrated are especially valuable.

Reviewed in Bost Trans p6 Aug 23 1916; Ind 88:30 Oct 2 1916; N Y T 21:367 Sep 17 1916.

* Morse, Hosea Ballou. The International Relations of the Chinese Empire. The Period of Conflict 1834-60. Lond, N. Y. , Langmans, Green, and Co. , 1910. xxxix, 727, lp, front. , plates, maps, diagr. 23cm.

A full and impartial record of events from the early Canton factory days down to the close of our last War with China in 1860. The author's effort is to give an original authority or reference for every statement made and this object has been completely carried out. Its arrangement and references are very suitable for reference purposes.

Reviewed in Eng Hist R 26:610 July 1911; Na 93:263 Sep 21 1911; Sat R 111:304 Mar 11 1911.

* Reinsch, Paul Samuel. Intellectual and Political Currents in the Far East. Boston & N. Y. , Houghton Mifflin Co. 1911. viii p. 1 1. ,396p. ,1 l. 21cm.

"A valuable work for readers who desire not an object study of present conditions, but an unprejudiced examination. Of their underlying intellectual causes."A L A Bkl Mar 1912.

Reviewed in Am Pol Sci R 6:268 May 1912; Dial 52:87 Feb 1 1912; Lit D 44:830 Apr 20 1912; Na 95:104 Aug 1912.

Simpson, Bertram Lenox. The Coming Struggle in Eastern Asia. Lond. Macmillan and Co. , Ltd. 1908. xiv p. ,1 l. ,656p. incl tables. 16 pl. fold. map. diagrs. 23cm.

"Apart from his political argument the book is of value for the large amount of information it gives of the present condition and future prospects of Eastern Siberia and Manchuria and the financial and commercial statistics of Japan and China."Ind. Apr 1908.

The author believes that it is the military Japan which forms the new problems in Eastern Asia.

Reviewed in Ann Am Acad 32:466 Sep 1908; Dial 45:58 Aug 1 1908; Ind 64:748 Apr 1 1908.

* Simpson, Bertram Lenox. The Re-shaping of the Far East. N. Y. The Macmillan Co. , Lond. , Macmillan and Co. ,Ltd. 1905. 2v. fronts. plates, ports. 22.5cm.

"The author, combining the knowledge of the student with the knowledge of the man on the spot, present the Far eastern question exhaustively in almost every imaginable aspect. In spite of the manner in which the Russian debacle has upset some of his calculations his book is the most valuable of recent contributions to the education of Far eastern problems. "Lond. T. Dec 1905.

Reviewed in Ath 1:193 Feb 17 1906;Bookm 23:556 Aug 1906;Lond T 4:438 R of Rs 33:253 Feb 1906.

Simpson, Bertram Lenox. The Truce in the East and Its Aftermath. N. Y., Macmillan Co., Lond., Macmillan and Co., ltd. 1907. xv,647p. front.,15pl.,2 fold,maps,chart,fold tab. 22.5cm.

This admirable volume of Oriental politics resolves itself into three distinguished parts: Japan and the new position; China and the Chinese and the powers and their influence. Various documents concerning the political chapters are included in the appendices. The whole presentation indicates that the author possesses keen observation in combination with his thorough knowledge of the Eastern problems.

Reviewed in Ann Am Acad 30:189 July 1907; Ath 1:433 Apr 13 1907; R of Rs 35:636 May 1907.

Smith, Arthur Henderson. China and America Today: A Study of Conditions and Relations. New York, Chicago. F. H. Revell Co. 1907 256p 20cm.

"In the main the present volume is a discussion of China's relations, present and future, with the United States, in which an exceedingly interesting historical sketch is given, incidentally of the Chinese empire. "Lit D. Oct 1907.

Reviewed in Ind 63:842 Oct 17 1907; Lit D 35:490 Oct 5 1907; N Y T 12:499 July 20 1907.

Tyau, Min-chien Tuk Zung. The Legal Obligations Arising out of Treaty Relations between China and Other States. (Thesis approved for the degree of Doctor of Laws in the University of London) with prefaces by Sir John MacDonell and Hon. Wu ting-fang. Shanghai, Commercial Press,1917. 304p. 23.5cm.

Tyau, Min-Chien Tux Zung. Legal Obligations Cont'd.

This is the first attempt in its field to deal with the subject of China's relations or legal obligations arising out such conventional relations. As the author says " Not a few, indeed, have dealt with, in the form of a brochure or monograph, one or more of the topics discussed herein, but an all-embracing survey of China's treaty obligations in the light of present day world conditions is still lacking. "Very systematic in treatment and the appendices and the tables are very valuable for the students of world politics and international law.

Williams, Frederick Wells. Anson Burlingame and the First Chinese Mission to Foreign Powers. N. Y., C. Scribner's Sons,1912. x p.,2 1.,3-370 p. front. (port). 21.5cm.

In 1860 Anson Burlingame was appointed by President Lincoln as minister to China. After seven years he was accorded the unique distinction of being asked to return to his own country as a representative to it and to the other powers of the western world of the Chinese government. This is the story of the mission together with an account of Anson Burlingame.

Reviewed in Ind 73:1173 Nov 21 1912; Outk 102:381 Oct 26 1912; R of Rs 46635 Nov 1912.

BOXER UPRISING 1900

Chamberlain, Wilbur J. Ordered to China: letters of W. J. Chamberlain written from China while under commission from the N. Y. Sun during the Boxer Uprising of 1900 and the international complications which followed. N. Y. Stokes 1903 340p. 19cm.

"Probably no book thus far written gives from the inside such a vivid and truthful picture of Peking during the boiling of the diplomatic cauldron in 1900 and the petty squabbles for social and diplomatic procedure among the foreign diplomats."

Reviewed in Crit 44:95 Jan 1904; Na 77:347 Oct 29 1903; Spec 93:332 Sep 3 1904.

Clements, Paul Henry. The Boxer Rebellion: A Political and Diplomatic Review. N. Y., Columbia University 1915. 243p. 25cm.

"It might be urged by way of criticism that the author has paid too little attention to secondary accounts. The references are very complete. The bibliography is unusually will selected and satisfactory. The book is well indexed would that the same could be said of every such study. This monograph will be useful to students of modern history and contemporary politics, and it is to be hoped that its practical value and possible less to statement will not be overlooked." S. K. Hornbeck.

Reviewed in Am Hist R 21:501 Apr 1916; Na 102:143 Feb 3 1916.

Landor, Arnold Henry Savage. China and the Allies. N. Y. Charles Scribner's Sons, 1901. 2v front., illus., plates, maps, plans, 22cm.

"These two big volumes consist of the descriptions of the Boxer uprising and the story of the siege of Peking legations. The tone is critical as well as descriptive. It is a book of the irregular information about the Boxer Uprising and the author's judgments are rather hasty and colored."

Reviewed in Bookm 14:88 Sep 1901; Na 73:73 July 25 1901.

* Pott, Francis lister Hawks. The Outbreak in China: Its Causes. N. Y., J. Pott & Co., 1900. vi, 124p. fold map. 19.5cm.

A logical and calm inquiry into the causes of the Boxer uprising of 1900 and the anti-foreign movement at that time.

Reviewed in Dial 30:45 Jan 16 1901.

* Simpson, Bertram Lenox. Indiscreet Letter from Peking; Being the Notes of an Eye-witness, Which set forth in some detail, from day to day, the real story of the siege and sack of a distressed capital in 1900 the year of great tribulation; ed. by B. L. Putnam Weale pseud...N. Y. Dodd, Mead and company,1917. Vii. 447P, front. , maps. 21. 5cm.

The reader cannot help fell that the picturesque narrative is too highly colored and the real facts cannot have been so horrible. Nevertheless, this work is considered by many to give the very faithful account of the siege of the legations, as seen by the author in 1900.

Reviewed in Ath 1:635 May 25 1907; Na 84:570 June 20 1907; Spec 97:256 Feb 16 1907.

* Smith, Arthur Henderson. China in Convulsion. N. Y. Chicago, F. J. Revell Co. , 1901. 2v. fronts. , plates. ports, maps, fold. plans. 23cm.

"These who want reading for pleasure only must and will have Landon's 'China and the allies.' Those who would know just what did happen will read 'China in convulsion.' Dr. Smith is not only a narrator of events, but also a philosophic historian...of the 28 chapters in the two volumes thirteen are devoted to the causes of the trouble of 1900 ...The following 15 chapters, describing the siege of Peking." Na Dec 1901.

Reviewed in Na 73:480 Dec 19 1901; Spec 119:398 Mar 19 1902.

Thomson, H, C. China and the Powers: A Narrative of the Outbreak of 1900. London, N. Y. and Bombay, Langmans, Green, and Co. ,1902. xii,185p. front. ,plates, maps,23cm.

The author treats the event of the Boxer outbreak under three main lines, military operations, policies. Adopted by the various powers and position and the rights of the Christian missionaries in China. A lengthy description devoted to the capture of Tientsin.

Reviewed in Acad 62:360 Apr 1902; Ath 119:592; May 1920.

REVOLUTION 1911

* Blakeslee, George Hubbard. Recent Developments in China. N. Y. G. E. Stechert and Co., 1913. xi, 413p. 24cm.

　　Containing twenty-two addresses, they are written by representatives of the United States, England, China and Japan. All the contributors are authorities in their respective callings. In regard to the causes of the Chinese revolution and the present problems, it supplies a large amount of valuable information and clear insight of the satisfactory solution.

　　Reviewed in Am Pol Econ 22:910 Nov 1914.

Bland, John Otway Percy. Recent Events and Present Policies in China. Philadelphia, J. B. Lippincott Co., 1912. xi, 481p, 1p. front, plates, ports., 2fold map. 25cm.

　　Mr. Bland's career in China and remarkable power of writing on Eastern topics entitles his personal and partial views to respectful examinations. As Dr. Wannamaker remarks, 'Though possessing unusual value as a scholarly study, the discussion in too deeply tinged with pessimism to be convincing.' China's fate will be doomed, if the Chinese would follow the author's ideals for a despotic monarchy and for the insatiable Indian opium Vampires.

　　Reviewed in Ath 2:683 Dec 7 1912; Dial 54:138 Feb 16 1913; Na 96:179 Feb 20 1913; Spec 109:965 Dec 7 1912.

Brown, Arthur Judson. The Chinese Revolution. N. Y. Student volunteer movement 1912 x, 217p. front., plates, ports., fold, map. 19.5cm.

　　This volumes is an excellent review of the present conditions of China for general readers.

　　Reviewed in Ann Am Acad 44:145 Nov 1912; Lit D 45:683 Oct 19 1912; Na 95:331 Oct 10 1912.

Dingle, Edwin J. China's Revolution: 1911-1912. A Historical and Political Record of the Civil War. Shanghai, China the Commercial Press, Ltd., 1912. xiv, 358p. plates, ports, maps. 23cm.

　　It is a record studying the overthrow of the Manchu dynasty and the establishment of the Republic in China. More than one-half of the volume is devoted to the description of the fighting at Wuchang Hankow and Hanyang from Oct 10th to Dec. 4, 1911.

　　Reviewed in Ath 2:335 Sep 28 1912; N. Y. T 17:672 Nov 17 1912; Spec 109:337 Sep 7 1912.

* Farjenel, Fernand. Through the Chinese Revolution: my experiences in the south and north, the evolution of social life, interviews with party leaders, an unconstitutional loan, the coup d'etat...tr by Margaret Vivian. N. Y. Frederick A. Stokes, So. ,1916. xii ,352p. 22cm.

"When the author gives us as such authors never fail to do, remarks on China as a whole, his works must be taken with reserve. Of his proper subject, the Chinese revolution, Prof. Farjenel gives a clear and interesting account and this English version is one of the most readable book on China that we have seen of recent years. "Ath Nov 1915.

Reviewed in Ath 2:363 Nov 20 1915; Bost trans p24 May 29 1916; R of Rs 53:626 May 1915.

Harding, Gardner, Ludwig. Present-day China: a narrative of a nation's advance. N. Y. The Century Co. 1916. x. p. ,3 1. ,3-250p. front. , plates, ports. 18cm.

It is a very readable volume, entertaining in its picturesque narratives, valuable in its clear account of cotton factories, coal mines, railroads, school, modern prisons, etc. But its chief drawback is too condensed.

Reviewed in Bost trans p4 June 14 1916; Dial 61:316 Oct 19 1916; R of Rs 54:106 July 1916.

* Kent, Percy Horace Braund. The Passing of the Manchus. Lond. , E. Arnold, 1912. xi, 404p. front. plates, ports. maps. 23cm.

"Though we must wait a long time before an inner history of the revolution can be written, the present work is complete so far as available material will allow. Nothing of importance has been omitted, and the impartiality and fairness throughout is refreshing. It has almost the value of a first hand authority because of a copious citation of the accounts of eyewitness; While at the same time it brings all the unfolding events together into a complete well-proportioned panorama. "W. J. Hail

Reviewed in Am Hist R 18:432 Jan 1913; Ath 2:510 Nov 2 1912; Pol Sci Q 28:160 May 1913; Yale R n. s. 2:782 July 1913.

McCormick, Frederick. The Flowery Republic; London, Murray 1912. 489p. pl. ports. maps. 22.5cm.

The author was in China when the revolution started and ended in the overthrow of the Manchu monarchy. The information in this book is reliable and the style is impressive, but the treatment is rather hastily done.

Reviewed in Am Pol Sci R 7:482 Aug 1913; Ath 1:514 May 10 1913; No Am 198:421 Sep 1913.

Pott, Francis Lister Hawks. The Emergency in China. N. Y. Missionary education movement of the United States and Canada. 1913. xii, 309p. front. , illus. , plates, ports. , fold, map. tab. 19.5cm.

"A brief account of the recent events from the standpoint of the Christian missionary."

K. S. Latourette. Dr. Pott is the president of St. John's University, Shanghai, for nearly thirty years and he knows the things Chinese and Chinese mind thoroughly well. What is his judgment is usually sound and impartial.

* Simpson, Bertram Lenox. The Fight for the Republic in China. N. Y. Dood, Mead and Co. 1917. xiii p. , 1 l. ,490p. front. plates. (part fold) ports. 23.5cm.

This book is Mr. Simpson's latest production on China. It deals solely with the Chinese republic from 1911 to 1917. The author knows Peking as no other foreigner does and he is certainly in the preface clearly indicates the scope of the book. He says "This volume tells everything that the student or the casual reader needs to know about the Chinese question." In a position to speak with authority. As the first sentence.

It also includes excellent photographic reproduction and interesting biographies of the heroes and traitors of the republic. The appendices give "every document of importance for the period covered." An indispensable volume for any library.

Reviewed in Bookm 46:267 Nov 1917; Nil R 5: No. 12 Feb 16 1918; N Y T 23:13 Jan 13 1918.

Thomson, John Stuart. China Revolutionized. Illustrated with maps and photographs. Indianapolis. The Bobbs-Merrill Co. 1913 5p. , l. ,590p. plates, port-22cm.

It is an up-to-date history of China. The style is fair, but the entire atmosphere of the book is spoiled by too many repetitions, blunders and a host of old illustrations.

Reviewed in Ath 2:227 Sep 6 1913; Na 97:266 Sep 8 1913; Spec 112:830 May 16 1914.

Waley, Adolf S. The Remarking of China. N. Y. Dutton, 1915 93p. 19.5cm.

This brief history of China begins with 1898 down to the fall of the Manchu dynasty the founding of the republic under Sun Tat-Sen and the rise of Yuan Shih-Kai, whom the author admires a great deal. It is an orderly and succinct account of China's recent political history.

Reviewed in Dial 59:280 Sep 30 1915; Na 101:474 Oct 14 1915; R of Rs 52:123 July 1915.

AUTHOR INDEX

The reference given after each brief title in this index is the class-reference, e. g. Martin, W. A. P. Kore of Cathay. Soc L & C. means that the book will be found under the class heading "Social life and Customs."

The author's name of a biography is in Curves.

INDEX

Allan, C. W. Makers of Cathay. Bio.

American acad. of Pol. & Soc. Science. China, social and economic conditions. Econ and Pol Organ.

Ayscough, H. G. C. Perry-, see Perry-Ayscough, H. G. C.

Backhouse, E. Annals and memoirs of the court of Peking. Hist.

Ball, J. D. Chinese at home. Soc. L & C.

Ball, J. D. Things Chinese. Gen work.

Bard, E. Chinese life in town country. Soc. L & C.

Bashford, J. W. China. Gen. Work.

Bashford, J. W. China and methodism. Miss.

Beach, H. P. Princely men in the heavenly Kingdom. Bio.

Beal, S, tr. Heuen Tsang. Phi & Rel.

Bell, A. Spell of China. Tra & Des.

Benoy, K. S. Chinese religion thru Hindu eyes. Phi & Rel.

Binyon, L. Flight of the dragon. Fine A.

Binyon, L. Painting in the Far East. Fine A.

Bitton, N. Regeneration of new China. Miss.

Blake, H. A. China. Soc L. & CM

Blakeslee, G. H., ed. China and the Far East. Int Rel.

Blakeslee, G. H., ed. Recent developments in China Rev.

Bland. J. O. P. China under the empress dowager. Bio.

Bland. J. O. P. Li Hung-Chang. Bio.

Bland. J. O. P. Recent events & present policies in China. Rev.

Boggs, L. P. Chinese womanhood. Soc. L & C.

Borel, H. New China. Tra & Des.

Broomhall, M., ed. E Chinese empire. Miss.

Broomhall, M., ed. Islam in China. Phi & Rel.

Broomhall, M., ed. Present-day conditions. Soc. L&C.

Brown, A. J. Chinese revolutions. Rev.

Brown, C. C. China in Legend & story. Lang & Lit.

Brown, C. C. A Chinese St Francis. Bio.

Budd, C., tr. Chinese poems. Lang & Lit.

Burlingame, Anson. (Williams) Int. Rel.

Burton, M. E. Education of women. Educ.

Burton, M. E. Notable women of modern China. Bio.

Bushnell, S. W. Chinese art. Fine A.

Byng, L. A. Cranmer-, see Cranmer-Byng, L. A.

Candler, E. Unveiling of Lhasa. Tibet.

Cantlie, J. Sun Yat Sen. Bio.

Carl, K. A. With the empress dowager. Bio.

Carruthers, A. D. M. Unknown Mongolia. Mon.

Carus, P. Chinese life and customs, Soc. L & C.

Cecil, Lord W. R. E. Gascoyne-, Changing China. Miss.

Chamberlin, W. J. Ordered to China. Box Up.

Chan, S. W. Chinese cook book. Soc. & U. A.

Chang, C. T. China's only hope. Hist.

Chau Ju Kua. Chu-fan-chi. Econ & Pol Organ.

Chen, H. C. Principles of Confucius. Econ & Pol Organ.

Chen, S. K. System of taxation. Econ & Pol Organ.

China. Inspectorate general of customs. Decennial reports. Econ. & Pol Organ.

China and the Far East. Int Rel.

China mission year book. Miss.

China, social and econ. conditions. Econ & Pol. Organ.

China year book. Econ & Pol Organ.

Chitty, J. R. Things seen in China. Soc. L & C.

Christie, D. Thirty years in Moukden. Man.

Chu, C. Tariff problem. Econ & Pol Organ.

Chu-fan-chi, see Chau Ju Kua.

Chu Yen. Chinese pottery & Porcelain. Fine A.

Chuang, Thsze. Phi & Rel.

Church, P. W. P. Chinese Turkestan. Turk.

Clements, P. H. Boxer rebellion. Box Up.

Clennell, W. J. Historical development of religion in China. Phi & Rel.

Colquhoun, A. R. China in transformation. Hist.

Confucius. Ethics. Phi & Rel.

Conger, Mrs. E. H. See Conger, Sarah(Pike)

Conger, Sarah(Pike) Letters from China. Hist.

Conger, Sarah(Pike) Old China and young America. Tra & Des.

Coolidge, Mrs. M. E. B. (Roberts) Smith. Chinese immigration. Econ & Pol Organ.

Cooper, Mrs. E. My lady of the Chinese court-yard, Soc L & C.

Couling, S. Encyclopaedia sinica. Gen work.

Curtin, J. The Mongols. Mon.

Curtin, J. The Mongols in Russia. Mon.

Curtis, W. E. Turkestan: "Heart of Asia." Turk.

Daly, R. L. (French). An Irishwoman in China. Tra & Des.

Dawson, M. M. Ethics of Confucius, see Confucius, Ethics.

Decinnial reports. Econ & Pol Organ. See China. Inspectorate general of customs.

Denby, C. China and her people. Tra & Des.

DerLing, princess. Two years in the Forbidden City. Soc L & C.

Dingle, E. J. Across China on foot. Tra & Des.

Dingle, E. J. China's revolution. Rev.

Dingle, E. J. New atlas. Gen work.

Dore, H. Researches into Chinese superstitions. Soc. L & C.

Dundas, L. J. L., earl of Ronaldshy, see ronaldshy, L. J. L., earl of.

Eames, J. B. The English in China. Int Rel.

Eddy, S. Students of Asia. Educ.

Educational directory of China. Educ.

Far eastern geographical establishment. New map of China. Gen work.

Farjenel, F. Thru the Chinese Revolution. Rev.

Farrer, RLJ. On the eaves of the world. Tra & Des.

Fenollosa, E. F. Epochs of Chinese and Japanese art. Fine A.

Fergusson, W. N. Adventure, sport and travel on the Tibetan steppes. Tibet.

Fryer, J. Admission of Chinese students to American colleges. Educ.

Gamewell, Mrs. M. N. (Porter) Gateway to China. Tra & Des.

Gascoyne-Cecil Lord W. R. E. See Cecil, Lord W. R. E. Gascoyne-

Gaunt, M. E. B. Woman in China. Tra & Des.

Geil, W. E. Eighteen capitals of China. Tra & Des.

Geil, W. E. Great Wall of China. Tra & Des.

Gibson, R. R. Forces mining and undermining, China. Econ & Pol Organ.

Giles, H. A. China and the Chinese. Soc L & C.
Giles, H. A. China and the Manchus. Hist.
Giles, H. A. Chinese-English dist. Lang. & Lit.
Giles, H. A. tr. Chuang Thsze, see Chuang Thsze.
Giles, H. A. Civilization of China. Soc L & C.
Giles, H. A. Confucianism & its rivals, Phi & Rel
Giles, H. A. History of Chinese literature Lang & Lit.
Giles, H. A. History of Chinese pictorial art. Fine A.
Giles, H. A. Relations of ancient China. Phi & Rel.
Giles, L. tr. Laotzu, see Laotzu.
Goodrich, J. K. Coming China. Soc L & C.
Gorer, E. Chinese porcelain & hard stones. Fine A.
Gowen, H. H. Outline history of China. Hist.
Griffis, W. E. China's story of myths, etc. Hist.
Groot, J. J. M. de, Religion in China. Phi & Rel.
Groot, J. J. M. de, Religion of the Chinese Phi & Rel.
Gulland, W. G. Chinese porcelain. Fine A.

Harding, G. L. Present-day China. Rev.
Hart, E. I. Virgil C. Hart. Bio.
Hart, Sir Robert. These from the land of Sinim. Hist.
Hart, V. C. (Hart) Bio.
Headland, I. T. tr. Chinese Mother Goose. Lang & Lit.
Headland, I. T. tr. Court life in China. Soc L & C.
Headland, I. T. tr. Home life in China. Soc L & C.
Hearn, L. Some Chinese ghosts. Lang & Lit.
Heding, S. A. Central Asia and Tibet towards the hold city of Lhasa. Tibet.
Hedleyl, J. Tramps in dark Mongolia. Mon.
Henke, F. G. tr. Wang Yang Ming. See Wang Yang Ming. Phi & Rel.
Hertslet, Sir Edward. China treaties. Int Rel.
Heuen-Tsang. Si-Wuaki. Phi & Rel.
Hirth F. Ancient history of China. Hist.
Hirth F. tr. Chau Ju Hua, see Chau Ju Kua.
Hirth F. Scraps from a collector's note book. Fine A.
Hiuen-Tsiang, see Heuen-Tsang.
Holdich, Sir T. H. Tibet, the mysterious. Tibet.
Hobson, R. L. Chinese pottery and porcelain. Fine A.
Hoei-li. Life of Hiuen-Tsiang. Phi & Rel.
Holcombe, C. China's past and future. Int Rel.

Hornbeck, S. E. Contemporary politics in the Far East. Int Rel.
Hosie, Sir Alex. Manchuria. Man.
Hsiang, Y. P. Chinese porcelain. Fine A.
Hsu, M. C. Railway problems. Econ & Pol Organ.

Imperial Japanese Government railway. Official guide to eastern Asia. Gen work.

Jack, R. L. Back blocks of China. Tra & Des.
Jefferys, W. H. Diseases of China. Sc & U. A.
Jernigan, T. R. China in law and commerce. Econ & Pol Organ.
Jernigan, T. R. China's business methods & policy. Econ & Pol Organ.
John, Rev. Griffith. (Thomson) Bio.
Johnston, L. E. China. Tra & Des.
Johnston, R. F. Buddhist China. Phi & Rel.
Johnston, R. F. From Peking to Mandalay. Tra & Des.
Johnston, R. F. Lion and dragon in northern China. Soc L & C.
Jones, J. The fall of Tsingtau. Int Rel.

Kemp, Miss E. G. Face of China. Tra & Des.
Kemp, Miss E. G. Face of Manchuria, Korea, Russian & Turkestan. Man.
Kendall, E. K. A Wayfarer in China. Tra & Des.
Kent, P. H. B. Passing of the Manchus, Rev.
Kent, P. H. B. Railway enterprise. Econ & Pol Organ.
King, F. H. Farmers of forty centuries. Sc & U. A.
King, E. D. Educational system. Educ.
Koo, V. K. W. Status of aliens in China. Int Rel.
Kuo, P. W. Chinese system of public education. Educ.

Lanton, P. Opening of Tibet. Tibet.
Landon, P. Opening of Tibet. Tibet.
Landor, A. H. S. China and the allies. Box Up.
Landor, A. H. S. An explorer's adventure in Tibet. Tibet.
Lanning, G. Wild life in China. Hist.
Laufer, B. Chinese clay figures. Sc & U. A.
Laufer, B. Chinese pottery of the Han dynasty. Fine A.
Laufer, B. Jade. Fine A.
Lesdain, Count de. From Peking to Sikkim. Tra & Des.
Letters from a Chinese official (Anon) see Dickinson, G. L. Soc L & C.
Li, U. B. Outlines of Chinese history. Hist.

Liang, Y. K. (Tao, L. K. X Village and town life. Soc L & C.
Liddel, T. H. China. Tra & Des.
Lin, S. Y. Chinese appeal to Christendom. Miss.
Little, A. H. N. (Bewicke.) Li Hung-Chang. Bio.
Little, A. H. N. (Bewicke.) Round about my Peking garden. Tra & Des.
Little, A. J. The Far East. Tra & Des.
Little, A. J. Gleaning from 50 years in China. Tra & Des.
Little, A. J. Mount Omi & Beyond.
Little Mur A. J. See Little A. H. N. (Bewicke)
Lockhart, Sir J. H. S. Chinese copper coins. Fine A.

McCormic, F. Flowery republic. Rev.
McGowan, J. Men and manners of modern China. Soc L & C.
McGowan, J. Sidelights on Chinese life. Soc L & C.
Mao, Cheng. (Brown) Bio.
Martin, W. A. P. Awakening of China. Hist.
Martin, W. A. P. Lore of Cathay. Soc L & C.
Merwin, S. Drugging a nation. Soc L & C.
Meyer, F. N. Agricultural exploration in the fruit and nut orchards. Sc & ULA.
Millard. T. F. F. American & the Far eastern question. Int Rel.
Millard. T. F. F. Our eastern question. Int Rel.
Miller, G. A. China inside out. Soc L & C.
Morse, H. B. Gilds of China. Econ & Pol Organ.
Morse, E. S. Glimpse of China and Chinese homes. Tra & Des.
Morse, H. B. International relations of the Chinese empire. Int Rel.
Morse, H. B. Trade and administration. Eco & Pol Organ.
Moule, A. E. Half a century in China. Tra & Des.

New atlas and commercial gazetteer of China. Gen work.
New map of China, Gen work.

Official guide to eastern Asia. see Imperial Japanese government railway. Gen work.
Ollone, H. M. G. vicomte d'ollone. In forbidden China. Tra & Des.
Osgood, E. I. Breaking down Chinese walls, Miss.

Paker, E. H. Ancient China simplified. Hist.
Parker, E. H. China, her history, diplomacy & Commerce. Hist.
Parker, E. H. China & religion. Phi & Rel.
Parker, E. H. Students in Chinese religion. Phi & Rel.

Perry-Ayscough, H. G. C. With the Russians in Mongolia. MON.
Pott, F. L. H. Emergency in China. Rev.
Pitman, N. H. Chinese fairy stories. Lang & Lit.
Pott, F. L. H. Outbreak in China. Box Up.
Pott, F. L. H. Sketch of Chinese history. Hist.

Rawling, Capt. C. G. Great plateau. Tibet.
Reinsch, P. S. Intellectual & political currents in the Far East. Int Rel.
Richard, L. Comprehensive geography. Gen work.
Richard, T. 45 years in China. Tra. & Des.
Rijnhart, Mrs. S. C. With the Tibetans in tent and temple. Tibet.
Rockbill, W. W. tr. See Chau Ju Kua.
Roe, A. S. China as I saw it. Tra and Des.
Ronaldshay, L. J. L. Dundas, earl of. A wandering student in the Far East. Tra & Des.
Ross, E. A. Changing Chinese. Soc L & C.
Ross, John. Original religion of China. Phi & Rel.

Sargent, A. J. Angle-Chinese commerce and diplomacy. Econ & Pol Organ.
Scidmore, E. R. China. Tra & Des.
Scott, C. E. China from within. Miss.
Sergeant, P. W. The great empress dowager of China. Bio.
Shaw, N. Chinese forest trees and timber supply. Sc & U. A.
Simpson, B. L. Coming struggle in eastern Asia. Int Rel.
Simpson, B. L. Fight for the republic in China. Rev.
Simpson, B. L. Indiscreet letters from Peking. Box Up.
Simpson, B. L. Manchu & Muscovite. Hist.
Simpson, B. L. Re-shaping of the Far East. Int Rel.
Simpson, B. L. The truce in the east and its aftermath. Int Rel.
Smith, A. R. China & America to-day. Int Rel.
Smith, A. R. China in convulsion. Box Up.
Smith, A. R. China, Uplift of. Miss.
Scothill, W. E. Three religions of China. Phi & Rel.
Sowerby, A. de Carle. Fur & feather in north China. Sc & U. A.
Speicher, J. Conquest of the cross, Miss.
Stanford, E. Atlas of the Chinese empire. Gen work.
Stein, M. A. Ancient Khotan. Turk.
Stein, M. A. Ruins of desert Cathay. Turk.
Strehlneek, E. A. tr. Chinese pictorial art. Fine A.
Sun Yat Sen. (Cantile & Jones) Bio.

英文著作

Thomson, H. C. China & the powers. Box Up.

Thomson, J. S. China revolutionized.

Thomson, J. S. The Chinese. Tra & Des.

Thomson, R. W. Griffith John. Bio.

Tisdale, A Pioneering where the world in old. Man.

Tokyo. Imperial university. Decorations of the imperial palace of Peking. Fine A.

Tokyo. Imperial city of Peking. Fine A.

Tredwell, W. R. Chinese art motives interpreted. Fine A.

Trubner's oriental series. Heuen-Tsang. Phi & Rel.

Tsu, Y. Y. Spirit of Chinese philanthropy. Econ & Pol Organ.

Tzau, M. C. T. Z. The legal obligations arising out of treaty relations between China and other states. Int Rel.

Tzu Hsi, empress dowager of China. (Bland) (Carl) (Sergeant) Bio.

Waddell, H. Lyrics from the Chinese. Lang & Lit.

Waddell, L. A. Lhasa and its mysteries. Tibet.

Wagel, S. R. Chinese currency and banking. Eco & Pol Organ.

Wagel, S. R. Finance in China Econ & Pol Organ.

Waley, A. S. Remarking of China. Rev.

Wallace, H. F. Big game of central & western China. Sc & U. A.

Wang Yang Ming, Philosophy. Phi & Rel.

Weale, Bertram Lenox Putnam (Pseud). See Simpson, B. L.

Wei, W. P. Currency problem. Econ & Pol Organ.

White, Mrs. T. C. see Princess Der Ling,.

Wieger, L. Chinese Characters. Lang & Lit. .

Wieger, L. Chinese characters. Phi & Rel.

Williams, F. W. Anson Burlingame. Int Rel.

Williams, S. W. Syllabic dictionary of the Chinese Language. Lang & Lit.

Willis, B. Research in China. Sc & U. A.

Wilson, E. H. A naturalist in Western China. Sc & U. A.

Wisdom of the East series.

  Chung Thsze. Phi & Rel.

  Feast of lanterns. Lang & Lit.

  Sayings of Laotzu. Phi & Rel.

  Tang Chu's garden of pleasure. Phi & Rel.

Yang Chu, Garden of pleasure.

Yen H. L. Survey of constitutional development. Eco & Pol

Yule, Sir Henry. Cathay and the thither. Tra & Des. Organ.

Yung Wing. My life in China and America. Bio.

后 记

20世纪初,中国最早一批留学海外的图书馆学家发起了一场以强调图书馆的社会教育功能、引进和创办近代新式图书馆为特征的图书馆运动,促进了古代藏书楼向近代图书馆的转型,这场疾风暴雨式的运动推动了中国近代图书馆的建立和发展。

20世纪80年代,全球化时代到来,电子化、网络化、虚拟化、数字化技术发展占据了主导地位,技术的进步改变了人们的学习和阅读习惯,也改变了图书馆的运行模式。进入21世纪,随着政治民主化、法制化的发展,图书馆的发展从内容到形式进入了又一个巨大的变革时代。人们在追踪世界技术发展足迹的同时,对图书馆的本质属性进行了反思,2005年《图书馆》杂志社发起了"以人为本,弘扬公共图书馆精神,倡导图书馆走近平民,关心弱者,平等服务,缩小数字鸿沟,建立一个信息公平和信息保障的制度"为中心的大讨论,掀起了一场21世纪的新图书馆运动,这种与时俱进的新观念,促进了中国传统图书馆向现代图书馆的转型。

20世纪的图书馆运动和21世纪的新图书馆运动,对于中国图书馆及图书馆学的发展产生了深远的影响。今日学者在为21世纪"寻找失落的公共图书馆精神"的同时,也从20世纪图书馆运动中汲取思想财富。20世纪的图书馆学家倡导的平等、开放、免费等图书馆理念,在21世纪仍然是图书馆学者追求的目标。前辈学者闪光的思想,今日仍然在大放异彩。所不同的是,在继承前辈学者思想的同时,今日学者更进一步,树立了"图书馆是实现社会平等的一种设施"的新观念,使得"现代图书馆精神正在以更为厚重的方式回归中国图书馆界"。

温故才能知新,继承才能超越。中国图书馆事业和图书馆学由幼稚走向成熟,是一代代图书馆学者前赴后继、不懈努力的结果。了解前人,是为了更好地继承,站在前人的肩头上可以站得更高,看得更远。正如戴志骞所说:"人们总是对自己的祖先感兴趣,对于很多学者来说,宗谱学是一个很有吸引力的研究课题,现代图书馆员也不例外。对过去图书馆员的研究,能够使现代图书馆员感到自豪,因为他们的祖先出身不凡,为人类的文明和进步提供了有益的专业服务。这个观念能够激励现代图书馆员切实行动起来,追随他们的祖先,取得更大的成就。"在百年图书馆发展历程中,先贤学者探索和积累了丰富而宝贵的思想和经验,研究和总结这些思想和经验是开创未来的基础。

戴志骞是20世纪初中国图书馆运动的代表人物,是研究近代中国图书馆发展史不可缺少的人物,尽管戴志骞职业生涯的后半段转职教育和银行界,但他对图书馆学界的贡献是最闪亮的,超过了其他职业。他的图书馆学术著述,体现了图书馆开放、服务、教育等思想,这正是20世纪初期中国社会迫切需要更新的思想。

但是,从20世纪后半叶开始,戴志骞长期淡出图书馆人的视线,其文章论著散在各处不为人知,学界无法深刻了解他的思想和贡献。2007年开始,我有机会从事清华校史和图书馆史的专业研究工作。作为中国近代著名的图书馆学家,也是清华图书馆历史上最重要的掌门人,戴志骞引起了我极大的关注,从那时起,我就开始搜集有关戴志骞的资料。

戴志骞于1914年来到清华学校任图书室主任,从一个小图书室开始,经之营之,到1928

年离任,在清华工作14年,是执掌清华图书馆时间最长的馆长之一,他的主要图书馆学思想和对图书馆事业的贡献,都是在清华图书馆工作期间产生的;他两次留学美国均由清华学校派出,最终获得博士学位也是在清华期间实现的。

戴志骞在清华图书馆工作时期,不仅是清华图书馆处于起步阶段,也是中国近代图书馆事业的起步阶段,戴志骞作为最早到西方学习图书馆学的专业学者之一,回国后做了很多开创性的工作,他最早组织创办图书馆专业组织,并担任重要领导职务;最早建立完备的图书馆管理秩序,设立分支部门;最早开办新图书馆暑期学校,使中国图书馆学界由学习日本转向学习美国;他在图书馆管理上和业务上的思想和实践活动,为发轫时期的中国近代图书馆事业指明了发展方向。

戴志骞在清华图书馆的影响极为深远,是清华图书馆的精神领袖。在他的主持下,从1922年至1927年,每年都有中国唯一的一所图书馆专业学校文华大学图书科的毕业生到清华学校图书馆工作,他们积极思考,勇于探索,发表专业学术论文,在戴志骞的带领下,形成了实力强大的清华图书馆员学术群体。在浓厚的学术氛围中馆员成长很快,查修、孔敏中、徐家麟、顾子刚、曾宪三、章新民、刘廷藩、刘中藩等都在当时或后来成为图书馆专家或图书馆馆长,有一定的全国性影响。戴志骞所提倡的服务精神,在清华图书馆生根开花,出现了金大本、毕树棠、唐贯方、马文珍等服务明星。著名剧作家曹禺回忆到:"我怀念清华大学的图书馆,时常在我怎样想都是一片糊涂账的时候,感谢一位姓金的管理员允许我,进书库随意浏览看不尽的书籍和画册,我逐渐把人物的性格与语言的特有风格揣摩清楚。"曹禺笔下的金管理员即是金大本先生,后来成为天津有名的藏书家。著名学者季羡林回忆到:"我在校时,有一位馆员毕树棠老先生,胸罗万卷,对馆内藏书极为熟悉,听他娓娓道来,如数家珍。学生们乐意同他谈天,看样子他也乐意同青年们侃大山,是一个极受尊敬和欢迎的人。"毕树棠自学成才,成为著名作家,出版了散文《昼梦集》。著名植物学家吴征镒回忆到:"图书馆里有一个善本书库,管理这个书库的是马文珍先生。他管理古籍图书很有经验,对古籍图书的编目很是熟悉,查找古籍图书手来即到。清华南迁至昆明时……清华文科所成立后,马文珍管理的古籍书库随之搬迁到昆明小坝施家营。马文珍先生成为闻一多、李公朴二位老师的主要助手。"马文珍是著名诗人,出版了诗集《北望集》。唐贯方被誉为"清华图书馆的活字典",清华老校友到了80多岁,还来找唐贯方帮助查找资料,因为他是最信得过的人。金大本、毕树棠、唐贯方、马文珍都是在戴志骞任馆长时来馆工作的,他们曾亲身感受戴志骞提倡的服务精神。据唐贯方的儿子唐绍明(曾任国家图书馆党委书记)回忆,唐贯方去世前两年,唐绍明曾拿给唐贯方1927年清华图书馆员工的名录,唐贯方的名字也在其中,他指着戴志骞等名字,一一说出当时各人的情况,最后,不无感伤地说:"如今恐怕就剩下我一个人了。"清华图书馆藏龙卧虎,但他们没忘服务的初心,务本务实,成为后来的服务明星。戴志骞占据清华图书馆的精神高地,一呼百应,对于这样一位受人尊敬、贡献卓著的著名学者,整理他的遗著是我们义不容辞的责任。

2012年11月,清华大学图书馆百年馆庆时,在中山大学图书馆馆长、中山大学资讯管理学院程焕文教授的鼓励下,我开始动议编辑《戴志骞文集》。2013年,我向馆里申请立项计划出版文集,得到馆领导的大力支持,成立了课题组,并组织成立了编委会。2013年10月,在南京东南大学举行"纪念洪范五先生诞辰120周年暨图书馆学思想与实践论坛"期间,我再次与程焕文教授及华东师范大学范并思教授谈到文集的编写工作,得到他们的鼓励,同年年底,《戴志骞文集》进入实质性编辑阶段。

尽管在中国图书馆近代化初期戴志骞位高功大,成为业界公认的领袖,但因他后来淡出图书馆学界,尤其是新中国成立后移居海外,他本人及家人消失在同胞的视线中,这给查找其著述资料带来了极大的困难。由于无法找到他的后人,只能通过查找档案中的蛛丝马迹和翻检旧图书报刊来拼接验证,逐渐厘清戴志骞的生平轨迹及搜集他的中英文著述资料。

其中:清华图书馆文献资料丰富,通过本馆馆藏查找到戴志骞的一些著述;本馆馆际互借的同事们也提供了大量的帮助,从国外借阅了国内难以查找到的英文著述;从清华档案和早期报刊中,收集整理了一部分资料;编者还曾二赴南京、三赴上海,从民国著述、期刊、档案中尽力搜集各种资料。本书除收录戴志骞的著述资料外,还收录了戴志骞夫人,也是戴志骞事业上的重要助手戴罗瑜丽的资料。尽管尽了最大努力,难免还有遗漏。比如,俞君立先生在《20世纪我国分类学名著研究》(见俞君立主编《中国文献分类法百年发展与展望》武汉大学出版社,2002:167)中,提到杜定友在1925年出版的《世界图书分类法》,何日章、洪有丰、戴志骞曾为之作序,戴志骞在序中写道:"世界图书分类法……该著简括而切实用,诚非普通著作所可企及。"但查找1922年广东全省教育委员会出版的《世界图书分类法》和1925年上海图书馆出版的《图书分类法》(出版时杜定友将书改名),均未找到戴序,本书仅将霍怀恕文章中的一段节选照录。再如,据《民国总书目》载:"《南开大学校图书馆中西图书目录合编》(王文山编,南开大学图书馆,1925年12月):书前有张伯苓、戴志骞、袁同礼序,编者引言。"但在该书中亦未发现戴序。戴志骞自述文献中亦有未找到者,如 *Chinese Wood-Block Printed Books and Provincial Libraries*. New Education. (Proceedings Number) Feb., 1922。其他文献也有可能遗漏,只能留待未来发现后补充。

作为与美国图书馆学界交流最多的学者,戴志骞留下的英文著作与论文占其全部文献的大半,为了方便业内同行阅读参考,我们请课题组成员翻译了戴志骞的重要英文著作和论文,并请本馆教授及研究馆员参加审稿。由于我们水平有限,不当之处,敬请方家指正。

与其他中国近代图书馆学家有所不同,戴志骞职业生涯的前20年活跃在图书馆学界,为近代图书馆事业的发展做出了重要贡献;后20年则转职教育和银行界,亦有一些著述,为了保持人物的完整性,本文集除收录戴志骞关于图书馆学的论著外,亦收录了关于教育与银行专题的著述和言论。

戴志骞的全部著作、论文、照片均由韦庆媛搜集。为了便于读者了解戴志骞著述的背景,每篇前有【编者按】,由韦庆媛撰写。全书由韦庆媛统稿。本书作为国家社科基金项目"民国时期图书馆学者群体研究"(项目编号:15BTQ003)的研究成果之一,课题组组长韦庆媛及课题组成员胡冉、武丽娜、郭兰芳、庄玫、董琳承担了全部中文文稿和部分英文文稿的校对工作。

本书的出版,得到了业界学者以及清华大学图书馆领导和老师的大力支持,中山大学图书馆馆长、中山大学资讯管理学院程焕文教授给予诚恳的鼓励,并不吝赐序,本馆蒋耘中书记亦慷慨为本书作序,邓景康馆长在百忙之中抽出时间亲自参与审稿,审稿专家认真审读译稿,编委会、课题组成员反复审校译稿和文字录稿。国家图书馆出版社的支持使本书得以顺利出版。在本书即将付梓之际,向所有关心、指导、支持和帮助我们的师长、同事表示衷心的感谢!

韦庆媛

2016年10月

戴志骞文集

上 册

韦庆媛 邓景康 主编

国家图书馆出版社
National Library of China Publishing House

图书在版编目(CIP)数据

戴志骞文集：全2册/韦庆媛,邓景康主编. --北京：国家图书馆出版社,2016.12
ISBN 978－7－5013－5951－6

Ⅰ.①戴… Ⅱ.①韦… ②邓… Ⅲ.①社会科学—文集 Ⅳ.①C53

中国版本图书馆 CIP 数据核字(2016)第 224529 号

书　名	戴志骞文集（全二册）	
著　者	韦庆媛　邓景康　主编	
责任编辑	高　爽　唐　澈	
出　版	国家图书馆出版社(100034　北京市西城区文津街7号)	
	(原书目文献出版社　北京图书馆出版社)	
发　行	010－66114536　66126153　66151313　66175620	
	66121706（传真）　66126156（门市部）	
E-mail	nlcpress@ nlc. cn（邮购）	
Website	www. nlcpress. com ──▸投稿中心	
经　销	新华书店	
印　装	北京鲁汇荣彩印刷有限公司	
版　次	2016 年 12 月第 1 版　2016 年 12 月第 1 次印刷	
开　本	787 毫米×1092 毫米　1/16	
印　张	53	
彩　插	1	
字　数	1314 千字	
书　号	ISBN 978－7－5013－5951－6	
定　价	300.00 元	

本书编委会

主　　编：韦庆媛　邓景康

编　　委（按姓氏拼音排序）：

邓景康　董　琳　范莹莹　冯立昇　冯　璐
管翠中　郭兰芳　贺维平　胡　冉　姜爱蓉
蒋耘中　林　佳　任　奕　王　媛　韦庆媛
武丽娜　肖　燕　杨　玲　张　秋　庄　玫

审稿专家（按姓氏拼音排序）：

邓景康　冯立昇　姜爱蓉　林　佳　肖　燕

戴志骞摄于1917年

1912年戴志骞获圣约翰大学文科学士的毕业照

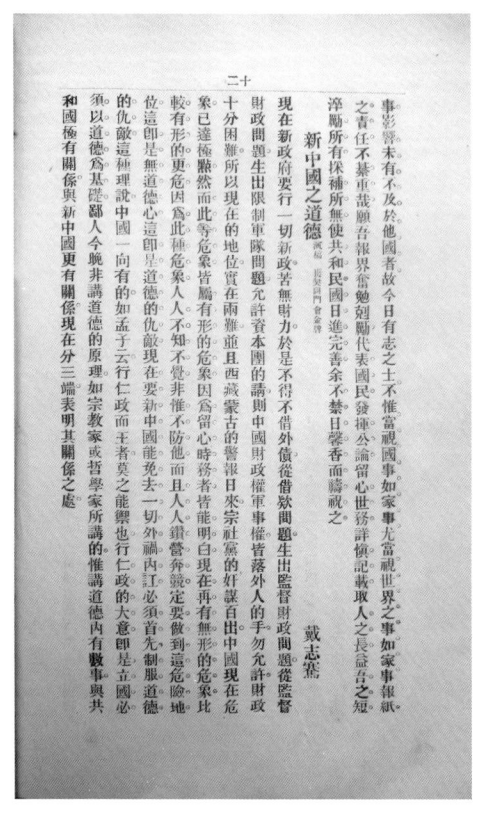

戴志骞于1912年发表于《约翰声》的第一篇论文《新中国之道德》

戴志骞于1909—1912年任圣约翰大学罗氏图书馆馆长。图为1910年圣约翰大学罗氏图书馆外部

圣约翰大学罗氏图书馆内部

圣约翰大学罗氏图书馆内部

1913年圣约翰大学职员合影,后排右三为戴志骞

1920年北京圣约翰大学同学会合影,后排左四为戴志骞

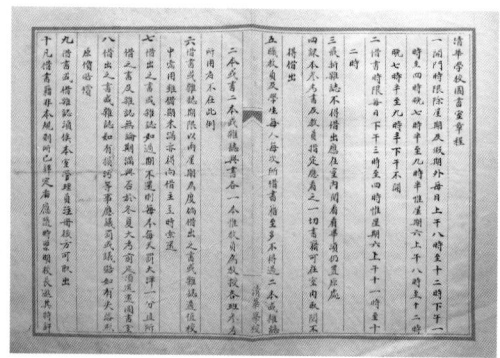
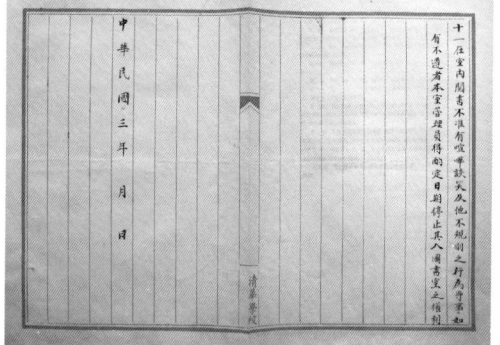

1914年戴志骞任清华学校图书室主任时制定的《清华学校图书室章程》

1916年清华学校临时图书室内部

1916年清华学校临时图书室内部。地点在同方部西面的平房内,有大房一间,小房两间

1917年清华学校职员合影,后排左五为戴志骞

1920年戴志骞在北京高等师范学校创办图书馆学讲习会,这是中国首个图书馆学夏季学校,参加者共78人。图为讲习会师生合影,第一排右六戴志骞,右七沈祖荣,右八李大钊

1921年清华图书馆员合影,前立者为戴志骞

1919年清华学校新图书馆建成,图中"T"字形建筑为图书馆

新图书馆外观

新图书馆书库

新图书馆阅览室

新图书馆大厅

1922年4月,戴志骞在上海结婚。图为戴志骞夫人,挪威人,原名Julie Rummlehoff,中文名戴罗瑜丽,纽约州立大学图书馆学院学士,曾任清华图书馆编目主任、协和医学院图书馆主任

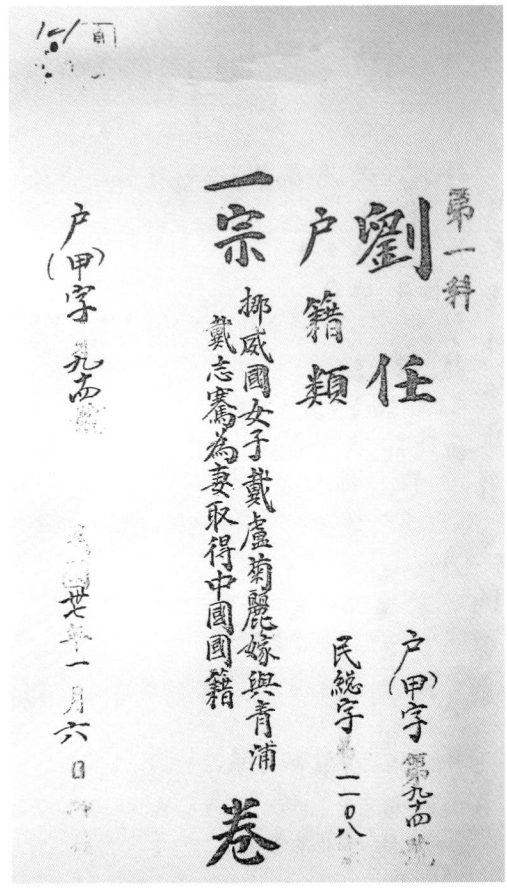

1948年1月6日,戴志骞夫人正式加入中国国籍,户籍名:戴卢菊丽。此为入籍文件

1921年竣工的清华学校照澜院甲种洋房,戴志骞住照澜院7号。图为照澜院7号洋房旧址

1923年戴志骞在清华图书馆　　1923年的清华图书馆主任戴志骞，圣约翰大学文科学士，纽约州立大学图书馆学士

1922年中华教育改进社"图书馆教育组"成员合影，左起：洪有丰、孙心磐、朱家治、戴罗瑜丽、杜定友、沈祖荣、戴志骞

1922年中华教育改进社第一届年会职员合影，前排右一为戴志骞

1923年中华教育改进社第二届年会在清华学校举行,图为年会委员合影,左起:陶行知、戴志骞、曹云祥、陈主素、张仲述、张企文、李仲华

1923年第二届图书馆组代表在清华学校科学馆前合影,前排左一戴志骞夫人,左二冯陈祖怡,右一韦棣华女士。第二排左三朱家治,左四戴志骞,左五施廷镛

1924年中华教育改进社年会图书馆教育组举办展览,右侧墙上是清华图书馆图片展览

1924年戴志骞任北京图书馆协会会长

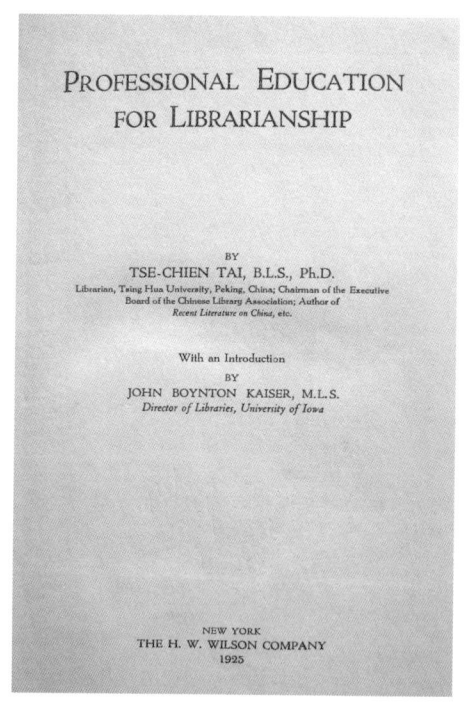

戴志骞于1925年6月获得爱荷华大学哲学博士学位。图为由美国威尔逊出版公司出版的戴志骞博士论文 Professional Education for Librarianship(《图书馆学专业教育》)

1923年清华学校职员合影,第一排右一为戴志骞,右五为校长曹云祥

1923年清华童子军领袖,后排右三为戴志骞,前排中为曹云祥校长

1924年清华校友会成员在清华学校科学馆前合影,第二排右二为戴志骞

1926年清华学校图书馆员合影,左上角为图书馆主任戴志骞
前排左起:唐贯方、曾宪三、孔敏中、戴志骞、余光宗、樊济宽、戴志骞夫人
后排左起:刘廷藩、顾子刚、陆震平、吴钰祥、茅宗藩、刘中藩

1927年戴志骞任《清华年刊》社经理

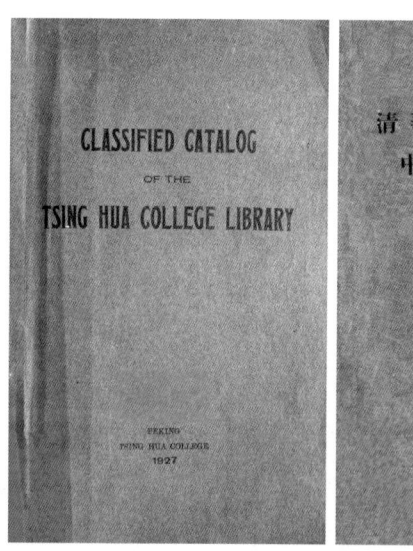 

1927年戴志骞主持编辑的清华学校中、英文书籍目录出版

1929年中华图书馆协会第一次年会代表在国立中央大学图书馆前合影,前排左八为年会副主席戴志骞

1929年中华图书馆协会第一次年会代表合影,前排右七为戴志骞

1928年11月至1929年9月戴志骞任国立中央大学图书馆馆长。图为国立中央大学图书馆外观

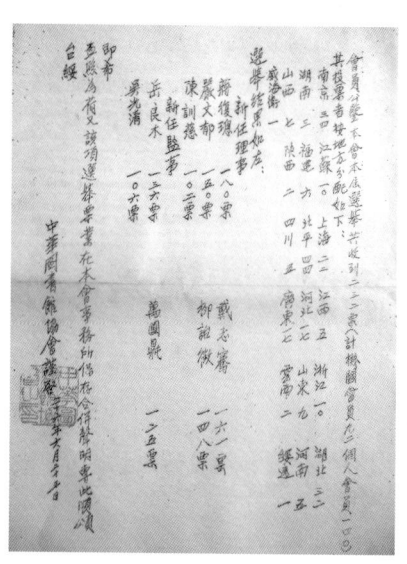

1937年中华图书馆协会选举理事、监事选票,戴志骞获得理事选举161票,高票当选为中华图书馆协会理事

1930年刊登在《中国图书馆名人录》上的戴志骞照片

1936年刊登在《中国名人录》上的戴志骞照片

1933年参加中国银行行务会议成员合影

前排左起：粤行经理郑铁如、代理沈行经理汪翊唐、总稽核汪楞伯、总经理张公权、董事长李馥荪、常务董事冯幼伟、常务董事宋汉章、鲁行经理王仰先、闽行经理黄伯权、滨行经理卞仲荜、沪行经理贝松荪

后排左起：代理总秘书戴志骞、浙行经理金润泉、津行经理卞白眉、宁行经理吴震修、常务董事陈光甫

1934年戴志骞与银行同事，右二为戴志骞

1934年戴志骞与银行同事，中为戴志骞

1947年戴志骞在中国银行

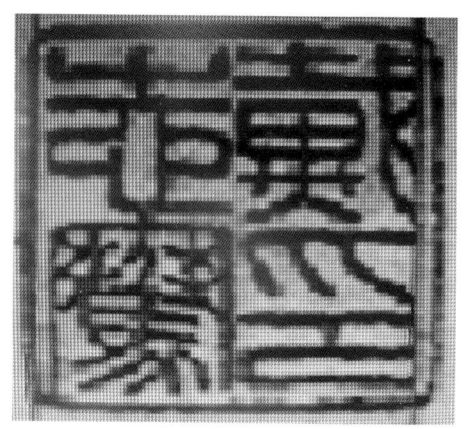

戴志骞印章

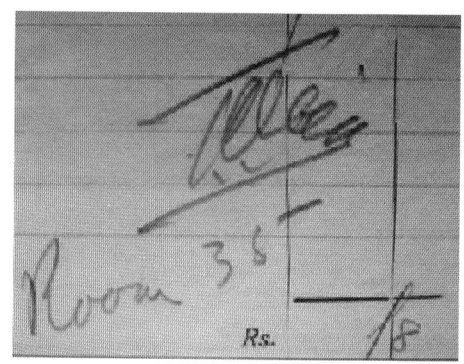

戴志骞英文签名(T. C. Tai)

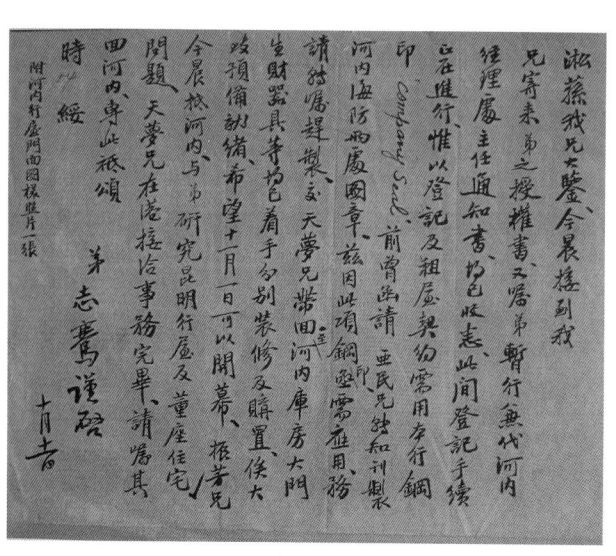

1939年戴志骞写给中国银行副总经理贝松荪的书信手迹

戴志骞在上海的住所：南京西路770号德义大楼内55号

序 一

程焕文*

20世纪初,在中国社会风起云涌的大变革时代,涌现出"清一色留美"的第一代中国图书馆人,他们传播欧美图书馆观念,创办新式图书馆,研究图书馆学术,开展图书馆学教育,开创了中国现代图书馆事业和图书馆学学科。

自20世纪80年代以来,关于第一代中国图书馆人的研究一直颇受图书馆学界重视,有关"中国现代图书馆运动之皇后"——韦棣华女士(Mary Elizabeth Wood,1861—1931)、"中国图书馆学教育之父"——沈祖荣先生(1884—1977)、"20世纪图书馆学大师"——"北刘南杜"[刘国钧(1899—1980),杜定友(1898—1967)],以及洪有丰(1893—1963)、李小缘(1897—1959)、袁同礼(1895—1965)等中国现代图书馆先驱和奠基者的专题研究、学术研讨、周年纪念和文集出版赓续不辍。然而,有关戴志骞(1888—1963)和胡庆生(1895—1968)的系统研究则一直阙如。

戴志骞和胡庆生都是20世纪初中国新图书馆运动中叱咤风云的卓越领袖人物,二人有着惊人相似的经历:

其一,二人都就读于美国圣公会在中国创办的大学:戴志骞1912年毕业于上海圣约翰大学;胡庆生1915年毕业于武昌文华大学。

其二,二人大学毕业后都供职于大学图书馆:戴志骞1909年在上海圣约翰大学读书期间就任图书室主任,1912年毕业后继续任圣约翰大学图书室主任,1914年转任清华学校图书室主任;胡庆生1915年毕业后任武昌文华大学文华公书林协理。

其三,二人其后又都被公派到美国攻读图书馆学:戴志骞于1917—1919年被清华学校派往纽约州立大学图书馆学院攻读图书馆学;胡庆生于1917—1919年被文华大学派往美国纽约公共图书馆学校攻读图书馆学。

其四,二人回国后都在全国各地演讲,发表图书馆学专业论文,宣传新式图书馆,成为新图书馆运动的领袖人物。

其五,二人同时开办图书馆学教育:1920年,戴志骞在北京主持开办北京高师图书馆讲习会,邀请李大钊、沈祖荣、程伯卢、李贻燕、程筱庄、邓翠英等担任讲师,开创中国图书馆学短期培训的先例;1920年,胡庆生在武昌文华大学与韦棣华、沈祖荣一起开办文华图书科,开创中国图书馆学专业教育的先河。

其六,二人同时受中华图书馆协会邀请向1929年在意大利罗马召开的国际图书馆协会联合会(IFLA)第一次国际图书馆及目录学会议(The First Congress of Libraries and Bibliography)提交学术论文:中华图书馆协会将向大会提交的4篇英文论文印成 Libraries in China(《中国图书馆》)在会上分赠各国代表,其中包括:顾子刚撰 The Evolution of the Chinese Book

---

* 程焕文,中山大学资讯管理学院教授、图书馆馆长、校长助理,中国图书馆学会副理事长,教育部高等学校图书馆学学科教学指导委员会副主任委员,教育部高等学校图书情报工作指导委员会副主任委员。

(《中国图书制度之变迁》)、戴志骞撰 Development of Modern Libraries in China(《中国现代图书馆之发展》)、胡庆生撰 Library Training in China(《中国图书馆教育》)、沈祖荣撰 Indexing Systems in China(《中国之索引体系》)。

其七,二人最后都因客观原因几乎同时离开图书馆界供职于银行业:戴志骞于1929年9月辞去国立中央大学图书馆馆长职务,1930年7月辞去国立中央大学副校长职务,8月赴哈尔滨担任哈尔滨工业有限公司经理,从事东北垦殖开发的金融商行业务,1931年7月任中国银行总管理处(上海)人事室主任,1933年后任中国银行总秘书;胡庆生于1928年11月辞去武昌文华大学文华图书科主任职务,1930年正式辞去武昌文华大学文华图书科教授职务,转任武昌上海银行行长。

虽然戴志骞和胡庆生在20世纪中国新图书馆运动中功勋卓著,但是由于他们相继离开图书馆界转职于银行业,在图书馆界的贡献和影响力主要集中在20世纪20年代,只有十余年的短暂时光,因此,时至今日,图书馆学界虽然偶有提及,但鲜有系统的专门研究。

令人欣慰的是,近年来清华大学图书馆韦庆媛一直潜心研究清华大学图书馆历史和清华大学校史,相继发表了一系列有关清华大学图书馆历史的研究论文,并在史料整理的基础上编辑出版了《清华大学图书馆百年图史》(清华大学出版社,2013年),成果丰硕喜人。近年来,笔者一直在收集整理和编辑出版20世纪图书馆学家的著述,并以《图书馆学家文库》为丛书名陆续出版图书馆学家的文集,更希望图书馆界同人能够在此方面有所作为,以共襄盛举。2012年11月清华大学图书馆百年馆庆时,因有感于韦庆媛在清华大学图书馆史研究上的成就,特别是有关戴志骞研究资料的积累,笔者建议韦庆媛百尺竿头更进一步,编辑出版《戴志骞文集》,以纪念先驱,填补学术研究史料的阙如。在清华大学图书馆馆长邓景康教授的大力支持和亲自参与下,韦庆媛与清华大学图书馆同人齐心协力,历经数个春秋寒暑,整理编辑了这部《戴志骞文集》。

《戴志骞文集》分上下两册:上册收录论文、报告、采访、序言等共62篇中文文章,18篇英文文章,另有附录:①戴志骞撰写的书报介绍(4篇);②戴志骞主持的图书馆和中国银行会议记录及议决案选(6篇);③其他相关文章(3篇);④戴志骞夫人著述(2篇);正文前有韦庆媛撰写的《戴志骞先生传略》,详细记述戴志骞的生平事迹。下册收录戴志骞的著作,包括中文著作《图书馆学术讲稿》和英文著作 Professional Education for Librarianship(《图书馆学专业教育》)、Bibliography on China:1900—1918(《关于中国的书目:1900—1918》),面面俱到,蔚为大观。

《戴志骞文集》是一部极其珍贵的图书馆史与图书馆学史史料著作,不仅第一次向学界全面揭示了戴志骞的著述,为今人研究戴志骞提供了丰富的史料,而且填补了中国图书馆史与中国图书馆学史研究的史料空白。长期以来,有关戴志骞的研究一直比较滞后,究其原因主要在史料的匮乏和收集的困难。从《戴志骞文集》来看,戴志骞的著述有两个重要特点:其一,英文著述甚多,且多发表在海外,国人难得一见;其二,中文著述有的发表于非专业学术期刊之上,或散见于他人学术专著之中,一般学人难以想见。能够将如此分散的戴志骞著述汇集在一起,而且几乎没有什么遗漏,这是一件十分了不起的事情,值得赞赏!

《戴志骞文集》的编辑整理者并不满足于著述的收罗全面,还着力于史料的普及利用。为此,清华大学图书馆同人对戴志骞的全部英文著述进行了中文翻译,韦庆媛、王媛、杨玲、郭兰芳、张秋、胡冉、任奕、董琳、武丽娜、冯璐、管翠中、范莹莹、庄玫、贺维平分别承担了相关英文著述的中文翻译，邓景康、冯立昇、姜爱蓉、肖燕、林佳则承担了中文译文的审校，蒋耘中作序，总计参与编辑整理者多达20余人。由此可见，《戴志骞文集》亦是清华大学图书馆同人集体智慧的结晶。

作为中国现代图书馆的先驱，戴志骞在20世纪的中国图书馆史上虽然只是昙花一现，但是鲜艳夺目，光彩照人，足以垂名青史。

戴志骞是清华大学图书馆的卓越奠基人。1912年，清华学堂更名为清华学校，8月20日清华学校图书室（一间大房两间小房）成立，黄光担任清华学校图书室第一任主任。1914年8月，戴志骞被聘为清华学校图书室主任；1916年4月，清华学校图书馆开工建设，10月清华学校图书室正式改名为图书馆，戴志骞担任清华学校图书馆第一任主任，直到1928年9月离开清华大学，在清华学校图书馆担任主任长达14年之久（其中，1917年8月—1919年8月，1924年8月—1925年夏在美国留学），为清华大学图书馆的创办和发展做出了不可磨灭的卓越贡献。20世纪30年代，国立清华大学图书馆能够成为与国立北京大学图书馆和国立中山大学图书馆齐名的三大国立大学图书馆，戴志骞的奠基之功永不可没。

戴志骞还是中华图书馆协会的卓越奠基人。1921年，中华教育改进社成立，1922年戴志骞成为中华教育改进社图书馆教育委员会（后改为图书馆教育组）的六位委员之一。1923年，中华教育改进社第二届年会在清华学校举行，戴志骞任会务主任，并提出"组织各地图书馆协会案"，倡导建立各地图书馆协会。1924年3月30日，戴志骞与袁同礼、蒋复璁等发起成立北京图书馆协会，会址设于清华学校图书馆，戴志骞担任首任会长，是为中国第一个地方图书馆协会。1925年4月25日，中国第一个全国性图书馆组织——中华图书馆协会在上海成立，选举蔡元培、梁启超、胡适、丁文江、沈祖荣、钟福庆、范源廉、熊希龄、袁希涛、颜惠庆、余日章、洪有丰、王正廷、陶知行、袁同礼15人为董事，戴志骞为执行部部长，杜定友、何日章为副部长，戴志骞成为中华图书馆协会第一位执掌人。

抚今追昔，饮水思源，戴志骞在20世纪中国图书馆史上的历史贡献永远值得我们纪念，而编辑出版《戴志骞文集》嘉惠学林，传之后世，实为利在当代，功在千秋之举。衷心地感谢韦庆媛和清华大学图书馆同人，祝贺《戴志骞文集》出版。

是为序。

2016年9月18日凌晨
完稿于中山大学康乐园竹帛斋

序 二

蒋耘中*

戴志骞先生1888年出生于江苏青浦,1912年毕业于上海圣约翰大学,获文学学士学位;1917年赴美国纽约州立大学图书馆学院学习,并获图书馆学学士学位;1925年在美国爱荷华大学获哲学博士学位。先后担任上海圣约翰大学图书馆馆长、清华学校图书室主任、清华学校图书馆馆长,还担任中华教育改进社图书馆教育委员会主席、北京图书馆协会会长、中华图书馆协会执行部部长等职,是中国现代图书馆事业的早期重要开拓者之一。戴志骞先生在图书馆领域从业的历史不长,20世纪30年代以后,他就转入金融领域了。这大概是他不为人熟知的一个重要原因吧。

作为一个文明古国,中国藏书楼的历史可以追溯到2000多年前的汉代,历史上也涌现出很多著名的藏书家。但是这种藏书楼更多的是出于对书籍的收集和保存。现代意义上的图书馆在中国的出现不过是100多年前的事情,而为图书馆建设服务的图书馆学出现的就更晚一些。经过100多年的发展,我国图书馆学已经有了长足的发展,早已脱离了筚路蓝缕的阶段。但是我们回顾历史,研究和整理图书馆学的发展脉络,对于图书馆学今后的发展还是非常有意义的。

戴志骞先生不仅是中国现代图书馆事业的早期开拓者,也是中国图书馆学研究的开拓者。作为中国图书馆界最早获得博士学位的人,他对国外图书馆学理论有比较深入的了解,在图书馆建设的实践中,他将所学到的理论知识与图书馆建设相结合,对图书馆进行改革,明确学校图书馆的性质和定位,改进学校图书馆的管理,初步建立了现代图书馆的管理制度。这些,在他所处的时代是具有开创性意义的,也为后来大学图书馆的发展奠定了基础。开展对戴志骞图书馆学理论的研究,无疑是研究中国现代图书馆发展历史的一个重要方面。

戴志骞先生的著作留下来的很少,而且散落在各种文献之中,查找起来也很困难。近年来,清华大学图书馆组织力量,开展了戴志骞著作的编辑整理工作,我们手上的这本《戴志骞文集》就是这项工作的成果。《戴志骞文集》收录了戴志骞先生自1912年至1948年间的著作、论文和讲话,内容涉及图书馆、教育、银行等领域。而图书馆学则是其中的主要内容,从中可以看到戴志骞先生在图书馆学方面所做出的思考和贡献。这项成果填补了戴志骞研究的空白。我相信它会对相关领域的研究产生积极的作用。

2016年9月

---

* 蒋耘中,清华大学图书馆党委书记。

戴志骞先生传略

韦庆媛

戴志骞先生是近代早期图书馆学家,是中国图书馆事业的先驱。1909—1917年,他直接从事图书馆工作,作为一个旧式管理者,在中国图书馆事业发轫之初摸索前行,在实践中探寻工作方法。1917—1929年,在学习外国经验的基础上,他站在全国的高度,领导了中国的新图书馆运动,在近代早期图书馆的重要事件中都有他的足迹。他热爱图书馆事业,曾坦言"我对于图书馆学问有无穷兴趣",即使在离开图书馆界后,仍然对他曾倾注极大热情、付出艰苦努力的图书馆事业留有无限眷恋,一直参加中华图书馆协会的领导工作。戴志骞是中国第一位获得图书馆学博士学位的学者,他置身于改良中国社会、建立新图书馆秩序的社会潮流之中,从一个旧式管理者,到新图书馆事业的领导者,完成了时代变迁的华丽转身,为中国近代图书馆事业的发展做出了重要贡献。在他职业生涯的后半段,先后转职教育和银行界,担任重要职务,同样做出了贡献。然而,由于他在新中国成立后迁居海外,长期淡出图书馆学人的视线,著述多用英文在海外发表,国内对他知之不多。作为近代图书馆学家,戴志骞的新图书馆思想与实践在今天仍然具有积极意义,追踪他的生平经历,是我们全面了解和认识他的基础。

1 江南俊彦傲,蕙质兰心娇

戴超,字志骞,又名戴丙庚、戴子骞,英文名 Tse-chien Tai,简写 T. C. Tai,1888年2月27日生于江苏青浦珠溪镇,父亲戴造梁(1853—1929),母亲沈氏(?—1929)。

珠溪镇现隶属于上海市青浦区,20世纪50年代改称朱家角镇,是江南有名的古镇。朱家角镇位于今上海市青浦区中南部,紧靠淀山湖风景区。东与西大盈接壤,南与练塘镇、松江科技园区、佘山镇交界,西依淀山湖,与金泽镇相连,北与昆山市淀山湖镇毗邻。朱家角镇历史悠久,早在1700多年前的三国时期就已形成村落,村内河湖纵横,具有典型的江南水乡风貌。后因水运方便,商业日盛,宋、元时期形成集市,名朱家村。明万历年间正式建镇,名珠街阁,又称珠溪。曾以布业著称江南,号称"衣被天下"。明末清初,米业兴起,再次带动百业兴旺,镇上老店林立,南北百货,各业齐全,素有"长街三里,店铺千家"之说,江浙百里之外远近闻名。

清宣统二年(1910年),珠溪实行地方自治,改称珠葑自治区。民国初年,称珠葑市,设市公所,民国二十年(1931年)列为青浦县八个区公所之一,称第二区公所。民国二十九年(1940年),属汪伪青浦县第六区;民国三十四年(1945年)9月,恢复第二区公所;民国三十五年(1946年),撤销区公所,改称区署,名珠溪镇。1949年5月14日,成立苏南行政公署松江专区青浦县朱家角市,1954年改为朱家角镇。

自形成繁华市镇后,朱家角文儒荟萃、人才辈出。明代办有书院、义塾。清代以后,兴建众多学堂。明清两代共出进士16人、举人40多人,其中有清代学者王昶、御医陈莲舫、小说家陆士谔、报业巨子席裕福、画僧语石等,留下了丰富的文化遗产。民国时期,镇上有民众教育馆、书报社、戏院、书场等文化场所,有咏珠社、韵声社等文艺结社,民间艺人也相当活跃。

小桥流水、书院飘香孕育了水乡人家的灵性。6岁时,戴志骞进入上海的私塾读书,经过9年的私塾教育,打下了坚实的国学功底。1904年,16岁的戴志骞考入上海圣约翰学院预科学习。圣约翰学院是上海有名的教会学校,建于1879年,1896年得到美国圣公会的批准,正式成立由文理、医学、神学组成的大学部,1905年改为圣约翰大学。1907年,戴志骞从该校预科毕业,此时该校已由圣约翰学院改为圣约翰大学。

戴志骞学识渊博,口才极好,圣约翰大学预科毕业时,获得了该校奖给最优学生的"溥贝子奖"(the Prince Pu Medal),并因出众的演说获得"圣约翰大学校友奖"(the St. John's Alumni Medal)。

圣约翰大学预科毕业后,1907年1月26日,19岁的戴志骞赴温州瑞安高级中学任教,讲授历史和英文,同事评价其"人极丰雅",岁俸一千元,可谓厚聘矣。其时,瑞安高级中学监督项申甫提出修改校章,教课按日记分,每小时60分钟,教师20分钟授课,学生20分钟复习,余20分钟考试,戴志骞与学校教师们认为授课时间太短,考试太过频繁,学生知识学习不够扎实,此种考核方法不可行,一起抵制不合理的修改方案。

戴志骞好学上进,学习深造一直是他努力的方向。在瑞安高级中学任教时,他没有满足当前的学业,积极准备进行本科学习。1896年,美国圣公会批准圣约翰学院办大学部时,规定文理学院学制三年,学生完成圣约翰预科或与之同等的课程学习,可报考圣约翰大学本科。戴志骞已经在圣约翰大学预科毕业,符合报考条件,1909年他又考入圣约翰大学本科,学制三年,同时兼任图书馆馆长,1912年毕业,获得文科学士学位。

圣约翰大学本科毕业时,他参加圣约翰大学同门会(即校友会)演讲比赛,演讲题目是"新中国之道德",他从个人道德、社会道德、民主国道德三个方面,论述了刚刚建立的中华民国应兴应革之事,受到一致好评,获得金牌,讲稿刊登在圣约翰大学学报《约翰声》上,这是他公开发表的第一篇文章。毕业后,留校继续任图书馆馆长。

1914年8月,戴志骞从上海转到美丽的清华园,任清华学校图书室主任。初到清华园,住在宫殿式建筑学务处(工字厅)22号。他的初婚时间和原配妻子情况不详,只知他于1916年曾得一女。另据清华学校英文教授王芳荃的女儿桂碧清回忆:"清华图书馆戴馆长(戴志骞)的前任太太是个中国人,去世后留下三个孩子,一男两女,其中的两个女孩和我们姐妹关系很好。"由此可知,戴志骞的原配妻子是中国人,后因故去世。据查,戴志骞的儿子叫戴士明,小女儿戴士琛,大女儿名字不详。

戴志骞的第二位妻子是与他志同道合的戴罗瑜丽。戴罗瑜丽生于1896年,挪威人,原名Julie Rummlehoff(朱莉·儒门霍夫),婚后一般称为Mrs. T. C. Tai(戴志骞夫人),早年毕业于挪威克烈斯丁逊大学校,曾任克烈斯丁逊图书馆助理员、克列斯希亚那图书馆员,1917年赴美留学,就读纽约州立大学图书馆学院,与戴志骞同班学习,留学期间曾到纽约公共图书馆实习,任编目员,1919年夏与戴志骞一起获得纽约州立大学图书馆学院图书馆学学士学位。那一年,该校共有六名毕业生获得学位,他们是Tse-chien Tai(戴志骞)、Julie Rummlehoff(戴罗瑜丽)、Harris Rachel A.、Hinesley Pearl、Reed L. Ruth、Stauffer Robert E.。戴志骞的好友约翰·博因顿·凯撒(John Boynton Kaiser)于1917年获得该校硕士学位。

毕业后,戴罗瑜丽回到挪威,任国立农专学校图书馆馆长,共同的志趣使她和戴志骞最终走到了一起。1922年4月26日,时任清华图书馆主任的戴志骞到上海与戴罗瑜丽完婚。之所以选择在上海结婚,一是因为戴罗瑜丽乘船而来,轮船靠岸码头即是上海;二是戴志骞家乡江苏青浦珠溪镇离上海较近;三是刚刚在清华学校参加完世界基督教学生会的该会主席穆德,赴上海参加(中国)全国基督教大会,戴志骞请他为证婚人。

婚后,戴志骞惦记清华图书馆的工作,未在上海久留,5月携戴罗瑜丽回到清华学校,9月戴罗瑜丽被聘为图书馆名誉职员,主要负责英文编目工作。图书馆学的专业背景使她成为当时不可多得的专业人才,充实了清华图书馆的专业队伍,由她主持编辑的 Classified Catalog of Tsing Hua College Library 成为清华图书馆的宝贵遗产。

由于家庭人口增加,戴志骞原在学务处的房屋不敷使用,恰逢1921年清华学校在校门以南(现称二校门)建筑教师住宅,即今之清华大学校内照澜院住宅,分为甲、乙两种,甲种为西式洋房,乙种为中式平房。戴志骞迁居甲种西式洋房,住照澜院7号。

戴罗瑜丽悉心照顾戴志骞前妻留下的孩子们,与孩子们感情很好。据桂碧清回忆:"老三戴士琛和我同班,她挪威籍的后妈最喜欢她,因为她长得漂亮。她家里种葡萄树、草莓,那葡萄是玫瑰葡萄,吃到嘴里满嘴都是玫瑰香,她每天上学都会带几颗葡萄、草莓给我吃。她后妈待她很好,冬天给她准备春天的衣服,夏天给她准备秋天的衣服,她总是穿得很漂亮,我们都羡慕她,可她总是不快活。她对我说:'你们都有自由,我却没有,连衣服都是妈妈给准备的,吃饭的时候都不能随便,还得穿得整整齐齐。'因为她妈妈有一套洋规矩。后来我妈妈看她穿得漂亮,也照着她衣服的样子给我们做。她家里也很漂亮:地毯、外国家具,还专门有穿白大褂的炊事员给他们开饭。"幸福的家庭生活使戴志骞心无旁骛,专注于他的事业。

2 在图书馆界的职业生涯

2.1 任圣约翰大学图书馆馆长

1909年8月,戴志骞进入圣约翰大学本科学习,不久开始兼任该校图书馆馆长,边学习、边工作。

圣约翰大学图书馆始建于1888年,卜舫济接任校长时建立。最初的图书来自于捐赠,圣约翰学院的施主教将自己私人收藏的中文图书数十部捐给学院,文主教私宅有一所圣公会藏书室,均为英文书,也捐给了学院,两批捐赠合在一起,即是圣约翰大学图书的源头,地址仍设在文主教私宅的圣公会藏书室。1894年藏书室迁至圣约翰学院西北隅二层楼,1899年迁至该楼下层。1900年冬,美国传教士韦棣华女士曾短暂留沪,帮助圣约翰学院整理图书,开始使用《杜威十进分类法》进行分类和编目。1904年秋,藏书室迁入新落成的思颜堂西南隅,为纪念纽约罗氏兄弟慷慨捐助兴建此堂,将此命名为罗氏藏书室。

1909年秋,学校聘请戴志骞任图书馆馆长,数学教授华克(Prof. M. P. Walker)任图书馆顾问。当时西文书有3000余册,中文书190部1900册。戴志骞接任后,对管理工作进行改革,增加了开放时间,每天开放7小时,星期六上午和晚间也开放。

1911年秋,圣约翰大学新购兆丰园,并建校长住宅,图书馆迁至卜舫济校长住宅楼下,占屋三间,聘请该校英语、神学教授都孟高任顾问,添聘陈灿勋为助理。为了提高图书馆的利用效率,戴志骞进一步延长开放时间,每天开放7个半小时。图书也有所增加,英文书增至5000余册,中文书391部4432册,比戴志骞接手时增加一倍。1912年,戴志骞对该馆中西文图书全部采用《杜威十进分类法》进行分类和编目,并借鉴西文图书的装订方式,将中文图书全部改为西式装订,还尝试编制分类卡片目录。

在圣约翰大学图书馆的工作,已经初见戴志骞对图书馆工作的改进和兴趣。1912年,他以优异的成绩从圣约翰大学本科毕业,决定继续留在该校任图书馆馆长,1912年9月—1913年年底,他同时在圣约翰大学学习研究生课程,包括哲学、社会学和教育学等专业课程。1913年年底,由于身体健康原因,暂时放弃了继续攻读研究生学位的想法。

戴志骞从1909年秋开始任圣约翰大学图书馆馆长,到1914年8月离开圣约翰大学图书馆,5年的馆长经历为他后来从事图书馆管理工作积累了丰富的经验。

2.2 任清华学校图书(室)馆主任

2.2.1 初识清华园

1914年8月,戴志骞被聘为清华学校图书室主任。清华学校始建于1911年,是利用美国退还庚子赔款创办的留美预备学校,校内一切设施均仿照美国学校建立,建校之初就计划建造图书馆。清华学校图书室于1912年8月20日正式开放,但在独立馆舍建成之前,一直借住同方部(今仍存)西面的平房,为临时图书室,仅有大房一间,小房二间,归庶务处管辖。

清华图书室第一任主任为本校学生黄光,黄光以学生身份兼任图书室主任本为临时性质,最终将出国深造,为图书室选定一位有才华、有能力的管理者成为当务之急。毕业于圣约翰大学的清华学校校长周诒春慧眼识人,认定圣约翰大学校友、管理得法的戴志骞为理想人选。黄光出国后,戴志骞开始执掌清华学校图书室,脱离庶务处,自成学校直属管辖的一个行政单位。在戴志骞的主持下,图书室的管理工作颇有成绩。

图书大量增加。图书是图书馆之本,1912年图书室初建时,仅有中、西文图书2000余册,购书经费无一定数额,由学校随意拨给。1912—1913年,每年只有1000多元,戴志骞接手后,图书经费逐年增加,1914年4000多元,1915年9000多元,1916—1919年,除1918年4000多元外,其余均在1万元以上。不断增加的购书经费,保证了图书的稳定增长。1914年1万多册,1915年1.3万多册,到1919年增加到3万余册。除大批购买图书外,也有部分捐赠,并与其他图书馆建立了最早的馆际交换关系。美国一些图书馆(如美国国会图书馆、纽约国家图书馆、纽约公共图书馆)都有书刊赠送,清华图书室也收集本校各种出版物赠予相应各馆。

建立规章制度。1914年,戴志骞制定了《清华学校图书室章程》,对开馆时间、借书时间、借书期限、借出图书保管、阅览参考书规则等都有详细规定。图书室每到学期终,都要清理本学期借书账目,要求读者把本学期所借图书还回,如想继续阅览,要到图书室重办手续。刊物亦是如此,每年的期刊都要装订成册。1917年正式制定了《图书馆规则》,1919年又制定了《图书馆借书规则》。

开展读者服务。1914年以前,因书籍较少,为保证读者使用,图书室规定,书籍概不外借,只可在图书室阅览。戴志骞任主任后,书籍增加很快,加之图书室狭小,读者又多,阅书室非常拥挤,遂将邻室并入,仍显拥挤,开始实行外借,规定每人一次借书三册,以两个星期为限,如没有他人需要,可续借一次。1914年共借出800多册,以后外借数量逐年增加,1918年借书量增加到1.1万多册。

分类编目工作。尽管戴志骞在圣约翰大学已经有了使用《杜威十进分类法》的经验,但到清华后,并没有急于彻底改革,而是采取改良的方式。戴志骞刚执掌清华图书室时,由于书籍较少,图书仍沿袭旧制,仅按顺序编号。随着图书增加,1916年开始实行"将书名用字母分类,另作一表,悬于图书室内",方便读者查询检索。

建设一座与美国学校相当的图书馆,一直在清华学校管理者的计划之中。1914年6月,周诒春校长聘请年轻的美国建筑师亨利·墨菲为清华学校设计校园规划,并设计了图书馆、大礼堂、体育馆、科学馆四个单体建筑,成为后来著名的清华校园四大建筑。1916年4月新图书馆开工建设,1916年10月图书室改称图书馆,1919年3月新馆舍开始使用。

早在戴志骞来清华之前,建设一座先进图书馆馆舍的计划就已经开始实施,戴志骞被给予管理这座先进图书馆的厚望可想而知。这一时期,戴志骞虽然对图书馆工作进行了很多革新,但总体来说仍然属于对旧式管理方式的改良。为了进一步提升自己,提高新馆建成后的管理水平,戴志骞决定出国深造。

2.2.2 二次赴美留学

在清华学校,戴志骞两次赴美留学。第一次是1917年8月—1919年8月。1917年8月18日,戴志骞与当年赴美留学的清华学生42人,以及通过其他途径赴美留学的24人,一起乘坐太平洋公司的委内瑞拉号轮船驶向大洋彼岸,护送员为清华学校校长周诒春、赴美书记员周辨明。戴志骞半自费、半受学校资助赴美留学,亦在旅途中承担护送任务。

到美国后,戴志骞进入纽约州立大学图书馆学院学习。他用一年的时间学完了学校规定的专业课程,1918年夏到哥伦比亚大学图书馆实习,并加入美国图书馆协会。当时正值第一次世界大战期间,美国图书馆协会号召图书馆员开展战时服务,1918年10月,戴志骞报名参加了纽约爱布顿军营图书馆的工作,先后任该馆参考部主任、副馆长、代理馆长等职。1919年7月正式获得纽约州立大学图书馆学院图书馆学学士学位,1919年8月回到清华图书馆,此时新馆舍已经建成开放。

戴志骞回国后,积极领导中国的新图书馆运动,将美国先进的图书馆管理理念和方法介绍到中国,并以清华学校图书馆作为实践基地,大力进行改革创新,使20世纪20年代的清华图书馆成为中国新图书馆运动的先锋,创立了国内多项最早和第一,戴志骞也从一个旧式管理者转变为新式图书馆的倡导者和领导者。1923年,他还因给丹麦政府提供了特殊服务,而获得丹麦国王授予的丹尼勃罗格骑士勋位(The Order of Knighthood of Dannebroge)。

第二次留学美国是1924年8月—1925年6月。按照当时清华学校的惯例,教职员在校工作满五年,可以申请休假或赴美考察研究一年。戴志骞第一次留学是1919年8月回国,到1924年8月已满5年,他第二次申请出国,获得学校批准。同时戴罗瑜丽也应纽约公共图书馆之聘赴美工作一年,担任该馆编目工作。1924年8月22日,戴志骞与戴罗瑜丽乘坐提督公司杰佛逊总统号轮船(S. S. President Jefferson),由上海启程赴美,同行的还有当年清华派赴留美的应届毕业生61人,上届毕业生3人,以及当年社会各界招考的其他自费留学生81人,共计145人,学生中有后来成为著名物理学家的周培源、大律师梅汝璈、作曲家黄自、语言学家李方桂等,戴志骞及同船教师承担护送任务。在途中,自费生团与清华学生团合作建立协会,戴志骞被推举为会长。

初到美国,据戴志骞的好友凯撒介绍:"戴先生的计划是不确定的,他希望可以到一些大学演讲介绍东方文献。"然而这个计划很快就改变了,因为爱荷华大学(The University of Iowa)的校长杰赛普(Jessup)建议他到爱荷华大学继续攻读研究生学位。戴罗瑜丽也放弃了纽约公共图书馆的工作,而在爱荷华大学图书馆担任助理编目员。

在爱荷华大学,戴志骞学习了教育统计、心理测量、学校管理、大学管理、现代哲学和图书馆教育等课程,并提交了博士学位论文《图书馆学专业教育:在爱荷华大学建立图书馆学院的建议》(*Professional Education for Librarianship:A Proposal for a Library School at the University of Iowa*),以及他的著述清单、研究背景等资料。1925年6月5日,爱荷华大学为戴志骞举行申请哲学博士学位论文答辩会,Kaiser 及 Packer、Ruch、Patrick、Taeusch、Cousins、Thomas 等教授为答辩委员,6月9日该校评委会一致推荐,授予戴志骞哲学博士学位。

获得学位后,戴志骞与戴罗瑜丽走访考察了美国、英国、法国、比利时、荷兰、挪威、瑞典、丹麦、德国、俄国、日本等国的图书馆,拜访了戴罗瑜丽的故乡,1925年9月回到清华图书馆。1925年11月,戴志骞的博士论文由西方最大的书目文献出版公司纽约威尔逊出版公司正式出版,出版时删除了副标题,以《图书馆学专业教育》(*Professional Education for Librarianship*)为题出版。

戴志骞的《图书馆学专业教育》(*Professional Education for Librarianship*)为他在美国图书馆界赢得了极高的声誉。曾任普林斯顿大学图书馆馆长的理查德森(E. C. Richardson)在《图书馆杂志》上评价这是一部"优秀的和实用的著作"。正如1988年旅美学者骆传华在《中国学术研究指南》(*Notable Books on Chinese Studies*)中所说,戴志骞的研究有两点值得铭记:第一,他发现那时美国的23所图书馆学校并非设备齐全或有足够的教师来培训专业图书馆员以满足全国的发展需求,地域分布不平衡。他建议在爱荷华大学新开一所图书馆学校,提供研究生课程和本科生课程。第二,他审视了当时的图书馆学校课程后,提出了多方面的改进建议。现在美国380多个图书馆专业机构的基本要求和课程设置,基本上和戴博士60年前设想的一样。

2.2.3 清华园的图书馆学思想家和活动家

2.2.3.1 开展与外国图书馆界的交流

参加美国图书馆协会的活动。戴志骞利用二次到美国留学的机会,与美国图书馆界建立了友好的关系。最早与美国图书馆界的交往始于1918年,这一年,还是纽约州立大学图书馆学院学生的戴志骞加入了美国图书馆协会,1918—1931年戴志骞始终是该会会员。1918年夏参加了在纽约散落托加泉举行的年会(Saratoga Springs Conference),后又参加了纽约图书馆协会在泼澜雪湖(Lake Placid)举行的会议。1919年6月参加了在艾斯博瑞公园举行的美国图书馆协会战时图书馆服务展览会(Asbury Park Conference)。1924年12月受美国图书馆协会"图书馆学教育董事会"(Board of Education for Librarianship)的邀请,参加建立美国图书馆学高等学校可行性计划公开会议,1925年4月再次受到该会邀请,第二次参加建立美国图书馆学高等学校可行性计划的公开会议。

率先向国外同行介绍中国图书馆界的情况。1919年,戴志骞分别在《公共图书馆》(*Public Libraries*)2月号上发表了《中国图书馆的现状》(*Present Library Conditions in China*),在《图书馆学刊》(*The Library Journal*)6月号上发表了《中国图书馆概述》(*A Brief Sketch of Chinese Libraries*)两篇文章,介绍中国图书馆发展的历史及现状,引起了美国图书馆学界的重视。1920年美国图书馆协会负责报告东方图书馆发展情况的韦德女士从华盛顿回到中国南京,无法按时完成中国图书馆的报告,美国图书馆协会邀请戴志骞代表中国撰写图书馆发展报告,戴志骞撰写了《中国的图书馆运动》(*Library Movement in China*)一文,刊登在

1920—1921年的《美国图书馆协会委员会报告》上,让美国图书馆学界更加了解中国图书馆的发展。1923年,由美国教育会发起的"万国教育会议"(即世界教育联合会)在旧金山俄克兰召开成立大会,中国教育界派代表参加了此次有世界影响的大会,并推举各专业的名人撰写论文,中国共提交了17篇论文,戴志骞代表中国图书馆界提交了《中国的图书馆运动》的学术论文。1929年国际图书馆协会联合会(IFLA)在罗马召开规模宏大的代表大会,戴志骞提交了论文《中国现代图书馆的发展》(Development of Modern Libraries in China)。戴志骞以各种机会向外国同行传递中国图书馆学界的信息,是近代早期中国图书馆学界与外国图书馆学界交流的主要使者。

推动庚款基金用于发展中国的图书馆事业。1925年,为了获取美国第二次退还的庚款用于发展中国的图书馆事业,戴志骞借助在美留学的机会,协助美国友人韦棣华女士奔走呼吁,宣传中国文化,向美国图书馆界与普通民众介绍中国国内的图书馆运动,得到美国同行的支持,声援中国的图书馆从庚子退款中受益。他以中华教育改进社图书馆教育组主席、图书馆教育研究委员会主任之职,促成中华教育改进社邀请美国图书馆协会派员前往中国调查图书馆的发展情况,最终美国图书馆协会派该会前主席、圣路易斯公共图书馆馆长鲍士伟博士(Dr. Arthur E. Bostwick)来华调查访问,促使部分庚款基金用于发展中国的图书馆事业。

编制西人论中国书目。1918年夏,戴志骞到哥伦比亚大学图书馆实习,从那时起,他就注意收集西方人论中国的书目,他先后查阅了美国图书馆协会、波士顿图书馆、宾夕法尼亚卡内基图书馆、哥伦比亚大学图书馆等各大图书馆的图书目录,以及《图书评论文摘》刊载的图书目录,同时也参考了高迪爱的《中国书目》(Bibliotheca Sinica),收集到一些最新的西方汉学书目,陆续在《中国学生月刊》(The Chinese Students' Monthly)上发表介绍,并编辑完成了《关于中国的书目:1900—1918》(Bibliography on China:1900—1918),该书不同于其他同类书目只提供作者、题名、刊物、刊期等简单信息,而是在书目信息之外,增加了内容简介、图书评价等,开创了编辑书目的新体例,十分便于读者使用。

2.2.3.2 近代中国图书馆事业的领导者

创立中华图书馆协会。从美国学习归来后,戴志骞一直在思考如何推动中国的新图书馆运动,在1920年给美国图书馆协会的报告中,他阐述了一直在头脑中计划的几件事:建立中国的图书馆协会,宣传图书馆,规范图书馆管理;鼓励各个城市建立图书馆协会;在高等教育机构中建立图书馆学校;鼓励每个地区建立小型图书馆和阅览室;鼓励中国学生赴美学习图书馆学等;在他的不懈努力下,一些计划得以实现,其中最重要的成果就是创建了早期中国图书馆协会组织。1921年12月,戴志骞参加由蔡元培、郭秉文、陶行知等发起成立的"中华教育改进社",创立"图书馆教育组",这是中国第一个全国性的图书馆专业组织,戴志骞任"图书馆教育组"主席。1922年,在中华教育改进社第一次年会图书馆教育组会议上,戴志骞提议"组织图书馆管理学会",学会虽未成立,但促成了"图书馆教育研究委员会"的成立,戴志骞任"图书馆教育研究委员会"主任。1923年,在中华教育改进社第二届年会上,戴志骞提案"组织各地方图书馆协会"在图书馆教育组获得通过。1924年3月30日,戴志骞率先领导成立北京图书馆协会,这是第一个组织完备的地方图书馆协会,戴志骞任会长。1925年4月25日,成立中华图书馆协会,戴志骞远在美国,缺席被选为中华图书馆协会首任执行部部长。1929年,中华图书馆协会在南京召开第一次年会,戴志骞任年会筹备委员会主任、大会副主席、图书馆建筑委员会主席,一直到新中国成立之前,他始终担任中华图书馆协会的领导工作。图书馆协会组织的建立,使图书馆员有了精神归宿,图书馆员群体有了交流的机会,提高了馆员的整体水平,有助于图书馆事业的发展。

引进先进管理模式,创立分部门管理制度。1919年8月,戴志骞第一次留学回国,积极投身中国的新图书馆运动,将在美国所学的图书馆理论与方法应用到实际工作中,他以清华图书馆为实践基地,实施一系列改革创新的措施:①健全组织系统;②确定学校图书馆的定位;③建立预算制度;④采用先进的图书分类编目方法。戴志骞率先把分部门管理的概念引入中国,创立分部门制度,他在清华图书馆设立了参考部、购置部、编目部、出纳部、登录部、装订部,工作人员分工负责,工作更加专业细化,使清华图书馆成为近代早期中国第一个采用分部门管理方式的图书馆。通过这些改革,使清华图书馆成为当时国内设施最先进、管理最完备的图书馆,在全国起到了示范作用,各地争相派人前来参观学习。

创立图书馆暑期学校,培养图书馆学人才。1920年,戴志骞在北京高师举办了图书馆学讲习会,也称图书馆暑期学校,这是中国第一个图书馆暑期学校,所有讲稿均由戴志骞编译,听者极为踊跃,起到了很好地宣传新图书馆的作用,提高了民众对新式图书馆的认同感。讲习会引进了美国式图书馆管理理念,学习美国式管理方法与技术,标志着中国图书馆学界由学习日本转向了学习美国。

2.2.3.3 中国近代图书馆学的奠基人

提出"图书馆为终身学校"。1918年,戴志骞首次提出"图书馆为终身学校",他说:"学校即教育之初步也,教少年人民以温故知新之识。然学校不能教育国民之终身,人人有出学校之一日;若社会中无图书馆,则多数离学校后,即于智力上不能生长。如要国民有终身智力生长之机,除图书馆外别无较良美之法;故图书馆可称国民之终身学校也。"终身学习改变了单纯接受学校教育的学习途径,从阶段学习扩展到终身学习,从被动学习扩展到主动学习,从少数人扩展到所有人。"终身教育"作为现代教育概念,由前联合国教科文组织(UNESCO)官员保罗·朗格朗在1965年提出,他在《终身教育展望》一文中说"任何年龄阶段的所有人都能得到学习的机会",而早在40多年前,戴志骞就提出了"图书馆为终身学校"的概念。

提出"六要素"说。1920年8月,戴志骞在北京高师图书馆暑期学校的演讲中,首次提出了图书馆管理的"六要素"说,归纳起来为馆舍、环境、书籍、方法、服务、馆长。"要素说"是新图书馆运动最重要的理论依据,新型图书馆与封建藏书楼的明显不同,就是要素的不同。后来经杜定友、陶述先、刘国钧等不断阐述,"要素说"成为民国时期影响最大的图书馆学理论流派。戴志骞最早提出"要素说",且与后来的"要素说"相比更加具体和全面。

构建中国近代图书馆学理论体系雏形。戴志骞在其主持开办的北京高师图书馆讲习会上,系统讲述图书馆的组织法、管理法、分类法、编目法、图书馆建筑等,最早构建了中国近代图书馆学理论体系的雏形。据北京《晨报》报道:"中国自从开办图书馆以来,大家只知道图书馆,不知道什么是图书馆学。到了这会讲演图书馆组织法、管理法、分类编目以及图书馆教育科学,一切听的人,都知道图书馆是一门科学,大有研究的价值。"

"知识组织"概念的先驱。戴志骞在1925年出版的《图书馆学专业教育》中,提出了"动的"和"静的"图书馆的概念,他把图书馆分成为科学研究服务的静态图书馆和为当前经济发展服务的动态图书馆。静态图书馆类似传统图书馆,收藏的文献包罗万象,主要功能是保存文化,供学者和研究人员使用。动态图书馆是适应工业化时代的要求,收藏的是最新的工业和商业信息文献,主要满足工业社会对信息的需求,解决现实遇到的实际问题。美国著名图书馆学家亨利·埃韦林·布利斯(Henry Evelyn Bliss)受此启发,在20世纪20年代末最早提出了"知识组织"的概念。然而,直到20世纪末,"知识组织"的概念才引起中国同行的重视。

此外,戴志骞还设计了图书馆民主管理制度,主张建立公共的、平民化的图书馆,提出图书馆员的职业标准等,为后世图书馆学思想的发展打下了基础。

2.2.4　告别清华园

1928年6月,北伐军攻克北京,奉系张作霖派出的清华学校军人校长温应星去职。6月4日,国民政府外交部派余日宣暂行代理清华校长,一星期后外交部及裁撤教育部后设立的大学院来电,派原教务长梅贻琦暂代校务,等待接管。争夺清华领导权的暗流涌动,波及清华校园,8月3日,学生评议会通过"组织校务改进委员会,全权办理改进校务事宜"的决议。8月17日,南京国民政府任命罗家伦为清华大学校长,9月3日,学生校务改进委员会发动"清校运动",当晚,学生评议会召集全体学生大会,通过议案,驱逐作为学校领导机构的评议会成员余日宣、杨光弼、赵学海、戴志骞、虞振镛五位著名教授,罪名是"把持校务"。当时的京沪各大报纸都登载了关于这一事件的消息,据《申报》载,学生会"并推代表(偕同全体同学)持函至上列五人家中,声述同学之意见,当经五人亲向全体学生答复,以后决不再在清华任职",学生始散。上述五人均为校内有威望的教授,此事在校内引起不安,教师人人自危,学生会为稳定事态,发表对教职员声明书,声言不会波及其他教授。罗家伦上任的障碍被清除,9月18日,罗家伦宣誓就任国立清华大学校长。

戴志骞无奈辞职,离开了他工作14年的清华学校。戴志骞离去后,他本人和清华图书馆领导人都进入动荡时期,造成一定的损失。1928年10月28日,戴志骞与清华大学的梅贻琦、赵元任同乘平沪特别快车启程南下,梅贻琦为从上海乘船赴美就任留美监督,赵元任为受中央研究院历史语言研究所及清华大学国学研究院的委托赴广东调查方言,而戴志骞则受南京国立中央大学之聘,前往担任国立中央大学图书馆馆长兼江苏大学区督学。戴罗瑜丽也随之离开清华,就任北京协和医学院图书馆主任,移住大方家胡同27号。

2.3　任国立中央大学图书馆馆长

1927年6月,南京国民政府按照蔡元培的建议,仿效法国教育制度,中央取消教育部,代之以大学院,直隶于国民政府;各省裁撤教育厅,划定大学区,区内设国立大学一所,由大学校长综理区内一切学术与教育行政事宜。大学区制实际上只在江苏、浙江和北平实行,前后仅两年时间。

国立中央大学是江苏大学区制中的国立大学,领导区内学术、教育等一切事务。该校是由国立第四中山大学改定而来,1927年6月9日,江苏9所专科以上的公立学校合并,组建为国立第四中山大学。1928年5月16日,原第四中山大学奉令改为国立中央大学,图书馆馆长由皮宗石担任。1928年9月,皮宗石应邀到国立武汉大学任社会科学院院长、教授,戴志骞受聘为国立中央大学图书馆馆长兼江苏大学区督学。

戴志骞任馆长的时间是1928年11月—1929年9月,虽然时间短暂,但对中大图书馆工作多有考虑和改进。他在中大总理纪念周演讲中说:"图书馆方面,觉书库太空,观众太少,设备不周,阅报处之不妥,就诸点观察,亟待改良者也。现在隆冬时期,寒风习习,装设之火炉,颇多危险,今拟改设汽管。电灯不明,在校中新电机装成后,再加台灯。阅书室太小,拟再扩充之。以我校有八院之多,二千学生之众,如购二、三万元之书籍,未免太少。其他如管理问题,千头万绪,都在筹划中,要之物质与形式,均应注意及之也。"

对于馆内的管理工作,戴志骞从整理书目入手。原国立中央大学图书馆采用洪有丰分类法进行分类和编目,分为八类,戴志骞在此基础上,对分类法进行了补充,将革命文献列为第九类,主持编纂了《国立中央大学图书目录》,全书共分为四册,1929年12月出版。

在国立中央大学图书馆馆长任上,戴志骞还承担了筹备召开中华图书馆协会第一届年会的任务。1928年10月,戴志骞准备由清华学校转职国立中央大学,临行前与袁同礼商议在南京举行年会,并任年会筹备委员会主任。到南京后与金陵大学的刘国钧、李小缘等加以讨论,赴沪与商务印书馆王云五接洽,取得教育部蒋梦麟、中央研究院蔡元培、杨杏佛的支持,从教育部、铁道部、外交部、内政部、卫生部、工商部、中央大学、北平大学、清华大学、燕京大学、江苏省政府等处筹款。1929年1月28日—2月1日中华图书馆协会第一届年会在南京盛大召开,戴志骞任年会副主席,并致开会词,被选为执行委员会委员、建筑委员会主席。

3 教育职业生涯

3.1 任国立中央大学高等教育处处长、副校长

1929年2月,因原国立中央大学高等教育处处长张贻惠赴北平,中大校长张乃燕聘戴志骞兼任中大高等教育处处长,主要协助校长处理大学本部事务。1929年5月,张乃燕"援浙江大学例,由校长聘副校长,以前高等教育处长戴超充任"。同年9月,国立中央大学聘崔莘村代理图书馆馆长,戴志骞专任副校长。

1929年5月—1930年7月,戴志骞任国立中央大学副校长,在副校长任上,他的工作受到好评,据中大校友董德鉴回忆:"副校长戴志骞精明能干,也比较开明,那时中大能有所改进,不能抹杀他善于采纳意见的优点。"

3.2 告别南京

大学区制的实行,并没有得到广泛的支持。大学区中等学校联合会指出:"这种采用学术机关与行政机关合二为一的大学区制,只能使清高的学府变为政客角逐的场所,恳请设法变更。"1928年10月,大学院恢复为教育部,1929年6月,各地停止实行大学区制。戴志骞仍然任副校长,1930年1月,国立中央大学校长张乃燕在呈送给教育部的《中央大学组织规程》中规定:"本大学设副校长一人襄理校务,由校长聘任之,并呈报行政院、教育部备案。""校长不在校时,副校长代行校长职务。"

虽然大学区制被取消,但由于遗留问题太多,仍然矛盾重重。实行大学区制时,国立中央大学综理区内所有教育机构,中小学经费均由大学统一拨给。停止大学区制后,大学经费由国家拨给,中小学经费由地方拨给,但中央和江苏省互相推诿,大学经费迟迟不能到位,出现了大学与中小学对地方财政争利的状况,矛盾几近不可调和。1929年7月,戴志骞提出辞职,赴青岛避暑,暑假期间,回到北平家中休养。7月29日,中大电请戴志骞回校继续主持校务,8月回到中大,8月19日开始主持中大行政院会议。

1929年秋,戴志骞父戴造梁先生和母沈太夫人先后去世。1930年5月,戴造梁先生和

沈太夫人开吊安葬,戴志骞请假两周,返里治丧。假满刚刚返校,校内就出现了张贴标语,攻击校政,校长张乃燕公告澄清。5月23日,又出现了毁谤戴志骞的标语,校长张乃燕发布公告痛斥之,肯定戴志骞"学识品性,夙为士林所推重,自任职本校以来,治事精勤,态度诚恳,襄理校务,公正和平,本校长方庆辅助得人,即各同学亦多深钦佩"。

戴志骞悲愤请辞,学校多次挽留。1930年7月,经第4次请辞后,戴志骞最终辞去了中大副校长的职务,此后中大再未任命副校长。1930年9月,张乃燕上呈行政院、教育部,裁撤了副校长一职。

4　参与其他图书馆和社会活动

北京图书馆委员会委员。1926年,在韦棣华女士和戴志骞的共同努力下,管理美国第二次退还庚款的中华教育基金会决定将部分退款用于发展中国的图书馆事业,并决定创办"北京图书馆"。1926年3月1日成立"北京图书馆委员会",委员有范源濂、任鸿隽、周诒春、张伯苓、戴志骞等人。1927年7月"北京图书馆委员会"改组,委员有周诒春(委员长)、任鸿隽(书记)、李四光(会计)、张伯苓、戴志骞、袁同礼;1927年9月成立"北京图书馆建筑委员会",聘周诒春、李四光、戴志骞、袁同礼、安那为委员;1928年7月北京图书馆改为北平图书馆,10月又改为北平北海图书馆,原"北京图书馆委员会"改组,由任鸿隽(委员长)、袁同礼(书记)、胡先骕(会计)、周诒春、丁文江、陈垣、张伯苓、戴志骞、叶企孙任委员;1929年2月北平北海图书馆成立购书委员会,委员有任鸿隽(委员长)、胡先骕(会计)、袁同礼(书记)、周诒春、张伯苓、戴志骞、陈垣、丁文江、叶企孙。1926—1929年,北京图书馆委员会几经改组,人员数次变动,但戴志骞始终担任委员职务。

担任中华图书馆协会的领导职务。戴志骞在离开图书馆界后,仍然一直担任中华图书馆协会的领导职务,参加协会的活动。1930—1944年,历年协会领导机构选举,均被选为中华图书馆协会执行委员(1937年以后改为理事)或监察委员及建筑委员会主席等职。1933年被选为中华图书馆协会募集基金委员会委员、基金保管委员会主席,1944年5月参加中华图书馆协会第六次年会,当选为协会监事。

松坡图书馆馆务委员会委员。松坡图书馆是梁启超为纪念反袁领袖蔡锷(字松坡)将军而倡议建立的,1923年11月4日正式成立,梁启超出任馆长。1920—1928年,戴志骞担任松坡图书馆馆务委员会委员。

南开大学图书馆顾问。1919—1922年,戴志骞担任天津南开大学图书馆顾问。1921年11月,应南开大学邀请,戴志骞先后三次用英语为南开大学学生做了题为《如何使用图书馆及参考书》(*How to Use the Library and Reference Book*)的长篇演讲,其间用幻灯片展示西方各国的图书馆,听众获益甚多。

中国科学社成员。该社由赵元任、任鸿隽、杨铨等人创办,最初只发行《科学》杂志,1915年10月25日改组为中国科学社,宗旨是"联络同志,共图中国科学之发达",是中国近代史上影响最为深远的科学社团,影响波及海内外。1918年,戴志骞加入该社。

中国国防会会员(The Advisory Committee of the National Defense League of China)。这是中国留学生在美国建立的学生组织,1915年为反对日本强加给中国的《二十一条》,哈佛和麻省理工学院的中国留学生发起成立国防会,主张唤起国人,团结民众,以达救亡图存之目的,会长张贻志,副会长尹寰枢,出版《国防报》季刊。戴志骞到美国后加入了国防会。1919年8月以后,随着会友先后回国,活动逐渐转入国内。

戴志骞还参加了一些其他图书馆界的活动。1932年7月,上海创制中学添设女子部图书馆科,戴志骞、戴罗瑜丽、杜定友、洪有丰、李小缘、沈祖荣、刘国钧等人受聘为指导委员。1935年4月,戴志骞当选为上海市图书馆临时董事会董事,并与王云五、杜定友、洪逵等董事一起,草拟了上海市图书馆第一年预算。1936年,戴志骞作为文华图专的校董,捐赠该校特等新式打字机一架,以供实习之用。

5 短暂的东北之行

1930年7月,戴志骞回到北平大方家胡同27号的家中,1930年8月赴哈尔滨,开始从事东北垦殖开发的金融商行投资业务。戴志骞离开图书馆学、教育学领域,成为一名金融与投资领域的拓荒者。

多年领导中国图书馆事业的经验,使戴志骞能够站在全国的高度思考中国的发展大计,对东北的开发有深刻的认识。当时,日本和俄罗斯长期觊觎中国东北的黑土地,其狼子野心昭然若揭,强烈的爱国情结和责任感使他意识到要自立自强,才能摆脱日、俄的控制,他在给好友凯撒的信中说:"满洲和蒙古合起来比中国本土还要大,而如果中国忽略这些边远地区的发展,30或40年后,它们就将不属于中国了。满洲(东北)四省蕴藏特别丰富的各类矿产,而且那些未经垦殖的土地很适合种植谷物和豆类。将山东与河北两省的壮年汉人迁往满洲,并引进国际资本(日本与俄国资本除外),是阻止日本与俄国渗透影响的根本性政策。"1931年,日本发动"九一八事变",疯狂掠夺东北的资源,应验了戴志骞的预言。

"九一八事变"前,在奉系军阀主政下的东北,社会相对稳定,尤其是20世纪20年代,关内连年军阀混战,自然灾害频繁,而同期的东北由于采取了一系列鼓励垦田的措施,使耕地面积不断扩大,粮食产量不断提高,经济形势较好,吸引直、鲁两省出现移民大潮,大量移民迁往东北从事垦殖农业,东北的垦殖公司不断增加。

迅速发展的垦殖业对资金的需求量很大,促进了东北金融业及民族资本主义的发展。戴志骞出于"引进国际资本(日本与俄国资本除外),是阻止日本与俄国渗透影响的根本性政策"的信念与梦想,"决心放弃我的专业,努力在荒凉的满洲(东北)边疆四省充当一名金融与投资领域的拓荒者"。1930年9月,他受邀担任哈尔滨工业有限公司经理,开始在哈尔滨、奉天(沈阳)、上海、南京之间来回奔波,处理金融业务。从图书馆界、教育界转到银行界,在一年的时间里,戴志骞强势完成了角色转换。

6 在银行界的职业生涯

6.1 任中国银行人事室主任、赴外稽核、总秘书

1931年7月,戴志骞回到上海,由陈长桐(清华校友,中国银行国外部营业部主任)、蔡承新(清华校友,中国银行上海分行副总经理)、陈隽人(中国银行济南分行经理)推荐,进入中国银行工作,任人事室主任兼赴外稽核。1931年7月25日,戴志骞参加由孔祥熙发起成立的"工商管理协会"聚餐讨论会,"因戴志骞先生曾在东北经营实业,请其讲演东三省之经

济问题,均极详尽"。

中国银行是从大清银行发展来的,曾在很长一段时期里扮演国家银行的角色。赴外稽核是中国银行的重要业务工作,1915年开始设立,专司检查各行账目。期间历经变迁,"直至二十年(1931年),总处设立检查室,始恢复赴外稽核名义,而以人事室主任(戴志骞)、总账室主任(刘攻芸)关系,皆兼赴外稽核"。

1931年12月,中国银行修订组织大纲,规定"中国银行设总管理处,总揽全体行务"。"总管理处设总稽核一人,总秘书一人,承总经理之命,分掌全行一切业务事务。其任免由总经理提出,商同董事长、常务董事提交董事会定之。"戴志骞受聘为代理总秘书兼人事室主任,1933年正式任总秘书,1934年6月由原总务课课长林旭如接替人事室主任,戴志骞专任总秘书。

中国银行总秘书的职责是:"掌管全行各项事务如下:1. 掌管全行机要文卷及总务事项。2. 掌管重要印信、图章及电报密码。3. 掌管印制及销毁兑换券,并关于处理兑换券及代理公债本息票一切事项。4. 掌管关于本行股票一切事项。5. 审定全行房屋、地皮买卖租赁契约。6. 审定全行建筑计划。"由上述职责可知,总秘书担负全行的重要责任,参加高层行务会议,参与重要事件的讨论及决策,负责对下辖国内外众多分行的管理指导。在戴志骞服务中行的近20年里,4位总经理或董事长张嘉璈、宋子文、孔祥熙、宋汉章都是中国著名金融界人物,宋子文、孔祥熙还是活跃在中国政坛上的重要人物,戴志骞作为总秘书,与他们多有合作,互有往来,参与了很多重大事件的处理。

从1931年代理中国银行总秘书,1933年正式任总秘书,直到1942年,戴志骞一直在中国银行总秘书岗位上工作,1942年11月,"戴(志骞)总秘书调充赴外稽核,以王韧代理总秘书兼人事室主任"。抗战胜利后,1945年9月,戴志骞奉派协助中行总稽核霍宝树主持东北中国银行的复业工作,10月23日到达长春,三周后,因与苏联驻军交涉无进展而回到北平。1945年12月负责接收中国银行天津分行并兼代该行经理。

1946年5月,中国银行"调派赴外稽核暂行兼代津行经理戴志骞充任总秘书兼人事室主任,所遗津行经理一职,调现任代理总秘书兼人事室主任王韧代理"。此后,中国银行再未更换过总秘书兼人事室主任,直到1949年年底。

6.2 中行的管理工作

6.2.1 建立考试录用制度

戴志骞任中国银行总秘书,一直兼管人事工作,他非常注重用人,建立了通过考试择优录用的用人办法。考试程序非常严格,分为笔试和口试,录用的标准是:①考进时要中文通顺,中文之外,要懂一国外国语文,如日文、英文、法文或德文等;②在柜台上没有算盘的时候,亦要笔算快;③算盘要精,养成能同顾客口中说话,手下已把数目算出;④须会用计算机;⑤英文打字必须熟;⑥试用员亦要会用计算尺。笔试通过后,要经过4个人面试,评判合格后,总经理还要亲自面试。中国银行录用的一般为大学生,考试对所有的人都一视同仁,机会均等。经过考试录取的途径,使入行新人很快就能适应工作的需要。

6.2.2 主持搬迁

1937年8月13日,日军发动"八一三事变",大规模进攻上海。为躲避战事,中国银行总管理处由上海汉口路五十号中国银行大楼,迁至霞飞路办事处楼上办公。1937年11月

12日上海沦陷,中国银行总管理处人员逐步移至香港办公。1937年12月1日,国民政府迁都重庆,1939年9月,中国银行总管理处奉令迁往重庆。

戴志骞主持了整个中行的搬迁工作。中行总管理处迁往重庆后,先在重庆两路口予园办公,后迁至上清寺二楼办公。由于重庆遭到轰炸,行屋受损,以及迁渝人员增多,中行在重庆郊外石桥铺玉灵洞购地建筑简单办公用房,并开凿防空洞备用。同时建造了员工宿舍,解决住宿问题。

玉灵洞地处重庆郊区,物资匮乏,为了解决员工的生活问题,他们想了很多办法,比如,租用附近田地约十亩开荒种地,开筑蓄水堰塘一方以裕水源;购置柴油发电机一具,以供电灯及电台之用;置备交通车数辆,以便同人暨眷属往返城乡之用;开办各种福利事业,设立员工消费合作社、眷属公共食堂、同人俱乐部及医务室等,帮助同人渡过难关。通过这些有效的措施,稳定了员工队伍,为战时金融服务提供了保障。

6.2.3 积极开拓海外市场

抗战期间,由于日军占领了中国东南大部分地区,原有中国银行的很多分行、支行不能正常营业,为了保证业务工作的开展,戴志骞受中国银行的委托,积极开拓海外市场。1938年戴志骞主持在安南、河内、海防筹设中国银行分行经理处,1940年开辟了仰光经理处。抗战期间,中国银行海外分支行努力争取侨汇,积极支持抗战,1942年中国银行成为国际贸易专业银行,主要承担外汇经营管理工作,戴志骞主持建立的海外经理处发挥了作用。

6.2.4 主持接收工作

1945年8月15日,日本宣布无条件投降。日军侵华期间,敌占区的中国银行分、支行全部被日军霸占或控制,抗战胜利后戴志骞两次参加从敌军手中接收中国银行并准备复业的工作。第一次是1945年9月,戴志骞奉派赴东北接收,10月到达长春,会见当地中国银行留守人员,筹划复业办法。但是由于东北政局发生变化,接收未果,回到关内。1945年12月,戴志骞第二次接受接收任务,负责接收中国银行天津分行,任天津分行经理。在接收过程中,戴志骞积极征调人员,使天津分行很快恢复了营业秩序。

7 最后归宿

在戴志骞任职中国银行期间,戴罗瑜丽于1936年辞去北平协和医学院图书馆主任之职,移居上海,全家搬入上海的中国银行员工宿舍,住上海市南京西路770号德义大楼内55号。卢沟桥事变爆发后,中国开始全面抗战,1937年11月12日上海沦陷,戴志骞只身赴香港、重庆任职,戴罗瑜丽与孩子们留守上海。抗战胜利后,戴志骞随中国银行总管理处回到上海。戴罗瑜丽自1922年4月26日与戴志骞结婚,已经把中国当成了第二祖国。1947年4月26日,戴志骞与戴罗瑜丽携手走过了25个年头,按照西方婚俗,迎来了银婚庆典,这一天,同人前来祝贺,"共祝志骞夫妇银婚"。在戴罗瑜丽的悉心照顾下,孩子们健康成长,小女儿于1942年10月在上海结婚,大女儿于1947年1月5日在上海结婚。1947年11月15日,戴罗瑜丽向江苏省青浦县提交了入籍申请,1948年1月6日得到批准,戴罗瑜丽正式加入中国国籍。

1948年年底,国民党在大陆大势已去,1948年12月28日"志骞夫人来港",暂住中国银行香港分行经理郑铁如处,后移住香港福利别墅10号,这也是戴志骞在香港的最后住所。

在此期间,戴志骞仍奔波于香港和内地之间处理行务,1949年2月24日抵达香港,3月5日乘船回到上海处理公务,4月初再到香港。1949年4月26日,在宋子文的运作下,上海金融界高级人员南下,中国银行总经理席德懋、副总经理陈长桐及重要职员霍宝树、徐广迟等抵达香港,在此之前,金融界人士张公权、李蘸蒜、陈光甫、戴志骞亦已到港,不久中行董事长宋汉章也抵港。

1949年5月27日,上海市军管会接收了上海中国银行总管理处,委派龚饮冰为中国银行总经理,6月6日新总管理处宣布复业。

面对国民党的溃败,戴志骞对国民政府非常失望,他在1948年12月视察中行新加坡分行时说:"国内战局,国民党已经没有希望,新加坡中行不要再迁移了,最多是改朝换代,(中行)还是中国人的。"他没有跟随原国民政府迁往台湾,但也没有选择回到大陆。1951年7月下旬,戴志骞偕夫人戴罗瑜丽同赴阿根廷,住在阿根廷首都布宜诺斯艾利斯奥利弗斯区罗克·萨恩斯·培纳街851号(R. S. Pena 851 Fondo, Olivos FCNGBM, Buenos Aires, Argentina.)。关于戴志骞去世的时间有两种记载,一是原中国银行副总经理卞白眉于1963年5月收到戴志骞生前同事兼好友姚崧龄的来信,报告戴志骞于1963年3月初在阿根廷逝世;二是据旅美学者骆传华所记,戴志骞于1963年3月19日在布宜诺斯艾利斯逝世,他的名字和贡献将被永远铭记。

凡　　例

一、本书收录戴志骞先生所著的中英文论著、单篇文章、书评、演讲词与序言；戴志骞所编的关于中国的书目也被收入文集之中。

二、本书依类编排，上册为中、英文文章，下册为中、英文著作。中文文章按主题类聚，按照戴志骞职业生涯的经历，分列图书馆事业篇、教育事业篇、银行事业篇，每篇排列以发表时间为序。

三、文集收录的均为戴志骞或与戴志骞有关的著述，中文文章除有特殊说明需要署名外，一般不再署名；英文文章，因中英文对照，故署名均有保留。

四、原载于某著作卷首的序言，原题往往为"序"或"preface"，本书酌改为"某书序"格式。

五、诸文原散载于报章杂志或书刊卷首，版式不尽一致。此次结集，以尽可能保留原初版式为原则，以见文稿原貌；但也进行了一些必要的改变，将原刊本中文竖排者改为横排，表格版式也相应略做调整。

六、原刊本中的中文繁体字，均改用规范简体字，对原文标点符号不合者，本书根据现代行文习惯进行了适当修正。

七、原刊中一些文章为未标点的文言文，本书均加以标点。

八、本书对原文明显印刷错误，包括错字、别字、丢字等进行了订正，异体字一般改为通用字，补字一般用（ ）表示。

九、作者注释以【原注】示之。原文译名，包括人名、地名、组织机构名称等，保持原貌，确有说明需要，以【编者注】【译者注】示之。

总目录

上册

序一 ································ 程焕文(1)
序二 ································ 蒋耘中(1)
戴志骞先生传略 ······················ 韦庆媛(1)
凡例 ··································· (1)

中文文章

图书馆事业篇

论美国图书馆 ································ (4)
图书馆学 ····································· (8)
图书馆与教育——在北京高师图书馆的演讲 ··· (11)
图书馆与教育——在南京高师的演讲 ·········· (13)
《图书馆学》戴志骞先生序 ···················· (16)
图书馆与学校 ································· (17)
图书馆学简说 ································· (19)
图书馆学——在清华学校的演讲 ··············· (27)
图书分类法几条原则的商榷 ···················· (33)
欧美图书馆概况 ······························· (35)
清华周刊记者与戴志骞谈话记 ················· (39)
《图书分类法》序(节选) ····················· (41)
清华周刊记者采访戴志骞 ······················ (42)
清华学校图书馆概况 ·························· (44)
十五年来之中国图书馆事业 ···················· (50)
服务图书馆的甘苦 ···························· (53)
清华学校图书馆之过去,现在,及将来 ·········· (54)
图书馆的变迁与利用 ·························· (58)
《清华学校图书馆中文书籍目录》序 ············ (59)
中华图书馆协会第一届年会开幕辞 ············· (60)
中华图书馆协会第一届年会筹备主任报告 ······ (61)
《国立中央大学图书馆图书目录》序 ············ (62)

《中国图书馆名人录》序 …………………………………………………… (63)
图书馆员职业之研究 ……………………………………………………… (64)
【附录Ⅰ】戴志骞撰写的书报介绍 ……………………………………… (66)
　　【附录Ⅰ-1】《清华周刊·书报介绍副刊》第一期 ……………… (66)
　　【附录Ⅰ-2】《清华周刊·书报介绍副刊》第二期 ……………… (73)
　　【附录Ⅰ-3】《清华周刊·书报介绍副刊》第四期 ……………… (76)
　　【附录Ⅰ-4】《清华周刊·书报介绍副刊》第十二期 …………… (78)
【附录Ⅱ】戴志骞主持的会议记录及议决案 …………………………… (79)
　　【附录Ⅱ-1】中华教育改进社第一届年会"图书馆教育组"会议纪要 …… (79)
　　【附录Ⅱ-2】中华教育改进社第二届年会"图书馆教育组"会议纪要 …… (84)
　　【附录Ⅱ-3】中华教育改进社第三届年会"图书馆教育组"会议纪要 …… (96)
　　【附录Ⅱ-4】中华图书馆协会第一届年会图书馆建筑组会议纪要 ………… (105)
【附录Ⅲ】其他相关文章 ………………………………………………… (106)
　　【附录Ⅲ-1】图书馆 ………………………………………………… (106)
　　【附录Ⅲ-2】如何利用图书馆 ……………………………………… (109)
　　【附录Ⅲ-3】中华图书馆协会第一次年会筹备及经过报告 …………… (112)

教育事业篇

新中国之道德 ……………………………………………………………… (116)
人与蚊之竞争 ……………………………………………………………… (119)
留别之言 …………………………………………………………………… (122)
在国立中央大学总理纪念周上的演讲(1928年12月17日) ……………… (124)
在上海家庭日新会上的演讲 ……………………………………………… (126)
国立中央大学半月刊发刊词 ……………………………………………… (127)
对于《国立中央大学日刊》今后之希望(1929年1月1日) ……………… (128)
在国立中央大学总理纪念周上的报告(1929年3月4日) ………………… (129)
在国立中央大学总理纪念周上的报告(1929年3月18日) ……………… (130)
在国立中央大学总理纪念周上的报告(1929年4月1日) ………………… (132)
在国立中央大学总理纪念周上的报告(1929年4月22日) ……………… (133)
在国立中央大学五三纪念仪式上的报告(1929年5月3日) ……………… (134)
在国立中央大学纪念五四运动大会上的演讲(1929年5月4日) ………… (135)
在国立中央大学双五节纪念大会上的致辞(1929年5月5日) …………… (136)
在国立中央大学总理纪念周上的报告(1929年5月6日) ………………… (137)
在国立中央大学总理纪念周上的报告(1929年6月11日) ……………… (138)
在国立中央大学总理纪念周上的报告(1929年9月23日) ……………… (140)
在国立中央大学师长欢宴留京毕业同学大会上的致辞(1929年10月17日) ……… (142)
在国立中央大学总理纪念周上的报告(1929年12月9日) ……………… (143)
在国立中央大学总理纪念周上的报告(1929年12月30日) ……………… (144)

在国立中央大学总理纪念周上的报告(1930年3月10日)……………………(145)
在国立中央大学总理纪念周上的报告(1930年4月28日)……………………(146)
《国立中央大学学生会刊》序 …………………………………………………(147)

银行事业篇

东北经济问题 ……………………………………………………………………(150)
人与事 ……………………………………………………………………………(152)
有业者乐业的理论和实验——本能说的职业指导 ……………………………(154)
戴志骞刘焘关于在东北接洽关盐两税情形报告 ………………………………(156)
本行对于练习生的期望——鲁行练习生谒师典礼训词之一 ………………(159)
如何推进我行之业务——在宁行新屋落成典礼演讲 ………………………(161)
视察中国银行闽粤分支行演讲录 ………………………………………………(162)
戴志骞赴闽粤考察记述 …………………………………………………………(167)
银行人事调查与训练 ……………………………………………………………(169)
银行界同人进修服务社工作简报——在三十四区党部党员代表大会报 …(173)
中国银行行务会议戴总秘书报告(1946年) …………………………………(176)
中国银行行务会议戴总秘书人事报告(1946年) ……………………………(178)
中国银行行务会议人事报告(1947) ……………………………………………(179)
中国银行董事长孔庸之先生致股东总会报告书 ………………………………(181)
本行沿革概要 ……………………………………………………………………(183)
【附录】戴志骞主持的会议记录及报告 ………………………………………(186)
　　【附录Ⅰ】1942年中国银行行务会议人事委员会会议记录及议决案 …(186)
　　【附录Ⅱ】1946年中国银行行务会议人事组戴召集人志骞报告 ………(191)

英文文章

Present Library Conditions in China ……………………………………………(197)
中国图书馆的现状　　　　　　　　　　　　【译文】任奕译　姜爱蓉审(203)
A Brief Sketch of Chinese Libraries ……………………………………………(208)
中国图书馆概述　　　　　　　　　　【译文】董琳、郭兰芳译　邓景康审(216)
English Books on China: Preface ………………………………………………(222)
《关于中国的英文书目》序　　　　　　　　　　【译文】张秋译　肖燕审(223)
Libraries Aid in Educating China: Review ……………………………………(224)
评《图书馆对中国教育的支持》　　　　　　　【译文】武丽娜译　林佳审(225)
Libraries Aid in Educating China ………………………………………………(226)
图书馆对中国教育的支持　　　　　　　　　　【译文】冯璐译　林佳审(233)
Library Movement in China(一) ………………………………………………(239)
中国的图书馆运动(一)　　　　　　　　　　【译文】管翠中译　邓景康审(246)

Library Movement in China（二） ……………………………………………………（252）
中国的图书馆运动（二） ……………………【译文】管翠中译　邓景康审（265）
Library Movement in China（三） ……………………………………………………（275）
中国的图书馆运动（三） ……………………【译文】管翠中译　邓景康审（280）
The Library ……………………………………………………………………………（283）
清华大学图书馆 ………………………………【译文】武丽娜译　姜爱蓉审（286）
Supplements to the Dewey's "Decimal Classification & Relative Index"：Preface …………（289）
《杜威书目十类法补编》序 ……………………………【译文】戴志骞自译（291）
An Advanced School of Librarianship—Aim of Curriculum ……………………（292）
高等图书馆学校——课程宗旨 …………………【译文】郭兰芳译　肖燕审（295）
Modern Library Development and Its Relation to Scholarship ……………………（298）
现代图书馆发展及其与学术的关系 ……………【译文】范莹莹译　林佳审（308）
Classified Catalog of the Tsing hua College Library：Preface ………………………（315）
《清华学校（英文）书籍目录》序 …………………【译文】庄玫译　肖燕审（316）
Development of Modern Libraries in China ……………………………………………（317）
中国现代图书馆的发展 …………………………【译文】贺维平译　姜爱蓉审（323）
China's Finance and Banking ……………………………………………………………（327）
中国的金融与银行业 ……………………………………【译文】贺维平译（334）
Recent Literature on China（一）
最新关于中国的书目（一） ………………………………………………………（339）
Recent Literature on China（二）
最新关于中国的书目（二） ………………………………………………………（349）
Recent Literature on China（三）
最新关于中国的书目（三） ………………………………………………………（356）
【附录】戴志骞夫人著述 …………………………………………………………（362）
　　【附录Ⅰ】北欧四大女文豪 …………………………………………………（362）
　　【附录Ⅱ】Medical Libraries in China：A Survey ……………………………（369）

下　册

中文著作

图书馆学术讲稿

序言……………………………………………………………………………………（5）
第一章　图书馆组织法…………………………………………………………………（7）
第二章　图书馆管理法………………………………………………………………（10）
　　第一节　图书选择法……………………………………………………………（12）

第二节　图书出纳法 …………………………………………………………（13）
　　第三节　杂志书籍登录式 ……………………………………………………（15）
　　第四节　管理、出纳、选择、装订等之参考书 ………………………………（18）
第三章　图书馆之建筑 ……………………………………………………………（19）
第四章　论美国图书馆 ……………………………………………………………（23）
第五章　图书馆分类法 ……………………………………………………………（27）
　　第一节　勃郎氏分类法（Brown Classification）……………………………（30）
　　第二节　美国国会图书馆之分类法 …………………………………………（31）
　　第三节　克脱氏展开分类法（Cutter's Expansive Classification）…………（31）
　　第四节　杜威氏十分分类法（Dewey's Decimal Classification）……………（33）
　　第五节　清华学校图书馆分类法 ……………………………………………（36）
　　第六节　日本帝国图书馆分类法 ……………………………………………（43）
　　第七节　图书馆分类法之评断 ………………………………………………（47）
第六章　图书馆编目法 ……………………………………………………………（48）
和汉图书目录编纂概则 ……………………………………………………………（57）
西书著者、书名目录编纂略则 ……………………………………………………（59）

英文著作

Professional Education for Librarianship

Preface …………………………………………………………………………………（69）
Introduction ……………………………………………………………………………（71）
Part I　The Development of Modern Libraries and Librarianship ………………（80）
Part II　Training and Education for Librarianship ………………………………（109）
Part III　A Proposed Scheme of Professional Education for Librarianship ……（164）
Appendix I　Suggested Curriculum for the Proposed Library School at the State
　　　　　　University of Iowa …………………………………………………（193）
Appendix II　A Budget for the Proposed Library School at the University of Iowa ………（200）
译文：图书馆学专业教育 ……………………………………冯立昇、司宏伟审（223）
　　前言 ……………………………………………………………………王媛译（227）
　　序言 ……………………………………………………………………王媛译（229）
　　第一部分　现代图书馆与图书馆事业的发展 ………王媛、杨玲、郭兰芳、张秋译（237）
　　第二部分　图书馆学专业教育与培训 ………………………………韦庆媛译（261）
　　第三部分　图书馆学专业教育的提案 ………………………………胡冉译（313）
　　附录Ⅰ …………………………………………………………………胡冉译（337）
　　附录Ⅱ …………………………………………………………………胡冉译（343）

Bibliography on China:1900—1918(关于中国的书目:1900—1918)

Preface ····· (348)
Abbreviations ····· (349)
Bibliographical Aids ····· (352)
General Works ····· (354)
Philosophy and Religion ····· (356)
Missions ····· (361)
Economic & Political Organizations ····· (363)
Education ····· (368)
Social Life & Customs ····· (370)
Science and Useful Arts ····· (375)
Fine Arts ····· (378)
Language and Literature ····· (382)
Travels & Description ····· (384)
Manchuria ····· (391)
Mongolia ····· (392)
Tibet ····· (394)
Turkestan ····· (397)
Biography ····· (399)
History ····· (402)
International Relations ····· (406)
Boxer Uprising 1900 ····· (411)
Revolution 1911 ····· (413)
Author Index ····· (416)

后　　记 ····· 韦庆媛(425)

目　录

序一 ··· 程焕文(1)
序二 ··· 蒋耘中(1)
戴志骞先生传略 ··· 韦庆媛(1)
凡例 ·· (1)

中文文章

图书馆事业篇

论美国图书馆 ··· (4)
图书馆学 ··· (8)
图书馆与教育——在北京高师图书馆的演讲 ················ (11)
图书馆与教育——在南京高师的演讲 ························ (13)
《图书馆学》戴志骞先生序 ····································· (16)
图书馆与学校 ·· (17)
图书馆学简说 ·· (19)
图书馆学——在清华学校的演讲 ····························· (27)
图书分类法几条原则的商榷 ·································· (33)
欧美图书馆概况 ··· (35)
清华周刊记者与戴志骞谈话记 ······························· (39)
《图书分类法》序（节选） ····································· (41)
清华周刊记者采访戴志骞 ····································· (42)
清华学校图书馆概况 ··· (44)
十五年来之中国图书馆事业 ·································· (50)
服务图书馆的甘苦 ·· (53)
清华学校图书馆之过去，现在，及将来 ····················· (54)
图书馆的变迁与利用 ··· (58)
《清华学校图书馆中文书籍目录》序 ························ (59)
中华图书馆协会第一届年会开幕辞 ·························· (60)
中华图书馆协会第一届年会筹备主任报告 ················· (61)
《国立中央大学图书馆图书目录》序 ························ (62)
《中国图书馆名人录》序 ······································· (63)
图书馆员职业之研究 ··· (64)

【附录Ⅰ】戴志骞撰写的书报介绍 ……………………………………………… (66)
　　【附录Ⅰ-1】《清华周刊·书报介绍副刊》第一期 ………………………… (66)
　　【附录Ⅰ-2】《清华周刊·书报介绍副刊》第二期 ………………………… (73)
　　【附录Ⅰ-3】《清华周刊·书报介绍副刊》第四期 ………………………… (76)
　　【附录Ⅰ-4】《清华周刊·书报介绍副刊》第十二期 ……………………… (78)
【附录Ⅱ】戴志骞主持的会议记录及议决案 ……………………………………… (79)
　　【附录Ⅱ-1】中华教育改进社第一届年会"图书馆教育组"会议纪要 …… (79)
　　【附录Ⅱ-2】中华教育改进社第二届年会"图书馆教育组"会议纪要 …… (84)
　　【附录Ⅱ-3】中华教育改进社第三届年会"图书馆教育组"会议纪要 …… (96)
　　【附录Ⅱ-4】中华图书馆协会第一届年会图书馆建筑组会议纪要 ……… (105)
【附录Ⅲ】其他相关文章 …………………………………………………………… (106)
　　【附录Ⅲ-1】图书馆 ………………………………………………………… (106)
　　【附录Ⅲ-2】如何利用图书馆 ……………………………………………… (109)
　　【附录Ⅲ-3】中华图书馆协会第一次年会筹备及经过报告 ……………… (112)

教育事业篇

新中国之道德 ……………………………………………………………………… (116)
人与蚊之竞争 ……………………………………………………………………… (119)
留别之言 …………………………………………………………………………… (122)
在国立中央大学总理纪念周上的演讲(1928年12月17日) ………………… (124)
在上海家庭日新会上的演讲 ……………………………………………………… (126)
国立中央大学半月刊发刊词 ……………………………………………………… (127)
对于《国立中央大学日刊》今后之希望(1929年1月1日) …………………… (128)
在国立中央大学总理纪念周上的报告(1929年3月4日) …………………… (129)
在国立中央大学总理纪念周上的报告(1929年3月18日) ………………… (130)
在国立中央大学总理纪念周上的报告(1929年4月1日) …………………… (132)
在国立中央大学总理纪念周上的报告(1929年4月22日) ………………… (133)
在国立中央大学五三纪念仪式上的报告(1929年5月3日) ………………… (134)
在国立中央大学纪念五四运动大会上的演讲(1929年5月4日) …………… (135)
在国立中央大学双五节纪念大会上的致辞(1929年5月5日) ……………… (136)
在国立中央大学总理纪念周上的报告(1929年5月6日) …………………… (137)
在国立中央大学总理纪念周上的报告(1929年6月11日) ………………… (138)
在国立中央大学总理纪念周上的报告(1929年9月23日) ………………… (140)
在国立中央大学师长欢宴留京毕业同学大会上的致辞(1929年10月17日) … (142)
在国立中央大学总理纪念周上的报告(1929年12月9日) ………………… (143)
在国立中央大学总理纪念周上的报告(1929年12月30日) ………………… (144)
在国立中央大学总理纪念周上的报告(1930年3月10日) ………………… (145)

在国立中央大学总理纪念周上的报告(1930年4月28日) …………………………（146）
《国立中央大学学生会刊》序 …………………………………………………（147）

银行事业篇

东北经济问题 ……………………………………………………………………（150）
人与事 ……………………………………………………………………………（152）
有业者乐业的理论和实验——本能说的职业指导 ……………………………（154）
戴志骞刘焘关于在东北接洽关盐两税情形报告 ………………………………（156）
本行对于练习生的期望——鲁行练习生谒师典礼训词之一 …………………（159）
如何推进我行之业务——在宁行新屋落成典礼演讲 …………………………（161）
视察中国银行闽粤分支行演讲录 ………………………………………………（162）
戴志骞赴闽粤考察记述 …………………………………………………………（167）
银行人事调查与训练 ……………………………………………………………（169）
银行界同人进修服务社工作简报——在三十四区党部党员代表大会报 ……（173）
中国银行行务会议戴总秘书报告(1946年) ……………………………………（176）
中国银行行务会议戴总秘书人事报告(1946年) ………………………………（178）
中国银行行务会议人事报告(1947) ……………………………………………（179）
中国银行董事长孔庸之先生致股东总会报告书 ………………………………（181）
本行沿革概要 ……………………………………………………………………（183）
【附录】戴志骞主持的会议记录及报告 ………………………………………（186）
　　【附录Ⅰ】1942年中国银行行务会议人事委员会会议记录及议决案 …（186）
　　【附录Ⅱ】1946年中国银行行务会议人事组戴召集人志骞报告 ………（191）

英文文章

Present Library Conditions in China ……………………………………………（197）
中国图书馆的现状 ……………………………………………【译文】任奕译　姜爱蓉审（203）
A Brief Sketch of Chinese Libraries ……………………………………………（208）
中国图书馆概述 ………………………………………【译文】董琳、郭兰芳译　邓景康审（216）
English Books on China：Preface ………………………………………………（222）
《关于中国的英文书目》序 ………………………………………【译文】张秋译　肖燕审（223）
Libraries Aid in Educating China：Review ……………………………………（224）
评《图书馆对中国教育的支持》 …………………………………【译文】武丽娜译　林佳审（225）
Libraries Aid in Educating China ………………………………………………（226）
图书馆对中国教育的支持 …………………………………………【译文】冯璐译　林佳审（233）
Library Movement in China(一) ………………………………………………（239）
中国的图书馆运动(一) …………………………………………【译文】管翠中译　邓景康审（246）

· 3 ·

Library Movement in China(二)	(252)
中国的图书馆运动(二)	【译文】管翠中译　邓景康审(265)
Library Movement in China(三)	(275)
中国的图书馆运动(三)	【译文】管翠中译　邓景康审(280)
The Library	(283)
清华大学图书馆	【译文】武丽娜译　姜爱蓉审(286)
Supplements to the Dewey's "Decimal Classification & Relative Index": Preface	(289)
《杜威书目十类法补编》序	【译文】戴志骞自译(291)
An Advanced School of Librarianship—Aim of Curriculum	(292)
高等图书馆学校——课程宗旨	【译文】郭兰芳译　肖燕审(295)
Modern Library Development and Its Relation to Scholarship	(298)
现代图书馆发展及其与学术的关系	【译文】范莹莹译　林佳审(308)
Classified Catalog of the Tsing hua College Library: Preface	(315)
《清华学校(英文)书籍目录》序	【译文】庄玫译　肖燕审(316)
Development of Modern Libraries in China	(317)
中国现代图书馆的发展	【译文】贺维平译　姜爱蓉审(323)
China's Finance and Banking	(327)
中国的金融与银行业	【译文】贺维平译(334)
Recent Literature on China(一)	
最新关于中国的书目(一)	(339)
Recent Literature on China(二)	
最新关于中国的书目(二)	(349)
Recent Literature on China(三)	
最新关于中国的书目(三)	(356)
【附录】戴志骞夫人著述	(362)
【附录Ⅰ】北欧四大女文豪	(362)
【附录Ⅱ】Medical Libraries in China: A Survey	(369)

中文文章

图书馆事业篇

论美国图书馆

【编者按】戴志骞于1917—1919年赴美留学,就读纽约州立大学图书馆学院,在此期间,除完成学业外,还访问了美国多个图书馆,参加美国图书馆协会的活动,担任《留美学生季报》的编辑,本文为发表在《留美学生季报》上的文章。

西人游历中国城镇,普通所见者,城隍庙也,省有省城隍,县有县城隍,市乡有市乡之城隍。吾人游美国城乡,普通所见者,有四特色:即教堂、邮政局、学校及图书馆也。以前三者,为各文明国国民必要之物,而图书馆亦林立其中,不得不有疑问焉。盖国民教育已操之于学校,而图书馆之设立,如星罗,如棋布,用意何在?而有益于国民教育之关系亦何在?作者请暂不论图书馆与学校及国民教育之密切关系,先言美国图书馆发达史之梗概,以飨留心图书馆诸君。

一六七九年,有英国牧师勃兰氏(Dr. Thomas Bray)始创图书馆于新大陆之教堂内,如曼尔兰一省(Maryland),创教堂图书馆三十所,共有书籍二千五百四十五册,为教士参考而设,惟亦允每教堂区域内之人民,自由借阅。此可谓美国图书馆史之开辟时代。至一八零三年,始有学校区域图书馆之设。如纽约省在一八三五年,立专律以维持各学校区域之图书馆,教士学生有专所观览典籍。然而当时普通人民仍未免有向隅之叹,故法兰恩格林(Benjamin Franklin)集股创合股图书馆(Subscription Library)于费立特城(Philadelphia),不但认股诸人有借览该馆图籍之权利,而近处人民亦能同受该馆之利益焉。各埠商人,悯商铺学徒无从研究学问,而商人图书馆(Mereantile Library)于一八二〇年亦创于纽约、波士顿、圣路易三城矣。至于大学校图书馆之鼻祖,首推哈佛,此馆之设立,始于 Rev. John Harvard 在一六三八年,迄今为全国大学校图书馆之冠。至美国公共图书馆者,向以税饷维持,亦可谓人民之图书馆。英国国会议员(William Ewart)通过一议案,此公共图书馆之根本也。一六九七年,美国有 Sir Francis Nichilson 者发起,由曼尔兰省市政厅上禀于英皇惠廉第三,请抽军火税之一分,为设公共图书馆之用。不意此禀竟遭无结果之打消。至一八三三年纽哈姆省(New Hampshire)首创公共省图书馆①。二十六年后,纽极才省(New Jersey)亦创公共省图书馆。至十九世纪之初,人民稍稍知公共图书馆有益于社会,南加落立那省(South Carolina)设省图书馆于一八一四年,纽约省(New York)于一八一八年,始设省图书馆,二年后,本薛佛尼 Pennsylvania 省图书馆成立。今首都华盛顿之国立图书馆,始创于一八〇〇年,虽已二次被焚,然迄今藏书之富,不但为全国之冠,而已为全世界之冠矣。

美国图书馆受个人捐资而成立者,始于波士顿之迭格拿氏(George Ticknor)一八五一年之义举。迭氏愿建一图书馆,与公共图书馆不同,愿多数之人民,能同时读一种有益之书籍。盖当时美国图书馆,亦如现今中国之藏书楼,专为保藏书籍,非为人民自修而设也。以图书

---

① 【编者注】原文为177年。现在一般认为美国的第一个公共图书馆是1833年在新罕布什尔州(New Hampshire)的一个小镇成立的,原文应为印刷错误。资料来源:陈同丽.追求卓越:美国公共图书馆的绩效评估.山东图书馆学刊,2010(6)。

馆为普通人民自修之所，为普通人民教育之关键，始于一八七六年。介绍此图书馆之新理想于人民之脑海中者，皆美国图书管理员会之力也。

美国图书管理员会，首由 Professor Charles Jewett 在纽约城于一八五三年发起，到会者共八十人，在闭会时，Jewett 虽云愿该会作永久图书管理员会之母，然无教育界中人相助，而受一顿挫。直至二十三年后，该会始正式成立。会纲由全会会员一〇三人选定，并出图书管理月刊一种，作该会之出版物，以后每年有年会一次，以互相研究图书管理法，而以普及教育为目的。故现今美国图书馆之发达，而人民得无限之利益者，均此会之力也。该会对于图书管理法，详细研究，不厌烦屑，对于如何设立图书馆，如何购办书籍杂志，如何分类编目，均详细印成最简明之小本，分发于各处之有意设立图书馆者，并请驻会书记一人，筹划通信事。除此全国图书管理员会外，现各省有各省图书管理员会。骞初应美国图书管理员会之请，今夏特赴该会年会于纽约之散落托加泉（Saratoga Springs），默察该会会员之精神，皆悉心擘画图书管理法，会员互相切实砥砺。后又应纽约全省图书管理员会之招，而再赴泼兰雪湖（Lake Placid）之会。该会会员之团结精神，互相砺磨，研究图书管理之法，实令人崇拜。该会之种种出版物，关于该省之图书管理法，亦详细研究，且助各图书馆改正管理上之缺点。

全国图书管理员会，始创于美国，后一年英国亦创立斯会，发起于英国国立图书馆长 John Winter Jones。近年来，欧洲诸邦，如法、德、意均有全国图书管理员会之建设矣。美国图书管理法之完备适当，亦全仗诸发明家，如 Cutter, Dewey, Winsor, Bowker 等之力居多。至南北美战争时，方有美国妇女崛起，而为图书馆管理员矣。如将三十年前美国图书馆之数目，书籍之多寡，与现在之图书馆及书籍之数目比较，有天地之别。现不但省有省图书馆，市乡有市乡图书馆，而大城如纽约、芝加哥、波士顿等，一城之中有数十之图书馆，并有无数幼孩图书馆、盲人图书馆、医院图书馆、旅行图书馆、银行图书馆、工艺图书馆、大学校图书馆、高等学校图书馆、中学校、小学校图书馆及种种专门职业图书馆。自去年美国加入欧战以来，全国图书管理员会，即全力提倡军营图书馆、战场图书馆。美陆军总长 Baker 云，此次战争之胜负，非枪械之精，战术之娴，能决最后之胜利，其真能决最后之胜利者，在兵士能用书与否耳。骞为美国图书管理员之精神所动，故今夏毕业后，竭力思得军营图书馆之阅历，现已蒙政府许可，将赴军营图书馆为实地之练习矣；希日后还国有所贡献于我国之健儿也。

美国图书馆林立，得力于富翁慨捐者甚多。如纽勃兰氏（Walter Newberry）之三百万元之图书馆，建于芝加哥；飞斯刻氏（Fiske's）以一百五十万元之图书馆，赠于康奈尔大学；泼兰忒氏（Enoch Pratt's）一百五十万元之图书馆，设于排尔跌城（Baltimore）；卡纳奇氏（Carnegie's）二百五十万元之图书馆，建于 Pittsburg；天尔登氏（Tilden's）之一千万元，赠于纽约图书馆。诸富翁中捐资建筑图书馆之最豪者，惟推卡纳奇氏，几乎各城各乡，均有卡纳奇氏之图书馆。去年军营图书馆，需一百七十万元之款，卡氏立助其半。若将美国富翁，曾捐助图书馆之芳名汇刻，必成一巨册。然而图书馆如此之多，藏书如此之富，则需有人理其事，是则图书管理学学校之设尚矣。在一八八七年，纽约省大学列图书管理科，为大学院之一专门科。在此三十一年内，全国设立专门图书管理学学校十四处。欧洲诸邦，均逐年遣有阅历、有心得之图书管理员，到美国专门图书管理学学校留学矣。故各国之图书馆管理，均取法于美国。由此可见美国图书馆，实甲于天下，而否则欧洲各国多典章文物之旧邦，岂肯俯首推重。今请细察下方纽约全省图书馆及二十五年来流通书籍之比较表，则可知美国图书馆尚有日增月盛之势焉。

纽约全省图书馆及流通书籍二十五年之比较表 1893—1917

年份 Year	图书馆数目 No of Libraries	书籍册数 Volumes in Libraries	流通书籍之总数 Total circulation	每日流通书籍数目 Circulation per day	每千个人中使用流通书籍之人数 Circulation per 1,000 population
1893	238	849995	2293861	6285	352
1894	293	1049869	2766973	7581	425
1895	309	1127199	3146405	8620	483
1896	351	1313299	3933623	10777	604
1897	375	1446874	4904793	13438	753
1898	408	1755036	6439999	17644	989
1899	431	1979319	7395527	20262	1135
1900	460	2187125	8452445	23157	1163
1901	529	2425260	9232697	25350	1290
1902	550	2598472	10063703	27571	1385
1903	555	2804628	10897126	29855	1500
1904	573	3108365	11347802	31089	1561
1905	*377	*2953177	*11685889	33115	1663
1906	678	3645662	13835639	37906	1715
1907	661	3782609	14968722	41010	1855
1908	686	4050563	16479457	45146	2043
1909	689	4227665	18749849	51364	2324
1910	710	4341103	19254729	52753	2387
1911	661	4635716	20122745	50131	2208
1912	*464	*4421901	*20309176	55641	2228
1913	*477	*4707472	*21530294	58987	2362
1914	*493	*5074650	*22918026	62762	2515
1915	*536	*5330826	*26003009	71241	2853
1916	*544	*5570271	*28223898	77326	2913
1917	*551	*5775115	*27259840	73693	2814

*高等学校图书馆不包括在内。

图书馆与教育,有极密切不能分开之关系。教育者,智力生长之义也;如不生长,即至灭绝。学校即教育之初步也,教少年人民以温故知新之识。然学校不能教育国民之终身,人人有出学校之一日,若社会中无图书馆,则多数学子出学校后,即于智力上不能生长。如要国民有终身智力生长之机,除图书馆外,别无较良美之法,故图书馆,可称国民之终身学校也。美国人民因知此义,故不惜数亿兆之金钱,造就全国国民终身之大学校,今者途人问答皆曰,"该村之图书馆在何处?"而不问"该村有无图书馆?"于此语,则知美国人民之教育与图书馆如手足,有不能分离之势矣。美国图书管理家 Dewey 云:学校者,锥也,图书馆者,大理石也,二者缺一,虽能工刻者,亦不能产美丽之石像。夫图书馆既为国民之终身学校,则该学校之教授法,不得不悉心研究。因该校学生程度之不齐,年龄之不一,各种职业,莫不代表,自专门有心得之大学教员,至目不识字之工人小贩;自耄耋之士,至四五龄之婴孩,故当此特制学校之教员者,须有适当之教授法,而应以上种种学生之要求,否则虽有国民终身学校之设,而于事实上,则等于无有。故设立图书馆之至要者,不在屋宇之宏丽庄严,亦不在藏书有汗牛充栋之富,首要者,在图书之管理法。管理适当,虽少数之有用书籍,皆能应多数人民之参考。管理不完备,虽有极多之书籍,而不能应少数人民之参考。仆在中国时,参观数处之公立图书馆,及通俗图书馆,管理法曾注重于保藏主义,而轻忽书籍流动主义。善本希珍之书籍保藏之,亦图书管理员之天职,然切不可不注意书籍流动主义焉。馆长应想种种法则,诱劝地方多数之人民,日常到馆;并于离馆时,多借流动书籍回家,为茶余饭后之消遣品,则该馆虽每年书籍因用而损坏之数不少,然而该馆馆长之天职尽矣!造福于社会,岂可胜数哉?

现我国最缺少亦最要者,莫如管理良美之图书馆。吾全国有无数之藏书楼,而可谓无一处有良美图书馆。中国历年来,派留学生之数,可称甲于天下;而留学生之在各国者,于学问上,均有极深之心得。然观近来三十年之留学史,虽为总长、局长者,比比皆是,然真能于科学上、文学上、工艺上,而有所发明,而能造福于国民,并能造福于世界者,其数少若晨星。鄙见非谓我中国学生之智力迟钝,实缺乏良美图书馆,为回国后参考之用,是一大原因也。留学诸君回国后,因无适当之图书馆,并于幼时未养成好读之习惯,故一遇此境,智力生长,骤遭停顿。而数年在异邦所得之学问,亦日退而无进境矣,故极愿我诸同学于设立良美之图书馆,希慷慨出全力相助,为发育国民智力日进之基础。

如欲设立有实用之图书馆,希留意以下诸事:

(一)切不可设在偏僻交通不便之处。

(二)虽不必有极华丽之屋宇,然终要整齐、清洁、干燥、空气流通、光线充足之所。

(三)若限于款项,所购书籍,不必出重价购善本希珍之书籍,应先购有实用而多参考资料之书籍。

(四)所购之书籍,应详细分类编目,以便检查,以省阅者宝贵之时光,以免书籍陈列架上,终无与阅览者。

(五)开门借书时刻,应日夜、星期、假日皆不闭馆,为利便人民起见;惟此项于人民极有益,而于图书馆款项上,稍有妨碍,因须加增馆员人数,并值星期及假日馆员之薪金应稍优,以示鼓励。然于人民有益,此层终须力行。

(六)馆长之对于书籍,切不可有守财奴对于金钱之观念。应想各种方法,使人民多用书籍杂志,而少窖藏书籍;须具商铺掌柜之资格,望每日夜皆有主顾,愈多愈善。切不可具局长之威严,有"图书馆为重地,闲人莫入"之牌示。

以上六项,实普通图书馆管理法之要素,希有意捐资设立公共图书馆者,三注意焉。美国图书馆管理员会格言之一云:"出少数之金钱,购多数有用之书籍,与大多数人民享受。"此格言每图书馆管理员应当作金科玉律。骞参观美国各种大小图书馆百余处,而反顾我国图书馆之状况,不禁受无穷之感触,拉杂书此,希我国人于图书馆问题,有所激动,则于中国之教育前途,有厚望焉。

原载:《留美学生季报》 1918年第4号

图书馆学

【编者按】 1920年第4期圣约翰大学出版的《约翰声》上刊登该文。文章未署名，但从文章的内容和戴志骞专著《图书馆学专业教育》中提供的戴志骞著述列表所示，1920年戴志骞在《约翰声》上发表过文章，且文中列出了"爱布顿军营图书馆"的借书信息，该馆是戴志骞曾在美国工作过的图书馆，因此判断该文为戴志骞所著。

多数的人，往往以为图书馆是一个贮藏室，专为保存各种图书而设，至于人民阅览并不是重要的目的。此种误解，不但多数中国人常有；就是西方人民在十九世纪时候亦有同样的误解。英国牛津大学的波德立图书馆，用铁链将各种书籍锁起来，不许人阅览。波德立捐赠此馆时曾说过，"此馆专为有学问的人而设"，所以偶然平常人到该馆阅览，一律拒绝。一八七六年美国组织图书馆协会。英、日、德、法、比等国，全国图书馆协会相继成立，为图书馆开一新纪元。二十世纪初，欧美人渐渐知道图书馆不是一种专为保存书籍的贮藏室，实是一种与社会有密切关系的事业，因为他是传播新思潮的中心点。

中国图书馆事业，尚在萌芽的时代。现在我说图书馆与社会，有极重大的关系，多说人必不能信我的话。然试问曾到美国留学或游历过的人，他们在美国的时候，不论到大城，乡村，小镇，常见的是什么？他们常见的必是教堂，学校，图书馆。美国虽是新建的国家，然图书馆之多，欧洲各国不能与其抗衡。欧洲每年均送学生到美国学图书馆学。请诸君细细的想一想，为什么英美创办这许多的图书馆，大学内并设有图书馆学科？（伦敦大学，于一九一九年秋始立图书学专科。）

美国图书馆之多，仿佛中国的城隍庙，大约可分十类：

（一）公立图书馆。如纽约，波士顿，芝加哥，各大城都设一大公立图书馆为该城图书事业总机关。其未设有大公立图书馆的城，如薄洛克林必设事务所一处。其内中办法，将一城分数区，每区设分馆一处，扩张一切。全以该区居民的需要为标准。如纽约市东二街，为犹太人住处。该处的图书馆，便藏些希伯来文的书籍。总馆与分馆的组织法、管理法，均非常周密。公立图书馆的费用，都以本城租税维持之。

（二）大学图书馆。大学图书馆都藏皆系高深的书籍，可供参考的居多。并且各校图书馆各有特长。如哥伦比亚大学图书馆，关于教育学的书籍，搜藏极富。哈佛大学的威得诺图书馆，关于初版的书籍。勃郎大学图书馆，关于国际公法的书籍，均无不收藏。现各大学竭力扩张图书馆，因为要使学生，多有心得。图书馆实在是不可少的。

（三）国立或省立图书馆。美国国立图书馆，搜藏之富；为全国图书馆之冠，亦为全世界三大图书馆之一（其余二大图书馆，为英法二国国立的图书馆）。美国省立图书馆，为全省图书馆事业的模范，并为市乡图书馆的总机关。对于该省的名人传记，采购尤为注意。

（四）股分图书馆。系一种私立的性质，其组织法，略似股分公司。股东有享该馆借书及阅书种种权利。在美国西方，此种私立图书馆颇多。除书报外，并收藏话匣片及电影片等等。

（五）专门图书馆。专为某种特别研究而设，如纽约的银行图书馆，施奈克退狄的电学图书馆，波士顿李德的化学图书馆等等。现因专门图书馆一天比一天多。已设立专门图书馆协会，专研究管理、编目及一切设施。

（六）游行图书馆。隶属于省立图书馆，或省立图书馆委员会，以补市乡图书馆之不足。其游行法，用一种大汽车，内可置书架，约容书籍二千本。除汽车夫外有管理员一人，每到一村，任村民到车内选择，依法借出。此种游行图书馆在美国西方最多。

（七）儿童图书馆。多为公立图书馆之一部分，惟家具书报，都能与儿童的身体及心理适宜，并聘请于儿童图书馆学素有研究的女子，充任其事。

（八）残疾人的图书馆。此类中最有兴味的是盲人的图书馆，各种有名书籍及小说等。多按"盲人识字法"印成，故盲人亦有利用图书馆之机会。

（九）各种俱乐部及会社的图书馆。大半系一种私立性质，能享此等图书馆之权力者，以会员为限，取不开放主义，现在此种图书馆已在淘汰之列。

（十）军营图书馆。美国加入欧战后，美图书馆协会即创设军营图书馆。军营三十二所，均设有图书馆。半年之内，共设海陆军营图书馆二百三十余处。美兵至法战地，军营图书馆随之迁至战地。其组织法，国立图书馆长为军营图书馆总裁，图书馆协会，为一种立法机关，在军营内费用及执行一切事务，均由海陆军部委人掌之。又设副总裁一席于巴黎，管理设在法国的海陆军营图书馆。美国创设此种组织，实历史上破天荒之举，每日来馆借阅图书者，不下数百人。证以下列爱布顿军营图书馆一年的流动书籍统计表，可见兵士读书之多。

爱布顿军营图书馆及十七处分馆借出书籍统计表

1918 年	总馆	分馆	总数
二月	1665 本	6467 本	8132 本
三月	2582 本	5665 本	8247 本
四月	1971 本	6640 本	8611 本
五月	2235 本	11418 本	13653 本
六月	3107 本	8706 本	11813 本
七月	2985 本	10520 本	13505 本
八月	3765 本	4364 本	8129 本
九月	4677 本	4891 本	9568 本
十月	4676 本	8254 本	12930 本
十一月	4009 本	5148 本	9157 本
十二月	3886 本	4952 本	8838 本
1919 年			
一月	5680 本	6114 本	11794 本
总数	41,238 本	83,139 本	124,377 本

美国人民是极善于理财的，但是每年各处图书馆耗去极大的款，此中必有极重要的理由。图书馆学发明家杜威博士曾说过，"图书馆是平民的学校"。我们详细研究这句话，觉得图书馆与人民教育，实在有极密切的关系。学校教育有时期的，譬如由小学而至大学，或再

出洋留学,到留学回国,学校教育的时期便算完了。但图书馆是无时期的教育。自小孩以至老人,都有用图书馆之需要。图书馆是助智力生长的养料。图书馆是无时期的学校教育。吾人要有终身智力生长的机会,除图书馆外,再无较良的方法。

图书馆不但是吾人终身教育的学校,并且亦能增进职业上的技能。譬如美国银行图书馆,关于银行的书籍很完备。若问他五年前某种股票的价值,他就能立刻查出来。我曾在美国参观橡皮公司的图书馆,他关于橡皮的出产、价值、制造、种类,都有很详细的记载。照上几个例子,图书馆与吾人职业上的技能,关系很深,除以上二种功用外,图书馆还有一种修养的功用。

吾人工作不能像机械一样,一天到晚,工作不息。精神的养修,比体力的修养更重要。往往人家独注重体力的修养,譬如设立公园、球场等等,但是对于脑力的修养,容易忽略。人常有失眠病,或神经衰弱症,多是用脑过度,修养不足所致。如劳心的人,工事完毕后,读几章有趣的小说,或传记,精神立刻觉得舒服。因为小说等书籍,有修养精神的功用,所以英美的公立图书馆搜罗此种书籍极多。每日借出的书籍统计表,小说占百分之五十三四,由此晓得图书馆是智力修养的公园了。

从上面所说的理由看起来,人家费了许多的钱,设立各种图书馆,并不是做国家或地方的装饰品,实在是做平民终身教育的机关,亦是增进平民职业上的技能,并且补助智力的修养。图书馆既有许多的好处,大家竭力设法组织图书馆,是造福人生及社会最好的方法。然而有了图书馆,不讲究管理的方法,钱耗了许多,恐怕人民得着的益处很少,所以管理方法,必须讲求。英美设图书馆学专科,造就专门图书管理员,并且师范及高等学校,亦授浅近图书馆学一科,就是教学生如何用图书馆,教将来的教员如何用参考书。美国大学如纽约省大学、伊利诺、威斯康新、西余等,都有图书馆学专科,须在大学毕业,专门二年方能卒业。现在美国图书馆管理员有数千人,并有一极完备的图书馆协会为图书管理研究的总机关。

中国近来教育家颇注意,打破阶级教育的制度。然而在最短的时间,用较少的银钱,普及到大多数的国民,除设立管理良善的图书馆外,没有别种更好的方法。中国人近年来,渐渐晓得要良好的教育,必须采良好的教师,所以男女的高等师范学校,逐渐的设立。现在我们要办图书馆。有了图书馆而无专门管理的人员恐怕收效必不能完美。许多人以为管理图书馆,无论哪一种人都可以的。一次有位学生对我说:"一天我到图书馆里去,要找罗斯福的著作。我一问馆员,罗斯福的著作有没有?他从来未曾听见过罗斯福的名字。找了半天,仍是找不着。岂不是白费了他的光阴及我的光阴么?"所以图书馆的人材,不但要有图书馆学的学问,必须要有普通的常识,并须具有和蔼的性情,愿意帮人的忙。所以我的意见,现在男女高等师范的本科,可加图书馆学一科。如有愿学图书馆学的,即可选图书馆学的科目,预备将来作图书馆的事业。儿童图书馆及各图书馆的编目员,女子是最相宜的,亦是最有用的职业。希望我国教育家,对于此问题,加以注意。图书馆与教育问题,最为密切。研究图书馆学,即是解决社会问题的一部分。

原载:《约翰声》 1920年第4期

图书馆与教育
——在北京高师图书馆的演讲

图书馆在各国都很注重，大战后更加注意。现在先就美国说一说：就国家而论，美为新建国，一切学术，都从西欧传来；但是论到图书馆，他是最新的，可推为世界第一。美国图书馆和别国古代不同的地方，在于他带有平民主义的色彩，是社会教育的机关。美国各地都有图书馆，和中国的城隍庙差不多一样多。欧战的时候，图书馆在社会服务很有功效。现在先说他的略史：1697年，英国牧师 Thomas 在美国设了一个图书馆，供教士们参考，这就是图书馆的起源。1803年，才按区域设立学校图书馆，区内的人民可以来阅览。1820年，因为学校图书馆不十分便利，于是商人自己合股设立。但是那时的情况，和中国差不多，只知道储藏，不知道利用书籍。1876年，成立图书馆协会，讨论关于图书馆一切设施的事情。所以1876这一年，不仅开美国图书馆的新纪元，可以说是开世界图书馆的新纪元。从这年以后，才讲求开放的方法，才现出长足的进步。后来英国于1898年，德国于1900年，日本于1901年，都成立了图书馆协会，其余法、意各国，也相继的成立。

美国图书馆可分十类：（一）公共图书馆，用地方租税维持；（二）大学或高等学校图书馆；（三）国立或省立图书馆；（四）股份图书馆；（五）专门图书馆，如银行、电车等；（六）游行图书馆，书籍可以邮寄借阅；（七）儿童图书馆；（八）残疾人的图书馆；（九）各种会社的图书馆；（十）军营图书馆。

关于图书馆与教育的问题，有三个疑问：一、为什么要有图书馆？二、怎么样才能设立图书馆？三、什么是图书馆所必要的？

（一）为什么要有图书馆？古代有些教育家说："图书馆的性质，一半是奢侈的，一半是应用的；好像装饰品，并不是必要的东西。"这话我很不赞成，我觉得图书馆不但不是装饰品，并且比教育的关系更重大。狭义教育，是有时期的，譬如一个人，从幼稚园经过小学、中学、高等专门，或是大学，再出洋留学，等到留学回国，那教育的时期就算完了。但是图书馆，自小孩到老人，自博士工程师到皮匠，无论什么年龄职业，都是需要的。现代哲学家柏格森说：人生是变动的。易卜生说：人生不动就死。所以二十世纪的人生，是要变的、动的，并且要有组织的。人生是什么呢？What is Life？人生有三种表现：（1）教育，无教育的人，只可说是存在（Existence），不能说是人生（Life）；（2）职业，拉车的也算是一种职业；（3）休养，因为人生不能像机器一样，一天二十四小时老是工作，全不休息。所以人生必定要有教育、职业、休养三种。那么世界上什么东西能够包含这三种呢？我是学图书馆的，当然推举图书馆了。学校里面，从小学一直到大学，想得点参考或帮助，都离不了图书馆。那么，图书馆和教育的关系，不生疑问了。职业和图书馆，也有密切的关系，不过中国现在还不到这步情形。美国有银行图书馆，关于一切银行的书籍很完备；你若问他五年前的今天股票价值是多少，他就能立刻查出来。我去年在美国参观一个橡皮公司的图书馆，他关于橡皮的出产制造价值，都有详细的记载。在现行商业竞争的时代，那专门职业的图书馆，更其紧要。美国又有个化学图书馆，因为关于军事上的制造，所以须有参观证才行。由以上几个例子，可见职业和图书馆的关系了。至于休养一层,因为图书馆有小说、报纸、画片等,都可以恢复神经的疲劳。图书馆对于教育职业休养三种,都很紧要,可见和人生有密切的关系了。所以我回答第一个问题为什么要有图书馆,因为他和人生有密切的关系。

(二)怎样才能使中国设立图书馆?图书馆的必要,已经知道了,那么再进一步,用什么方法去设立呢?在英、美、日本等国,多由政府设立,但是现在中国的情形,既不能靠政府去办,也不靠有钱的人捐助,因为人民没有图书馆的需要,虽然办起来,恐怕没人去看,不过把书籍去供蛆蠧就是了。现在我有几种办法:(1)现在念书是很费钱的?譬如诸位研究教育,那关于教育的英文、德文的书籍,非常之多,就杂志而论,已经有六十多种,你想个人怎么能有这样的财力去买呢?所以最好的办法,是集合几个朋友,拿自己所有的书籍,放在公共地方,成立个小图书馆的规模。(2)诸位将来到学校里任教的时候,就要他设法成立图书馆,若是担任别的职业,也一定要他们设立图书馆或阅报室;若都按这样办,那么图书馆也就可以渐渐的多起来了。(3)诸位回到家乡的时候,约几个同志,组织一个阅书室,我想中国许多的古书,一定很可以罗致的。美国图书馆的起源,也是这样,这是很方便的方法,只要有毅力去办,决没有什么困难的地方。

(三)什么是图书馆所必要的?有了图书馆,应该怎么去管理呢?现在只能说个大概。因为图书馆性质不同,一切设施,也随他不一样。譬如公共的和学校的不同,而大学的和小学的又不一样。所以现在不能说那些特殊的,只能说那些普遍可以应用的:(1)美国图书馆有句格言说:"买最好的书,给最多数人看,出最少的价值"(The best books for the great number of people at least cost)。这条条件,无论哪一个图书馆,都可以应用的。因为买书不是储藏,是要让多数人看的;所以一切装订目录规例,都要有条理要经济。他所谓最少的价值,也是这个意思。(2)诸君是在学校里的,现在说点学校图书馆应该注重的事体。学校图书馆,切不可多买小说;并不是说小说全不可买,但是应该多买些关于科学参考的书籍。(3)图书馆不可排斥某种主义或学说。譬如现在许多人反对波尔雪委克(Bolshyviki)①,但是波尔雪委克的书籍,不能排斥。美国儿童有看波尔雪委克的书,问他们从什么地方借来,他们说是从纽约公共图书馆借来的。这是什么意思呢?因为图书馆是研究学术的地方,决不能拿管理者的个人意见,来代表大家,决定去取的。(4)图书馆不可多设禁止的规则,因为禁例太多,人家就不愿意看了。所以宁可由馆员多费些气力去整理,决不怕阅览者的乱翻或损坏。就是学校图书馆,也应该用积极的手段,引导他们去研究,决不可用消极的手段去禁止。我在美国参观儿童图书馆。有个小孩很吵闹,旁边一个七八岁的儿童就干涉他,说:"这是公共的地方,不许你吵闹的。"可见图书馆很可以养成自动的能力。此外对于一切设备,如空气光线等,都很应该注意。诸君若想办图书馆,应该学商店的掌柜,欢迎主顾。切不可学守财奴,把所有的东西牢牢的藏起来。所以美国图书馆,都有广告,招人来阅览。

原载:《民国日报副刊·觉悟》 1920年3月9日

---

① 【编者注】即布尔什维克。

图书馆与教育
——在南京高师的演讲

戴志骞先生讲　何兆清记

【编者按】 此为戴志骞在南京高师的演讲，讲稿刊登在教育汇刊1921年第1期上。

今蒙诸君相邀，得与诸君共话一堂，兄弟非常荣幸。当初本拟携带影片来，帮助说明各国图书馆的建筑和设施，惜竟未带来，只能就普通的略说罢了。所说的很不详尽，一定要使诸君失望。

今所讲的，为"图书馆与教育"问题。大概可分两层说：（一）先比较观察中外各国的图书馆。（二）次说儿童图书馆和教育。

（一）先讲我国图书馆。我国素有图书馆吗？有的！即所谓藏书楼。但这藏书楼的目的，实际很狭，不配称图书馆。他的目的，只重"保藏"一方面，将一切有用可贵的书籍，专门藏之高阁，以免损毁散失而已，全不知怎样利用，怎样扩充，换言之，全不知图书馆目的及用处。所以现在北京图书馆，仍带"保藏主义"，他的地址，要设在偏僻地方，他的阅书的手续，又非常限制；凡阅书的都要买票，一铜元阅一册，十铜元阅十册，直如玩把戏一样，务期常人不易来看。这样情形，怎能望教育普及呢？

试观各国对于图书馆又何如？各国对于图书馆事业，都很注意，大战后尤为提倡。就美国言，美虽为新建之国，然其图书馆之发达，今日却可称为先进。据各国统计，能有二十五万册以上之最大图书馆，为数至二十七所之多者，厥为美国；其次英国，仅有十七所；其次德、俄、意各国，依次递少；如日本，此种大图书馆亦有两所；惟有我国，直等于零。

再就图书馆总数言，亦以美国最多，有谓美国可以平均一人一图书馆，可见其数之多了。其种类约可分为十类：（1）公共图书馆，用地方经费维持。（2）高等学校图书馆。（3）国立或州立图书馆，对于各州或一州风土之记载书籍特详。（4）游行图书馆，用汽车或邮局传递。（5）专门图书馆，如波士顿有一化学图书馆，各国化学书籍，都搜罗完备（惟无中国的），且在旁边设一实验室，以备阅者之实验。试思其设备为何如？又如其银行图书馆，一切股票皆分类排列，随可查出。即此一端，亦可见其商战之易于取胜了。（6）股份图书馆。（7）儿童图书馆。（8）残疾人的图书馆。（9）各种会社图书馆。（10）军营图书馆，此为欧战时成立，当创办之初，即倡用捐助法，如各图书馆可捐赠书籍，慈善家可捐资补助，普通人可将每日阅过之报纸或书籍由邮捐赠。于是一倡百和，未六阅月，即已得一最大图书馆载赴欧场，随营应用了。

所以图书馆之多，无出美国右，其图书馆随处林立，惟有我国城隍庙、土地庙可以比方。良由社会提倡最热，所以图书馆的建筑，也非常雄壮，直如学校礼拜堂的建筑一样，其规模之大，真令人欣羡不置。

再者美国图书馆既如是宏大，其中的管理员如何造就呢？因他们很注意图书馆，他们在各处大学中，特设有此一科，专门研究。甚有此处长于研究儿童图书馆管理法的，他处又长于公共图书管理法的,因而学的人,也可以在此处研究,又可到彼处研究。听说去年英国伦敦大学也特设图书馆管理一科。诸君试想,外人对于图书馆的提倡是怎样呢?

再看他们的编目法,多取划一制,各图书馆皆同,多少国家亦相同。至其编制目录的人物,多为社会上大专门家、学问家,所以很能研究得详审周到(美国近有种最新的叫做杜威编目法出现。——但此杜威非来吾华之杜威),又设有图书委员会,常派委员至各州各乡指导监督,且得互相联络一贯。

总之,美国图书馆的目的,(1)在流通,用汽车等为传递之具。(2)重在设法使人来看,从前日本,则只重使人来看,今亦渐仿流通的办法了。惟有我国图书馆,不惟不想流通,有时还要禁止闲人看,真可叹啊!

由上看来,诸君得毋疑于美人对其图书馆,毋乃太糜费、太奢侈吗?实则不然。世间许多大科学家、大事业家,其知识学问,未能由正式学校得来,则多半得力于图书馆。如安迪生①、佛郎克林②,从未受过学校教育,仅由图书馆研究得来。试思此二人对于人类幸福之贡献为如何呢?是可知图书馆的益处了。并且学校教育为有时期的,有年级限制的,不适于自由研究。如图书馆,则无此患,一切书籍无论深浅都有,均能随意选习,又因收罗宏富,参考便利,尤良于专门之研究。

再者,人类终日劳动,身体必感疲弊。到休息时,实不能不有小说、报章、画片等,以为赏心悦目、恢复精神的方法,图书馆既专门设备书籍,实为人生劳动后一极良于休息的地方了。

所以图书馆一物,实为国家教育上一重要机关,惟念我国,既无专门、乡村等等图书馆之设立,并且专门大学或普通中小学校中,亦复有书无多,设备不全;试问我国各图书馆教科书、杂志有几种,就可推知国内中小学校所设备的书籍了。且我尝观外国人,极喜阅览书籍、报章,我国人却很与之相反,惟有喜好麻雀、纸烟,尚或足以相仿。此等不喜阅书的习惯,都皆由于图书馆甚少,人民未得时常观书,所以闲暇之时,无所消遣,惟有习于赌博一途了。故兄弟以为今日图书之提倡,实为不可稍缓。至于提倡的方法,窃以为:(1)现有之图书馆及各处藏书楼之尚实行保藏主义者,宜劝其开放,劝其扩张。(2)凡属团体研究的,各人所备的书籍必多,亦可实行公开,互相交换阅览,亦可成一小图书馆。(3)年假回乡时,亦可约数同志办一阅报室,然后渐次罗致群书,这也很容易进行的。总之,惟望诸君努力罢。

(二)儿童图书馆和教育

应办的图书馆很多,惟诸君既学教育,则觉与诸君有密切关系,尤为儿童图书馆。所以兄弟再说儿童图书馆和教育。

兄弟这一年来,觉得有种现象,很足令人悲观。因见许多图书馆中,阅书的人很不讲卫生和公德。他们来阅书时,或任意吐痰,或任意将书涂抹损毁,或任意将书窃去,或任意将书藏着他处,以便自己来时得看。种种弊端,直令管理者防不胜防,疲于奔命。但是外国图书馆中何尝有是!他们又喜看书,每日无论何处图书馆中,阅者不下五六百人,然每至年终,计算损毁之书籍,尚不到百分之一,何以我国阅书的人既少,而书籍之损毁散失特多?岂中国国民性根本不及外人吗?抑或有他种缘故?据兄弟想起来,由于外人有儿童图书馆,中国素来没有图书馆。

---

① 【编者注】今译爱迪生,大发明家。
② 【编者注】今译富兰克林,十八世纪美国最伟大的科学家和发明家。

因外国儿童图书馆中，非仅供给设备儿童用书，且负种种训育之责。(1)当儿童入图书馆中，管理人常教以取书的方法，看书的方法，以及看书的种种规则。儿童天真烂漫，听着即行，所以容易养成守纪律、重公德、喜读书的种种好习惯，并且儿童虽很喜欢喧闹，但到图书馆中，自然会知喧闹足以妨害他人，大家都能各守静默。有时有些儿童不合规则时，其他儿童会群起干涉，或迳诉之管理员。所以有了儿童图书馆，又可养成儿童互相监督、信守规则的好习惯。俗话说得好，"习惯成自然"，所以他们长成时，自然没有损书窃书的恶习了。(2)外国儿童图书馆，其管理员且需负讲解之责。当儿童入图书馆中，其管理员即为他们讲典故，务使浅而有趣，恰合儿童之程度，使其懂得。儿童能懂得，能尝到图书馆中的兴味，就易养成好读书的习惯了。所以外国儿童图书馆的管理员，不仅要能知道管理图书，并且又要善于辞令，又要耐心，能为儿童讲故事才行。所以外国儿童图书管理员多为女子。

由上看来，儿童图书馆的效力，直不亚于小学教育了。我国若求教育普及有效，这儿童图书馆之设，实为不可稍缓。不过我国欲办儿童图书馆，困难殊多，而其中尤为困难者，即儿童图书是也。试问国中各图书馆，有几种儿童用书？童话、画片等即或间有一二，又试问其适于儿童心理否？现在的图书馆，除只知营业投机外，尚有谁能想到儿童心理方面。所以目前中国不惟忧患无法设立儿童图书馆，纵设有儿童图书馆，当儿童进馆看书时，亦不知将何书可与儿童看？这真令人难于下手了。不过兄弟以为诸君既学教育，关于编制儿童用书、儿童画片等，尚属易事。不想提倡儿童图书馆则已，若想提倡儿童图书馆，惟望诸君努力啊！

原载：《教育汇刊》 1921年第1期

《图书馆学》戴志骞先生序

【编者按】1920年戴志骞在北京高师首次举办中国图书馆学讲习会,在全国影响很大,杨昭悊为听讲的学生之一。其时杨昭悊即主张翻译外文图书馆著作,以指导中国的具体工作,但在经过对外文著述进行反思后,认为其不完全合于中国实际情况,于是决定自编图书,1921年9月开始编辑,1921年11月28日杨昭悊乘坐日本大洋九号轮船赴美留学,赴美途中仍在校对书稿,并请蔡元培、戴志骞等作序,船到日本靠岸后,杨昭悊将书稿寄回,1923年该书由商务印书馆出版,这是我国第一部《图书馆学》专著。此为戴志骞序。

我国旧有之图书馆,对于搜罗保存,固已尽其能事,而欧美之于图书馆也,则不独加意于搜罗保存,而尤能使之活用于个人、学校,以及于社会,俾人人藉以增长智识,获其利益,其法诚美备矣。美国图书馆协会之格言有云,"集最有用之书籍,施以最和经济之方法,以供给大众之应用",诚近时图书馆管理之南针也。自欧美文化东渐以来,中国教育逐渐推广,各种学术,均须参考研究,平民教育之声浪愈唱愈高,欲达普及教育研究学术之目的,则活用图书馆尚焉。庚申夏,北高师办有图书馆讲习会,虽值直皖之战,而各省图书馆员,前来听讲者,仍形踊跃,此可见国人对于改良旧有图书馆之积习,固甚亟也。讲演者只能就西文或日文图书馆学中之教材译而编之,以为讲演之资料,故对于改良本国图书馆一方面,未尽得其领要。杨君能见及此,不惮其烦,编有图书馆学,对于图书馆之原理,及应用之方法,无不条分缕析,而于建筑上及管理上,亦适用于我国之图书馆,吾知是书一出,其有裨于中国图书馆之前途者,实匪浅勘。

十,十二,二十 珠溪戴超序

原载:杨昭悊《图书馆学》序

图书馆与学校

【编者按】1921年北京高等师范学校校长邓萃英（1920/12—1921/10任职）动议建设新图书馆，聘请戴志骞帮助筹划设计建馆事宜。1921年9月开始在北京和平门外的校园内兴建图书馆大楼，1922年10月完成。在新馆开馆之际，北京高等师范学校举行了新图书馆开幕式，邓萃英等发表演讲，戴志骞文章《图书馆与学校》刊登在《北京高师周刊》1922年第176期上，此外还刊登在《教育丛刊》第三卷第六集《图书馆学术研究号》（1923年1月出版）上。

吾国一般人之图书馆观念，与现在欧美人对于彼等图书馆之影像，甚多相异之点。我国人心目中之图书馆，系一藏书楼，其为用仅等于守财奴之金库耳。但知一味收藏书籍，而其功用极少普遍于国民，只求保存而不愿为人享用，此种守财奴金库式之图书馆，对于国民及学生知识上之补助，能力固属极微；即与学校及教授应用上，亦毫无互助关系之可言。欲求图书馆与学校互相为用，须先确定今日设图书馆之目的而后可。

图书馆之设，由广义而言，其目的与办学校无异，目的唯何？即使人民有机遇得最新之学识，藉以发展人民之知识，而因各种之利便，且得阐扬文化之本能耳。论其办到目的之方法，则亦有相异之点焉。学校授学生以新知识，其时期为连续而有一定者也。比如由初等而至大学，受新知识之时期，继续约有十五六年之久；由大学毕业后，受新知识之时期于此告终。图书馆授国民以新知识，其方法虽不连续，然无一定时期，而为继续不断者也。学校发展学生知识，其教授方法，有论理及统系之特点；而图书馆则侧重个性自动之能力，故其组织及管理，不便用有统系之方法以发展人民知识。盖学校灌输知识，重在年幼之国民，因幼年脑筋活泼，易于印感，且其印感之影像，亦能永久保存，至图书馆之传播新知识，则不论求知识者之老幼，均可在图书馆用自动能力以研究新知识，其所受印感，虽不若在学校之深；而日积月累，亦不难受同等之感化也。综上各节观之，则对于传播新知识及发展人民之知识，与其自动之能力，学校与图书馆二者，实有互相补充之功用焉。

更进言之，学校先散播知识欲之种子于人民之脑中，及养成年幼人爱读书之习惯（好用图书馆者必具此二种要素）。然后图书馆再养成读书者之自动研究，而深求各科之参考，试观欧美学校所以能发扬新学术，使其逐渐进步者，胥赖图书馆辅助之力焉。今再举一浅例以显明学校与图书馆补助之处。比如：某学生读地理书内非洲一课，当时该生对于非洲风土人情之兴趣极浓，如学校内有一完备之图书馆，则凡关于非洲风土人情之图书必多，该生稍加披览，即觉兴味更浓；日后在校或出校遇有他种疑难问题，辄往图书馆费一番自动之研究。学生如此，教员亦何独不然？教员偶讲及一典故或一问题，有课内未能尽述者，即指导学生往图书馆作有次序之参考；于是图书馆之目录，及架上之书籍，乃有应用之主顾，不至徒为收藏而无活用流通之利焉。且图书馆与学校犹文化之两半球也，缺其一则不成其为球矣。

文化之发展，人民知识之进步，端赖学校与图书馆互相提携之精神，即如上所述；而求二者之团结力坚固有效，教员与图书管理员不可不注意下列二事。

（一）教员与图书管理员应先了解双方办事之方法与目的，然后乃能互相辅助而无隔阂之虞。教员能了解图书目录之效用，并能随时利用图书馆准备之参考书，则其指导学生利用图书馆之能力，较之不明图书馆之办法者为强，而其指导之方法亦必透切。至图书管理员，更宜研究学生之心理，按其发育之程序，不但知学生在图书馆之需要，尤须设法增进学生阅书之兴味，并宜随时提高其兴味之程度。提高之法，在使学生所研究之学术，趋于高尚之一途；久之学生便觉图书管理员实有辅助其阅书之能力。是故馆员能明白了解学生心理之发达，胥赖教员之指导，而教员能应用图书馆之目录及书籍，则又须馆员扶助之力焉。

（二）馆员与教员应持坚忍之精神，共同合作；且宜随时讨论一切，预定一种有程序之方法，引导学生参考图籍杂志及应用图书之目录。英美各国于师范学校，设图书馆教育科，其目的不在造就管理图书人才，而在造就一种教员能领导学生按程序应用图书馆所有之图籍，同时图书馆教员学校，亦注重教员心理及原则者，在使馆员能了解学生心理及其意向耳。图书馆与学校如能共同合作，在较短时期内，能使学术易于发展，文化易于进步，而教育程度亦易于增高。

北高师生，鉴于学校与图书馆互相提携必有大造于中国教育之前途，不惜在校费饥荒之中，竭力筹措，建设新图书馆；屋宇求坚固而朴实，收罗求普遍而适用，管理求简易而明了，书籍杂志，流存兼顾。北高图书馆落成之日，即中国文化学术发展之时。此篇之作，深望北高诸君，在校用有程序之方法，应用新图书馆内历代世界名人之经验；出校服务时，提倡建设学校图书馆，并指导他人如何活用之，则庶几全国人民，亦得享诸君已享之福矣。

原载：《北京高师周刊》 1922年第176期
另载：《教育丛刊》 第3卷第6集（1923年1月出版）

图书馆学简说

图书馆沿革

皮藏图书及管理方法,既非近年之时新学术,亦非西方之新文化,其肇端殆远在数千年以前。中国藏书最早者则为大禹藏书于洞庭,老聃守书于柱下。汉唐以来,天禄、石渠、四库,是为娜嬛福地。宋之崇文馆,明之文渊阁,清之文澜、文汇、文宗三阁,皆藏有四库全书,俾胶庠好古之士,得入而涉猎焉。惟上述诸阁,皆官家藏书之处,非缙绅先生,概无披览之机会也。至私家搜藏古籍,专供硕学鸿儒之浏览者,则以昆山徐氏之传是楼,鄞县范氏之天一阁,杭州汪氏之振绮堂,乌镇鲍氏之知不足斋为最著。同光以还,惟吴兴陆氏之丽宗楼,首屈一指,陆氏另建守先阁以供一郡人士之浏览,此为公开私家藏书楼之先导也。中国古代藏书之目的,专供学术高深者之涉猎,既如上所述,而考诸西洋各国之藏书记载,与中国殆出一辙。古代各国藏书最早,除中国外,首推埃及、希腊,罗马次之。埃及开亚洛城之藏书处,尤擅盛名。惟自古代迄于十九世纪,其藏书之观念,仅为少数学术高深者而设,正与我国官守者无异,例如英国牛津大学之波得力(Bodlian)图书馆,限止普通人入馆阅书,公然见诸明文,意盖谓图书馆之设,专为有学问者起见。再查美国图书馆历史,在 1697 年有牧师勃兰氏(Thomas Bray)始创图书馆于教堂内,考其本意,亦专为教士参考而设。

观于上述各节,可知古代东西洋各国之设图书馆,盖纯为研究高深学术者探讨之所,而未尝就平民着想者也,此其效用所为不广欤。时至今日,普及教育之潮流,弥漫欧美,于是向为智识阶级独享之藏书处,逐一变而为国民共享知识之宝藏焉。

图书馆趋势

教育之普及,端赖学校,而不赖图书馆、演讲所及露天学校等附属机关,此普通一般见解也。察其故,则以附属机关之效用,不若学校之远大耳。然彼贫寒子弟,衣食且不暇给,安有余力攻书,受教育者,若仅属少数家计充裕之子弟,而求教育之普及,必不可得。苟欲普及教育,则附属各机关尚焉。图书馆为辅助普及教育之惟一机关,已为社会教育家所公认,而欧美各国,且以图书馆为国民终身学校,亦有至理存焉。

吾人试就狭义教育而言,则人生所受学校教育,有时期之限制,譬如一人从幼稚园经小学、中学、而高等、而大学,于是学校教育之时期乃毕。图书馆则既无时期之限制,且无阶级之判别,上自博士工程师,下逮一般艺徒工匠,莫不以图书馆为供给知识之渊薮。应用图书馆既如是之多,图书馆若无完善之参考部,实不足应其要求。学校图书馆之设参考者,所以供学生及各教授之研究者也。通俗图书馆设有职业参考部,亦所以供研究职业教育之参考者也。然吾人终日孳孳于学问,或劳碌于职业,脑力有所不逮,则可藉小说、传记、图画作为消遣品。图书馆对于此类图籍,亦宜多备,以应不时之需。欧美大图书馆为阅者及管理员双方便利起见,特将图书馆分为各部,如参考部、儿童部、工程学部皆是;亦有设立专门图书馆者,如纽约城之银行图书馆,波士顿之化学图书馆,第曲劳哀①城之汽车图书馆,此皆应阅览者之需要而设也。

图书馆种类

美国教育政策注重于普及,故公开公用之图书馆,独早于欧洲各国。自1876年,美国组织图书馆协会后,而全国图书馆,乃相继崛起。欧洲各国,终不能与之抗衡。自1891年后,英、日、德、法、比各国之图书馆协会先后成立,遂为欧洲图书馆事业开一新纪元。二十世纪初,图书馆最发达之国家,莫英美若。兹将二国图书馆之种类,胪列于左:

(一)公立图书馆　如纽约、波士顿、芝加哥、伦敦、孟恩却斯忒各大城,均设一规模较大之公立图书馆,作为全城图书馆事业之总机关。其未设有大公立图书馆之各城,如薄洛克林等,必设事务所一处,其办法系将一城分为数区,每区设分馆一处,分馆所备图书,纯以该区居民所需为标准,如纽约市东二街为犹太人居处,该处图书馆所藏之图书,大都为希伯来文,即其例也。总馆与分馆之组织法及管理法均异常周密。公立图书馆之经费,则以本城之租税为抵项。

(二)学校图书馆　学校图书馆专庋藏高深之书籍,可供参考者居多,且各校图书馆各擅特长,如哥伦比亚大学图书馆,关于教育学之书籍搜藏极富,勃郎大学图书馆关于国际公法之书籍无不应有尽有。现各校图书馆仍竭力从事扩张,盖求学生多具心得,图书馆实为刻不容缓之举。

(三)国立或州立图书馆　英国国立博物院图书馆及美国国立议会图书馆,搜藏之富,为全国图书馆之冠。美国州立图书馆为全州图书馆事业之模范,且为市镇图书馆之总机关,对于采购该州之名人传记,尤特别注意焉。

(四)私立图书馆　其组织法略似会社或股份公司,凡社友及股东皆得享该馆借书及阅书各种权利,有时阅书部亦取公开主义,迩来此类图书馆逐渐淘汰矣。

(五)专门图书馆　专为某种特别研究而设,如伦敦之银行图书馆,纽约之工程学图书馆、施奈克退狄之电学图书馆等皆是,现因专门图书馆日多,已设立专门图书馆协会,专研究管理编目及一切设施。

(六)巡回图书馆　隶属于州立图书馆,以补市镇图书馆之不足,其巡回法系用一种大汽车,内可置书架,约容书籍二千本,除汽车夫外,有管理员一人,每到一村,任村民到车内选择书籍,依法借出。此种巡回图书馆,在美国西方最多。

(七)儿童图书馆　多为公立图书馆之一部,所备家具书报,均与儿童之身体及心理相吻合,并聘请于儿童图书馆学素有研究者充任其事。

(八)残疾人之图书馆　此种图书馆最有兴味者,厥惟盲人图书馆,各种有名书籍及小说等,多按"盲人识字法"印成;二目虽失明,而亦得利用图书馆之机会,经营图书馆者,用心亦苦矣。

(九)军人图书馆　美国加入欧战后,美国图书馆协会即创设军人图书馆,军营三十二

---

① 【编者注】疑为今译底特律城。

所,均设有图书馆,半年内共设海陆军营图书馆二百三十余处。美兵至法战地,军营图书馆亦随之迁入,其组织法,国立议会图书馆长,为军营图书馆总裁。图书馆协会为一种立法机关,凡在军营内费用及执行一切事务,均用海陆军部委人掌之;又设副总裁一席于巴黎,管理驻法海陆军营图书馆一切职务。及欧战告终,在法一部分海陆军营图书馆因之取销,而在美国则规定常备军区域,设图书馆若干所。美国创设此种组织,实为破天荒之举也。

图书馆学校

欧美图书馆之多,规模之大,已如上述。至其管理方法,不能如曩日之简单,亦势所必然。图书馆在未公开时代,馆中事务异常简单,只须聘一略具常识者主理其事,即属措置裕如。今日之图书馆迥非昔比,规模既大,而内部一切经营,日趋繁复,馆内每年开支动辄数万(取之于地方税或普通税)。向之聘用管理员一二人即足者,今则数十人不为多。他如建筑合适屋宇、书架排列、选购书籍、编目、分类以及出纳书籍各种问题,均须主持其事者,惨淡经营,始能收效。是以今日之充图书馆管理员者,不有数年之练习,数年之经验,必不能胜任。图书馆管理科,即所以造就此项管理员者也。为管理员者,对于一切管理方法固应洞悉,即对于普通教育如普通参考书之内容及其用法,应宜略识梗概。美国图书馆专门学校,只收纳大学毕业之学生,宁非注重普通教育之微意欤?

图书馆学校,约分三类,缕述于左:

(一)(甲)图书馆专门学校 入学资格须大学毕业,得有学位或程度相等者,毕业期限,定为二年。第一学年授以普通图书馆管理方法,学完一年,无意继续第二学年之学科者,即可在图书馆充当馆员。第二学年注重欧美各国图书馆之沿革,及编目、分类、参考等学之比较法,兼讨论各项未经解决之问题。以下二校成立最早,在该校毕业者,给于图书馆学学位:

University of the State of New York, Library School, Albany, 1887.

University of Illinois, Library School, Ill. , 1893.

(乙)图书馆学专科设在大学或师范学校内,亦有附设于规模极大之图书馆内者,毕业期限二年或三年,学科与第一类相等。

Pratt Institute Library School, Brooklyn, N. Y.

Drexel Institute, Philadelphia, Pa.

New York Public Library School, New York, Los Angels Public Library School, Cal.

Carnegie Library School of Pittsburgh, Pa.

Carnegie Library School of Atlanta, Pa.

St. Louis Public Library School.

University of California, San Francisco, Cal.

University of Wisconsin, Madison, Wis

University of Washington, Seattle, Wash.

University of Texas, Texas.

University of London, England.

Simmons College, Boston, Mass.

Western Reserve University, Cleverland, Ohio.

Syracuse University, Syracuse.

（二）图书馆普通学校设在州立或公共图书馆内，修业期间一年或半年不等，入学资格须曾进过大学或高级中学校者，所学科目均属普通图书馆应用学识，及初步编目、分类等法。其实习毕业后，能在普通图书馆任事者，以下数校成绩颇佳：

Riverside Library Service School, Cal.

Boston Public Library, Boston, Mass.

Brooklyn Public Library, N. Y.

Indiana Library School, Indianapolis, Ind.

Cautaugua Library School.

Ontario Library School, Canada.

Library Association Library School, London.

（三）著名大学校图书馆或大图书馆，在每年暑假期中，特开数星期夏季学校，教授数门图书馆学之普通学科，既可以广造市镇图书馆馆员，而中小学教员有志研究图书馆学者亦可得相当之知识。例如下列各大学及大图书馆，皆设有此项夏季学校：

Columbia University, New York.

University of the State of New York, Library School, Albany.

University of Michigan, Michigan.

Colorado Library Summer School, Colorado.

New Hampshire Library School.

图书馆学科

专门图书馆所设各科课目，互有异同，惟各校均有擅长之学科，如 Carnegie Library School of Pittsburgh 长于管理儿童图书馆及工程学图书馆。而纽约州之大学，则以图书馆管理、图书参考以及分类、编目等法见长。再如惠斯康新大学，则于法律学之图书参考，尤擅盛名。

兹将纽约州立大学及伊利诺爱大学之图书课程分列于后：

纽约州立大学第一学年课程

I. 图书管理	每科积点
（1）小图书馆管理	½
（2）美国图书馆史	½
（3）图书馆建筑	1
（4）儿童图书馆	½
（5）图书馆研究	3½
（6）调查报告	2
	共 8 积点
II. 目录科学	
（1）书目学	4

(2) 图书参考　　　　　　　　　　　5
　　(3) 图书选择法　　　　　　　　　　12
　　　　　　　　　　　　　　　　　　共 21 积点

Ⅲ. 实习　　　　　　　　　　　　　　共 8 积点
Ⅳ. 学术科目
　　(1) 装订　　　　　　　　　　　　1½
　　(2) 印刷　　　　　　　　　　　　1½
　　(3) 编目法　　　　　　　　　　　7
　　(4) 分类法　　　　　　　　　　　3
　　　　　　　　　　　　　　　　　　13

　　(5) 出纳法　　　　　　　　　　　1
　　(6) 编档法　　　　　　　　　　　2
　　(7) 购置登录法　　　　　　　　　1½
　　(8) 书籍顺序法　　　　　　　　　½
　　(9) 纲目编制法　　　　　　　　　3
　　　　　　　　　　　　　　　　　　共 21 积点

　　　　　　　　　　　　第一学年应学必修科共 58 积点

第二学年课程

Ⅰ. 图书管理　　　　　　　　　　　　每科积点
　　(1) 大图书馆管理　　　　　　　　5
　　(2) 图书馆研究　　　　　　　　　3½
　　(3) 调查报告论文　　　　　　　　3½
　　　　　　　　　　　　　　　　　　共 12 积点

Ⅱ. 目录科学
　　(1) 公刊参考　　　　　　　　　　2
　　(2) 图书馆史　　　　　　　　　　1
　　(3) 图书选择法　　　　　　　　　12
　　(4) 目录学　　　　　　　　　　　8
　　　　　　　　　　　　　　　　　　共 23 积点

Ⅲ. 实习　　　　　　　　　　　　　　共 8 积点
Ⅳ. 学术科目
　　　分类比较　　　　　　　　　　　共 3 积点

　　　　　　　　　　　　第二学年应学必修科共 46 积点

纽约州立大学选择科(第二学年在选择科中至少须选八积点方能毕业)

	每科积点
(1)书目实习	2
(2)编目比较法	4
(3)检字索引法	2
(4)法律图书参考	2
(5)法律图书馆实习	2
(6)扩充图书馆	2
(7)图书馆调查	8
(8)书目论文	8
(9)图书参考法	3
(10)图书参考实习	2
(11)学校图书馆管理	4

一个积点等于二十五小时上课及自修时间,一学年须读三十六星期,每星期上课及预备约须四十二小时。

伊利诺爱图书馆学课程

第一学年第一学期　　　　　　　　　每周时间
　(1)图书参考　　　　　　　　　　　3
　(2)书籍选择　　　　　　　　　　　2
　(3)登录法　　　　　　　　　　　　2
　(4)分类法　　　　　　　　　　　　3
　(5)编目法　　　　　　　　　　　　3
　(6)出纳法　　　　　　　　　　　　1
　(7)图书管理　　　　　　　　　　　<u>1</u>
　　　　　　　　　　每周授课共 15 小时

第二学期　　　　　　　　　　　　　每周时间
　(1)图书参考　　　　　　　　　　　3
　(2)书籍选择　　　　　　　　　　　2
　(3)实习　　　　　　　　　　　　　3
　(4)图书馆史　　　　　　　　　　　2
　(5)书坊书目　　　　　　　　　　　1
　(6)印刷装订与索引　　　　　　　　2
　(7)扩充图书馆　　　　　　　　　　3
　(8)图书馆管理　　　　　　　　　　<u>1</u>
　　　　　　　　　　每周授课共 17 小时

第二学年第一学期　　　　　　　　　　　　每周时间
　(1)科目书目学　　　　　　　　　　　　　1
　(2)高级图书参考　　　　　　　　　　　　2
　(3)实习　　　　　　　　　　　　　　　　3
　(4)公刊参考　　　　　　　　　　　　　　2
　(5)图书馆研究　　　　　　　　　　　　　2
　(6)书籍选择　　　　　　　　　　　　　　2
　(7)图书馆管理　　　　　　　　　　　　　3
　(8)编目学的机关　　　　　　　　　　　　1
　　　　　　　　　　　　　每周授课共16小时

第二学期　　　　　　　　　　　　　　　每周时间
　(1)科目编目学　　　　　　　　　　　　　1
　(2)图书沿革　　　　　　　　　　　　　　2
　(3)实习　　　　　　　　　　　　　　　　3
　(4)公刊参考　　　　　　　　　　　　　　3
　(5)图书馆研究　　　　　　　　　　　　　2
　(6)书籍选择　　　　　　　　　　　　　　3
　(7)图书馆管理　　　　　　　　　　　　　3
　(8)实习　　　　　　　　　　　　　　　1或4
　(9)高级分类法　　　　　　　　　　　　　2
　　　　　　　　　　　每周授课共19或22小时

结论　现时中国图书馆已至改革及扩充时代,然求改革扩充,必须图书馆专门人才,近日习此项学科者异常缺乏,俱以为此种学问,与个人将来之前途,无若何远大之发展。殊不思共和国家成立之要素,首在推广社会教育,教育一普及,民智乃大开;民智既开,然后始有适当之舆论;舆论既治,则国治矣。图书馆者,推广社会教育唯一之机关也。兹将关于图书馆学及中国图书馆状况之书报,介绍数种,俾初学者得窥其门径焉。

　　Bostwick,A. E.：American Public Library,N. Y.,Appleton.
　　Bostwick,A. E.：Library and School,N. Y.,Wilson & Co.
　　Bostwick,A. E.：Library and Society,N. Y.,Wilson & Co.
　　Brown,J. D.：Small Library,Lond.,Routledge.
　　Dana,J. C.：Library Primer,Chicago,A. L. A.
　　Dewey Melvil：Decimal Classification,N. Y.,Forest Press.
　　Hitchler,Theresa：Cataloging for Small Libraries,Chicago.
　　Plummer,M. W.：Hints to Small Libraries,Chicago.
　　Sayers,W. C. B.：Introduction to Library Classification Grafton.
　　Stearns,L. E.：Essentials in Library Administration,Chicago,A. L. A.
　　Ward,G. O.：Practical Use of Books and Libraries,Boston Book Co.

Wilson, M.: School Library Management, N. Y., Wilson & Co.

教育丛刊图书馆研究号	北京高师
新教育	中华教育改进社
图书馆与市民教育	广东省教育委员会

原载:《新教育》 1923年第7卷第4号

图书馆学
——在清华学校的演讲

戴志骞讲　毕树棠记

【编者按】清华学校是一所留美预备学校,鉴于学生赴美留学选择专业时较为盲目,1916年周诒春校长主持开展职业演讲活动,开展职业指导,旨在激发学生的职业兴趣,正确地选科择业。1924年3月,戴志骞先生演讲"图书馆学",向学生介绍新兴的现代图书馆学,鼓励学生学习图书馆学。此篇为戴志骞在清华学校的演讲稿,记录者毕树棠先生,为1921年来馆工作的老馆员,是民国时期的知名作家,1973年退休,1983年逝世。

　　图书馆学,现在各国,尚是一种最新的学问,研究的人正在日求进步。至于中国,则更在幼稚时代。吾校同学多已了解这门学问,至少也该比旁的学校同学了解些;所以今日我讲起来,比较容易得多。我要讲的内容,大约可分为两项:(一)图书馆学的起源与图书馆学校的情形;(二)我个人在中国图书馆事业上所得的经验与所抱的将来的希望。

　　我们都知道:必是先有图书馆,然后始有图书馆学;因为一种具体事业必先有发起草创,然后始有研究这种事业的学问的要求。所以要讲图书馆学,不得不先讲图书馆本身的来源和经过。在十五年前,只有藏书楼,没有图书馆。图书馆的初形,只是一种藏书楼的性质。这个中外都是相同的。中国各朝代的书库,各地方的书院和私家的藏书室,由来都很久,藏书都甚富。然而他们只是死藏不活用,所以只能说是藏书楼,不能称为图书馆。外国如古代埃及、巴比伦、希腊、罗马皆有大规模的藏书机关。后来各国大学也注意藏书,但是仍然不能称为图书馆。譬如在英国牛津大学,卜德立图书馆是一个很著名的藏书机关,但他却有一句格言"禁止无学识的人用他的藏书"。凡捐书给他的都有指定权,将书用铜锁铁链封固起来。只有高明的学者,始能阅读,普通人是不能的。如此可见彼时的藏书机关,与现在图书馆的性质相差的远了。

　　自十九世纪以来,普及教育与社会教育的运动盛行。一般人觉悟了图书馆与普及教育有密切的关系,于是把图书馆一变而为一种社会机关,他在美国最为发达,这却也有原故。各国的教育,各有一种主义,法、德各国注重专门人才的造就,普通教育次之。美国则抱普遍主义,务使人民平均发达,所以社会教育最发达,图书馆发展亦最早。他国内各地方都设立图书馆,造就出来的图书馆专门人才亦最多。有人说美国有自创的两种学问:一是牙科(dentistry),一是图书馆学,这话确实是事实。

　　图书馆的最大功用,就是补学校教育之不足,因为他的搜藏无穷无尽,所有的学问都涵括在内。他可算是研究学问的一个渊薮,上自大学问家,下至车夫、孺子都要用他。美国有很多大人物,都是从图书馆里成就出来的。如钢铁大王卡纳奇,他自己说他的学问,不是从学校里得来的,完全是从图书馆里得来的。他因为有这种经验,所以看到图书馆有发达的必要,而把家产的三分之二,都捐办图书馆。美国卡纳奇图书馆和中国北京的政治学会图书馆,每年都有一部分图书是他捐的。又如兰克林费和爱狄生诸大科学家,都是全赖图书馆以成就学问的,观此可知图书馆效用之大。

美国图书馆之多,有如中国的城隍庙;都会城市不消说,即乡村僻壤,亦都有小图书馆。大图书馆的规模极大,如纽约公共图书馆每年用费达美金二百四十万元之多,每日阅览者无不满座。至于他的图书馆的种类亦甚多,第一是专门图书馆——如银行图书馆,法律图书馆,化学图书馆——其中搜藏最富,编制最精。这种专门图书馆最便利,譬如美国纽约时报馆记者要查一种难找的参考材料,他就可以依着种类打电话到那个材料所属的专门图书馆去问,马上就可以查得明明白白,此不过举其一端。第二是普通图书馆,他的性质广泛,人人可用。因为图书馆有这样神妙的功效,并且他的性质又是公开的、公有的、公用的,所以图书的分类、编制、购置、出纳等等复杂问题也就生了,势不得不有科学的研究。这种研究于是就促进了图书馆管理法的出现。管理法是什么呢? 就是图书的购置、保存、应用的方法。因为要研究管理法,所以方有图书馆学校的设立。

图书馆学校有四种:(一)图书馆专门学校;(二)大学,或师范学校,或大图书馆所附设的图书馆专科;(三)普通图书馆学校;(四)夏季图书馆学校。

(一)美国专门图书馆学校最老的有两处:一为纽约州立大学图书馆学院(University of the State of New York, Library School, Albany)创设于一八八七年。一为伊列诺大学图书馆学校(University of Illinois, Library School),创设于一八九三年。入校资格须高等或大学毕业,与入医科或法科的限制相同,因为必得基本的学问有素,始能有完全的造就。所习的方言除英文外须选习德文、法文任何一种(详细课程见后)。此是美国情形。他国除英国伦敦大学将于一九二〇(?)年设立专校外,法、德诸国尚无此种学校,只有一种 Apprentice Course,专为造就急用的人员而设。

(二)图书馆学专科设在大学或师范学校或大图书馆内的,毕业期限是二年或三年,学科与第一类相等。美国现有的此种学校如下:

Drexel Institute, Philadelphia, Pa.

Pratt Institute, Library School, Brooklyn.

New York Public Library School, New York.

Los Angeles Public Library School, Cal.

Carnegie Library School of Pittsburgh, Pa.

Carnegie Library School of Atlanta, Ga.

St. Louis Public Library School.

University of California, San Francisco, Cal.

University of Wisconsin, Madison, Wis.

University of Washington, Seattle, Wash.

University of Texas, Texas.

Simmons College, Boston, Mass.

Western Reserve University, Cleveland, Ohio.

Syracuse University, Syracuse.

(三)图书馆学普通学校,有州立的,有大公共图书馆立的。毕业期限一年或半年不等,入学资格也须曾进过大学或高等学校。所学科目有图书馆学普通科和初步编目法、分类法、目录学等,并有实习。毕业以后能在普通图书馆任事。下列数处学校成绩颇佳:

Riverside Library Service School, Cal.
Boston Public Library, Boston, Mass.
Brooklyn Public Library, N. Y.
Indiana Library School, Indianapolis, Ind.
Chautauqua Library School, Canada.
Ontario Library School, Canada.
Library Association Library School, London, England.

(四)图书馆学夏季学校,是著名大学图书馆,或大图书馆,或专门学校在每年暑假期内所设立的学校;时间只有数星期,仅教授几门图书馆学的普通科学以广造普通人才。凡市镇图书馆员,及中小学校教员,有志研究图书馆学的,皆可入此类学校:

Columbia University, New York.
University of The State of New York, Library School, Albany.
University of Michigan, Michigan.
Colorado Library Summer School, Colorado.
New Hampshire Library School.

以上几种学校,除在专门图书馆学校完全毕业的以外,其余的(在专门学校一年级毕业的亦在此类)都得先有学校发给的凭照,到所分发的省份去考试,取凭证,并且注册,然后才能到任办事。此项考试非常严格,就和作医生的手续一样。

现在把美国著名图书馆学校的课程约略一述:

(甲)纽约州立大学图书馆学院

第一学年课程:

一、图书馆管理法	共八积点
1. 小图书馆管理法	$1/2$
2. 美国图书馆史	$1/2$
3. 图书馆建筑	1
4. 儿童图书馆	$1/2$
5. 图书馆研究	$3\frac{1}{2}$
6. 调查报告	2
二、目录学	共二十一积点
1. 书目学	4
2. 图书参考	5
3. 图书选择法	12
三、实习	共八积点
四、学术科目	共二十一积点
1. 装订法	$1\frac{1}{2}$
2. 印刷	$1\frac{1}{2}$
3. 编目法	7
4. 分类法	3
5. 出纳法	1

6. 编档(?)法   2

7. 购置登录法   1½

8. 图书顺序法   ½

9. 目录编制法   3

总计第一学年应学必修科共五十八积点。

第二学年课程：

一、图书馆管理法   共十二积点

  1. 大图书馆管理法   5

  2. 图书馆研究   3½

  3. 调查报告及论文   3½

二、目录学   共二十三积点

  1. 公刊参考   2

  2. 图书馆史   1

  3. 图书选择法   12

  4. 目录学   8

三、实习   共八积点

四、学术科目   共三积点

  分类法比较   3

共计第二学年应学必修科目四十六积点。

第二学年在选科中至少须选八积点，方能毕业。选科科目如下：

  1. 书目实习   2 积点

  2. 编目比较法   4 积点

  3. 检字索引法   2 积点

  4. 法律图书参考   2 积点

  5. 法律图书馆实习   2 积点

  6. 图书馆发展策   2 积点

  7. 图书馆调查   8 积点

  8. 书目论文   8 积点

  9. 图书参考发   3 积点

  10. 图书参考实习   5 积点

  11. 学校图书馆管理法   4 积点

一个积点的课程要上课和预备至少二十五小时。

一学年须读三十六个星期，每星期上课和预备至少须用四十二小时。

(乙)伊利诺爱图书馆学校

一、第一学年第一学期——每周授课共十五小时

  1. 图书参考   三小时

  2. 图书选择法   二小时

  3. 登录法   二小时

4. 分类法　　　　　　　　　三小时
　　5. 编目法　　　　　　　　　三小时
　　6. 出纳法　　　　　　　　　一小时
　　7. 图书管理法　　　　　　　一小时

二、第二学期——每周授课共十七小时
　　1. 图书参考　　　　　　　　三小时
　　2. 图书选择法　　　　　　　二小时
　　3. 实习　　　　　　　　　　三小时
　　4. 图书馆史　　　　　　　　二小时
　　5. 书坊书目　　　　　　　　一小时
　　6. 印刷装订与索引　　　　　二小时
　　7. 图书馆发展策　　　　　　三小时
　　8. 图书馆管理法　　　　　　一小时

三、第二学年第一学期——每周授课共十六小时
　　1. 科目书目学　　　　　　　一小时
　　2. 高级图书参考　　　　　　二小时
　　3. 实习　　　　　　　　　　三小时
　　4. 公刊参考　　　　　　　　二小时
　　5. 图书馆研究　　　　　　　二小时
　　6. 图书选择法　　　　　　　二小时
　　7. 图书馆管理法　　　　　　三小时
　　8. 编目学的机关　　　　　　一小时

四、第二学期——每周授课共十九或二十二小时
　　1. 科目编目学　　　　　　　一小时
　　2. 图书沿革　　　　　　　　二小时
　　3. 实习　　　　　　　　　　三小时
　　4. 公刊参考　　　　　　　　三小时
　　5. 图书馆研究　　　　　　　二小时
　　6. 图书选择法　　　　　　　三小时
　　7. 图书馆管理法　　　　　　三小时
　　8. 实习　　　　　　　　　　一或四小时
　　9. 高级分类法　　　　　　　二小时

　　以上是讲的外国图书馆的发达和图书馆学校的情形。现在要说说学图书馆学的人的性格。大概有三种人不宜学图书馆学：

　　第一：在政治方面或位置方面志向太高的人不应当学图书馆学，因为图书馆事业是社会服务，容不得有什么升官发财，鹏飞骥腾的雄心与希望。

　　第二：性情暴躁的人不宜学图书馆学，因为图书馆是一个复杂的组织，手续次序非常精细，处处得精心静意持温和的态度。

　　第三：作事忽略的人不宜学图书馆学，因为图书馆的事情是草率不得的，敷衍不得的，忽

略不得的。作事浮躁的人如何办得来呢?

以上是我个人的经验,也是众人所承认的事实。大家若有意学图书馆学,事前应先详细自察一番。现在要讲到中国方面了。

在中国办图书馆,比较在其他各国尤为困难。第一,事在草创。从前一点根基没有,马上着手开办,自然有很多困难。第二,旧书难以整理。中国以往的旧书很是不少,搜集既不容易,编制尤其不易;内容杂乱之至,若按着新编目法做去,简直莫有办法。第三,人才缺乏,组织无助。现在中国人在外国习图书馆的很少,本国大半人尚不知注意,办起来,孤手独呼,没有多大效果。第四,社会方面多不了解图书馆所以重要的原因,大多数都没有图书馆常识,创办起来没有多少人表同情。最大的原因,就是这事在生活上,没有什么大发展,人们都不乐为。凡此种种都是些不易举办的困难。

其实这个事业,虽不算舒服,却也不算苦。依我个人十几年来的经验看来,倒觉得是很快活。

第一,精神上快乐,因为这个事是可以协助多数人作事作学问的。即以最近的事实而论,财政部调查各国统计,到我们清华图书馆来请问,结果都查得了,而他处则无法可想。其次为北京各大学校的学员也到我们这里来查参考资料。我们能这样的协助人,岂不是一件大快事?

第二,多认识人。以前说过图书馆是什么人都得用他的,无论是政客、学者、企业家,都要和图书馆发生来往。我们交接这样多的人,形形色色,什么样的都有,岂不又是一件乐事?

第三,生活上也有希望,因为中国现在尚缺少这样的人才。中国人在美国学图书馆的只有八个人。中国境内只有一个文华大学有图书馆科,造就的人也很有限。既少则贵,所以现在学图书馆学总有发展的余地。将来纵然不能发财,也不至于饿死,这是可以断言的。

至于中国将来的希望,那是很大的。现在虽正在创造,十年后当很有可观。只看捐钱的日多,就是一个铁证:如齐巡阅使捐款建设东南大学图书馆;萧督军动议捐款办理湖北省立图书馆;又如日本退还赔款将提出几千万,办北京图书馆。如此看来,中国图书馆事业的前途,不是很有发展的希望吗?留心的满可及时努力。

原载:《清华周刊》 1924 年第 305 期

图书分类法几条原则的商榷

十三年五月十八日在北京图书馆协会的演讲

【编者按】 1924年3月30日，戴志骞主持成立北京图书馆协会，这是在中华教育改进社下创立的第一个地方性图书馆协会，会所设在清华学校。该会定期举行年会，此为第三次会议，戴志骞发表的演讲。当年8月，戴志骞第二次赴美留学。

鄙人赴美在即，敝馆诸事，急待结束，故无充分预备，请各位勿以讲演看待；此次所讲为"图书馆分类学的原则"。

对于分类书籍所具之眼光，不可太小（以我是为是）。按中国图书分类法，自《汉书·艺文志》以下，大都通用经、史、子、集四大类；而西方分类书籍方法，则五花八门，种类极多，故择善而从，实为分类学之至要。兹将"图书分类法的原则"略举于后：

（一）我国学者向来对于编目的方法，注重学理的分类，兼及版本校勘等事，而不以编目之能事尽于注重分类，实为一种极是的态度。近来往往有人以分类为编目之唯一方法，其见解不甚妥当。盖编目与分类，二者应相辅而行，其于图书馆目录之功效，犹人之有手足，手足缺一，则成残废；编目与分类不相辅而行，则失图书目录之功效。兹编但讲分类、编目一层，俟有机会，再与诸君讨论之。

（二）世界上事物之分类，不论其为学问，或为书籍，概各从性所同，而自然有其类别。例如化学中同性原子之吸引力，较不同性者为强。照自然分法，同本性者归一类，不徒考察其形色，亦必察其性质之异同，然后方可归类。譬如辨别人种，不可纯以头发之颜色为标准，而必察其为扁的或椭圆的。再如分花瓶之种类，应察其质料，而不可徒观其大小。

按本性归类犹不足，且须于一类之中，又可复分数小类，其程序则由渐而入，小分类应互相衔接而有统系。例如生物学一类，可复分为植物类、动物类；而植、动两类，又有各个的小分类，例如动物之分为有脊骨的与无脊骨的是也。类与类须有连贯性，且每类应有各个的完全可能性。

（三）以上所述，是几条分类学问的原则。如完全用分类学问的原则来分类书籍，是不可能的；因为书籍系由抽象之学问，变成有形体之物质。譬如化学在原子的时代，或汽体的时代，是纯粹的；一变液体，或固体，其中便混有许多杂质，而不易复分了。书之内容，包罗极广，故其分类，决不能如学问分类之精确（因学问分类须侧重一个"真"字）。于是分类书籍之目的，不得不侧重一个"用"字，但其方法，亦不可与分类学问之方法相去太远。

（四）图书分类法既侧重一个"用"字，则各种应用之手续，须研究最简便之方法，于是欧美各国便产生五花八门之分类方法了。今将历来分类方法的原则，简单说一说：

1. 按书籍性质相似者归为一类，如中国之经、史、子、集分类法。
2. 按著者字母相同者归为一类。
3. 按出版日期之先后，或收藏日期之先后归类。
4. 按地理区分者——如欧洲的历史、地质、农林等，概归欧洲一类。

5. 按书帙大小归类者——如二开等,四页八页。

6. 按书面颜色归类者——如 Every Man's Library。

7. 按装订归类者——即最好之书,用精致之装订,放在最便利之地点。

8. 按体裁归类者——如医学百科全书、政治百科全书及各种百科全书,均归在百科全书之一类。

9. 按方言归类者。

(五)以上单独分类,皆不完全,必混合"与论理相合的"及"人为的"数种分类法的原则而成者,方为完全适用之分类法。如下表:

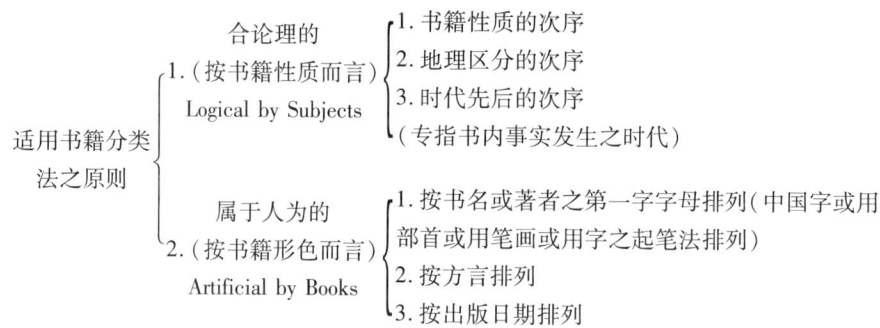

(例)Carlyle French Revolution 1865,(In French)

1.(历史)系书籍性质,(法国)系地理区分,(革命)系事实发生之时代。

2.(Carlyle)按作者字母排列,(法文译本)按方言排列,而(1865)按出版日期排列。

(又例)中华民国宪法史　吴宗慈编　民国十三年出版

1.(宪法史)系书籍性质,(中华)系地理区分,(民国)系事实发生之时代。

2.(吴宗慈)的"吴"字,按作者"吴"字画笔,或"吴"字部首排列。(中文)按方言排列。

(民国十三年)按出版日期排列。

(六)以上所说皆书籍分类法的原则,尚有附则三条,亦为研究分类法者所宜注意。

1. **常识**　分类书籍,应具有常识的眼光,且须斟酌图书馆本身性质,与环境情形而变通之。切不可拘于成法,囿于我见,此就分类书籍而言。若书籍之排列,亦不可板照分类号码,有时须应用常识而加以变通。例如有许多图书馆,为便利阅书人起见,常将文字、语言两类书籍排在一处。

2. **分类记号法**　分类后应用分类记号法,便于在书架上排列。普通所用分类记号法,约有四种:

(甲)字母法。(乙)数目法。(丙)代名字法(如天,地,元,黄等字)。(丁)代名字或字母及数目混合法(如天十一,A23)。关于此四种分类记号法优劣之标准,不外易读、易写、易记、易识、易增减而已。

3. **用目录卡片**　一书在架上仅占一位置,亦只有一分类记号;然书之内容,每兼及数类,故不妨多写分析目录片,分门别类,标出该书之内容,而排列此分析目录片于多数有关系之一类目片中,使阅书者能由类目片中,觅到一种书籍内容之节目。

原载:《北京图书馆协会会刊》　1924 年第 1 期

欧美图书馆概况

戴志骞博士讲　孔敏中先生记

【编者按】1924年8月22日，戴志骞第二次赴美留学。在美国一年的时间里，戴志骞在爱荷华大学学习了教育统计、心理测量、学校管理、大学管理、现代哲学和图书馆教育等课程，6月5日通过爱荷华大学哲学博士论文答辩，6月9日，获得该校一致推荐，获得哲学博士学位。6月25日，戴志骞与夫人戴罗瑜丽赴欧洲，考察了英国、法国、比利时、荷兰、挪威、瑞典、丹麦、德国、俄国、日本等国图书馆，1925年9月回到清华图书馆。此篇为戴志骞回国后，就他在欧洲考察各国图书馆的见闻，在北京图书馆协会所做的演讲。

本题是戴博士在欧美各国研究图书馆学一年后的经验谈。博士是我们所知道的，是中国图书馆界有经验的人才，并大有功于图书馆事业的专门学者。去年他特地再往美国研究更新更完善的大学图书馆管理法，同时竭力宣传中国固有文化，并谓倘得友邦协助，当于世界文化上大有贡献。美国的退还庚款余额，美人承认以其中之部分为提倡中国公共图书馆用者，韦棣华女士一人外，博士与有力焉。博士于深造专门学术之余，复从事于此类要事，已属难得，而又不以为满意，周游世界列强，详细考察各邦施行现代图书馆之结果，由日至美，并及欧亚，其志亦大矣。博士倦游归来，今日以此题赐我同志，并享以各国各大图书馆之相片，岂偶然之盛事哉！（北京图书馆协会十二月份常会演说题）惜此讲因时间关系，不得不从简，殊为憾事；但所述多为要言，所有批评，亦无不中肯，谓非有价值之演讲而何？

记者附识

因为我对于图书馆学问有无穷兴味，所以在去年秋初我再往美国研究图书馆学，并往欧洲各国调查他们的图书馆事业，忽忽已是一年有余。今日回国，自是快活，但除了原有的归家乐之外，觉得更加可乐的是，我国在这一年之中，对于这一个国家内极重要的图书馆事业，已有极快的进步——例如北京、上海及其他各地，都已有了协会成立，中华图书馆协会的组织，也在这一年内告成。并蒙举鄙人为这全国协会的执行部部长，自惟学问浅薄，毫无贡献，受诸位好意，实不敢当。追想我在外一年余所费的光阴与金钱，曾否得到相当代价，那也是我极虚心的。

今天又蒙诸位及北京图书馆协会会长袁守和先生等嘱鄙人对于这个"欧美图书馆概况"一题说几句话，我觉得又荣幸又抱歉。

我去欧美研究图书馆的目的有二：（一）可说为我自身学问起见。（二）这第二个使命要说是清华学校；因为清华在这二三年之内，预备建设一个较完善一点的大学图书馆，供给将来的大学应用。所以我在研究专门的学识时间外，我又用了许多考察功夫，去调查各大学图书馆的实际情形，及其他各种问题。这个演讲题，就是这一项研究上产生出来的。我现在就路程上所经过各地的先后，来说各国图书馆的大概情形。

回忆六年前在美时，美国各地的图书馆的发达，当时虽然已经不是他国可比，但与今日相比，又有天壤之别。形式方面、组织方面，都有极大的进步。大学图书馆、中小学图书馆及公共图书馆,全是如此,所差的不过是规模上大小的不同而已。收藏方面,也是各不相同,那是各图书馆的经费不同所致,而利用图书馆来普及教育,增进学术的目的,可说全是相同的。讲到美国的大学图书馆,六七年前,哈佛大学图书馆、加州大学图书馆、及米希更大学①图书馆,算是三个有大规模的图书馆,但现时米尼沙太大学②所改造的大学图书馆,比上述三大学的图书馆更胜一筹。目下美国各大学图书馆,你我的竞争的气焰,非常之高。米尼沙太州立大学有很好很大的大学图书馆,伊利璃埃州立大学③也将要产生一个很大很好的大图书馆出来了。听说今年耶鲁大学得到司德林氏一笔捐款,约有美金四百余万,议定要建设一个空前绝后的大学图书馆(Leupp, H. L: The Library the Heart of the University. Library Journal Vol. 49, No. 13, July 1924——美国各大学以图书馆为一校荣辱之竞争,岂争红斗绿之作为耶)。收藏一事,也竭其全力,如钞本、古本等册页,尽量收藏无遗。目下美国各大学对于图书馆的建筑,也有改变的情形,例如取"管理集中"与减少建设无数的分馆起见,主张在建筑方面改良多购重本,以备分馆之用,而管理仍属总馆,这也是一个主张(Centralization of Administration and Decentralization of Books)。这个对于在一大学之内设专科分馆的赞成与否认的说数,各有利弊,此处从略。

至于美国公立图书馆的事业,亦即普通民众图书馆的工作,以前虽已有极可观的成绩,但是进行到现时,依旧日进不已。拿西亚图④一地讲,以前西地的图书馆,可说寥若晨星,这六年来的进步,确是一日千里了。再拿纽约公共图书馆说,也有惊异的进步,馆员加到一千二百人上下,每年经费需二百二十余万美金,分馆有五十余处之多。总之现在美国的公共图书馆的目的,比以前更加十倍,最看重的是:(一)对于没有设立图书馆的地方,非设不可;(二)已有而仍嫌其稀少者,设支馆于其地。这许多公立图书馆所做的工作即所谓现代图书馆的工作或称责任,与昔日也有不同的地方。最显明的是:以前公共图书馆有出借参考书、小说等到人家家中阅读的权利,现在他们的办法,除此之外,兼办现时各大教育家所注目的成人教育。凡社会中有年至十五六岁,而尚未得到学校教育的幸福的少年,他们若要再想得到求学机会,那就全靠这一批公共图书馆和服务于公共图书馆的人,他们多有这个责任。这是现在美国公共图书馆第一宗旨。其二就是注重积极的帮助儿童的校外教育。设立儿童图书馆部,常开故事演讲会等。这是今日美国利用"现代图书馆意义"的趋势。(记者按:图书馆的原则,本为助学校教育之不足,今于一人智识初开时即施以补助,其为益更不待言而喻矣)。

以前美国卡纳奇基金会对于图书馆极其尽力,这是我们都知道的。所以往往一个图书馆的成立,里面的书籍,外面的房屋,多由卡氏基金会包办,但是现在卡氏基金会的补助,也有革新的方针。眼前他所帮助的,专在图书馆人才的训练及增进图书馆服务社会的效率上着眼。所以目下美国图书馆学校能逐日扩充,一小半也根据这一点。

此外我在美国除了竭力为我国固有的文化宣传之外,再为图书馆学术上尽了一些义务。其他便是为美国图书馆界与普通民众解释中国国内图书馆运动的事业。这一点很得彼邦人士的同情,他们极希望我们中国也成为一个受到图书馆实益的国家。

---

① 【编者注】今译密歇根。
② 【编者注】今译明尼苏达。
③ 【编者注】今译伊利诺伊。
④ 【编者注】今译西雅图。

图书馆事业在欧洲各国,有极古的历史;图书馆的发明活用法,欧洲可说也是一个极早的发源地。欧洲各国中,英国的有图书馆事业,也可说是很早的国家,但被美国实行普遍的利用法所胜。至今英国还追不上美国的缘故,我们可以说是根本上与人民的性格有关系,因为他国内的人,有一些和我国人极着重无用的旧习惯的根性相同。因守旧而妨碍进步,这是很可惜的事。英、法、德的学校图书馆,以馆舍而论,也远不及美。英国的大学图书馆,牛津推为第一;各大城内有"人民图书馆"的设立,——总算可以。人民图书馆者,就是普通称的公共图书馆的相等者——英文是 Peoples' Library(有人民图书馆,乃可有"国家"或"皇家"等图书馆之称,鄙哉——记者言),但这类图书馆,并无一种蓬勃气象,这一层或者与大战极有关系。

法国国立图书馆的收藏,比欧亚各国多胜一筹,可惜缺乏现代图书馆的管理法。他们的组织可分做四部:(一)手钞本及古刻本(Manuscripts and Incunabula),有列代帝皇手谕、名人日记等真迹,(二)现代的书籍(Imprints),(三)地图及其他图样(Cartography),(四)钞币及印章等类的东西(Numismatics and Sigillography)。所以法国的图书馆严格论起来,依旧不脱博物院的性质。

法国现在有一所由美国图书馆协会所立的图书馆学校;学校中的训练,完全采用美国图书馆管理法。所以将来法国的图书馆,管理上定有变通办法发明。

比国的图书馆事业,也比不上美国,不过他国内普通图书馆的管理法,很有些采用美国式,所以形式上也算可以过去,但是馆所的形式很小,这大约是因为经济的关系所致的。

荷兰国的普通图书馆,和比国不相上下,但学校图书馆中,兰顿大学的图书馆,确很可观。

北欧的三国——那威①、瑞典、丹麦——确多采用了美国的现代图书馆制度。在收藏上,抄本、古书亦酌量采集;在管理上,主要馆员的学问,多很深博,有根底。对于各类学术书籍的采择,都聘请各大学的教授兼理之,并评论书籍的内容。

那威国家的西南二面,差不多全在洋海之中,海岸线极长,海边有无数船户。那威公立图书馆为这些人民设想,就产生出一个无微不至的图书馆事业。譬如海边的人民的生活有一种不可免的牺牲,就是当海中发生大风浪时,船户及其他居民,只能闲散起来。在这时期内,他们的公共图书馆就尽他们的责任——送书给这一班须要一种娱乐以消磨时光的人去看。至于在海口上看守灯塔的人,也享到这个无上的权利。办法是每七日调换一批新书报。

葛立斯希那亚的图书馆所藏的书籍,不及瑞典戈登堡图书馆所收藏的富,规模也不及丹麦的可本海艮②图书馆之大,但普通图书馆比丹麦为多。

丹麦国立图书馆的收藏各国书籍,也很丰富,中国线装书,他们也收集了不少。在北欧国立图书馆中,可称是最大的一个,但丹国的普通图书馆不及那威之多——已有各馆的管理法,也很从看书人的便利方面着想;将来也有很大进步的余地。

德国也可说是一种发达的国家,但图书馆事业与美国又不相同。勒不士格一地的图书馆,对于新闻纸的收藏,极出众,可以说是全世界之冠,因为这是德国一国中印刷最发达的城市,他也是全世界之模范。勒不士格城内,有一个图书馆——(Deutsche Beucherei 书局图书馆),德国所发行的书籍,在这个书局图书馆内都能找到,因为全德国的书局出版的书报,都要送一份存放在这个各书局合办的图书馆内。她并且是公开于大众,所以实在可说是世界上独一无二的

---

① 【编者注】今译挪威。
② 【编者注】今译哥本哈根。

"书局图书馆"。中国出版书籍的书局并不算多,其实很可以仿办一个"中华全国书局图书馆"。最好请上海的商务印书馆扩充他们的涵芬楼,使中国将来也有这样一个出版界的图书馆。(这个创作,在中国的创作,定大有益于中国的教育,同志当急起图之——记者言)

柏林大学图书馆及普鲁士州立图书馆的规模与收藏,也可算得伟大与丰富二者俱全;但据这二处的馆长说,欧战之后,因经济实在不足,故不能大大的从事于发展。德国对于书籍的收藏,也很讲究版本的年代。

当我进这个自治力极强的国家内,因为他有极多的学者生产,我特地到威马尔地去拜望歌德、席勒尔等的家园,那几处古迹满目的妙境,也使我得到了几件宝贵的知识。威马尔地有一歌德与席勒尔的图书馆,馆内所有的收集,全是这两大家的著作和对于这两大家有关的书籍。这个图书馆在图书馆界中可算是少见的。

目下去参观俄国境内的事物,有不可不知的几件事。俄国现在因为政治关系,外方人要到俄国境内是不很容易;就手续上说,他们对于分发入境护照极严,此时要去调查或考察他们的实业和社会状况,更是难事。我这一次去参观他们的国立等图书馆,事先虽已经我国驻俄公使与他们的外交部接洽妥当,但也稍还费了一些周折。他们要问去的人有什么目的,懂哪一国语言——我们那天是英、法、德三国。但是在他们招待我们的时候,极其殷勤;我们那天又很幸福,受着他们很厚的待遇。他们知道我们懂三国文字,就为我们预备了三国文学的说明书——但是他们不给我们带出国外,单说将来寄给我们。

在莫斯科有七个图书馆,设备均很完备。其中列宁纪念图书馆的房屋很大,设备也可说过得去,藏书很多。但因看书的人非常之拥挤,所以很大的地位,还有不舒畅情形发生。除这列宁图书馆外,有医学、工艺、共产等图书馆。

日本的图书馆状况,虽然受了大地震的损失,但他们明白图书馆的利益,所以很有生色。譬如他们在大地震之后三星期内,他们就恢复了东京市立图书馆的旧观——并且可说,他们虽然房屋没有好的,书籍也有不全备的,而供给民众的读书乐,竟是胜于昔日。日本的帝国大学,现在得到了美国煤油大王洛克斐勒氏和英国议会的金钱帮助,并且再得英美各国图书馆书籍的捐助,将来馆舍落成,很可以有称作亚洲唯一的大图书馆的可能。

上面所讲,是我一路所见闻的事实,我想这也是我应当报告于国内的同志的。乘便请诸位知道一件事:今夏美国图书馆界代表鲍士伟博士来华参观我国图书馆之后,对于我们图书馆界的批评和赞美,有一段原文载在十一月份的美国图书馆杂志上。他说:中国人对于文字上改革的方法不下十数种,每种方法各有独到之处,但个人不愿牺牲一己之说,而公推一个比较上可行的方法。这句话就是说吾们中国人多个人主张,不去联在一处合作——譬如图书馆的编目,各种编法都有合理之处,但欲求阅览人的便利,不能不筹划出一个通一的编目法。这也是他批评中国人重于个性的话。各人有这种观念,因此不易产生一个通一合作的法则,这点希望同人注意之。其他鲍博士赞美中国文化之处,诸位有工夫,读一读该杂志,便能明白一切。在座诸君,今天为鄙人费了许多时间,是很感谢的。

民十四,十二,十三
清华园

原载:《晨报副镌》 1925 年 12 月 29 日

清华周刊记者与戴志骞谈话记

与图书馆主任谈话记录 伸

【编者按】这是一篇采访稿。戴志骞第二次留美回国后,接受了《清华周刊》记者伸的采访,介绍了清华图书馆的当前状况,以及未来的计划。

- 与北大、燕京及协和的图书馆商酌互相利用
- 中文编目部与研究院合作
- 中英文图书目录不久可以刊印
- 购买书籍费之分配
- 有希望挪二千元作买新思潮书籍之用
- 扩充计划及另建中文图书馆二者将采其一

图书主任戴志骞先生,自欧回国以来,对于图书馆之各方面,积极进行,顾此中情形,同学中尚有未尽悉者。周刊新闻栏请伸往,询伸于上星期六上午特往访戴先生,请教关于图书馆方面之各种事务,蒙戴先生详为解释,其盛意至为可感。兹将谈话结束,用戴先生之语气,摘要记之于下。

图书馆现在的困难情形——

编目难 从前积下来未经编目之书籍,为数颇多,加以新买之书籍,日益增加,工作人员无多,但管理经费有限,不能增加人员,故极感困难。且中国刻下缺乏图书馆学人材,即使能增加人员,尚须费许多时候去教练他,然后能作正当之工作。

性质之难定 外国图书馆,多是专门性质,管理与组织,无大困难,且外国互相临近之图书馆,皆互通声气,互相利用,此馆所有,则彼馆可缺,彼馆所有,则此馆可缺,至为方便。北京方面,图书馆无多,甚难得到可以互相利用之图书馆。若本馆采用专门参考性质,则诸多困难,同学既不能利用,财力亦办不到。若完全采取普通性质,则本馆经费有限,且每年购买书籍费中,有一部分是购买"各科教员所指定之参考书及杂志"(Teaching Subjects,另详购买书籍费之分配一节),虽欲多买普通书籍,亦所不能。再者,本馆若不稍买专门书籍,则将来清华大学设立各种专门部时,参考书必不敷用。本馆目光,看到将来,故每年斟酌购买专门书籍,及中国故籍,盖现在不买中国故籍,将来价值日高,实不经济,有此种种情形,本馆性质,现在不能决定采取专门性质或普通性质。本馆现在正与北京大学、燕京大学、协和医学校等商酌互用图书馆事,大概将来北大采买中国文献的书籍,燕京采购讲中国事情之西文书,协和采买医学书籍,清华采买各国文参考书,此事若成,则北京教育界,受益不浅矣。

中文编目部——"图书是一种宝库,而目录者,宝库之键也"(戴先生语,见《教育丛刊》第三卷图书馆学术研究号戴先生讲演)。本馆编目,现在虽发生困难,亦积极进行,使目录能早日产生,以利阅览者。中文编目部,现在与研究院合作,正从事于书名之编录及书籍之分类。

西文编目部——该部正从事于英文及英文参考书之分类及编目,将来编好,再及于法德

文之书籍。现在书库内之英文书,都事已经编好目录之籍。将来全部英文书籍编好目录后,即可刊印书目。

购买书籍费之分配——本馆从前购买书籍费,从前是每年二万元;近因本校经费支绌,一九二四——一九二五年购书籍费,改为一万二千元。此一万二千元之中,各科教员指定购买之课本及参考书之费,占去三千一百元;订购中外杂志费,占去二千五百元;普通参考书费,占去一千元;购买中国书籍费,占去二千元;其余之五千四百元,为购买普通参考书籍之费。此种分配,原为旧制各级学生打算,因为去年预算时,大学部尚未招考,我又不在学校,故关于大学部应用之书,未能购买。现在本馆发现大学部学生不能如旧制各级学生之能力,用本馆固有之参考书籍,又不能用研究院各股之专门书籍,困难实多。本馆有鉴于此,曾筹有补救之方:

一、与各科教员商酌,以后略减指定购买课本及参考书之费,以该项余款,购买适于现在及将来大学部学生之用之书籍。

二、购买中国书籍费二千元,因研究院已有二万元之买书费,对于重要的中国书,已收搜不少,研究院移置研究室之书籍为数不少,但一部分书籍本馆亦可让及旧制及大学学生应用,则此二千元之数,可以作购买适于大学部学生之用之书籍。

三、本馆现在所有之书籍,已足供旧制各级学生之用,况今后旧制学生,年年减少,每年购买书籍费,当可渐次购买适于大学部学生之用之书籍。

四、目前之办法,本馆惟有候十四年至十五年六月底之预算批准后,本馆仍能如前领得一万二千元之购买书籍费,则上言二千元之数,则以全数购买关于新思潮的书籍。至于购买此种书籍,本馆不敢自定,将与大学普通科主任商量选择书籍之办法。

两大计划——本馆拟定下列二计划,与学校当局讨论之。

一、扩充计划　本馆拟将现在之房屋,大加扩充,设备特别阅览室,例如,研究教育的,可以在教育阅览室内阅览,研究社会学的,可以在社会学阅览室内阅览。

二、另建中文图书馆　所有中文书籍,均庋藏此馆,西文书籍,仍存放旧馆。惟新馆建筑费,恐较扩充旧馆为大,且将来常年费用,亦须增多,盖两馆须用两部办事人也。

脱稿后蒙戴先生检阅一遍,至为可感,特在此鸣谢(伸识)。

原载:《清华周刊》　1925年第358期

《图书分类法》序(节选)

【编者按】1925年杜定友出版《图书馆分类法》,戴志骞、何日章、洪有丰分别作序,但编者未找到原序,仅从霍怀恕论文中节选部分,照录如下。

杜君于六十页中云:"各国图书馆,有各个不同情形与需求,则分类法亦势难统一。世界图书分类法虽以'世界'为名,其宗旨在容纳中西书籍于同一分类法之下。而编纂之时,仍以适合我国之情形,供给中国图书馆之采用为目的。"按各国人民以言语习惯之不同,其需求亦不能无异。图书及其他文化机关,亦只求本国人民之需求而已。例如杜君云:"诗文别集之英文著作者(美国文亦在内),除翻译品外,均可归入英国文学类"(参阅148页),按此法于排列书籍,并无不便。惟一国文学家决不愿他国文人之著作并列其间。尝闻英美著作家云:"英美文学之不同,几如法之与德。"设有图书馆为便利办事起见,将英文著作之诗文别集,不论著作之国界,而并置一处,则英美文学家必谓其不舍(合)逻辑。可知书籍分类法,无论如何完备,其不能尽合于世界各国之图书馆,殆无疑义。且不独世界各国大图书馆分类法,难统一也。即同在一国之各大图书馆,亦每以历史环境之不同,需要之各异,而不得不变通其分类法焉。欧美各大图书馆,虽办理完善,而欲求图书分类之统一,竟为事实所不许。今以美国大图书馆而论,有采用DC者焉,亦有用JC或EC者焉,要由历史习惯之不同耳。(见杜定友《图书分类法》戴序)

转引自:霍怀恕 《图书分类的面面观》
原载:《学风(安庆)》 1934年第4卷第5期

清华周刊记者采访戴志骞

球

【编者按】1926年,戴志骞再次接受清华周刊记者的采访,谈到清华图书馆的大政方针、分馆、书库、扩充图书馆等问题。

球久承新闻栏主任之嘱,访问本学期图书馆各种进行计划,因于本月十二日下午二时访图书馆主任戴志骞先生于主任室,当蒙接见,并以极肫挚之态度,教示一切,盛意令人心感。兹记其大略如下:

图书馆大政方面,本学期将有变更者数端:其最重要者为支配购书预算办法之改变。以前支配各科购书预算之办法,先由图书委员会将一部分购书预算,分配与各科。然后由各科教师介绍须购之新书。惟有数科之教师,人数甚多,若各人直接介绍,遂发生无统系之流弊。校中现正改组,以前办法,势在必改。大约俟各系成立后,所需添购新书之预算,由各系自行规定,提交校中最高立法机关通过,然后各系教师即可介绍需购书籍于各学系会。俟通过该会,再交图书馆购置。将来情形,到底如何,此刻虽不敢断定,但以前办法,势在必改。

第二为分部图书馆(Departmental Library)之商酌。此种问题,目前似乎尚谈不到,但按他处先例,及校中将来状况,势必发生。盖校中实行分系后,各系有设立分部图书馆之倾向。此事欧美各国,亦有行者;其办法亦有善足取。如分部图书馆设立太多,于阅书者,不甚方便;因书籍性质,多不能划分清楚,何书应归何系,每每此系学生,同时需用他数系中之书籍。分部图书馆既分立于各处,则学生东奔西走,枉费时间,损失太大。故欧美各国,现正力求改良。吾校在未设立分部图书馆之先,自不能不从长计议;一俟改组定后,予(戴先生自称)当会同各系主任,开一会议,详细讨论一种妥当划一的办法。

第三为关闭书库问题。开放书库,流弊甚大,欧美学校及中国南开师大,皆曾实行,其成绩均不佳,故现已关闭。最通行之弊病,为入库寻书者不知按号放置书籍,翻阅之书,随手乱插,后来者不得按号取书,此书即等于遗失,完全失其效用。其次,书中精美插图,每多被人剪去;而全本书籍,亦间有遗失者。此等情事,于图书收藏方面,实有不利。本校图书馆,现正设法扩充屋宇,另设特别阅览室,有多数书籍,皆可按类分置各阅览室中;如关于教育书籍放入教育阅览室中,社会学书籍,放入社会学阅览室中。其余教师指定参考书籍,放入参考书架,普通必读书籍,亦另行放置一书架。如此:则书库中所藏书籍,十九皆非常人所必需,阅书自无入库之必要,爱读者仍可借出馆外,如此办理,阅书藏书,两得其便。

第四为扩充图书馆之进行。本校图书馆在未改大学之前,尚可敷用;内中能藏书籍不过十万本。现既改为大学,至少须有能藏五十万本书籍之图书馆,方可足用。办事房间,亦须增加。目下办事职员,有三四人同居一室,地方狭小,不便作事。现在扩充计划,虽已定妥,而经费未有着落,不能立刻实行。故望校中改组事业,早日告成,使此种计划,得早日实现。扩充图样,亦已绘成,较之原有阅览室约增一倍,书库之容量,约增三倍。——戴先生言此,即于室之西隅,抽出蓝色图样一幅,披开共览;并一一解释。计于现有图书馆两侧,各加特别阅览室及杂志阅览室各一所,面积与现有阅览室约相等;书库后面,亦增加书库一所,面积较现在书库大三倍。房屋虽加多,光线仍极合宜。阅毕,球因戴先生事忙,即兴辞而出。

原载:《清华周刊》 1926年第372期

清华学校图书馆概况

【编者按】1925年4月25日中华图书馆协会在上海召开成立大会,1925年6月2日在北京举行成立仪式,其宗旨是,"研究图书馆学术,发展图书馆事业,并谋图书馆之协助"。创办了学术刊物《图书馆学季刊》,此篇文章刊登在《图书馆学季刊》第一卷第一期上。

清华学校在民国元年时,仅有小规模之图书阅览室。每日上午九点至十二点为阅览时间。当时学校行政之组织,图书室隶属于庶务处之下。缘该处乃由前清游美学务处之提调处改组而成,故其权限极大,学校行政,除教务外,几尽属于该处之范围。至民国三年夏,学额加增,课程提高,于是图书室始离庶务处而自成学校行政之一部。其时每日阅览时间,比前增加二倍,书籍亦许借出,惟购书经费,只有五千元。何种书籍应否购置,须得校长之许可。二年后,书籍增加数倍,原有图书室遂不敷庋藏之用。嗣将邻室并入,犹嫌局促。爰于民六春间开工建筑新馆①。二年后,阅览室成,乃将旧图书室迁入焉。

图书馆委员会之组织,始于民国七年。一年后复改组为五人图书购置委员会,而以图书馆主任为其主席。购书预算,乃由每年五千元增至两万元。选购书籍之办法,先由各科教员介绍拟购之书,俟通过图书购置委员会后,迳由图书馆购办。民国十年钢架书库竣工,始有余架存放书籍,然未数年书架又不敷用矣。

凡建筑图书馆,须先注意下列数种标准:(一)拟定每年购书经费。(二)确定图书馆之性质——现每年出版之中外书籍杂志极多,无论何种图书馆,均不能尽量购置,故每种图书馆须确定本身之性质,而采购书籍,否则必难免宽泛之弊。(三)内部之配置及容积,亦须于建筑之先有详细之计划。有此三种标准,始能定出图书馆容积之大小,否则不数年,即觉书库阅览室之狭小矣。本馆建筑时,未计及此,现距建筑期尚不满七年,已无余架可存放书籍,现又拟添筑馆宇。须知此种办法,极不经济,且于管理上尤感不便。用将此种缺点表出,以为后来建筑图书馆者之殷鉴。

清华学校自民国十四年后,已改变教育方针。现除旧制外,特添设大学部及研究院。二年后,即开办大学专科。本馆采购书籍之方针,遂不得不因学校之改定教育方针而变通其办法。现拟扩充之馆宇较前大一倍又半,计划时曾详细按以上三种标准,悉心研究。俾实行此计划后,能容扩充十年之书籍(参阅扩充计划平面图)。

关于图书购置法,现已组织七人图书委员会,由该会负责,决定预算之支配,及购书事宜。其委员之分配法如下:

主席一人,由图书馆主任充之;国学及东方语言文学一人;外国语言文学一人;生物、植、动、微生物及医、农一人;数、理、化及工程一人;哲学、心理、名学②及教育一人;历史与社会科

---

① 【编者注】据庄俊文章记载,新馆舍于1916年4月开工建设。后因进入冬季暂时停工,1917年春继续建设。

② 【编者注】名学,"逻辑学"的旧译。一般认为因逻辑学与中国古代着重研究名实关系的名家学说有类似之处而得名。中国最早使用"名学"一词指称西方逻辑,是在1824年出版的《名学类通》的译著中。影响较大的是严复于1903年翻译的《穆勒名学》和1908年翻译的《名学浅说》。20世纪40年代起,作为译名已不用,但仍有称中国古代逻辑学为"名学"的。

学一人,共七人。

凡各科应购之专门书籍及杂志,既得该科教授之同意,且书价未超过图书委员会之预算者,可由各该科或数科教授自行推举代表一人,直接与图书馆主任接洽购置之。至采购各种普通参考书、自然科学、传记、游记、美术、音乐等书,则由图书委员会酌量其性质,自行负责购置,或就商各科教授以定行止。惟学校图书馆之选购书籍最易受各教授之指摘,盖学者往往对于一书之学理,观点各异,故选择时取舍亦有不同。即同科之教授,其所选书籍亦难得其余多数之同意,此殆各大学教授选择图书之常情也。故学校图书馆之采购书籍,应详细斟酌,务使不偏于某科。本馆按以往之历史,并参酌欧美各大学图书馆采购书籍之方法,组织一图书委员会,并由各科自推代表一人管理该科应购之书籍、杂志,此法比较尚妥当。今国内各大学图书馆相继成立,对于采购书籍谅多善法,兹将本馆已行之办法,略记于此,以供参考。

本馆选购书籍,先由教授、学生日常必需参考者入手,至于古刻珍本,暂无余力搜罗。盖教授与学生所用之书端重实用;尤需检查方便。故本馆向採公开书库之办法,所有书籍(除少数珍贵书籍另存贮藏室外)任人检阅。俟本馆经济稍宽,亦拟略备珍本书籍作为陈列之品。最好在吾国各大都市,创设博物院式之图书馆,专藏珍贵书籍,俾学校图书馆及普通图书馆得致力于购办中西文应用之书。如此分头办理,方得两全,否则一馆之财力有限,欲兼顾珍贵及实用两类书籍,终不可得也。

清华学校图书馆管理之组织如下:

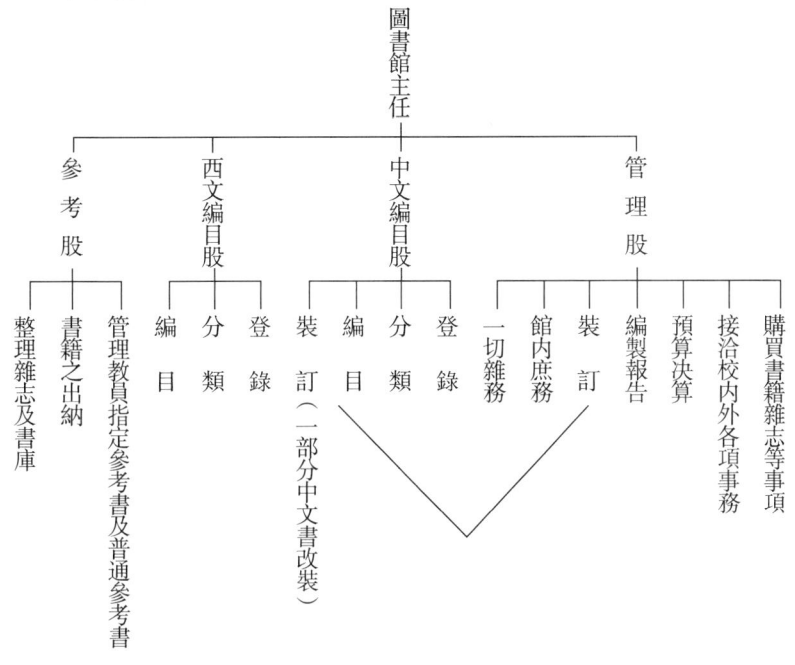

编目分中西二股,为事实上所不可避免。其故有二:(一)人才问题。(二)方法问题,兹分述之。欲求一中西文并优而兼通图书馆管理及编目法之人才,颇不易得。即以编目股之事务员而论,如能用西文打字机而兼能在线装书书头上写宋体字者,已不可多得,遑论其他重要之职务乎?中西文书籍之编目方法,其不同之点甚多。若混在一处,易生错误,且难于察觉。吾国今日之图书馆,凡兼藏中西文书籍者,最好将编目事务分为二股也。

本馆西文书籍之分类,采用杜威十分法,而加以数处之补正。中文书籍之分类,采用本馆修订之《杜威书目十类法补编》,编目专重书籍内容,除著者、书名、类名卡片外,另备有各种分析细目卡片。西文目片,按字典式排列,中文目片,先按首字笔画之多寡为序,同笔画之字则按永字八法之点、横、直、直钩等笔法之次序排列之。

本馆书本目录尚未编就付印。其所以暂缓付梓者,良以本馆现正添购书籍。今日将目录付印出版,而明日新增之书即无处安插。若求完备,除出目录补编外,别无善策。然屡出补编,检查亦甚不便。今拟俟中西书籍购至于应用上可称敷足时,再移一部分购书费,作刊印书本目录之用。明知此种办法,极不经济(二年即需付印一次),且其结果亦不如卡片之便利,而易于扩充。然吾国学者多以此种书目为不可少,故不得不备之以应其需。

本馆管理手续(如登录、出纳等事),务求便捷。所有应用之卡片、表格等物,均备有印成者,临时即可取用。例如有人欲借某书,而该书已为他人借去。如此人欲预定该书,只须填一"预借书证",俟书还来时,即按预借书证所填日期之先后,通知预定者借用。今略取三种卡片式样附后:

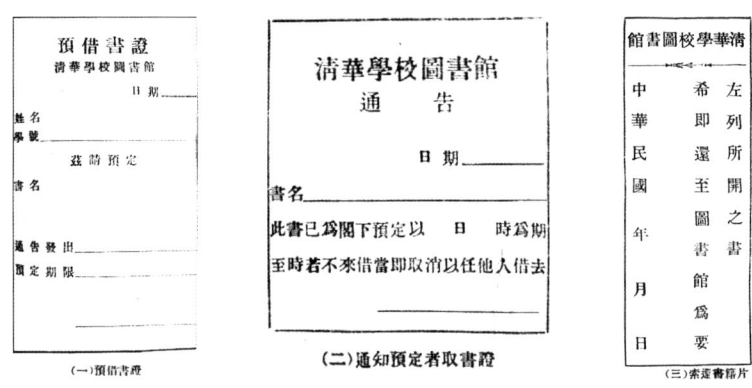

本馆馆宇之容积,现藏书籍之数目,每月借出馆外书籍之统计,均逐项用表格式记载于下:

清华学校图书馆
馆宇之大小　　长 190 英尺
　　　　　　　宽 41.5 英尺
书库之容量　　长 49 英尺
　　　　　　　宽 46.5 英尺(计有钢架三层)
阅览室之容量　同时可坐 300 人
房间之类别　　大阅览室 2 间
　　　　　　　教员研究室 13 间
　　　　　　　图书馆办公室 9 间
　　　　　　　装订室 1 间
　　　　　　　新闻纸阅览室 1 间
　　　　　　　储藏书籍室 2 间
　　　　　　　衣帽室 2 间
　　　　　　　厕所 4 间
　　　　　　　火炉室 1 间
　　　　　　　杂用室 2 间
馆员　　　　　共 16 人
购置书籍杂志费(民国十四年至十五年)
　　(1)研究院　　$20,000

|杂志| (2) 新旧制　$12,000
共计　$32,000 |
|---|---|

杂志
(1) 中文杂志76种
(2) 日文杂志6种
(3) 英法德文186种
(有价值之杂志现正设法搜集,由第一卷第一号补起,以便参考。)

新闻纸
(1) 中文新闻纸22种
(2) 西文新闻纸11种

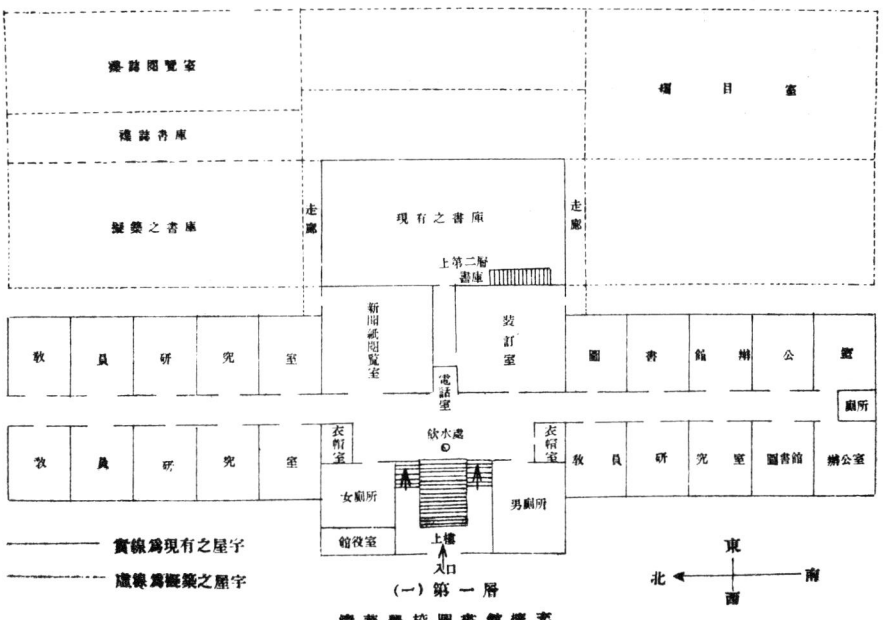

(一) 第一层
清华学校图书馆扩充

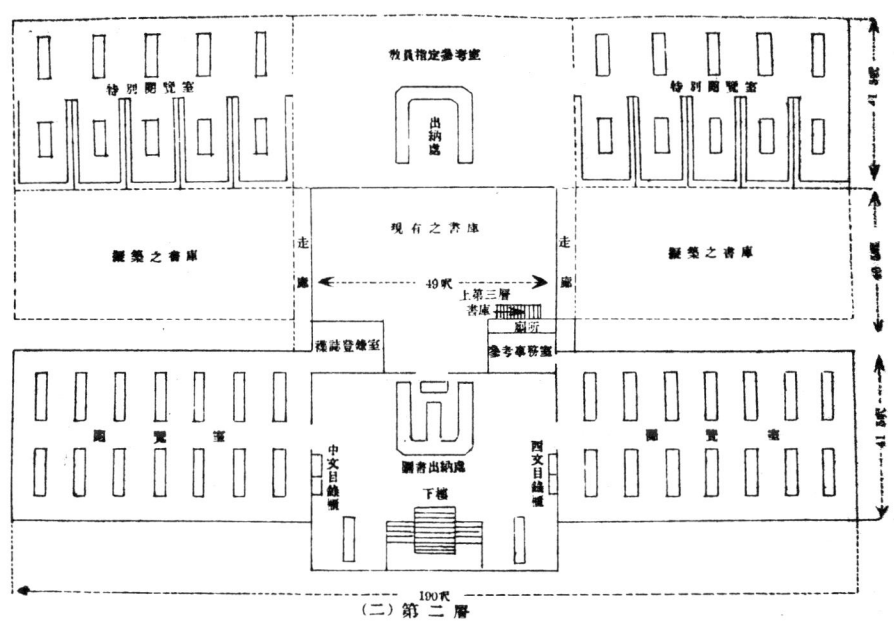

(二) 第二层

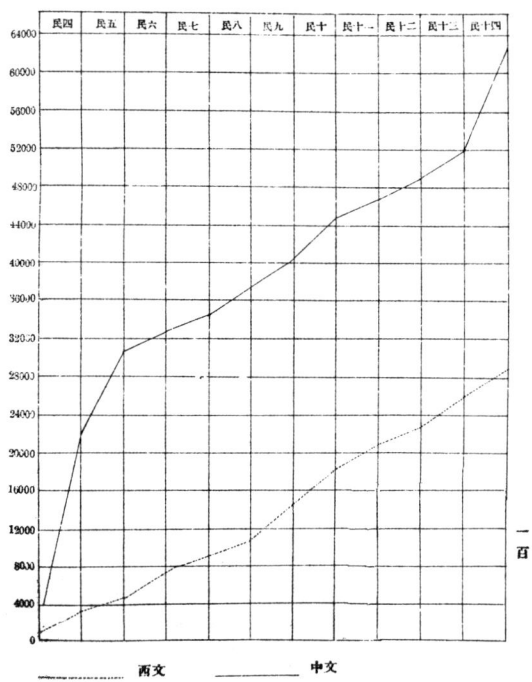

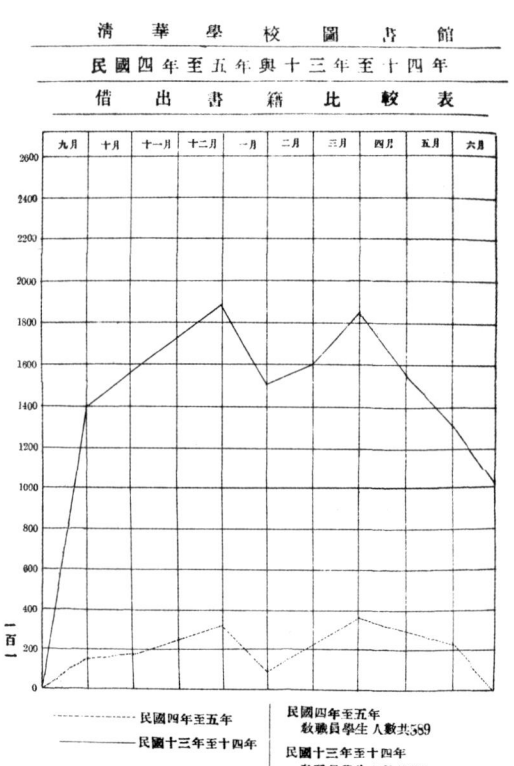

吾国大学校,创设图书馆,本在幼稚时代,各种管理方法均属试验性质。今以线装书之出纳方法而论,即为难问题之一。譬如借书处只有馆员一人,而五分钟内,借线装书者有十人之多,欲在此时间内应付周到,手续亦丝毫不紊,诚非易事。他如排列中文书目片,如何可使阅者便于检查,亦属不易解决之问题。本馆对此,现正研究适当方法,能否得圆满之结果,则未可知。仅略述清华学校图书馆之颠末及组织之大概如上,以供我国留心图书馆事业者之参考。

原载:《图书馆学季刊》 1926年第1卷第1期

十五年来之中国图书馆事业

本校成立,已十有五年。周刊社拟出一增刊,作为纪念,并嘱超略述中国之图书馆事业。兹就管见所及,将民国十五年来中国图书馆事业之发展拉杂写来。挂漏之处,在所不免。尚希海内明达有以匡正之。

溯自辛亥鼎革以还,政象日趋混沌,而民众求智之心,则较前弥切。举凡近代风行之学说,例如:马克思、克鲁泡特金、罗素及爱因斯坦诸家之论著,多有遥译其文,或加以研究,以为革新民众思想之工具者。

革新思想之工具,端在灌输智识。灌输之法首重国民能阅读书报,俾可自动的研究一种学说。欲使国民得阅读书报或研究学说之便利,除推广平民教育及开放旧有之藏书楼外,并需多设通俗图书馆,俾人民随地有读书之机会焉。

民国四年十月间,教育部为合于自动教育思潮,曾颁布《图书馆规程》十一条,着各省尽力推行,以期普及。并开放京师图书馆,以为各省开放省立图书馆之先导。民国十三年四月五日政府复颁明令,拟创设四立图书馆,嗣为内争所阻,未成事实。民国十四年秋。教部与中华文化基金董事会订立契约,拟设国立京师图书馆,并任新会梁任公先生为馆长。乃教育部忽于四月七日下一部令,其文云:"本部直辖京师图书馆所藏图书,在未经迁移北海庆霄楼以前,仍由该馆主任金事徐鸿宝督同馆员暂行妥为保管,此令。"按此部令推测,则教部曩与文化基金董事会合建国立京师图书馆之计划,纵能实现,恐难收一帆风顺之效也。

中央政府几番欲设一规模较大之国立京师图书馆,而终未能如愿以偿,良堪叹惜。所幸各省各县之图书馆,较其他文化事业,差称发达。今将国内已成立之图书馆别为四类略述其大概焉。

(一)公立图书馆(此名之定义,根据民国四年教部所颁《图书馆规程》第三条之规定,其文云:"各省、及各特别区、及各县所设立之图书馆,称公立图书馆。") 自民国成立后,各省书院及官家所藏典籍,汇藏于一处,以供民众阅览,是为创设省立图书馆之初步。例如南京、杭州、济南等处之省立图书馆皆是。所有管理、购书等费,皆由各省教厅指拨。惟频年内争不息,各省之财力,多半耗于军用。公立图书馆欲沾少数之维持费,亦不可得。以故设备简陋,而新书要籍,概无力购置。所藏书籍,限于馆内阅览,不得贷出馆外,且不准阅者入书库检查参考资料。至阅书收费,则为馆章所规定。重要馆员,大都挂名兼差之辈。而常川办事人,每有枵腹从公者。处此窘迫景况之下,实无发展能力,但求其能维持公开主义,俾民众稍沾利益,已属难能可贵。

凡公立图书馆所搜藏者,大都线装之善本书。其合于普通人民阅读之新书,或译本书则甚少。苟欲珍藏善本书于省立图书馆,专供博学者之用,而又希望民众得免费阅览书之机会,则不如多设通俗图书馆,以补其不足。但我国通俗图书馆之书,亦不能外借,此宜改良之点也。又国内各省立及通俗图书馆之馆舍,大都由旧屋改造。对于藏书之安全,阅览人之舒畅,以及管理之是否合宜,多未顾及,良属遗憾。查中华图书馆协会会报第一卷第三期所载

"全国图书馆调查表",计国内已成立之公立图书馆八十八所,通俗图书馆二百九十余所。若以省与省比,江苏有通俗图书馆六十二所,山东四十九所,直隶二十八所,广东二十三所,河南十八所,奉天十七所,山西十四所,其余各省,均不出十所。夫以天灾人祸更迭而起之中国,在十五年内竟产生三百七十余所略具雏形之图书馆,不得谓非吾国文化事业之一线光明也。

（二）学校图书馆　近来设备较完善之大学校,均设有图书馆,与学者以自动研究之机会,诚辅助教学之唯一良法也。美国芝加哥大学校长哈拍于一八九四年曾云:"二十五年前之大学校图书馆,大都藏书无几,馆舍狭隘。教授间或一去,学生则多中(终)年不至者。至今日而情形为之一变。全校屋宇最华丽且为教授学生所夸耀者,厥惟图书馆。书库内之书籍汗牛充栋;阅览室则金壁辉煌;借书处则山阴道上;而研究室之琳琅满目,尤足厌学者探索之苦心。今日之学校其为学校生活之中心点欤?再二十五年后,学校图书馆及学校试验室将为全校之结晶处。"

大学自动教育之潮流澎湃以来,学校图书馆为最不可缺之设备。我国在此十五年中学校图书馆逐渐发达。大学图书馆亦成立数处,所藏书籍,有多至十万册者。外人所办之大学,其图书馆之书籍,西文恒多于中文;本国官私立或公私立大学校之图书馆,其所备中文书则较西文为多。中文书之类目录,泰半采用四库分部法,西文书则用改定杜威十分法者居多。据中华图书馆协会"全国图书馆调查表"所载,统计大学、专门学校、及高中学校之图书馆,约共一百七十所。其中有单独之馆舍及合宜之书库者,仅有学校图书馆十二处。至书库为避火险而用钢架者,只有东南及清华两校之图书馆。东南大学图书馆为齐抚万捐资所设。此在吾国可称捐财设图书馆之先导。

近读美国二月十五号《图书学报》内载一文,述及耶鲁大学将建之图书馆,其建筑费超过六百万美金。该馆能容书五百万册,同时能容阅书者一千五百人。大学院之学生,每人有书桌及书架各一座。此在世界大学校图书馆中,可称规模最大者矣。

（三）团体图书馆　此为公共团体所设。惟尚在萌芽时代,馆数有限,统计全国连外人所办者,不过二十七所。外人所办之上海亚细亚协会图书馆,藏书甚富。关于西文中论述中国情形之书籍,搜罗最广。凡该协会会员,均得讲(将)书籍借往家中应用。进(近)来该馆限制阅书人之资格,已不如往日之严。无论中外人士,均可入馆阅书。本国人团体所办之图书馆,其藏书既富,管理亦得法者,莫如上海之总商会图书馆、南京科学社图书馆及北京之政治学会图书馆。而政治学会图书馆能有现在之规模者,实赖美使芮恩斯氏及纽约卡纳奇基金会辅助之力。芮使于民国七年移挪美国退还庚款中之十万两,作为该馆之开办及维持费。纽约卡纳奇基金会每年复捐赠该馆关于历史、社会及政治之书籍一千册。现该馆藏书已有可观。惜地道略偏曲,阅览者甚属有限耳。查近来团体图书馆已推行至内地,此亦图书馆界之好现象也。

（四）机关图书馆或称衙门图书馆　建设此类图书馆之用意甚善,盖欲增进机关人员之办事能力及专门学识,非有完备之专门图书馆供其探讨不为功。查国内已成立之机关图书馆,不出十所,而北京占其七。如大理院、外交部、交通部、教育部、修订法律馆、京师学务局及农商部地质调查所等图书馆是也。其所收书籍,大致与各该机关性质相似。就中农商部地质调查所图书馆,收藏甚富,且有标准,管理亦井井有条,足为机关图书馆之规范。十五年中,此类图书馆之发展,比较最为迟缓。

我国旧有之图书管理家,对于搜罗保存,已尽其能事。至如何便利阅书人,如何能引起阅书者之兴趣,则多未讲求,故当日之管理方法,重在"藏"！而不重在"用"。近来自动教育之声浪,几布满全国。于是管理图书之方针,亦不得不应时代潮流而变更之。从事图书馆事业者,颇欲采开放主义。但苦于不得其法,国内又无训练之处。除往外国留学外,别无长策。数年来继续往美国或他处研究斯学者,约有十人。惟外国之学识,只足作为考镜,终非持久之道,且不能在短期内造就多数图书馆管理家。于是国内仍（乃）有图书馆学校之设。创办最早者,为武昌华中大学（前名文华大学）之文华公书林图书管理学校。该校成于民国九年,大学二年级生方准入该校肄业。三年后毕业①,六年以来,毕业者二十三人,均在各地图书馆服务,成绩颇佳。同年夏季北京高师（现名师大）应各省之请,设暑期图书馆讲习会。其时虽逢直皖之战,交通中断,而各省遣来听讲者,仍甚踊跃。计男生六十九,女生九人,两共七十八人。其中三分之二,均为各省公立及学校图书馆之职员。民国十一年春,广东全省教育会主办全省图书馆管理员养成所,期限为三星期,专为养成广东全省中等以上学校图书馆之管理人才,报到学习者计四十余人,大都中等以上学校之教员或职员。

综观以上各节,可知近来办理图书馆事业者,有两种目的:（甲）欲使人民知图书馆之重要,故对于已成立之图书馆,则扩充其范围；未设图书馆之处则提倡创办之。（乙）馆数虽增,而无合宜之管理人才,亦不能引起阅书者之兴味。此图书馆管理学校及各种讲习所由创办也。

中华教育改进社为促进各类教育问题起见,特于每年开年会时,聚全国教育家及学术专家于一处,分组讨论。全国图书馆管理家因得会聚一堂,研究图书馆教育及各项管理问题。第一次于民国十一年七月初集会于济南商埠公署,第二次在北京清华学校,第三次在南京东南大学,第四次在太原山西大学。查改进社四年年会报告所载图书馆教育组之议案不下四十余条。由推行而成事实者,亦有七案。就中关于"图书馆界之组织各地方图书馆协会"一案,自通过大会后,不两年,而各地正式成立之图书馆协会,已有六处。十四年夏,复创设中华图书馆协会于北京,此为全国图书馆事业之总枢纽。该会已出会报三期,专为报告图书馆事业之进行状况。第一期图书馆学季刊,现已出版。各地方图书馆协会进行尚顺利。上海图书馆协会近刊行图书馆学丛书一种,于图书管理上,具有相当之价值。

数年来,国内战事频仍,而办理图书馆事业者,犹努力进行,未尝稍懈。灼见夫图书馆与平民教育、学校教育及专门教育,胥有密切之关系也。吾国教育家对于图书馆事业,果始终努力进行,则将来必能为我国文化界发一奇光异彩,是在海内同志之自勉而已。

原载:《清华周刊十五周年纪念增刊》 1926 年

---

① 【编者注】文华大学图书科学制二年。

服务图书馆的甘苦

戴志骞[①]

【编者按】此篇为戴志骞作为清华学校职业指导计划之一对清华学校学生所做演讲的一部分,《生活》杂志节选后登载于此。

戴君系北京清华学校图书馆长,本文系戴君在清华演稿之一部分。

说到学图书馆学的人的性格,大概有三种人不宜学图书馆学:

第一,在政治方面或位置方面志向太高的人不应当学图书馆学,因为图书馆事业是社会服务,容不得有什么升官发财,鹏飞骥腾的雄心与希望。

第二,性情暴躁的人不宜学图书馆学,因为图书馆是一个复杂的组织,手续和次序非常的精细,处处要静心静意,持温和的态度。

第三,作事忽略的人不宜学图书馆学,因为图书馆的事情是草率不得的,敷衍不得的,忽略不得的。作事浮躁的人如何办得来呢?

以上是我个人的经验,也是众人所承认的事实。大家若有意学图书馆学,事前应先详细自察一番。现在要讲到在中国办图书馆的困难了。

在中国办图书馆,比较在其他各国尤为困难。第一,事在草创。从前一点根基没有,马上着手开办,自然有很多困难。第二,旧书难以整理。中国以往的旧书很是不少,搜集既不容易,编制尤其不易;内容杂乱之至,若按着新编目法做去,简直没有办法。第三,人才缺乏,组织无助。现在中国人在外国习图书馆的很少,本国大半人尚不知注意,办起来,孤手独呼,没有多大效果。第四,社会方面多不了解图书馆所以重要的原因,大多数都没有图书馆常识,创办起来没有多少人表同情。最大的原因,就是这事在生活上,没有什么大发展,人们都不乐为。凡此种种都是些不易举办的困难。

其实这个事业,虽不算舒服,却也不算苦。依我个人十几年来的经验看来,倒觉得是很快活。

第一,精神上快乐。因为这个事是可以协助多数人作事求学问的,即以最近的事实而论,财政部调查各国统计,到清华图书馆来请问,结果都查得了,而他处则无法可想。其次为北京各大学的学员也到这里来参考资料。我们能这样的协助人,岂不是一件大快事?

第二,多认识人。图书馆是什么人都得用他的,无论是政客、学者、企业家,都要和图书馆发生来往。我们交接这样多的人,形形色色,什么的都有,岂不又是一件乐事?

第三,生活上也有希望,因为中国尚缺少这样的人才。中国人在美国学图书的只有八个,中国境内只有武昌文华大学有图书馆科,造就的人也很有限,既少则贵,所以现在学图书馆学总有发展的余地。

原载:《生活》 1926年第1卷第40期

---

① 【编者注】原文署名为戴志赛,根据内容判断,此篇为戴志骞所作,原文署名印刷有误。

清华学校图书馆之过去,现在,及将来

【编者按】1927 年在清华学校十六周年校庆日,《清华周刊》出版清华介绍,戴志骞应《清华周刊》编辑之约,撰写此篇。

清华之有图书馆,自民国元年始。当时之馆址,即现下同方部之游艺室。仅大房一间,小房二间。每日上午九点至十二点为阅览时间。按当时学校行政之组织,图书室隶属于庶务处之下。缘该处乃由前清游美学务处之提调处改组而成,故其权限极大,学校行政,除教务外,几尽属于该处之范围。至民国三年,购书经费,增至每年五千元,所藏图书,乃数倍于昔。书籍既准借出室外阅览,而每日阅览时间,亦视前增加二倍,于是图书室始离庶务处而自成学校行政之一部焉。嗣后书籍逐渐增加,原有图书室不敷庋藏,虽将邻室并入,犹嫌局促,爰于民六春间开工建筑新馆。两年后,阅览室成,旧有图书乃系数迁入。又二年,书库钢架竣工。书库之容积,原拟供本馆扩充十五年书籍之用。至民国十四年后,本校改变教育方针。除旧制外,添设大学部及研究院。本馆购书费比前增加约五倍。购入之书一多,书库之容量顿嫌狭小矣。现拟扩充之阅览室及书库,较本馆原有之地位大一倍有半,约能容扩充十年之书籍。(参阅扩充计划平面图)

图书馆现下管理之组织如下:

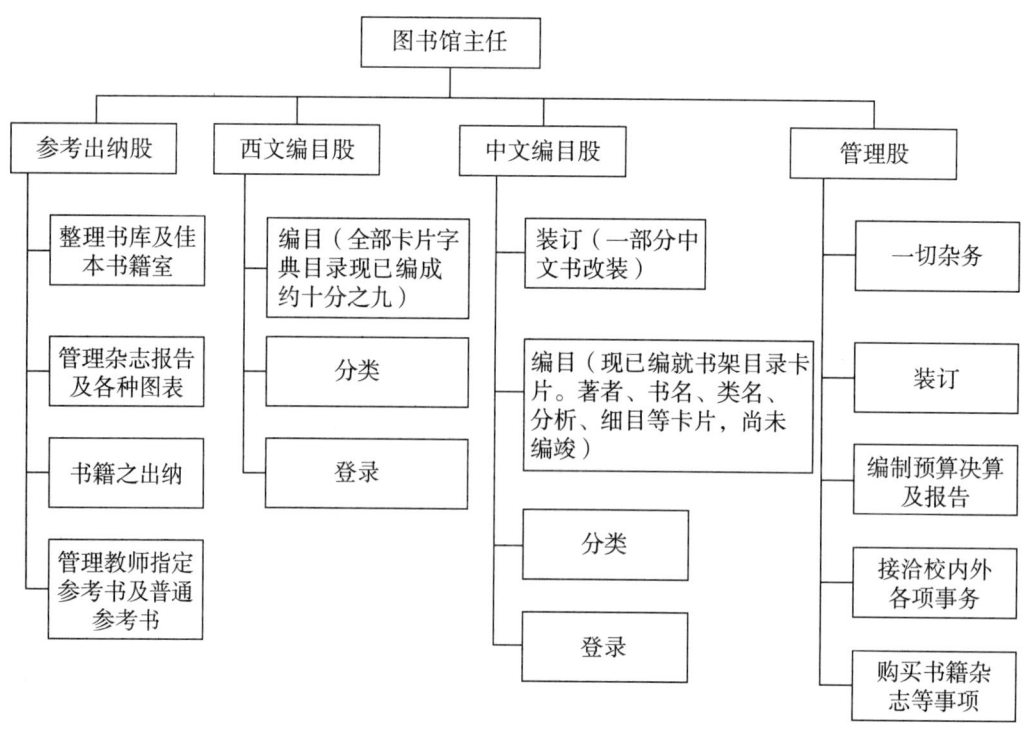

自十四年起,本馆选购书籍之方法,及每年购书费之多寡,除订购普通杂志及普通参考

书外,均由各学系及研究院教授自定之。例如新出版一本化学书,本校教师及同学,均能介绍,惟决购与否,应先等化学系之许可,书款亦在化学系之图书费中扣除。本年度本馆各学系及研究院之图书费如左表:

十五年至十六年度图书费表

图书馆订购普通杂志、普通参考书目及不属学系之书籍、杂志等装订费	$7,200
国文学系	1,000
西洋文学系	1,500
数学系	1,000
物理学系	1,000
化学系	1,000
生物学系	1,000
历史学系	600
政治学系	600
经济学系	600
社会学系	350
哲学系	300
教育心理学系	450
农学系	550
工程学系	1,000
体育军事	100
音乐	200
东方语言学系	50
研究院	14,500
	$33,000

　　本馆中文书籍之分类,采用本馆修订之《杜威书目十类法补编》。西文书籍,则采用杜威十分法,而加以数处之补正。编目专重书籍之内容,除著者、书名、类名卡片外,另备各种分析细目卡片。西文目片,按字典式排列。中文目片,先按首字笔画之多寡为序,同笔画之字,则按永字八法之点、横、直、直钩等笔法之次序排列之。本馆中西文书本目录,现已付梓。因页数较多,一时不能印就。中文书本目录,约一千五百余页。西文书本目录,约七百余页。希望暑假时能印齐出版。

　　本馆管理、参考、出纳等手续,务求便捷。所有应用之借书券、阅览室借书证及各种卡片、表格等物,均备有印成者。临时即可取用。

　　本馆馆宇之容积、现藏书籍之数目、每月借出馆外书籍之统计,均逐项用表格式记载于左:

清华学校图书馆

馆宇之大小	长 190 英尺,宽 41.5 英尺
书库之容量	长 49 英尺 ⎫ 计有钢架三层 宽 46.5 英尺 ⎭
阅览室之容量同时可坐	300 人

馆内房间之类别:——

大阅览室	2 间
教师研究室	12 间
图书馆办公室	10 间
装订室	1 间
新闻纸阅览室	1 间
储藏书籍室	2 间
厕所	4 间
火炉室	1 间
馆员	17 人

杂志

中文杂志	89 种 ⎫ 有价值之杂志,现正设法搜集(由
日文杂志	16 种 ⎬ 第一卷第一号补起),以便参考
英、法、德文杂志共	326 种 ⎭

新闻纸

中文新闻纸	19 种
西文新闻纸	10 种

本馆现时之组织及管理方法,虽略具规模,而欲令教职员与同学阅书报时,得较多之便利,并增进馆员办事之效率,是非完成以下诸事不为功:

(一)图书馆管理上,最忌书多地狭。盖图书过多,即不能按类陈列架上,惟有将书籍捆扎,搁置一处。检觅时殊觉困难,因此消耗管理者及阅书人之光阴,实属不少。本校近年竭力添购书籍,凡馆内可藏书之处,均已储满。若再继续增购,非先扩充书库不可。按本校大学部已成立两年,而各系同学应研讨之书籍,概无专室陈列,以便阅读。又订购之杂志,逐年增加,现已达四百余种,亦未开杂志阅览室,以陈列之。此扩充本馆馆宇所为刻不容缓者也。扩充馆宇之平面图于次。(图见另页)①

(二)图书馆之行政费与购书费,应成相当之比例。在德、比、英、日各国图书馆,其比例约为六与四。即每年经费一千元,行政费占六百元,购书费占四百元。美国图书馆约为七点

---

① 【编者注】原文未附图。

五与二点五之比例。而我国图书馆能得五与五之比例。购进之书,在相当时期内,可完成登录、分类、编目等手续。若购书费与行政费之比例失调,则购进之书,必日积月累,而登录、分类、编目等手续,一时遂不能完成。于是图书之效用,失去其大半矣。尝谓图书馆一时购书太多,致减管理上之效率,与人之进食过量,致积于胃中而不能消化,身体转受其害一也。观于本校现下购书之情形,大有食多不易消化之势。故此后宜设法调和购书费与行政费之比例,使书籍购入校,能于最短时期内,整理完毕,陈列架上,以便阅者。

(三)本馆中文书本目录,七月间虽能出版,而于检觅书籍。恐亦无多大补助。盖欲与馆员检书之便利,每书须有一"书号"(分类号与著者号合并为书号)。欲与阅书者查书之简易,须有一完全卡片目录。本校近年购入之线装书极多,中文编目股日惟从事于登录、查缺页及编制书架目录片等手续,安有余力编制书号及卡片目录。故由下学年起,此二种工作,拟竭力促其实现。否则进书愈多,觅书愈难。管理人及阅书者无形中损失之光阴,何可胜计。

(四)本馆馆宇扩充后,各科均有专门阅览室,杂志有杂志阅览室。书库内之书籍,纯属普通性质,均可借出馆外。如须参考,可至各专门阅览室,或杂志阅览室。此等阅览室,均采"开架制",室内书报,任人翻阅。至书库内之书籍,则属于可出借之范围,且辅以卡片目录,可供检查,似不必采"开架制"。盖书库内藏书甚多(今以十万册而论),且均按书号排列架上。如采"开架制",阅者偶不经意,将某书插入不同书号之书内,则检觅大感困难,于馆员及阅者两无裨益,此大书库不采"开架制"之一种理由也。惟书库既不开,则须辅之以各种专门阅览室及杂志室,俾阅书人对于所攻之学说,有随意翻阅之机会焉。

上列四端,皆本馆应逐渐推行之事,故特表而出之。

兹为本校周刊社拟出"新清华介绍号"征稿于本馆。爰撰写此篇,聊以塞责。凡本馆过去之情形,现下之概况,及将来之计划,略具于是,倘亦留心本馆事务者所乐闻乎?

原载:《清华周刊》 1927年第408期

图书馆的变迁与利用

【编者按】戴志骞在清华学校多次对学生举办了解图书馆、利用图书馆的演讲，此为本学期第二次演讲，题目为编者所加。

（演讲）举行于三号下午，讲者图书馆长，戴先生也。是日因同班座号皆已排定，故到人甚齐。戴先生口齿清明，气采俊逸，人人皆有不得不倾心聆听之概，戴先生演讲，可析述如下：

（一）清华图书馆之萌芽，在今之同方部、阅报室等处。书籍甚缺，规模亦小。

（二）出洋游历，遍考各国图书馆组织，而悟（吾）廿世纪新伟大事业，图书馆创办其一也。如工人有工人图书馆，铁路有铁路图书馆，报社有报社图书馆等。书籍分类，概按杜威十种法。又阅览者之剪裁偷窃之陋习，遍见于各国，并非国人特别无公德心。

（三）清华图书馆之扩大于（与）组织。戴先生考察回国后，清华对图书馆需要亦益甚，遂建今日之大楼。年年添购书籍，尽量发展，在中华教育界中，亦颇有声誉。西文书籍，用杜威法分类，中文用"永"字八法列之。

（四）开放书库之宗旨及同学之义务。书是要了读的，广藏着不如无书。戴先生极端主张开放，任同学翻览。爱护同学苦心，亦云甚矣！惟同学应帮忙者，即书籍取于何处，放于何处，万勿乱放，乱放不易寻觅也。

（五）大学成立，迄已二载，需要图书馆益急。先以为充足有余裕者，今且不敷应用。现正积极策划，建筑新楼，努力发展。

戴先生演讲历一时有半，讲毕，暮色朦胧矣。

原载：《清华周刊》 1927 年第 416 期

《清华学校图书馆中文书籍目录》序[①]

【编者按】戴志骞于1919年留学回国后,即聘请美籍狄玛夫人任英文编目员,采用《杜威十进位分类法》,对英文书进行编目,狄玛夫人辞职回国后,请戴夫人(戴罗瑜丽)主持英文编目工作。中文编目则于1922年聘请文华大学图书科首届毕业生查修到清华图书馆,对中文书籍进行编目。戴志骞鼓励查修改进《杜威十进分类法》中不适用于中国书籍之处,查修编制了《杜威十进分类法补编》,使清华图书馆中英文新书均采用杜威十进分类法,1927年出版了《清华学校图书馆中文书籍目录》和《清华学校图书馆(英文)书籍目录》,此为戴志骞为中文书籍目录撰写的序言。

本馆自民八迁入今馆后,即采开架制,以便阅者。惟此制于管理上较多困难,加以近年学校购入之书极多,致分类、编目、登录等手续不能循序完成。此种困难,凡大学校图书馆管理者类能道之。咎在学校支配购书费极丰裕,而于管理上之用度转觉悭吝。此书籍所以愈积愈多,而整理愈无头绪也。他校图书馆如此,本馆已往之历史,亦何独不然。

图书馆购书一多,编目之手续乃绝不可少之工作。否则于馆员及阅书者之检查书籍,两感不便。本馆有鉴于此,费数年之光阴,始将编目股组织就绪。并拟制目录三种,即"字典目录"、"书架目录"及"书本目录"是也。字典目录系以著者、书名、类名条列于卡片,然后按"永"字起笔法,排列目录匣中,陈列于借书处,以供检查。书架目录之排列,系按分类号码,乃编目员分类书籍时之指针也。

至书本目录之编订,其利有三:(一)易于明了每类书籍之多寡。大学图书馆有此目录,则搜集图书,得以平均发达;(二)教师及同学得此目录,随时随地皆可检查书籍;(三)财力有限之图书馆,如不能聘请有专门训练之图书管理员,即可用本馆书本目录为选择图书及分类编目之参考。惟新增之书不能随时载入,此其缺点。今就本馆增购书籍之猛进言之,书本目录尚未出版,已有甚多图书不能列入。其功用盖仅及于当时而已。补救之方,惟有每年或每二年印续编一次。本馆现下每月出油印之新书报告数页。如阅者能汇集此项报告,则于续编未出以前,亦可补旧目录之不足也。本馆藏书日多,卡片字典目录一时不能编就。又虑读者检查不易,特由中文编目股在最短时期内编成书本目录一种,俾全校教授及同学于检查书籍时有所凭依,并非以此自炫炫人也。海内大雅幸洞察斯旨。

中华民国十六年六月戴志骞序

原载:《清华学校图书馆中文书籍目录》 1927年

[①] **【编者注】**原标题为《戴主任序》,现标题为编者所加。

中华图书馆协会第一届年会开幕辞

今日本会第一次年会开幕，诸君远道来此，冒雪与会，极堪钦佩。本会于十四年四月成立于上海，而事务所设于北平，此数年来，因国家多故，以致年会延未举行。现在全国统一，训政开始，不能再事延搁，此次年会在首都召集，盖以此也。而将来在图书馆历史上之价值，亦可于是观之。图书馆在学术上、文化上、风俗上、社会上均有密切之关系，而尤以在训政时期为刻不容缓之图。此次承蔡、杨诸先生[①]极力赞助，大会始克顺利举行；蔡先生并允为大会主席，同人等至深感幸！但蔡先生于前二日因事赴沪，今日未能出席；本请杨杏佛先生临时代表致开会词，兹杨先生谦逊有加，志骞敢致数语，敬祝大会顺利！

附：开幕大会纪事

中华民国十八年一月二十八日下午二时，中华图书馆协会在南京金陵大学大礼堂，举行开幕典礼。时，梅雪争春，新都郁丽，会员及来宾约二百人，莫不踊跃欣忭。国民政府特遣代表与会，内政部为杜曜箕君；工商部为杨铎君；外交部为黄仲苏君；卫生部为余梦莊君；教育部为朱经农、陈剑修二君。中央大学为俞凤岐，巢仲觉二君：江苏省政府为章警秋君。外宾则有德国图书馆协会代表莱斯米博士（Dr. G. Reismuller）。都下名宿毕集，济济一堂，允称盛会。大会主席蔡孑民先生因要事赴沪，托杨杏佛先生为代。由副主席戴志骞报告开会，何日章君司礼如仪。戴君致开会词后，杨杏佛先生暨教育部陈剑修（蒋梦麟部长代表）、江苏省政府章警秋（钮惕生主席代表）、中央大学俞庆棠（张君谋校长代表）、中华教育改进社陶知行，及金陵大学校长陈景唐诸先生，相继演说，各指示图书馆事业改进上当认定之趣向，奖勉有加。最后由执行部长袁同礼君致答词，申感谢之意。主席报告会序之进行，遂宣告散会。于六花飘漫中，会众莫不欣欣然色喜焉。

原载：中华图书馆协会执行委员会编
《中华图书馆协会第一次年会报告》 1929 年

---

① 【编者注】指蔡元培、杨杏佛先生。

中华图书馆协会第一届年会筹备主任报告

　　年会之动议,在十七年十月二十一日晚,袁同礼先生北平寓宅之筵席上。后志骞赴京,与刘国钧、李小缘两先生加以讨论,又赴沪与王云五先生见面接洽。此时感觉筹划经费之必要,遂返京向各方奔走募集。至十一月底,尚无把握,乃电请袁同礼先生先汇三百元来京办事,复向教育部蒋梦麟先生、中央研究院蔡孑民、杨杏佛两先生磋商,结果由教育部转呈行政院拨助一千元。

　　此外铁道部捐二百元,外交部捐二百元,内政部捐五十元,卫生部捐三十元,中央大学捐一百元,北平大学捐一百元,清华大学捐五十元,燕京大学捐五十元,工商部捐五十元,江苏省政府捐二百元,以上共有二千元之诸。

　　筹备委员会共开会四次,决定年会日期及地点,初不料近日之阴雪连绵,同人等至以为歉。年会之举行,有下列三种原因:

　　a 图书馆事业亟须宣传。

　　b 图书馆事业有诸多待决之问题。

　　c 本会章程,有修改之必要。

　　关于筹备诸事,多赖刘国钧、李小缘两先生及金陵大学图书馆馆员之力,志骞不过略事奔走而已。此次诸君赴会之精神,十分踊跃,倘闭会后仍抱此种精神,办理图书馆事业,预料明年年会,必更盛于今年也。

　　又据杜定友先生言,戴季陶院长允提议由中央党部捐助本会年会会费洋二千元,以后并每月捐助本会经常费一百元,尚望杜先生再向戴院长作一底之接洽,此议当可实现也。

原载:中华图书馆协会执行委员会编
《中华图书馆协会第一次年会报告》 1929年

《国立中央大学图书馆图书目录》序

【编者按】 1928年11月,戴志骞就任国立中央大学图书馆馆长,除改进图书馆外在条件,创造良好的环境外,戴志骞还主持编制目录,1929年12月出版,此为戴志骞为该目录撰写的序言。

近世大学教育,咸注重于自动研究,承学之士非徒登讲堂,缮笔记,手讲义课本耳。教师提命即足,尽其能事也,必将运用脑力,并利用多数人之脑力,以为己助。多方探讨,穷源竟委,就前人所已发者而贯穿之,举前人所未发者而抉启之,以解答问题,阐明奥奥。为教师者,亦必广事搜罗,细心研究,以应学子之质疑,而求真理之会通,于以贡献社会,蔚成学府无难焉。欲达此程,非入图书馆不为功。盖古今中外,卷轶浩繁,私人财力不能致,即致矣,而讲堂几案不能容。图书馆者,古今中外无量数人脑力之所萃,而便学者探索之地也。然非有良好之分类、编目,则虽有极浩博之图书,而茫无头绪寻检,为难故图书馆为智识之宝库。而良好之图书馆目录,又此宝库中最适用之键钥也,键钥不灵,宝库奚启,然则图书馆目录,其可忽乎!本大学承东南大学之后,扩充购置,对于图书馆事业,向悬二义以为鹄:一充实其内容;二精良其编目。前者与时俱增,后者亦粗有就绪。西文书目录既已刊行,今复新编中文书目录,以为教师学子研求之助,是编也。门类攸分取便,寻检持以,较古来目录之学,虽不敢谓有所心得,而分别部居,有条不紊,或犹足供入宝库者键钥之用也。

中华民国十八年十二月　戴超

原载:《国立中央大学图书馆图书目录》 1929年

《中国图书馆名人录》序

【编者按】 1930年3月上海图书馆协会出版了宋景祁编辑的《中国图书馆名人录》，其中收录了143人。人物介绍以姓氏笔画为序排列，内容包括姓名、籍贯、年龄、求学经历、工作经历、学术著述、性格特点以及工作特长等。此为戴志骞为该书所写的序言。

汇萃大多数之人名，依其所守，别派分流而著之书，国之人按类索骥，莫不称便，人名录用是固也。东西各国每年必有多数之人名录出版，其性质范围较普遍者，不外以下二种：一为一国内普遍之人名录，如《谁是谁》，其人名之排列用字典式，如美国之 Who's Who，英国、加拿大等地之 Who's Who，几家喻户晓，人置一编。其销售之广，用途之大，竟有不可思议者。小之如一城市，亦有城市人名录，如 Who's Who in New York。一为一国内之人名录，而以学位、职业分类汇编者，如日本出版之博士录，有医学博士、法学博士等编。此种亦有不限国界只限职业者，如 International Who's Who in Music，其意盖欲使一国内或全世界某项职业、某项专门学识之人才，罗列其姓氏于一书之内，使阅者一索即得，诚至便也。惟以上二种，均限于生人，其已亡者，另入名人传记或专门职业传记，此各国编人名录之大概情形也。

中国对于各种人名录，均付阙如，近年美国人主办之密勒氏评论报，出版中国名人录，仅及于政治方面之人物，遗漏太多，未满人意，然除此而外，未见其他矣。夫以同一职业之人，散布全国，各为各事，不独老死不相往来，且并不知有其人，则其事业之不能相谋而益善，从可知也。比如，今日欲设立一图书馆，或欲为图书馆觅一相当之编目员，竟有百思不得其人之感。夫图书馆事业，在中国尚为草创时代，欲将国内之藏书楼，一一变为供给民众公览之图书馆，更其组织，慎其守藏，务使与全世界最适用之制度相吻合，非合全国图书馆界人物群策群力以赴之不可。宋君景祁有见于此，罗列为图书馆事业者之姓名于一册，附以相片略历，便阅者一览而知某为何人，某长何事，由是以沟通同志间之友谊，传达图书馆事业之消息，研究图书馆管理之方法，此书之功用，诚不可以屈指数。因是书而中国图书馆事业得以蒸蒸日上，而文化于以大进，岂不懿欤。是为序。

十九年一月　戴超

原载：《中国图书馆名人录》　1930年

图书馆员职业之研究

【编者按】1930年美国友人韦棣华女士来华三十周年,文华图书馆专科学校拟举办纪念活动,向全国图书馆界征集纪念文章,戴志骞作为韦棣华女士的朋友撰写了此篇文章,遗憾的是,1930年5月1日,韦棣华女士不幸辞世,此篇竟变成祭文。

天禄石渠之蕴,曹仓邺架之储,地秘娜嬛,林荟翰墨,藏书之盛,千古艳称;虽无图书馆之名,似已有图书馆之实。然而自古以来,未有以图书馆员职业一名词,定为专称而加以研究者,何哉?盖图书馆性质,古今绝异;古尚保藏,其性质为陈列的,有近于博物馆;今重应用,其性质为公开的,实同于教育馆;古为贵族式,今为平民化。此古之图书馆,所以无须研究其职员之事业,而今则必须研究也。

今日中国之图书馆,其制度仿自欧美,谈社会教育者,辄首屈图书馆,顾自外国来之事业,入中土每感迁地勿良。三十年来,新政新学,往往利未见而害已形;图书馆盖亦不能外此,名曰公开,实同虚设;甚至主其事者侵占剽窃,以利其私,簿目夥颐,诸成缺简;纵不至是,而登记不完,管理不善,散碎纷拿,徒饱虫鼠,亦何贵有此图书馆为?欲救此弊,而实现公开的、教育的、平民的图书馆之精神,其责任全在于图书馆员,此图书馆员职业之所以亟待研究也。

图书馆员职业之应注意者,管见所及,约有七端:

(一)有丰富之常识:图书馆所有图书,包含至广,为图书馆员者,必具普通之学问,裕各科之常识,方能泛应曲当,有条不紊;且图书馆员兼有指导阅览人之职务,若非己身常识丰富,何能指导他人?此图书馆员职业之应注意者一也。

(二)有管理之能力:图书馆为文化之宝库,而图书馆员则为司此宝库键钥之人。对于各种图书,须有整理、皮藏、编目、分类、流通诸手续,语其详细,实为一专门之学,非有充分之能力,何能管理此浩如烟海之宝库?此图书馆员职业之应注意者二也。

(三)有淡泊之性情:图书馆员事务既繁,责任亦重,较之他种事业,劳瘁相当,或且过之;而物质之报酬,远逊他业。为图书馆员者,必捐除世俗之成见,牺牲一己之荣利,而后能精神愉快,不生厌倦之心。诸葛公所谓"淡泊明志,宁静致远",图书馆员之性情,殆近是焉。此图书馆员职业之应注意者三也。

(四)有勤劳之习惯:从前一般人误解,以为图书馆员乃清闲之职,外国亦有此观念,学校中每有年龄较老之教授,俾膺斯职,义取尊贤,事同养老。而为图书馆者,亦自以为静坐观书,苟适一己,无他预焉,不知图书馆员实一勤劳之职司,非有耐劳苦肯作事之习惯不可。盖图书,死物也,而利用之使发生活动之价值者,厥在图书馆员。能利用则遗文坠简,皆是奇珍,不利用则充栋汗牛,俨等废物;而利用与否,胥视图书馆之勤劳如何,此图书馆员职业之应注意者四也。

(五)能随时浏览以增新知:现代新知,层出不穷,即新图书亦日增而月异;为图书馆员者,既以图书馆为职志,自应以知识为生命,勤劳虽已备至,仍须于暇时浏览各种书籍,以增新知而便应付,此图书馆员职业之应注意者五也。

（六）能具有为人服务之热诚:流通知识,灌输文化,为图书馆员之天职。浏览人有所询问,纵极匆忙,必罄其所知以告之,无畏难,无惧烦;即使图书馆偶缺此书,亦当代谋替品,使人如入宝山,非同空。盖图书馆固为人介绍知识文化之区,图书馆员即宜尽此介绍之义务,非有为人服务之热诚,何能胜任,此图书馆员职业之应注意者六也。

（七）宜以和蔼可亲之面目引人入胜:今之图书馆为公开的、教育的、平民的,前既言之矣。故为图书馆员者,不第孜孜焉尽其本质已也;必须循循善诱,使人乐于亲近而不自知,然后闻风禽集,文化可昌;否则訑訑拒人,人将远避,何必设此图书馆？比如商店,店员须善于招徕,设肆之目的乃可达,此图书馆员职业之应注意者七也。

综上七端:图书馆员之职业,顾不重哉？环顾国中,能合此条件者盖寡。

韦棣华女士来华三十年,专心一志以为图书馆服务,且办图书馆学校,又慨中国图书馆事业之未臻发达,常在美国募捐补助,其于图书馆之热心可谓至矣;而核其生平行事,实与上述七条相符合,足为图书馆员之模范。今值韦棣华女士来华三十年纪念之期,爰述图书馆员职业之研究,以志钦佩,而励国人,兼以自励焉。

原载:《文华图书馆学专科学校季刊》 1930年第3卷第3期

【附录Ⅰ】戴志骞撰写的书报介绍

【附录Ⅰ-1】

《清华周刊·书报介绍副刊》第一期

【编者按】 1923年3月1日《清华周刊》出版《书报介绍副刊》第一期，附在《清华周刊》第271期之中，以后不定期出版，到1925年5月29日出版《书报介绍副刊》第十七期，附在《清华周刊》第349期之中，是《清华周刊》出版的最后一期《清华周刊·书报介绍副刊》。1925年下半年以后，《清华周刊·书报介绍副刊》改为单行本出版。《书报介绍副刊》第一期刊登了戴志骞和清华图书馆另一位老馆员余光宗合作撰写的《英文杂志介绍》和《西文书籍介绍》。

英文杂志介绍

志骞　光宗

杂志介绍，范围极广，门类又极复杂，一人担任搜集，事实上有所不能。且人各有所好，若强勉一人阅其不爱阅之杂志，是徒费光阴，于事毫无所补者也。某杂志既非某阅者所好，而令其作一种评论，则其文字亦各隔靴搔痒，痛痒莫关。是以杂志内文章介绍，最好各人分作评论，庶可透切。譬如一人认定其爱阅之数种杂志，择其较好者做几篇评论，公诸大众，此事于个人学问及他人读书兴味上，长进不少。读杂志内文章，有时含糊读去，就算完事，如要做一种札记，读时须有运化这篇文章之能力，他人得着有心得的介绍，然后再读这篇文章，必兴味横生。故能由自己喜读之几种杂志内介绍数篇好文章，既利己而又利人，益处实在不少。希望同学时常在周刊内，介绍著名文字。

图书馆共有西文杂志二百余种，有些是关于专门的杂志。研究此种专门学术者，必能与此类杂志时常会面。对于该杂志之内容，想亦熟悉。但有许多同学，进了图书馆阅览室，见杂志架上满放杂志，不知看哪一种是好。有时取到一本关于专门学术之杂志，一见书面上之书名，便没精打采的放下，以后决不再去与他会面了。因此选择一点有兴味的杂志，介绍于诸位同学，请稍留意焉。

中等科的同学们，对于下列六种杂志，尽可时常看看，看毕择优做几篇评论，送到书报介绍栏内，本刊极其欢迎。

（一）*American Boy* 月刊。一八九九年出版。

近来常有很好的著作，论户内外各种游戏方法，并注意时事、历史、各国名人传记，内中小说一部分亦是有价值的。

（二）*Boy's Life* 月刊。一九一一年出版。

为美国童子军的杂志，故对于童子军所有情形，说得很详细，故人多称之为 Boy Scouts

magazine。关于户外生活、邮票收藏、新闻及各种少年生活,请有名人担任著述。惟其中小说一部,比之 American Boy 的,稍有逊色。

(三) Captain 月刊。一八九九年出版。

英国童子军的生活、运动足球等游戏之著作,均用浅近并优美的文字表现出来。画图插画亦甚切当,其中小说,多属理想而乏实事的,人名亦系伪造者。

(四) Popular Mechanics 月刊。一九零二年出版。

各种机械的用法,新发明的机件,均用最浅近的英文字说明。在美国年轻人及平常的机器工人,最爱读这种杂志。其中"手工摘要"一项,很有价值。每次印就另册,专门发行。机器工匠,能常读此类杂志,对于机械一方面,得益不少。

(五) St. Nicho'as 月刊。一八七三年出版。

此杂志在英美少年中,销路极广。小说、历史、地理、游记、名人传记、户外生活及自然科学等文章,均在收罗之列。著述者均属当世名人,插画照片,亦甚精致。此报订成的过期卷数,爱读者甚多。现由英国纽约惠尔逊图书公司,将该杂志自第一卷至三十六卷,编置索引目录,以便阅旧卷数者之用。

(六) Youth Companion 周刊。一八二七年出版。

少年杂志中,此为出版最早之一种。内中甚多长篇小说,重印为书。短篇小说,亦甚有趣。时事、工艺、游记、历史、传记故事,亦本杂志之特长。每期并有男童应读的文章,及女孩居家应知之事实。

下列二十种杂志,对于普通应知之时事,均已列入。除去很专门的杂志外,差不多各类学问之杂志都有了。这些种杂志内的英文都写得很美丽。图画照片,要算杂志中最上乘。议论不偏激,新书评论,都很精到。同学如能择几种看看,增长见识不少。

(一) Atlantic Monthly 月刊。一八五七年出版。

在美国杂志界,富有文学价值者也。小说、诗、文学、各类批评均佳,而尤以文艺栏之论说为优。关于哲学、社会、政治、经济等事,叙述雅纯,易于了解。无图画,间有数种精美活版式之广告。至其言论之见解,概从宽大,而不吹毛求疵,未受普通教育者,不易得其利益。而各图书馆以之作参考资料者,则甚多。富有思想之学者,亦喜读之。

(二) Bookman 月刊。一八九五年出版。

此有图画之杂志也。所述多为文艺家之传记、各类批评、文艺史。至美术上之讨论,间或有之。文辞敏捷,有用于学者,诚非浅显。其与 Book Reviews 不同之点,在前者有详细批评,而后者则仅有简洁之注释也。

由一九一七年起,大肆扩充,加入许多政治及社会问题。

(三) Century 月刊。一八七零出版。

所载多当时之史事。图书及印刷具佳,已过各期,可作参考资料。内载小说,亦饶有价值。

(四) Current History 纽约时报所出之一种月刊。一九一四年之十二月出版。

大战时所载多为战事重要消息。其目次之门类甚多,而又注意实事一方面。小图书馆购之,最为合宜。战事告终后,仍继续出版。

(五) Dial 月刊。一八八零年出版。

内容所载,多为书籍详细评论。其无关重要之书籍,则批评甚简。文艺著作及图书馆事务,亦时有记载。

至其每月报告上所载主要杂志,尤便于检查。此种杂志,对于研究当代文学者,功用尤大。

(六)*Forum* 月刊。一八八六年出版。

Vol. 1-33 对于政治、经济及社会各问题之参考,或辩论材料,大有公用。

Vol. 34-39 为财政、政治、算术及各时代文艺活动之撮要,普通条项,不多见也。此类卷颇似一种文艺杂志,其特别注意之点,则为社会向上发展,及最近美术与文艺之趋向。至对于反对现时经济及社会状况之参考资料,尤有特别之效用焉。

(七)*Harper's Magazine*。一八五零年出版。

普通杂志之一种,其与 *Scribners* 及 *Century* 之价值,不相上下。此杂志注意旅行及通俗科学,并记载时下之文艺及名人之传记。内载小说颇多,最近数篇,多为长篇文字。言论栏所载,有时事、文艺、评论及谐谈数项。图画甚精美,著色亦考究。

(八)*Illustrated London News* 周刊。一八四二年出版。

图画杂志中之巨擘,爱阅图画者,宜时常翻阅。

(九)*Illustrated World* 月刊。一九零四年出版。

篇幅上满布图画,其形式最为普遍。所载为实业上、科学上之发明,及时下应用之创作。对于此门学术上价值甚微,而读此者多为少科学经验者也。

(十)*Independent* 两周刊。一八四八年出版。

往日为宗教周刊。现在此杂志,多载最近时事,及各国政治上之方针,至时事辩论文学,亦常在收罗之列。

近来所出各期,对于参考上尤饶价值。高等学校研究文学历史及公民学者,多选用之。

(十一)*International Studio* 月刊。一八九七年出版。

关于美术之一种杂志。各种绘画及解剖之说明,颇令读者注意。而关于建筑、雕刻、家庭之装饰、陶器及各类美术,亦均搜罗尽致。黑白各色之图形,及着色之印版,最为美观。美术教授及习美术者,均宜手执一篇。

普通人因其图画美而多,故亦爱读之。

(十二)*Literary Digest* 周刊。一八九零年出版。

由美国及各国新闻纸杂志及书籍上摘来之材料,汇为一编。包含各种时事、科学、宗教、哲学、美术以及文学各类条目。讨论公平,而无言论栏。其收罗广而简括,故最宜于事务纷忙者之披览。又以其子目繁多,故亦为参考不可少之材料也。

(十三)*National Geographical Magazine* 月刊。一八八八年出版。

此种杂志,关于旅行记述、风土人情、物产、植动物及商业情形,罗列无遗。所述不涉于专门,文字流利,足以引起读者之兴趣。对于教授地理学、商业地理学,或科学者,均有实在之价值焉。

(十四)*New Republic*。一九一四年出版。

所讨论者,为社会及文艺上活动之重要情形。关于文艺戏曲之批评,该报亦甚注意。报内所载各项文字,公平而不稍讳,常引起阅者之批评。而其价值,即在独守己见,不事阿谀。读者有谓其论调近乎普拉德哲学者,亦有称道其文体清晰,批评恰当者。总之受过高等教育者,均爱读之。

(十五)*Outlook* 周刊。一八六九年出版。

述当时新闻惟一之周刊也。每号均有插画,内载社论政治方略,及一二较长之文艺书籍。批评之短者甚佳,但不甚紧要。其言论一项,颇有精彩,全杂志能将编辑部各人之心理完全显出。且竭力主张社会改造,但不趋向于剧烈之手段。应时之新闻记载,亦足为高等学校参考之用。

(十六)*Scientific American* 月刊。一八四五年出版。

此杂志记载最近科学的、机械的及工艺的各新闻,颇为确切而明显。其解释各类科学,措词浅近,关于人种学、考古学等问题,亦时有记载。最新发明之事实,及新版书籍之评论,亦在搜罗之中。此种杂志,记载科学新闻而非专门科学家之正当资料也。

(十七)*School & Society* 周刊。一九一五年出版。

记载教育事实,及其关于社会服务之情况,其用途在公共社会,较在小团体为广。以要求此种杂志者,仅少数之学者。惟其富于思想,而讨论公平,对于热心社会之改良者,实有莫大利益焉。

(十八)*Scribner's Magazine* 月刊。一八八七年出版。

此为美国杂志中于文学上及图画上,均有价值者。内容尤多美术及文艺之批评,最近销行渐广,而未尝稍失其本来面目。

(十九)*Survey* 周刊。一八七九年出版。

论述公家,或私人之活动,其主义在促进社会,好打笔头官司。然其议论均属建设一方面的,窥其趋向,多袒护劳动家,而攻击资本家。但两方面之文章,同时并载,以取阅者之评鉴。近来措词稍微和平,故其左袒劳动家,亦不若往日之显露。公共学会、宗教机关及学校辩论方面用之者甚多。

(二十)*World's Work* 月刊。一九零零年出版。

所有记载时论者均为当时富有名望之人,其专论甚佳。其目的在增进社会幸福,及物质的进步。图画甚美,文字用流行的笔法,英美各学校学生,阅之者亦甚多。

西文书籍介绍

志骞　光宗

此次西文书籍介绍,不限清华图书馆所有的书籍。

其选择之标准有五:(一)均属近年出版之书籍;(二)专门科学书不在其内;(三)此种书籍,英美盛行,为人人所乐于翻阅或诵读者;(四)文法不深奥而且透彻;(五)中国人能读英文者闲时尽可披览。

(一)科学

Thomson, J. A. ed., *Outline of Science*, N. Y. Putnam 一九二二年出版,共三卷,附图解。

汤姆生之最近名著科学大纲一书,现正风行欧美。

其成功无异韦尔斯之历史大纲。该书阐发科学思想,浅而易明。文笔通畅,令人喜读。书中图解鲜明,阅之益增兴趣。作者意在使人人能读,故少用专门名词。凡读社会科学之人,欲求学问之渊博,此书万不可不读也。兹将其目录摘录如下:

第一卷:关于天象之说明——天演之记闻——环境之适宜——生存之竞争——人类之

进化——天演之继续进行——性灵之发端——宇宙之根原。

第二卷:显微镜检查之奇异——身体机械及其工作——达尔文主义何以能存在今日?——1.自然物质史;2.哺乳动物;3.昆虫界;4.植物学。

第三卷:Sir Oliver Lodge 所著灵魂科学——性灵学;新心理学;心理的分析——生物互相关系——生物学——生物之特性——化学之裨史——化学家犹创造者——气象学——应用科学:1.电气之奇异;2.无线电报及电话;3.飞行术。

(二)社会学

(1) Eucken, Radolf, *Socialism: An analysis*, tr, by Joseph McCabe, N. Y. Scribners. 一九二二年出版,计一八八页。

倭肯谓社会主义与理想生活不甚适合。世人多所争取,均未知理想主义之安易泰然,著者行文平和,亦注意社会主义优长之处,故读者无论信其说与否,均觉其说实有见到之处。

(2) Rathenau, W., *In days to come*, tr. By Eden and Cedar Paul, Lond. Allen and Urwin. 一九二二年出版。计二八六页。

最近德国重组 Wirth 内阁之秘书著有《现存之社会及经济秩序》一书,脱稿于一九一五年,而在一九一七年始刊行于德国。Rathenau 之作,专为指斥该书之非者也。按德秘书之宣讲"因人类及劳工而牺牲之哲学。"以为非求实际之报酬,不过乐观厥成耳。此种理想,易为读者所忽略,盖有三端:(一)经济方面,(二)道德方面,(三)情欲方面是也。

(三)教育

Scott, M. F., *Meeting your child's problems*, Bos. T Little. 一九二二年出版。计二三一页。

此书系就"How to know your child"稍加扩充者也。书中所述具属实用问题。例如因循之小儿,小儿何故诳语,如何破坏规则,及小儿之恶由其父母本属恶劣性者。此外常识多根据于健身场及小儿有益工作各种经验得来。此篇曾载 Good house keeping。

(四)政治

Merriam, C. E., *The American party system*, N. Y Macmillan 一九二年出版。计四三九页。

学者初研究美国政党制度,能以此书作教本,获益必多。本书所讨论者为:政党之分子及其组织、分赃制度、政党之领袖、制度之原理及其方略、官员自身之选择、委任制度。此书分析清楚,命意坦白无私。

(五)历史—欧战史

Carpenter, A. F. B., *The blocking of Zeebrugge: with an introduction by admiral earl Beatty and appreciations by Marshal Foch, Rear-Admiral Simp and Count Visart*, Boston, Houghton. 一九二二年出版。计二七六页。

此书所述为英国当大战时之最活泼而有精彩之事迹。其内容颇饶兴趣。第一部陈述当时所处地位、战事之目的,及战时准备之情形是也;第二部叙述攻击时之情形,另有补录载明战时所用各种军舰,末附地图索引及像片图画等。

(2) Zimmern, A. E., *Europe in Convalescence*, N. Y. Putnam 一九二二年出版。计二三七页。

著者先申述欧洲之政治经济概况,然后分析言之。自武装解除以来,徒以协约国诸领袖之见识短狭,只图私利,致世界大局难以收拾。所幸在经济上尚能相互协助。是一线希望犹存。令者农民日见增加,统辖全欧之大权,将由老辈而移诸新国民之手矣。至老辈之所以利令智昏者,在受实际主义之蛊惑耳。

（六）传记

Eckardstein, H. freiherr Von, *Ten Years at the Court of St. James*; tr. and ed. by George Young. London, Butterworth. 一九二二年出版。计二五五页。

本书不特将王公大人及各类外交家、政治家之形形色色描写纸上,即酿成战祸之英德协定,亦为坦然缕述。

（2）Lucy, H. W. *Lords and Commons*, Lond. T. F. Urwin

此书用小说之笔法描写一般英国政治家。著者曾充当议会内五十年之报告员。至其叙述 Disralli, Gladstone, Lloyd George, Balfour and Chamberlain 诸公之事实尤熟,如数家珍焉。末将国会及众议院开会秩序及手续,互相比较之。书中插画,神奇莫测,系出诸著名艺术家 Alma Tadema, Abbey, Phil-May 等之手笔。

（七）文学

（1）Alden, R. M. *Shakespeare*（Master Spirits of Literature）, N. Y. Duffield 一九二二年出版。计三七七页。

此书所述为莎士比亚著名事迹之摘要,近世文学界盛行之批评。内容极简明,一般读者既无虑其蓄有专门字句之繁难,而评论事实者又具各抒所见,丝毫不剽窃他人之牙慧。

（2）Davis, O. *The Detour*, Boston, Little 一九二二年出版。计一二二页。

此书形容一操守坚固之女子,与其狭窄之生活奋斗,而决意为其女造就圆满之生活,惟其计划终难遂意,末后但希望其幻梦或能由其孙女成功之耳。剧情极能写出英伦农家之生活风味,现在纽约风行此剧。

（3）Garnett, E. *Friday Nights*; first series, Lond. Cape 一九二二年出版。计三七七页。

此书评论近世之文学家,如 Hudson, Tchekof, Ibsen, Conrad 诸文豪之著作,皆在评论之列。此书对于英美之小说,美国诗家之评注,及最近百年之批评,收罗尽致。有数篇已在各类文学杂志上登载。

（4）Strachey, G. L. *Books and Characters*, French and English, Lond. Chatto 一九二二年出版。计三二四页。

书中论著体材各异,惟所述多不出英法文学界之范围。二十年前已分见于英国各杂志。此类论说能将 Mr. Strachey's 文字之特长表现纸上,而其所著 Eminent Victorians and Queen Victoria 尤擅盛名。

（八）小说

（1）Belloc, H. *The Mercy of Allah*, Lond. Chatto 一九二二年出版。计三三五页。

对于贸易方法之一种讽刺文。其描模方法与《天方夜谈》内摩哈穆德①训诫其因竞争而贫困之七位阿侄之神味甚相类似。此篇除间有一二处略嫌深刻外,实有趣之小说也。

（2）Fletcher, J. s. *Ravenadene Court*, Lond. Ward 一九二二年出版。计三一五页。

此为 Fletcher 别具一种体裁之侦探小说。其叙事与寻常著述迥乎不同,盖其诡谲事实之锻炼,煞费工夫。其精彩部分。在行刺两兄弟之凶手莫辨谁何,盖一在 Northumbrian 河畔,而一在 Devonshire 河畔也。爱读侦探小说者,最欢迎此书。

---

① 【编者注】今译默罕默德。

(3) Frazer, E. , *Secret Partner*, N. Y. Holt 一九二二年出版,计二零六页。

叙述一王(wall 街之一大汉)与其女之亲爱者(一幼年发明家)之撞突,卒因王之贪眠而为小发明家所败。原系无味之事实,经其穿凿,乃成惊人之故典,思想可谓超绝。

(4) Hansen, R, *Two Dead Men*; tr. from the Danish of Jens Anker, by Frith of Toksvig, N. Y. Knopf 一九二二年出版,计二一一页。

一种侦探小说,内容富于特异之点。两重行刺者之结果,以疑案作结束,小说界之佳构也。

(5) Hutchinson, A. S-M. , *This Freedom*, Boston, Little 一九二二年出版,计三七二页。

叙述一女子名 Rosalie 者如何增进其生活状况。书中历述其往日之生活及其谋经济与知识二者之独立奋斗精神。此篇曾载 Delineator。

(6) Lewis, S. , *Babbitt*, N. Y. Harcourt 一九二二年出版。计四零一页。

此书为美国贸易家所必读。盖其所述均吾人日用不可缺少之经验。至其事实类皆率真,无虚设之词,诚美国城市生活之大观也。此书较 Main Street 意味既长,而叙述亦较详切也。

(7) Rinehart, Mrs. , *Mary(Roberts) The Breaking Point*, N. Y. Doran 一九二二年出版。计三五六页。

未受猛烈之震悸以前,一切记忆完全失去,乃此书之要点。著者能将以往之奇叙述透切;而自首至尾,未失去小说之体格,尤为难事。

原载:《清华周刊·书报介绍副刊》 1923 年第 1 期

【附录Ⅰ-2】

《清华周刊·书报介绍副刊》第二期

【编者按】 戴志骞在1923年3月30日出版的《清华周刊·书报介绍副刊》第二期上,在"中文定期刊物中的论文"栏目中,介绍了《教育丛刊·图书馆学术研究号》上,关于北京高师新图书馆落成情况及戴志骞在北京高师暑期学校上所用的《图书馆学术讲稿》。在"英文书籍"的"长篇介绍"栏目中,介绍了 *This Freedom* 和 *Kimono* 两部外文小说,在"短篇介绍"中,分别介绍了(1)北京社会状况,(2)中国风俗,(3)政治,(4)社会政治,(5)经济,(10)日本海军等方面的书籍。

中文定期刊物中的论文

(4)图书馆学术研究号(教育丛刊第三卷第六集)

北京高等师范学校出版之图书馆研究号,亦即北高新图书馆落成纪念号。前三篇:通论北京高等师范学校图书馆之历史及造成新图书馆之一切经过情形。自第四篇至末着重两点:(一)图书馆教育与学校之关系;(二)图书馆学术——此篇计六十七页,系戴志骞在北高暑假图书馆讲习会之讲演稿。

末附广东图书馆教育计划,中华教育改进社第一次年会图书馆分组议决案汇录、北京高师图书馆目录之种类及其利用法,及北京高师附中图书馆一览表。欲知图书馆教育之梗概,不可不读图书馆研究号。

英文书籍

(一)长篇介绍

(4)Hutchinson,A,S. M. *This Freedom.* London,Hodder and Stoughton,1922.

在一九二一年八月至一九二二年九月一年之内,作者之名著 If Winter Comes 再版有三十八次之多。当 This Freedom 出版时,其销数与 If Winter Comes 相等,实近时小说界之杰作也。著者谓目下各类问题时有变迁,或迁至善境,或移至恶境,乃借小说之体裁,而评论当今妇女问题。至此书之题目,系得之《新约圣经使徒行传》"With a great Aum obtained I this Freedom"。书中所述,略谓某妇人极怀恨男女不平等,乃决然抛弃其妇女事业,而专力于可与男子竞争之事,且报独身主义。然情海无限,岂能令其独渡,遂结婚焉。既婚,而仍抱平日与男子事业相竞争之宗旨,至家庭生活、儿童教育概不惜为之。卒至子女三人相继死亡。于是始悔悟世间男女各有专责,所谓男女平等、不平等皆不成问题者也。此书文字优美,布置精密,爱读小说者,宜手执一编。

(5)Paris,John,*Pseud*,*Kimono.* London,Collins,1922.(标点两处修改)

巴黎约翰乃著者假姓名也。此小说内之布置,大都采用日本风景。其事迹为一日本有遗产之女孩名 Asa-ko 者,生长于欧洲家庭之下,其父亲遗嘱禁止其女返日本。后其女嫁给一英国人,完婚后,违父亲之遗训,而夫妇相偕返日本。归国后,夫妇之感情为一英父日母的妇人所离间。而此妇人之种种不道德行为,书中描写尽致。未几,英国少年探悉 Asako 之遗产,皆其父操妓业所得,乃嵩返英国,效力于欧战军役。Asako 则受其亲属之虐待,身历各种危险,结束夫妇重圆。此书专描写东京社会之罪恶,出版后风行欧美。各种著名杂志,均著有专篇评论。

(二)短篇介绍

(1)北京社会状况

Gamble & Burgess: *Peking, A Social Survey.*

New York, Doran Co, 1921.

北京实中国历史上为(惟)一名胜之地。西方人凡到远东者,莫不争先以一睹北京为快。好著书者亦以北京为搜集文章资料之地。无论历史家、政治家、美食(术)家、文学家、诗家、戏剧家以及考古家旅行家,既来北京,必做几篇文章发表其意见,及对于北京各类景况之评论。至专为描写北京多数人民之生活状况、社会情形及其组织,此书实为创作。北京警察统计,毫不可靠。四百页事实之调查统计,著者费时之多,概可想见。第十五章教会调查,为全书最精确之文字。欲知北京之现状及居民之生活者,能读此书,所得必多。

(2)中国风俗

Cormack, Mrs, *Chinese Births, weddings and Deaths.*

Peking, 1923.

中文书名为《北京的生礼婚礼丧礼》。此书系著者之演稿,始在"Things Chinese Society"演讲此题,嗣后要求重行演讲者甚多,乃由著者托《华北正报》将演稿印成。而在出版后数月内,销路极广。著者叙述北京人生三大礼,纯用叙事的笔法,而不杂以评语。中国版图极广,交通不便,故生、婚、丧之礼节,南北异点甚多。此书调查北京及直隶各县之礼俗甚详。西方人读之固可领略许多北地风俗,即中国南方人读之,亦可稍广见闻也。

(3)政治

(a) Ogg, F. A. *Introduction to American Government.* New York, Century, 1922.

此为关于英国联邦制之准鹄。凡中央政府及州、市政府,论之甚详。后幅附有美国宪法,并注明何条何项已修改或废止。此书所载(较)一九一九年出版之 Munro, S "Government of the United States" 更详。

(b) Krabbe, Hugo. *Modern Idea of State*; translated by Sabine and Shepard. New York, Appleton, 1922.

克拉勃为荷兰莱登大学之法学教授。此书推论国家观念之新思想。出版后,风行欧美,已译成英法各文。关于此书之详细而公平之评论,可参阅一九二二年十月十八日之 New Republic 第二百零三页内该评论,为 Hf. Laski 所作。

(4)社会政治

(a) Beard, C. A, *Economic Basis of Politics.*

New York, Knopf, 1922.

全书以 Aristotle, Machiavelli, Locke, Madison, Webster, Calhoun 政治哲学六家为起点。并谓上述各家之同一误点,在未能顾及劳动团体之经济状况。深望后起政治家之眼光,务必虑到此节。尤应设法将劳动团体之幸福,兼纳于政治范围以内,为将来政策之指归。此书系 Beard 在亚母斯大学之演稿。

(b) Burns, C. D. *Principles of Revolution.* London, Allen and Unwin, 1921.

该书专为阐明 Rousseau, Marx, Mazzini, Morris 及 Tolstoi 诸家之革新学说,而加以评论者也。且申言不用过分激烈手段,而能改革社会之组织者,胥赖在社会中传布一种普及改革之自觉心而已。此书探索卢骚马克斯等之学说,极其深邃。好其学说者盍一读。

(c) Johnsen, J. E., Comp. *Selected Articles on Social Insurance*
(Handbook Series) New York, Wilson, 1922.

此书内容关于各种社会问题之保险利益及其害处。两方面之理由备载无遗。至关于此类问题之各种书报,亦节录于书末,有四十五页之多,实研究社会保险之津逮也。其目录则有(一)社会保险,(二)工人之损伤赔偿案,(三)公家强迫保险案,(四)健康保险案,(五)产母饷银案,(六)年老保险案,(七)残弱案,(八)无业保险案,(九)拯救孀孤案,(十)兵士水手保险案。此外并研究劳工待遇之理论,综各家之说,汇为一编,诚佳构也。

(5) 经济

Lee, Mabel Ping-Hua. *Economic History of China with Special Reference to Agriculture*. New York, Columbia University, 1921.

此书为李女士在纽约哥伦比亚大学得博士之毕业论文。李女士留美有年,实中国女子留学美国得博士学位之先导也。本书自首页至四二一页,追溯中国历朝以来之农业及经济史。大致谓中国农业实不让欧美各国。盖中国农夫耕种虽无机器,而每亩田地之收获,则交(较)欧美各国为多。中国土地之肥沃,不言而喻。然中国仍不免于饥荒者,不在出产之歉,而实人口过于食料故也。著者希望中国每年限制增加人口。移民至他处,亦限制增加之一法也。尤望中国采用机器,增加收获,若不急起直追,则民平(贫)国困之症不可救也。末附中国书目十页,乃此书采集资料之参考书籍也。

(10) 日本海军

Ballard, C. B., Vice-Admiral. *Influence of the Sea on the Political History of Japan*. New York, Dutton. 1921.

日本海军政策,关系太平洋之国际问题,实为重要。著者为英国海军提督,费极长时间,追溯日本向来之决心,端在维持广大之海军政策而已。此书前半叙述日本之海军历史,自战胜元成吉斯汗①起,直至歼尽俄国波罗的海舰队为止。著者以为日本海军政策思逞雄于太平洋上及亚细亚沿海岸各国者,远在十三世纪,以迄于今,始无一日忘怀也。读此书者可知英国留心远东问题,实无微不至。

原载:《清华周刊·书报介绍副刊》 1923 年第 2 期

---

① 【编者注】今译成吉思汗。

【附录Ⅰ-3】

《清华周刊·书报介绍副刊》第四期

【编者按】戴志骞在1923年6月1日出版的《清华周刊·书报介绍副刊》第四期上,在"英文书籍"栏目"长篇介绍"中,介绍了《一九二三年中华年鉴》、《中国戏剧》、《游记》三部图书。

一九二三年中华年鉴

China year Book, Ed. By H. J. W. Woodhead 1923. 一二四三页。天津印字馆出版。

《一九二三年中华年鉴》实为参考书出版界之一大杰作。近来当局既无暇顾及各种事业之统计,即各界亦无一定调查之记载,而此书于各种事业之详情,缕述无遗,实为难得。参考书之优劣,端在调查之精确与否。是书所有统计表格,虽不能谓为尽确,然对于中国各种事业之调查,固甚有头绪焉。黎总统之序语云:"殚见洽闻",实为该书最适当之评语。书内数章,如中国之地质、动物、矿产、矿质、交通、关税、财政等,均系重写,较之一九二一年出版之《中华年鉴》详细多矣。至如中国、语言、航运、医学、收还青岛、中东铁路、华盛顿会议诸章,皆新近加入年鉴之特点。此书内容极富,各类问题,无不搜罗尽致。例如版图、人口一章,所述为"中国人口除蒙古、西藏外,有四万二千七百万。而全国人口最繁密之省,首推江苏。据邮务局调查,江苏每方英里有人口八百七十五。"再如二百四十九页所述,"海关收入,在前清时,各处清关收入,应缴之款,存于海关道。自民国以来,各处关税之收入,直接管辖于总税务司矣。"余如铁路、无线电及各种工厂之调查,亦甚详细。兹将其细目抄录于左,阅者一望而知是书包括之广矣。如欲参考中国各种问题,不可不备此书。

(一)中国版图及人口统计;(二)舆地;(三)地质;(四)动物;(五)植物森林;(六)气候;(七)矿产;(八)人种言语;(九)新闻纸杂志;(十)出产品;(十一)权度;(十二)贸易;(十三)币制;(十四)法律;(十五)教育;(十六)交通(铁路道路类);(十七)交通(邮电类);(十八)海运;(十九)制造;(二十)海关;(二十一)水利;(二十二)军备;(二十三)中东铁路;(二十四)蒙藏;(二十五)财政;(二十六)人名录;(二十七)鸦片;(二十八)宗教;(二十九)医学;(三十)贸易统计;(三十一)租借地;(三十二)中央政府;(三十三)华盛顿会议;(三十四)青岛交涉。

中国戏剧

Buss, Kate. *Chinese Drama*. Boston, Four Seas Co. 一九二二年出版

近时英美人论中国戏剧之书籍,稍知门径而评论不失之偏激者,厥惟上海别发出版之Johnston's "*Chinese Drama*"与本书而已。著者谓欧美人观中国戏剧,往往具西方之眼光,故未能得其优美之处。至其批评中国戏剧之弱点,则在乐器之振耳、声调之不和以及服饰之不当耳。然观者如能抛弃其西方文化的主观,并稔知中国几千年来之历史及各地风土人情,则中国戏剧之善于描摹,实不亚于欧美各国之戏剧。此书之作,即启迪西方人观中国剧之钥也。观于本书首数章所述中国戏之起源及其种类,即知著者对于中国剧具有一种分析的研究。书中图画照片计十三张,而艺员梅兰芳之虹霓关、嫦娥奔月等照片,独占五张之多,则著者亦可谓嗜梅者矣。全书之纸色、印工、装订,均甚雅致。

游记

Sowerby, Arthur de C., Naturalist in Manchuria. Vol. 1
Travel and Exploration. Tientsin. Tientsin Press. 一九二二年出版

美国国立博物院,现从事搜集关于各国之生物及地理。凡与人类风土进化上有关系者,往往派人实地调查。此书即著者调查东三省及黑龙江流域之人种进化、地理沿革之结果。此书出全,计有五卷。第一卷只述著者调查时旅行之景况,所旅行各地之风土人情,种种困难之境遇以及向未查得之各类动物。第一卷行文,系用普通笔法,令一般读者觉有兴味。其余四卷,专论各种动物之性情及变迁之问题。殆为习动物学者所立论。此四卷尚未出版。第一卷书内,有图画及照片共六十幅,其三幅着色之图画,乃著者自绘,尤为精致。书末有参考书目单及亚细亚北部地图一张。图上有红线者为著者曾经历之地。

原载:《清华周刊·书报介绍副刊》 1923年第4期

【附录Ⅰ-4】

《清华周刊·书报介绍副刊》第十二期

图书馆学书目

Bostwick, A. E. : *American Public Library*, N. Y. , Appleton.
Bostwick, A. E. : *Library and School*, N. Y. , Wilson & Co.
Bostwick, A. E. : *Library and Society*, N. Y. , Wilson & Co.
Brown, J. D. : *Small Library*, Lond. , Routledge
Dana, J. C. : *Library Primer*, Chicago, A. L. A.
Plummer, M. W. : *Hints to Small Libraries*,
Stearns, L. E. *Essentials in Library Administration*, Chicago, A. L. A.
Ward, G. O. *Practical Use of Books and Libraries*, Boston Book Co.
Willson, M. *School Library Management*, N. Y. , Wilson & C
Library Economy Series, American Association.

教育丛刊图书馆研究号	北京高师
新教育	中华教育改进社
图书馆与市民教育	广东省教育委员会

本刊曾请戴先生介绍关于图书馆学的书,以供同学有兴趣者阅读,先生以事忙,无暇多作,故仅将此书目寄示。此书目曾登《新教育》七卷四期先生所作《图书馆学简说》之后,此次稍有修改,取消三本书,又加入 Library Economic Series, 此类丛书,对于图书馆各项问题,均分类讨论,为参考最好资料。此书目中所列各书,大部分均为图书馆所未有,惟戴先生私人则完全购置,同学欲看者,可到戴先生家里借阅。

铨识

原载:《清华周刊·书报介绍副刊》 1924 年第 12 期

【附录 Ⅱ】戴志骞主持的会议记录及议决案

【附录 Ⅱ-1】

【编者按】1921年,在北京成立了在美国时期很有影响的中华教育改进社,在该社下设"图书馆教育组",戴志骞于1922—1924年担任该组主席,主持该组三届年会,并于1922年起担任图书馆教育研究委员会主任,直至该会停止活动。此处照录戴志骞主持的三次年会的记录。

中华教育改进社第一届年会"图书馆教育组"会议纪要

书记　朱家治

第一次会议

地点　年会事务所应接室

时间　七月四日上午八时

到会　戴超 沈祖荣 洪有丰 杜定友 戴超夫人 朱家治 孙心盘

主席　戴超

主席发言:谓本组议案太多,讨论当首先择定标准。杜定友君提议,各人议案有与杜君相同之处,拟将各议案归并成一个议案。众人以为杜君之议案范围太广,当由沈祖荣君提出标准,逐渐讨论,其标准为:

一、何种图书馆最为紧要

二、经济如何支配

三、管理员如何养成

四、图书馆如何推广

戴超、洪有丰二君谓标准应以与教育有关系者为去取。于是即阅洪有丰君之议案加以讨论,内容略有修改,并增入理由及办法,决议为各校应添设教导用图书方法案通过。时已十时半,遂散会。

第二次会议

地点　年会事务所应接室

时间　七月五日上午八时

到会　沈祖荣 杜定友 洪有丰 朱家治 孙心盘 程伯庐

旁听　王倬民

主席　沈祖荣

戴超君因病不能到会,由沈祖荣君主席;戴君之议案则由洪有丰君代表提出讨论,其议案为:

一、中国师范学校及高等师范学校应添设图书馆管理科案

将此案详加讨论,各人均发抒意见,并拟有理由及办法加入,遂决议通过。

二、通俗图书馆内应设儿童图书部案

三、组织图书馆管理学会案

此二案因无复议,暂不讨论。

四、各学校应有图书馆讲演案

此案与洪有丰君前案相同,当然包括在洪君案内。时十点一刻,遂散会。

第三次会议

地点　年会事务所应接室

时间　七月六日上午八时

到会　沈祖荣 杜定友 洪有丰 戴超夫人 朱家治 孙心盘

旁听　王倬民

主席　沈祖荣

戴超君病尚未愈,仍由沈祖荣君主席,讨论杜定友及沈祖荣二君之议案。杜君之议案为:

一、大学应添设图书馆教育专科案

此案因设备经济有种种需审虑之处,故多数主张缓提,决议将此案保留。

二、添设图书馆教育行政机关案

此案须由提案人重行修改再提,决议将此案保留。

三、呈请教育部推广学校图书馆案

此案经全体讨论拟有理由及办法,并将沈祖荣君议案之一并入作为一种办法,决议通过。

继续讨论沈君之议案,其议案为:

一、拟呈请教育部通咨各省省长转饬各教育厅长,除省会内必须建设省立图书馆外,凡所属之重要商埠(如上海、汉口等处)亦必有图书馆之建设案。

此案办法稍有讨论,决议通过。

二、设立京师图书馆案

讨论此案理由与办法,将杜定友君改组京师图书馆理由加入,原文略有修改,决议通过。时十点半散会。

第四次会议

地点　年会事务所应接室

时间　七月七日上午八时

到会　沈祖荣 洪有丰 朱家治 孙心盘 戴超 戴超夫人

旁听　傅盛德　王倬民　王冷庆芙

主席　戴超

杜定友君因事回粤,由孙心盘君代表提出议案:

一、大学添设图书馆专科议案

此案因提议人缺席,尚有种种事须斟酌,故多数主张暂为搁置,决议将此案暂为搁置。

二、请教育部添设图书馆教育司案

讨论此案咸以现在尚非其时,故亦主张暂为搁置,决议将此案暂为搁置。

沈祖荣君提议凡学校未附设图书馆者,不宜举办图书馆科或图书馆员训练所案,讨论此案,孙心盘君提议,将此案全文附于戴超君中国师范学校及高等师范学校应增设图书馆管理科案办法之后;众赞成,决议通过。

沈祖荣君提议著作家出版书籍,须存一部于教育部,存一部于国立图书馆案,讨论此案结果,决议通过;一方面当附于建设国立图书馆案之后。

洪有丰君提议各市区小学应就近联合,于校内创设巡回儿童图书馆,以补充教室内之教育案,讨论此案照原文略有修改,决议通过。

戴超君提议请中华教育改进社组织图书馆教育研究委员会案,此案经众人讨论后,拟有理由及组织大纲,决议通过。

以上系连日讨论各种议案之经过情形,并将议决各案举出,另作表录。本组以为各事均已收束,主席乃宣告休会,时已十一点矣。

图书馆教育组议决案汇录

一、各校应添设教导用图书方法案

理由:

(一)现在学生不知馆中图书,以致阅书发生困难。

(二)养成一种好读书习惯及自动的教育。

(三)学生毕业后对于学校服务,当明参考图书之方法。

(四)学生中途无力升学,藉此可以利用图书馆修养。

(五)为备学校图书馆之建设。

办法:

各校如得相当教员,得列为正科。(中等以上学校)如校中不能得教员长期教授,则另寻专家课外演讲;总期学生能得利用图书馆之知识。

附利用图书之方法:

(一)图书之保护

(二)利用参考书之方法。

(三)图书馆分类法大纲。

(四)目录之用法。

(五)图书之出纳法。

二、中国师范学校及高等师范应增设图书馆管理科案

理由:

(一)予以图书馆常识,以管理图书馆。

(二)使师范毕业生能利用图书馆,提倡公共生活。

(三)与师范学校课程无矛盾。

(四)予师范毕业生将来教授时,有指导学生用图书之能力。

(五)设立此科应学生之需要。

办法：

(一)师范学校选择图书馆重要教材,编入学校管理法中。此外仍得附设图书馆学科,令学生选习;以有图书馆学识者担任教授。

(二)教材大概授以各种参考书用法,简单分类法,编目审择用书法,儿童图书馆之购书登入法,图书馆办理法等等。

(三)编入学校管理法者,每星期授课一小时,半学年完毕。编入选科者,每星期授课一至二小时,一学年完毕。

附注:凡学校未附设图书馆者,不宜举办图书馆科,或图书馆员训练所。

三、呈请教育部推广学校图书馆案

理由:

(一)补助学校教育之不足。

(二)养成学生读书习惯及自习能力。

(三)以应师生心理及生理需要。

(四)增加学校中之共同生活。

办法：

(一)拟呈请教育部通饬全国国立、公立、私立大学及高等专门,于五年内必须设立图书馆,备置中西应用书籍两万册以上。一面派员视察其设备成绩。此外凡新设立而呈请备案之大学专门,无相当之图书馆者,不予认可。至常年经费及购书费,宜列入大学预算案内,其数目至少须占大学常年经费十分之一。

(二)中等学校至少有千册以上及经费百分之五。

四、拟呈请教育部通咨各省省长转饬各教育厅长,除省会内必须建设省立图书馆外,凡所属之重要商埠(上海、汉口等处)亦必有图书馆之建设案。

办法：

关于通商口岸分七区,广东、上海、天津、汉口、重庆、南京、奉天,共需费五百万元,为建筑购书设备之用。

五、拟呈请教育部会同财政部筹拨相当款项建设京师国立图书馆案

理由:

(一)京师代表中华全国之文明。

(二)今京师图书馆湫隘褊狭。

办法：

(一)设立改组京师图书馆委员会。

(二)聘请专家为馆长。

(三)改建图书馆馆所。

(四)改良管理法,以整理原有书籍,并添购中外之新图籍。

六、凡著作家出版书籍欲巩固版权,须经部审查备案,注册者宜将其出版之书籍,尽两部义务,一存教育部备案,一存国立图书馆,以供众览案

七、各市区小学校应就近联合于校内创设巡回儿童图书馆以补充教室内之教育案

理由:

(一)读书习惯及用参考书之习惯,均宜自幼养成。

（二）可供给适合儿童个性之读物。

（三）可资儿童课外之正常消遣。

办法：

各市区小学之地点相近者，宜结合为一团体，购置适合儿童之图书，分为数份，更番轮置于此诸小学中，以备学生阅览。其经费可由此各小学校筹拨若干，以为开办费；嗣后每年酌摊经常费三五元，即可敷添置书籍之用。而此种办法仅为目前教育经费困难时之一种，若照常理言，各学校皆宜自有其图书馆，另立办法。

备注：凡加入此团体各小学校之教职员，均负保管其校内所陈列图书之责。

八、请中华教育改进社组织图书馆教育研究委员会案

理由：

（一）图书馆教育与改进问题，本有密切之关系。例如美国图书馆协会与教育会互相独立，原非妥当办法，以致常生隔阂。

（二）中华教育改进社已设立各处办事机关，并以图书馆教育为新教育问题之一，设立图书馆教育研究委员会于中华教育改进社内，对于经济上既属节俭，而与教育事实上亦大有裨益。

组织：

（一）定名

中华教育改进社图书馆教育研究委员会。

（二）宗旨

本会以研究图书馆教育问题为宗旨。

（三）委员

委员名额暂定十五人，由改进社函请国内研究图书馆教育及热心研究教育者充之。

（四）职员

本委员会设干事一人，副干事一人，书记一人，由本委员会互选之；并由中华教育改进社聘任之。

（五）研究计划

本会研究计划分二种：

（甲）共同研究　以分组研究之结果，应由全体委员讨论决定之。

（乙）分组研究　暂分四组，遇必要随时增减之：

（1）图书馆行政与管理。

（2）征集中国图书。

（3）分类编目研究。

（4）图书审查。

（六）出版

研究结果暂由新教育发表。

原载：《新教育》　1922年第5卷第3期

【附录Ⅱ-2】

中华教育改进社第二届年会"图书馆教育组"会议纪要

本组会议四次,自八月二十日起,至二十四日止,惟二十三日休息,其余各日,每日各开会一次;本组提议案共十四件,通过者五案,保留者七案,移交者一案,至目录中之第三案(即筹划图书馆经费案),则未经讨论。兹将本组到会人名列左:

戴志骞　何日章　朱家治　洪有丰　施廷镛　周良熙　刘廷藩　熊景芳　冯陈祖怡
许卓陆秀　许达聪　王文山　陈家登　胡庆生　裘开明　韦棣华　张嘉谋　查修
王警宇　戴罗瑜丽　刘昉　陶怀琳

第一次会议(八月二十日下午二时开会)

出席会员十五人。

旁听员十一人。

主席戴志骞君报告:书记程时煃君缺席,请会众推选一人补充。陶怀琳君乃提议请主席指派。王警宇附议。

结果:查修君为临时书记。

主席报告下列事项:

(1)旧岁年会本组经过情形。

(2)文华大学图书馆长韦棣华君代表该大学图书科全体,呈请中华教育改进社转请美国政府,以其将要退还之庚子赔款三分之一作为扩充中国图书馆事。并及沈祖荣、胡庆生、洪有丰与戴志骞四君,会为此事致函美国图书馆协会年会,请其在美国方面给以相当之赞助;复函亦已收到。

(3)主席于去岁曾与本组委员会委员程时煃君讨论关于本组事业进行办法,稿已拟定,以程君缺席,故不能公诸会众。

(4)主席曾为本社著有《中国之图书馆运动》,交中国代表携赴美国世界教育会议。

(5)沈祖荣君每年有关于中国图书馆事业报告,在《新教育》杂志登载。

(6)议案由本组会议通过后,须俟本社大会通过,方为有效。

主席发表以本日会议,为时颇短,似应将提议案件,择其重要,关系图书馆事业全体者,如本届年会议案第一编所载本组案第九"呈请中华教育改进社转请美国政府以其将要退还之庚子赔款三分之一作为扩充中国图书馆案——文华大学图书科全体"先付讨论。其他关于图书馆内部问题,如议案第一编所载本组议案第一、二、五、六、八等,则可从缓计议。何日章君乃发表请将议案第一、二、五、六、八等从缓计议。张嘉谋君又发表请将议案第九提前讨论。

主席宣读议案第九主文并其理由及办法。经会众详细讨论后,结果如下:

(1)胡庆生君提议,朱家治君附议,修正议案主文,其经修正者如下:

呈请中华教育改进社转请政府及美国政府,以美国将要退还之庚子赔款三分之一作为扩充中国图书馆案。一致通过。

(2)朱家治君提议,胡庆生君附议,将议案办法段中第一项(建设)删除,而以下列一项代之：
于此后二十年内，就尚未退还之庚子赔款项下，每年提出美金二十万元。其第一年提出之全数，另行存储，作为久远基金。以年利六厘计，每年可得息金美金一万二千元，专供中华图书馆委员会之用。第二年提出之二十万金元，应存妥实之银行生息。俟第三年之款提出（连第二年之母子金共计金元四十一万二千元）可拨金元二十一万二千元，以充大图书馆一所建筑及设备之用。余剩之金元二十万元，以六厘生息年得金元一万二千元，可供维持之费。此后每间一年，可增设类于第一次所建之图书馆一所。迨至各最大城市已有大图书馆五所后，其后九年，可于较小城市中，年增图书馆一所。每所拟用金元十万元，作建筑及设备之用。而以余剩之金元十万元作为基金，以六厘生息，年得金元六千元，藉供维持。

(3) 戴志骞君提议，朱家治附议，将议案办法段中第二项（经费之支配）完全删除，而以第一及第二项并成修改之第一项。第三项移前作为第二。

主席将修正之议案付表决。结果：一致通过。

散会　三时五十分。

第二次会议（八月二十一日下午一时三刻开会）

出席会员十五人。

旁听员十人。

书记查修君宣读前次会议记录，无异议，通过。

主席戴志骞君将本届年会议案第一编所载本组议案第四"拟在海关附加税项下酌拨数成建设商业图书馆案——朱家治"付会众讨论。经会众详细讨论后，结果如下：

(1) 戴志骞君提议，会众通过，将本议案办法段中第一项（由中华教育改进社备具说帖，说明图书馆在中国商业上之需要，送交海关附加税委员会讨论，指拨款项。）修正为：
由中华教育改进社请中国总商会同具说帖，说明图书馆在中国商业上之需要，送交海关附加税委员会讨论，指拨款项。

(2) 胡庆生君提议，王文山君附议，会众通过，将办法段中第二项（由海关附加税委员会聘请专家办理之）修正为：
由海关附加税委员会请总税务司每年就附加税拨出四十万元，以作开办及维持商业图书馆之用。

(3) 戴志骞君提议，会众通过，加入下列一项，为办法段中之第三项：
商业图书馆所在地之商会，应担任该图书馆之常年经费十分之三。
并将办法段中第四项（购备中西文商业书籍，使中外人士均得阅览。）删除，五、六两项仍旧。

主席询会众以本议案其他字句有无修正之必要，无异议，通过采纳原文。

主席将本组议案第五"省立图书馆应征集省县志书及善本书籍案——洪有丰施廷镛"付讨论。经会众详细讨论后，结果如下：

朱家治君提议，冯陈祖怡君附议，将本议案办法段中第一项（由省立图书馆筹款，留心访察，设法归公，以保国粹。）修正为：

由省立图书馆留心访察,设法归公,或筹款购置,以保国粹。一致通过。

主席发表以本组议案颇多,而会期则颇短,故对于议案之能合并或参议者,似应从速办理。后韦棣华君发表以中国各图书馆中之善本及普通书籍,均应设法保存开放。主席乃请陈家登君、许达聪君将主席所拟在下次会议提出之本组议案第六"图书馆善本书籍应行酌量开放以供参考案——洪有丰"研究一番,将韦棣华君之意拟成一案,俟下次会议提出讨论。

冯陈祖怡君又发表以中国图书馆收费办法,与教育本旨背道而驰,改良之需,急若燃眉;故对于洪有丰君所提议案内,主张亦应有免费之规定。主席乃请冯陈祖怡君将此意拟成一案,俟下次会议提出,与洪有丰君之议案,及韦棣华君所拟提出之议案,并同讨论。

散会　三时四十分。

第三次会议(八月二十二日下午一时三刻开会)

出席会员十六人。

旁听四人。

主席戴志骞君将前次会议所拟在本次会议提出之议案"图书馆善本书籍应行酌量开放以供参考——洪有丰",并陈家登君(王文山君代)、许达聪君为韦棣华君所拟之提议,及冯陈祖怡君所拟之提议,并同交付讨论。经会众详细讨论后,由张嘉谋君提议,王警宇君附议,多数通过,将修正之下列议案收纳:

呈请中华教育改进社转请全国各公立图书馆将所藏善本及一切书籍严加整理布置酌量开放免除收费案

理由经修正者如下:

(1)现有全国各公立图书馆,大多数均呈萎靡不振之现象。苟欲弥补此弊,则应严加整理布置。

(2)善本书籍,其所以可贵,非徒其名而已,实以其有可贵者在也。或为校雠精确,秘本未传,可供学者之研究;或为刻刷精美,得之不易,发挥历史之精华。但此种书籍,收藏苟不得其法,固恒以饱蠹鱼之腹;而或代远年湮,纸张脆碎,不能仅有功效,则亦何贵之有。今各省图书馆收藏书籍,不无善本,大率秘而不宣,致学者无研究之机。国学何由而昌,我中华固有之文明因之而衰。

(3)扩充阅览人数,增加读书机会。

办法经修正者如下:

(1)在六个月内,本社即将此案函请各省省长,转知各该属图书馆委员会,或其他管理该属图书馆团体机关,从速整理图书馆事业。

(2)善本书籍,宜存列玻璃架内,如遇人来馆申请阅览,当酌许之。

本案原文办法段中第一、二、三等项,改为第三、四、五等项。原文第四项删除,而代以下列一项:

易收费限制,为保证限制。各公立图书馆应备有阅览券。凡受有保证者,迳可领取,凭券入览。

主席将本组议案第七"组织各地方图书馆协会案——戴志骞"提出。经会众详细讨论,由胡庆生君提议,朱家治君附议,多数通过,将修正之下列议案收纳:

组织各地方图书馆协会

理由经修正者如下:
(1)由中华教育改进社将地方图书馆协会组织之紧要通告各地方图书馆。
(2)依本案原文所载。
(3)在某地方图书馆协会未能成立以前,或遇必要时,中华教育改进社图书馆教育研究委员会——由社员报告——应委派本社社员在该地方充当发起人或交际员。
(4)社员于收到上项委派书后,六个月内,须将该地图书馆协会进行情形(如调查、统计、报告、困难、疑问等)详细呈报图书馆教育研究委员会,以便有所资助。
(5)图书馆教育研究委员会应于前期时间内,尽力回答各委派员所提出之疑问、困难等项;并须将本年地方图书馆协会经过情形,在第三届年会时,报告本组社员,以便明了得失,藉可改良进行。

主席将本组议案第十"请规定'图书馆年',并请本社图书馆教育研究委员会速制中等学校图书馆建筑图式及馆中设备计划案——程湘帆"请朱家治君修正提出。经会众详细讨论后,由胡庆生君提议,何日章君附议,多数通过,将本案保留。

主席将本组议案第十一"请本会图书馆组分期编制各种中小学校需用图书目录以便各校酌量采用案——许本震、何巽"提出。经会众讨论后,结果:通过修正本案主文;并将理由段中第二行"拟请本部先行"本部二字删除。主文经修正者如下:

请分期编制各种中小学校需用目录以便各校酌量采用案

次由胡庆生君提议,朱家治君附议,将本案移交本社中等及初等教育二组讨论。移交之理由,则为新学制课程尚在研究之中,本组对于中小学校所需之图书,茫无标准可藉规定。主席付表决之结果,为通过移交。

主席将本组议案第八"交换重本图书——戴志骞"提出。经会众讨论后,结果:通过保留。

主席将本组议案第三"策划图书馆经费案——参见新教育第五卷三期五五九至五六零页图书馆教育组议案第四——查修"提出。惟本案之内容,与本届年会本议决案第一"呈请中华教育改进社转请政府及美国政府以其将要退还之庚子赔款三分之一作为扩充中国图书馆案"及议决案第二"拟在海关附加税项下酌拨数成建设商业图书馆案"根本一致。故本案由原提议人撤回。

主席将本组议案第一"图书馆事业办法及应用名辞(词)等等应有规定之标准案——查修"提出。经会众详细讨论后,结果:以中华图书馆委员会尚未实现,关于图书馆事业一切之标准,无从规定,通过保留。

主席将本组议案第二"书籍装订改良案——查修"提出。经会众详细讨论,未得解决。胡庆生君提议,王文山君附议散会。结果:通过。

散会 三时四十分。

第四次会议(八月二十四日下午一时半开会)

出席会员十九人。

旁听七人。

主席戴志骞君将前次会议未得解决之本组议案第二"书籍装订改良案——查修"提出复议。讨论结果,佥以本案内容复杂非常,一时难以议定。胡庆生君乃提议保留。裘开明君复修正胡庆生君之提议,而主张保留此案,同时本组须有一书籍装订分委员会产生,以从事研究书籍装订改良问题。主席乃付表决,结果:通过。次,许达聪君提议,何日章君附议,请主席指派本组会员为该委员会委员。主席乃指派下列五人充任:

冯陈祖怡　朱家治　裘开明　许达聪　查修

主席将临时提议案一件"请中华教育改进社备函向国内各大图书公司接洽凡各地学校公立及私立公开之图书馆购书应与以相当折扣案——裘开明"提出。经会众详细讨论后;办法段中第一项完全删除。第二、三两项移前作第一及第二。次,主席付表决,结果:通过。

主席报告国际教育组移交来之议案一件"世界图书馆案——世界教育会议中国代表团"请会众讨论。结果:以本案范围过大,设施之举尚毫无把握,通过保留。

主席报告有冯陈祖怡君及陆秀君之临时提议案一件"呈请中华教育改进社转请各省教育厅增设留学图书馆学额培植师资案"交进已逾期限,请会众讨论。会众乃请冯陈祖怡君宣读该案全文。宣读既竟,一致主张收纳。后经详细讨论,由裘开明君提议,朱家治君附议,将此案保留,俟后再提。主席付表决。结果:通过保留。

散会三时五十分。

备注:本记录中所载各议决案,其最后修正之主文、理由及办法,具详本组议决案汇录。

议决案汇录

(I) 通过案五件

(一)呈请中华教育改进社转请政府及美国政府以美国将要退还之庚子赔款三分之一作为扩充中国图书馆案(文华大学图书科全体提议)

理由:

(1)图书馆为普及教育之利器。

　　(A)图书馆不限程度之高下——较之贵族式之学校,或其他为最少数人谋利益之组织,不可同日而语。(如谓图书馆为平民大学校也可,谓为专门学者之知识宝库也亦无不可。)

　　(B)图书馆不限职业之贵贱——无论士、农、工、商,均得同享图书馆之利益。

　　(C)图书馆不限年龄之大小。

　　(D)图书馆不限男女之差别——能调剂男女教育不平等之现象。

　　(E)图书馆能使(a)未受教育者,受相当之常识(如通俗演讲等);(b)已受教育者,继续求学,得与时并进(就智识方面言。)

(2)希望我国政府推广图书馆事业现在已如泡影,绝无成为事实之可能。故吾人如欲发展中国图书馆事业,舍仰给于"美国退还赔款"外,并无第二捷径。

(3)各省公立图书馆之经费,异常拮据。整顿无从着手。故不得不假"美国退还赔款",用为改良中国原有之图书馆(此项图书馆须收藏较富,成绩较优,地点适宜,并能履行特别条件者。)

(4)今日中国人士之"捐助"观念日渐发达;惟对于图书馆事业,较之西人,甚形冷淡。推原其故,实因中国图书馆收效未著,不易引起多数人之同情。为今之计,应藉"美国退还赔款"建设若干设备完善之图书馆。速尽图书馆所应尽之服务,早著图书馆所应著之功效,以博国内多数人士之赞助。如是,则图书馆事业庶可普及于中华民国矣。
(5) 中国尚无模范图书馆堪足取法者。一旦得此巨款,则可经营若干模范图书馆,划一各种制度标准,管理手续,以为全国公、私、省、县、市、村图书馆之赞助。
(6) 中国各界领袖对于图书馆事业甚表赞同。
(7) 美国为图书馆事业发达最盛之国家。故该国人士对于"退还赔款"用为扩充中国图书馆事业,势必尽力襄助。
(8) 图书馆在欧美教育界所占位置之重要,识者尽知,不待赘述。今中华教育改进社既以改进中华教育为宗旨,理应以改进图书馆事业为前提。
(9) 中华教育改进社为中国教育界惟一代表,故该社所提出之议案,极易得中外人士之信仰。

办法:
(1) 于此后二十年内,就尚未退还之庚子赔款项下,每年提出美金二十万元。其第一年提出之全数,另行存储,作为久远基金,以年利六厘计,每年可得息金美金一万二千元,专供中华图书馆委员会之用。第二年提出之二十万金元,应存妥实之银行生息,俟第三年之款提出(连第二年之母子金共计金元四十一万二千元),可拨金元二十一万二千元,以充大图书馆一所建筑及设备之用。余剩之金元二十万元,以六厘生息,年得金元一万二千元,可供维持之费。此后每间一年,可增设类于第一次所建之图书馆一所。迨至各最大城市已有大图书馆五所后,其后九年,可于较小城市中,年增小图书馆一所。每所拟用金元十万元作建筑及设备之用。而以余剩之金元十万元作为基金,以六厘生息,年得金元六千元,藉供维持。
(2) 凡接收此项公共图书馆之城市,须履行以下条件:
  (甲)拨给为建筑该图书馆基地一块。
  (乙)每年拨该馆津贴费若干元。其数目之多少由图书馆委员会详定之。但其用途,须半作购置新书费,半作扩充等费。
(3) 组织:
  (A)选举部——由美国驻京公使、中国外交部、教育部及全国高等教育联合机关(如中华教育改进社、中华职业教育社、中国科学社)总商会等组织之。
    选举部之职权概略如下:
    选举图书部、董事部(人数多少,由选举部另定之。)
  (B)董事部——由选举部推选之(但能代表中美两国者方为合格。)
    董事部之职权概略如下:
    (a)对于图书馆计画(划),担负完全责任。
    (b)监督各种款项及其用途。
    (c)议决图书馆一切进行事宜。
    (d)交付议决案件于委员会,并监督其实行。
    (e)受理图书馆委员会各种建议。
  (C)图书馆委员会——由董事部派选之。
    图书馆委员会之职权概略如下:
    (a)委员会执行董事部议决案件。

(b)委员会得建议于董事部。

(c)委员会应编制每年预算表及各种进行计划,送呈董事部审定。

(d)委员会得扶助中国图书馆协会组织及其发展。

(e)委员会得随时审查各地图书馆进行情形。

(f)委员会如得同意时得资助各地公私图书馆进行事业。

(g)委员会有辞聘各地"赔款"所建设之图书馆馆员之全权等等。

备注:本案系修正通过。

(二)省立图书馆应征集省县志书及善本书籍案(洪有丰、施廷镛提议)

理由:

(1)省县志为研究乡土史地者必要之参考书。

(2)可为旅行家及考古家之指南。

(3)为地方文献之特征。

(4)善本书籍咸由私家收藏,但终难保持不变。非遭火,即因子孙滥售,流入他国。今竟有书籍为他国所有,而本国反无者,诚可痛惜!

办法:

(1)由省立图书馆留心访察,设法归公,或筹款布置,以保国粹。

(2)劝人捐款购置,存于图书馆以作不朽之事业。

(3)劝藏书家将善本书籍捐赠,或存置图书馆,由公家为之保存。既可免于损伤及散佚,而他人亦得藉以参考。

备注:本案系修正通过。

(三)呈请中华教育改进社转请全国各公立图书馆将所藏善本及一切书籍严加整理布置酌量开放免除收费案(洪有丰、冯陈祖怡、韦棣华提议)

理由:

(1)现有全国公立图书馆,大多数均呈萎靡不振之现象。苟欲弥补此弊,则应严加整理、布置。

(2)善本书籍,其所以贵,非徒其名而已,实以其有可贵者在也。或为校雠精确,秘本未传,可供学者之研究。或为刻刷精美,得之不易,发挥历史之精华。但此种书籍收藏,苟不得其法,固恒以饱蠹鱼之腹;而或代远年湮,纸张脆碎不能保有功效,则亦何贵之有。今各省图书馆收藏书籍,不乏善本,大率秘而不宣,致学者无研究之机会。国学何由而昌,我中华固有文化因之而衰。

(3)扩充阅览人数,增加社会读书机会。

办法:

(1)在六个月内,本社即将此案函请各省省长转知各该属图书馆委员会,或其他管理该属图书馆团体机关,从速整理图书馆事业。

(2)善本书籍宜存列玻璃架内,如遇人来馆申请阅览,当酌许之。

(3)宜由馆中雇员影印,或任人抄写,以广流传。

(4)如遇人来馆申请借阅时,倘得相当介绍,当酌许之。

(5)仿博物院陈列法,选择数部,开卷陈列;非但供人流览研求,是亦引人入胜之一法。并于每周或每月轮换一次。

(6)易收费限制,为保证限制。各公立图书馆应备有阅览券。凡受有保证者,迳可领取,凭券入览。

备注:本案系冯陈祖怡君及韦棣华君将洪有丰君所提议案(图书馆善本书籍,应行酌量开放,以供参考案。见议案第一编四二页)慎加研究,各拟一案,经会众讨论,合并成一案如上,通过。

(四)组织各地方图书馆协会案(戴志骞提议)

理由:

(1)研究适中管理法。现各处图书馆逐渐成立,而同一处之二三图书馆毫无联络。管理办法及手续均不一致,此于阅书者及图书管理,颇有阻碍。

(2)节省图书馆经费。同一地方之二三图书馆可合作购置新书,搜罗旧籍。譬如:甲图书馆专心搜集经、史、教育、历史、社会各类之书籍;则同时乙图书馆即可搜集子、集、自然科学、丛书等类书籍。于是同一地方有二图书馆,所出购置费与前相等,而同一地方之书籍,则种类必倍蓰于前。近来各图书馆每缺乏经济,如能通力合作,实节省经费惟一之妙法。

(3)促进图书馆学问。我国图书馆管理事业,正在萌芽,诸待创作。同一地之各图书管理员,凡关于友谊上、学问上,应有一种组织,藉以互相研究。

办法:

(1)由中华教育改进社将地方图书馆协会组织之紧要,通告各地方图书馆。

(2)各地方各图书馆管理员,可召集首次会议,选举职员。其召集事由,则可云"某处图书馆协会聚会",开会次数可定为每月一次或二次,会议地点则在各图书馆轮流,章程可由各处图书馆协会自定之。

(3)在某地方图书馆协会未能成立以前,或遇必要时,中华教育改进社图书馆教育研究委员会——由社员报告——应委派本社社员在该地者,充当发起人或交际员。

(4)社员于收到上项委派书后,六个月内,须将该地图书馆协会进行情形(如调查、统计、报告、困难、疑问等)详细呈报图书馆教育研究委员会,以便有所资助。

(5)图书馆教育研究委员会应于前期时间内,尽力回答各委派员所提出之疑问、困难等项,并须将本年地方图书馆协会经过情形,在第三届年会时,报告本组社员,以便明了得失,藉可改良进行。

备注:本案係修正通过。

(五)请中华教育改进社备函向国内各大图书公司接洽凡各地学校公立及私立公开之图书馆购书应与以相当折扣案(裘开明提议)

理由:

(1)图书馆为公共教育机关之最重要者,其所藏书籍乃供诸众览。故各界人士对之,应负有见义勇为之责。

(2)书业界与图书馆有密切关系。盖书籍藏于图书馆者,不啻为书业界之广告;而书业界亦可赖之以广销其出品焉。

(3)吾国现今图书馆甚不发达。其原因虽不一端,而因书籍昂贵,窘于经济,不能多备良册,亦为一大阻碍。书业界若能克己减价,以特别折扣售书于图书馆,则各地图书馆既可多添佳籍,亦能另设分馆。其造福于中国前途,岂可限量耶。

(4)各国图书公司对于各该国及国外之图书馆,均与特别折扣。

办法:

(1)图书馆购置书籍,应得书业界同行之折扣。

(2)由中华教育改进社备具公函,请求国内各大图书公司给与以上之利益。

备注:本案系修正通过。

(Ⅱ)移交案一件

请分期编制各种中小学校需用图书目录以便各校酌量采用案(许本震、何巽提议)

近年来国内各中小学校,对于图书馆之设立,咸知注意。惟图书馆目录,急宜编制,以便各校采用,庶几经费、图书,两得经济。鄙意拟请先行编制下列各图书馆目录。

(1)中小学校开办图书馆时之图书目录:

  (甲)小学校:

    (A)三百元之图书馆所需之目录。

    (B)五百元之图书馆所需之目录。

    (C)一千元之图书馆所需之目录。

  (乙)中学校:

    (A)一千元之图书馆所需之目录。

    (B)二千元之图书馆所需之目录。

    (C)三千元之图书馆所需之目录。

(2)中小学校分年添置之图书目录(自十二年起)。

  (甲)某年度小学校添置之图书目录。

  (乙)某年度中学校添置之图书目录。

备注:本案系议决以新学制课程尚在研究之中,对于中小学校所需之图书,茫无标准可藉规定。结果:通过移交中等教育及初等教育两组讨论。

(Ⅲ)保留案七件

(一)拟在海关附加税项下酌拨数成建设商业图书馆案(朱家治提议)

理由:

(1)以商业上进项,办理增进商人知识事业。

(2)提高国际商业程度。

(3)藉以陶镕性情,修养道德。

办法:

(1)由中华教育改进社请中国总商会同具说帖,说明图书馆在中国商业上之需要,送交海关附加税委员会讨论,指拨款项。

(2)由海关附加税委员会请总税务司每年就附加税拨出四十万元,以作开办及维持商业图书馆之用。

(3)商业图书馆所在地之商会,应担任该图书馆之常年经费十分之三。

(4)此种商业图书馆宜设在通商大埠。

(5)征集商品标本、统计,以供参考。

(6)设立图书馆数目应逐渐增加。

备注:本案原为本组议决通过案之一,但经大会讨论与整理议决案委员会之审查,佥认为与义务教育组之第二案同属要求拨海关增加税,似有冲突之处,故议决保留。

(二)请规定学校"图书馆年",并请本社图书馆教育研究委员会速制中等学校图书馆建筑图式及馆中设备计划案(程湘帆提议)

理由:

按学校图书馆为学校教育之中心。今日我国各校,除少数的专门大学尚能渐次设立图书馆外,多数的中等以下学校,对于此端殊不注意。虽或设有图书室,亦不过藏书之所,未能予学生自动的读书机会。近来学校教育之少进步,学生之少修养,多喜参与无味的运动者,原因虽不止一种,其无学校事业中心之图书馆则甚显著。故提倡图书馆事业,实为本社改进教育之首要职务。

办法:

拟一方由本社商准教育部,规定民国十三年为教育界之"图书馆年"。本年中,全国公私学校一律注重图书馆。学校临时经费,宜有一定分配用于图书馆事业。其已经建筑者,竭力增加图书及设备,并规定每年购书经费。未建筑者一律设法募请专款建筑。总之,办教育者,本年一律以建设或扩充图书馆事业为首务。

一方由本社图书馆教育研究委员会从速制定中学校图书馆建筑图式,并拟定馆中各项设备。其建筑与设备二者,宜按经费多寡分定等差,图式不妨略多,设备务求实用。照个人意见应制定以下各种样式:

(1)一千元之建筑式。
(2)一千五百元之建筑式。
(3)二千元之建筑式。
(4)二千五百元之建筑式。
(5)三千元之建筑式。
(6)四千元之建筑式。
(7)五千元之建筑式。
(8)一万至数万元之建筑式。

以上估计不过略示端倪,非确数也。各式图书馆中应有设备,按照经济的及科学的标准,详为拟定,画成图样,一律精印为单行本子,分送全国学校及教育机关。于是一方可引起社会及教育界之注意,一方作为办学者之参考。

备注:本案议决保留。

(三)交换重本图书案(戴志骞提议)

理由:

图书馆庋藏某种书籍,只须一二部即敷应用。若所藏重本图书多至三四部,则反觉不便。盖赠与他图书馆既非所愿,而转卖书店又碍馆章。若令其储积一处,则所占地位亦甚广。

书籍原为读书者之用,欲免重本过多之弊,莫善于与他图书馆交换相当价格之图书。既无损失,且便读者。欧美图书馆多行此法。

办法:

英美各国全国图书馆协会出版之杂志专论图书馆管理学,兼登图书馆交换重本图书之广告。中国全国图书馆协会尚未产生,当然无此类出版物,为目前计,如有欲登交换重本图书之广告,可暂由《新教育》杂志代为声明,然后各图书馆可互通信息,以便交换。

备注:本案系通过保留。

(四)图书馆事业办法及应用名词等等应有规定之标准案(查修提议)

理由:

(1)可使全国图书馆有一致进行之方针。

(2)可使职员任事收驾轻就熟之功效。

(3)可使人民实用得简单准确之便利。

办法:

(1)由中华教育改进社图书馆教育研究委员会厘定新法公布之。

(2)由同上委员会采纳国内图书馆成绩最佳之办法公布之。

备注:本案系以中华图书馆委员会尚未实现,关于图书馆事业一切之标准,无从规定。结果:议决保留。

(五)书籍装订改良案(查修提议)

理由:

(1)旧籍装订,纯取平放法,纸张松薄,易于破烂,抽取困难,外观不美,与图书馆书籍流通办法,殊觉不便。

(2)近来出版中文书籍仍间用旧法装订。图书馆购到后,势必改订一番。然改订,则于人工、经济、时间,均靡费过甚。

办法:

(1)由中华教育改进社图书馆教育研究委员会函请国内各书馆,采用中西二法,同时装订出版书籍,以便购者选取。

(2)旧籍装订由同上委员会厘定新法公布之。

(3)旧籍装订由同上委员会采纳国内图书馆成绩最佳之办法公布之。

备注:本案系通过保留。同时并通过请主席指派下列五人为本组书籍装订分委会会员:

冯陈祖怡　朱家治　裘开明　许达聪　查修

(六)世界图书馆(世界教育会议中国代表团提议)

世界之进步赖乎教育之普及,尤有赖于智识之传播。然传播智识非藉图书馆不为功,故有以下之决议:

(1)设一世界图书馆局,以后或与世界大学相联络。

(甲)此项世界图书馆局如遇有各国请求时,供给关于国际问题之书报。

(乙)此项世界图书馆局为各国现有之公立图书馆作定一定之标准。

(2)各国教育团体应立一全国图书馆局,供给全国之需要,并为该国人民与世界图书馆局之媒介。

备注:本案系国际教育组移交本组讨论。本组以中华图书馆局尚未产生,加入世界图书馆局更属不能办到。结果:议决保留。

(七)呈请中华教育改进社转请各省教育厅增设留学图书馆学额培植师资案(冯陈祖怡、陆秀提议)

理由:

(1)图书馆之设立日见增加,而缺乏曾经训练之馆员。推原其故,实以无专门学校以培植之,今之从事斯业者类皆知之。欲补此缺憾,惟有急行筹备设立图书馆专门学校,以广育人才,普及全国图书馆事业。惟以现在情形而论,除少数专门家现在从事于图书馆事业之实行,奔走于宣传之不暇,何能分身兼任教授。纵使设立学校,亦缺乏教师。此不得不先行培植师资之理由也。

(2) 我国向无图书馆专门学问。原有旧法失于简略,是否合用,亦有待于研究而后始能规定施行,以期统一之效。研究之标准,则不能不借取先进国以为鉴镜。此必须遣派留学外国之又一理由也。

办法:

(1) 由教育部及各省教育厅于每年派送留学名额内,加派图书馆科。

(2) 先行选派国内已有图书馆经验人员,以便随时研究本国图书馆应行采取或改良方法。

(3) 毕业人才归国后,或任教师,或办图书馆,应实行负责。

备注:本案之交进已逾期限,主席乃付表决。结果:通过收纳;经讨论后复通过保留。

原载:《新教育》 1923 年第 7 卷第 23 期

【附录 II-3】

中华教育改进社第三届年会"图书馆教育组"会议纪要

本组自七月四日至七日,共开会议五次,计提议案九件,读论文两篇。结果:通过者五案,保留者一案,退还国际教育组者二案,退还教育行政组者一案;读过论文两篇。

第一次会议

七月四日

出席人数:二十四人。

主席:戴志骞。

书记:朱家治。

主席报告本年各组会议注意事项;并宣读分组会议职员联席会议决之八项(见四日年会日刊议案组通告二)。当即讨论支配研究议案及读论文之时间,其结果为:四日宣读论文,五日研究议案,六日宣读论文,七日八日研究议案。主席即请查修君当众宣读论文,查修君将其论文"中文书籍编目问题"印成大纲分散今日出席会员,其大纲为:

(A)方针

 (一)分类与目录须分两事。打破旧式目录以分类及目录淆为一谈的观念,而认清双方都有自成一种学术之必需。

 (二)治分类法的道路。摈斥四库法,舍去改变的仿杜威书籍十类法,而努力于扩充杜威书籍十类法的进行,使图书馆事业,此后分类法的应用万众一致。

 (三)目录的性质。

  (1)指南的。

  (2)客观的。

  (3)有条理的。

  (4)有伸缩性的。

  (5)适大多数人用的。

(B)目录编制前的关隘

 (一)购求 孙从添曾提到六难,购求这事,最宜谨慎。其须注意者,至少有十四点。

 (二)整理 登录及应注意的各项,排比厚薄以备装订盖图章,制购置目录片及应注意的各项等等。

(C)目录的编制

 (一)改造 目录之目的,废除装订牢之书本式而采用片子或活叶式之必要,及片子上所应载的各项。

 (二)手续 编目手续颇为繁杂。每部书所经过的为数约有十八。

(D)版本的研究

 (一)原起 版本二字的古用及沿革。

 (二)历代刻书概况 唐、五代、宋、金、元、明、清的刻书者及风尚。

 (三)历代刻书比较观 宋元刻之精粗,明刻之谬误,清刻之优劣,撮要条举以明梗概。

  （四）版本学的入门途径　关于版本的书籍之选择，及实际之应用，须理论与经验相辅并行。

（E）书籍装订问题的进行

  （一）中华教育改进社图书馆教育组书籍装订分委员会各委员意见的汇集。

  （二）清华学校图书馆书籍改订的成效。

  出席会员对于上列大纲有所发言，章箴君谓分类与编目不必分为两事，于四库分法之内加添门类则可，若将四库法入杜威十类分法未免不便。谭新嘉君谓须讨论"治分类法的道路"一项。惟查君之论文系本研究及经验而作，篇幅太长，设使挨次讨论，恐为时间所限，故王文山君提议不如选读其中最要之点，然后加以讨论。裘开明君提议其中要点甚多，不如请查君自行选其最有兴趣之作，宣读于众。查君乃将其论文中"目录编制前的关隘"一节宣读。此节中之最堪注意者，为购求书籍之六难及十四点，其六难为：（一）知有书而无力购求；（二）求非所好；（三）价钱之不定；（四）来路困难；（五）知近不知远；（六）不知鉴识真伪。其十四点为：（一）书籍之非常相似；（二）类别相同；（三）书完整而名不现；（四）补编续编；（五）是否完整；（六）是否夹杂他种；（七）版本优劣；（八）书目与内容是否相符；（九）名同而内容不同；（十）页数；（十一）同样书籍以价贱而得劣本；（十二）书名更换而内容未改；（十三）书名更换而内容差缺；（十四）字迹蒙混。以上各项查君均各为举例，将来其全文发表时，可以见之。

  杨劼弦君提议查君读论文时，有因语言关系不能了解明白者，似宜先将本组议案先行讨论，完结后再行宣读，以免耽误议案进行时间，何日章君复议，故将暂请查君将论文留待下次再读。当时即讨论章箴君所提之议案"请中华教育改进社转请部省凡公立图书馆应一律免除券资案"。洪有丰君谓此案理由充足应提出讨论。主席问会员各处公立图书馆是否都收券资。答案有三：（一）有收券资者；（二）有不收券资者；（三）有从前收券资而现在已免去者。戴志骞君谓此议案系意见之发表可以备供斟酌施行。裘开明君提议，众赞成，今日散会，明日续行讨论。

  散会时九点五十分。

第二次会议

七月五日

出席人数：二十人

主席：洪有丰。

书记：朱家治。

  （一）继续讨论昨日未毕之议案"请中华教育改进社转请部省凡公立图书馆应一律免除券资案"，讨论结果，照原文连同理由办法一致通过。

  （二）讨论"刊行图书馆学季报案"，主席问举办季报对于经费一项，是否应有预算计划，经众讨论后，由主席指派施廷镛、裘开明、查修三人调查印刷需费若何情形，俟明日报告之后，再行妥定办法。

  对于组织上经众讨论，咸以为应有编辑部及经理部二部，各部细则自行另定；惟对于征集稿件，则除组员著作及投稿而外，兼搜集各地方图书馆协会之报告、国内外图书馆消息，故本季报实为图书馆界之耳目。当时并举定本报职员:编辑部——主任沈祖荣,副主任戴志骞。经理部——主任洪有丰,副主任朱家治。本议案一致通过。

(三)"各省公立图书馆得附设古物陈列所案",此案主文中之"得"字系原提案中"应"字之更改,又主文中之"古"字系原提案中"博"字之更改,其外办法中照原有亦稍有增加修正,余无异议,一致通过。

(四)"各省教育行政机关应设图书馆教育科案"经众讨论,佥以为图书馆事业尚未臻发达时期,且于经济人才等项诸多困难,现时不易办到,故议决将此案保留。

散会时九点五十分。

第三次会议

七月六日

出席人数:二十二人。

主席:戴志骞。

书记:朱家治。

(一)"世界图书馆案"。

(二)"世界图书馆事业案"。

上列第一案系去年保留之案,其第二案系国际教育组移交之案,并要求连同第一案重提讨论。惟本组同人对于此二案所拟理由及办法多有未明了之处,如"图书局""图书馆局"究何所指,且其办法离题过远,未能清晰,似非现时所能办到,故议决不如将此二案退还国际教育组,请原提议人妥拟详细办法。结果:将此二案备函退还。

(三)"请中华教育改进社转请教育部及各省教育厅于留学学科内添图书馆教育科案",此案去年因交议逾时故为保留,此次经众讨论均以为关系重要,有提议之必需。但上述主文已经较去年原文有所修改,理由照去年所议决无异议,办法修正如下:

(1)由教育部及各省教育厅于每次派送留学名额,就各学科加一图书馆教育科。

(2)先行选派国内已有图书馆经验人员,以便随时研究本国图书馆应行采取或改良方法。

本议案经此修正遂一致通过。

(四)"请政府设立自然科学研究院提高文化培植专门人才案",此案系教育行政组移交,本组同人以此案非属本组讨论范围,议决将此案备函退还。

(五)"各县宜酌设农村图书馆案",此案主文中之"酌"字系原提案中"普"字之更改,经众讨论对于理由尚无异议。惟将其办法修正如下:

(1)建议各省署通饬各县,就市乡教育实业等机关所在设立农村图书馆。

(2)照原文办法第三。

(3)照原文办法第二。

(4)仍照原文办法第四。

本议案经此修正,遂一致通过。

附录

本组第二次会议之关于"刊行图书馆学季报案"内所派施廷镛、裘开明、查修三君调查经费一节,兹施君报告如下:

假定本季刊每次印八百本,每本一百页,则需印刷费二百元。公议请本组社员商务印书馆交际股股员黄警顽君,再向商务印书馆接洽。

散会时九点四十分。

第四次会议

七月七日

出席人数:十九人。

主席:洪有丰。

书记:朱家治。

本组议案俱已讨论完毕,主席乃请查修君继续读其论文,查修君即读论文"中文书籍编目问题"中之"目录的编制"项下"手续"一节,其注意点有十八:(一)鉴定书名;(二)鉴定版本;(三)分类书籍;(四)查著者姓名;(五)查著者号码;(六)书背上透明质;(七)写借书片;(八)书袋;(九)写书中检查号码;(十)书背写书名及检查号码;(十一)书背上第二次透明质;(十二)不借出馆外之书特标出字样;(十三)制书架目录片;(十四)制正式目录片;(十五)校对书片、书袋,书内检查号码,登录总数书背书名,及检查号码等等,有无错误;(十六)排列书架目录片;(十七)排列正式目录片;(十八)制目录片的导引片。

查君读毕,并谓在《东方杂志》二十卷、二十二、二十三两号内详载查君著作,举例目录片之格式约三十种。

主席问对于查君论文有无讨论,众无言。即请王文山君代表宣读沈祖荣、胡庆生二君之论文"中学图书馆几个问题",其大纲为:

概论——中学校与中学图书馆之调查

(A)中学是否需要图书馆

 (甲)中学之现象——急待图书馆补济。

  (一)黑板教育。

  (二)课本教育。

  (三)被动教育。

 (乙)中学难办图书馆之原因。

  (一)不明了图书馆在教育上之价值。

  (二)因循敷衍。

  (三)限于经济之支配。

(B)中学图书馆之经济如何维持

 (甲)经济支配法(下表系为中学图书馆计算学生约二百名左右)。

  (一)开办费总目。

   (1)设备费。

   (2)书籍费。

   (3)薪资。

   (4)杂费。

  (二)常年经费。

 (乙)经济筹措法。

（一）列入学校预算案。

（二）规定为学校的例费（如健身费等）。

（三）学生公费购书。

（四）学生乐捐购书。

（五）学生毕业纪念捐。

（六）学生开游艺会筹捐。

（七）旧生或其友人纪念捐。

（八）学校特别纪念时筹捐。

（C）馆员选择问题

（甲）专门人才。

（乙）校中热心图书馆之教职员。

（丙）师范生或中学毕业生。

（丁）学生助手。

（D）图书选购法

（甲）依学校性质。

（乙）视学生程度。

（E）引导学生利用图书馆法

（甲）标明新书名目。

（乙）关于时事问题。

（丙）关于功课。

（丁）利用学生会社。

（戊）馆员亲自导引。

王文山君将全文读过，主席问对于沈、胡二君之论文有无讨论，众无言。

施廷镛君提议前次本组所通过之"刊行图书馆学季报案"，虽系中华教育改进社之议决案，但实际上须本组同人自办，今趁大多数同志在此，不如议一办法。兹将讨论办法录下：

（一）出版。

自十四年一月起，以后每季各出版一次。

（二）经费（开办时经费）。

（甲）广告费收入。

（乙）社员担任认募。

关于二，乙项，主席问可否由本年本组出席社员今日先行担任认募，众即踊跃，争先报认下列数目，且限今年十一月以前缴齐，交到经理部。

洪有丰三十元，黄警顽五十元，裘开明五十元，蒋复璁、查修合五十元，朱家治三十元，王文山二十元，杨绍思十五元，陈长伟十五元，施廷镛十五元，章箴十元，陈梦觉五元，刘维屏五元，周贺章五元，戴志骞五十元，钟叔进十元，冯绍苏五元，冯陈祖怡五十元，何日章三十元。

关于募捐一事，公推章箴君草募捐启，俟印成后即分寄各组员及各处图书馆协会，以便着手劝募，使《图书馆学季报》得以如期出世。

散会时九点四十分。

第五次会议

七月七日

出席人数:十八人。

主席:戴志骞。

书记:朱家治。

此会专为修正本组组员而集,借南京图书馆协会在东南大学孟芳图书馆欢迎本组社员之便,修正本组组员如下:

(甲)委员会委员

主任:戴志骞。

副主任:洪有丰。

书记:朱家治。

委员:沈祖荣(武昌文华),胡庆生(武昌文华),杜定友(上海复旦),程时煃(北京师大),冯陈祖怡(北京师大),查修(清华),谭新嘉(京师图书馆),陈长伟(南京金陵),何日章(河南第一图书馆),冯绍苏(南京一女师),裘开明(厦门),王文山(南开),施廷镛(东南),袁同礼(北大),章箴(浙江公立图书馆),吴汉章(清华),许达聪(燕京),陈宗登(北京)。

(乙)志愿加入本组之社员

王洪策,宋还吾,邵鹤举,陈益谦,陈广埙,徐莲清,桂质柏,章元善,张嘉谋,张庆昇,张宪承,彭清鹏,冯梅先,董作实,杨劫弦,杨树达,赵焕文,刘乃章,刘廷藩,龚自知,周贺章,黄警顽,芮慕城,陈梦觉,陈佩忍,陆秀,杨绍忠,蒋复璁,刘维屏。

本组以议案、论文及其他各事俱已完全结束,主席乃宣告休会,时已五点矣。

议决案汇录

一、通过案五件

(一)请中华教育改进社转请部省凡公立图书馆应一律免除券资案。

理由:

图书馆收取券资,无补于公家,徒阻社会读书之机会。故虽有谓参考图书馆可收者,要之终以不收为善。况我国京外各馆,大率成立未久,阅览人无多,正宜多方招徕,讵容故意限制。乃调查所及,尚有采用收费制者,甚至多分等级,最高者每券须铜元十五枚,致寒士为之裹足,实与设馆本旨背道而驰,非一律免除不可。查去年本组会通过,请全国公立图书馆应将善本书籍酌量开放免除收费案,但仅及于善本而未及于非善本,爰提议及之。

办法:

(1)凡国内以公款设立图书馆,上自国立下至乡立,一律免除券资。

(2)由中华教育改进社分函教育部,及各省省长转饬所属图书馆照办。

(二)刊行图书馆学季报案

理由:

(1)近来国内研究图书馆教育者日见增加,关于斯学文字颇多发表;惟散见于各种杂志之中,研究者欲作参考,不易检阅。

(2)本组于第一次年会时,曾设有图书馆教育研究委员会,并规定将所研究结果印刊出版。有此季刊则不但可作图书馆教育研究委员会之言论机关;更能鼓励此种研究,而促进吾国之图书馆事业。

(3)吾国现今图书馆究有若干,现状如何?及各地办理图书馆者之景况又若何?虽有少数私人及机关之调查,然无应时报告及记载,故各处图书馆管理员颇感隔膜,不能互通声气。若有季报之刊行,则可作通讯之机关,得以彼此联络感情。

(4)凡一种新创事业,欲求发达坚固,必借组织宣传之力。图书馆事业之在欧美及日本所能如此发达者,虽原因众多,大要不外此一途,故各国皆有图书馆协会及学报之行世。吾国图书馆事业虽已有组织(指中华教育改进社图书馆教育组而言),而宣传则无专刊,故急宜筹备出版图书馆学季报。

办法:

(1)由中华教育改进社图书馆教育组选举数人(需要几人临时议定)组织编辑部,担任编辑事宜。

(2)编辑部得向本组组员随时征求稿件。

(3)经费暂由本组组员及热心图书馆教育者捐助,俟季报能自立时为止。

(4)此种季报刊行后,中外书肆及与图书馆有关系者来登广告必多,故可望其渐渐自给。以后除开销之外,如有盈余,应留作将来筹备中华图书馆协会之用。

(5)暂拟季刊性质及内容如下:

(子)此时暂出季报,将来改为月刊。(丑)凡关于图书馆学、目录学、印刷事业种种学理及实际问题,皆在本报讨论范围之内。(寅)仿《中国社会学杂志》体例,发刊文字应用中、英二种,中文门以作国人讨论研究之利器,英文门以联络国外图书馆及图书馆专家为目的。

附注本季报组织如下:

(1)职员(细则由各部另订)。

编辑部——主任沈祖荣,副主任戴志骞。

经理部——主任洪有丰,副主任朱家治。

(2)出版。

自十四年一月起,以后每季各出版一次。

(三)各省公立图书馆得附设古物陈列所案

理由:

(1)各种古器古物金石字画等,为研究一国文化最好之资料。

(2)现欲求各省市立博物院,所需经费必甚浩大,故一时不易成功。

(3)各地因无博物院,所有古器古物类多散失,或遭私人损弃,或流入外人之手,诚可痛惜。

(4)借现有图书馆另开一间为博物陈列所,所费不大,举办甚易。

办法:

(1)各省区若有发现古物,得由省立图书馆保存之。

(2)劝各地寺院及私人藏有古物者,捐赠或放置图书馆,由公家为之保存而供众览。

(3)由省立图书馆留心采访各种古物,如私人发现古物,不愿赠置图书馆时,应以相当价值购得之。

(4)由中华教育改进社呈请教育部通令施行。

（四）请中华教育改进社转请教育部及各省教育厅于留学学科内添图书馆教育科案

理由：

(1) 图书馆之设立日见增加，而缺乏曾经训练之馆员。推原其故，实以无专门学校以培植之，今之从事斯业者类皆知之。欲补此缺憾，惟有急行筹备设立图书馆专门学校，以广育人才，普及全国图书馆事业；惟以现在情形而论，除少数专门家现在从事于图书馆事业之实行，奔走于宣传之不暇，何能分身兼任教授。纵使设立学校，亦缺乏教师，此不得不先行培植师资之理由也。

(2) 我国向无图书馆专门学问。原有旧法失于简略，是否合用，亦有待于研究而后始能规定施行，以期统一之效。研究之标准，则不能不借取先进国以为鉴镜。此必须遣派留学外国之又一理由也。

办法：

(1) 由教育部及各省教育厅于每次派送留学名额，就各学科加一图书馆教育科。

(2) 先行选派国内已有图书馆经验人员，以便随时研究本国图书馆应行采取或改良方法。

（五）各县宜酌设农村图书馆案

理由：

通俗图书馆各城市多已设置，办理虽未尽善，然基础已具，不难逐渐改良；至于农村人每忽视，鲜有设置图书馆者。其实风气蔽塞之区，尤需开发。我国农村社会远逊欧西，近亦有提倡农村教育者，图书馆之设乃当务之急，其理由分述如下：

(1) 已识字之村民得以增长普通知识。

(2) 未识字之村民藉以引起读书观念。

(3) 增加平民继续读书之便利。

(4) 辅助学校教育之不足。

(5) 规模简单易于设置。

办法：

(1) 建议各省署通饬各县，就市乡教育实业机关所在设立农村图书馆。

(2) 经费如充足，可以：(a) 增设广场，莳种花木；并陈列美术物品及简单运动器，供众游息；(b) 附设巡回文库，使附近小学教师得阅书之便利；并备简单标本模型及简单试验器具，辅助学校教育之进行。

(3) 馆内购置日报、地图及关于公民常识各种浅近书籍。

(4) 事业未发达之市乡，可暂与邻区合租。

二、保留案一件

（一）各省教育行政机关应设图书馆教育科案

理由：

(1) 欲谋各省图书馆之改良及图书馆教育之发达，非有正式机关督促其进行不可。

(2) 前二次年会本组对于各省图书馆及图书馆教育所建议之案件，大多数未见诸施行，缘各省教育厅无专科以掌管其事。

(3) 各地图书馆协会乃团体性质，非由政府特设机关，故无督促进行之权。

办法：

在各省区教育厅或教育委员会设图书馆教育科,聘请专家充任之。专司关于图书馆及图书馆教育之调查、统计、设计、研究、视察等事。其详细职务依各省区地方情形自定之。

三、退换国际教育组移交案二件

(一)世界图书馆案

(二)世界图书馆事业案

理由及办法不具录。

四、退换教育行政组移交案一件

(一)请政府设立自然科学研究院提高文化培植专门人才案

理由及办法不具录。

原载:《新教育》 1924 年第 9 卷第 3 期

【附录Ⅱ-4】

中华图书馆协会第一届年会图书馆建筑组会议纪要

【编者按】1929年1月,中华图书馆协会在南京举行第一届年会,戴志骞任图书馆建筑组主席,主持讨论会。

时间:一月三十一日上午十时三十分
出席会员:十四人
主席:戴志骞
书记:施廷镛
开会如仪
(一)主席报告图书馆设备不能太过简陋之理由
 (1)图书馆馆舍须超过使用图书者之上。
 (2)内部支配须适当。
 (3)先有房屋而后办图书馆往往不可实用,办图书馆者对于董事或支款者,必须参加建筑设备上之种种意见,有第三点然后前两点方可实现。
(二)讨论议案:
 甲、关于建筑设备者
  (1)拟为中等学校图书馆筹划图式案   集美学校图书馆
  (2)请协会组织设计建筑委员会案   孔敏中
  (3)请协会函中华工程师协会注意图书馆之建筑术案 孔敏中(不成立)
 议决:修正为请协会组织建筑委员会研究计划图书馆建筑案,表决通过。
 乙、关于用品者
  (1)本会应特约图书公司或特设公司制造图书馆应用物件案 陆秀
  (2)组织图书馆用品公司案   耿精民
  (3)请协会设法经营图书馆文具用品案   洪有丰
  (4)协会于最近期内开办图书馆用品商店以便各图书馆采购案 山西图书馆
 议决:修改为本会应指导特约图书公司制造图书馆应用物品案,表决通过。
 丙、关于中文书籍者
  本协会应请专门家研究中文书籍排架法,并定平排、直排之标准容量及架之深浅案 李小缘
 议决:照原文通过交建筑委员会办理。
 丁、关于图书馆用品免税者
  请国民政府财政部对于图书馆用品应予免税案   北平图书馆协会
 议决:修改为请国民政府财政部对于各国图书馆呈请图书馆用品免税,应予免税执照案,表决通过。

原载:《中华图书馆协会会报》

【附录Ⅲ】其他相关文章

【附录Ⅲ-1】

图书馆

【编者按】此篇根据清华学校学生刘聪强的文章"清华图书馆"改编而成,原篇载于《新教育》1920年第4卷第1期上,文中"自从戴志骞先生任馆长以来"指的是1919年8月戴志骞第一次赴美留学归来后。

自从戴志骞先生任馆长以来,该馆日见发达,如书籍加多及管理法改良。现在把该馆过去和现在的情形及将来的计划,分述如下,八年至九年①之过去大事记:

一、书籍的增加　西文书由八千本加至一万三千本,中文书由三万二千本加至三万五千二百余本,购费约一万元。

二、书籍的编号及分类　从前该馆的书,只编收入总数(Accession No.)。自狄玛夫人管理此事后,除原有的收入总数外,另照杜威分类法,编号分类。一年来中西文书籍大半均已编就。现在检书已不如从前之难。

三、书目的编制　书目正在编制之中。现采用 Card System 以便临时增加。中文拟备二种书目,一照作者名字编列(Author's Catalog),一照分类编列(Classified Catalog);西文书则照字母之先后编列(Dictionary Catalog)。此事大概至少须一二年告竣。

四、借书方法的改良　从前所用之借书证,只照借者姓名排列,极难找出哪一本书是哪一人借去,或哪一本书已借出去没有。现在的借书证是放于书后的一个袋中,上有该书的号数及书名;借者填名于上,交图书管理极为便利。

五、借出书籍　中文书每月平均借出三百三十六册,西文书七百六十八册。

六、介绍图书的办法　从前购书自各科主任选定,现在大家可以介绍。介绍者可将该馆特印之介绍纸填好投戴馆长门前小柜中。

七、书库的建筑　前铁书架运来时遗失螺旋二箱,致不能开工。现已设法开工,惟尚在建筑中。该书库分三层,可容书十五万册。

现在书籍、日报及杂志的总数

一、书籍
　　　　中文　三五八一五本(二七九一部)
　　　　西文　一三八零六本
二、杂志
　　　　中文　七四种

---

① 【编者注】八年即民国八年,1919年;九年即民国九年,1920年。

英文　一九四种

法文　七种

德文　五种

三、日报

中文　四五种

英文　一一种

法文　一种

将来的计划

一、印行手册　一俟编制书目大致就绪后,该馆将印一种手册,名 *Handbook on the Use of the Tsing Hua Library* 以便阅者。

二、新书　自下年起,新书到校后,先置入陈列架中,任人翻阅,惟不得携出馆外。二星期后,方能借出。

三、阅者　阅书桌椅,以后一律编号。要书时,可指名向管理员要,由听差送至阅者桌上。如此则阅者检书时间可省,而十万卷以上之书库不致翻乱——以后书籍全放于书库内,阅者不得入内。

四、借书　借书分长期、短期及参考书三种。参考将来改置于借书桌里面,阅者可借出置于所坐号数之桌上,他人不得妄动。

五、一九二〇年拟购书籍之预算表

中文书籍及杂志	三千元
新闻纸	四百元
普通杂志及装订	一千元
关于中国的西文书	五百元
目录片	五百元
普通及参考书	一千六百元
德文英文书之关于德国者亦在内	七百元
法文	三百元
英文文学书	五百元
物理	三百元
化学	三百元
数学	三百元
手工	一百元
动植物学	三百元
社会学	二百元
经济	二百元
国际公法	二百元
体育	一百元
历史	二百元
医药	一百五十元
职业及农业	三百元

美术	一百元
心理学	一百元
儿童及童子军用书	二百五十元
法律	一百五十元
工程学	一百五十元
图书馆学	一百元
共计一万二千元	

（这篇记载是得刘君聪强的允许后，由他的《清华图书馆》内摘下来的。）

原载：《清华周刊》 1920 年第 6 次增刊

【附录Ⅲ-2】

如何利用图书馆

孔繁祁

【编者按】 此篇为清华学生孔繁祁写的介绍图书馆的文章,刊登在《清华周刊》上,其中多处提到戴志骞对图书馆的要求。

中国各学校图书馆之最完善的,也只怕就是我们学校里的这一个了。我们有这样好的图书馆,要不想法利用,未免可惜。所以使我们知道如何用他,也是一件最要紧的事情,但是现在目录还未编成,许多书还未分类,又有好些书的号数还未写上,因为这样,所以多数同学一进图书馆,就差不多沉入大海一样,不知看哪一本是好,就是有人知道书名,至少也要费半小时才寻着,要是知道法子,一分钟内一定可以找出来,去补救这暂时的要求,就是我作这篇的第一目的。第二个目的就是要请那些少数人存一点公德心为大家蒙利便,这又是我对于一些少数人特别的盼望。

(一)怎样找书和杂志

要知道怎样找书,一定要知道书的分类法,我们学校用的是杜威分类法。这是用数目次序定各书类别,大致如下:

000-090　普通著作类(如百科全书、字典、杂志)
100-190　哲学类(形而上学、心理、伦理、论理学)
200-290　宗教类(神道学、宗教、历史)
300-390　社会学类(统计、政治、经济、教育等)
400-490　言语类(英、法、德、意等)
500-590　自然科学类(数学、天文、化学、物理、动植物)
600-690　有用艺术类(医药、工程、农艺等)
700-790　美术类(图画、音乐、雕刻)
800-890　文学类(美、英、法、德等)
900-990　历史类(地理、自传、古史及各洲历史等)

这个类别号数,总是写在书的侧面。这类别号数底下又有一个英文字母,字母后面又有一个号数。那字母即指这书著作者姓的第一个字母,那后面的号数是指某著作家的号数,每一著作家都有一定的号数。譬如 *An Introduction to High School Education by Colvin* 这本书是属于教育的,一定在社会学类里,精细分起来,类别号数应当是371,著者的姓的第一个字是C,这位著作者在C字的第72号,所以这本书的侧面就写371 C72。既然知道了这个法子,诸君要找什么书,先拿书名来裁判一下,知道是属哲学的就可以到架上去,从100寻到190一定可以找着,这是已经知道了书名的办法;但是譬如我要看几本关系园艺的书,这园艺种花是关于风景的,含有美术的意思,所以属于美术类,他的类别号数是700—710,那么到架上去寻这号数就得了。(上面说的都是在目录没有成功以前的简单办法。)

类别号数000到090都是参考书,如字典、百科全书、读者指南(专指杂志的著作),及各种丛书如 Cyclopedia of Am. Agriculture；Cyclopedia of Education 等等，——馆内南屋靠东壁及北壁全是。

杂志的次序是用其名的第一字母照字母的次序编列的。较大的杂志是放在馆内南屋靠北壁抽屉内，次序是从西到东，较小的杂志是放在馆内南屋靠东壁和西壁书架下面的抽屉里面，次序是东边起（北到南）一直到西边（南到北）为止。要知道这个次序，至少可以省许多时候，并且不致于有找不到的苦处。

（二）怎样尽个人责任去蒙大家的幸福

凡是关于大家的事，有二点我们要注意的，就是：（甲）凡公共的事只要每个人多作一点，要省办事人许多手续；（乙）每个人都守章程，则事事如意，反转来说，就是我个人要捣乱，人人都可以捣乱，结果大家有害。我这儿说的也就不外请大家注意上列甲、乙二项，大约分三端：

（1）取书和杂志的时候务请记着我是打哪儿取来的，放回的时候不要放错了，这事说来很简单很小的，但是好些人不注意，这事的害处就是多给管理人麻烦，使他们不能另外作一点较好事情。第二就是遗害大家，因为人人如此，把全馆的书籍弄得乱七八糟，人人不利。诸君中想已受了这样的苦处不少。这就是许多图书馆不让人还书到架子上的缘故，这儿既然是公开的，为什么大家不好好享受呢？

（2）要是不知道应该放在什么地方，宁可放在桌上，虽然有甲项坏处还不致有如乙项致遗害大家。

（3）窃取书籍是万万不可的。我知道有许多人故意私自取出书去，他们的理由我不十分知道，但我猜想是学生、教员不平等，有教员一人借四十本的，但是学生一人只能借三本。这个也未免过于主观了。我以为学生每人三本书已经很足用了，并且借出来的三本还不见得他打算都看。至于教员呢，因为参考教材或编辑讲义，因此之故不能加以一定限制。又有人说这是因为我们要求图书馆改订借书章程，不能满我们的意，所以就只有各行其是。这样见解未免太不卓越，试想哪样事可以使人人满足他的欲望？凡事总有不满意的人，照这样，一来人人都各行其是，其结果是怎样？所以我很诚恳的劝这几位终止这样的行为。以上是指普通书籍，此外参考书也有不经正当手续私取出馆的。现在礼拜日上午关门时，及平常晚间关门时都可以借，难道还有什么不方便的地方？要是怕他人借去自己不能用，所以才如此，那么我请问如果你同他人异地而处，你怎么办呢。况且参考书总是一班二十多人用的，哪能一个人自私自利？

（三）"希望养成一种风气"

这是图书馆主任戴先生说的。他希望同学对于图书馆应守的规则成为一种风气，如甲看见把书放错了，甲似乎有纠正乙的责任。看书的人都有干涉那说话的人的责任，并且对于特别的事应当报告管理员。这种风气要是养成，一个可容千余人的图书馆，就虽然只有一个看守管理员尽足矣。又有人以为那进门梯上用绳悬的"关门"似乎没意思，并且还近乎傻，殊不知这都是为养成一种美满风气的利器。譬如现在关门，管理人员及仆役都可以不在馆内。人人只要看见"关门"自然不入馆去，那么简直是大好世界。谁不愿意如此，其实说来也不是难事。外国杂货店掌柜的，每每一个人把"吃饭去了"的牌子挂起，就离店去了，也没人进去。

他们(市民)可以办到,我们(学生)还办不到吗？劝那些不按时入馆的快改罢,听差固然没奈何,你自己心里未免难受。

结束起来,第一愿大家不要丢掉这个机会,好好的利用他,看他可以帮助你好多,也是人生少不了的一个益友,第二愿大家都互相监督,养成一种优良美好的风气,感化那不谋公益自私自利的少数同学。

原载:《清华周刊》 1921 年第 205 期

【附录Ⅲ-3】

中华图书馆协会第一次年会筹备及经过报告

本会成立,于兹三稔,乃以时局关系,致会章规定之年会,久未举行,殊属憾事。今者革命告成,训政开始,图书馆事业,尤为重要建设之一端。因此执行部乃议决在南京举行第一次年会,各地方协会亦纷纷要求,实属刻不容缓。故协会即聘定袁同礼,戴志骞,刘国钧,李小缘诸君,为年会筹备委员,于十八年一月二十八日至二月二日,在首都金陵大学召集第一次年会大会。兹谨将重要筹备及经过事项,分述如下:

(一)筹备委员

筹备委员系由执行部函聘,其人选如左:(以姓氏笔画多寡为先后)

王云五　朱家治　李小缘　何日章　杜定友　沈祖荣　柳诒征　洪范五　胡庆生
俞庆棠　袁同礼　徐鸿宝　陶知行　陈长伟　陈剑翛　崔苹村　曹祖彬　章警秋
万国鼎　杨杏佛　刘季洪　刘国钧　钱端升　钟福庆　戴志骞　顾斗南

并推定戴志骞、刘国钧、李小缘、章警秋、刘诒征诸君为常务委员,戴志骞为筹备会主席,刘国钧为书记。

(二)筹备会开会经过

自十七年十二月一日起至十八年一月廿日止,共开筹备会四次,谈话会一次,当时记录均曾用誊写版油印发表;会议结果,叙述于本会会报第四卷第三期中,兹不赘录。

(三)经费

此次年会经费,预计所需甚巨,筹备之时,颇觉踌躇。惟幸北方有袁君同礼从事筹备,而南方则多赖戴君志骞之力,不惮劳辛,奔走接洽,得国民政府各机关以及教育部当局之慨予补助,始达举行年会之目的,兹将收到各机关之津贴列后:(以收到日期为先后)

(1)国民政府行政院　　洋壹仟元　　十二月廿二日
(2)国民政府卫生部　　洋叁拾元　　十二月廿一日
(3)国民政府铁道部　　洋贰百元　　十八年一月四日
(4)中央大学　　　　　洋壹百元　　一月十四日
(5)江苏省政府　　　　洋贰百元　　一月廿五日
(6)国民政府外交部　　洋贰百元　　一月廿五日
(7)清华大学　　　　　洋伍拾元　　一月廿六日
(8)北平大学　　　　　洋壹佰元　　一月廿八日
(9)燕京大学　　　　　洋伍拾元　　一月廿八日
(10)国民政府工商部　 洋伍拾元　　一月廿八日
(11)中央党部　　　　 洋贰仟元　　二月廿一日
(12)国民政府内政部　 洋伍拾元　　二月廿日

(甲)来源

除上列各项津贴外,尚有中华图书馆协会事务所拨来洋叁佰元,及会费杂费等收入。(详见会计报告)

(乙)收支

(1)总收五千四百三十贰元。

(2)总支壹仟六百贰拾伍元叁角。

(丙)存余

(丁)净存叁仟柒佰伍拾陆元七角。(除拨付季刊费及拨交协会外,实存贰拾六元七角。)

(四)会址

因接各地会员报到通知单,届时到会者颇呈踊跃,故须觅相当地点以便居住。后经筹备会商议结果,肯借金陵大学礼堂、教室、宿舍三处为会场、办公处及招待膳宿之用。女会员则借用金陵女子大学各宿舍。

(五)聘定年会职员(以姓氏笔画多寡为先后)

丁晓元　何汉之　曹祖杰　曹祖彬　刘贵生　谢湘

此次年会为第一次举行,各事俱须创办,而筹备时期尤以文件一项,拟稿缮写,异常冗忙,故以上诸君,均酌送津贴,藉作微酬。

(六)推定主席及各组干事

蔡元培(主席)　袁同礼(副主席)　戴志骞(副主席)　刘国钧(总务)

注册组　朱家治(主任)　曹祖彬　吴光清　陈祖规　汪兆荣　于震寰　曹祖杰　洪有章

招待组　崔苹村(主任)　余舜芝　冯绍苏　严文郁

编辑组　顾斗南(主任)　朱家治　金敏甫　黄警顽　赵吉士

文书组　曹祖彬(主任)　丁晓元　周雁石　何汉三　陈杰夫

庶务组　陈长伟(主任)　刘纯甫　向培豪　俞家齐　俞宝书

会计组　谢　湘(主任)　于震寰

(七)事务

筹备之时,终日多忙于寄发各机关会员、个人会员及其他机关开年会之通知函,并用函接洽各项事宜,今将所发各处函件,计数如左:

筹备委员函	二百七十二件
机关会员函	二百六十二件
个人会员函	三百五十四件
各院部公函	二十件
各省教育厅公函	十六件
地方图书馆协会函	廿六件
各省公私立图书馆函	三百六十二件

江苏各县通俗教育函　　十四件
非会员及其他机关函　　三十件
共计　　　　　　　　　一千三百五十六件

收到机关及个人会员又其他来件共计九十五件。

庶务组于大会开幕前数日,则忙于布置总办公处及各组办事室暨会场等。会场有三处:(1)开幕典礼在金陵大学大礼堂;(2)分组会议在该校行政厅二层楼各教室;(3)会务会议及讲演等在该校科学馆。宿舍亦分数处,男会员则宿于金陵大学之行政院第一层楼、东楼宿舍及养蜂园;女会员则宿于金陵女子大学。膳厅用金陵大学膳堂。至于会员需要各项用具,均由庶务组筹备,一切尚觉便利。

(八)招待

自一月廿四日起会员遂陆续报到,招待组即派招待员安置宿舍及导引用膳等事,并派工役在各指定所,以便随呼随应。至若招待会员游览事,原拟南京各名胜逐日分队遍游,籍增会后兴趣。奈时值严寒,积雪盈尺,以致路途泥泞,行旅艰难,不克如顾。只得变更初衷,仅至车辆所能到之地,游览参观焉。今将所到各地列下:

一月卅一日下午　　中央大学图书馆　　科学社图书馆　　通俗教育馆　　国学图书馆
二月一日下午　　　金陵女子大学　　　清凉山　　　　　北极阁

(九)宴会

一月廿八日下午六时　　南京图书馆协会欢迎聚餐会(在金陵大学膳堂)
一月廿九日下午四时　　金陵大学图书馆欢迎茶会(在金陵大学图书馆)
一月卅一日十二时半　　中央大学图书馆欢迎聚餐会(在中央大学体育馆)
　　　　　下午五时　　国学图书馆欢迎茶会(在龙蟠里国学图书馆)
二月一日下午四时　　　中央党部欢迎茶会(在中央党部)
　　　　　下午六时　　教育部欢迎聚餐会(在安乐酒店)

(十)誌谢

金陵大学校长、金陵大学图书馆、金陵女子大学图书馆、中央大学图书馆、国学图书馆及外交部图书馆各职员,对此次年会,均竭力襄助,殊深感激。再中央党部、教育部、中央大学等各机关,俱蒙赞助指导,庶此次年会得有圆满结果,此尤为同人所深誌谢者也。

附录　会计报告(下略)

教育事业篇

新中国之道德

演稿　获奖同门会[①]金牌

【编者按】戴志骞于1912年获得圣约翰大学文科学士学位,当年参加圣约翰大学中文演说竞赛,获得第一名,荣获同门会赠送的演讲金牌,讲题为《新中国之道德》,演讲稿刊登在圣约翰大学出版的《约翰声》上。

现在新政府要行一切新政,苦无财力,于是不得不借外债。从借款问题,生出监督财政问题,从监督财政问题,生出限制军队问题。允许资本团的请,则中国财政权、军事权,皆落外人的手;勿允许,财政十分困难,所以现在的地位,实在两难。并且西藏、蒙古的警报日来,宗社党的奸谋百出,中国现在危象,已达极点。然而此等危象,皆属有形的危象。因为留心时务者皆能明白,现在再有无形的危象,比较有形的更危。因为此种危象,人人不知不觉,非惟不防他,而且人人钻营奔竞,定要做到这危险地位。这即是无道德心,这即是道德的仇敌。现在要新中国能免去一切外祸内讧,必须首先制服道德的仇敌,这种理说,中国一向有的。如孟子云:行仁政而王者,莫之能御也。行仁政的大意,即是立国必须以道德为基础,鄙人今晚非讲道德的原理,如宗教家或哲学家所讲的,惟讲道德内有数事,与共和国极有关系,与新中国更有关系,现在分三端,表明其关系之处。

（一）个人道德

自从欧西文化与耶教普及东方以来,个人主义的说大盛。诸君皆知个人主义,为基督的道德。中国向不讲个人主义,虽孔子曰:欲平天下,必先齐家;欲齐家,必先修身;欲修身,必先正心。孔子讲到修身正心,似乎个人主义,其实不是。因孔子最高的目的在平天下,看修身正心,可当为平天下的一法,非看修身正心,为人人应做到的目的,所以个人主义,在中国是一新理说。

个人主义与共和国民的思想,有密切关系。因个人主义,着重人人有自主性质,独立理想。中国人无此理说,所以没有新思想发达,偶有新思想者,即为旧风俗所摧折。诸君岂不常闻人曰:汝所为的事,前人未曾做过,尔祖尔父亦未做过,汝所做者必须效法前人或尔祖尔父。鄙人非说效法的不善,但只有效法,而无独立的理想,则永不能长进。现在共和时代,国民必须发达其独立性质、自主理想,然后思想能活泼,文化易长进,但是鄙人欲忠告诸君,若惟发挥个人主义,而无道德为根本,则此极好的个人主义,一变为自私自利的主义,什么缘故？因个人皆谓,人有自主性质,独立理想,自私自利,是我自主的性质,独立的理想。如此驱全国国民,皆为杨子一流人物,而且不及杨子,因杨子为我,尚不侵害他人,自私自利的结果,都是损人利己了。所以欲除个人主义的弊,必须重个人道德,个人道德如何,则有三

[①] **【编者注】**即校友会。

要素。

（甲）自制。何谓自制，即不可随自己的私欲而做，必须谨守一最完全、最高尚之目的而做。

（乙）自修。即个人自己的德、智、体三育。若三中缺一，即不能为完全品格的国民。

（丙）自重。从根本上说起，即不求他人的赞美，惟求自己的良心无责备。古时希腊圣人说：人不可辱我，惟吾独能辱我也。

以上三端，是个人道德的根本，个人有道德，然后行个人主义，有利而无弊。

（二）社会道德

社会与国家，极有关系。社会有高等程度之道德，该国一定富强，所以要一国兴盛，必须注意社会道德。论到社会道德，最要的有二端，即公平仁爱是也。

或问曰：新中国内，有此二种社会道德否？鄙人曰：有是有的，惟讲公平仁爱者多，本身奉行者少，现在以二事为证。

奴婢的风俗，虽上海渐渐减少，然仍有人家畜的，各处内地，虐待奴婢的甚多，敝处珠溪，有一富家畜女婢二，女主人性极凶悍，稍不合意，即以皮鞭鞭之，或以针刺之，遍体鳞伤，终夜啼哭，地方自治会毫不干涉，似乎该女主人有天然的权利。珠溪与上海毗连，新文化易传染的地方，尚有此等无人道的举动。再皖南江北的饥荒，饿夫满道，待毙者不下数十万。虽沪上诸大善士、各处一视同仁的教士，慷慨捐助，但此等仁人君子，实中国社会内一小分，岂可代表全国的社会心理。虽华洋义振会印出许多惨苦的小照，然能受其感动，而慷慨解囊者极少。

呜呼！畜奴婢的，为个人快乐，以人为牛马，是摧残人道。坐视饥饿待毙的同胞，狠心不救，并不想一策，是天良澌灭，尚有公平仁爱的心理乎？社会道德既如此，新中国命运，能享受长久者，鄙人实不敢信。希腊罗马之亡，亡于无社会道德心，现在在坐诸君，欢喜共和国政，祈诸君极力发挥同胞的社会道德心，则新中国幸甚。

（三）民主国道德

民主国与专制国的大分别，民主国有自由平等的道理，专制国没有的。去年起义时候，爱国志士，热血英雄，昌（倡）言自由平等，欲脱去政府压制，所以推翻满人，易如反掌。然革命的直接结果，颇极紊乱，因革命后新旧交界，旧思想、旧风俗，已经破坏，而新思想却未增进，新风俗却未成就。如法兰西1789年革命之后，全国紊乱，杀戮无度。今年中国各处亦有兵变，地方绅士意见分歧，几比前清更乱。即因革命后，人民已脱旧法律监督，而误用无规则的自由，无秩序的平等，若长此不变，是万不能立国的，欲完全组织民国，须知人民。对于民主国的真相，有二大要端：

（甲）服从多数。帝国法律是君造的，民国法律是民造的，是人民多数造的，第一立法是国会，凡议一案，议员多数赞成，即成法律，虽总统不能变更，降而下之，有省议会、县议会、市乡议会。凡一省、一县、一市、一乡，单行章程，但无背于全国普通法律，亦得以该议会的多数议员赞成，为该地方的单行法律，所以议会议决的法律，行政员必须服从，人民亦必须服从，这即是服从多数。若不服从,便是乱民了。

(乙)勿侵权限。权限者,法律的范围,治安的保障。以大者言,立法、行政、司法为三权限,以小者言,一人有一人的权限,一事有一事的权限,在我权限中,我可自由行动,若他人欲侵我权限,而使我失其自由,为文明法律所不许。若我欲侵他人的权限,而使人失其自由,岂文明法律所许乎?曲礼云:并坐不横肱,即是不侵他人的自由,即是法律,即是道德,现在做民国的民,只要明白权限,自然办事有秩序,没有争权争利的风潮,凡百事业,可以渐渐建设,渐渐进步,成个真心共和国。

夫振兴实业,扩张海陆军队,原可富国强兵,但尚是表面上计策,不是根本上计策。我们岂不知前清亦行新政么?非但不能得新政的益,反受新政的害。只因做事人没有道德心,件件借公济私,多一个名目,即多一层弊病。现在新中国,岂可蹈其覆辙。鄙人所以要把三种道德,唤起国民心理:第一个人道德,第二社会道德,第三民主国道德。总之,有道德心,才能实事求是,件件有些效力。因为民主国道德,着重国民必须有服从法律、纯正爱国的性质。今能着重此三端,则新中国之强,可预定,新中国之永久,可与日月同。若勿着重此三端,虽然极力振兴实业,扩张武备,新中国必不能强,必不能长久。诸君与鄙人皆国民,做国民有国民的责任。美国著名大律师林文史登(Robert R. Livingston)说:专制政体的错,可归于君主,民主政体的错,要归于国民。所以鄙人欲与诸君研究这新中国的根本问题,还请诸君指教。

原载:《约翰声》 1912 年第 5 期

人与蚊之竞争

【编者按】 1913年4月10日物理学硕士顾斐德先生在上海环球学生会演讲此题,提倡灭蚊,预防传播疾病。顾斐德毕业于英国皇家学院,1894年任圣约翰学院理科主任。4月15日圣约翰大学校长卜舫济博士又以此题在上海益智会演讲,戴志骞先生根据两次演讲内容,加入己见,整理而成,故收入文集。

蚊,人之仇敌也,不独扰清梦,亦为传染病之媒介。其病分三种:一疟疾(Malaria),一黄热病(Yellow fever),一红斑热症(Dengue fever)是也。中国境内,黄热病、红斑热症尚不恒见,疟疾则往往而有。轻者,废时失业,重者至死。其贻害社会,诚非楮墨所能罄。尝读欧、非二洲历史,而知彼邦人民,所以今盛于昔者,灭蚊亦其一端也。吾论灭蚊法,先述蚊之种类。

蚊之强者,约分三种:(一)曰阿诺反力司(Anophales),俗称尖头蚊;(二)曰使塔格米亚(Stegomyia),俗称花蚊,西人谓之虎蚊,盖其足上有黑白花条如虎纹也。(三)曰科力克司法跌更司蚊(Culex Fatigans)。凡此三种,具有雌雄二类,雄蚊吸树木之液,不为人害。雌蚊则吮动物之血,实为传染病之媒介。

蚊之过程分四时期,凡雌蚊,每次约可产卵二百枚,入水中,历一日夜而成孑孓,俗称倒跂虫,或称打拳虫。食腐烂水草,尾有管,为浮于水面时呼吸空气之用。经一星期而成蛹,再历二日,始裂壳而成蚊。综计前后为时约旬日而已。

上述各种之蚊,均能传染病症。如阿诺反力司蚊,能传疟症;使塔格米亚蚊,能传黄热病;科力克司法跌更司蚊,能传红斑热症。今急须研究者,乃阿诺反力司蚊,盖中国为多疟疾之国也。

古人不知疟疾之由来,咸谓为秽气所感,故名疟疾曰Malaria,意即臭气也。故热带中人相戒不夜出、不露宿,后乃知其不然,盖实因人体血液中有寄生虫之故。始查明此理者,为法医兰佛伦氏。渠常发问题曰:寄生虫如何至人血中,一人血中元寄生虫,如何至他人血中,后为英医洛司氏所答。洛氏居印度,于兵丁聚集之处,用显微镜悉心考察,于蚊之腹内发见此种寄生虫,始知蚊实为疟虫之媒介也。此蚊即阿诺反力司蚊,其状与他蚊有别,头尖而翼有斑,栖时直立,身与口几成一直线,此即传疟之恶魔也。

此蚊吸疟者之血液,疟虫即随血液而入蚊腹。渐次繁衍为生殖子,转达蚊之口管涎腺内。苟此蚊再刺无病之人,其涎腺之生殖子,输入血管内,此人遂亦染疟矣。疟虫至血管后,其形色如变形虫(Amoeba),以红血轮为滋长之所,滋长后再分裂成许多之生殖子,该时受其毒者,即觉冷气侵骨,疼痛难言。重者数小时,轻者约一时后,此无数之生殖子,再散布于全身血液之中,于是身如炽炭,而成热矣。然此分裂之生殖子,再能入红血轮相聚而复其初,为一种之变形虫,其时间或二十四小时,或四十八小时,或七十二小时,由此成日疟、间日疟或三日疟也。设此阿诺反力司蚊,复刺此患疟症者,而疟虫再入蚊腹,变成生殖子而至涎腺,复刺他人,则疟虫又传一人矣,此即疟疾与寄生虫循迭生之故也。以是推之,一人有疟,即传至千万万人,亦易事耳。西历一千九百年,英医孟司氏嘱意大利人,收集会刺患疟者之蚊,寄至伦敦,使刺其友,而其友亦染此疟,于是疟由蚊传染之证据为确凿矣。

天下疾病虽多,惟疟疾最易阻人进化,最易耗人体质而得他症。以二三事表明之,因疟而死亡,而损失财产者,其数等于兵燹。白人至热带工作为疟死者,其数占百分之六十九。非洲之不振,罗马之致败,疟疾亦其一大原因。盖非洲、罗马皆易产蚊之地也。昔合众国之南方有塔克山司省,铁路工人因疟病而不能工作者,每年耗费工资有墨洋267,620元之数。每年美国因工人疟疾而耗费各种工资,有墨银10,666,640元之数,学生为疟疾而荒学业者亦然。

疟之为害如此,则如何可以扫除之,曰:必先设法灭去阿诺反力司蚊。此蚊灭,而疟症与之俱灭矣。灭蚊之法有二:一、保守;二、攻击是已。

保守法:(甲)疟者之卧床,必用珠罗纱帐,使空气流通而蚊不能入(洋布洋纱等料为帐,蚊虽亦不能入,而空气不易流通,于病者不相宜),蚊既不能近疟者刺取疟虫,则无传染之原料。(乙)建屋必远避产蚊之地,如已建筑,必须装铅沙于窗牖,勿使蚊入。夜则用帐以避蚊刺。(丙)常服白药,即金鸡纳霜,此药能杜绝血液中之寄生虫。

攻击法:(甲)养鱼于池沼内,以食孑孓。盖鱼蛙皆蚊卵天然之仇敌,昔西印度有一岛名曰排片驼(Barbadoes)①,虽有死水而不生蚊。后经考察,始知此死水中有无数小鱼也。(乙)浇火油于水面。孑孓恒至水面,呼吸空气,若遇火油即死。(丙)阴沟中、檐溜下,及一切积水之处,皆可生蚊。积水之处,宜用砂土填之,沟头檐际,勤加拂拭,倘有积水之器,则每星期必有一次以火油浇之。(丁)旧铁盒、破磁器、花盆、花瓶等项,能盛雨水者,必须毁去。如缸井等不能毁去,必须妥实闭盖,免蚊虫落水育卵。(戊)设法律罚积水生蚊之家。因此事关系公众卫生,不特个人之安康也,各处地方自治会宜选派职员或结合同志,设灭蚊队,以排除上言之各种积水为务。遇愚暗者尽力劝导,俾知蚊虫之为害,而共担灭蚊之责任。

本校近年来患疟疾者日少,其效全在用以上诸法。非作者之附会,实缘灭蚊除疟之效力,早著全球也。试观下列之表,知各国未灭蚊之前与已用灭蚊法之后,其疟死之数,相差为甚远也。

蚊害一览表

地名		未用灭蚊法	初用灭蚊法	灭蚊法之功效	
意大利	年份	1887	1902	1903-1907	
	疟死之数	21033	16000	4000	
希腊之麦兰霜	年份	1906	1907	1908	1909
	疟死之数	90%	47%	20%	2%
非洲之邑司蛮利亚,户口八千名	年份	1903	1904	1905-1908	
	疟死之数	214	90	无人患疟症,惟前曾患此而复发则有之	
香港	年份	1901	1905	1906-1908	
	疟死之数	574	285	死于疟者不过百人	

---

① 【编者注】疑为Barbados,巴巴多斯岛。位于东加勒比海小安的列斯群岛最东端,西距特立尼达岛322公里。巴巴多斯岛原是南美大陆科迪勒拉山脉在海中延伸部分,大部分由珊瑚石灰岩构成。

续表

地名		未用灭蚊法	初用灭蚊法	灭蚊法之功效	
苏彝士运河① 附近	年份	1903	1904	1905-1908	
	疟死之数	214	90	死于疟者无	
巴拿马运河	年份	1903	1906	1907	1908
	虐死之数	2174	821	424	282

法人在1881年即欲开巴拿马土腰,至1903年,事仍不果,因法人在该处做工者,于二十二年中死于疟及黄热病者有五万人之多,故至1904年,将该土腰售于美人。美人在兴工之前,极力设法灭蚊。而死者即少,于是巴拿马运河成矣。人谓美之成功,因财政较富于法人,岂知实赖灭蚊之功。黄热病之传布,由使塔格米亚蚊。中国亦生此蚊,然无黄热症者,盖无黄热症之寄生虫也。美国前亦无之,惟数年前南方大城有曰纽俄尔连丝者(New Orleans)始发见此症,经人考察知病源由巴拿马传染,盖病者适从巴拿马归也。或云,巴拿马运河通,中国亦将有此症。此虽理想之词,然语非无因也。

此蚊产于水桶之底,或隙缝中,及破碎花盆之内,其灭之法,多与灭疟蚊法同。此外则烧硫磺于室中,以消灭墙壁间之蚊子。惟烧硫磺时,须严扃其窗户,以免气泄而力若。科力克司法铁更司蚊,传红斑热症,中国亦有之,其生产地及消灭法均与前二者同。

或问曰:中国多产米之区,田无积水,稻焉能长,若欲洒以火油,必使水溢田面,油不及苗,乃可无害。而后逐渐宣泄,使水复其旧,此无论农人无此财力,即手续亦太繁矣,鸟能实行。则答之曰:稻田之中,害虫甚多,固尝利用此法,惟蚊独不易生长。因田内有青蛙,能食子孓,蚊卵不易生存也。且蚊之飞力,并不甚强,于夜气清朗之时,其飞不能及远,故稻田之蚊,不足传疟。

或又问曰:子言诚然矣,然隆冬时蚊尚未生,而亦有患疟者,其故何欤。曰:隆冬之疟,是疟之复发,若向无疟者,决不能染。盖疟疾愈后四五年,红血轮内之疟虫,尚有复发之能力,体弱者不易消灭之,故疟疾无间冬夏也。

若吾国各地方有户口生死册,当知一年中死于蚊之害者,不下数十万,则统全国言之,因而致疾病、耗资财者,当亦不可胜数。今世富绅巨贾,惟汲汲求一己之名利,而不顾公益,抑知公共卫生之不讲,而欲得一家之幸福,犹衣冠而立厕旁,岂能不臭哉。英儒斯宾赛氏曰:社会之机体,如人身之机体。谅者斯言,且灭蚊非甚难,并不须用多金,无富贵贫贱,皆可尽力。若人人以灭蚊为任,则蚊不难除,疾病少而心力强,心力强而经济足,不亦快乎,又何惮而不为。

(附志)此事实为当今急务,研究卫生学者,莫不苦口贡献于社会。四月十号,格致②硕士顾裴德先生演讲此题于上海环球学生会,命余口译。四月十五号,本校校长卜舫济博士复以此题演讲于益智会,于蚊患及灭蚊法之必要,两先生均已畅发无遗,骞不揣梼昧,略参己意,译成是篇,非敢自炫,藉以志名训于不朽,并望社会之努力进行云。

原载:《约翰声》 1913年第4期

---

① 【编者注】今译苏伊士运河。
② 【编者注】格致:现在称物理学。

留别之言

【编者按】1919年8月戴志骞第一次留学回国,1924年8月在清华学校工作已满5年,按照清华学校的规定,申请一年学术休假获得学校批准,第二次赴美留学。在赴美之前,戴志骞应《清华周刊》编辑包华国之约,深情地写下留别之言。

清华周刊编辑包君华国,以超将于七月底与予所爱之清华学校,及诸同事同学等,暂时离别,乃请予作一临别赠言。溯超自民国三年夏来校任事以来,迄已十载。虽期间赴美一次,然亦时与清华同学互相砥砺。清华课堂上及寝室内生活,予虽未尝过,而朝夕与众同学切磋,各种情形,尚无多大隔膜,用特掬诚以数言为我诸同学告。

我校同学,好国学者,固不乏其人;惟就图书馆借出中西文参考书比较之,似乎好读西文者较中文为多。平时与同学闲谈时,亦间闻有许多同学在国学课堂上,想各种方法翻阅西文书籍;此于求学修养方面,殆尚欠功夫焉。夫求学一事应出诸个人之心愿,读书而须教员强迫,则其收效与个人之发愤读书,必不可同日而语矣。用功能出于自动,定能收事半功倍之效。中国现在教育之趋势,国民之心理,及一般社会所希望,大都渴望吾辈留学归来之学生,能沟通中西文化,有适当之著作,以建言于中国社会及国民。欲遂此愿,如于国学无功夫,虽其人学问渊博,亦不易传达于多数人民。且国学无根底者,其浏览书籍,必不如阅西文书之一目数行,于是个人之学问,不期然而偏重于西方思想,而于中国固有之学术,反疏忽焉。予为年少求学时忽略国学之一人,至今急思补前此之非,然终觉时间与精神上有所未逮,此予经验之谈,深望诸同学引为前车之鉴,而自动的研究国学,多读国学书籍,则将来必大有造于中国也。

中国交通不便,一般人多存畛域之见,吾校同学对于省界观念,虽不较别校为深,而存此观念者,亦在所不免。清华同学,乃各省优秀分子集合而成,在校时理应消除省界观念,时相过从,交换各地风土人情,既增智识,又敦友谊,此同学等所应注意者也。近年吾校同乡会,不及往年之盛,此诚一种好现象,盖可以免除同乡小团体之不良习惯也。近日厦门大学发生罢课风潮,内分福建学生与非福建学生之两派。夫知识界犹存此种畛域观念,则欲为将来中国领袖而不发障碍,胡可得耶?所冀吾校同学竭力捐除此种浅见,而融合全校同学,成一大同乡会焉。

本校学生会对于学生群众,应有勇敢公正之言论,切勿存"学生会为学校管理之对敌"之意见。比如学生对于学校管理上有不满意之处,即提出于学生会,学生会明知所提出之理由不充足,或证据不确实,然亦不愿出勇敢公正之言论,批评学生之提议。有时欲博得学生群众之欢心,且贸然从事鼓吹之,于是提议通过矣。及与学校当局开始交涉,当局之意,或以为某种提议实行后,害大利小,而不愿采纳。因此学生会与学校管理方面合作之精神,遂逐渐萎靡,而对峙之态度乃成,此诚不好之现象也。"五四"运动以来,各校时起罢课或驱逐校长之风潮,虽曰潮流如此,然大半由于学生会对学校当局过存对峙之偏见耳。本校在"五四"后,虽经几次风潮,然终不至如他校之不可收拾者,良以本校学生有时真能为学校谋幸福,亦且对学生群众发为公正之议论,决不令一般政客派之学生,借题遂其私欲也。深望清华学生会嗣后与学校当局和衷共济,俾学务日臻完善焉。前阅东方时报,载有英首相麦克丹纳耳氏在下议院声明云,不能以萨懋尔所提议"延缓退还中国庚子赔款案二读直至中国政府更改商标注册条后为止"为适当,麦氏云,商标案应以商标案内曲直是非,另与中国政府交涉,不能与退还庚子赔款案混为一事。盖中国认退还庚子赔款为友邦亲善之举,而非一种交换条件耳。麦氏此种公正言论诚足以折服同党,而不愧为其领袖矣。本校学生会,对于学生群众,亦宜大公无私,果敢评判,方不愧为学生之模范也。

以上临别之言,拉杂成篇,虽属"老生常谈",确系今日学者之通弊,希留意焉。

原载:《清华周刊》 1924 年第 10 次增刊

在国立中央大学总理纪念周上的演讲

(1928年12月17日)

【编者按】1928年10月28日,戴志骞与清华学校梅贻琦、赵元任同乘平沪特别快车,到南京就任国立中央大学图书馆馆长,兼任江苏大学区行政督学。按照国立中央大学的惯例,学校每周一举行总理纪念周仪式,在仪式上聘请行政要员或本校教职员演讲,1928年12月17日总理纪念周仪式由国立中央大学校长张乃燕主持,仪式结束后,拟请江苏省政府委员缪丕成到校演讲,缪丕成因事未到,转请戴志骞演讲。

【张乃燕讲话】

每逢星期一举行纪念周礼时,请党国要人,或本校教职员讲演。今日本请苏省府委员缪丕成先生讲演,缪先生因事不克来校。特请本校图书馆主任戴志骞先生讲演。戴先生系纽约州立(大学)图书馆学院学士,爱我华大学①教育院哲学博士,美国哥伦比亚(大学)图书馆参考部职员,纽约曷不顿军营②图书馆副馆长,清华大学图书馆主任,北京师大图书馆学校暑期学校主任,丹麦王家图书馆顾问,北平北海图书馆委员。明年(民国十八年)正月二十八日将开全国图书馆会议,戴先生被推为筹备委员会主席。今戴先生为本校图书馆主任兼大学区督学,此后对区内各校及本部之图书馆定多发展改进之计划也。

【戴志骞讲话】

戴先生讲演大意:今日缪先生不能来校讲演,兹将余对于图书馆之问题,报告于诸君:在上星期,曾至本校图书馆视察一周,以不甚熟悉,未能作详细之谈话。今就大学教育与大学图书馆之关系,约略述之。我国在三十年前,外国在六十年前,对于图书馆,不甚注意,以为装饰品、休息室而已。实太不知图书馆之作用,与应用之方法。在今日之欧美各国,对于大学校之图书馆观感大变,七十年前之大学教育,惟一以课本讲义为治学方法,以教授为百科全书,现在之大学教育,一变昔态,注重自动之研究,如教授出一题目,指定研究之范围,使学生作自动之探讨,如欧战以后道斯计划之如何? 则非仅在课本上能了解者也。学生方面,应将有关于此题者,无论经济、政治种种,搜集之,研究之,再本个人之理解,在上课时,公开讨论。先生方面,亦应详加预备,作充分之解答,如是之教育法,方有进步也。

学校之对于图书馆,应有充分之经济,然后可购多量之书籍,对于大学校之图书馆,尤应特别注意。如国内之南开大学、清华大学、中山大学等校,对于图书馆之发展,均在积极进行中。国外如法德诸国素抱守旧主义,学生大半埋首于希腊文、拉丁文及几何学中,但今日对于图书馆设备,亦极力扩充。近耶鲁大学出六百万金,筑一完美之图书馆,此我国诸大学所望尘莫及者也。

图书馆之应用问题,不在管理之人,而在用书之人。每因院系之不同,将书籍分为某院

---

① 【编者注】今译爱荷华大学。
② 【编者注】即爱布顿。

某系之图书室,如《近世史》一书,法学院所须用者,文学院亦须用者也。就理应置一处,则时间与经济,便利殊多。又如讲师指定参考书籍,每感书少人多之弊,于是为自利起见,预为藏置。甚至书籍中之插图等等,私自割取,此种均关道德问题,管理者力所不及也。

在二十五年前,有人谓:大学校最重要者有二事,第一试验室,第二图书馆。今日可谓:第一图书馆,第二试验室。因试验失败与成功,须先阅览书籍,然后知其利弊之所在也。又谓参观学校之优劣,只须注意三点:(一)参观图书馆,可知公德之如何?(二)参观饭堂,可知清洁之如何?(三)参观厕所,可知自治之如何?今日大学校与图书馆之重要有如此。

就本校情形言之:各院图书馆之合并与否?另一问题,如图书馆方面,觉书库太空,观众太少,设备不周,阅报处之不妥,就诸点观察,亟待改良者也。现在隆冬时期,寒风习习,装设之火炉,颇多危险,今拟改设汽管。电灯不明,在校中新电机装成后,再加台灯。阅书室太小,拟再扩充之。以我校有八院之多,二千学生之众,如购二三万元之书籍,未免太少。其他如管理问题,千头万绪,都在筹划中,要之物质与形式,均应注意及之也。

原载:《国立中央大学教育行政周刊》 1928年第73期

在上海家庭日新会上的演讲①

（上海）家庭日新会于昨（25日）下午3时，在霞飞路1048号周宅，欢迎中央大学副校长戴志骞博士，及新自美归国之沈公健博士，到者戴、沈二君外，有陆礼华、彭望芬、周静涵、沈叔逵、潘仰尧等五十余人。首由主席周静涵致欢迎词，次戴、沈等演讲，关于改造新家庭之欧美办法，极有价值。直至6时始散会，兹将演词录下：

戴志骞演词略谓

二十年来南北奔走参观，观察中，每有不愉快之感想。自庚子以来，种种情形，均觉有改革之必要，可是军备、铁路、轮船、矿业、教育等等，在中国试行总无进步，甚至失败者比比，何以在外国行之甚好，而一至中国，动辄无效者，此则最为扼腕。因之颇有人以为种种失败，无一不由于缺乏人才所致，而造就人才之学校，其情形尤可慨叹，推究最大原因，实在家庭。德国（育）之教育，不外三点：（一）厨房。妻子欲得丈夫的欢心，不但知其心，（亦能）知其肠胃。（二）教堂。（三）幼稚园。中国最坏之习惯为"随便"，外国民族之精神，在一定的仪容内，如果未得其好处，先学其坏处，那便糟了。如小孩子买物时随便取物，其母非但不禁，反加奖励，此种影响甚巨。今日救济教育之失败，当从女子教育始，从幼稚教育始。吾东游丹麦，其儿童图书馆之发达，至为敬佩，家庭教育发达，学校教育，易见功效。所谓贤妻良母主义，实为颠扑不破之说，将来改良教育之责任，当惟家庭之贤妻良母是赖，对于日新会实有无穷之希望。

（下略）

原载：《申报》 1929年8月26日第17版

---

① 【编者注】原题目为"昨日欢迎两博士纪 中大副校长戴志骞 新自美归国沈公健博士"，现题目为编者所加。

国立中央大学半月刊发刊词

【编者按】戴志骞于1929年2月兼任高等教育处处长,1929年5月任国立中央大学副校长,他倡导学术,鼓励创办学术刊物,此文为1929年10月16日出版的《国立中央大学半月刊》创刊号的发刊词。

自来好学深思之士,潜心研几之余,辄纵笔载述,或十年数十年,华首弥固,未敢自足,或兴到墨随,朝作夕竟,随时有修短,均是昭灼文明,觇国者每视一国出版事业之盛衰,断其国之隆替也。吾国承凋敝之余,干戈连年,潜修未遑,以云著述,可称仅有,方诸欧美各国,名篇钜著,汗牛充栋,岁新而月不同者,真不可以道里计。欧战以还,若德若英若美,名著辈出,如惠尔斯之世界史纲,汤姆生之科学大纲,司宾葛拉之西方文化之衰落,爱因斯坦之相对论等,尤昭昭在人耳目。迥视吾国著作之林,其真有价值,真能于学术上有所贡献者,能有几何,出版物如此,国事可知,有心之士,怒焉忧之。本校窃不自量,集全体师生之述作,出版半月刊一种,凡属研究有得之作,部(不)分学科,尽量登载。夫学问以观摩而益精,事业藉文字为传播,则斯刊之作,虽不敢谓于国家文化有所贡献,于国家建设有所裨补,而提倡高深之学术,发皇固有之文化,实具宏愿,凡诸明达,幸辱匡教。

原载:《国立中央大学半月刊》 1929年第1卷第1期

对于《国立中央大学日刊》今后之希望

(1929年1月1日)

今日何日,非青天白日旗由中国本部进而飞扬于久思收复之辽沈诸部后之第一元旦耶? 在此全国统一,训政开始,万众腾欢,普天同庆声中,而吾最高学府日刊,亦届两周岁诞辰。浩浩前途,亿万斯年,则今后使命之重大,可想而知,吾人应如何奋发努力,更不待言。爰就个人对于本刊之希望略贡刍荛,用质高明。

本刊过去之成绩,在传播校闻、交换思想、鼓励求知与发表诸方面所负之使命,尚称克尽厥职。唯严格论之,本刊既系中央最高学府之言论机关,其内容当如何宏伟充实,表现本大学之特殊使命,方足以矜式全邦。是则以往之本刊又仅为将来理想日刊之雏形而已,更何敢固步自封哉?诚以本大学为全国文化之中心,其任务之重大,在上次双十特刊校长之言辞中,已阐发其端矣。窃以为除本三民主义教育尽力实施外,其在增长学者研究方面,于领导学者对于正确思想之认定,鼓励学者对于精深学理之阐扬,均负有绝大使命,职是之故。将来本刊更当本此旨趣,分门别类,尽量搜辑是项材料,庶几成为新闻、思想、学术诸方面正确之指车,俾阅吾刊者今后工作有正轨可遵,不以寻常校刊相看也。

原载:《国立中央大学日刊》 1929年1月1日

在国立中央大学总理纪念周上的报告

(1929年3月4日)

【编者按】1929年2月,国立中央大学高等教育处张少函处长赴北平,戴志骞暂代高等教育处处长。5月国立中央大学校长张乃燕聘戴志骞为副校长,1929年3月至1930年4月,戴志骞曾多次主持国立中央大学每周举行的总理纪念周仪式,并发表讲话。

【张乃燕讲话】

此次本人欲报告者,可分两方面,述之如次:(一)建筑方面:(略);(二)行政方面:高等教育处长张少涵先生已接渠由平来函,不久即回,现请戴志骞先生暂代。(下略)

【戴志骞讲话】

张处长俟北平学潮解决后,即来校。现时暂由本人代理,惟本人甫由去年十一月到校,各种观察,完全凭个人之推测,容有隔膜之处,未必悉符事实。兹就对于学校及同学两方面,略贡希望之词,权作报告,分述之如次:

(甲)对于学校之组织上,可析言之如下:

一、现在中央大学,共分八院,同学数达一千九百余或至二千余人,在表面上观之,不可谓非发达之盛,惟就实际言之,不能以规模之巨大,即认为圆满。良以大规模之组织,非用严密二字以贯彻之不可。以全校论,最大之重心,固在校长,由是而分析之,一部分之重心,则在院长、主任。学问自当力求实在,而人格之陶冶,尤关紧要。故最妙全校应有密切之合作,(次)第组织上各院既各有重心,高等教育处系形成一互相配置之机关。

二、建设一层,顷聆张校长言,业已诸事毕举。惟就本人意见所及,经费之来源有限,并且得之匪易,譬如有款洋二百万元,不能完全充作费用,须与他项建设用途,定一相当之比例率,方称万全。并须由消费上极力撙节,将所余之款项,从事建设,尤属难能可贵,即如女生宿舍,将来亦须设法建筑。

(乙)对于同学方面,约言之如下:

一、学校如家庭,然同学对于教职员,莫善于事事相见以诚。就本人在校之经验,觉有大多数同学,尚能各以信孚相感,犹不免有极少数之人,偶染隐讳旧习。要知学校对于同学,既已视若家人,纵有为难之处,不妨直说。但令学校力所能及,无不为之设法臂助。又若学校应做的事,不必同学要求,自当毅然做去。不应去做的事,即有要求,亦万不能做,是故希望诸同学,嗣后凡有建议,须出于积极一方面,至于消极的批评,总以减少为是。

二、本人在张处长未来以前,虽任暂代期内,亦必负责处理一切,决不存五日京兆之想,推诿搪塞。

原载:《国立中央大学教育行政周刊》 1929年第83期

在国立中央大学总理纪念周上的报告

(1929年3月18日)

【编者按】1929年3月18日,国立中央大学在该校体育馆举行总理纪念周活动,主席张乃燕,行礼如仪毕,即由高等教育处长戴志骞报告。

【戴志骞报告】

今天纪念周,本请薛子良先生来校讲演,上星期五由兄弟与彼接洽,时薛先生方自豫、陕、甘调查灾情回京,当蒙允许,今日纪念周来校向诸同学报告豫、陕、甘灾情。讵今晨忽得来讯:谓今日将出席第三次全国代表大会,不能来校,以后无论何时见召,均可到校,同时并有函致张校长。以时间忽遽,另请殊觉不恭,故今日讲演只可暂付缺如。校事甚繁,本学期第一次纪念周时已报告概略,今日再以教务及内部整顿情形为诸同学告:

本校同学为数甚多,惟向无准确统计,故校外有以校内学生人数见询者,每苦无准确之答复。最近已统计就绪,京报上已为披露,诸同学阅京报者,当知其详。计截至最近为止,在注册组注册者,共一千五百二十人,此数商学院除外,因该院报告尚未到校,一俟函到,当即送登日刊也。以省别而论:江苏籍最多(九七五人),数近一千,辽宁省籍者一人为最少。以院别而论:除商学院外,计文学院二八〇人,理学院三〇四人,法学院三八一人,教育学院一二〇人,艺专科六〇人,体专科三四人,农学院六五人,医学院四二人,工学院二三四人,此为关于统计方面者。

至本学期所聘教授,日刊上虽略有记载,然语焉不详,兹将各院添聘教授作一详细报告:

理学院:(算学系)副教授朱公瑾,(化学系)郑兰华、曹任远(具副教授)。

文学院:(外国语文系)讲师张松度,(哲学系)讲师冯文潜,(史地学系)讲师叶来青、陈庆祺,(社会学系)副教授孙本文。

法学院:(经济系)副教授邵元冲、雍家源,(政治系)副教授梅思平,(法律系)于能模。

教育学院:(教育系)副教授张耀翔、赵迺传、顾树森,(艺术学系)讲师邱广。

农学院:代院长王善佺,副教授唐仰虞、唐启宇、孙恩麐,讲师曾宪章、宣霞章。

工学院:(土木科)副教授沈在善,(电机科)副教授杨简初,(机械科)副教授钮因梁,(建筑科)副教授卢树森,(化工科)主任曾昭抡、副教授贺闿。

理学院院长一席,原拟请孙洪芬先生担任,惟孙先生已赴平就文化事业委员会之聘,本校曾五次电促来校,并函任叔永、赵元任两先生婉商,至今理学院长问题延未解决。因此院内教授缺少,不敷分配,前曾走访王季梁先生挽其来校,王先生已允担任分析化学及实验,并已到校授课矣。化学系主任,现请张江树先生担任,物理系主任,请方光圻先生担任。

上学期寒假中,理学院忽有许多教授离校,本学期已筹有妥善办法,教授任职问题拟提前四、五月内确定,以免开学时临时发生恐慌。至教授待遇,亦拟从长计议。现在国内好教授到处争聘,大率欲聘好教授应有两个(重)要条件:其一,地点优越,从前好教授集中北大,即因北大为京都所在,现本校地处首都,地点优越,故聘请好教授较诸其他大学为易。其二,设备充实,教育部拟在汉西门筹建中央研究院,将来于本校教授研究上殊多便利。此外,教授薪俸过菲不可,然尚非主要条件也。

本(大)学现拟组织委员会,讨论学则问题。讨论学则,断不可拘泥于死的不适用的章程。例如:同学欲请假回里结婚,而请假条例,不许其结婚,于事实上必不适用也。现在本校学则,多系东大沿留下来者,不适用处甚多,亟待改弦更张,以谋根本彻底之改革。

吾人一方面,固应努力建筑事业之进行,他方面应已就成之建筑物中充实其设备。除从前已经报告者不计外,现在图书馆中水汽管,业已装置,数日后即将试验一次,今冬可以应用。再者校内自来水,敷设完竣后,于卫生工程,当有一番改进。将来拟设,两压浴器,以便同学运动后沐浴之用。厕所亦亟待改良,用自来水冲涤,拟先就图书馆地下装设新式厕所,将来逐渐推行于各处,以谋天雨时同学之便利。现在开学未久,各事纷至沓来,一俟少暇,即当会同张校长赴各宿舍实地调查,何者应兴,何者应革,以便积极进行。新校舍落成后拟用铁床,因木床既不雅观,复易损坏也。要之一切建设事业,假使学校经济可以办到者,无不努力做去!

化工科近以制革需用皮料一千元,其他设备一千五百元,图书馆编印目录需用一千五百元,凡此皆在预算以外,而属必不可省者,应请校长设法筹划。本学期开学已过两周,同学中颇能作积极之建议,殊堪欣慰!今后望再随时建议,在可能范围之内者,无不酌量采纳也。

原载:《国立中央大学教育行政周刊》 1929 年第 86 期

在国立中央大学总理纪念周上的报告

(1929年4月1日)

【编者按】 1929年4月1日,国立中央大学在学校体育馆举行总理纪念周活动,戴志骞任主席。

【戴志骞主席讲话】

诸位同学,在演讲之前,有数事欲向诸君报告:度诸君必不愿闻此项报告,顾以集全校同学于一堂之机会,极为难得,故纵诸君不愿闻,亦不得不趁此机会为诸君告也。余今日在此,并非责备诸同学,乃希望诸同学,能帮助学校进行一切!我校建筑,虽不能称为庄皇典丽,然范围甚广,校内人杂,常有失窃破坏等不幸事发生。此不能责备诸君!然深望诸君能协助学校注意防范查察!

今日报告有三点:

第一点,日来天气渐趋温暖,为防制蚊蝇等虫害计,拟就各宿舍等处装制纱窗。纱窗装制后,或有些微不方便处,然终望诸君能注意爱惜,勿任意损坏!

第二点,言之殊为痛心!图书馆中,因从前电灯不明,因另装台灯,上加绿罩以防有损目力,不图日来频有窃去灯泡,并损坏绿灯罩事发见!似此举动,直使以后许多设备不敢着手。此或由于门岗不严之故。此后拟整顿门岗,加紧防察,如有此项事件发察后,非本校人交公安局法办,如系本校者,另订惩处办法。

第三点,校徽现有铸就运到,刻正赶制练子,一星期后当可分发。至于分发手续,则由事务组拟订,另行通知。此后一切闲杂人等,无故概禁通行!虽不能说"校内重地,闲人莫入",然亦不可无相当限制。终求一方(面)能使教职员学生便利,一方面于外来人等,不可不加防备。此事虽属积重难返,然学校非一二人之学校,乃二千余人之学校,大家肯努力,则事无不举矣。校徽颁发后,诸君如偶尔忘带校徽,望婉言向校警声明,最好能勿忘佩带,庶几校外人无可冒充也。总之,学校当局于应进行各事,无不努力,但不得不嘱属望诸同学能帮助进行,消弥前此缺憾。

今日报告已毕,请龚贤明先生演讲!龚先生于时事观察极深,诸同学上次已经聆悉,诸同学关心时事,谅必乐闻也。现在请龚先生登台演讲。

(下略)

原载:《国立中央大学教育行政周刊》 1929年第88期

在国立中央大学总理纪念周上的报告

(1929年4月22日)

【编者按】 1929年4月22日,国立中央大学在学校体育馆举行总理纪念周活动,由高等教育处长戴志骞任主席。

【戴志骞主席报告】

希望同学注意三事:

(一)本校面积广辟,人数众多,近查外间时有人来校内赛车骑马,草地道路,俱为损坏,不能不加以限制,现为慎重门禁起见,凡外人入校者,须经校警询明后方得通行。闲杂人等,无故不准入校。希望全体教职员、同学,皆佩戴徽章,以资识别。

(二)据图书馆报告,孙本文先生指定人口统计班参考之《东方杂志》中有数篇,竟被撕去,阅书者川流不息,管理员安能一一监视?此事虽不能确定是校内同学所为,但亦不能说一定非校内同学。堂堂大学生,如有此不道德之行为,诚可引为憾事。现图书馆除筹周密办法保护,并将被撕书籍,揭出篇章,陈列馆内,俾众周知外,并望同学尊重公德,共同爱护。并振作勇气,告发败类,以除众害,不宜有"自扫门前雪"之观念也。在欧美各国图书馆,凡偷书撕书者,须受刑法处分,拘禁一月。盖此关乎社会公益,非严限不可,希同学注意焉。

(三)本校定于四月二十七日举行春季运动会,五月中旬江南大学运动会又将在校举行,希望同学踊跃参加。虽不能参与比赛,而加入跑一跑、跳一跳,亦可鼓运动员之勇气,助兴不少也。

关于校务之报告,暂止于此,现请教育部普通教育司长朱经农先生讲演。朱先生之学问道德,同学早已深悉,毋庸介绍。朱先生本日须赴北平,于万忙之中,指教吾人,谨致谢意。继由朱先生演讲。

(下略)

原载:《国立中央大学教育行政周刊》 1929年第91期

在国立中央大学五三纪念仪式上的报告

(1929 年 5 月 3 日)

【编者按】1929 年 5 月 3 日,国立中央大学本部在体育馆举行五三纪念仪式,主席戴志骞。

【戴志骞主席报告】

今年是"五三惨案"的一周纪念,回想到去年今日,诸位得到惨案消息后,一定是悲愤填膺,非常愤慨,当时各地纷起组织反日会,全国各地民气,激昂异常,各地努力反对日本侵略,实行对日经济绝交,论功应归诸各地青年者为多。今天早晨听到一个消息,诸君或已看报知道,就是久未解决的宁案、汉案和济案,已经在昨天晚上签字协定,从此暂得一个结束。在六个月以前,上海日本馆事夏达(译音)因为签订中方所提草案,被日本政府开缺,经过中国方面六个月继续不断的努力,听说这次双方正式签订的内容,仍旧同六个月以前中国所提的一样,这样的圆满解决,可以说完全是国内青年们一致努力的结果,去年本校同学在首都领导民众,积极反日,工作极紧张,所以今天举行"五三惨案"一周纪念尤有意义。在此一年中,全国反日运动,始终各一,从前外国人往往讥诮我们中国人"五分钟热度",可是这番已今非昔比,继续努力已有一年,且努力的程度,无不是以一年为已足,我们反对帝国主义的精神应当再接再厉,永久不断的努力。

今天请立法院委员、法制委员会主席焦易堂先生演讲,焦先生是党国先进,追随先总理革命多年,大家平日颇很知道焦先生的学问道德,无用多述,今天本校敦请到会,起初焦先生以连日开会极忙碌,辞谢,后经再三挽商,今天能得来校与诸位相见,实在是荣幸的事,现在就请焦先生演讲。

(下略)

原载:《国立中央大学日刊》 1929 年 5 月 6 日

在国立中央大学纪念五四运动大会上的演讲

(1929年5月4日)

【编者按】1929年5月4日,国立中央大学及首都各学校联合会在中大体育馆举行五四纪念演讲大会,主席团报告开会宗旨:(一)纪念过去光荣的五四运动。(二)请党国先进及曾参加民八(1919年)五四运动之学生领袖指示今后的方向。并请戴季陶、罗家伦、桂崇基、戴志骞等相继演讲。

【戴志骞先生演讲辞】

诸位同学,对于十年以前的五四运动,已经听到罗先生[①]详细讲过,兄弟今天只有很简单的两点,贡献给诸位。

第一点,从今日起,青年们要去做罗先生所讲的民众运动。兄弟在民众运动的上面,再加上两个字,改为民众救国运动。要诸位去指导民众,要诸位到城市以外、乡村中去指导民众。因为五四运动,并不仅在打倒曹、陆、章[②]。罗先生已经讲过,讲起远因来,自从鸦片战争,中国民众很感到帝国主义压迫的痛苦,于是大家努力民族自权运动。辛亥革命成功以后,在军事上变成北洋军阀专制,政治上人民更痛苦得欲哭无泪,但苦没有人去指导他们。五四运动,就是学生界第一次领导民众的表现。在五四以前国际上的交涉,外国人只知道中国政府,只要把政府钳制住了不生问题。五四以后,外国人才知道中国尚有民族的势力存在。我们现就在天天读总理遗嘱,但是取消不平等条约的工作,还是没有成功,如果要达到目的,必定要拿民众做后盾,而领导民众的责任,完全在诸位的身上。

第二点,五四运动以后,中国思想界发生了重大的变迁,对于人生观、男女平等、劳资协调,都发生了一种新思想,对于宗法社会、建设思想,发生了革除的观念,对于一切旧的文化,根本上发生疑问,但是对于合于过渡时代的新思想尚待建设。这种责任,责之其他民众是不兴的,惟有诸位青年能担当得了。今天奉赠给诸位的意见,概括说起来是两点,第一,领导民众救国运动。第二,建设足以适应环境的新思想。

原载:《国立中央大学日刊》 1929年5月7日

---

① 【编者注】即罗家伦先生。罗家伦(1897—1969),现代教育家。字志希,浙江绍兴人。1917年入北京大学,积极投身五四新文化运动。1920年赴欧美留学,1928年任清华学校首任校长。1932年任中央大学校长。

② 【编者注】即交通总长曹汝霖、币制局总裁陆宗舆、驻日公使章宗祥。

在国立中央大学双五节纪念大会上的致辞

(1929 年 5 月 5 日)

【编者按】 1929 年 5 月 5 日,是孙中山先生在广州就任非常大总统八周年纪念日,国立中央大学于是日上午在校体育馆举行纪念大会,请胡汉民先生演讲,戴志骞任主席,并致开会辞。

【戴志骞先生的开会辞】

今天是民国十年总理在广州就职非常大总统纪念日,这个纪念日,在革命的历史上,占很重要的位置,在民族生存上也有很大的关系。那时候的境光,非常恶劣,北方军阀的恶势力,正在鸱张;欧战刚完,有共管之说。在此严重的时期,故总理本大无畏的精神,召集非常国会,选举非常大总统,巩固革命的基础。今天特请党国要人胡汉民、余井塘先生来校讲演,余先生因事不果来,胡先生精通中西学问,对于革命,尤有悠久的历史,现在任立法院院长,预备宪政时期的一切工作。于百忙中抽空指教我们,非常革命,仅以至诚,代表学校,感谢胡先生。

原载:《国立中央大学日刊》 1929 年 5 月 6 日

在国立中央大学总理纪念周上的报告

(1929年5月6日)

【编者按】 1929年5月6日上午十一时至十二时,国立中央大学本部在体育馆举行总理纪念周活动,由戴志骞先生主席,率全体同学行礼如仪。

【戴志骞主席报告】

今天在未演讲之前,对于本校事业略有报告:

第一,关于建设方面的,生物馆业已开标着手建筑,诸君想已知道,校内马路,一到了下雨的时候,有几处很泥泞难行,亟待从事开浚阴沟,现在正在请工学院的先生们测量校外河道的深浅,计算将来校内阴沟中的水,能否向河内流去(因为有人报告,校外的河身要比图书馆的地下为低),每到了夏初,图书馆地下的积水,往往有二三尺之深,今后阴沟开好,一定可以免除前此困难。

商学院方面,上届行政会议已经议决,拨款购基,兴筑校舍。

农学院方面,在江浦县从前向棉纱联合会租借一片农场,现在该会已允出让,计共有田四百多亩,田价共一万四千余元。

大学本部,缺少礼堂及办公厅,开会和办公都感不便,张校长在外募捐,据说已经募到四万多块钱。大学本部,因为会计年度将届结束,预拟撙节其他用途,节省下来的钱,悉数充作建筑大礼堂的费用,总期于最短期内,把这一座大礼堂建筑起来。

第二,关于下半年计划方面,全校的各项章程,都正在预备重新修订一下,至于各院各系的计划,要请各院院长、各系主任帮忙擘划,希望能够在五六月以前,计划就绪,不要像从前,到了七八月之后,方才开始筹划。

此外,还有几件小事情,要请同学注意的,每逢纪念周或举行其他纪念仪式集会时,大多(数)同学很守卫生秩序,不过少数人应注意,下次开会时各带手帕,吐痰纳入帕中,不要随意吐痰。来听讲的同学们,既已到会,最好终会而去,即使因为时间过长,亦望在演讲告一段落时离席,如果有两个人以上的演讲,要走应该在第一人讲完的时候出去,否则中途纷纷离座,很是扰乱演讲者的思想,听演(讲)时,务须将帽子脱(掉),凡此,虽然多属小节,然而与秩序有关,要请大家注意。

今天本校特请史尚宽先生演讲,史先生从前留学日本,后来又遍历法、德各国,现任立法委员,担任民法及劳动法的起草,今天的讲题是:劳动法概观。史先生读书很多,工作亦很多,史先生实行他的和农工接近的主义,所以住在洪武门外的乡间,前次我为了本校请史先生演讲,特地跑到史先生的府上去,史先生正在外面和工友们一起工作,他的精神我们很佩服的,今天能请史先生来此,实深荣幸。

原载:《国立中央大学日刊》 1929年5月7日

在国立中央大学总理纪念周上的报告

(1929年6月11日)

【编者按】 1929年6月11日上午十一时至十二时,国立中央大学本部在体育馆举行总理纪念仪式,主席副校长戴志骞,率领全体同学,行礼如仪。

【戴志骞主席报告】

建筑方面,生物馆即日动工,以说明书寄将洛氏基金委员会去后,曾接到捐款五千元,其后当再陆续设法。

礼堂亦拟于十日内开标,然江苏省政府方面,建筑费迄未领到,校长曾拟捐四万元,然亦同洛氏基金,不建筑此项房屋,亦当不捐纳此款也,故当冒险为之。即当开标动工,再议其后。此项建筑,若告成功,则开会可以有一定之地点,然后再肆力宿舍。关于宿舍现在计划十所,每所能容二百五十人,则十所当可容二千五百人矣。

下学年计划,理学院长七月回校,各主任、各教授及课程,皆于暑期前早定,当不似十七年度局促也。唯计划虽有,无经济仍不能实现。江苏省于本大学经费之供给,困难异常,如江苏实拨教费三百五十万,本校用百六十八万,外人不察,咸以本校滥用为口实,农工各院实各年支十三万元,竟有浦乱听闻之事,有谓本校每一学生年费公帑五千元,然实在计之,每人只四百九十八元耳。与他校较,北平大学每月须三十一万元,本校则月糜十万零八千元,清华每一学生,年须二千元,实皆倍蓰于我。苏省每年于本校以六万五千元之建筑费,然终不可得也!下学期仍有一事足为恐慌者,即苏省府会议,十八年预算案中教费,中等学校占二百八十万元,扩充教育占七十万,三百七十万元中,仅此所余二十万,以之充大学经费,用办一院犹不足乎,况全校乎。其声言以国款办国校,省款办省校,未尝不合理论,然当财部罗掘既穷之中,且攫捲烟税以为己有,积欠本校至六十万元者,殊无办法。再上海屠宰牙税每年可得百万元,中央、地方争执良久,结果因地方代征,征而不付,奈何奈何!

下年计划之实施,于此学期将了时,约略言之,然非暑间努力交涉,使根本有立,计划诚难实现也!

明日,在去年大学院公布学历,曾订放假一日,惟今年奉安①后,中央政治会议议决,推翻前案,故本校方面,曾以此询教部,教部答以此次议决,系属机关方面者,非对学校,当未规定以前,仍因昔规,放假一日。

再本学期虽较长,然学校制则,不容轻改,曾以此旨达各学院,非特别事故者,不得提前考试,致引纠纷。盖规定早立,自当依排定日期举行考试,计七月十日放假,毕业典礼择日举行之。

---

① 【编者注】1925年3月12日孙中山在北京病逝,1929年移柩南京,6月1日在南京举行葬礼,亦称奉安大典,葬于紫金山南麓。

本日并请本校副教授胡文炳先生演讲,胡先生系留学法国巴黎大学,研究法律经济者,继由胡先生登台讲演。

原载:《国立中央大学教育行政周刊》 1929年第98期

在国立中央大学总理纪念周上的报告

(1929 年 9 月 23 日)

【编者按】 1929 年 9 月 23 日,国立中央大学举行总理纪念周活动,由戴副校长主席,朱培基纪录,行礼如仪。

【戴志骞主席报告】

今日为开学后第二次纪念周,张校长在上次纪念周上,已将学校情形,详细报告。今日所报告者:

第一,院长方面。本学期略有变动。理学院院长请动物系主任蔡作屏先生代理,工学院院长请陈懋解先生担任,教育学院院长请韦捧丹先生担任,其余各学院均仍旧,各系主任及各教授亦略有更变。本年教授之聘请,大为不易。如物理系教授张钰哲先生,系研究天文专家,在美时本校即去电聘定,乃开学后,南开又一再争聘。其余尚有几位教授,亦有此同样情形,虽终未他去,亦可见得一教授之难矣。

第二,本校经费。照行政会议议决暂定一百九十二万,惟财政部之款,须自九月份起。将来全数领到后,对于三种费用必须增加:

(一)图书费,图书为研究学术最重要之工具,本校图书甚形缺乏,亟宜增加。

(二)设备费,视各院需要之程度而定,欠缺者尽先添加。

(三)建筑费,关于此层,有几点应当注意:

第一,现在校内建筑,均有具体计划。前东大时曾聘美人孟菲①,设计全校图样,现在新添建筑,大概均照此图进行。将来大礼堂建造时,平房宿舍须拆去。以后添造男生宿舍,集中于成贤街之东,即现在新宿舍附近,女生宿舍集中于来复女学一带。全校建筑,对于地形之高低,极应注意,现请工学院林教授作全校测量,不日即可完成。

第二,今年设立建筑委员会,建筑图样,必经该委员会审查,现在已经实行。如此次李工程师所绘大礼堂图样,光线声浪,均有未合,业经委员会审查,请李工程师重绘。

第三,本校拟创办小规模研究室,择各系设备较全者,尽先成立。本校毕业生经院系审查核准后,可以入内研究,暂时不收学费。又本学期本拟创办新闻学系,系主任一职,亦已聘请戈公振先生担任,后以戈先生不能专任,遂致停止,下学期或可成立也。新宿舍下月大约可以住入,惟现在宿舍中,校外之人,借住在内者颇多。现庶务组正在设法清查,望诸君予以援助。现在到校同学,除医、商两院外,据注册组报告,共有一千六百余人,已缴费者一千四百三十余人,已注册者九百零六人,其余之人请速注册,以便上课。最近浙省政府拟派送一百五十人至本校农学院肄业,闻不久即可决定,惟本校只能容一百人。

---

① 【编者注】即美国著名建筑师墨菲。亨利·墨菲(Henry Killam Murphy,1877—1954 年),美国建筑设计师,20 世纪上半叶曾在中国设计了雅礼大学、清华大学、福建协和大学、金陵女子大学和燕京大学等多所重要大学的校园,并主持了南京的城市规划。

本校系整个的,各学院情形,有使全校同学明了之必要,故以后拟请各院院长,轮流报告。今日先请工学院薛绍清先生报告。

原载:《国立中央大学日刊》 1929 年 9 月 24 日

在国立中央大学师长欢宴留京毕业同学大会上的致辞

(1929年10月17日)

【编者按】 1929年10月,成立南高、东大、中大留京毕业同学会,在成立会上,戴志骞发表了演说,10月17日,国立中央大学张乃燕校长、戴志骞副校长等在南京三牌楼国际联欢社宴请留京毕业同学会执行委员会部分委员,戴志骞致辞,号召毕业同学帮助母校建设。

【戴副校长致辞】

关于购地建筑毕业同学会所情形,刚才张校长已经报告过,我可以不必多讲,我所要讲的,是报告本校经费概况。本校经费自确定之后,各院院长已经开过会议,将来收数或多或少,均以比例成数分配,庶不致像从前东大一样,有争夺经费之举。我想将来毕业同学亦能如外国著名大学之毕业同学一样地帮助母校,则不管他一个月拿到两万块钱,就是只拿到两块钱,亦是不要紧的,所以我很希望诸位毕业同学,对于本校的发展,能极力帮助。

原载:《国立中央大学日刊》 1929年10月21日

在国立中央大学总理纪念周上的报告

(1929年12月9日)

【编者按】1929年12月9日,国立中央大学举行总理纪念周活动,由戴副校长主席,行礼如仪。

【戴志骞主席报告】

大礼堂图样,现由英国工程师打就,已经上星期六校务会议通过。该工程师经验甚富,所绘图样,对于声音光线,均称完善。堂中可容二千余人,所需经费,约二十余万,现已决定本学期内动工,明年暑假前落成。

又本校八学院,均已有负责之人。现在各项规程,亦已逐渐完成,以后院与院及院与处之关系,皆有明文厘定,行政上可不致紊乱。至于国内有名教授,当更努力徐图罗致也。

再唱校歌一事,务请诸位注意,校歌之词与谱,均极清雅,惟音调略高,不易唱习,如能熟习之,自亦不难。此事在公共集会之时颇关重要,望诸位切勿忘却。继由孙本文先生演讲"文化改造与优生政策"。

原载:《国立中央大学日刊》 1929年12月10日

在国立中央大学总理纪念周上的报告

(1929 年 12 月 30 日)

【编者按】 1929 年 12 月 30 日,国立中央大学举行总理纪念周活动,由戴副校长主席,行礼如仪。

【戴志骞主席报告】

今日系本年最末之纪念周,普通商店,均于年终时结一总账,以见盈亏,现在鄙人亦总汇一年本校进行概况,作一简括之回忆,以与他年比观,望同学们有以自勉焉。

物质方面,本年度比上年进步,颇为显明,如新教室、新宿舍之建筑,自来水、热汽管之设备,均在本年内落成,因而物质环境,改善不少。但此种进步,并非最关紧要。鄙人所以首先将其提出者,不过为叙述上之便利而。

学术方面,本年度亦较上年进步,出版物如半月刊及丛书等,均为今年所产生,现在丛书之付印者,已达五六种,半月刊已出至第五期(本学期内出到第八期),且该刊稿件,非常拥挤。如文艺专号稿件,已选中再选,而仍有过剩,此可见同学对于学术热心,实为可喜现象。至于同学功课方面,鄙人日昨曾与各院长及系主任谈起,均觉本年程度,比往年整齐,亦引以为慰也。

学校管理方面,就鄙人所经验者,确较往年为有系统,虽尚有多事未能尽如人意,而以后逐步改良,颇觉头绪厘然。以上各点,均较往年进步。然亦有两点不如去年者,一即经费问题,一即毕业生之出路。此两事皆受大学区制取消之影响,因而时有捉襟见肘之困难,此种困难则有待今后之战胜者也。

关于操行方面,尚有数事提出,请同学自勉。假造文凭,非独有关道德,抑且触犯刑网,希望以后不再发见。匿名揭贴,攻击个人,或送匿名信于教授,均与学校声名有关。以后如对某教授怀抱不满,尽可直陈当局,当局必能设法改善,务望勿出以卑劣手段为要。又图书馆书籍,不得私自携出,久已悬为定章。取缔办法,以后当更从严,方能保持公共利益,亦望同学特别留意。

今日请文学院院长谢次彭先生演讲,谢先生留法十七年,擅长戏剧,法国文坛上,且负盛名,现得聆其演讲,欢幸之至!

原载:《国立中央大学日刊》 1929 年 12 月 31 日

在国立中央大学总理纪念周上的报告

（1930年3月10日）

【编者按】 1930年3月10日，国立中央大学举行总理纪念周活动，由戴副校长主席，行礼如仪。

【戴志骞主席报告】

演讲之前，鄙人有四事为诸君报告：

一、大礼堂建筑工程，已于上星期六开标，标价系照最小之数决定，但连同钢骨、窗户、座椅等设备，已逾三十五万元，比照原定预算，约超过五万余元之谱。张校长对于经费筹集，颇感困难，现拟援广东省政府之例，向其他各省政府募款，一面并向蒋主席捐募。庚款委员会方面，亦拟请款，以资挹注。大礼堂两翼房屋，现因经费关系，暂不建筑。堂内蒸汽管及卫生管，亦留待经费充裕时装设。建筑地基，因依照学校将来全部计划，须与科学馆、图书馆等保持适当距离，比原定地址，移后五十五尺，故开工后，第一宿舍第一进东首之一部分房屋，及前面一部分走廊，皆须拆除。所有该屋内原设之阅报、办公等室，当设法移至他处。

二、明晚本校特请美国培琪氏演讲，（培琪）氏于明日始可到京，校中已去函邀请。诸君听讲时，请注意秩序为要。

三、体育之于人生，颇关重要。大概北方体育，比南方发达。吾校亦受风气影响，运动方面，不甚优良，希望全体同学，一致注意，踊跃参加，练成优胜队伍。

四、十二日为总理逝世五周纪念日，是日上午九时，本校在体育馆举行纪念式，然后须在体育馆前集合，由指挥引导赴飞机场参加纪念典礼，各人需要黑纱，可向庶务组领取。今日特请乔万选先生演讲"法律与自由"。乔先生系内政部司长，并兼本大学副教授，学问渊博，向为同人所钦敬，今得莅临讲演，殊深荣幸。

原载：《国立中央大学日刊》 1930年3月11日

在国立中央大学总理纪念周上的报告

(1930 年 4 月 28 日)

【编者按】 1930 年 4 月 28 日,国立中央大学本部举行总理纪念周活动,由戴副校长主席,行礼如仪。

【戴志骞主席报告】

本校春季运动会,已于上星期六举行,成绩甚佳。撑杆跳高,且能打破全国记录,此实可喜之事。不过鄙人尚有须请诸君注意者,即张校长在运动会特刊上所提出之普遍的健康与团体的训练二点。健康生活与学业颇有关系,英谚云:"All the work without Play makes jack a dull boy",故健康之体格,非求之于少数运动员,且当求之于全体同学。上星期六定上午八时开运动会,等半小时,始开会。其时除运动员外其他同学到者甚少,当知学校每在春、秋两季开运动会,并非专为运动员运动,尤望多数同学参加,即不参加,亦须及时临场参观,以鼓励运动,增进一种活泼之精神。

本校运动风气,较南北各大学为逊。今后全校师生,均当各尽其责,努力发扬,使健康得普遍之增进,而学业亦因此有不断之发展。再纪念周之用意,原所以使全校师生,有每周一度之聚会,除纪念总理之伟大人格,及吾人对党国应尽之责任外,并可聆普通之讲演,以补功课之不足;同时全校师生,聚于一堂,精神方面,不无油然兴奋之处。故纪念周之意义,在学校生活上,殊为重大。在校同学,望勿忽视为要。今日特请农学院院长王尧臣先生演讲"近十年中国农业上之变迁"。王先生对于此题,曾作精确之调查。现得莅临演讲,必有宏论,以启迪吾人也。

原载:《国立中央大学日刊》 1930 年 4 月 29 日

《国立中央大学学生会刊》序

本大学学生团体,向只有各院学生会、各宿舍学生会之组织,其范围仅及于一学院一宿舍;自本年度上学期开学之始,全校同学感于大团体精神之不可或缺,于是群相应求,而有整个的中央大学学生会之组织,于十八年十一月十二日"总理诞辰"宣告第一届代表大会成立继续进行,以迄于今。当第一届代表大会成立之日,同学且举行同乐大会,以相庆祝,于追念伟人之中,附带而为团体成立之纪念,吾同学之所以重视此学生会,而期以为党国之扶助者,其用意概可想见。

学生会之组织,其注重在自治二字;最近中央颁布法令,学生会须正名学生自治会,亦以此也。大学学生为各级学生之领袖,就学校方面管训而言,为大学学生者尤须扩重自治。自治之能力,贵在锻炼,苟不锻炼,势必以放荡不羁为自由,同人自由过度扩张,而团体之自由反以退缩,其结果仍不能得自由,故必能自治而后能自由。民族之恢宏,民权之发展,胥由此致。学生会之产生、代表讨论开会等等,皆须遵守会章,服从公意,正极好练习自治之机会也。练习熟则使用易,他日出而参预国事,指导社会,必能游刃有余,斯大学学生会之使命一也。

大学生受高深教育,所得之各种知识较广,又已身未入社会,观察社会状况亦较为纯洁而无私,推己立,立人己达,达人之惜,应将一己所得,贡献于学术界,贡献于社会,引起社会上民众对于学术之趣味。故大学生除研讨学术修养、自治能力外,尤必对社会有一种优良之贡献,对民众为学术上之先觉,方不负国家、社会之培养。此所贡献,不离刊物,而所出之刊物,要贵精确真实,而有学术上相当之价值,以表现高深之智识,斯大学学生会之使命二也。

本校学生会成立以来,业经数月,凡所以增进全校同学自治能力,兴起同学专心研究学术,以达上文所述之第一种使命者,既于历次会议中练习而进行矣。今又将各种研究之结果,汇集刊行,谨献社会以合乎上文所述之第二种使命,而问序于余。余意同学诸君,既知学生会地位之重要,必能确尽其应负之责任,而有以副社会人士之期望。凡所刊行,精确真实,无愧首都学府之名。爰于其刊行之始,敬志缘起,并述个人之所希望,以为之序。

中华民国十九年四月　戴超

原载:《国立中央大学学生会刊》 1930 年第 1 期

银行事业篇

东北经济问题

【编者按】1930年7月,戴志骞辞去国立中央大学副校长之职,8月赴哈尔滨,9月任哈尔滨工业有限公司经理。1931年7月,戴志骞从东北回到上海,参加由孔祥熙发起成立的"工商管理协会"在联华总会举行第十三次聚餐讨论会,并演讲东北问题。1931年12月潘文安、殷师竹翻译出版神原周平(日)所著《日本经济与中国东北问题》,在序言中,潘文安写到:"最近吾遇到两位朋友,都是熟于东北情形,积有研究的,一位是戴子骞(超)博士,一位是何醉帘(廉)博士,他们研究东北,是十分深切,观察东北,是十分精细。"他记录了戴志骞谈到的东北问题。题目为编者所加。

戴先生说:

到了沈阳,便知东北之大,过了长春,到了哈尔滨,更知东北之富。到了那边,正是什么都有。在车上,举目远眺,两旁黑土,沃野千里,恍如置身沪宁、沪杭车上,桑麻万顷,到处黄金,比那津浦线的黄土,和西北铁道的灰色土,真是大大不同。东北唯一的产物,便是大豆,大豆在东北,即是金钱;东北的财源,都是靠此。去年大豆没有销路,钱也没有了。东北的经济,也入于窘乡了。

东北有那样的财源,而目前东北人还这样的穷困,似乎有些矛盾,其实便由国人向来不注意东北问题的缘故。这大概由:(一)国人大都对东北不肯切实研究,观念中完全对于东北不了解而起的误会。(二)东北的人民,一大半由山东等地移殖去的,所以智识太差,程度多幼稚。(三)关外人不信任关内人,不免有排斥意味,而关内人好弄聪明,常常行诈使骗,以致不为东北人所信任。

在黑龙江省的煤矿很多,比了抚顺的还要质地良佳,而矿区也大,这是有人调查而证明过的。森林农产,那边什么都有的。而金矿在黑龙江,尤其是世界闻名久了。东北有这样的富源,而现在穷得这个地步,实在不知开发之故。现在黑龙江的富源开发的,不过十分之一,吉林不过十分之五,辽宁十分之七,黑龙江什么都比吉、辽二省好,可惜没有人去。

关于经济问题,在东北的利息,是很厚的,通常二分的利息,是法律所许可的。回看南方,上海、广东等地利息很薄,那么为何不投资到东北去呢?在东北呢,因为关内的人很少,他们那边没有一定的币制基金,所以发行了几种不兑现的纸票,因而日本人的金洋,操纵了全东三省,这也在关内的人不去的缘故。如果关内能把兑现的银洋,去改造他们的币制,日本人的金洋,也可打倒。所以现在我们应该有严密的组织,准备到东北去,要知道东北,不但日本在积极的谋我,侵略我,就是俄国也决不肯放弃,他们知道东北是很富的,所以老早就想来谋我了,百年来对于黑龙江的侵略,锐意经营,不遗余力,整个的东三省,被双重帝国主义的践踏觊觎,其危殆的程度如何啊?所以要讲到东北,便不可不知道她现在处境的危险,更不可不知道必须要由关内的人去经营,才可以谋她危险程度的渐次降低。譬(如)大豆应该用什么方法去救济改良,以恢复这一宗大生产,矿产的调查开采等等,都是极重要而宜急行的事。有了这样的土地,禁止别人的去,是不妥当,因为你不去,人家要代你去啊。如果我们切实地能把东北的富源开掘,则无论投资在金融上、实业上,我们的资本决不会亏折的。况且那边的利息,是非常之厚,这实在是一件自助、助人、助民族、助国家的一件事。

至于日本的侵略我们,自然比了俄国更厉害,我国向来是以农立国的,在东北种水稻的,本来只有山东人,可是日本驱使韩人,也来抢种,这几年从水稻上被他们获的利息,实属不小。这次万宝山事件①,也全是强抢的冲突啊。譬如这种高丽人,到了那块田中,日本的警察,也就跟了来,狼狈为奸,其心太恶,所以这种高丽人的所至,就是日本势力的所及。因为如此,所以我们要谋交通的建设,为最要的一点。东北的铁道,如果努力进行,何尝不可以打倒日本的南满势力。所以我主张:(一)我们当认清东北的事,非由本部的中国人去帮同整理不可。(二)改良那边的经济与投资,如果说那里的经济制度改良了,即以投资地产而论,其利息也有二分半至三分之厚。(三)是移民,有组织的移民,是急需的,黑龙江省仅开垦了十分之一,余则都是货埋于地,宝藏未辟,土地是你的,必须要你自己去,必须要使那块土地,完全真正成为你的,那么你何致为暴日侵略到这般地步?

原载:张研,孙燕京主编 《民国史料丛刊》 225
《政治·对外关系》 大象出版社 2009 年

---

① 【编者注】1931 年九一八事变前,中国人郝永德将农田违法转租给朝鲜人耕种水稻,朝鲜人开掘水渠,截流筑坝,损害了当地农民的利益,中国政府干预,日本警察强行到现场"保护朝鲜人",为发动侵占东北三省的战争制造舆论。

人与事

戴志骞讲　陆贻记

这是中国银行人事科科长戴子骞博士[①]所发表的意见,中间指示青年职业上不少的途径,是一篇很有价值的著作。

职业指导,有很长的历史。譬如中国从前考八股,以定官职,就是一个例证,这不但中国如此,就是世界各国,也是如此。不过以前的方法,和现在的不同罢了。从前的方法是以事就人,不是像现在以人就事的。从前的方法好像用一只绷筛去筛择豆米,不管三七二十一的,所以这种方法,于学理上讲来,是不合逻辑而有弊病的。职业指导有新的觉悟,是在1900年。正式成立职业指导所,在1907年。当时美国纽约有个波森氏,他见每日踯躅街道之失业儿童及成人就发生感触。后来,他就设法训练他们,再介绍他们去从事于相当的工作,这就是职业指导所的滥觞。最近二十年来,世界各国,对于职业指导事业,都有相当的注意。即关于职业指导事业的国际会议,也已开过三次。尤其对于职业指导方面,着重于个人的本能,并不着重于机关的本身,这也是一个小小的变迁。当工业时代,盛行泰娄氏的科学管理的方法,这个方法是注意于三个部分:一、组织的改进,二、工具的改进,三、对于人的工作,如何使效能增加至最高度,而如何把消费减至最低度。而这三部中,尤以最后的一个为最重要,因为如果有了好的组织,好的器具,但若没有好的人去干,那么试问有什么效果呢？因为人的选择,占着最重要的地位,于是职业指导也增加他的重要性了。譬如制造自由车工厂中,最难的一部工程,就是选择轮轴的珠子。这种珠子,在我们这般普通人手上遴选起来,差不多觉得每粒都是圆的,而在一般感触较强于常人的工人手中经过时,立可分别其圆正与否,而定其取舍。这就是因为这种工人,有这样的本能,再加以训练,那么就可达到效能大、消费小的产业原则。欧洲大战,可谓科学战争。科学方法,最重要的原则,就是把人用在相当适合的地方,当时美国临时征集百万大军,至欧洲作战。当征集时,军界方面聘了许多大学校的心理学教授,来选择这般志愿从军的健儿,用了种种测验,分别派定其入飞机队、陆军、炮兵、交通队、辎重队等。欧战以后,职业指导,又有进一步的新发展,因为有许多因战争而成残疾的人,要有相当的安置。世界各国本来以为欧战可以解决世界上各种问题,而结果呢,不但不能解决问题,并且酿成更难解决、更复杂的状态。各种竞争,比较战前更为厉害,事业的人更是一天天的增加,所以对于选择人的问题,更是注意。讲到选择人的问题,就是先要明了机关本身的分析,究竟要用具有何种特长的人,譬如电话公司的接线生,则应用听觉力、耐力较长于常人的人。信差,则有特别走路的技能,薄记员,则应有明晰的头脑、不苟且的精神。经理则应有组织力,有判断力、勇毅的精神。经理对于所用的人应有深切的了解,常常去做访问的工作,第二步应多去观察。说到问呢,第一就是去问他自己,关于学历经验方面,不过这也不能完全信任,因为在现代,一个人自己讲的话,决不会十分正确的。第二

---

① 【编者注】即戴志骞。

就是去问他的教师或亲戚等,不过这也只能把这种材料做种种参考而已。第三就是观察,看他的能力。譬如电车公司要需用卖票员时,先叫许多人坐在一电车中,然后叫这应征的人,去周旋于各乘客之间,看他的活动能力如何。此外,就是现在各国所通用的测验。讲到测验的方法,那是很多的,现在我们也可不必去谈他。总之,一个机关,如果要用人,那么先要对于这机关中的事,有相当的分析,明了究竟需用具有哪种技能的人,那么这人将来做起工作来,可得心应手,而机关本身的业务,也可蒸蒸日上。从前美国某工厂内有一工人,在厂中的工头和工人,都说他不好,这所谓不好,就是他的脾气太坏。后来厂主叫这工人进来谈话,一谈有二小时,厂主极钦佩他的主张,就马上升他做了工头,管理全厂的工人。由此可见"用其所长",是发展各种机关业务的不二法门,现在世界各国对于用人,非常注意,惟有我国事事落后,仍是醉生梦死。有人以为我国地大物博,人口众多,可无亡国之患,其实人多而无用,仍依旧与无人一样。讲到多,则苍蝇蚂蚁,其数目之多,较人类如何?然试问有什么用处和能力?所以我国事事应急起直追,运用科学方法,注重职业指导,使各种事业能"人尽其才",使各种人都能"用其所长"。

诸位现在各机关中服务,有的也许不能发展自己的抱负,埋没本能,但也应一心一意忍耐着,等待着贤明的领袖。我觉得现在我们中国各种机关中,也都渐渐注重用人和职业指导,可见诸位的前途,并不是没有一些曙光的。再进一步说,我国各种事业尚在草创时期,将来的发展,比外国更大。愿诸位各就本业,从事努力于学术经验的修养工作!

原载:《机联会刊》 1932 年第 49 期

有业者乐业的理论和实验
——本能说的职业指导

职业指导,这个富有价值的问题,对于个人的经济发展、国家的前途昌盛,都有很密切的关系。有才而无业,或者有业而不能乐业,这种畸形社会象征,对于国家前途,实有莫大的戕害。所以无业者有业,有业者乐业的职业指导工作,对于"国"和"人"的两大单位上,都有重大的贡献。

在二十世纪尚未开幕,职业指导,就占据社会历史上的重要地位了。1907年,美国纽约富翁派森斯先生,目击许多踯躅街头的无业青年,很替本国社会担忧,他就送给许多书籍,供给他们自由阅读,后来,由"问"而"答"的结果,各人个性,完全熟悉。他便根据平时的本能调查,介绍以相当位置,成绩果然非常满意,从此,他们成为职业指导的开山鼻祖。

二十年来,世界各国,都先后成立职业指导机关,国际间也开过了几次关于职业指导的会议,此后对于职业指导,应当很快的进展了。欧战以前,工业时代,火车电车常常出险,研究下来,始知开车者犯了色盲病,红绿色分不清,以致误会信号,于是主事者拣选,能辨别得出颜色的人,才准他开车,这也算是职业指导史上的一页。

工业发达以后,潘以太猎希斯把职业指导分成三种要素:第一,良善工厂的组织。第二,工具的改进,这点,我们孔子也说过,"工欲善其事,必先利其器",所以工具的改进,确是重要的。第三,减少工作时间,增加工人读书机会。潘氏更认为第三部分人的问题最重要,我呢也深信"人"是一切组织中的重要分子,很像自行车工厂内,器具很好,组织也好,要拣一个精于判别自行车车球的人才最是要紧,最是困难。因为车球不圆,车子效用,势必减少的,所以职业指导中之"人的问题",诚为中心问题。

工业发达的原则,是出产要多,所费却少,然而要达到这种目的,不能不注意个人本能的职业指导。我们试看欧战时代,他们征集了许多兵士,其中有大中学毕业的学生、工商农夫,各种都有,聚集几种人在一起,训练上要多么困难?但是他们在最短期内,居然能够致用。那时我也在美国军营里,看他们请了几个著名的心理学教授,加以心理的测验,因此他们就很能明白各人的本能,何人应派飞机队工作,何人应派炮兵队服务,所以欧战期中,美国能有最大的贡献。欧战告终后,有的腿打坏了,有的手轰毁了,这些人的生活处置,不是一个很难解决的问题吗?然而他们仍旧根据各人实存的本能,量才录用,譬如眼睛尚可看的,便给以用目的工作,职业指导的本能说,到了那时实在已到最高的效用。直至1931年,世界趋重于商业竞争,竞争愈利害,更不能不注意本能,所以职业指导在今日,已成为最重要问题,而进展历史大概是这样。

测验本能的效果,归纳起来,可以人得其位,才得其用,确是有业者乐业的舟楫。

更进一步的讨论,我认为倘使职业指导要与社会发生最高效率,那么从事职业指导者,不但是要注意个人本能,并且要指导机关,因为机关的领袖,也须无大能力,尽可由专家分析机关和指导机关,否则还是不能达到最大效用的。即于分析个人本能,比较最普通的方法,有以下三种:

（一）发问　就是假借发问而得知个人的本能，他的学问，经济状况……但是有许多人，一时不便说，有的不愿说，结果你要知道的，还是没有知道，那么再用间接的方法，去问他的教师们，这虽是比较的进一步了，然而也有流弊，也许这个人，他的环境，他的性质，已经大大的改变了，所以这个方法，只可作一种辅助，只可说发问总比不问好些。

（二）观察　对于对方的一言一动，都加以实地的观察，去考察他的本能，而定事业上的需要；好像电车公司考试卖票员，就在开车时候，自己坐在电车上，观察他卖票的手术快慢，这种方法最为妥当。

（三）测验　这个方法，应用最多，是比较最好的方法，有了这样的科学职业指导，可以：

1. 依事的分析就可以指导所需要的是什么人才？
2. 这人本能，配做什么事，据我个人的经验，这确是最有效益的方法。

从前外国某纸厂，规模很大，工人很多，其中有一个工人，几为全体工人所排斥，经理考察了三四天，实在查不出什么缘故来，他的私德，他的工作，并无过失，不过和同事间的意见不同罢了。经理就召他去谈话，谈了二点钟，才知道所有的工人，不知进取，他是有意识的工人。他还说："假使采取我的方法，出产可以多，时间可以短，材料可以省"，经理立刻升他做工头，予以改革全权，果然过了一月，成绩已经可观，原来他是不善于工作，而善于思想的人物，才得其用，所以该厂才有今日的发展。

关于"本能说"的理由，我已介绍许多事实来证明。总之，无论何人，一定有可取的本能，不过用他的人不知道罢了。所以在上者要平时和他谈话，留意他的工作，各人都要用在适当的地位，庶几在雇员方面，可以才得其用，极力向他自己本位上发展，在雇主方面也可以得到各分子的优越成绩，这样才是职业指导最大目的。

现代的社会，真使人气沮！机关里紧要位置，一味的占据亲戚朋友，以致有才者，英雄无用武之地。结果，在机关方面，找不到好的人才，工作退化。所以职业指导，对于这些问题，确是要用学理或实验，来分析，来挽救。职业教育专家潘仰尧先生观察这种恶像，一时不易解决，便用缓冲的手段，对一般不能乐业的青年说："你们不要嫌薪金不多，其实最怕的，是你学问不够，经验不足。倘使你一心一德的做去，总有达到你希望的时候的。"的确，社会现象如此，倘使不离冲突地点，回到安全区域去，积极图强，反恐要发生意外之危险呢。所以，一般青年，既不要患失业，只怕你没有应世的学问，更不要患目前不能发达，须知学问上进，和职业上进是一个正比例的。况且中国已经有"使无业者得业，有业者乐业"的研究机关，尽力指导雇主和雇员两种阶级发展效用，同时，人才主义也已经有实行的趋势了。不见近来的银行工厂，有二千人以上，总有人事一科，这样看来，诸位只要努力做去，忍耐现状，决不会感叹"生不逢时"，要知道国家元气，丧失殆尽，吾人为国家着想，也应振奋精神，努力生产，增加国家的经济力量。何况青年尚在事业开始时代，岂能不以服务观念为事业信条？

原载:《通问月刊》　1931年第11期

戴志骞刘焘关于在东北接洽关盐两税情形报告

1932 年 6 月 3 日

【编者按】鸦片战争后,中国的海关大权一直掌握在外国帝国主义手中。英国作为老牌帝国主义国家在中国海关的角逐中一直占据绝对优势。九一八事变前,中国海关由上海总税务司掌管,由英国人负责。总税务司所辖各关的收入,直接用于清偿外债。总税务司在东北设有七个海关,下属六个分关,十个分卡。各关还设有海关监督公署,隶属于南京财政部关务署。海关虽然在形式上存在着两套相对立的领导机构,但实权掌握在总税务司手中。在东北,日本操纵"伪满洲国",向各海关派遣日本顾问,封锁税收,没收关税,而总税务司英国负责人向日本顾问屈从,使日本一步步夺取海关的税收权。至 1932 年 10 月,"伪满"政权将海关改为"税关"。自此,日本彻底劫夺了中国东北的海关。此篇为戴志骞等报告在东北接洽关盐两税的情况。

谨将在东北接洽关、盐两税情形缮具报告,陈候钧核。

甲、关税

一、营支行经收关税办法

营支行经收山海关税款,系于民国九年六月间由正金银行移转,与山海关税务司订有合同。惟正金银行以交还营口条款内订明,日本银行有储存税款之权,故另订有分存协定,凡本行经收税款,均按日分存该行,半数作为税务司正钞存款。至汇出时,再凭税务司支票提回并汇。

在营接洽情形

骞等于四月五日到营后,即查询营支行对抗强提关税经过,与其函电陈报情形尚属相符。监督署日顾问小泽因请示长春财政部尚未得复,故本行仍照常征收汇沪,惟被勒迫必须每日将收支数目报告监督署备案。并闻满洲政府规定四月一日以后,无论何种税收,均须归入新国家岁入项下。则本行业已汇沪之税款既已具报有案,万一武力强提,总税务司须予赔偿,否则本行损失堪虞。六日早,骞即偕营支行沈经理往访山海关税务司 Mr. SHAW,当与研究各事甚详。结果议定电陈总税务司请示,一面骞即分访代理监督及日顾问,亦允暂事观望再定。乃骞等离营后,长春财部即派顾问夏绍康到营,仍拟即将税款提归官银号。复经沈经理会同税务司、代理监督及日顾问与夏绍康会商,交换意见。结果税款暂存本行,不汇不提,以待解决。

二、安支行经收关税办法

安支行经收安东关税款,系于民国三年十月与安东关税务司订立合同,税务司将税款完全提归安东朝鲜银行存解。本行因与朝鲜银行订立协定书,除现镇银交存朝鲜银行外,其余以各币折合之银数,以日金交存该行,作为押金。所有现镇银向凭税司支票,向朝鲜银行提回做汇,而各币折合之银,俟汇交沪朝鲜银行后,始可收回押金。自今年起,税司改变办法,统合现镇银存入朝鲜银行。汇款时仍凭税司支票提汇,所有本行对于朝鲜银行缴纳押金一层,已无形取销。

在安接洽情形

四月八日晚到安东,因安东关税办法与滨、营迥殊,故安支行于接到长春三月二十六日部令后,即以本行只收不存函复关监督署,一面仍照常办理收税事务。九日,骞与安支行刘经理访安东关税务司 Mr. TALBOT,研究之后,认为彼方既无进一步之动作,自应照常办理。为维护税款计,骞当时即商之税务司,如彼方再来催提,最好由税司借用本行收税员自行收税以为抵制之计,安税务司允加考量。十日,骞等见日顾问崎川,其态度颇为傲慢,对关税手续亦极不明了,惟断然以本行不服从长春财部命令相诘责。经一再申明安东收税及税司存款办法,析辩历三小时,始略谅解,云请示长春财部再定办法。骞等离安东时,尚系照常收汇。惟夏绍康自营到安后,即径访税务司说明其使命,一面即与各方面会谈,勒令暂时不汇沪,亦不解长。刘经理当以税款向存朝鲜(银行)为辞,说明本行不能代为保管。夏即以违抗新国家命令相恫吓,几至决裂。继乃由夏与税司言明,税款改交本行代存,于是遂与山海关办法趋于一致。此骞等在辽宁时,据刘经理当面所述之实况推测,彼方必须迫令本行保管,恐即为将来强提改存东三省官银号地步。

三、滨行经收关税办法

滨行代收滨江关税款,系于民国十年四月间与滨江关税务司订立合同,连同爱珲等分关八处,收存汇解均由本行一并办理。

在滨接洽情形

滨江关监督署之日顾问加藤,较之小泽、崎川狡猾精刻,而税务司 Mr. PRETTIJOHN 对于本行地位初亦未加谅解。本行原以十分诚意帮同税司维护关税,首先税司那行收回自办,以防强提,未得容许,而日顾问已窥见本行隐衷,于是百端威胁,以危害本行东北全体地位为要挟,始有迫签党书及强制逐日将税款交东三省官银号之举动。骞于四月十七日到哈,十八日即偕卞经理同访滨税司,研究之下,幸蒙谅解本行困难,允暂止汇沪。其时日顾问一面亦已由哈市长鲍观澄介绍会晤税司,订明四月八日以后税款亦暂不解长,惟三月二十八日至四月八日之款必须要求税司开给关员职务、人名、薪水清单为交换条件,始肯缓提,否则并海关经费亦不允拨。税司知其意在接收,坚不肯照办。嗣经调停,由税司开给经费清单,内列内班薪水共若干,外班薪水共若干,日用杂费若干,加藤始允将经费照付,其三月二十八日至四月八日之税款亦即暂止汇长。至此则本行党书签字一节,即等于无形取消,三关一致办理,不汇不提,以待解决。所不同者,营、安税款存于本行,滨关税款存于东三省官银号,此则限于势力,无可如何也。

总之,三关收税办法原有差别,而对方手段强弱亦异,但本行尊重合同,委屈求全,力护税款之意,则绝无二致。滨关对方最难交涉,而滨行办理最为强硬,故结果被迫最烈。滨、辽两行陈报经过情形函电綦详,惟症结所在,实如上述,目下能办至如此地步,洵已煞费周章矣。

就接洽经过而推测其趋势,除大连关目前无问题,滨、营、安三关现均暂行停止汇解,将来彼方在短时期内必先取以下之态度,即(一)外债可以承认,内债绝对不认;(二)海关经费可以照给;(三)海关关员恐须经长春财部加一复委任手续;(四)关余归满政府收入。如再不能如(愿),必须提前强制接收。但即使照以上条件暂时默认,如仍无根本解决办法,听其自然,结果迟早亦必出于全部接收。此时不即接收之大原因,大抵为缺乏关员人才也。

乙、盐税

骞等到营口时,稽核分所业经运署接收,各处分局事务,亦均由各场公署接管,绝无转圜希望。经向长春、营口关系各方日人探询,其意大致谓:

一、满洲政府既以独立国家自居,与从前各省独立情形不同,当然不能容许其他国家之关、盐行政机关存在于其行政权之下。

二、据称,总所似未能明了目下东北之情势,亦为促成其提早接收稽核分所之原因。

三、关、盐外债部份,满洲国可以承认,惟须直接交债权团,不愿经过任何方面之手。此点并恐牵连国际承认问题,日人则不肯完全明示。

现在辽宁盐税之外债部份及三角附税,运署顾问永田虽曾口头允许仍交本行汇沪,三月份已汇来,四月份现正催汇,尚无复电。但以上述情形衡之,将来亦恐有变局。至恢复分所一层,在最近期间更恐不易着手也。

又,据长春财政部总务司长坂谷谈话,关、盐两税征收税款移转东三省官银号,自系当然举动,本行无权参预。并云:各地中国银行不遵长春财部命令,仍代南京政府汇沪税款,并多所奔走,现正对此搜集证据。如证据充分,或有没收本行东北全部财产之可能。虽属恫吓之辞,不能不事先慎防,合并陈明。

戴志骞 刘素
海关总税务司署档案

原载:《中华民国史档案资料汇编》 第 5 辑第 1 编《财政经济2》 1994 年

本行对于练习生的期望
——鲁行练习生谒师典礼训词之一

戴志骞讲　曹尔龙记录

　　今天为鲁行练习生举行谒师礼式，王经理前曾电请总经理莅青。总经理刚由南阳回沪，事繁不克分身，鄙人承王经理之约，代表参加，得此机会与诸位相见一堂，非常愉快。本行练习生指定业师训练，并规定谒师礼式，其中意义何在呢？盖以练习生均属青年，初入社会，如何服务？如何为人？若不绳以纪律，有误入歧途之虑，是在指导有人，表率有人，方能遵循走上轨道，所以前人对于师道与天、地、君、亲并尊。中国自革命以后，新思潮澎湃而来，礼教大防，因之溃决。一般青年，往往误解自由平等，非独师道之不讲，即父兄训诲之言，亦目之为顽固腐败，此种不良风气，纠正无方，社会遍受影响，遂致纪律荡然，紊乱日甚。世界上无论任何国家断无不守纪律之社会，而能长治久安者。如苏俄那样现状的国家，而革命亦能成功，因有"纪律"足以维持之也。至于个人持身涉世，亦何独不然？诸位舍弃学业来银行练习，自身固抱有一种希望，而为家长者希望之心尤切。银行顾念各家长之委托，以及本行人材之需要，训练责任，自属义无可辞。银行之学识经验，为练习生服务之要素，"言忠信，行笃敬"尤为练习生接近社会、处世为人之基础。凡此种种，非指定业师专任指导之则，不足以总其成。

　　北平教育界近来有句俗话：教授讲师，如同拉人力车夫一样，学生是坐车的大爷，教授讲师是拉车的车夫，坐车大爷说，要快拉，车夫就得快拉，说要慢，就得慢拉，学校教育破产到如此地步，再有什么尊师之道可说？至此当然有许多复杂原因。总之，先生权利微薄，学校纪律荡然，因此青年误入歧途者不少，工商界应以此为前车之鉴。

　　我国从来工商业收受生徒，向有拜师之礼，关于学徒言行宿食一切事宜，均由业师监督教诲之。又如英国牛津大学、剑桥大学，亦有导师之制，除担任日常功课外，每个导师必另率有七、八个学生，由其专任指导，立法甚为美善。本行从前对于练习生，本定有训练办法，现在指定业师，俾专责成。规定谒师典礼，用尊师道。精神、仪式并重，严格训练，以期诸生将来为本行之中坚份子，国家之善良国民。

　　诸位今日谒师后，诸事均有遵循，将来持身涉世，无不具有纪律化，胥于今日基之，但师资以外，友助亦不可无人，大凡人与人，人与事，有联络之关系，互助之精神，方能成功。譬如社会与国家，必先有良善之国体，一心一德，勇往迈进，然后始能有纯洁之社会，完整之国家。诸位到行练习有一年者，有二年、三年者，其后来之练习生，对于先入行者，均须表示相当敬意，因为到行既先一年，必多一年经验，咨询求教，足为他山之助。先入行者，遇事指告，互相友好，感情日密，团结之力，即由此生焉。

　　我觉得本行将来最为得力的，就是练习生。譬如带兵的官，收编他人军队，杂凑成军，必不足恃。必须亲自训练，情同家人，利害与共，始能成为基本军队。本行对于练习生，实事求是加以训练，亦是希望练习生养成纪律化的基本行员，将来与本行发生一种不愿相离之关系。

　　诸位在三年中练习时期，对于学识经验，悉心研讨，必能日有进益。但学无止境，最忌浅尝辄止,如笔算一项,商业上不甚便利,就得学珠算及计算机器。本国文字固应有相当程度,而时会所趋,英文亦不得不习,如有余暇,不妨再兼习他国文字,多一学问,即多一用途。希望诸位抱此毅力,日求精进,由是而助员、而办事员,则今日之练习生,即为他日本行之中坚份子。诸位前途,未可限量。鄙人希望亦无穷期,其各勉旃无懈。

原载:《中行生活》 1932 年第 1 卷第 6 期

如何推进我行之业务
——在宁行新屋落成典礼演讲

今日宁行新屋落成,方才总经理报告已多,兹从吾人做人的观点上,如何推进我行之业务?略为诸君告。

一、观念的构成

无论做什么事,首先要有一个观念。比如造这座房子,在未造之前,我们已有一个观念去造。假使以前没有这个观念,决不会有这座房子出现。现在既有这样一座伟大的房子,有这样的物质享受,我们就得于业务上加倍努力,构成发展业务的观念。假使我们有了这样好的一个观念,将来一定也能有伟大的事实出现。

二、思想的运用

我们有了造房子的观念,然后对于这座房子如何造法,外部如何建筑,内部如何布置,方能美观合用,必须运用思想,加以设计与规划,所以单有观念而没有思想,也不中用的。我们既具有发展业务的观念,必须要运用思想,想尽方法来研究,来推进,来谋其实现。

三、训练的工夫

我们做事,有了观念,有了思想,假如要用手足的,我们就得用手去做,用足去跑。我们用手数钱记账,我们用足跑出去和人家接洽,还得用口和人家说话。凡事如何能做到身到、眼到、手到、心到、口到,最为难事。这必须要有一番训练的功夫。假使我们能有这样的训练,定可增进业务上的效率不少。

所以,我们要想发展我行的业务,应当根据上面三点:第一要有发展业务的观念;第二要运用思想,想出发展的方法;第三要训练功夫,来训练自己,以谋发展业务的实现。如果我们有了深刻的观念、系统的思想和良好的训练,必能创造我们中国银行伟大的业务。希望大家共此信念,共同努力,那么也可以同建筑这一座伟大的房子一样,造成一个伟大的中国银行!

原载:《中行生活》 1934年第30期

视察中国银行闽粤分支行演讲录[①]

月前戴志骞先生有闽粤之行,三月七日由沪动身赴粤,十日抵港,十六日赴广州,二十二日由港搭轮赴汕,二十六日由汕乘轮赴厦,二十九日复由厦乘轮赴福州。四月六日由福州乘飞机回至上海。所至各处,均有演讲,兹承粤闽同人寄示记录,特汇刊如下:

1. 银行员应有德性及学识之修养　粤　黄芷湘　叶绍棠

总处总秘书兼人事室主任戴志骞先生,对于人事管理,备极精密,任用人员,选择尤为严格,更不惮跋涉之劳,亲履各行,实地考察,目的在使我行人事前途,日益精进也。

先生未尝履粤地,但闻久有南来之心,以事冗迟迟其行,直至三月七日始由沪乘"Pres. Mckinley"总统号轮船南下,于十日早晨抵港。同行者有汕支行代理襄理陶少松君、广处营业员李云阶君。登岸后,时方八句钟,即与接船诸人,一同来行,从事各种视察工作,并与各股人员,逐一接谈,历时半日始毕其事。旋由粤行经、副、襄理、各股主任,暨全体同人三十余人,于是日午后五时,在行内会客室设备茶点,开会欢迎,并请即席演讲。对于我行实施人事训练方针,及业务上过去事实,凡资表现我行之精神与毅力诸端,均历述无遗。兹录其演讲要旨如下:

麦金兰总统船今晨八时抵港,承郑经理[②]诸人招待来行。其时粤行正开始办公,见全行规模齐整,各同人办事精神,均极勤奋,深为粤行前途庆幸!诚以粤行为粤属之管辖行,自应有精密之组织,以为粤属各行之表率也。

自总经理国外考察回国,以外国大银行多有人事管理课之设备,而我行全体行员不下二千三百六十人,分支行处多至一百六十余处,如是广阔之范围,欲全体同人服务上精神团结一致,非用科学管理,难期收效。为适应环境之需要,故于民国二十年总处有人事室之成立,对于人事之训练,已取积极进行之步骤。盖我行之业务,能否日臻发达?荣誉能否垂久不朽?全视同人于服务上能否尽职为断。人事室之使命,在指导同人能尽服务之责任,智识之培植,及德性之修养也。智识不完备,责任上缺憾必多。试就棉业而言:不仅应知国内棉价,印度、美国之棉价亦应明了也;更就放款于工厂而言:工厂组织内容,固应明了,而经理人之才能及其办事精神,亦应考察,若无德性学识之修养,则处此社会竞尚浮华,外诱纷繁,易出越轨之行动。故银行员应有刻苦、任劳、俭朴、自奉之态度,以为社会之榜样。反之,如生活以奢侈是尚,用度又漫无节制,易招外界物议,固非银行之福,亦非行员个人之利。此外尚有应与同人个别谈话之处,现因限于时间,明日再与诸位逐个相见……

[①] 【编者注】原题名为"戴志骞先生闽粤演讲录",现题名为编者所加。
[②] 【编者注】即郑铁如,中国银行香港分行经理。

2. 中国银行现在的精神和将来之趋势　汕支行

诸位同仁,这一次南下视察,每到一处,为时虽暂,同仁统要我说几句话,我也想聚晤之机会难得,能随便谈谈几句,倒亦是一件很愉快的事情。

我现在想和诸位所谈的题目,是:"我行现在的精神和将来之趋势"。在未说到本题之前,我先谈谈此次南下视察之比较。我所到过的分支行,可说很多。我觉得汕支行同仁,对于治事精神上,都很活跃,工作亦很敏捷,即柜台之布置,亦很整洁有序。若从各行多方面比较起来,汕支行虽未能达到纯粹的科学化,却已步入新的途径。关于汕支行前途,这是值得有希望的!努力前进,再接再厉,这是兄弟所期望于同仁的,亦同仁之所应奋斗前进的。

现在来和同仁谈本题。说到"精神",这个名词是很抽象的。从前有人说:西方是物质文明,东方是精神文明,这亦未必尽然。譬如汕头地方,马路洋房,电灯电话,应有尽有。谓非物质文明,倒说不过去。不过比较西方文明,膛乎其后罢了。至于精神文明,亦是很抽象的,尤其是银行之制度和组织,银行员治事之才具和合理化,在在均足表现一个银行的精神。我对于银行精神之所在,第一次深刻之印象,即是民五①住北平的时候。当时我尚未进行,但我的朋友在行服务的很多。我有时到行汇款,听他们一部分少数行员在那里讲话,对于柜台顾客,必等他们高谈阔论后,始来应付。这种治事的精神,合理化吗?又当时我行钞票,经民四停兑后,恢复兑换,但兑换是有限制的,而行中一部分少数人,日以买卖京钞是谋。这种想发横财、先私后公之才,合理化吗?差幸民四京津两行停兑,沪行毅然照常兑换,博得社会之信仰,行誉藉以撑住。直到民十六,北伐成功,总处南迁,总经理深觉得本行虽有商股,原有利益,已强半非属我有,恐有崩溃之一日。又以银行之制度和组织,关系银行之精神,至重且钜,爰有躬自出国考察,借他山之石,供我切磋。所以从民十八到现在,挣扎图存,专以服务社会为主旨,扶植工商业为职志。一方面打开新的途径,一方面振发行员精神,这是多么苦心呀!但是制度和组织虽好,要是无人运用制度,或者运用的人不合理化,当亦不能得到良好的效果。再进一步说,假定已经有合理化之人才办事,效率虽亦很好,而精神不专对于银行,反怕比没有才具的还要有害。从前有人说:一个人要是所受的教育愈高,他的物质思想也愈高,私欲也愈大,这是任何人都是如此的。西谚说:有智识的强盗,犹两面锋利的刺刀,确是至理名言。所以总经理常说:"如有精神不自私,不利用银行找钱,喜欢尽其本能,为社会服务的人,本行当然欢迎,"否则他决不招致。总经理是以身作则的,从前政府曾几度要总经理就财长,总经理总是予以拒绝。盖他全副精神和事业,整个的寄托在本行。所以从民二十一以后,我行钞票发行,就达到一万九千万,存款就达到五万万。每股股票,由四五十元,现在涨到七十二三元。这种收获,固然是总经理之惨淡经营,亦算是我行近年来精神的胜利品。

其次说到我行将来之趋势。我行原有二十余年之历史背景,历年改革方策,是採演进的,不是採革命的。因为革命策略,不适用于经济,尤其是不适用于银行,不适用于有悠长历史之银行。现在我行关于会计制度,已上轨道。关于人事方面,亦较从前增加效率不少,可说已有六十分之程度。但因历史背景的关系,对于旧的行员,虽然有的效率较低,亦应念其

---

① 【编者注】即民国五年,公历1916年,下述纪年方法类推。

过去的相当之劳绩,惟对于新进行员,则应予以严格甄别,期适于用,勿使滥竽。盖现代银行林立,竞争日烈,稍一疏忽,颠踬随之;潮流所趋,自不能不慎之于始。我行将来之势趋,自可蒸蒸向上。同仁之待遇,亦可逐步改进。

3. 吾人要有科学的思想与合作的精神　闽　张纪歆

三月二十六日,接汕支行来电,谓总秘书戴志骞先生即日乘轮来厦,计程当于二十七日早晨可到。不意天不作美,是日沿海弥天大雾,轮船不能行驶,因之戴总秘书在海上停留了一天。时黄经理已赴沪出席行务会议,闽行同人,尤其是贺副经理①,由渴望而焦急,由焦急而失望,整天陷于不安的状态中!二十八日清晨,我们所盼望的戴总秘书终于到来了。他的庄严而和蔼的态度,给予我们以深刻的印象!他原拟与各同人逐一谈话,以示亲切,只以行务会议开会在即,须于二十九日乘轮赴福州,然后转程返沪,在厦仅能停留一天,逐一谈话已为时间所不许;贺副经理乃设欢迎会于下午五时公毕之后,请戴总秘书训话。届时在行同人全体出席,座为之满。首由贺副经理致欢迎词,大意说:他欢迎戴先生有两个愿望,第一是私的愿望,他以前在总处与戴先生同事,曾闻总经理说:"我行之得戴先生,如同得一保姆"。盖因戴先生之治事精神,甚足为同人效法。今日得戴先生亲临指示,觉得非常荣幸。第二是公的愿望,戴先生带着总处使命南来,好像从我们家里出来的伯叔兄弟,我们急欲问问家中消息,听听公公婆婆有什么吩咐?俾我们得所遵循,努力发展云云。旋请戴总秘书训话,兹记其大意如次:

刚才贺副经理说我好像是从家里出来的人,希望我对诸位讲些家里的情形,和这回出来的使命。不错,我们都是一家人!我现在对诸位不是演说,不是训话,不过如家人聚首,谈叙家常罢了。

诸位第一要问,我这回出来的使命是什么?例如从总账室出来的,他的使命是查问账目和改良会计制度等等;在我出来之前,我曾经和总经理谈论过我的使命的问题。简单说是考察行务和视察同人,可是我这种使命是抽象的。即如观察同人这一项,我和诸位初次见面,怎能够从外表上观察出各个的个性呢?查现在本行的分支行办事处计有一百六十余所,行员有二千三百六十余人,组织虽然这样庞大,但是中国银行比其他本国人办的银行更为进步,这是可以从成绩上看出来的;但是现在的成绩可够得上说好吗?其实是不够的!若和英美的银行相比,则相形见绌了!所以我们当努力与世界各大银行相比才是。

有人说:"中国银行已遍设于全国,这么大的组织,非有科学的管理不可。"这话是对的,因为管理得法,才能增加工作的效能;但谈到组织的科学化,却关系于人的问题。假如个人的脑筋不科学化,怎样能够增加工作的效能?譬如我国的铁路,便没有经过科学的计划。何以哈尔滨出的面粉价格高于美国运来的呢?说是因为交通不便,转运艰难,以致成本过重吗?那末,计划铁路的人怎不想到这一层呢?可知道管理人的思想不科学化,其组织当然不行!又如我国的金融,因各地的币制不统一,常受投机家的操纵,执政者为什么不以科学的方法去整理呢?所以归根到底,还在人的思想要科学化,然后才能增加工作的效能。我现在要和诸位说的,就是希望大家思想科学化,其次是要有合作的精神!行中同事大都不嫖不

---

① 【编者注】闽行副经理贺自畏。

赌,不做投机事业,于此可见本行同人都是很好的,惟仅仅个人好还是不够,必须达到整个行好;一个行好还是不够,必须达到全中国银行都好;而欲达到这个目的,便非有合作的精神不行。现在各联行方面,还有些地方观念没有完全除掉,以致调拨营运,尚不无窒碍!故希望各联行此后能以合作的精神,打破以前因袭的观念。先由股与股间合作,次由行与行间合作,终则全中行打成一片,这样才能与外国银行相颉颃。

大凡一行之兴起,必有所凭藉。中国银行之所以有今日,亦自有其所凭藉者在。在前清和北京政府时代,中国银行——前清为大清银行——乃是国家银行。其所凭藉的是经理国库,有如现在的中央银行所享受的种种特殊利益。那时候的中国银行,是政府属下的一个机关,政府亦并不以这个机关,视为替社会服务的机关,对于生意是可做可不做的!民国初年我住在北京,中、交两行里头,都有我的朋友。他们大都是以应酬过日的。我见他们用得这么阔,便发生一个疑问:他们花的钱究竟伊于胡底呢?我此时还想起了一件事:大约是民国四年吧?我在清华学校执教,那时清华领到一笔庚款,存在某某银行;不意该行忽然停顿,于是清华的存款,便没法子领出来了!因此那年的应派遣出洋留学的费用,遂发生问题。到了第二次领得庚款的时候,不得不慎重从事,将款改存于花旗银行了!以后京钞,定期限制兑现,在兑现的时候,有一天早上,我经过前门,见地上瞩着许多人。询之他们,说是恐怕迟到挤兑不着,所以在那里露宿。我当时目击这种凄凉状况,不觉有感,人类不平的观念,自然要因此而加深了!

上面所说,中国银行所凭藉的是经理国库,及至革命军北伐成功,国民政府定都南京之后,中央银行亦已经成立了。中行已改为国际汇兑银行,从前的凭藉已经失了!张总经理早见及此,在做副总裁的时候,便主张召集商股,脱去国家银行之名,以免受政潮影响,并时时计划保持本行种种利益。中国银行之有今日,赖总经理之力居多,现在中行所凭藉的是什么呢?无疑的就是信用,诸位大概是知道的了。

从前大清银行,听说有许多是官僚式的行长。若问他们关于行务的情形,他们是不知道的;因为经营生意是营业主任的事,管理账目是"洋账房"的事,而行长呢?是专为应酬官场的!后来改为中国银行之初,仍未免积习相沿。可是近年开行务会议,出席的各分行经理,对于行务莫不条分缕析,今昔相比,迥不相同,可见本行人事方面的进步。再看我国的社会,亦确已进步很多了。以前存支款项的人,多不愿意亲自到行,只派仆人去办,且多拒用钞票,现在则存支款项的多系本人到行,而且喜用钞票了。从前银行职员对于顾客,不免傲慢;现在呢?行员办事稍为迟缓,顾客便要催问;行员对顾客倘不客气,他们也要发话了。故现时应付柜台情形,和以前已大不相同!去年上海银行,曾因为不付有一点小问题的支票,被顾客所控,以致涉讼,结果,上海银行的官司打输了!于此足见人民的智识程度之进步。我们服务于社会,应与潮流俱进,才不会落伍!上海设有银行学会,专研究银行学识,以适应社会之需要。希望诸位亦力求进步,跟着潮流走!

我对于新进行的行员,必问他为什么要进中国银行?假如他的志愿不是服务社会,而是想求舒服,或是想发财,我必劝他不要进中国银行来,进来必会失望的!各人有个人的志趣,不必勉强,尔有能力尽可向他方面活动,何必要进中国银行?有一句谚语说:"浑水里捉鱼",意思是碰幸运。现在中国银行已经走上了轨道,没有什么幸运可碰,而上了轨道的中行亦决不让那些不安分的分子混进来"捉鱼"!

仅有服务的志愿,而没有相当的技能,还不够进中国银行的资格。必须算盘纯熟,中文清通,有丰富的商业常识,而又懂得英文才算合格!从前总处不要用的人,便搪塞到分行去;分行不要用的人,便搪塞到支行去;而以办事处为其尾闾!殊不知办事处,更需要有干练的人材!因为在分支行用人较多,可以随各人的兴趣而分配其工作;至于办事处呢?因人少之故,非兼办各股的事务不可。故办事处的职员,有类于学校中擅长全能运动的学生,都是很难得的呢。

谈到认识方面,有人说:要增加办事的效能,必须淘去陈旧的份子,实行人事革命,我实在不敢赞同。要知道革命的反面就是反革命,革命精神,每易促成反动。革命愈激烈,则社会愈遭殃,不独中国如是,世界各国亦莫不然!且金融界以信用为重,根本不宜採用革命手段。今举一例,以说明人事上不能革命之理由:譬如有一个三十岁进行,现年五十岁的行员,在二十年前他的思想亦是很新的,但没有随着时代进步而进步,遂慢慢的变成老朽。此种过失,不能全责诸其个人,而银行实应负一半的责任。理由是:如果认为他的办事才能不够,则应当于他进行半年或一年后知道,何以沿用至二十年之久,才革其命呢?人和汽车一样,走的路多,必会破坏的,这是自然的结果。行员年老不能办事,还得给他养老金!对于养老金的章程,已加改善,使年老行员得安全的保障。又查本行同仁的存款,计有一千一百八十余万元,每年供息之巨,殊可惊人。而实受其惠者,不过五百余人。盖大多数的行员存款额都是很小的,每见下级职员存款累万,其所得利息,常超过于责任繁重而没有巨额存款的上级职员的入息,此种不平现象,实为社会思想之导源。故去年行务会议,本行有改订行员存款办法。只因此种改革,关系各方面很大,不能不採取逐步改良的办法:第一存款额应有相当限制,以防不均之弊;第二照原息减低二厘,以此息款作为行员人寿保险基金,凡到行未满五年者,规定保险额为一千元;五年以上定为二仟元;而月薪在三百五十元以上者,无论年期久暂,一律保一千元;因薪俸大者,比较有能力自己投保的缘故。此种办法,于行无损;而于全体行员,则利益均沾,至为公平。

总处在人事方面,不采取革命手段,已如上述。对于老行员且力为设法保障,对于新进的行员,则主张严格训练。老行员经验比较丰富,应为新进员做领导;新行员皆系年富力强的青年,总处当给予以发展的机会。将来中行拟深入内地,做刻苦的工作。那时正需要一般青年来担当这种使命!

我此次南来,先到粤行,次到广处,然后来到这里。现因时间匆促,未能尽量观察,刚才到本市游览一周,仅以所得的感想和诸君谈谈。

厦门的风景,比青岛、大连更好;因大连、青岛的风景虽好,大半亦靠人力;而厦门天然的风景,比大连、青岛尤佳。厦门是华侨的故乡,金融极为活动。闽行处此优越的环境,又有巨额的发行,根基之稳固,自非粤行、广处所能比拟。古人云:"地灵人杰",闽行已得地之利,希望从人事上作更进一步之迈进!

原载:《中行生活》 1934 年第 26 期

戴志骞赴闽粤考察记述

【编者按】戴志骞此次闽粤之行，所到之处受到热烈欢迎，各分、支行撰写了其在各地的旅况，特录于此。题目为编者所加。

总处戴志骞君此次南下视察行务，兹承粤、汕、厦、闽各行同人将戴君所经各地旅况，写寄本刊（公务接洽情形，概从省略），特为刊载如下，俾读者藉可知天南景物之一斑也。

一、戴志骞先生于三月十日抵港，十六日午后四时半由九龙乘车至广州，曾参观岭南大学、白鹅潭（白鹅潭之码头系填土筑起，大轮可傍岸，大阪及太古之货栈皆在焉）、芳村、花埭、黄沙及广三、广韶等车站，花埭有本行栈房，系向永其昌栈租来，正储有花生米甚多。并游览公园、纪念堂、黄花岗、黄婆洞、飞机场等处。二十二日由港乘怡生轮"Norviken"赴汕。该轮系由广州开来，适遭洗劫者，故此次开行，搭客仅有三人。港埠有所谓"酒差"者，上船搜查，志在需索，翻箱倒箧，缠扰不清，予以犒赏，则立呈恭顺之态，实为行旅之大害！三时启椗，闻六时行至大鹏湾，该地为海盗出没之区，而机器忽告损坏，停泊多时，幸修好出险，二十三日上午安抵汕埠云。（云寄）

二、汕支行同人闻戴志骞先生将乘怡生轮来汕，遂于二十三日由陈襄理与各主任雇小轮往接。抵埠后，即驱车往适宜楼休息。午后莅行视察同人工作，并召各主任谈话，傍晚汕支行同人开茶话会，并请演讲（词另见本期）。二十四日上午视察收税处，及参观汕支行运动场，旋往商业街口，勘视筹建行员宿舍之地基。回行中膳后，即在本行楼上召各同人个别谈话，垂询同人生活状况及工作感想至详。二十五日为星期日，乘早车赴潮州（即潮安城），往游湘子桥十八梭船，旋渡桥赴韩山，谒韩文公祠，祠祀韩愈，建自唐代，祠侧有韩山师范学校。嗣渡桥参观唐开元寺及省立四中学校，校建于金山之上，遥望全城，了如指掌。下金山后，往游西湖，旋乘潮汕火车赴枫溪，调查瓷器。潮瓷出口，除高陂外，全部产自枫溪。最盛时，年产约二百万，现因遭南洋不景气及日货倾销之影响，已锐减为五十万矣。翌日（二十六日）乘广东丸赴厦，计在汕共留四日。（汕支行寄）

三、二十七日早，戴总秘书乘船抵厦门港外，因大雾不能进港，次晨始达目的地，由闽行副经理贺自畏君等偕至屿处。稍事休息后，赴港仔勘视闽行新置宿舍地址，背山临海，风景宜人。顺道游日光岩，是日仍大雾，为近年所罕见。旋返屿处视察一周，继至闽行及看新行址。午后往观购备货仓码头之海地（货仓位长一千二百尺，阔一百尺，码头低潮深三十尺，能舶大船二艘），并参观厦门大学、自来水池、南普陀、中山公园及虎溪岩。午间天色清明，在虎溪山上得俯视厦、鼓全景，归途周览街市，即赶赴五时之同人欢迎会。席间演说，七时散会。旋至屿处聚餐，与各主任谈话，十时始散。次日上午复与同仁谈话，午餐后登轮赴福。频行至码头，泉支行经理方耐尘君赶至晤谈，随送上船而别。（公量来稿）

四、戴志骞先生三十日来福州，适逢大风雨，船至傍晚五时，始抵马尾。八时到福州，晚膳后到行查勘新近被焚之行屋。连日与各主任及同人晤谈，并视察城处，至鼓山，观戚继光之平安台及祠堂，沈葆桢之祠堂亦在此。二日电汽公司邀往参观并午宴，洽谈各事，饭后参观电灯新厂及福州造纸厂等。电灯新厂所用机器,为捷克国出品,造纸厂为陈希庆君经理,出品颇佳,有求过于应之势。三日与各行员个别谈话,晚全体行员聚餐,举行摄影。即席演说,对同人服务精神,以放远眼光、增进效能、力行合作三点相勉。四日午后至科贡、石仓乡,科贡有一农村,系以电气灌溉,收成加倍,石仓乡办有农事试验场,亦颇具成绩。五日十二时半乘水上飞机飞沪,飞约三刻钟,风云陡变,东南风忽变为东北风,风势极大,时接温州无线电,告以不能前飞,遂又折回福州,福州亦有大雾,是晚福州航空公司经理约聚餐,六日晨再登飞机,天仍有雾,九时始飞向上海云。(杰寄)

  此次戴志骞先生闽粤之行,以船往,以飞机回,据所闻知,殆极"乘风破浪"之险! 何以言之? 志骞先生由港乘方遭洗劫之怡生轮,复以机损在海盗出没场所之大鹏湾停留多时,其险一;在汕、厦航程之广东丸中,同舟有一疯子,持刀纷哎,几欲杀人,嗣经加以捆缚乃止,其险二;飞机师曾云:此次遇罕见之大雾,在厦门停留四日,今飞沪又在温州阻于风雾,尚不知何日能行,其后行经 Air Pocket 中,空气稀薄,五脏六腑,几有冲夺口腔而出之势。其险三;但仅此三者,尤未足以云险也! 志骞先生所乘之飞机,为塞可斯机十六号"Sikorsky NO.16",亦即此次飞抵上海后不幸于飞回闽粤途中遇险失踪之飞机,飞机师为 Mr. Gast,无线电师为 Mr. Filink,飞机师驾驶之术甚精,夙称审慎,此次由粤飞回,其夫人曾挈其爱女迎候于沪站,并经介见于戴先生,讵不数日后,人与机殉,良可惋惜! 据闻于飞回福州之夕,机师对连天风雾,蹙额不怡! 志骞先生笑慰之曰:"南海航行,相传不易,中国习惯,航海须虔拜'观世音',方可无碍,如准本人将所有行李随带,(飞机乘客每人重量有一定限度,不能携带行李,惟是日乘客仅仅一人),则余此次在潮州枫溪购有'观世音'一座,置在行装中,定可佑护通行也。"经此一番交涉,机师于笑颜中,准为捆载全件而行,竟一路顺风,安抵上海。又闻沪闽途中,天台雁荡,为航线必经之路,经过雁荡时,曾绕飞"天柱峰"一周,俯视"大龙湫",瀑布高数百丈,盘旋三折,如水银下泻,峰峦树石,悉收眼底;名山胜景,全境豁露。此次志骞先生行途虽险,而得此宇宙之奇观,其亦足游目骋怀,少慰履险如夷之况矣! 编者近有浙游之约,限于时日,未能一至,闻此益为神往! 山水之乐,人同此情,特信笔志之于末,以告同人中之同好者,得勿亦振衣跃跃欲试耶?(编者)

原载:《中行生活》 1934 年第 26 期

银行人事调查与训练

(人事管理学会第一次演讲会讲稿)
戴志骞先生讲　朱钟正速记

【编者按】 1934 年 4 月 19 日,中华职业教育社在上海召开成立中国人事管理学会筹备会,提倡与研究科学的人事管理问题,戴志骞参加会议。5 月 26 日召开中国人事管理学会成立大会,戴志骞任名誉理事。从 1934 年 10 月开始中国人事管理学会每月举办演讲会,请名人专家演讲人事管理问题。10 月 21 日在八仙桥青年会九楼食堂举行首次演讲会,由该会名誉理事戴志骞主讲"银行人事调查与训练"。

　　主席,各位先生,今日承人事管理学会之命,叫兄弟来演讲人事管理问题。人事管理问题,方才主席何清儒先生也曾说过,是一个很复杂而不容易讲的问题。因为什么呢！诸位都知道,一个人在吃饭以前与吃饭以后的情绪都是不同的,在一天二十四小时之内,无时无刻没在变化的,单单一个人尚且如此,讲到机关上有集合性的问题,其千变万化,不亦更多？我可以肯定的说,天下的事情,没有一件可比人事更有变动性的。因为人事问题根本是一件复杂的事情,今天欲作此演讲当然很感困难,因此兄弟今天来不能说是演讲,只好说是大家共同讨论讨论,倘要作为演讲,势难面面都能谈到,因为各个机关的性质不同,管理的方式也随之而异。同是一个机关,在两个不同时间与空间上,其管理方法又不尽相同了。所以若要为人事管理,下定一个天经地义的原则,是绝不能推行尽力的。必须因地制宜,随时有共同讨论的机会,方能研究出适当的办法,所以今日能与诸位聚首一堂,共资切磋,实为荣幸！

　　主席给我决定的题目,是"银行人事调查与训练"。我方才已经说过,同一性质的机关,其各个内部的管理就不相同。即以银行而论,甲银行与乙银行不能相提并论,因为甲乙二方营业方针与人才需求标准很有不同,兄弟现在讲银行人事的调查与训练,只能从狭义方面讲,专指中国银行人事的调查与训练,一得之愚,亦聊以供诸位参考而已。

　　讲到银行人事管理,不能说是像一个空屋子,要怎样陈设,就怎样陈设,因为银行是一天一天发达出来的,所以要讲人事管理时,必须要顾到他的历史、沿革,以及他现在和将来所要做的事。中国的银行历史并不很久,姑舍钱庄而不论,在中国的银行设立最早者,为中国通商银行,其次,即为中国银行,成立于民国元年,垂今二十三年,他是没有什么特别的组织,不过在最早时,所有总裁都是由政府财政部长或财政总长等兼任的。本行存款的,也是官方居多,商界甚少,民国十四五年,还不能完全脱此情形,当时对于人事管理以及训练工作,尚不如今日之重视,顾现在如何能引致大家注意人事管理的问题呢？有几个原因：

　　从前一般的银行是靠政府借款,利息厚,或者买卖地产、公债；因为做这些事,无关行员之有无训练,所以没有训练与调查的需要。因此在柜台上的行员,对待顾客都是冷面孔,等他吸完水烟,等他自己的事做完之后才来接待顾客,弄得大家都怕进银行,以顾客的热气换行员的冷气。至于稍有身份的人,都是直接走到行长,或者是总裁的房间里去接洽。进去之后,烟茶有人很恭敬地送上来,拿钱也不要自己直接去,有茶房代拿。行长、总裁等也从来不到柜台上去察看察看行员的工作,所以上级人员不知下级人员的情形,行员也就随便起来了。行长也很随便,一天到晚花天酒地,无所底止。这是兄弟当洪宪年间①,在北平亲眼看见的。现在的情形不同了,(一)债券的利息不如从前好,地产事业有行无市。以前完全靠做政府的往来,就可以赚钱,现在必须要做生意了。因为要做生意,必须要扶助工商业,服务社会,使生产者,成本减轻,效率增加,才可以赚钱。因此银行的工商放款,自不可与政府放款,同日而语了。(二)因为要放款,一方面就不得不吸收存款,要吸收存款,不可不研究顾客的心理,譬如银行设化妆室于保管库旁,使得太太小姐们欢迎,诸如此类,都要不断的设计与研究。(三)受了世界不景气的影响,商业竞争,日甚一日,如果再照以前的方法做去,必致落伍。因为大家有了这三种原因,于是对于人事管理,认为像饮食一般的需要了。因为在这种情势之下,一个行员的知识,不充分是不能做生意的。譬如有一个棉花主顾上门来做押款,这行员不但要知道某地方出多少棉花,能纺几支纱,值多少钱,还要知道中国市价之外的印度棉的市价、美国棉的市价以及埃及棉的市价,凡此必须精密的研究方能智珠在握,万无一失,如果没有这种知识和头脑,贸然应接,则不啻"盲人骑瞎马",危险孰甚? 又如从前发行钞票的银行,并自己都不知道发行的数目有多少,更不必谈自己有多少的准备金,现在发行钞票,必须有六成现金保证,四成证券保证,还要缴纳相当的发行税。各种营业都很难做了,想要维持营业的前途,银行的生命,就不能不在人事管理上用功夫,因为在目前无论哪一个普通的银行,都不能保得住除了股利之外每年还能有若干大数的盈余,其原因在以前放款能高至一分二或一分三的利息,现在要扶助工商业,调剂金融,尽现代银行的使命,利息不能那样大了。譬如收进存款给人家八厘半利,放款出去收人家利息,期间只赚半厘钱。银行要拿这半厘利润来维持全行的开支,试问除了在用人方面,力求效率的增加,以减轻自己的成本之外,更有什么完善的办法? 讲到这里所谓组织健全化,管理合理化,自然是关系银行前途兴替的最重要问题。

现在既要有人事管理,就有许多问题发生,因为一个机关,是先有人事而后有管理,尤其是在中国,往往到了半途中间,才觉有管理的需要,像中国银行里有不少二十多年历史的老职员,年纪总在五六十岁相近,他现在的效能一定稍为低一点,但假使因为他的效能低,而就舍弃他,决非人情之常,我们留他在行里有两个理由:(一)当他效率高的时候,已在行里用过了。(二)他为行里曾出过很大的力,现在年纪大了,不能照以往一样的努力,乃因其智力、体力的衰退而然,并非由于他自己的过失,所以我们仍旧要优待他,一方亦所以使年青的职员可以安心努力工作,知道自己将来老了,他的位置亦不发生问题。所以要整理一个机关,断不能用革命的方式,像快刀斩乱麻一样的干,必定要用渐进的方式,随着事实与环境的推演而谋以改善。现在讲到新行员进来的时候,以中国银行而论,练习生必须高中毕业;内地偏僻的支行练习生,可以初中毕业;但必须有三年商业的阅历才准许投考。因为银行的事业不是单纯的,普通知识必须要充分具备,因为柜台上来的顾客,有士农,有工商,有军政各界,倘要面面应付周全,非有充分的普通知识不可。我们考取的练习生,就要用作将来的基本人员,决不能等闲视之。但是练习生考取之后,必定要经过相当时期的训练,才能应用,在这人才青黄不接的中国,我们便征用一般大学生充任试用员,他们教育程度比中学生要高一级,给他较短时期的训练,便可应用。大学生考取进行的时候,最少要见四个重要人员,每一人

---

① 【编者注】指袁世凯称帝时期。

谈话,有一回记录,共同评判认可之后,最后总经理还要亲自和这个尚未进行的行员谈话;人事室还要到同他有关系的人那里去详细调查,然后决定是否任用。我们对于新行员的取用是要介绍的,从来不登报。对于老行员也随时有很详细的调查,每一个行员的经济状况如何,有多少亲戚朋友来往,有几个小孩子,他每天晚间出门的次数多不多,去的是哪几处,全有很详细的调查记载。有了这种调查,对于训练方面就有莫大的关系。譬如一个行员家里有十个八个小孩子,负担很重,要是给他月薪一百元,在行方不算少,可是叫那个行员拿了一百元就不够开支。我们一定要想方法使他能解决他全家的生活问题,而一无内顾之忧。可是又不能直接给他加薪水,如若给他二百元一月,他多出来一百元,上焉者用以为投资,下焉者就不免出之浪费,及养成他有不好的习惯。所以我们与其直接的增加薪水,毋宁设计为种种间接的待遇,比如行员的小孩子读书有学校,全家住在本银行自建的住房里,比外面的学校的学费和房价便宜得多,朝夕往返,行中自备大汽车接送,不要花很多的车钱。此外,每年年终有奖金,平时有储金制度,年纪老了,六十岁不能工作退职时,按他工作的年数,与薪水的多寡,算出一个数目来,每月照数付给他,一直到死亡为止。我们平时对于人事上详细的调查,就可以随时决定每个行员适当的待遇。有一种性情静的人就可以分配他做记账工作,有种性情活动而无家累的人,就不妨分配他到营业上去。

讲到防弊的事很难,俗语说得好:"只有千日做贼,没有千日防贼。"因为有周密防弊的方法,即有十二分灵巧舞弊法子出现,如果决心要作弊的话,真是防不胜防,只不过是能防则防,不能防则唯有想法子早使之发现。一个经历深的行员假使存心不良而想做坏事,他的机会一定更多,也很容易。做到分、支行经、副、襄理职务时,要保人也不易请人保。譬如像我们苏州支行,亦有一千余万存款,叫这经理到哪里去找这样大的保人,我们能升他做到这种位置时,一定知道他历年工作的情形,与他的个性道德、品格非常详细,才能付之以重任而一无可虞。

现在讲训练问题,中国银行对于进来的练习生,要给他基本的训练。我们训练他,像训练全能运动员一样,使他各种工作都要会做,另外还要有几种基本才能。

A 技术上的才能,大致可分六种:

(一)考进时要中文通顺,中文之外,要懂一国外国语,如日文、英文、法文或德文等;(二)在柜台上没有算盘的时候,亦要笔算快;(三)算盘要精,养成能同顾客口中说话,手下已把数目算出;(四)须会用计算机①;(五)英文打字必须熟;(六)试用员亦要会用计算尺②。我们所以要这样训练,不是叫他在中国银行能用,将来出中国银行到别处去时,随便到哪一家,也能用。即大学生、留学生,也要派到各部学机械工作,譬如每人都要派到钞票间点票子,假使没有练习过,将来到办事处去做主任或办事员时,有顾客上门问起这张票子是真的还是假的,便回答不出来,岂不是一桩大大的笑话?在钞票间能训练到八小时之内能点好、整理好五万张杂票,辨别真伪,叠扎完整好,盖好印章,才可以说点钞票的事毕业了。

大学生进来的时候,领他到各处走,叫他看几个星期,看不懂,讲给他听,同时便叫他在这地方实习,这一个银行对内、对外的事,都要能明了熟习,总要一年的时期。

以前各地方考进来的行员都在各地训练,现在要集中上海总行训练。因为上海的工作最忙,能在忙的工作时间内,把一切事应付裕如,将来派到内地去工作时,感觉非常舒适。如

---

①② 【编者注】疑为计算器。

果在内地训练,比较是闲惯的,派到上海行来,他便不易应付。训练的时期,每人还要天天做日记,送交人事室主任看过,再时常要轮流召集谈话,借以明了其工作进步的情形。这是关于技术训练方面的。

B 精神训练:

讲训练方式,各业不同。制钢厂有制钢厂的训练方法,工厂有工厂的训练方法,商业有商业的训练方法,银行有银行的训练方法,然而人事训练有一个总的根本的训练,便是精神训练。假使技术训练尽美尽善,而忽略精神训练,那无异于一个没有灵魂的形骸,有什么用处?一个人技术训练越好,倘没有精神的修养来主宰,那么它做坏的方法也越巧。譬如一个人管汇款,今天汇来三千元,这人用钱,他留下来,晚一天通知收款人,因为明天又有人汇三千元来,拿明天的钱给昨天的人,后天的钱,给明天的人,这样他总有三千元在手里用,很难查出来。譬如中国银行精神训练的办法,是每星期有一二小时由总经理、总稽核、总秘书等演讲告诉他怎样做人?怎样做事?以及如何进德?如何修业?都有剀切说明。同时并告诉他进中国银行是不能存心享受。中国银行与社会国民经济,息息相关,我们尽力于中国银行,就等于尽力于社会,尽力于国家。我们不但训练下级人员是如此,就是上级人员亦要各种精神上的陶冶。因为这班新进的行员都是大学生、中学生,很有头脑,很有思想的人;如果上级人不能以身作则,一天到晚吃、喝、嫖、赌,乱用钱,下级人员决难有以感化的。以中国银行的总经理张公权先生而论,他个人立身处事就十分的严格,他有时在外面宴客,对于公私方面分得最清楚,同一时间内,有的为公事,开公账;为私事,开私账。他也从来没有随便引荐过一个亲戚朋友到行里来,有这榜样精神训练,才会有风行草偃的好效果。

所以要讲管理、训练,必定要上者以身作则,这是一个最根本的问题,丝毫没有例外,更千万不容忽视。

原载:《工商管理月刊》　1935 年第 2 卷第 2 期

银行界同人进修服务社工作简报
——在三十四区党部党员代表大会报

【编者按】戴志骞为国民党党员,入党时间不详,在国立中央大学工作期间参加国民党的活动。国立中央大学是国民政府直属的大学,作为该校图书馆馆长、高等教育处处长、副校长,加入国民党是很正常的。抗战时期戴志骞为重庆国民党三十四区党部负责人。

本社自民国三十一年四月间社址落成,荏苒迄今,瞬逾一载,检讨社务进展情形,深觉已作之事,去理想计划尚远;今后推动,尚待努力,兹将过去一年中重要工作,列举于次:

(一)关于文化工作者

本社精神,首重进德修业,进德修业之意义,不外人格之培养,知识增进;而进修之方式,又分为直接、间接两种;例如丰富的图书设备,及各种学术讲演会、座谈会、研究会等,是为直接的进修;例如各种正当娱乐之提倡,裨益身心,是为间接的进修,兹逐项缕述之。

甲 图书方面:本社为经费所限,仅有简单图书室一所,经常开放,备有自修书籍二百余册,杂志二十余种。近拟大加扩充,使成为比较完备的银行界公共图书馆。

乙 学术讲演方面:本社直接举办或与其他机关合办者,先后请吴雅晖、谷正纲、翁文灏、张继、冯玉祥、朱学范、邵力子、王芃生、老舍、陈耀东、凌其翰、顾维钧、章桐、沈鸿烈诸先生,演讲二十余次;尤以与中法比瑞文化协会合办之"废约讲座"及"新约讲座",适当不平等条约取消,平等新约成立之时机举行,极博社会好评。

丙 关于文艺研究方面:本社近组"文艺小集",内分诗文、书画、金石三组,聘曾履川、乔大壮、潘伯鹰、沈尹默、黄君璧、彭醇士、曾绍杰、张冷僧诸先生为导师,各银行同人参加者,甚为踊跃。

丁 本社并为提倡银行界同人读书写作之风气,借以交换智识起见,近编印《银行通讯》月刊,创刊号六月一日出版,月刊内容,将以各同人对于银行实务之讨论,业余读者之心得,及对于三民主义之研究为主。

戊 关于正当娱乐之提倡:本社曾组织音乐研究会,及象棋研究会两种,前者由金律声、李俊二先生任教授;后者由棋王谢侠逊先生指导,各同人参加者极众。最近本社与中华交响乐团合作,每周举行星期音乐会一次,银行界同人,一律享受减价之优待,至电影戏剧方面,曾放映介绍科学常识之影片五次,免费招待同人,民国三十二年岁首,曾举行社员新年同乐大会一次,成绩甚佳。本社自今年二月份起,与中国艺术剧社合作,每月上演话剧十余场,曾两度招待同人观剧。今后更当力促该社专演有裨世道人心及抗建宣传之剧本,俾使完全符合双方合作之原旨。

(二)关于体育工作者

伟大之事业,基于健全之体魄。我银行界同人,日常工作八、九时以上,缺乏运动之时间及环境,本社于此特加注意,兹将过去工作,略述于后:

甲 经常举办者,为太极拳练习团,由郑曼青、金侣琴二先生分任正、副团长,每日清晨练习,始终不辍,每三个月为一期,现已毕业三期,毕业同人,共达五百余人。

乙 去年十二月间,对于室内运动之乒乓球,曾举办行际竞赛一次,各银行参加者,达十四队之多。

丙 去年五月初,本社又发起行际篮球"庸之杯"锦标赛,各银行参加,更为踊跃,并有女子队两队,现正举行竞赛中。

丁 本社为重庆市银行界同人热心体育,锻炼身体之精神,资为其他各大都市银行界之模范起见,近又组织本市银行业联合篮球队(简称银联队),远征昆明,预料此次结果,并可为本社募集相当经费,备不久为建筑本社体育馆之用。

(三)关于服务工作者

本社对于进修工作,虽提倡不遗余力,但本社根本目标,实在为银行界,乃至一般社会服务;进修之目的,亦在培养吾人服务之能力,惟本社限于经费,且社址除一会场外,并无余裕,以致种种服务计划,如创办民众夜校,设立银行同人公共理发室、沐浴室、寄宿舍等等,均无法实现,过去一年中之工作,均属消极性质,兹简述如下:

甲 本社会场,原只能容六百人,讲台亦只能供演讲会,及小规模音乐会之用。自与中国艺术剧社合作改建后,已能容八百人以上,舞台设备,亦完备适用,在本市各公共集会场所中,堪称后来居上,本社对于会场之出借,完全以服务为目的,收费极少,对于各银行,及各同人之租借,尤予以优先之便利;至若四联夜校,借用会场,因本社与中剧社订约在前,时间分配方面,稍感不便。统计本社自民国三十一年十月,至本年五月底止,共出借一百六十次以上。

乙 关于银行界同人,对于业务、人事、法律等问题之咨询,本社原列为重要服务工作之一,过去格于人力财力,仅获举办法律问题之咨询一种,曾拟定本社服务组法律咨询办法八条,特约法学博士陈耀东先生,担任解答,现此项工作,正在积极开展中。

(四)关于社员及支社之发展者

本社为本市银行界同人唯一业余公共团体,希望同人踊跃入社,并希望本社组织,能普及于各金融机构,多设分支社,俾本社进修服务工作之精神,能充分而普遍发挥,截至现在止,社员已达五百二十人,三十四区党部所属党员八百余人,并为本社当然社员,共达一千余人;至分支社之组织,尚仅邮运储金汇业局(邮政储金汇业局)方面,已成立支社一所,经常聘请党国名流,做学术演讲,工作殊为努力。

(五)关于联络员之活动者

本社成立之初,为使本社工作能与各金融机构密切联系配合起见,曾拟订各金融机构遴选联络员办法,函请各银行选派联络员,共五十八人,可代表本市每一金融单位,联络员之任务,在沟通社与社员间之意志,联络社员相互间之感情,用意甚善,惜过去未做有计划之组织与推动,致无显著成绩,最近本社召集联络员,开会商讨,佥以加紧工作,必先有章则做依据,业经推出人选,草拟本社联络员会议组织简则一种,一俟通过,转请核准,即可施行,此项办法,并规定每半年必须选出驻社联络员八人,参加本社各组工作,对于本社今后与各银行之联系配合,必有裨益。

(六)关于本社财务状况者

本社既属服务机构,一切工作,非人力莫办,非财力莫举,后者尤为根本问题。本社工作人员,除主任、副主任为无给职外,总干事、副总干事各一人,各组主任干事四人,兼任干事三人,仅支少数之交通津贴,其余专任干事四人,工役四人之薪津、伙食及电水、杂费等,每月开支已达两万元左右。至本社收入方面,在本年二月未与中国艺术剧社合作以前,根本无固定收入,经济拮据已极。去年十一月底,即员工伙食,亦有断炊之虞。当时承中央银行借给五万元,勉维现状,尚待筹还。本年二月份起,中国艺术剧社每月演剧十六夜场,四个日场,共纳租金二万八千元左右,本社经济状况,始获稳定,所有一年来收支情形,现已造具详表,送请三十四区党部查核备案矣。

（七）关于本社与中剧社合作问题

本年二月以前,本社会场舞台,不合用情形,已如前述。当时每月利用会场,平均不过十二次,其余时间完全空闲,去年十一月间,中国艺术剧社社长赵志游商请合作,出资改建会场舞台,本社基于以下原因,予以同意。

甲 该剧社系沪港撤退剧人所组织,其工作目的,在以话剧方式,效力抗建宣传,与本社精神,及工作计划,尚属吻合。

乙 舞台会场之改造,需费四十余万元,全由该剧社自行筹资,本社可坐享其利。

丙 该剧社每月只演十六个夜场,四个日场,且分两期演出,核以本社过去每月实际只利用十二场之数目,并不影响本社本身工作。

丁 该剧社每晚场付租金一千五百元,日场一千二百元。月计二万八千余元,本社经济困难,立获解决,本身工作,并可赖以推动。

本社根据以上四点,于去年十一月秒,与该剧社签订合同,定期二年,经提请三十四区党部通过,转报市党部,并奉市党部指示,应行修改之点,完全遵照修改,合同满期时,所有该剧社投资改造之处,均无条件归本社所有。

（八）关于本社所租银行公会地基问题

本社筹创之初,借用银行公会地基,修建社址,系由总干事陈天表经办,本社主任、副主任,初未据报有订立租约情事,至本年初,因本社与中剧社合作问题,银行公会来函查询,方悉真像,是项租约,几经严询,陈君始行交出。为使租约能融合银行公会与本社合作精神计,除请示上级党部外,并拟向银行公会洽商。

以上诸端,业将一年来工作情形,暨重要社务,略陈梗概,抑尤有进者,本社为我国银行史上新兴的事业,承金融界最高指导者孔庸之先生①之奖掖,市区党部之督导,银行界同人之协助,始获创立,柏园等谬荷重任,主持社务,过去殊感心余力绌之苦,良以公共事业,必赖群策群力,独木难支,众擎易举,检讨一年来工作未克开展之原因,实人力不臧所致。我银行界同人,如能全体参加本社,各竭智虑,共策进行,则来日成绩之灿然可观,自可预卜,此柏园等检讨之余,衷心企盼,热诚祷祝者也。

报告人　戴超
　　　　徐柏园
　　　　范鹤言

原载：《银行通讯》　1943年第2期

---

① 【编者注】即孔祥熙。

中国银行行务会议戴总秘书报告（1946年）

【编者按】1946年，中国银行举行抗战胜利后的第一次行务会议，戴志骞总秘书在会上做了报告。

抗战期间，与承平之时情形不同。在此期内，本行总管理处对于事务之措施不特须体察情形，随时随地谋办公之便利。一方面复应顾到同人食住行问题，不断研讨做合理之解决。今幸战事结束，关于复员事宜亦告一段落。爰将历年办理经过简备报告于后：

（一）总管理处由沪迁港办公

民国二十六年八月十三日沪战发生①，总处先由上海汉口路五十号行址迁至霞飞路办事处楼上办公。旋于是年十一月间因上海沦陷，乃开始逐步迁移香港办公，并有一部分人员由沪移往汉口，再经渝滇转港，集中一地办公。

（二）总处由港移渝办公

民国二十八年九月总处奉令开始由港分批陆续内迁至重庆办公，一面在港成立总驻港处，迄民国三十年十二月太平洋战事爆发，乃全部移渝办公。

（三）总处在渝情形

民国二十八年十月总处首批人员抵渝，先在两路口予园办公，旋即迁至上清寺办事处二楼办公。嗣以渝市轰炸频仍，上清寺行屋遭受震损不能应用，又因总处由港内迁人员抵渝者日见增多，乃另在重庆郊外石桥铺玉灵洞购地建筑简单办公房屋及宿舍。并以空袭频繁，为谋同人及公物安全起见，经开凿防空洞以策安全。嗣因同人眷属纷纷内迁至渝，遂分次租地建筑极简单之草顶竹壁眷属宿舍二批，共约容纳八十余家。唯以玉灵洞僻处乡郊，不特治安方面须自行雇用警卫多人，以资防卫。即水电两项亦俱感缺乏。经租用附近田地约十亩，开筑蓄水堰塘一方，以裕水源；并购置柴油发电机一具，以供电灯及电台之用。又因玉灵洞距离城区颇远，交通至形不便，乃陆续置备交通车数辆，以便同仁暨眷属往返城区之用。又以物价不断高涨，同人生活艰苦，经先后举办各种福利事业，如设立员工消费合作社、眷属公共食堂、同人俱乐部及医务室等。当时内地物资缺乏，各同人暨眷属赖有上项种种设施，故虽局促乡间，仍勉获衣食住行上之便利。此于工作上，不无具安定因素，可为诸君告慰者也。

（四）总处复员情形

民国三十四年八月抗战胜利结束，各地本行纷纷复业，总处亦奉命准备复员。先由少数同人来沪，筹备上海总处办公处所。嗣于民国三十五年四月由渝包机载运一部分同人来沪，其余大部分同人及眷属因江水涸浅，轮只稀少，乃均取道川陕公路，再循陇海、津浦、京沪等路来沪，大都业已先后到达。所有在渝雇用之工友大多就地资遣。玉灵洞、汪山等地总处房屋及器具等均交由渝行接收保管。大部分账券公物箱件亦暂寄存渝行仓库中，俟江水涨后，设法交轮运沪。总处在渝事务于焉告一结束。上项复员工作情形与其他各行及各机关相

---

① 【编者注】即1937年8月13日上海"八·一三"事变。

较,进行尚称迅速。

(五)总处迁返上海后行屋及宿舍情形

总处迁沪后,先在汉口路五十号旧址办公。嗣以外滩新厦房屋已有空余,乃全部迁入办公。关于同人眷属宿舍,除先到沪同人业已分别在原有各处房屋如中行别业、德义大楼及虹口大楼等处居住外,后到同人及眷属为数甚多,因房屋不敷分配,乃暂就汉口路旧址及虹口大楼一部分作为临时安顿之所。目前正在计划同人眷属宿舍办法,拟先将各处宿舍及住户情形切实调查,加以整理,借谋公平之分配。一面积极进行设法购置现成房屋或自行建筑眷属宿舍,务使各携眷同人不久均能获得适当之住所。

(六)附带报告——总处办理各地行处房地产及损款案件情形

查抗战期间,总处及各分支行处因当地各界时有为救济难民,或慰劳将士,以及举办地方公益等募捐,为应付环境起见,均已分别酌量捐助。关于各地分支行处房地产之处理,亦就各行处实际需要情形,酌为建筑或租赁,均经陈报常董会核准。各地复员以后,因地方经过兵燹,原有房屋大都损毁,各行处纷纷陈请修理及建筑。值此物价昂贵之际,所有建筑及营缮费用为数似觉巨大,关于较大之建筑均先陈奉董座核准后再行办理。

原载:《中国银行行史资料汇编(上编)(二)》

中国银行行务会议戴总秘书人事报告(1946年)

一年以来,本行对于人事之设施,力求适应环境并配合业务事务之需要,办理至为困难。兹就经办情形举其大者,如复员之处理、待遇之改进,略述如下:

(一)复员之处理

民国三十四年春夏之交,敌势已颓,我国胜利期近,总处即考虑到复员伊始人手缺乏,应如何设计以期配合复业行之需要。几经人事委员会执行小组会研讨,顾以内地设备关系,既难预招多数新员训练以备,只好就内地各行管辖较广者先与商洽,抽调若干人以应急需。幸荷渝行徐经理、雍行朱经理、滇支行王经理尽量协助,调出多人,湘、桂两行亦有分调。赣支行则以辖内机构渐次复业需员正殷,浙行属人手历经资遣退休,本甚紧缩,益以辖内亦正谋复业,只能就本辖内酌予量移。闽行则因地理关系,行员多调往粤属及台湾,总处亦尽量选择相宜之人材调为复业行之用。现在各复业行行员除由后方调往服务者外,尚将接收行内原充本行旧员甄别复用,故目前差堪应付。俟业务逐渐发展之后,可能尚须添用人员。去年十一月行务谈话会,人事小组曾有建议,略以是项人手之估计是否准确,端视各行同人松紧之是否齐一,以及各收复区支行办事处等如何分期恢复而定。拟由总处按照各行实际情形,根据业务事务数量规定用人多寡之准绳,通函各行以作估计用人多寡之标准。一面由各行将逐步恢复旧有机构之计划函报,俾作逐步补充人员之参考。至如何实施是项方策,尚有待精密之研讨。

(二)待遇之改进

历年物价步涨,民国三十四年春已有剧烈变动,各行感到同人生活困难,申请四联总处将原有待遇加以调整,乃有国家银行行员战时待遇补助办法之颁布。所列补助项目计有:(1)生活补助费(仿照公务员分基数及薪俸倍数两项);(2)眷属食米;(3)特别办公费;(4)膳费;(5)宿费五种。当时本行会同他行局力争,以公务员分区核给生活补助费办法与银行行员情形稍有大(不)同,希望酌予改动。四联总处以法令所在,不容两歧,只陈明行政院将原定分区略予归并,以期简化。迨至是年八月又将生活补助费内所列基数、倍数重订,俾与物价上涨情形不至相差过巨。迨至今春物价又有剧烈波动,公教人员待遇又有改进,四行一局会商之下,乃有最近之改订。所难者无论如何改善,终难追随物价,而开支方面又须顾到,是诚目前最足研讨之问题也。

原载:《中国银行行史资料汇编(上编)(二)》

中国银行行务会议人事报告(1947)

去年五月,举行召开行务会议以来,又及一年,关于人事各案,深感各行经理及与会各同人详为研讨,大部分经董事长、总经理、副总经理核定已次第实施,惟其中最感困难者厥为征用人员及待遇问题,兹分别报告如下:

(一)用人问题

本行复员以后,各复业行所用人员多系向内地行商调或复用旧员,去年虽有训练及培养人才之提案,除国外部已考用一批大学毕业生及各行间有考用练习生外,因限于训练设备及训练地方尚未能积极进行,而各行迫于业务需要,不免随时酌予征用。一年以来,增加的一千五百余人,四联总处根据报告,对于各行局征用新员深加注意,特于去年十一月,在京召集各行局人事主任人员,前往会议,其主要论题为:

(甲)各行局今后录用新进人员应事紧缩,如业务上确有必要时,应先按实际需要,拟定名额,报请核准后再行征选。(乙)嗣后各行局录用新进人员应参照考试法规分别考选,此外,并嘱于每月月终填具重要职员动态表及员生人数统计表,送处查核。

关于(甲)点,四联总处为推行事前核准之权,自有其立场所在,而各行局用人孔(恐)急,如每用一人,均须先得四联总处之核准,事实上恐有困难,结果只得在员生人数统计表内,将加增人数,理由分别说明,但仍不免常有来函质问。关于(乙)点,各行局用人集中按考试法规考选,用意固佳,事实上亦有困难。本行方面,只得遇有某分行申请考用练习生,特将需要理由及考取名额报请四联总处核复,再行定期考试,所以现在征用新人外顾环境,内审行力,实值得研究,应如何期得妥善计划,当另案提请研究。

(二)待遇问题

年来物价暴涨,如何维持同人生活俾得安心工作,实属严重之问题,去年行务会议虽有改善方案,顾以闭会不久,政府即发表改订公教人员生活补助费基数倍数,各行局立即仿照办理,情形变更,如将本行所拟方案同时实施,势所难能,复虑引起政府及四联总处之注意,是以有一部分只得从缓,迨至今年二月,上海发生金潮,物价扶摇直上,政府采繁急措施,同时复发表公教人员配售实物办法,各行局有鉴于情形之迫切,先函致上海市政府询问各行局职员配售实物问题,未有结果,而职员生活之救济之急不能待,不得已,比照银行员生活补助费,较诸公教人员得加三成之规定,将膳费公厨各加三成,并将配售实物差额加入公厨之内,更因政府所定配售实物差额,只限于京沪区,而银行员待遇,秦具全国性故规,实各分支处职员应得之数,以总行为标准,据知此项办法备受四联总处之责难,谓银行员所领差额数目与规定不符,经于四月间召集各行主管人事人员赴京讨论,幸得善为解释,提出理事会研究,终未得正式之核准,所以最近因公教人员生活补助费基数倍数已予调整,不日公布,各行局公议,兼此取消原定差额之办法,以免指责,嗣后如何办理,尚须统盘筹划,总而言之,现在物价时有波动,如何将一般行员生活水准、高级职员与普通职员如何差别,俾符既禀称事之用意,如何求得各行局办法,能期相近,容易推行,如何不致引起政府及四联总处之诘责,同时并须考虑行力之担负,具有以上种种因素,故待遇问题实为近期办理人事者最感困难之关节,深望与会诸君详为指教。

原载:《中国银行档案》 未刊稿

中国银行董事长孔庸之先生致股东总会报告书

【编者按】1944年2月至1948年4月孔祥熙任中国银行董事长。1948年4月24日中国银行计划召开第二十四届股东大会,1948年4月2日远在美国的中国银行董事长孔祥熙电告戴志骞,请为其起草股东报告书。4月6日,戴志骞拟好报告书,孔祥熙仅对第(六)点稍加修改,准备在股东大会上宣读。然而,1948年4月16日,蒋介石在南京召见宋汉章,毫无商量地要其同意接替孔祥熙担任中国银行董事长,孔祥熙的报告也未能在会上宣读。

此为戴志骞起草的报告书原稿,孔祥熙在大会报告及印行时,将第(六)、(七)对调,在第(六)点中增加了个人活动:

"(六)上届股东会开会之日,本人曾引'不问收获,但问耕耘'二语,作为本行全体同仁应有之工作态度,今后自当仍本此旨,与各同仁互勉,抑尤有进者,现时局未靖,建国方殷,本行既为国际贸易银行,对于推广国际贸易,稳固国家金融,扶助侨胞海外发展,倡导国人民主精神,种种使命,实极重大,为完成此项使命,必须巩固行基,推广信誉,本人有鉴于此,常深自惕励,未敢疏懈,此次赴美考察,除向美方商讨促进合作外,并向中南美及南洋各地,调查工商侨务情形,业已陆续收到报告,现正研究推广国际贸易之计划,以供政府措施之参考,并做发展本行之准备,俾加强保障股东诸君之权益,再查年来物价腾涨未已,本行同仁生活虽异常困难,但其忠诚勤劳之精神,始终未懈,本行得有今日之成绩,实为同仁努力之结果,惜其所受艰苦,外界多未深知,股东诸君认识较深,想能洞察,尚望随时指导勉励,俾其精神上有所慰藉,本行职责所在,对同仁生计务须力求改善,使各同仁能安心服务,并应加紧收罗人才,培植本行后进,俾增强组织,发展行务,期以点滴之贡献,协助政府,使建国大业,得以早日实现。"其余未改动。

此处将戴志骞起草的原稿照录。

(一)诸位股东先生,今日为本行召开第二十四届通常股东总会之期,平日本行同人因职务关系,不克时向股东诸君有所请益,深以为歉,惟本行同人在执行任务时,莫不警惕于股东诸君托付之重,而股东诸君对于本行行务设施,亦必深致关切,是则今日之会,其意义之重大深远,当不待言。

(二)金融事业,与国内外经济环境,息息相通,世界大战结束,虽过两年,而和平康乐之境,尤待创造,各国经济情况,除极少数国家外,大率生产萎缩,物价上涨,贸易失其平衡,民生仍虞匮乏,大西洋宪章所揭橥之四大自由,尚难计日以待,至于国内经济,则因我国产业基础,素欠坚强,抗战期间,受创尤重,兼以战后政治局势,未臻安定,以致生产萎缩之程度,物价上涨之速率,国际贸易之逆差,民生困苦之普遍,较其他各国为尤甚,自抗战结束以来,本年度实为我国经济情况最艰苦之一年。

(三)政府为适应环境,一切设施,均以针对现实为指归,奖励生产,平抑物价,厘订外汇政策,管理国际贸易,凡此种种,均系在困难中求出路,动荡中谋安定,施行结果,虽未能如预期之美满,而其苦心孤诣,实为国人所共鉴。

（四）银行为整个国家之有机组织，国家经济情况之演变，对于本行业务之进展，固有重大影响，而政府为针对现实所厘订之政策，对于本行进展之方向，尤具指导作用，易言之，即本行一切设施，均应遵照政府规定，努力推动，以冀协助政府，改善我国经济地位，借尽本行所负之使命，而慰股东诸君之期望。

（五）兹就本行业务设施经过，举其荦荦大者，向股东诸君简略报告，生产事业之盛衰，与产品运销之滞畅，原因虽不止一端，然资金融通之便利与否，实为基本原因，本行为国际贸易银行，积极方面，应以便利出口贸易，增加外汇收入之业务为主，消极方面，凡能抵消进口，减少外汇支出之业务，均应尽力协助，故本行本年度主要放款对象，即为物资之生产与运销，对于出口贸易之推广，及外汇支出之减少，实收相当效果，此堪告慰于股东诸君者一也。我国以时局关系，财政收支不能平衡，通货逐渐增加，游资日趋庞大，治本有赖于政府，治标有赖于银行，本行为吸收游资，减轻其对于物价之压力，曾以最大努力，吸收存款，在物价逐月上涨之际，增加存款，原非易事，本行既不能以过分高利吸引存户，唯有改善办事手续，以服务精神争取顾主之好感，使其乐于将剩余资金，存入本行，施行结果，虽不能谓尽如预期，而本行同仁之心血，似尚未虚耗，综计本年底全行存款总额，达五万九千二百七十一亿，其中国币存款，计一万六千三百五十三余亿，外币存款，按基准价折合国币，计四万二千九百十八亿，较诸上年之国币存款二千三百六十亿，外币存款折合国币一千九百九十五亿，增加各在七倍与二十一倍之间，此堪告慰于股东诸君者二也。汇款方面，本年度数字十倍于上年，惟值兹币值未臻稳定，资金之埠际移动，就全国经济言，每易发生流弊，例如内地资金之大量集中东南少数都市，非特无补于物资之流通，反足使原已充斥于各该都市之游资，益趋庞大，而为投机事业推波助澜，政府有鉴及此，不得不厉行紧急措施，一面以收购成品代替货款，一面并限制汇款，在此种环境下，本行汇款业务，虽不免减色，然对于整个国家经济，裨益实多，良以本行职责，端在奉行国策，凡于国家有利之事，自当尽力以赴，此可告慰于股东诸君者三也。本年度内，本行经收出口外汇，约合美金四千七百三十余万元，占全国出口总值五分之一，经付进口外汇，约合美金八千七百五十余万元，其在进口总值内所占比率，与经收出口外汇相等，经收出口外汇中，包括华侨汇款，但全年侨汇总额，尚不及美金一千万元，较上年殊为逊色，平日本行为侨胞及侨眷服务，虽已竭尽心力，惟因受其他因素之阻挠，仍不免事倍功半。

（六）至本行在三十六年度内，各种设施之详细情形，宋总经理当另有报告。

（七）上届股东会开会之日，本人曾引"不问收获，但问耕耘"二语，作为本行全体同仁应有之工作态度，今后本行处境纵属艰苦，本行同仁仍当一秉过去精神，克服困难，努力迈进，以期点滴贡献，协助政府，使国家经济由动荡趋于安定，由安定臻于繁荣，唯一切仍有赖于政府及股东诸君之督导。

民国三十七年四月六日

原载：《中国银行档案》 未刊稿

本行沿革概要

【编者按】此为在戴志骞档案中发现的打印稿。1942年12月3日，中国银行成立"银行人员训练所"，戴志骞任所务委员。1943年2月8日，"银行人员训练所"开学，戴志骞主讲"本行先进发展史"。1944年6月8日，中国银行渝分行举办"初级人员训练班"，聘请戴志骞讲授"本行先进服务史"，6月15日，中国银行渝分行再次聘请戴志骞为"初级人员训练班"讲授"本行先进服务史"。本稿疑为戴志骞的讲稿。

中国银行系前清户部银行及大清银行递嬗而来，当辛亥革命告成，各地大清银行因战事影响相继停业，乃由大清银行商股联合会呈准南京临时政府，就上海大清银行旧址改设中国银行，并设分行于南京，迨南北统一，中央政府将大清银行清理，由财部另拨股本，设中国银行筹备处于北京，八月一日，北京行开始营业，至二年四月，参议院公布"中国银行则例"，成立总行，为全行总辖机关，而于各省分设分行、分号等机构，中国银行于以成立。

中国银行开业之始，实收股本甚微，而发荣滋长，以至今日，实基于重视信用及服务效能，期间兴革应付有足述者，兹为撮举数事，以为鉴往知来之助。

一、民初之承还大清银行商股商存

大清银行商股共有库平银五百万两，存款银六百七十余万两，中国银行于成立之初，概即担任代还之责，所有商股换给存单，分四年还清，存款亦定分年摊还之办法，其在两千两以下者一年还清，两千两以上者三年还清，此项整付之款再由政府陆续拨还，当时本行基础薄弱，而毅然担任代还之重责者，盖以认清信用之重要。

二、民五之维持兑现

民国五年洪宪政变，南北军兴。五月，袁氏下令停兑中、交两行钞券，全国骚然，本行上海分行首先反抗，主张组织股东联合会，由律师代表股东接收该行之资产负债，一面与上海绅商各界合作，维持兑现，继而江、浙、津、汉、豫、晋各省亦闻风响应，人心赖以安定，而袁氏希冀任意取借，不兑现纸币之图谋因未得遂，此举不独使本行之社会地位愈臻巩固，实亦为我国树立钞信基础。

三、民六之改制

由于民五之停兑，本行有鉴于发行银行不可不求业务上之独立，爰于民国六年十一月呈准政府修改则例，以股东总会为本行最高组织，原由政府简任之总裁、副总裁改由政府于股东总会选出之董事中简任，营业方针亦自政府方面转注于商业，迄至北伐告成之十年中，国内干戈时起，政变频仍，本行之得以维持其独立精神不受政潮波动之影响，且能发挥服务效能于社会有所贡献者，民六之改制实有以致之。

四、国际汇兑业务之创办

我国自前清开埠通商以后，国际间汇兑及贸易业务，无不操纵于在华外商银行、洋行及其买办之手，例如，商民以货物售予洋行，取回洋行之汇票既不明汇兑手续，又无法以之周转损失綦重，本行鉴于商民需要之殷切，于民初即由上海分行办理有关国际汇兑之业务，收受国外汇票贴现抵押,其设立于通商口岸各分行,如津、鲁、闽、广等行亦均办理,一时商民称便,惟起初此种业务仍须经过洋行买办之居间,历经困阻,卒以本行信誉昭著,深受外国各银行之信仰,始能直接经办。外国商家夙与我国银行不通,闻问者亦多,乐与本行往来,至此,洋行买办之气焰亦为之稍敛,其于国(民)族利权颇有挽回。民国十七年国府特定本行为国际汇兑银行者,盖有由来。

组 织

本行为股份有限公司组织,民国六年以前,以总裁与副总裁为首长,总理全行行务。自民国六年十一月第二次修正"中国银行则例",扩充商股,依照公司条例,以股东大会为全行最高组织,而总裁、副总裁原由政府简任者,改由政府于股东大会选出之董事中简任,并于民国七年二月召开第一届股东大会于北京,选出董事十一人,监事五人,分组董、监事会,以行使职权,以至民国十七年本行总管理处南迁至沪,除董、监事因任期届满而依法改选外,其名额及组织均无变更。

民国十七年,国民政府订颁"中国银行条例",特定本行为国际汇兑银行,其组织仍为股份有限公司,董事名额增至十五人,设常务董事五人,由财部指派,其中一人为董事长,以总理全行事务,监察人名额仍为五人,设常务监察一人,主席监察一人,以执行监察事务,取消总裁、副总裁制,改设总经理。民国二十四年,增加官股,董事、监事人名额亦以增加:订董事名额增至二十一人,监察人名额增至七人,其中由财政部指派之董事九人、监察人三人,其余董事十二人、监察人四人,则由股东总会之商股股东就百股以上之商股股东中选任之,分组董事会及监察人会,并各推常务董事七人,常驻监察人一人,以执行会务。由财政部于常务董事中指派一人为董事长,设总经理一人,承董事长之命办理全行事务,并执行董事会议决事项。民国二十六年十二月设副总经理一人,民国三十一年十二月增设副总经理一人,共为二人,民国三十三年二月举行第二十一届股东总会,改选商股董事,因民国三十二年财部增加官股,故本行董事名额增为二十五人,监察人名额增为九人,其中官股董事为十三人、官股监察人为五人,所有商股董事、监察人名额及常务董事、常驻监察人名额俱无增减。

业 务

一、民国元年至十七年

自民国元年至民国十七年之一阶段中,本行履行国家银行之职务,除一般性之存放款汇兑业务外,其主要者有:(甲)代理国库;(乙)协助整理币制;(丙)发行钞券;(丁)外汇业务及外债经付。

二、民国十八年至二十六年

本行于民国十七年十月改为国际汇兑银行,自民国十八年迄二十六年对日抗战发生时止之一阶段中,本行除赓续原有之一般业务,继续发行兑换券及代理一部分国库外,因鉴于国际汇兑业务实基于国际贸易之发达,而国际贸易之发达,必须促进国内农工商业之繁荣,故于国内各项经济建设颇多,致力此一阶段中,本行业务工作方面,其要者约有:(甲)设置国外行处及办理国外业务之专部;(乙)辅助新兴工业;(丙)农业放款;(丁)协助铁路建设;(戊)安定金融市场;(己)调查及研究工作;(庚)服务辅助之增多与工作效率之增进。

三、民国二十七年以来

自民国二十六年"七七"对日抗战发生以来,本行力行国策,凡百设施均求与国家战时需要相适应,自民国二十七年至三十二年止之一阶段中,本行除赓续原有之一般存汇业务,并继续发行兑换券,以至民国三十一年七月发行集中停止外,业务工作之重要者有:(甲)外汇行市之维持与需要之供给;(乙)军政汇款之应付;(丙)侨汇之沟通;(丁)后方工业生产及国营事业之协助;(戊)农贷及工业合作贷款之推进;(己)节约储蓄之推行;(庚)捐款之经收与公债之募集;(辛)收兑硬币金银,(壬)国外及后方机构之增设。

原载:《中国银行档案》 未刊稿

【附录】戴志骞主持的会议记录及报告

【附录 I】

1942年中国银行行务会议人事委员会会议记录及议决案

【编者按】中国银行行务会议成立人事委员会,贝淞孙、卞白眉、金涌泉、束云章、徐广迟、黄伯权、戴志骞为委员。

戴志骞君报告上次大会议决关于人事各案组织永久性之小组会讨论,今日列席诸君,均系指定委员,现在先将各案逐次讨论:

一、调剂人才案

众议可照原案将优秀行员向人事室登记,其有员缺需要人手者,亦可先在人事室登记,并议及资遣人员办法,凡在行服务一年以上者,给予薪津两个月作为遣散费,每在行服务增加一年,所发遣散费之薪津亦进增一个月,遇有特别情形者,如眷属人口多、回籍地方远之类,并得由当地行经理斟酌情形,另予加发薪津,但至多不得过两个月,以上所述之薪津,即按月所发总数,除去房租津贴及膳食代金之数。

二、关于家用汇款案

众议可仿照中央及农民银行办理。

三、退职人员之恤养金应如何支给案

众议应比照在职行员战时生活补助金固定及指数部分加给补助金,另给本人两市斗米,有配偶者加发两斗,指数部分及米代金,均以付款行所在地为准,支领之后,如需汇往他处,汇水概由自理。

四、本行同仁团体保寿案

众议:(1)应改定保额,凡在行在五年以下,保额三千元,满五年以上,保额六千元,满十年以上,保额一万元;(2)保费先在现存基金项下支付,一面另筹集福利基金,将来保费有不足时,即在福利基金拨付。

五、筹集福利基金并组织基金委员会案(临时动议)

众议先拟组织委员会之委员,拟请总经理、副总经理、总稽核、总秘书、副总稽核、总账室主任、人事室主任及沪渝处史海峰副经理为委员,俟委员会成立后,再议如何筹集福利基金方法及福利基金总额。

六、雍行所提拟具全行人事整个计划意见案

众议由人事委员会详拟具体办法见诸实施。

七、渝行及赣支行提案已分别并入上列各案讨论

议决事项：

本届行务会议关于人事部分，历次所讨论者，除已有结论外，本小组会应继续讨论者分列如下：

一、调剂本行人才案

（原案摘要）：1. 设法少用新员；2. 对于撤退人员之安插，应由人事室设法介绍于各行，尽先安插，其实无可安插者，只好依照撤退人员遣散办法资遣；3. 各行人才应互相调用，将可调之才填表送人事室登记，再由人事室通知联行，以备随时商调，俾人得其用，职无闲员。

（上次小组会意见），拟照原案并添入，"凡各行人手有余或不足者，均先报人事室登记，如有相当缺出，先尽登记人才选用"。

（大会意见）除照小组会拟增以上两句外，对于调剂人才及资遣庸碌等问题，应组织永久性人事小组，详为讨论。此案似可将雍行所提"提高员生工作效率，务使人尽其才，并认真减少冗员，俾一人可办兼人之事，即以所省之薪津，增厚其余努力服务者之待遇，以免人事开支膨胀，而同时可收节用废人之功"并案讨论。

二、同仁家用汇款应研究适当办法案

（原案摘要）本行行员在自由区服务者，其家属现住沦陷区数尚不少，因交通不便及服务行近战区之处，常有移动，故一时不能悉数迁入内地，而接济家用遂生困难，对于汇款不予帮助，不免分心，于促进工作效率不无影响，但汇水日高，本行担负甚重，汇往北方者，贴水比前益增，汇往上海者，自当地禁用法币，后汇率亦与前不同，究应如何办理。

（上次小组会意见）拟定办法三项，勿（无）论汇往何处，一律通用，（一）汇额按本人全月实得之一切薪津总数百分之八十为限；（二）汇水按百分之八十由行付账，百分之二十由汇款本人负担；（三）汇水之计算，第一办法如不能直接通汇，只以国币能通汇最近之地点应付之汇水为限。第二办法不论汇往何处，行方只担负定额之汇水，最多不得过若干，其数目请大会公定。

（大会意见）交上述人事小组会研定后再为核定。

三、退职人员之恤养金应如何支给案

（原案摘要）养老金及终身恤金照三十年七月三十日行务会议之决案，系按旧章，甲等时津贴加倍支给，现住沦陷区者时，因改用当地货币，各退职人员不足以维生活，且亦无法汇给，应如何办理。

此案应与渝行所提调整退职养老金案并案讨论，渝行提案大意，以在职人员另有其他津贴以资弥补，但退职人员对于各项津贴均不能享受，相差过巨，似应予调整，以维生活。

（上次小组会意见）关于退职人员养老金、终身恤金，比照人字六十号通函"改善员生生活办法"第三条所定，战时生活补助金固定部分加倍支给，养老金、终身恤金均应在非沦陷区本行分支行支领，但在沦陷区者，可委托本行行员代领，仍经总处核准后代领。

（大会意见）决定原则如下：除原领恤养金外，再照本人退职时本俸，比照现时同等薪给者应得之战时生活补助金固定部分，加倍支给，另给本人及其配偶米代金各两斗，并比照现行房租津贴办法最高额半数支给或另定固定金额，所有该项详细办法，交由上述人事小组会研订后再为核定。

四、本行同仁团体保寿增加保额案

（原案摘要）（一）现行办法保额太少，职员不幸身故，尚不足以殡殓，适满还族之存恤，拟改为到行未满三年者,保额国币二千元,到行满三年或三年以上者,保额国币五千元;(二)保险基金渐次减少,如保额增加,基金更见锐减,应如何筹补。

此案与渝行所提改订人寿保险额度并案讨论,渝行提案大意拟增加保额自五千元至一万元,并拟请将保险改为带储蓄性之定期普通寿险,至退休时可以取款,其增加之保费,拟请将行员存款利率提高二厘,以为补偿。

(上次小组会意见)(一)照原案所拟改保额度办理;(二)希望保费减低与中国保险公司商洽办理,并将行员定期存款另加息二厘,提作保险基金;(三)凡加入团体保寿者,以已到自由区之行处,并已派定职务者为限。

(大会意见)除原定保额二仟元及五千元两种外,并增加一万元一种,其年限交由上述人事小组会议研订后,再为核定。

五、渝行所提调整同仁各项待遇案

(原案摘要)(甲)调整米贴;(乙)改订特别办公费;(丙)调整旅费及选调携眷旅费;(丁)调整储金年金及年间津贴;(戊)明确规定办事处主任及办事分处主管员之待遇;(己)改订人寿保险额度;(庚)调整退职养老金。

(上次小组会意见)(甲)仿照中央银行办法办理;(乙)(己)(庚)已并案讨论,见前;(丙)改订旅费、日用费已有通函;(丁)(戊)俟四联总处漾(样)定后,再行办理。

(大会意见)甲乙决定仿照中央银行办理,自十月份实行。其余各案除经声明因牵涉其他各行局有连带关系者外,均已并入上列各案讨论。

六、雍行所提拟具全行人事调整计划意见案

(原案摘要)1.本行应建立中心思想,由总处通信、训话,或由总处领示方针,由各行高级人员阐发演讲;2.总处对于人事管理机构宜更求充实,并严定人事考核制度;3.总处对于高级人员之养成,或低级员生之训练等,宜有通盘计划。

(上次小组会意见)原则极表赞同,拟请另组委员会,详拟具体办法,再行讨论。

(大会意见)并交人事小组会议详拟具体办法。

七、赣支行所提汇寄留居沦陷区内同人眷属家用所差升水由行方负担案

(原案摘要)为体会同人生计,并使安心工作起见,对于接济家用汇款,允宜予以维持,并规定请汇款额以不得超过每月所入薪津之若干成为限,由服务行最高主管员负责从严审核。

(上次小组会意见)拟与总处提案并案讨论。

(大会意见)与人事小组会议并案讨论

此案似可与上列第二案并案讨论。

关于人事问题的大会议决案:

第七案　调剂人才案　　　　　　　　　　　　　　总处提出
第十八案　第五项　第三目　提高员生工作效率　　雍行提出

以上两案经人事委员会并案讨论,拟具办法,提经大会通过如下:

应照原案将优秀行员向人事室登记,其有员缺需要人手者,亦可先在人事室登记。

又议定资遣人员办法,凡在行服务一年以上者,给予薪津二个月作为遣散费,每在行服务增加一年,所发遣散费之薪津亦递增一个月,遇有特别情形者,如眷属人口多,回籍地方远之类,并得由当地行经理斟酌情形,另予加发薪津,但至多不得过三个月,以上所述之薪津,

即按月所发总数,除去房租津贴及膳食代金之数。

  第八案 住居沦陷区退职人员之恤养金应如何支给案   总处提出

  第十七案 (庚)项 调整退职养老金   渝行提出

  以上两案经人事委员会并案讨论,拟具办法,提经大会通过如下:

  应比照在职行员战时生活补助金固定及指数部分,加给补助金,另给本人两市斗米,有配偶者加发两市斗,指数部分及米代金均以付款行所在地为准,支领之后,如须汇往他处,汇水概由自理,自本年十月份起实行。

  第九案 同人家用汇款应研究适当办法案   总处提出

  第二十二案 汇济(寄)留居沦陷区内同人眷属家用款项所差升水请由行方负担案

                         赣支行提出

  以上两案经人事委员会并案讨论,拟具办法,提经大会修正,应仿照中央银行办法办理,自本年十一月份起实行。

  第十案 改订公费案   总处提出

  第十七案 (己)项 改订特别办公费   渝行提出

  以上两案经人事小组会议并案讨论,拟具报告,提经大会修正通过如下:

  除应将总处原案所订办事分处主管员、办事处主任公费数目,修改为分行副主任直辖支行及支行各系主任或专员办事分处主管员,月支公费国币六十元至一百二十元,分行各股主任或专员办事处主任,月支公费国币八十元至二百元外,其余均照原案通过,自本年十月份起实行。

  第十一案 改订房租津贴数目范围案   总处提出

  经人事小组会议讨论,拟具报告,提经大会修正通过如下:

  除应将原案简易储蓄处主管员房租津贴删去,并将原案第二项改为"支行各系主管或专员月支房租津贴至多不得超过一百四十元",第三项改为"支行经理月支房租津贴至多不得超过二百元,支行襄理、分行各股主任或专员办事处主任月支房租津贴至多不得超过一百六十元"外,其余均照原案通过,自本年十月份起实行。

  第十二案 同仁团体保寿增加保额案   总处提出

  第十七案 (己)项 改订人寿保险额度   渝行提出

  经人事委员会并案讨论,拟具办法,提经大会修正通过如下:

  (1)应改订保额,允在行在五年以下,保额三千元,满五年以上保额六千元,满十年以上保额一万元,但雇员保额最多不得超过六千元。

  (2)保费先在现存基金项下支付,一面另筹集福利基金,将来保费有不足时,即在福利基金拨付,自本年十二月份起实行。

  第十七案 (甲)调整米案   渝行提出

    (丙)调整旅费及迁调携眷旅费

    (丁)调整储金年金及年间津贴

    (戊)明确规定办事处主任及办事分处主管员之待遇

  经人事小组会议讨论,拟具报告,提经大会通过如下:

  (甲)仿照中央银行办法办理,定于十月份起支给。

  (丙)关于旅费日用费之改订,只能仿照中央银行现行限额办理,总处已有通函公布。

(丁)四联总处人事制度设计委员会小组会正在讨论,俟议定并由中央银行实行时,再行照办。

(戊)俟四联总处人事制度设计委员会议后,再行办理。

  第十九案 拟具全行人事整个计划意见案   雍行提出

  议决:由人事委员会详拟具体办法,见诸实施。

  临时动议:福利基金并组织基金委员会案

  议决:先组织委员会,请总经理、副总经理、总稽核、总秘书、副总稽核、总账室主任、人事室主任、各部经理、各分行经理及沪渝处史海峰副经理为委员,俟委员会成立后,再议如何筹集福利基金方法及福利基金总额。

  第十八案 第六项 由总处遴派赴外稽核分赴各地检查账目,并考核营业、人事以及开支等实况   雍行提出

  议决:原则甚是,由总处随时注意实行

  临时动议:电台报务员管理问题   浙行金经理提出

  查电台报务员应归当地行处文书股管理,前有通函规定,兹经议决,应将电台服务规程再发通函饬遵。

                     原载:《中国银行档案》 未刊稿

【附录Ⅱ】

1946年中国银行行务会议人事组戴召集人志骞报告

【编者按】 1946年6月14日中国银行行务会议闭会,人事组召集人戴志骞作人事报告。

(甲)关于人事者

(一)维持同人生活问题

原提案16——各级主管人员公费核给标准拟加改订案

原提案55——建议调整同人待遇原则案

原提案73——请厘定各级人员水、电、灯费,住宅、家具、工程等之供应标准案

原提案65——本行行员公厨供应一项,应如何调整案

原提案84——拟请放宽同人子女教育奖励金(金)标准案

原提案85——同人子女在小学肄业者,拟请援照中学办法,给予贷金及奖金案

原提案66——本行行员定量供应周转金如何支配案

原提案96——请速举办收复区同人福利事业案

行员部分:

(1)生活补助费 再增支百分之二十,作为"技术津贴",关于基数倍数,以管辖行行员所支基数倍数为原则,其辖内有特殊区域经政府规定基数倍数比管辖行所在地为高者,得另案申请总处核准,照特殊区域之规定。又粤行系支港币,其辖内行员应支基数倍数以广州为标准,粤行本身待遇照香港当地情形另定之。

(2)膳费 按照向例,由行供膳,每月餐费最多不得超过当地市石一石中等米之市价。

(3)日用必需品 指定日用必需品四项(米、煤、布、油),按一定标准价及一定之数量售与同人,负责之职员及直系亲属超过六人者,可在定量以外,分别增加一份或半份,对于高级职员,并有相当之供应,其公费并得照本俸应加之倍数加给之。

(4)福利 福利部分如子女教育费及医药费等均照原拟办法加以改善。

雇员、试用员、练习生部分:

(1)雇员待遇按行员待遇百分之八十办理。

(2)试用员试用雇员之待遇在到行三个月以内按行员待遇百分之五十办理,到行满三个月以上,按行员待遇百分之七十五办理。

(3)练习生之待遇,限正项津贴生活补助费,按薪加倍数基本数,及加成数膳费、本人宿舍等项,其公厨部分或售给实物部分不予支给。

(二)调整行员俸级问题

原提案15——请将本行中级及初级行员俸级酌予调整,请核议案

原提案56——复员人事流动,拟请调整行员本俸或提前办理考绩,放宽晋升级数,以适应需要案

审查意见:仍照原定薪俸规则办理,再各处复员调动人员已有半数将薪俸调整,至于考绩一节,由总处酌定办理。

(三)训练及培养人才问题

原提案12——拟请培养人才案

原提案 53——训练外汇人才案

审查意见：

较高级干部人才及外汇人才，由总处训练培养中级人员，由各分支行分别办理，本年各处如有需要，可酌招练习生一批。

(四)行员内外互调问题

原提案 42——建议会计人员内外互调，以利会计制度之推行

原提案 89——抗战期内在后方服务人员，应陆续与收复区征录进行人员互调案

审查意见：

原则通过，至如何调动，应草拟办法，由各行提出意见，交人事室汇总统筹。

(五)恤金及养老金问题

原提案 13——拟请改定现行恤养办法案

原提案 81——拟请提高养老金及抚恤金数额案

审查意见：

养老金及终身恤金办法，仍照行员恤养规则第十九条、第二十条、第三条之规定分别办理，但值此时期，得按月支数目比照付款行(即领受养老金终身恤金人员居住所在地)行员所支取之基数倍数加成数支给有配偶者给米一石，无配偶者六斗，另关于配售日用必需品米、煤、油、布四项，亦可比照办理，但成分应予酌减，其月支养老金或终身恤金自愿一次支领者，得一次给予之，又一时(次)恤金仍照行员恤养规则第十五条办理，在此时期可比照其生前所支之基数、倍数加成数，加入计算，并得由行酌量批给棺殓费，其支领养老金终身恤金人员死亡时，亦得酌批棺殓费。又资遣费，其给薪津之月份，仍照现行办法办理，并加支基数、倍数，终身人员于支领资遣费之外，并照上述标准加给二个月，省①眷属者，加给三个月作为旅费。

(六)奖慰战时服务同人及边区同人问题

原提案 57——本年度为奖慰同人战时服务忠勤，凡因有省亲扫墓而请假者，拟请特给假期免予扣支考勤奖慰案

原提案 88——对行员回籍给假，拟特订办法，核给旅费，其应享有之待遇，仍行照给，以优待外省籍留在后方工作同人案

原提案 101——为使服务边区同人安心工作起见，拟请按照邮汇局例另订边区津贴及特准返籍假，并支给旅费办法案

审查意见：

第 57 案由各行斟酌办理，1. 以不妨碍工作为原则；2. 每人准请假一次，次(此)项办法适用至明年六月底止；3. 今年计算不请假奖金从宽办理，边区津贴规定至为困难，拟从缓议，至准给假省亲一节，拟照第 88 案渝行所提办法办理。

(七)提高行员因公旅费问题

原提案 80——拟请提高行员因公旅费案

审查意见：

因公旅费办法已由总处改订颁布，本案不讨论。

(八)批给雇员不请假奖金问题

---

① 【编者注】即探望。

原提案82——拟请批给雇员不请假奖金案

审查意见：

雇员不请假奖金由当地行批给，为最多不得超过行员应得之半数。

(九)划一国外行处待遇问题

原提案99——划一国外行处待遇案

审查意见：

留供人事室及国外部厘订国外行待遇时之参考。

(十)治装费及补助费截止期限问题

原提案67——本行所定调往收复区工作人员治装费及补助费应否定一截止期限案

审查意见：

由总处斟酌办理。

(十一)提高集团致赙金额问题

原提案86——提请提高集团致赙金额案

审查意见：

致赙金额加十倍，同仁每月扣提之数照加十倍。

(十二)加拨福利基金问题

原提案87——拟请总处加拨福利基金案

审查意见：

请由福利基金委员会酌议增加，由总处统筹办理，但以(一)各行人数多寡；(二)各处物价高低为筹拨金额之标准。

(十三)处理同人借支薪津问题

原提案100——本年二、三月份同人借支薪津及春节借款(沪行十万元，其他各行二个月薪津)应如何处理案

审查意见：

本年一、二、三月份薪津按四月份新定办法调整扣抵借支，其公厨部分以四月份所支之数为标准，其计算方法比照上海四月份米价三万一千元、公厨五万元之比例，依各地米价将原支之数予以调整后重新支给，以之扣抵前借之款，其不足扣抵者分别缴还。

(乙)附事务部分

(一)改编电本问题

原提案47——拟请改编本行成密电本案

原提案75——拟请彻底重编本行成密电本以切实用案

审查意见：

本行电本正在重编中，各行如有心得，请提供总处参考。

(二)调整电台问题

原提案40——为调整本行电台及改进电务手续以利业务案

审查意见：

原则照办，由总处积极办理。

(三)定期编印通函问题

原提案74——拟请总处将发出通函每隔半年编印分类摘要以便参考案

审查意见:
照办。
(四)订立营缮费标准问题
原提案78——营缮费用应事前陈准订立标准案
审查意见:
照办。
(五)集中管理行产问题
原提案79——行产之移转与让售应集中管理案
审查意见:
由各行建议总处酌办。

原载:《中国银行档案》 未刊稿

Present Library Conditions in China[①]

T. C. Tai, B. A., B. L. S. librarian of Tsing Hua college Peking, China

SINCE the Revolution of 1911, China has undergone a movement of change. Politically the outlook is still very dark, but social and educational works have bright prospects. In 1912 the Ministry of Education laid great emphasis on social education, and he regards the public library as one of the powerful agencies in the diffusion of knowledge among the people. The government turned the imperial library of the late Manchu dynasty at Peking into a public library and ordered the authorities of different provinces and districts to establish public libraries. Some of the districts have carried out the order, but some, owing to lack of funds, are still in the period of preparation. At present the library conditions in China are in their infancy.

This article is not a general survey of present Chinese libraries, but a sketch of a few so-called leading libraries. These can be roughly classified into three types, namely, society libraries, college libraries, and public libraries. The society library has been mainly established by westerners and maintained by membership fee. The acquisition chiefly depends upon donation, exchanges and complimentary copies from authors. The best known is the Library of the North China Branch of the Royal Asiatic Society at Shanghai.

This library was founded about 1860 and the collection on China given by Mr Wylie formed its nucleus. Now it has about 4000 volumes in foreign languages and about 2000 in Chinese. Although the collection is not large, it is fairly strong in works on China. The section of Eastern Asiatic languages was enlarged by Messrs Kingsmill and Morse. The famous bibliographer, Henri Cordier, compiler of "Bibliotheca Sinica," was once the librarian of this society library.

The Dewey decimal classification with the Cutter author numbers and the card dictionary catalog were adopted in 1907, upon the strong recommendation of Dr Bolton of the Boston Athenaeum. The library is open daily and the privilege of taking out books is enjoyed by members only. Members not resident in Shanghai can have books by mail.

As a model for establishing society libraries in different parts of China for meeting special needs, it is a very good example for the foreigners who are in the service of Chinese governmental, commercial, industrial and other corporations, and for the Chinese students who have received their technical education in this country or in Europe. It will require generations yet for the Chinese public libraries to have strong collections of scientific books.

Almost every college now has a sort of library. A few of the could-be-called college libraries

---

[①] Mr. Tai will be very glad to answer any inquiries relating to Chinese library topics or, indeed, any Chinese subject, within his knowledge and ability. A letter addressed to him at Tsing Hua college library, Peking, China, will receive his prompt attention.

are as follows:

    Hongkong Queen's college library.

    Huangchow ChiKiang college library.

    Lin-Nan college library.

    Nanking High Normal college library.

    Nanking university library.

    Pei Yang university library.

    Peking Government university library.

    Peking Medical college library.

    Peking Methodist university library.

    Peking Tsing Hua college library.

    Shanghai Baptist college library.

    Shanghai Polytechnic institute library.

    Shanghai St John's University, Low library.

    Shanghai Siccawei Catholic college library.

    Shangtung university library.

    Shensi university library.

    Soochow university library.

    Tungchow Union college library.

    Wuchang Boone university library.

    All the libraries named above have two collections, one in English and the other in Chinese. Among the 19 libraries, so far the writer knows only three which are run according to the systems of modern American libraries with modifications.

    1. Wuchang Boone university library. This was extended and reorganized through the effort of Miss M. E. Wood about 1907. It has two collections, one of 6000 volumes in English and the other of 9000 in Chinese. As Mr Seng, the assistant librarian says: "The former is largely made up of theological and literary books; the latter, of classics and histories. Though the collection is too small to meet all the needs of that city, the books have been well selected." This library has been adequately organized and has done a great service not only to the students and alumni of that university, but also to the community of Wuchang at large.

    2. The Low library of St John's university, Shanghai, was begun about 1890. Mr Low's donation formed the nucleus of the collection. It has gradually and steadily grown year after year, until now it has its own quarters in the Anniversary Hall which was a gift from the alumni, students and friends, to the present president, Dr Pott, in commemmoration of the 25th anniversary of his presidency. The writer was then the librarian of the Low library and had the pleasure of watching its progress personally from 1909 to 1914. Its yearly growth necessitated the removal from the Yen Hall to the beautiful building in the ChaoFeng garden in 1911.

    For the sake of convenience in charging, shelving and cataloging, all the Chinese books in 1912 were bound in the style of English books. This was a great innovating advance in the history of Chinese libraries. Both English and Chinese books were classified according to Dewey decimal classification and the experiment was introduced of having a card classed catalog for the Chinese books. The section of Chinese history, 951, was also expanded in 1913. According to the 1916 report the library has 8000 volumes in English and 5000 volumes in Chinese. It is now well organized and ably administered under Mr Hsu, once a student in the New York public library school.

3. Peking Tsing Hua college library. This institution was a recent production of 1908 and became a college in 1911. Before the summer of 1914 the library had about 11,000 volumes in Chinese and 500 volumes in English and two dozen periodicals. On account of the rapid needs of the college and the amount of reference work done by the faculty and students, the library was, has been, and is always in thirst of new books. Within the last four years the collection grew to 25,000 volumes in Chinese, 6000 volumes in foreign languages and 150 periodicals. In 1916 the accessioning and classification were properly completed and organized. A mimeograph catalog of Chinese books was issued. According to the library report of February, 1918, the circulation in February reached the figure of 1389 volumes. In order to accommodate the rapidly increasing number of books, an up-to-date library building has just been completed in August, 1918, and its two big reading rooms can take more than two hundred readers at a time, and the stack capacity for 150,000 volumes in foreign languages was planned for the development of the next 15 years. The books are well selected and aim to have a strong collection on China in different languages.

Since 1914 I have been the librarian of that young but hopeful institution. Now it is my duty to point out a serious danger in such a rapidly growing library. The present-day Chinese educators begin to know the importance of a library, but are still ignorant of its administrative questions. They are willing to assign big appropriations for acquisitions, but are extremely stingy in the expenses of maintenance and administration. Economically and scientifically it is much better for a library to have a steady growth, but at the same time with an efficient system of administration.

On account of lacking statistics, I am able to give only a few well-known public libraries in four provinces, viz., Chihli, Shangtung, Kiangsu, and Chekiang. In those four provinces there are 16 organized public libraries, and the few well-known ones are as follows:

The Peking public library established in 1912 has about 80,000 volumes besides a big collection of ancient and valuable transcript copies. The systems of classification and cataloging are in accord with the "Imperial descriptive catalog of the Manchu dynasty." It has two branch libraries, the Peking branch public library and the Peking *free* public library.

The public libraries in China sell tickets for using books. The amount of ticket charges is different in different localities and also varies according to the kind of ticket you buy. There are six grades of tickets in the Peking public library, namely 1) one penny ticket for ordinary books, 2) one penny ticket for periodicals and newspapers, 3) one penny student ticket for ordinary books, 4) free student ticket for periodicals and newspapers, 5) one nickel ticket for incunabula, 6) half nickel ticket for the manuscript copy of the famous "Imperial descriptive catalog of the Manchu dynasty." Certainly the public is not admitted to the stack rooms. There are many reading rooms, as special reading room for special ticket holders, ladies' reading room, periodical and newspaper reading room, etc. There is much red tape in drawing books.

Besides the six ordinary tickets, there are two classes of special tickets, first and second. Those who hold the special ticket of the first class can enjoy the privilege of inspecting and using ordinary books, periodicals, newspapers, incunabula, etc., without charge in addition to having access to the stacks. Those who hold the special ticket of the second class can enjoy only the free use of ordinary books, periodicals and newspapers. The *free* public libraries in China mean to let the people use their collections without any charge, but you cannot draw out the books for home use. In connection with those libraries there are generally playgrounds and public lecture halls.

The second well-known public library is situated in the metropolitan city of Soochow, Kiangsu province. It has 85,000 volumes and the books are very well selected. The red tape in that library is comparatively better and less than in the Peking public library and the amount of charge has two grades instead of six. The penny special ticket holder can use the special reading room and the half penny ticket holder the ordinary reading room.

The third public library requiring special mention is the Wusih public library. It was founded in 1914 and now has about 30,500 volumes. According to the 1915 annual report the average number of readers in each month is about 300. The ticket charge is the same as in the other public libraries, but has only one grade, the half penny ticket. The other public libraries in different provinces have almost the same features as the Wusih public library, but not so well organized. The following two tables illustrate the comparison between a Chinese district library and an American city library.

Annual report of Wusih public library for 1915

Expenses	Chinese Currency
Salary for 5 members	$690
Two servants	60
Board for the library staff	248.888
Acquisition of books	636.834
Stationery, printing	159.515
Other	158.195
	$1953.432

Equal to $1302 U. S. Currency roughly.

Income	
General fund	$2126.129
Ticket charges	65.975
	$2192.104

Equal to $1538 U. S. Currency roughly.

Annual report of Troy, N. Y. public library, 1916

Expenses

Salaries	$7293.26
Supplies	470.92
Heat and light	894.62
Binding	551.02
Books	1147.73
Periodicals	391.36
Librarian, expenses	274.46
Repairs	311.00
Insurance	151.20
Other	933.13
	$12,418.70

Income

General fund	$1407.01
Special fund	1032.93
State of New York	100.00
City of Troy	8500.00
Fines, etc	639.92
Rents	1002.24
	$12,682.10

The population of Wusih is about one and half as large as that of Troy, but the library income and expense are only one-tenth those of the latter city. It is quite ridiculous now to compare the Chinese college libraries with those of Columbia, Harvard, and other American colleges, and the public libraries with those of New York, Boston, and other American public libraries.

A republic cannot be a true republic unless her citizens are properly educated. What have the libraries to do with the education of the people? The people of my country are not awake enough to answer this question, but you, the American librarians, can answer this question not only with pride but already prove to the world the good fruits of your actual deeds. I do not write to flatter you, but I do write to speak the truth. When the Prussian imperialism comes to the dust, the historian will say that American spirit and civilization saved the world. The American spirit and civilization were, are, and will be, carefully cultivated in the deeds of the American libraries and the American Library Association War Service. Any one who attended the A. L. A. Conference this year at Saratoga and visited the camp libraries will be my witness to the truth of my statements.

Since the treaty of Wanghia, between China and the United States on July 3, 1844, the history of the relations between these two great republics is one of unbroken friendship. We, the Chinese, always feel grateful towards your many a hearty and friendly help in political, social, educational and missionary works. We trust you because you are not the avaricious devourers of territory, but the loyal followers of democracy, fearless protectors of liberty, and true lovers of humanity. Now, I appeal to you, the American librarians and the Americans, that once more you win from us an everlasting gratitude by helping your young sister republic to educate her citizens by a library movement. I know you will not fail to answer the call by taking up the pleasant motherly duty of nourishing the four hundred millions with intellectual food after your manly work of slaughtering the "Brute of Kultur."

原载:*Public Libraries*(*Monthly*) Vol. 24 February 1919

【译文】任奕译　姜爱蓉审

中国图书馆的现状

戴志骞,B. A. ,B. L. S. 北平清华学校图书馆,中华民国①

自 1911 年辛亥革命以来,中国正经历一场变革运动。国内政治仍一片晦暗,但社会与教育工作却展露出令人欣喜的前景。1912 年,教育部十分重视社会教育,更是将公共图书馆视为向民众传播知识的重要机构。国民政府将位于北京的大清皇家图书馆开辟为公共图书馆,同时督促各省及地区政府建立公共图书馆,但由于各省财政状况不同,有些已贯彻执行,有些则仍在筹建。因此,目前中国的图书馆仍处发展初期。

此文并非是对中国图书馆现状的一般性评价,而是对业内佼佼者的概况简介。此佼佼者大致可分为社团图书馆、大学图书馆和公共图书馆三类。社团图书馆多由西方人创建并依靠会费维持,图书来源主要为捐赠、交换和作者的赠阅本,其中最著名的一所是位于上海的亚洲文会北中国支会图书馆。

该图书馆创建于 1860 年,伟烈亚力先生(Mr. Wylie)的私人藏书构成该图书馆收藏的核心。目前,该馆已拥有外文藏书四千余册,中文藏书两千余册。虽然藏书量不是很大,但它却在中国发挥了重大的作用。金斯米尔(Kingsmill)和摩尔斯(Morse)两位先生扩充了东亚语言类的藏书部分。《西人论中国书目》(*Bibliotheca Sinica*)的作者,著名书志学家高第(Henri Cordier)也曾是这家社团图书馆的馆员。

由于波士顿图书馆波顿博士(Dr Bolton)的大力推动,1907 年起亚洲文会图书馆开始采用《杜威十进分类法》、卡特著者号和卡片辞典目录。该馆每日开放,只有会员才可借阅图书,非上海市的会员可通过邮寄借阅。

全国各地面向不同需求的社团图书馆可将亚洲文会图书馆视为学习的楷模,在华供职于政府、工商业和其他团体的外国人,以及接受本国或欧美教育的中国学生都会因此受益。中国的公共图书馆还需要未来几代人持续不断地丰富科技类图书馆藏。

几乎每所大学都设有某种类型的图书室,其中可称为"大学图书馆"的有如下一些:

香港皇仁书院图书馆

杭州之江大学图书馆

岭南大学图书馆

南京高等师范学校图书馆

金陵大学图书馆

北洋大学图书馆

国立北京大学图书馆

国立北京医学专门学校

---

① 【原注】戴先生非常愿以他的知识尽其所能地解答关于中国图书馆或有关中国的任何疑问,通讯地址是中国北京清华学校图书馆,他会尽快回复。

北京汇文大学图书馆

北平清华学校图书馆

上海浸会大学图书馆

上海工业专门学校图书馆

上海圣约翰大学罗氏图书馆

上海徐家汇耶稣会总院图书馆

山东大学图书馆

陕西大学图书馆

东吴大学图书馆

通州协和大学图书馆

文华公书林

以上所有图书馆都拥有中文和英文馆藏,但就笔者所知,19家图书馆中只有3家大致按美国现代图书馆的方式运营。

1. 文华公书林

1907年,在韦棣华(Miss M. E. Wood)女士的努力下,该图书馆在原藏书室的基础上得以扩展和重建。该馆馆藏包括两部分,6000册英文藏书和9000册中文藏书。如助理馆员僧先生所言:"英文馆藏大部分是技术类和文学类书籍,中文馆藏则主要为古籍和历史类。"该馆的藏书组织布局合理,不仅为该校学生和校友的阅读使用提供便利,也服务于整个武昌地区。

2. 上海圣约翰大学罗氏图书馆

创建于1890年。罗氏兄弟的捐赠构成了该馆馆藏的核心,其后数年,馆藏数量在持续而稳定地增长。在校友、学生和朋友为校长卜舫济博士举行任职25周年纪念会时曾捐资兴建纪念讲堂,目前该讲堂已作为图书馆馆址。1904—1909年,笔者曾为罗氏图书馆的馆员,因此有幸感受该馆期间的发展,由于馆藏的逐年增加,图书馆不得不从思颜堂迁往兆丰花园内。

为便于图书的编目、上架和管理,1912年时,所有的中文书籍都借鉴西文书的方式进行装订,这在当时的中国图书馆界是一项创新之举。该馆中西文书籍都采用了杜威十进分类法分类,并试验性地引入了卡片分类目录管理中文图书。1913年,中国历史类藏书在原951卷的基础上也获得了极大的扩充。该馆1916年的报告称,西文馆藏8000册,中文馆藏5000册。目前,罗氏图书馆在徐先生的管理下蒸蒸日上,而徐先生曾就读于纽约公共图书馆学校。

3. 北平清华学校图书馆

该学校于1908年②设立,1911年正式成为留美预备学校。截至1914年夏,该校图书馆拥有中文书籍11,000余册,西文书籍500余册,期刊20余种。由于学校需求的迅速增长和

---

② 【译者注】1909年设立游美学务处,开始招生。1911年建清华学堂,1912年改称清华学校。

师生参考业务量的增加,其时图书馆的资源已捉襟见肘。随后的四年间,馆藏中文增至25,000 册,西文 6000 册,期刊 150 余种。1916 年,馆内图书的分类登记进行了完善,后发布油印的中文图书目录。该馆 1918 年 2 月的报告显示,当月的流通已达 1389 册次。为适应馆藏数量的快速增长,一座现代化的馆舍已于 1918 年 8 月竣工,其中两个大阅览室可供 200 名读者同时使用,可容纳 150,000 册西文书籍,以满足未来 15 年的发展。入藏图书都经过精心挑选,旨在国内创建丰富的多语种馆藏。

自 1914 年起,笔者开始在这个年轻而充满希望的图书馆任馆长,笔者觉得有责任指出这个迅速成长的图书馆面临的一系列风险。目前,中国的教育家已经认识到图书馆的重要性,但图书馆的行政管理并未因此得到重视。他们愿意将大笔经费用于采购,却在运营管理方面极其吝啬。无论从经济角度还是科学发展的角度考虑,对于一所图书馆来说,在拥有高效管理系统的同时,稳定而持续地发展将是更为明智的选择。

由于统计的缺乏,笔者只能给出直隶、山东、江苏、浙江四省较著名的一些公共图书馆的数据。上述四省中,共有组织得当的 16 家图书馆,其中尽人皆知的几家是:国立京师图书馆,始于 1912 年,馆藏达 80,000 余册,包括大量古籍和珍贵的善本。该馆仿照"四库全书"的方法对图书进行分类与编目。其下设京师图书馆分馆(Peking branch public library)和京师免费公共图书馆(Peking free public library)两个分馆。

国内公共图书馆需购券入览,所需费用因各图书馆及购券种类不同而异。京师图书馆阅览券分六个等级:甲,普通书阅览券,一张收铜圆一枚;乙,新闻杂志阅览券,一张收铜圆一枚;丙,学生阅览普通书券,一张收铜圆一枚;丁,学生阅览新闻杂志券,不收费;戊,善本书阅览券,一张收铜圆十枚;己,四库全书阅览券,一张收铜圆五枚。当然,读者不能进入书库,但馆内设有多个阅览室,例如,对购善本及四库全书阅览券者开放的特别阅览室,妇女阅览室,报刊阅览室等等。外借书籍也有许多繁琐规定。

除上述六种阅览券外,还有甲、乙两种优待券。持甲等优待券者,可浏览使用馆内普通书籍、报纸、杂志、善本等馆藏,可进入书库,且无需付费;持乙等优待券者,只可免费使用普通书籍、报纸和期刊。中国的免费图书馆,为民众提供无偿服务,但书籍不可外借。与此类图书馆毗邻的,通常是运动场或公共集会场所。

另一著名的公共图书馆坐落于江苏省苏州市③。该馆馆藏达 85,000 余册,入藏书籍经过精心挑选。与京师图书馆相比,该馆的各项规定更加简明且人性化,付费阅览券只有两种。持有一铜圆卷者可使用特别阅览室,持有半铜圆卷者则可使用普通阅览室。

无锡县立图书馆也是一所值得关注的图书馆。该馆创立于 1914 年,目前馆藏 30,500册。1915 年年报显示,平均每月入馆读者达 300 人次。该馆阅览券的价格与其他公共图书馆相当,但只有半铜圆一档。国内各省公共图书馆现状大抵如此,无锡图书馆管理运营得当,可称其中翘楚。

下列两张表格比较了中国地方图书馆与美国城市图书馆:

---

③ 【译者注】江苏省立第二图书馆。

无锡县立图书馆 1915 年年报

支出

	民国货币
五位工作人员工资	690
两名仆人	60
工作人员膳食费	248.888
采购书籍	636.834
文具、印刷	159.515
其他	158.195
	1953.432
	大致折合为 1302 美元

收入

普通基金	2126.129
阅览券收费	65.975
	2192.104
	大致折合为 1538 美元

纽约州特洛伊市公共图书馆 1916 年年报

支出

工资	$7293.26
供给	470.92
供热照明	894.62
装订	551.02
书籍	1147.73
期刊	391.36
馆员支出	274.46
维修	311.00
保险费	151.20
其他	933.13
	$12,418.70

收入

普通基金	$1407.01
特别基金	1032.93
纽约州	100.00
特洛伊市	8500.00
罚款等	639.92
租金	1002.24
	$12,682.10

  无锡的人口规模约为特洛伊市的 1.5 倍,但图书馆的收入和支出仅是后者的十分之一。目前,将中国的大学图书馆与美国的哥伦比亚、哈佛或其他大学图书馆相比,或是将中国的公共图书馆与美国的纽约、波士顿或其他公共图书馆相比,都很荒谬。

  受教育的国民才是国家之根本,图书馆在推进国民教育中可有哪些作为呢?中国人对此并未完全认清,但诸位美国图书馆工作者完全可以回答这个问题,你们已经用实际的工作成果向世界证明了这一点。这并非笔者奉承,乃实至名归。当普鲁士帝国主义灰飞烟灭时,史学家曾预言,美国精神和美国文化将会拯救世界。而美国精神与美国文化的成长,不管是过去、现在还是未来,都得益于美国各家图书馆及美国图书馆协会(A.L.A.)的努力工作。出席这次萨拉托加ALA会议并访问军营图书馆的参与者,都将在不久的将来见证此言的真实性。

自1844年7月3日中美签订《望厦条约》起,牢固的伙伴关系使两国关系进入历史新阶段。中国人民感谢你们在政治、社会、教育、宗教等方面给予我们许多热忱而友好的帮助。我们信任贵国,因为你们并非贪婪的殖民者,你们忠实地追求民主,无畏地保护自由,并热爱人权。现在,我向所有美国图书馆馆员和美国人民呼吁,用图书馆运动帮助你们年轻的姊妹共和国以教育她的国民,你们会赢得我们永恒的谢意。我知道你们将一定会回应这个请求,在以英雄气概杀戮了"军国主义禽兽"之后,履行这个令人愉快的、母亲般的责任,用精神食粮养育中国的四亿公民。

原载:《公共图书馆(月刊)》 1919年第24卷第2期

A Brief Sketch of Chinese Libraries

By T. C. TAI, B. L. S. , Librarian of Tsing Hua College, Peking, China

The history of Chinese libraries really begins with the invention of Chinese writing. But the word "library" in China always means strictly a place for storing books instead of a place for educating the public. It is only recently that educators have begun to know the library not only as a place for taking care of books but also as a melting pot for diffusing knowledge to the ignorant as well as to the learned.

Owing to the remoteness of the invention of writing, references in the historical records of twenty-four dynasties, which occupy the period of 4651 years, are widely scattered. Lack of statistics and different methods in recording dates by different emperors also increase the difficulty. This sketch is therefore merely as a pebble along the seashore.

Roughly the history of Chinese libraries can be divided into six periods which are arbitrarily set in this paper to serve the purpose of narrating their development. The first period extends from the appointment of a royal custodian by Huangti down to the burning of books and the persecution of scholars by the great emperor, Shih Huangti of Ch'in dynasty. This period covered the years 2697 to 206 B. C.

Many historical references relate that a royal custodian was usually appointed by a ruler to look after the archives of former reigns and to keep the records of the important events of the emperor's own reign. About the sixth century B. C. the staff of the royal custodian was increased till it included five separate offices under the supervision and direction of the chief royal custodian. From this it is inferred that the material in the royal library must have increased rapidly.

The head royal custodian, T'ai Shih[1], or "librarian," recorded the ruler's actions (something like a modern court circular) besides his duty of supervising the library. The Hsiao Shih's (assistant librarian in modern sense) duty was to take care of the records of the important events of the country and the Wai Shih[2] (reference librarian) was to keep archives and geographical records. The Nei Shih was a librarian's secretary in the modern sense. The Yü Shih watched and recorded the actions of various officials and the Hsiao Yin Jen were the assistants.

In this period there was not only a royal library but each feudal prince (or duke) had a place for storing his books. Confucius's great work, "Spring and autumn annals," was compiled from the official records of one hundred and twenty pretty principalities. At that time Laotzu, the founder of Taoism, was the custodian of the royal library of the Chou dynasty about 53 B. C. and Confucius consulted him for material for his works. Another instance shows clearly that each petty principality had its own library. The books of K'un-Jih and Yin Yang (philosophy of positive and negative elements) were seen by Confucius at the library of the principality of Sung.

The flourishing period of various philosophical systems advanced by the different classical philosophers and Confucius came to a disastrous end, because the ambitious Shih Huangti, the first great emperor of Ch'in dynasty, 249 B. C., desired to be known as the originator of all human knowledge. There are various accounts of his sweeping policy of persecuting literati and of burning all the books except the Yi Chang, or "Book of Changes," and works on agriculture, medicine and divination[3].

His thoro method of destroying literature, classics and history, and his consolidation of the feudal kingdoms into an empire arrested the development of the numerous libraries of the principalities for a short time.

This unfortunate end of the first period fortunately lasted only forty-three years. Then came the downfall of the great empire of Ch'in and the rise of Han dynasty which took place about 206 B. C. This marked the beginning of the second period of the history of libraries. The first emperor of the Han dynasty, Liu Pan, was a man of practical action and military tendency, but he was willing to take advice from his ministers of the literati. In one instance they persuaded him to collect the Confucian classics and other books. The emperor said that there was no good reason to collect them and he won the empire on horse-back but not by books. His ministers replied, "Yes, but you cannot rule your empire on horse-back." By the constant encouragement of the successive emperors of the Han dynasty, numerous ancient books were dug out from walls of houses where they had been secreted and the revival of interest in classics and literature at once was manifested in every branch of intellectual activity.

The famous "Historical records" by Ssü Ma-Chu'an, "the Herodotus of China," appeared in 90 B. C. The science of lexicography was invented by Hsu Shen, and philosophy and poetry flooded the book-market. In order to encourage the people to study, three buildings, namely, Tien-Lu, Shih-Ch'u and Pai Hu Kuei, were erected as the imperial libraries. According to the Annals of the Han dynasty, about the first half first century of the Christian era, the imperial library had 3123 volumes on the classics, 2705 volumes of philosophy, 1318 of poetry, 790 on warfare, 2528 on mathematics, and 868 on medicine[4].

Besides the collections in the imperial library, famous scholars always had their own private libraries. The ancient Chinese always took pride in having books in their homes and they took interest and pleasure in seeing that their friends and relatives would use their private collections. Special attention was paid to editions and early manuscript copies, and even now the Chinese scholars still insist on having good early editions instead of cheap reprints made by movable types.

From A. D. 67, the collections both in the Buddhistic literature and philosophy, hence Chinese philosophy and literature from the second century and on were greatly influenced by the mystic philosophy of Gautoma. It was, has been, and is still a usual practice for the Buddhist monastery always to have a place for storing Buddhistic books, well arranged, classified and preserved.

After the Han dynasty there was a period of four centuries of political turmoil. In spite of the turbulence, the development of libraries was not without steady progress. The rapid increase of production of new books in this period may be explained by the invention of the brush pen and hemp paper as well as the strong reaction in favor of the old and forgotten Confucian classics.

A few words on the writing material of the first and second periods of the history of the libraries will indirectly cast some light upon library developments. In the days of Confucius the sharpened bamboo stylus which served to carve the texts on palm leaves and reeds was the usual practice. Later cloth and silk were introduced for use with the brush pen. About the first century paper was invented and later ink was manufactured. Hence the second period of the history aided by all these new materials took a great stride toward the systematic development of libraries and their collections.

The third period began with the glory of Tang dynasty 618 A. D. This dynasty is regarded as the Augustan age in Chinese history. The second emperor T'ai Tsung (627-650 A. D.) made the name of China respected beyond its own frontiers. His policy of tolerance and hospitality towards the foreign missionaries made China a place of harmony between various antagonistic creeds. Zoroasterism came to the magnificent capital, Si-An-Fu, in 621 A. D., and seven years later Mohammendans and Magians also settled down in the metropolitan city in peace. In 631 A. D. the Nestorian Christian missionary, Olupum, was enthusiastically welcomed and in order to perpetuate his doctrine a memorial tablet with suitable inscription was erected in the capital in A. D. 781[5]. Several of the sacred books of the Nestorian were translated into Chinese[6]. Various people with different religious beliefs frankly interchanged their opinions. The documents relating to these marvellous happenings filled an entire cell at Tung Huang. Dr Stein called this collection the "Polyglot temple library."

Not only did the illustrious emperor tolerate the various missionaries and encourage them to publish their respective religious writings, but he was also a grand patron of learning and a promoter of the founding of libraries. His attitude toward the usefulness of the library was admirably expressed in one of his sayings in the imperial library, Shih K'u, "Four treasuries." The saying runs, "With a mirror of brass you can adjust your cap, with a book as a mirror you can forecast the rise and fall of empires." A literary academy of high standing was founded in the capital and the system of civil service examination was inaugurated. By his and his successors' enthusiastic encouragement, manuscript works in literature, philosophy and poetry were issued in large quantities.

Poetry under the Tang dynasty reached its perfection and its anthology published in 1707 A. D. contained 48,900 poems in thirty great volumes. Immortal poets, distinguished essayists, and profound scholars were numerous. The collection in the imperial library contained 53,915 volumes of all kind of works of former dynasties and 28,469 volumes of works issued during this golden era of Chinese history.

As classification can be termed the daughter of big collections, the Tsang dynasty began to classify the books in the imperial library under four main classes: Classics, History, Philosophy and Belles Lettres. This system of classification was immediately and widely adopted by the libraries of the imperial districts and many private libraries. On account of the civil service examination in literature each district began to have a place for competitive examination, where the books were kept as a sort of district library for the use of scholars and students. This magnificent period was closed with the perfection of block printing by Feng Tao, a versatile politician (881-954 A. D.). The wonderful productions of literature and poetry and the great demand for them by the people there seems to have certainly tended to make some process of printing necessary. We are certain that before Feng Tao crude printing had been known in the early and middle part of Tang dynasty. About A. D. 960 the practical application of printing books from blocks was carried out under the enlightened rulers of Sung dynasty. This begins the fourth period of the history of the libraries.

Among the numerous private libraries, there were three prominent ones, which in size and value of their collections could almost rival the imperial library. Those were the libraries of Wu Ch'in, Tu Sin and Li Fan.

This period 960-1815 A. D. may be considered the period of the largest production of books, including numerous dictionaries, encyclopedias and other general reference works printed from blocks[8]. Nearly five hundred years before Gutenberg cut his matrices at Mainz, the honor of being the first inventor of the movable type belongs to a Chinese, name Pi Sheng, who lived about 1000 A. D. As to its process I quote a paragraph in full from Dr. Williams's "Middle Kingdom."

"They were made of plastic clay, hardened by fire after the characters had been cut on the soft surface of a plate of clay in which they were moulded. The porcelain types were then set up in a frame of iron partitioned off by strips, and lime to fasten them down. The printing was done by rubbing, and when completed the types were loosened by melting the cement, and made clean for another impression."

Nevertheless, this invention was never developed to any practical application in superseding the printing from blocks which predominated until the reign of Kang Hsi, second emperor of the Manchu dynasty, 1661-1722, when movable copper types began to be used for printing the government publications. This period may therefore be called the period of block printing.

Before attempting to describe the size of the imperial and private libraries, mention of some few of the remarkable sets of reference books published during that period may be interesting. Besides numerous philological works of more or less value, a phonetic dictionary "Chi Yün" by Sung Ch'i (998-1061 A. D.) in conjunction with several other eminent scholars was published in the twelfth century. It contains 53,000 characters.

Another remarkable work on "Liu Shu Ku," or "Six scripts," an examination into the origin and development of the writing by Tai T'ung was published about A. D. 1250. The first encyclopedia, "Shih Lei Fu," by Wu Shu, a poverty stricken scholar (A. D. 947-1002), dealt with celestial, and terrestrial phenomena, mineralogy, botany and natural history. It is arranged under categories on account of the lack of an alphabet. Later a more extensive work of the same nature under the name "T'ai P'ing Yü Lan" was published, and reprinted in 1812. It consists of thirty-two large volumes with 800 authorities and 400 pages of index.

Ma Tuan-Lin's large and famous encyclopedia with five supplements of Bibliography, Imperial Lineage, Appointments, Uranography and Natural Phenomena, made him widely known even among present-day European scholars. It is a rich storehouse of antiquarian lore in regard to things Chinese. It was published about the fourteenth century.

In order to relieve the burden of the reader's memory of those unfamiliar romanized names, only three more reference works will be mentioned. The first, probably the most gigantic encyclopedia ever known in the world, is the Yung Lo Ta Tien. The work was compiled by 2169 scholars under five chief directors and twenty subdirectors during a period of something more than three years. On account of the huge expense of block cutting, it was never printed and the beautiful manuscript copy consisted of 22,937 folio volumes. In the fifteenth century there were three transcripts of this great work. Two of them were destroyed by fire at the fall of the Ming dynasty, 1644, and the third imperfect copy containing 20,000 pages was kept in the Peking Han-lin College until 1900 A. D. Then it met its fate in the looting, murder and fire of the civilized troops of the allied nations after the relief of the legations. [9&10]

The K'ang Hsi Tzu Tien, the greatest standard dictionary of the Chinese language and the Tu Shu Chi Ch'eng,[11] a profusely illustrated encyclopedia in 5020 volumes, were published about A. D. 1728. In addition to the above literary enterprises, there was a considerable increase of books in prose, verse, fiction, drama, philosophy and various branches of knowledge. All these treasures were properly arranged and well cared for in the libraries.

In the year 980 A. D. the imperial library of the Sung dynasty, Chung Wen Tien or "The Hall for Respect of Culture," was erected. In A. D. 1036 the emperor, Jen Tsung, ordered the librarian to appoint a number of prominent scholars to classify and catalog the books. The four main classes started under the Tang dynasty, were sub-classified and the sub-headings were again minutely classified.[12] The system of classification and the books of the imperial library were published in a descriptive catalog, "Chung Wen Catalog," which occupied about 100,000 sections. Prominent private libraries during the year A. D. 960-1278 attained a size of from 50,000 to 60,000 volumes each. Gi Library of Puchow, Wu Library of Yauchow, Dien Library of Chin-chow, Li Library of Lu Shan, Shen Library of Lien Yang, Chen Library of Kiukiang, and others were all considered by the scholars of that time much as the Bodleian Library of Oxford, and the Boston Athenaeum are at present. Most of the libraries were anxious to secure manuscript copies of old books. Some of the collectors valued their books as much as Sir Thomas Bodley did his famous collection. For example, Ssu Ma Kuang (1019-1086 A. D.), the scholarly statesman, the historian and the author of the "Tung Ch'ien" or "Mirror of history," was extremely particular in the handling of his books. He would not permit his disciples and friends or anybody else to turn the leaves by scratching them up with their nails. (Owing to the thinness of the paper, it is a usual practice to turn over the leaves by scratching them up with the nail of the middle finger.) He made every user of his library promise to turn over the leaves by using the forefinger and the second finger of the right hand. His library was famous for manuscript classics.

The flourishing empire of Sung attained its chief glory in the development of philosophy and literature, but lacked military strength. In the year 1260 A. D. it was dominated by Kublai Khan, the first emperor of the Mongul dynasty. He built himself a new capital which he called Khanbaligh and later the capital received its present name of Peking, or "Northern Capital." Altho he was a barbarian depending chiefly on brute force, yet all his life he remained the faithful patron of the *literati* of China. The new capital was adorned with a grand building for the imperial library, named Hung Wen Yuan, or "A Place for Lofty Culture." The great collection was composed of the books removed from the capital of the Sung dynasty and other principal cities. It had about 2309 sets of different subjects and also spent a great deal of money in collecting old manuscripts.

There were three very prominent private libraries in Kiangnan and the best known one was Chuang Library. The founder was at one time the assistant librarian of the imperial library of the Sung dynasty. The range of the collection was so wide that it included everything from the cheap fiction to the ancient classics. Most of the books were the original handwritten copies. It is curious enough to say that the system of classification adopted in the Chuang Library had many points of similarity with the system of the Dewey Decimal Classification. It arranged the field of knowledge under ten main classes in logical order and used the characters of the Chinese Cycle as notations.

After the expulsion of the Mongols by Hung Wu, the founder of the Ming dynasty, he established his capital in Nanking, or "Southern Capital," and he sent his minister, Hsu Dah, to remove the Yuan imperial library to his new library, Wen Yuen Koh, or "A Place of the Source of Culture," in A. D. 1370. His son, Yung-lo, made Peking again the capital and consequently in 1420 A. D. the Nanking imperial library was again removed to Peking. In 1442 A. D. the descriptive catalog of the imperial library was published in 43,200 folio volumes. This catalog was thoroly revised with critical notes and published in the reign of Ch'ien Lung. It contained 3460 works in 8000 volumes under the arrangement of five main heads, Classics, History, Philosophy, Belle Lettres and General Encyclopedias. The vastness of the work required eighteen years' labor by hundreds of scholars. It was begun in 1772 and finished in 1790. In order to cultivate the learning of the people, the emperor, Ch'ien Lung, ordered the erection of three great imperial libraries in the cities of Tseng Kiang, Yangchow and Huangchow. The first two were destroyed by the T'ai-Ping rebellion. Only the imperial library in Huangchow has been preserved to the present time and now it has been turned to a public library and removed to an up-to-date building on the shore of the beautiful West Lake.

Four important features mark the development of the library history of the fifth period. The first event was the practical application and preparation of Chinese movable types for filling the demand for the rapid manufacture of evangelical works of the Christians. The first fonts were made by P. P. Thoms, for the East India Company's office at Macao in 1815, to print Dr. Morrison's Dictionary. Thru nearly forty-five years' various experiments in Paris, Berlin and other missionary presses, making matrices by the electrotype process was perfected by Mr. Gamble at Shanghai in 1859. By means of different fonts Chinese books are now printed in any style. Lately the government has opened an extensive printing office in Peking and this new printing business has been taken up in different provinces with wonderful progress. For instance, the Commercial Press in Shanghai is one of the largest printing presses in the world and it issues cheap text-books in editions of several millions. Most of the elementary text-books cost two pence for a volume of about fifty leaves with clear illustrations. This rapid production of books has recently influenced the policy and usual method of the Chinese libraries to a great extent.

The second feature of this period is the earnest restoration and erection of libraries and government printing offices in provincial capitals, prefectural and district cities after the suppression of the T'ai-Ping rebellion. Those governmental libraries were mostly situated in a hall where literary examinations took place. They were the libraries for scholars and students, but not for the common people. The size of the collections varied in various localities. In general the collection rated from a few hundred to a few thousands of volumes.

Numerous private libraries with large collections formed the third typical feature of this epoch. More than a dozen famous private libraries are scattered far and wide in the empire and the value and size of their collections have been recognized as surpassing any private library in the former dynasties. The best known one belongs to the Lu family of Wu Hsing, Chekiang. "Siu Sien Koh" or "A place for Preserving the Source of Culture," is the name of their private library. In 1880 the library began to be opened for the public without any entrance charge.

Thru the various periods, altho there were no free public libraries as those in this country, the private libraries always welcomed the poor students who desired to use their treasurese. The owners rather generously provided the poverty-stricken research students with free board and room, because they always took pleasure in helping the poor students to perfect their studies. Such instances were not rare in the history of any period. It is probably no exaggeration to say that most of the brilliant scholars, poets, essayists, philosophers and artists in this long history of China came from poor families. The private libraries certainly contributed a great share in the civilization of the "Flowery Republic."

After the woeful results of the Chino-Japanese War of 1894-95 and the Boxer Uprising of 1900, China gradually recognized the importance of western learning and the inefficiency of the old educational system. This awakening started the movement for founding schools and colleges, academic and professional. Several western educators, as Dr. Martin, Dr. Richard, Dr. Hayes, Dr. Tenney, and others, were appointed by the government as the presidents of some of the universities.[14] In 1905 an edict was issued abolishing the old system of examinations and modern education was vigorously carried into practice.

By the strong desire of the Chinese people for modern education and the evangelistic efforts of the Christian missionaries, many missionary institutions of learning of various kinds have been founded all over the country.[15] Their influence in social education and library development are too great to be neglected. Their founding formed the fourth essential feature of the fifth period of the Chinese library history.

Missionary institutions, modern school systems, and western learning are the powerful factors in determining the nature and policy of Chinese libraries of the present. By the influence of missionary institutions the library, besides the enormous collections of literature of other religions, are pressed to acquire numerous works on Christianity. The modern school system advocates popular and social education. The old order of the Chinese library system for scholars and students has to give place to the needs of all the classes of the people. It is not a place for hiding books but a powerful agency in education.[16] On account of lack of translations of scientific works, compulsory study of foreign modern languages in schools and the general thirst for western learning, make the libraries not only have books in Chinese, but also have a workable collection in foreign languages. All those inevitable tendencies have given birth to the sixth period of Chinese library history.

The present period began with the significant birth of the young republic on Oct. 9, 1911. One of the innumerable innovations was to turn the places for storing books and for privileged *literati* only into free public libraries. In order to set an example for the provinces to follow the government turned the imperial library of the late dynasty in Peking into a public library in 1912.[17] The educators are beginning to realize that the library is one of the powerful factors in building the conduct of the citizens of the republic. Now not only the universities, colleges and learned institutions are anxious to have libraries, but also like to have an efficient system for administration. Since 1914 four Chinese librarians have come to this land of libraries and book lovers to receive the instruction of library science from the library schools of the New York State Library and New York Public Library. There are three more to enroll themselves for such education next year. Two are the scholarship students of Tsing Hua College, Peking, and one of the Polytechnic Institute of Shanghai.

The writer took up this profession in 1909, since then he has always had a vision that a gigantic library movement in China will take place in the near future. As the above sketch shows clearly, in spite of the mediaeval system of Chinese libraries and many defects, the development thru thousands of years is a slow but steady and encouraging one. As a result of the present educational systems, the library movement is bound to come. I hope the American librarians will extend their hands to help a library movement in the young sister republic as earnestly as the American educators have done to accomplish their wonderful work in other educational problems.

1. Li Chi, or Book of Rites.
2. Chou Li, or Book of Rites of Chou Dynasty.
3. Gowen's Outline History of China, v. 1, p. 83.
4. Douglas's Literature of China, p. 82.
5. William's Middle Kingdom, v. 1, p. 151.
6. William's Middle Kingdom, v. 2, p. 169.
7. Seng's Can the American library system be adopted to China? Lib Journal, v. 41, p. 385.
8. Bashford's China, an interpretation, p. 110.
9. Giles's Chinese literature, p. 296.
10. Gowen's Outline History of China, v. 2, p. 170-71.
11. Swingle's Chinese Book and Libraries, A. L. A. Proceedings, 1916-17, p. 122.
12. Wylie's Notes on Chinese literature.
14. Bashford's China, an interpretation, p. 97-123.
15. Kuo's Chinese System of Public Education, p. 136-40.
16. Kuo's Chinese System of Public Education, p. 112.
17. Tai's Present Library Conditions in China, *Public Libraries*, Feb. 1919.

原载：*Library Journal* June. 1919

【译文】董琳、郭兰芳译　邓景康审

中国图书馆概述

戴志骞　图书馆学士　中国北京清华学校图书馆主任

　　中国的图书馆史是伴随着汉字书写的产生而正式开始的。但从严格意义上讲,一直以来,"图书馆"一词指代的是存储书籍的地方,而非教育公众的场所。直到最近,教育工作者们才开始认识到图书馆不仅是保存书籍的地方,而且是向大众传播知识的场所。

　　由于书写诞生的年代久远,史料又历经24朝、横跨4651年,这使得参考文献非常散乱。统计资料的匮乏以及各朝代的纪年法相异也为本文的撰写增加了难度。因此,本文只可算作沧海一粟。

　　为了方便讲述其发展历程,本文冒昧将中国图书馆史粗略划分为六个阶段。第一个阶段从黄帝任命史官到秦始皇焚书坑儒,跨越的年代是从公元前2697年至公元前206年。

　　据史料记载,史官往往由统治者亲自任命,其职责是管理前朝文献并记录当朝重大事件。约公元前6世纪,史官数量增加,分成五个独立的部门,统一接受主管史官的监督和领导。由此可以推测,在此期间,皇家图书馆的文献资料一定是得到了快速增加。

　　主管史官被称为太史①,即"图书管理员"②,除了要监管图书馆,还要记录当朝皇帝的言行(类似现代的宫廷公报)。小史(现代意义上的助理图书馆员③)的职责是管理记录着国家重大事件的文献,外史④(参考馆员)负责管理档案和地理文献。内史从现代意义上讲是图书管理员的秘书。右史观察并记录官员们的活动,小尹仁为助手。

　　在这个时期,不仅有皇家图书馆,每个分封的诸侯(或公爵)都有其用于存储书籍资料的地方。孔子的伟大著作《春秋》就是根据120个诸侯国的官方记录编制而成。大约公元前53年⑤,道家创始人老子任周朝史官,孔子曾为著书向其问礼。另一个事例也足以证明各个小诸侯国都拥有自己的图书馆。孔子曾在诸侯国宋国的图书馆看到了《乾坤》⑥和《阴阳》(哲学的两个因素)二书。

　　公元前249年,秦朝伟大的开国皇帝秦始皇为了成就自己成为人类文明鼻祖的雄心,制定了各种政策迫害文人学者,并下令焚烧除《易经》和有关农业、医药、占卜之外的书籍⑦,百家争鸣的繁盛时期就此结束。

　　秦始皇对文学、典籍与历史的毁灭性破坏,加上他对六国统一后大秦帝国政权的巩固,

---

①　【原注1】《礼记》。
②　【译者注】应为"图书馆长",古代还没有现代意义上的图书馆,那时一般只有一个人管理图书,称为图书管理员,直到近代亦是如此,下同。
③　【译者注】应为"馆长助理"。
④　【原注2】《周礼》。
⑤　【译者注】实为公元前523年。
⑥　【译者注】依据胡怀琛(1886—1938)的《古今读书法》,古为"坤乾",周代改为"乾坤"。
⑦　【原注3】高恩的《中国历史大纲》,第1卷,第83页。

在一段时间内阻碍了诸侯国图书馆的发展。

好在这段不幸的历史只持续了43年。大约公元前206年,大秦帝国灭亡,汉朝建立,中国图书馆发展进入第二个历史阶段。汉朝的开国皇帝刘邦是注重实践的军事家,但他也愿意听取文官的建议。一次,文官们想说服他收集儒家经典和其他典籍。刘邦说他从马背上得天下,而非靠书籍,所以没有理由去收集。大臣接着说,"是的,但你不能继续靠武力治理天下"。在历代汉朝皇帝的支持下,大量古籍从房屋墙壁中挖出来,对经典和文学的兴趣很快在各学派中复兴并活跃起来。

公元前90年,司马迁撰写的《史记》问世,他本人被后人誉为"中国的希罗多德"⑧。许慎首创了词典编纂学,哲学和诗歌书籍大量涌现。为了鼓励民众学习,朝廷兴建了天禄、石渠、麒麟三阁用作皇家图书馆。据汉代年鉴记载,约公元1世纪上半叶,皇家图书馆藏有典籍3123卷、哲学类书籍2705卷、诗歌类书籍1318卷、军事类书籍790卷、数学类书籍2528卷以及医药类书籍868卷。⑨

除了皇家图书馆的馆藏,著名学者也通常有私人藏书楼。中国古人以家中藏书为荣,并且非常乐意亲友前来借阅。版本和早期手稿备受重视,时至今日,中国学者依然偏爱收藏善本古籍,而非廉价的印刷本。

自公元67年起,藏书大都关于佛学和哲学,因此自公元二世纪以来的中国哲学和文学都深受乔达摩⑩神秘哲学的影响。一直以来,佛教寺院设藏经阁用以收藏、分类、管理佛经已成为惯例。

汉代之后的四百年一直是动荡时期。尽管如此,图书馆事业依然稳步发展。在此期间,可能由于毛笔和麻纸的发明加上对曾被遗忘的儒家经典的热衷,新书大量涌现。

在图书馆发展史的第一、二阶段,书写工具的发展间接地促进了图书馆的发展。孔子时代,人们通常用竹尖在棕榈叶和芦苇上刻字撰文,后来用毛笔在布和丝绸上写字。大约在公元一世纪,纸和墨相继被发明。第二个阶段里,有了上述新型书写工具,图书馆及其藏书就进入了快速、系统的发展时期。

第三个阶段始于公元618年的唐朝。荣耀的唐王朝被认为是中国的"奥古斯都时代"⑪。唐朝的第二个皇帝唐太宗(公元627—650年)使中国名扬海外。他采用怀柔政策对待外国传教士,使大唐国土上各种信仰和谐共存。公元621年,古波斯拜火教传入大唐宏伟的首都西安府,七年后,伊斯兰教徒和拜火教徒也在此安居。公元631年,基督教传教士阿罗本⑫受到了热烈的欢迎,公元781年,人们在都城为他树碑立传以纪念其人并传承其教义⑬。一些基督教的圣书被翻译成中文⑭。不同种族的人宗教信仰不同,但都可以坦诚交

---

⑧ 【译者注】希罗多德(Herodotus,约公元前484—425年),伟大的古希腊历史学家,史学名著《历史》一书的作者,西方文学的奠基人。人文主义的杰出代表。从古罗马时代开始,希罗多德就被尊称为"历史之父"。

⑨ 【原注4】道格拉斯的《中国文学》,第82页。

⑩ 【译者注】乔达摩·悉达多,佛教的创始人。被后世尊称为释迦摩尼佛。

⑪ 【译者注】罗马帝国最辉煌的时代,统治范围横跨欧亚非三洲。

⑫ 【译者注】已知的第一个到中国传教的基督教教士,实际到达中国的时间应为公元635年。

⑬ 【原注5】威廉姆斯的《中国》,第1卷,第151页。【译者注】碑名为《大秦景教流行中国碑》。

⑭ 【原注6】威廉姆斯的《中国》,第2卷,第169页。

流。记载有当时这些不可思议的事情的文献整整塞满了敦煌的一个屋子。斯坦因博士[15]称这批藏书是"多语种寺庙图书馆。"

唐太宗不仅包容各国传教士,鼓励他们出版各自的宗教著作,他还倡导学习、支持图书馆建设。他对图书馆用途的重视令人钦佩,皇家图书馆四库中皇帝语录中有云:"以铜为镜,可以正衣冠,以古为镜,可以知兴替。"唐朝还设立了翰林院,推行科举考试制度。在唐太宗和他的继任者的大力提倡下,文学、哲学和诗歌原创作品大量涌现。

唐代诗歌水平达到顶峰,公元1707年出版的唐诗集包含48,900首诗歌,分为30卷。不朽的诗人、杰出的散文家、渊博的学者数不胜数。皇家图书馆藏有前朝各类文献作品53,915卷,当朝盛世作品28,469卷。

巨大的藏书量催生了图书分类法。唐朝皇家图书馆开始将藏书分为四类:经、史、子、集。这种分类体系很快在皇家所辖图书馆和私人藏书楼广泛流传和应用。考虑到科举考试的需要,各地区为学者和书生开设地区图书馆。这个辉煌的阶段因冯道(杰出政治家,公元881—964年)完善了雕版印刷术而得以终结。文学和诗歌的兴盛及人们对这类作品的追捧促进了印刷术的发展。可以确信的是,在冯道之前,原始印刷术已在唐朝初期和中期为人们所熟悉。大约公元960年,宋朝的开明统治者促使雕版印刷术用于书籍印刷。图书馆历史的第四个阶段开始了。

在众多的私人藏书楼中,Wu Ch'in, Tu Sin and Li Fan[16]的藏书楼闻名天下,其藏书规模和价值几乎可以媲美皇家图书馆。

公元960—1815年间可能是书籍出版量最大的时期,许多辞典、百科全书和其他通用工具书通过雕版印刷得以面世[17]。古腾堡[18]在美因茨发明活字印刷术前的500年,生活于约公元1000年的中国人毕昇就在世界上首次发明了活字印刷术。关于活字印刷的过程,我想通过引用威廉姆斯博士[19]在《中国》一书中的一整段落加以说明。

"在胶泥做成的毛坯上刻上字符,然后用火烧硬做成字模。排字的时候把字模放进带框的铁板上并胶着固定。通过摹拓的方式完成印刷后,使胶融化取下字模,并清洗以备下次再用。"

然而,活字印刷术在实际应用中并没有取代雕版印刷术,直到满清王朝的第二个皇帝康熙年间,公元1661—1722年,铜活字开始被用于朝廷出版物。因此这个时期可被称为雕版印刷时期。

在介绍皇家图书馆和私人藏书楼的规模之前,我想先谈一下在此期间出版的几套优秀工具书。公元12世纪,除了多部价值各异的语言学著作外,宋祁[20](公元998—1061年)与一些知名学者合作编写出版了语音字典《集韵》,共收字53,000个。

---

[15]【译者注】斯坦因(Marc Aurel Stein,1862年—1943年),著名考古学家、艺术史家、语言学家、地理学家和探险家,国际敦煌学开山鼻祖之一。

[16]【译者注】无法确认三个藏书楼的中文名称。

[17]【原注8】贝施福的《中国述论》,第110页。

[18]【译者注】Johannes Gensfleisch zur Laden zum Gutenberg(1400—1468年),德国发明家,是西方活字印刷术的发明人。

[19]【译者注】威廉姆斯(S. Wells Williams),19世纪上半叶传教士兼印刷商。

[20]【译者注】宋祁(998—1061)字子京,安州安陆(今湖北安陆)人,北宋文学家。

大约公元 1250 年，戴侗[21]所著《六书故》出版，这是一本分析汉字产生和发展的字书。穷苦潦倒的学者吴淑[22]（公元 947—1002 年）作《事类赋》，这是中国第一部百科全书，内容涉及天体、地理、矿物、植物和自然历史，因当时还没有字母表，全书按专题分类。之后，收录更广泛的一部类书《太平御览》问世，全书 32 大卷，800 个重要引用，400 页索引，于 1812 年重印。

马端临[23]所著的著名大型类书增加了五个门类：经籍、帝系、封建、象纬、物异，它是研究中国古文物、古文化知识的宝库。这部类书大约出版于 14 世纪，它的出版使作者本人广为人知，甚至在现今的欧洲学者中也广为流传。

为了减轻读者因不熟悉罗马化书名所带来的负担，下面仅再介绍三部作品。第一部是《永乐大典》，它可能是世界上迄今所知最为庞大的百科全书。这部宏伟著作由 5 名总纂修、20 名分纂修主持，2169 名纂修历时三年多的时间合力完成。考虑到雕版印刷耗资巨大，《永乐大典》并未印刷，精美的手抄本包括 22,937 对开卷。公元，其抄本有三个，其中两个在 1644 年毁于明末战火，剩下一个含有 20,000 页的不完整抄本被保存在北京翰林院。然而在 1900 年八国联军的烧杀抢掠中，这最后一个抄本也惨遭焚毁，所剩无几。[24][25]

大约公元 1728 年，《康熙字典》[26]和《古今图书集成》印制完成，前者是汉语最高标准的字典，后者是插图丰富、共 5020 卷的百科全书。除了上述文化成就外，散文、诗歌、小说、戏剧、哲学及其他各类知识的书籍也大幅增加。所有这些珍宝均被妥善保存于图书馆。

公元 980 年，宋朝兴建皇家图书馆崇文院。公元 1036 年，宋仁宗下令崇文院管理者委派一批著名学者为书籍分类并编目。四部分类法从唐朝就已开始，而今被再次细分并给予子目。[27] 分类体系和皇家图书馆馆藏在"崇文总目"中得以体现，该总目大概含有 10 万卷。公元 960—1278 年间，知名私人藏书楼的藏书量达到 50,000 到 60,000 册。亳州祁氏藏书楼、Yauchou 的吴氏藏书楼、荆州田氏藏书楼、庐山的李氏藏书楼、历阳沈氏藏书楼、九江的陈氏藏书楼[28]，和其他一些藏书楼对于当时学者的意义堪比今日的牛津大学博德利图书馆和波士顿图书馆。大多数图书馆都极力收藏古籍手稿。有些收藏家看重藏书的程度堪比托马斯·博德利先生[29]。司马光（公元 1019—1086 年），博学的政治家、历史学家，《资治通鉴》的作者，对待藏书极其特别。他不允许其弟子、朋友或其他任何人用指甲翻书（由于纸张薄，用中指指甲翻书是惯用方法）。他要求每位读者用食指和右手的第二手指来翻书。他的藏书楼因经典手稿而闻名。

繁荣的宋代在哲学和文学方面取得了辉煌成就，但缺乏军事实力。公元 1260 年，蒙古

---

[21] 【译者注】戴侗（1200—1285 年），字仲达，浙江永嘉人，南宋文字学家。

[22] 【译者注】吴淑，字正仪，润州丹阳人，宋代文学家。

[23] 【译者注】马端临，(1254—1323 年)，字贵舆，饶州乐平人，宋元之际著名的历史学家，本中所指为《文献通考》。

[24] 【原注9】翟里斯的《中国文学史》，第 296 页。

[25] 【原注10】高恩的《中国历史大纲》，第 2 卷，第 170—171 页。

[26] 【译者注】《康熙字典》的印行年代实际是康熙五年，即 1716 年。

[27] 【原注12】伟烈亚力的《中国文献录》。

[28] 【译者注】Chen Library of Kiukiang 应该是陈振孙，浙江安吉人，并非九江人。

[29] 【译者注】托马斯·博德利（1545—1613 年），英国外交家，牛津大学博德利图书馆创始人。

王朝的第一位皇帝忽必烈汗推翻宋朝。他建立了一个新的都城,称之为汗八里,后来改名为北京,或"北都"。虽然忽必烈是个依靠蛮力的未开化之人,但他穷其一生热衷于中华文明。新都城兴建了宏伟的皇家图书馆,命名为宏文院,取意"恢宏文化之地"。其藏书主要来自宋朝都城和其他主要城市,依据主题来分共计约 2,309 套。宏文院同样在收集旧手稿方面耗资巨大。

江南有三座非常著名的私人藏书楼,最负盛名的是庄氏藏书楼㉚。创办人曾是宋朝皇家图书馆的助理馆员。该藏书楼的藏书范围广泛,从便宜的通俗小说到经典古籍无所不有。大部分藏书是原始手抄本。十分稀奇的是它所采用的图书分类体系与《杜威十进分类法》有许多相似之处。它把知识领域按照逻辑顺序分为十大类,并使用中国汉字纪年法作标记。

洪武驱逐蒙古人,建立明朝,把都城建在南京,或称"南都"。公元 1370 年,他派大臣胡大海把元朝皇家图书馆的馆藏,移到他的新图书馆文渊阁(意为"文化源流之地")。公元 1420 年,洪武皇帝的儿子永乐皇帝再次将北京定为都城,南京皇家图书馆藏书也因此又移到北京。公元 1442 年,皇家图书馆目录出版,共 43,200 对开卷。后来,根据评论意见该目录被修订,并于清朝乾隆时期出版㉛。它收录作品 3460 部,共 8000 卷,由经、史、子、集和丛书五个主要部分组成。这项浩瀚工程由数百名学者历时 18 年完成,始于 1772 年,完成于 1790 年。为了教化民众,乾隆皇帝下令在镇江、扬州和杭州开设三大皇家图书馆㉜。前两个在太平天国起义中被摧毁。只有在杭州的皇家图书馆一直保存至今,现在它已被移到了美丽西湖畔的一座新式建筑内,成为了一家公共图书馆。

图书馆的第五个发展阶段有四个重要特征。首先,因基督教传播福音需要快速印刷,活字印刷术就终于被运用到了实际当中。为了打印马礼逊博士㉝的字典,汤姆斯为东印度公司澳门办事处委托制作了金属活字。近 45 年间,在巴黎、柏林和其他传教士印刷馆进行了各种实验,1859 年,姜别利先生㉞在上海通过电铸处理完善了制作活字模具的工艺。现在,中国的书籍可以按照字体的不同印刷成任何风格。近来,政府在北京开设了一个大型印刷馆,这项新的印刷业务也在多个省份取得了可喜进展。例如,上海商务印书馆是世界上最大的出版商之一,出版发行的廉价教科书版本达几百万个之多。大部分配有清晰插图的 50 页左右的初级课本,每本价格 2 便士。这种快速印刷方式在很大程度上影响了中国图书馆的政策和惯常做法。

这一时期的第二个特征是,太平天国运动被镇压后,各省会、县及地方城市的图书馆和政府印刷局都得以火热修复和重建。这些图书馆大多位于科举考试的考场内,面向学者和学生提供服务,与普通老百姓无关。藏书规模各地不同,从几百卷到几千卷不等。

众多收藏颇丰的私人藏书楼形成这一时期的第三个特征。全国各地分布有十多家著名的私人藏书楼,所藏书籍的价值和规模均超越前朝任何私人藏书楼。最著名的私人藏书楼当属浙江吴兴陆氏㉟"守先阁",意为"保护文化源流之地",1880 年开始免费向公众开放。

㉚ 【译者注】庄氏藏书楼的主人庄肃为江南三大藏书家之一,储书画八万卷。宋亡后隐居不仕。

㉛ 【译者注】应为《四库全书》。

㉜ 【译者注】被称作"江南三阁"的扬州大观堂之文汇阁、镇江金山寺之文宗阁和杭州圣因寺之文澜阁。

㉝ 【译者注】马礼逊(Robert Morrison,1782—1834 年)。1805 年,英国伦敦布道会选派基督教新教传教士马礼逊来中国传教,1807 年 9 月 8 日到达广州。

㉞ 【译者注】姜别利(William Gamble,1830—1886 年),美国人,1858 年来华。

㉟ 【译者注】陆心源(1834—1894),字刚甫、潜园(一作号潜园),号存斋,浙江归安(湖州)人。

虽然在各个阶段都没有像美国那样的免费公共图书馆,但是私人藏书楼却始终欢迎好学的穷书生。藏书楼主人一般都乐于帮助穷书生提高其学业水平,对于穷困潦倒的秀才,他们大多会提供免费食宿,这种事例在各个历史阶段并不罕见。毫不夸张地说,在悠久的中国历史长河中,才华横溢的学者、诗人、散文家、哲学家和艺术家大都出身贫寒。私人藏书楼无疑为灿烂的华夏文明做出了不可磨灭的贡献。

1894年至1895年中日甲午战争和1900年义和团运动给中国带来了沉痛打击,国人逐渐认识到了西学之重要和中国传统教育体制之落后,从而开始了洋务运动,创办各类专业技能学校。朝廷任命了一批西方教育学家,如马丁博士、理查德博士、海斯博士、坦尼博士等,担任大学校长。㊱ 1905年科举制度被废除,近代新式教育制度得以实行。

由于当时人们迫切向往新式教育,加上基督教传教士的努力,全国各地建立了很多教会学校。㊲ 这些学校对社会教育以及图书馆发展产生了巨大的影响。它们的成立也成为了中国图书馆史第五阶段的第四个主要特征。

教会、现代学校制度和西学是决定当今中国图书馆性质和政策的强有力因素。受教会影响,图书馆除了收藏有大量其他宗教的资料外,还特别采购了大量基督教相关的作品。现代学校制度倡导通俗而大众化的教育。中国图书馆在旧制度下的服务对象仅是学者和书生,而在新制度下则要满足社会各阶层的需要。图书馆不再是藏书之地,而是教育机构。㊳ 由于科技译作匮乏、外语是学校的必修课以及西学的需求极大,因而图书馆不仅收藏中文书籍,也收藏实用外文书籍。这些必然的发展趋势孕育了中国图书馆的第六个历史阶段。

第六个历史阶段(现阶段)开始于1911年10月9日㊴,年轻的民主共和国诞生之日。此阶段的创新之一是把原来用于存储书籍和服务文人的图书馆转变为免费的公共图书馆。1912年,为了给各省树立榜样,政府将晚清在北京的皇家图书馆改为公共图书馆。㊵ 教育家们开始意识到,图书馆可以在民众行为导向中起到重要作用。现在,大学、学院及学术机构不仅渴望拥有图书馆,而且也希望建立高效的行政管理体制。1914年至今,已有四位中国图书馆员来到这片图书馆和图书爱好者的热土,在纽约州立图书馆和纽约公共图书馆的图书馆学校接受图书馆学专业培训。明年还将有三名学生前来学习,其中两名是北京清华学校的奖学金获得者,另一名来自上海理工学院。

笔者于1909年进入图书馆行业,从那时起就一直预感,在不久的将来中国将会发生一场规模宏大的图书馆运动。根据上文我们可以看到,虽然中国的图书馆体制老旧、弊病诸多,但在几千年的历史长河中,它的发展脚步缓慢却不失稳健、鼓舞人心。目前的教育体制必然会促发图书馆运动的诞生。我希望美国的图书馆员能够伸出援手,用美国教育工作者在处理其他教育问题时所表现出来的热诚,来帮助年轻的姐妹共和国开展图书馆运动。

原载:《图书馆学刊》 1919年6月号

㊱ 【原注14】贝施福的《中国述论》,第97—123页。
㊲ 【原注15】郭秉文的《中国公共教育体系》,第136—140页。
㊳ 【原注16】郭秉文的《中国公共教育体系》,第112页。
㊴ 【译者注】1911年10月10日爆发武昌起义,即辛亥革命。
㊵ 【原注17】Tai(戴志骞)《中国图书馆现状》,公共图书馆,1919年2月刊。

English Books on China: Preface

(Selected and annotated)

By

TSE-CHIEN TAI, B. A., B. L. S.

Assistant Librarian

Camp Upton Library, Camp Upton New York

Since the unfortunate Boxer uprising in 1900, the Russo-Japanese war of 1904, and the Chinese revolution of 1911, the English speaking people have been more interested in the affairs of the "Middle Kingdom". Naturally the printed matter increased with this interest and attention. Thus the book-market is flooded with books and articles on China. Some who happen to read pessimistic books biased by personal grievance against, China are led to think that country should be wiped off the map. Others who read the works of successful adventurers and sympathetic missionaries are led to think that China is the utopia of the East. However there are books impartial in view and accurate in statements. This list has been compiled with a view of aiding the reader in choosing and comparing the best and most accurate accounts of all activities in China.

Books published since 1900 are much more interesting to the present reader, so that date (1900) has been selected as the starting point. However, revised editions of books published before 1900 have been included. In order to keep the list within usable limits only books in English and certain selected documentary publications having close connections with important subjects are included. Magazine literature has been entirely omitted because of its accessibility through the various indexes and guides to that material.

The titles selected are arranged in classed order. This seeming more practical since the reader is generally interested rather in a subject and its related topics than in the works of any particular author. The classification is primarily arranged according to Decimal Classification with minor variations. The table of contents shows the system in outline and an author index has also been added.

Entries are annotated with descriptive and critical notes, these so far as possible having been taken from critical reviews of the book in question, whether condensed or quoted exactly. Other views are also noted. As a further aid to the reader these books considered excellent by authorities are marked with an asterisk. Most of the books in this bibliography have been examined by the compiler.

原载: *The Chinese Students Monthly* Vol. 14. 1919, No. 3

【译文】张秋译　肖燕审

《关于中国的英文书目》序

戴志骞　文科学士　图书馆学士　美国爱布顿(军营)图书馆副馆长

　　自义和团运动失败,1904年的日俄战争和1911年的辛亥革命以来,英语世界的人对这个"中央王国"的事务越来越感兴趣。相应地,关于中国的纸质印刷品也随着对中国的兴趣和关注的增加而增加。因此,图书市场上充满了关于中国的书籍和文章。那些碰巧读过悲观主义书籍的人带有强烈的个人不满情绪,认为中国应该从地图上被抹去;而那些读过成功探险家和富有悲悯情怀的传教士的作品的人士则认为,中国是东方的乌托邦。尽管如此,有些书仍不失观点公允,陈述精准。本目录的编辑旨在帮助读者选择和比较对中国史实最佳和最准确的著述。

　　由于现在的读者对1900年以来出版发行的书籍更感兴趣,故本目录所收著述出版日期始于1900年。尽管如此,1900年之前出版著述的修订版也囊括在内。为使本目录便于使用,仅收录英文书籍和与某些重要主题密切相关的特定的纪实性出版物。而杂志文章则被完全忽略,因为它们可以通过各种索引和指南获取。

　　所选出版物按内容进行归类,这样看起来更具有实用性,因为读者通常对一个主题及其相关的话题更感兴趣,而不是任何特定作者的作品。分类主要根据《杜威十进分类法》展开,仅对少数类目做细微调整。目次列出了分类系统纲要,后附作者索引。

　　每个条目都有描述和评注,它们尽可能摘自书评,包括摘要性的引述和精确引述。其他观点也进行了注释。为进一步辅助读者阅读,我们将权威认定的优秀图书做了星号标注。本书目编者也核查过收录书目的大多数图书。

原载:《中国学生月刊》　1919第14卷第3期

Libraries Aid in Educating China: Review

By T. C. TAI,
Librarian of Tsing Hua College.

Under this title Mr. Tai most attractively presents the present library situation in China in the February number of the TransPacific. China has sent four students to American library schools since 1914, and these young men have now become the leaders of this new movement for the scientific management of libraries. The movement originated, Mr. Tai tells us, in 1914, the third year of the Republic. That it is a thoroughly healthy movement, holding within itself the seed of success, is shown by the progress it has made in six short years, years of trouble and doubt the world over. In the summer of 1920 the first library summer school of China was held in the Pekin High Normal College. The enrollment numbered 78, 69 men and 9 women.

The Tsing Hua Library took the lead in forming a Pekin Library Association in 1918. Under the auspices of this Association a system of inter-library loans has been introduced, and Mr. Tai comments on the spirit of co-operation which now exists among the librarians of the city. Seeing the need of more modern libraries in China, a group of librarians and educators in Pekin is now organizing a Chinese Library Association. An organizing committee was elected in the autumn of 1920 and it is planned to hold the first conference in the summer of 1921. Mr. Tai's article is attractively illustrated with a picture of the students attending the first summer school, interiors of various public libraries, and a corner of the children's reading room of the Free Public Library, West City, Pekin.

原载:*Special Libraries* Vol. 12 February, 1921

---

① 【编者注】原标题为"Libraries Aid in Educating China",现标题为编者所加。

【译文】武丽娜译 林佳审

评《图书馆对中国教育的支持》①

戴志骞
清华学校图书室(馆)主任(馆长)

在2月份的《泛太平洋》②上,戴先生以"图书馆对中国教育的支持"为题,极富感染力地介绍了中国图书馆的现状。自1914年以来,中国已派送4名学生前往美国图书馆学校学习,现在这几位青年学子已经成为图书馆科学管理新运动的领导者。戴先生告诉我们,这项运动始于1914年,即民国三年。这是一场孕育着成功并且势不可挡的运动,在经历了全世界充满动荡与怀疑的短短六年时间后,它向世人展示了其取得的进步。1920年夏天,在北京高等师范学校举办了中国第一个图书馆暑期学校,共有78人参加学习,即69名男性和9名女性。

1918年清华图书馆组建了北京图书馆协会。在这个协会的帮助下,开始实行馆际互借。戴先生还评价了当下北京的图书馆馆员之间的合作精神。鉴于中国更加现代化图书馆的需求,一些在北京的图书馆馆员和教育工作者发起成立中国的图书馆学会③,并于1920年秋季推选出组织委员会,筹划将于1921年夏季召开的第一次学会大会。戴先生的文章用照片生动描述了学生参加第一届暑期学校的场景、多个公共图书馆的内景以及北京西城免费公共图书馆儿童阅览室的一角。

原载:《专业图书馆》 1921年第12卷第2期

---

① 【译者注】原文刊登在 Special Libraries,12(2),Feb. 1921。原标题为"Libraries Aid in Educating China",现标题为编者所加。
② 【译者注】原文为"The Trans-Pacific"。
③ 【译者注】应为中华教育改进社图书馆教育组,1922年成立图书馆教育研究委员会,戴志骞任主任,正式的中华图书馆协会于1925年成立。

Libraries Aid in Educating China

Movement To Convert Storehouses of Books Into Universities of the People Grows

By T. C. TAI

Librarian of TsingHua College

Since the Revolution of 1911, China has undergone a movement of change in intellectual problems as well as in politics. The people have not only tried hard to shake off the yoke of despotism, but they are also fully determined to free themselves from the oppression of intellectual bondage. Today on the bookstalls the translated works of Karl Marx, Kropotkin and Russell are demanded like hot-cakes, while critical essays on Chinese classics are even welcomed by scholars of the old type. The intellectual class has seen the failure of numerous reforms and has come to the conclusion that the Chinese process of thought should be revolutionized.

To introduce the use of a Chinese phonetic alphabet and to publish books and periodicals in *PehHwa*, or colloquial language, are present day means of diffusing new knowledge to the masses. In order to supply the new Chinese intellect with fresh vital energy, famous American and British philosophers, like Mr. John Dewey and Mr. Bertrand Russell, are now touring China giving lectures in most educational centers. And among institutions whose existence depends upon their ability to meet the public demand, the library is now face to face with rapidly changing conditions.

China even today is full of places for storing books. Although scholars continue to be interested in editions of bygone dynasties, like the Sung or Yuan or Ming, and only librarians know how to collect valuable incunabula, yet the tendency is daily growing stronger in favor of converting the book-museum into a living library. During the last two years especially the new library movement has taken great strides.

Roughly, there are three kinds of libraries in China-public libraries, society libraries and college libraries. The public library was started towards the end of the late Manchu dynasty. An imperial edict ordered the different provincial authorities to establish public libraries. That order, however, was not implicitly carried out, and only a few provinces obeyed it. It was not until 1914, the third year of the Republic, that the modern system of public libraries was introduced. Owing to lack of funds most of these have been unable to do their best to help the people.

Two kinds of such public libraries exist. The first is maintained by either the capital of a province or a principal city. This generally requires a small sum for admission. It has no circulation and the number of daily patrons is very small. It has no works of recent publication and it is only a storehouse for the old Chinese books. The Peking Public Library, for instance, sells tickets of six kinds to those who wish to go in to read, namely: (1) Two-copper tickets for ordinary books, (2) 1-copper tickets for periodicals and newspapers, (3) 1-copper students' tickets for ordinary books, (4) free students' tickets for periodicals and newspapers, (5) 10-copper tickets for Incunabula and (6) 5-copper tickets for the manuscript copy of the famous "Imperial Descriptive Catalog of the Manchu Dynasty." The public is not admitted into the stack rooms.

FIRST LIBRARY SUMMER SCHOOL IN CHINA, AT THE PEKING HIGH NORMAL COLLEGE

The Peking Public Library has many reading rooms, such as a special reading room for special ticket holders, a ladies' reading room, a periodical and newspaper reading room, etc. These rooms are bare, and the seats are not comfortable. Lighting and heating facilities are naturally out of the question. There is much red tape in drawing out books.

Besides the six ordinary kinds of tickets there are two special classes, first and second. Those who hold special tickets of the first class enjoy the privilege of inspecting and using ordinary books, periodicals, newspapers, incunabula, etc., without charge and also that of having access to the stacks. Those who hold special tickets of the second class have only the free use of ordinary books, periodicals and newspapers.

Three years ago the provincial public libraries had a system similar to that in the Peking Public Library. At that time many people thought that it was already a great advance towards democratic education, since only scholars were supposed to have the privilege of being near books. By selling tickets the books could be used by any who would pay a nominal sum.

Today people are getting wiser. The public library, they feel, should be free to everybody. Hence the system of free libraries is being introduced. The public libraries in provincial capitals and principal cities are gradually either discarding the policy of selling tickets or are establishing branch free libraries…

Generally a free library in China allows the people to use its collections without any charge, but one cannot draw out books for home use. In connection with these libraries are playgrounds and children's reading rooms. In spite of the financial difficulty, free libraries are better administered than public ones. In addition to old Chinese books the former also have newly published volumes on many subjects. Children's rooms are supplied with pictorial tales and juvenile books, and the playgrounds are well patronized by the children.

The libraries are open on Sundays just as on week days. Some of them close on Mondays as a holiday to the members of the staff. There are altogether 30 organized free libraries of medium size.

Several free libraries, including those in Peking, I have visited and investigated. They are well patronized and their reading rooms are always crowded to the utmost. Of course, there is yet plenty of room for improvement. For instance, the budget for the annual acquisition of books should be greatly increased so that a circulation department can be established for promoting the use of books at home. Secondly, the rooms are too bare and unattractive, and the furniture in children's reading rooms especially is not suitable.

Attractiveness of reading rooms and attention to the comfort of readers are necessary factors in inducing people to use libraries. Of course, all the above improvements hinge on the question of money, but the money will come if public sentiment demands comfortable and attractive free libraries. There are already signs in different prosperous localities pointing toward a movement in favor of fine free libraries.

The second type of libraries in China is better equipped than the free public libraries, but their use is only enjoyed by a few privileged groups. These are not maintained by the Government or by provincial authorities but depend for their chief income upon the funds of some society.

COURTYARD, FREE PUBLIC LIBRARY, WEST CITY, PEKING

These collections of books of course, reflect the nature and purposes of the fostering association. Thus, the Library of the Chinese Social and Political Science Association in Peking has its chief collection of books on history, government, social and political sciences.

The best-known society library maintained by Westerners in China is the Library of the North China Branch of the Royal Asiatic Society, at Shanghai. This library was founded about 1860, and the collection on China given by Mr. Wylie formed its nucleus. Now it has about 5,000 volumes in foreign languages and about 2,000 in Chinese. Although the collection is not large, it is fairly strong in works on China. The section of Eastern Asiatic languages was enlarged by Messrs. Kingsmill and Morse. The famous bibliographer of "Bibliotheca Sinica," Prof. Henri Cordier, was once its librarian. The Dewey decimal classification system, together with the Cutter author numbers and the card dictionary catalog, was adopted in 1907, upon the recommendation of Dr. Bolton of the Boston Athenaeum. The library is open daily, though the privilege of taking out books is enjoyed by members only。 Members not resident in Shanghai may borrow books by mail.

READING ROOM, LIBRARY OF THE CHINESE SOCIAL AND POLITICAL SCIENCE ASSOCIATION, PEKING

Another society library now rapidly coming to the front is the above mentioned Library of the Chinese Social and Political Science Association. It was founded and is maintained largely by a group of returned students who feel the need of a good library with Western books, journals and magazines in Peking. It owes its success to the United States of America, the late Imperial Manchu family and the Carnegie Endowment Corporation. The first, through its representative in Peking, Dr. Paul S. Reinsch, set apart the sum of Tls. 100,000 from the remitted Indemnity Fund for initial and maintenance expenses of the library. The second kindly donated a centrally located site for the library building, while the Carnegie Corporation of New York has already contributed about 2,000 volumes on history, social and political sciences, etc. I believe this is the first endowment of English books from that corporation to a library in China.

The reading rooms of this library are comfortably furnished. With big windows, both the light and air are excellent. A dictionary catalog with decimal classification is now on the way of accomplishment. It will be one of the most up-to-date society libraries in North China, and the members of the association as well as the reading public in general will have an ideal place for doing research work.

In addition to the above two society libraries, there are about a dozen others of similar character scattered among the coast cities of China. The movement towards founding libraries of this type is slowly extending into the interior.

Almost every college in China now has some sort of library. Among the few noted ones, the Low Library of St. John's University, Shanghai, is one of the oldest college libraries in the country. It was begun about 1890, with Mr. Low's donation as the nucleus of the collection, and it has grown steadily year after year, until now it has its own quarters in the Anniversary Hall which was a gift from the alumni, students and friends to the present president, Dr. Pott, in commemoration of the twenty-fifth anniversary of his presidency.

For the sake of convenience in charging, shelving and cataloging, all Chinese books in this library were in 1912 bound in the style of English books. This was a great advance in the history of Chinese libraries. Both English and Chinese books were classified according to the Dewey decimal classification, and the experiment was introduced of having a card catalog for Chinese books. The reading rooms are divided into cosy alcoves, furnishing an attractive place for students for study and research.

CORNER'S OF CHILDREN READING ROOM, FREE PUBLIC LIBRARY, WEST CITY, PEKING

MARBLE HALL, CHARGING DESK AND CHINESE READING ROOM, TSINGHUA COLLEGE LIBRARY, PEKING

Another well-known college library is the Boone University Library at Wuchang, which was extended and reorganized about 1907, and has done a great service not only to the students and alumni of that university, but also to the people of Hupeh and the neighboring provinces at large. It is the first institution in China to introduce a regular course of library science, and many young librarians now working in various places are the products of the Boone Library School. Besides producing regularly trained librarians every year, the Boone University Library serves through its system of traveling libraries. It has already established more than 20 centers to handle the circulation of such collections. The school has now undertaken the Herculean task of translating the Dewey decimal classification and its relative index into Chinese.

In 1912 a small library had its birth about a mile from the eventful spot of the old Summer Palace of Peking, on the beautiful campus of TsingHua College. After the summer of 1914 it began to grow rapidly. Now, in the course of only eight years, its collections in Chinese as well as in foreign languages, are easily the most pretentious of all libraries in China, as it has 56,000 volumes of well selected books. It subscribes to 290 leading periodicals of the world and to 50 dailies. The circulation figure generally reaches to 1,200 books every month, besides a much bigger figure for books used in the library. The library not only provides reference facility for the faculty and students but also answers many reference questions from teachers of various schools in Peking and Tientsin as well as from the scattered alumni of the college.

In order to accommodate the rapidly increasing number of books, an up-to-date and beautiful library building has been erected. It is the first library in China to use steel standard stacks, glass and cork floors, and other scientific equipment. This institution is responsible for a great deal of initiative in promoting a movement for scientific management of libraries. In the summer of 1920 it co-operated with the Peking High Normal College to found the first library summer school. It was a great surprise to all that the enrolment numbered 78 men and women—69 men and 9 women. Most of these were the librarians of various libraries in different provinces. Even the PublicLibrary of Amoy, Fukien Province, delegated its librarian to attend lectures, in spite of the great distance and the civil war between the Chihli and Anfu military parties around Peking. The lectures being strictly professional, the school was open to both sexes. Undoubtedly the innovation has exerted a strong influence in support of the movement towards co-education.

The TsingHua Library took the lead in forming a Peking Library Association in 1918, so that now the librarians of the capital city have an opportunity to discuss questions of importance in connection with library administration. Under the auspices of the association, the system of inter-library loans of books has been introduced. A spirit of genuine co-operation between the various libraries of the city is, indeed, a good sign of the times。.

Seeing the need of modern libraries in China, a group of librarians and educators in Peking are now organizing a Chinese Library Association. The first step is to ask each province or city to form a local library association to promote library science in that particular locality. The Chinese Library Association will have an annual conference with the representatives of the library associations, librarians and educators of different cities who are interested in the library movement. An organizing committee was elected last autumn, and it plans to hold the first conference in the summer of 1921.

Since 1914 four Chinese librarians have been graduated from the New York Public Library

School and the New York State Library School, and it is they who are the promoters of this library movement in China. At present there are two men studying library science at the New York State Library School. Before they left for the United States to further their knowledge and experience, these men had all had years of practical experience in administering libraries in the homeland.

The responsibility, however, of converting storehouses of books into active centers for diffusing knowledge to the reading public should belong to every educated Chinese. A republic cannot become a true republic unless its citizens are properly educated. What have libraries to do with the education of the people? This question was once answered by Dr. Melvil Dewey, father of the modern American library movement, that the library is the people's university.

To help establish libraries in every city and in every village and to launch the present library movement over the top is therefore the responsibility of every loyal son and daughter of the Republic of China.

原载:*Trans-Pacific* February,1921

【译文】冯璐译　林佳审

图书馆对中国教育的支持
从藏书之所向人民的大学转变

戴志骞

清华学校图书馆主任

　　自1911年辛亥革命开始,中国无论在政治格局还是思想意识方面均发生了一系列的改革变迁。中国人民不仅试图极力摆脱封建君主的专制统治,而且坚定迫切地要从压抑的旧传统文化束缚中解放出来。书报摊上,有关卡尔·马克思、克鲁鲍特金和罗素的译作仍然非常畅销,甚至于那些针对中国古典文学的评论文章也会受到一些旧派学者的关注与赞同。知识分子阶层见证了中国无数次改革的失败并因此得出结论:中国人的思维方式需要彻底革新。

　　引入汉语拼音字母的使用、用白话或口语出版书籍和期刊,是目前向普通大众传播新知识的手段。为了给新生的中国知识分子提供鲜活的生命力,一些美国和英国的著名哲学家,如约翰·杜威和贝特郎·罗素,正在中国的许多教育机构巡回授课。作为靠自身实力满足公众需求而存在的机构,图书馆正处于瞬息万变的环境中。

　　藏书之所遍及今天的中国。尽管学者们仍持续关注诸如宋朝、元朝或明朝等前朝版本的书籍,但只有图书管理员懂得如何储存收集这些早期有价值的古籍。支持将单纯藏书的博物馆变为有生命力的图书馆的趋势日益增强。并且越来越多的人愿意到图书馆里寻求知识而不仅仅把它当成一座藏书的博物馆。值得一提的是过去两年新图书馆运动取得了很大的进步。

　　中国的图书馆大体可分为三类——公立图书馆,社团图书馆和学校图书馆。公立图书馆最早起始于满清王朝的末期,当时朝廷发布公告命令各省各区域建立当地的公立图书馆。然而,这个公告并没有被有效的遵守和实施,只有极少省份在本地建立了公立图书馆。一直到1914年,民国三年,现代化图书馆理念才被正式引入到中国。但是由于缺乏资金的支持,大多数的公立图书馆其实于普通民众并无太多帮助。

　　这样的公立图书馆有两种。第一种存在于省会或大城市,通常需要交纳少许费用方可进入,馆内书籍一般不外借,每天光顾的读者也寥寥无几。这种图书馆没有近期出版的作品,充其量不过是个储藏中文旧书的地方罢了。例如,北京公立图书馆向公众出售6种不同价位的阅览门票:(1)2铜圆门票,阅览一般图书;(2)1铜圆门票,阅览期刊和报纸;(3)1铜圆学生门票,阅览一般图书;(4)免费学生门票,阅览期刊和报纸;(5)10铜圆门票,阅览古籍;(6)5铜圆门票,查阅著名的《钦定四库全书总目》原稿。公众是不允许进入储藏书库的。

北京高等师范学校开设的中国第一个图书馆暑期学校

北京公立图书馆有很多阅览室,例如特别门票持有者可使用的特色阅览室,女士专用阅览室,期刊和报纸阅读室等等。这些阅览室设施简陋,座椅不舒服,照明和取暖条件更是不必谈了,取书的规定也有很多的繁文缛节。

除了上述六种普通门票之外,另有两种高级别门票——一等和二等。持有一等门票的读者可以免费享有优先取阅一般书籍、期刊、报纸、古籍的特权,并且可以自由进入书库。而二等门票持有者能够免费阅读一般书籍、期刊和报纸。

三年前省级公立图书馆有着和北京公立图书馆类似的体制。那时许多人认为这已经是通向民主教育的一大进步了,因为过去只有学者才有特权使用的图书馆在当时可以向购买门票的任何人开放。

现如今,人们越来越聪明,他们认为公立图书馆应该面向公众免费开放。从这时起,免费图书馆的理念被引入。在各省会和各主要城市的公立图书馆逐渐或是取消了购票入馆的制度,或是建立免费的图书馆分馆。

通常情况下,中国的免费图书馆允许读者免费使用馆内藏书,但是仅限内部阅览而不外借。和这些图书馆相配套的有儿童阅览室和活动场地。虽然有经费方面的困难,免费的图书馆却在管理经营上比公立图书馆要好多了。另外除古旧的汉语书籍外也有涉及各个学科的最新出版读物。儿童阅览室里还提供画报故事与少年读物,孩子们也经常光顾所属的游乐区。

多数图书馆在周日也像工作日一样对外开放,但也有些馆会在周一闭馆一天让员工放假。这类中等规模的免费图书馆一共有30家。

我走访并调查了其中的几家免费图书馆,包括位于北京的,它们很受读者欢迎,阅览室读者人数总是接近极限。当然,即使这样也仍然存在很多需要改进的空间。例如,应该大幅增加年度购书的预算,这样就可以建立图书流通部门,方便读者可以借书回家阅读。其次,阅览室的设施因太过简陋而不吸引人,儿童阅览室里的家具也不适合儿童使用。

阅览室的吸引力和读者对阅览环境舒适度的关注,是吸引人们利用图书馆的必要因素。当然,所有上述问题的改进需要资金支持。如果公众需要舒适、有吸引力的免费图书馆,资金的问题终归会得到解决的。在繁华地区,已有迹象表明,免费图书馆设施日趋精良。

与免费公立图书馆相比,中国的另一类图书馆的设施要好得多,但是仅供小部分特权团体享用。它们不受国家或地方政府管辖,资金主要来源于一些学会的基金捐助。当然,这类图书馆的馆藏内容也体现了出资学会的性质和发展目标。例如,位于北京的中国社会及政治学会①图书馆,馆藏图书主要集中在历史、政体、社会和政治领域方面。

免费公共图书馆的庭院,西城,北京

中国社会及政治联合会图书馆阅览室,北京

中国最有名的社团图书馆是设立在上海由西方人管理的上海皇家亚洲文会北中国支会图书馆。这个图书馆大约是在1860年由伟烈亚力先生捐赠的书籍为基础建成的,目前的馆藏大概有5000册的外文书籍和2000册左右的中文书籍。虽然它的藏书量不大,但是它在中国题材方面的作品收藏是相当强的。之后金斯米尔(Kingsmill)和莫尔斯(Morse)先生进

---

① 【译者注】原文为"The Chinese Social and Political Science Association"。

一步扩展了其中的东亚语言部分,著名的《中国学书目》②编制人高迪爱(Henry Cordier)教授曾经是这家图书馆馆长。1907年在波士顿图书馆博尔顿(Bolton)博士的推荐下开始采用《杜威十进分类法》和卡特著者号码表及卡片式目录。图书馆每天开放,图书外借仅限有特权的会员,非上海会员可以通过邮寄的方式借书。

另外一个迅速崭露头角的社团图书馆是前面提到的中国社会及政治学会图书馆。它主要是由一群留学归国的学生创办并监管的,这些学者需要北京有这么一个收藏西方书籍、期刊和杂志的高水平图书馆。它的成功落成归功于美国、后满清王朝家族以及卡内基基金会的支持。首先是通过在京代表保罗·赖施(Paul S. Reinsch),从美国退还中国的赔偿款中拨出总额十万元,作为筹建图书馆和日常运营的资金。第二笔慷慨的捐赠是位于市中心的图书馆建筑,捐资者纽约卡内基基金会当时已经捐赠了大约2000册有关历史、社会、政治学等方面的书籍。我相信这是在中国第一次由外国组织向中国的图书馆捐赠英文书籍。

这家图书馆内的阅览室也都装修得非常舒适考究,大窗户使得光线充足、空气流通顺畅,使用《杜威十进分类法》的目录即将完成。它将会是华北最现代的社团图书馆,将会成为大批会员和普通读者学习、研究的一个理想之所。

除了上述两个社团图书馆,有着类似特征的图书馆广泛分布在中国的一些沿海城市。建立此类图书馆的行为已逐渐延伸到中国内陆地区。

现在几乎所有的中国院校都有自己某种形式的图书馆。在为数不多的几个知名图书馆中,位于上海圣约翰大学的罗氏图书馆是中国最早的大学图书馆之一。它始建于1890年,以罗氏家族的赠书为馆藏基础,之后逐年持续稳步发展。为纪念校长卜舫济任职25年,该校校友、学生及各界友人捐建了一座纪念堂,图书馆在该纪念堂中拥有自己的一隅之地。

1912年,为了便于流通、排架和编目,罗氏图书馆按照与英文书相同的方式管理中文书籍,这是中国图书馆史上的一大进步。不管是中文还是英文书都采取了《杜威十进分类法》,尝试为中文图书编制卡片目录。阅览室分成舒适的小隔间吸引学生来此学习和研究。

儿童阅览室一隅,北京西城的一所公共图书馆

---

② 【译者注】原文为"Bibliotheca Sinica"。

清华学校图书馆内的大理石厅、出纳台和中文阅览室,北京

另外一个著名的大学图书馆是1907年扩建并重组的位于武昌的文华大学图书馆,它不仅面向在校学生和校友,同时也对湖北及相邻各省普通民众提供优质服务,并且是中国第一个开设图书馆学课程的教育机构,遍布各地的许多年轻图书馆馆长都源自文华大学图书科。这个图书馆除了每年举办例行的图书馆馆员培训之外,也通过其流动图书馆系统提供服务,并已建立了20多个中心来处理这些流动图书馆的流通管理。文华大学图书科学校正在花大力气将《杜威十进分类法》及相关索引翻译成中文。

1912年,在距离历史悠久但实属多事之地的北京颐和园一公里以外的美丽的清华学堂校园内,一个不起眼的图书馆诞生了,并在1914年夏天以后迅速发展。在仅仅八年时间内,其中外文馆藏量已遥遥领先于所有中国其他图书馆——拥有5.6万册精心挑选的图书,订购290种世界主要期刊和50份日报。除了大量的馆内阅览,每月的图书外借量逐步增加到1200册。图书馆不仅向教职工和学生提供参考工具,同时也向来自北京和天津其他院校教师及分散在各地的校友提供参考咨询服务。

为了适应快速增长的图书数量,清华大学一座漂亮的新式图书馆竖立起来,这是中国第一个使用钢架书库、玻璃和软木地板,以及其他科学设备的图书馆,肩负着推动图书馆科学管理运动向前发展的重大责任。1920年夏天,它与北京高等师范学校一起举办了第一届图书馆暑期学校,令人惊讶的是,竟然有共计78位学生(69名男同学和9名女同学)报名参加,他们中大多数供职于不同省份的各类图书馆,甚至连福建省厦门公立图书馆,也不畏路途遥远,冒着北京周围直皖军阀混战的危险,派代表参加课程学习。严格的专业课程同时面向男女生开放,这一创新无疑对支持男女同校运动产生重大影响。

1918年,清华图书馆发起成立了北平图书馆协会,因而首都的图书馆员们现在有机会共同探讨有关图书馆管理重要性的问题。在协会的帮助下,建立了图书馆之间的图书互借系统(馆际互借),同一城市内各类图书馆之间精诚合作的精神,对于那个时代来说的确是一个很好的迹象。

鉴于中国现代化图书馆的需求,在北京的一些图书馆馆员和教育工作者开始着手组建中华图书馆协会,第一步便是要求各省各市在本地建立图书馆协会以促进当地图书馆学的发展。中华教育改进社图书馆教育组每年将与不同省市有志于图书馆发展的协会代表、馆员一起举办年会。去年秋天选举成立了组织委员会,这个委员会将在1921夏天举办第一次年会。

自1914年始,中国先后有4位图书馆员从纽约公共图书馆学校和纽约州立大学图书馆学院毕业,正是他们积极推动着中国图书馆运动的进程。目前还有两位在纽约州立大学图书馆学院学习图书馆学,去美国继续深造之前,他们已有数年管理国内图书馆的实际经验。

无论如何,将藏书楼转变成向广大读者传播知识的有生命力的中心是每个中国知识分子的责任。一个国家成为一个真正的共和国,须以公民接受良好教育为前提。图书馆应该为国民教育做些什么?美国现代图书馆运动之父麦维尔·杜威(Melvil Dewey)博士曾经很好地回答了这个问题——图书馆是人民的大学。

因此,帮助每个城市和每座村庄建立图书馆,推动图书馆运动发展,是每个中华民国儿女义不容辞的责任。

原载:《泛太平洋》 1921年第2期

Library Movement in China(一)[①]

By T. C. Tai, Librarian of Tsing Hua College

Since the Revolution of 1911, China has undergone a movement of change in politics as well as in intellectual problems. The people have not only tried hard to shake off the yoke of despotism, but also fully determined to free themselves from the oppression of intellectual bondage. Today on the bookstalls the translated works of Karl Marx, Kroptokin and Russell are demanded like hot-cakes while the critical essays on Chinese classics are even welcomed by the scholars of the old type. The intellectual class has seen the failures of numerous reforms and come to the conclusion that the Chinese process of thought should be revolutionized.

To introduce the use of a Chinese phonetic alphabet, and to publish books and periodicals in Peh Hwa or colloquial language are present day means of diffusing the new knowledge to the general masses. In order to supply the new Chinese intellect with fresh vital energy, famous American and British philosophers like John Dewey and Bertrand Russell are now touring China giving lectures in most educational centers. And among institutions whose existence depends upon their ability to meet the public demand, the library is now face to face with rapidly changing conditions.

China even today is full of places for storing books. Although scholars continue to be interested in the editions of bygone dynasties, like the Sung, or Yuan or Ming, and librarians only know how to collect the valuable incunabula, yet the tendency is daily growing stronger in favor of converting the book-museum into a living library. And during the last two years especially the new library movement has taken great strides.

Roughly there are three kinds of libraries in China-namely, public libraries, society libraries and college libraries. The public library was started towards the end of the late Manchu dynasty. An imperial edict ordered the different provincial authorities to establish public libraries. That order however was not implicitly carried out, and only a few provinces obeyed it. It was not until 1914, the third year of the Republic, that the modern system of the public libraries was introduced. Owing to the lack of funds most of these libraries have been unable to do their best to help the people.

There are two kinds of such public libraries. The first is maintained by either the capital of a province or some principal cities. This generally requires a small sum for admission. It has no circulation and the number of daily patrons is very small. It has no books of recent publication and it is only a storehouse for the old Chinese books.

For instance, the Peking Public Library sells tickets to those who wish to go in to read. There are six kinds of such tickets-namely, (1) two-copper ticket for ordinary books, (2) one-copper ticket

---

① 【编者注】戴志骞先生分别在1921、1923、1926撰写《中国的图书馆运动》一文,发表在不同的期刊上,三篇论文题名一致,内容有部分一致,但三篇均有不一致之处,因此本文集将三篇文章全部收录,并分别译出。

for periodicals and newspapers, (3) one-copper student ticket for ordinary books, (4) free student ticket for periodicals and newspapers, (5) ten-copper ticket for incunabula, (6) five-copper ticket for the manuscript copy of the famous "Imperial Descriptive Catalog of the Manchu dynasty." The public is not admitted into the stack rooms.

The Peking Public Library has many reading rooms, such as a special reading room for special ticket holders, a ladies' reading room, a periodical and newspaper reading room, etc. These rooms are bare and the seats are not comfortable. Lighting and heating facilities are naturally out of the question. There is much red tape in drawing out books.

Besides the six ordinary tickets there are two special tickets, first and second. Those who hold special tickets of the first class can enjoy the privilege of inspecting and using ordinary books, periodicals, newspapers, incunabula, etc., without charge and also that of having access to the stacks. Those who hold special tickets of the second class can enjoy only the free use of ordinary books, periodicals and newspapers.

Three years ago the provincial public libraries had a system similar to that in the Peking Public Library. At that time many people thought that it was already a great advance towards democratic education, since only scholars were supposed to have the privilege of being near the books. By selling tickets the books could be used by any one who would pay a nominal sum.

Today people are getting wiser. The public library, they feel, should be free to everybody. Hence the system of free libraries is being introduced. Hence the public libraries in the provincial capitals and principal cities are gradually either discarding the policy of selling tickets or establishing branch free libraries.

Generally a free library in China allows the people to use its collections without any charge, but you cannot draw out the books for home use. On the other hand, in connection with those libraries there are play-grounds and children's reading rooms. In spite of the financial difficulty the free libraries are better administered than the public libraries. In addition to old Chinese books the former also has newly published books on different subjects. Children's rooms are supplied with pictorial tales and juvenile books, and the play-grounds are well patronized by the children.

The libraries open on Sundays just as on week days. Some of them close on Mondays as a holiday to the members of the staff. There are altogether thirty organized free libraries of medium size.

Several free libraries, including those in Peking, I have visited and investigated. They are well patronized and their reading rooms are always crowded to the utmost capacity. Of course there is yet plenty of room for improvement. For instance the budget for the annual acquisition of books should be greatly increased, so that a circulation department can be established for promoting the use of books at home. Secondly the rooms are too bare and unattractive and the furniture in the children's reading rooms especially is not suitable.

The attractiveness of the reading rooms and attention to the comfort of readers are necessary factors to induce people to use the libraries. Of course, all the above improvements hinge entirely on the question of money. The money will come, if public sentiment demands comfortable and attractive free libraries. There are nevertheless signs at present in different prosperous localities for promoting a movement in favor of fine free libraries.

The second type of libraries in China is better equipped than the free public libraries. Their use is only enjoyed by a few privileged groups. They are not maintained by the government or provincial authorities. Their chief income depends upon the funds of the society. Their collection of books is of course similar to the nature of the parent society. So the Library of the Chinese Social and Political Science Association in Peking has its chief collection on history, government, social and political sciences.

The best known society library maintained by westerners in China is the Library of the North China Branch of the Royal Asiatic Society at Shanghai. This library was founded about 1860 and the collection on China given by Mr. Wylie formed its nucleus. Now it has about 5,000 volumes in foreign languages about 2,000 in Chinese. Altho the collection is not large, it is fairly strong in works on China. The section of Eastern Asiatic languages was enlarged by Messrs. Kingsmill and Morse. The famous bibliographer of "Bibliotheca Sinica", Professor Henri Cordier, was once its librarian.

The Dewey decimal classification system, together with the Cutter author numbers and the card dictionary catalog, was adopted in 1907, upon the recommendation of Dr. Bolton of the Boston Athenaeum. The library is open daily and the privilege of taking out books is enjoyed by members only. Members not resident in Shanghai can borrow books by mail.

Another society library now rapidly coming to the front is the above mentioned Library of the Chinese Social and Political Science Association. It is founded and maintained largely by a group of "Returned" Students who feel the need of a good library with western books, journal and magazines in Peking. Its final success in 1918 depends upon the United States of America, the late Imperial Manchu family and the Carnegie Endowment Corporation. The first, through its worthy representative in Peking, Dr. Paul S. Reinsch, set apart the sum of taels 100,000 from the remitted indemnity fund as the initial and maintenance expenses of the library. The second kindly donated a centrally located site for the library building. The third is the Carnegie Corporation of New York which has already contributed about 2,000 volumes in history, social and political sciences, etc. I believe this is the first endowment of English books from that corporation to a library in China.

The reading rooms are comfortably furnished. With big windows both the light and air are excellent. A dictionary catalog with decimal classification is now on the way of accomplishment. It will be one of the most up-to-date society libraries in North China. The members of that Association as well as the reading public in general will have an ideal place for doing research work.

In addition to the above two society libraries, there are about one dozen other society libraries scattered along the sea coast of China. The movement towards founding libraries of this type is slowly extending to the interior of the country.

Almost every college in China now has a sort of library. Among the few noted ones, the Low Library of St. John's University, Shanghai, is one of the oldest college libraries. It was begun about 1890. Mr. Low's donation formed the nucleus of the collection. It grew steadily year after year, until now it has its own quarters in the Anniversary Hall which was a gift from the alumni students, and friends to the present president, Dr. Pott, in commemoration of the twenty-fifth anniversary of his presidency.

For the sake of convenience in charging, shelving, and cataloguing, all the Chinese books in 1912 were bound in the style of English books. This was a great advance in the history of Chinese libraries. Both English and Chinese books were classified according to Dewey decimal classification and the experiment was introduced of having a card catalog for Chinese books. The reading rooms are divided into cosy alcoves. It is an attractive place for students to study and research.

Another well-known college library is the Boone University Library at Wuchang. It was extended and reorganized about 1907. This library has been adequately organized and has done a great service not only to the students and alumni of that university, but also to the people of Hupeh and the neighboring provinces at large.

It is the first institution in China to introduce a regular course of library science. Many young librarians now working in the different libraries are the products of the Boone Library School. Besides producing regularly trained librarians every year, the Boone University Library introduced the serviceable system of traveling libraries. It has already established more than twenty centers to handle the circulation of traveling libraries. The school has now undertaken the Herculean job of translating the Dewey Decimal Classification and its Relative Index into Chinese.

In 1912 a small library had its birth about a mile from the eventful spot of the ruined old Summer Palace of Peking(Yuan Ming Yuan), in the beautiful campus of Tsing Hua College. After the summer of 1914 it began to grow rapidly. Now in the course of only eight years, its collections in Chinese as well as in foreign languages, are easily the most pretentious of all libraries in China. At present it has 56,000 volumes of well selected books. It subscribes to 290 leading periodicals of the world and 50 dailies. The circulation figure generally reaches to 1,200 books every month besides a much bigger figure of books used in the library. The library not only provides reference facility for the faculty and students but also answers many reference questions from the teachers of various schools in Peking and Tientsin as well as the alumni of the college.

In order to accommodate the rapidly increasing number of books, an up-to-date and beautiful library building was erected. It is the first library building in China to use steel standard stacks, glass and cork floors, and other scientific equipment. According to the present rate of annual acquisition it will in five years become the largest college in China.

This Library is responsible for a great deal of the initiative in promoting a movement for scientific management of libraries. In the summer of 1920 it co-operated with the Peking High Normal College to found the first library summer school. It was a great surprise to all that the enrollment numbered seventy-eight men and women. Most of these are the librarians of various libraries in different provinces. They were sent up to attend the summer school, and even the Public Library of Amoy(Fukien)delegated its librarian to attend lectures in spite of the great distance and the civil war between the Chihli and Anfu military parties around Peking. Among the seventy-eight students, nine were girls. The lectures being strictly professional, it was open to both sexes. Undoubtedly the innovation has exerted a strong influence in support of the movement towards co-education.

The Tsing Hua Library took the lead in forming a Peking Library Association in 1918. Now the librarians of Peking have an opportunity to discuss questions of importance in connection with library administration. Under the auspices of the association the system of the inter-library loans of books has been introduced. A spirit of genuine co-operation between the various libraries in Peking, is certainly a good sign of the times.

Seeing the need of modern libraries in China, a group of librarians and educators in Peking are now organizing a Chinese Library Association. The first step is to ask each province or city to form a local library association promoting the library science of that particular locality. The Chinese Library Association will have an annual conference with the representatives of the library associations, librarians and educators, who are interested in the library movement of different cities. An organizing committee was elected last Autumn and it plans to hold the first conference in the summer of 1921.

Since 1914 four Chinese librarians have graduated from the New York Public Library School and the New York State Library School. They are the promoters of a library movement in China. At present there are two men studying Library Science at the New York State Library School. They are fully equipped to introduce a new era into the Chinese library world. Before they left for the United States to further their knowledge and experience, they all had years of practical experience in administering libraries. So we hope that these men who have the opportunity to see and study the library systems of the great powers will innoculate the old Chinese librarians with the serum of modern libraries.

The responsibility however of converting the storehouses of books into active centers for diffusing knowledge to the reading public should belong to every educated Chinese. A republic cannot become a true republic unless its citizens are properly educated. What have the libraries to do with the education of the people? This question was once replied by Dr. Melvil Dewey, father of the modern American library movement, that the library is the university of the people. To establish libraries in every city and in every village and to launch the present library movement over the top, are therefore the responsibility belonging to every loyal son and daughter of the Republic.

To sum up the plans regarding a library movement in China at present are simple and not ambitious. For there are two factors obstructing the way of having an ambitious plan: (1) The central government is very unstable and nearly to the verge of bankruptcy. Hoping to get some governmental subsidy for the movement is no more than a mere dream. (2) The public opinion of the people is not keen enough yet to have libraries established everywhere. In view of these two difficulties we have to go along steadily and cautiously but with hope and patience.

There are several things now in my mind:

1. Organize a Chinese Library Association which will publish a periodical and other pamphlets on library topics. The work of advertisement and propaganda can be successfully accomplished through such an organization, but above all to standardize library administration.

2. Encourage to have a local library association in every city. As a matter of fact those two

plans since last summer have been discussed; but owing to financial difficulty, only a few of their activities have been put into practice.

3. Influence a few high educational institutions to establish library schools. I have discussed that plan with the presidents of Peking High Normal College and the South Eastern University at Nanking. They fully endorse my suggestion. Again due to shortage of fund the plan is temporarily suspended.

4. Encourage to establish small libraries and readings rooms in every district. Many cities along the Yangtze Valley have taken up that movement.

5. Try to influence Chinese students to study library science in the United States of America. We want trained librarians to give the public efficient library service.

Above all the most imminent need is a Chinese Library Association, through which we can standardize the system of library administration. My aim is to see all those plans put into force as extensively as possible.

A List of Libraries Having Foreign Books and Modern Library Service

Names of Libraries	Volumes in Chinese	Volumes in foreign languages	System of Classification
Anking Provincial Library, 1912	34,000	1,000	Chinese classification. (C. C.) i. e. Classics, history, philosophy, belle lettres and general works
Canton Christian College Library	5,000	9,000	No system yet
Chengsha Yale College Library	1,000	3,000	Decimal classification (D. C.)
Chekiang Public Library, 1912	372,188	2,000	C. C.
Foochow Public Library, 1912	26,480	1,000	C. C.
Hupeh Provincial Library, 1912	140,000	1,500	C. C.
Kiukiang William Nest College Library	3,000	2,500	Classified according to subjects taught
Kwangsi Public Library, 1913	60,000	2,000	C. C.
Nanking Science Society Library, 1918	900	1,500	Modified Harvard classification
Nanking Teachers College Library, 1914	10,000	5,600	D. C. & C. C.
Nanking University Library, 1905(?)	3,000	10,000	D. C. & C. C.
Nantung School Library, 1913	130,000	1,000	C. C.
Peking Chinese Social & Political Science Association Library	1,000	4,000	D. C.
Peking Christian Univ. Library, 1919	1,000	2,000	D. C.
Peking Government Library, 1904	60,000	10,000	C. C.
Peking High Normal Col. Lib., 1910	8,000	7,000	Tokyo Library system

续表

Names of Libraries	Volumes in Chinese	Volumes in foreign languages	System of Classification
Peking Public Library,1912	128,000	2,000	C. C.. (Has many valuable mss.)
Peking Tsing Hua Col. Lib.,1912	42,000	18,000	D. C. & Modified C. C. For Chinese Books
Peking Union Medical Col. Lib.,1919	300(?)	9,000(?)	Subject classification.
Shanghai St. John's Univ. Lib.,1890	3,000	16,000	D. C.
Shanghai Baptist Col. Lib.,1915(?)	1,500	3,000	D. C.
Shanghai Poly. Institute Lib.,1909(?)	20,000	4,000	C. C.
Shantung Public Library,1908	12,000	2,000	C. C.
Shantung Christian Univ. Library	10,000	8,000	D. C. & C. C.
Soochow Univ. Library,1904(?)	2,500	9,000	
Sung Kiang Public Library,1915	55,000	1,000	C. C.
Tientsin Nankai Col. Library,1911	4,000	5,000	D. C. & C. C.
Tientsin Public Lib.,1908	13,500	3,600	C. C.
Tientsin Peiyang Univ. Library	25,000	10,000	Lib. Congress classification
Wuchang High Normal Col. Lib.,1911	21,000	2,000	C. C.
Wuchang Boone Univ. Library	15,000	10,000	D. C.
Wuchang Wesley Col. Lib	2,000	3,000	D. C.
Wusih Public Lib.,1912	41,000	2,500	Modified C. C.

1. Most of the provincial public libraries were established in 1912.
2. The numbers of volumes of each library is approximate.

原载:*American Library Association Committee Reports* Vol. 1921,1920-21

【译文】管翠中译 邓景康审

中国的图书馆运动(一)

戴志骞 清华学校图书馆主任

　　1911年辛亥革命以来,中国在政治和文化上经历了一系列变革。中国人民挣脱了封建专制的束缚,也决心要从文化樊篱中解放出来。现在书店里马克思、克鲁泡特金和罗素的译作非常畅销,就像中国古典文学评论受到老学究追捧一样。

　　知识分子目睹无数改革的失败后意识到必须彻底颠覆中国人的传统思想。

　　引入汉语拼音的使用、用口语化的白话文出版书籍和期刊现在是向广大群众传播新知识的手段。

　　著名的美国和英国哲学家约翰·杜威、伯特兰·罗素等到中国许多教育中心讲学,为中国先进知识分子带来新的生命力。图书馆作为满足公众需求而存在的机构,现在正面临着快速变化的环境。

　　中国现在依然有很多藏书楼。尽管学者们依然对宋元明等朝代的古籍感兴趣,尽管图书馆员仅知道如何收藏这些珍贵的古籍,然而如今将藏书楼变为充满生机活力的图书馆的趋势日益增长。在过去的两年中,新型图书馆的发展取得了很大的进步。

　　在中国,图书馆大致分为三类,公立图书馆、社团图书馆和学校图书馆。公共图书馆起始于晚清末期,清政府颁布诏书命令各省政府建立公立图书馆。然而诏书并没有彻底执行,仅有少数省份建了公立图书馆。直到民国三年(1914年),才引入现代公立图书馆制度。由于缺乏资金,大多数图书馆都不能尽其最大能力来服务民众。

　　有两类公立图书馆,第一类是由省会或某些重要城市维持的,通常只允许少数人入内。所藏书籍仅限于馆内阅览,不得带出馆外,而且每日来馆人数很少。馆内没有最新书籍,更像是古籍的储藏室。

　　例如,京师图书馆需要购券进入。券分为六个等级:(1)普通书阅览券,铜圆币两枚;(2)期刊和报纸阅览券,铜圆一枚;(3)普通书学生阅览券,铜圆币一枚;(4)期刊和报纸学生阅览券,免费;(5)善本书阅览券,铜圆十枚;(6)著名的《四库全书总目》原稿阅览券,铜圆五枚。阅览者不能入库查看书籍。

　　京师图书馆有很多阅览室,比如特殊券持有者的特殊阅览室、女士阅览室、期刊和报纸阅览室等。阅览室较为空旷,座位也不舒服,照明和取暖设施自然也存在问题,借书的时候还有很多繁琐手续。

　　除了这六种常规阅览券之外,还有两种特殊阅览券。拥有第一类特殊阅览券的人,不用交费就享有查阅和使用普通图书、期刊、报纸、善本等的特权,还能进出书库。拥有第二类特殊阅览券的人仅享有免费使用普通图书、期刊和报纸的权利。

---

① 【编者注】戴志骞先生分别在1921、1923、1926撰写《中国的图书馆运动》一文,发表的不同的期刊上,三篇论文题名一致,内容有部分一致,但三篇均有不一致之处,因此本文集将三篇文章全部收录,并分别译出。

三年前省级公立图书馆都有类似京师图书馆的制度。那时候很多人认为这已经是民主教育的一大进步，因为以前只有学者才有靠近书籍的特权。用出售阅览券的方式任何人都可以通过支付象征性的费用来使用书籍。

今天，人们变得更加明智了，他们认为公立图书馆应该免费向公众开放。因此引入了免费图书馆制度，省会和一些主要城市逐渐舍弃售卖阅览券的政策或者设立免费图书馆分支。

通常情况下，中国的免费图书馆允许人们不用交费就可以使用其馆藏，但是不能将书借回家使用。另一方面，免费图书馆还有游乐场和儿童阅览室。尽管经费困难，免费图书馆相比较于公立图书馆管理的更好。免费图书馆除了中国古籍外，还有新出版的不同学科的书籍，儿童阅览室还提供图画故事书和少年读物，也有游乐场地供孩子们光顾。

图书馆在周日也正常开放，一些馆周一闭馆让工作人员休息。总共有30个中等规模的免费图书馆。

我曾经去过几个免费图书馆，包括在北京的那几个。入馆的人很多，阅览室常常挤满了人。当然免费图书馆还有许多改进的空间，如每年采书的预算应大大增加，以便能够建立促进书籍外借的流通部门；其次阅览室太空旷，没有吸引力，儿童阅览室中的家具尤其不舒服。

阅览室的吸引力和对环境舒适度的关注是诱导人们利用图书馆的必要因素。当然，上述所有问题的改进完全取决于经费。如果公众觉得需要舒适的和有吸引力的免费图书馆，那么自然会得到经费。然而目前可以看到的迹象是，尽管经济实力有差异，但各地都在尽力推广和宣传免费图书馆的概念。

在中国第二种形式的图书馆比免费公立图书馆有着更好的设施，它们仅为少数特殊人员使用。这类图书馆并不是由政府或者地方当局出资，其主要收入来源于协会资金，藏书当然也和协会的性质相似。北京的社会政治学会图书馆主要收藏历史、社会和政治科学方面的图书。②

最有名的社团图书馆是上海皇家亚洲文会北中国支会图书馆，由在华西方人主持，该馆约建于1860年，伟烈亚力捐赠的有关中国的藏品是它的核心，目前大约有5000册外文图书和2000册中文图书，虽然收藏量不大，但是关于中国的藏品很有价值，东亚文种部分通过尊敬的马士（H. B. Morse）③、金斯密（T. W. Kingsmill）④的努力得以扩展，著名的《西人论中国书目》的作者亨利·高第曾经是这里的图书馆员。

1907年，在波士顿图书馆的博尔顿博士（Dr. Bolton）推荐下，该馆开始使用杜威分类法以及卡特著者号码和字典目录，图书馆每日开放，会员可以享受将图书借出馆外的特权，不在上海的会员还可以通过邮寄借书。

另一个迅速崭露头角的社团图书馆是上面提到的北京社会政治学会图书馆，该馆主要

---

② 【译者注】中国社会政治学会于1915年在北京成立。美国驻中国公使芮恩施博士（Dr. Paul S. Reinsch）提议仿效美国政治科学协会（American Political Science Association），成立了中国社会政治学会，旨在研究国际法与外交，是中国最早的全国性的社会科学专业协会。

③ 【译者注】马士（H. B. Morse，1855—1934），美国人，1874年毕业于哈佛大学，后应聘到中国海关任职长达35年，1909年因健康原因辞去中国海关职务，致力于远东与中国史研究，著有《中华帝国对外关系史》等多部学术论著，被公认为西方汉学的先驱之一。

④ 【译者注】金斯密（T. W. Kingsmill，1837—1910），汉学家，曾任上海皇家亚洲文会主席，1899年将《道德经》译成英文。

由归国留学生创立与管理,他们认为北京需要一个拥有西文图书、期刊和杂志的优秀图书馆。1918 年,该馆借助于美国政府、晚清政府和纽约卡内基基金会的支持最终建成。美国政府通过其在北京的代表芮恩施博士从美国退还的庚款中移挪十万两白银作为开办及维持费。晚清政府捐赠市中心位置作为馆址。纽约卡内基基金会捐赠大约 2000 册历史、社会、政治等书籍,我相信这是该基金会第一次向中国图书馆捐赠英文书籍。

阅览室陈设很舒适,有大窗户,光线和通风都极好。采用十进位分类法的字典目录即将完成,这将是华北最现代的团体图书馆之一,该会会员和普通民众将有一个理想的地方去做研究工作。

除了上述两个图书馆外,中国还有很多其他的社团图书馆分散在东南沿海,这种创办社团图书馆的运动正慢慢地延伸到中国内地。

目前,中国的每个大学几乎都有图书馆,在少数几个有名的大学图书馆中,上海圣约翰大学的罗氏图书馆是最古老的学校图书馆之一,该馆约建于 1890 年,罗氏兄弟的捐赠形成了馆藏的核心,图书逐年稳定增长,现在已经有了独立馆舍,该馆舍是为了纪念卜舫济校长(F. L. Hawks Pott)任职 25 周年,由该校校友、学生及卜氏好友捐资建造的。⑤

为了整理、排架、编目的方便,1912 年该馆所有的中文书均改为西式装订,这是中国图书馆历史上的一大进步。中英文图书均采用《杜威十进分类法》,并尝试编制中文图书卡片目录。阅览室分成舒适的隔间,对于学生学习和研究来说,这是一个有吸引力的地方。

另一个有名的大学图书馆是武昌的文华大学图书馆⑥,约在 1907 年筹备扩建和重新整理。该馆管理得当,不仅为本校学生、校友服务,而且为湖北及周边省份提供服务。

它是中国第一个开设图书馆学专业课程的机构。很多现在在不同图书馆工作的馆员都是文华图书馆学校培养出来的,除了每年正规培养途径外,文华大学图书馆还引入巡回文库服务制度,已经建立了二十多个中心,负责巡回文库的图书借阅。学校正在承担把《杜威十进分类法》和相关索引译成中文的艰巨任务。

1912 年,在距北京旧夏宫遗址(圆明园)⑦约一英里的美丽的清华学校校园内,诞生了一个小型图书馆,1914 年夏以后迅速发展,现在仅仅过了八年时间,它的中外文藏品是中国所有图书馆中最值得夸耀的,目前有 56,000 册精选的图书,订购 290 种世界领先的期刊和 50 种日报,每月借阅图书达 1200 册,在阅览室中阅读的图书更多,图书馆不仅为本校教师和学生提供参考,而且回答北京和天津很多学校的教师以及校友提出的问题。

为了容纳迅速增长的大量图书,一座典雅华丽的现代图书馆建筑拔地而起,这是中国第一个有钢制书架、玻璃地面、软木地板以及其他科学设备的图书馆建筑。依照现在每年购书的速度,未来五年它将成为中国最大的学校图书馆。

该馆还承担促进图书馆科学管理的责任。1920 年夏与北京高等师范学校合作,创立了

---

⑤ 【译者注】1913 年 12 月 20 日,约大同学和校友举行校长卜舫济任职 25 周年纪念会,募集资金 2 万元,捐建纪念室作图书馆之用,称为纪念室(Anniversary Hall),又因纽约罗氏兄弟亦捐赠图书,故又称为罗氏图书馆(Low Library)。1915 年初奠基,1916 年夏落成。

⑥ 【译者注】1903 年,美国圣公会韦棣华女士(Miss Mary Elizabeth Wood)在文华书院八角亭建小阅览室。1907 年,她赴美募资筹建新馆舍,1910 年 5 月 16 日举行新馆舍开幕典礼,定名为"文华公书林"。

⑦ 【译者注】圆明园建于 1709 年,因清朝皇帝每到盛夏来此避暑、听政,因此也称为夏宫。

第一个图书馆暑期学校,让人们大吃一惊的是,有78名男女学生注册,大部分是来自不同省份各个图书馆的图书管理员,尽管路途遥远,北京附近还有直皖战争,⑧他们还是来参加暑期学校,甚至还有厦门(福建)公共图书馆的代表。在78位学员中有9位女生,完全专业化的课程向男女学生同时开放。毫无疑问,这一创新对支持男女合校运动产生深刻的影响。

1918年,清华图书馆领导建立了北京图书馆协会,现在北京的图书馆员有机会在一起讨论一些重要的有关图书馆管理的问题。在协会的支持下,已经引进图书互借制度,北京各种图书馆的合作精神必定成为一个时代的标志。

考虑到中国现代图书馆发展的需求,北京的图书馆员和教育工作者正在组织中国的图书馆学会,⑨首先请每个省或城市在本地建立图书馆协会,促进当地图书馆学的发展。中国的图书馆学会将召开由关注中国各城市图书馆运动的图书馆协会、图书馆员、教育工作者为代表的年会,去年秋天选举了组织委员会,计划于1922年夏举行第一次会议。⑩

1914年以来,已经有4名中国图书馆员从纽约公共图书馆学校和纽约州立大学图书馆学院毕业,他们是中国图书馆运动的推动者。目前有2人在纽约州立大学图书馆学院学习图书馆学。他们受过全面教育,将把中国图书馆引入一个全新的时代。在去美国深入学习知识和经验之前,他们已经有多年的图书馆管理经验。所以我们希望这些有机会见识和学习西方大国图书馆制度的人能为古老的中国图书馆注入现代图书馆的血液。

将藏书楼转换成向公众传播知识的活动中心是每个中国知识分子的责任。只有其公民受到一定的教育,中国才能成为真正意义上的共和国。图书馆应该为人民的教育做些什么呢?现代美国图书馆运动之父麦维尔·杜威博士曾经回答了这个问题:图书馆是人民的大学。在每一座城市和村庄建立图书馆并推进图书馆的发展是每一个中华儿女的责任。

总而言之,当代中国图书馆发展的计划是简单和平实的,究其原因主要有两个:(1)中央政府极不稳定并几乎濒于破产的边缘。图书馆发展想要得到一点政府的补贴比做梦还难。(2)公众舆论还不够激烈来推动每一处都建立图书馆。鉴于这两个困难我们还要稳步谨慎但是充满希望和耐心的继续下去。

现在我脑海中有几件事:

1. 组织一个中华图书馆协会,将来可以创办以图书馆为主题的期刊或小册子。广告宣传工作可以通过这个组织成功完成,但是最要紧的是规范图书馆的管理。

2. 鼓励每个城市都有一个地方图书馆协会。事实上,这两个计划去年夏天就已经讨论过了;但是由于资金困难,只有少数的活动已经付诸实践。

3. 建议一些高等教育机构成立图书馆学校。我曾经和北京高等师范学校和南京东南大学的校长讨论过这个计划,他们对我的建议完全赞同。但是又一次由于资金短缺的问题计划暂时被搁置。

---

⑧ 【译者注】1920年7月,以段祺瑞为首的皖系军阀"安福军"和以吴佩孚、曹锟为首的直系军阀为争夺北京政府的统治权,在京津地区发动战争,最后皖军大败,直、奉两系军阀控制了北京政权。

⑨ 【译者注】1921年12月,蔡元培、陶行知等在北京创设教育研究团体——"中华教育改进社",下设图书馆教育组,即戴志骞提到的"中国图书馆学会",是中国最早的全国性图书馆专业组织,戴志骞任主席。

⑩ 【译者注】原文为"计划于1921年夏举行第一次会议",实际为1922年,原文印刷错误,此处订正。1922年7月,中华教育改进社在济南召开第一次年会,图书馆教育组参加者有洪有丰、沈祖荣、朱家治、孙心盘、杜定友、戴罗瑜丽等,戴志骞任主席。

4. 鼓励在每个区建立小型图书馆和阅览室。长江流域边上的很多城市已经采取了这一行动。

5. 设法让中国学生去美国学习图书馆学知识。我们希望训练有素的图书馆员为公众提供高效的图书馆服务。

综上所述,最迫切的需求是成立中华图书馆协会,通过它我们可以规范图书馆管理制度。我的目标是看到所有这些计划能够尽可能广泛地实施。

有外文书籍和先进图书馆服务的图书馆名单:

图书馆名称	中文图书卷数	外文图书卷数	语言分类系统
安庆省立图书馆,1912	34,000	1,000	中文分类法(C.C.),例如经史子集和一般著作
岭南大学图书馆	5,000	9,000	暂无分类法
长沙雅礼大学图书馆	1,000	3,000	杜威十进分类法(D.C.)
浙江公立图书馆,1912	372,188	2,000	C.C.
福州公立图书馆,1912	26,480	1,000	C.C.
湖北省立图书馆,1912	140,000	1,500	C.C.
九江南伟烈大学图书馆	3,000	2,500	按主题分类
广西公立图书馆,1913	60,000	2,000	C.C.
南京科学社图书馆,1918	900	1,500	改进的哈佛分类法
南京高等师范学校图书馆,1914	10,000	5,600	D.C. & C.C.
金陵大学图书馆,1905(?)⑪	3,000	10,000	D.C. & C.C.
南通大学图书馆,1913	130,000	1,000	C.C.
北京中国社会政治学会图书馆	1,000	4,000	D.C.
北京基督大学图书馆,1919	1,000	2,000	D.C
北京政府图书馆,1904	60,000	10,000	C.C.
北京高等师范学校图书馆,1910	8,000	7,000	日本图书馆系统
京师图书馆,1912	128,000	2,000	C.C..(有很多珍品)
北京清华学校图书馆,1912	42,000	18,000	D.C. & 中文图书为修订后的C.C.
北京协和医学院图书馆,1919	300(?)	9,000(?)	主题分类法
上海圣约翰大学图书馆,1890	3,000	16,000	D.C.

---

⑪ 【译者注】金陵大学实际创立于1910年。

续表

图书馆名称	中文图书卷数	外文图书卷数	语言分类系统
上海浸会大学图书馆,1915(?)	1,500	3,000	D. C.
上海格致书院图书馆⑫,1909(?)	20,000	4,000	C. C.
山东公立图书馆,1908	12,000	2,000	C. C.
齐鲁大学图书馆	10,000	8,000	D. C. & C. C.
东吴大学图书馆,1904(?)	2,500	9,000	
松江公立图书馆,1915	55,000	1,000	C. C.
天津南开大学图书馆,1911	4,000	5,000	D. C. & C. C.
天津公共图书馆,1908	13,500	3,600	C. C.
天津北洋大学图书馆	25,000	10,000	国会图书馆分类法
武昌高等师范学校图书馆,1911	21,000	2,000	C. C.
武昌文华大学图书馆	15,000	10,000	D. C.
武昌博文书院图书馆	2,000	3,000	D. C.
无锡公立图书馆,1912	41,000	2,500	修改后的 C. C.

1. 大多数省级公立图书馆建在1912年。
2. 各图书馆的图书册数为近似数。

原载:《美国图书馆协会委员会报告(1921卷)》　1920-21

---

⑫ 【译者注】上海格致书院实际创立于1876年,由英国驻沪领事麦华陀倡议,由麦华陀、傅兰雅、唐廷枢等中外人士共同创立,建有博物馆和藏书楼,开设物理、化学、地理、医学等科目。1914年10月,格致书院的经营权被上海公共租界工部局收归己有,改名为"华童公学",1917年改为"工部局格致公学",是今上海市格致中学的前身。

Library Movement in China(二)

T. C. TAI, B. L. S.
LIBRARIAN OF TSING HUA COLLEGE
BULLETIN 3   1923   VOLUME II
CHINESE NATIONAL ASSOCIATION FOR THE ADVANCEMENT OF EDUCATION
PEKING, CHINA

INTRODUCTION

Since the Revolution of 1911, China has undergone a movement of change in intellectual problems as well as in politics. The people have not only tried hard to shake off the yoke of despotism, but also fully determined to free themselves from the oppression of intellectual bondage. Today at the bookstalls the translated works of Karl Marx, Kroptokin, Russell, Einstein and others are demanded like hot cakes, while the critical essays on Chinese classics are even welcomed by the scholars of the old type. The intellectual class has seen the failures of numerous reforms and come to the conclusion that the Chinese process of thought must be revolutionized.

Our present day means of diffusing the new knowledge to the general masses are to introduce the use of a Chinese phonetic alphabet, and to publish books and periodicals in Peh Hua or colloquial language. In order to supply the Chinese intellect with fresh, vital energy, famous philosophers like Dewey, Russell and Driesch have been and are still touring China, giving lectures in most educational centers. Among institutions whose existence depends upon their ability to meet the public demand, the library is now face to face with rapidly changing conditions.

ATTITUDE OF GOVERNMENT

China even to-day is full of places for storing books. Although scholars continue to be interested in the editions of bygone dynasties, like the Sung, or the Yuan or the Ming, and many libraries only know how to collect the valuable incunabula, yet the tendency is daily growing stronger in favor of converting the book vault, jealously guarded by thick doors and heavy locks, into a living and attractive library. And during the last decade the new library movement has taken great strides.

On April 11, 1915, the Ministry of Education issued an order embodying eleven regulations which emphasize promotion, organization and administration of libraries throughout the different provinces of the country.

They are translated as follows:

1. Every province and special district shall establish public libraries for the use of the people.

When the inhabitants of a city call for a library, let it be established without unnecessary delay.

2. Any school, public or private, or any society or individual person may establish a library by following the library regulations promulgated by the Ministry of Education.

3. Libraries maintained by cities and special districts shall be called public libraries. Libraries maintained by schools and societies shall be called respectively school libraries and society libraries, while libraries maintained by individuals shall be called private libraries.

4. (a) The public library shall at the time of establishment submit to the Ministry of Education through the district officer or the educational commissioner the following data:

   1. Name.
   2. Location.
   3. Expenditure.
   4. Number of volumes.
   5. Plan of the building.
   6. Regulations.
   7. The date of opening.

(b) Private libraries shall register at the district officer with the same seven data as in (a).

(c) School and society libraries shall report those data through the authorities of the school or the society to the district officer or the educational commissioner.

   Discontinuation of the operation of any library, or any change of name, etc., shall be reported to the district officer or educational commissioner.

5. Every library is required to have a librarian and also assistants. The qualifications of the librarian and the assistants shall at the time of their assumption of duties be reported to the Ministry of Education through the district officer.

6. The salaries and privileges of the librarian and assistants of any public library shall follow the regulations for the educational officers of that district.

7. Every public library is required to submit to the district officer an annual report which shall be published in the general annual educational report of that province.

8. The budget of a public library shall at the beginning of the fiscal year be submitted for approval to the Ministry of Education through the district officer or the educational commissioner.

   The budget of a school library must be incorporated in the school budget.

9. Libraries may collect a nominal assessment from the readers.

10. When an individual person establishes or donates a library, the district officer shall report the matter to the Ministry of Education, so that the donor shall be duly rewarded according to the regulations governing "Establishment and Donation of Schools."

11. The above regulations shall take effect at the date of publication.

In order to add weight to the proclamation, the government turned the Imperial Library of the late Manchu dynasty at Peking into the Peking Metropolitan Public Library. Some of the provinces and special districts have carried out the order, but others owing to lack of funds are still in the period of preparation.

CLASSES OF LIBRARIES

At present the Chinese libraries, excluding private ones, can be roughly divided into four main classes, namely public libraries, school libraries, society libraries, and special libraries.

PUBLIC LIBRARIES

In old days many provincial capitals kept large collections of books printed from wooden blocks.① They were stored in some public hall for the use of scholars. Since 1913 these places have been turned into public libraries. Some of them are maintained by endowments, but the majority by the educational funds of the districts and are thus under the control of the Commissioner of Education of that province.

As to the administration, nearly all of the public libraries not only have adopted the closed shelf-system in reading rooms, but also allow no circulation. Some of them require a small fee for admission, with the purpose of keeping away vagabonds and ruffians. Asseting charges for use of books in reading rooms are also practiced in many a public library.

For instance, the Peking Public Library sells tickets to those who wish to go in to read. There are six kinds of such tickets—namely, (1) two-copper ticket for ordinary books, (2) one-copper ticket for periodicals and newspapers, (3) one-copper student ticket for ordinary books, (4) free student ticket for periodicals and newspapers, (5) ten-copper ticket for incunabula, (6) five-copper ticket for the manuscript copy of the famous "Imperial Descriptive Catalogue of the Manchu dynasty."

The Peking Public Library has many reading rooms, such as a special reading room for special ticket holders, a ladies' reading room, a periodical and newspaper reading room, etc. These rooms are bare and the seats are not comfortable. As yet there have not been sufficient funds for lighting and heating facilities. There is much red tape in drawing out books.

Besides the six ordinary tickets there are two special tickets, first and second. Those who hold special tickets of the first class can enjoy the privilege of inspecting and using ordinary books, periodicals, newspapers, incunabula, etc., without charge and also that of having access to the stacks. Those who hold special tickets of the second class can enjoy only the free use of ordinary books, periodicals and newspapers.

Generally the public libraries have no recent publications, and there is much red-tape before admitting readers to the stack rooms.

FREE PUBLIC LIBRARIES

During the last decade the medieval idea of a library for a learned few has broken down and the intellectual kingdom has opened its gates for the plebians, who are daily getting bolder and wiser. The public library, they feel, should neither collect admission fee nor asset charge for use of

---

① See Tai, T. C. Brief sketch of Chinese Libraries in Library Journal, July, 1919, pp. 423-429.

books. This public feeling has been duly recognized, hence the system of free public libraries are introduced. Now many public libraries in the provincial capitals and cities gradually either discard the policy to charge fees for admission and use of books or establish free public libraries.

The policy of a free public library in China is to allow the readers to use its collections without any charge, but not to permit them to draw out books for home use. In connection with these libraries there are children's reading rooms and playgrounds. In spite of the financial difficulties the free public libraries are better administered than public libraries. In addition to old Chinese books they have newly published books on various subjects. Children's rooms are supplied with pictorial tales and juvenile books and the playgrounds are always well patronized.

The libraries open on Sundays just as on week days. Some of them close on Mondays to give a holiday to the members of the staff. There are about 51 public libraries and 219 free public libraries. [2] Quite a number, the writer has visited and investigated. They are all well patronized, as to improvement there is yet plenty of room. For instance the budget for the annual acquisition of books should be greatly increased, so that circulation departments can be established for promoting the use of books at home. Secondly the rooms are too bare and unattractive, and the furniture is not suitable especially in children's reading rooms. Fortunately in many prosperous localities at present there is a growing tendency toward establishing attractive and comfortable libraries.

TRAVELING LIBRARIES

Under the administration of some public libraries, also traveling libraries[3] have been organized. At present about thirty traveling libraries are scattered over five provinces, namely Fengtien, Kiangsu, Kansu, Szechwan, and Yünnan. They are operated on a small scale. During the last few years the progress of these traveling libraries in the interior and mountainous regions has been much retarded due to the continuous disturbance of petty civil fights.

Name of Province	Number of traveling libraries	Volumes
Fengtien	17	354
Kiangsu	4	338
Kansu	4	300
Szechwan	1	400
Yünnan	4	420

---

[2] Chinese Library Statistics, published by Peking Law College, 1922.
[3] The 4th statistical Report published by the Ministry of Education.

PUBLIC AND FREE PUBLIC LIBRARIES

Name of Province	Number of Public Libraries	Volumes	Number of Free Public Libraries	Volumes
Peking	2	25,000	1	1,400
Chihli	2	14,160	4	900
Fengtien	4	12,402	35	7500
Kirin	1	2,200	3	700
Heilungkiang	2	1,830	3	650
Shantung	1	3,000	23	10,000
Shansi	7	10,000	9	2,700
Honan	1	5,500	22	9,000
Kiangsi	1	850	5	1,500
Kiangsu	11	30,000	5	1,600
Anhwei	1	1,100	4	1,200
Fukien	1	1,240	21	600
Chekiang	6	8,000	21	5,350
Hupeh	1	7,310	44	18,000
Hunan	1	4,500	14	3,500
Shensi	1	1,250	1	600
Kansu	2	3,000	2	500
Singkiang	---	---	4	1,200
Szechwan	1	4,500	4	1,600
Kwangtung	1	3,065	6	1,800
Kwangsi	1	6,930	1	300
Yünnan	1	4,740	6	1,500
Kweichow	1	1,880	---	---
Jehol	1	390	1	300
	51	72,400	239	152,847

The figures including the number of volumes in the different libraries are inaccurate, for some libraries consider pamphlets as books and others not. Furthermore some count the number of volumes in "pu" and others in "Pên." "Pu" means a set of books, sometimes one "pu" consists of hundreds of "pên" which is a folio volume.

COLLEGE LIBRARIES

Almost every college in China now has a sort of library. According to the available statistics there are 37 college libraries maintained by various educational institutions. A few of the well known college libraries are as follows:

	I. *Peking*:	
	*Volumes in Chinese*④	*Volumes in foreign languages**
1. Peking National University Library	65,000	15,000
2. Peking Teachers College Library	10,000	8,000
3. Tsing Hua College Library	50,000	25,000
4. Union Medical College Library	500	9,000
5. Yen Ching University Library	1,000	3,000
	II. *Chihli*:	
1. Nankai College Library, Tientsin	6,000	7,000
2. Pei Yang University library, Tientsin	25,000	12,000
	III. *Shantung*:	
Shantung Christian University Library, Tsinan	10,000	9,000
	IV. *Shansi*:	
Shansi University Library, Taiyuan	(?)	(?)
	V. *Kiangsu*:	
1. Fu Tan University Library, Shanghai	(?)	(?)
2. Nanking University Library, Nanking	4,000	10,000
3. St. John's University Library, Shanghai	3,500	17,000
4. Nang Yang University Library, Shanghai	20,000	5,000
5. Shanghai Baptist College Library, Shanghai	1,500	3,500
6. Soochow University Library, Soochow	2,500	9,000
7. National Southeastern University Library, Nanking	10,000	7,000
	VI. *Hupeh*:	
1. Boone University Library, Wuchang	15,000	12,000
2. Wuchang Teachers College Library, Wuchang	21,000	3,000
3. Wesley College Library, Wuchang	2,000	3,500
	VII. *Hunan*:	
Yale College Library, Changsha	1,000	3,500
	VIII. *Kwangtung*:	
1. Canton Christian College Library, Canton	5,000	9,000
2. Canton Teachers' College Library, Canton	(?)	(?)

---

④ The numbers of volumes in each library are approximate.

续表

IX. *Fukien*:		
Amoy University Library, Amoy	(?)	(?)
X. *Chekiang*:		
Chekiang College Library, Hangchow	(?)	(?)
XI. *Kiangse*:		
William Nest College Library, Kiukiang	3,000	3,000

The libraries named above are scattered over eleven provinces. They all have two collections, one in Chinese, the other in foreign languages. All colleges maintained by the Chinese possess invariably a larger collection of Chinese books, while institutions supported by missionaries and western philanthropists always have more foreign books. Several reach the figure about 80,000 volumes.

As to classification most libraries classify books in foreign languages according to the Dewey Decimal System and Chinese books according to four main divisions, viz., (1) Classics (2) History (3) Philosophy (4) Belle Letters. It is nearly unavoidable to have two paralled systems of classifications used side by side in the same library. The nature of the old Chinese books is quite different from that of the western books. The ancient and comprehensive system of the above four main divisions with subdivisions is therefore inadequate for western books, as well as for the new Chinese books. For instance there is no place for a book on such a subject as gasoline engines. On the other hand the headings provided by the western library systems are not comprehensive enough for the old Chinese books. So the difficult task of working out a system of classification suitable for the old Chinese books as well as the new is at present confronting the Chinese librarians.

Beside the question of classification, there are other problems connected with books in the Chinese language, such as binding, lettering, cataloguing, indexing, filing cards, etc. Libraries and library commissions have undertaken a few of these problems and try to find satisfactory solutions.

The Boone University Library has published a modified Dewey system adapted to Chinese books. It works fairly well but is not detailed enough for big libraries. The Tsing Hua College Library supplements this modified system with three tables to be used for books on China, one for language, one for the period divisions of the Chinese history, and the third a table of geographical divisions. The Kwangtung Library Commission has initiated two undertakings, one a list of author numbers for Chinese names, and the other a method of indexing Chinese characters. The last is still in the age of experiment. The characters of the Chinese language are themselves the very obstacles for introducing a workable system of indexing. The college libraries in China are not only centers for promoting a library movement, but also laboratories trying to solve some of the technical questions of library administration. Almost every college library has made some contribution to the development of modern libraries in China.

The Peking National University Library is considered as one of the best college libraries in China. It has a very fine collection of Chinese books among which are manuscripts and original imperial edicts most valuable for historical research. As to books in foreign languages the collection was originally well selected, but unfortunately not kept up for a number of years. At present the authorities feel the great need of a workable collection of western books, so a liberal annual budget has been provided for the purpose of buying new books. Partly due to Chancellor Y. P. Tsai's efforts, and partly due to the good will and generosity of The Library of Congress, the National University Library has been given a complete set of Library of Congress depositary card catalogues. This much valued gift will undoubtedly be of great benefit to research students. The authorities are now planning to erect a fire-proof building for these depositary catalogues and other national bibliographies.

Not far from the eventful spot where the ruins of the old Summer Palace of Peking (Yuan Ming Yuan) still can be seen, a humble library was founded in 1912 in the beautiful campus of Tsing Hua College. After the first few years it began to grow rapidly, now in the course of only nine years its collections in Chinese as well as in foreign languages are among the largest libraries in China.

The Library has at present 75,000 volumes of well selected books. It subscribes to 310 leading periodicals of the world and also 50 dailies. The circulation figure generally reaches to 2,500 books every month, besides a much bigger figure for books used in the reading rooms. The library not only provides reference facilities for the faculty and students, but also answers many reference questions from the alumni of the college as well as the teachers of various schools in northern China.

In order to accommodate the rapidly increasing number of books, an up-to-date and beautiful library building has been erected, the first library building in China to have Italian marble in the lobby, steel standard stacks, glass and cork floors, and other scientific equipment. According to the present rate of annual acquisition it will in the next ten years become the largest college library in China.

Tsing Hua College Library is also responsible for taking the initiative to promote a movement for scientific management of libraries. In the fall of 1918 it played an active part to form a Peking Library Association. The purpose of the Association is to further the interests of libraries in Peking. Under its auspices the system of inter-library loans of books have been introduced in the capital.

The missionary colleges in China have also much interest and desire in developing college libraries. Among the few noted ones, the Low Library of St. John's University, Shanghai, is one of the oldest. It was founded about 1890. Mr. Low's donation formed the nucleus of the collection. It grew steadily year after year, until now it has its own quarters in the Anniversary Hall which was a gift from the alumni, students, and friends to the present president, Dr. Pott, in commemoration of the twenty-fifth anniversary of his presidency.

For the sake of convenience in charging, shelving, and cataloguing, all the Chinese books in 1912 were bound in the style of English books. This was a great advance in the history of Chinese libraries. Both English and Chinese books were classified according to the Dewey decimal classification, and the experiment was introduced of having a card catalogue for Chinese books. The reading rooms which are divided into cosy alcoves, are attractive places for students to study and research.

Another well-known missionary college library is the Boone University Library at Wuchang. It was extended and reorganized about 1907. This library has been adequately organized and has done a great service not only to the students and alumni of that university, but also to the people of Hupeh and the neighboring provinces at large. It is the first institution in China to introduce a regular course of library science. Besides producing a class of trained librarians every year, the Boone University Library has also introduced the serviceable system of traveling libraries. It has already established more than twenty centers to handle the circulation of traveling libraries.

About nine college libraries at present have their own library buildings, as a rule the most beautiful and comfortable buildings on the college campus. The South Eastern University in Nanking is thus erecting a large and magnificent building which will after its completion be one of the most imposing libraries in the region of the Yangtze valley. It is safe to assert that in every respect the college libraries in China are more efficiently administered, richer in collection and better in service than the public libraries.

SOCIETY LIBRARIES

The third type of libraries in China, generally known as society libraries, is now only in the period of dawning. They are now only a few in number, scattered in Peking and in cities along the coast. The annual expenditures and initial expenses of these libraries are secured either from donations or from the funds of the respective societies. They are generally only used by the members of the society. The collection of books is of course similar to the nature of the parent society. It will not be out of place here to describe very briefly a few of the well-known society libraries.

The best known is the library of the North China Branch of the Royal Asiatic Society at Shanghai, founded about 1860. The collection on China given by Mr. Wylie formed its nucleus. Although the library is not very large, it is fairly strong in works on China. The Dewey Decimal Classification system was adopted in 1907 upon the recommendation of Dr. Bolton of the Boston Athenaeum. The library is open daily and the privilege of taking out books is enjoyed by members only.

Another society library now rapidly coming to the front is that of the Science Society at Nanking, entirely maintained by the Chinese. Its collection emphasizes the various subjects of science. The catalogue and equipment are all up-to-date; it has a fine building and renders efficient library service to its members and the students in Nanking.

A famous memorial society library, formerly situated in Shanghai, was recently removed to Peking. It was founded by a group of well-known politicians in memory of General Tsai Ao[5] who in 1915 managed to get down from Peking to Yünnan, there rallied his troops around him and frustrated Yuan Shih Kai's long cherished and ambitious plan of converting the Chinese Republic into his own personal dynasty. General Tsai thus saved the Republic. Having accomplished this task, he succumbed to the rigors of his superhuman effort.

This library will occupy a large building in the beautiful Pei Hai, a part of the Winter Palace.

---

[5] Weale, Putnam: Fight for the Republic in China, Chapter 12, pp. 242-248.

The necessary arrangements, such as installing shelves, etc. , are being made at present. It is intended soon to open Pei Hai to the public, and this memorial library will then constantly inspire the readers to follow the uplifting example of this immortal general.

The library has a well selected collection of books in Chinese and foreign languages and the Dewey Decimal system has been adopted, and it is planned to extend the privilege of using books also to the general public.

The fourth society library belongs to the Chinese Social and Political Science Association, Peking. It was started largely by a group of "Returned Students," but its final success in 1918 depended upon the United States of America, the late Imperial Manchu family and the Carnegie Endowment Corporation of New York. The first, through its worthy representative in Peking, Dr. Paul S. Reinsch, set apart the sum of taels 100,000 from the remitted fund of the Boxer Indemnity as initial and maintenance expenses of the library. The second kindly donated a centrally located site for the library building, and the third is the Carnegie Corporation to contribute every year about a thousand volumes in history, social and political sciences. I believe this is the first endowment of English books from that corporation to a library in China. The movement of founding society libraries is now slowly extending to the interior of the country.

SPECIAL LIBRARIES

In order to increase the efficiency and knowledge of the component factors of certain organizations and bureaus, special libraries have been founded. Again, cities like Peking, Shanghai and Canton are in the lead. There are four special libraries in the capital, namely, the Library of the Bureau of Geological Survey under the Ministry of Agriculture, the Library of the Railway Association under the Ministry Communication, the Library of the Ministry of Education, and the Library of the Ministry of Foreign Affairs.

Their collections are naturally along the lines of their respective spheres. Only the members of these ministries have the privilege of using the libraries. The Imperial system of classifying the books into classics, history, philosophy and belle letters is adopted in shelving the Chinese books. The collection in foreign languages are roughly grouped according to subjects. Generally no books can be loaned for home use.

In Shanghai there are two very interesting special libraries, one under the Chinese General Chamber of Commerce and the other established and maintained by the Commercial Press. The Library of the Chinese General Chamber of Commerce was founded in the Winter of 1921 under the leadership of Mr. C. C. Nieh, then the Chairman of the General Chamber of Commerce. He feels very keenly that the business men should not only have a thorough understanding of Chinese affairs, but also a general acquaintance of the conditions of the foreign societies and a thorough knowledge of the trade-problems of various mercantile nations. He persuaded the merchants to open their pockets to found a special library for their use. The writer had the privilege of organizing this library and of compiling a bibliography of books and periodicals suitable for industrial magnates, merchants and business men.

The Library of the Commercial Press has a unique feature, namely, its rare editions of many famous books; they are collected for the purpose of producing reprints. In addition to this the company has a good general collection for the use of the editorial staff-members and other employees. The relative location is used in shelving books which are classified according to the Dewey Decimal System.

In spite of the constant political troubles in Canton a special library for the use of educators was founded in January, 1922, by the Canton authorities. It has two parallel collections of books, one in Chinese and the other in foreign languages, chiefly on education and general reference. It acts as a laboratory for the short term library school in Canton. The administration is up-to-date, and this library intends to be the model library in the province of Kwangtung.

LIBRARY SCHOOLS

Since the gradual disappearance of the old idea regarding the librarian as only a page to the scholars, the beginning of demanding trained librarians has been on foot; hence library schools in one form or another have been inaugurated to give courses in library science and administration.

The Boone University at Wuchang as mentioned before is the first institution in China to introduce a regular curriculum of library science. It gives a three years' course and admits only students of sophomore standing. Many young librarians now working in different libraries all over the country are the products of the Boone University Library School. The demand for trained librarians is larger than the Boone University can supply and many a library finds it impossible to await the employment of a trained librarian before transforming its storing place into a serviceable institution; hence library trustees and educators wish to introduce apprentice courses of library science and also summer schools in order to give the present library workers a general knowledge of library service.

In the Summer of 1920 the Peking Teachers College opened the first library summer school in China. It was a great surprise to all that the enrollment numbered seventy-eight men and women. Most of these were the librarians of various libraries in different provinces and sent up to attend the summer school. Even the Public Library of Amoy (Fukien) delegated its librarian to attend the lectures in spite of the great distance and the summer heat. Among the seventy-eight attendants, nine were girls. The lectures, being strictly professional, were open to both sexes. Undoubtedly the innovation has exerted a strong influence in support of the movement toward co-education.

In the Spring of 1922 a short term course of library science was introduced in Canton by the Provincial Educational Committee. This apprentice course of three weeks was under the authority of the Kwangtung civil governor who asked all schools above the middle school to send an instructor or a staff-member to the capital to attend the lectures. The school was opened on March 27th and attended by sixty-five representatives from various high schools in the province. The forenoons were occupied by lectures on the principal points of classification, cataloguing, order and accession work and library administration, while in the afternoons the students did practice work. All the attendants would take charge of their native libraries after the expiration of this three weeks' course of library science.

The Peking Teachers College for Women, the Peking Teachers College, and the National Southeastern University are planning to introduce a regular library course. Probably in the near future the plans will be realized, and there will be three more institutes to supply trained librarians.

LIBRARY MEETINGS

In order to accelerate the library movement a Committee on Library Education was organized under the auspices of the Chinese National Association for the Advancement of Education. In July, 1922, at Tsinan, Shantung, the librarians of the principal educational institutions came together under one roof to discuss the many problems related to the question of launching a nation-wide library movement. Of the following resolutions passed by the Association, items number 2, 3, 7 and 8 have been carried out.

1. That all schools shall have instruction in the use of books.
2. That the normal schools in China shall offer courses in Library science.
3. That extension of school libraries shall be emphasized.
4. That the chief places, such as Shanghai, Hankow, etc., including provincial capitals, shall establish libraries.
5. That a National Library shall be properly established in Peking.
6. That the publishers of new books shall present one volume to the Ministry of Education, and one volume to the National Library.
7. That primary schools, within certain regions, shall unite to establish circulating libraries.
8. That a committee for the study of library science shall be organized by the national Association for the Advancement of Education.

Considering the rapid growth of modern libraries in various parts of China, a few common principles and practices should be followed by all for sake of the systematic development of libraries and library economy. Now the first step in the minds of the trained librarians is to form a national library association and in turn to ask each city to form a local library association. Meetings have already been called by the Library Committee of the National Association for the Advancement of Education to discuss several important problems such as cooperative buying, inter-library loans of books, consolidated catalogues and others. A spirit of coöperation between the various libraries of the same locality is a sure way to success for a library movement.

AMERICAN LIBRARY SCHOOL GRADUATES

Since 1914 five Chinese librarians have graduated from the New York Public Library School, New York City, and the New York State Library School, Albany. They are the promoters of the library movement in China. At present there are four more men studying library science in the American library schools. They all had years of practical experience in administering libraries in China before they left for the United States of America to continue their studies.

CONCLUSION

As the writer reviews the situation of the Chinese libraries, the progress during the last nine years has been a slow but steady one in spite of many difficulties, as civil wars, famines, and other calamities. If the educators and social workers will actively support a wide library movement in China, its result will be immeasurably great and deep. True democracy cannot be attained unless the bulk of the people can enjoy and utilize the printed material with easy access.

原载：*Chinese National Assiciation for the Advangement of Education* Bulletin 2,1923

【译文】管翠中译　邓景康审

中国的图书馆运动(二)

戴志骞,图书馆学学士,清华学校图书馆主任
中华教育改进社　北京,中国

引言

1911年辛亥革命以来,中国在政治和文化上经历了一系列变革。中国人民挣脱了封建专制的束缚,也决心要从文化樊篱中解放出来。现在书店里马克思、克鲁泡特金、罗素、爱因斯坦等人的译作非常畅销,然而有关中国古典著作的评论更受到旧学者的欢迎。先进的知识分子目睹无数改革失败后,意识到必须彻底颠覆中国人的传统思想。

引入汉语拼音的使用、用口语化的白话文出版书籍和期刊现在是向广大群众传播新知识的手段。著名哲学家杜威、罗素、杜里舒等来到中国许多教育中心讲学,为中国的先进知识分子带来新的生命力。图书馆作为满足公众需求而存在的机构,现在正面临着快速变化的环境。

政府的态度

中国现在依然有很多藏书楼。尽管学者们依然对宋、元、明等朝代的古籍感兴趣,尽管图书馆员仅知道如何收藏这些珍贵的古书,然而如今将小心翼翼用厚门重锁守护的藏书楼变为充满活力和吸引力的图书馆的趋势日益增长。在过去的十年中新型图书馆的发展取得了很大的进步。

1915年4月11日教育部颁发《图书馆规程》11条,[①]要求全国各省加强图书馆的推广、组织和管理。

规程如下:[②]

1.各省、各特别区域应设图书馆,储集各种图书,供公众之阅览。各县得视地方情形设置之。

2.公立、私立各学校、公共团体或私人,依本规程所规定得设立图书馆。

3.各特别区域及各县所设立之图书馆,称公立图书馆。公众团体及公私学校所设者,称某团体、某学校附设图书馆。私人所设立者,称私立图书馆。

4.(a)公立图书馆应于设置时开具下列事项,由主管长官咨报教育部:名称;位置;经费;书籍卷数;建筑图式;章程规则;开馆时日。

(b)私立图书馆应照前项所列各款,禀请地方长官核明立案。

---

① 【译者注】据1915年第八期教育公报载,《图书馆规程》发布于1915年10月23日。
② 【译者注】译文参照《图书馆规程》原文。

（c）附设之图书馆,由主管之团体、学校照前项具报于主管长官。

任何图书馆中止开放或者更改名称等,都需要向主管长官报告。

5. 图书馆得设馆长和馆员,图书馆馆长及馆员均于任用时,开具履历及任职日期,具报于主管公署,并转报教育部。

6. 公立图书馆馆长及其馆员关于任职、服务、俸给等事项,准各公署所属教育职员之规定。

7. 图书馆馆员每届年终,应将办理情形报告于主管公署,发布在该省的年度教育报告中。

8. 公立图书馆之经费,应于会计年度开始之前,由主管公署列入预算,具报于教育部。公立学校附设图书馆之经费,列入主管学校预算之内。

9. 图书馆得酌收阅览费。

10. 私人以资财设立或捐助图书馆,由地方长官依照捐资兴学褒奖条例,咨陈教育部核明给奖。

11. 上述规定自公布之日起施行。

为了增加该规程的份量,政府将北京的晚清皇家图书馆改名为京师图书馆。部分省和特别区已经执行了该公告,但是其余地方由于经费缺乏仍然在准备阶段。

图书馆类别

除了私立图书馆之外,现在中国的图书馆可以分为四个主要类型:公立图书馆,学校图书馆,社团图书馆和机构图书馆。

公立图书馆

过去很多省会有大量木活字印刷的藏书,它们存储在一些公共会堂中供学者使用③。1913年以后这些会堂变成了公立图书馆。部分公立图书馆是靠捐赠维持,但是大多数是靠教育经费维持并由省教育厅行政长官掌管。

管理上,几乎所有的公立图书馆在阅览室中采用闭架管理,而且也不允许图书的流通。一些馆为了防止流浪者和闲杂人员入馆,需要对入馆的人收取少量费用,许多公立图书馆对在阅览室中看书也要收费。

例如,京师图书馆对那些想要入馆读书的人售卖阅览券。阅览券分为六个等级:(1)普通书阅览券,铜圆两枚;(2)期刊和报纸阅览券,铜圆一枚;(3)普通书学生阅览券,铜圆一枚;(4)期刊和报纸学生阅览券,免费;(5)善本书阅览券,铜圆十枚;(6)著名的《四库全书总目》原稿阅览券,铜圆五枚。

京师图书馆有很多阅览室,如特殊阅览券持有者的特殊阅览室、女士阅览室、期刊和报纸阅览室等。阅览室较为空旷,座位也不舒服,没有足够的资金用于照明和取暖设施,借书的时候还有很多繁琐手续。

除了这六种常规阅览券之外,还有两种特殊阅览券。拥有第一类特殊阅览券的人不用

---

③ 【原注】See Tai, T. C. Brief sketch of Chinese Libraries in Library Journal, July, 1919, pp. 423-429.

交费就享有查阅和使用普通图书、期刊、报纸、善本等的特权,还能进出书库。拥有第二类特殊阅览券的人仅享有免费使用普通图书、期刊和报纸的权利。

通常公立图书馆缺乏新出版物,并且在允许读者进入书库前还有很多繁文缛节。

免费公共图书馆

过去的十年中图书馆仅为少数精英学者服务的中世纪思想已经被打破了,知识王国的大门已经向日益聪明的平民敞开。他们认为公共图书馆既不能收取入馆费,也不能对使用书籍收费。这一想法被正式认可,因此引入了免费公共图书馆制度。现在很多省会和城市的公共图书馆逐渐舍弃对入馆和使用书籍收费的政策或者成立免费公共图书馆。

中国免费公共图书馆的政策是允许读者不交费就可以使用馆藏,但是不允许他们将书借回家使用。免费图书馆还有儿童阅览室和游戏场地。尽管经费困难,免费图书馆比公立图书馆管理得更好。免费图书馆除了中国善本外,还有新出版的不同学科的书籍,儿童阅览室还提供图画故事书和少年读物,孩子们也经常光顾游戏场地。

图书馆周日也像工作日那样正常开放。一些馆在周一闭馆休息。总共有大约51个公立图书馆和219个免费公共图书馆。④ 作者曾经去过很多免费图书馆,到馆的人很多,然而免费图书馆还有很多有待改善的空间。例如每年采书的预算应大大增加,以便能够建立促进书籍外借的流通部门。其次阅览室太空旷,没有吸引力,家具也不舒服,尤其是儿童阅览室中的家具。幸运的是现在很多富裕的地方都在建立舒适宜人的图书馆。

流动图书馆

在一些公立图书馆的管理下,流动图书馆⑤也建立起来了。目前有约三十个流动图书馆分布在五个省,分别是奉天、江苏、甘肃、四川和云南,他们的规模较小。在过去几年中由于连续不断的战争,很大程度上滞后了内地和山区流动图书馆的发展进程。

省	流动图书馆的数量	卷
奉天	17	354
江苏	4	338
甘肃	4	300
四川	1	400
云南	4	420

公立图书馆和免费公共图书馆

省	公立图书馆数量	卷	免费图书馆数量	卷
北京	2	25,000	1	1,400
直隶	2	14,160	4	900
奉天	4	12,402	35	7500

---

④ 【原注】Chinese Library Statistics, published by Peking Law College, 1922.

⑤ 【原注】The 4th statistical Report published by the Ministry of Education.

续表

省	公立图书馆数量	卷	免费图书馆数量	卷
吉林	1	2,200	3	700
黑龙江	2	1,830	3	650
山东	1	3,000	23	10,000
山西	7	10,000	9	2,700
河南	1	5,500	22	9,000
江西	1	850	5	1,500
江苏	11	30,000	5	1,600
安徽	1	1,100	4	1,200
福建	1	1,240	21	600
浙江	6	8,000	21	5,350
湖北	1	7,310	44	18,000
湖南	1	4,500	14	3,500
陕西	1	1,250	1	600
甘肃	2	3,000	2	500
新疆	- - -	- - -	4	1,200
四川	1	4,500	4	1,600
广东	1	3,065	6	1,800
广西	1	6,930	1	300
云南	1	4,740	6	1,500
贵州	1	1,880	- - -	- - -
热河	1	390	1	300
	51	72,400	239	152,847

  图表中不同图书馆的卷数是不精确的,因为一些图书馆将小册子算作书籍,而另一些却没有计算在内。另外一些将卷数计为"部"而其他的是"本"。"部"的意思是一套书,有时一"部"包含数百个对开本的"本"。

学校图书馆

  现在几乎每个中国的大学都有图书馆。据统计,在不同的教育机构中有37个大学图书馆。一些著名的大学图书馆如下:

英文文章

	Ⅰ.北京：	
	中文书卷数⑥	外文书卷数[22]
1.国立北京大学图书馆	65,000	15,000
2.北京高等师范学校图书馆	10,000	8,000
3.清华学校图书馆	50,000	25,000
4.协和医学院图书馆	500	9,000
5.燕京大学图书馆	1,000	3,000
	Ⅱ.直隶：	
1.南开大学图书馆,天津	6,000	7,000
2.北洋大学图书馆,天津	25,000	12,000
	Ⅲ.山东：	
齐鲁大学图书馆,济南	10,000	9,000
	Ⅳ.山西：	
山西大学图书馆,太原	（?）	（?）
	Ⅴ.江苏：	
1.复旦大学图书馆,上海	（?）	（?）
2.金陵大学图书馆,南京	4,000	10,000
3.圣约翰大学图书馆,上海	3,500	17,000
4.南洋大学图书馆,上海	20,000	5,000
5.上海浸会大学图书馆,上海	1,500	3,500
6.东吴大学图书馆,苏州	2,500	9,000
7.国立东南大学图书馆,南京	10,000	7,000
	Ⅵ.湖北：	
1.文华大学图书馆,武昌	15,000	12,000
2.武昌高等师范学校图书馆,武昌	21,000	3,000
3.博文书院图书馆,武昌	2,000	3,500
	Ⅶ.湖南：	
雅礼大学图书馆,长沙	1,000	3,500
	Ⅷ.广东：	
1.岭南大学图书馆,广州	5,000	9,000
2.广东高等师范学校图书馆,广州	（?）	（?）
	Ⅸ.福建：	
厦门大学图书馆,厦门	（?）	（?）
	Ⅹ.浙江：	
浙江高等学校图书馆,杭州	（?）	（?）
	Ⅺ.江西：	
南伟烈大学图书馆,九江	3,000	3,000

---

⑥ 【原注】这里所给的每个图书馆的卷数都是大概的数字。

以上图书馆分布在十一个省,均有中外文藏书。由中国人管理的大学总是有更多的中文藏书,而由传教士和西方慈善家管理的大学总是有更多的外文书籍。有几个图书馆的馆藏达到了 80,000 卷。

在分类上,大多数图书馆将外文书籍依据《杜威十进分类法》分类,中文书主要分为经、史、子、集四类。在一个图书馆内同时使用两套不同的分类法几乎是不可避免的。老的中文书籍的性质和西文书籍完全不同,划分为经、史、子、集四类的古老的综合分类法不适用于西文书籍,同样也不适用于新出版的中文书籍,例如无法将主题为汽油发动机的书进行归类。另一方面西文图书分类法对中文古籍而言也不够全面。因此制定一个同时适用于中文古籍和新书的分类法是现在中国图书馆员面临的艰巨任务。

中文书除了分类法问题外,还有其他问题,比如装订、印刷、编目、索引、排卡工作等等。图书馆和图书馆委员会已经注意这些问题,并尝试找到满意的解决办法。

文华大学图书馆发布了适合中文书的改良杜威分类法,用起来很方便,但是对于大型图书馆来说不够详细。清华学校图书馆对这个改良后的分类法在中文书的应用上,通过三个表来补充,一个是语言,一个是中国历史年代划分,一个是地理区域划分。广东图书馆委员会引入了两个工作,一个是中文著者号的列表,另一个是汉字索引。后者仍旧在摸索尝试阶段。汉语的特点使得引入可行的标引体系非常困难。中国的大学图书馆不仅仅是促进图书馆运动的中心,而且是试图解决图书馆管理技术问题的实验室。几乎所有的大学图书馆都对中国现代图书馆的发展有所贡献。

北京国立大学图书馆是中国最好的大学图书馆之一,有很好的中文书馆藏,其中对历史研究最珍贵的是手稿和原始诏书。对于外文书籍其馆藏最初也是通过精心挑选的,但不幸的是此举并没有维持几年。现在当局感觉到很有必要有足够的西方书籍馆藏,所以提供了宽松的年度预算来购买新书。部分出于校长蔡元培的努力,部分出于美国国会图书馆的善意和慷慨,国立北京大学图书馆获赠一套完整的美国国会图书馆的馆藏卡片目录。如此珍贵的礼物无疑对做研究的学生非常有益。现在,官方正在准备建造防火建筑,存放这些目录和其他国家文献目录。

距圆明园遗址不远的地方,1912 年,一个小型图书馆在美丽的清华学校校园内诞生了。在开始的几年中它发展迅速,现在仅仅过了九年时间,其中文书和外文书的馆藏已经跻身于中国最大图书馆之列。

图书馆现在有 75,000 卷经过精挑细选的书籍,订阅了 310 种世界领先期刊和 50 种日报。每个月流通书籍的数量达到 2500 卷,在阅览室中被使用的书籍更多。图书馆不仅为教师和学生提供参考咨询,而且为校友和中国北方各个学校教师提供咨询。

为了适应迅速增加的书籍数量,一座典雅华丽的现代图书馆建筑拔地而起,这是中国第一个拥有意大利大理石大厅、钢制书架、玻璃地面、软木地板以及其他科学设备的图书馆建筑。依照现在每年采书的速度,它在未来十年内将成为中国最大的大学图书馆。

清华学校图书馆还主动促进图书馆科学管理的发展,在 1918 年秋成立北京图书馆协会过程中起了积极作用。协会的目的是增进北京各图书馆的协助互益,在其主持下将图书互借系统引入到北京。

中国的教会大学也对发展大学图书馆有着很强的兴趣和欲望。其中一个最古老著名的是上海的圣约翰大学罗氏图书馆。它大约建立于 1890 年,罗氏兄弟的捐赠形成了馆藏的核心。它逐年稳步增长,现在已经有其自己的新馆。这是为了纪念校长卜舫济任职25周年,由校友、学生及卜氏好友捐资建造的。

为了整理、排架、编目的方便,1912年所有的中文书都用英文书的方式装订。这是中国图书馆历史上的一大进步。中英文书均采用《杜威十进分类法》分类,并尝试为中文书引入目录卡片。阅览室分成舒适的隔间,吸引学生来此学习和研究。

另一个有名的教会大学图书馆是武昌的文华大学图书馆,大约在1907年扩建和重组。该图书馆管理得当,为该校学生、校友和湖北及周边省的人们做了很多工作。它是中国第一个开设图书馆学专业的机构。文华大学不仅每年培养一批训练有素的图书馆员,而且还引入巡回文库服务制度,已经建立了20多个中心来管理巡回文库的图书流通。

现在大概有9个大学图书馆有其自己的图书馆建筑,通常都是大学校园里最漂亮最舒适的建筑。南京的东南大学将建一个大型而雄伟的建筑,竣工后将是长江流域最宏伟的图书馆之一。可以断言,中国的大学图书馆在各个方面都要比公立图书馆管理更有效、馆藏更丰富、服务更好。

社团图书馆

在中国图书馆的第三种类型通常称为社团图书馆,现在尚处在萌芽阶段,仅有少量分布在北京和沿海城市。这些图书馆每年的支出和初始费用的来源是捐赠或者是各个协会的基金,一般仅供协会会员使用,馆藏量当然也与其协会性质相关。这里简要介绍几个著名的社团图书馆。

最著名的是成立于1860年的上海皇家亚洲文会北中国支会图书馆,其馆藏核心是来自于伟烈亚力先生的有关中国的馆藏。尽管图书馆不是很大,但收藏的中国作品相当可观。在波士顿图书馆博尔顿博士的推荐下,1907年采用了《杜威十进分类法》。图书馆每日开放,借书的特权仅会员享有。

另一个快速发展的社团图书馆是由中国人管理的南京科学社图书馆。其馆藏着重于科学的各个学科。它的目录和设施都是最新的,建筑也非常精美。为其协会会员和南京的学生提供服务。

还有一个著名的纪念图书馆,原位于上海,最近搬到北京了,是一些著名政治家为了纪念蔡锷将军而建立的。1915年蔡锷⑦由北京回到云南召集自己的部队,挫败了袁世凯妄图将中华民国变为个人帝国的野心,蔡将军因此拯救了共和国。完成这一使命后,他被过度辛劳压垮了。⑧

该图书馆将占据美丽的清廷冬宫北海中的一座大建筑。⑨ 安装书架等工作现在正在进行,计划很快向公众开放,该馆将继续激励读者以蔡将军为榜样。

图书馆精心挑选中文和外文书籍,采用《杜威十进分类法》,还计划向普通公众开放。

---

⑦ 【原注】Weale, Putnam: Fight for the Republic in China, Chapter 12, pp. 242-248.
⑧ 【译者注】1916年11月8日,蔡锷(字松坡)将军病逝于日本福冈医院。12月5日,梁启超在上海为蔡将军举办了公祭与私祭,并倡议创办松坡图书馆。当年11月4日,松坡图书馆正式成立,梁启超出任馆长。
⑨ 【译者注】松坡图书馆位于北海的快雪堂,曾是慈禧冬天赏雪的地方。

第四个社团图书馆属于北京的中国社会政治学会。图书馆最初由归国留学生创立，1918年借助美国、晚清和纽约卡内基基金会之力建成。首先，芮恩施博士从庚子赔款基金中得到10万两白银作为图书馆开办和维护费用；其次，图书馆获赠市中心的建筑地点；第三，卡内基基金会每年向图书馆捐赠约一千卷历史、社会和政治科学书籍。我相信这是第一次由基金会向中国的图书馆捐赠英文书籍。社团图书馆的发展现在正慢慢地延伸到中国内地。

机构图书馆

建设此类机构图书馆的用意是为了增进机构人员的办事能力和专门学识。北京、上海、广州等城市再次走在了前列。在北京有四个机构图书馆，分别为农商部的地质调查所图书馆、交通部的铁路协会图书馆、教育部图书馆，以及外交部图书馆。

它们的馆藏自然与其机构性质相似，仅机构人员有使用书籍的特权。在中文书的排架上按照经、史、子、集分类法，外文书馆藏大致按照主题分类。通常情况下书不能借回家使用。

在上海有两个非常吸引人的机构图书馆，一个设在上海总商会下，另一个由商务印书馆建设和维护。上海总商会图书馆成立于1921年冬季，由当时上海总商会会长聂云台先生领导。他敏锐的感觉到商人不仅需要对中国事务有全面的了解，而且需要对外国社会状况有普遍的认识，以及对各个商业国贸易问题有全面的了解。他建议商人们出资建造并利用图书馆。笔者有幸参与了该图书馆、为收集适合于商业巨头、商人和生意人的图书和期刊而展开的组织、编制书目活动。

商务印书馆图书馆有一个独特的特征，即藏有很多著名书籍的善本，可用来再版。另外印书馆有很好的馆藏供编辑和其他员工使用。该馆使用《杜威十进分类法》分类排架。

尽管广州不断有政治问题，1922年1月广州当局成立了机构图书馆供教育工作者使用。有中外文两类馆藏书籍，主要涉及教育和综合参考类。它在广州为短期图书馆学校充当实验基地，采用了最新式的管理方式，将会成为广东省的示范图书馆。

图书馆学校

自从图书馆员只为学者服务这个老观念逐渐消失后，对训练有素的图书馆员的需求开始显现。图书馆学校是一种培养方式，另一种是提供图书馆学和图书馆管理的课程。

之前提到的武昌文华大学是中国第一个引入图书馆学正规课程的机构。它提供三年课程，并只从二年级以上的学生中招生。⑩ 现在在全国各个图书馆工作的很多年轻馆员都是由文华图书馆学专科学校培养的。然而对训练有素的图书馆员的需求要远超文华大学的培养

---

⑩ 【译者注】1920年3月，美国韦棣华女士和沈祖荣创办文华大学图书科，仿美国纽约州立大学图书馆学院办学制度，招收大学毕业或肄业二年以上的学生学习图书馆学专业。1925年，文华大学改称华中大学。1927年，华中大学暂时停办，图书科单独成校，韦棣华任校长。1929年8月，经湖北省政府教育厅及国民政府教育部批准立案，成立私立武昌文华图书馆学专科学校。1953年并入武汉大学，成为武汉大学图书馆学专修科。

速度，许多图书馆意识到在将藏书室变为可供使用的图书馆前，等待聘用训练有素的图书馆员是不可能的，所以图书馆教育研究委员会[11]和教育工作者希望引入图书馆学入门课程和暑期学校，为图书馆工作人员提供有关图书馆服务的一般常识。

1920年夏，北京高等师范学校开办了中国的第一次暑期图书馆讲习会，共有78名男女学生注册，这让大家大吃一惊。大部分人是不同省份的各个图书馆送来参加暑期学校的图书馆员，甚至还有福建省厦门公共图书馆派其图书馆员，不畏路途遥远和暑期炎热来参加课程。78位报名者中有9名是女性，严格的专业课程向男性和女性都开放。毫无疑问，这一创新会为共同教育的发展产生深远影响。

1922年春，广东全省教育会将短期图书馆学课程引入广州。广东省政府授权开展三周的见习课程，并要求中等以上所有学校送教员或职员来省会参加课程学习。学校于3月27日开学，有省内各个中等以上学校的65名代表参加。上午通常是讲座，主要内容为分类、编目、排架和登记工作以及图书馆管理，下午是学生实习工作。所有参与者在三周图书馆学课程结束后，将负责其各自图书馆的工作。

北京女子高等师范学校、北京高等师范学校、国立东南大学也正在计划引入正规的图书馆学课程，这些计划会在不久的将来得以实现，届时将再有三个培养训练有素的图书馆员的机构。

图书馆会议

为了加快图书馆的发展，在中华教育改进社的支持下成立了图书馆教育委员会。1922年7月在山东济南，主要教育机构的图书馆员齐聚一堂，讨论开展全国范围内图书馆发展的问题，并通过了以下议案，其中2、3、7、8条正在进行中。[12]

1. 各校应提供图书使用方法指导。
2. 中国的师范类学校应设图书馆学科。
3. 加强学校图书馆的推广。
4. 上海、汉口、省会等主要城市需要建图书馆。
5. 国家图书馆最好建在北京。
6. 新书出版时，需要送交一部存教育部，一部存国家图书馆。
7. 各市区小学校应就近联合，于校内创设巡回儿童图书馆。
8. 请中华教育改进社组织图书馆教育研究委员会。

考虑到现代图书馆在中国的各个地方快速发展，为了图书馆和图书馆经营的系统发展，应当遵循一些共同的原则和做法。我考虑，现在的第一步是培训图书馆员，建立全国图书馆学会，并随后在各个城市成立地方图书馆学会。中华教育改进社的图书馆委员会已经开会讨论了几个重要的问题，比如联合采购、图书互借、编制联合目录等。同一地区各个图书馆的合作精神是图书馆成功发展的可靠之路。

---

[11] 【译者注】1922年在济南召开的中华教育改进社第一次年会图书教育组会议上，通过了成立图书馆教育研究委员会的议案，会后该委员会成立，戴志骞任主任。

[12] 【译者注】译文参照议案原文。

美国图书馆院校毕业生

1914年以来有五名中国图书馆员从纽约市的纽约公共图书馆学校和奥尔巴尼市的纽约州立大学图书馆学院毕业,他们是中国图书馆发展的推动人。现在又有四个人在美国图书馆学校学习。这些人在离开中国去美国继续深造之前都有多年的管理图书馆的实际经验。

结 论

作者回顾了中国图书馆的概况,尽管有战争、饥荒和其他灾害等困难,中国图书馆在过去的九年里缓慢但持续地发展着。如果教育工作者和社会工作者积极支持在中国大范围的图书馆发展,其结果将是不可估量的、巨大而深刻的。只有广大人民群众能够很容易地使用图书资料,才能达到真正的民主。

原载:《中华教育改进社通报》 1923年第2期

Library Movement in China(三)

By T. C. Tai, Ph. D.,
Librarian of Tsing Hua College, Peking, China.

Since the Revolution of 1911, China has undergone a movement of change in politics, as well as in intellectual problems. The people have not only tried hard to shake off the yoke of despotism, but also fully determined to free themselves from the oppression of intellectual bondage. To-day at the bookstalls the translated works of Karl Marx, Kropotkin, Russell, Einstein and others are demanded like hot-cakes, while the critical essays on Chinese classics are even welcomed by the scholars of the old type. The intellectual class has seen the failures of numerous reforms and come to the conclusion that the Chinese process of thought should be revolutionized.

Our present-day means of diffusing the new knowledge to the general masses are to introduce the use of a Chinese phonetic alphabet, and to publish books and periodicals in Peh Hua or colloquial language. In order to supply the Chinese intellect with fresh vital energy, famous scholars like John Dewey, Bertrand Russell and others have been invited to China and to give lectures in most educational centres. Among institutions whose existence depends upon their ability to meet the public demand, the library is now face to face with rapidly changing conditions.

China, even to-day, is full of places for storing books. Although scholars continue to be interested in the editions of bygone dynasties, like the Sung, or the Yuan or the Ming, and libraries[1] only know how to collect the valuable incunabula, yet the tendency is daily growing stronger in favour of converting the book-vault jealously guarded by thick doors and heavy locks into a living and attractive library. And during the last decade the new library movement has taken some strides.

On April 11, 1915, the Ministry of Education issued an order embodying eleven regulations which emphasize promotion, organisation and administration of libraries throughout the different provinces of the country. In order to add weight to the proclamation, the government turned the Imperial Library of the late Manchu dynasty at Peking into the Peking Metropolitan Public Library. Some of the districts have carried out the order, but others owing to lack of funds and fightings between military leaders are still in the period of preparation.

At present the Chinese libraries, excluding private ones, can be roughly divided into four main classes, namely, public libraries, college libraries, society libraries and special libraries.

In old days many provincial capitals kept large collections of books printed from wooden page-blocks. They were stored in some public hall for the use of scholars. Since 1913 these places have been turned into public libraries. Some of them are maintained by endowments, but the majority by the educational funds of the districts and are thus under the control of the Commissioner of Educa-

---

[1] Tai, T. C. Brief Sketch of Chinese Libraries. Library Journal. 44:423-429. July, 1919.

tion of that province.

As to the administration: nearly all of these public libraries not only have adopted the closed shelf-system in reading rooms, but also allow no circulation for home use. Some of them require a small fee for admission, with the purpose of keeping away vagabonds and ruffians. Asseting charges for use of books in reading rooms are also practised in many a public library. Generally they have no recent publications, and there is much red-tape before admitting readers to the stackrooms.

During the last decade the mediaeval idea of a library for a learned few has been broken down, and the intellectual kingdom has opened its gate for the plebians, who are daily getting bolder and wiser. The public library, they feel, should neither collect admission fee nor asset charge for use of books. This public feeling has been duly recognised, hence the system of free public libraries has been introduced. Now many public libraries in the provincial capitals and large cities gradually either discard the policy charging fees for admission and use of books, or establish free public libraries.

Generally a free public library in China is to allow the readers to use its collections without any charge, but not to permit them to draw out books for home use. In connection with these libraries there are play-grounds and children's reading rooms. In spite of the financial difficulties the free public libraries are better administered than public libraries. In addition to old Chinese books, they have newly published books on various subjects. The libraries open on Sundays just as on week days. Some of them close on Mondays, as a holiday to the members of the staff. There are about 88 organized public libraries and 291 free public libraries. ②

Almost every college in China now has a sort of library. Practically all the college libraries have two collections, one in Chinese, the other in foreign languages. All colleges maintained by the Chinese possess invariably larger collections of Chinese books, while educational institutions supported by missionaries and western philanthropists always have more foreign books. Several reach the figure about 100,000 volumes.

The books in foreign languages are generally classified according to the system of the Decimal Classification, and Chinese books according to four main divisions, viz. , (1) Classics; (2) History; (3) Philosophy; (4) Belles-lettres. It is nearly unavoidable to have two paralleled systems of classifications used side by side in the same library. The nature of the old Chinese books is quite different from that of the western books. The ancient and comprehensive system of the above four main divisions with subdivisions is, therefore, inadequate for western books, as well as for the new Chinese books. For instance, there is no place for a book on such a subject as gasoline engines. On the other hand the headings provided by the western library systems are not comprehensive enough for the old Chinese books. So the difficult task of working out a system of classification suitable for the old Chinese books as well as the new is at present confronting the Chinese librarians. Many a Chinese librarian has attempted to expand and to modify the system of the Decimal Classification to be

---

② Library Association of China. A Statistical Table of the Chinese Libraries. (In its Bulletin, I: 7-19. Sept. - Oct. ,1925.)

suitable for the old Chinese books as well as the books in foreign languages.

About twelve college libraries now have their own library buildings, and several are trying hard to get enough funds for erection of modem library buildings. Among them the South-Eastern University, Nanking, and Tsing Hua University Library, Peking, are the only ones equipped with metal stacks. It is safe to assert that in every respect the college libraries in China are more efficiently administered, richer in collection and better in service than the public libraries.

The third type of libraries in China, generally known as society libraries, is now only in the period of dawning. They are now only a few in number, scattered in Peking and in cities along the coast. The annual expenditures and initial expenses of these libraries are secured either from donations, or from the funds of the respective societies. They are generally only used by the members of the society. The collection of books is, of course, similar to the nature of the parent society. The best-known society libraries are the library of the North China Branch of the Royal Asiatic Society at Shanghai, the library of Science Society at Nanking, General Tsai-Soong-Poo Memorial Library at Peking, and the library of the Chinese Social and Political Science Association at Peking. [3]

The last-named library belongs to the Chinese Social and Political Science Association, Peking. It was started largely by a group of "Returned Students," but its final success in 1918 depended upon the United States of America, the late Imperial Manchu family and the Carnegie Endowment Corporation of New York. The first, through its worthy representative in Peking, Dr. Paul S. Reinsch, set apart the sum of taels 100,000 from the remitted fund of the Boxer Indemnity as initial and maintenance expenses of the library. The second kindly donated a centrally located site for the library building, and the third is the Carnegie Corporation to contribute every year about a thousand volumes in history, social and political sciences. I believe this is the first endowment of English books from that corporation to a library in China. The movement of founding society libraries is now slowly extending to the interior of the country.

In order to increase the efficiency and knowledge of the component factors of certain institutions or bureaux, special libraries have been founded. Again, cities like Peking, Shanghai and Canton are in the lead. There are six special libraries in the Capital, namely, the Library of the Bureau of Geological Survey under the Ministry of Agriculture, the Library of the Ministry of Communication, the Library of the Ministry of Education, the Library of the Ministry of Foreign Affairs, the Library of the Supreme Court and the Library of the Bureau of Codification.

Their collections are naturally along the lines of their respective spheres. Only the members of these ministries have the privilege of using the libraries. The Imperial system of classifying the books into classics, history, philosophy and belles-lettres is adopted in shelving the Chinese books. The collections in foreign languages are roughly grouped according to subjects. Generally no books can be loaned for home use.

In Shanghai there are two very interesting special libraries, one under the Chinese General

---

③ Tai. T. C. Description of the Chinese college, society and special libraries. (In his Library Movement in China. Chinese National Association for the Advancement of Education, Peking, 1923, p. 8-17.)

Chamber of Commerce, and the other established and maintained by the Commercial Press.

In spite of the constant political troubles in Canton, a special library for the use of educators was founded in January, 1922, by the Canton authorities. It has two parallel collections of books, one in Chinese and the other in foreign languages, chiefly on education and general reference. It acts as a laboratory for the short term library school in Canton. The administration is up to date, and this library intends to be the model library in the province of Kwangtung.

Since the gradual disappearance of the old idea regarding the librarian as only a page to the scholars, the beginning of demanding trained librarians has been on foot. Hence library schools in one form or another have been inaugurated to give courses in library science and administration.

The Boone University at Wuchang, Hupeh, now known as Central China University, is the first institution in China to introduce a regular curriculum of library science. It gives a three years' course and admits only students of sophomore standing. Many young librarians now working in different libraries all over the country are the products of the Central China University Library School.

In the summer of 1920, the Peking Teachers' College opened the first library summer school. It was a great surprise to all that the enrolment numbered seventy-eight men and women. Most of these were the librarians of various libraries in different provinces and sent up to attend the summer school.

In the spring of 1922 a short term course of library science was introduced in Canton by the Provincial Educational Commission. This apprentice course of three weeks was under the authority of the Kwangtung civil governor, who asked all the schools above the middle school to send an instructor or a staff-member to the capital to attend the lectures. The school was opened on March 27th and attended by sixty-five representatives from various high schools in the province.

In order to accelerate the library movement, a Committee of Library Education and Development was organised under the auspices of the Chinese National Association for the Advancement of Education. In July 1922, at Tsinanfu, Shantung, the librarians of the principal educational institutions came together under one roof to discuss the many problems related to the question of launching a nation-wide library movement. More than ten resolutions were passed, and a few most important ones have been carried out. One of them was to urge the metropolitan cities of each province to form local library associations and in turn to organise a national library association. Within the last three years, nine local library associations were organised, and the Library Association of China was inaugurated in Peking on June 3rd, 1925. The delegate of the American Library Association, Dr. Arthur E. Bostwick,[④] who was invited to China to make a survey of the Chinese libraries and to prepare a report with a view to its presentation to the Committee of the China Foundation, was also present at the occasion. He delivered an inspiring address.

The Government appropriated a sum of $5,000 to the newly formed national library association as initial expenses. Besides the task of compiling bibliographies and editing pamphlets on li-

---

④ Bostwick, A. E. Report of his mission to China as A. L. A. delegate, reprinted from Bulletin of the American Library Association, Feb., 1926.

brary administration and economy, it at present issues a bi-monthly bulletin and a quarterly library journal. Due to financial difficulty, it is not in a position to carry out many projects at once.

As the writer reviews the situation of the Chinese libraries, the progress during the last ten years has been a slow but steady one in spite of many difficulties, as civil fightings between different war-lords, famines and other calamities. If the educators and social workers will actively support a library movement in China, its result will be immeasurably great. True democracy cannot be attained unless the bulk of the people can utilize the printed material with easy access.

原载:*The Librarian and Book World* Vol. XIV Aug 1924-July 1925

【译文】管翠中译　邓景康审

中国的图书馆运动(三)

戴志骞博士　中国北京　清华学校图书馆主任

  1911年辛亥革命以来,中国在政治和文化上经历了一系列变革。中国人民挣脱了封建专制的束缚,也决心要从文化樊篱中解放出来。现在书店里马克思、克鲁泡特金、罗素、爱因斯坦等人的译作非常畅销,然而有关中国古典著作的评论更受到旧学者的欢迎。先进的知识分子目睹无数改革的失败后意识到必须彻底颠覆中国人的传统思想。

  引入汉语拼音的使用、用口语化的白话文出版书籍和期刊现在是向广大群众传播新知识的手段。约翰·杜威、伯特兰·罗素等著名学者来到中国著名的教育机构讲学,为中国先进知识分子带来新的生命力。图书馆作为满足公众需求而存在的机构,现在正面临着快速变化的环境。

  目前,我国仍旧有很多藏书楼。尽管学者们依然对宋、元、明等朝代的古籍感兴趣,尽管图书馆员[①]仅知道如何收藏这些珍贵的古籍,然而如今将小心翼翼用厚门重锁守护的藏书楼变为充满活力和吸引力的图书馆的趋势日益增长。在过去的十年中新型图书馆的发展取得了很大的进步。

  1915年4月11日教育部颁发《图书馆规程》11条,[②]要求全国各省加强图书馆的推广、组织和管理。为了增加该规程的份量,政府将北京的晚清皇家图书馆改名为京师图书馆。部分地区已经执行了该公告,但是其余地方由于经费缺乏和战争影响仍然处于准备阶段。

  除了私立图书馆之外,现在中国的图书馆可以分为四个主要类型:公立图书馆、学校图书馆、社团图书馆和机构图书馆。

  过去很多省会有大量木活字印刷的藏书,它们存储在一些公共会堂中供学者使用。1913年以后这些地方变成了公立图书馆。部分公立图书馆是靠捐赠维持,但是大多数是靠地区教育经费维持并由省教育厅行政长官掌管。

  在管理上,几乎所有的公立图书馆在阅览室中采用闭架管理,而且也不允许将图书借出。一些图书馆为了防止流浪者和闲杂人员入馆,需要对入馆的人收取少量费用,许多公立图书馆对在阅览室中看书也要收费。通常这些公立图书馆没有新的出版物,并且在允许读者进入书库前还有很多繁文缛节。

  在过去的十年中,图书馆仅为少数精英学者服务的中世纪思想已经被打破,知识王国的大门已经向日益聪明的平民敞开。他们认为公共图书馆既不能收取入馆费,也不能对使用书籍收费。这一想法被正式认可了,因此引入了免费的公共图书馆制度。现在很多省会和大城市的公立图书馆逐渐放弃了对入馆和使用书籍收费的政策,或者建立了免费的公共图书馆。

---

 ①　【原注】Tai,T. C. Brief Sketch of Chinese Libraries. Library Journal. 44:423-429. July,1919.
 ②　【译者注】据1915年第八期教育公报载,《图书馆规程》发布于1915年10月23日。

中国免费公共图书馆的政策,通常是允许读者不交费就可以使用馆藏,但是不允许他们将书借回家使用。免费图书馆还有游乐场和儿童阅览室。尽管经费困难,免费图书馆相比较于公立图书馆管理得更好。免费图书馆除了中文旧书外还有不同学科的新出版书籍。图书馆周日也像工作日那样正常开放,一些馆周一闭馆让工作人员休息。总共有大约 88 个公立图书馆和 219 个免费公共图书馆。③

现在几乎每个中国的大学都有图书馆。所有的大学图书馆几乎都有中外文两类藏书。由中国人管理的大学总是有更多的中文藏书,而由传教士和西方慈善家支持的大学总是有更多的外文书籍。有几个图书馆的馆藏达到了 100,000 册。

外文书籍一般依据《杜威十进分类法》分类,而中文书主要分为经、史、子、集四类。在一个图书馆内同时使用两套不同的分类法几乎是不可避免的,旧的中文书籍的性质和西文书籍完全不同。划分为经、史、子、集四类的古老分类法不适用于西文书籍,同样也不适用于新出版的中文书籍。例如无法将主题为汽油发动机的书进行归类。另一方面西文图书分类法对中文古籍而言也不够全面。因此制定一个同时适用于中文古籍和新书的分类法是现在中国图书馆员面临的艰巨任务。许多中国图书馆员试图修订《杜威十进分类法》来同时适合中文古籍和外文书籍。

现在大概有 12 个大学图书馆有其自己的图书馆建筑,7 个正在试图筹集足够的资金来建先进的图书馆建筑。他们之中仅南京东南大学和北京清华学校的图书馆是有钢制书架的。可以断言,中国的大学图书馆在各个方面要比公立图书馆管理更有效、馆藏更丰富、服务也更好。

在中国图书馆的第三种类型通常称为社团图书馆,现在尚处在萌芽阶段,仅有少量分布在北京和沿海城市。这些图书馆每年的支出和初始费用来源于捐赠或者各个协会的基金,一般仅供协会会员使用,馆藏当然也和其协会性质相近。最著名的是上海亚洲文会图书馆、南京科学社图书馆、北京松坡图书馆和北京中国社会政治学会图书馆。④

最后一个图书馆属于北京的中国社会政治学会。图书馆最开始由归国留学生创立,1918 年借助美国、晚清和纽约卡内基基金会之力获取成功。首先,芮恩施博士从庚子赔款基金中得到 10 万两白银作为图书馆开办和维护费用;其次,图书馆获赠市中心的建筑地点;第三,卡内基基金会每年向图书馆捐赠约一千卷历史、社会和政治科学书籍,在中国,我相信这是第一次由基金会向图书馆捐赠英文书籍。社团图书馆的发展现在正慢慢延伸到中国内地。

为了增进机构人员的办事能力和专门学识成立了机构图书馆。北京、上海、广州等城市再次走在了前列。在北京有六个机构图书馆,分别为农商部的地质调查所图书馆、交通部图书馆、教育部图书馆、外交部图书馆、最高法院图书馆和法律修订局图书馆。

它们的馆藏自然与其机构性质相似,仅机构人员有使用书籍的特权。在中文书的排架上按照经、史、子、集分类法,外文书馆藏大致按照主题分类。通常情况下图书不能借回家

---

③ 【原注】Library Association of China. A Statistical Table of the Chinese Libraries. (In its Bulletin, I:7-19. Sept.-Oct., 1925.)

④ 【原注】Tai. T. C. Description of the Chinese college, society and special libraries. (In his Library Movement in China. Chinese National Association for the Advancement of Education, Peking, 1923, p. 8-17.)

使用。

在上海有两个非常吸引人的机构图书馆,一个设在上海总商会下,另一个由商务印书馆建立和维护。

尽管广州不断有政治问题,1922年一月广州当局成立了机构图书馆供教育工作者使用。有中外文两类馆藏书籍,主要涉及教育和综合参考类。它在广州为短期图书馆学校充当实验基地,采用了最新式的管理方式,将会成为广东省的示范图书馆。

自从图书馆员只为学者服务这个老观念逐渐消失后,对训练有素的图书馆员的需求开始显现。图书馆学校是一种培养方式,另一种是开办图书馆学和图书馆管理的课程。

武昌文华大学(现在改名为华中大学)是中国第一个引入图书馆学正规课程的机构。它提供三年课程,并只从二年级以上的学生中招生。现在全国各个图书馆工作的很多年轻图书馆员都是由华中大学图书馆学校培养的。

1920年夏天,北京高等师范学校开办了第一次图书馆暑期学校。共有78名男女学生注册,这让大家大吃一惊。大部分人是不同省的各个图书馆送来参加暑期学校的图书馆员。

1922年春天,广东全省教育会将短期图书馆学课程引入广州。广东省政府授权开展三周的见习课程,并要求中等以上所有学校送教员或职员来省会参加课程学习。学校在3月27日开学,有省内各个中等以上学校的65名代表参加。

为了加速图书馆的发展,在中华教育改进社的支持下成立了图书馆教育委员会。1922年7月在山东济南,主要教育机构的图书馆员齐聚一堂,讨论开展全国范围图书馆发展的问题。通过了十余条议案,最重要的几个正在实施。其中一条是督促各省的大城市组织当地图书馆协会,进而组织中华图书馆协会。过去的三年中,九个地方图书馆协会形成,中华图书馆协会也于1925年6月3日在北京正式成立。⑤ 美国图书馆协会的代表鲍士伟博士⑥也出席了成立仪式,他受邀来华调查中国图书馆事业,并对中国庚款基金委员会的表现准备一个调查报告。

政府为新成立的中华图书馆协会提供了总额达5000美元的初期经费。除了编制书目和编辑图书馆管理和经营的小册子外,协会还发行双月刊中华图书馆协会会报和图书馆学季刊。由于财政困难,无法同时开展多个项目。

作者回顾了中国图书馆的概况,尽管有战争、饥荒和其他灾害等困难,中国图书馆在过去的十年里缓慢但持续地发展着。如果教育工作者和社会工作者积极支持中国图书馆的发展,其结果将是不可估量的。只有广大人民群众能够很容易地使用图书资料,才能达到真正的民主。

原载:《图书馆员和图书世界》 卷14 1924年8月至1925年7月

---

⑤ 【译者注】中华图书馆协会于1925年6月2日在北京举行成立仪式,宣布正式成立。

⑥ 【原注】Bostwick, A. E. Report of his mission to China as A. L. A. delegate, reprinted from Bulletin of the American Library Association, Feb., 1926.

The Library

One of the most important accomplishments of the College is the erection of the new library. It was completed in January 1919 and not until then did both the student body and the faculty have comfortable and convenient library facilities. The present building contains a handsome lobby, spacious reading rooms, and steel stacks, with a collection of books, and periodicals, for study and research. There are at present about 20,000 volumes of books in foreign languages and 50,000 in Chinese. The current periodical both in Chinese and other languages number 305 and dailies, 41. With a yearly allowance of $12,000(mex), it is hoped that in a few years the collections can meet the growing need of the users.

The administration of the library is divided into five divisions, namely, reference and loan desk, order and accession, periodicals and newspapers, binding, and cataloguing, Chinese and western. At present the cataloguing of books in foreign languages has been temporarily suspended. We hope before long the library will have a trained and experienced cataloguer to look after the foundation work of a rapid growing library.

RULES FOR THE TSING HUA COLLEGE LIBRARY

I. *The Reading Rooms.*

1. Until further notice the Library is open according to the following schedule:

(a) Mondays-Fridays: 8 – 12 a.m. 1 – 4 p.m. 5 – 6.30 p.m. 7.30 – 10 p.m.

(b) Saturdays: 8 – 12 a.m. 1 – 4 p.m. 5 – 6.30 p.m. (c) Sundays: 9 – 12 a.m. 5 – 6.50 p.m. 8 – 10 p.m.

(d) Single Holidays: Same as Sundays.

(e) Other Holidays: Separate announcement will be made in each case.

2. Reference books, periodicals, and newspapers may be consulted in the reading room, and must be returned to their original places after reading.

3. Books for circulation and bound volumes of periodicals which are kept in the stack-room, may be had upon presenting the number of each as shown in the card catalogue to the charging desk. Admission to the stack-room is only by special permission of the person in charge.

4. No one is permitted to make any correction in a book or periodical. Any mistake found during reading should be reported to the Librarian.

5. Any one who mutilates or damages a book will be required to make full payment for same.

6. Loud talking or reading, smoking and spitting are not allowed in the Library.

7. Coats, hats and umbrellas should be left in the cloakroom.

8. Visitors may have use of the Library upon being introduced to the Librarian.

Ⅱ. *Loaning of Books.*

1. Books may be borrowed and exchanged daily (Sunday and holiday excepted) from 8 – 12 A. M. and 1 – 4 P. M.

2. Books of value can under no circumstance be taken out of the Library.

3. The number of books that may be borrowed at a time is limited to three. Books loaned to teachers for the work of their classes do not come under this ruling.

4. Before any book leaves the Library, registration of the loan must first be made.

5. Books borrowed may be kept out for a period of two weeks. A fine of one cent a day will be charged for delay in the return of each book.

6. In case a book is wanted for the use of the school before the period of loaning expires, the borrower must return it at once to the Librarian on notice being given to that effect.

7. Anyone who mutilates or damages a book will be penalized by fine. In case a book is lost or the damage is of a serious nature, full payment for same must be made.

8. Periodicals, textbooks, encyclopedias, reference books, reports, bound volumes of periodicals, and reserved books are not to be taken out of the Library.

9. On special application to the Librarian books on the reserved shelf for collateral readings can be taken out after the close of the Library at 10 p. m., but they must be returned on the following morning before 9. When a reserved book is not returned on time, an initial fine of five cents on the first hour and an additional fine of two cents on each succeeding hour will be charged. In case the borrower infringes this rule three times, his privilege of borrowing reserved books will be withdrawn for the rest of the term.

Ⅲ. *Loan of Books: Summer Vacation.*

1. Each student is allowed to borrow three books for the summer vacation.

2. Four Chinese books (bound volumes excepted) are considered as the equivalent of one foreign book.

3. Applications for loan of books must be addressed to the Librarian. All important books are not to be taken out of the Library (see Section Ⅱ. Article 8).

4. In case a. book is lost or damaged, full payment for same must be made.

5. A deposit of two dollars for each book should be made against any damage.

Ⅳ. *Circulation of books in the College Hospital.*

1. Certain books and periodicals are specially set aside for the use of students in the Hospital.

2. One member of the Library staff will be in attendance in the Hospital for one hour each afternoon.

3. All books must be returned before leaving the Hospital.

4. Students with infectious diseases are not allowed to borrow any of the books.

V. Circulation of Books among College Servants.

1. Certain books are for the use of College servants.

2. Books may be borrowed and exchanged daily from 10 – 12 A.M.

3. College servants are allowed to borrow one book at a time.

4. Before any book leaves the Library, registration of the loan must first be made.

5. Books borrowed may be kept out for a period of two weeks. A fine of one cent a day will be charged for delay in the return of each book.

6. In case a book is wanted for the use of the school before the period of loaning expires, the borrower must return it at once to the Librarian on notice being given to that effect.

7. Any one who mutilates or damages a book will be penalized by fine. In case a book is lost or the damage is of serious nature, full payment of same must be made.

VI. Miscellaneous Rules.

1. Gifts of books, paintings, scripts, etc., to the Library will be duly acknowledged, and kept in the Library with the donor's name.

2. A letter-box is put up outside the Librarian's Office to receive recommendations for books, etc.

3. Valuable books, paintings, etc., belonging to individuals may be exhibited when sent to the Librarian with a description.

4. Such exhibits are subject to the regulations of the Library. In case they are lost or damaged, the Library will be responsible.

Information.

The following information in brief will help users of the library to get more acquainted with the present system of operation:

1. Loan system: Books are loaned to the users on presentation of a borrower's card—one for each book. These cards, differentiated by colors—students in blue and members of the faculty and staff in white—are given on application. Each person is entitled to three and they can be used throughout the year.

2. Special permits for borrowing books outside the three allowed may be granted to students on recommendation of their teachers.

3. Reserved books are books assigned by teachers for collateral reading. They are placed in separate cases and may be obtained at the reserved desk; and only to be read in the library.

4. Users of the library are at present allowed free access to the stack-room. In case any book should be taken out to the reading room, it must be checked at the desk on a special slip for the purpose.

T. C. TAI,
Librarian.

原载:Tsing Hua College Bulletin of Information 1922—1923

【译文】武丽娜译　　姜爱蓉审

清华大学图书馆

　　学校图书馆最显著的成就之一是建立了新图书馆。直至1919年1月图书馆落成,师生才享受到舒适便利的图书馆设施。图书馆有美观的大厅、宽敞的自习室和钢制书架,收藏用于学习研究的书刊,约收藏中文图书50,000册、外文图书20,000册;中文和其他语种的期刊305种、日报41种;在每年最高12,000美元的经费支持下,经过几年的建设,馆藏资源有望满足读者日益增长的需求。

　　图书馆包括五个部门,分别为参考和出纳股、采访股、报刊股、装订股、中西文编目股。目前外文编目工作暂停。我们希望不久的将来图书馆会有一支经过培训、有经验的编目员队伍,为快速发展的图书馆做好基础性工作。

清华学校图书馆规章制度

Ⅰ.阅览室

1. 如无特殊通知,图书馆开馆时间如下:
   (a)周一至周五:上午8:00—12:00　下午1:00—4:00;5:00—6:30　7:30—10:00
   (b)周六:上午8:00—12:00　下午1:00—4:00　5:00—6:30
   (c)周日:上午9:00—12:00　下午5:00—6:50　8:00—10:00
   (d)单日假期:开馆时间同周日。
   (e)其他假期:另行通知。
2. 工具书、期刊和报纸可以在阅览室阅览,但阅毕须放回原处。
3. 可外借的图书和期刊合订本收藏在书库,读者在出纳台出示与目录卡片上一致的书目信息后可以借出。如要进入书库,还须获得相关主管人员许可。
4. 如发现图书或期刊上有错误,请勿涂改,您在阅读过程中发现的任何错误都可报告给图书馆员。
5. 图书如有破损或残缺,需全额赔偿。
6. 馆内禁止大声喧哗、大声阅读,禁止吸烟、吐痰。
7. 外套、帽子和雨伞需存放在衣帽间。
8. 校外来访人员获得图书馆员许可后方可利用图书馆。

Ⅱ.图书出借

1. 上午8:00—12:00,下午1:00—4:00可办理图书借还手续(周日和节假日除外)。
2. 珍贵图书严禁带出图书馆。
3. 一次最多可借出图书三册(教师因为教学原因借出的图书除外)。
4. 携书离馆前须办理借书手续。

5. 图书借期两周,超期未归还图书须按照每天1分钱交纳罚款。
6. 图书借期内,如学校需使用该书,持书读者收到归还通知后须立即将图书归还图书馆员。
7. 任何人损毁图书都须交纳罚款。一旦图书遗失或损毁严重,读者须交纳全额赔偿。
8. 期刊、教科书、百科全书、工具书、报告、期刊合订本以及预约书不能带出图书馆。
9. 向图书馆员提交申请后,读者可以在晚上10:00闭馆后取用预约架上的课外读物类图书,但须在次日早上9:00前归还。如未能及时归还预约图书,图书馆将在超期的第1个小时执行5分钱罚款,从第2小时起执行每小时2分钱罚款。如图书持有者违反规定3次,图书馆将停止其在该学期内借阅预约书的权限。

Ⅲ. 暑假借书规则

1. 暑假期间每个学生允许借出三本图书。
2. 一本外文图书等同于四本中文图书(合订本除外)。
3. 重要图书不允许带出图书馆(参见第二部分第8项内容),如需外借须向图书馆员提出申请。
4. 一旦图书丢失或损坏,图书持有者须交纳全额赔偿。
5. 为避免图书损坏,每本书需交纳2美元押金。

Ⅳ. 校医院图书流通

1. 指定图书和期刊专门预留给医院的学生使用。
2. 图书馆一位工作人员须每天下午在医院值班一个小时。
3. 离开医院时必须归还所有图书。
4. 患传染性疾病的学生不可以借任何图书。

Ⅴ. 校役图书流通规则

1. 校役可以借阅指定图书。
2. 每天上午10:00—12:00可借出图书。
3. 校役一次可借一本图书。
4. 携书离馆前,必须办理借阅手续。
5. 图书借期两周。超期未归还图书须按照每天1分钱交纳罚款。
6. 图书借期内,如学校需使用该书,持书读者收到归还通知后须立即将图书归还图书馆员。
7. 任何人损毁图书都须交纳罚款。一旦图书遗失或损毁严重,读者须交纳全额赔偿。

Ⅵ. 其他规定

1. 图书馆接受图书、绘画、手稿等捐赠,捐赠物连同捐赠者的信息将被一并保存在图书馆中。
2. 馆长办公室外悬挂的信箱用于接收图书荐购等信息。
3. 个人有价值的图书、绘画等资料可以在图书馆展览,但需向馆长提供相关展览信息。

4. 这些展览活动应该遵守图书馆有关规章。如有丢失或损坏,图书馆承担相应责任。

相关信息

下面的简要信息有助于图书馆使用者对当前的运行制度有更多了解:

1. 借书制度:读者经过相关申请可获得借书证;出示借书证后方可借书,每张卡可借书一本。这些卡用不同的颜色区分——学生卡是蓝色的,教职工卡是白色的。每人有三张卡,可以全年使用。
2. 经他们教师的推荐,学生可以获准借出三本以上图书。
3. 预留图书指的是教师指定的教辅资料,这些资料单独保存,可以在预留台找到并仅限馆内阅读。
4. 目前图书馆读者可以自由进入书库。任何图书被拿出阅览室须在借书台填写索书单办理借出。

图书馆主任　戴志骞

原载:《清华学校信息通报》　1922—1923

Supplements to the Dewey's "Decimal Classification & Relative Index": Preface

To the mind of modern librarians, the idea of classifying all Chinese books according to the four main divisions as provided by the Ssu K'u Ch'uan Shu(四库全书)does not seem very practical. In the first place, the number of divisions is not sufficient to cover the present day books on various subjects. Secondly, there is no logical arrangement among the subdivisions under each of the four main divisions. Thirdly, the whole system does not provide for flexibility, and fourthly, the system provides no place for scientific works as D. C. , E. C. , or L. C. docs. Fifthly, it has never taken into consideration of shelving and the procedure of the loan desk. Priinarily. it is a system of subjective classification and was never intended to be applied to the methods of modern library management.

Since as a system of classification of books the discrepancies of the Ssu K'u Ch'uan Shu have been too obvious, the idea of adopting Dewey's "Decimal Classification" for the classification of Chinese books, has been suggested. . For fear of the impossibility of entire application, the Boone University Library School has proposed that a modified system of D. C. might be workable.

After a couple years' experiment in the Tsing Hua College Library we have been brought face to face with a few drawbacks which any modified system of D. C. in our opinion has to encounter.

The D. C. system has been the result of many years' patient labor by specialists. The imperfect and arbitrary in the arrangement of the main divisions and subdivisions, its comprehensiveness, practical utility and economy overbalance the defects. Whether a modified D. C. system which only rearranges the order of the divisions, improves the original D. C. is questionable and whether such a modified D. C. is more applicable to Chinese books is also doubtful. Our experience in using modified D. C. to classify Chinese book has been a disappointing one.

Many libraries in China have already adopted the D. C. system. If some libraries use the new modified D. C. which in fact is not so full and comprehensive as the original D. C. , this would create a confusion among the readers as well as among the librarians. The present need of the Chinese libraries is for a definite practical system whereby to arrange the books systematically on the shelves, with simple call numbers for the loan desk assistants, not so much for a scientific classification. The new modified D. C. has not only been unable to remove the defects of the original. D. C. , but creates also unnecessary confusion in the mind of the layman.

A modified D. C. seems more applicable to Chinese books, but less adaptable to the books in western languages. Hence any library which has a collection of both Chinese books and western books has to classify its books in two different D. C. classes. This practice will be most confusing and illogical to the readers, as for-example, a book on education in Chinese has a D. C. number quite different from that of a book on the same subject, written in English. Therefore the work of the modified D. C. system has neither improved the original D. C. nor is it entirely applicable to Chinese books. So we turn our mind to find a solution of classifying Chinese books in the original D. C. once more.

T. C. Tai, Librarian.
Tsing Hua College Library,
Peking, China.

原载:*Supplements to the Dewey's "Decimal Classification & Relative Index"*

【译文】戴志骞自译

《杜威书目十类法补编》序

　　中国书籍按四库全书以四大部分类,在近代图书管理家视之,不甚合于实用,其故有五:(一)四部类别不足概括现代各类书籍;(二)统属于四大部之小分类,其排列不按论理之规则;(三)四部分类法不便委转取用;(四)四部分类法非如杜威开展及美国国会图书馆各分类法可以安置科学书籍;(五)四部分类法于书架排列法及借书管理法多未计及焉。

　　按四部纯属主观之学术分类法,原非为近代图书管理法而设,不合实用,固其所也。四部之法既不适用,于是,采用杜威十分类法以整理中国书籍之议,乃应运而生焉。文华大学图书科又虑杜威十分法不尽合用,复取杜威原法,变更其类目之排列号曰《杜威书目十类法》,以为此法或较利于实用矣。乃清华图书馆积数年编目之经验,觉任何修订杜威十分类法终不免发生困难。

　　杜威十分类法乃各科专家经长时间之苦工而成之结晶品也,虽于大小类别之排列,不免有武断及遗漏之弊,而其广博切用与夫用号之经济殆蔑以加已。

　　所谓改订杜威十分类法,不过将杜威原分类重行排过,其于原法是否有所改良或于编制中文书籍果否较便,均属疑问,于是应用改订杜威十分类法以编制中文书籍之办法,又不足厌吾人之望矣。

　　查近来中国图书馆已多数采用杜威原法,若少数图书馆骤用改订之分类法(不如原法完密而广博)转令读者及图书管理员发生误会,且学术分类在我国今日之图书馆,尚非急务,而迫不容缓者,厥惟一种适用之排书方法,使管理借书者能按极经济之分类号码安置各类书籍于架上是已。

　　改订杜威分类法非惟不能免除杜威原法之缺点,且足紊乱一般读者之头脑,用以编制中文书籍似较便利,而又不适用于编制西文,坐令兼有中西书籍之图书馆不得不并用两种相异之杜威十分法矣。然此种办法,既不合论理又易生读者之误会。例如,关于教育之中文书籍,其分类号迥异于同类之英文书籍,其不便于检查,可知所有改订杜威十分法既不能改良杜威原法,又不尽适用于编制中文书籍,遂不得不转向杜威原法中觅一编制中文书籍之适当方法焉。

戴志骞序

原载:《杜威书目十类法补编》

An Advanced School of Librarianship—Aim of Curriculum

By T. C. TAI, librarian, Tsing Hua College, Peking, China

I am not going to present you a schedule of courses for an advanced school of librarianship. First, a foreign student with a smattering knowledge of library training and education is not competent to lay down the curriculum of a professional advanced library school. The curriculum of any advanced professional school is one of the most difficult and most complex problems to be tackled. Second, several prominent librarians have already treated this topic in detail. You have the criticisms of the curricula of existing library schools from Dr Williamson's report, Training for library service; the views and reasons expressed by library school directors and faculty members in their comments on Dr Williamson's report; many authoritative statements of the experts in the Professional Training section of the forty-sixth annual conference of the A. L. A., and the constructive program of courses of library training from Mr Reece's Some possible developments in library education.

I hope, however, it will not be out of place to present again this topic, a curriculum for an advanced school of librarianship, from a new angle which emphasizes the fundamental aims of making a curriculum of a professional school. If the aims would be better embodied in a prescribed curriculum, let the curriculum of an advanced school of librarianship be prescribed. Were they more suitable to a curriculum arranged to fit students for definite types, let it be so arranged. It is a question dealing with the aims of a curriculum of an advanced library school rather than its external composition. A curriculum either prescribed or arranged to fit students for definite types will yield beneficial results, provided it contains the essential requisites of a curriculum for a professional school.

According to Dean Russell of Columbia University, the curriculum of a professional school should have three fundamental aims, namely, specialized knowledge, technical skill and high ideals. Permit me to quote his excellent statements in the address delivered at the inauguration of Dr Lotus D. Coffman as president of the University of Minnesota.① He says, " In its curriculum it should strive to organize and systematize the knowledge available in its particular field so that its students may get the essential facts needed at the beginning of their career; in its teaching, it should give inspiration to creative effort and altruistic service; and at some stage of its training provision must be made for gaining technical skill. The pedagogical problems of all professional schools grow out of those three fundamental requisites. These factors, however, are all variable quantities…Right proportion in the adjustment of these essentials is the crux of administration in every type of professional school. "

---

① Russell James Earl, Trend in American education, N. Y. AM. Bk. co, 22, p. 223-237.

Let us apply these aims to the curriculum of an advanced school of librarianship. First, the specialized knowledge of the library profession should be so organized and systematized that, within the minimum period of time, it will give the graduate student the maximum amount of the advanced knowledge of the profession. This means two definite things in the making of a curriculum, viz. : 1) Do not crowd the curriculum with introductory and elementary courses of the professional subjects. Any member of the faculty who tries to introduce a new course which lengthens the curriculum by extending its standard downward should be prohibited from doing so.

2) Emphasis should be laid on the completion of prerequisite courses of any graduate student who wishes to enter the advanced school of librarianship. For example, a graduate student in the school of history, specializing in the movements of the Renaissance and the Reformation, must have the prerequisite courses of ancient, mediaeval and modern history. Therefore, a graduate student in an advanced library school wishing to specialize in incunabula cataloging must have a thorough knowledge of general cataloging as a prerequisite.

The curriculum of an advanced school of librarianship should have the distinctive feature of high standard of quality in the courses offered. It is simply preposterous to have a curriculum which composes a set of high-sounding, conglomerate courses, but in quality does not differ very much from the courses offered by the existing library schools and academic subjects of undergraduate standing. We want to have an advanced school of librarianship with the high ideals of raising out professional standard comparable to those of other professions, with the consequence that we may be able to give better service to society.

Second, technical skill. Many think that men and women with first class mental calibre and ambition refuse to enter the library profession because, in the first place, many courses in the curricula of the existing library schools, and in the second place, the library work is chiefly of clerical nature. I do not believe this is so serious an obstacle as to deter ambitious young persons from joining the library profession. We all know that every profession demands technical skill. For instance, in medicine, a skilled surgeon knows how to place a bandage when the interne or the nurse is not around. When and how the teaching of technical skill should be introduced in the curriculum of a professional school is the keynote of the question.

The length of its time, the content of its subject-matter and the method of its teaching vary in various professional schools. For instance, law, medicine, and engineering give the students competent instruction in professional subjects and some teaching of technical skill in schools but leave them to acquire the thorough technical skill in an office, a hospital or a shop under the guidance and instruction of a master. In other professions as teaching, agriculture and social work, the graduates of those professional schools must make good the first day on the job. In my opinion, the library profession is similar to those of teaching, agriculture and social work. Every library that employs a library school graduate expects that he or she possesses specialized knowledge as well as technical skill. Under such conditions, the curriculum of a library school has not to provide the students with the art of walking, because as soon as they graduate, every employer expects that they can move about freely on their own feet on the job. So the advanced school of librarianship is brought face to face with the real question of acquisition of technical skill in its curriculum. When and how can it best be administered? In other words, the curriculum should provide the instruction of technical skill on the professional plane. As to its importance in library work, Dr Anderson wisely remarked in his address on Training for library service, delivered before the Pennsylvania library club at Atlantic City, "A reasonable amount of the routine or drudgery is wholesome in that it compels the professional man to keep his feet on the earth and not become enveloped in clouds of theory."[②]

Third, high ideals. I am not going to take more of your time on this topic, "high ideals," in the making of a curriculum, not because it is less important than the other two principles, but both the existing library schools and the librarians have fully exemplified their spirit of altruistic service. In the art of teaching there are two essentials, i. e., giving inspiration to individual creative thinking and inducing the students to open their minds to learn during the rest of their lives.

From the above outlined principles and their applications in the making of a curriculum for an advanced school of librarianship, it follows that it is comparatively better, in my opinion that a curriculum be arranged to fit students for definite types of service. Nevertheless, this statement cannot be regarded as conclusive without hearing the opinions about individual research in specialized fields and the adjustable proportion of a curriculum of library subjects as major, and other academic subjects as minor, in the advanced school of librarianship.

原载：*Public Libraries* Vol. 30 1925

---

② Anderson, E. H. Training for library service. Lib. Jour., v. 49, May 15, 24 p. 462-466.

【译文】郭兰芳译　肖燕审

高等图书馆学校
——课程宗旨

戴志骞　中国北京清华学校图书馆主任

　　本文并非要为高等图书馆学校提供课程表。首先,作为一名对图书馆培训和教育认知尚浅的留学生,我还没有能力为高等图书馆专业学校设置课程。任何高等专业学校的课程设置都是个既困难又复杂的问题。其次,一些杰出的图书馆员已详尽地探讨过这一话题。威廉姆森博士[①]在其报告《图书馆服务培训》一书中,批评了现有图书馆学校的课程;一些图书馆学校负责人和教师在对上述报告做点评时,表述了他们的见解和理由;在美国图书馆协会[②]第四十六次年会期间举办的职业培训分会上,许多专家做过权威性论述,里斯[③]在其《图书馆教育可能出现的发展》一书中,对图书馆培训课程提出了建设性规划。

　　然而,我还是想从一个全新的角度,即着重于专业学校课程设置的基本宗旨,就高等图书馆学校的课程谈一下个人观点,希望不要不合时宜。如果统一设定的课程能够更好的体现上述宗旨,那就统一来设定课程;如果根据学生类型而设置的课程更能与宗旨相符,那就按学生类型来设置课程。总之,需要探讨的是高等图书馆学校课程的宗旨,而非其外在构成。不论是统一设定的,还是按学生类型而定的课程,只要它符合专业学校课程的基本宗旨,就都能取得有益成效。

　　在哥伦比亚大学拉塞尔院长看来,专业学校的课程应该涵盖三个基本宗旨:专业知识、专业技能以及崇高理想。请允许我援引其在明尼苏达大学校长洛特斯·德尔塔·科夫曼[④]博士就职典礼上的精彩演讲[⑤],他提到:"设置课程时,应注重组织并系统化特定领域的有关知识,以便学生掌握职业生涯伊始所需的基础知识;教学中,应激发学生的创造灵感并鼓励其无私服务的精神;在某些训练环节中,应设定规范,以便学生掌握专业技能。所有专业学校的教育问题皆出自此三项基本宗旨。这些要素[⑥]均为可变量……正确分配这些要素的比

---

① 【译者注】Charles Clarence Williamson(1877—1965),生于美国俄亥俄州西北部,是近代普世图书馆推展运动的关键人物。他认为图书馆不只是藏书楼,同时也是将书目按条理分类,能够有效服务公众的场所。通过他的努力,图书馆成了近代启迪民智的教育单位,更成了普世资讯交流与知识管理的中心。其被后人称为"图书馆学之父"。

② 【译者注】美国图书馆界的专业组织,世界最大的图书馆协会之一,成立于1876年,总部设在芝加哥。

③ 【译者注】Ernest James Reece(1881—1976),生于美国俄亥俄州克利夫兰,做过图书馆员、图书馆专业教师等,终身从事图书馆理论和实践研究工作。

④ 【译者注】Lotus Delta Coffman(1875—1938),生于美国印第安纳州,拥有法学博士学位和古典文学博士学位。曾任明尼苏达大学第五任校长,经过他的努力,明尼苏达大学成为了当时全美第三大大学。

⑤ 【原注】Russell James Earl,Trend in American education,N.Y. AM. Bk. co,22,p.223-237.
【译者注】Russell James Earl(1864—1945),生于美国纽约哈姆登,一生致力于教育事业的发展,曾任职于纽约师范学院,该学院并入哥伦比亚大学后,担任学院院长。

⑥ 【译者注】即前文提到的基本宗旨。

重是各类专业学校行政管理的关键任务。"

让我们把这些宗旨运用在高等图书馆学校的课程中。首先,将图书馆专业的专门知识加以组织并系统化,让学生在最短的时间内学到最多的高等专业知识。这意味着在课程设置时需要明确两件事情:一、不可让专业科目里介绍性和基础性的课占满课表。绝不允许任何教师以延长整个课程并降低其水平为代价而开设新课程。二、强调那些希望入读高等图书馆学校的毕业生必须完成预备课程的学习。例如,想进历史学院,以文艺复兴和宗教改革运动为研究方向的毕业生,必须先完成古代史、中世纪史及近代史等预备课程的学习。同理,打算入读高等图书馆学校,专研古版本目录学的毕业生,就必须预先对一般目录学知识有透彻的理解。

高等图书馆学校的课程表设置应该特征鲜明,课程表里的所有课程质量应有着很高的质量标准。如果课程表是由成堆的名头虽响亮,而水平却几乎与现有图书馆学校所开设的课程,甚至本科专业课相当的课程所组成,那只能是荒谬可笑的。我们想要的是有着崇高理想、专业水准可以与其他专业学校相匹敌,从而可以更好服务于社会的高等图书馆学校。

其次,专业技能。许多人认为,那些智力超群、胸怀大志的人拒绝进入图书馆专业的原因有二,一方面现有图书馆学校的课程设置存在问题⑦,另一方面图书馆工作主要以事务性工作为主。我不认为这些原因是阻止胸怀大志的年轻人加入图书馆行业的决定性障碍。我们都知道,每种职业都有相应的技能要求。比如,在医疗行业,没有实习医生和护士的情况下,外科医生也会打绷带。什么时间、以何种方式将专业技能教学引入到专业学校课程中是问题的关键所在。

不同专业学校的教学时长、教材内容以及教学方式也都不同。比如,法律、医学及工程专业,教给学生的仅是专业技能要义,而要彻底掌握这些技能则还需要在律所、医院或车间,经过师傅指导才可完成。而另一些专业,如教育、农业及社会工作,学生走上工作岗位后必须马上就可以上手。在我看来,图书馆专业与教育、农业及社会工作相类似。对于聘用来的图书馆学校毕业生,图书馆期望他们既要有专业知识也要有专业技能。在这种情况下,图书馆学校的课程需要培养学生胜任工作的能力,因为参加工作后,雇主都期望他们可以马上进入角色、游刃有余地完成任务。所以,高等图书馆学校所面临的一个现实问题,就是如何通过课程安排来让学生掌握专业技能。什么时间、以怎样的方式安排将会取得最好的效果?换言之,课程安排应该提供职业技能训练。关于职业技能训练对于图书馆工作的重要性,安德森博士在为大西洋城宾夕法尼亚图书馆俱乐部致辞时,对《图书馆服务培训》做过精辟的评论:"图书馆工作要求专业人员脚踏实地干活,而不是沉迷在理论中,所以一定量的周而复始、单调沉闷的工作是合理的。"⑧

再次,崇高理想。关于体现在课程设置中的崇高理想,我不打算占用太多时间去讲,这并不是因为它没有前两点重要,而是目前的图书馆学校及图书馆员已充分展现出了无私服

---

⑦ 【译者注】原文可能缺单词,此句为猜测翻译。

⑧ 【原注】Anderson, E. H. Training for library service. Lib. Jour., v.49, May 15, 24 p.462-466.

【译者注】Anderson Edwin Hatfield(1861—1947),是 20 世纪前 30 年美国杰出的图书馆事业领导者,曾任匹兹堡卡耐基图书馆馆长、纽约公共图书馆馆长和美国图书馆协会主席。因在匹兹堡和纽约创立了图书馆员教育课程而被后人所纪念。

务的精神。在授课技巧方面,需要注意两个要点,即激发学生的创新思维和引导学生养成终身学习的习惯。

根据对以上几个要素的论述,以及对其在高等图书馆学校课程设置中应用的探讨,我认为,相比较而言,课程安排较好的做法是着眼于特定服务类型,适应学生的专业方向。然而,此观点并非定论,高等图书馆学校的课程设置还需结合个体在专业领域的研究需求,以及主副科目,图书馆学专业课程和其它非专业学术课程的比例调整来综合考虑。

原载:《公共图书馆》 1925 年第 30 卷

Modern Library Development and Its Relation to Scholarship

By T. C. Tai, Ph. D. (戴志骞)

(Paper read before the Wen Yu Hui, Peking, November 4th, 1926)

Scholarship and the library from the historical past to the present day were and are in intimate relationship. If we glance over the early historical tales of China, we would be interested to notice that already Confucius was a great user of libraries. The libraries of that early time were probably archives of official records. The story runs that Confucius once consulted Laotse as to material for his works. The latter was then the keeper of the royal archives of the Chou dynasty. In the ancient history of the Near East and Greece many references point to the truth that the scholars were patrons and keepers of libraries. The researches which followed the discoveries of P. E. Potta and H. Layard in 1850 at Kouyunjik, on the Tigris, have revealed the fact that the ancient Babylonians and Assyrians had magnificent libraries. Clay tablets with cuneiform characters were the "book" of the palace-library of Assu-bani-pal, King of Nineveh. These tablets have been arranged according to subjects. From such orderly arrangement we can infer that there must have been a keeper who classified the tablets for the convenience of the readers.

Anyone who reads the history of the Egyptian civilization cannot help but admire the numerous brilliant grammarians and profound scholars. The libraries also occupied a conspicuous place in the cultural history of Egypt. The four famous Alexandrian libraries were always well patronized, and even the present day librarians would admire their administration. The librarians of that time not only preserved the collections with great care, but also took inventory and revised the library catalogs once in every five years. Two of the Alexandrian booklists on tragedies and comedies were prepared by famous scholars. Callimachus, one of the best known scholars at that time, compiled a catalog of all the principal books in Alexandria under 120 classes. A fragment of that catalog, containing the philosophical works from a papyrus found near Alexandria, is now in the Library of Leningrad.

According to Edwards' "Memoirs of Libraries," Prof. Boyd's "Public Libraries and Literary Culture in Ancient Rome" and Clark's "Care of Books," the number of libraries under the Roman emperors were greater and the scholars more numerous even than in Alexandria. Some authorities have claimed that there were twenty-eight, possibly 29, public libraries in ancient Rome. The use of the libraries increased in proportion as the literary and cultural tendencies of the Roman citizens developed. The practice of lending books from libraries was also introduced.

The splendid Roman public libraries fell into decline upon the repeated invasions of the northern barbarians. Literary activity at Rome as well as at Constantinople rapidly collapsed. Books were either burnt or destroyed and scholars were not wanted. This marks the end of the library development and scholarship among the ancients.

The library development during the Mediaeval and the early modern age had an insignificant beginning, but a splendid later history. The mediaeval age in Europe covers the growth of the monastic libraries. The scholars of that age nearly all wore the garb of monks. Biblical literature, theological dogma and biographies of saints and martyrs were the principal collections of the monastic library of that period. The modern era covers the great strides made by libraries in institutions of learning, after the invention of printing had multiplied the number of books, and after a revival of true learning and science had made the library an indispensable tool for the scholar. In the 17th and 18th centuries books were rapidly multiplied by the use of movable types. Freedom of thought budded forth as the first fruit of the Renaissance and the Reformation. Authorship in literature and science was much more prolific than under the ecclesiastic yoke of monasticism.

Now let us have a hasty glance over the historical development of the library and scholarship in China. Since the epoch of burning books and burying scholars alive by Shih Huang Ti, the Han, the Pei Wei and the T'ang dynasties have been regarded as epochs of producing essayists and poet. In poetry and literature the T'ang dynasty reached full brilliancy. As to scholarship, profound in quality as well as great in number, the Sung dynasty was far superior to all the previous dynasties. One of the chief causes might be well attributed to the usage of woodblock printing. From that time emperors often issued edicts of collecting books to form imperial libraries and scores of well-to-do scholars from Sung dynasty to the later part of 17th century had large private book collections. But the prosperity of private libraries reached the climax during the first few reigns of the Manchu emperors. Scholars of that period were especially learned. Most of them were well-known bibliographers or renowned(训诂家 commentators), or careful(考订家 editors). The production of Ch'ung Shu(collective works) and bibliographies outshadowed all the previous ages. All these scholars made constant use of private libraries. Scholars like 顾亭林(Koo Ting-lin), 黄梨州(Huang Li-chow), 黄丕烈(Huang Pei-lieh) and others had many fascinating stories about their habit as bibliophiles.

From the above brief sketch, our mind can be clarified as to the relation between library development and scholarship in the past. The cultural history of any nation indicates clearly that the relation between these two factors is an intimate one.

In discussing our subject tonight, I realize that I am exposing myself to criticism for talking too much about the library development and scholarship from the ancient time to the end of the 18th century. However, we must not forget that to approach the past is also a method of understanding the present.

In the history of library development up to the end of 18th century in Europe as well as in China, the relation of the library to scholarship was a passive and static one. It was passive, because the library was a place for storing books, and often an exhibition of vanity and pride. The use of such libraries was only granted to scholars. Sometimes to be given permission to use the royal libraries was a very great favour. Such an act could be regarded as an expression on the part of emperors of their love for literature and science. Though the relationship between library and scholarship was intimate, yet the library had never tried to be an active force in stimulating the ordinary persons who had an inclination towards learning. In China as well as in Europe an ordinary person was not supposed to have the privilege of using a library.

It was static, because the concept of the functions of a library was regarded as an elegant concomitant of prosperity and peace in a community. The libraries were reservoirs but not fountains of knowledge. They were museums of rare books. The scholars valued them because they stored and preserved authenticated, though not current, material on special subjects. The libraries never attempted to attract students there to make investigation and to secure information, they were only a treasure house for the genius.

In the second half of the 19th century, libraries of the museum type were gradually changed into centers of diffusing knowledge and of disseminating ideals among the people. There were many forces, such as improvement of printing machinery, reduction of the cost of paper, increase of reading material, library philanthropy, democratic ideal in education, and spirit of research to develop the modern library movement. The most important ones are the democratic ideal in education and the spirit of research.

The United States of America is the first country to put the democratic ideal of education into the development of modern libraries. The American educators knew that the period of formal schooling was limited. The method of teaching in schools was limited. The method of teaching in schools was only to teach pupils how to read, to spell, and to write, but seldom taught the pupils how to educate themselves. The educators also saw clearly that it would be unfortunate if young people, after leaving the schools and becoming bread-winners, were to have no agency to furnish them with good and desirable reading. Many great educators felt the need of some educational agency which would continue what the school had begun. They desired to have something which could exert a continuous educational influence over the young as well as the old; which could supply a stimulus for the development of scholarship among the citizens; and which could gratify those who had a strong love for reading. This something was bound to be the public library. Since the 19th century, modern public libraries have been gradually founded side by side with the public schools. The public schools not only taught pupils the rudiments of learning, but also began to give them the tools with which to educate themselves in the form of books available in the more modern type of public libraries. From that time chiefly in America, to a certain extent in Great Britain and in Europe, schools and libraries joined together to do their educational work. The library became a natural complement of the school. The democratic ideal of education would not have fully developed if there had been instituted only the schools without their natural and necessary complement, modern public libraries. Without the library the work in schools and colleges would become the rigid method of memorizing textbooks, and the desire for knowledge awakened in classrooms and lecture halls would have to go unfinished. Melvil Dewey, one of the pioneers of the modern library movement, emphasized this very point in his address before the convocation of the university of the State of New York in 1888:

Our schools, at best, will only furnish the tools; but in the ideal libraries towards which we are looking today, will be found the materials with which these tools may be worked up into good citizenship and higher living. The schools give the chisel; the libraries the marble; there can be no statues without both.

Thus the movement of education for the masses resulted in the founding of public schools which, in turn, was one of the influential factors in bringing about the development of modern public libraries. The students who are educated in the schools must continue their training after they leave the classroom or the endeavours of their teachers will not have been of much use. But, besides the young, there are adults in every community to be educated. Therefore it is the duty of the state to establish and to maintain not only schools for the young but free public libraries both for the young and the mature. For the young the modern public library in the very process of helping the school education creates a taste for books and thereby makes for the necessary foundation towards scholarship. For the mature the modern public library in the method of conserving and disseminating knowledge gives convenience and opportunity to all the people and not to a small intellectual elite of each generation. The modern public library is founded on the corner stone of intellectual democracy which means all that is knowable is to be made accessible to all who desire to know and to study. When we make knowledge accessible to all, it will be a sure way of finding what minds and hearts are among us.

For instance, Horace Mann and Andrew Carnegie both confessed to the public that they got their attainments from modern public libraries. In Mr. A. E. Winship's "Great American Educators," he said:-"As this library (a little library at Franklin, Mass.) furnished the only books that Horace Mann had in his boyhood and youth, without it he would probably have developed no taste for scholarship, and the world would not have known this most brilliant American educator. Mr. Mann was so much indebted to this library, that in speaking of it in later years, he said he would like to scatter libraries broadcast over the land as a farmer sows his wheat."

Mr. Andrew Carnegie wrote strongly about the benefit he received from the modern public library in an article, "The Best Field for Philanthropy" in the North American Review, December 1889, or in Andrew Carnegie's Autobiography Chapter 4. Mr. Carnegie said:

The result of my own study of the question, what is the best gift which can be given to a community, is that a free library occupies the first place, provided the community will accept and maintain it as a public institution, as much a part of the city property as it public schools, and, indeed, an adjunct to these. It is, no doubts possible that my own personal experience may have led me to value, a free library beyond all other forms of beneficence. ……No millionaire will go far wrong in his search for one of the best forms for the use of his surplus who chooses to establish a free library in any community that is willing to maintain and develop it.

Dr. Ernest A. Baker of the University of London remarked in his book "The Public Library" that the development of the modern public libraries in Great Britain was as a consequence of the new democratic ideal in educational problems. Space will not permit me to quote more authorities to the effect that the strong factor, Democratic Ideal in Education, makes the development of modern libraries a success. The modern library is different from that of yesterday, because it opens its gates to everybody, because it tries as actively as possible to attract people to its treasures, because it makes its collection accessible to every person of the community. It is a dynamic force to create scholars out of the general mass. It is a people's university.

Now has such an important movement ever taken place in China? Since the Revolution of

1911 the people not only have tried and are trying hard to shake off the yoke of despotism, but are also fully determined to free themselves from the oppression of intellectual bondage. Problems of mass education have been tackled and the inarticulate body of millions are realizing that they also have the birthright to be brought into contact with the rudiments of learning. Among institutions whose existence depends upon their ability to meet the new ideals, the library is now face to face with rapidly changing conditions.

China, even today, is full of places for storing books. Although scholars continue to be interested in the editions of bygone dynasties and libraries only know how to collect the valuable incunabula, yet the tendency is daily growing stronger in favour of converting the bookvault jealously guarded by thick doors and heavy locks into a living and attractive library. According to the statistics in a bulletin published by the Chinese Library Association, such a change has already taken place in many provinces. Right in this city not very long ago you may have already read the news about the amalgamation of the Ching Ssu T'u Shu Kwan with the newly established Peking Metropolitan Library. Probably this will form the nucleus of a modern Chinese national library with branches as popular libraries. During the last decade the new library movement in China has made some strides.

On April 11, 1915, the Chiaoyupu (Ministry of Education) issued an order embodying eleven regulations which emphasize promotion, organization and administration of modern libraries throughout the different provinces of the country. Some of the districts have carried out the order, but others, owing to lack of funds and fighting between military leaders, are still in the period of preparation. There are at present about 88 organized public libraries and 291 T'ung su (通俗) or people's libraries.

The second important factor in the development of modern libraries I want to discuss tonight is the Spirit of Research in higher education. The conception of college studies a century ago was quite different from that of the present time. In former days students regarded their teachers as a sort of walking encyclopedia. They took down all the sayings of their professors and studied their textbooks word by word without looking further into other authorities. The subjects were limited mainly to Latin, Greek, mathematics, and philosophy, Theology, law and medicine were the only so-called special subjects for postgraduate students.

The early university libraries under a limited curriculum of classical courses and cultural studies did not have need of enormous collections of books. The rigid method of textbook teaching required very little use of a college library. A library in a university was a museum of rare books. The librarian was generally a professor with regular work in class instruction. The office was a sinecure. Opening the library three or four hours per week to loan a few books of interest was a courteous act to the professors. The library was virtually a place for storing and hiding books. Under such an atmosphere the students had no pleasure in or desire to use the college libraries and, furthermore, they were neither welcome to nor wanted by the librarians. The eminent librarian of Harvard University, Justin Winsor, well illustrated the vogue of the university libraries at the time in his address before the American Social Science Association at Saratoga, September 10, 1879:

Time was when the student in college came up to the library once or twice a week on sufferance, under the impression that it would never do to have too much of a good thing. "Boys!" cried the warder of one of the first of our college libraries, within the memory of the present generation; "Boys! What are you doing here-this is no place for you!" The poor craving creatures slunk away to Euclid and Horace in the seclusion of their bedrooms.

The enlargement of the field of knowledge in the last century has had a profound effect on the methods of academic teaching. The students, in view of the very rapid increase of new subjects for study, realized that they could not pursue all. The administrators and professors recognized the situation and hence pushed forward a set of new methods of instruction with all effort. They accelerated the wide adoption of the elective system, they introduced the topical study by syllabi and emphasized collateral readings. All these methods encourage and direct the the students not to confine themselves to their text-books alone. The students select the subject they like. The professors aim more to suggest than to direct their pupils to the various authorities on the subject. This result in a much freer expression of opinions and judgments in the classroom, for the topic taught is no longer restricted to recitations from a single textbook. Besides these innovations in instruction, the German form of seminary method conducted in the university libraries was also introduced.

These new methods of instruction were based on the deep conception of freedom of thought and breadth of view which are the essentials in the spirit of research. No view will be broad and no thought impartial without studying the works of various authorities. Such changes in instruction have necessitated an unavoidable change in the administration of a university library and concurrently contributed an important factor in the development of modern university and special research libraries. As President Thwing remarked: "The causes of the growth of the library of the college are comprehended in a single movement. It is the movement toward research. The college has come to stand for scholarship. Scholarship is at once the cause and the result of the book. The continuity of learning is embodied in the library. The library gathers up the wealth of the past. It represents all that man has struggled for or achieved. The library is, therefore, the treasure-house of the linguist, the philologist, the philosopher, the historian. Even the scientist finds in the library the records of experiments, be they successful or of failures."

This theory regarding the growing significance of modern libraries is well sustained by the established facts concerning the greater use and rapid growth of college libraries during the last fifty years. There are striking contrasts between a college library of today and that of about the middle of the nineteenth century if we compare the hours open, the size of collections, and annual expenditure for the purchase of books. For instance, take Harvard College Library which was founded as early as 1638, but after more than two hundred years, through the efforts of many faithful and enthusiastic librarians, it only contained about forty-one thousand volumes. Professor John Langton Sibley effectively remarked in his address to the American librarians in 1879: "It was open for consultation from 9 o'clock to 1, and from 2 until 4, on the first four secular days of the week, and on Fridays in the forenoon. There was one hour when the sophomores on Tuesdays and the freshmen on Wednesdays took out books, and one on Mondays and on Thursdays for seniors and juniors. There were no shelves in the galleries, and Gore hall was considered large enough to accommodate all the additions that would be made during the century. The total income from the permanent fund for purchasing, repairing and binding books was exactly $250 a year. The modern college librarian would take such a condition as a joke. Nevertheless, it actually existed in one of the most renowned American colleges only eighty-four years ago. Harvard College Library was at that time the leading institution in the length of hours kept open. It also advocated liberal principles for the use of books by students. As to the other college libraries, their collections were less accessible than those of Harvard."

Now let us take a look at most famous college library in England and see whether the spirit of research has affected its development. In 1602 the Bodleian Library in Oxford was opened with a collection of 2500 volumes — a fairly large collection for those days. Most of the books were chained to the shelves, a custom which was finally given up only in 1769. Scholars were required to pay a deposit in cash when borrowing books. But the deposit was so trifling that some of the unscrupulous scholars willingly forfeited the money and kept the manuscripts. In a manuscript copy there is an imprecation like that on a book-plate of a book belonging to the house of St. Mary of Robert's Bridge: "This book belongs to St. Mary of Robert's Bridge: Whosoever steals it, or sells it, or takes it away from the house in any way, or injures it, let him be anathema-maranatha." Underneath another hand has written: "I, John, Bishop of Exeter, do not know where the said house is: I did not steal this book, but got it lawfully." The gist of such incidents illustrates the museum type of college library.

Anyone who reads the history of the Bodleian Library cannot help thinking that the college library at that time adopted an attitude of absolute indifference to study. Let me quote Prof. Koch's remarks on the Bodleian in his "On University Libraries":

The records of the Bodleian substantiate the low point to which the intellectual life of the university had ebbed. The registers of books borrowed for the decade 1730-1740 show that only rarely were more than one or two books asked for in a day. In some cases a whole week is passed over without a single entry being made.

As to the opening hours the Bodleian was more irregular than its American contemporary college libraries.

There is preserved in the Bodleian a scrap of paper which an angry scholar posted on the door of the library in the early 19th century, when he found the library closed against the statutes. The words on the paper are: "Woe unto you who have taken away the key of knowledge! Ye enter not yourself and hinder those who come." One who visits the Bodleian and studies its management will be interested to notice that the library now is very well patronized by teachers and students during very hour that it is open.

As the spirit of research in the universities intensifies the method of instruction in every branch of scientific and professional subjects, the momentum of acceleration of growth of university libraries is and will be increased. The slogan now-a-days is "use and more use" of the college and university libraries. The present methods of college teaching increase the use of the university libraries. They have become mental laboratories for every phase of human knowledge.

About 15 years ago most of the colleges in China did not have any library. Some of them happened to have one, which was invariably a store-house for old books. Now almost every college has a library. Practically all of them have two collections, one in Chinese, the other in foreign languages. All colleges maintained by the Chinese possess larger collections of Chinese books, while educational institutions supported by missionaries and Western philanthropists always have more foreign books. Several reach the figure of over 100,000 volumes. About 12 college libraries now have their own buildings, and several are trying hard to get enough funds for erection of modern library buildings. At present the college and university libraries in China are more efficiently administered, richer in collection and better in service than the average public libraries.

The important role to be played by the modern university and college libraries in the sphere of university teaching functions was well described by President William Rainey Harper, of the University of Chicago, in his "Trend in Higher Education." He said:

A quarter of a century ago the library in most of our institutions, even the oldest, was scarcely large enough, if one were to count volumes; or valuable enough, if one were to estimate values, to deserve the name of library. So far as it had location, it was the place to which the professor was accustomed to make his way occasionally, the student almost never…… Today the chief building of a college, the building in which is taken greatest pride, is the library. With the stack for storage purposes, the reading room for reference books, the offices of delivery, the rooms for seminar purposes, it is the center of the institutional activity. The director of the library is not infrequently one of the most learned men of the faculty; in many instances certainly, the most influential. Lectures are sometimes given by him on bibliography, or classes organized for instruction in the use of books. The staff of assistants is often larger than the entire faculty in the same institution thirty years ago. Volumes are added to the number of 3000; 5000; 10000; or 20000 in a single year; the periodical literature of each department is on file; the building is open day and night…… That factor of our college and university work, the library, fifty years ago was almost unknown, to lay already the center of the institution's intellectual activity, half a century hence——with its sister, the laboratory, almost equally unknown fifty years back——will, by absorbing all else, have become the institution itself.

This is a very enthusiastic statement. As the spirit of research advances in the universities the university library will be the heart of intellectual activities and it will constantly supply life and strength in the process of creating scholarship.

In this country of chronic disturbance during the last fifteen years the democratic ideal in education and the spirit of research have taken root in the development of modern libraries. The libraries of the museum type used only by famous scholars have gradually disappeared and modern libraries for the people have grown in different provinces as well as educational institutions. How much influence has the modern library development exerted in the contemporary scholarship in China? It is still too early to be gauged. All we can say is that the present age already outshines any of the previous ages in the quantity of publications.

Take newspapers for instance. Most of us will not consider them as scholarly production, nevertheless, they are indicative of the mental activity of the generation. There are 435 dailies distributed in various places as follows:

Anhwei	4
Chekiang	11
Chihli-Peking	87)

Rest	20）107
Fukien	16
Honan	6
Hunan	13
Hupeh	39
Kansu	1
Kiangsi	8
Kiangsu-Shanghai	39）
Rest	61）100
Kwangsi	10
Kwangtung	31
Kirin & Heilungking	10
Mukden	8
Kweichow	2
Shansi	11
Shantung	28
Shensi	2
Szechuan	22
Yunnan	6
Total	435

As to the weeklies and monthlies the market has been flooded with all kinds of publications since the appearance of the "New Youth" （新青年）in September 1915. Again, according to the statistics in the China Year Book for 1925, the publications whose circulation amounts to 300 or more per issue now number about 750. Bulletins, society reports and students' ephemeral publications are not all included in this total. They can be roughly classified into four main classes, namely：

（1）Along the line of the "New Culture Movement"（新文化运动）. As Dr. Hu Shih has said："Hundreds of tiny periodicals, modeled after the one-sheet form of the Weekly Review（星期评论）, were published by student organizations in various places, and practically all of them were in the spoken language of *pai hua*." This class includes a great deal of writings of "cheap iconoclasm and blind faddism"（Hu Shih's phrase）. The popular ones are 政治生活, 向导, 评论之评论, 改造 and others. Due to suppression, most of them have now been suspended from publication.

（2）Along the line of constructive criticism and high grade literature and philosophy. This class represents the work of the saner and older people. Publications like 现代评论, 国闻周报, 民铎 are the popular ones.

（3）Along the line of scholarly effort. The writers of this class have patience and energy in introducing Occidental science, philosophy and literature into China, or else they apply the Western methods of scientific research to the painstaking labour of systematizing the old learning of China. The latter work is popularly called 整理国故, 国学季刊 and 国学丛刊 and possibly 学衡 are leading ones of this class. 华国 and 国学辑林 may be regarded as the reflections of the old type scholars. Society publications such as 心理(Psychology), 科学(Science), 法律评论(Law Weekly Review), 社会学杂志(Chinese Journal of Sociology) and others are daily increasing in number.

(4) Along the line of commercialized enterprise. The publications of this class are chiefly published by the big printing companies in China. The represented ones are 东方杂志, 妇女教育, 小说月报 and others.

Within the last ten years more publishers have come into existence. A great number of social novels and essays have been produced, and besides many Western books have been translated into Chinese. Pamphlets on various subjects and modern textbooks are also published. Several great and voluminous books, such as 正统道藏, 续藏经, 四部丛刊, 四部备要 and other 丛书 are all carefully edited and reprinted.

From many library reports the users of libraries are growing daily in numbers. By chance if you drop into the Peking Public Library, No. 1 inside of Shun chih Men, the statement will not be far from the truth. Recently I received a Library Weekly from one of the libraries in Chengtu, Szechuan province. Several persons residing in the northern part of that city petitioned the Chengtu Central Library to open its fourth branch library in that district. The General Chamber of Commerce Library and the Commercial Press Library in Shanghai are always well patronized. The college libraries in China are now the most crowed and the most used buildings in every college community.

Scholarship is a product and crystalization of many social forces and the modern library can certainly claim to be one of the most essential factors in moulding man with scholarly attainment. The library is a dynamic force in all grades of education. It is the great agent in the betterment of society and culture and it is the spiritual delight of the human soul.

原载:*The Chinese Social and Political Science Review* Volume xi . 1927

【译文】范莹莹译　林佳审

现代图书馆发展及其与学术的关系

戴志骞

（1926 年 11 月 4 日在北平文友会上宣读）

自古以来,图书馆与学术密不可分。如果浏览中国早期历史故事,我们会发现孔子是一位了不起的图书馆用户。在那个遥远的时代,图书馆可能就是官方的档案馆。据说孔子为了撰写著作曾向老子请教一些相关资料的问题,而老子当时恰巧负责周朝的类似国家档案管理的工作。古代近东和希腊也有史料表明,当时的学者们通常都是图书馆的用户或管理者。P. E. 波塔和 H. 莱亚德于 1850 年在底格里斯河流域的库云吉克所做的研究发现,古巴比伦人、亚述人都有非常宏伟的图书馆。陶土块烧制的一个个楔形文字泥板就是尼尼微王室阿苏尔巴尼帕图书馆的"书",并且按照主题排列起来。从这些排列有序的字块可以推断出,当时肯定有管理者将这些字块进行分类编排,方便读者进行查找。

凡是读过埃及文明史的读者无不钦佩那些造诣高深的语法学家和学者,同时也发现在埃及的文化历史中图书馆占据了非常重要的地位。当时四个著名的亚历山大图书馆相当受欢迎,甚至当今的图书馆员也很欣赏他们那时的管理。那个时代的图书馆员不仅非常小心细致地维护馆藏,而且每五年会重新修改馆藏目录。亚历山大图书馆关于悲剧和喜剧推荐书目中,有两个是由知名学者编著的,其中一个非常著名的学者卡利马科斯,将该馆最重要的书目分成了 120 个类别。现存列宁格勒图书馆的一份在亚历山大附近发现的纸莎草纸上所列哲学著作就是此目录的一部分。

据爱德华兹的《图书馆纪要》、博伊德教授的《古罗马的公共图书馆与文学文化》和克拉克的《照管图书》,古罗马皇室所拥有的图书馆和学者的数量甚至大于亚历山大大帝。据权威统计,古罗马的公共图书馆有 28 个（也可能是 29 个）。随着罗马民众文学和文化素养的提升,图书馆的使用比例也随之提高,图书外借的行为也越来越普及。

曾经辉煌的罗马公共图书馆在北方蛮族的反复入侵下走向没落,文学活动在罗马和君士坦丁堡快速消亡。在这种社会状况下,大量书本被烧毁,学者们的研究失去了存在的依靠,因而成为古代文明社会图书馆发展和学术研究的终止标志。

虽然没有很好的开端,但图书馆在中世纪和现代早期却有辉煌的发展历史。中世纪时代的欧洲修道院图书馆发展迅速,那个时代的学者几乎都是修士的装束。圣经文学、神学教条、圣徒和殉道者的传记都是那个时期修道院图书馆的主要藏品。印刷术的发明使书籍数量大幅增长,科学研究的复兴使现代的图书馆成为学者探求科学的必备工具,也使学术型图书馆取得了跨越式进步。在 17 和 18 世纪,由于活字印刷的使用,书籍数量成倍增长。文艺复兴和宗教改革产生了自由思想的萌芽,继而出现了大量文学和科学方面的著者,且数量远大于精神束缚下的神职人员。

现在我们来看一下图书馆和学术的关系在中国的发展历史。自秦始皇焚书坑儒以来,汉、北魏和唐代被视为盛产散文家和诗人的时代,在唐代更是达到了顶点。在学术方面,无论在数量上还是质量上,宋代都远远超过其以前所有朝代,其主要的原因可能是木版印刷的使用。从那时起皇帝经常发布法令收集书籍以建立宫廷图书馆,从宋代到17世纪后期许多富裕的学者都拥有大量的私人藏书。私人藏书在清朝前几个皇帝统治时期达到鼎盛,而这一时期的学者也都具有颇深的造诣,他们中大部分都是书志学家、评论家或考订家。于此同时,汇编文集丛书和图书目录的数量较之前大幅增加。学者们充分利用私人藏书,像顾亭林、黄梨州、黄丕烈等学者在藏书爱好方面都有有趣的故事。

以上所述,清晰地反映出我国古代历史上图书馆的发展与学术之间的关系。其实任何一个民族的文化历史都清楚地表明图书馆的发展与学术之间的关系是十分紧密的。

到此为止我们一直在讨论18世纪末之前图书馆发展与学术的关系,但探索历史是为了更好地研究现在。

在18世纪末之前,无论在欧洲还是中国的图书馆发展史上,图书馆与学术的关系都是被动和静态的。被动是因为图书馆是用来藏书的地方,象征着虚荣和骄傲,只有学者才能使用图书馆,被允许使用皇家图书馆甚至是非常荣幸的事情,这同时也说明了皇室对文学与科学的喜爱。虽然图书馆和学术之间的关系紧密,但图书馆却从未对普通的热爱学习的民众产生过积极影响,因为在中国和欧洲普通民众是没有权利使用图书馆的。

静态是因为图书馆只是被看作繁荣而平静的藏书之地,是珍贵书籍的博物馆,而非知识的创造之源。学者们认为图书馆有着极高的价值,因为图书馆保存了某些领域极为权威的资料,尽管这些资料不是某一领域的最新资料。那时的图书馆并不会吸引学生去做科学研究,因为它只是少数精英的知识宝库。

19世纪下半叶,博物馆类型的图书馆逐渐转变为向民众传播知识和理念的中心。有很多因素推动了现代图书馆运动的发展,例如印刷业的进步、纸张成本的降低、阅读材料的增加、图书馆慈善事业、教育民主理念和研究精神等,其中最重要的当属教育民主理念和研究精神。

美国是第一个把教育民主理念融入到现代图书馆事业发展的国家。美国教育家意识到,日常的学校教育是有限的,学校的教学方法也是有限的。当时学校的教育仅仅教学生如何阅读和书写,却很少教导学生如何进行自我教育。教育工作者也清楚地看到,年轻人离开学校后开始养家糊口,不再有机构提供给他们良好和理想的阅读条件,这是一件非常遗憾的事情。许多伟大的教育家逐渐认识到持续教育的必要性,他们希望有一些东西可以发挥对年轻人和老年人持续教育的影响力,可以激发民众的学术能力,并能满足对阅读有强烈愿望的人的需求,这样的东西只能是公共图书馆。自19世纪以来,随着公办学校的创办,现代公共图书馆逐渐建立起来。公办学校不仅教会学生学习的基本原理和技能,同时教他们如何利用现代公共图书馆进行自我教育,这种情况当时在美国比较普遍。在英国和欧洲,学校和图书馆在一定程度上开展联合教育,图书馆教育成为学校教育的有益补充。现代化的公共图书馆作为学校教育的有效补充形式促进了教育民主理念的充分发展。如果没有图书馆,学校内的教学将成为记忆课本的死板方法,而那些于教室和讲堂中所激发的求知欲也将无法得到满足。1888年,现代图书馆运动先驱之一的麦维尔·杜威在纽约州立大学的演讲中曾强调:

> 我们的学校充其量只能提供工具,而我们今天正在寻找的理想图书馆将会提供材料,利用工具加工这些材料能够获得更高的公民权和生活品质。正如要想修

建一座雕像,学校提供的是凿子,而图书馆提供的是大理石,两者缺一不可。

民众教育的普及促进了公立学校的建立,也成为影响现代图书馆发展的因素之一。学生从学校毕业后,或者教师意识到教学能力有限,都需要接受继续教育。除了年轻人以外,各个不同社会群体的成年人同样需要教育,因此政府有责任为民众设立学校和免费的公共图书馆。对于年轻人来说,现代公共图书馆可以辅助学校教育,让学生阅读大量的书籍从而为他们打下学术基础;对于成年人来说,作为收藏书籍和传播知识的现代公共图书馆为广大民众的学习提供了便利和机会。使用图书馆不再是少数社会精英的特权,现代公共图书馆的基石是知识民主,任何渴望知识、渴望学习研究的民众都可以使用它,当知识在普通民众中得以普及时,它也成为了解民众内心和思想的一个可靠途径。

贺拉斯·曼和安德鲁·卡内基都曾向公众讲过,他们能取得今天这样的成就应该归功于现代公共图书馆。在 A.E. 温希普先生《伟大的美国教育家》中说道:"这个图书馆(马萨诸塞州富兰克林县的一个小图书馆)的书籍陪伴贺拉斯·曼度过了他的童年和青年时代,图书馆带给他学术成就,也让世界认识了这位伟大的美国教育家。贺拉斯·曼先生非常感激这个图书馆,若干年后他谈到此事,说他会像农民播种一样在祖国各地广泛建立图书馆。"

安德鲁·卡内基先生在 1989 年 12 月发表于《北美评论》上的《最佳慈善领域》一文和其自传的第 4 章中都提到他从现代公共图书馆中获益匪浅:

> 什么是给社会最好的礼物?对于这个问题我的答案是一座免费图书馆。如果社会认可它作为一个公共机构来维护和发展,应将其同公立学校一样视为社会公共资产的一部分,甚至视为公立学校的附属机构。毫无疑问,我的经历让我意识到,任何一个百万富翁都想有效利用自己的盈余资产投资建立一座免费图书馆。在所有慈善事业中,免费图书馆的社会价值远大于其他任何慈善形式。

伦敦大学的欧内斯特·贝克博士在他的著作《公共图书馆》中写道:英国现代公共图书馆的发展是教育问题中新民主思想推动的结果。由于篇幅有限,我在此不再引用更多权威资料来证明教育民主理念促进了现代图书馆的成功发展。现代图书馆与以往的图书馆有所不同,它向所有民众开放,并尽可能积极主动地让读者利用其馆藏资源,它以一种动态的影响力从民众中培养出学者,是一所广大民众的大学。

中国有这样的运动吗?1911 年辛亥革命以来,人们努力摆脱专制主义的枷锁,试图从思想和知识的束缚中解放出来。随着民众教育问题的解决以及民众学习意识的觉醒,作为依靠实力不断适应新观念而存在的机构,图书馆正面临着不断的变革。

现在中国仍有很多藏书的地方。尽管学者们对古籍充满了浓厚的兴趣,而图书馆也只是将其作为主要馆藏资源,但图书馆由一个有着厚重的门锁的书库向着充满生机和吸引力的方向转变的趋势越来越明显。据中华图书馆协会发布的统计数据显示,这样的转变发生在中国的很多省份。不久前你可能听到关于京师图书馆与新建的北平图书馆合并的消息,这可能就是国家图书馆的核心组成部分。在过去的十年中,中国新图书馆运动已经取得了一定的进步。

1915 年 4 月 11 日教育部签发了 11 项规则条例,在全国范围强调现代图书馆的宣传、组织和管理。一些地区已经实施,但其他地区由于缺乏资金和军阀之间的争斗,仍然处于准备阶段。目前大约有 88 家有组织的公共图书馆和 291 家通俗图书馆或民众图书馆。

今晚我要论述的第二个推动现代图书馆发展的重要因素是高等教育的研究精神。大学学习研究的观念古今有较大差异,以前的学生把老师当作一部活的百科全书,他们认真记录教师所说的每个字,除了认真学习自己的笔记以外不再学习其他知识,学习的科目也仅仅局限于拉丁文、希腊文、数学、哲学、神学、法律和医学等被称为所谓的特殊科目。

由于受课程设置和文化研究的限制,早期的高校图书馆对馆藏的需求量并不大,僵硬的课本教学模式对图书馆的需求极低,高校图书馆只是一个珍藏善本的博物馆,馆员也由有日常教学工作的教师兼任,图书馆的工作较为清闲,每周开放三四个小时提供借阅服务,因此图书馆实际上仅是藏书的书库而已。在这种情形下,学生对使用图书馆没有兴趣和意愿,而且馆员们也不大愿意让学生来图书馆。1879年9月10日,哈佛大学的著名图书管理员贾斯汀·温莎在萨拉托加的美国社会科学协会的演讲中较好地阐述了高校图书馆在当时的情况:

> 在这一代的大学生们勉强获准每周去一两次图书馆的时候,他们对图书馆基本没留下什么好印象。图书馆的看守人会大声叫喊:"你们在这里干什么!这不是属于你们的地方!"于是,这些对图书馆有一丝渴求的可怜学生们只有溜回了封闭的宿舍里去研究欧几里得或贺拉斯。

19世纪知识领域的拓宽对学校的教学方法产生了深远影响。鉴于学科种类的快速增长,学生们意识到他们无法对所有领域都进行学习研究。在这种情况下,管理者和教授们采用了一套新的方法加以应对,他们迅速启用了全面的选课系统,根据课程设置推出专题研究大纲,并强调了辅助阅读的重要性。所有这些措施鼓励并引导了学生摆脱教科书的束缚,学生们可以选择自己喜欢的科目,而教授们则给予学生更多的建议而非指导,帮助他们接触某一学科的权威书籍。在这样的课堂中,学术氛围变得更加自由,教学内容也不再仅仅局限于单一的教科书了。除了这些创新的教学举措,高校图书馆还引入了德国神学院的教学方法。

这些新的教学方法是基于思想自由的深度和视野的广度,而这正是研究精神的本质。只有广泛开展学习研究才能有更加广阔的视野和全面的思想。教学方法的改变不可避免地推动高校图书馆的管理的变化,并且对于现代高校图书馆和专业图书馆的发展起到了重要的作用。特温校长说过:"高校图书馆增长的原因可以理解为一场简单的学术研究运动,高校开始作为学术的代表,学术成为书籍增长的原因和结果。学习的持续性在图书馆体现,图书馆汇集了已有的知识财富,代表了人们曾经为之奋斗的或已经实现的目标。因此,图书馆是语言学家、语文学家、哲学家和历史学家的宝库,甚至让科学家在此找到成功或失败的实验记录。"

随着过去50年高校图书馆的利用率和增长速度明显提高,有关现代图书馆存在意义的理论持续增长。如果我们把开馆时间、馆藏规模和每年的购书经费这几个方面做个比较,会发现现在的高校图书馆与19世纪中叶相比有显著的差异。以早在1638年就建立的哈佛大学图书馆为例,在很多忠实和热心馆员的努力下,经过200多年的发展,其馆藏量仅达到4.1万册。约翰·兰登·西布利教授于1879年在对美国图书馆员的演讲时说过:"哈佛大学图书馆的开馆时间为每周一至周四的9:00—13:00、14:00—16:00以及每周五上午。每周周一至周四都有一个小时对学生开放借书业务,周一对大四学生开放、周二对大二学生开放、周三对大一学生开放、周四对大三学生开放。图书馆的书库内没有书架,戈尔大厅能够容纳本世纪以来的所有馆藏。每年的固定购书、维护和装订经费为250美元。以现在的高校图书馆员来看,那样的条件简直就是个笑话,然而,这确实是仅仅发生在84年前的这一美国知名大学中的实际情况。从开馆时间的角度来看,哈佛大学图书馆在当时已经名列前茅了,并且倡导实行对学生提供自由借阅的政策,而其他高校图书馆供读者借阅的文献量远小于哈佛大学图书馆。"

现在我们来看一下英国最著名的高校图书馆的发展是否同样受到了研究精神的影响。1602年牛津大学博德利图书馆对读者开放,虽然当时的馆藏仅有2500册,但在那时已经算很有规模了。当时大部分的书籍都被锁在书架上,这一惯例终于在1769年被终止。学者们借书需要交纳押金,但由于这些押金与书籍的价值相比微不足道的,一些无道德原则的学者们为了把这些书籍手稿留为己有而宁愿舍弃押金。在罗伯特桥圣玛丽修道院的一份手稿的藏书标签上有这样一段诅咒的话:"这本书属于圣玛丽罗伯特·桥:凡偷书、卖书、以任何方式把书从这个房子里带走或者损害书的人都会被诅咒。"而在这些话下面有人又写道:"我,约翰,埃克塞特主教,不知道你所说的房子在哪里:我没有偷这本书,只是通过合法途径得到了它。"此事例描述了当时博物馆型的高校图书馆。

任何读过牛津大学博德利图书馆历史的人都会认为当时图书馆对学术研究的态度是淡漠的。我引用科赫教授在"关于大学图书馆"中对牛津博德利大学图书馆的描述:

> 牛津大学博德利图书馆的记录证实了大学学术的低迷状态。在1730年至1740年间,该馆每天的借书量只有一两本,甚至有时一周都不会有人去借书。

在开馆时间方面,牛津大学博德利图书馆远不及同时期的美国高校图书馆有规律。

牛津大学博德利图书馆保留着一张小纸片,这是19世纪早期一个愤怒的学者发现图书馆违反条例闭馆时贴在图书馆门上的,上面写道:"你们带走了知识的钥匙,阻碍别人使用图书馆。"访问过牛津大学博德利图书馆并研究过其管理方式的人会注意到,现在图书馆开馆期间有大量的教师和学生光顾。

研究精神带动了高校的各个学科专业教学方法的极大改进,高校图书馆的增长势头逐渐加强。现在,"使用图书馆、更多地使用图书馆"已成为高校图书馆的口号,高校的教学方法促进了高校图书馆利用率的提升,图书馆已成为人类知识各个阶段的精神实验室。

大约15年以前,大部分的中国高校都没有图书馆,而偶有图书馆的高校也只是存放一些老旧的书籍。现在几乎所有的高校都有自己的图书馆,而且有的图书馆有中外文两类馆藏。由中国人资助创建的高校,其馆藏资源主要为中文图书,而由传教士和西方慈善家资助创建的教育机构,其馆藏资源主要为外文书籍。部分图书馆的馆藏甚至超过10万册,大约有12个高校图书馆拥有自己独立的馆舍,还有一些正在努力寻找更多的资金用以建立现代化图书馆。目前我国的高校图书馆与普通的公共图书馆相比,其管理更加高效,馆藏更为丰富,服务更加优质。

现代高校图书馆在高校教学领域所起的重要作用可以用芝加哥大学校长威廉·雷尼·哈珀在《高等教育的趋势》一书中的内容来描述:

> 25年前大部分学术机构的图书馆,甚至包括最有历史的图书馆,从馆藏规模上来说都不够大,就其价值来说也不算大,就其空间位置而言,它只是教授偶尔光顾的地方,而学生则几乎从未去过。今天,高校内的主要建筑并且是引以为傲的建筑就是图书馆。图书馆有藏书的书库、参考书阅览室、加工馆藏的办公室和进行学术研讨的房间,图书馆已经成为高校的活动中心。通常,图书馆馆长不是少数的教师精英,而是最有影响力的人物之一,馆长有时会开设文献学的讲座或开展如何使

用图书馆馆藏的课程,普通馆员的数量大于 30 年前全校的教工总数。图书馆馆藏数量快速增长,每年新增藏书 3000、5000、10,000 或 20,000 册,各个院系的期刊也全部集中管理,图书馆的工作时间延长,早晚全部开放。50 年以前,高校图书馆基本不为人所知,现在已成为高校学术活动的中心,与同样在 50 年前不为人所知的姐妹——实验室不同,图书馆并没有被其他机构吸收,而成为了一个独立机构。

这是一个激情满溢的陈述。由于研究精神在高校中的不断发扬,图书馆将作为高校学术活动的中心,不断地为学术创造提供生命和力量。

在这个经历了过去 15 年长期骚乱的国家内,教育民主理念和研究精神扎根于现代图书馆事业的发展中。仅限知名学者使用的类似博物馆的图书馆已经逐渐消失,供广大民众使用的现代图书馆以及教育机构在不同省份不断涌现。在中国,现代图书馆的发展对当代学术有多大影响? 现在衡量还为时过早。我们所能说的是在出版物的数量方面,现在的时代已经远超出以往任何时代了。

以报纸为例,大多数人都不把其归为学术产物,不过报纸却揭示了一代人的精神活动。如下是分布在各地的 435 份日报:

安徽		4
浙江		11
直隶—北京	(87)	
其他地区	(20)	107
福建		16
河南		6
湖南		13
湖北		39
甘肃		1
江西		8
江苏—上海	(39)	
其他地区	(61)	100
广西		10
广东		31
吉林 & 黑龙江		10
奉天		8
贵州		2
山西		11
山东		28
陕西		2
四川		22
云南		6
总计		435

至于周报和月报,自 1915 年 9 月《新青年》出版发行以来市场上涌现出了各种出版物。据 1925 年的《中国年鉴》统计数据显示,发行量大于或等于 300 份的出版物约有 750 个,简

报、社会报告和学生的非正式出版物未计其中。这些出版物大致分为4个主要类别：

(1)以"新文化运动"为主线。正如胡适先生所说："由各地的学生组织出版发行的、以单页期刊《星期评论》为蓝本的数百微小期刊都是使用的口语化的白话文。"这类出版物包含了大量的"圣像破坏运动和盲目跟风"的著作。其中较为著名的有《政治生活》《向导》《评论之评论》《改造》等，由于受到压制，其中大部分已暂停出版。

(2)以建设性的批评为主线，及高水准文学与哲学。这类出版物的读者思想更加理性和成熟，其中较为著名的有《现代评论》《国闻周报》《民铎》等。

(3)以学术成就为主线。这类出版物的作者为将西方科学、哲学和文学引入中国花费了大量的精力，还有一部分致力于将西方的科学研究方法应用于中国传统知识的系统化。后者的代表刊物主要有《整理国故》《国学季刊》《国学丛刊》和《学衡》。《华国》和《国学辑林》是旧学派学者的主要代表，社团出版物，如《心理》《科学》《法律评论》《社会学杂志》等，发行量与日俱增。

(4)以商业化企业为主线。此类刊物主要由国内大型印刷企业出版发行，主要代表刊物有《东方杂志》《妇女教育》《小说月报》等。

在过去十年中，出版机构大量涌现，社会小说和散文的产量大增，许多西方书籍被翻译成中文，也出版了不同主题的小册子和现代教科书。大量的知名著作如《正统道藏》《续藏经》《四部丛刊》《四部备要》等其他丛书得到了精心的编排和重印。

许多图书馆报告中都反映出图书馆用户的数量与日俱增。如果你偶然进入位于顺治门内1号的京师通俗图书馆，便能证实这一点。最近我收到了一份四川成都一家图书馆的《图书馆周刊》，该市北部居民请求成都图书馆在该区开设第四家分馆。上海总商会商业图书馆和商务印书馆受到了读者的欢迎。现在中国的高校图书馆是校园内人员最集中、使用最频繁的地方。

学术是众多社会力量和现代图书馆的产物和结晶，现代图书馆被看作是以学术成就塑造人的最重要的因素之一。图书馆对各个阶段的教育来说都是一个积极的动力，它能够改善社会和文化并陶冶人类灵魂。

原载：《中国社会及政治学报》 1927年第11卷

Classified Catalog of the Tsing hua College Library: Preface

Since the Library was moved to its present building in 1919, the open shelf-system has been installed for the benefit of the readers. In addition to this hard-to-handle system the college has bought and is still buying too many books for the present library staff to handle and make accessible through the channels of accession, classification and cataloging. It is an old tale to most college librarians that a college library is usually supplied with generous funds for buying books but rather parsimonious in its appropriation for administrative purposes. The Tsing Hua College Library was no exception until recent years.

Consequently the books were rushed into the library and the readers were not able to use them extensively due to the lack of a key to the collection. So the library has tried hard during the last few years to get a properly organized catalog department. We wanted to have a dictionary card catalog, a shelf-list and a printed catalog. A dictionary card catalog with analytical entries is now placed near the loan-desk for the use of the public. A complete shelf-list as a guide to the future classification work has been prepared for the use of the staff.

Besides the two lists mentioned above this classified book-form catalog is now printed with three purposes. First it shows clearly the extent of the collection on any one subject. A proportionate growth of all subjects is necessary for a university library. Secondly a catalog in book-form is most convenient for teachers and students to use in office or class-room or whatever place they like. Thirdly a classified printed catalog may be helpful to any other library which is financially unable to engage a trained librarian to look after the problems of book selection, classification and cataloging. But a book-form catalog gets soon out of date in a fast growing library. Many new acquisitions are left out, before this catalog is out of press. This defect may be remedied to certain extent by issuing an annual or bi-annual supplement. The library at present issues a mimeographed monthly bulletin of new acquisitions. If a reader would save these bulletins he could have a fairly complete list of new books before the issue of a supplement.

In the compilation of this catalog thanks should be extended to Dr. C. S. Yeh, Mr. T. F. Tsen, Dr. G. H. Danton and other professors for revising and extending the classification pertaining to their respective departments. To Mrs. C. G. Dittmer who first started the work of cataloging, and to Mrs. T. C. Tai who has organized the catalog department and is supervising all the work, grateful acknowledgment is returned. Finally it is a great pleasure to acknowledge the industrious and painstaking work of the members of the catalog department. Without their effort, this catalog would not have been possible in its present condition.

Tse-Chien Tai
Librarian
July 1927.

原载: *Tsinghua University Library Classified Catalog of the Tsing hua College Library*

【译文】庄玫译　肖燕审

《清华学校（英文）书籍目录》序

自图书馆1919年迁至现址以来，为了方便读者，图书馆采用了开架借阅制度。在艰难推行开架借阅制度的同时，现有图书馆工作人员还要处理过往和当下持续采购的图书，通过登记建账、分类和编目使之得以借阅使用。高校图书馆一般购书经费宽裕，行政管理费拨款严格从俭，这对大多数高校图书馆而言是传统惯例，清华大学图书馆在这方面也不例外，只是近些年才有所改观。

由此带来的结果是图书馆购进了大量的图书，但读者却因为缺乏有效的了解途径而不能实现对图书的广泛借阅。鉴于这样的状况，图书馆在过去几年一直在努力组建井然有序的编目部门。我们希望编制一套字典式卡片目录，一套排架目录和一份印刷型书本式目录。目前，我们将带有分析款目的字典式卡片目录摆放在借书处附近供读者查询。供图书馆馆员使用的完整的排架目录已经编制完毕，它可作为未来分类工作的指南。

除上述二套目录外，当下印制的分类书本式目录具备三方面用途。首先，本目录清晰展示了馆藏对所有学科的覆盖程度。对于高校图书馆而言，所有学科的馆藏应当成比例地增长。其次，对于教师和学生而言，书本式目录尤其便于在办公室、教室或他们喜欢的任何地方使用。第三，印刷型分类目录或许对其他图书馆有所助益，此类图书馆往往由于经费所限无法雇佣受过专业培训的图书馆员处理选书、分类和编目问题。然而，对一所快速发展的图书馆而言，书本式目录很快就会过时。在目录还没有印制完成的时候，已出现许多不包括在目录之中的新增馆藏。这一缺陷，可通过每年或每两年印制增补本的方法得到一定程度的补救。目前，本馆每月发布油印本新书通报。如果读者保存上述新书通报，那么，就会在增补本印制之前拥有相当完整的新书目录。

本目录的编辑要特别感谢叶企孙博士（Dr. C. S. Yeh），郑之蕃先生（Mr. T. F. Tsen），谭唐博士（Dr. G. H. Danton）和其他教授们的鼎力相助，他们对相关院系专业的图书分类进行了修改和拓展。同时还要衷心感谢狄玛夫人启动了编目的工作，戴志骞夫人负责组建编目部并指导所有编目工作。最后，我由衷地向各位编目部同仁在编辑过程中的勤勉付出和努力工作表达诚挚的谢意。没有他们的辛劳，这份目录在当前的条件下是无法顺利完成的。

戴志骞
图书馆主任
1927年7月

原载：清华学校图书馆编　《清华学校（英文）书籍目录》序

Development of Modern Libraries in China

By T. C. TAI B. A. ,B. L. S. ,PH. D.

Director of Higher Education ,Kiangsu Educational District
Dean of National Central University ,Nanking
Director of the National Central University Library ,Nanking

Since the Revolution of 1911, China has undergone a movement of changes in intellectual problems, as well as in politics. The people have not only tried to shake off the yoke of despotism, but have also determined to free themselves from the oppression of intellectual bondage. The intellectual class, seeing the failures of numerous reforms, has come to the conclusion that the Chinese process of thought should be revolutionized. In order to attain the object, the government as well as educational leaders have taken up the task of examining the educational methods used and of pushing the spread of people's education.

The new methods in schools lay stress on the pupil's initiative rather than rigid following of texts. Hitherto, students regarded their teachers as a sort of living dictionary and walking encyclopaedia. They blindly committed to memory what they read in a text-book and what they heard in a class of recitation. Nowadays, the colleges and universities have all adopted the elective system and emphasize the topical study of a subject by syllabus and collateral reading. These methods not only encourage the students to do more reading, but have also affected the development and management of Chinese libraries.

China, even to-day, is full of places for storing books. Although old scholars continue to be interested in the Sung, Yuan or Ming editions, and old fashioned libraries wish to collect only valuable incunabula, yet the tendency is daily growing stronger in favour of converting the book-vault, jealously guarded by thick doors and heavy locks, into a living and attractive library.

This change has been brought about by the democratic ideal of education for the people. Hitherto, education was open only to a few who intended to enter the rigid imperial examinations. But recently, the Chinese people have realized the importance of mass education and have tried to diffuse new knowledge by introducing the use of a Chinese phonetic alphabet, and by publishing books, periodicals and newspapers in the colloquial language. The old libraries intended for storing books are now face to face with rapidly changing conditions. They are obliged to discard their traditional policy and to throw their doors wide open to the masses. During the last fifteen years, the modern library movement has taken great strides.

On April 11,1915, the Ministry of Education, realizing the importance of libraries, issued an order embodying eleven regulations which emphasized the promotion, organization and administration of libraries throughout the different provinces of the country. In order to add weight to the proclamation, the government turned the library of the late Imperial Board of Education into a public library, now known as the National Peping Library. Some of the districts in the provinces did carry out the order, but there were still many others, owing to the lack of funds and civil disturbances, which did not do anything towards the erection of libraries. However, the attitude of the government is worth remembering in the development of modern libraries in China.

After the installation of the National Government in Nanking, the Ta Hsueh Yuan (University Council) on December 20, 1927, promulgated fifteen regulations for the promotion of modern libraries, which indicate the keen interest shown by educational authorities in the improvement of the library service.

At present, the Chinese libraries, excluding private institutions kept by individuals, may be roughly divided into four main classes, viz., public libraries, college libraries, society libraries, and special libraries.

In the old days, many provincial capitals kept large collections of books printed from wooden blocks made by provincial printing establishments. They were stored in some public hall for the use of scholars. Since 1913 these places have been turned into public libraries. Some of them are maintained by endowments, but most of them are supported with the educational funds of the provinces and are thus under the control of the Commissioners of Education.

The administration of these provincial libraries is mostly not very modern. Not only do they adhere to the closed-shelf system but also they allow no circulation for home use. Some of them even require a small fee for admission. Generally, they have not kept up with recent publications, and there is much red-tape before admitting readers to the stackrooms.

In Peping, there are two large public libraries which serve as good examples illustrating the recent changes and development of modern libraries in China. The National Peping Library is now situated in Chu Jen T'ang, one of the palace buildings in the beautiful Middle Sea. Having a wonderful collection of valuable manuscripts and rare books, it may be compared favorably with the Bibliotheque Nationale or the Vatican Library. It has put up signs along the main streets and has advertised in papers asking the public to go to its reading rooms. It shows how a public library of the old type is changing its traditional policy. The old practice of discouraging the people to use the library has been discarded. The new view of stimulating the love of books and the diffusion of knowledge among the masses is taken up by the present administrators.

Another great institution in Peping is the Metropolitan Library with its site west of Peihai Park. This library has been recently founded and has been supported by the China Foundation for the Promotion of Education and Culture. It is a modem public library. To supplement the existing collection of Chinese books in the National Peping Library and to collect standard books in foreign languages are its main aims. The building, now under construction, is an up-to-date and fireproof structure and the administration is organized along the line of the modern occidental public libraries.

During the last decade the mediaeval idea of a library for the learned few has been broken down, and the intellectual kingdom has opened its gates for the plebians, who are daily getting bolder and wiser. The public library, they feel, should neither collect admission fee nor assess any charge for the use of books. This public feeling has been duly recognized, hence the system of free public libraries has been introduced. Now many public libraries in the provinces and large cities have gradually discarded the policy of charging fees for admission or the use of books.

Generally, a free public library in China allows the readers to use its collections without any charge, but does not permit them to draw books out for home use. In connection with these libraries, there are playgrounds and children's reading rooms. In addition to old Chinese books, many newly published books on various subjects have been bought. The libraries are open on Sundays just as on week days. There are about 88 organized public libraries and 291 free public libraries. Within the latter class, travelling libraries are included.

Side by side with public libraries, many college libraries have sprung into existence. Practically all the college libraries have two parallel collections, one in Chinese and the other in foreign languages. The books in foreign languages are generally classified according to Dewey's Decimal Classification, and Chinese books, according to four main divisions, viz., (1) Classics; (2) History; (3) Philosophy; (4) Belles-lettres. It is nearly unavoidable to have two systems of classifications used side by side in the same library. On the one hand, the nature of old Chinese books is quite different from that of the western; and on the other hand, the ancient classification system of four main classes with subdivisions is by no means adequate for western books. So the difficult task of working out a system of classification suitable for old Chinese books as well as for foreign books is at present confronting Chinese librarians. Many a Chinese librarian has attempted to expand and modify the Decimal Classification to enable it to meet the special situation in China.

About fifteen college libraries now have their own library buildings, and several are making efforts to get enough funds for the erection of modern buildings. Among them the National Central University Library, Nanking, Tsing Hua University Library, Peping, and the Nankai University Library, Tientsin are the only ones equipped with metal stacks.

The third type of libraries existing in China, generally known as society libraries, is only in its early period of development. There are but a few scattered in Peping and in other cities along the coast. The annual expenditures and initial expenses of these libraries are secured either from donations or from the funds of the respective societies. They are, as a rule, used by the members of the society, and their collections of books fall generally into the special fields in which the societies are especially interested. The best known society libraries are the library of the North China Branch of the Royal Asiatic Society (foreign) at Shanghai, the library of the Science Society at Nanking, General Tsai-Soong-Poo Memorial Library, and the library of the Chinese Social and Political Science Association at Peping.

The last named library belongs to the Chinese Social and Political Science Association. It was started largely by a group of "Returned Students", but its final success depended upon the friendly interest taken by the United States of America, the late Imperial Manchu Household and the Carnegie Endowment for International Peace. Dr. Paul S. Reinsch, then the American Minister to China, acting on behalf of his government, agreed to set aside a sum of taels 100,000 from the remitted fund of the Boxer Indemnity as an endowment fund for the library. The Imperial Household kindly donated a centrally located site for a library building. The Carnegie Endowment made a contribution of several thousand volumes in history, social and political sciences, which formed the nucleus of the steadily growing library.

The library of the Science Society at Nanking is now rapidly coming to the front. Its speciality is in the field of natural science. The catalogues and equipment are all up-to-date. It has a fine building and renders efficient library service to its members and the students of science in Nanking. The movement of founding society libraries is now slowly extending to the interior of the country.

In order to promote the knowledge of special subjects, special libraries have been founded. Cities like Peping, Shanghai and Canton are in the lead. There are several well-known special libraries in Peping, namely, the Library of the National Geological Survey, the Library of the Ministry of Communications, the Library of the Ministry of Education, the Library of the Ministry of Foreign Affairs, the Library of the Supreme Court and the Library of the Bureau of Law Codification. The collections of some of these libraries have been removed to the respective offices at Nanking, the new capital of the National Government. The collections thus built up are naturally along the lines of their respective spheres. Only the members of these ministries have the privilege of using the libraries. Generally no books are loaned for home use.

In Shanghai, there are two very interesting special libraries, one under the Chinese General Chamber of Commerce, and the other established and maintained by the Commercial Press.

The library of the Chinese General Chamber of Commerce was founded in the winter of 1921. The Shanghai merchants felt keenly that the business men should not only have a thorough understanding of Chinese affairs, but also a general knowledge of the conditions of foreign commerce. So a business library was established in the building of the Chinese General Chamber of Commerce. This movement has been followed by the Banker's Association of Peping and chambers of commerce in other large cities.

The Library of the Commercial Press, known as the Oriental Library, has a unique feature in that it possesses a large number of rare editions of old books, which have been collected for the purpose of producing facsimile reprints. In addition, the Library has a fine collection of occidental and oriental books for the use of the editorial staff. It has a special building and the books are classified according to the Decimal Classification. It is also open to the public.

A special library for the use of educators was founded in January, 1922, by the Canton authorities. It has two parallel collections of books, one in Chinese and the other in foreign languages, chiefly on education and pedagogy. It acted as a laboratory for the short term library school in Canton. The administration has been up-to-date, and serves as the model library in the province of Kwangtung.

Since the gradual disappearance of the old idea of the librarian as a page to scholars, the demand for trained librarians has been keenly felt. Hence library schools in one form or another have been established to give courses in library science and administration.

The Boone University at Wuchang, Hupeh, now known as Central China University, is the first institution in China to introduce a regular curriculum of library science. It gives a two years' course and admits only students of sophomore standing. Many young librarians now working in different libraries all over the country are the products of the Boone Library School.

In the summer of 1920, the Peking Teachers' College opened the first summer library school. It was a great surprise to all that the enrollment numbered seventy-eight men and women. Most of them were librarians in the various libraries in the different provinces, and were sent up to attend the summer school by local authorities.

In the spring of 1922, a short term course of library science was introduced in Canton by the Provincial Educational Commission under the authority of the civil governor, who ordered all institutions above the middle school grade to send an instructor to the provincial capital to attend the lectures. The school was opened on March 27th and attended by sixty-five representatives from various high schools in the province.

The former National Southeastern University offered courses of library service in its summer schools. The University of Nanking and the College of Education in the National Central University are also giving courses in library service and administration. The aim of these courses is to teach the university students how to use books and libraries rather than to train them as professional librarians.

In order to accelerate the library movement, a Committee on Library Education and Development was organized under the auspices of the Chinese National Association for the Advancement of Education. In July 1922, at Tsinanfu, the librarians of the principal educational institutions came together to discuss the problems relating to the launching of a nation-wide library movement. More than ten resolutions were passed; and a few of the most important ones have been carried out. One of them was to urge the libraries in the metropolitan cities of each province to form local library associations, which were in turn to organize a national library association. Within the last few years, many local library associations have been organized, and the Library Association of China was inaugurated in Peking on June 3rd. 1925. The delegate of the American Library Association, Dr. Arthur E. Bostwick, who was invited to China to make a survey of Chinese libraries and to prepare a report for presentation to the Board of Trustees of the China Foundation, was also present at the occasion.

The Government appropriated a sum of $5,000 to the newly formed national library association to meet initial expenses. Besides the task of compiling bibliographies and editing pamphlets on library administration and economy, the Association issues a bi-monthly bulletin and a quarterly library journal. Due to financial difficulty, it has not been in a position to carry out as many projects as one would wish.

The first Annual Conference of the Library Association of China took place from January 28 to February 1st, 1929, at the University of Nanking. The National Government extended warm receptions to the delegates, besides giving financial support to the Conference. About one hundred and seventy members were present and many important problems of library service and administration were thoroughly discussed. The Conference proved to be a great success.

Since 1914 about twelve Chinese librarians have graduated from the library schools in the United States, and two from the University of the Philippines. They have introduced many new methods of library administration. They are the pioneers in advocating free access and home use of the books in the libraries.

  The progress of the library movement during the last eighteen years has been a slow but steady one, made in spite of financial difficulties and civil wars. The government and the educational leaders now realize that to establish modem libraries all over the country is one of the surest ways to educate the general masses. Modern public libraries are peoples' universities and they will play an ever increasing part in the educational world of China.

        原载：*Libraries in China by Library Association of China* 1929

【译文】贺维平译　姜爱蓉审

中国现代图书馆的发展

戴志骞　文学士、图书馆学学士、哲学博士
（南京）江苏大学区教育行政院督学、
国立中央大学高等教育处处长、国立中央大学图书馆馆长

  1911年辛亥革命以来，中国在政治和文化上经历了一系列变革。中国人民挣脱了封建专制的束缚，也决心从文化樊篱中解放出来。知识分子目睹了许多次革命的失败后，认识到传统思维方式必须彻底转变，为此，政府及教育界领导者担负起了审查现有教育方法和推动全民教育的任务。

  学校的新式教育思想强调学生的自主性而不是生搬硬套课本知识。过去，学生把老师看作是活字典或行走的百科全书，他们盲目信奉从课本或教室里死记硬背下来的东西。今天，高校都采取了选修课制度，重视在课程大纲框架下进行专题研究和相关资料阅读。这种方式不仅鼓励学生进行更多阅读，也推动了我国图书馆的发展与管理。

  目前我国仍有很多收藏图书的场所。尽管年长的学者们仍旧对宋、元、明代珍本感兴趣，老式图书馆也希望只收藏珍贵古籍，但人们希望将厚重门锁阻隔的藏书楼转变为生机而富有吸引力的图书馆，而且这一愿望日益强烈。

  这种变化伴随着"平民教育"这种民主思想而来，之前教育仅对少数打算参加科举考试的人开放，但近年来人们已经意识到大众教育的重要性，并通过采用汉语语音体系、出版白话文书报来传播新知识。那些旨在藏书的旧式图书馆面对外部环境的快速变化，不得不抛弃传统政策，向普通大众打开大门。在过去的15年里，现代图书馆运动已经取得显著进步。

  教育部意识到图书馆的重要性，于1915年4月11日颁布了一道包含11项规定的命令，加强对全国各省份图书馆的创办、组织与管理。为了扩大影响，政府将清代学部附属的京师图书馆改成了公共图书馆，也就是现在的国立北平图书馆。一些省份落实了这一命令，但还有许多地区由于资金有限和受内乱局势影响，未曾建立图书馆。尽管如此，政府在发展现代图书馆方面的努力是值得铭记的。

  南京国民政府成立后，大学院（大学委员会）于1927年12月20日颁布了15项规定来推动现代图书馆发展，这表明了教育当局在改善图书馆服务方面的迫切愿望。

  目前中国的图书馆，不含个人所有的私立机构，大致可以分为四大类：公共图书馆、学校图书馆、社团图书馆和专业图书馆。

  之前，省会城市收藏了大量由省印刷厂木版印刷的图书，这些图书存放在公共大厅供学者使用。1913年以来，这些场所被改造成公共图书馆。一些图书馆依靠捐赠来维持运营，大部分依靠省里的教育经费支持，因此由教育专员掌管。

  这些省立图书馆的管理谈不上现代化，不仅坚持闭架管理，也不允许把图书借回家，有的还收取少量入馆使用费。通常这些图书馆不能及时入藏最新图书，并设有各种条条框框限制读者进入书库。

在北平,有两家大型公共图书馆堪称是彰显现代图书馆变革与发展的典范。国立北平图书馆位于居仁堂——美丽的中海的一座宫殿里,拥有许多贵重手稿和珍本,也许可与法国国家图书馆或梵蒂冈图书馆媲美。该馆在主要街道沿路挂牌及在报上刊登告示邀请人们去其图书馆,彰显了一座旧式的公共图书馆如何改变它的传统政策。以往限制人们使用图书馆的旧式做法已经被摒弃了,管理者们已经接受了要激发人们热爱图书、向大众传播知识的新观念。

在北平的另一家大型图书馆是位于北海公园西边的北海图书馆。该图书馆新近成立,由中华教育文化基金会支持,是一座现代化的图书馆。它主要是补充收藏国立北平图书馆没有的中文书籍,以及收藏权威性外文图书。该图书馆建筑目前正在修缮中,是一座现代化的防火建筑,其管理符合西方公共图书馆的理念。

在过去十年里,图书馆仅为少数精英学者服务这一中世纪以来的观念被打破,知识宝殿的大门朝日益智慧的平民百姓敞开。人们认为公共图书馆不应当收取入馆费或图书使用费。这一想法被及时认可,免费使用公共图书馆的制度开始实行。现在大城市的许多图书馆也逐步取消了入馆费或图书使用费。

我国免费的公共图书馆通常允许读者不花任何费用使用其收藏,但不允许他们把书借回家。这些图书馆还设立了儿童游玩场所和儿童阅览室。除了老的中文书外,还购买了许多新近出版的各科图书。图书馆周日也像平时那样开放。目前约有88座有组织的公共图书馆和291座免费的公共图书馆,后者包括了旅游类图书馆。

在公共图书馆快速发展的同时,许多大学图书馆也不断涌现。几乎所有大学图书馆都并行发展两部分馆藏:中文馆藏和外文馆藏。外文图书主要按照《杜威十进分类法》分类,中文图书分为四大类:经、史、子、集。同一个图书馆几乎不可避免地需要使用两套分类体系。一方面,老式中文图书的特点不同于西文书;另一方面,四个大类加细目的古老分类体系完全不能满足西文书的要求。因此开发一套既适合中文图书又适合西文图书的分类法是摆在中国图书馆员面前的难题。许多中国图书馆员尝试扩充、修改十进制分类法以满足中国图书馆的特殊需要。

约有15所大学图书馆拥有自己的馆舍,还有一些在争取足够资金来修建现代化大楼。其中国立中央大学图书馆(南京)、清华大学图书馆(北平)和南开大学图书馆(天津)采用的是金属书架。

我国的第三类图书馆通常认为是社团图书馆,尚处在早期发展阶段,零星分布在北平和一些沿海城市。这些图书馆的年度经费和主要开销或者来自捐赠或者来自某些社团,图书馆也通常由社团成员使用,收藏基本上限于社团感兴趣的领域。最有名的社团图书馆有:设在上海的(英国)皇家亚洲文会北中国支会图书馆、设在南京的中国科学社图书馆,以及北平的松坡图书馆(为纪念蔡锷将军而建)、中国社会政治学会图书馆。

最后命名的中国社会政治学会图书馆隶属于中国社会政治学会,主要由一群"归国留学生"发起,但其最终成立有赖于美国、前清皇室以及卡内基世界和平基金会的友好支持。时任美国驻华公使的芮恩施(Paul S. Reinsch)博士代表美国政府,同意从返还的庚子赔款中拨出10万银两捐赠给图书馆。前清皇室热心捐出了中心地带的一个处所作为图书馆大楼,卡内基基金会捐赠了数千册历史、社会学和政治学图书,这些作为后来图书馆馆藏稳步发展的起点。

位于南京的科学社图书馆发展迅速、崭露头角。收藏领域为自然科学,编目和设备均是新式的,建筑设计精巧,为南京的会员和该学科领域的学生提供高效服务。建立社团图书馆的风潮逐渐延伸到内陆地区。

为了促进专业学科知识的传播建立专业图书馆,以北平、上海、广州三个城市领先。在北平有几个知名的专业图书馆,例如国家地质调查所图书馆、交通部图书馆、教育部图书馆、外交部图书馆、最高法院图书馆、法律编纂局图书馆。这些图书馆中有些图书馆的收藏被转移到国民政府的新首都南京的各个办事处,并相应地根据各个领域来发展收藏,只有各个部委的成员才有资格使用,一般不外借。

上海有两个很有意思的专业图书馆,一个属于中华总商会,一个由商务印书馆建立和运营。

中华总商会图书馆成立于1921年冬。上海的商人们敏锐地意识到商人不仅要对中国事物有透彻了解,还要对外贸情况有大体认识,因此在中华总商会的大楼里成立了商业图书馆。这一行动为北平银行家协会以及其他大城市的商会效仿。

商务印书馆图书馆,即东方图书馆,其独特之处是拥有大量用于制作复印本的古籍珍本。此外,还拥有供编辑人员使用的优质中西文图书,以及设计独特的建筑大楼。图书依据十进制分类法分类,面向大众开放。

1922年1月广州当局专门为教育工作者建立了一座特别的图书馆,拥有中外文两类馆藏,主要是有关教育和教学法的。该图书馆用作广州短期图书馆学校的实习场所,采用现代化管理,在广东省起到样板作用。

对图书馆员的旧式看法逐渐改变,学者们很快意识到对训练有素的图书馆员的需求。因此各种形式的图书馆学校建立起来,开设了图书馆学与管理方面的课程。

位于湖北武昌的文华大学,即如今的华中大学,是我国第一个引进正规图书馆学课程的机构,提供两年的课程,只接收大学二年级及以上学生。如今许多在全国各处图书馆工作的年轻馆员都是从这所学校毕业。

1920年夏天,北京高等师范学校(1923年更名为北京师范大学)开辟了第一个暑期图书馆学校。招生人数意外地达到78人,大部分是来自不同省份各个图书馆的馆员,由地方当局选派。

1922年春,在省长督导下,广东省教委在广州引入了短期图书馆学课程,规定初中以上级别的所有机构均派一名教员到省城参加课程学习。学校3月27日开学,全省各个高中的65位代表参加了培训。

前国立东南大学在暑期提供图书馆服务方面的课程,南京大学和国立中央大学教育学院也提供图书馆服务与管理方面的课程,目的是教育学生如何利用图书和图书馆,而不是培训他们成为专业的图书馆员。

为了加速图书馆事业的发展,在中华教育改进社发起成立了"图书馆教育组"。1922年7月,主要教育机构的图书馆员汇聚在济南探讨发起全国性图书馆运动的相关事宜。会议通过了10余项决议,部分重要决议得以实施。决议之一是敦促各省主要城市的图书馆成立图书馆协会,这些协会再组成一个全国性的图书馆协会。近几年,许多地方性图书馆协会已经成立,1925年6月3日中华图书馆协会正式成立。美国图书馆协会派出的代表鲍士伟博士(Arthur E. Bostwick)出席了大会,他曾应邀来我国考察图书馆状况,为向中华基金理事会汇报作准备。

　　政府拨出5000美元给新成立的中华图书馆协会作为启动经费。除了编纂书目和制作图书馆管理与运营方面的小册子外，协会还发行《中华图书馆协会会报》和《图书馆学季刊》。由于经费困难，不能如愿开展更多项目。

　　中华图书馆协会第一届年会于1929年1月28日至2月1日在南京大学召开。国民政府除了对会议给予经济支持外，还热情招待了与会代表。约170名会员出席，深入讨论了图书馆服务与管理方面的许多重要问题。会议非常成功。

　　1914年以来约有12名中国图书馆员从美国图书馆学校毕业，以及2名从菲律宾大学毕业。他们带回了许多图书馆管理的新方法，是倡导免费借阅与外借服务的先行者。

　　18年来，图书馆运动发展缓慢却平稳，尽管期间遇到经济困难和国内战争。政府官员和教育界领导者都认识到在全国建立现代化图书馆是教育民众的最可靠方式之一。现代化的公共图书馆是人民群众的大学，将发挥越来越大的教育作用。

原载：中国图书馆协会编　《中国图书馆》　1929年

China's Finance and Banking

By T. C. TAI

In presenting this brief account of American university men in China's finance and banking, I have constantly kept in my mind a rigorous standard of selection. I have followed consistently the principle that quality is better than quantity. Although it happens that all the representatives mentioned in this article have held or are holding very important positions, mere exaltation in official rank is not the primary reason for their selection. My chief emphasis has been placed upon the constructive influence a person has exerted in the realm of financial thinking as well as action. I have taken into special consideration initiative of, or responsibility for, certain financial and banking reforms that have contributed to the transformation of China from a medieval to something near a modern economy. With this object in view, I shall limit my narration to the following men who, historians will probably agree, have made contributions which will undoubtedly be remembered in China's finance and banking for years to come.

1. CHEN CHIN-TAO(陈锦涛). Courtesy name: Lan-sheng(澜生).

Dr. Chen was born in Nanhai, Kwangtung, 1870. He graduated from Queen's College, Hongkong, and for sometime was professor at Peiyang University, Tientsin. He went to America as a government student in 1901. Having received his Master's degree in mathematics and social sciences at Columbia University in 1902, he went to Yale University where he majored in political economy and was graduated with Ph. D. degree in 1906. He returned to China in the same year and was made in Hanlin Compiler by the Imperial Court. Under the Manchu regime, he held the following important positions: inspector of the Ta-ching Government Bank, chairman of the Currency Reform Commission, vice-governor of the Ta-ching Government Bank and vice-president of the Board of Finance. In 1912 he was made minister of finance of the Provisional Republican Government and director of the Audit Bureau under the cabinet. In that year he also represented China at the International Conference of Chambers of Commerce in Boston, Massachusetts, USA. In 1913 he went to Europe as China's financial commissioner. During 1916-17 he was minister of finance and concurrently director-general of the Salt Administration. From June to October, 1916, the portfolio of the minister of foreign affairs was added to his already heavy responsibilities. In 1920 he was minister of finance of the Canton Military Government and in 1926 was reappointed minister of finance of the Peking Government. From 1926 to 1935 his official career had a temporary eclipse. In January 1935 he was called from his retirement to be chairman of the Currency Committee under the Ministry of Finance of the National Government.

Dr. Chen is author of *Societary Circulation*, *Public Schools in the Four Countries* and *Distribution of Wealth*, the first one being his doctoral dissertation. However, it is in his comprehensive memorandum presented to the Peking Government, while Minister of Finance, that he showed his statesmanship and his penetration into the pressing problems of China's finance and banking. In this memorandum he suggested many important reforms, such as: curtailment of military expenditure, tax reforms, adoption of budgetary procedure, unification of the national treasury, improvement of national credit, centralization of note issue and strengthening of the Bank of China and the Bank of Communications by increasing their capital. Due to the brevity and the frequent interruptions of his tenure of office and the chaotic conditions of the country at that time, his plans were not carried out. His far-sightedness however has been amply proved by the fact that most of his suggestions have been embodied in the reforms executed in the past few years.

2. CHEN HUI-TEH(陈辉德). Courtesy name: Kuang-fu(光甫). Prefers English rendering: K. P. Chen.

Mr. Chen was born at Chinkiang, Kiangsu, in 1880. He studied at the University of Pennsylvania from which he received the degree of B. S. in commerce in 1909. After his return to China, he was chief of Foreign Affairs Department of the Nan-yang Industrial Exhibition, deputy director of the Financial Re-organization Bureau of Kiangsu, assistant commissioner of finance of Kiangsu, supervisor of the Kiangsu Bank, director of the same bank and advisor to the Bank of China.

In 1915 he organized, with the help of a small number of friends, the Shanghai Bank Commercial and Savings Bank, popularly known as the Shanghai Bank, of which he became one of the managing directors and the general manager. These posts he has held up to the present without interruption. Other concurrent positions, which he has held at one time or another, include: advisor to the Financial Rehabilitation Commission of Peiping, chief advisor to the Tariff Commission, chairman of the Financial Commission for Kiangsu, director of the Central Bank of China, managing director of the Bank of China, the Bank of Communications and the Chekiang Industrial Bank, member of the Kiangsu Financial Commission, the Kiangsu Reconstruction Commission and the Commission for the Irrigation of the Hwai River, supervisor of the Kiangsu Agricultural Bank, representative at the International Labor Conference at Geneva and the international Commercial Conference in Holland, and president and general manager of the Kuo Ming Bank at Hsuchow which is affiliated with Shanghai Bank.

In 1929 and 1930 he toured the world to study banking, industrial and commercial conditions and practices in foreign countries. At the time of this writing, Mr. Chen, as head of the Chinese Bankers Mission to Washington, has just completed his negotiations with the United States Treasury on currency matters. He has been offered the post of vice-minister of finance and other high positions by the Government since 1926, but he has persistently declined positions which would prevent him from concentrating his attention upon his bank for any length of time.

Though Mr. Chen has rendered meritorious service in connection with the many capacities in which he has been called to serve, his outstanding contributions are naturally connected with the Shanghai Bank of which he is the life and soul. It may be said that, under Mr. Chen's progressive leadership, his bank blazed the way of modern banking in China. It introduced the teller system so that the waste of time involved in the old practice of handing in checks at one place on the counter and collecting cash at another place was eliminated. It established a special school for the training of staff members, and it is the first banking institution in China to recognize the usefulness of returned students from Europe and America. In 1923, it organized a Travel Service Department, which has evolved into the present China Travel Service with its network of branches in all principal cities in China. It has also made special provisions to grant loans to customers on a credit basis and to open small savings accounts as low as one dollar, thus making the service of the Shanghai Bank accessible to the masses of the population. Finally, it pioneered in granting loans for agricultural relief, the necessity of which has now been recognized by both the Government and other banks. The fact that in the past twenty years the capital of the Shanghai Bank has increased from $100,000 to $5,000,000 and its deposits from $50,000 to $150,000,000 bears ample testimonial to its phenomenal growth and the fulfillment of a vision long entertained by its founder and general manager.

3. SUNG TSE-WEN(宋子文). Prefers anglicized Shanghai rendering: T. V. Soong.

Dr. Soong was born in Shanghai in 1894. He received his early education under private auspices and at St. John's University. He went to the United States in 1915, attending Harvard University from which he received the degree of B. A. He did graduate work at Columbia University, and at the same time served on the staff of several New York leading banking houses. Upon returning to China, he joined the Han-Yeh-Ping Coal and Iron Works at Hankow as secretary. Later he was made general manager of the International Trading Corporation. He went to Canton at the time of the organization of the Nationalist Government and served as director of the Department of Commerce and organizer and general manager of the Central Government Bank. Later, he was commissioner of finance for Kwangtung and in 1926 was appointed minister of finance of the Nationalist Government. In the spring of 1927, he resigned from the Nationalist Government at Hankow and in the fall of that year joined the Nanking Government as minister of finance, a position which he held, with only a brief interruption, till October, 1933. It was during his term as minister of finance that St. John's University in Shanghai conferred on him an LL. D. degree(1929) in recognition of his meritorious service. While he was minister of finance of the National Government, he also served for sometime concurrently as vice-president, later acting president, of the Executive Yuan and the governor of the Central Bank of China. In 1933 he attended the World Economic Conference at London as the head of the Chinese delegation. He has been an executive member of the National Economic Council since 1932 and chairman of the board of directors of the Bank of China since 1935.

Dr. Soong's contributions to China's finance and banking are numerous. Only the most important ones will be mentioned here. In 1928 he established the Central Bank of China with a paid-up capital of $20,000,000 appropriated from the National Treasury. This bank was granted special rights to issue bank notes, to mint and issue coins, to act as a fiscal agent of the Government and to raise, collect, or manage domestic and foreign loans of the Government. In 1934 the capital of this institution was increased to $100,000,000. It has recently assumed the functions of a central reserve bank and it now stands as a powerful stabilizing force in China's financial structure.

Another notable contribution to Chinese currency and banking made by Dr. Soong is the abolition of the tael. Prior to this memorable event, the Shanghai money market was the most complicated affair with its simultaneous use of the tael, the transfer tael, the dollar and the transfer dollar. Dr. Soong's bold stroke marked the first step in the simplification and rationalization of Chinese currency.

In the field of government finance, Dr Soong's contributions are also significant. He brought about the demarcation of the central and local revenues. He unified and simplified the Chinese taxation system. In 1930 he adopted the Custom's Gold Unit in the calculation of China's tariff duties so that customs revenues were freed from the erratic fluctuations in the price of silver. In 1931 he abolished likin so that a serious impediment to internal movement of trade was removed. In 1932 he adopted a plan whereby the interest rate of Government bonds was reduced to a flat 6% per annum and the current payments for amortization of principal were also reduced through lengthening the terms of the loans. By this operation the Government saved almost $100,000,000 annually in debt charges. Finally, he introduced budgetary reforms and early in 1932 achieved the surprising feat of being able to balance the national budget for the first time in the twenty-one years of the Republic at a time of world economic depression when practically every government had large deficits and when, in addition to depression, the Chinese Government had to confront the colossal burden of the 1931 flood, the slump in silver, the Japanese seizure of the revenue in Manchuria and the attack on Shanghai.

4. KUNG HSIANG-HSI(孔祥熙). Courtesy name: Yung-chih(庸之). Prefers English rendering: H. H. Kung.

Dr. Kung was born at Taiku, Shansi, in 1881. He is the 75th descendant of Confucius. He received his B. A. from Oberlin College in 1906, M. A. from Yale University in 1907, and LL. D. from Oberlin College in 1926. He was in command of the volunteers of Shansi during the Revolution in 1911 which overthrew the Manchu Dynasty. Upon the establishment of the Republic, he introduced many reforms into Shansi under the administration of General Yen Shih-shan, including the establishment of the Oberlin Shansi Memorial School in his own city. After the Washington Conference when Shantung was returned to China by Japan, he served as chief of the Industrial Department of the Shantung Rehabilitation Commission. Upon the conclusion of this important commission, he was appointed assistant director of the Sino-Russian negotiations. When Dr. Sun Yatsen set up his Military Government in Canton, Dr Kung became finance commissioner of the Provincial Government of Kwangtung, holding concurrently the offices of minister of finance as well as minister of industry of the Nationalist Government. In 1927 when the Nationalist Government was formally inaugurated in Nanking, he was made the first minister of industry, commerce and labor, which office he held up to December, 1930. When the Ministries of Industry, Commerce, and Labor and of Agriculture and

Mining were amalgamated into the Ministry of Industries, he was appointed minister of the same, which post he held up to the end of 1931. In 1932 he was appointed industrial commissioner to Europe and America. Upon the resignation of Dr T. V. Soong from his concurrent post as governor of the Central Bank of China, Dr. Kung was appointed governor of that bank. In November 1933 he became minister of finance of the National Government and concurrently vice-president of the Executive Yuan.

As a minister of finance, Dr. Kung executed several important reforms in Chinese finance and banking. From July 1934 to May 1935 he abolished over 5,000 kinds of exorbitant and miscellaneous levies, and in this way saved for the taxpayers of China some 49,000,000 dollars. He reformed the Salt Administration and local taxation practices. He consolidated and converted Government bonds(1936), securing for the Government a sorely needed relief by postponing interest and amortization payments. He established the Manufacturers' Bank of China(1928), the Central Trust of China(1935) and the Central Saving Society(1936).

It was with his currency reforms, however, that Dr. Kung's influences were felt not only locally but internationally as well. Due to the severe drain of China's silver reserve brought about by a persistent unfavorable balance of trade and America's silver-purchasing program, Dr. Kung ordered in October 1934 a tax on the export of silver and an equalization charge equal to the deficiency existing between the theoretical parity of London silver and a rate of exchange officially fixed after making allowance for the export duty. This step checked the outflow of silver and marked the beginning of the departure of the Chinese currency from a metallic base. In November 1935, this process was consummated by a decree of the Ministry of Finance nationalizing silver and making the notes of the Central Bank of China, the Bank of China and the Bank of Communications legal tender. Dr. Kung, therefore, achieved the distinction of being the minister of finance who definitely put China on a "managed currency basis".

In conclusion I must call the attention of my readers to the fact that though so far only a few American university men—I have confined the scope of my article to Chinese—have come to the front and have won national reputation in China's finance and banking, time is still too short for the majority of American returned students to demonstrate in a spectacular way their usefulness to their country. In the field of government finance, conditions favorable for constructive statesmanship have prevailed only in the past seven or eight years. During this period outstanding contributions have been made by two American university men, whose careers have already been mentioned. Lesser lights in this field, who deserve honorable mention include: Mr. F. Chin, secretary-general of the National Economic Council; Mr. F. Y. Chang, former superintendent of the Customs Administration and now director of the Research Department of the Bank of China and Mr. Loy Chang, superintendent of the Customs Administration. In the realm of financial thinking worthwhile contributions have been made by Dr. Y. C. Ma and Messrs. T. S. Wei, C. H. Chen, Y. C. Ku and D. K. Lieu. In local finance, American university men have also made considerable headway. Messrs. J. S. Yin, Y. F. Chen, H. J. Ho, T. H. Chao and T. C. Chen have all reached the status of provincial commissioners of finance.

Due to the advantage of earlier start, Japanese returned students greatly outnumber American returned students regarding leadership in the field of banking. However, the influence of American university men in the banking field has been growing very rapidly. Even if one should forget for the time being the remarkable achievement of Mr. K. P. Chen, one will still find American university men an immense force, actual as well as potential, in Chinese banks. Among those who have reached managerial positions I may mention Mr. Jian Chen, deputy governor of the Central Bank of China; Mr T. L. Soong, general manager of the Manufacturers' Bank and concurrently general manager of the China Development Finance Corporation; Mr. Z. S. Bien, manager of the Tientsin Branch of the Bank of China; Mr. Fredrick Sze, assistant general manager of the Joint Savings Society; Mr. T. S. Wong, general manager of the Sin Hua Trust and Savings Bank; Mr. Lane Van, manager of the China Development Bank; Mr. Stone Lok, general manager of the Kiangsu Bank; Mr. U. B. Hsu, manager of the Chekiang Provincial Bank; Mr. Y. T. Miao, general manager of the New Fu Tien Bank, Yunnan, and Mr. S. C. Wei, general manager of the Frontier Bank, Tientsin. Mr. Percy Chu, manager of the Joint Reserve Board of the Chinese Bankers' Association has been a very energetic promoter and organizer of inter-bank clearings and acceptance, and in this way has contributed his share in modernizing the banking system in China.

Many American university men are occupying positions as specialists in one filed or another connected with banking operations. To give a sample of this type of ability, I may mention Messrs. L. T. Shen, T. When Chu and Chester Huang of foreign exchange and Messrs. T. S. Wong, P. W. Tsou and C. C. Chang of rural economy.

Nor are American university men inadequately represented in the brokerage field. Here we find Messrs. Tom Z. Wang, and K. S. Lee among those who have already made their names known.

There are many more American university men of first class ability who are occupying secondary positions at present and who will naturally come to the front in the next ten or fifteen years. In fact, when one thinks of this class of reserve material, one cannot help marveling at the vast influence which will be exerted by American university men in China's finance and banking in the near future.

Shanghai, June, 16, 1936.

BIBLIOGRAPHY

1. Bankers' Year Book, Research Department, Bank of China, 1935.
2. Recent History of Banking and Finance in Shanghai, by Hsu Chi-Chin, Commercial Press Ltd. Or the Bankers' Association, Shanghai. Hsu Chi-Chin.
3. History of Finance of the Republic of China, by Chia Shihyi, Vol. I., Commercial Press Ltd., Shanghai, China.
4. Report to the Plenary Session of the Central Executive Committee of the Kuomintang for the 19 and the 20th Fiscal Years, (July, 1930 to June, 1932), by T. V. Soong, Minister of Finance.
5. Report to the political Council of the Central Executive Committee of the Kuomintang for the 21st and 22nd Fiscal Years (July, 1932 to June, 1934) by H. H. Kung, Minister of Finance.
6. The China Press, July 19, 1831.

7. The China Year Book, edited by H. G. W. Woodhead, year 1926-35, the North China Daily News & Herald Ltd., 17 the Bund, Shanghai. H. G. W. Woodhead.
8. The New Monetary Policy of China, Currency Reserve Board, Shanghai, 1935.
9. Two years of Nationalist China, by M. T. Z. Tyau, Chapter IV, Kelly & Walsh Ltd., Shanghai.
10. Who's Who in China, The China Weekly Review, Shanghai.

原载:*American University Men in China*. The Comacrib Press. Shanghai, 1936 年

【译文】贺维平译

中国的金融与银行业

本文简述了中国金融与银行业的留美人士。在人物选取时一直遵循严格的标准,质量重于数量。尽管文中选取的代表人物曾经或仍然在很重要职位上,但其职位高低不是选择的主要标准,着重看他们是否对金融理论或实务有重大影响,特别是是否发起或负责过某一项金融或银行改革,推动了中国经济从封建旧经济模式向现代化经济模式转变。因此,本文记述了这些人:他们曾在中国金融与银行业做出了值得铭记的贡献——史学家也多半会认可这一点。

1. 陈锦涛,字澜生

陈博士 1870 年生于广东南海,毕业于香港皇仁书院,曾在天津北洋大学担任过一段时间教习。1901 年他由政府公派留学美国,1902 年在哥伦比亚大学获得数学与社会学硕士学位,然后在耶鲁大学主修政治经济学,1906 年获得博士学位。他同年回到中国,入清廷翰林院。在清朝政权下,他担任了如下重要职务:大清银行稽核、币制改良委员会会长、大清银行副监督、度支部副大臣。1912 年他被任命为中华民国临时政府的财政总长及财政部审计处总办。同年他代表中国出席了在美国马萨诸塞州波士顿举行的商务部国际会议。1913 年他作为中国财政专员外派欧洲。1916—1917 年,他担任财政总长和盐务署督办。1916 年 6—10 月,他业已繁重的职务中又添了外交总长一职。1920 年他担任广州军政府的财政总长,1926 年被重新任命为北平政府的财政总长。1926—1935 年,他的职业生涯出现暂时黯淡,1935 年 1 月,他从隐退状态被召回担任南京国民政府财政部币制委员会主席。

陈博士是《社会循环》、《四国公立学校》(*Public Schools in the Four Countries*)、《均富》的作者,其中第一部是他的博士论文。然而,他是在任财政部部长时提交给北平政府的众多内容丰富的便函中,展示了自己的政治才干和对中国金融与银行业紧迫问题的洞察力。在便函中,他提出了很多重要的改革建议,比如缩减军费、改革税务、采用预算制度、统一国库、提高国家信用、通货发行权的中央集中,以及通过增加资本金来提高中国银行和交通银行的实力。由于他的任期短暂并被频繁打断,以及当时国内局势动乱,他的这些计划没能实施。然而,大部分的这些建议在后来的改革中被采纳,这充分证明了他的远见卓识。

2. 陈辉德,字光甫,喜欢用英文译名 K. P. Chen

陈先生 1880 年生于江苏镇江,曾在宾夕法尼亚大学(沃顿商学院)学习并于 1909 年获得商学学士学位。回国后,他担任南洋劝业会外事科主任、江苏金融重组局副局长(Deputy Director of the Financial Re-organization Bureau of Kiangsu)、江苏助理财政司长(Assistant Commissioner of Finance of Kiangsu)、江苏省银行监督和总经理、中国银行顾问。

1915 年,在几个朋友的帮助下,他组建了上海商业储蓄银行,即大众熟知的上海银行,他是常务理事之一,并担任总经理之职。这些职位他没有间断地一直担任。期间他陆续担任的其他职务包括:北平金融复苏委员会顾问(Advisor to the Financial Rehabilitation Commission of Peiping),关税委员会首席顾问(Chief Advisor to the Tariff Commission),江苏财政委员会主任,中央银行理事,中国银行、交通银行和浙江实业银行常务理事,江苏财政委员会、江苏重建委员会和导淮委员会委员,江苏农业银行监督,在瑞士日内瓦召开的国际劳工大会和在荷兰召开的国际商务大会的代表,位于徐州、隶属于上海银行的国明银行总裁兼总经理。

1929年和1930年他出访国外,了解国外银行业、工业与商业的状况及运作。本人撰写此文时,陈先生作为中国银行家代表团团长出访华盛顿,刚结束与美国财政部就货币问题的谈判。自1926年起,政府曾授予他财政部次长及其他高级职位,但他一律婉辞了这些可能妨碍他专注于银行业的职位,哪怕时间很短。

尽管陈先生在委任给他的许多其他职务上也取得了令人赞许的功绩,但他的突出贡献当然还是与被他视为生命和灵魂的上海银行紧密相联。也许可以这么说,在陈先生卓有成效的领导下,上海银行开拓出了一条中国现代银行业之路。上海银行通过引进出纳系统,淘汰了旧模式下在柜台的一处验收支票而在另一处领取现金的做法,节约了时间。创建了一所专门学校来培训工作人员,这是中国第一家认识到欧美归国留学生价值的银行机构。1923年,组建了旅行部,后来演变为现在的中国旅行社,网络遍布全国主要城市。它制定了专门条款,基于信用为客户提供贷款,开通低至1美元的存款账户,因此普通大众都能够使用上海银行的服务。最后,它首次为农业救援(agricultural relief)提供贷款,政府及其他银行现在也认识到了这种必要性。过去20年,上海银行的资本金从10万美元增加到500万美元,存款从5万美元增加到1500万美元,这充分显示了它的惊人成长,以及它的创始人、总经理实现了自己的长期抱负。

3. 宋子文,喜欢用英国式上海化的名字:T. V. Soong

宋博士1894年生于上海,在私立学校圣约翰大学接受教育。他1915年去了美国,进入哈佛大学学习并获得文学士。他在哥伦比亚大学读研究生,同时在纽约几家主要银行兼职。一回到中国,他加入位于汉口的汉冶萍煤铁矿产公司,担任秘书,后来被任命为商务所(the International Trading Corporation)的总经理。在广州国民政府成立时期,他去了广州,担任商务厅长以及中央银行的筹办者和总经理。后来他担任广东省财政厅长,1926年被任命为国民政府的财政部长。1927年春他从汉口国民政府辞职,同年秋加入南京政府担任财政部长,在这个职位上直到1933年10月,期间仅有一次短暂的中断。在此期间,位于上海的圣约翰大学于1929年授予他法学博士学位(LL. D.)以表彰他的突出业绩。担任国民政府财政部长的同时,他也担任过行政院的副院长和代理院长,以及中央银行行长。1933年他作为中国代表团团长去伦敦参加世界经济会议。从1932年以来他一直是国家经济委员会的执行委员之一,自1935年以来是中国银行董事会主席。

宋博士对中国金融与银行业的贡献不计其数,这里仅记述最重要的几项。1928年他建立了中央银行,实收资本为国库拨来的2000万美元。该银行被授予一些特殊权利:发行钞票,铸造和发行硬币,承担政府的财政代理,发行、回收和管理国内外公债。1934年中央银行的资本金增加到1亿美元,近年来承担着中央储备银行的功能,成为中国金融体系中一支强大的稳定力量。

宋博士对中国货币和银行业的另一项著名贡献是废止了银两的使用。在这一具纪念意义的事件之前,上海货币市场十分混乱,同时流通银两、银元、硬币(dollar)和纸币(transfer dollar)。宋博士的大胆举措标志着中国货币简化与合理化的开始。

宋博士在政府财政方面也有很突出的贡献。他将中央收入与地方收入分开,还统一和简化了中国的税收体系。1930 年他采用了海关金单位制度来计算关税,这样海关收入不再受银价无序波动的影响。1931 年他废除了厘金制,消除了这一严重阻碍内部贸易的障碍。1932 年,他实施了一项计划,将政府公债的利率降至固定的年利 6%,通过延长贷款期限来降低本金分期偿还的当前支付额,政府因此每年在债务支出上节省了 1 亿美元。最后,他推行预算改革,早在 1932 年就取得了惊人成果,中华民国 21 年来第一次实现国家收支平衡,而且当时正处世界经济危机,几乎所有国家都有大量赤字,除此之外,中国政府还面临 1931 年洪灾、银根疲软、日本攫取了满洲里收入并进攻上海等巨大困难。

4. 孔祥熙,字庸之,喜欢用英文译名 H. H. Kung

孔博士 1881 年生于山西太古,是孔子的第 75 代嫡孙。1906 年他从欧柏林学院获得文学学士学位,1907 年在耶鲁大学获得文学硕士学位,1926 年接受欧柏林学院授予的法学博士学位(LL. D.)。在 1911 年推翻清朝政权的辛亥革命中,他领导着山西的义勇队。中华民国建立后,他为当时处在阎锡山将军政权下的山西引进了许多项革新,其中包括在家乡建立铭贤学校。华盛顿会议后山东从日本手里归还中国,他出任山东复兴委员会产业部主任(Chief of the Industrial Department of the Shantung Rehabilitation Commission),该重要任期一结束,他被任命为中俄谈判的助理主任。当孙逸仙博士在广州建立军政府时,孔博士担任广东省财政厅长,同时担任广州国民政府的财政部长和产业部长。1927 年国民政府在南京正式成立,他被任命为第一任工商部长,这个职位他一直担任到 1930 年 12 月。当该部门与农矿业部合并为实业部,他继续担任部长,直到 1931 年底。1932 年他被任命为实业特使去欧美。当宋子文博士辞去中央银行行长一职后,该职位由孔博士担任。1933 年 11 月,他成为国民政府财政部长兼行政院副院长。

作为财政部长,孔博士完成了中国金融界几项重要的改革。1934 年 7 月到 1935 年 5 月,他废止了 5000 余种苛捐杂税,为中国的纳税人节约了 4900 万美元。他改革了政府及地方税收做法,合并与调换公债(1936 年),通过延缓利息和分期偿还来缓解政府财政上的燃眉之急。他创立了中国国货银行(the Manufacturers' Bank of China,1928 年)、中央信托局(1935 年)和中央储蓄会(1936 年)。

不过孔博士的影响遍及海内外还是因为他的货币改革。由于持续的贸易逆差和美国推行银两收购计划,我国的白银严重外流,1934 年 10 月孔博士对白银出口实行征税,以及加征平衡税,即"如伦敦银价折合上海汇兑之比价与中央银行当日照市核定之汇价相差之数,除缴纳上述出口税,而仍有不足时,应按其不足之数,并行加征平衡税"。这项措施遏制了银两外流,标志着中国通货开始脱离银本位的格局。1935 年 11 月,财政部颁发通告:将银两收归国有,规定以中央银行、中国银行和交通银行所发行之钞票为"法币",这为货币改革划上了完满的句号。为此孔博士赢得了美誉,他作为财政部长,无疑带领中国进入了可控货币轨道。

最后,必须提醒读者,尽管到目前为止只有少数留美归国人士——本文将其范围局限在中国人——在中国金融界崭露头角、赢得声誉,但对于大多数留美归国学生来说,有利于他们为国家做出突出贡献的时间仍然太短了。在政府金融领域,也就最近七八年时间才具备条件供他们施展建设性政治干才。在这段时间里,两位留美人士已经取得了杰出贡献,他们的经历上文已经记述。在这一领域值得一提的人士还有:国家经济委员会的秘书长秦汾(Chin F.),前任关务署署长、现任中国银行经济研究室主任张福运(Chang F. Y.),现任关务署署长 Chang Loy。在金融思想领域做出重要贡献的有:马寅初(Ma Y. C.)、魏易(字冲叔,Wei T. S.)、陈振先(Chen C. H.)、Ku Y. C. 和刘大钧(Lieu D. K.)。在地方金融领域,留美人士也取得了很大进展,Yin J. S.、Chen Y. F.、Ho H. J.、Chao T. H. 和 Chen T. C. 均做到省财政厅长的位置。

由于去日本留学开始得更早,在银行业担任领导职务的留日学生大大超过了留美学生,不过银行业留美学生的影响力发展很快。即便一时忘了陈光甫先生的非凡成就,人们还是会发现留美人士在我国银行中现实的和潜在的巨大力量。在已经取得管理职位的人士中还要提到这几位:中央银行副行长陈行(Chen Jian)、中国国货银行和中国建设银公司的总经理宋子良(Soong T. L.),中国银行天津分行经理卞寿孙(Bien Z. S.),联合储蓄会的助理总经理 Sze Fredrick,新华信托储蓄银行总经理 Wong T. S.,中国开发银行(The China Development Bank)的经理 Van Lane,江苏银行总经理 Lok Stone,浙江省银行经理徐恩培(Hsu U. B.),富滇新银行行长缪云台(Miao Y. T.),天津边业银行总经理韦锡九(Wei S. C.)。上海银行业同业公会联合准备委员会经理朱博泉(Chu Percy),是一位银行间结算与验收的积极推动者、组织者,为我国银行系统的现代化做出了贡献。

许多留美归国人士成为与银行业相关的某个领域内的专业人士,例如外汇领域的 Shen L. T.、Chu T. When 和 Huang Chester,农村经济领域的 Wong T. S.、邹秉文(Tsou P. W.)和 Chang C. C.。①

留美归国人士在经纪领域也同样可圈可点,这里列举 Wang Tom Z. 和 Lee K. S. 作为众多知名人士的代表。

目前,还有许多拥有一流才干的留美人士处在二流的岗位上,在未来十年或十五年他们自然会引人注目。事实上,考虑到这么好的人才储备,人们不禁要为不远的将来留美归国人士对中国金融与银行业产生的巨大影响而惊叹。

(上海,1936 年 6 月)

参考文献

1. Bankers' Year Book, Research Department, Bank of China, 1935.
2. Recent History of Banking and Finance in Shanghai, by Hsu Chi-Chin, Commercial Press Ltd. Or the Bankers' Association, Shanghai. Hsu Chi-Chin.
3. History of Finance of the Republic of China, by Chia Shihyi, Vol. I., Commercial Press Ltd., Shanghai, China.
4. Report to the Plenary Session of the Central Executive Committee of the Kuomintang for the 19 and the 20th Fiscal Years, (July, 1930 to June, 1932), by T. V. Soong, Minister of Finance.
5. Report to the political Council of the Central Executive Committee of the Kuomintang for the 21st and 22nd Fiscal Years (July, 1932 to June, 1934) by H. H. Kung, Minister of Finance.

---

① 【译者注】部分人名无法确定中文名字,故未译。

6. The China Press, July 19, 1831.

7. The China Year Book, edited by H. G. W. Woodhead, year 1926-35, the North China Daily News & Herald Ltd., 17 the Bund, Shanghai. H. G. W. Woodhead.

8. The New Monetary Policy of China, Currency Reserve Board, Shanghai, 1935.

9. Two years of Nationalist China, by M. T. Z. Tyau, Chapter IV, Kelly & Walsh Ltd., Shanghai.

10. Who's Who in China, The China Weekly Review, Shanghai.

原载:《留美的中国人》 上海:商务印书馆 1936 年

Recent Literature on China(一)①
最新关于中国的书目(一)

T. C. Tai, Camp Upton Library, N. Y.
戴志骞　纽约爱布顿(军营)图书馆

Alsop, Gulielma F.
　　MY CHINESE DAYS. Boston. Little Brown, 1918. 271 pp. illus. pls. $2 net
　　Vignettes of Chinese life, giving episodes which came under author's observations during her four years' work as physician in China. Partial contents: the mandarin's bride; the Coolie's wife; glowing needles; a romance of the East; the song of the coolies.

Andrews, Roy Chapman, and Andrews, Yvette Borup.
　　CAMP AND TRAILS IN CHINA; a narrative of exploration, adventure and sport in little known China. N. Y. Appleton, 1918. 334 pp. illus. pls. ports. folded maps, $3 net.
　　Mr. R. C. Andrews, who is the associate curator of mammals in the American Museum of Natural History, was missioned as leader of the American Museum's Asiatic Zoological expedition of 1916-1917. Mr. Y. B. Andrews was the photographer of this expedition. The book is full of entertaining stories of delightful explorations and dangerous adventures in northern China and along the border of Tibet. Its scientific value is immensely increased with a workable index.

Burton, Margaret E.
　　WOMEN WORKERS OF THE ORIENT. Central Committee on united study of Foreign Missions, West Medford, Mass., 1918. 240 pp. illus. pls. ports. pap. 35 c. cl. 50 c.
　　A very fascinating book to tell the works of the "Women Workers" of the Orient. It gives much encouragement to the women missionaries of this country.

　—EDUCATIONAL REVIEW, v. 10, no. 3, July 1918.
　　A quarterly journal published by the China Christian Educational Association. This number consists of many valuable articles and well studied reports of the Chinese educational problems and systems.

Fahs, Mrs. Sophia Lyon.
　　RED, YELLOW AND BLACK; tales of Indians, Chinese and Africans. N. Y. Methodist Book

---

① 【编者注】戴志骞在美国学习和在爱布顿军营图书馆工作期间,于1918—1919年陆续在《中国学生月刊》上介绍有关中国的书目,本书分(一)、(二)、(三)照录。

Concern, 1918. 209 pp. illus. pls. port 75 c.

Missionary tales about American Indians, Chinese and Africans written for girls and boys.

Farrer, Reginald John.

ON THE EAVES OF THE WORLD. London, Arnold, 1917. 2 v. fronts. pls. ports. folded maps. 23 cm.

The author spent two years 1914 and 1915 at the Kansu-Tibet border for searching plant life adaptable to the British climate. This two volume work not only gives you many interesting descriptions of customs and social life of that loessland, but brings to notice many new species of the plant kingdom. Mr. Farrer has succeeded in this work to satisfy both the general reader and the student of the botany.

Gamewell, Mrs. Mary Ninde (Porter).

GATEWAY TO CHINA; pictures of Shanghai. N. Y. Revell, 1917. 252 pp. illus. pls. ports. 21. 5 cm.

A descriptive book of Shanghai, "Paris of the East" with very simple and entertaining style. The author reviews the history of that city from the time that Great Britain opened it as a port in 1842 to the present day. Everything, ancient and modern, of that popular seaport is vividly portrayed.

Huang, Han-liang.

THE LAND TAX IN CHINA. N. Y. Longmans, 1918. 180 pp. $1.50. (Studies in history, economics, and public law. Vol. 80, Columbia University Faculty of Political Science, pt. 3.)

A very good history and survey of the land tax in China and quite indispensable to the students of economics.

Madrolle.

CHINE DU NORD ET VALLÉE DU FLENVE BLEU. Corée 39 cartes et 21 plans. 2 ed. Paris, Librairie Hachette, 1913.

—CHINE DU SUD, JAVA, JAPON, PRESQ'ILE MALAISE, SIAM, INDOCHINE, PHILIPPINES, PORTS AMERICANS. 54 cartes ou plans. Deuxième ed. Paris, Librairie Hatchette, 1916.

This two volume guide book is excellent, but their value is somewhat lessened on account of having no corresponding names in the original language.

Strehlneek, E. A.

CHINESE PICTORIAL ART; illustrated by colored and collotyped reproductions from the author's collection. Shanghai, Commercial Press $20.

The descriptions and notes on the history of drawing, writing, etc., are very well done. Attractively bound in light blue Chinese silk and the colored collotyped reproductions are excellent.

ARTICLES

AGRICULTURE.

China and her food problems. Far Eastern Review, v. 14, 228-9 p., June 1918.

The food output can be largely increased, if the scientific system is adopted in fertilizer use and very necessary of having a fertilizer program.

—*Partnership between railways and agriculture in China.* Far Eastern Review, v. 14, 209-14 p. June 1918. Illus.

A very good article telling you why and how government railways could further agricultural development.

ATHLETICS.

Development of modern athletics in China. By Richard H. Ritter. Millard Review, v. 5, 93-4 p. June 15, 1918.

Shows the value of athletics in democratizing China and emphasizes the importance of clean sportsmanship and friendly rivalry in athletics.

—*Modern Athletics in the Far East.* By Thomas Gregory. World's Work, v. 36, 197-206 p. June 1918. Illus.

A sketch of the Far Eastern Athletic Association with many interesting photographs, especially the picture of Chinese girls at the Tokyo games is very fascinating and inspiring.

COLONIZATION.

Japanese Situation in North China and Korea. By H. P. Shastri. Millard Review, v. 5, 134-36 p. June 22, 1918.

The Japanese aggressive policy in China is a shortsighted one and for sake of humanity and civilization Japan better defines her definite goal of Japanese rule in Korea.

—*Your Chinese Neighbours.* By John K. Winslow. World Outlook, v. 4, 4-9 p. Aug. 1918.

A brief survey of the Chinese life in the Chinatowns of New York and San Francisco.

COMMERCE.

Japan Seeking China's Tobacco Monopoly. By Hollington K. Tong. Millard Review, v. 5, 49-52 p. June 8, 1918.

Lays blame both on Chinese officials who give away China's potential resources and Japan's loan policy to bankrupt China by getting concessions after concessions.

—*Our Great Field for Trade in China.* Literary Digest, v. 58, 86-88 p. July 13, 1918.

The belief of the Foreign Trade Department of the San Francisco Chamber of Commerce of the possibilities of a great afterwar trade with China is thoroughly discussed. This is an extract

—*A Successful Chinese Tobacco Co.* By T. C. Tsang, Millard's Review, v. 5, 92-93 p. June

15, 1918.

"In view of the article published last week explaining how Japan was seeking a tobacco monopoly in China and in view of the fact that the principal Chinese tobacco company in China is, according to common report, indebted to Japanese for loans advanced, this article is of exceptional interest." Ed. of M. R.

—*Trade of Shanghai and District.* Trade Journal of the Far East, v. 3, 9-11 p. July 1918.

Much information on trade conditions between Japan and China can be secured from this article. The internecine war has cast a very dark effect on business. A good general survey of the various markets in China with current prices.

—*Trade possibilities of the Far East.* By M. A. Oudin. Millard Review, v. 5, 32-33 p. June 1, 1918.

It is an extract from an address before the National Foreign Trade Convention, Cincinnati, Ohio, April 19, 1918. The chief point emphasizes John Hay's Open Door Policy. Any deviation from this fixed policy would mean to injure the American economic position and interests in the Pacific Ocean.

CRIME AND CRIMINALS.

Bandits still unchecked are terrorising China. Literary Digest, v. 58, 50-54 p. July 20, 1918.

A fair statement regarding to the lawlessness of the Chinese soldiers of the militarists government now established in Peking.

—*The Making of Hunghutze.* By Prof. Joseph Bailie, University of Nanking. Far Eastern Review, v. 14, 287-88 p. July 22, 1918.

Although short, yet having some interesting points and practical remedies to make "Hutze" into law abiding citizens.

CURRENCY.

China's Efforts at Currency and Coinage Reform. By Hollington K. Tong. Millard Review, v. 5, 112-116 p. June 15, 1918.

A sketch of the history of the Chinese currency reform and its difficulties.

DESCRIPTION AND TRAVEL.

Camps in China's Tropics. By R. C. Andrews. Harper's Monthly, v. 137, 124-37 p. June 1918. Illus.

A vivid description of the interior province of Yun-nan and its borders near Burmah. Very interesting to explorers as well as to hunters.

—*Tracking the Chinese Chamois.* By R. C. Andrews, Asia, v. 18, 473-79, June 1918.

An account of the Asiatic Zoological Expedition and its aim is to conduct a mammalian survey of Yun-nan Province, with many interesting photographs.

EDUCATION.

An Appeal to American Returned Students. By Ida Khan. Millard Review, v. 5, 131-34 p. June

22, 1918.

The writer enthusiastically and unmistakably points out the way to take the Chinese Republic to the land of salvation.

—*Chinese Students in the United States.* By William Hung. World Outlook, v. 4, 6-7 p. Aug.. 1918.

An excellent article illustrating the various phases of Chinese students' life in America.

—*Educated Man's Opportunity in China.* By Julean Arnold. Millard Review, v. 5, 292-93 p. July 29, 1918.

"The following are extracts from an address delivered by Julean Arnold, American Commercial Attache, before the graduating classes of Soochow University and of McTyeire School." M. R. Emphasizing the importance of education.

—*When the Chinese Girl Breaks with the Old Convention.* By Tyler Dennett. World Outlook, v. 4, 13 p. Aug. 1918. Illus.

An account about the life of Chinese women and emphasizes the imminent need of woman education.

FINANCE.

China's Salt Tax. By A. W. Ferrin, U. S. Special commercial agent. Millard Review, v. 5, 213-14 p. July 6, 1918.

The writer believes that the salt surplus is the biggest free salt asset of the Chinese government, and if it should continue to grow, it would be able to solve China's financial problems.

—*The New Chinese Loan.* By John Foord. Asia, v. 18, 729-31 p. Sept 1918.

A clear outline of the present American policy towards the Chinese loan and the whole point of the article needs the American government to aid American bankers and investors in every way possible to secure the execution of equitable contracts, made in good faith by the Chinese citizen and the Chinese government.

—*Peking to Issue* $80,000,000 *Gold Notes.* By Hollington K. Tong. Millard Review, v. 5, 253 p. July 13, 1918.

It is a new clever plan of Japan for the economic penetration of China.

T'ang and Sung Paintings; from the collection of Vladimir G. Simkhovitch. Asia v. 18, 561-68 p. July 1918.

The reproductions of 12 famous Chinese paintings are fairly good, but the explanations cast lots of light upon the good qualities of the pictures.

FOREIGN RELATIONS.

American Policy in China. By James F. Abbott. Asia v. 18, 711-14 p. Sept. 1918.

A splendid article suggests ways to solve the chronic chaos in China. Mr. Abbotts diplomacy and advocacy of the recognition of rights of other people towards the international problems in China are not only the means to rehabilitate the Chinese Republic, but to kill the potentialities of having a possible war far greater than the present European conflict in future.

—*Hongkew and the Chinese-Japanese Riots.* By J. B. Powell. Millard Review, v. 5, 328-30 p. July 27, 1918.

A riot by rowdy element of some nationality simply means an ordinary riot, but especially a riot created by the irresponsible and snobbish Japanese rowdy elements in China always give the Tokio government a good international advertisement on the subjects of "Anarchy and disorder in China" and result in a splendid chance for Japan to do something in China as what she did in Korea.

—*Is China Worth Helping?* By Hollington K. Tong. Millard Review, v. 5, 331-33 P-July 27, 1918.

The points outlined in this article are sound and hope that the world great statesmen and diplomats will give them some consideration.

—*The Recent Sino-Japanese Agreement.* Far Eastern Review, v. 14, 236-39 p. June 1918.

The writer points out that if China is not developing a concrete and effective national organization now and given sufficient hold in the next few years it will be easy enough for Japan to expand in China to the extent of her ambitions.

—*Violating the "Open Door" in Manchuria.* Millard Review, v. 5, 294-96 p. July 20, 1918.

Lots of instances mentioned herein showing the close of the "Open Door" policy by Japan in Manchuria.

—*Voice of an Oriental Nation.* By Peter S. Jame. Millard Review, v. 5, 13-15P. June 1, 1918.

Shows the inadvisability of Japan's baiting policy toward China.

INDUSTRIES AND RESOURCES.

Chang Chien, a Man who Would Reform a Nation by Precept and Practice in a Model City. By Frederick R. Sites. Asia, v. 18, 587-92 p. July 1918. Illus.

A well written article about Chang Chien's life and his practical work of industrial problems.

—*China's Silk Industry and Reforms.* By Y. L. Chang. Millard Review, v. 5, 318-22 p. July 20, 1918.

A well written article on the history and development of the Chinese silk industry.

—*First Experiment in American-Chinese-Japanese Co-operation.* By J. B. Powell. Millard Review, v. 5. 208-09 p. July 6, 1918.

Shows the advisability of such an establishment.

—*Great Manchurian Coal Seam.* Far Eastern Review, v. 14, 273-77 p. July 1918. Illus.

I request every Chinese should pay a little attention to the following quotations: "When the Chinese failed to develop the great coal seam at Fushun, 20 miles east of Mukden, Manchuria, thru superstition in the first place and willful negligence in the second they allowed to pass out of their hands the richest fuel deposit in the three Eastern provinces."

—*Improving China's Tea Industry.* By Yu Sin Chang. Millard Review, v 5, 228-31 p. July 6, 1918.

A sketch of the exports of Chinese tea and also points out the common defects of packing and preparing of tea leaves.

—*Scratching the Scales Off the Dragon's Back.* By James Lewis. World Outlook, v. 4, 8 p. Aug. 1918.

The author gives a very general idea about the natural resources of China.

LABOURERS.

Coolieship. By O. Gilbreath. Asia, v. 18, 459-64 p. June 1918.

A fine description of the superstitions and customs of the Chinese coolie class with illustrations.

LANGUAGE.

Direct Method of Teaching English. By Mrs. E. W. Sawdon. Education Review, v. 10, 230-41 p. July 1918.

A paper read at the annual meeting of the West China Christian Educational Union, Chungking. Well written and practical in the methods suggested, with a very good bibliography on phonetics.

—*Teaching English to Chinese Students.* By F. B. Lenz. Educational Review, v. 56, 12-18 p. June 1918.

The author points out definitely the failure of scholastic method in teaching a language to any foreign student. This is an exposition of the direct practical, natural way of teaching English to Chinese Students.

MEDICINE.

China Builds Modern Hospital at Peking. By Hollington K. Tong. Millard Review, v. 5, 209-11 p. July 6, 1918.

A description of the founding and establishment of the Central Hospital, Peking.

NATIONAL CHARACTERISTIC.

John Chinaman By Carl Crow. World Outlook, v. 4, 3 p. Aug. 1918.

The author has not overlooked some good points of John Chinaman, but they are sufficiently overshadowed by that implied contemptuous term "John Chinaman."

—*The Problem of Patriotism in China.* By M. T. Z. Tyau. New East, v. 3, 123-24 p. Aug. 1918.

A well written article on Chinese patriotism.

OPIUM.

China Going Back to Opium. Extract from "The Pharmaceutical Era." Aug. 1918. Literary Digest, v. 58, 24-25 p. Sep. 21, 1918.

It is a curse worse than the rape of Belgium and the bombing of hospitals and ambulances.

—*China Revives the Opium Trade.* Far Eastern Review, v. 14, 264-272 p. July 1918.

It is shameful to indicate here again that the official purchase of stock and sale to Syndicate nullify ten years' work of suppression of using the poisonous drug and also gives you a very clear outline of the history and formation of the Shanghai Opium Combine.

—*The Great Opium Scandal.* By David Fraser. New East, v. 3, 145-149 p. Aug. 1918.

A brief survey of the opium questions, its history and present development

POLITICS AND GOVERNMENT.

Chang Hsun Again Centre of Peking Intrigue. By Hollington K. Tong. Millard Review, v. 5, 4 p. June 1, 1918.

An outline shows the underplots of the various military parties in the capital.

—*China and World Democracy.* By R. A. Ward. World Outlook, v. 4, 4-5 p. Aug. 1918.

Educational and moral character of the people will uplift China to a permanent democratic country.

—*Education and Politics.* Far Eastern Review, v. 14, 242-43 p. June 1918.

A great and immediate need to the Chinese people is the political education of the common people.

—*The Futile Political Game.* Far Eastern Review, v. 14, 284-85 p. July 1918.

Shows the contemporary political upheavals in China.

—*No Prospect of Internal Peace for China.* By Hollington K. Tong. Millard Review, v. 5, 129-31 p. June 22, 1918.

The government tries every means to bankrupt China in order to continue the terrible internal turmoil

—*Who Is to Be China's Next President.* By Hollington K. Tong. Millard Review, v. 5, 289-91 p. July 20, 1918.

A sketch of the movements of the various political parties for the election of the next president.

PUBLICITY.

China Needs Publicity. By C. Y. Chiu. Millard Review, v. 5, 54-55 p. June 8, 1918.

Shows the importance of publicity, giving some good suggestions of establishing "International Intelligence Bureau" and "Welcome Association."

RAILWAY.

Another Link Between Korea and Chinese Railways. Far Eastern Review, v. 14, 277 p. July 1918.

A line from Kirin to Hueining is proposed to be built and such a link making Kirin-Changchun railway now under the control and management of the South Manchurian Railway Co. is complete.

—*Chinese Poverty Largely Due to Lack of Roads and Railways.* Engineering and Contracting, v. 50, 50-51 P-July 17, 1918.

Several good points in this article suggested, but the treatment is rather too short and inexhaustive.

—*Chinese Railway Reports.* Far Eastern Review, v. 14, 278-80 p. July 1918.

Two reports, viz. : Peking-Mukden Line in 1917 and Peking-Suiyuan Railway, 1917.

—*A Low Grade Route to Szechwan.* Far Eastern Review, v. 14, 249-263, p. July 1918.

A very valuable article on the products and resources of Szechwan in addition to the description of the proposed route. Many painstaking tables of products and the statistics of imports and exports of that province besides many photographic illustrations.

RELIGIOUS INSTITUTION AND AFFAIRS.

A Buddhist Priest Gives Up His Job. By Theodore M. Inglis. World Outlook, v. 4, 11 p. Aug. 1918.

An instance of a buddhistic monk turned to be an ardent Christian.

—*Factors in China's Crisis.* By Sherwood Eddy. Missionary Review, v. 41, 676 p. Sep. 1918.

A clear announcement of the failure of all worldly means, as foreign and domestic loans, secular education, classical and moral precepts, etc, to satisfy the deep need of the Chinese. As Dr. Eddy says, China "has reached the position where a great religious revival is imperatively needed and it is in just with the condition in which such movements have often started in past history in other parts of the world."

—*Is Idolatry Dead in China?* By Carl F. Kupfer. Missionary Review, v. 41, 500-506 p. July 1918. Illus.

According to Mr. Kupfer's idea the only salvation for China is in the Christian education of the children.

—*Summering With the Gods in China.* By Boardman Pickett. Asia, v. 18, 667-71 p. Aug. 1918.

A delightful description of the monasteries around the Western Hill, Peking.

SHIP-BUILDING

New Ship Built in Shanghai. Far Eastern Review, v. 14, 283 p. July 1918. Illus

The description of the two ships, Solvaer and harbor collier for Manila. They can be considered as a new chapter in the history of Chinese engineering.

SOCIAL LIFE AND CONDITIONS

Chinese of the Inner Courts. By Ida Belle Lewis. World Outlook. v. 4, 18 p. Aug. 1918.

A description of woman life in China.

—*Conquering Chinese.* By Walter E. Weyl. Harper's, v. 137, 153-163 p. July 1918. Illus.

A real picture of Chinese coolie class. Whether the author's theory of the unconquerable Chinese on account of quiet expansion of the Chinese vast population holds good or not, we the Chinese should wake up for avoiding the fate of the Koreans and Indians.

—*Emancipating the Women of China.* By Tyler Dennett. Asia, v. 18, 596-575 *p.* July 1918. Illus.

The section on Chinese feminine life and customs are hasty in observations and snappy in judgments.

—*New Codes for Old.* By Tyler Dennett. Asia, v. 18, 657-664 p. Aug. 1918.

The quotation of Yung Tao regarding to the evils of concubinage is well portrayed. The polygamy in family life is undoubtedly a great obstacle to impede the progress of a nation.

原载：*The Chinese Student Monthly* November, 1918. Volume XIV. Number 1

Recent Literature on China(二)
最新关于中国的书目(二)

T. C. TAI, B. A. , B. L S.

Camp Library, Camp Upton, New York.

戴志骞　文科学士　图书馆学士

纽约爱布顿(军营)图书馆

COLLINS, WILLIAM F. *Mineral Enterprise in China.* —London, Heinemann 1918. 308 p. 5 folded maps, illus.

This volume supplies a sketch of the mining development in China besides thoughtful discussions of the various phases of the mining enterprise. Much valuable information regarding to taxation, regulation and agreements of mining between China and other countries are all contained in the 8 appendices. The material is systematically arranged in addition to a very minute index.

Returns of trade and trade reports. —Vol. 4—Southern coast ports and vol. 5—Frontier ports; published at the Statistical Development of the Inspectorate General of Customs.

These reports issued by the Maritime Customs cover many facts about trade in the districts covered during 1917.

TAI, EN-SAI. *Treaty ports in China.* (a study in diplomacy) N. Y. Columbia Univ. 1918. 202 p. 24. 5 cm.

This scholarly dissertation outlines the treaties between China and other countries and the discussion on the Commercial policy is also well written. A useful book for the students of diplomacy and international law.

TYAU, M. T. Z. *China's new constitution and international problems.* — Shanghai, Commercial Press, 1918.

This work is not as important a book to juristic literature as is his first book entitled the Legal Obligations arising out of Treaty relations between China and Other States. However the problems of treaty revisions, the entitled claims of China at the great Peace Conference and the discussions of Provisional Constitution are scholarly summarized and analyzed. It will be very valuable to those who interest in the Chinese problems.

ARTICLES

Agriculture.

China officially adopts American cotton seed as standard. H. K. Tong Millard's Review. V. 6, 514-6 p. Nov. 30, 1918.

First agricultural train in China. H. K. Tong. Millard's Review V. 6, 118-9 p. Sep. 21, 1918.

Practical agriculture and missions in China. J. H. Reisner. Millard's Review. V. 6, 370-2 p.

Nov. 2,1918.

    Romance of the Soya bean. L. S. Palen. Asia. V. 19,68-74 p. Jan. 1919. Illus.

A very interesting article on the history of the Soya bean.

Asiatic Problems.

    Democratic tendencies in Asia. Tyler Dennett. Asia. V. 18,911-17 p. Nov. 1918. Illus.

In this article Mr. Dennett treats China as the very center of the whole Asiatic problems.

Commerce

    China's 1917 trade breaks all records. Thomas Sammons. Millard's Review. V. 6,218-21 p. Oct. 12,1918.

    This article is a summary of Consul-general Sammons report on the trade of China. The original report appeared in the American "Commerce Reports" Aug. 6,1918.

    Chinese markets from the inside. T. G. White. System. V. 34,350-68 p. Sep. 1918.

    Opening the 'kingdom' of Mongolia to the world trade. H. K. Tong. Millard's Review. V. 6, 238-42 p. Oct 12,1918.

Crime and criminals.

    Assassination of Tong Hua-Lung at Victoria, B. C. H. K. Tong. Millard's Review. V. 6,52 p. Sep. 14,1918.

Description and travel.

    Across Mongolia by motor car. Far Eastern Review. V. 14,437-41 p. Nov. 1918.

    It is "a romantic region, marvellously rich in pasture, with great cattle and sheep raising potentialities awaits development."

    China's neglected monuments. Illus. Review of Reviews. V. 58,317-8 p. Sep. 1918.

    Temple of the four patriots. Far Eastern Review. V. 14,492 p Dec. 1918.

    This temple was erected by His Excellency Lu Tseng-tsiang in commemoration of the four far sighted patriots and martyrs of the Boxer Uprising,1900.

Education.

    Asiatic woman in America. M. E. Burton, Missionary Review. V 41,760-3 p. Oct. 1918.

Engineering.

    "Dry Ford" instead bridges. Far Eastern Review. V. 14,380 p. Sep. 1918.

European War-Peace Conference.

    China and the Peace Conference. Far Eastern Review. V. 14,503-4 p. Dec. 1918.

    China and the Peace Conference. T. R. Jernigan. Millard's Review. V. 6, 296-8 p. Oct

26,1918.

China must receive full justice at the Peace Conference. J. O. Y. Millard's Review. V. 6,434-6 p. Nov. 16,1918.

China's claims in Peace Settlement. Christian Science Monitor. V. 11. No. 32, Dec. 31,1918.

Southern China to be represented at the Peace Conference. Christian Science Monitor. V. 6, No. 32, Dec. 31,1918.

Why Japan is apprehensive regarding the Peace Conference H. P. Shastri. Millard's Review. V. 6,473-5 p. Nov. 23,1918.

Siberian Expedition.

China's full participation in the Siberian Expedition. Ida Kahn. Millard's Review. V. 6,16-20 p. Sep. 7,1918.

—*War Aims.*

China as effected by allied war aims. C. L. Prescott. Millard Review. V. 6, 56-8 p. Sep. 14,1918.

—*War Work.*

United war work campaign in China. R. H. R. Millard's Review. V. 6,392-3 p. Nov. 9,1918.

Finance.

American finance in China. Far Eastern Review. V. 14,371 p. Sep. 1918.

Economic development of Japan a lesson for China. H. P. Shastri. Millard's Review. V. 6,12-16 p. Sep. 7,1918.

How Japan finances China. Far Eastern Review. V. 14,362-4 p. Sep. 1918.

"Japanese officials publicly outline the various steps taken to enable the conclusion of recent loans with 'Secrecy and despatch.'"

International control of China's finances is needed now. H. K Tong. Millard's Review. V. 6, 172-6 p. Oct. 5,1918.

Japanese efforts to gain control of the Chinese banks. H. K. Tong. Millard's Review. V. 6,261-3 p. Oct. 1918.

Loans and more loans. Far Eastern Review. V. 14,421-2 p. Oct 1918.

Loan craze in China. Far Eastern Review. V. 14,335-38 p. Aug. 1918. A complete list of financial transactions made between Chinese and Japanese.

New loan forecasts extension Chinese-American trade. J. B. Power. Millard's Review. V. 6,4-6 p. Sep. 7,1918.

Plans for gold currency in China. Far Eastern Review. V. 14,382-6 p. Sep. 1918.

Summarizing the history of a currency reform scheme promulgated by presidential mandate.

Foreign Relations.

America protests against the Chinese-Japanese trading monopoly. H. K. Tong. Millard's Review. V. 6, 388-91 p. Nov. 9, 1918.

Anglo-American friendship in China. C. Lane Prescott. Millard's Review. V. 6, 345-6 p. Nov. 2, 1918.

Exchange of notes between the United States and Japan concerning their mutual interest relating to the republic of China; with declaration of Chinese government concerning the notes. American Journal of International Law. V. 12, Supplement 1-4. Jan. 1918.

Exterritoriality—Revision of China's laws. T. R. Jernigan. Millard's Review. V. 6, 87-90 p. Sep. 21, 1918.

Japan's conditions for remitting her share of Boxer indemnity. H. K. Tong. Millard's Review. V. 6, 303-6 p. Oct. 26, 1918.

This article should be carefully read. Mr. Tong thinks that there are sinister motives behind the good offer for remitting the share of the Boxer indemnity by Japan.

Japan's last effort to control China. Millard's Review. V. 6, 430-1 p. Nov. 16, 1918.

Principle and practice of exterritoriality in China. Charles Denby. Far Eastern Review. V. 14, 493-4 p. Dec. 1918.

Sino-Japanese military conventions. R. Machray. Fortnightly Review. V. 110, 245-55 p. Aug. 1918.

What can President Wilson do for China? H. K. Tong. Millard's Review. V. 6, 431-4 p. Nov. 16, 1918.

Forestry

Relation of forests to floods. D. Y. Lin. Far Eastern Review. V. 14, 482-5 p. Dec. 1918.

Emphasizing that the permanent effect of the engineering works to check the flood must be supplemented by a system of tree-planting.

Industrial Arts.

China's great porcelain and pottery industry. Y. L. Chang. Millard's Review. V. 6, 455-8 p. Nov. 16, 1918.

Where the Chinese get their rug, pottery and art designs. J. C. Houston. Millard's Review. V. 6, 414-5 p. Nov. 9, 1918.

Industries and Resources.

Accounting and industry. J. E. Baker. Far Eastern Review. V. 14, 393-5 p. Oct. 1918.

The author emphasizes that the sound accounting practice is fundamental to the growth of manufacture and industry in China.

China's efforts in modern industry. R. W. Child. Asia. V. 18, 962-7 p. Nov. 1918. Illus.

China's great fishery industry. H. K. Tong. Millard's Review. V. 7, 31-4 p. Dec. 7, 1918.

Chinese wines a misnomer. Y. P. Sun. Far Eastern Review. V. 14, 365-6 p. Sep. 1918.

Discussing the manufacture and use of spirits by the Chinese.

Development of the canned goods industry in China. Y. L. Chang. Millard's Review. V. 6, 286-89 p. Oct. 16, 1918.

Hydro-electric development in South China. Prof. Middleton Smith. Far Eastern Review. V. 14, 378-9 p. Sep. 1918.

Industrial electrical development by the Chinese. Illus. F. W. Allonby. Far Eastern Review. V. 14, 494-5 p. Dec. 1918

Japanese coal mine at Ta-King and Chinese enterprise-observations. T. R. Jernigan. Millard's Review. V. 6, 384-6 p. Nov. 9, 1918.

Wolfram in China. Far Eastern Review. V. 14, 344-5 p. Aug. 1918.

Law.

China's progress toward legal reform. H. K. Tong. Millard's Review. V. 6, 53-6 p. Sep. 14, 1918.

Manchuria.

Development of Manchuria. Far Eastern Review. V. 14, 323-8 p. Aug. 1918.

It is an authoritative report by officials of the Chinese maritime Customs.

Economic conditions in Manchuria and Chosen. Far Eastern Review. V. 14, 426-7 p. Oct 1918.

National characteristics.

American ways and Chinese ways. W. H. Shith. Missionary Review V. 41, 674 p. Sep. 1918.

Study of the mental and physical characteristics of the Chinese W. H. Pyle. School and Society. V. 8, 264-9 p. Aug. 31, 1918.

Opium.

America and Britain must stop opium revival in China. E. W. Wright. Millard's Review. V. 6, 92-5 p. Sep. 21, 1918.

Opium revival. Far Eastern Review. V. 14, 343-4 p. Aug. 1918.

Opium scandal and the Chinese mind. C. Lane Prescott. Millard's Review. V. 6, 266-8 p. Oct 19, 1918.

Politics and Government.

Chinese Bolshevik. Far Eastern Review. V. 14, 340-1 p. Aug. 1918.

Constitutional situation in China. W. W. Willoughby. Far Eastern Review. V. 14, 433-6 p. Nov. 1918.

An expert's opinion as to how the present dispute between the North and South may be adjusted and settled.

Imminent collapse of the military policy. Far Eastern Review. V. 14,341-2 p. Aug. 1918

Need of allied mediation in China. Far Eastern Review. V. 14,416-7 p. Oct. 1918.

Present prospects for peace in China. H. K. Tong. Millard's Review. V. 6, 301-3 p. Oct. 26,1918.

Principles for which America and England should stand on China. W. C. Dennis. Millard's Review. V. 6,393-5 p. Nov. 9,1918.

Prospects for China's unification. H. K. Tong. Millard's Review. V. 6,133-5 p. Sep. 28,118.

A Republic with two parliaments. Far Eastern Review. V. 14 387-9p. Sep. 1918.

Time for foreign intervention has arrived. C. Lane Prescott. Millard's Review. V. 6, 97-100 p. Sep. 21,1918.

Trying to solve China's difficulties *by* "Friendship." H. K. Tong. Millard's Review. V. 6,341-3 p. Nov 2,1918.

Vice-presidential election scandal. Far Eastern Review. V. 14,465-6 p. Nov. 1918.

Railways and roads.

Chinese railways reports for 1917. Far *Eastern Review.* V. 14,356-9 p. *Sep.* 1918.

New *Japanese railways in* Manchuria and Shangtung. Far Eastern Review. V. 14,449-53 p. Nov. 1918.

Opening of Peking-Tungchow Red Cross *Highway. Roger S. Greene. Millard's* Review. V. 6,10-12 p. Sep. 7,1918.

Pioneering over the new Changsha-Wuchang railway. Edward H. Hume. Millard's Review. V. 6,306-8 p. Oct. 26,1918.

Ship-building.

How China plans to build ships for America. H. K. Kwong. Millard's Review. V. 6,494-5 p. Nov. 23,1918.

Social life and conditions.

China's second childhood. Illus. Scientific American. V. 119,339 p. Oct 26,1918.

China's social challenge. J. S. Burgess. Illus. Survey. V. 38,501-3 p. V. 39,41-44 p. 311-16 p. V. 40,633-8 p. Sep. 8, Oct. 13, Dec. 15,1917. Sep. 7,1918.

Chinese officials,, agriculture and treatment of women. T. R. Jernigan. Millard's Review. V. 6, 429-33 p. Nov. 16,1918.

"Coney Island" amusement idea comes to China. Y. L. Chang. Millard's Review. V. 6, 242-4 p. Oct. 12,1918.

Uplifting the women of China. Far Eastern Review. V. 14,472-3 p. Nov. 1918.

Where the Shanghai Chinese amuse themselves. Illus. Far Eastern Review. V. 14,510-11 p. Dec. 1918.

Work for Chinese women. Far Eastern Review. V. 14,342-3 p. Aug. 1918.

Lacking of women-education and occupation will plunge the Chinese society into a general moral disintegration.

Waterways.

    Can Shanghai become a world harbor? Far Eastern Review. V. 14,367-9 p. Sep. 1918.

    Floods in South China. D. S. Williams. Far Eastern Review. V. 14,409-11 p. Oct. 1918.

    Foochow plans port improvement. North China Daily News. July 15 and 16,1918.

    Grand Canal restoration. Far Eastern Review. V. 14,361 p. Sep. 1918.

    Improvement begins on China's famous Grand Canal. Pao-Ling Yang. Millard's Review. V. 6, 158-64 p. Sep. 28,1918.

    Motor boats in South China. Far Eastern Review. V. 14,400 p. Oct. 1918.

    The paragraphs on the Yunnan trade in this article have lots of up-to-date information.

    Scheme to improve the Canton River. Far Eastern Review. V. 14,486-8 p. Dec. 1918.

原载：*The Chinese Students Monthly*　　Volume XIV　　February,1919　　Number 4:266-271

Recent Literature on China(三)
最新关于中国的书目(三)

T. C. Tai, Assistant Librarian, Camp Library, Camp Upton, N. Y.

戴志骞 纽约爱布顿军营图书馆副馆长

RECEMT BOOKS

Alsop, Gulielma Fell. *My Chinese Days.* Illus. Boston, LittLe, 1918

  This book is a sketch of things Chinese, but mingles fact and fiction in many an interesting and imaginative episodes. The story is full of the gorgeous color of the East. The author is a medical missionary in China and the illustrations are very attractive.

~ *China Maritime Customs.* Treaties, conventions, etc. between China and foreign states; supplementary volume to edition of 1908; Russia, Great Britain, international protocol (Whanghoo conservancy) United States of America, France, Sweden, Portugal, The Netherlands, Japan, Brazil; published by order of the Inspector General of Customs (miscellaneous series, No. 30), 199 p. Half mor. N. Y. Stechert, 1917,

Coleman, Frederick. *Far East Unveiled.* Cassell, 1918. A sketch of complicated events in Japan and China in the year, 1916.

Davis, Sir John Francis, *tr. Chinese Moral Maxims.* 46p. Boston Phillips, Le Roy, 1918.

Ferguson, J. C. *Outlines of Chinese Art.* Chicago, University of Chicago, 1919. $3.

Gautier, Judith. *Chinese Lyrics from the Book of Jade;* translated from the French by James Whitall. 53 p. N. Y. Huebsch, 1918.

Giles, Herbert Allen, tr. *Chinese Fairy Tales.* Boston, Phillips, Le Roy, 1918. 30c.

Morse, Hosea Ballou. *International Relations of the Chinese Empire.* 479P. illus, London, Longmans, 1918.

  VoL 1. Period of conflict, 1834-1860, was published in 1910.
  See descriptive note under Morse in the chapter *of* "international relation"
  In "250 English Books on China."
  Vol. 2. Period of submission, 1861-1893.
  Vol. 3, Period *of* subjection, 1894-1911.

Overlach, T W. *Foreign Financial Control in China.* 295 p. N. Y. MacMillan, 1919. Bibliography,

p. 283-87.

Tomimas, Shutaro. *Open-door Policy and Territorial Integrity of China*; with verses in Japanese. 161-134p. N. Y. Seiler, 1919. Partial contents: Helpless East and the policies of the western powers; Position of the United States; Discussion of the open-door policy; American diplomacy and the territorial integrity of China. Author is instructor in Japaness, Columbia University.

Waley, Arth. *170 Chinese poems*. N. Y. Knopf, 1919.

Wheeler, William Recinald. *China and the World War*. 263P. illus N. Y. MacMillan, 1919

ARTICLES

AGRICULTURE.
Chinese petsai as a salad vegetable; by D. Fairchild. Illus. Journal Heredity, v. 9, p. 290-5. Nov. 1918.
On the existence of a growth-inhibiting substance in the Chinese lemon; by Reed & Halma. Illus. Cal. Univ. Pub. Agri. Sci. , v. 4, No. 3, 99-112. 1919.

COMMERCE.
 China's commerce needs explained. Christian Sc. Monitor, p. 3. Mar. 15, 1919.
 Montgomery, Ward and Company and the missionaries; by H. H. Ballard. Millard's Review. v. 12, p. 143-3. Dec. 28, 1918.

CRIME AND CRIMINALS.
 Chinese confesses to triple murder; Z. S. Wan says motive for slaying Dr. T. T. Wong was burglary. Sun, Feb. 11, 1919.
 Student taken in Chinese murders. Sun, Feb. 2, 1919.
 Three Chinese officials slain at Washington. N. Y. Times, p. 1. Feb. 1, 1919.

CUSTOMS SERVICE.
 Mr. Taylor and Customs scrvice. Far Eastern Review. v. 15, p. 37-38. Jan. 1919.

DESCRIPTIVE AND TRAVEL.
 China and the cross roads; a review of the year 1918 and the outlook for 1919; by L. Hodous. Illus. Missionary Review. v. 42, p. 16-18. Jan. 1919.
 Naturalist's journey across little known Yunnan; by R. C. Andrews. Illus. Far Eastern Review. v. 15, p. 1-12. Jan. 1919.

EDUCATION.

Assisting China in Education. Christian Sc. Monitor, p. 16. Feb. 7. 1919.

Development of vocational education in China; by C. H. Chuang. Manual training, v. 20, 170-3. Jan. 1919.

Education of modern China. Christian Sc. Monitor, p. 14. Jan, 31, 1919.

Hope for Chinese illiterates. Missionary Review. v. 42, p. 82-4. Feb. 1919.

Object lesson for China-education in the Philippines; by T. R. Jernigan. Millard's Review. v. 7, p. 197-201. Jan. 11, 1919.

Shall China have an alphabet? H. P. Beach. Illus. Missionary Review. v. 42, p. 127-30. Feb. 1919.

EUROPEAN WAR-PEACE CONFERENCE.

China and the international Peace Conference; by H. K. Tong. Millard Review. v. 7, p. 164-170. Jan. 4, 1919.

China and the Peace Conference; by T. R. Jernigan. Millard's Review. v. 7, p. 341-342. Feb. 8, 1919.

China fights for life in Peace parley. New York Tribune, p. 1. Feb. 3, 1919.

China's attitude to war problems. Christian Sc. Monitor, p. 7. Apr., 4, 1919.

China's claims: she wants a complete revision of her relations with the Power; by K. P. Wang. New York Times, sec. 3. Feb. 2, 1919.

China's delegates to Peace Conference. Christian Sc. Monitor, p. 2. Feb. 10, 1919.

Peace claims of China laid before Paris Conference. Christian Sc. Monitor, p. 1-2. Mar. 7. 1919.

Wants to right wrongs to China; by Dr. G. Reid. The World, p. 2. Mar. 10. 1919.

EUROPEAN WAR-SIBERIAN EXPEDITION.

Japanese occupation of Siberia; by G. E. Sokolsky. Millard's Review v. 7, p. 174-76. Jan. 4, 1919.

Trouble with Japan averted before the armistice: Lansing's protest on behalf of the United States stopped aggression in Siberia and was followed by victory of the peace-party in Tokio. New York Times, Sec. 4. Mar. 16, 1919.

EUROPEAN WAR-SINO JAPANESE SITUATION.

Alien forces working against China's unification; by H. K. Tong. Millard's Review. v. 7, p. 306-08. Feb. 1, 1919.

Bashfulness of Japan. Christian Science Monitor, p. 16, Mar. 8. 1919.

Can Japan successfully gag China at the European Conference? Millard's Review. v. 7, p. 377-382. Feb. 15, 1919.

China: Colony or nation; by "Asiaticus." Asia. v. 19, p. 209-220. Mar. 1919.

China and Japan: former's appeal to the powers resented by the latter. New York Times. Feb. 7, 1919.

China urges voiding of Japanese demands. New York Times, p. 2. April 7, 1919.

China wants treaty with Japan revised. New York Times, p. 3. Jan. 24, 1919.

China's crucial state exposed in Peace debate: *her vast wealth and territory*; Prof. Willoughby tells world, will go to Japan unless future is settled now. N. Y. World, p. 1. Feb. 14, 1919.

China's president rejects Tokio demand. New York Times, p. 1. Feb. 11, 1919.

Chinese army for the Japanese conquest of China. Millard's Review. v. 7, p. 345-46. Feb. 8, 1919.

How Japan plans to "Return" Tsingtao to China. J. B. Powell. Millard's Review. v. 7, p. 160-64. Jan. 4, 1919.

Iyenaga denounces Dr. Wellington Koo's statement that treaty of 1915 is negatory. New York Times, sec. 2. Feb. 2, 1919.

Iyenaga impugns motives of China. Sun, Feb. 2, 1919.

Japan and China at odds; by J. W. Harrington, New York Times, Sec. 7, Feb. 16, 1919.

Japan-China crisis is watched here. China wants Conference to rid her of onerous terms of 1915 treaty with Tokio. The World, p. 4, February 12, 1919.

Japan completing control of China's means of communication. H. K. Tong, Millard's Review. v. 7, p. 201-03, January 11, 1919.

Japan rests on secret pledges: contention advanced is that agreements with China all antedate war and are not now subject to arbitrament. Christian Science Monitor, p. 1, Feb. 27, 1919.

Japan threatens force in shaping policy of Chinese. The World p. 4, February 12, 1919.

Japan threatens to keep islands. New York Times, p. 1 and 3, February 12, 1919.

Japan will hold China to treaty. Sun, February 2, 1919.

Japanese occupation of Tsinan: by Upton Close. Millard's Review. v. 7, p. 236-40, January, 18, 1919.

Japan's newest intrigue for possession of China's iron work; by H. H Tong. Millard's Review. v. 7. p. 233-35, January 18, 1919.

Nanking, Shanghai or Tokio. Millard's Review. v. 7, p. 170-2, January 4, 1919.

Outlines Japan's ideals of peace; *by Baron Makino.* (Looks to China for outlet.) New York Times, February 10, 1919.

Sino-Japanese treaty of 1915. Christian Science Monitor, p. 16, February 10, 1919.

FINANCE.

Chinese loan. Living Age, v. 299, p. 639 December 7, 1918.

Control of China's finances. Review of Reviews, v. 58, p. 657, Dec., 1918.

Optimistic view of China. Christian Science Monitor, p. 3, Mar. 24, 1919.

Review of China's finances in 1918; by H. K. Tong. Millard's Review. v. 7, p. 272-76, Jan. 25, 1919.

FINE Arts.

Asiatic art: the Far East; A. K. Coomaraswamy. Illus. Art World, v. 10, p. 71-4. Dec. 1918.

Treatise on Chinese porcelain; R. M. Chait. Illus. International Studio, v. 66, p. 120-4, supplement. Feb. 1919.

FOREIGN RELATIONS.

Allied note to China. Nation. v. 108, p. 149. Jan. 25, 1919.

Attitude of Americans and Britons in China toward Japan. Millard's Review. v. 7, p. 89-94. Dec. 21, 1918.

China among the nations. Nation. v. 107, p. 750-1. Dec. 14, 1918.

Constructive plan for China. Asia. v. 19, p. 221-2. Mar. 1919.

Fair chance for China; by Putnam Weale (pseud.) Asia. v. 19, p. 223-30. Mar. 1919.

President Wilson's message to China. Review of Reviews. v. 58, p. 88. Jan. 1919.

Principle and practice of exterritoriality in China; by Charles Denby. Millard's Review. v. 7, p. 52-54. Dec. 14, 1919.

Solving the Far Eastern problems. Christian Science Monitor, p. 1, April 3, 1919.

Void Ishii-Lansing deal, China urges; by Charles A. Selden. New York Times. Feb. 8, 1919.

INDUSTRIES AND RESOURCES.

China's great hide and skin industry; by Y. L. Chang. Millard's Review. v. 7, p. 221-2. Jan. 11, 1919.

Chinese production of sugar; by Y. L. Chang. Millard's Review. v. 7. p. 332-33. Feb. 1, 1919.

Chinese products of interest to Americans; by J. Arnold. Commerce Reports, No. 299, Dec. 21, 1918. No. 10, Jan. 12, 1919.

Flour mills industry, a purely Chinese enterprise; by Y. L. Chang. Millard's Review. v. 7, p. 256-57. Jan. 18, 1919.

Japan and the industrial development of China. Millard's Review. v. 7, p. 382. Feb. 15, 1919.

Throttling industries in China. Far Eastern Review. v. 15. p. 19-20. Jan. 1919.

LABOR AND LABORING CLASSES.

Conditions of the Chinese labor corps in France; by H. K. Tong. Millard's Review. v. 7, p. 70-72. Dec. 14, 1918.

Estimate of the standard of living in China; by C. G. Dittmer. Quarterly Journal of Economics. v. 33, p. 107-28. Nov. 1918.

Human cab horse of China; by Gerard King. Far Eastern Review. v. 15, p. 27. Jan. 1919.

No unions wanted here. Survey. v. 41, p. 730-1. Feb. 2, 1919.

LAW.

Recent progress in the Chinese administration of Justice; by W. K. Lo. Far Eastern Review. v.

15, p. 12-4. Jan. 1919.

LEAGUE OF NATIONS.

China and the League of Nations; by Carl W. Ackerman. New York Times, Mag. Sec. Mar. 2, 1919.

Kang Yu-wei as Chinese advocate of League of Nations; by H. K. Tong. Millard's Review. v. 7, p. 342-46. Feb. 8, 1919.

President Wilson and the League for Peace; by Dr. W. C. Dennis. Millard's Review. v. 7, p. 85-89. Dec. 21, 1918.

LITERATURE.

Chinese poems, trans. by A. Waley; reviewed by J. G. Fletcher, Poetry. v. 13, p. 273-81. Feb. 1919.

Chinese written wall pictures, poems; trans. by F. Ayscough. English version by A. Lowell. Poetry. v. 13, p. 233-42. Feb. 1919.

Inn at the Western Lake; poem. Poetry, v. 13, p. 242. Feb. 1919.

Recluse; poem, Chang-ling Wang. Poetry. v. 13, p. 239. Feb. 1919.

Tell me now; poem. Wang Chi. Living Age. v. 300, p. 192. Jan. 18, 1919.

Two Chinese poems; trans. from Li Po, by Sasaki and M. Bodenheim. Touchstone. v. 4, p. 398. Feb. 1919.

Written pictures; by F. Ayscough. Poetry. v. 13, p. 268-72. Feb. 1919.

MEDICINE.

Chinese chemists' shop; by G. King. Far Eastern Review. v. 15, p. 25. Jan. 1919.

MISSIONS.

Putting mission on a new basis; by Paul Hutchinson. Millard's Review. v. 7, p. 346-48. Feb. 8, 1919.

Result of the war upon missionary work in China; by J. L. Childs. Millard's Review. v. 7, p. 46-51. Dec. 14, 1918.

Studies in missionary psychology. Millard's Review. v. 7, p. 51-2. Dec. 14, 1918.

来源：*The Chinese Students Monthly* Volume XIV May, 1919. Number 7:456—460

【附录】戴志骞夫人著述

【附录 I】

北欧四大女文豪

戴志骞夫人（戴罗瑜丽）讲 蒋逸霄译

【编者按】戴志骞夫人，原名 Julie Rummlehoff，挪威人，中文名戴罗瑜丽，1919 年毕业于纽约州立大学图书馆学院，获图书馆学学士学位，1922 年 4 月与戴志骞结婚，1922 年 9 月到清华图书馆工作，从事英文编目，1924 年 8 月戴志骞第二次赴美留学，戴罗瑜丽与戴志骞一起赴美，任爱荷华大学图书馆编目助理，1925 年 8 月至 9 月与戴志骞一起考察欧美 11 国图书馆，1925 年 9 月下旬回到清华图书馆。1928 年 9 月，戴志骞在学潮中离开清华图书馆，戴罗瑜丽也随之离开，就任北京协和医学院图书馆主任，1936 年辞职。

戴志骞夫人原籍是脑威人①，对于北欧文学很有研究，她任职北平协和医校图书馆。最近应天津国际妇女俱乐部之请，在利顺德饭店演讲"北欧四大女文豪的传略"。她介绍的是楷密拉·柯莱脱（Camilla Collett）、爱伦·凯（Ellen Key）和曾得诺贝尔奖金的两位女作家西玛·莱葛洛芙（Selma Legerlof）同锡葛立特·恩特赛（Sigrid Undset）四人。演词很饶兴味，现在把它翻译在下面，以饷读者。

今天，所以选脑威和瑞典的四位女作家来做演讲的题目，因为我想到诸位听着文学界妇女的故事，一定比听着男作家更感兴味。而且我们谈到女性的成就，也是给妇女界增添脸面。

* * * * *

楷密拉·柯莱脱，是我第一个所要说的，她出世的时候，正当国家多难之秋，接着在一八一四年脑威脱离了丹麦宣布独立。她的父亲是路德教堂的主管，他是对于政治文化问题的短文写作家，因此他被选为非常国会里的议员，这国会在一八一四年为脑威制定了现在的宪法。楷密拉的青年时期，都住在乡村中的宏大的牧师住宅之中，其中只有两年在丹麦的一个学校里完成她的学业，她常到克立斯兴尼亚（Christiania，脑威京城，现改名叫做奥斯洛 Oslo）去游历，那里只有几小时路程的距离。她在社会之中是漂亮有才智而且为群众所欢迎的一个女子，她自幼年至成人为当时一切限制所包围着，她深感到苦痛。"当我同我的兄弟去溜冰的时候，深感到苦痛，"她在她的日记中这样写，"但我从没有发生过反抗我父母的命令的能力。"

她跟她的母亲没有多少同情。"母亲对于她的女儿的将来的观念正和那时候的一切的母亲一样。女子必须要出嫁，而男子能供给女子的便是适合的伴侣。"这是无足奇异的，她在

---

① 【编者注】今译挪威。

她的孤寂之中,转向到写短札以及日记,因此在她的作品刊行以前,早已成熟了她文字的结构。

在十九世纪之初,脑威脱离丹麦以后,在国内争论最热烈的问题,便是对于丹麦的文化应当保持着怎样的关系。两国联合几乎有四百年,这当然是个很足注意的问题,当时发生了极有力而主张极不相同的两派。一派是楷密拉的兄弟名叫亨立威格伦特(Henik Mergeland)做领袖,他是一个诗人而又是一个著名的教育家,他主张说,脑威人建设他们自己的传统的时机已到,不应当仍旧因袭着丹麦统治时代的文化。他的反对派的领袖是查斯显关威尔海文(Schastian Welhaven),他也是个诗人,他极力怂恿着国人在旧有的基础上去建设文化,因为没有一个国家可以离开了过去,割断了传袭而创造出文学来的。这两派各走一端,甚至于在后来开始笔战,而经过了长期的争斗,双方都坚持着自己的论断。楷密拉对亨立很为友爱,但是她的天性是倾向保守一方。不特如此,而且她跟威尔海文有很密切的联结,在某一个时期,双方都希望着从友谊关系上,更进一步。他为她写了许多诗,直传诵到现在;她仗着自己的力量想设法感化她的哥哥,以冀两派的争斗稍趋缓和。到后来经过了五年,威尔海文决定了不能容忍威格伦特做着他的大舅,因为他"恨他的品格正如恨他的诗一样",这是她生平最感失望的一件事情。"在我青春之中一个很短的美梦已经幻灭",楷密拉在她的日记里写着,"一个长久的烦闷的日子在我的面前"。

两年后,那时她二十八岁,她跟彼得柯莱脱(Peter Collett)结了婚,他是脑威大学的法律教授,是保守派很有势力的份子。他真实地认识她的才能,而且对于她的需求予以同情与鼓励。于是她开始做她文学的工作,在报章杂志上发表了很多的写实派的小品文字以及小说。在幸福的结婚十年之后,她的丈夫便告逝世,在她丈夫未去世时,她写了一本使她成名的小说,叫做《县长之女》(The Magistrate's Daughter)。这是那时期的灰色生活的写照,一个中等家庭的女儿,只受了一些初级的教育,毫无机会可以发展,这样以至于成长,这样一个无知的妇女并没有立脚之点,而不为社会所齿及,于是只有把结婚视作唯一的出路。因此悲剧发生,在这些女子的最可爱之点之上,因为她做出来的事情对于她所爱的人处处现着不合妇道之处。《县长之女》是描写脑威生活的第一部小说,也是脑威讨论重要社会问题的第一部小说,至今尚列入文学作品里面。

这是很奇怪的一件事,楷密拉只写了这一本小说,似乎这样格局的作品不适宜于她后来的发展。她刊行了些短篇小说,隔了几年又出版了一册《在长夜中》(In the Long Nights),这是参合叙述着她童年及青年时的回忆。渐渐地她对于妇女解放的兴味遮盖了其他一切,而她后来的作品如 Last leaves 以及 Against the Stream 都是根源于这类的叙述。直到那时,她的书都是不署名的,这样她可以很勇敢的走到前线为她伟大的信仰而奋斗,后来书坊店都不敢把她的书刊行,但她对于这经济上的牺牲,毫不犹豫。她对于宗教具有确信,因此使她后来得到了生命的工作,而且做着极大的牺牲使群众对她的观念有所改变。当她晚年的时候,很得了同时代的脑威作家的认识,有些非常地钦佩于她。她对于青年作家常予以帮助与鼓励,他们受她的人格上的感化,或者更胜于受她的书籍上的感化。楷密拉·柯莱脱的名字虽然在她的祖国之外,不很有人知道,因为她没有一本书被译成外国文字,然而在前一百年的脑威,确把她视作一个出类拔萃的妇女。在奥斯洛皇宫周围的花园之中,她的铜像兀然矗立。那铜像的形态在表示她挣扎于狂风暴雨之中,衣服呈被风吹拂之状,这凛然之气,直达到围绕那纪念物的栏栅之外。

* * * * *

一八六二年,在瑞典有一个年青姑娘做十三岁生辰的纪念,她的母亲便把一册《县长之女》送给她做礼物,她到了二十五岁,第一篇作品,便写着楷密拉·柯莱脱,因为她使她得了极深的印象。这姑娘便是爱伦·凯,她后来以著作关于社会和道德问题名于世。她是生在瑞典贵族之家的女儿,她生长于美丽的环境之中,又是爱情美满的父母的长女,家庭充满着高尚尊严之气,爱伦因此受了很完善的教育。然而她的日常生活非常简单,直到十二岁,她总是同着她的弟弟妹妹站在一张只放着牛奶面包的桌畔,吃着早餐与晚膳。直到十六岁,她吃饭的时候,没有人向她说话,她从不启齿,她自己这样告诉人。她生长在这样的生活之中,我们很易了解她为何要把苏格拉底一句话当作格言:"一个人欲望愈少,便愈能与神接近。"自幼至老,她的生活是永远刻苦朴素,这是一个很当注意的重要之点,世人往往说她是矫枉过直。

当她二十岁,她做着她父亲的秘书,那时他正充当瑞典的国会议员。又过了几年,她开始写她的评论文字以及传纪研究。她亦曾试作过小说,然而非常留意监护她的教育的母亲,具着惊人的远大的眼光,极力地打消她从事著作小说的勇气。爱伦·凯在那时梦想着要在故乡创办一所平民女子中学,模仿着丹麦的学校,她在家里甚至屡次到外国游历,悉心研究而且工作,都是为着想要实现她的梦想,这样经过了好几年。

当她父亲失却了他的财产之时,这便是她生活上的旋转之点,逼迫着她不得不到 Stockholm 学校去充当着教师。她除了日常的学校工作以外,她通常到公民会社(people's Institute)去演讲,对于恋爱问题她继续研究了二十年。

有一时期,爱伦·凯曾在首都服务,当一八八零年,易卜生的《傀儡家庭》正在上年出版,对于这剧本的激烈的争论,依然在汹涌澎湃着。一位瑞士贵妇甚至于在她请客的帖子上写着"赴宴时请弗讨论易卜生的新剧"。你们或者都能记得一句常被引用的名句:"你只是一个妻子与母亲,"郝茂尔说。"不,"戏里面的女主角娜拉说,"无论如何我是个人,最低限度我现在要去做一个人。"

当妇女解放呈着《傀儡家庭》的现象而闹着很大的风潮的时候,爱伦·凯似乎觉得女性被引入了歧途。很多的妇女把易卜生的句子日夕诵读,而且加重其语气,以为一个女子必须要和男子享受同等的权利,而且要和男子一样地过着自由生活。一言以蔽之,要给予政治上、法律上以及社会上的平等,这般女权的战士,以为将来必操胜利。爱伦·凯的意见便有不同,她了解平均的妇女的内心生活是一件很集中的东西,她需要恋爱远胜过于需要其他一切。这种观念,爱伦·凯在她的一本小书叫做《妇女能力之误导》(*Woman's Energies Misdirected*)里面坚持主张着,不久又接着刊行《恋爱与结婚》、《恋爱与伦理》、《儿童的世纪》以及其他。哈佛洛克·谒理斯(Havelock Ellis)已把爱伦·凯对于妇女运动的态度总合起来过,我不能比他说得更完善一点,所以只好把他的话转述一下:"妇女是母亲,她执掌着种族的将来,而妇女是人类,因为她对于整个的自由的发展和人权运用的能力两俱需要。并不是去仿效做着适宜于男子所做的工作,只是使她能做些自己的工作,满足自己的本能冲动,而且行着母亲的职责,这所谓母亲的职责是指广义而言,这是世间至高无上的地位。"

爱伦·凯自己从未结婚,她具有这样优美的内性,当然很难得到一个相当的男子,因着她处于未婚的地位,许多人便觉得她这样很坦白地写着关于性、恋爱与结婚的文字,很不相宜。在实际上她的思想,是超过时代,有许多她的理想,在三十年前,也不能不受人们严重的指摘(责)。但是要和现代所谓社会改造家来比较,她确是异常和平了。我们可以不赞同她的言论,但我们不能不钦佩它在《妇女的道德》里所说的话:"新道德观念的最简单的方式可以用几句话总括起来:结婚即未经法律的承认,只须有爱情便为道德,假如结婚而没有爱情,即不得谓之道德……最后将要发生,没有一个温柔多情的妇女,没有互爱,可以成一个母亲;由双方恋爱而结合的母性,不论在法律上已否承认,都可视为真正的母性……因此假如人类,对于续嗣的感觉有了醒悟,而以为结婚只是根源于肉的冲动,或者为了审慎的缘故,或者觉得这是应尽的责任,这便可视作人生最高价值的大罪人。法律的保障未尝不可期望,但这对于真正的恋爱并不能稍稍增加一些庄严神圣,正如她对于其他缺少内容的事件不能增加庄严神圣一样。"

在德美两国,对于爱伦·凯的思想特别发生了影响,著作家如梅德林克(Maeterlink)、萧伯纳(Bernard Shaw)以及丹麦的批评家乔治勃伦特斯(Gorge Brandes)都承认受了她很大的赐予。她逝世去今只有四年,享年七十七岁。

楷密拉、爱伦·凯二人之间,有很多的相似之处,两位著作家都受了那时社会问题的感应,她们的著作都有一个目标。西玛·莱葛洛芙却是和他们不同,她是瑞典现代著名的小说家,在她的世界之中,好似没有任何问题存在。她出现在一个很幸运的舞台之上,在那十九世纪之初,一般人对于写实派文学专写着社会的罪恶而且寻求着新的事物,已怀有厌倦。莱葛洛芙的家族在瑞典农村居往了有几百年之久,她的家族出了不少职业界杰出人物,她常想做一个伟大的女诗人,当她在她的青年时代,常练习着写作词章,在三十岁以前,她对于自己的才能,还没有得相当的认识。她会发表些诗词,参与教员考试,并且教了两年书,她老是梦想着要做一本伟大的书籍,在里面表现一个世界,反映她对于所爱的农村英雄儿女之事以及美曼的处在。从她童年时代,心意中便珍藏着很丰富的圣徒列传以及惊人冒险之事,她记着曾经听人传述的许多奇异的人物,以及她附近各大地区活泼快乐的生活。她把这美丽的材料用盛行的写实方法去描写,她在这努力上遇了失败,直到后来,她才决定用着她自己所发现的最好的方法去著作。结果便写成《歌史泰巴林的傅说》(*Gosta Berling's Saga*),这本书立刻使她享了盛名,而且她后来的著作未曾超过此书之上。在这部书里所写的大部分文字的结构,实际不是传奇,而很是一部伟大的近代诗史。中心人物歌史泰巴林是一个俊美而年轻的牧师,因着犯了饮酒之戒,而离开了教堂,住在一位富妇的家里,那妇人家先已有一班快乐的退伍军官和潦倒的贵族——欧克彼(Ekeby)的武士住在那里。他们整天的生活享乐,沉浸在歌舞,以及浪漫的里面。这样的生活,度了一年,歌史泰巴林觉得非常满足,因为他获得其中一个美女郎的爱,于是他和她决定拿生命奉献给人类的幸福。

莱葛洛芙书里的布景,大部分是农村,而她用着很高的艺术描写着瑞典人田舍的生活与习性。她的特点便是运用她所造的神仙故事以及奇异的事迹,她具有惊人的想象力,她从未犹豫去引用非常不足信的事实,例如人死之后又复还阳。有时用着这迷信的事情,更可使故事生动得神,但有时使人感觉得有些画蛇添足,因此很多读者以为她的书太嫌空幻。她的道德上的万物皆善说,也常在人物的个性上表现出来,意欲教人慈悲与亲善,并对宗教有深切的信仰。凡能读瑞典原文的读者,对于她美丽的抒情体裁,没有一个不陶醉的。

在歌士泰巴林传说之后,她的第二部伟大作品便是《耶路撒冷》。她写这书的动机,因为在瑞典一个山谷中,达拉那居民笃信宗教,于是集群移往圣地,意欲在那里觅得一所殖民之地,和初期的教徒一样地互相博爱。这惊人的移民使西玛·莱葛洛芙得了极深的印象,所以她在一八九九年亲自到巴勒士丁去实地考查。在那书第一卷里,叙述一个年老而傲慢的农民家庭的生活和遗传,以及惊人的复活宗教,第二卷叙述瑞典的人民在耶路撒冷,每人都易看出第一卷远胜于第二卷。西玛·莱葛洛芙用着巧妙绝伦的方法,把那些瑞典农民内心的两种冲突,写得逼真,他们一方面抱着宗教的热情,一方面爱着故乡的土地。她后来又写了一部圣经故事,叫做《耶稣轶事》(Legends of Christ)。

因着瑞典教员联合会委托她写一部瑞典地理,而又须以小说为体裁,以备作学校课本之用,她于是在一九零六年又产生一部《尼尔士漫游记》(The Wonderful Adventures of Nils)。在这里面,她的幻想优美到了极点。一个年幼的孩子,名叫尼尔士(乌有),他因着地理不熟而感困难,于是变成一只知更鸟,骑在天鹅的背上,周游瑞典全境。西玛·莱葛洛芙在这故事上得了十分的成功,在幻想的描写之中,显出了优美的风景和瑞典的伟大,一般孩子们看了这本书,只视作这是奇异的神仙故事。

我在上面所提的四本书是她著作中最重要的书籍,但她此外还写了很多的书,几乎都被译为各国不同的文字。

一九零九年因为她理想派文学的成功,得了诺贝尔奖金,那时她便赎回了她曾住过的农村旧宅。她从未结婚,一九一四年她被推选入瑞典学院,后来一九二八年决定把诺贝尔奖金给锡葛立特·恩特赛的时候,她也是委员之一。

* * * * *

在早年时,锡葛立特·恩特赛并无何等惊人之处。她的父亲是一个研究古物的学者,在脑威大学充当教授,因为他逝世很早,所以逼得她不得不在年轻时便离了学校而到公事房去谋得一席之地。一九零七年,她二十五岁的时候,出版了她的第一部小说,得了很丰富的报酬,她因此决定弃了她公事房的工作。她又得着一笔游学奖金,到了一次外国,不久回到脑威,于是安心从事于文学事业。她嫁了一个脑威的画家,叫做斯洼司泰特(Svarstad),他是一个毫无才能的艺术家,生了四个孩子,结了婚没有几年,她决定和她的丈夫离异。此后她带着她的孩子家居在丽莉哈玛(Lillehammer),这是在国境中央的一个美丽清雅的小城。

在她因作历史小说而闻名于世界之前,她已经因着描写近代的生活的美妙绝技而得了斯干的纳维亚人士的赞仰。她喜欢描写的人物是脑威很普通的一种人,曾受完善教育,但处于可怜的中等阶级。她从她自己个人的经验很深切地了解他们的生活,我们常在古旧的街道之上,看见拥挤的寄宿舍。其中为母者在那里劳苦工作,希望能挣得微资,以维持人的模样儿。这种人并不能正确的说是贫苦可怜,不过为着经济的原因艰难奋斗,只有极微的享乐。男子在恩特赛的小说之中,比较的不甚重要,她喜欢描写妇女,特别赤裸裸把她们的感情生活呈显现在读者之前。她描写一个能够自给、骄傲而又守旧的女子,最有精采,她在公事房工作,憧憬着恋爱,想能一天得到美满愉快的生活。但是等到有人爱她,那男子又不合她理想的标准,结婚的生活,与她的理想相反。但不问这些零碎幻想,恩特赛小说里的女主角是始终不承认自己失败的,她们很明白一个人不能逃出乎天命。家庭成了安全的屏蔽,女子的幸福在寻求为儿女工作与生存之中。在她一切的著作之中,她宣述着"为儿女尽责的福音"以及尊崇母性是妇女最高的成就。

她的第一部伟大的小说叫做《约纳》(Jenny),这是脑威人时常诵读而且讨论的一本书,里面很勇敢的研究着女性心理。约纳是一个幸运的艺术家,在罗马研习图画,她用着伟大的技巧写着这故事的奇异的开展。这书再版了很多次,而且是恩特赛的近代小说的唯一被译成英文的。她又写了一本长篇小说叫做《春天》(*Spring*)，这是一部关于婚姻的小说，还有许多小说如 *The Happy Age*、*Humble Destinies*，都是写着劳工阶级。她的最近的一本小说叫做《*The Wise Virgins*》，描写良善、能牺牲自己，但是姿色不能摄引男子的妇女，她显示给我们一所具有各色各样妇女的展览室。

在一九零九年她已试作了一本以圣教为根据的小说，过了几年，又编述了一册《亚述王传奇》(*King Arthur*)，以供脑威人诵读。这两册历史书并不引人多大的注意，但 *Kristin Lavransdatter* 这本小说，在脑威的作品之中得了空前的同情，这是她所做的中古时期的最有威力的一部小说，第一卷出版于一九二零年，第二卷出版于一九二二年。

这书的背景是在脑威，时期在十四世纪初叶，我们考求女主角克立司丁的生平，她是一个大地主的女儿。她和恩特赛以前描写的女主角十分相像，但是个性较强而且感情较盛。她的父亲具有北方刚健之气，然为宗教所陶冶而趋于柔和，她违了父亲的意志，嫁给一个武士叫做欧尔伦(Erland)，他长得俊俏动人，但弱于责任心。这两位性情不同的男主角，相形之下，更为引人注意。克立司丁和欧尔伦的结婚生活是很不安定的，虽是他们都觉得很纯正的相爱着。他因着政治的牵涉，他的大地区郝斯贝被充了公，而且禁止他服务一切公共的机关。欧尔伦感觉到一切都属无望，便逃到一个小的山间的农村之中，这是他仅有的留下的产业，而克立司丁还是辛勤地工作，她因为受到了她父亲的遗传，她要尽着她的能力去抚养她的孩子。欧尔伦恳求她放弃了一切，也跑到他那里去，但她觉得她肩上所负的责任很重，她回答他说，年幼的孩子还需要母亲的抚育。到后来发生了诽谤，欧尔伦便去救她，但是反被毁谤者把他害死，死在她的臂中。克立司丁度过了几年寡居生活，她隐居在一个修道院里以终余年，到一三五零年罹黑死病而亡。

这本书的特色便是令读着忘却是一部历史小说，而文学上的批评都认为这是纯粹的由历史构成的新事物。当时的政治的趋势很正确的在这里解释着，她虽没有把真的历史事实呈显出来，但描写的都是十四世纪的日常生活，因此她把那时代的整个的社会文明活跃在我们的眼前，她的丰富的历史智识融会得十分美妙，她毫不费力地描写着中世纪的礼节、习惯以及仪典，写得生动如画的高大的木建的会堂，火把的光焰把四室照得很亮，装点着绣帷和籘牌，还有宏壮的天主教堂，这是那每人生命上统治的要素。书中的人物活动于灵的空气之中，跟我们很不相同，但仍使我们感觉得根本上和我们并无大异，在感情上是一样。所以 *Kristin Lavransdatter* 成了我们日常生活的一个故事，虽则布景是在中世纪，但是内中用了很多的脑威原来的方言，使这书的文字，更有力量，而近乎一个奇突的古旧的传说体裁。

她后来又写了一本长的历史小说，叫做 *the Master of Hestviben*，文体很相似，不过宗教上罪恶的观念、忏悔与赎罪，在 *Kristin Lavransdatter* 已写过的，在这里更写得更深远一点，但是沉闷而少精彩，所以不及第一本书那样流传得广。

这是很有趣味去观察的一件事情，恩特赛怎样度着她自己的生活，而能吸收许多材料，把它重行表现出来。我信她迁移到丽莉哈玛的主因，是为着要收集那地方罕有的历史材料，那处起始由一富人开辟，后来归了政府。有几世纪前的古旧的木材农舍，甚至有一个著名的龙穴木材教堂。这些建筑里面陈设的家具什物以及习俗，都表示着古旧而神奇，使人对于过去时代的生活得了一个明了的观念。考察了很久，她自己便在一个很远的山谷之中继续建了两所木房。这两所房子互相毗连着，于是再进一步做中古的式样布置内部，甚至她所穿的衣服也模仿中古的式样，只在出门与人交接时，穿着近代流行的服装。因着她研究中古时期,于是而使她对于天主教堂非常赞美,甚至在数年前加入了这教会,在这时候在脑威国内对她发生了很多的批评,她的反对者说她守旧而且是反动力,但她对于这些批评,却丝毫不介意呢。

——一九三零年 Xmar 夜译完

原载:《国闻周报》 1931 年第 8 卷第 1 期

【附录Ⅱ】

Medical Libraries in China: A Survey

By Julie Rummelhoff Tai, B. L. S.

Librarian, Peiping Union Medical College

【编者按】此为戴罗瑜丽为1935年世界图书馆大会(IFLA)所写的论文,1935年中国共提交给世界图书馆大会9篇英文论文,编入《中国图书馆》,在大会上发放。

Medical libraries are invariably associated with medical education and research. In order to understand the present medical library situation in China, it is necessary to survey briefly the development of western medicine in this country.

Dr. Wu Lien-teh, who has made extensive studies on this subject, claims that the introduction of western medicine was made at an early date by European physicians, particularly the Jesuit fathers, who successfully treated Emperor Kang Hsi(1662-1772) with quinine. The Jesuits, however, failed to take advantage of this opportunity to further the cause of western medicine in China. For practical purposes it is, therefore, safe to say that western medicine was introduced into China at the beginning of the last century. In 1805 the practice of vaccination had already been started by Dr. Alexander Pearson in South China; in 1827 Dr. Thomas Colledge opened the first eye hospital in China in Macao, and in 1834 Dr. Peter Parker, the pioneer medical missionary arrived in Canton. Gradually medical missionaries took up work in various parts of the country, and with the development of foreign trade, a number of western physicians settled down as practitioners in the chief ports.

Even the first medical missionaries realized the importance of giving western medical training to young Chinese men and women. Student classes were gradually organized in various parts of the country in connection with mission hospitals, and a few selected students were sent abroad for advanced medical studies. The first Chinese medical graduate from a foreign university was Dr. Wang Fun who returned to China in 1857. In 1850 appeared the first Chinese translation of a western medical text and the important work of translating the medical books of foreign authors has been continued ever since.

Although a beginning towards a modern medical school was made in Tientsin already in 1881, it was not until after 1900 that a real need was felt for a systematic medical education on a broad basis.① Missionary societies of various denominations combined their efforts and during the period 1900-1913 eight union medical colleges were organized, far too many for the limited finances and personnel. At the same time a small group of keen Chinese doctors, some trained in mission schools, some trained abroad, called to the attention of the Chinese Government the need for up-to-

---

① It should be noted that the British had already in 1887 established a medical college for Chinese in Hongkong.

date medical instruction. Provincial governments began to open medical schools and to cooperate with some of the missionary medical colleges.

Important development took place during 1914-1915 when the Rockefeller Foundation of New York sent out to China two commissions "to enquire into the condition of medical education, hospitals and public health". A report called *Medicine in China* was submitted to the Rockefeller Foundation in 1914. As a result of the findings of these commissions the Rockefeller Foundation decided to undertake medical work in China, and the China Medical Board was created in order to put the various recommendations into effect, one of which was to provide for a first class medical school. The old Union Medical College in Peking was submerged into the new Peking Union Medical College which was opened in the fall of 1921. Housed in a group of beautiful buildings in modem Chinese style, the College possesses all the facilities for up-to-date medical work and compares favorably with the leading medical institutions of other countries. The China Medical Board has, in addition, given substantial grants to a number of other medical schools, hospitals, and universities in China.

Outstanding events in later years were the establishment by the National Government of a Ministry of Health[②] in Nauking in 1928, and the opening of the well endowed Henry Lester Institute of Medical Research in Shanghai in 1930. Of considerable importance was the visit of Dr. Knud Faber in 1930 and his *Report on Medical Schools in China*, which was presented to the League of Nations in 1931. Much thought and effort is being spent upon the problem of evolving a system of medical education suitable for China. Since there are still far too few Chinese graduates of medicine, most medical schools are short of personnel. The world depression, the depreciation of the Chinese dollar, and the disturbed political situation have so seriously effected finances that nearly all medical schools are short of money. Definite progress is however being made. Encouraging events are the amalgamation in 1932 of the National Medical Association[③] and the China Medical Association[④] to form the Chinese Medical Association, and the Congress of the Far Eastern Association of Tropical Medicine held in Nanking in 1934.

It is not surprising that books on the history of western medicine in China do not refer to medical libraries; even Wong and Wu's exhaustive study, *History of Chinese Medicine*, scarcely mentions this subject. Probably for many years there was no collection of medical books that could be called a library. The early medical missionaries must have had for their own use small collections of medical handbooks, gradually supplemented, as the translation work progressed, with Chinese editions for their assistants and students. The early medical workers, as already mentioned, realized the importance of creating a Chinese medical literature—that is by translation—but they were not particularly interested in recording their original observations and thus building up material relating to diseases in China. In 1880 an attempt was made to start a small medical periodical, which lasted

---

② Since November 1930 called the National Health Administration.
③ Organized by Chinese graduates of medicine in 1915.
④ Originally the China Missionary Medical Association, founded in 1886.

only two years. In 1887 finally appeared the *China Missionary Medical journal*, which still continues to-day under the title, *Chinese Medical Journal*.

It is probable that some attention was paid to the establishment of medical libraries after 1900, as part of the equipment of the medical colleges founded at that time, but one gathers that due to the lack of funds not much was done. ⑤ The report, *Medicine in China*, submitted in 1914 to the Rockefeller Foundation, contains the following recommendation: " One need emphasized by many of the best medical men in China is some means of getting hold of medical literature. At least one, probably two, extensive libraries containing especially files of medical journals should be established in connection with medical schools. These libraries should be provided with competent librarians and such assistance as will enable them to send books anywhere in China."

Below is a list⑥ of the twenty-seven medical schools existing in China today, arranged according to the method of support:

	NAME	Location	Date of Establishment	Medium of Instruction
National	National Tung Chi University, College of Medicine	Woosung, Shanghai	1908	German
	National Peiping University, College of Medicine	Peiping	1912	Chinese
	National Chung Shan University, College of Medicine	Canton	1926	Chinese and German
	National Shanghai Medical College	Shanghai	1927	Chinese and German
	Army Medical School	Nanking	1902	Chinese
	Yunnan Army Medical School	Kwun-Ming, Yunnan	1931	Chinese
Provincial	Chekiang Provincial Medical and Pharmaceutical School	Hangchow, Chekiang	1912	Chinese
	Hopei Provincial Medical School	Paoting, Hopei	1916	Chinese
	Kiangsi Provincial. Medical School	Nanchang, Kiangsi	1921	Chinese
	Honan University, College of Medicine	Kaifeng, Honan.	1928	Chinese
	Shantung Provincial Medical School	Tsinan, Shantung	1932	Chinese

⑤ Dr. W. R. Morse in his Three Crosses in the Purple Mists, p. 175-79, waites amusingly about the early days without books of the Medical School of the West China Union University, Chengtu.

⑥ This list has been taken from Dr. T. Lee's article. Some Statistics on Medical Schools in China for 1932—1933, in the Chinese Medical Journal, 47: 1029-39, Oct. 1933.

续表

	NAME	Location	Date of Establishment	Medium of Instruction
Private	Hackett Medical College	Canton	1899	Chinese and English
	St. John's University, College of Medicine	Shanghai	1906	English
	Peiping Union Medical College	Peiping	1906	English
	Aurora University, College of Medicine	Shanghai	1909	French
	Cheeloo University, College of Medicine	Tsinan, Shantung	1909	Chinese and English
	Kwang Wah Medical College	Canton	1909	Chinese
	Mukden Medical College	Mukden	1912	Chinese and English
	Nantung University, College of Medicine	Nantung, Kiangsu	1912	Chinese
	West China Union University, College of Medicine	Chengtu, Szechuan	1914	Chinese and English
	Hsiang Ya Medical College	Changsha	1914	Chinese and English
	Tung Teh Medical College	Shanghai	1918	Chinese
	Shansi Chwan Chih Medical School	T'aiyuan, Shansi	1919	Chinese
	Manchuria Medical College	Mukden	1921	Japanese
	Women's Christian Medical College	West Gate, Shanghai	1924	English
	Harbin Medical School	Harbin	1926	Chinese
	Tung Nan Medical School	Shanghai	1926	Chinese

The fact that medical teachers in China have received their training according to the medical systems of various countries is reflected in this table. In addition to the American and English methods of education, French, German and Japanese methods are found. Generally English is the foreign language adopted. Although only one school uses the German language exclusively, many of the government schools and some of the private ones are strongly influenced by German methods as the teachers originally studied in Japan where the German system is used. This again means that the libraries of these institutions may be arranged according to German methods, that most subscriptions would be to German and Japanese journals and that the greater part of the books would be in these two languages. As a matter of fact, even in those institutions where Chinese is the medium of instruction, medical libraries in China tend to have most volumes in foreign languages. This is particularly true of the larger libraries. Since usually original medical observations are published in English, occasionally in German and French, medical publications in Chinese are likely to be translations or else rather elementary material. As medical education in China progresses, and Chinese scientific and medical nomenclature is further developed, a medical literature in the Chinese language, aside from translations, may be built up.

It is well known, of course, that China has an extensive literature on the old Chinese system of medicine which goes back several thousand years. But except for a collection used in connection with research on Chinese native drugs or illustrating the history of medicine, books on Chinese medicine are not usually to be found in a modern medical library.

A detailed questionnaire and, when required, two follow ups were sent by registered mail to the Dean or Librarian of each medical school, allowing ample time for an answer. At the time this article was written twenty-four answers had been received. The 1934 Chinese Medical Directory and the Announcements of the medical schools themselves were consulted for figures about the remaining three libraries. The result has been tabulated below, the libraries which failed to answer the questionnaire are marked with an asterisk. For one library no statistics or general information are available.

	NAME	Total number of volumes (Books, periodicals and pamphlets)	Number of periodicals subscribed to	Annual budget for new purchases and binding	Seating capacity of library
National	Library, National Tung Chi University, College of Medicine	5,558	19	M＄16,800	72 persons
	Library, National Peiping University, College of Medicine	9,453	36	500	80 persons
	Library, National Chung Shan University, College of Medicine	5,200	91	14,700	20 persons
	Library, National Shanghai Medical College	5,224	130	16,416	40 persons
	Library, Army Medical School	1,007	13	1200	20 persons
	∗ Library, Yunnan Army Medical School				
Provincial	Library, Chekiang Provincial Medical and Pharmaceutical School	10,775	46	2000	60 persons
	Library, Hopei Provincial Medical School	34,352	53	2,800	80 persons
	Library, Kiangsi Provincial Medical School	2,050	16	Library not yet organized	
	Library, Honan University, College of Medicine	600	35	5,000	
	∗ Library, Shantung Provincial Medical School	300			

续表

Privite	Library, Hackett Medical College	6,945	32		
	Library, St. John's University, College of Medicine	1,880	50	750	10 persons
	Library, Peiping Union Medical College	59,225	412	M $2,110 G $12,550	115 persons
	Library, Aurora University, College of Medicine	10,000	60	7,000	
	Library, Cheeloo University, College of Medicine	6,000	100	1,750	36 persons
	Library, Kwang Wah Medical College	5,373	32	1,000	38 persons
	Library, Mukden Medical College	2,000	30	Library under reorganization	
	Library, Nantung University, College of Medicine	683	76	1,500	80 persons
	Library, West China Union University, College of Medicine	3,484	113	1,475	
	Library, Hsiang Ya Medical College	2,340	34	5,000 (for current year only)	30 persons
	*Library, Tung Teh Medical College	3,000	10		
	Library, Shansi Chwan Chih Medical School	8,122	34	2,400	
	Library, Manchuria Medical College	41,000	464	Yen 47,350	
	Library, Women's Christian Medical College	1,500	43	M $500 G $1,000	
	Library, Harbin Medical School	Library not yet organized			
	Library, Tung Nan Medical School	4,720	127	7,160	50 persons

(Note:) The Medical Faculty of Hongkong University has not been included in the survey. In a report issued in 1934 the Medical Library is said to occupy a room in the Pathology Building. About the size of the Medical Library nothing is mentioned, but the total collection of the university libraries at the end of 1933 is stated to consist of 36,467 volumes. 189 periodicals were received regularly.

The questionnaire was also sent to the following institutions:

NAME	Total number of volumes (Books, periodicals and pamphlets)	Number of periodicals subscribed to	Annual budget for new purchases and binding	Seating capacity of library
Library, Chinese Medical Association, Shanghai. Founded 1932.	1,200	290	M $2,800	12 persons
Library, Henry Lester Institute of Medical Research, Shanghai. Founded 1930.	3,825	138		40 persons
Library, National Health Administration, Nanking. Founded 1928.	6,916	142	8,775	16 persons
Library, Shanghai Municipal Council, Public Health Department. Founded 1900. (reorganized 1922)	1,955	65		16 persons
Library, National Quarantine Service, Shanghai. Founded 1930.	Library not yet organized			

It was decided to send the questionnaire to hospitals having 150 beds or more. The 1934 Chinese Medical Directory lists only thirty-one such hospitals though probably there are more. As twelve of these are teaching hospitals connected with medical schools the questionnaire was sent to nineteen hospitals. Answers were received from nine. The time was too short to allow follow ups to be sent to the institutions that had failed to answer.

Only one of the nine hospitals reports an organized library with a classification and a card catalog. Eight hospitals report a small reading room seating 6-12 persons. All of the ten hospitals have a small collection of standard medical textbooks and subscribe to a few medical journals.

Although these figures give some indication of the size of the existing medical libraries in China, most of them are probably far from being accurate. It was evident, as the answers to the questionnaire came in, that some were written by persons unfamiliar with library terminology and library methods. Various libraries also have different ways of counting their volumes and pamphlets, especially their Chinese books. Instead of giving the actual number of journals currently subscribed to, several libraries seem to have included periodicals sent as gifts. Some of these often of very slight value, and may consist only of a few numbers.

Of the eight medical schools connected with universities only one, namely, the College of Medicine of the National Peiping University, has an independent library. The remaining medical schools with the possible exception of that of Honan University, seem to have separate reading rooms where at least a part of the medical collection is kept.

It should be noted that the libraries of the National Tung Chi University and the National Shanghai Medical College would be considerably larger but for the bombardment of Woosung, early in 1932, when both institutions suffered heavily.

All libraries which answered the questionnaire report a card catalog. As for classification, three libraries use the Boston medical library system, three the Dewey, one the Library of Congress system and one Doo's universal classification system (based on Dewey). Three libraries employ two different systems. Two libraries are considering changing to Cunningham's medical classification. One library reports a "general" classification system, another a "simplified systematic system". A foreign doctor in charge of one library aptly remarks that Dewey is hopelessly unsuitable for a medical library.

Shanghai has most medical libraries as eleven of the institutions mentioned in this survey are located there. Three of these have issued small printed catalogs of their books and periodicals. A union catalog of medical books and journals available in Shanghai libraries is in preparation. The library of the Henry Lester Institute has shown considerable development during the short period of its existence. One cannot help thinking that there must be in Shanghai much duplication of effort as far as medical libraries are concerned. There seems to be an urgent need for a large medical library having extensive back files of medical periodicals and possessing a good collection of important medical reference works. Such a library might well be organized to serve not only Shanghai, but South China.

A rapidly growing collection, giving great promise for the future, is that of the National Health Administration, Nanking. So far, however, very little has been done towards completing periodical files. It is hoped that in due course this library may be able to assume the role of the national medical library of China and conduct an extensive inter-library loan service.

The Manchuria Medical College is a purely Japanese institution. Its library which is reported to have a staff of 13 persons has recently outgrown its quarters and a new library building is under construction. It is of considerable interest to note that one third of the students in this institution are Chinese, drawn from all over the country.

As one would expect, the largest medical library in China at present is that of the Peiping Union Medical College. This library not only has been fortunate in having sufficient funds for steady growth but has been under the care of a trained librarian since 1918. Its staff of eight persons includes two library school graduates. Special emphasis has been put on acquiring back files of journals and large medical reference works such as the German "Handbücher" and the American looseleaf series. Recently a collection of books on the history of medicine has been started. Many requests for inter-library loans, usually for back volumes of periodicals, are constantly received from medical and scientific institutions all over the country. During the past two years twenty-eight such institutions have been served. Typewritten or photostated copies of articles can be arranged for if a journal cannot be sent. It is felt, however, that medical libraries should aim at possessing their own files of the more common and inexpensive periodicals, and turn to the Peiping Union Medical College Library only for material not easily obtainable.

As already stated, most medical schools in China at present suffer from lack of money, of equipment and of personnel. If expenses have to be curtailed in an institution, often the library is the first to suffer. Medical books and especially journals are very expensive, and many publications go quickly out of data. When a library has no definite budget or a very inadequate sum, progress is hardly possible. An adequate yearly budget providing for books, periodical subscriptions, binding and salaries continued over a period of years is essential in order to build up a collection. It is gratifying to note that two of the libraries in our series reported recent special appropriations in addition to the usual grant.

"The training of the librarian and library staff is also of great importance. Perhaps the most outstanding fact the survey has brought out is that most medical libraries in China are in charge of persons without professional library training. Of the eight university libraries containing a medical collection it would appear that only two are headed by trained librarians. Of the independent medical libraries only two or three have librarians who are library school graduates, although several are college graduates. Several medical librarians have had a little library experience, but no special training and a limited general education. A few libraries are directed by a physician of the institution, aided by one or two young assistants; two such libraries report that they hope to engage a trained librarian in the near future. The assistant librarian of one of the national medical schools in Shanghai is on leave of absence in order to take the two year library course at Boone Library School, Wuchang. Another medical institution in Shanghai has recently sent its Chinese librarian north for special instruction at the Peiping Union Medical College Library and at the National Library of Peiping. It seems highly desirable that a medical librarian should be a graduate of a library school, Chinese or American, and in addition should have a few months experience in a good sized medical library. Although this may seem to high a standard for a small institution, it is certain that a collection of highly technical books in several languages such as the average medical library generally contains, cannot be properly looked after except by a professionally competent and well educated librarian. The trouble, of course, is that there still are far too few Chinese library school graduates.

It has not yet been possible to develop a system of close cooperation among the medical libraries of China, but much would be grained if medical librarians would work together on certain important problems. A regular exchange of duplicate journals as recently proposed by Dr. H. E. Campbell, Foochow,[⑦] might help considerably to build up back files of periodicals. It would be highly desirable to have a union list of journals in medical libraries, should it not be possible in the near future to compile a regular union list of serials in the libraries of China. Medical libraries in the same vicinity might have a definite agreement so that each library would specialize along certain lines. This would prevent unnecessary duplication of expensive books and journals and at the same time provide for a greater variety of medical publications. The larger libraries might conduct short courses in medical library administration and methods.

---

⑦ See the Chinese Medical Journal 47:1100, Oct. 1934.

Perhaps the time has arrived for organizing a Chinese Medical Library Association as a division of the Library Association of China.

SOURCES:

Balme, Harold: China and modern medicine. London, United council for missionary education, 1921.

Chinese medical directory, 1934.

Greene, R. S: General considerations for medical curriculum requirements in China. Chinese medical journal 49: 59-62, Jan. 1935.

Hongkong. University: Annual report 1932-1933. 1934.

League of Nations. Health organization: Report on medical schools in China; by Knud Faber. 1931.

Lee, Tao: Some statistics on medical schools in China for 1932-1933. Chinese medical journal 47: 1029-1939, Oct. 1933.

Morse, W. R: Three crosses in the purple mists. Shanghai, Mission book company [1928].

Rockefeller foundation. China medical commission: Medicine in China. N. Y. 1914.

Wong, K. Chimin and Wu, Lien-teh: History of Chinese medicine. Tientsin [1932].

Wu, Lien-teh: Memorandum on medical education in China. 1914.